De Mackenzie King à Pierre Trudeau

Quarante ans
de diplomatie canadienne

From Mackenzie King to Pierre Trudeau

Forty Years
of Canadian Diplomacy

1945~1985

De Mackenzie King à Pierre Trudeau

Quarante ans
de diplomatie canadienne

From Mackenzie King to Pierre Trudeau

Forty Years
of Canadian Diplomacy

1945-1985

Sous la direction de
PAUL PAINCHAUD
Editor

LES PRESSES DE L'UNIVERSITÉ LAVAL
Québec, 1989

Cette publication a bénéficié de l'aide du Conseil
de recherches en sciences humaines du Canada,
du ministère des Affaires extérieures du Canada
et du Secrétariat d'État du Canada

CONCEPTION GRAPHIQUE: NORMAN DUPUIS

RÉALISATION GRAPHIQUE: NORMAN DUPUIS ET CATHERINE DUGRÉ

RÉVISION LINGUISTIQUE: DOMINIQUE JOHNSON

TABLE DES MATIÈRES   CONTENTS

TROISIÈME PARTIE   PART THREE
Les systèmes régionaux   *The Regional Systems*

QUATRIÈME PARTIE   PART FOUR
Les politiques sectorielles   *The Sectorial Policies*

INTRODUCTION

Paul Painchaud
Université Laval

En 1945, le Canada n'est plus un pays jeune du point de vue de son développement politique interne. Ses rapports avec l'ancienne métropole britannique ont été définis sur la base d'une souveraineté complète, le régime fédéral a trouvé sa vitesse de croisière, les institutions parlementaires sont solidement établies, l'administration publique se développe, les grandes politiques d'intervention de l'État dans la vie économique et culturelle sont déjà en place, et la fin de la guerre marque un répit dans la confrontation entre Canadiens de langue anglaise et de langue française. Même si de nombreux problèmes demeurent, le décor de l'État canadien, pour l'essentiel, est planté. Le système s'est doté de mécanismes d'adaptation et d'une légitimité qui lui permettent désormais de relever l'immense défi d'aménager politiquement la partie septentrionale de l'Amérique du Nord. Que l'on accepte ou non la vision et les intérêts qui supportent ce processus de développement politique, il s'agit là d'une étape majeure dans la formation de l'État canadien.

Mais sur le plan de son insertion dans le système international, le Canada d'avant la Deuxième Guerre mondiale est un pays encore jeune. Certes, dès la Confédération, le Canada obtient un statut à l'intérieur de l'Empire britannique qui lui permet de faire ses premières armes sur la scène internationale. Sans rompre formellement le lien colonial, il se fait même admettre à la Société des Nations, et met peu à peu sur pied un mince filet de représentation à l'étranger. Mais l'attitude qui prévaut à Ottawa jusqu'à 1939 consiste à pratiquer une politique du moindre engagement, le Commonwealth naissant et le commerce international demeurant les principaux centres d'intérêt de sa diplomatie.

La Deuxième Guerre modifie cette situation en profondeur. À partir de 1945, le Canada se dote, et cela très rapidement, d'un «système de politique étrangère» qui complète le processus de «state-building» amorcé au XIXe siècle. Tant au niveau des champs d'intervention dans les affaires internationales que des modes de participation à la vie internationale, des mécanismes de gestion, des ressources déployées, de l'élaboration d'une pensée internationale, des instruments d'influence et de la mobilisation sociale, le système politique canadien connaît une expansion qui, plus que tout autre aspect de son développement antérieur, contribue à définir son identité. C'est là une incontestable réussite. Les Canadiens, davantage absorbés par leurs conflits internes, ou plus étroitement identifiés à leur région immédiate, sont rarement conscients de l'importance qu'a eu la politique étrangère dans la consolidation et l'unification de leur système politique au cours des 40 années qui se sont écoulées de la fin de la Deuxième Guerre mondiale à la fin de l'ère Trudeau. C'est cette dimension du développement politique canadien que cet ouvrage cherche à analyser.

Car l'État canadien, la culture politique canadienne et le développement socio-économique du Canada ne seraient pas les mêmes sans les articulations, nombreuses, diversifiées et désormais permanentes, que la politique étrangère a créées, au cours de cette période, entre le Canada et le système international. La politique étrangère a donné, pour ainsi dire, un nouvel espace à ce pays dont les contours internes étaient encore incertains. Les relations extérieures, par exemple, avaient divisé Canadiens anglais et Canadiens français depuis la Confédération. Après 1945, elles deviennent un instrument d'unité, non seulement parce que les deux communautés relèvent ensemble les nouveaux défis qui s'imposent au Canada à l'extérieur, mais aussi parce que la politique étrangère elle-même assume officielle-ment la dualité canadienne. Les politiques d'immigration ont pour objet d'accroître la population du Canada en période d'expansion industrielle – facteur important de développement pour un pays comme le Canada –, mais donnent à la société canadienne cette dimension multiculturelle qui la distingue des États-Unis. Certaines politiques économiques extérieures – le Pacte de l'automobile, la création de marchés d'exportation pour le blé – ont non seulement des conséquences politiques pour la diplomatie canadienne, mais contribuent également à la prospérité de certaines régions. Les exemples pourraient être multipliés – et ils sont nombreux dans les différents chapitres de cet ouvrage – où la politique étrangère d'après 1945 a non seulement contribué au progrès du pays, mais, surtout, a donné à celui-ci les moyens d'une cohésion nouvelle à divers niveaux.

Cette expansion de l'État canadien n'a pas seulement été le fruit des circons-tances et des pressions externes. Celles-ci, certes, ont imposé des choix très tôt après la guerre. Mais ces choix auraient pu être différents, n'eut été la vision de quelques individus remarquables dont l'action a créé un effet d'entraînement jusqu'à nos jours. Une dynamique a alors été enclenchée, que l'alternance des partis au pouvoir ne modifiera pas, comme le montre très bien Peyton V. Lyon dans le premier chapitre de cet ouvrage. En d'autres termes, un système de politique étrangère a été mis en place, donnant graduellement au Canada sa configuration spécifique sur la scène internationale en même temps que les moyens d'affronter les immenses défis de l'après-guerre.

Il y a plusieurs façons de définir un système de politique étrangère. Pour les fins de cette présentation, nous retiendrons qu'un système de politique étrangère est composé de quatre éléments: les rôles, les méthodes, les doctrines et les institutions d'une diplomatie. À ces quatre titres, la politique extérieure canadienne d'après 1945 témoigne d'un niveau de développement qui la démarque nettement de la période antérieure.

En politique étrangère, le rôle définit la place qu'entend occuper un État à l'intérieur du système international, ses principales articulations avec celui-ci, et par là le type de comportement et les instruments qui caractériseront son action. Après la guerre, le contexte géopolitique du Canada a changé: d'une part son isolement – et donc sa dépendance – face aux États-Unis s'est accru, et d'autre part, il se trouve exactement au centre d'une confrontation possible entre les deux superpuissances qui émergent du deuxième conflit mondial. Cette situation conduit la diplomatie canadienne, par étapes successives, à développer trois rôles nouveaux pour le Canada sur la scène internationale.

Le premier est d'amener le Canada à se définir comme un *acteur global* sur la scène internationale. Non, certes, dans le sens où le Canada se considère comme une superpuissance dont l'influence s'exercerait aux quatre coins de la planète, mais dans le sens où ses intérêts exigent désormais qu'il fasse sentir sa présence d'une manière active dans les dimensions centrales de la vie internationale, et au premier chef, dans les questions de sécurité. La conjoncture dans laquelle il se trouve après la guerre s'y prête, et le gouvernement saisit l'occasion pour secouer les traditions provincialistes et isolationnistes qui ont dominé sa démarche diplomatique jusque-là. Ce que, d'une autre façon, on appelle l'approche internationaliste dans la politique étrangère canadienne. La conséquence pratique de cette nouvelle orientation a été d'amener le Canada à développer une façon de penser et d'agir qui a poussé la diplomatie canadienne au cœur de tous les grands dossiers de notre époque. Cette démarche s'est d'abord appliquée aux organisations internationales universelles qui ont vu le jour après la guerre, aux différents dossiers des relations Est-Ouest, au désarmement, à la question nucléaire, puis, progressivement, aux autres problèmes globaux: le dialogue Nord-Sud, le commerce international, les droits de l'homme, etc. À partir de cette date, le Canada n'est plus un observateur distant dans les affaires internationales.

Cette tradition de penser globalement est établie par Pearson, mais poursuivie par Trudeau en dépit des critiques de celui-ci à l'égard de son prédécesseur: l'un de ses derniers gestes en politique étrangère, son «Initiative de paix», en est le symbole le plus éloquent. Ainsi, le tournant pris en 1945 est-il irréversible. En dépit de ses moyens limités, le Canada ne serait plus un État replié sur lui-même, la diplomatie canadienne ne cesserait pas d'articuler ses intérêts immédiats aux conditions générales de la vie internationale. On ne soulignera jamais assez l'importance de ce changement de cap, dont l'une des conséquences est de donner aux Canadiens une nouvelle image d'eux-mêmes, et à la diplomatie d'Ottawa des moyens d'influence qu'elle n'aurait osé espérer en 1939.

Le deuxième tournant de la diplomatie canadienne au cours de cette période est de sortir le pays de l'étau trop étroit de ses relations avec la Grande-Bretagne et les États-Unis pour l'ancrer au système plus large qui prend forme après la guerre: le système occidental. Celui-ci s'est peu à peu défini, et il s'exprime désormais dans le cadre d'institutions variées. Très tôt le Canada y joue un rôle actif en décidant, en particulier, de considérer l'Europe occidentale comme essentielle à sa sécurité.

Là encore, on retrouve la «continuité expansionniste» de la diplomatie mise en place en 1945. L'influence de Pearson apparaît au moment de la création de l'Alliance atlantique, mais aussi, plus tard, celle de Trudeau dans l'établissement du «Lien contractuel» avec la Communauté européenne et la participation du Canada au Sommet des pays industrialisés. C'est en acceptant cette interdépendance étroite et en l'assumant de diverses façons sur le plan bilatéral – notamment avec les États-Unis – que le Canada est en mesure de jouer le rôle global qu'il s'est assigné – par exemple en matière de sécurité européenne, ou dans la solution des problèmes régionaux, comme à Suez – et qu'il peut assurer la défense de ses intérêts propres. On peut, évidemment, débattre de son influence réelle à l'intérieur du système occidental, mais on peut également s'interroger sur ce que serait une diplomatie canadienne qui s'en serait isolée. La situation géopolitique du Canada n'est pas celle des États européens, ni celle du Japon. La grande réussite de la diplomatie canadienne est d'avoir pu, en effet, surmonter les contraintes qui sont les siennes en Amérique du

Nord pour s'amarrer à un système qui lui assure une indispensable couverture de sécurité ainsi qu'un espace d'interdépendances conforme à ses valeurs et à ses besoins.

Le système canadien de politique étrangère connaît également une autre phase d'expansion avec son ouverture sur le tiers monde. Peu de choses, à vrai dire, ni par l'histoire ni par les intérêts, ne prédisposent la diplomatie canadienne à s'impliquer activement dans des régions comme l'Afrique, l'Asie ou l'Amérique latine. En fait, il faut un certain temps avant que le Canada ne manifeste un intérêt réel à certaines parties du monde comme le Moyen-Orient ou l'Amérique centrale. Dès la fin de la guerre, cependant, en raison de la décolonisation et du contexte de la «guerre froide», le Canada est amené à développer des instruments d'intervention qui en feront un acteur significatif dans ce qui deviendra le dialogue Nord-Sud.

Les voies par lesquelles le Canada fait l'apprentissage de ces régions sont multiples. Elles sont politiques par le biais de l'ONU, des opérations de maintien de la paix, des crises régionales, et du Commonwealth. Elles sont économiques, d'abord par les programmes d'aide, et progressivement plus globales au sein des conférences internationales sur les problèmes du développement, comme celle de Paris en 1975. Là encore doit-on noter la continuité dans l'élargissement du champ de la diplomatie canadienne. D'abord avec Pearson, dont la relation spéciale avec Nehru a été à l'origine de l'ouverture du Canada sur le tiers monde, et plus tard avec Trudeau, qui fera de la crise du sous-développement l'un des axes dominants de son action internationale.

En réalité, le Canada s'est taillé une place dans le dialogue Nord-Sud dont il existe peu d'équivalents dans le monde industrialisé. Non seulement, en effet, a-t-il très tôt mis sur pied une politique d'aide, notamment avec le plan de Colombo – qui devait conduire aux programmes diversifiés de l'ACDI –, mais il établit avec les pays du Sud des relations très larges sur le plan politique et culturel. Son absence de passé colonial et d'ambitions géopolitiques y sont évidemment pour beaucoup, mais aussi le leadership qu'il a su exercer au sein d'institutions multilatérales, comme le Commonwealth, et plus récemment la Francophonie. À bien des égards, la situation du Canada vis-à-vis du tiers monde diffère donc de celle de la plupart des pays de l'Ouest, dont les programmes d'aide sont pourtant plus importants, parce qu'il a su profiter d'une conjoncture favorable à un rôle d'articulateur entre aspirations, régions et cultures diverses.

Certes, on peut critiquer tel ou tel aspect des politiques canadiennes, à l'égard du tiers monde, par exemple en matière de niveau d'aide, de droits de l'homme ou de politique commerciale. Mais un fait essentiel demeure: la diplomatie canadienne s'est liée structurellement à l'avenir des pays en développement. Un tel choix ne s'imposait pas d'emblée en 1945. Désormais, aucun gouvernement, quelles que soient ses préférences idéologiques, ne pourrait remettre en cause ce choix sans menacer la situation globale du Canada sur la scène internationale. Ce qui, bien entendu, n'interdit pas des modulations dans la mise en œuvre de cette politique d'un gouvernement à l'autre.

Ces trois ancrages fondamentaux – un rôle global, une solide insertion à l'ouest, un rôle actif dans le système Nord-Sud – constituent la toile de fond du développement de la diplomatie canadienne après 1945. Mais le système canadien de politique étrangère s'est aussi enrichi d'autres éléments. On en mesure moins l'importance à notre époque tant ils semblent faire partie du paysage politique. Nous en mentionnerons ici quelques-uns parmi les plus significatifs du point de vue de la conduite des relations extérieures.

Au-delà de ses objectifs et de ses intérêts spécifiques, en effet, toute politique étrangère doit s'exprimer par une ou des méthodes d'intervention dans les affaires internationales. Le choix des méthodes est fonction de la culture politique du pays, de sa situation géopolitique, des contraintes qu'il doit surmonter. Par ailleurs, les méthodes ne s'improvisent pas. Elles supposent un apprentissage dans le temps. Au cours de la période qui a suivi la guerre, le Canada a ainsi développé un mode d'intervention sur la scène internationale qui ne lui est pas unique, mais qui le caractérise hautement: le multilatéralisme, c'est-à-dire la participation active à des organisations internationales.

Certes, tous les États, à notre époque, doivent s'engager d'une manière ou d'une autre dans les organisations internationales. Celles-ci sont devenues un des traits dominants du système international contemporain. Mais pour le Canada, le multilatéralisme est un choix délibéré de méthode. Non seulement fait-il du développement des organisations internationales une condition de réalisation d'un certain nombre d'objectifs valables pour l'ensemble de la communauté internationale, mais le multilatéralisme, sous toutes ses formes, est poursuivi comme moyen spécifique pour assurer la défense de ses intérêts propres. On le voit au moment de la création de l'ONU, dans la formation de l'Alliance atlantique, au sein du Commonwealth, à l'OCDE, auprès des diverses instances qui se créent en Europe, dans un grand nombre d'organisations techniques, au GATT, au sein de conférences *ad hoc*, dans ses efforts pour participer à des institutions de concertation comme le Sommet des démocraties industrielles, et plus récemment dans le rôle qu'il cherche à jouer au sein de la Francophonie. Bref, le Canada est non seulement présent dans de nombreuses instances multilatérales, mais il cherche très souvent à en susciter.

Il ne s'agit pas là d'un accident. Le choix en est fait d'une manière délibérée dès 1945 comme moyen pour multiplier les éléments de puissance à la disposition du Canada. Il en résulte un savoir-faire, des techniques – comme sa participation aux opérations de maintien de la paix –, des instruments de pénétration du système international dont le niveau est impressionnant pour un État de la taille du Canada, surtout si l'on met cette situation en parallèle avec celle qui prévaut après la guerre. Cette méthode, en un sens, définit le style de la politique étrangère canadienne, et parce qu'elle fait désormais partie de la culture internationale canadienne, on peut dire qu'elle en conditionne l'efficacité.

Le développement de cette méthode, par ailleurs, s'appuie sur la formation progressive d'une pensée internationale au Canada, c'est-à-dire l'élaboration de *doctrines de politique étrangère*. Avant 1945, le Canada a peu de traditions diplomatiques. Son inspiration lui vient surtout de Londres. Dans le contexte nouveau qui naît après la guerre, le gouvernement canadien doit définir une approche aux affaires internationales qui lui soit propre. Il le fait par étapes, d'une manière pragmatique. La doctrine s'élabore d'abord à la lumière des circonstances, mais peu à peu prend forme et s'articule autour d'un certain nombre de principes qui doivent déterminer, d'une manière souple, les grands choix de politique étrangère. Il a été fait état précédemment de l'approche internationaliste, et de son corollaire, la doctrine du *middlepowermanship*, c'est-à-dire le comportement spécifique dans les affaires internationales que doit avoir une moyenne puissance comme le Canada. Ces approches servent durant toute la période Pearson à la détermination de choix concrets. Mais surtout, elles jettent les bases d'un développement doctrinal qui prendra plus d'importance au cours de la période subséquente.

Avec l'arrivée au pouvoir de Pierre E. Trudeau, en effet, les contextes interne et international changent. Le nouveau premier ministre cherche à asseoir la diplomatie canadienne sur des bases plus explicites. Très rapidement, il suscite un effort de réflexion sur différents aspects des relations extérieures, qui doit à son tour générer la définition de principes directeurs, dont l'utilité immédiate, sur le plan pratique, n'est pas toujours évidente, mais qui ont pour avantage de structurer la démarche diplomatique autour de quelques axes. On n'en jugera donc pas ici le mérite, mais on prendra acte de ce développement dans le système canadien de politique étrangère: la formation d'un corps de pensée plus articulée au niveau gouvernemental. C'est ainsi que naissent des principes comme celui du biculturalisme en politique étrangère, le respect des droits de la personne comme critère des relations extérieures, la primauté des intérêts internes dans la conduite des affaires étrangères, la doctrine de la «troisième option», la définition de priorités régionales, et en particulier la redécouverte de l'Europe occidentale comme l'un des piliers de la diplomatie canadienne. Ces éléments de doctrine n'innovent pas toujours. La réflexion sur les relations canado-américaines, par exemple, est précédée de l'affirmation de la *quiet diplomacy* sous Pearson, mais elle prend sous Trudeau une ampleur théorique qui conduit à une démarche permanente et s'élargit à d'autres dimensions de la politique étrangère.

L'impact de cette démarche est considérable à l'intérieur du système politique canadien. Elle force l'appareil diplomatique à plus de sophistication dans son activité courante. Elle entraîne les parlementaires à s'impliquer davantage dans la formulation de la politique étrangère, et si elle n'est pas à l'origine des progrès considérables que la discipline des relations internationales dans les universités canadiennes a connus, elle contribue à donner à l'étude des relations extérieures canadiennes une légitimité nouvelle, de même qu'elle suscite nombre de débats publics. C'est d'ailleurs pour répondre à ces besoins nouveaux que plusieurs institutions de recherche sont créées au Canada: l'Institut Nord-Sud, l'Institut canadien pour la paix et la sécurité internationales, l'Institut canadien d'études stratégiques, le Centre québécois de relations internationales, pour n'en mentionner que quelques-unes. Bref, le système canadien de politique étrangère passe à l'âge adulte, et ce n'est pas l'un des moindres acquis de cette période que d'avoir suscité l'émergence d'un corps de doctrine propre au Canada, même si des éléments importants lui font encore défaut (par exemple, une véritable pensée stratégique). Le gouvernement conservateur qui suivra pourra s'appuyer sur cette tradition et la développer (comme l'initiative du ministre Joe Clark de soumettre à la population canadienne un livre vert sur l'avenir de la politique extérieure du pays).

Une méthode, une doctrine, mais aussi des instruments de gestion, c'est-à-dire des institutions. Au cours de cette période, l'administration des affaires étrangères connaît en effet une expansion considérable. Le ministère des Affaires extérieures est encore une petite organisation en 1945, les autres ministères – sauf le ministère du Commerce et celui de la Défense –, ne portent qu'un intérêt marginal aux questions internationales, et les missions à l'étranger sont peu nombreuses. Pourtant dès cette époque, le Canada doit faire face à des défis de taille et les tâches qu'il doit assumer à l'extérieur dans tous les domaines se multiplient rapidement. Qu'il s'agisse des politiques d'immigration, de sécurité, de promotion commerciale, des programmes d'aide, de concertation économique, de coopération culturelle et scientifique, le Canada doit être présent à l'extérieur sur tous les fronts pour assurer la défense de ses intérêts. Les organisations internationales se multiplient, le nombre d'États indépendants s'accroît, les grandes négociations absorbent de plus en plus d'énergie, et les problèmes deviennent de plus en plus techniques. Il faudra donc créer des structures, dégager des ressources, engager du personnel, mettre sur pied des mécanismes de concertation interne, cela dans un domaine où le Canada a à cette époque peu d'expérience, et dans un laps de temps relativement court.

C'est là une des grandes réussites de l'administration publique canadienne. Sans ce soutien, et sans l'inventivité qu'il suppose, la politique internationale du Canada n'aurait jamais pu atteindre les objectifs qu'elle s'était fixés. En peu d'années, le Canada s'est doté d'une tradition diplomatique et d'un corps de représentants d'une qualité reconnue. Il a en outre procédé à plusieurs réformes administratives dont certaines, comme l'intégration aux affaires extérieures du commerce international, des services externes de l'immigration et de l'ACDI, constituent des solutions originales à des problèmes de coordination auxquels doivent faire face tous les gouvernements en matière de politique étrangère.

Ces réformes s'imposaient d'autant plus que c'est l'ensemble de l'administration fédérale qui a dû s'impliquer dans la gestion des affaires internationales. On pourra constater dans la quatrième partie de cet ouvrage la diversité des politiques sectorielles internationales que le Canada a développées au cours de cette période. Qu'il s'agisse de finance, d'agriculture, de pêcheries, de relations culturelles et scientifiques, de l'espace, d'immigration, d'environnement, le gouvernement canadien s'est imposé avec vigueur et compétence dans tous ces domaines. Le champ de la politique étrangère, en s'élargissant rapidement à des dimensions qui n'étaient pas que techniques, mais souvent très politiques par leurs conséquences sur le pays, posait des problèmes de gestion inusités. Le défi a été relevé plus qu'honorablement. Si l'on ajoute que les provinces n'ont pas été absentes de ce processus de gestion, et qu'elles ont elles-mêmes développé des mécanismes de plus en plus sophistiqués de participation aux affaires internationales, on ne peut être que frappé par l'ampleur des mutations que le système canadien de politique étrangère a connues au cours de cette période.

Comment conclure ce bilan général? On peut, certes, critiquer tel ou tel aspect de la politique internationale du Canada. La politique de défense n'a pas été poursuivie avec la ténacité et la cohérence qui s'imposaient. La politique d'aide n'a pas été à la hauteur des engagements moraux du Canada. La politique européenne n'a pas été administrée en fonction de son importance stratégique. Une véritable politique à l'égard de l'Amérique latine n'a pas vraiment démarré. Mais surtout, le Canada n'a pas su se doter, au cours de cette période, d'une politique arctique qui devrait occuper le premier rang dans ses priorités: les différents gouvernements qui se sont succédé à Ottawa depuis 1945 ont ici manqué de vision et de réalisme.

Quant aux États-Unis, les Canadiens en ont fait une obsession parfois malsaine. Il a fallu un certain temps – en fait pas avant les dernières années de l'ère Trudeau – pour que s'articule une approche quelque peu intégrée à ce problème qui déborde largement la politique étrangère et touche à divers aspects de la politique intérieure du pays. Les relations canado-américaines ont dominé l'horizon international des Canadiens au cours de cette période, et de ce fait elles ont souvent obscurci les possibilités d'initiative dont disposait le Canada sur la scène internationale. Mais ce problème touche à des dimensions idéologiques si profondes et à des intérêts si divers dans la vie politique canadienne qu'il appartient, en quelque sorte, à une catégorie à part dans la politique étrangère. L'approche pragmatique qui a prévalu après la guerre pour y faire face peut porter flanc à diverses critiques, mais on voit mal par quoi on pourrait la remplacer. C'est peut-être la leçon qu'en ont tiré les Canadiens après les tentatives désordonnées du régime Trudeau pour y substituer une méthode plus conflictuelle, supposément plus rationnelle, et en principe davantage inspirée par la primauté des intérêts canadiens. Les ambiguïtés et les contradictions, auxquelles ont conduit cette approche nationaliste mal pensée (par exemple l'abandon de la «troisième option», vaisseau amiral de la pensée trudeauiste en matière internationale, l'incohérence de la position canadienne dans l'Arctique, l'échec de l'Initiative de paix), démontrent que les relations canado-américaines ne se prêtent pas à des approches globalisantes et théoriques. La fin du régime Trudeau ramène donc la diplomatie canadienne au réalisme et à la lucidité.

Mais toutes ces critiques ne peuvent obscurcir le fait d'un développement assez remarquable depuis 1945. Le Canada s'est taillé une place qu'on peut considérer comme stable dans le système international. En peu de temps, il s'est équipé de méthodes de gestion et de participation à la vie internationale. Sa pensée a mûri. La politique étrangère, sans cesser d'être débattue, a cessé de diviser les Canadiens, comme elle l'avait fait avant et pendant la guerre. Mais surtout, la diplomatie canadienne a accumulé un capital politique au sein de la communauté internationale qui permet au Canada d'exercer une influence que ses moyens limités, sur le plan économique et militaire, ne lui permettraient pas autrement. C'est là le résultat d'une gestion prudente qui n'a pas interdit, à l'occasion, les initiatives audacieuses.

D'aucuns trouveront ce jugement trop optimiste. Mais si l'on salue, avec raison, la réussite de certaines entreprises, pourquoi faudrait-il s'interdire de le faire lorsqu'il s'agit d'un État? La diplomatie canadienne, certes, n'a pas gagné toutes ses batailles, elle a eu des ratés, des erreurs de tir, à l'occasion des déficiences morales et des oublis importants. À long terme, l'essentiel n'est pas là, mais dans l'architecture d'ensemble qu'elle a su créer à partir de matériaux très limités au départ.

C'est ce que cet ouvrage veut rappeler. Il nous a semblé que la période s'étendant de la fin de la guerre jusqu'au départ de Pierre E. Trudeau forme un tout assez cohérent pour en dresser un premier bilan. L'ouvrage ne cherche donc pas à couvrir les années les plus récentes de la diplomatie canadienne depuis l'arrivée au pouvoir des Conservateurs. L'entreprise serait futile car les événements ne cessent de s'accumuler et il serait impossible d'en rendre compte d'une manière satisfaisante. Il existe à cette fin des instruments d'information courante. À l'inverse, la politique actuelle repose sur des assises qui se sont progressivement développées au cours des 40 dernières années. C'est cette synthèse qu'il paraît utile de présenter. Une autre édition mettrait l'ouvrage à jour pour la période plus immédiate.

Une telle entreprise impose qu'il s'agisse d'une œuvre collective. Tout d'abord en raison de la diversité des sujets abordés qui dépassent la compétence d'un seul individu. Sur chaque question, nous voulions une mise à jour des connaissances aussi complète que possible. De plus, il importait de laisser s'exprimer à travers l'ouvrage une certaine diversité de perspectives théoriques ou idéologiques. L'ouvrage ne repose donc pas sur une grille unique d'interprétation. Il y a pour cela d'excellentes études auxquelles on peut se référer. Enfin, il nous paraissait significatif que l'entreprise soit le résultat d'une coopération à peu près égale d'universitaires anglophones et francophones. Que le défi ait pu être relevé constitue une bonne illustration de la maturité nouvelle des sciences sociales au Canada, en même temps que la confirmation de l'importance qu'a prise la réflexion collective sur la politique étrangère au Canada. Pour cette raison, cet ouvrage a été pensé et réalisé comme un projet bilingue, et nous le proposons au lecteur sous cette forme. Il s'adresse à un public pour qui, normalement, cette présentation linguistique ne devrait plus être un problème au Canada.

Enfin, si aucune démarche théorique n'a été imposée aux collaborateurs, la matière a été organisée d'une façon qui permette une vue cohérente des diverses politiques internationales du Canada. La première partie traite des fondements de la diplomatie canadienne après 1945, sujet très général qui permet de présenter une synthèse de la période, des facteurs qui la déterminent, et de son environnement institutionnel, notamment le rôle nouveau des provinces.

La deuxième partie aborde les politiques canadiennes à l'égard des systèmes globaux qui sont apparus à cette époque: les relations Est-Ouest, les relations Nord-Sud, la place du Canada dans l'économie mondiale ainsi que sa participation à l'institution universelle qu'est l'ONU. Nous y avons ajouté les politiques du Canada à l'égard du Commonwealth et de la Francophonie, non pas parce que ces deux organisations sont mondiales dans leur caractère, mais parce qu'elles transcendent l'une et l'autre les découpages régionaux et qu'on y trouve des États appartenant aux différents systèmes globaux. La multiplicité de leurs fonctions interdisaient aussi qu'on les classe avec les politiques sectorielles du Canada.

La troisième partie analyse les diverses politiques régionales internationales du Canada. Le concept de politique internationale régionale n'a jamais été déterminant dans l'élaboration de la politique étrangère canadienne. Néanmoins, l'importance croissante de la régionalisation dans les relations internationales après 1945 justifiait que la politique extérieure du Canada soit aussi considérée sous cet angle. Un tableau complet des politiques du Canada dans divers espaces géographiques internationaux aurait supposé une distribution des sujets plus diversifiée. Les contraintes d'espace ont imposé certains choix.

Enfin, un autre niveau d'analyse devait être introduit dans cette vue d'ensemble de la diplomatie canadienne après la guerre: le rôle très actif que joue le Canada dans divers domaines des relations internationales contemporaines. Ces politiques sectorielles sont sans doute la dimension la plus significative des politiques extérieures canadiennes, car c'est là où l'expérience et le savoir-faire des Canadiens pouvaient le mieux s'exprimer. La liste qui en a été faite ici n'est évidemment pas complète. On aurait pu y ajouter d'autres dimensions, comme l'environnement, les questions énergétiques, le transport aérien, etc.

La préparation de cet ouvrage a été une entreprise complexe. Je tiens ici à remercier tous les collaborateurs qui y ont participé et qui ont poursuivi la route avec nous jusqu'au bout, faisant preuve d'une patience dont je leur sais gré. Un tel projet méritait d'être terminé.

PREMIÈRE PARTIE   PART ONE

Les fondements   *The Foundations*

1

The Evolution of Canadian Diplomacy since 1945

Peyton V. Lyon
Carleton University

Canada emerged from World War II under the same party, the Liberals, and the same Prime Minister, Mackenzie King, as when it entered. But its attitude towards international involvement was radically different. Largely gone was the juvenile concern over status for its own sake, coupled with a myopic reluctance to make international commitments in times of peace. A struggle for preferred status in a number of international organizations was waged with vigour, but a major concern was not, as during the interwar period, to limit Canada's obligations. Rather it was to share fully, confidently, and responsibly in managing the common affairs of the community of nations.

For the second time Canadians had made a massive contribution in men and matériel towards winning a world war. They were willing and able to assist in the reconstruction of battle-scarred Europe. Primary responsibility for maintaining global security, they recognized, would have to rest with the major military powers. Canada, however, was now fully committed to collective security, and demanded a voice in its management. In other issue areas, notably the economic, it was more certain of its relative strength, and even less inclined meekly to accept the leadership of the great powers.

The architects of our postwar foreign policy had on their conscience the knowledge that Canada's earlier refusal to make firm commitments had helped bring about the costliest war in history. They also believed that the protectionism of the 1930s had not only been economic madness, but a major cause of war. Such beliefs were not uniquely Canadian. Similar thinking was transforming the policies of other nations, notably the once isolationist United States. In the case of the Canadian policy makers, however, the determination to improve upon past performance was exceptionally strong.

In the past, external relations had frequently imposed a severe strain on domestic cohesion; now a source of unity, especially as both English and French speaking Canadians had come to see the world in much the same light[1]. The economy was robust, and Canadians from coast-to-coast were prepared to support, or at least tolerate, a generous, outward-looking approach. The Ottawa «mandarins» of the 1940s comprised the ablest group of men ever to serve Canada in the external realm; despite the fatigue and erratic behaviour of an aging Prime Minister, the Cabinet was also unusually strong.

These factors, coupled with the temporary exhaustion of almost all the traditionally great powers, and the colonial status of most of Africa and Asia, contributed to a foreign policy remarkable both in its internationalist quality and in its impact. The postwar years became known as the «Golden Decade» in Canadian diplomacy, and not only among Canadians. Barbara Ward went so far as to speak of Canada as the first «international nation», and in 1957 its External Affairs Minister was awarded the Nobel Peace Prize. The Conservative Opposition, while critical on secondary issues, supported the broad thrust of Canadian policy. Indeed, in their brief turns in office, their chief aim was apparently to outshine the Liberals at the internationalist game. They did not succeed. International politics, in fact, became for them a considerable source of embarrassment. This was the result, however, of ministerial incompetence, and a more competitive international environment, rather than change in basic orientation.

Doubts about Canada's foreign policy, especially its close alignment with the United States, began to surface after the death of Stalin in 1953 had brought about a modest easing in Cold War tensions[2]. The doubts became a serious political factor in the mid-1960s, and even invaded the Cabinet[3], as the increasing American involvement in the morass of Vietnam aroused questioning, and even repugnance. As late as 1968, however, an in-house review requested by Prime Minister Pearson confirmed the continuing soundness of the foreign policy charted in the postwar decade[4].

Unconvinced by this review was Pearson's chosen successor, Justice Minister Pierre E. Trudeau. On becoming Liberal leader in 1968, he initiated the most intensive, and most public, inquest on foreign policy in the nation's history – perhaps in the history of any nation[5]. The outcome brought comfort neither to the Pearsonian internationalists nor to the vocal critics who had wanted to couple a drastic cut in alliance involvement with augmented activity in the Third World and the United Nations, increasingly the Third World's club. Instead, the new «Trudeau Doctrine» promised a more modest, self-interested approach; the pursuit of international roles and even influence was to be shunned; priority would be given the projection abroad of domestic interests; Canada, in future, would perform more as a nation like all the others.

Long before its demise in 1984, the Trudeau Government was acting almost as if there had been no review and no new doctrine. Although he may at times have sounded like a throwback to the isolationism of Mackenzie King, the Prime Minister acted, and even came to talk, increasingly in the internationalist tradition of St. Laurent, Pearson, Green and Martin. On his second coming to office in 1980, Trudeau embarked on a personal crusade to keep alive the flagging dialogue between the rich, industrialized North, and the poverty-ridden South. A second crusade, launched in the final months of his prime ministership, sought to revive the East-West dialogue intended to tame the nuclear arms race. Although success in either crusade seemed sadly improbable, it was no longer inconceivable that a second Canadian leader would be awarded the Nobel Prize.

*   *

*

This brief overview suggests that in Canada's post-1945 foreign policy, the elements of continuity dwarf the changes. The chapter will feature the talents and ideas of the parties, politicians and officials, but it should not be inferred that these are necessarily decisive in the determination of national policy. When first in office,

Trudeau complained that preceding governments had merely «reacted» to external events. His Government, he said, would act differently but in fact it had little success, as we shall see, in breaking free of environmental and bureaucratic determinants.

That there have been major changes since World War II cannot be questioned. Most obvious is the sheer growth in the scale and complexity of Canada's international involvement and the corresponding increase in its diplomatic establishment. Most departments of the Federal Government are now engaged, and the external activity of the provinces has become a major complication. The increase in transnational relations, especially within North America, is at least as striking as the increase in interaction between governments. The breakdown of the wartime alliance, and the spread of nuclear weapons, soon upset many of the optimistic assumptions of 1945. Despite intervals of détente, in 1985 we are no longer as confident as in the early 1970s that the Cold War is history; the arms race remains a scandalous extravagance, and deadly threat. The political emancipation of the Third World, however, and its augmenting capacity to disrupt the global economy, have transformed the bipolar simplicity of the postwar decades. Two new economic giants, Japan and West Germany, loom large, and international trade has increased enormously. It would be little short of miraculous if, in the light of such developments, Canada's foreign policy had remained unchanged. More interesting is the way which Canada's response to global change may have differed from that of other countries, and also the alteration in its external behaviour that may be attributed to changes in the action initiated by Ottawa politicians and mandarins.

*　*
*

Canada's post-1945 internationalist orientation owed nothing to the continuance in office of Mackenzie King. He had learned little, and remained apprehensive about external commitments. Although losing his remarkable capacity to control day-to-day developments, King could still retard, or even veto, as he did plans far advanced in 1947 for a free trade arrangement with the United States. He was worried about Soviet power and intransigeance however, and tolerated Canada's early advocacy of a North Atlantic alliance. While hanging onto the prime ministership until 1949, King surrendered in 1946 his second portfolio, that of Secretary of State for External Affairs, to Louis St. Laurent, an able corporation lawyer whom he had conscripted for wartime Cabinet service as his Québec lieutenant. St. Laurent, by his rapid comprehension, sterling character, and instinctive courtesy, quickly won a preeminent position in the Cabinet. He developed a particularly constructive relationship with his Deputy Minister, Lester B. Pearson, whom he subsequently lured into active politics as his successor in 1949 when he himself assumed the prime ministership. St. Laurent was more prone than Pearson to display temper; he was harsher, for example, in his reaction to the 1956 British-French-Israeli invasion of the Suez. The two men agreed on basics, however, especially in rejecting the prewar isolationism that had been particularly strong in St. Laurent's home province, and they backed one another loyally; to this teamwork should be accorded considerable credit for Canada's diplomatic success during its «golden decade».

Nor did Pearson experience difficulty working with the Ottawa mandarins from whose ranks he had sprung. His outlook had been strongly conditioned by the two world wars; having observed at close quarter the failure of the Chamberlain appeasement policy, and the catastrophic breakdown of the League of Nations' system of collective security, he believed that Canada's most elementary interest lay in strong international structures, with wholehearted Canadian participation. Energetic, imaginative, open in manner and ready with a quip, as a participant in United Nations politics, Pearson won an unrivalled fund of confidence and goodwill. He proved to be a superb tactician, and worked so closely with the United Nations Secretariat that its senior officials almost forgot that Pearson was the representative of a national government[6]. Although best known for his Suez peacekeeping initiative in 1956, the action that earned the Nobel Prize, he had earlier played a central role in establishing such specialized agencies as UNRRA and FAO. He had twice been nominated to be Secretary-General of the United Nations, only to be vetoed by the Soviet Union. Clearly there is substance in the conventional judgment that Pearson's personal commitment and talent contributed greatly to Canada's internationalist image.

But he was far from alone. Nor was he the most profound thinker within the Ottawa mandarinate. Hume Wrong earned an awesome reputation for being right about global trends and was exceptionally influential in Washington. Norman Robertson displayed comparable knowledge and a strikingly fertile imagination. Escott Reid, unusual among Ottawa mandarins for his faith in grand designs, proved extraordinarily effective as a drafter of international constitutions. Dana Wilgress was a dominant figure in the formative years of the GATT, while Wynne Plumptre and Louis Rasminsky made outstanding contributions in the founding of the IMF and World Bank[7]. This list, which could be much extended, helps explain the widely-held belief that Canada had fielded one of the world's most impressive foreign services. Indeed, in his declining years, Norman Robertson was wont to complain that Canada had concentrated too many of its «brightest and best» in international affairs, to the neglect of the threat to domestic cohesion that became fully apparent only in the 1960s.

The task of the mandarins was facilitated by the seemingly sound Canadian economy that rarely made it necessary to stress narrowly national concerns, or to seek special favours in Washington. Canada did obtain preferential treatment in placing purchase orders under the American Marshall Plan, but only because a serious payments problem had been created by its own more generous financial aid to Britain. Canada was a major contributor to many UN undertakings, to the rearming of its European allies, and to the Commonwealth's Colombo Plan for developmental assistance. Its exceptional dependence upon trade, and reluctance to become exclusively reliant upon the US market, induced it to support a liberal trading regime, and to be generous toward traditional and potential customers.

The early postwar record was good, but not perfect. Canada's attitude towards the millions of refugees seeking new homes was often restrictive, and its spokesmen too readily invoked the BNA Act as an excuse to ignore the international aspects of individual rights. Nor, in retrospect, did Ottawa pay adequate heed to the plight of inconvenient little peoples, such as the Eritreans and the Palestinians, whose claims appeared to stand in the way of the more tranquil world we so eagerly desired. The challenges of decolonization, and economic development in what became known as the «Third World», were largely unanticipated by Ottawa's postwar planners. Their faith in «collective security»[8], understandable in view of the experience of the 1930s, was soon exposed as irrelevant in the era of ideology and the bomb, and it yielded to the promotion of an old-fashioned military alliance, and UN peacekeeping.

But which other country was more enlightened or realistic? No nation exceeded Canada in devotion to the United Nations and its specialized agencies. Only when it became obvious that bipolarity and nuclear weapons were frustrating the achievement of the UN's primary purpose, collective security, did Canada resort to the expedient of a regional military alliance, NATO. It did this in part to save the UN from itself being converted into an anti-Soviet military bloc; and it continued to promote practical innovations, such as peacekeeping, to augment the utility and authority of the UN in the security realm. Samplings of foreign elite perceptions in 1975 and 1983 suggest that Canada's image as a constructive participant in world affairs is exceeded only by Sweden's, India's, and perhaps Yugoslavia's[9]. The policies that earned Canada this internationalist image were well established in the «Golden» postwar decade.

Canadian foreign policy of the period was often explained, and to a degree inspired, by the theory of «functionalism». This prescribes that the road to peace should begin with a concentration on the economic and social issues closest to the common man, and least encumbered by national sovereignty and pride; grand designs for overarching world Government are to be avoided, and progress is envisaged as a series of modest, pragmatic steps from existing reality; as the need for cooperation in specific fields becomes apparent, as in the control of transborder airlines, old institutions should be adapted or new ones created. Function should dictate form. A profusion of flexible, overlapping organizations, with varied rules and memberships, should be fostered as the most sensible way to meet evolving human needs, and also to erode the dangerous monopoly of the nation state without recreating the «state writ large» on a regional scale[10]. The functionalist emphasis on workability and adaptation reinforced Canada's instinctive pragmatism. Its functionalism was displayed in many ways, but never more usefully than when improvising UN peacekeeping after the Korean War had exposed collective security as a chimera.

The theory of functionalism was invoked most prominently to strengthen Canada's bid for an international status superior to that of the multitude of small states. It would only be functional, the Canadians argued, if duties and rights were assigned in accordance with a state's willingness and capacity to serve in specific international undertakings, and this might well vary greatly in different issue areas. Since the major military powers could not be denied primary responsibility for global security, they had to be conceded permanent membership on the Security Council, and even the use of the veto. However, it would be unnecessary and inappropriate to extend the veto beyond the strict needs of the security function, or to permit the Security Council to behave as a global executive for any purpose except security. It also followed that the major military powers would not necessarily be those with the requisite characteristics for an executive role in other issue areas. The Canadians were thus able to employ functionalist theory to combat the pretensions of the major powers, and advance Canada's claims to status, without becoming as unrealistic as other non-great powers, for example Australia[11].

Having contributed substantially to the military victory over the Axis powers, and being willing to support collective security measures, the Canadians claimed semi-permanent membership on the Security Council; they were even more assertive in the specialized agencies. They failed to obtain formal acceptance of their claims and lost out to Australia in the first election to the Security Council. Since then, however, they have served once a decade on the Council, and were elected to a considerable number of other positions on executive bodies. Even after the UN expanded to include the host of Third World nations, a development for which Canada bears primary responsibility[12], it often filled influential roles, such as Chairman of informal drafting committees. Rather than a formal recognition of the functionalist creed, however, this was generally a tribute to the personal qualities of the Canadian representatives, coupled with Canada's inoffensive international image.

Subsequently, Canada's international activity came to be articulated in terms of «middle-powership», especially when it emerged in the mid-1950s as the UN's most innovative and reliable peacekeeper. Often «middle power» is used to refer simply to the structural characteristics of being somewhere between the major and minor powers in terms of strength; geographically located between contending forces; or ideologically moderate. Canada, despite its «western» culture and commitment, qualified as a middle power by all three tests.

The term came to have important behavioural implications. To be a «middle power» meant that the state should assume a «middle-power» role in the international system. Typically this role consisted of bridge-building, mediating, moderating or peacekeeping. The link between the structural and behavioural definitions is that while minor powers lack the requisite diplomatic and military resources to play the role, major powers are generally disqualified because their very strength arouses apprehension[13]. Canadians came to view their country as the prototype «middle power», and there may be a little truth in Trudeau's complaint that the impulse to play roles had become excessive in the determination of Canada's external policies.

Although the notion of Canada as a bridge between London and Washington has often been exaggerated, Canadians did assist in maintaining a constructive dialogue between the Americans and the British during the difficult adjustments to the post-1945 world. A bridge-building role between East and West never seemed as feasible and the possibilities in the North-South dialogue are also limited. Canadians have rarely served, despite Trudeau's energetic attempt in 1983-1984, in a formal mediatory capacity, but informally they have worked hard at the role in a multitude of international contexts, a fact widely appreciated by foreign diplomats. Belief that mediation is a major Canadian responsibility, one arising out of its middle-power status, helped account for the carefully bland tone of many of its public pronouncements.

Of greater significance was the Canadian policy elite's conviction that Canada serves everybody's interest by playing the role of moderator, especially within the western camp. The purest example was Canada's persistent attempt, during the Korean War, to persuade the Americans to implement their essential leadership responsibilities in a manner consistent with the authority of the United Nations and the avoidance of all-out war with China and the Soviet Union[14]. Pearson exhausted much of the goodwill he had enjoyed in Washington, and it is difficult to prove that the selfless Canadian diplomacy made a significant difference. The experience, however, did much to intensify the Canadian elite's conviction that as moderators of US behaviour, they were performing a service vital to mankind. The role was played in a variety of other contexts, and not always directed towards the Americans; Canadians, for example, tried to moderate British and French behaviour in the Middle East, and were the first allies to encourage the West Germans to abandon their rigid, legalistic approach to their eastern neighbours[15]. In order to maximize Canada's capacity to moderate, Canadian diplomats found it essential to convice their allies of their basic loyalty. This in turn emphasized the importance of quiet diplomacy and a substantial military contribution to western defence.

Peacekeeping became the middle-power role that most engaged Canadian enthusiasm. (This is the interposition between contending forces of lightly armed troops from a number of countries not engaged in the dispute.) Canadian involvement in the Arab-Israel conflict had begun long before the Suez Crisis of 1956, and was never as disinterested or enlightened as most Canadian imagine[16]; the successors to Mackenzie King displayed a decidedly pro-Israel bias, Pearson's role in defusing the Suez Crisis was nevertheless criticized by many Canadians who would have preferred wholehearted support for the British, French and Israeli aggressors. International acclaim symbolized by the Nobel Prize, altered Canadian attitudes and expectations, and there was little opposition to subsequent peacekeeping operations. Most of these, notably those in Cyprus and the Congo, owed much not only to Canada's highly skilled professional soldiers but also to its innovative UN diplomacy in improvising the conditions under which each would operate. Opinions differ as to the utility of the peacekeeping function, but not concerning Canada's claim to have become the UN's most reliable practitioner.

Another Canadian propensity, already noted, was the promotion of new institutional structures. This did not extend, however, to Canada's two closest bilateral relationships, those with the United States and the United Kingdom. Despite the continuing success of the International Joint Commission in dealing with water related problems along the Canada-US border, and the huge increase in continental interdependence, Canadians remained apprehensive about formal institutions that must – or so it seemed – be dominated by the superpower member. Almost all the wartime bilateral committees were disbanded, and few new ones were installed in their place. The two Cabinet level committees established to discuss defence and economic issues have long ceased to meet. Although most Canadians appeared to agree with the economists that free trade with the Americans would be good for their standard of living, the irrational fear that it would lead to formal political integration proved to be even more persuasive[17].

By most material tests, especially trade, Britain and Canada had become far less relevant to one another. Relations remained intimate, however. As the two became more equal in power, old complexes faded. The style of Canadian diplomacy still revealed its British origins, and Ottawa long relied on London for information about much of the world; but British assessments were not accepted uncritically, and Ottawa led the Opposition to proposals to tighten the Commonwealth organization and give it a single voice. On the other hand, Canadians promoted close informal consultation and practical innovations, such as the Colombo Plan for cooperation in economic development. Canadian leaders suggested the formula that enabled India, and most of the other ex-colonies, to remain within the Commonwealth – and another formula that persuaded South Africa to depart. A Canadian, Arnold Smith, became the first Secretary-General of the Commonwealth Secretariat. Canada thus became the principal architect of the new Commonwealth that, although now virtually devoid of military or economic significance, is one of the very few organizations fostering intimate consultation and collaboration between nations of varied races, continents and levels of development. In the 1970s, Canada came to play a leading role in the formation of L'Agence de coopération culturelle et technique, in some ways the francophone equivalent of the Commonwealth, and another Canadian, Jean-Marc Léger, served as its first Secretary-General.

On one point London and Ottawa agreed totally: the bilateral relations that each maintain with Washington had to be given first priority. Sentiment could not obscure the hard fact that the United States now mattered most to their defence and also their economic well-being; Britain, because of its war-wrought exhaustion, was the more dependent in this respect. Both also concurred that a repetition of the American retreat into isolation must be avoided; active, responsible American leadership had become essential to the health of the international system.

The United States appeared even more vital as the growing rift with the Soviet Union exposed the inadequacy of the United Nations as a security mechanism. It was quickly obvious that the United States was not going to ignore the Soviet challenge, but prominent Americans urged measures, such as a unilateral extension of the Monroe Doctrine to Western Europe, that were palatable to neither Britain nor to Canada. The Canadians recognized that they could hardly escape close military collaboration with the United States, but preferred that it occur within a multi-nation alliance; this would reduce the risk of total domination by the Western champion, and improve Canada's capacity to moderate American policies by mustering support among the other allies.

In 1947, St. Laurent, then Secretary of State for External Affairs, became the first western leader publicly to propose a regional alliance, and Canadian spokesmen subsequently «crusaded» for the North Atlantic Treaty that established NATO[18]. It was London, however, that proposed to Washington and Ottawa the secret trilateral talks that first deliberated the treaty subsequently negotiated with nine other European governments. The Canadian negotiators strove, with some success, for the strongest possible American commitment. A clearer Canadian achievement, but one that subsequently caused embarrassment, was the insertion of Article 2, the «Canadian article», in the face of strong American opposition and European indifferences; by committing the allies to foster economic cooperation and democratic values, this article sought to ensure that NATO would be more than a mere military alliance. So it is, but economic collaboration among the allies rarely occurs within the NATO forum and, for most of its history, one or two military dictatorships were numbered among its members. Canadian critics of NATO frequently cite the failure of Article 2 to live up to its full promise as an excuse to leave the alliance.

NATO's greatest achievement has been in the realm of political consultation, and for this Canada deserves considerable credit. The occasional failure, as in dealing with the Soviet invasion of Afghanistan, has always received more publicity than the routine observance of consultative practices unprecedented in history, and found in no other contemporary group of sovereign powers. The systematic exchange of information and views on critical East-West issues often results in common policies; even when it fails, confidence between the allies, and the ability to act together in an emergency, is fostered by discussions in advance of initiatives that could affect the interests of the others. Pearson is acknowledged to have been the principal author of the «Three Wise Mens'» report of 1956 that remains the definitive statement of the «club» rules regarding consultation, and many other Canadians have laboured to make the system work. Whatever one's sentiments about alliances, NATO must be ranked high among Canada's achievements in the role of community builder.

Initially it was not anticipated that membership would entail more than a Canadian commitment to assist in the defence of any ally under attack. With the outbreak in 1949 of the Korean War, however, rearmament was greatly accelerated and the decision taken to underscore the Canadian guarantee by stationing in Europe 10 000 fighting men, half in the form of an army brigade based with the British Army of the Rhine, and the other an air force division located in Southern Germany and France. Although modest in number, the contribution was appreciated as a means to counter the image of NATO as dependent upon just one non-European power. From Ottawa's perspective, Canada's purpose was always more political than military. In the early years, however, the Canadian air division comprised a major part of the fighter aircraft in Europe and the high quality of Canada's soldiers, the most professional in the alliance, frequently set NATO standards. They certainly augmented the persuasiveness of the Canadian voice in NATO diplomacy.

That voice, along with the Scandinavians', was the voice of moderation. Canadians consistent urged military caution and diplomatic imagination. They argued, for example, that a Polish plan for disengagement in the heart of Europe be seriously considered, and that every effort be made to negotiate viable measures of disarmament and arms control. NATO is frequently portrayed as a means by which American views are imposed upon its allies. For the Canadians, it was seen rather as a useful channel through which to insert Canadian common sense into the Washington decision-making process. Many Americans, notably in the State Department, held views similar to those of Ottawa mandarins; others advocated a simplistic, muscular approach that seemed almost as likely to cause world war as the presumed designs of the men in the Kremlin. In Washington, the Canadians often allied with the sensible elements against the «wild men» in Congress and the Administration; their tactics in NATO were essentially similar, and they could generally count on the support of at least some of their allies. No Government allows itself to be bound by a NATO consensus. But neither can Governments fail to be influenced by the frank discussion of the «destiny» agenda that occurs around the NATO table.

* *
*

Canada's international prestige was never higher when, in 1957, the St. Laurent Government was toppled at the polls by the Progressive Conservatives under John Diefenbaker. Foreign policy, however, had not loomed large in the campaign and there was little reason to anticipate a significant change in orientation. Nor did one occur. The biggest differences were in style, skill and accomplishment.

Canada's sudden prominence on the global stage in 1956 had fostered the demand within the country for Canadian leadership. From undue modesty in its expectations, the public had become excessively demanding. The new Cabinet was eager to oblige. Unfortunately, with the recovery of the war-torn nations of Europe, and the emergence of a host of newly independent Third World countries, Canada's opportunity to play an influential role had sharply declined. Moreover, the diplomatic skills of the Diefenbaker Cabinet, as well as its experience, were decidedly inferior to those of the St. Laurent team. Rising public demand, coupled with diminishing opportunity and talent, resulted in a tendency to substitute posture for policy, to stress appearance at the expense of more substantial interests. The sound precepts of quiet diplomacy were often ignored in order to demonstrate the initiative, independence and influence of the new Government.

Prime Minister Diefenbaker's interest in external affairs was not new. He had served as Opposition critic in the field and, with some justification, he claimed authorship of the proposal for a Middle East peacekeeping force. As a staunch anti-communist, he took even greater pride in his fiery denunciation of Soviet imperialism from the UN rostrum in 1960. In the Conservative tradition, he was an ardent supporter of the Monarchy and Commonwealth, and was determined to keep the British despite their increasingly serious flirtation with Europe. Notwithstanding his patriotic rhetoric, Diefenbaker's denial that he was anti-American had substance. Indeed, he acceded too quickly to a number of Washington requests, such as the one in 1957 for a hasty signature of the NORAD Agreement, and the adoption of a nuclear strike role for our air squandrons in Europe. He did advocate a 15 % shift in Canada's trade from the United States to Britain, but rejected out-of-hand London's bluff-calling proposal of a free trade arrangement. And the trade shift that occurred during his tenure was *from* the UK *to* the US.

For four of his six years in office, Diefenbaker's foreign policy was generally sensible, confident and consistent with both his own long held views and well established Canadian positions. The performance of the final two years, by contrast, was erratic, hesitant and self-destructive. Diefenbaker's problem was Pearson. Although he had trounced the Liberal leader in the House and on the hustings, he was often reminded that the world regarded Pearson as a statesman and Diefenbaker as a backwoods politician. The resultant complex was intensified when Pearson's Nobel Prize dominated the headlines on the very day Diefenbaker had persuaded the Queen to open her Canadian Parliament. It became acute when he learned that President Kennedy considered him a bore.

Diefenbaker related uncomfortably with most foreign leaders, and he made no effort to conceal his suspicion of the Ottawa mandarins whom he had inherited from the Liberals. His first External Affairs Minister, Sidney Smith, commanded considerable respect in the academic world but had little political experience or confidence. His views inclined to be activist, notably in seeking to moderate the Cold War, but timidity in standing up to the Prime Minister severely limited his influence.

Very different was Howard Green, Smith's successor. A homespun manner, and simplistic approach, rendered him one of the least probable of foreign ministers. He was confident of Diefenbaker's friendship, however, of his own standing in the party, and of the support of the civil servants. Within weeks he had abandoned a life-long unquestioning acceptance of British leadership, and soon emerged as the boldest and most dedicated advocate of disarmament within the NATO community. He frequently embarrassed his officials, and exasperated his fellow foreign ministers, but his commitment to peace was admirable. He was warmly encouraged, moreover, by some of the most thoughtful Ottawa mandarins, notably Norman Robertson and E.L.M. Burns. Green appears to have exercised little influence in UN and NATO circles. As Diefenbaker's resentment of Kennedy mounted, however, he became increasingly receptive to his foreign Minister's apprehension about the nuclear policies of the US-led alliance. Green's principal antagonist was Defence Minister Douglas Harkness, another man of conviction and political courage. His perception of the Soviet military threat was close to Diefenbaker's, but he was never an intimate. His stock declined as Green's ascended.

The first Diefenbaker years passed without major upset. Professional diplomats deplored his anti-communist rhetoric as inconsistent with Canada's moderator image and also Green's crusade to disarm the world, but it went down well with the electorate, especially the part that was of East European extraction. Diefenbaker's anti-communism did not stand in the way of large, popular, grain sales to China

—under a regime that Canada refused to recognize. Diefenbaker's role in precipitating South Africa's departure from the Commonwealth was widely applauded[19]. London resented his efforts to impede its negotiation for membership in the European Community, but many in both Canada and Britain welcomed his resistance as evidence of loyalty to the British connection.

Diefenbaker claims to have enjoyed his encounters with world leaders such as Eisenhower, de Gaulle, Adenauer and Macmillan. His first visit with President Kennedy he also reported to have gone well. The return meeting in Ottawa, however, was quite another story. Kennedy seemed more interested in hearing Pearson's views, and he carelessly left behind a confidential briefing paper that, according to Diefenbaker, proved he had come to Ottawa «to push Canada around». A year later, incensed by Kennedy's well reported attention to Pearson at a White House dinner for recipients of the Nobel Prize, Diefenbaker threatened to publish the paper. Kennedy coldly rejected this attempt at what he called «blackmail», and Diefenbaker backed down. Relations between Ottawa and Washington approached their historic nadir, and Diefenbaker's behaviour during his remaining year in office bordered on the bizarre. His appalling hesitancy during the Cuban Missile crisis of October 1962 was in sharp contrast to his prompt, firm, response a year earlier during a crisis over Berlin, and the hesitancy seems largely attributable to his resentment of Kennedy. After several days he did authorize an advanced state of military alert, but only when it had become obvious that this was demanded by a large majority in caucus, the media, and the country. It was too late to erase the shock in Washington that, at the moment of supreme Cold War crisis, the weakest support had come from the Government of the country supposed to be the United States' closest ally. Even neutral countries had been more cooperative.

Tension had already been built up over Diefenbaker's reluctance to accept warheads for the four nuclear weapons systems his Government had readily accepted several years earlier. These were now largely installed, two in Canada and two with the forces in Europe. The delay did not constitute a major threat to western security, but Diefenbaker's misleading explanation for the delay angered Washington and NATO headquarters. The State Department took the unprecedented step of issuing a press release bluntly challenging his veracity. Ottawa pundits at once concluded that Washington had rescued Diefenbaker by providing him an issue on which he could call and win an election. The State Department's crude intervention did trigger three resignations from the Cabinet, the defeat of the Government in the House, and a general election. As expected, Diefenbaker exploited the issue to the full and, aided by large Créditiste gains in Québec, he managed to keep the Liberals from winning an overall majority. To the extent that the nuclear issue influenced the outcome, however, the principal benefactors appeared to have been the Liberals whose leader, Lester B. Pearson, had shortly before abandoned his opposition to the acquisition of the warheads.

Did this mean that Washington had successfully manipulated the outcome of a Canadian election? Although this is widely believed, there is no evidence that Pearson and Kennedy had struck a deal, or that Washington intervened on Pearson's behalf during the campaign. Had Diefenbaker appeared to be in control of his Government, and had the Americans not had the better of the nuclear argument, the outcome might well have been different[20].

This is not to say that Washington, and indeed the other NATO allies, were anything but pleased with the Liberal victory. Diefenbaker's uncharacteristic softness on the nuclear issue, and during the Missile crisis, had dismayed them all. On becoming Prime Minister in 1963, Pearson quietly armed the weapons because he believed that Canada was committed to do so, but he promised to revert to a purely conventional role as soon as this became feasible[21]. His action produced none of the adverse international consequences predicted by his critics. Indeed, by permitting the weapons to be fused, he had defused the issue. The ugliest controversy in the history of Canada-US relations was shown to have been the least necessary. Had Diefenbaker performed as he had up to his humiliating clash with Kennedy, or after his defeat at the polls[22], the controversy would have never arisen.

A major event in Canada's external relations is thus only explicable in terms of the idiosyncratic behaviour of a highly idiosyncratic individual. Personality in this case clearly mattered. On the other hand, the long-term significance of the controversy was probably exaggerated, by this author and many others. The Diefenbaker Government was already heading for an early defeat. Most of the damage done to Canada's relations with its allies was speedily and easily repaired by the Pearson Government. Moreover, even during the worst of the controversy, much of the extensive interaction between Ottawa and Washington continued unaffected. Gordon Churchill, who replaced Harkness as Defence Minister, maintains that the Canadian forces in Europe had in fact already been assured access to nuclear warheads, while Harkness has revealed that, from the very start of the Missile crisis, the Canadian forces had quietly implemented virtually all the emergency measures that the Prime Minister had refused to authorize. Diefenbaker's behaviour had soured the atmospherics but the substance of the continental relationship had been spared.

We shall never know what might have developed had Diefenbaker survived the 1963 election. Good old Pearson was back, and for a while it seemed just like the good old days. The welcome accorded Pearson by allied leaders, and also by the Ottawa mandarins, bordered on impropriety. He quickly embarked on a series of fence-mending visits. In London, he assured the British that Ottawa would cease resisting their bid to joint the European Community. During an exceptionally congenial visit to Hyannisport, Pearson informed Kennedy that Canada would honour its nuclear commitments, and the two leaders commissioned a study of the Canadian-American relationship by two former ambassadors. Not surprisingly, they came out in favour of «quiet diplomacy»[23].

Pearson had become deeply disturbed by the growing rift between English and French-speaking Canada. He recognized that a contributing cause had been the neglect of the «French fact» in Canada's external relations. In Paris, he assured de Gaulle that henceforth Canada would accord its other Motherland equal treatment with Britain. He was rewarded by a toast to Canada's «federal» state, but there had in fact been little meeting of minds. Perhaps it had been unreasonable to expect rapport between one of the world's most ardent internationalists and its staunchest champion of national sovereignty. Pearson, moreover, although representing in Parliament the constituency hardest hit by the prevailing slump in the demand for nuclear fuel, was obliged to deny France terms comparable to those conceded in Britain and the United States before Canada had become a leading advocate of nuclear safeguards. De Gaulle was soon rolling out the red carpet for Québec ministers and fostering the separatist movement. His historic shout of «Vive le Québec libre» in 1967 nevertheless came as a rude shock. Pearson earned applause, mostly among English-speaking Canadians, for his firm rebuke to the French President, and the Government intensified its efforts to cultivate ties with the other countries of the Francophonie in order to demonstrate that the «French fact» really did matter in Canada's foreign policy. The incident, however, dramatically underlined one of Pearson's two great failures in international diplomacy.

The second involved another President, Lyndon Johnson of the United States. During the post-Hyannisport euphoria, Pearson permitted Finance Minister Walter Gordon to introduce a budget containing restrictions on US investment. An instant fiasco, it was quickly redrafted to meet massive criticism from within Canada as well as the United States. Washington had nevertheless been reminded that not all of its problems with Canada had originated with John Diefenbaker. Kennedy, had he lived, might still have continued to communicate easily with Pearson, and also have escaped earlier from the tragic overinvolvement in Vietnam.

His successor, however, was a Southerner with little feel for Canada, or indeed most other foreign countries, and he became increasingly intolerant of criticism, especially of his conduct of the war in Indochina. Initially, President Johnson seemed friendly to Canada. He was effusive in his gratitude for Canada's role in initiating the UN peacekeeping operation in 1964 that headed off imminent war over Cyprus between two NATO allies, and he helped complete the Auto Pact of 1965 that facilitated a rapid growth in the Canadian industry[24].

Johnson's crudity of manner, however, and even more his simplistic approach to global issues, disturbed Pearson. For his part, the President came to dislike his northern counterpart. He saw through Pearson's genial attempts to win his confidence in order to change American foreign policy. He was outraged when Pearson, violating his own precepts of quiet diplomacy, recommended from an American rostrum the suspension of the bombing of North Vietnam. External Affairs Minister Paul Martin related better to Johnson, and laboured hard to moderate the US tactics, and also to mediate between Washington and Hanoi. His efforts, however, were equally vain. Johnson and his entourage treated peace-makers with contempt, and even misused Canadian reports to justify continued reliance on force[25].

Involvement in the Korean War had strengthened the conviction of the Canadian elite that they served mankind, as well as Canada, by exploiting their special relationship with the Western superpower. Other events, such as Suez, had further inflated the conceit that Canada played a vital role in the international system. The Canadians had undertaken in 1954 peace supervisory duties in Indochina with reluctance, but were confident their influence would again be on the side of sanity. By the mid-1960s, however, the involvement was proving as destructive of their moderating vocation as Korea had been inflationary. Not only was it costly in popular support for Canada's policies but divisive within the ranks of the Ottawa mandarins; virtually all the hundreds of Canadians to serve on one of the three control commissions in Indochina became more sympathetic to the American intervention, and more hostile to the North Vietnamese, than their home-based colleagues. A decade later, Hanoi's brutal treatment of its own minorities, and its expansion in Laos and Cambodia, helped restore consensus within the Department of External Affairs. From the mid-1960s until the 1972 American decision to withdraw, however, Vietnam not only imposed a severe strain on Ottawa relations with Washington but sapped the Canadian self-image of being an objective and useful member of the international community. Many were thus disposed to welcome the Trudeau decision of 1968 to conduct a searching review of Canada's foreign policy.

Pearson was more effective in Commonwealth meetings where he helped defuse African impatience with Britain's failure to discipline, or replace, the white minority regime in Rhodesia. Especially congenial was the role of host during Canada's joyful Centennial to a stream of foreign dignitaries. The nation's greatest internationalist took particular satisfaction in giving Canadians their own flag; Pearson could see no conflict in being both a good Canadian and a good citizen of the world. Indeed, he recognized that Canadians were likely to be effective in the world only if they were confident of their own national identity.

Domestic preoccupations limited Pearson's external role. Negotiating with the increasingly assertive provinces was exhausting; his diplomatic conditioning made it difficult for him ever to say «enough», «never», or «no». Several political scandals weakened his reputation; the Munsinger case, which had embarrassed Diefenbaker, in the end hurt Pearson even more[26]. Pearson left the conduct of External Affairs very largely to Paul Martin, a friend of many years who shared his internationalist philosophy and belief in quiet diplomacy. Martin coped well with several tough issues, such as the renegotiation with Washington of the Columbia River Treaty, and setting up the UN peacekeeping force for Cyprus. The failure of his Vietnam initiatives, however, and his characteristic circumlocution, fostered the mounting skepticism about Canadian foreign policy in both country and Cabinet. Even Pearson complained privately that his Minister's approach was passé.

One whose doubts grew as he listened to Martin was Pierre E. Trudeau. Before entering public life in 1965, he had travelled extensively. While fascinated by foreign societies, however, he seemed uninterested in the relations between Governments. He had not considered World War II to be his concern, or Canada's, and although dogmatically anti-nationalist, he had not become an internationalist[27]. The most scathing attack on Pearson's decision to accept nuclear warheads had come from Trudeau's pen[28], and he found it difficult to believe in the existence of a Soviet military threat to Canada. He had entered the Liberal Party, and active politics, to save Canada's federal structure. Foreign policy was at best a minor concern. His resolve to alter Canada's orientation in global affairs probably evolved while he served as a bored delegate to the UN General Assembly in 1965; listened to Martin in Cabinet; and took counsel from a number of skeptical mandarins, notably Michael Pitfield and Allan Gotlieb. Apart from a promise to conduct a review, little was said about foreign policy during Trudeau's first campaign as Party Leader in 1968. While the review was on, his own statements were frequently contradictory, and he encouraged his ministers to articulate opposing positions in public, notably on NATO.

For years Trudeau had displayed impatience to recognize the Beijing Governement as the rightful Government of China. Once he was in office, the Department of External Affairs lost no time in initiating the appropriate negotiations. Fortuitously the timing was right, and Canada was able to lead the second wave of recognitions that brought the real China back to international society.

Trudeau early complained that defence policy was dominating foreign policy, and he promised to reverse this situation. Well before the conclusion of his review, however, the Government was obliged to take a stand on the major bone of current contention, membership in NATO. Trudeau wanted Canada to withdraw, or at least repatriate, its 10 000 troops based in Europe. Resistance to this course in the country, reflected both in caucus and Cabinet, forced a draw; Canada remained in the alliance but ostentatiously cut its European contingent in half, removed it from the front line, and dispensed with its nuclear weapons[29]. Defence priorities, Trudeau explained, were being reversed: henceforth the defence of national sovereignty would come first, followed by defence of the continent, the North Atlantic region and, finally, a contribution to global security. Superficially logical, these priorities overlooked the fact that the only serious security threat to Canada stems from instability in the international system. Although the reversal of priorities was fortunately watered down in the implementation, Canada's overall military strength, and influence in alliance diplomacy, were sharply reduced.

The full «Trudeau Doctrine», the result of the review, emerged a year later. This stressed the national interest and implied that «economic growth» would take precedence over «social justice», «peace and security» and even «sovereignty and independence». That the national interest would in fact take precedence over a more equitable distribution of global resources, and also Canada's traditional support of international law, seemed to be confirmed by the Government's aggressive and remarkably successful, diplomacy in the negotiation of a new regime for the oceans[30]. In most other ways, however, Trudeau's actions belied the hard-boiled, national interest thrust of his Doctrine. He emerged as one of the most eloquent champions of the underdeveloped Third World, and Canada's development assistance increased significantly during most of his tenure. His Government's response to the more significant demands of the developing countries, such as the removal of barriers to their exports, was far less generous but, especially after returning to office in 1980, Trudeau's energetic promotion of the North-South dialogue, especially at the annual Western summits, removed any doubt about his personal commitment to a more equitable international system. It received international recognition in 1981 when he was invited to serve as co-chairman of the first, and possibly last, North-South summit at Cancun, Mexico.

More surprising had been his earlier change of attitude towards NATO. Having taken part in its Council in 1974, and a Heads of Government meeting in 1975, he became for a time the most ardent advocate of alliance summitry. The withdrawn Canadian troops were not replaced, but Trudeau authorized a significant increase in defence spending and the re-equipment of the NATO contingent with a modern German tank. His delighted officials nevertheless maintained a modest posture in most NATO deliberations, including the disarmament talks with the Soviet bloc. In the Conference on Security and Cooperation in Europe (CSCE), especially in the actual drafting of the Helsinki Final Act, the Canadian delegation, disregarding Canada's «moderator» tradition, emerged as one of the toughest in pressing for Soviet concessions. Canada's standing in the alliance was substantially restored, and Trudeau, the *enfant terrible* of 1969, had become a respected elder statesman.

Had he changed his mind about the Soviet military threat? Probably not. The first speech to the United Nations that he was persuaded to deliver was to the 1978 Special Assembly on Disarmament (UNSSOD I), and it took the form of a cogent appeal to «suffocate» the nuclear arms race[31]. In 1981, he incurred widespread criticism for suggesting that military rule in Poland might well be preferable to civil war or Soviet occupation. His personal inclination was clearly that Canada resume its moderator role in East-West relations, an inclination strengthened by the adoption by the new Reagan administration of a hard-line posture towards the Soviet bloc.

Trudeau's commitment and concern became fully apparent in the dramatic personal crusade that occupied much of his time and energy during his final months in office. This was a valiant but vain attempt to invigorate the East-West negotiations on arms control, and entailed visits to Washington, London, Paris, Beijing, Prague, East Berlin, and Bucharest; Moscow had to be excluded because of Premier Andropov's illness. No one can doubt Trudeau's seriousness of purpose, and the peace mission, especially when considered along with his earlier contribution to the North-South dialogue, qualified him as a front runner for the Nobel Prize.

One might still wonder, however, if the slight prospect of the mission's success might not have been a degree greater if Trudeau had not initiated his term in office by offending Canada's allies, and his own diplomatic service, by appearing to repudiate so much of our post-1945 internationalism? His early national-interest doctrine did less than justice to his own global commitment. It also diminished the contribution that an internationalist foreign policy might make to domestic cohesion. Pride in Canada's active internationalism has at times been a source of national unity. It could be again. Trudeau did learn, but too late to be fully effective.

The principal reason for Canada's improved military contribution to NATO, and also the moderating of its moderator role, had been the traditional quest for counterweight in Canada's relations with the United States; to strengthen ties with Western Europe, still the most obvious source of this counterweight, it appeared imperative that Canada demonstrate anew its commitment to European defence. The disadvantages of dependence upon the United States had been brought home by the traumatic shock of the Nixon-Connally economic offensive of August 1971. The measures, directed at all the trading partners of the United States, were especially disturbing to Canada, the country with the largest share of US trade; even more jolting was Washington's unprecedented refusal to consider exemptions for Canada. Many in the Ottawa establishment who had previously been relaxed about the high level of continental integration, were obliged to face up to the fragility of the cherished «special relationship». External Affairs Minister Mitchell Sharp, for long an opponent of economic nationalism, became in 1972 the author of the «Third Option», an approach intended to diminish Canada's vulnerability to changes in US policies and societal conditions. This called for the restructuring of Canadian industry, something that was never seriously attempted, but was more widely interpreted as a pro-gramme for increased economic ties with other regions, notably Western Europe.

Overcoming his initial boredom with Western Europe, Trudeau travelled extensively to support the energetic campaign that in 1975 resulted in the Framework Agreement (or «Contractual Link») with the European Community. The desired in-crease in economic relations failed to occur. Increase in trade to the Pacific rim, notably Japan, was far more impressive, even if largely confined to raw materials. Overall trade statistics, however, and the outcome of the Tokyo round of GATT negotiations, confirmed that Canada would remain largely dependent upon the American market.

The Foreign Investment Review Agency (FIRA), set up in 1974, invoked a good deal of American criticism, and even more European, but appeared to have little impact upon capital flows. More serious was the Government's national energy policy, introduced in 1980. Its provisions to foster Canadian ownership were attacked on the grounds that they retroactively changed the rules under which foreigners had been encouraged to invest. During the 1980 election campaign, and for some months following, it seemed that the Government had embarked on a course of economic nationalism. By 1981, however, the relatively benign administrations of Gerald Ford and Jimmy Carter had been replaced by the muscular Reagan regime, and Congress became quick to retaliate against Canadian innovations. Faced with high unemployment and inflation, Ottawa deemed it wise to postpone indefinitely the steps to strengthen FIRA, and promised that the principles underlying the national energy policy would not be extended to other industries. The Liberals continued to be somewhat more nationalistic in their economic orientation than the Conservatives (a striking reversal of the historic positions of the two parties) and the sweeping restructuring of the Department of External Affairs in early 1982, especially its merger with the trade component of the defunct Department of Trade and Commerce, implied renewed resolve to increase and diversifty Canadian trade. Despite this, prospects for a reduction in economic dependence upon the United States seemed little better than at the beginning of the Trudeau era. When the Foreign Affairs Committee of the Canadian Senate recommended in 1982 the negotiation of a free trade compact with Washington, its report was received with surprising warmth by a substantial portion of the business elite. Although the proposal was quickly dismissed by Trudeau and his External Affairs Minister, Mark MacGuigan, senior officials opined that continental free trade was in fact approaching through the multilateral negotiation in the GATT and bilateral efforts to limit the increasingly salient non-tariff barriers.

Across the board, Canada's external policies in 1984 were closer to those inherited from Pearson than had seemed possible during the heady days of the Trudeau foreign policy review. Canada was no less reactive to external developments, such as the acceleration in the arms race and the retreat from detente marked by the Soviet intervention in Afghanistan. The few changes in Canadian policy that had become apparent are more easily explained as a response to the changing international environment than as the result of the pretentious policy planning of the early Trudeau years. The increase in the scale, complexity and salience of international interaction was matched by growth in Canada's diplomatic establishment. On the other hand, after more than a decade of structural innovations that often diverted attention from the substance of policy, the expansion of External Affairs to embrace the trade-promotion function presaged a further period of administrative turmoil and low morale. Partly because of his personal commitment to arms control and the North-South dialogue, and even more because of the longevity of his regime, Pierre E. Trudeau had emerged as a widely admired statesman. The historian, however, is likely to conclude that his impact upon international events, or even upon Canadian foreign policy, was relatively slight.

*   *

*

The nine-month Conservative interlude in 1980 was too brief to indicate the major differences, if any, between the foreign policies of the two major parties. The Clark Government seemed more concerned than the Liberals to keep in step with NATO and the United States, and less disposed to assist the developing nations of the Third World. These were matters of emphasis, however, rather than basic orientation. Joe Clark initiated his Prime Ministership with one of the most egregious gaffes in the history of Canada's external relations. During the election campaign, he attempted to gain Jewish votes by promising to transfer Canada's embassy in Israel from Tel Aviv to Jerusalem. The Arab world was outraged, and most Canadians appeared critical. It was opposition from Canadian business circles, however, that persuaded Clark to effect a humiliating retreat. Subsequently, the Ottawa mandarins found Clark to be intelligent and responsive. The media had conditioned the public to consider the mere absence of fiasco a success whenever Clark met his peers. In fact, he performed well at the summit and earned the praise of other delegations for modest but constructive contributions.

Flora MacDonald, Clark's Secretary of State for External Affairs, started out with greater public expectation, and bureaucratic goodwill, but proved disappointing[32]. Her strong opposition to the sale of nuclear technology to undemocratic countries was principled, and cost her a good deal of support in Cabinet. Despite her reputation for compassion, however, MacDonald appeared to be advocating cuts in Canada's economic assistance to the poor countries[33]. MacDonald stressed human rights, especially in their Cold War context. Her strident tone, however, very much in the Diefenbaker tradition, impressed professional observers as better calculated to win domestic applause than to assist the victims of Soviet oppression.

This brief, selective survey tends to confirm the proposition that the elements of continuity in Canada's post-1945 foreign policy exceed those of change. The differences between the parties, and the much more dramatic contrasts in the personalities of the leaders, have had relatively little impact on policy outputs. Canada's approach to the world become decidedly more internationalist as a consequence of World War II, and the diplomatic successes of the Golden Decade owed almost as much to the quality of our diplomats and leaders as they did to the temporary exhaustion of most of the traditional powers. Furthermore, during the final years of the Diefenbaker regime, and the first of Trudeau's, the behaviour of the Prime Minister caused sharp declines in Canada's prestige and effectiveness in international dealings. With the benefit of hindsight, however, these can be seen as but minor departures from a foreign policy that has been as steady since 1945 as those of the majority of nations, and among the most sensible and constructive.

The election in 1984 of a majority Conservative Government seems unlikely to upset this generalization. Prime Minister Mulroney made clear his Cabinet's intention to make improved relations with Washington its first priority, and also to stiffen Canada's support for the Atlantic alliance. On the other hand, the 1985 green paper indicating the Government's overall approach was more in line with Pearsonian internationalism than had been the early Trudeau Doctrine: «Plus ça change...»

NOTES

1. World War II, largely because of Mackenzie King's crafty handling of the Conscription issue, had proven far less devisive than World War I. Moreover, Québec, still strongly influenced by its conservative Church hierarchy, generally agreed with the rest of Canada concerning the international threat posed by athiestic communism. Foreign policy was still largely the preserve of English-speaking Canadians, however, and only in the 1960s was a serious effort begun to stress Canada's bicultural nature in its external relations.

2. The most influential statement of these doubts was James M. Minifie, *Peacemaker or Powdermonky,* Toronto, 1960.

3. The most prominent doubter was Finance Minister Walter Gordon. Although the Prime Minister reprimanded him for making his doubts public, privately Pearson indicated that he shared most of the Gordon misgivings about US policies in South-East Asia.

4. The review was conducted by a former Under-Secretary of State for External Affairs, Norman Robertson, and two serving officials, Geoffrey Murray and Geoffrey Pearson.

5. For a critical account of the review, see Peyton V. Lyon, «A Review of the Review», *Journal of Canadian Studies,* 1970, or «The Trudeau Doctrine», *International Journal,* Winter 1970-1971. A longer and more balanced treatement is in Bruce Thordarson, *Trudeau and Foreign Policy,* Toronto, c. 1970.

6. See Brian Urquhart, *Hammarskjold,* New York, 1972, p. 257 for the Secretary-General's fulsome tribute to Pearson – and Canada.

7. The best assessment of the men responsible for Canada's postwar policies is found in John W. Holmes, *The Shaping of Peace,* Volume 1, Toronto, 1979.

8. The term properly refers only to the universal approach to security as prescribed in the UN charter. Confusion is created when «collective security» is stretched to cover the very different approach embodied in regional military alliances, such as NATO.

9. See Peyton V. Lyon and Brian W. Tomlin, *Canada as an International Actor,* Toronto, 1979, p. 77-94.

10. David Mitrany, the high priest of functionalism, severly criticized this tendency as he saw it embodied in the European Community.

11. The strident tone adopted by Australia's Foreign Minister, H.V. Evatt, in the first meetings of the UN helped to make Canada appear reasonable.

12. Despite strong American opposition, the leader of Canada's delegation, Paul Martin, was instrumental in 1955 in negotiating the deal with the Soviet Union that broke the logjam blocking expansion of UN membership. The huge increase soon followed.

13. The United States, Britain and France did attempt the peacekeeper role in Lebanon in 1984, but the results were little short of disastrous.

14. See the admirable account of Canada's moderating role in Korea by Denis Stairs, *The Diplomacy of Constraint,* Toronto, 1974.

15. This was done so quietly that few Canadians were aware of it. For an indication of the views of Norman Robertson, at the time Under-Secretary of State for External Affairs, see Peyton V. Lyon, «The Case for the Recognition of East Germany», *International Journal,* Autumn, 1960.

16. See the M. A. thesis by Ann Hillmer, *Canada and the Palestine Question,* Carleton University, 1980. Pearson and Justice Ivan Rand both played major roles in the UN activity leading to the creation of the State of Israel. As Pearson was later to acknowledge, he and most other Canadians were relatively indifferent to the claims of the Arab inhabitants of the area.

17. For an optimistic assessment of the probable political consequences, see Peyton V. Lyon, *Canada-US Free Trade (CUFTA) and Canadian Independence,* The Economic Council of Canada, 1975.

18. The definitive account of Canada's part in the formation of NATO is Escott Reid, *A Time of Fear and Hope,* Toronto, 1977.

19. Curiously, Diefenbaker later denied that his actions had prompted the departure of South Africa. See House of Commons Debates, Novemver 7, 1962, p. 1377.

20. For a detailed account of the nuclear weapons controversy, see Peyton V. Lyon, *Canada in World Affairs 1961-63,* Toronto, 1968, p. 76-222.

21. The 1963 promise the abandon nuclear weapons was finally realized in 1984.

22. Once back in Opposition, Diefenbaker again became one of Canada's strongest supporters of American Cold War policies.

23. A.D.P. Heeney and L. Merchant, «Canada and the United States: Principles for Partnership», *Atlantic Community Quarterly,* Fall, 1965.

24. Although many Canadians later became critical, the accord was viewed at the time as a major American concession that would – and did – increase Canada's share of the North American auto industry.

25. For a fuller account of Canada's Vietnam involvement, see David Van Praagh, «Canada and South-East Asia» in Peyton V. Lyon and Tareq Ismael, *Canada and the Third World,* Toronto, 1976, p. 307-342.

26. Gerda Munsinger, who had been convicted in Germany on a minor espionage charge, was revealed to have been the mistress of Diefenbaker's Associate Minister of Defence. Pearson appeared eager to exploit this relationship to silence Diefenbaker.

27. For an explanation of this paradox, see the discussion of Trudeau's foreign policy philosophy in Thordarson, *op. cit.,* p. 55-76.

28. «Pearson ou l'abdication de l'esprit», *Cité libre,* April, 1963, p. 9-10.

29. The best account of the NATO debate is in Thordarson, *op. cit.,* p. 121-163.

30. A critical treatment of Canada's oceans policy is in Lyon and Tomlin, *op. cit.,* p. 179-86.

31. May 26, 1978. His only other address in the United Nations forum was to UNNSOD II on June 18, 1982; it dealt with the same theme.

32. In an apparent admission that her tenure had been less than a complete success, MacDonald subsequently alleged that her officials had conspired to resist her wishes and limit her influence. «The Minister and the Mandarins», *Policy Options,* September-October, 1980, p. 29-32.

33. See, *e.g.,* her speech to the Empire Club of Toronto, October 4, 1979.

BIBLIOGRAPHY

Canada in World Affairs, various authors, Canadian Institute of International Affairs, Toronto. Series complete from «previous years» to 1965, and 1971-1973.

Canadian Annual Review, Toronto, from 1960 to present; see chapters on foreign and defence policy.

BOTHWELL, R., DRUMMOND, I. and ENGLISH, J. *Canada after 1945,* Toronto, 1982.

DEWITT, David and KIRTON, John. *Canada as a Principal Power,* Toronto, 1983.

EAYRS, James. *In Defence of Canada,* Toronto, five volumes, 1964-1984.

HOLMES, John W. *The Shaping of Peace,* Toronto, 1979 and 1982.

LYON, Peyton V. and TOMLIN, Brian W. *Canada as an International Actor,* Toronto, 1979.

MACKAY, R.A. and ROGERS, E.B. *Canada Looks Abroad,* London, 1938.

PAINCHAUD, Paul, ed. *Le Canada et le Québec sur la scène internationale,* Montréal, 1977.

REID, Escott. *Time of Fear and Hope,* Toronto, 1979.

SHARP, Mitchell. «Canada-United States Relations; Options for the Future», *International Perspectives,* Autumn, 1972.

STACEY C.P. *Canada and the Age of Conflict,* Toronto, 1977.

STAIRS, Denis. *The Diplomacy of Constraint,* Toronto, 1974.

THORDARSON, Bruce. *Trudeau and Foreign Policy,* Toronto, c. 1970.

TUCKER, Michael. *Canadian Foreign Policy,* Toronto, 1980.

2

The Determinants of Canadian Foreign Policy

Garth Stevenson
University of Alberta

INTRODUCTION

To attempt to catalogue, let alone to evaluate, the «determinants» of Canadian foreign policy is a formidable task. Almost any political, social or economic characteristic of Canada might, and probably does, influence foreign policy, but the very vastness of the subject makes difficult the task of imposing some order on the data and some intellectual rigour on the analysis. John Kenneth Galbraith may have had this fact in mind when he observed that foreign policy was the only field of study in which good tailoring and an elegant manner could serve as substitutes for thought.

Let us begin with a definition, and say that Canada's foreign policies, or those of any State, are a function of its objectives and of its capabilities. Both terms require more precision; its objectives mean the objectives considered important by those who make policy in its name, or perhaps by others who are in a position to influence them, and its capabilities are those that can be effectively mobilized by the State for the purpose of pursuing the objectives. Objectives and capabilities are also not independent of one another, for the former will normally be adapted to some more or less realistic evaluation of the latter.

When the problem is stated in this way, the vastness and complexity of any attempt to identify the «determinants» become apparent. Some of the determining factors would be conditions or circumstances within the society over which the State has jurisdiction, while others would be external to it. Some, such as trade or investment flows across its borders, might be dealt with under either of these broad categories, more or less at the discretion of the analyst.

The internal factors that might affect both objectives and capabilities might be loosely classified into the broad categories of economic, social and political. (Political is to be understood in the narrow sense, *i.e.*, directly related to the institutional framework of the State.) Both the economic and social phenomena have, in Canada, important external linkages. In the case of the economic phenomena, these would include foreign ownership of industry, dependence on imported technology, and trading relationships with other countries. In the case of the social phenomena, they would include the ethnic, ideological and sentimental ties between certain Canadians and other countries such as the United Kingdom, France, the United States, or Israel.

Determining the relative importance of the economic, social and political determinants, or of particular determinants within those broad categories, is a difficult and perhaps impossible exercise. Some areas or types of foreign policy are influenced by certain factors, some by others. Most factors will influence a number of aspects of Canadian foreign policy, but to varying degrees. The relative importance of the different aspects is itself a matter of judgement. Is defence policy (and therefore its particular set of determinants) more important than commercial policy (and therefore its particular set of determinants), or is it less important? By and large, one is attempting to measure what cannot be measured. Like the hero of *Fiddler on the Roof,* one is tempted to say: «On the one hand... but, on the other hand», rather than arriving at any clear decision. Perhaps that is as it should be.

Attempts to weigh, measure and evaluate the various determinants are fated to be controversial, and for reasons not always of a strictly scientific nature. Attributing great influence to external determinants may bias the analyst in the direction of determinism, pessimism, and the status quo (*e.g.*, there is a Soviet «threat» and therefore adherence to NATO is «inevitable», or, as a former leader of the Social Credit Party once observed, «the United States is our best friend whether we like it or not»). Conversely, a preoccupation with economic determinants of foreign policy will be viewed by some as evidence of radical or even revolutionary tendencies on the part of the analyst. All observers may tend to overestimate the impact of those domestic influences which they view with suspicion, and to underestimate the influence of those which they view with sympathy. Business-people profess to believe that policy makers are too sensitive to the concerns of impractical academics, and vice versa. Provincialists believe that provincial interests are ignored, while Macdonaldian federalists believe that they are taken too seriously. Anglo-Saxons attribute foreign policies which they consider irrational to the political influence of Jewish, French or Ukrainian lobbies, while non-Anglo-Saxons believe that an unrepresentative WASP establishment still dominates the policy-making process.

In the last analysis, how does one demonstrate that a particular factor or circumstance influences Canadian foreign policy? The easier and less satisfactory approach is strictly inductive: observing a similarity between some aspect of foreign policy and some circumstance that seems to correspond with it, it elevates the latter into an explanation for the former. A hypothetical, but not far-fetched, example might be the following chain of reasoning: Canada pursues policies more sympathetic to the United States than to the USSR; public opinion is more sympathetic to the United States than to the USSR; therefore, public opinion determines policy.

The more difficult but more reliable approach requires the analyst to identify deductively some logically coherent reason why the circumstance might be expected to have certain consequences for policy, and then to verify that the policy which actually takes place does correspond with the anticipated consequences of the determinant identified earlier. While more rewarding, this approach is also subject to a loss of reliability as imponderables and complexities accumulate.

A final problem in identifying and evaluating the determinants of policy is the measurement of continuity and change. No doubt in Canada, as elsewhere, many things change only slowly, if at all; the writings of Goldwin Smith and of André Siegfried, for example, can still provide insights into Canadian society. Yet it is equally obvious that some of the determinants of Canadian foreign policy, both internal and external, have changed considerably in the four decades covered by the present volume. The analyst must convey a sense of the relevant importance of continuity and change, and must also try to distinguish long-term trends from minor short-term fluctuations.

THE EXTERNAL ENVIRONMENT

The external determinants of Canadian foreign policy can be outlined quite briefly in this chapter, since a number of other chapters will treat particular aspects of them in greater detail. Nonetheless, they are not unimportant, for as they have changed over the years since 1945, Canadian policy has changed with them.

Canada's geographical position places it on three oceans: the Atlantic, the Arctic and the Pacific, in close proximity to the world's most powerful nation, the United States, and relatively close to the northern and western parts of the Eurasian landmass. Other industrialized countries, including those more powerful than Canada itself, are relatively near neighbours in global terms. The poorer and weaker countries, collectively known 20 years ago as the «Third World» and more recently as the «South», are with few exceptions far distant.

Geography and location may appear to be factors not subject to change, but in fact their significance is decisively determined by changes in the distribution of power among nations and by technological developments in weaponry, transport and communication. Moreover, the impact of geography and location are to some extent the consequences of the way in which these factors are perceived by the policy makers. All of these intervening factors are subject to change.

Since most Canadians have always lived in the Southeastern part of the country, and since the federal capital is located there, it is natural that Canadian policy makers have been more aware of Canada's position on the Atlantic than of its position on the Pacific and the Arctic oceans, although this is probably less true in recent years than formerly. Political and economic ties with the United Kingdom, and the European cultural backgrounds of the overwhelming majority of Canadians, helped to preserve this Atlantic perception. The notion of the «North Atlantic triangle» (The United Kingdom, Canada and the United States) was a part of this perception, and was also related to the fact that in the early part of Canada's existence as a federal state, the United Kingdom and the United States were approximately equal in power and importance.

For most of Canada's history, the United States were viewed, for better or for worse, as being the only geographically close neighbour, and among the general public, although not to the same extent among policy-makers, this perception still survives. (Few Canadians have ever thought of Mexico as part of North America, although it is so in fact.) Until World War II, Canadians, like Americans, considered their continent to be isolated from the rest of the world, an attitude epitomized by the celebrated metaphor of the fireproof house, once used by a Canadian delegate to the League of Nations. The illusion may have been fostered by the popularity of maps drawn to Mercator's projection, which make Canada appear both considerably larger and more distant from Eurasia than it actually is. The operation of German and Japanese submarines near Canada's coasts in the 1940s and the development of the Soviet long-range air force in the 1950s, helped to shatter these illusions, as did the growth of long-range commercial air transport and electronic means of communication.

The distribution of military and economic power in the world is also a part of Canada's external environment. Until World War II, Canada's neighbour, the United States, was only one of several great powers, roughly comparable in status to the United Kingdom and France. Since 1945, only the United States and the USSR have enjoyed first-rate military capabilities, with the United Kingdom and France relegated to the status of junior allies of the United States. Economic power has remained somewhat more widely distributed, with the United Kingdom, France, the Federal Republic of Germany, possibly Italy, and certainly Japan, having significant capabilities. The first four of these countries are grouped (the United Kingdom only since 1973) in a European Community that for certain purposes can perhaps be perceived as a single unit on the international chessboard; insofar as it can be, its economic although not military capabilities are comparable to those of either of the superpowers. China has also emerged as an important power, although it remains relatively poor and technologically backward. India is a somewhat similar case, although weaker than China in every respect. In the 1970s, the oil-exporting countries gained considerably in wealth, but many of these have backward social structures, exceedingly small populations, or both.

For Canadian foreign policy, the most significant change since 1945 in the international distribution of power has been the relative decline of the United Kingdom. Until 1945, that country was comparable to the United States, if not superior to it, in terms of military forces and economically strong enough to absorb one-third of Canada's exports. Canadian policy-makers, beginning with Sir John A. Macdonald, more or less consciously pursued a policy of promoting ties with the United Kingdom as a counterweight to the otherwise overwhelming influence of the United States. The United Kingdom was particularly well suited for this purpose because of its historical, ideological and sentimental ties with Canada. Its decline, which became dramatically evident soon after 1945 and has continued inexorably up to the present, has left a vacuum which has been difficult to fill. Economic and military integration between Canada and the United States increased sharply in the decade that followed the conclusion of World War II, a situation that some Canadians viewed with concern although most, at the time, appeared indifferent. Ideological hostility to the USSR ruled that country out of consideration as a potential counterweight, even if it had been willing and able to play the part. The Diefenbaker Government, between 1957 and 1963, tried to reinforce Canada's ties with the United Kingdom, which it alleged had been neglected by the previous Government, but it discovered that the United Kingdom was no longer strong enough to serve as an effective counterweight to the United States.

After 1963, the European Community came to be viewed as the only possible replacement for the old British connection, although its actual performance of this role has been a severe, and perhaps inevitable, disappointment. Japan surpassed the United Kingdom as a trading partner in the 1970s, but its relationship with Canada remains narrowly focused and few if any Canadians have a warm regard for their Pacific neighbour.

The failure to develop an effective external counterweight to the United States means that Canada's external environment is dominated by the preponderant influence and power of that country. It impinges directly and inescapably on almost every aspect of Canada's external relations, from fisheries to foreign investment and from cultural diplomacy to the choice of weapons for the Canadian armed forces. It is safe to say that no initiative in Canadian foreign policy is ever undertaken without considering its impact on Canadian-American relations, and a very large part of the substance of Canadian foreign policy consists of bilateral disputes and problems that involve Canada and the United States exclusively.

So intense and multifaceted is the Canadian-American relationship that it is analytically useful to view Canada as participating in two international systems of relationships: the global system and a regional system in which the United States and Canada are the only sovereign state actors. Herman Kahn's celebrated comment that Canada was a regional power without a region should really be rephrased to say that Canada's region is unique in that it contains only two sovereign state actors of which Canada is by far the smaller, with the additional disadvantage that the dominant power in Canada's region is one of two dominant powers in the global system as well. Canada's capabilities, although far from negligible, are inevitably overshadowed by those of the country with which it is most frequently compared, and must be devoted mainly to managing a bilateral relationship in which Canada cannot expect to win easy victories. There are no weaker and smaller neighbours to constitute a Canadian sphere of influence, in the sense that New Zealand, Papua-New Guinea and the Pacific Islands constitute an Australian sphere of influence.

Both of the international systems in which Canada participates, the global and the regional, have remained the same in some respects since 1945 but have undergone important changes in others. At the global level, the major element of continuity has been the bipolar distribution of military power between the United States and the USSR. The significant elements of change, familiar to anyone even slightly interested in world politics, include the disappearance of European colonial empires, the development of the European Community, the rapid advances in military technology, the cycle of revolutions in China, Cuba, Vietnam, and elsewhere, the sudden rise of petroleum prices in the 1970s with all its economic and political consequences, and the demands of the less industrialized countries for new international economic order.

Similarly, in the North American system, there has been one obvious element of continuity in the overwhelming disproportion of power between Canada and the United States. Elements of change, in some cases related to those at the global level, include the decline of the old New York-based financial-industrial establishment that dominated both the continent and the capitalist world between 1945 and 1965, the rise of ethnic politics (Blacks, Natives, Francophones and Hispanophones), the growing economic power of the southern and western peripheries, the weakness of traditional industries (*e.g.*, automobiles) in the face of overseas competition, and the fact that the continent (excluding Mexico) has become a major importer of crude oil.

CAPABILITIES AND STATUS

No discussion, however brief, of its place in the world, can avoid the difficult problem of assessing Canada's capabilities in relation to those of other states. While the sources of capabilities are essentially internal, and will be referred to again when the economic, social and political determinants of Canadian policy are considered in due course, some preliminary observations are in order at this point.

Canada has often been referred to as a middle power, sometimes as a small power, and on one or two occasions even as a «foremost nation»[1]. The lack of consensus reflects the general difficulty of measuring the capabilities of nations, and also some specific problems: the overshadowing of Canada by the United States and the obsolescence of the traditional category of «great powers», as opposed to «superpowers». Moreover, as the subject of international relations has grown more and more heterogeneous, it becomes more plausible to assert the functionalist position that relevant capabilities vary from one issue to another and that an overall ranking of nations is neither useful nor possible.

A fairly recent study by two political scientists demonstrates some of the difficulties of measuring capabilities, and the curious conclusions that can result from inappropriate criteria. Peyton Lyon and Brian Tomlin assert that between 1950 and 1975, Canada never ranked lower than sixth among the nations of the world in terms of its capabilities, and that it consistently ranked higher than either France or Japan[2]. These unexpected conclusions become more explicable when it is discovered that no less than four of the ten criteria employed are related to energy. Two of them indeed measure energy consumption, so that the vast distances, cold climate and wasteful habits of Canadians, which common sense would suggest are sources of national weakness, are instead interpreted as sources of national strength. On the other hand, Lyon and Tomlin fail to measure production of food, production of manufactured end products, or any indicator of scientific and technological advancement. Precision in measuring capabilities is never possible, since there is no objective way to determine the relative weight that should be assigned to various criteria, but a more suitable set of indicators would doubtless determine that Canada ranks well behind either France or Japan. Probably it would rank about even with Italy, and not very far ahead of India, Brazil, or the German Democratic Republic. This is nonetheless a respectable showing, and Canada is clearly closer in strength to the traditional European «great powers» than to the vast majority of members of the United Nations.

Closely related to, but distinct from, capabilities is the even less easily measurable quantity of Canada's reputation in the world. Reputation in part influences, and in part reflects, Canada's ability to achieve its objectives in dealing with other states. Lyon and Tomlin also provide some data on this subject, based on a survey of foreign journalists, academics, and policy-makers[3]. The data suggest that Canada is on the whole viewed favourably, although the fact that Canadians administered the questionnaire may have biased the responses somewhat in that direction. Adjectives such as «generous», «modest», «principled» or «disinterested» were frequently used. When asked to name another State similar to Canada in its international behaviour, respondents most frequently selected Australia, Sweden, Norway or the Netherlands in that order. On the delicate question of Canada's relations with the United States, the opinions expressed were generally reassuring although not overwhelmingly so. 63 % said that Canada's autonomy in foreign policy was not significantly limited by the influence of its giant neighbour, and 59 % agreed with a statement that compared to most countries, Canada acts independently in international relations. (Significantly, fewer were convinced that Canada enjoys complete freedom of action in its domestic policy, a perception perhaps explained by Canada's failure, up to that time, to reduce the level of foreign ownership in its economy.) On balance, one can at least say that Canada's reputation does not seem to be an obstacle to the achievement of its objectives, and may possibly be of some assistance.

Since this chapter is based on the premise that most, although not all, of the determinants of foreign policy are to be found within the society over which the State has jurisdiction, the remainder will be devoted to examining those internal characteristics of Canada that appear to have a significant influence on its foreign policy. For convenience, these characteristics will be classified into the broad and possibly somewhat artificial categories of economic, social, and political.

ECONOMIC DETERMINANTS

The first and most obvious observation that must be made about Canada as an economic system is that it is a capitalist economy. The production of goods and commodities, as well as the circulation of capital, is mainly in the hands of enterprises owned by individual shareholders, either domestic or foreign, and not by the State. Decisions as to the investment of capital are made by private individuals in expectation of profit either for themselves or for the corporations whose interests are entrusted to them. The State influences such decisions through its control over taxation, interest rates and so forth, but those who act on behalf of the State generally view its role as one of supporting and assisting the goals of private enterprise. State ownership is not unknown but with few exceptions is confined to unprofitable sectors of the economy or those with abnormally low rates of return.

The second and perhaps equally obvious characteristic of the Canadian economic system is its modern or «developed» character, in the sense that practically all of the employed population is involved in a modern economy characterized by wage labour, the application of modern technology to production, and a high degree of interdependence between individuals and between sectors. As a result, national income is high in relation to the size of the population.

These observations may appear trite, and also pitched at a rather high level of generality, but they are nonetheless of the greatest importance. Taken together, it would seem that they largely explain the character of the Canadian state, political process and ideology, at least in broad terms, all of which have an impact on foreign policy. They place Canada firmly within an identifiable and relatively small group of nation-states that might be collectively referred to as advanced liberal democracies, although less flattering descriptive labels for them are not unknown. Whether or not such states exhibit generally similar behaviour patterns in international politics, their policy makers appear to assume some degree of common interest between them, as suggested by the presence of organizations and institutions such as the OECD, which includes all the major states of this type, or NATO, which includes the majority of them.

Moving to a somewhat lower level of generality, we can say that, while Canada undoubtedly belongs to this category, it has some unusual although not unique features. Unlike most members of the group, it produces more resources and raw materials, at least of certain kinds, than can be absorbed by its own relatively small industrial sector. Conversely, it is a major net importer of manufactured end products. In both respects, it appears to resemble the underdeveloped «southern» countries more than it resembles its fellow members of the OECD, the chief difference being that Canada's resource base is large enough, and its resource industries productive enough, to pay for sufficient imports to support a high material standard of living.

Canada also resembles some of the «southern» countries, and differs from most other OECD countries, in the fact that a rather large proportion of its industries are owned by foreigners, and particularly by residents of the United States.

These facts are as controversial as they are important, and the reasons for them, as well as the relationships between them, have been extensively debated by Canadian political economists, economic historians, and other commentators. Without attempting to enter these controversies, it can be asserted that they are associated in some way with other characteristics of Canada: relatively large geographical area, relatively small and unevenly distributed population, concentration of secondary manufacturing in a small core area of the country, uneven development of the different areas of the country and consequent resentment in some areas manifesting itself as «regionalism», an early history of colonial rule that established a tradition of dependence on external sources of capital, technology, and management. The liberal democracy that comes closest to resembling Canada in all of these characteristics is Australia, and it will be recalled that, according to Lyon and Tomlin, that country was the one most frequently cited by foreign observers as resembling Canada in its foreign policy behaviour. While this does not in itself demonstrate a relationship between these economic characteristics and the character of Canadian foreign policy, it may suggest the possibility of such a relationship. It is safe to say at any rate that these characteristics of Canada are associated, whether as causes or consequences or both, with the character of its economic relations with the outside world. Since the focus of the present volume is on the period since 1945, little can be said about the previous history of these relations, the broad outlines of which are generally familiar. Canada originated as an economic and political colony of France, and then passed under the control of the United Kingdom in 1763. After the economic ties of the British Empire were loosened about 1849, Canada drifted gradually, although not continuously or consistently, into the economic orbit of the United States, a process that accelerated after 1945 when the United Kingdom ceased to be a first-rate power. In the process of passing from one sphere of influence to another, Canada acquired enough political and economic autonomy to begin to conduct its own diplomacy and to be generally recognized as a sovereign State. Yet the extent and nature of Canada's economic relations with the United States since World War II has caused some observers, both Canadian and foreign, to question whether Canada enjoys a sufficient measure of real as opposed to formal independence.

Long before World War II, the United States had become the major source of Canada's imports, and since World War II, it has assumed a similar predominance as a market for Canadian exports, so that almost 80 % of Canada's trade in both directions is now with that country. The United Kingdom share of Canada's trade has declined inexorably, mainly as a result of that country's economic problems. Japan has gained in importance as a market for raw materials and a source of manufactured end products.

Canada's trade with other OECD countries mainly consists of selling raw materials and semi-processed commodities, and buying manufactured end products. In the case of the United States, this picture is modified somewhat (since 1965) by the rough balance of bilateral trade in automotive products, a result of the treaty which allows manufacturers to integrate their production on both sides of the border. There is also a long-established Canadian tradition of importing both coal and food products from the United States. However, the overall pattern of trade with the United States, apart from the special case of automotive products, has changed little during the period under consideration. Commodities based on Canada's mineral and forest resources still account for most of our non-automotive exports to that country. Canada exports grain to a variety of countries, with China as an important market since the 1950s, and the USSR since the 1960s. Canada also exports some manufactured end products, apart from motor vehicles, particularly to semi-industrialized countries such as Mexico, Brazil and Australia. Like most other OECD members, it imports substantial quantities of crude oil from the OPEC countries, and more recently from Mexico.

The distribution of Canadian trade by sectors and commodities has changed gradually since 1945, with agricultural exports as a proportion of all exports tending to decline. Apart from the impact of the automotive agreement with the United States in 1965, the most dramatic changes have been with regard to energy commodities. In 1945, Canada exported few of any significance, but between the early 1950s and the early 1970s it was a significant exporter of crude oil to the United States, although it continued to import the same commodity from Venezuela and later from Africa and the Middle East. Although exports of crude oil to the United States have since tapered off, exports of natural gas continue to be important. Exports of hydroelectricity to the United States became important in the 1960s and significant exports of coal to Japan and other overseas countries began soon afterwards. Throughout the period, Canada has been an important producer of uranium, so that on balance it has a considerable surplus of trade in energy products, in sharp contrast to its situation in 1945.

Another characteristic of Canadian trade is the tendency of the country's different regions to specialize in particular commodities and markets. Since 1945, Ontario has come to specialize increasingly in manufactured end products and Alberta in oil and gas, while British Columbia and Saskatchewan have somewhat reduced their dependence on lumber and grain respectively. At the beginning of the period, central Canada exported mainly to the United States and the peripheries to the United Kingdom. Today, British Columbia's trade is heavily oriented towards Japan, while Alberta and Ontario are almost entirely dependent on the United States market. Québec is close to the Canadian average in the proportion of its exports that go to the United States, while Saskatchewan is below the average.

The pattern of Canada's external trade and the structure of its domestic economy are closely linked in a reciprocal relationship. Because the economy depends heavily on trade, trade plays an important part in setting the agenda and determining the goals of foreign policy. A not particularly important example of its effect was the reversal of the Clark Government's ill-considered promise to recognize Jerusalem as the capital of Israel, a reversal largely prompted by a belated consideration of the impact on Canadian access to Arab markets. Far more significant is the impact on Canada's political relations with its major trading partner, the United States. It is true that in the early 1970s, the protectionist policies of the Nixon administration caused the Department of External Affairs to produce the ill-fated policy of promoting trade with Europe as a counterweight, the so-called Third Option. However, a more characteristic Canadian response to American protectionism has been to seek a special arrangement with the United States, as recommended by the Macdonald Royal Commission in 1985. More generally, Canadian Government departments concerned with economic matters tend to argue that Canada should not imperil its economic ties with the United States by adopting either foreign or domestic policies that would antagonize the US administration or Congress. In general, the promotion of exports, particularly of manufactured end products, is a major priority of external policy. It is also an area in which provincial governments, responding to the particular needs of their specialized economies, have become active, giving the Federal Government an additional incentive to be active so as to retain its primacy in the field of external relations.

Imports as well as exports affect Canada's political relations with other countries. Dependence on imported oil from a variety of sources is an incentive for Canada to cultivate friendly relations with OPEC countries and with Mexico. Importation of end products and consumer goods involves political complications of a different kind. Although Canada is vaguely committed to the principle of opening its market to the industrial products of poorer countries in Asia and Latin America, its commitment to this goal is lessened considerably by concern for the vulnerable and labour-intensive (and mainly Canadian-owned) industries that would be threatened if the goal were pursued seriously. Canada's relations with Japan have also been affected by domestic demands for protection, particularly from the automobile industry. The agreement by two Japanese automobile firms to establish factories in Canada has removed an irritant from the relationship, but Canadian-Japanese trade in manufactures is still almost exclusively in one direction.

Closely related to commodity trade are international transactions in capital and services, including the politically sensitive question of foreign direct investment. In the 1950s, the inflow of direct investment capital into Canada more or less balanced what was then a chronic deficit in commodity trade. Today, commodity trade shows a surplus, but there is a chronic deficit in services, a large part of which is the outflow of dividends and interest as a result of foreign investment in earlier years. Canadian direct investment in the United States and external borrowing by Canadian governments are other important elements of the equation. Borrowing by provincial governments in the 1960s complicated Canada's political relations with the United States, and there is some evidence that provincial governments heavily dependent on the American money markets use their influence to discourage the Federal Government of Canada from pursuing policies to restrict foreign direct investment.

The political and economic implications of American direct investment in the Canadian economy have been endlessly discussed. It grew rapidly between 1945 and 1970, so that by the latter year, about half of all Canadian manufacturing and mining was under foreign, and in most cases American, control. Some sectors, such as petroleum refining, rubber products and the automobile industry, had fallen almost entirely under foreign control. In the 1970s, foreign control of Canadian industry levelled off, and in recent years there have been some notable cases of foreign-controlled enterprises being transferred to Canadian control, and in some cases to the public sector. The National Energy Programme announced in October 1980 set a target of 50 % Canadian control in the petroleum industry, which has now virtually been achieved. However, foreign control seems likely to remain substantial in the resource industries, and preponderant in some sectors of manufacturing.

Policies towards foreign investment are really domestic rather than foreign policies, insofar as the distinction can be made, but the subject may have implications for foreign policy. As long as extensive foreign, and especially American, control of Canadian industry persists, it will complicate relations between Canada and the home countries of the foreign-controlled enterprises. American firms in particular tend to integrate their Canadian with their domestic operations, increasing the flow of commodities and services between the two countries. American investors in Canada and, to an even greater degree, Canadian investors in the United States have a vested interest in minimizing any divergence between either the domestic or the foreign policies of the two countries. Protests by the United States Government against the National Energy Programme, and previously against the takeovers of potash companies by the Province of Saskatchewan, suggest the responsiveness of the United States Government to the interests of American capital operating in Canada. On the other hand, it is at best an oversimplification to assert that American direct investment causes Canada to pursue a foreign policy of subservience to the United States. Canadian foreign policy is not entirely a carbon copy of American foreign policy, and to the extent that resemblances exist, they are in large part a result of the similarities between the two countries (both are rich, conservative, capitalist, and largely Anglophone liberal democracies) rather than subservience of one to the other. Insofar as Canada is motivated to pursue some policies and avoid others by fear of adverse reactions in the United States, it is mainly dependence on American markets for commodities and American purchasers of Government bonds that explains the caution of Canadian foreign policy-makers, rather than American direct investment as such. Also it must be emphasized that Canadian direct investment in the United States, which at times is celebrated as though it were an antidote to the reverse phenomenon, is actually worse in terms of its likely impact on the independence of Canadian foreign policy. The biblical assertation that «where your treasure is, there will your heart be also», has a certain relevance to foreign policy, and a relatively small country whose most influential citizens invest heavily in a larger and more powerful neighbouring country is likely to find itself locked into a particularly intractable form of dependence.

As suggested earlier, Canada occupies a complex and ambiguous position in the world economy, having some characteristics of an industrialized metropolitan country and some characteristics of a resource-exporting hinterland country. While the latter characteristics are associated with Canada's neo-colonial ties to the United States, it is paradoxically they that may account for those aspects of Canadian foreign policy that diverge from the norms of Washington, NATO and the OECD. Like Australia, Ireland and the Scandinavian countries, which share some of its ambiguous characteristics, Canada appears relatively sympathetic to the economic and political demands of the «South», despite its high level of income and its devotion to capitalist principles of economic organization[4].

If Canada becomes significantly more industrialized and less dependent on the United States and other advanced countries, it may be at the cost of coming to resemble those countries more, and the developing countries less, than it does at present. As a result, Canada's foreign policy might become more, rather than less, committed to the international *status quo.*

SOCIAL DETERMINANTS

The social determinants of foreign policy are in some ways less easily defined than the economic determinants, and their influence is less easily measured. By social determinants are meant basically those characteristics of the people of Canada, or of Canada as a society, which appear to influence foreign policy, if only by forming a relevant part of the environment within which foreign policy is made. Behaviour, values, attitudes, political culture, national character and public opinion are some of the terms, not necessarily mutually exclusive, that attempt to define various aspects of this set of phenomena. Social realities are of course related to economic ones. The division of a society into classes, for example, is clearly a product of economic forces, and the ethnic divisions in Canada are related to its economic history, and specifically to the fluctuating demand for labour that caused immigration to occur on a large scale at particular times.

The relevance of all this to foreign policy may appear questionable if one considers that the vast majority of Canadians play little or no part in the making of foreign policy, and indeed appear to take little interest in it. Nonetheless, the social determinants of policy may be important in two ways. First, those who do participate in making and implementing policy are drawn from, and continue to form a part of, the larger society. Their values, attitudes and perceptions are at least related to those of the general population. Second, the values, attitudes and perceptions of the general population, and the circumstances and characteristics from which they arise, are part of the environment within which policy is made.

Using terminology employed by Denis Stairs, it can be said that public opinion influences Canadian foreign policy by agenda-setting (influencing the selection of issues that are considered important) and parameter-setting (establishing limits to the freedom of action of policy-makers). Stairs also suggests that its influence has in-creased as domestically-oriented departments have become more influential in Canada's external policies, challenging the traditional dominance of External Affairs and of National Defence, both of which are not tied to any domestic client-groups and are therefore relatively insensitive to public opinion[5].

For the social as well as for the economic determinants of foreign policy, one can distinguish between general characteristics which Canada shares with other similar countries and those which are unique to Canada itself. The characteristics in the first category, while possibly obvious, cannot be ignored. Canada's level of economic development ensures that the population is, relatively speaking, well-informed and literate. Most Canadians live in urban areas and the nine urban areas with populations of more than 500 000 account for almost half of the total population. Opinions and attitudes are formed in large part by exposure to the commercial and quasi-commercial media of communication, and to some extent through contacts at work with others of similar class and occupation. The prevailing ideology propagated through the media, schools, and other agencies is broadly similar to that prevailing in other liberal democracies with high levels of economic development. Certain aspects of this ideology, notably a pronounced hostility to communism, have a direct bearing on foreign policy. Other aspects have a less obvious but perhaps equally important significance. For example, the assumption in bourgeois ideology that prosperity is the reward of initiative and hard work probably has a negative effect on Canadian percep-tions of less developed countries in Asia, Africa and Latin America. A Canadian of conservative inclination is likely to feel that the poverty of such countries is largely their own fault.

It is only fair to add, however, that Canadian ideology, and Canadian views on foreign policy, are by no means monolithic. Contrasting orientations towards foreign policy exist and in Canada, as in other liberal democracies, their bases are largely to be found in different occupational sectors within what is loosely termed the «middle class». Self-employed persons and the owners and managers of business enterprises, as well as those involved in the police or the armed forces, tend to espouse a fundamentalist conservative view of international politics which equates freedom and virtue with capitalism and prosperity, regards communist states as evil by definition, and is critical of post-colonial countries in Africa and Asia. Academics, teachers, persons involved in cultural activities, and some of the clergy of the major churches (Roman Catholic, Anglican and United) are inclined to be far more tolerant of socialism and cultural diversity, to regard world poverty and racism as worse evils than communism, to support disarmament, external aid, and demands for a new international economic order, and to be critical of right-wing regimes in Latin America. Political decision-makers and members of Parliament may fall into either of these camps, with their previous occupational background having considerable influence on the outcome. Bureaucratic decision-makers tend to vary in their attitudes from one department to another. Those in National Defence, Finance, or Industry tend to have a conservative outlook on foreign policy while those in the Canadian International Development Agency are in the opposite camp and those in External Affairs, somewhere in the middle[6].

Of the social determinants more specific to Canada, the most obvious is the division of the country into two distinct linguistic communities, Anglophone and Francophone, each of which is too large and too deeply rooted in a network of institutions to be absorbed by the other, as well as the fact that the Francophone group is heavily concentrated within one province where it comprises the majority, while the Anglophone group is dominant everywhere else.

Anglophone and Francophone Canadians differed profoundly from one another in their views on foreign policy in the period when the major problem of Canadian foreign policy was to define Canada's relationship to the British Empire. The conflicts over Conscription during two world wars, and particularly during the first, were the most dramatic but not the only symptoms of a fundamental dispute. Anglophone Canadians, or at least the more influential among them, were convinced that Canada must support the United Kingdom to the fullest extent whenever that country was in danger. Francophone Canadians, not perceiving any direct threat to Canada itself, took a more detached view.

This conflict has ceased to be significant as Canada's ties with the United Kingdom and the importance of the United Kingdom in world politics have both declined. It last emerged at the time of the British invasion of Egypt in 1956, and the controversy in Canada over that event was happily no more than a pale shadow of those that occurred on earlier occasions. Canada's involvement with the United States, although it produces controversy within both of the major linguistic communities, has not produced conflict between them to any significant extent. The Korean War, NATO and NORAD were as readily accepted in Québec as in English Canada, and there has been little anxiety in Québec about the implications of Canada's close economic ties with the United States.

This is not say, however, that the differences between the two linguistic groups in their orientations towards foreign policy have entirely disappeared, or that the bilingual and bicultural character of Canada has no consequences for its foreign policy. Attitudes not only towards the United Kingdom, but towards France and to some extent towards the United States continue to differ. Anglophone Canadians are not on the average more friendly towards the United States than Francophones, but they are more preoccupied with that country and more heavily influenced by it[7]. Language affects the sources of information about the outside world that are available to Canadians. The Anglophone media rely heavily on their American, and to some extent on their British, counterparts, for their coverage of international affairs. The Francophone media rely to some extent on information from France. Anglophone Canadians also have direct access to American magazines and, in most localities, to American television. Certain periodicals from the United Kingdom are also read in Anglophone Canada, although much less widely, and certain periodicals from France have a counterpart audience in Francophone Canada. Thus Canadians, including policy-makers, have their perceptions of the world filtered through foreign sources and are subtly influenced to adopt the American, British or French view, as the case may be, of international events and problems[8]. This is a potential danger to both Canadian unity and Canadian independence.

Canadian foreign policy, and to some extent domestic policy, is constrained by the fact that important foreign governments can influence Canadian public opinion, and thus exercise leverage over the Government of Canada. The influence of the United States is by far the most important. In Canadian-American disputes over nuclear warheads in the early 1960s and over energy policy and economic nationalism more recently, large numbers of Canadians sided with the United States Government rather than with their own Government and in both cases the official Opposition party in Canada attempted to exploit this fact by adopting a pro-American position. The influence of France is also important, as can be demonstrated by recalling the events of the 1960s. The fear that the French Government would publicly support the cause of Québec's independence, which it eventually did, led the Canadian Government of Lester B. Pearson to avoid publicly condemning Gaullist policies concerning NATO, the European Community and other matters, although it was in fact strongly opposed to those policies[9].

The incoherence often attributed to the Canadian «identity» may also be influenced by the fact that almost one out of every six Canadian residents, at the time of the 1981 census, had been born outside of Canada. Within the general category of the foreign-born, the largest group were those born in the United Kingdom, but substantial numbers had been born in the United States, Italy, Germany, China and a variety of other countries. Some of these foreign-born Canadians are very hostile to the present regimes in their countries of origin, while others are inclined to be supportive of them. For better or for worse, few can be entirely indifferent to the countries in which they were born.

Sentimental interest in or preoccupation with various foreign countries is not confined to those who were born outside of Canada, although usually it is based on some real or imagined ethnic and cultural ties with the country in question. The curious Canadian practice of recording ethnic origins in the census (the USSR and South Africa are among the few other industrialized countries that do so) encourages this tendency, as does the recent political preoccupation with «multiculturalism». Many Canadians of British origin (and some who are not) still cherish the «British connection» even if, or especially if, they are generations removed from any direct connection with the United Kingdom. The past, if not present, relevance of such attitudes to foreign policy has already been referred to. Jewish Canadians, and more recently Arab Canadians, have sought to influence Canadian policies towards the Middle East. Canadians of Ukrainian and other Eastern European origins are believed by many politicans to respond favourably to anti-Soviet rhetoric, although it is possible that the politicians are underestimating the intelligence of the people concerned. However, the influence of ethnic groups on foreign policy is probably limited to cases in which the group is relatively large and relatively cohesive, and in which Canada's relations with the country in question are both important and controversial. Only a few of the many ethnic groups recorded in the census meet all of these conditions.

Ethnicity may affect Canadian attitudes towards foreign policy in another way, however. Prejudices which Canadians have about various ethnic groups, including their own, may determine their perceptions of foreign countries even if, as is possible, the source of the prejudices is to be found in the internal dynamics of Canadian society. One recent study ranked 26 ethnic groups according to the extent to which a representative sample of Canadians associated the groups with positive characteristics. English, Scottish and French were shown to be viewed most favourably. Japanese had a relatively high rating. Russians and Chinese were viewed much less favourably, while Blacks and East Indians had extremely low ratings, being ranked 25th and 26th[10]. It is hard to believe that such attitudes have no bearing on Canadian perceptions of international relations.

In concluding this section, it should be emphasized that the conduct of foreign policy, and indeed the very concept of foreign policy, is based on the assumption of a conceptual boundary between «us» and «them», between those who are a part of the society over which the State had jurisdiction, and those who are not. Foreign policy is supposed to defend the interests of «us» against «them». In Canada, however, the conceptual boundary between «us» and «them» is vague and at times controversial. Certain foreign countries are not regarded by all Canadians as truly foreign. The Canadian identity is threatened by two powerful forces in the modern world: ethnic nationalism and geopolitical continentalism. English Canadians who succumb to the temptation of ethnic nationalism will identify not with their own country but with a larger Anglophone world whose centre was formerly in London but is now for all practical purposes in Washington[11]. French Canadians who are ethnic nationalists will feel more solidarity with France than with Anglophone Canada, while Canadians of miscellaneous ethnic origins will feel a variety of foreign attachments. North American continentalism is perhaps less destructive of Canadian unity, at least in the short run, but tends to destroy any Canadian identity by causing Canadians to identify their interests with those of the United States. For Anglophone Canadians, ethnic nationalism and continentalism tend to reinforce one another (those who are hostile to bilingualism tend to be strongly pro-American and vice versa), while for Francophones and unassimilated minority groups the two forces operate at cross purposes. Both forces, insofar as they exist, threaten the purpose and coherence of Canadian foreign policy. Neither of them should be underestimated.

POLITICAL DETERMINANTS

It is not proposed in this section to discuss the process by which Canadian foreign policy is made and implemented, since that is the subject of the following chapter. Rather, the intention is merely to mention some general characteristics of the Canadian political system that have an impact on foreign policy. The obvious fact that Canada is a liberal democracy has already been mentioned several times, and need not be discussed at any greater length. Some more specific aspects of the Canadian political system are worth noting.

In the first place, Canada has a parliamentary system of Government, «similar in principle to that of the United Kingdom», to quote from the preamble to the Constitution Act of 1867. Legally, this means that the making, although perhaps not the implementation, of foreign policy is considered the prerogative of the Crown. In practice, the powers of the Crown are exercised by the Prime Minister, the Cabinet, and the bureaucracy, whose influence over foreign policy is thus paramount. On the other hand, the influence of the House of Commons and of the Senate is correspondingly reduced, although not entirely non-existent. Certainly, there is no equivalent to the important role in foreign policy which the United States Senate derives from that country's constitution.

This consequence of parliamentary Government is reinforced by two other circumstances to which it has contributed. One is the existence of an essentially permanent bureaucracy whose continuity is hardly affected at all by the vicissitudes of electoral politics or the demands of elected legislators. A new Government wishing to undertake new foreign policies can make changes only slowly, if at all, since it cannot place its own supporters in positions of influence within the bureaucracy. The existing bureaucracy will tend to be committed to existing policies, not so much because they are those of the former Government as because the bureaucracy itself almost certainly contributed decisively to their formulation. Thus, foreign policy is, to a large extent, divorced from «politics».

The second circumstance is the existence of disciplined and cohesive political parties in the House of Commons, the individual members of which are unlikely to deviate publicly from the views and policies of the party leaders. For reasons already stated, there are few opportunities or incentives for the House to discuss foreign policy, but when occasions do arise, the discussion is likely to be predictable and lacking in spontaneity.

Whether Canada's political parties differ significantly from one another in their views on foreign policy is a subject on which it is difficult to reach a definitive conclusion, although we have attempted to do so elsewhere[12]. Insofar as politicians make foreign policy only within limits set by economic and social circumstances, and by the bureaucracy, it could be argued that the existence or otherwise of party differences is not particularly important, and it is made even less important by the infrequency with which the Government changes hands. Between 1945 and 1984, the Liberals formed the Government for all but six and a half years. Thus, it is hard to separate the Liberal Party's policies from those of the bureaucracy, and hard to know how the other parties would have contributed to policy had they been in office.

Broadly speaking, it can be said that until about 1963, the Liberals tended to be somewhat more pro-American and the Conservatives somewhat more pro-British, but as American and British foreign policies converged, these tendencies declined in significance. Since 1963, the Progressive Conservative Party has been influenced by, although never entirely captured by, the view of foreign policy that was described in an earlier part of this chapter as «fundamentalist conservative», a fact that reflects the importance of professionals, farmers, and small busines-people within the Party. It is thus now more pro-American than the Liberal Party. The New Democratic Party, with its predominance of teachers, academics, and clergymen, has taken the opposite view. The Liberal Party has steered a middle course between the extremes, although it is difficult to say to what extent this reflects the views of the Party itself as opposed to its leaders on the one hand, and the bureaucracy on the other.

Neither parliamentary institutions nor political parties, however, have as much influence on foreign policy as does Canadian federalism. Since another chapter considers the role of the provinces, only a few brief observations need be made here. One effect of Canadian federalism, as interpreted by the courts, is that the power of the Federal Government to implement foreign policy is limited by the functional division of legislative powers between the federal and provincial levels. Some treaties can only be made effective through provincial legislation. Less frequently noted, but equally important in practice, is the fact that federalism limits the financial resources available to the central Government for expenditures on diplomacy, external aid, or military defence. A large share of tax revenue, and almost all natural resource revenue, is collected by the provinces for their own purposes, while a large part of the revenue that the Federal Government does acquire must be handed over to the provinces in equalization payments or contributions to shared-cost programmes. Thus, the effective capabilities of the Canadian State as an international actor are considerably lower than Canada's population, resources and level of economic development would suggest.

The Canadian provincial governments enjoy greater powers than their counterparts in other federations such as Germany or the United States. This fact, as well as the distinctive economic and, in the case of Québec, cultural interests which they allegedly represent, has encouraged them to undertake external initiatives and policies of their own, often in competition with the federal authorities. Carried to its logical conclusion, this practice would cause the Canadian Federal State to disintegrate, as the British Empire disintegrated for all practical purposes when the Dominions challenged the imperial Government's exclusive control over external policy.

So far at least, disintegration has been avoided, but provincial external activities have influenced Canadian foreign policy nonetheless. Provincial efforts to promote exports of manufactured goods and resources have probably stimulated the Federal Government to do the same more vigorously than it would have done otherwise, so as to undercut the rationale for provincial activity. Similarly, and more clearly, Québec's efforts to conduct its own diplomacy from about 1965 onwards stimulated the Federal Government to recruit more Francophones into the Department of External Affairs and to promote relations with France and with former French colonies.

Thomas Hockin, a Progressive Conservative MP, once argued that federalism affects the style and procedure of Canadian foreign policy, as well as the substance. Because the Canadian Federal Government must frequently rely on reaching agreement with provincial governments in order to achieve its domestic goals, federal politicians and officials acquire habits of negotiation, compromise, flexibility and, at worst, willingness to sacrifice substantive goals for the sake of preserving the lowest common denominator of agreement. As a result of this experience, Canadians engaged in international negotiations tend to act in the same way as they are accustomed to act domestically. Hockin was critical of the results, arguing that Canadian diplomacy tends to underestimate the importance of substantive conflicts of interest, to regard organizations (*e.g.*, the Commonwealth, NATO or the UN) as ends in themselves rather than as means to achieve other ends, and to assume that all differences can be resolved through negotiation. On the other hand, he admitted that the lessons learned through our domestic experience might «generate ideas of real relevance for the international system», if they were applied more critically and selectively[13].

NOTES

1. Normand Hillmer and Garth Stevenson (ed.), *Foremost Nation: Canadian Foreign Policy and a Changing World,* Toronto, McClelland and Stewart, 1977. The expression was first coined by James Eayrs.

2. Peyton V. Lyon and Brian W. Tomlin, *Canada as an International Actor,* Toronto, Macmillan, 1979, p. 56-76.

3. *Ibidem,* p. 77-94.

4. This is explored more fully by Garth Stevenson, «Canada in the United Nations», in Hillmer and Stevenson, *op. cit.,* p. 150-177.

5. Denis Stairs, «Public opinion and external affairs: reflections on the domestication of Canadian foreign policy», *International Journal,* XXXIII, No. 1, Winter, 1977-1978, p. 128-149.

6. Some evidence may be found in R.B. Byers and David Leyton-Brown, «Canadian elite images of the international system», *International Journal* XXXII, No. 3, Summer, 1977, p. 608-639.

7. See for example The Canadian Gallup Poll Report of December 1, 1973, which compares the attitudes of Francophone and Anglophone Canadians towards France and towards the United States.

8. Joseph Scanlon, «Canada sees the world through US eyes: one case study in cultural domination», *Canadian Forum,* September, 1974, p. 34-39.

9. This interpretation is suggested by John B. McLin, *Canada's Changing Defence Policy,* Baltimore, Johns Hopkins University Press, 1967, p. 213.

10. The study is discussed in Raymond Breton, Jeffrey G. Reitz and Victor Valentine, *Cultural Boundaries and the Cohesion of Canada,* Montréal, Institute for Research on Public Policy, 1980, p. 351-356. See especially the table on p. 352.

11. For an interesting interpretation of how the «loyalist» tradition has been transformed into continentalism, see Ramsay Cook, «Loyalism, technology, and Canada's fate», in *The Maple Leaf Forever,* Toronto, Macmillan, 1971, p. 46-67.

12. Garth Stevenson, «Foreign Policy», in C. Winn and J. McMenemy (ed.), *Political Parties in Canada,* Toronto, McGraw-Hill Ryerson, 1976, p. 250-266.

13. Thomas Hockin, «Federalist Style in International Politics», in Stephen Clarkson (ed.), *An Independent Foreign Policy for Canada?,* Toronto, McClelland and Stewart, 1968, p. 119-130.

3

Elaboration and Management of Canadian Foreign Policy

John Kirton
University of Toronto

Most Canadians wondering how their country's foreign policy is formulated may well be forgiven for being confused about who within their federal Government is actually in control. Within the maze of modern Ottawa, the venerable doctrines of Cabinet solidarity, ministerial responsibility and the Official Secrets Act still conspire to keep most details about foreign policy-making confined to those who are insiders in the process. And for those on the outside, the media offer ever-changing images about who the dominant figures are. One day it is an internationally-respected Prime Minister meeting the world's major leaders in the annual Western Economic Summit; another, it is a Ken Taylor demonstrating the traditional excellence of Canada's Department of External Affairs and Foreign Service in the distant reaches of Iran. And in between, a host of officials and ministers from other departments and organizations issuing an endless stream of pronouncements about Canada's involvement in the globe.

An easy answer to the question of «who is in charge?» would exist if each of these claimants enjoyed primacy within its preferred sphere. In a simple world, External Affairs would manage general peace and security matters, other departments would cope with routine military, economic and functional issues, and the Prime Minister would save himself for momentous decisions or issues where others' jurisdictions overlap. But as the foreign policy agenda becomes crowded with complex issues mutating beyond conventional categories, and as each group expands to keep up with the changes and to control the overall flow, a myriad of connections and conflicts arise. For a major power in the modern world, there thus remains no easy answer to the questions of who dominates daily decision-making on matters with international implications, and who determines the country's foreign policy as a whole[1].

In such circumtances, considerable attention must be given at the outset to the portrait implied by the great liberal-internationalist traditions of Canadian diplomacy. Symbolized by the image of Lester B. Pearson as Secretary of State for External Affairs receiving a Nobel Peace Prize for his peacekeeping initiative in the Suez Crisis of 1956, this portrait assigns the Foreign Minister and his professional foreign service in the Department of External Affairs a predominant role. It gives other departments a secondary but still substantial complementary involvement and leadership in the more routine areas of low politics. And it offers the Prime Minister and his associates a passive, oversight function which reinforces as necessary, External's internationalist thrust. In such a system the widespread consensus about these internationalist precepts, the informal contacts among senior officials in a compact Government, and a legacy of success in responding to crises on an *ad hoc* basis renders unnecessary elaborate mechanisms for interdepartmental consultation and Government-wide coordination. In short, the lead departments are left alone to do their daily job in their assigned area and their leaders are trusted collectively to deal with ease with major matters when the occasion demands.

In traditional opposition to this comforting portrait stand those who see the fundamentals of Canadian foreign policy controlled by American imperialists abroad and their capitalist collaborators at home. To them, the decision-making game within the federal Government's executive branch is but a relatively powerless counter to (and pale reflection of) demands imposed by concentrations of power beyond. As a result, the «domestic» departments and agencies, and particularly those best positioned to service these outside masters, dominate the foreign policy decision-making process. Before them, the foreign office and prime ministerial groups get subordinate positions, happily assuming or reluctantly recognizing the very narrow room for manœuver which these outside faces allow. The overwhelming impact of these «realities» renders unnecessary an internal capacity for forward planning and tight, comprehensive coordination, as the smoothly ticking pieces contribute with minimum deviation to their single, simple objective. In short, the foreign policy apparatus operates like clockwork to aid its outside masters as they intended, devoid of the disruptions which internal exercises of autonomy might bring.

The antithesis of this discouraging vision comes, rather more tentatively, from those who believe that Canada might be large enough on the global scale to help define, rather be defined by, those «realities» beyond its borders. Arguing that the internal machinations of Ottawa matter profoundly in the specification of Canadian foreign policy, they see those at the apex of the overall process – the Prime Minister and his direct associates – as the leading figures in the fight. The domestic departments – closest to the abundant reserves of national power – also have a high salience, while the foreign office group retreats to a moderate level. Not surprisingly, the existence of three strong and somewhat equal competitors, all relatively free from outside constraints and overriding objectives, leads to a process of prolonged, complex conflict, and ultimately, to the creation of strong, central coordinative mechanisms to define the national interests and enforce its primacy in the struggle below. In short, because the parts now have the freedom to become involved in one another's job, those at the centre have the autonomy and the responsibility to continually define how the whole will be assembled.

Since the modern era of Canadian foreign policy began in 1948, the operation of Ottawa's foreign policy machinery has always conformed in some measure to all of these three portraits and has, at various times, given each some claim to a position of real strength. Yet throughout these three and a half decades, a striking pattern has emerged. For as the American-dominated international system has eroded, and Canadian freedom commensurably expanded, the «liberal-internationalist» and «dependence» visions of Canada's foreign policy decision-making process have increasingly lost their claims.

In Louis St. Laurent's Liberal Government of 1948-1957, the process was indeed based largely on External Affairs leadership, segmented policy-making and informal coordination, yet still affected by the small size and perceptual constraints of officialdom and its leadership. Yet John Diefenbaker's Conservative Government of 1957-1963 brought major conflicts over defence issues and prime ministerial intrusions, while the successor Liberal Government of Lester B. Pearson from 1963 to

1968 both broadened and deepened the conflicts and instituted the first systematic efforts at comprehensive coordination. In Pierre E. Trudeau's first two Liberal governments, from 1968 to 1974 countervailing capacity, interdepartmental conflict and strong central coordination were injected into the foreign policy process as a matter of philosophy. And from 1974 onward, there emerged within Ottawa a *de facto* central agency that was sufficiently strong on the whole to successfully manage this process, despite the disruptions of Joe Clark's short-lived Conservative Government in 1979-1980. This historic shift culminated with the return of Trudeau's Liberals in 1980, as a 1982 reorganization of the Government's foreign policy process and external affairs machinery gave broader and deeper institutional expression to the strong internal competition and coordination through which a State's autonomy is secured.

SEGMENTATION AND HARMONY, 1948-1957

The foreign policy decision-making system, which prevailed in Ottawa during the first postwar decade, rested on three foundations – stable executive branch leadership, a comfortable segmentation of the major departments involved in foreign affairs, and the common internationalist vision of the individuals most directly concerned. While the wartime Conscription legacy and current Cold War demands imposed some constraints, America's new international primacy and commitment, Canada's internal peace and prosperity and the Government's secure parliamentary majority and budgetary surpluses left the Government with considerable freedom to promote their newly-enshrined international ideals in a difficult world. In keeping with External's seminal role in the internationalist revolution, the enduring principle of individual ministerial responsibility, and its small size, the Government operated, in an easy division of labour, by having External exercise unchallenged leadership in peace and security matters, other departments assume predominance on international matters in their functional sphere, and the Prime Minister saved to intervene, if necessary, in a mediatory role. Reducing prime ministerial intervention and cementing the broader segmentation was the profound internationalist commitment of a tightly-knit group of men who had absorbed at first hand the lessons of World War II, decisively repudiated Prime Minister Mackenzie King's lingering quasi-isolationist instincts in 1947 and remained determined to forward their values in the unknown era of atomic weaponry and total war.

At the top of this edifice stood Prime Minister Louis St. Laurent, a man with firm Christian beliefs, an orderly legal mind, and a traditional French-Canadian antipathy towards imperial powers. St. Laurent had developed very early an intense personal attachment to internationalist precepts and as Secretary of State for External Affairs from 1946 to 1948, had crafted the inaugural initiatives of the new era. To be sure issues which threatened to produce large-scale Canadian commitments and casualties in distant locations such as Korea, the cautious instincts of the Conscription era could be aroused. But in general, St. Laurent as Prime Minister proved true to his intellectual commitments, pressing as a priority to have Canada adopt NATO, with a strong Article 2, discouraging France's efforts to retain its empire, and exploding at the hubric folly of the «supermen» of Europe in the Suez Crisis of 1956.

Sustaining St. Laurent's predispositions was Secretary of State for External Affairs Lester B. Pearson, a man who St. Laurent had twice chosen as his deputy in the Department. Pearson, knowing that he had received St. Laurent's full trust, and constrained only by a self-imposed obligation to inform the Prime Minister in advance of major initiatives, was free to lead External into undisputed preeminence in the formation of policy on politico-military issues. Under Pearson's creative leadership, External served as the fountainhead of the Golden Decade's internationalist initiatives (NATO 1949, UNEF 1956), prevailed where necessary against the conservatism of other ministers and departments (Korea 1950, Indochina 1954), and, on occasion, against St. Laurent's instincts themselves (French arms transshipments).

In a large measure, Pearson's primacy was sustained by the talented personnel, internal cohesion and operational ethos of his Department. As the preeminent Department within Ottawa, save possibly for Finance, External possessed the most talented officials in the public service, including generalists, such as Norman Robertson, with an intricate knowledge of trade and related economic affairs, and distinguished soldier-statemen such as Generals MacNaughton, Pope and Burns. Within External, highly fluid supervisory arrangements, a similarity social background and superior credentials, a practise of rapid rotation and generalist career pattern, and the proliferating responsibilities and rewards imposed on a small service bred cohesion, with intellectual differences among conservative, moderal and left-liberal tendencies serving merely to sharpen the analytical sophistication of departmental proposals. Of equal importance was a deep inbred consensus that Canada was a middle power with sufficient capability to help preserve peace, create a better global order, and defend western values within it, by diligent diplomacy within multilateral institutions. Accordingly, career incentives and concepts of professionalism were concentrated on sustaining global peace and security through the United Nations, and regional defence through the North Atlantic Treaty Organization. A decade of continuing success in the high calling of mediatory diplomacy testified to the propriety of this view.

Within the interdepartmental community, External faced an easy task. For in Ottawa the sphere of foreign policy, the area of global peace and security, and the imperatives of diplomacy were separated from their rivals and permitted to prevail when challenges arose. External thus played the major or exclusive part in the multilateral security realm, and even on the more functional and economic issues closer to home, notably relations with the United States, seldom consulted beyond the core group of Ottawa's other major powers – Trade and Commerce, Finance and National Defence. Routine interdepartmental consultation was confined to United Nations and defence-related subjects, with formal committees used by External to mobilize the specialized advice of others and give them central political direction[2].

Broadly speaking, it was the ministers and the mandarins rather than the bureaucratic mechanisms that ensured coherence in the foreign policy sphere. Within Cabinet, St. Laurent allowed his ministers to state their views freely, employing his stature, persuasive skill and commanding intellect to solidify an emerging consensus. Immediately below was the heart of the system for here potential disputes were resolved or massaged in advance by the three dozen members of the «Subcabinet», and before them by the 200 or so members of the «bureaucratic elite». Graduating from the same elite universities, maintaining informal, intimate contact in Ottawa, and moving easily among jurisdictional boundaries in conversation and career pattern, these men had an intuitive appreciation of one another's policy perspectives and the limits imposed by their long-serving ministers on the definition of the collective good. Committed to the precepts defined by St. Laurent in his 1947 Gray lecture, and relieved from squabbling over resource allocation by a rapidly expanding foreign service, both mandarins and ministers could move in unorchestrated unity to achieve the internationalist successes of the Golden Decade.

COMPETITION AND FRAGMENTATION, 1957-1963

During the six years of John Diefenbaker's Government, the internal harmony and overall consistency of the St. Laurent era were severely eroded by profound changes in the world beyond Ottawa. In particular, a highly ambiguous external environment brought the beginnings of détente and decolonization, even as sudden eruptions of Soviet intrusiveness in Berlin and Cuba imposed the old Cold War constraints in more rigid form. This changing world gave greater scope for initiatives from Ottawa and led, partly as a result, to unstable relationships and growing frictions among major departments. Primacy passed unevenly among National Defence, with its security and NATO objectives, External Affairs, with its global disarmament concerns, and the major economic departments, with their more pressing domestic imperatives. This instability was heightened by a strong-minded Prime Minister whose policy beliefs, electoral sensitivities, and distrust of the «pearsonalities» in External and Trade and Commerce impeded the reliable implementation of the old precepts of internationalism, the effective application of new varieties, and the emergence of a workable synthesis between the two[3].

John Diefenbaker entered office with a longstanding interest in foreign affairs, an equally enduring commitment to peacekeeping, the United Nations, and NATO, and a passionate attachment to Britain, the multiracial commonwealth and human rights. Yet his intensely political character, Western Canadian power base and minority situation in 1957-1958 and 1962-1963 led him to calculate foreign policy for its electoral advantage, respond to the direct concerns of Canada's eastern European minorities, and oscillate between a student anti-communism on the one hand and support for a non-nuclear Canada and disarmed world on the other. Thus Diefenbaker, suspicious of his professional foreign policy advisers, decided from the outset to take the leading role in foreign policy. He proved true to his word in a host of early issues – Middle East policy, South African Commonwealth membership, trade diversion to the US, Britain's Common Market membership, Canadian forces in Europe, Bomarc acquisition, Arrow cancellation, and NORAD establishment. Yet after 1960, the prime ministerial involvement, suspicions and indecisiveness increased, as Diefenbaker concluded that he had been poorly advised on the NORAD and Arrow decisions, ill-treated by the new US President Kennedy, and insufficiently sympathetic to the anti-nuclear sentiments of his Secretary of State for External Affairs, Howard Green. He thus led Canada's reluctance to support American behaviour in the Cuban Missile Crisis of 1962 and to oppose the introduction of nuclear weapons into Canada through to the fall of his Government over this issue in February 1963[4].

John Diefenbaker's convictions initially left little freedom for External Affairs. The Prime Minister occupied the portfolio himself on two occasions, chose as the first Minister the inexperienced Sidney Smith, and deliberately kept the Department's Under Secretary, Norman Robertson, outside of his inner circle of advisers. External's fortunes, however, rose considerably with the June 1959 ministerial appointment of Howard Green, a parliamentary veteran, trustworthy friend of the Prime Minister, and stout supporter of the British connection, of his new Department's officials and of global disarmament initiatives. Thus External began to make its presence felt, particularly in such security-related questions as intelligence monitoring, United Nation's Congo peacekeeping, the Cuban Missile Crisis and weapons procurement arrangements. Most importantly, Green, backed by a sympathetic Robertson, was able to hold up Cabinet approval of a draft agreement for Canadian acceptance of nuclear weapons, to counter DND's pressure for interdepartmental agreement on, and Cabinet consideration of, the issue, and to sustain John Diefenbaker's reluctance to accept the weaponry until the end.

In these security issues, External's primary antagonist after 1960 was the Department of National Defence. Yet, while it was the resignation of DND's Minister, Douglas Harkness, that led to the parliamentary defeat of the Diefenbaker Government in 1963, the increasing interdepartmental tensions also began to emerge in other policy spheres. Domestic economic considerations and departments began to make growing claims on defence resources and the framework of foreign policy as a whole. Trade and Commerce, particularly after Deputy Minister Mitchell Sharp's resignation and George Hees' assumption of the portfolio, was reoriented to focus on promoting Canadian trade with the United Kingdom, Latin America and other overseas markets. And Finance was left largely alone to impose constraints on Canadian representation and aid programmes abroad, deal with the problems of slow economic growth and Government austerity, to manage the exchange crisis with the United States in 1962.

The decline of the traditional internationalist consensus, reflected in the tension between defence and disarmament tendencies, and concerns over a close relationship with the United States, presented the Conservative problem with a major need to actively promote Government-wide foreign policy coordination. Yet given John Diefenbaker's distrust of officialdom and penchant for personal, politically-oriented decision-making, the available vehicles of the Cabinet process and attendent interdepartmental network operated much less reliably than in the past. John Diefenbaker chose not to involve his Cabinet in such major decisions as NORAD and South African withdrawal from the Commonwealth, rotated his major ministers far more frequently than his predecessors, and relied for policy advice within the Privy Council Office only on Robert Bryce and Basil Robinson. At senior levels of the civil service, the traditional Undercabinet group became somewhat less cohesive, as several leading officials left the economic departments and External Affairs before and shortly after Diefenbaker's arrival. When reinforced by a 50 % growth in the civil service since the early 1950s, and the creation of new institutions such as the National Energy Board, these trends severely reduced the easy relationships, psychological consensus and of the earlier era, and left the task of coordination to an increasingly isolated Prime Minister.

IDEOLOGICAL CLEAVAGE AND DOMESTICATION, 1963-1968

The advent of Lester B. Pearson's Liberal Government brought the first systematic attempt to impose such coherence, first through decisive prime ministerial action and, later, through the creation of a Cabinet Committee and foreign policy planning process. Yet at the same time, the competing policy tendencies of the Diefenbaker era slowly spread into broader economic and diplomatic areas and into newly-established departments. They were driven by a growing impatience at home and abroad with the old verities of Canada's role vis-à-vis the UN and NATO and the United States, and by an acute need to manage the stresses of minority Government, to counter Québec's assertion of greater autonomy within and beyond Canada's borders, and to respond to the internal economic and social demands which a rapidly growing bureaucracy, replete with a plethora of new domestically-linked departments, injected into the foreign policy process. The result was a set of deeply-rooted cleavages at the ministerial and senior official level over the treatment of Québec, Canada's international economic relationships, and the country's traditional relationship with the United States in NORAD, NATO, and in Vietnam. While the new coordinative processes tried to cope, adjustment to domestic concerns and the creation of a renewed foreign policy consensus remained an uneven, troubled and uncompleted process[5].

Prime Minister Lester B. Pea   driven to play a major role in foreign policy by his formidable reputation ir   at home and abroad, the desire of compatriots and foreigners for reassu   er the Diefenbaker debacle, the need to mediate between the competing vie   major ministers, and by his chairmanship of a Cabinet Committee on Ext   irs and Defence created n 1964. In addition, the uncertainties which the   is of Vietnam created for his minority Government, the severe threat which   's fused attack on the North American Alliance and Québec's place in Confe   osed to national and personal values, and his desire to adapt his internatio   victions to the changing international order, demanded his involvement. Y   ame time, the incessant demands of parliamentary management and el   ng, the escalating challenges from Québec City, and his own experienc ... ... St. Laurent Government, made for a highly circumscribed role. In the security sphere, Pearson tended to confine his attention to the summit diplomacy, peacekeeping initiatives and crisis mediation at which he excelled, and, particularly after 1965, to mediating the growing disagreements among prospective claimants to his leadership. Although he resisted Defence Minister Paul Hellyer's demands for large increases in defence expenditure in formulating the defence White Paper of 1964 and overrode Foreign Minister Paul Martin to call publicly for a pause in American bombing of North Vietnam at Temple University in Philadelphia in 1965, he tended to defer to his major ministers. Indeed despite his increasing reservations, he commissioned the «Robertson Review» of Canada's overall foreign policy, amid External Affairs' hesitations, only in 1967. In the economic sphere, his mediatory skills were fully employed in managing the conflicts between the nationalist Finance Minister Walter Gordon and the liberal Trade Minister Mitchell Sharp over the 1963 budget, the *Time* and *Reader's Digest* issues, the status of the Mercantile Bank, direct foreign investment screening and the Kennedy Round GATT negotiations. Indeed, prime ministerial leadership was reserved preeminently for the strains of managing the relationship with Québec and France, as Pearson decided that priority in Canada's external affairs must be given to strengthening and developing close ties with France expanded Canadian activities with France, and directed Canadian aid towards the Francophone world. By 1965, he again took the lead in producing a compromise policy on the sale of Canadian uranium to France, defining Canada's vigorous opposition to French withdrawal from the military component of NATO in 1966, and, with personal outrage, directing a Canadian protest against France's refusal to receive visits from Canadian representatives. And in 1967, he insisted upon a centennial year visit by de Gaulle to Ottawa as well as to Québec City, assumed personal responsibility for arrangements for the visit, and, over the objections of Paul Martin, produced the strong response to de Gaulle's declaration of support for a free Québec[6].

On most occasions, however, Secretary of State for External Affairs Paul Martin was left surprisingly free to assert leadership in the security sphere. Not only did Pearson desire such an arrangement, but he also felt reassured by Martin's status as a strong Minister, committed internationalist and highly experienced practitioner in the foreign policy realm. Martin was ably backed by Marcel Cadieux, appointed Under Secretary in 1964 on the grounds that he was a Francophone with a firm belief in strong federal Government. In addition, the creation of new division for Cultural Affairs, relations with French-speaking states, and federal-provincial coordination and the emphasis on recruiting Francophone offices began to broaden and re-orient External's interests to the fundamental challenges arising at home, even if such senior officials as Cadieux, and Canadian Ambassador to France Jules Léger could disagree over how relations with Québec and France were to be conducted. With these formidable assets, Paul Martin and his Department easily dominated NATO-related questions and peacekeeping involvements in Cyprus, Vietnam and the Middle East. Despite occasional checks, Martin overrode Pearson's doubts about Vietnam, his desire for an early NATO review, and his reluctance, shared by clerk of the Privy Council Gordon Robertson, to have Canada accept membership on the United Nations Security Council in 1966. Yet as doubts about the war in Vietnam and concern with the Franco-Québec challenge grew, Martin's preserve became increasingly subject to the criticisms of other ministers, who began to acquire some meaningful involvement in policy formulation[7].

The primary claimant of a voice in the foreign policy domain was Walter Gordon, Minister of Finance from April 1963 to December 1965, and leader of a left-wing coalition in Cabinet and Caucus, which included Allan MacEachen, Edgar Benson and, after 1965, Jean Marchand, Gérald Pelletier and Pierre E. Trudeau. Although this coalition favoured redirecting Canadian defence from its close association with the United States in NATO and NORAD, and transferring defence resources to foster social welfare objectives at home, its major energies were devoted to furthering Canadian economic independence from the United States and arresting Québec's movement towards an autonomous presence abroad.

Despite the growing intensity of such challenges to orthodox positions, conflicting ministerial perspectives, particularly in the security sphere, were seldom solved or even fully debated in the frequent Cabinet discussions held during this period. To be sure the Prime Minister and Cabinet had begun to develop their coordinative capacity through the appointment of Tom Kent as a policy adviser to Prime Minister Pearson, the work of Jean Beetz and Marc Lalonde on constitutional questions in the Prime minister's office, and the formation in 1964 of fixed array of nine Cabinet committees, including bodies for External Affairs and for Defence. Yet the decline in Pearson's authority as leader after 1965 led to an increasing disorder in Cabinet's business, a focus on reacting to crisis issues, and, with the exception of NORAD, an absence of broad reviews in the field of foreign policy or defence. These trends were exacerbated by the tendency of Paul Martin and other ministers to resolve all contentious issues in private discussion with the Prime Minister and only then bring them to Cabinet for ritual scrutiny and confirmation[8].

And at the official level, the old coordinate processes began to break under the strain of a rapidly growing bureaucracy, and the creation of new departments with focused missions, precise demands and domestic constituencies, notably Industry in 1963, Manpower and Immigration, and Energy, Mines and Resources in 1966. To be sure, the establishment of a Cabinet Committee and task force on foreign investment and the initiation of the Robertson Review towards the end of the Pearson Government marked a move towards special policy-planning exercises in particular areas[9]. Yet these initiatives were authorized with considerable reluctance, conducted in some secrecy and developed and dealt with at one remove from the Government's central decision-making process.

STRUCTURAL COORDINATION AND CONCEPTION OF THE NATIONAL INTEREST, 1968-1974

The first fundamental effort to contain these proliferating internal conflicts and impose an explicit conception of the national interest on them came with the Liberal Government of Prime Minister Pierre E. Trudeau. Particularly during its first four years in office, the rapid dispersion of power in the international system, combined with Trudeau's charismatic leadership and parliamentary majority, provided a refreshing freedom to re-orient Canadian foreign policy in a fundamental way, in considerable detail and in accordance with a precise, integrated conception of Canada's distinctive national interests. The vitality of this process was sustained by the proliferation, within a rapidly growing bureaucracy of new departments and bureau with organized expertise in international affairs, and External Affairs' expanding involvement in the full range of domestically-linked policy arenas. Although the convergence of these expansions created intense, persistent interdepartmental tensions, these processes no longer overwhelmed the coherence of overall Government policy. For stimulating, structuring and guiding these tensions were new, powerful and precise coordinative mechanisms, including an organized Cabinet Committee system, comprehensive policy-planning exercises on defence, foreign investment, foreign policy and Canada-US relations, a programme of foreign service integration and, finally, a new leadership role for the Department of External Affairs itself. Although less successful in practice than in the plans of their progenitors, these coordinative mechanisms produced a continuing incentive for coherence, and a discernable constraint on daily decision-making itself[10].

Initially, these thrusts towards redefinition and coherence were largely the work of Prime Minister Trudeau. Although he entered office with little knowledge of, or interest in, international politics, he possessed a particular impatience with the past concepts and conduct of Canadian foreign policy. His previous travels and activity in Québec's intellectual circles had provided him with considerable sympathy for the People's Republic of China's place in the world community, an emphatic rapport with the socio-economic imperatives of leaders in Third World states and a pronounced antipathy towards defence and nuclear involvements. More importantly, his entry into politics in 1965, his work as Pearson's Parliamentary Secretary and Minister of Justice, and his quest for the Liberal leadership had been motivated by a deep-seated belief in the need for a strong Federal Government, under which the oppressive strains of narrow nationalism could be contained, the virtues of ethnic pluralism registered, and the values of individual liberty expressed in full.

When applied to Foreign Affairs, this heritage translated into a de-emphasis on any systemically-oriented concern with fostering global peace and security through mediatory initiatives and the progression of international institutional promotion, in favour of policies derived from Canada's particular, domestically-linked national interests, and aimed at sustaining its existence as a strong Federal State. From this commitment, Trudeau's French-Canadian heritage and his generational perspective flowed a distaste for traditional military roles, a desire to reduce defence expenditure to promote economic growth at home and economic development abroad, and a concentration on the particular objectives of reducing international economic disparity, environmental degradation and nuclear proliferation[11]. Such objectives suggested a conception of Canada as a State, whose global relevance centered on the solution of its internal linguistic dilemmas as a means of removing a potential source of global conflict and inspiring others to equally enlightened responses to the dilemmas of modern society. At the same time, however, Trudeau's concern with creating counterweights to Canada's relationship with the United States, both for intellectual balance and to meet the genuine needs of Francophones, revealed a more ambitious belief. Reinforcing this belief was a view of Governement as a powerful instrument of innovation, capable of anticipating rather than reacting to environmental alterations and producing those new policies which met society's changing needs. This meant a commitment to a rational decision-making process in which the demands of foreign and domestic interests would be raised for balanced consideration and integrated under a defined policy framework that ensured central political control. When reinforced by Trudeau's distaste for the disorder of the Pearson Government, these predispositions dictated a continuous, wide-ranging, countervailing debate among a much broader group of officials, strong central agencies to ensure competing bureaucratic proposals flowed to Cabinet, and a revised array of Cabinet committees and procedures in which political leaders could determine policy in an autonomous, coordinated and creative fashion.

These preferences were rapidly registered in far-reaching decisions initiated and determined by the Prime Minister himself. With support from a small group of sympathetic individuals, a strengthened Prime Minister's Office, and, after 1970, his full-time Special Adviser on International Relations, Ivan Head, Trudeau produced a statement entitled «Canada in the World», that initiated a full-scale review of Canadian foreign policy, defined several policy areas to be re-examined and announced definitive decisions on several significant issues notably, diplomatic recognition of the People's Republic of China. His office actively supervised and shaped the foreign policy review that culminated in *Foreign Policy for Canadians*, and sustained his predisposition to reduce Canadian NATO forces in Europe, and review defence policy as a whole. Trudeau and Head were also dominant in formulating Canada's «functional» claim to jurisdiction in the Arctic Waters controversy of 1970 and in securing from a divided Cabinet an agreement to exclude its application from the jurisdiction of the International Court of Justice. Perhaps the tightest prime ministerial control was exercised in all matters related to Québec, where Trudeau, his closest advisers, and his Québec ministerial colleagues, notably Gérald Pelletier and Jean Marchand, defined in detail Canada's response to Québec's relationship with France, Canada's suspension of diplomatic relations with Gabon, and its actions on the international dimensions of the October Crisis of 1970[12].

Not surprisingly, prime ministerial preeminence and predispositions propelled the Department of External Affairs, in turn, into a position of painful irrelevance, a revolutionary re-orientation and, ultimately, a renewed effort to regain relevance over a much broader policy sphere. To facilitate this process, Trudeau gave the External Affairs portfolio to Mitchell Sharp, a highly-experienced former civil servant and economic Minister, and a decisive supporter of Trudeau at the 1968 Liberal Leadership Convention. Yet despite Sharp's credentials, External's desire to retain Canadian forces in Europe at existing levels, its views on the Arctic waters issue and its advice on other overseas matters were overturned or countered by recommendations from central agencies and Cabinet. Moreover, the Prime Minister publicly challenged the reporting functions, military priority and internationalist emphasis at the heart of External's traditional mission forced External Affairs to close missions and release personnel during a 1969 austerity programme and imposed on it a new interdepartmental procedure for administering posts abroad that seemed to prophesy a permanent reduction in the Department's financial resources and administrative autonomy. This attack on DEA's essential organizational mission devastated the morale of those traditional departmental officials who viewed overseas «peace and security» diplomacy as their central mission and sphere of influence within Ottawa. However, after the initial shock, and attendant senior-level resignations and rotations, External responded with several initiatives designed to demonstrate its awareness of the new comprehensiveness, interrelatedness, and priorities of foreign policy and its determination to acquire a leading role in this potentially unlimited policy sphere[13]. A Policy Analysis Group (PAG) was formed to define the diplomat's function and the overall foreign policy framework the Prime Minister desired. The Department assumed direction of the integrated procedures for managing operations abroad. In 1971, it conducted a full-scale reorganization of its headquarters structure, designed to enhance, *inter alia* its influence in a broad range of internationally-related functional and domestic issues and its links with organization outside the bureaucracy. And in the autumn of 1972 was given responsibility for drafting and directing Canada's first comprehensive policy towards and statement of its «Options for the Future» in, its relations with the United States.

However, despite their far-reaching character, these changes did not enable External to re-establish its traditional preeminence. One reason was the weakness of its traditional associate in politico-military affairs, the Department of National Defence, which was headed by three different ministers during Trudeau's first four years in office, similarly overriden on major issues, and restored to some influence only with the adoption of the more civilianized mission codified in *Defence in the Seventies*[14]. A far more fundamental brake on External's re-emergence was the Trudeau Government's major expansion of the foreign affairs components of domestic departments. These departments were given direct authority over the international aspects of their national activity, allowed to establish internal units to act as focal points for foreign-related matters and permitted to recruit officers with competitive foreign affairs expertise. This simultaneous expansion in the roles of DEA and the other departments soon replaced the many segmented processes of the past with a new nest of interconnected policy-making «systems». In the economic policy area, debates within the inner triumvirate of Finance, Industry, Trade and Commerce and External, and the regular challenges from such «secondary» members as Agriculture, Manpower and Immigration, Consumer and Corporate Affairs, Labour, National Revenue, and Regional Economic Expansion, usually gave the Cabinet Committee on Economic Policy and its supporting Privy Council Office secretarial a substantial voice in decisions. Elsewhere, energy, scientific and classic diplomatic matters also for Cabinet consideration and resolution. Environmental and defence questions were handled in a close, cooperative, senior-level relationship between External and its Domestic counterpart. And communications, transportation and immigration issues were controlled by the lead functional Department. Only in the rather new and more amorphous field of public diplomacy was policy-making centered in the Department of External Affairs alone.

This diversity in policy-making processes provided a major challenge to the coordinative ambitions of the Prime Minister. The Trudeau Government's search for a reliable method began at the Cabinet level. In order to achieve «a greater degree of planned, *collective*, political control over a large and complex Government apparatus», the Government separated the Prime Minister's Office from the Privy Council Office, provided the latter with the resources to continually monitor all policy sectors and directed the Treasury Board Secretariat to focus on allocating funds among programmes and departments in the light of Government-wide priorities[15]. Within the Cabinet, an orderly process of adversarial policy-making and central coordination was introduced, the number of ministers increased, Cabinet committees reduced in number and rationalized in structure into a network of five operative and four coordinating bodies, and meetings were scheduled at fixed times, with agendas, documents, and briefings given in advanced. To ensure broader coordination, ministers were allowed to receive all agendas and documents and to attend meetings of all bodies, with the exception of the key Priorities and Planning Committee, a small group of senior ministers focused on maintaining an overview of policy, defining priorities and planning strategies.

The impact of the new committee system was soon seen throughout the security sphere, notably in the six specific options, four separate policy reviews, and open disagreement among a large number of ministers in the NATO forces reduction decision of 1969. Moreover the advent of minority Government added a further incentive to greater, if less orderly, Cabinet control, as reflected in Cabinet's decisions on Vietnam in the spring of 1973. However, under the impact of an increased workload and minority government, the Cabinet system began to experience increasing difficulty in performing the integrative role its founders envisaged. The Government's move towards rapidly rotating deputy ministers and senior officials among departments engendered, not only countervailing, debate, but tendencies towards compromise at the higher reaches of the civil service. Within the Prime Minister's office only Ivan Head had a continuous, major involvement in foreign affairs, and concentrated on those overseas issues which aroused major domestic sensitivities or were of particular concern to the Prime Minister himself. The Privy Council Office rarely used its formidable powers of assembling agendas, writing and interpreting Cabinet decisions, and briefing the Prime Minister, to provide advice that directly countered or replaced proposals from below. And Treasury Board Secretariat focused primarily on screening foreign operations with a particularly high expenditure content. With Cabinet itself, matters were not routinely assessed as to their foreign impact and neither the Priorities and Planning Committee nor the full Cabinet moved to fill this vacuum.

These constraints soon shifted emphasis to the mechanism of comprehensive policy planning, notably a review of foreign policy as a whole, conducted from 1968 to 1970, and a 1972 paper on Canada's «Options for the Future» in its relations with the United States. However, this unprecedented effort to prepare and publish papers aimed at producing a comprehensive, coherent statement of its foreign policy objectives, quickly became overwhelmed by organization consideration, with both the content and continuing relevance of the documents directly reflecting the inter-ests and power of the actors that had sponsored them. Thus, the five sector studies outlining Canada's policies with regards to Europe, the Pacific, Latin America, the United Nations, and International Development, each prepared through a laborious process of interdepartmental consultation, served as a reference for subsequent policy deliberations and stimulus for interdepartmental cooperation. In marked con-trast, the general booklet which set out framework for Canadian foreign policy as a whole, prepared by a small component of External Affairs alone, had little continuing impact. A somewhat similar process occurred in the review of Canada-United States relations, where External Affairs alone wrote the final document and consulted other departments only at a rather late stage.

These exercises in comprehensive policy-planning thus quickly shifted from cooperative interdepartmental efforts at policy coordination to means for acquiring a leadership role for the Department of External Affairs. A similar result occurred in the Government's programme for enhancing coordination by integrating the administra-tion of departmental operations abroad[16]. At the initiative of officials in the central agencies, a carefully selected task force with a pro-integrative mandate was estab-lished in 1968 to examine the question and in 1969 forwarded proposals for combin-ing the separate foreign services of External Affairs, Industry, Trade and Commerce, Manpower and Immigration, and the Canadian International Development Agency into a «single comprehensive system of accountable management», unifying support staff at Canadian posts abroad and then instituting an interdepartmental country-programming procedure at home. The strong opposition of the various foreign service departments forced this integration programme to be introduced without its central «superministry» feature. Lacking a strong organizational centre, and with little con-tinuing attention from its Cabinet sponsors, integration was left to proceed on an incremental basis, enabling External Affairs, as the most generally-oriented foreign service departments, to slowly acquire lead responsibility. This assertion led other departments, notably Industry, Trade and Commerce, to resist vigorously any exten-sion of integrated procedures under the existing framework, and in turn prevented the integration programme from developing into an effective means for planning or coordination.

As a result, the Government turned increasingly to External Affairs, as its foreign office, to serve as the primary centre for surveying foreign-related activity throughout the bureaucracy, combining it into a coherent policy approach, and con-trolling all its aspects so as to bring this approach into effect[17]. Recognizing the unreliability of the Department's normal working practices, the Government moved to a much more ambitious programme of coordinative reform, directed at the hitherto elusive sphere of relations with the United States. Here it attempted the unprece-dented task of having External address Canada's extraordinarily broad and pervasive relationship with the United States on an ongoing basis, coordinate it to a greater degree than its other foreign relations, and creating a distinct executive procedure for this purpose. By late 1974, after considerable ministerial and bureaucratic effort, Ex-ternal Affairs was given a clear mandate to manage the relationship with the United States as a whole, the power to clear all United States-related issues taken to Cabinet, the responsibility to report periodically on the state of the relationship and the best way for Canada to approach it, and the lower-level bureaucratic resources to make these powers effective.

With these new resources, External soon achieved a comprehensive monitoring of the Government's full array of dealings with the United States, developed a considerable capacity for assessing the impact of Canadian proposals and responses on the United States and an ability to provide otherwise separated officials with the direct assessment of the linkages among, and the cumulative effect of, Canadian activities vis-à-vis the United States. Beyond the balancing stage, however, integrative achievements were extremely rare, as External was forced to concentrate on such immediate questions as reducing the general level of friction in the relationship over the next few months.

CENTRAL AGENCY COORDINATION, 1974-1980

External's move to secure a more pervasive coordinative effectiveness formed the central dynamic of the foreign policy decision-making process from 1974 to 1980. The need for such a coordinative centre stemmed from several factors. Within Ottawa, a declining civil service complement, the imposition of austerity in 1978 and the institution of an «envelope» system of financial expenditure heightened conflicts over allocating real resources. The preoccupation of both Prime Minister Trudeau and Clark, with a few priorities and their consequent emphasis on the individual ministerial prerogatives, reduced the strength of personally-based coordinative instincts at the top. And outside Ottawa, the challenges of a separatist Québec, resource-rich provinces and stagnant economy, together with the tensions bred by America's decline, demanded new foreign policy initiatives. As a result, External Affairs moved, with forceful intellectual and bureaucratic leadership, to transform its role to that of a modern central policy agency operating throughout the policy universe as a whole. And with the consistent support of Prime Minister Trudeau and his closest associates, it largely succeeded in exercising creative leadership over the expanded range of issues which Canada's heightened international stature produced[18].

With a secure parliamentary majority, the confidence of a renewed mandate and six years of experience, Pierre E. Trudeau returned to office in July 1974 with a considerably more sophisticated understanding of the type of decision-making system he wanted and of the way in which it could be obtained. His revised conception began with a stress on the need to conserve scarce ministerial time, a view of Government as a «confederacy of institutions [...] not rigidly commanded but enriched by a certain degree of countervailance», and a realization that «selection, training, promotion and demotion [of personnel] are in the final result as determinant of policy formation as techniques and instruments as likely to be»[19]. At the Cabinet level, a greater emphasis was soon placed on the responsibility of *senior* ministers, leadership by committee chairmen, and the use of special *ad hoc* committees for such complex time-consuming questions as the Tokyo Round of GATT negotiations, the Canada-US Alaska gas pipeline and the East Coast fisheries and maritime boundary dispute. In September 1976, Allan MacEachen was appointed Government House Leader and acting Prime Minister in the absence of Trudeau. And as the threat of the separatist *Parti québécois* and personal concerns came to preoccupy the Prime Minister, he withdrew, in the summer of 1977, from actively guiding all policy spheres save those of national unity economic recovery, and North-South international affairs. At the central agency and deputy ministerial level, a correspondingly greater reliance was placed on the transfer into influential positions of senior civil servants sympathetic to the Prime Minister's style of thinking and on procedure changes to enhance their influence. Three months after the 1974 election, Michael Pitfield replaced Gordon Robertson as Secretary to the Cabinet, thus placing in the most senior and sensitive post in the civil service an individual much closer to the Prime Minister in generational perspective, decision-making style and personal rapport. In the two years beginning in December 1974, early retirements, resignation and rotations brought changes in 22 Government departments and agencies. In February 1977, a career foreign-service officer assumed the presidency of CIDA. And over the next year changes were made, *inter alia,* at External Affairs and the Economic Council of Canada. Accompanying this flow of younger individuals into deputy ministerships was a shift of older, ex-deputy ministers into a series of short-term, special assignments.

This emphasis on individual ministers and prime-ministerially sensitive deputies allowed Trudeau to focus his influence on his paramount priorities, by directing the federal response to Québec's attempts to secure autonomous recognition abroad, playing an increasingly active role in the seven-power Western economic summits after 1976, and focusing on resource-transfer questions following Canadian co-chairmanship of the Conference on International Economic Questions in Paris in 1975. In other areas, however, he tended to assert a presence only where the demands of electioneering and summitry, his increasingly formidable reputation as an international leader, and long-standing personal beliefs, dictated.

The increasing selectivity of prime ministerial involvement gave greater prominence to the role of individual ministers and departments. Under Allan MacEachen, External Affairs played a major role, in support of the Prime Minister, in furthering the quest for a North-South dialogue and the Canadian contractual link with Europe. After Don Jamieson's appointment in September 1976, the Minister's deep attachment to friendly relations with the United States and close personal relationship with US Secretary of State Cyrus Vance led him to take the lead in a broad range of areas as well. The effort to sustain traditional conceptions of individual ministerial responsibility was also reflected in the increased prominence of other major departments, even in the formerly uninfluential Department of National Defence.

These reassertions of departmental autonomy, exacerbated by the strains of financial austerity and the pull of new priorities at home and abroad considerably reduced the coordinative impact of the Cabinet-Committee process. As Prime Minister Trudeau focused on responding to the November 1976 election of the *Parti québécois,* his three priority areas, and the demands of an impending election, his personal leadership and coordinative influence became concentrated through the newly-fused Priorities and Planning Federal Provincial Committee, on disbursing the scarce dollars which this body alone controlled, regulating issues with a high conflicting impact on economic recovery, national unity and North-South relations, and intervening in unpredictable fashion to forward these priorities and the Government's re-election concerns. The broader impact of such activity was restricted by the increasing power, if largely convergent views, of Allan MacEachen, Jean Chrétien and the functional committee chairmen. And with the 1978 resignation of Ivan Head, and preoccupation of central agency officials on expenditure constraint, the broader coordinative burden was increasingly thrust on senior PCO officials and those deputy ministers with particular sensitivity to, and ability to penetrate, Priorities and Planning's closed processes, variable preoccupations and electoral concerns.

To some extent, coordination was left to a revived planning process at the bureaucratic level. After the Trudeau Government's year-long ministerial effort to define overall Government priorities, and its subsequent preoccupation with the Québec situation, the Government returned to the foreign policy planning task in 1977, under the initiative of External Affairs' new Under Secretary Allan Gotlieb. The Undersecretary's first step was to create a Committee of Deputy Minister on Foreign Policy, which was a very restricted group of senior officials allowed to conduct a relatively free informal exchange of views, on issues of immediate importance, under the firm leadership of External Affairs. The Under Secretary also revived the External Affairs planning group, giving it the new name of Policy Planning Secretariat (POL), and an opportunity to participate in all important deliberations before final departmental decisions were made. And in early 1979, the Under Secretary requested POL to write a paper outlining the options for Canadian foreign policy for the 1980s, and to conduct a policy review in which specific individuals, largely in External Affairs, were to prepare papers in such areas as relations with the United States, federal-provincial relations, human rights, energy, NATO, the United Nations, and the contractual link. The primary paper, thematic in orientation, posed the basic question of how Canada as a middle power could influence the great powers, and sought to identify how all instruments of policy could be best used for Canada's advantage. Constrained by Mr. Jamieson's lack of interest, the constraints of the Liberal Government's public attachments to *Foreign Policy for Canadians,* and the uncertainties of an imminent federal election, the eight papers neared completion only by the time of the Conservative Government's assumption of office. A far more direct coordinative impact came through a series of efforts to revise the Government's overall expenditure process and its mechanism for dealing with foreign operations abroad. In 1976, Cabinet accepted a recommendation from the deputy ministerial-level Interdepartmental Committee on External Relations (ICER) that there be three years of no-growth in the foreign service abroad. The resulting redeployment of officers to less expensive positions within Canada, and the greater tension introduced into the budgetary process, induced External Affairs to take a much greater initiative in the 1977-1978 Country Programming process, by defining initial foreign policy objectives, engaging in greater interdepartmental consultation and forwarding the combined requests for new resources to the Treasury Board. Faced with the need to protect its own man-years and manage interdepartmental reductions for the Government-wide austerity programme in the summer of 1978, External also took the lead in reviving ICER, allocating the existing reductions and guiding the process of foreign service integration, with the assistance of the PCO, to a higher level.

These initiatives from External Affairs were not isolated actions. They had their origins in, and represented part of, a broader concept of the leadership role which the Department could exert on behalf of the Prime Minister in coordinating the foreign policy process. As this concept was developed by External's Under Secretary, Allan Gotlieb, it crystallized into a view of External as a modern central policy agency whose horizons and knowledge extended throughout the Government at home and its network of posts abroad, and whose role embraced the identification of the Government's overall priority framework and larger national interests, and the direction of crucial issues of national policy[20].

To enable External to perform this role, the Under Secretary, with a firm mandate from, and the consistent support of, those at the centre of Government, moved in several directions. Within the Department he created a new array of deputy under secretaries with the status to deal with other deputy ministers, gave assistant under secretaries and new Special Advisors responsibility for negotiations and policy formulation in designated areas, and established new divisions to deal with emerging functional subjects. Within the interdepartmental community he freed himself to serve as the Senior Foreign Policy Adviser to the Government as a whole, to give advice to groups of ministers on a regular basis, to contact all ministers directly, and to clear in practice all Cabinet memoranda with international implications. And abroad, he sought to give practical force to External's formal right to conduct communications with foreign governments and international organizations, provide visible evidence of External's position as the key prime ministerial advisor at summit conferences, be kept informed of direct head-of-Government communications, increase External's managerial voice in the appointment of Canadians to international organizations, and manage more actively Canada's operations and foreign service personnel abroad.

It was during the seven-month long minority Government of Progressive Conservative Prime Minister Joe Clark that this concept of External's role faced its most severe challenge and secured its most spectacular vindication[21]. Prime Minister Clark had entered office with little experience or interest in foreign affairs, beyond such strong beliefs as Canadian support for Israel, a close alliance with the United States, increased defence expenditure, sympathy for NATO, and a skeptical view of the UN. Procedurally, he was determined to shift the focus of power from the PCO and career bureaucracy to Cabinet, Caucus and Parliament, by ruthlessly controlling Government expenditures, depressurizing the central decision-making process, and having individual ministers as the channel for exercising control over, and transmitting advice from, their particular departments. As a result, he chose not to appoint a Special Adviser on Foreign Policy, and called for the widest possible review of policy in the foreign affairs realm. Although his desire to fulfill campaign promises and demonstrate control over the civil service led him upon entering office to announce his intention to move the Canadian embassy in Israel to Jerusalem, he readily acceded to Secretary of State for External Affairs Flora MacDonald's advice to appoint Robert Stanfield to study the issue and to the latter's advice not to proceed with the move. Afterwards, he involved himself in foreign policy issues as little as possible. Only with the support of an unanimous inner Cabinet did he override Flora MacDonald to authorize Canada's attempt to sell a nuclear reactor to Argentina.

Joe Clark's reluctance left the foreign policy field free for Secretary of State for External Affairs Flora MacDonald[22]. MacDonald's claim to leadership stemmed from her provision of crucial support to Clark at the Conservative Leadership Convention, her chairmanship of the Cabinet Committee on Foreign and Defence Policy and membership in inner Cabinet, and her strong attachment, somewhat compatible with the Prime Minister, to «rectory» principles, and such values as public participation in foreign policy, nuclear non-proliferation and human rights. With these assets she skillfully secured an acceptable outcome to the Prime Minister's Jerusalem initiative, succeeded on formulating and securing the adoption of Canada's programme to accept a large inflow of Indochina refugees, forwarded a proposal to create a United Nations Deputy Secretary General for Human Rights and helped define Canada's approach to the Tokyo Western Economic Summit, Lusaka Commonwealth Prime Minister's Conference, Iranian revolution, and Soviet invasion of Afghanistan.

Yet there soon appeared major limitations to her leadership in the broader foreign policy sphere. On defence-related issues her deference to DND sensitivities produced a restrained involvement in policy and budgetary questions. Although she denied the proposal of her deputy minister, Allan Gotlieb, to create a «mirror committee» of deputy ministers on foreign policy to advise the Cabinet body, she was force to accept the Prime Minister's refusal to remove him as her Deputy Minister. And on the issue of a Canadian bid on the Argentinian nuclear reactor sale, she stood, and lost alone.

With the Prime Minister uninterested and Flora MacDonald's field of influence limited, coordinative demands fell back on the Cabinet apparatus. The Ministries of State developed in the PCO in the latter days of the Trudeau Government, and the active debates in Cabinet's Foreign Policy and Defence Committee had some effect, as did the creation of a system of expenditure management which ensured that policy formulation and resource allocation were done together within fixed financial «envelopes»[23]. However, the absence of the three largest Government spenders from inner Cabinet, the focus of this body on only major disputes and priorities, and the respect for spheres of influence with the Foreign Policy and Defence Body exercised a powerful force in the opposite direction. And the Government's distrust of civil service advisers, as reflected in PCO and deputy ministerial appointments, threatened to reduce the coordination secured at this level. In the foreign policy planning sphere, the Government quickly replaced the previous process with a review of Canada's aid and foreign policy, to be conducted in Cabinet Committee and parliamentary hearings[24]. And while Clark gave approval in principle to a PCO-prepared paper on foreign service consolidation, in response to, aware of ITC's opposition and CIDA's desire for a separate rotational foreign service, he created a carefully-constructed task force to undertake further work, and delayed implementing its recommendation of a major move towards integration.

This vacuum at the centre placed a greater burden on the ability of External Affairs to perform its recently articulated role as a central agency, even as it placed heightened obstacles in External's path. These obstacles included a Government committed to individual ministerial prerogatives and suspicious of senior civil servants, the removal of PCO officials who had provided support for the central agency concept, and a Secretary of State for External Affairs who had strong views on policy, and relied heavily on a much strengthened team of personal advisors. Yet while Flora MacDonald prevented her Undersecretary from contacting other ministers directly, he succeeded, not without difficulty, in briefing the Prime Minister in preparation for summit occasions, and in withstanding Flora MacDonald's request for his resignation. Indeed, the Under Secretary proved able to register his views directly at the centre, and to transcend the difficulties caused by his strained relationship with his Minister.

CONTINUOUS CENTRAL MANAGEMENT SINCE 1980

These coordinative initiatives emanating from External Affairs were more fully developed, and embodied in institutional form, during the ensuing Liberal Government of Pierre E. Trudeau. Trudeau returned to office not only with a secure majority but also with several additional assets. His twelve years of experience, juxtaposed with the inept foreign policy performance of the Clark Government, gave him an unusually large area of freedom to undertake fundamental reform. And propelled by his formidable reputation as a statesman, he proceeded to take a leading role in major areas of personal concern, notably the Ottawa Western Economic Summit of 1981 and the subsequent Cancun meeting on the North-South dialogue.

Underscoring the centrality of the Prime Minister in the foreign policy realm was his selection of Mark MacGuigan as Secretary of State for External Affairs. With no previous ministerial experience and a professional, intellectual style, MacGuigan relied much more than Flora MacDonald on the advice of his departmental officials and the directions that his Prime Minister set. And with no intimate knowledge of the latters' instincts he depended heavily on the device of formal memoranda through the Cabinet system as means of securing clearance. Such a precaution was reinforced by the fact that his general attachment to the principles of international law and his firm anti-communist views made his instinctive approach to a host of East-West and North-South issues discrepant with that of the Prime Minister. And while Mark MacGuigan had a personal interest in Canada-US relations, there were clear limits to his influence in this sphere. The most formidable, as shown in the introduction of the National Energy Policy and the dispute over strengthening the Foreign Investment Review Agency, was the presence in major economic portfolios of close Trudeauvian associates, notably Marc Lalonde in Energy, Mines and Resources and Allan MacEachen in Finance.

As a result, foreign policy coordination was left to senior officials in External Affairs and the PCO who were sensitive and sympathetic to Trudeau's own approach. In the field of formal foreign policy-planning, even before the return of the Liberal Government, Under Secretary of State for External Affairs, Allan Gotlieb, had begun to prepare a philosophically-oriented concept paper addressing such questions as what foreign policy was, how appropriate policies were defined, and what themes could best guide Canadian foreign policy in the 1980s. Within the broader framework, the concept of bilateralism was identified as one of a very small number of appropriate themes. Following an analysis and revision of the paper, at the Under Secretary's request, by the Department's Policy Planning Secretariat, bilateralism was selected by Allan Gotlieb as the one key foreign policy theme, partly on the grounds that it could be followed through into more specific definitions of policy and resource allocations. Following this, a decision was made to develop the concept into a more extensive, detailed and operational form, and the paper was discussed with the new Secretary of State for External Affairs, Mark MacGuigan. He very quickly became convinced of the need to organize his Department, and its governmental and private sector associates, to deal simultaneously with a highly competitive international environment in the commercial sphere. As a result, he readily accepted the concept and commissioned a series of studies designed to elaborate its elements and implications.

With this ministerial approval, the Under Secretary's paper was returned to the Policy Planning Secretariat which, in August and September of 1980, began to develop the general framework into more specific factors of concern, lists of priorities, plans of action for individual countries and the implications for financial and personnel resources. From that point, the general framework and concept were taken through the «mirror» Committee of Foreign Policy deputies, the Cabinet Committee on External Policy and Defence, Cabinet's Priorities and Planning Committee and full Cabinet itself. Within the Cabinet process the concept aroused some debate as ministers sought to ensure that traditional dimensions of Canadian foreign policy were taken into account, played devil's advocate, offered departmental suggestions, and attempted to clarify the implications for their departmental responsibilities.

However, there was neither sustained conflict over, nor major objections to, the central concept or policy thrust, and in the end the framework received general support. Thus, by mid-autumn of 1980, the general concept of bilateralism had been given Cabinet approval, and External Affairs returned with renewed vigour to the task of working out implications and giving the policy public expression. This latter process culminated on January 22, 1981, when MacGuigan announced the policy in an address to the Empire Club in Toronto[25]. Subsequently, a second theme contained in the Undersecretary's initial concept paper, focused on Canada-US relations, was developed by External's Policy Planning Secretariat and given public expression as well[26].

Within the Government itself, these expressions of more comprehensive and detailed foreign policy coordination were given institutional force. The new Liberal Government immediately created a «mirror» Committee of Deputy Minister on Foreign and Defence Policy, with a Secretariat located in External Affairs, to service the Cabinet Committee in a way comparable to that of Ministries of State in other policy spheres. The new Government also moved almost at once to consolidate all the foreign service, save for ITC's Trade Commissioner Service, under the *de facto* leadership of External Affairs. And as Canada-US issues became more prominent, it gave the Department an enhanced freedom to undertake comprehensive policy reviews in this realm.

These developments culminated in January 1982 when the Government conducted a major reorganization of External Affairs, centered around the «absorption» into the Department of the Trade and Commerce components of the former Department of Industry, Trade and Commerce[27]. This reorganization, devised for the Prime Minister by Secretary to the Cabinet, Michael Pitfield, was prompted by several factors which converged to produce a change of unprecedented speed and scale. The most general was the need for the Government to further its overall priority on economic development and concern with supporting the private section by giving economic considerations a more integral place in its foreign policy. More particularly, the need for economic development at a time of Government expenditure restraint required a system that would allow ministers to define their priorities more sharply, that would eliminate recent cases of competitive spending between ITE and Regional Economic Expansion, and that would redirect trade policy to the resource sectors that promised to be the most vibrant sources of future growth. Externally, the growing interaction of economic and political issues, their tighter relationship with domestic forces, and the Government's policy of bilateralism suggested such an institutional amalgamation, particularly as an increase in global instability promised a more demanding environment abroad. In addition, the implementation of the incremental organizational reforms of the past few years – notably foreign service consolidation, the envelope system and the proposals of the Royal Commission on Terms and Conditions of Foreign Service – suggested that further steps were necessary if their anticipated advantages were to be repeated. And the leaders of both DEA and ITC, burdened with heavy line responsibilities and a large programme load, had faced difficulties in developing the broad overarching policies – on such issues as Canada-US relations, Canadian sovereignty and national unity – that were needed in a large, complex Government.

Thus, after careful consideration of several alternatives, the Government decided to disband ITC, place its Industry component along with Regional Economic

Expansion into a new Department of Regional Industrial Expansion, and transfer its Trade and Commerce components to External Affairs. The resulting External Affairs federation was given three ministers – the Secretary of State for External Affairs, a Minister for International Trade and a Minister for External Relations. This ministerial triumvirate was reproduced at the deputy ministerial level. The newly-appointed Undersecretary of State for External Affairs, Gordon Osbaldeston, was charged not only with managing his Department and advising his three ministers but acting in an integrative central agency policy role across all areas of foreign policy, defence, aid and trade. The incumbent of the newly-created position of Deputy Minister (International Trade) was responsible for the Department's trade and economic functions generally and also named Coordinator, International Economic Relations, with a mandate to meld economic-foreign policy and domestic-international considerations throughout the Government's economic community as a whole. And the incumbent of the newly-created position of Deputy Minister (Foreign Policy) was not only assigned responsibility for the classic foreign office political functions but also the task of serving as the Prime Minister's personal representative for the Western Economic Summit.

Beneath these senior managers, the new Department was divided into two sectoral wings and a central management core. The Trade and Economic Sector embraced ITC's former units for Trade Development and for Trade Relations and External's existing units for Sectoral and Economic Relations. The Foreign Policy Sector joined External's Bureaus dealing with Political Affairs, Multilateral and Cultural Affairs and Security and Intelligence. And the new central management core included separate units for Sector and Corporate Planning, Management and Programs, and Personnel.

In addition to integrating economic and political considerations more closely within the new Department, the reorganization of External had two crucially important effects. It endowed the Department with the expertise and influence to interact and compete more effectively with the other departments of Government, particularly the dozen or so departments which inhabited the economic sphere. And most significantly by extending and institutionalizing External's central agency functions, it enabled the new departmental federation to perform *de facto* the role of a Ministry of State for Foreign Affairs. At lower levels this role was sustained by the absorption of the Trade Commissioner Service into a now single, and unified Foreign Service and by the creation of the central management core with functions broadly similar to those of the Government's existing Ministries of State. At the deputy ministerial level, it was strengthened by giving all three incumbents coordinating and policy responsibilities on a government-wide basis. And at the top it was furthered by having the ministerial triumvirate assume a dominant position in the Cabinet Committee on External Policy and Defence and represented on all Cabinet Committees in other policy spheres. And finally, by bringing all foreign operations within a single budgetary envelope and management regime, and by giving External primacy on an annual foreign policy planning exercise linked directly with government-wide priority setting, it gave External most of the essential powers of a government-wide Ministry of State.

To be sure the performance of the new system in its coordinating role depended critically on the creation of close working relationships forged between the Trade and Foreign Policy wings, among the three deputy ministers, and among the three ministers at the top. To facilitate the first, the Government gave central senior

positions in the new Department to individuals respected and trusted by trade officers and commissioners and by those in economic departments in the Government
at large. To ensure the second, it deliberately staffed the most senior positions with
individuals who were the most talented in the entire Government, broadly sympathetic to the new regime and known to be capable of working together. And to help
alleviate initial problems in the third factor, the Government in September 1982
shuffled the relevant portfolios, naming Allan MacEachen Secretary of State for
External Affairs, Gerald Regan Minister of State for International Trade and Charles
Lapointe Minister of State for External Relations. With a strong Minister guiding an
integrated departmental federation, Ottawa had achieved the institutionalized capacity for comprehensive coordination required by, and common to, the principal powers
of the globe.

NOTES

1. This distinction between ongoing policymaking and overall coordination is drawn in John Kirton, «Foreign Policy Decisionmaking in the Trudeau Government: Promise and Performance», *International Journal*, 33, Spring, 1978, p. 287-311. This current account also draws heavily in many places from the treatment in Chapter Six of David Dewitt and John Kirton, *Canada as a Principal Power: A Study in Foreign Policy and International Relations*, Toronto, John Wiley and Sons, 1983.

2. On the Department of External Affairs during this period, see John J. Kirton, «The Conduct and Coordination of Canadian Government Decisionmaking Towards the United States», unpublished Ph.D. dissertation, Washington, D.C., The Johns Hopkins University, 1977, p. 16-29, and James Eayrs, *The Art of the Possible*. See also Douglas Ross, «In the Interests of Peace: Canadian Foreign Policy and the Vietnam Truce Supervisory Commission», unpublished Ph.D. dissertation, Toronto, University of Toronto, 1979, and Don Page and Don Munton, «Canadian Images of the Cold War», *International Journal*, 32, Summer, 1977, 577-604.

3. The major sources for this period are: James Earys, *The Art of the Possible, op. cit.*; Bruce Thordarson, «Posture and Policy in Canada's External Af-fairs», *International Journal*, 31, Autumn, 1976; John McLin, *Canada's Changing Defence Policy, 1957-1963: The Problem of a Middlepower in Alliance*, Baltimore, Johns Hopkins Press, 1957; Peyton Lyon, *Canada in World Affairs, Volume 12, 1961-1963*, Toronto, Oxford University Press, 1968; Trevor Lloyd, *Canada in World Affairs: Volume 10, 1957-1959*, Toronto, Oxford University Press, 1968; Jocelyn Ghent, «Canadian-American Relations and the Nuclear Weapons Controversy, 1958-1963». Unpublished Ph.D. dissertation, University of Illinois, 1976; and Howard Lentner, «Foreign Policy Decisionmaking: The Case of Canada and Nuclear Weapons», *World Politics*, 29, October, 1976, p. 29-66. Memoir material, while less useful than that from the earlier period, includes John Diefenbaker, *One Canada: Memoirs of the Right Honourable John G. Diefenbaker: Volume Two: The Years of Achievement: 1957-1962 and Volume Three: The Tumultuous Years: 1962-1967*, Toronto, University of Toronto Press, 1976; R.H. Roy, *For Most Conspicuous Bravery, a Biography of Major-General George R. Pearkes, V.C., Through Two World Wars*, Vancouver, University of British Columbia Press, 1977; and Lt.-Gen. E.L.M. Burns, *A Seat at the Table: The Struggle for Disarmament*, Toronto, Clarke, Irwin, 1972; and Jack Granatstein, *A man of Influence: Norman A. Robertson and Canadian Statecraft, 1929-68*, Ottawa, Deneau Publishers, 1981.

4. The characterization of the Government being poorly advised by the military is that of General Foulkes, as cited in McLin, *op. cit.*, p. 45-46. Diefenbaker's much later account is provided in *One Canada, op. cit.*

5. The basic literature for this period consists of: Robert Bothwell, Ian Drummond and John English, *Power, Politics and Provincialism*, Toronto, University of Toronto Press, 1981; and Peter Dobell, *Canada's Search for New Roles: Foreign Policy in the Trudeau Era*, Toronto, Oxford University Press, 1972, p. 10-12. John McLin, *Canada's Changing Defence Policy, op. cit.*, p. 193-220; Rod Byers, «Canadian Civil-Military Relations and Reorganization of the Armed Forces: Wither Civilian Control», in Hector Massey (ed.), *The Canadian Military: A Profile*, Canada, Copp Clark, 1972, p. 197-229; Vernon Kronenberg, *All Together Now: The Organization of the Department of National Defence in Canada, 1964-1972*, Toronto, Canadian Institute of International Affairs, 1973; and Bruce Thordarson, *op. cit.* Material on individuals, in addition to that previously cited includes John Munro and Alex Inglis (ed.), *Mike: The Memoirs of the Right Honourable Lester B. Pearson, Volume 3, 1957-1968*, Toronto, University of Toronto Press, 1975; Walter Gordon, *A Political Memoir*, Toronto, McClelland and Stewart, 1977; and Judy LaMarsh, *Memoirs of a Bird in a Gilded Cage*, Toronto: McClelland and Stewart, 1969

6. Bothwell *et al.*, *C.D. Howe: A Biography*, Toronto, McClelland and Stewart, 1979 and John English, *Canada in World Affairs, 1965-1967*, Toronto, Canadian Institute of International Affairs.

7. A.E. Gotlieb, «Canadian Diplomatic Initiatives: The Law of the Sea», in Michael G. Fry (ed.), *Freedom and Change: Essays in Honour of Lester B. Pearson*, Toronto, McClelland and Stewart, 1975, and John Kirton, *op. cit.*, p. 30.

8. Walter Gordon, *op. cit.*, p. 279. Hellyer also maintained a direct relationship with Paul Martin who had suggested, when the Cabinet was formed, that divisive defence issues be reconciled in advance, private discussions between the two, as a means of avoiding the Defence Minister foreign conflict that had led to the fall of the Diefenbaker Government.

9. On the Roberson Review see Granatstein, *op. cit.*, p. 374-379.

10. Within the voluminous literature on this period, the best summary accounts are provided in Peter Dobell, *Canada's Search for New Roles: Foreign Policy on the Trudeau Era*, Toronto, Oxford University Press, 1972, especially p. 10-22, Harald von Riekhoff, «The Impact of Prime Minister Trudeau on Foreign Policy», *International Journal*, 33, Spring, 1978, 267-286, John Kirton, «Foreign Policy Decisionmaking in the Trudeau Government: Promise and Performance», *International Journal*, 33, Spring, 1978, 287-311, and Bruce Thordarson, «Posture and Policy», *loc. cit.* More detailed empirical information is contained in Bruce Thordarson, *Trudeau and Foreign Policy: A Study in Decisionmaking*, Toronto, Oxford University Press, 1972, Garth Stevenson, «L'élaboration de la politique étrangère canadienne», in Paul Painchaud, ed., *Le Canada et le Québec sur la scène internationale*, Montréal, 1977, p. 51-79; and Michael Henderson, «La gestion des politiques internationales du gouvernement fédéral», in *ibidem*, p. 81-107. «Defence and Foreign Policy in the 1970s: the Demise of Trudeau Doctrine», *International Journal*, 33, Spring, 1978, 312-338, Albert Legault, «The New Canadian Defence Policy», *Le Devoir*, George Radwanski, *Trudeau*, Toronto, Macmillan, 1978, Michael Tucker, *Canadian Foreign Policy: Contemporary Issues and Themes*, Toronto, McGraw-Hill Ryerson, 1980, John Kirton, «The Conduct and Co-ordination of Canadian Government Decisionmaking Towards the United States, 1970-1975», *loc. cit.* and Peter Dobell, *Canada in World Affairs, 1971-1973*, Toronto, Canadian Institute of International Affairs. For initial interpretation of the Trudeau Government initiatives, see Peyton Lyon, «The Trudeau Doctrine», *International Journal*, 36, Winter, 1970-1971, p. 19-43, James Hyndman, «National Interest and the New Look», *International Journal*, 26, Winter, 1970-1971, p. 5-18, and Peter Dobell, «The Management of a Foreign Policy for Canadians», *International Journal*, 26, Winter, 1970-1971, p. 202-220.

11. Harald von Riekhoff, *op. cit.*

12. Canada, Department of External Affairs, «Canada and the World: A Policy Statement by Prime Minister Pierre Elliot Trudeau, Issued on May 29, 1968», *Statements and Speeches*, 68/17.

13. Kirton, «Foreign Policy Decisionmaking», *op. cit.*

14. Canada, Department of External Affairs, «The Relation of Defence Policy to Foreign Policy: Excerpts from an address by Prime Minister Trudeau to a Dinner of the Alberta Liberal Association, Calgary, April 12, 1969». *Statements and Speeches*, 69/8; Canada, Department of External Affairs, «A Defence Policy for Canada: Statement to the Press by Prime Minister Pierre Elliot Trudeau on April 3,

1969», *Statements and Speeches*, 69/7. See also Colin Gray, «Defence in the Seventies: A White Paper for All Seasons», *Canadian Defence Quarterly*, 1, Spring, 1972, p. 30-34.

15. Marc Lalonde, «The Changing Role of the Prime Minister's Office», *Canadian Public Administration*, XIV, Winter, 1971, p. 521, Gordon Robertson, «The Changing Role of the Privy Council Office», *Canadian Public Administration*, XIV, Winter, 1971, p. 504-506, and A. W. Johnson, «The Treasury Board of Canada and the Machinery of Government in the 1970s», *Canadian Journal of Political Science*, IV, September, 1971, p. 346-349. Also relevant are Thomas D'Aquino, «The Prime Minister's Office: Catalyst or Cabal Aspects of the Development of the Office in Canada and some Thoughts about its Future», *Canadian Public Administration*, XVII, Spring, 1974, p. 55-79, and Michael Hicks, «The Treasury Board of Canada and its Clients: Five Years of Change and Administrative Reform 1966-71», *Canadian Public Administration*, XVI, Summer, 1973, p. 182 and 205.

16. The foreign policy planning exercises and their impact are discussed in Bruce Thordarson, *Trudeau and Foreign Policy: A Study in Decision-Making*, Toronto, 1972; André P. Donneur, «Politique et technique: Le rôle du groupe d'analyse politique du ministère canadien des Affaires extérieures», *Res Publica*, XVI, 1974, p. 209-220; Daniel Madar and Denis Stairs, «Alone on Killers' Row: The Policy Analysis Group and the Departement of External Affairs», *International Journal*, XXXII, Autumn, 1977, p. 727-755; G.A.H. Pearson, «Order out of Chaos? Some Reflections on Foreign Policy-Planning in Canada», *International Journal*, XXXII, Autumn, 1977, p. 756-768; and Harald von Riekhoff, «The Third Option in Canadian Foreign Policy», in Brian W.Tomlin, ed., *Canada's Foreign Policy: Analysis and Trends*, Toronto, 1978, p. 87-109. The introduction and results of the Foreign Service Integration Programme are examined in J.R. Maybee, «ICTR and its two-Year Search for an Approach to Integration», *International Perspective*, September-October, 1972, p. 40-43; Michael Henderson, prepared for the Canadian Political Science Association, Toronto, 3-6 June 1974; and Arthur Andrew, XXX, Winter, 1974-1975, p. 45-56.

17. For a public statement of some of the logic behind this thrust see Canada, Standing Senate Committee on Foreign Affairs, Canada-United States Relations, 1: The Institutional Framework for the Relationship, Ottawa, 1975.

18. The basic literature on this period consists of John Kirton, «Les Contraintes du milieu et la gestion de la politique étrangère canadienne de 1976 à 1978», Études Internationales, 10, juin, 1979, 321-349; W.M. Dobell, «Interdepartmental Management in External Affairs»,

Canadian Public Administration, 221, Spring, 1978, 83-102; Denis Stairs, «Responsible Government and Foreign Policy», *International Perspectives,* May-June, 1978, 26-30 and George Radwanski, *Trudeau,* Toronto, Macmillan, 1978; for the Trudeau Government and the Honourable Flora MacDonald, «Notes for Remarks», Address to the Annual Meeting of the Canadian Political Science Association, University of Québec and Montréal, June 3, 1980, Jeffrey Simpson, *Discipline of Power: The Conservative Interlude and the Liberal Restoration,* Toronto, Personal Library, 1980, and David Humphrey's *Joe Clark: A Portrait,* Ottawa, Deneau and Greenberg, 1978, for the Clark Government.

19. Michael Pitfield, «The Shape of Government in the 1980s: Techniques and Instruments for Policy Formulation at the Federal Level», *Canadian Public Administration,* 19, Spring, 1976, p. 8-20. See also M.J.L. Kirby, H.V. Kroeker, Policy-Making Structures and Processes in Canada», *Canadian Public Administration,* 21, Autumn, 1978, p. 407-417.

20. On the operation of central agents during this period see Colin Campbell and George Szablowski, *The Superbureaucrats: Structure and Behaviour in Central Agencies,* Toronto, Macmillan, 1979. See in particular Allan Gotlieb, *Canadian Diplomacy in the 1980s Leadership and Service,* Toronto, Centre for International Studies, University of Toronto, 1979.

21. David Cox, *International Journal,* Autumn, 1982.

22. Flora MacDonald, *op. cit.*

23. Details of the Cabinet Committee and envelope system are presented, respectively in Canada, PCO, «Cabinet Committee Membership», July 31, 1979 and Canada, Treasury Board, *Guide to the Policy and Expenditure Management System,* Ottawa, Supply and Services Canada, 1980. See also Canada, Office of the Prime Minister, *Release,* March 21, 1980, and «Background Paper on Foreign Service Consolidation», March 12, 1980.

24. Canada, Secretary of State for External Affairs, Discussion Paper, «Canada in a Changing World, Part 1, November 30, 1979, and Part II, Canadian Aid Policy».

25. Canada, Secretary of State for External Affairs, Statement, «Text as Delivered of an Address by the Secretary of State for External Affairs, Dr. Mark MacGuigan, to the Empire Club of Canada», Toronto, Ontario, January 22, 1981.

26. Allan Gotlieb and Jeremy Kinsman, «Reviving the Third Option», *International Perspectives,* January-February, 1981, p. 2-5.

27. On the reorganization of the Department of External Affairs, see Gordon Osbaldeston, «Reorganizing Canada's Department of External Affairs», *International Journal,* 37, Summer, 1982, 453-466, Arnold Smith, «The new Department of External Affairs», *International Perspectives,* May-June, 1982, 13-14, Robbin Frazer, «Canada enters a new trade era through a super ministry», *Canadian Petroleum,* 32, June, 1982, p. 71-77, and Canada, Office of the Prime Minister, «Reorganization for Economic Development», January 12, 1982. For some of the causes of the reorganization see Canada, Royal Commission on Conditions of Foreign Service, *Report,* October 1981 and Sir Geoffrey Jackson *et al.,* «Canada's Royal Commission on Conditions of Foreign Service», *International Journal,* 37, Summer, 1982, p. 378-412.

4

Les activités internationales des provinces canadiennes

Annemarie Jacomy-Millette
Université de Montpellier – France

Au cours des deux dernières décennies, un grand nombre d'ouvrages et d'articles ont traité de la question des relations internationales des provinces canadiennes[1]. Il convient de faire le point à l'aube des années 80, où tant au plan national qu'international les problèmes économiques constituent la donnée essentielle de la formulation de la politique étrangère[2]. Et dans ce domaine économique prioritaire, les provinces sont des acteurs nationaux et internationaux privilégiés, en particulier les plus puissantes d'entre elles. Nous retiendrons principalement les cas de l'Alberta, du Québec et de l'Ontario, la première en croissance économique continue et les deux autres marquant un temps d'arrêt, accentué dans ce contexte de récession économique mondiale. Le cas de la Saskatchewan sera également noté.

Le problème essentiel consiste à déterminer s'il y a partage des responsabilités dans la projection externe du Canada et plus précisément si aux deux niveaux – de la formulation de la politique étrangère du Canada au sens large du terme et de la gestion de cette politique – les gouvernements provinciaux peuvent être considérés comme des acteurs internationaux privilégiés, égaux ou subordonnés par rapport au gouvernement fédéral. Nous ne mentionnons pas le Parlement et les législatures puisque au Canada, de par l'héritage britannique, c'est-à-dire l'adoption du régime parlementaire, le pouvoir réside dans les exécutifs et est exercé essentiellement par les premiers ministres, en particulier lorsqu'il s'agit de fortes personnalités comme Pierre E. Trudeau et René Lévesque.

C'est donc dans cet environnement politico-économique national, continental et mondial, et au double niveau des événements et du processus décisionnel des acteurs impliqués, que s'inscrit essentiellement ce dossier. En premier lieu, nous situerons la politique internationale des provinces dans son contexte juridico-politique national. C'est la question du cadre constitutionnel et notamment de la répartition des compétences législatives en matière de relations internationales entre l'État fédéral et les provinces. À ces données, qui constituent la toile de fond, s'ajoutera la description à grands traits des structures gouvernementales chargées des relations internationales. En un deuxième temps, nous aborderons chacun des trois volets du tryptique-cadre, la représentation des provinces tout d'abord dans les pays étrangers; ensuite, aux conférences et organisations internationales; et les engagements internationaux ou «transnationaux» de ces entités, en soulignant, d'une part, l'aspect éminemment conflictuel des questions, et, d'autre part, la spécificité du Canada dans ce domaine – un État fédéral poussé vers des solutions de décentralisation, en sens inverse de l'orientation générale prise par les autres États fédéraux, avec cependant un tournant marqué au cours de la dernière décennie par une tentative de centralisation des pouvoirs entre les mains des autorités fédérales. Cette dynamique, qui va de l'unité (la lettre de l'Acte de 1867) à l'éclatement et à la multiplication des centres décisionnels, est freinée par les hommes au pouvoir, les mécanismes et le contexte mondial qui pousse à la centralisation.

*   *

*

Un bref rappel de la répartition des compétences législatives entre l'Union fédérale et les états membres, les provinces, s'impose en premier lieu car cette donnée éclaire maints aspects conflictuels et explique en partie les difficultés rencontrées pour l'établissement d'un consensus au niveau de la prise de décision en matière de politique étrangère du Canada. Les grandes lignes sont posées dans l'Acte de l'Amérique du Nord britannique de 1867 – aujourd'hui Loi constitutionnelle de 1867 – à une époque (l'époque coloniale) où le Canada naissait à l'autonomie interne mais avait encore de nombreux jalons à poser avant de devenir indépendant et ce, dans un système mondial très différent de celui de 1867. À l'Union fédérale étaient attribués les pouvoirs essentiels, à dimension «nationale», ainsi que, globalement, ceux qui n'étaient pas spécifiés (clause résiduelle de l'article 91 de l'AANB de 1867). Aux provinces ne revenaient que des pouvoirs d'intérêt local, précisés par le texte, comme le droit de propriété sur les terres du domaine public et sur les ressources naturelles, le droit de légiférer sur la propriété et les droits civils ou encore sur les questions administratives au sens large du terme[3]. L'aspect historique éclaire aussi la question. La répartition des pouvoirs collait donc au contexte politique, économique et social de l'apogée des empires occidentaux de la fin du XIXe siècle et du début du XXe siècle. De plus, des pouvoirs prépondérants étaient en fait attribués à la fédération, le pouvoir «national», à l'encontre des États membres, les provinces. Comme le souligne le constitutionnaliste Gil Rémillard, l'Acte de 1867 est «une Constitution quasi fédérative» qui comprend «des éléments qu'on retrouve beaucoup plus dans un État unitaire que dans une fédération»[4]. Une adaptation au contexte mouvant, national et international, s'imposait au cours des ans.

Elle fut le fait essentiellement de l'interprétation judiciaire et au plus haut niveau, tout d'abord le comité judiciaire du Conseil privé anglais, jusqu'en 1949, puis la Cour suprême du Canada. Dans un premier temps, en particulier dans les 20 dernières années du XIXe siècle et avant la crise économique des années 30, les décisions statuaient souvent en faveur d'une extension des pouvoirs des provinces. En un deuxième temps, particulièrement à partir de la coupure du lien avec le Conseil privé d'Outre-Atlantique, c'est la tendance inverse qui se précise[5]. On ne peut cependant pas parler d'un «gouvernement» des juges au sens américain du terme. Mais le troisième pouvoir, judiciaire, dans son rôle d'arbitre des conflits juridiques, s'inscrit dans une dimension politique et apporte sa contribution à la prise de décision des responsables. Les décisions juridiques servent souvent de tremplin pour la résolution des conflits qui se veulent des compromis politiques.

La Constitution fédérale ne traite pas de la répartition des compétences en matière internationale, à part l'article 132 de l'AANB qui, dépouillé de son contexte historique, n'est plus applicable. Il réglemente seulement la mise en œuvre interne des obligations engendrées par la conclusion des traités d'*Empire* qui relevaient de la compétence de la Couronne impériale, c'est-à-dire britannique. Depuis 1867, le

Canada a acquis la souveraineté internationale, entre 1919 et 1931, c'est-à-dire entre le traité de Versailles et le statut de Westminster[6]. La conduite des relations internationales du Canada est maintenant définie par le Cabinet fédéral. Juridiquement, elle relève des pouvoirs de prérogative de la Couronne[7], c'est-à-dire du monarque, et comprend les déclarations de guerre, de neutralité, la conclusion de la paix, l'établissement ou la rupture des relations diplomatiques, la conclusion des traités ou encore la présentation de réclamations internationales, en bref le faisceau des compétences et actes qui traduit la projection du Canada à l'étranger. Il convient d'ailleurs de distinguer le pouvoir de son exercice. Si en 1867 le monarque possède et exerce ces pouvoirs sur avis de ses ministres britanniques, lorsque le Canada acquiert la souveraineté internationale, ce sont les ministres canadiens qui prennent la relève. À partir de 1947, par de nouvelles lettres patentes, le gouverneur général du Canada est habilité à exercer ces pouvoirs sur avis du Cabinet fédéral. Cette délégation sera d'ailleurs précisée et en fait élargie en décembre 1977, pour inclure «toutes les fonctions de chef d'État canadien remplies par le souverain»[8].

*　*

*

Une question fondamentale se pose alors: Y a-t-il partage de l'exercice de ce pouvoir entre les deux niveaux de gouvernement, le fédéral et le provincial, correspondant notamment au partage de la compétence législative posé par l'Acte de 1867? Une controverse, diffusée tout d'abord par les médias d'information, puis les politiciens et la doctrine et littérature juridico-politiques, oppose Ottawa et Québec sur ce point au milieu des années 60, dans le contexte de la Révolution tranquille et des revendications «nationales» du Québec tendant à l'affirmation d'une spécificité à la fois culturelle, politique et économique, et tant sur son territoire que dans la projection de ses compétences et intérêts à l'extérieur. À la fin du XIXe siècle et jusqu'aux années 60, la question restait ouverte[9]. La Cour suprême du Canada a cependant statué sur ce point en 1981, en se référant d'ailleurs à des décisions antérieures, dont celle sur les droits miniers sous-marins. Elle ne reconnaît pas le partage entre les onze exécutifs – la reine du chef du Canada ou du chef de chaque province – des droits et pouvoirs de prérogative royale en matière internationale. Elle attribue donc ces droits et pouvoirs à la seule Couronne pour le chef de l'Union fédérale, c'est-à-dire en fait au seul exécutif fédéral[10].

Le Québec, pionnier des revendications provinciales dans la projection extérieure des questions provinciales dites nationales (il sera suivi sur ce plan, mais avec une approche différente, par les provinces les plus riches et puissantes dans les années 70 et 80), constitue cependant un «cas particulier»[11]. En effet, les provinces, dont la langue véhiculaire est entièrement ou majoritairement l'anglais, ne contestent généralement pas aux autorités fédérales la capacité et la suprématie en matière de politique étrangère du Canada dans sa traduction formelle ou officielle. Comme le déclare le sous-ministre des Affaires intergouvernementales de la Saskatchewan en 1981, «No one [...] seriously challenges the primary role of the federal government in developing Canada's foreign policy»[12], ce qui est confirmé par le document de travail albertain d'octobre 1978, en ces termes:

> It is generally accepted that the development of foreign policy and the conduct of international relations is the responsibility of the Federal Government[13].

Les provinces demandent néanmoins à être associées au processus décisionnel, c'est-à-dire à la formulation de la politique étrangère du Canada dans ses aspects qui touchent à: ou bien les domaines qui relèvent de leur compétence ou également leurs intérêts «sectoriels», essentiellement d'ordre économique et financier. Selon l'opinion exprimée collectivement par les premiers ministres provinciaux, notamment à deux des conférences annuelles qui les réunissent, l'une en 1977 à St. Andrews au Nouveau-Brunswick, l'autre à Victoria en Colombie-Britannique en août 1981, il est «hautement prioritaire de s'attaquer aux problèmes économiques actuels du Canada»[14]. Pour ce faire, le gouvernement fédéral est invité à collaborer avec les provinces en vue d'élaborer une stratégie économique canadienne. Les provinces ne souhaitent pas une simple consultation; elles réclament une «collaboration» et une «élaboration» collective entre égaux, ce qui devrait s'inscrire dans des structures et un mécanisme adéquats[15], comme, par exemple, une réunion annuelle des onze premiers ministres afin d'élaborer et de mettre en œuvre une stratégie économique nationale. Or cet aspect économique a une dimension internationale prioritaire, comme en témoignent tant les déclarations des hommes politiques fédéraux et provinciaux que les faits. Ainsi, le ministre Lumley rapporte que les exportations canadiennes constituent presque un tiers du produit national brut du pays et, partant, de celui de quelques provinces, l'Alberta et la Saskatchewan entre autres[16]. Les relations commerciales des provinces sont donc primordiales pour leur équilibre économique.

Les activités internationales des provinces englobent aussi les questions d'investissements étrangers, les emprunts, l'assistance au développement international, les échanges culturels, ainsi qu'une collaboration avec les États américains voisins en matière d'environnement et de réglementation routière, notamment. La question du «droit» de représentation provinciale à l'étranger et de la capacité de conclure des traités internationaux est posée par quelques provinces, les plus riches d'entres elles. L'Alberta demande même en octobre 1978 d'inclure dans la Constitution une clause confirmant «the established legitimate role of the provinces in certain areas of international relations»[17].

La position de principe d'Ottawa est cependant simple; c'est le refus au plan décisionnel en ce qui concerne l'objet de cette étude, la politique étrangère du Canada[18]. Mais son approche pratique est beaucoup plus souple. Reprenons ces deux points. Pour le gouvernement fédéral, la politique étrangère du Canada relève exclusivement de l'État fédéral seul habilité à exercer les pouvoirs de la prérogative royale dans ce domaine. Cette politique ne peut être fragmentée. Le premier ministre Pierre Elliott Trudeau l'a souligné avec force, lui-même ou par le truchement de ses ministres depuis les revendications du Québec dans ce domaine. De ce fait, le Canada n'a qu'une seule «personnalité» internationale; c'est le seul «acteur» international. La structure est donc «nationale» ou «fédérale», les deux termes ayant la même signification. Un livre blanc du gouvernement fédéral paru en 1968 «établit la responsabilité du gouvernement fédéral dans la conduite de la politique étrangère du Canada, et en particulier son pouvoir exclusif de conclure des traités [...], de participer comme membre aux organisations internationales et d'accréditer et de recevoir des représentants diplomatiques en vertu du droit constitutionnel canadien et du droit international»[19]. Les autorités fédérales intéressées étudient chaque cas et adoptent des solutions nouvelles, le cas échéant, en tenant compte à la fois des intérêts globaux du pays et des possibilités de compromis entre les positions provinciales parfois divergentes.

Cependant, comme le souligne le secrétaire d'État aux Affaires extérieures du Canada en 1981, «notre système fédéral et les réalités qui le sous-tendent (l'existence d'une majorité de langue anglaise et d'une minorité de langue française, d'une part; les différences régionales, tant économiques que culturelles, de l'autre) ont pesé et pèsent de façon constante sur l'orientation et le caractère de nos politiques au plan international, dans des domaines aussi variés que les échanges culturels, scientifiques, techniques, l'éducation, la coopération en matière de transport, de santé, de protection de l'environnement, l'aide au développement, la promotion commerciale et la coopération industrielle»[20]. C'est pourquoi les autorités fédérales ont une approche pragmatique. Elles étudient chaque cas et adoptent des solutions qui tiennent compte à la fois des intérêts globaux du pays et des possibilités de compromis entre les différentes positions provinciales souvent divergentes, en effet. Elles estiment donc nécessaire d'obtenir, le cas échéant, le concours des provinces, en fonction de la répartition des compétences ou même de considérations que l'on pourrait qualifier de politiques. Ce concours ne se présente pas d'une manière monolithique. Les solutions sont diverses; elles vont de la consultation officieuse à une sorte d'association dans les cas limites.

C'est pourquoi le ministère des Affaires extérieures crée dès 1967 une Direction de la coordination fédérale-provinciale, groupe de réflexion et de liaison avec les autorités provinciales. Dès le début des années 70, en réponse au désir exprimé par certaines provinces, l'Ontario et l'Alberta notamment, d'ouvrir un bureau à Washington, Ottawa confie à un diplomate canadien en poste à Washington le dossier des provinces. Cet agent est chargé d'informer les provinces des développements américains qui les intéressent particulièrement et de servir d'agent de liaison pour les contacts que les autorités provinciales désirent prendre avec les autorités américaines. Notons cependant que les contacts et échanges directs entre les hommes politiques provinciaux et américains – membres du Congrès notamment – ne sont pas éliminés. Toujours au plan de la structure bureaucratique, une autre formule est utilisée: un fonctionnaire provincial – québécois en l'espèce – est responsable d'un dossier provincial, immigration ou éducation au sein d'une mission diplomatique du Canada ou encore dans une maison du Québec, après entente fédérale-provinciale[21]. Quelle est la valeur ou la réussite de la formule? Elle diffère selon les ans en fonction du contexte politique, mais elle constitue un début de solution.

*   *

*

Les provinces ont mis en place des rouages administratifs pour la coordination des activités intergouvernementales, internes et externes, qui ont subi une évolution au cours des deux dernières décennies en fonction des besoins nouveaux répondant aux transformations du système mondial et de ses sous-systèmes[22]. Au Québec, le ministère des Affaires intergouvernementales, qui a succédé en 1967 au ministère des Affaires fédérales-provinciales créé en 1961, met progressivement l'accent sur cet aspect international qui devient aujourd'hui prioritaire au double plan politique et économique et ce, principalement dans deux directions: la France, et au-delà la francophonie, et les États-Unis[23]. Comme le soulignait le sous-ministre associé de ce ministère, Claude Roquet, «[...] à côté de la francophonie se discerne une autre ligne de force fondamentale, basée sur une symbiose économique et humaine avec les États-Unis»[24].

L'accent est bien mis traditionnellement depuis le début des années 60 sur l'ouverture à la francophonie. C'est le vice-premier ministre libéral, Gérard-D. Lévesque, qui souligne en 1972 que «l'histoire a voulu que [le Québec] soit le seul État à majorité francophone et le principal foyer de vie et de diffusion de la culture française au Canada et en Amérique». C'est encore le premier ministre péquiste, René Lévesque, qui en 1981 rappelle que sur le plan «existentiel», la France constitue «le premier partenaire» parce qu'elle «ouvre la grande audience internationale de la francophonie»[25]. En particulier depuis la nomination en février 1982 de Jacques-Yvan Morin au poste de ministre des Affaires intergouvernementales, et la création en septembre de la même année du poste de ministre du Commerce extérieur, la priorité des relations économiques, et de ce fait politiques, s'affirme avec les États-Unis[26]. La dimension francophone subsiste cependant, comme en témoignent les déclarations officielles et la création du nouveau poste de délégué à la Francophonie et aux institutions multilatérales en septembre 1982, dont le premier titulaire est l'ancien chef de Cabinet du directeur de l'Agence de coopération culturelle et technique[27].

La place de l'Ontario sur la scène internationale a évolué au cours des deux dernières décennies. Depuis l'envoi de délégués en mission à l'étranger avant même la création de la Confédération jusqu'à aujourd'hui, l'ouverture sur le monde de la province longtemps la plus puissante et la plus industrialisée du Canada a nécessité la mise en place de structures administratives. En 1972, le ministère du Trésor et de l'Économie s'est transformé en ministère du Trésor, de l'Économie et des *Affaires intergouvernementales,* avec un double objectif de planification et de coordination intergouvernementale aux plans interne et externe[28]. Les «activités extérieures» ne constituent alors qu'un des nombreux domaines d'activités du ministère. En 1978, un ministère des Affaires intergouvernementales, qui traite à la fois des affaires internes et externes, est créé. Une section du ministère est responsable des dossiers internationaux dans la dimension principale d'apport ontarien à la formulation de la politique extérieure du Canada, en particulier en matière économique; la priorité est donnée aux relations Canada-États-Unis. Comme le souligne en 1981 un fonctionnaire ontarien de ce ministère, « [...] la majeure partie de nos efforts est dirigée vers nos voisins du Sud. Pour l'Ontario, le reste est secondaire, il faut bien l'avouer»[29]. Il en résulte que la dimension économique est prioritaire.

En Alberta, le ministère des Affaires fédérales et intergouvernementales, créé en 1972[30], met sur pied en 1978 une *Division internationale,* en vue de coordonner les activités internationales de tous les ministères et établissements publics albertains où des agents se spécialisent dans ce domaine. Il a également pour tâche d'assurer la liaison avec les ministères fédéraux des Affaires extérieures, de l'Énergie, des Mines et des Ressources et de l'Industrie et du Commerce. Dans le rapport annuel du ministère au 31 mars 1981, il est souligné que son rôle de supervision des activités internationales de la province a pris une importance accrue au cours de la dernière décennie dans des secteurs variés (investissements étrangers, technologie, mais surtout commerce international)[31]. En 1979, l'Alberta a nommé un ministre responsable du Commerce international, soulignant de ce fait l'importance cruciale de ce domaine pour sa croissance économique et le bien-être de ses citoyens. Comme dans le cas précédent, les relations avec les États-Unis sont prioritaires tant au plan des exportations de la province que des investissements étrangers nécessaires à son développement économique. Le même rapport annuel de 1981 rappelle que «Canada-United States relations remained the dominant feature of both Canada's and Alberta's international relations during the 1980-1981 fiscal year».

En Saskatchewan, un ministère des Affaires intergouvernementales est constitué en 1979, en vue de planifier la politique du gouvernement avec les autres gouvernements, au Canada et à l'étranger[32]. La section des affaires internationales est chargée des dossiers internationaux toujours en vue d'une coordination des relations internationales de la province. Elle assure la liaison avec le ministère fédéral des Affaires extérieures et les autres ministères fédéraux intéressés. En Colombie-Britannique et au Manitoba, les activités internationales relèvent généralement des ministères responsables du développement économique et du Conseil exécutif provincial. Au plan régional des provinces de l'Ouest, une concertation s'établit principalement en matière économique au sens large du terme, c'est-à-dire sur le plan de l'énergie, des finances et du commerce international.

Dans les autres provinces, la coordination récente des relations internationales, principalement sous la poussée des impératifs économiques, se situe au niveau du Conseil exécutif, c'est-à-dire du Cabinet provincial. En Nouvelle-Écosse, une unité administrative a été créée en 1980-1981 au sein du Secrétariat du conseil des ministres, le *Service des affaires intergouvernementales,* qui traite des dossiers des relations fédérales-provinciales, et plus marginalement des affaires internationales. Comme le précise en 1980 le directeur des Affaires intergouvernementales, «Nova Scotia does not deal unilaterally with foreign countries.The Federal Government is responsible for the external affairs of Canada and we work closely with the Department of External Affairs on matters of direct interest»[33]. Les questions économiques internationales relèvent des ministères sectoriels, plus spécialement de celui du développement, en collaboration avec les ministères fédéraux des Affaires extérieures et de l'Industrie et du Commerce. L'avenir énergétique de la province peut amener des changements. À Terre-Neuve et à l'Île-du-Prince-Édouard, les structures sont à peu près similaires, tel le Secrétariat des Affaires intergouvernementales de Terre-Neuve et du Labrador au sein du Conseil exécutif. Un fonctionnaire de ce secrétariat écrit, en 1980: «The Province's involvement in the field of international relations is carried out in cooperation with the Government of Canada through the Department of External Affairs[34].» Si le Secrétariat de Terre-Neuve est appelé à jouer un rôle important dans le contexte des développements énergétiques de la province, à l'Île-du-Prince-Édouard, son homologue ne semble pas devoir suivre cette orientation. Cette province est en effet très peu peuplée et aujourd'hui tout au moins sans ressources naturelles pouvant assurer un certain coussin financier. Elle dépend et dépendra encore vraisemblablement demain d'Ottawa pour ses relations extérieures.

Au Nouveau-Brunswick, la coordination des affaires internationales s'effectue par le *Comité des politiques et des priorités* rattaché au Secrétariat du conseil des ministres, notamment pour les questions économiques. Cependant, dès le printemps 1980, le ministère de la Jeunesse, des Loisirs et des Ressources culturelles est chargé des dossiers internationaux de la culture et de la technique. Enfin, dans le cadre régional de l'Est du Canada et des États-Unis, provinces atlantiques dans le premier cas, Nouvelle-Angleterre dans le second, se tient depuis 1973 la *Conférence annuelle des gouverneurs de la Nouvelle-Angleterre et des premiers ministres de l'Est du Canada,* qui étudie les dossiers d'intérêt commun, essentiellement économiques, comme le souligne Lise Bissonnette dans ses écrits des dernières années[35]. À l'origine, cette institution envisageait globalement et largement l'établissement d'une sorte de groupe de pression auprès des autorités fédérales des deux pays, appuyée par un consensus des premiers ministres des provinces atlantiques et des gouverneurs de la Nouvelle-Angleterre, sur la politique étrangère «sectorielle» des deux régions et, de ce fait, des deux pays. Aujourd'hui cependant ce forum, foyer d'accueil et d'échanges au plus haut niveau, ne porte que sur quelques questions limitées, importantes, il est vrai, comme l'énergie – un Comité international du Nord-Est sur l'énergie est institué à la conférence de juin 1978 –, les pluies acides qui font l'objet d'ententes écrites et orales entre les provinces canadiennes et les États américains, en vue de faire adopter par les deux pays des législations de protection[36]. Il ne peut éviter les divergences de points de vues tant internes entre les provinces[37] ou entre les États, qu'entre États et provinces. Il conserve cependant l'utilité que possèdent les forums nationaux ou internationaux où les questions sont débattues et portées devant l'opinion publique nationale et internationale.

C'est pourquoi ces structures aident à promouvoir les contacts formels mais aussi «informels» au double plan interne et externe et, de ce fait, à résoudre les conflits entre les deux niveaux de gouvernement du Canada. Par contre, la prolifération bureaucratique, qu'elle soit voulue ou improvisée, multiplie les acteurs et ajoute à la complexité au niveau de la prise de décision. Les problèmes, à traiter au double plan de l'élaboration (de la conception et de la gestion), peuvent se regrouper en trois projections externes de la politique interne: la représentation internationale ou «transnationale», la participation aux conférences et organisations internationales, et enfin la conclusion des traités et accords internationaux ou transnationaux et leur mise en œuvre interne. Ces trois aspects mettent en jeu le concept juridique de personnalité internationale des états fédérés ou le concept politique d'acteur international sur la scène mondiale. Cette terminologie n'est intéressante à souligner que parce qu'elle traduit les luttes pour le pouvoir politique.

*   *
*

Tout d'abord, la représentation internationale ou transnationale, considérée sous l'aspect représentation d'un acteur international par ses agents. Au plan interétatique, il s'agit de relations diplomatiques[38]. Tout comme le premier ministre du Canada, les premiers ministres des provinces les plus importantes vont fréquemment à l'étranger, en particulier aux États-Unis, si l'on peut parler d'étranger dans ce dernier cas alors que des liens quasi familiaux ou internes, amicaux ou conflictuels, unissent les deux pays et les deux peuples[39]. En dépit d'une volonté de spécificité et d'identité canadienne, il est une culture nord-américaine; il est une adhésion à des valeurs communes que transcrivent et disséminent les médias d'information, au premier chef la télévision. Les premiers ministres provinciaux établissent des contacts directs avec leurs homologues étrangers, avec les chefs d'État des pays qui présentent pour eux un intérêt particulier d'ordre essentiellement économique. La dimension culturelle n'est cependant pas absente dans ces échanges, en particulier à partir de la décennie 60 pour le Québec, à l'égard de la francophonie et aujourd'hui dans une certaine mesure à l'égard des États-Unis (Québec, état nord-américain), de l'Italie et de la Grèce, par exemple, mais aussi pour les provinces à population multiculturelle, autrefois essentiellement les provinces de l'Ouest, aujourd'hui la plupart.

De plus, les provinces ouvrent des bureaux de représentation à l'étranger. Aux origines de la fédération, des agents provinciaux, par exemple de l'Ontario et du Québec, sont envoyés à l'extérieur, ouvrent parfois des bureaux en vue de promouvoir l'immigration et les relations commerciales. Ces bureaux sont toutefois fermés à la fin du XIXe et au début du XXe siècle[40]. À partir des années 60, des bureaux provinciaux sont à nouveau mis en place. Au début de la décennie 80, on en compte plus d'une quinzaine pour le Québec, une dizaine pour l'Ontario, et quelques bureaux (ou maisons) d'autres provinces comme l'Alberta qui en compte quatre, la Colombie-Britannique, trois, la Nouvelle-Écosse, deux, et la Saskatchewan, un. Ces bureaux ont donc développé leurs activités, principalement d'ordre économique, au cours des deux dernières décennies. La localisation géographique privilégie les États-Unis[41], l'Europe et l'Asie, avec une percée récente en Amérique latine. Il convient d'ajouter que, à part les États-Unis, prioritaires pour toutes les provinces[42], l'Est du Canada est plus tourné vers l'Europe, et l'Ouest, vers les pays du Pacifique.

Les maisons du Québec[43] sont tout d'abord des délégations générales ouvertes sur les différents aspects de la vie politique, économique, socio-culturelle. Elles œuvrent bien dans les secteurs d'activités qui sont de la compétence législative provinciale, mais dépassent largement ces limites, comme en témoignent les relations politiques établies à Paris par les différents délégués généraux qui s'y sont succédé, Jean Chapdelaine notamment; à Londres, où le délégué Gilles Loiselle a joué un rôle politique important à l'occasion de la question du «rapatriement de la Constitution»; à New York où depuis 1976, avec des hauts et des bas, le délégué général établit des contacts avec les milieux industriels et les marchés financiers et pilote les dossiers économiques – relations industrielles, financières, commerciales, technologiques, exportations d'énergie – mais porte aussi depuis novembre 1976, et d'une manière plus visible depuis mars 1982, une attention particulière aux liens politiques à établir avec les dirigeants officiels et officieux de Washington, le Congrès, les hauts-fonctionnaires, les groupes de pression; il semble avoir des difficultés cependant à établir des contacts directs avec la haute-administration américaine; les délégués du Québec à New York et à Boston poursuivent et accroissent leurs contacts avec les gouvernements des États voisins, de la Nouvelle-Angleterre et de New York et préparent les visites ministérielles[44]; il en est de même des délégations québécoises dans les autres régions des États-Unis; à Bruxelles où le délégué a un double objectif, resserrer les liens avec la Belgique notammant mais pas exclusivement avec la communauté wallonne, et en forger avec la Communauté économique européenne; enfin à Mexico, une des deux villes d'Amérique latine retenues par le Québec comme prioritaires. Le Québec crée aussi des délégations à vocation sectorielle répondant principalement à une ouverture économique à Tokyo, à Düsseldorf et à Caracas, notamment; touristique à Atlanta et à Washington; ou enfin avec un objectif qui redevient prioritaire en raison de la baisse des naissances (comme l'immigration) à Hong-Kong, Lisbonne et Rome.

Les délégations et bureaux du Québec s'inscrivent le plus souvent dans le conflit Ottawa-Québec, que ce soit à l'égard de leur création (le projet avorté de l'ouverture d'une délégation à Dakar en constitue une bonne illustration) ou de leurs activités. Les directives données par le ministère québécois des Affaires intergouvernementales varient bien selon les années en fonction du parti politique au pouvoir. Les revendications de spécificité, de cas particuliers, perdurent à travers les ans. En 1981-1982, les divergences fondamentales sur l'avenir du Québec demeurent la donnée essentielle posée à partir de novembre 1976. Elles sont projetées plus ou moins maladroitement devant l'opinion publique mondiale, par exemple dans le cadre des relations triangulaires avec la France ou avec les États-Unis.

L'Ontario avait établi une quinzaine de maisons à l'étranger, à objectif essentiellement économique, aux États-Unis, en Amérique du Sud et en Asie. La province a fermé onze bureaux en 1977[45], dans un double objectif d'efficacité administrative et financière et d'unité politique fédérale-provinciale sur la scène mondiale pour répondre au souhait exprimé par Ottawa. L'Ontario élargit cependant le mandat des anciennes missions qui subsistent ou des bureaux nouvellement créés, comme à Bruxelles ou à Paris en 1982, pour y inclure les questions culturelles d'éducation et intergouvernementales, tout en mettant toujours l'accent sur les liens économiques et les relations commerciales. «Depuis trois ou quatre ans on a réévalué sérieusement le rôle de ces bureaux étrangers et le Cabinet provincial est plus réceptif à l'idée d'une présence internationale importante[46].» En 1982, il y avait une dizaine de maisons ontariennes à travers le monde dont cinq aux États-Unis (ce qui traduit la priorité géographique de l'Ontario), quatre en Europe et deux en Asie. Ces maisons autrefois placées sous la responsabilité du ministère de l'Industrie et du Tourisme, relèvent maintenant du ministère des Affaires intergouvernementales.

L'Alberta avait quatre bureaux à l'étranger, l'un à Londres, les autres à Tokyo, Hong-Kong et Los Angeles; la province en a ouvert un cinquième à Houston. Le bureau de Londres, Alberta House, le plus ancien et le plus important, a un mandat général. Son champ d'action couvre le développement économique, le commerce, le tourisme, l'éducation et l'emploi. Le champ d'action géographique n'est pas limité au Royaume-Uni; il englobe toute l'Europe et le Moyen-Orient. Les bureaux de Tokyo, Hong-Kong, Los Angeles et Houston s'occupent essentiellement des relations économiques. Les cinq maisons albertaines maintiennent des contacts étroits avec les missions canadiennes de ces pays d'accueil. L'idée générale présentée par le ministère et ses représentants à l'étranger est bien l'unité de la politique étrangère du Canada, mais également la diversité et la spécificité de certains aspects de la politique économique de la province.

Dans le rapport annuel 1980-1981 du ministère des Affaires intergouvernementales de la Saskatchewan, nous retrouvons le même désir de jouer un rôle plus important sur la scène internationale, rôle qui est caractérisé comme légitime. Il est souligné que les provinces ont le «droit» d'ouvrir des bureaux à l'étranger[47]. Elles ont d'ailleurs commencé à le faire avec l'accord du gouvernement fédéral dès 1869, à Londres, en vue d'attirer des immigrants au Canada. De plus, la province exporte un pourcentage élevé de sa production. Enfin, c'est une province à population multiculturelle qui a de ce fait des liens historiques et de famille avec de nombreuses régions du globe. C'est pourquoi le rapport conclut que la Saskatchewan continuera à jouer un rôle croissant dans la communauté internationale.

C'est donc les provinces les plus riches et les plus industrialisées – aujourd'hui ou demain – qui ont ressenti et exprimé ouvertement cette nécessité d'élargir leurs relations avec l'étranger. L'ouverture d'un bureau ou d'une maison, qualifiée parfois de «représentation commerciale», constitue un outil pratique généralement nécessaire. Par contre, les provinces économiquement faibles, comme l'Île-du-Prince-Édouard et le Nouveau-Brunswick, comptent sur Ottawa pour les aider à augmenter leurs liens économiques avec l'étranger. Il y a donc divergence d'options et la ligne de démarcation passe par le seuil de la richesse économique, réelle ou potentielle.

Les agents provinciaux, tout comme les diplomates, ont pour fonction de représenter leur gouvernement, de faciliter les contacts (visites à et de l'étranger), d'observer et d'informer, c'est-à-dire de promouvoir le flux des renseignements, enfin de participer à des négociations ou à de simples conversations et échanges qui facilitent tant les liens transnationaux et régionaux que les liens formels de la fédération. Ce sont donc essentiellement des agents d'information, de relations publiques, des conseillers commerciaux chargés de la promotion et de la vente des «produits» provinciaux (donc canadiens) à l'étranger, ce qui s'inscrit dans la nouvelle ligne tracée par Ottawa en matière de politique étrangère au début de 1982: mettre l'accent sur le commerce international et plus globalement sur les relations économiques internationales. Ces agents sont aussi des courtiers en ce sens qu'ils facilitent les emprunts et la recherche d'investissements étrangers pour le développement économique de leur province. Ils œuvrent à la fois pour la province et pour l'ensemble du pays, la dimension régionale au sens interne du terme étant partie du tout, la dimension pancanadienne. Les observateurs oublient trop souvent dans cette atmosphère conflictuelle d'aujourd'hui que promouvoir le développement économique, social et culturel d'une province, c'est en même temps promouvoir le développement du Canada et que le même homme est à la fois un citoyen de la province et du Canada. Il apporte donc la dimension nationale à la province, et provinciale au pays. Comme le souligne John Buchanan, alors premier ministre de Nouvelle-Écosse, à la Conférence de Victoria d'août 1981, les provinces «sometimes become so preoccupied with [their] own individual affairs that [they] often are left with little time to reflect upon [their] collective responsibilities within confederation». Toutefois, elles constituent avec les territoires «the collective essence of what is Canada»[48].

Si les membres des exécutifs provinciaux visitent officiellement ou en privé l'étranger en vue d'augmenter les liens essentiellement économiques de leur province, les chefs d'État et de gouvernement, les ministres et les hauts-fonctionnaires étrangers visitent les capitales provinciales pour avoir des entretiens avec leurs homologues. Ils s'informent, entament souvent des pourparlers avec les autorités provinciales sur des sujets d'intérêt commun qui s'inscrivent généralement dans la dimension économique prioritaire de la politique étrangère du Canada[49]. Dans le rapport de 1980-1981 du ministère des Affaires intergouvernementales de l'Alberta, il est précisé que les points sur lesquels ont porté les entretiens touchent au commerce international, à l'agriculture, à l'énergie, à la technologie, aux investissements, à la culture, et enfin à l'éducation[50]. Ces visiteurs étrangers se rendent très souvent sur le terrain et visitent notamment les mines de charbon, les installations pétrolières et de gaz naturel et les usines pétrochimiques[51]. Un relevé des visites de chefs d'État ou de gouvernement ou autres responsables étrangers dans les autres provinces, en particulier au Québec, en Ontario et en Alberta, permet de constater un accroissement de cette catégorie d'échanges, en particulier au plan économique.

Il y a donc une «politique étrangère» des provinces qui appuie souvent les orientations de la politique étrangère du Canada en dépit des divergences qui opposent les provinces entre elles, une province ou encore un groupe de provinces et Ottawa. La politique étrangère du Canada dans son aspect économique ne peut être que compromis entre les différentes positions.

* *
*

La représentation internationale, transnationale ou officielle, joue un rôle important pour certaines provinces, en particulier le Québec – représentation officielle –, l'Alberta avec ses nombreux liens transnationaux américains, et l'Ontario, jouant sur les deux tableaux. Se pose également, et d'une manière plus urgente aujourd'hui, la question de la participation des provinces aux conférences et organisations internationales de la famille des Nations Unies, ou régionales, ou encore sectorielles, ou enfin *sui generis*. Cette question constitue un problème fort complexe. Elle met en jeu des éléments nationaux et internationaux au double plan des principes et règles juridiques, des oppositions politiques entre acteurs du système international et de ses sous-systèmes et de la scène nationale qui, en un sens, sont liés[52].

Pour le Québec, la position est claire. La participation aux activités des organisations et conférences internationales constitue «une ouverture sur le monde qui est loin d'être négligeable» aux différents plans: le politique, l'économique et le socioculturel[53]. En témoigne l'accent mis par le Québec sur la nécessité des liens à établir avec les institutions de la Francophonie, l'Agence de coopération culturelle et technique des pays francophones (ACCT) et les Conférences des ministres de l'Éducation des pays francophones (CONFEMEN), des ministres de la Jeunesse et des Sports des pays francophones (CONFEJES). Le Québec désire y jouer un «rôle fondamental» en tant que foyer d'une importante communauté de langue française[54]. Mais il rejoint les autres provinces dans leurs revendications à une participation – à négocier – aux travaux d'organisations internationales œuvrant dans d'autres secteurs, le secteur économique en particulier, et souvent au plan mondial. Comme le rappelle en 1979 le conseiller aux Affaires internationales du premier ministre du Québec, «le gouvernement du Québec doit être présent aux Nations Unies. Il doit en connaître les politiques, les programmes et surtout il doit être actif auprès des représentants des pays membres»[55]. Le politique et l'économique se rejoignent.

Pour les autres provinces, en effet, surtout les plus riches d'entre elles aujourd'hui ou demain, la dimension économique est primordiale mais les liens de politique générale font également leur apparition, en particulier dans le cas des deux provinces les plus impliquées dans les relations fédérales-provinciales, l'Ontario et l'Alberta, la première ayant des vues qui souvent coïncident avec celles des fonctionnaires et hommes politiques d'Ottawa, la seconde étant souvent en opposition avec les politiques préconisées par Ottawa, par exemple dans le domaine énergétique et son corollaire, le domaine financier. Il y a depuis plusieurs années un «front commun» des provinces de l'Ouest à l'égard de certains secteurs, ressources naturelles, énergie, économie dans son ensemble qui repose à la fois sur une perception négative, un sentiment d'aliénation à l'égard du gouvernement central, et une volonté, une stratégie autonome de développement économique[56]. Nous parlons essentiellement de l'Alberta, de la Colombie-Britannique et de la Saskatchewan et ce, en dépit du parti qui détient le pouvoir dans ces provinces. Le conservatisme albertain d'un Peter Lougheed, le créditisme de Colombie-Britannique d'un Bill Bennett, ou la sociale-démocratie NDP de Saskatchewan d'un Allan Blakeney, avant les dernières élections, se rejoignent à cet égard[57]. Terre-Neuve, la province atlantique qui s'est intégrée au Canada en 1949, rejoint ce groupe au cours des dernières années et le premier ministre Brian Peckford s'oppose au premier ministre du Canada, Pierre E. Trudeau, en ce qui concerne la question des hydrocarbures situés au large des côtes de cette province[58].

Comme le disait le premier ministre de l'Alberta, Peter Lougheed, en 1978, lors de la Conférence fédérale-provinciale des premiers ministres:

> Les provinces étant propriétaires de leurs ressources et ayant compétence dans les secteurs clés de l'économie, une politique nationale de l'économie ne peut se

résumer à une politique fédérale. Toute politique nationale de l'économie doit découler d'un fédéralisme fondé sur la collaboration dans son sens le plus large sur les politiques et les orientations économiques ayant recueilli l'assentiment de toutes les parties[59].

Les formules adoptées à l'égard des instances intergouvernementales internationales doivent être envisagées sur deux plans, la *formulation* de la politique «nationale» du Canada à ces instances, et la *participation*. À l'égard de la formulation, les problèmes se sont posés progressivement en liaison avec les transformations du système mondial. La politique étrangère des États s'articulait dans le passé sur deux aspects principaux: la guerre et la paix. Il n'en est plus de même aujourd'hui alors que de nombreux domaines, qui s'insèrent dans le quotidien économique vécu et planifié, ont une dimension internationale parfois prioritaire comme dans le champ d'action de l'économique et du financier. Or, le quotidien était perçu par la majorité en 1867 comme le «local», c'est-à-dire qu'il relevait de la compétence provinciale. Il y a donc aujourd'hui une source permanente de conflits internes dans ces transformations. C'est pourquoi les provinces réclament d'être associées au processus de formulation de la politique étrangère du Canada lorsqu'il s'agit de questions qui relèvent de leurs compétences internes ou qui les intéressent particulièrement[60].

Ainsi, en 1975, sous la poussée des gouvernements provinciaux, des mécanismes de consultation fédérale-provinciale sur les négociations commerciales multilatérales sont mis en place, dont un comité fédéral-provincial présidé par le coordonnateur fédéral de ces négociations. Il s'agit essentiellement d'informer les provinces. En 1978, Peter Lougheed, au nom des provinces de l'Ouest, demande une rencontre au double niveau, provincial et fédéral, en vue d'élaborer la position du Canada aux instances du GATT. À l'égard de la politique agricole, notamment, il souligne qu'il est important d'établir une collaboration maximale impliquant les producteurs et les gouvernements provinciaux. Cette concertation, selon le premier ministre albertain, ne doit d'ailleurs pas se limiter au domaine agricole, mais inclure tout le champ des relations commerciales internationales[61]. Dans le même sens, le premier ministre de la Nouvelle-Écosse en 1978, Gerald A. Regan, réclame une plus grande participation des provinces dans un autre secteur, la planification et la direction des pêcheries[62].

Tous les gouvernements provinciaux insistent sur l'importance des exportations canadiennes (et de ce fait provinciales), en particulier vers les États-Unis. Pour le premier ministre Bill Davis de l'Ontario, il est «crucial de comprendre que notre économie fait partie de l'économie mondiale» mais que la priorité va à une augmentation des exportations vers les États-Unis[63]. Ces questions étant traitées à l'intérieur des discussions du GATT, et les provinces ayant des intérêts divergents (libre-échange des provinces exportatrices de ressources naturelles contre protectionnisme des provinces à secteurs industriels menacés par la concurrence étrangère), le Québec, l'Alberta et Terre-Neuve, par exemple, désirent avoir des observateurs dans la délégation canadienne[64]. Les ministres fédéraux font remarquer en 1979 qu'«au cours des négociations, une collaboration étroite, de même que des arrangements de nature consultative, s'était créée entre le gouvernement, les provinces, le milieu des affaires et celui du travail, ainsi que les groupes d'intérêt de consommateurs»[65]. En 1982, cette consultation collective ne satisfait pas les gouvernements provinciaux. Certains demandent des rencontres périodiques institutionnalisées «au sein d'un conseil» et soulignent que le gouvernement fédéral doit maintenir le mécanisme de consultation, jusque-là *ad hoc,* comme un élément permanent de l'élaboration d'une politique commerciale internationale[66]. Le gouvernement fédéral et les gouvernements provinciaux sont cependant convenus de créer un comité de sous-ministres qui se réunirait régulièrement pour étudier les problèmes économiques internationaux[67].

En effet, en règle générale, les provinces ne sont pas véritablement associées à la formulation définitive de la position canadienne aux organisations et conférences internationales. Elles sont informées, consultées, ont même parfois une importance reconnue par les autorités fédérales pour la présentation de la position aux instances internationales. Les modalités varient dans le temps et surtout selon l'objet de la rencontre internationale. Elles sont établies principalement sur une base *ad hoc,* comme l'illustre l'exemple du GATT. L'input des provinces varie selon leurs forces et intérêts respectifs, dans ce domaine éminemment conflictuel qui voit s'accuser les oppositions entre provinces, entre par exemple les «sheiks aux yeux bleus de l'Ouest» et les provinces maritimes, beaucoup plus démunies. Ces divergences s'accusent au plan international dans le contexte de récession économique, alors que les accords du GATT sont bousculés ou détournés par des mesures de protection non tarifaires que réclament les provinces à secteurs mous (textile, chaussure, vêtement).

Dans le cas des conférences sur l'éducation organisées par l'UNESCO et l'OCDE, auxquelles le Canada participe, il y a, *avant la conférence,* consultation fédérale-provinciale à l'égard de l'adoption d'une position et non pas décision du conseil des ministres provinciaux de l'Éducation. Rappelons que l'éducation relève de la compétence provinciale. Il y a aussi consultation des provinces intéressées dans le cas de la préparation de la position canadienne aux organisations et conférences de la Francophonie, ACCT, CONFEMEN, CONFEJES. Dans d'autres domaines, santé (il s'agit de l'OMS), emploi (il s'agit de l'OIT), agriculture (il s'agit de la FAO), la consultation est établie entre les services ou les fonctionnaires provinciaux et fédéraux. Généralement, la Direction de la coordination fédérale-provinciale du ministère des Affaires extérieures participe à cette consultation-liaison.

La question de la *participation* aux conférences et organisations internationales soulève des problèmes majeurs aux plans international et national. L'organisation internationale en question, ou la conférence internationale, doit avoir réglementé, dans sa charte constitutive dans le premier cas, dans un accord pour le second cas, cette participation d'entités qui n'ont pas une pleine souveraineté internationale. À l'intérieur du Canada il y a, le cas échéant, négociation entre les deux niveaux de gouvernement. La contribution provinciale aux conférences générales se situe dans le cadre de la délégation canadienne. Elle fait parfois l'objet de négociations entre les deux niveaux de gouvernement. La perception qu'en a la province de Québec est formulée de la manière suivante: «Le gouvernement fédéral consulte et invite les gouvernements provinciaux selon qu'il le juge nécessaire et utile[68].» Aux conférences portant sur des domaines relevant de la compétence provinciale, l'éducation par exemple, des délégués provinciaux sont membres de la délégation canadienne. Ainsi, pour l'UNESCO et l'OCDE, lorsqu'il s'agit de conférences sur les questions relevant de la compétence provinciale, il y a plusieurs représentants provinciaux[69]. Pour l'OIT, la représentation provinciale s'intègre dans la représentation gouvernementale fédérale, c'est-à-dire canadienne, mais la consultation et la participation des provinces à la conférence annuelle et aux conférences spéciales de cette organisation est maintenant devenue une réalité (au moins deux représentants provinciaux sont membres de la délégation canadienne). Enfin, dans un certain nombre de conférences, les représentants provinciaux sont invités à titre de conseil-lers, comme dans l'exemple de la Conférence sur le droit de la mer[70].

Dans le cas de l'Agence de coopération culturelle et technique (ACCT), dont le rôle est limité en particulier devant l'opposition de la France à supprimer les liens privilégiés qu'elles maintient directement avec les anciennes colonies africaines, le Québec, depuis 1971, et le Nouveau-Brunswick, depuis 1977, ont le statut de *gouvernement participant* aux institutions, programmes et activités de l'Agence. Le Québec et le Nouveau-Brunswick participent donc depuis plusieurs années de plein droit aux activités et au budget de l'Agence[71]. L'entente conclue après de laborieuses négociations impliquant des acteurs étrangers (la France par exemple) entre le Québec et le gouvernement fédéral entre 1969 et 1971, sur les modalités de participation de la province à l'Agence comme gouvernement participant, ne lui accorde pas la pleine autonomie. Si le Québec peut avoir des relations directes avec les autorités de l'Agence, la province n'est cependant invitée que par l'intermédiaire du gouvernement fédéral à participer aux activités, tout comme le Nouveau-Brunswick. Les délégations des deux provinces font partie de la délégation canadienne, sous l'identification «Canada-Québec» et «Canada-Nouveau-Brunswick». La délégation canadienne, généralement présidée par un représentant fédéral, ministre compétent[72], comprend aussi des représentants de l'Ontario et du Manitoba. Elle n'a qu'un seul vote, les gouvernements du Québec et du Nouveau-Brunswick détenant une sorte de «droit de veto tacite» au sein de la délégation du Canada, droit qui, lorsqu'il en est fait usage, implique l'abstention du Canada. Ces arrangements-compromis engendrent une tension politique et un rapport de forces entre l'Union fédérale et le seul Québec.

Aucun statut spécial n'est reconnu aux provinces par les autorités fédérales dans le cas des Conférences internationales des ministres de l'Éducation et de la Jeunesse et des Sports des pays francophones (CONFEMEN et CONFEJES). Ces provinces sont le Manitoba, le Nouveau-Brunswick, l'Ontario et le Québec. Cependant, les arrangements qui président à la participation des provinces, y compris le Québec, découlent d'ententes *ad hoc*. L'une d'elles a été négociée avec le Québec lors de la Conférence des ministres de l'Éducation de Kinshasa en 1969. La délégation du Québec est identifiée au sein de la délégation canadienne; le Québec parle en son nom et lorsqu'un vote doit être pris, il est entendu que, d'une manière informelle, on adopte la solution retenue pour les conférences de l'Agence. La délégation cana-dienne est généralement présidée par un ministre provincial (Québec ou Nouveau-Brunswick) et comprend des représentants des provinces intéressées et des conseillers fédéraux et provinciaux[73].

D'autres programmes internationaux réunissent des représentants fédéraux et provinciaux. Deux exemples sont intéressants à mentionner: l'assistance au développement international et les activités des commissions mixtes qui planifient et concrétisent parfois les rapports bilatéraux du Canada. La première catégorie s'inscrit dans la dimension du dialogue Nord-Sud, privilégié par le premier ministre du Canada, Pierre E. Trudeau, la seconde dans le contexte des relations bilatérales sur lesquelles le Canada met l'accent aujourd'hui selon les déclarations du secrétaire d'État aux Affaires extérieures ou même du premier ministre[74]. L'aspect conflictuel interne n'est cependant pas absent de ces liens internationaux. Pour mémoire, rappelons les divergences entre Ottawa et Québec sur certaines questions – les relations avec la France et la Belgique, le mode de participation de la province à l'aide aux pays du tiers monde, le projet de création d'un Commonwealth francophone; et entre Ottawa et les provinces de l'Ouest à l'égard des relations avec les États-Unis –, les points de divergence portant principalement sur le programme énergétique national d'octobre 1980, les arrangements fiscaux, et la FIRA, l'Agence de tamisage des investissements internationaux.

Les événements politiques récents dans le contexte interne ont engendré un conflit ouvert entre l'Union fédérale et le Québec et également entre l'Union fédérale et les provinces de l'Ouest, l'Alberta principalement. Ces deux conflits sont peu propices à l'établissement de solutions rationnelles et définitives. Ce sont donc des réponses pragmatiques et en évolution qui s'imposeront au cours des prochaines années. Il n'en demeure pas moins que la participation aux organisations internationales, principalement fonctionnelles, est de plus en plus revendiquée par la plupart des provinces. Des formules devront donc être trouvées par les deux niveaux de gouvernement en se basant sur la distinction entre la loi et l'application de la loi, la lettre et l'esprit, et, notamment, entre l'établissement d'un certain accord sur des lignes directrices de base et la gestion, opérationnelle, à l'intérieur de ce cadre qui doit s'adapter à un contexte mouvant. De plus, des mécanismes nouveaux devront être mis en place pour servir de forums à ces échanges au plan interne[75].

$$* \qquad *$$
$$*$$

Les liens établis entre chaque province et l'étranger peuvent dépasser le stade de la simple représentation et se concrétiser dans des accords internationaux ou transnationaux. Et, en effet, des relations nombreuses et diversifiées sont tissées entre les provinces canadiennes et les subdivisions territoriales des États-Unis, États et municipalités. Il en résulte que des déplacements de personnes, des mouvements de capitaux, des échanges commerciaux, des flux culturels ou encore des consultations ou arrangements, ententes, accords dans les domaines les plus divers unissent les individus, les groupements privés et publics des subdivisions territoriales canadiennes et américaines[76]. Ce ne sont pas les seuls contacts, s'ils sont les plus importants et de loin les plus nombreux. Les provinces concluent des accords avec d'autres entités étrangères, privées ou publiques, en Europe, en Asie, en Amérique latine et en Afrique[77].

Dès le milieu des années 60, le Québec a revendiqué le droit de conclure des ententes internationales dans les domaines qui relèvent juridiquement de la compétence provinciale[78]. Les accords couvraient alors les questions culturelles (l'éducation, la coopération) avec la France tout d'abord. Un accord-cadre ou *ad hoc* conclu parfois le même jour par les autorités fédérales autorisait la conclusion de cet accord. Le Québec a conclu des ententes avec des entités étrangères dans d'autres domaines, la sécurité sociale, l'administration de la justice ou encore, tout comme d'autres provinces canadiennes, pour la réglementation des transports, la construction de ponts internationaux, la protection des feux de forêts; des domaines essentiellement d'ordre administratif, technique ou judiciaire.

Un autre champ d'activités, le développement économique, fait aujourd'hui l'objet d'un certain nombre d'accords, d'ententes ou d'arrangements provinciaux avec des pays étrangers ou leurs subdivisions politiques, ou encore des organes du secteur privé. Ces accords se placent parfois dans le contexte des commissions mixtes ou groupes de travail dont le nombre augmente[79]. Cependant, les provinces de langue anglaise, ou à majorité de langue anglaise, reconnaissent généralement et globalement aux autorités fédérales la compétence officielle en matière de traités internationaux tout en souhaitant parfois des changements. Elles n'en concluent pas moins de nombreux arrangements écrits ou oraux avec les subdivisions territoriales américaines[80]. La plupart du temps, en fait, les autorités fédérales ne sont pas informées de ces échanges.

Il y a donc une distinction très nette tracée entre les relations «transnationales», les flux «transnationaux», de toutes les provinces canadiennes en majorité orientés vers les États américains, et les relations «internationales» avec les autres pays étrangers ou leurs subdivisions politiques. Si les premières, imposées par la géographie, ne créent pas de véritables problèmes, excepté dans des cas limites ou à dimensions indubitablement nationales – comme les exportations d'hydrocarbures ou d'électricité –, la deuxième catégorie de rapports est source de conflits entre l'Union fédérale et les provinces.

Le conflit Québec-Ottawa à partir des années 60 de la Révolution tranquille, qui s'est accusé à partir de novembre 1976, date de l'arrivée au pouvoir dans la province d'un parti qui réclame l'indépendance, en témoigne. Il n'est en 1982 que l'expression, la transposition externe d'une vision fondamentale absolument opposée du destin du Québec entre les deux acteurs. Un conflit d'ordre essentiellement économique, le partage des recettes tirées des ressources naturelles, oppose également Ottawa à l'Alberta et dans une moindre mesure aux autres provinces de l'Ouest. Ajoutons qu'à l'est du Canada, Terre-Neuve s'oppose aussi à Ottawa pour des considérations similaires; ce conflit est politico-économique.

Nous avons évoqué antérieurement le contexte juridique canadien en matière de relations internationales. La Constitution de 1867 est muette sur ce point à part les dispositions générales sur le pouvoir exécutif et le seul article 132 qui réglemente le point particulier de la mise en œuvre interne des obligations engendrées par les traités d'Empire, confiée «au Parlement et au gouvernement du Canada». Or, la communauté internationale reconnaît aux États membres d'une fédération la capacité de conclure des traités «si cette capacité est admise par la Constitution fédérale et dans les limites» fixées par cette Constitution[81].

Dans l'état actuel du droit constitutionnel canadien, les provinces n'ont pas cette capacité[82]. Il ne s'agit cependant que de «formation» des engagements internationaux. Une fois conclu, le traité doit être mis à exécution. Si les obligations se situent exclusivement dans la sphère des relations internationales, les autorités fédérales peuvent agir. Par contre, si elles se situent partiellement ou entièrement dans l'ordre interne, la question de la répartition des compétences mentionnée précédemment se pose; elle est source de conflits. L'Union fédérale, le Canada, ne peut obliger les provinces à légiférer pour la mise en œuvre des traités et ne peut se substituer à la province défaillante. Selon l'image tracée en 1937 dans l'affaire des Conventions du travail, et toujours valable dans une certaine mesure, il s'agit de «compartiments étanches»[83]. Il y a donc une nécessité d'entente préalable à la conclusion de traités internationaux qui entrent dans cette catégorie.

Dans le long processus qui aboutit à la conclusion des traités et à leur application, la collaboration des provinces s'impose particulièrement à deux niveaux, à la phase des négociations officieuses ou officielles et, une fois l'accord conclu, à celle de la mise en œuvre, de la gestion. Reprenons ces deux points. Il n'y a pas de règle générale tendant à associer les provinces aux négociations des traités internationaux qui relèvent de leur compétence ou les intéressent particulièrement. L'approche est sectorielle ou *ad hoc,* du cas par cas selon le domaine couvert par le traité. Il est vrai que les provinces sont consultées lorsqu'il s'agit de traités portant sur des matières dont l'exécution ne peut se réaliser sans leur concours, et souvent consultées dans l'hypothèse de traités les intéressant tout spécialement, en dépit de la difficulté de définir cet intérêt particulier. Toutefois, une participation provinciale officielle aux négociations constitue l'exception dans les deux cas d'accords bilatéraux et multi-latéraux. On parle plutôt de consultation, souvent au même titre que les autres acteurs importants de l'activité socio-économique. L'exemple des accords conclus dans le cadre du GATT en constitue une illustration tout comme les accords sur l'environnement, la qualité de l'eau ou encore les exportations de pétrole, de gaz naturel ou de charbon liquéfié.

Il s'agit donc d'ententes fédérales-provinciales sur des points d'accord li-mités qui ne peuvent être étendus qu'à la suite de nouvelles négociations entre les différentes parties impliquées dans l'accord international dans des secteurs bien précis. Un des scénarios qui se présente est celui de négociations officieuses en-gagées par les provinces et qui seront poursuivies par les autorités fédérales com-pétentes. Le poids politique de quelques provinces s'impose à l'évidence, l'Alberta à l'égard des hydrocarbures, le Québec vis-à-vis des exportations d'électricité dans les États de la Nouvelle-Angleterre et de New York, l'Ontario dans le contexte des négociations sur l'industrie automobile ou également sur la pollution des Grands Lacs ou encore les provinces intéressées pour l'exploitation des fleuves qui coulent dans les deux pays, le Saint-Laurent et le fleuve Columbia, par exemple[84].

Les intérêts des acteurs nationaux et internationaux s'entrecroisent et, à ce stade des négociations officieuses, le scénario sera parfois une alliance d'un acteur sous-national, notamment l'Alberta, avec les États-Unis ou certains groupes de pression des États-Unis contre une politique du gouvernement fédéral, comme la nouvelle politique énergétique d'octobre 1980 ou les activités de FIRA. C'est pour lutter contre ces positions divergentes à l'intérieur d'un même pays que le gouverne-ment fédéral adopte progressivement des solutions qui se présentent comme centralisatrices, nationalistes et parfois «étatiques», c'est-à-dire créant des contrain-tes et obstacles au libre jeu des règles du marché économique. Au pays et à l'étran-ger, les acteurs et groupes de pression se divisent selon le clivage en faveur ou contre cet étatisme *(statism)* économique, voire la nationalisation, qui implique la canadia-nisation des secteurs touchés.

La deuxième phase requiert la collaboration des provinces ou l'application d'un fédéralisme coopératif en vue de l'introduction des dispositions des traités internationaux dans l'ordre interne. Elle soulève le problème général des rapports entre le droit national et l'international[85]. Héritage britannique, les traités interna-tionaux n'ont pas «force de loi» au Canada. Ils doivent donc être introduits, trans-formés en droit interne pour avoir des effets juridiques à l'égard des particuliers et être appliqués directement dans les affaires soumises aux tribunaux[86]. Si le traité par lui-même ne fait pas partie de l'ordre juridique interne, il y a des cas où la législation antérieure au traité est déjà conforme aux dispositions de cet acte international; la phase d'introduction ne se pose donc pas. Cependant, il peut y avoir divergence d'interprétation entre les deux législations, la nationale et l'internationale, et dans la sphère internationale, les acteurs internationaux peuvent réclamer des change-ments. L'exemple du traitement accordé aux Amérindiens au Canada en témoigne[87].

Les traités qui impliquent l'adoption de mesures législatives internes, pour avoir des effets juridiques à l'égard des particuliers, doivent se couler dans le moule de la répartition constitutionnelle des compétences législatives, telle qu'elle est fixée par la Constitution de 1867 et ses amendements successifs. Chaque province est en un sens souveraine dans sa sphère de compétence avec les réserves de compétence résiduelle attribuée à la fédération et reliée à la théorie des dimensions nationales et de compétence conjointe dont le champ s'élargit d'année en année, comme dans le cas des communications et des ressources naturelles. Ce phénomène s'accuse d'autant plus que dans le domaine des relations internationales, le seul acteur reconnu par la Cour suprême du Canada, au pays, est l'Union fédérale, aux termes mêmes de décisions récentes mentionnées précédemment.

*   *

*

Les discussions des années 60 sur la personnalité internationale du Québec, basées sur des considérations d'ordre juridique interne et externe, c'est-à-dire le droit canadien et le droit international ou les décisions des instances intergouvernementales internationales, apparaissent aujourd'hui comme une hypothèse d'école. Car ce qui compte dans le système mondial, c'est le jeu ou plutôt la lutte pour le pouvoir politico-économique engagée entre les acteurs nationaux et sous-nationaux et les réactions des acteurs internationaux et leurs prises de position. Avec un certain recul, les discussions purement juridiques s'estompent. Et des choix pratiques sont à faire, traduisant les forces respectives des parties en présence. Dans les scénarios pour l'avenir, on peut prévoir la mise en place de mécanismes *ad hoc* répondant à un besoin impérieux de coordination. Au sein de nouvelles institutions fédérales-provinciales, chargées des questions internationales, aux trois plans de l'étude, la consultation et la prise de décision, les solutions pourraient se dégager. Il n'en demeure pas moins que si au stade de la consultation, d'une sorte de concertation dans certains domaines bien définis, les difficultés peuvent être écartées, c'est à la phase de la prise de décision que les enjeux sont importants. Les divergences sont souvent irréconciliables, notamment de par le nombre élevé des acteurs au conflit et également l'influence de différents groupes de pression nationaux et internationaux. En matière de politique étrangère, il est difficile d'asseoir à la table des négociations du côté canadien des négociateurs dont les divergences font le jeu du partenaire ou des partenaires internationaux. Il est donc indispensable d'aboutir à des choix. Très souvent, le seul arbitre en la matière reste le gouvernement fédéral. Il convient cependant d'ajouter que si cette défense et cette illustration de la politique étrangère devant les instances internationales doivent être le fait du gouvernement fédéral, la gestion de cette politique étrangère, en particulier à l'égard des trois aspects que nous avons évoqués précédemment, pourrait être décentralisée et relever à la fois des provinces et de l'Union fédérale, selon des formules qu'il reste encore à définir, une fois l'accord établi sur les grands principes.

NOTES

1. Voir «Orientation bibliographique», dans *Le Canada et le Québec sur la scène internationale, Paul Painchaud, éd., 1977;* également, les publications de T.A. Levy, dont «Le rôle des provinces», *ibidem;* celles de I. Bernier, L. Bissonnette, J. Brossard, A. Dufour, E.H. Fry, P.R. Johannson, D. Latouche, L. Di Marzo, E. McWhinney, J.P. Meekison, G. Morris, P. Painchaud, A. Patry, P. Soldatos, G. Stevenson, R.F. Swanson, K. Valaskakis; Voir aussi Annemarie Jacomy-Millette (*infra* Jacomy-Millette), «Selected Bibliography» dans *Treaty Law in Canada,* 1975, p. 311; Annemarie Jacomy-Millette, «International diplomatic activities of Canadian Provinces with emphasis on Québec behaviour», 7 *R.G.D.,* 7-23 (1976); Annemarie Jacomy-Millette, «Le rôle des provinces dans les relations internationales», 10 *Études internationales,* 285 (1979); Annemarie Jacomy-Millette, communication au colloque de Bruxelles, février 1982, sur «Les États fédéraux et les relations internationales» organisé par la Société belge de droit international (*infra* Communication).

2. «The last decade has seen a dramatic increase in the international activities of the Western provinces [...]. The focus has been primarily in the economic sphere.» Wayne Clifford, «A perspective on the question with particular reference to the case of the Province of Alberta», dans *Le Canada dans le monde,* CQRI, 1982.

3. V. articles 91, 92, 93, 95, 109 et 117 de l'Acte de 1867 et les nombreux ouvrages des constitutionnalistes canadiens, en français et en anglais, dont ceux de A. Barbeau, G.A. Beaudoin, J. Brossard, G.P. Browne, H. Brun, R. McG. Dawson, W.P.M. Kennedy, B. Laskin, E. McWhinney, J.R. Mallory, G. Rémillard, F.R. Scott, A. Tremblay. Il y a d'ailleurs un 3ᵉ niveau de gouvernement, le municipal, dont l'importance est soulignée par le fait que la population de la région de Montréal est à peu près équivalente à celle de l'Alberta.

4. *Le fédéralisme canadien,* 1980.

5. *Cf.* J. Brossard, *La Cour suprême et la Constitution,* Montréal, 1968; G.P. Browne, *The Judicial Committee and the British North America Act,* 1967; W.R. Lederman, *The Courts and the Canadian Constitution,* 1971; A. Tremblay, «L'incertitude du droit constitutionnel canadien relatif au partage des compétences législatives», 29 *Revue du Barreau,* p. 197-209 (1969).

6. Aux termes mêmes de l'avis de la Cour suprême du Canada dans l'*Affaire des droits miniers sous-marins* (1967), R.C.S. 792, et du jugement du 28 septembre 1981 sur le rapatriement de la Constitution; v. aussi l'affaire des *Conventions du travail* en Cour suprême du Canada, J. Duff (1936), R.C.S. 461 et devant le comité judiciaire du Conseil privé, Lord Atkin (1937), A.C. 326.

7. «La prérogative de la Couronne est ce [...] pouvoir dont est revêtu le souverain et qui fait partie de cet ensemble de pouvoirs discrétionnaires dérivant du droit coutumier dont le monarque en personne avait l'exercice», rapport O'Connor, 1939.

8. *Cf.* Communiqué de presse du 30 décembre 1977, du Cabinet du premier ministre sur les nouvelles fonctions du gouverneur général.

9. *Cf. Hodge v. The Queen* (1883), 9 App. Cas. 117; *Liquidators of the Maritime Bank v. Receiver-General of New Brunswick* (1892), A.C. 437; *Bonanza Creek Gold Mining Co. Ltd.* (1916), A.C. 566; Affaire des *Conventions du travail*(1937), A.C. 326, et encore les affaires de l'*aéronautique* et des *radio-communications* (1932), A.C. 54, A.C. 304; V. *Treaty Law in Canada, op. cit.,* p. 49-59, 69-103, pour l'ensemble de la discussion.

10. «Les provinces [...] invitent cette Cour à déclarer que juridiquement la répartition interne des pouvoirs législatifs doit avoir des répercussions externes bien que [...] le pouvoir légal existant [comme à l'article 3 du Statut de Westminster] nie cette prétention des provinces.» Jugement du 28 septembre 1981 sur le rapatriement de la Constitution; V. aussi 1967, R.C.S. 792.

11. V. «Document de travail sur les relations avec l'étranger», notes préparées par la délégation du Québec à la Conférence constitutionnelle/Comité permanent des fonctionnaires, Québec, 5 février 1969; et les propositions présentées par les (autres) gouvernements provinciaux à la Conférence constitutionnelle de 1968-1971, doc. n° 355, CICS (Terre-Neuve: 0.1.2.; Nouveau Brunswick: 3.22.52; Ontario: 5.18.38; Saskatchewan: 7.2.14).

12. *Cf.* Howard Leeson, allocation devant les membres de l'ICAI, Saskatoon, 29 mai 1981.

13. «Harmony in Diversity: A new federalism for Canada, Alberta Government position paper on Constitutional Change», octobre 1978.

14. V. les documents de travail des conférences de 1977 et 1981, dont les remarques du premier ministre ontarien, W.G. Davis, en août 1981 (doc. 850-18/006): «Canadians have always given a high priority to issues related to our economic well-being [...]. There is one issue that I regard above all others as the first priority for Government action in the economy.»; ou le communiqué final de la conférence de 1981, où les premiers ministres «qualifient la situation économique de totalement inacceptable».

15. Communiqué final, 1981, *loc. cit.*

16. «The Trade Challenge for Canada in the 1980s», discours du ministre Ed. Lumley (Canada), 22 juin 1982, à la chambre de commerce de Toronto, Affaires extérieures, *Statements and Speeches,* n° 82/13.

17. *Supra,* note 13, «Harmony in Diversity».

18. V. les livres blancs du gouvernement fédéral sur les relations internationales de la fin des années 60, toujours applicables (*Fédéralisme et relations internationales,* 1968; *Fédéralisme et conférences internationales sur l'Éducation,* 1968); M. MacGuigan, «Le fédéralisme et les relations internationales du Canada», 12 *Politique internationale,* p. 189-200 (1981).

19. M. MacGuigan, *loc. cit.,* p. 195; V. aussi Jacomy-Millette, *L'introduction et l'application des traités internationaux au Canada* et *Treaty Law in Canada,* le chapitre correspondant.

20. M. MacGuigan, *loc. cit.,* p. 189-190.

21. Voir *Programmes et activités fédéraux-provinciaux,* répertoires 1980-1981 et 1981-1982, Bureau des relations fédérales-provinciales, Ottawa, p. 77, «Agents québécois d'immigration à l'étranger», p. 5, «Conseiller en éducation à Abidjan»; V.J.J. Kirton, «Les contraintes du milieu et la gestion de la politique étrangère canadienne», 10(2) *Études internationales,* p. 321 (1979).

22. V. les rapports annuels des ministères et organes provinciaux intéressés; la législation provinciale; les exposés des fonctionnaires provinciaux dans *Le Canada dans le monde, op. cit.;* ces développements s'appuient aussi sur un questionnaire adressé aux ministères provinciaux et un échange de correspondance ultérieur.

23. V. Statuts refondus, Québec, 1964, c. 56 (Loi du ministère des Affaires intergouvernementales); c. 208 (Loi des agents délégués généraux); Loi de 1974, c. 15; Lois refondues du Québec, 1977, c. M. 21.

24. *Le Canada dans le monde, op. cit.,* p. 67.

25. Allocution du 4 mai 1972 devant une délégation officielle du Maine; allocution du 22 août 1981 devant les associations Québec-France et France-Québec.

26. Lise Bissonnette, «The Evolution of Québec-American Diplomacy», dans C. Veltman, ed., *Contemporary Québec,* UQAM, 1981; J.L. Roy, «Les relations du Québec et des États-Unis», *Le Canada et le Québec sur la scène internationale,* 1977; et les communications de Lise Bissonnette et Bernard Bonin, au colloque des 1ᵉʳ au 3 septembre 1982, organisé à Harvard par le CQRI, et portant sur les relations Québec-États-Unis; V. aussi les récents discours des ministres québécois Bernard Landry, *Revue de presse-USA,* délégation du Québec à New York, 9 décembre 1981, et Jacques-Yvan Morin, *Globe and Mail* (Toronto), 20 février 1982, p. 3; *Le Soleil* (Québec), 12 mars 1982; *Le Devoir* (Montréal), 1ᵉʳ mars 1982, p. 9; *cf.* «Québec seeks more US trade», Transcript-Telegram (USA), 2 septembre 1982; *cf.* Joseph A. Lemay, «Québec and economic interdependence with the United States: A focus on Hydro-Québec», 10(1) *The American review of Canadian studies,* 1980, p. 94.

27. *Québec Inter,* vol. III, n° 2 (février 1982); *Le Soleil* (Québec), 1ᵉʳ septembre 1982: «Jean Tardif nommé délégué du Québec aux Affaires francophones».

28. Statutes of Ontario, 1972, c. 3, The Ministry of Treasury, Economics and Intergovernmental Affairs Act.

29. *Le Canada dans le monde, op. cit.,* p. 85.

30. Statutes of Alberta, c. 33, The Department of Federal and Intergovernmental Affairs Act.

31. *8th Annual Report* to March 31, 1981, p. 35.

32. Statutes of Saskatchewan, c. D-18.1, The Department of Intergovernmental Affairs Act.

33. Lettre du 13 juin 1980.

34. Lettre du 24 juillet 1980, Intergovernmental Affairs Secretariat, Executive Council, Newfoundland and Labrador.

35. «Orthodoxie fédéraliste et relations régionales transfrontières, une menace illusoire», *infra Orthodoxie,* 12 (4) *Études internationales,* 635, ss (1981); «La vocation tardive […]», communication au colloque d'Harvard précité.

36. *Cf.* ententes Québec-New York et Québec-Vermont, signées à l'automne 1981.

37. Par exemple à l'égard de l'exportation d'électricité alors qu'un contentieux Terre-Neuve-Québec oppose les deux provinces.

38. V. par exemple les chroniques d'*International Canada* (Toronto et Ottawa), et d'*Études internationales* (Québec).

39. V. «Canadian-American relations: distinctiveness and harmony», dans *Canada as an international actor,* P.V. Lyon et B.W. Tomlin, 1979; «North American Interdependence and Canadian Fuel Policies», J.N. McDougal, dans *Canada's Foreign Policy: Analysis and Trends,* 1978. Ce trait se vérifie même dans le cas du Québec (V. L. Balthazar, «La politique du Québec aux États-Unis», communication au colloque d'Harvard, *loc. cit.*). V. aussi «British Columbia's relations with the United States», P.R. Johannson, 21(2) *Can. Pc. Adtion,* 212 (1978); R.H. Leach, D.E. Walker, T.A. Levy, «Province-State transborder relations: a preliminary assessment», 16 CPA, 468 (1973); R.J. McLaren, «Les relations internationales de la Saskatchewan», *Perspectives internationales,* sept.-oct. 1978, p. 20; J.P. Meekison, «Les provinces et les affaires étrangères, une nouvelle dimension du fédéralisme», *Perspectives internationales,* mars-avril 1977, p. 8, et les trois brochures du Comité sénatorial permanent des Affaires

étrangères du Canada sur *Les relations Canada-États-Unis,* vol. 2, 1978, vol. 3, 1982.

40. Pour Claude Morin, alors ministre des Affaires intergouvernementales du Québec, ce fait est lié à la centralisation du Canada et à l'ouverture de hauts-commissariats et ambassades du Canada (allocution sur «La politique extérieure du Québec à l'ICAI», Québec, 7 mars 1978).

41. Cette priorité au plan des relations économiques et financières et transnationales est confortée dans les provinces par une opinion publique proaméricaine (V. le rapport n° 13 du 14 juillet 1982, *Opinion Update,* de la Canada West Foundation); ce n'est que dans une certaine «élite», généralement intellectuelle, que l'on relève un certain antiaméricanisme, dans une recherche de définition de l'identité nationale canadienne.

42. L'essentiel est cependant les liens économiques Nord-Sud pour toutes les provinces: *cf.,* par ex., «[...] relations with the United States remain the primary focus of the Western Provinces international interests», W. Clifford, *op. cit.,* p. 105.

43. Québec a quinze bureaux dont sept aux États-Unis et un dans chacun des pays suivants: France, Belgique, Royaume-Uni, Allemagne (RFA), Italie, Japon, Vénézuela et Mexique, plus un bureau de tourisme à Washington et un «délégué-conseiller ministériel» au Gabon; jusqu'à 1967, V. J. Hamelin, «Québec et le monde extérieur 1867-1967», dans *Annuaire du Québec,* 1968-1969.

44. Selon Lise Bissonnette, il n'y aurait pas de véritable politique étrangère du Québec à l'égard des États-Unis entre 1976 et 1982 (voir différents articles du *Devoir* (Montréal) pour la période considérée; *cf.* «Québec-Ottawa-Washington, the pre-referendum triangle», dans 11(1) *The American Review of Canadian Studies,* 64 (1981)); V. aussi la chronique trimestrielle des relations internationales du Québec, dans *Études internationales.*

45. Il y en avait alors 16, sept en Europe: à Londres, Bruxelles, Francfort, Paris, Vienne, Milan et Stockholm, une en Asie, Tokyo, six aux États-Unis: New York, Boston, Chicago, Los Angeles, Cleveland, Minneapolis, et deux en Amérique latine: Mexico, Sao Paulo, à comparer avec Québec qui en avait quinze; cinq en Europe: à Bruxelles, Düsseldorf, Londres, Milan et Paris, un en Asie, à Tokyo, et un à Haïti.

46. V. *Le Canada dans le monde, op. cit.,* p. 86, en particulier: l'Ontario a senti qu'une présence trop forte sur la scène européenne surtout entraînait beaucoup de confusion et menaçait même l'image canadienne si on la prend globalement (D. Massicotte).

47. H. Leeson, *op. cit.:* «A second area of legitimacy for provincial activities in international relations is the right of provinces to open offices abroad.»

48. Document 850-18/016, «Statement on Resource Income», Annual Provincial Premiers' Conference, 12-13 août 1981; *cf.* aussi *Communication, loc. cit.*

49. V. la publication mensuelle *International Canada,* ou chronique des faits internationaux qui intéressent le Canada, et pour le Québec, la chronique de la revue *Études internationales,* par ex.: visite du ministre thaïlandais de l'Industrie aux installations de pétrole et de gaz naturel d'Alberta, de potasse de Saskatchewan, juillet-août 1981; ou du ministre japonais de la Construction en Alberta et en Colombie-Britannique, *ibidem;* ou encore la rencontre François Mitterand-René Lévesque à l'ambassade de France à Ottawa en août 1981; les entretiens du ministre guinéen de l'Énergie avec des ministres québécois en juillet 1981; ceux du vice-président de la CEE avec les ministres provinciaux de l'Ontario, de l'Alberta et de la Colombie-Britannique à l'été 1981.

50. V. p. 34 du rapport.

51. Pour cette période, le rapport mentionne 265 visites, missions et délégations étrangères dont 47 pour les États-Unis, 38 pour le Japon, 24 pour la RFA, treize pour la Grande-Bretagne.

52. V. L. Sabourin, *Canadian Federalism and International Organizations: A Focus on Québec,* 1971; Jacomy-Millette, «Le rôle des provinces», *loc. cit.,* p. 304, ss.

53. V. par exemple la présentation le 4 juin 1974 du budget des ministères des Affaires intergouvernementales du Québec et les déclarations et discours des ministres de la Culture, de l'Éducation, des Affaires intergouvernementales du Québec, comme Paul Gérin-Lajoie, Jean-Guy Cardinal, François Cloutier, Claude Morin, Jacques-Yvan Morin, qui se sont succédé depuis la fin des années 60; celles de premiers ministres libéraux (Jean Lesage, Robert Bourassa), d'Union nationale (Daniel Johnson et Jean-Jacques Bertrand) et péquiste (René Lévesque).

54. Jacques-Yvan Morin, vice-premier ministre du Québec, *Le Canada dans le monde, op. cit.,* p. 12.

55. *Communication,* 22-23 février 1979.

56. V. par exemple les documents des Conférences des premiers ministres de l'Ouest; G.F. Rutan, «Western Canada: the winds of alienation», 12(1) *The American review of Canadian Studies,* 74 (1982).

57. V. par exemple les documents de travail des dernières années des conférences annuelles des premiers ministres provinciaux (*cf. Revue générale de la situation économique* par les premiers ministres de l'Ouest; *Les négociations commerciales multilatérales,* communiqués n°s 6 et 7 à la Conférence des premiers ministres de l'Ouest, Lethbridge, 22-23 avril 1980).

58. J.D. House, «Premier Peckford, Petroleum policy, and popular politics in Newfoundland and Labrador», 17(2) *Revue d'études canadiennes*, 12 (1982).

59. Notes pour une allocution prononcée par le premier ministre de l'Alberta Peter Lougheed à la Conférence fédérale-provinciale des premiers ministres, Ottawa, 13-15 février 1978; V. aussi le communiqué n° 6, *Revue générale de la situation économique, op. cit.*, doc. 850; doc. 850-15/012.

60. V. «Le rôle des provinces», *loc. cit.*, et *Communication, loc. cit.*

61. *Supra*, Conférence fédérale-provinciale, 13-15 février 1978.

62. 19ᵉ Conférence annuelle des premiers ministres provinciaux, Régina/Waskesiou, 9-12 août 1978, doc. 850-10/019: Economy-Position Paper by the Hon. Gerald A. Regan, Premier of Nova Scotia.

63. Conférence précitée de 1978.

64. V. T.A. Levy, «Le rôle des provinces», *loc. cit.*

65. Négociations commerciales multilatérales – Participation canadienne, 11 juillet 1979, communiqué du Bureau du coordonnateur à Ottawa.

66. Position de la Colombie-Britannique à la Conférence fédérale-provinciale des premiers ministres, sur l'économie, 13-15 février 1978; et L. Grossman, ministre ontarien, Industrie et Tourisme, *Globe and Mail* (Toronto), 12 juillet 1979.

67. V. *Le Devoir* et le *Globe and Mail* du 15 août 1982.

68. Interview au ministère des Affaires intergouvernementales du 30 novembre 1979.

69. Selon le Québec, «c'est par l'intermédiaire de la Conférence des ministres de l'Éducation que les provinces peuvent être représentées à l'UNESCO au sein de la délégation canadienne, au même titre que les organismes privés»; voir note précédente; à la Conférence générale de l'UNESCO de 1980, la délégation canadienne, présidée par un ministre fédéral, comprenait le ministre de l'Éducation de la Nouvelle-Écosse, le sous-ministre adjoint des Affaires culturelles du Québec, etc.; la délégation canadienne à la 8ᵉ Conférence du Commonwealth sur l'Éducation (1980) était présidée par le ministre de l'Éducation du Nouveau-Brunswick.

70. V. A/CONF. 62/INF 15, p. 8: des représentants de la Nouvelle-Écosse, du Nouveau-Brunswick, de l'Ontario et du Manitoba étaient conseillers.

71. La part du Canada au budget de l'ACCT est de 35 %, dont 31,7 % provenant du fédéral, 3 % du Québec, 0,3 % du Nouveau-Brunswick; soit en 1980-1981, 4 711 873 $.

72. En 1980, présidence du secrétaire d'État aux Affaires extérieures, à la Conférence générale extraordinaire de mars; en 1979, présidence du ministre d'État chargé de l'ACDI, à la Conférence générale.

73. Le Canada contribue pour 34 % (dont la moitié assumée par le Québec) au budget du fonctionnement du Secrétariat technique permanent conjoint de ces deux conférences.

74. *Cf.* par exemple les sessions des commissions mixtes France-Canada où les provinces sont représentées; Belgique-Canada – signalons l'existence de sous-commissions mixtes comme France-Québec; Belgique-Québec, et récemment Wallonie-Québec.

75. V. Jacomy-Millette, «Le rôle des provinces», *loc. cit.*; V. *8th Annual Report*, ministère des Affaires intergouvernementales d'Alberta: «The federal and provincial governments agreed in early 1981 to the establishment of regular quarterly federal-provincial trade policy consultations.»

76. V. «Le rôle des provinces», *loc. cit.*; *Communication, loc. cit.*; récemment, de nombreuses études font le point de ces relations dont celle de R.F. Swanson de 1974, poursuivie en 1976 et 1978 qui dénombre notamment 766 interactions entre les provinces et les États, *State/Provincial Interaction*, 1974; *Intergovernmental Perspectives on the Canada-US relationship*, 1978; A.B. Fox, A.O. Hero et J.S. Nye, ed., *Canada and the United States, Transnational and Transgovernmental Relations*, 1976.

77. V. listes compilées par les provinces, la liste québécoise se trouve au greffe du ministère des Affaires intergouvernementales; elle comprend tous les accords intergouvernementaux internes et externes; une liste albertaine «of international agreements which Alberta has concluded with foreign entities» était jointe à une lettre du 10 février 1982 du directeur exécutif de la Division internationale, elle comprend quinze «agreements» passés entre 1971 et 1981 (V. *Communication*).

78. Nombreux sont les ouvrages et articles qui ont traité de la question; V. Bibliographie dans *Treaty Law, op. cit.*, et *Le Canada et le Québec sur la scène internationale, op. cit.*, et lire le résumé d'A. Patry dans «Québec et relations internationales», dans *Dossier Québec*, livre Dossier-Stock, 1979, p. 377; V. aussi A. Dufour, «Fédéralisme canadien et droit international», dans *Canadian Perspectives on International Law and Organization*, 1974.

79. V. Rapport annuel 1980-1981 précité du ministère albertain des Affaires intergouvernementales, p. 39, et l'exemple du Resource Processing Working Group, dans le cadre du Canada-Japan Economic Framework; V. aussi rapport de la Saskatchewan (Affaires intergouvernementales), 1980-1981 et les exemples de liens avec la CEE, le Japon, le Mexique, la Chine populaire, les États-Unis (le fédéral et le Montana); ou encore rapports annuels du ministère des Affaires intergouvernementales du Québec.

80. *Cf.* Luigi Di Marzo, *Component units of federal states and international agreements*, 1980; Jacomy-Millette, *Treaty Law in Canada*, 1975; Jacomy-Millette, *Communication*.

81. Article 5, par. 2, du projet d'articles de 1966 sur le droit des traités élaboré par la Commission du droit international des Nations Unies; V. Jacomy-Millette, *Treaty Law in Canada, op. cit.*, et *biblio.* déjà citée.

82. Ce qui n'est cependant pas reconnu d'une manière définitive au niveau des gouvernements provinciaux; V. la controverse juridique dans les doc. officiels du fédéral et du Québec; et *Treaty Law in Canada, op. cit.*

83. (1937) A.C. 326, Lord Atkin; aussi les jugements de décisions ultérieures annonçant un revirement, Francis v. *The Queen* (1956), R.C.S. 618, *Offshore Mineral Rights* (1967), R.C.S. 792; *John Macdonald v. Vapor Canada* (1977), R.C.S. 134; aussi la doctrine, G.L. Morris, «Canadian Federalism and International Law», dans *Canadian Perspectives in International Law and Organization*; J-C. Bonenfant, «L'étanchéité de l'Acte de l'Amérique du Nord britannique», 18 *Cahiers de droit*, 383 (1977); G.V. LaForest, «The Labor Convention Case revisited», 12 *ACDI*, 137 (1974); R. St.J. Macdonald, «International Treaty Law and the Domestic Law of Canada», 2 *Dalhousie Law Journal*, 307 (1975).

84. N.A. Swainson, *Conflict over the Columbia, the Canadian background to an historic treaty*, 1978; P.R. Johannson, *op. cit.*, qui mentionne l'accord entre le premier ministre de Colombie-Britannique et le gouverneur de l'État de Washington sur les risques de pollution, qui a précédé un accord entre les deux pays.

85. R. St.J. Macdonald, «The relationship between International Law and Domestic Law in Canada», dans *Canadian Perspectives on International Law and Organization, op. cit.*

86. V. Jacomy-Millette, *Treaty Law in Canada, op. cit.*; Abel, *Laskin's Constitutional Law*, ch. III, Power to Implement Treaty Obligations, 4ᵉ éd., 1973; J.G. Castel, *International Law*, 4ᵉ partie: *International Agreements*, 3ᵉ éd., 1976.

87. V. l'Affaire *Lavell* (1973), 38 D.L.R. (3d) 481, par exemple; et R.L. Barsh and J.Y. Anderson, «Aboriginal rights, Treaty rights, and Human rights: Indian tribes and constitutional renewal», 17(2) *Revue d'études canadiennes*, 55 (1982).

Le système global   The Global System

5

Le Canada et les relations Est-Ouest

André Donneur
Université du Québec à Montréal

Les relations Est-Ouest ont dicté la configuration du système international d'après la Deuxième Guerre mondiale. La polarisation entre Washington et Moscou rendait le système international particulièrement rigide. Mais après la crise des missiles de 1962 qui marque la fin de la guerre froide – ou de la première guerre froide – le système international s'est considérablement assoupli. C'est à la même époque que la Chine, qui paraissait bien alignée sur Moscou, prit ses distances à l'égard de l'URSS et entra même en conflit avec elle. On ne pouvait plus la considérer dès lors comme relevant des rapports Est-Ouest, mais bien d'une autre dimension des relations internationales. Au sein du système international, les pôles chinois, européen occidental et japonais s'ajoutent aux pôles américain et soviétique dont ils contestent la suprématie sur les plans politique et économique. La crise pétrolière de 1973 marque l'avènement d'une autre structure du système international où les rapports Nord-Sud acquièrent une importance aussi égale aux rapports Est-Ouest. La structure du système international se fait plus complexe. Au domaine militaire qui domine les rapports Est-Ouest et aux rapports commerciaux traditionnels où Japon, Europe occidentale et États-Unis sont en tête, s'ajoute désormais toute la dimension de la restructuration des rapports économiques mondiaux pour amener la prospérité au Sud.

L'action du Canada s'insère dans ces trois structures successives du système international. Nous y verrons que, dans les rapports Est-Ouest, loin de s'aligner purement et simplement sur la position américaine, le Canada a joué sa propre carte. Il est évident que moins sont rigides les rapports Est-Ouest et plus fluide est généralement le système international, plus libre de ses manœuvres est le Canada.

LES RELATIONS EST-OUEST DURANT LA GUERRE FROIDE

L'équipe du ministère des Affaires extérieures, qui planifiait la politique étrangère de l'après-guerre, était animée par un désir profond et sincère de contribuer à la création d'un organisme international qui permettrait de garantir la paix. Elle y voyait là une priorité qui était d'ailleurs dans l'intérêt national du Canada[1].

Cette volonté se manifesta d'abord dans la préparation de la Charte des Nations Unies. Norman Robertson et Hume Wrong, les deux diplomates canadiens qui menaient ces négociations, étaient plus enclins que leurs collègues américains à obtenir une unanimité des grandes puissances. Sur la question du veto, ils comprenaient très bien le désir soviétique d'obtenir l'assurance de ne pouvoir être minorisé. Lors des pourparlers de Dumbarton Oaks, Mackenzie King envoya un message à Churchill pour le persuader d'accepter le point de vue soviétique sur le veto[2]. À la conférence de San Francisco, le Canada agit aussi dans le même sens[3].

Cette préoccupation était d'autant plus grande que les mêmes planificateurs avaient considéré, dès janvier 1944, la possibilité d'une autre guerre où l'URSS et les États-Unis seraient aux prises. Ils ne leur avaient pas échappé que le Canada serait alors la voie de pénétration des bombardiers russes vers les États-Unis. Maurice Pope, président de la mission militaire à Washington, évoquait en avril 1944 la possibilité que le dégoût idéaliste des États-Unis pour la Russie pourrait altérer leurs relations avec ce pays. Le Canada se trouverait alors dans une position difficile, puisque les États-Unis le presseraient de faire cause commune avec eux[4]. Le Comité de travail sur les problèmes d'après-guerre se préoccupait que les installations canadiennes bâties pour la défense de l'Alaska pussent être utilisées comme bases offensives contre l'URSS. Si les États-Unis demandaient le soutien du Canada, le choix serait d'accepter des installations de défense dans le Nord et d'encourir l'hostilité soviétique ou de refuser et d'être contraints de laisser les États-Unis agir malgré tout. La seule manière d'échapper à ce dilemme serait l'établissement d'une organisation mondiale de sécurité qui allégerait les suspicions entre les États-Unis et l'URSS et où le Canada pourrait travailler dans ce sens. Le Canada aurait un rôle d'intermédiaire ou d'interprète entre les deux pays[5].

Ce désir d'éviter toute confrontation avec l'URSS se manifesta également en juillet 1945, dans la satisfaction qu'éprouva Mackenzie King lors de l'élection du gouvernement travailliste au Royaume-Uni. Il y voyait là un gage de paix pour le monde, alors qu'un gouvernement conservateur aurait mené, selon lui, à un antagonisme entre Royaume-Uni et URSS[6].

Cependant, cette bonne volonté allait subir un violent choc le 6 septembre 1945 quand, peu avant l'ouverture de la Chambre des communes, Mackenzie King fut averti par le Sous-secrétaire d'État aux Affaires extérieures qu'un employé de l'ambassade soviétique venait de se présenter au ministère de la Justice avec des documents révélant l'existence d'un vaste réseau d'espionnage soviétique au Ca-nada. L'affaire Gouzenko, du nom de l'employé soviétique qui était le chiffreur de l'ambassade, était née. Sur le moment, Mackenzie King ne prit pas la chose au sérieux, mais lorsque les documents eurent été examinés, il fut horrifié. Des espions soviétiques étaient à l'œuvre aussi bien au ministère des Affaires extérieures qu'au Haut-Commissariat britannique et au Laboratoire de recherche nucléaire à Montréal[7]. Le spectre d'une attaque de l'Amérique du Nord par l'URSS se précisa. Mackenzie King était d'autant plus choqué que cet espionnage soviétique s'était découlé alors que le Canada apportait son aide à l'URSS et cultivait son amitié. Mais il décida de préserver ce qui subsistait de la coopération entre les deux pays. Il garda d'abord secrète l'affaire tant que dura l'enquête. Ensuite, le 8 novembre 1941, alors qu'il était en voyage au Royaume-Uni, il envoya le ministre de la Défense nationale, Douglas Abott, prendre la parole à une assemblée du Ralliement de l'amitié canado-soviétique. Celui-ci exalta l'amitié entre les deux grands voisins du Nord au même climat, aux mêmes ressources, aux mêmes problèmes de transport et de développement, aux populations toutes deux d'origines raciales diverses, qui avaient beaucoup à apprendre l'un de l'autre[8].

Toutefois, il fallut bien rendre publique l'existence du réseau d'espionnage. Mackenzie King le fit le 18 février 1946, sans révéler encore la puissance impliquée. Ce n'est qu'en mars qu'il se résigna à mettre en cause l'URSS. Le 18 mars, devant la Chambre des communes, après avoir fait le récit des événements, il écarta absolument toute possibilité de rupture des relations diplomatiques avec l'URSS. Il se déclara même persuadé que Staline et les principaux responsables soviétiques n'étaient pas au courant de telles pratiques. Il exprima enfin sa volonté que les relations entre les deux pays n'en fussent pas affectées. Mackenzie King favorisait une politique de patience et de prudence[9]. Les experts sur les affaires soviétiques du ministère des Affaires extérieures gardaient aussi une attitude ouverte à l'égard de l'URSS. Ils considéraient la politique soviétique comme non agressive à l'égard de l'Amérique du Nord et essentiellement défensive, quoique conduite avec des méthodes diplomatiques parfois brutales. La communauté politique canadienne conserva ce calme durant toute la guerre froide, en contraste avec les hommes politiques américains que soulevèrent les passions du maccarthysme[10].

À la Conférence du Commonwealth de mai 1946 à Londres, Mackenzie King, qui craignait de plus en plus une guerre, recommanda la patience à l'égard de la Russie[11]. À la conférence de Paris qui s'ouvrit le 29 juillet 1946, son souci était d'accommoder la Russie. Il manifesta cette volonté dès l'élection de la présidence de la conférence où il soutint le compromis tchécoslovaque en faveur d'une coprésidence belgo-soviétique, plutôt que la position britannique et américaine pour une présidence uniquement belge. Mais le Canada n'évita pas que les votes se prennent régulièrement sur un alignement est-ouest. Surtout, il s'attira l'ire de l'URSS pour avoir proposé d'accorder au bout de 18 mois (et non trois ans) la clause de la nation la plus favorisée dans les traités commerciaux à l'Italie[12].

Le Canada manifesta également son esprit de conciliation dans la question du contrôle de l'énergie atomique. Détenteur du secret nucléaire comme les États-Unis et le Royaume-Uni, il se retrouva membre de la Commission de l'énergie atomique, formée par la première Assemblée générale de l'ONU, avec les cinq membres du Conseil de sécurité. Lorsque la Commission se réunit le 14 juin 1946, le représentant américain Bernard Baruch présenta un plan pour le contrôle de l'énergie atomique. Les deux éléments essentiels de ce plan prévoyaient que les membres permanents du Conseil de sécurité abandonneraient leur droit de veto pour tout différend impliquant l'énergie atomique, et que des sanctions seraient appliquées contre tout État qui refuserait de se soumettre aux règles de la future autorité internationale de l'énergie atomique. L'Union soviétique refusait tout abandon du droit de veto et proposait plutôt une convention internationale qui interdirait la production et l'usage des armes atomiques ainsi que la destruction des bombes existantes dans un délai de trois mois suivant l'entrée en vigueur de la convention. La tactique de la délégation canadienne, dirigée par le général McNaughton, fut d'éviter une décision rapide et essayer, par l'étude technique des mesures de sauvegarde requises à chaque stade de la production et de l'utilisation de l'énergie à des fins pacifiques, de concilier les points de vue américain et soviétique. Le Canada chercha ensuite à rapprocher l'URSS des États-Unis en présentant des amendements au plan Baruch. Mais, finalement, l'URSS refusa cette médiation. On dut passer au vote sur le plan Baruch et sur instruction de Mackenzie King – mais contrairement à ses convictions–, le général McNaughton vota avec les États-Unis[13].

Durant l'année 1946, les États-Unis cherchèrent à amener le Canada à prendre conscience de l'acuité du danger soviétique pour l'Amérique du Nord et de la nécessité d'y faire face. Mackenzie King rencontra le président Truman à Washington le 28 octobre 1946. Il lui exprima sa préoccupation de ce que la Russie ne puisse prétendre en aucun cas que les deux pays d'Amérique du Nord faisaient preuve d'agressivité à son égard. À la mi-novembre 1946, le Cabinet canadien se mit d'accord sur le principe d'un plan de défense commun avec les États-Unis. Mais il fit entendre que sa mise au point devait suivre des conversations diplomatiques à un niveau élevé; ces discussions eurent lieu à Ottawa les 16 et 17 décembre dans le plus profond secret. Georges Kennan y expliqua son plan consistant à contenir l'expansionnisme russe jusqu'à ce qu'il s'émousse. Le Canada voulait éviter une détérioration des relations avec l'URSS. C'était toutefois impossible. En janvier 1947, l'ambassadeur à Moscou, Dana Wilgress, qui avait joui durant la guerre d'une position privilégiée venant immédiatement après celles des ambassadeurs britannique et américain, puis depuis l'affaire Gouzenko subissait toutes sortes de vexations, fut rappelé à Ottawa et non remplacé. Le 7 février, les *Izvestia* accusèrent le Canada de s'être joint aux cercles dirigeants américains pour leur apporter son aide dans leurs desseins impérialistes dans le Grand Nord. Molotov, ministre soviétique des Affaires étrangères, agitait le spectre de représailles. Le 18 février, les *Izvestia* faisaient état de la construction de baraquements militaires dans le Nord où les troupes américaines seraient prépondérantes. Pour rassurer les Russes, le gouvernement canadien invita les attachés militaires à Ottawa, notamment le soviétique, à visiter Fort Churchill. Il put se rendre compte que les installations étaient modestes et restaient entre des mains canadiennes[14].

D'une manière générale, tant les hommes politiques que les diplomates canadiens firent preuve, dans ces années 1946 et 1947, de beaucoup de sang froid. Certes, ils appréciaient le danger soviétique mais sans considérer la politique de l'URSS comme agressive en soi à cause de l'idéologie communiste[15]. La question de la sécurité était primordiale. Les espoirs mis dans l'ONU s'avéraient de plus en plus illusoires. Un éditorialiste du magazine *Saturday Night*, Wilson Woodside, ne s'était jamais fait d'illusions. Dès le 26 mai 1945, il avait lancé l'idée d'une union du monde démocratique contre l'impérialisme soviétique, qui seule pourrait garantir la paix. Le 6 octobre 1945, il était revenu à la charge, violemment attaqué par des lettres au *Saturday Night* et au *Toronto Star*. Chez les responsables de la politique étrangère, il fallut attendre le 13 mai 1946 pour remarquer, dans une conférence de Lester B. Pearson, ambassadeur à Washington, une allusion au fait que l'appartenance à l'ONU laissait la porte ouverte à la conclusion d'un arrangement spécial entre puissances désireuses de coopérer entre elles. Une année plus tard, Pearson, devenu entretemps sous-secrétaire d'État aux Affaires extérieures, précisait sa pensée dans une conférence prononcée à l'Université de Rochester. Si l'antagonisme entre les deux conceptions de la société ne pouvaient trouver accommodement aux Nations Unies, il recommandait une coopération entre les nations de l'Ouest. Devant la Chambre des communes, le ministre des Affaires extérieures, Louis Saint-Laurent, déclara le 4 juillet 1947 qu'il y avait place, au sein des Nations Unies, pour une association plus étroite comme celle du Commonwealth. Le 13 août, le Sous-secrétaire d'État adjoint aux Affaires extérieures, Escott Reid, se fit encore plus explicite lors de la Conférence annuelle de l'Institut canadien des affaires internationales. Il évoqua clairement la possibilité pour les États occidentaux de créer une organisation régionale de sécurité dans laquelle les membres mettraient en commun leurs ressources économiques et militaires. Au sein du ministère des Affaires extérieures, on travaillait à la préparation d'un plan d'action. Déjà le 30 novembre 1946, Charles Ritchie, chef de la première division politique, au terme d'une analyse sur le danger soviétique, avait insisté sur l'importance de l'unité des démocraties occidentales pour dissuader l'URSS. S'inspirant de ce document, Escott Reid écrivit un important mémorandum, daté du 30 août 1947, où il est expressément recommandé d'établir une alliance des puissances occidentales pour maintenir l'équilibre des forces face à l'URSS et la contenir fermement. Le Canada était ainsi prêt à prendre l'initiative qui allait donner un nouveau visage aux rapports Est-Ouest.

Le 18 septembre 1947, le ministre des Affaires extérieures, Louis Saint-Laurent, prenait la parole devant l'Assemblée générale des Nations Unies. Après avoir constaté l'impasse provoquée par l'usage abusif du veto, Saint-Laurent déclarait que les objectifs et les principes de la Charte des Nations Unies permettait la création d'une association des États démocratiques et pacifiques qui étaient prêts à consentir des obligations internationales plus spécifiques en retour d'une plus grande sécurité nationale. Aux questions posées par d'autres délégations en réaction au discours de Saint-Laurent, le Canada précisa qu'il avait à l'esprit un pacte de sécurité collective, selon l'article 51 de la Charte, qui affirme le droit individuel et collectif de légitime défense. Le 7 octobre, Saint-Laurent reprit à Québec, devant une audience populaire, les mêmes thèmes que son discours aux Nations Unies. À la mi-octobre, l'ambassadeur à Washington avertit Ottawa que le gouvernement américain donnerait durant l'année 1948 son appui à un pacte régional de défense. Escott Reid rédigea alors un projet inspiré à la fois par le Traité d'assistance mutuelle anglo-polonais du 2 août 1939, le Pacte interaméricain de Rio de 1947 et le protocole de Genève de 1924.

L'association prévue par ce projet aurait été ouverte à tous les membres des Nations Unies et aurait été régie par une assemblée appelée Conseil de légitime défense collective. À la mi-décembre 1947, c'est le ministre britannique des Affaires étrangères, Ernest Bevin, qui précisa l'idée d'un pacte d'alliance avec les États-Unis, la France, l'Italie, Le Bénélux et les dominions. Il s'en ouvrit au général Marshall, le secrétaire d'État américain, puis le premier ministre Attlee envoya un message au président Truman et à Mackenzie King. Le premier ministre canadien revenait alors à son isolationnisme d'avant-guerre et se méfiait de tout ce qui pourrait subordonner le Canada au Royaume-Uni. La persuasion de Saint-Laurent et Pearson s'avéra toutefois assez forte pour passer par-dessus ses réticences. Fort de l'appui américain et canadien, Ernest Bevin fit officiellement état de son projet devant la Chambre des communes le 21 janvier 1948. Le coup de Prague de février 1948, puis les menaces soviétiques à l'égard de la Norvège en mars, accélérèrent les choses. Attlee envoya le 11 mars un message à Mackenzie King en faveur de la création d'un Pacte atlantique d'assistance mutuelle. Le gouvernement canadien donna immédiatement son accord. Le 17 mars, Mackenzie King l'annonçait à la Chambre des communes. Saint-Laurent allait ensuite entreprendre une véritable croisade pour convaincre l'opinion publique du bien-fondé du traité. Sa campagne devait rencontrer l'opposition du *Devoir*, qui défendait la neutralité du Canada, celle du Parti communiste et de son appendice, le Congrès canadien de la paix, de quelques socialistes en rupture de ban avec leur parti et de quelques intellectuels de premier plan: l'économiste Harold Innis et les historiens Frank Underhill et Donald Creighton. Cependant, même au Québec traditionnellement isolationniste, Saint-Laurent devait remporter un succès complet que traduisait une avance de son parti aux élections fédérales de 1949. Les détails du traité de l'Atlantique Nord furent négociés pendant de longs mois[16]. Avec bien des difficultés face aux réticences américaines, le Canada put faire insérer l'article 2, qui prévoit que les parties au traité «s'efforceront d'éliminer toute opposition dans leurs politiques économiques internationales en encourageant la collaboration économique entre chacune d'entre elles ou entre toutes»[17].

Durant cette négociation et cette croisade eut lieu le blocus de Berlin. Le Canada prit une position originale et fit preuve de la plus grande prudence. Partant du fait qu'il n'était pas une puissance occupante en Allemagne, il refusa de participer au pont aérien que les trois grandes puissances occidentales mirent en place. C'est incontestablement Mackenzie King qui dicta cette attitude, mais il trouva un allié dans le ministre de la Défense, Brocke Claxton, alors que Saint-Laurent, conseillé par Pearson, son sous-secrétaire d'État, penchait pour une aide au Royaume-Uni comme le firent l'Australie, l'Afrique du Sud et la Nouvelle-Zélande. Pourtant Saint-Laurent, devenu premier ministre, maintint le Canada hors du conflit, malgré les critiques de l'opposition conservatrice, estimant qu'il était bien tard pour intervenir et que de toute façon la phase aiguë du conflit était passée[18].

Le dimanche 25 juin 1950, la Corée du Nord envahissait la Corée du Sud[19]. La Corée avait déjà retenu l'attention du gouvernement canadien, puisqu'il avait fait partie de la commission temporaire de l'ONU formée en novembre 1947, au grand déplaisir de Mackenzie King à qui Saint-Laurent et Claxton avaient forcé la main. Au sein de cette commission chargée de prévoir les modalités de réunification de la Corée, le Canada avait pris une position originale et minoritaire, refusant que la commission supervisât les élections uniquement en Corée du Sud devant le refus du Nord, puisque son mandat concernait la Corée entière[20].

Dès la nouvelle de l'invasion nord-coréenne, le 26 juin, Pearson déclarait à la Chambre des communes qu'il s'agissait d'une «rupture de la paix» et d'une «agression non provoquée»[21]. Le Canada insista immédiatement pour que les mesures d'aide à la Corée du Sud fussent prises dans le cadre des Nations Unies. Concrètement, l'ambassadeur du Canada à Washington, Hume Wrong, protesta le 7 juillet 1950 contre la formulation de la résolution présentée au Conseil de sécurité qui prévoyait que le commandement unifié des troupes des Nations Unies serait assuré par les États-Unis[22]. La contribution militaire du Canada fut modeste: trois destroyers dès le 12 juillet 1950[23], un escadron d'avions de transport[24] et une brigade envoyée tardivement sur le théâtre d'opérations[25]. C'est sur le terrain diplomatique que le Canada déploya sa plus grande activité. Et il fit preuve d'une grande prudence. Dès août 1950, le gouvernement canadien insista auprès du gouvernement américain pour que les questions de Corée et de Formose fussent nettement dissociées. Il suggérait même que le commandement des forces américaines dans la région de Formose soit enlevé à MacArthur, qui commandait les troupes des Nations Unies en Corée[26]. Lorsque le ministère des Affaires extérieures fut consulté par les États-Unis sur la permission que demandait MacArthur de bombarder des bases aériennes en Mandchourie, il s'y opposa dans les deux heures[27]. Le 4 décembre 1950, Pearson réagit de la même manière que Attlee à la suite de la conférence de presse du président Truman du 30 novembre où il déclarait que les États-Unis étaient prêts à employer n'importe quelle arme – y compris l'arme atomique – contre la Chine. Tandis qu'Attlee accourait à Washington, Pearson fit savoir clairement que le gouvernement canadien voulait éviter à tout prix un conflit majeur avec la Chine. Pearson craignait que des opérations militaires contre le territoire chinois n'amènent une intervention soviétique. D'autre part, le Canada partageait avec le Royaume-Uni le sentiment que le conflit coréen ne devait pas détourner les alliés du théâtre européen, principal enjeu de la guerre froide. Ils pressaient les États-Unis en faveur d'une stabilisation du conflit coréen et de l'ouverture de pourparlers pour un cessez-le-feu. Mais les États-Unis voulaient d'abord une amélioration de la situation militaire[28].

Leaster B. Pearson prit l'initiative le 5 décembre de faire une déclaration radiodiffusée de Lake Success par Radio-Canada dans laquelle il annonçait son soutien à des négociations avec la Chine qui devaient débuter dès que la situation militaire serait stabilisée. Un cessez-le-feu devrait alors intervenir, suivi d'un règlement de la question coréenne et d'autres questions concernant la région[29]. Le 12 décembre, le délégué de l'Inde présenta à l'Assemblée générale des Nations Unies une résolution de treize pays arabes et asiatiques proposant la constitution d'une commission de trois membres, incluant le président de l'Assemblée générale, et dont le mandat serait d'établir les conditions d'un cessez-le-feu satisfaisant en Corée. Approuvée par l'Assemblée générale le 14 décembre, la résolution amena N. Entezam, le président iranien de l'Assemblée générale, à s'adjoindre le délégué indien, B. Ray, et Lester B. Pearson pour constituer la commission. Pearson y alla avec réticence, convaincu que la commission allait au-devant d'un échec. En effet, le gouvernement chinois refusa de négocier avec la commission, arguant qu'elle avait été formée illégalement, puisque la Chine était absente de l'ONU. Le 3 février 1951, la commission fit état de son échec au comité politique de l'Assemblée générale. Les troupes chinoises avaient d'ailleurs lancé une offensive à l'aube de la nouvelle année, franchissant le 38e parallèle et acculant les troupes de l'ONU à la retraite. La commission du cessez-le-feu fut néanmoins chargée de préparer une déclaration de principes qui pourrait servir de base pour une nouvelle initiative du comité politique.

La commission présenta son rapport le 11 janvier. Sa déclaration reposait sur cinq principes: un cessez-le-feu immédiat, suivi d'étapes ultérieures vers une restauration de la paix, une Corée unifiée, indépendante et démocratique avec un gouvernement issu d'élections libres, durant la période intermédiaire entre cessez-le-feu et paix une administration de la Corée selon les principes de l'ONU avec sa sécurité garantie, un règlement des problèmes de l'Extrême-Orient, y compris Formose, par un organisme établi par l'Assemblée générale comprenant des représentants du Royaume-Uni, des États-Unis, de l'URSS et de la Chine. Cette déclaration de principes fut approuvée par le comité politique par 50 voix contre sept. Mais le gouvernement chinois la repoussa, déclarant que les négociations devaient précéder le cessez-le-feu; ces négociations devaient avoir lieu sur la base d'un accord pour le retrait de toutes les troupes étrangères de Corée et pour le règlement des affaires coréennes par le peuple coréen lui-même; devait être aussi négocié le retrait des forces armées américaines de Taiwan et du détroit de Taiwan, ainsi que les problèmes de l'Extrême-Orient; les négociations devraient avoir lieu en Chine et comprendre la Chine, l'URSS, le Royaume-Uni, les États-Unis, la France, l'Inde et l'Égypte, étant entendu que le gouvernement de Pékin avait le droit de siéger à l'ONU. Les États-Unis prirent fort mal la chose et introduisirent une résolution à l'Assemblée générale, déclarant la Chine agresseur en Corée, la sommant de retirer ses forces de Corée et requirent l'aide de tous les membres de l'ONU pour son action en Corée. Les délégués arabes et asiatiques voulaient une réponse moins hâtive à la proposition chinoise. Le Canada prit l'initiative d'envoyer un message signé par Saint-Laurent à Nehru, lui demandant de poser trois questions à la Chine par l'intermédiaire de l'ambassade indienne à Pékin. Il s'agissait de savoir si Pékin incluait, dans les troupes étrangères, les «volontaires chinois», si les négociations sur les grandes questions politiques étaient une précondition à un cessez-le-feu et enfin si la reconnaissance du gouvernement chinois comme représentant à l'ONU était une précondition à une réunion de la conférence. Parallèlement, les diplomates canadiens à New York et à Washington pressaient les États-Unis de différer leur résolution. La réponse chinoise arriva rapidement et fut présentée au comité politique de l'Assemblée générale par le délégué indien. Les troupes chinoises seraient retirées de Corée; un cessez-le-feu limité pourrait être décrété dès la première séance de la conférence et les problèmes concernant la Corée et l'Asie orientale discutés ensuite, et enfin, le droit du gouvernement de Pékin de siéger à l'ONU devrait être reconnu. Une résolution indienne demandant un ajournement de 48 heures fut acceptée par 27 voix contre 23. Les États-Unis étaient furieux, notamment que le Canada ait négocié avec la Chine derrière leur dos. Pearson répondit froidement que le Canada n'avait pas à avertir les États-Unis de chacune de ses démarches diplomatiques. Le Canada était particulièrement satisfait que la réponse chinoise laisse ouverte la possibilité d'un cessez-le-feu dès la première séance d'une conférence sur la Corée. Il jugeait donc la résolution américaine prématurée et dénuée de sagesse. Le 24 janvier, une résolution de douze États arabes et asiatiques fut introduite devant le comité politique. Elle recommandait une conférence des sept États mentionnés dans la réponse chinoise pour régler les problèmes coréen et d'Extrême-Orient. Le Canada refusa de la voter, la jugeant trop vague, et s'abstint. Il se résigna à voter la résolution américaine légèrement amendée parce qu'on ne pouvait nier que la Chine soit agresseur en Corée. Escott Reid, pour sa part, déplora que le Canada ne se soit pas abstenu sur la résolution américaine. La CCF, quant à elle, rendit public son mécontentement[30].

Alors que les troupes des Nations Unies avaient repris l'initiative et arrivaient à proximité du 38e parallèle, le général MacArthur, proclama que la Chine avait été vaincue et que, si l'ennemi ne voulait pas traiter, la guerre pourrait s'étendre au territoire de la Chine qui risquerait de s'effondrer. Le Canada exprima son «horreur» au département d'État; mais déjà, Truman rappelait à l'ordre le général avant de le démettre[31]. Le Canada joua encore un rôle modérateur dans la mise au point des propositions de l'ONU qui permirent enfin l'armistice, en juillet 1953. Au moment décisif, il intervint fermement pour assouplir la position américaine sur la question des prisonniers de guerre[32]. À la Conférence de Genève de 1954 sur la question coréenne, le Canada déploya une activité diplomatique dans un sens modérateur. C'est ainsi que, contrairement aux États-Unis, il cherchait un terrain d'entente avec les communistes en proposant une Commission de contrôle des élections coréennes composée de représentants d'États neutres plutôt qu'une commission de l'ONU qui n'avait aucune chance d'être acceptée. De toute façon, cette conférence fut un échec[33].

La guerre de Corée eut pour effet de stimuler les efforts militaires du Canada. La menace soviétique paraissait beaucoup plus concrète. La participation canadienne prit deux formes. D'abord, le Canada contribua à l'équipement des forces européennes[34] et dès octobre 1951, envoya une brigade en Europe et douze escadrons aériens les années suivantes[35]. Ensuite, il participa activement à la défense de l'Amérique du Nord. La ligne *Pinetree* de détection des bombardiers et missiles fut entreprise dès 1950, quand le Canada apprit que l'URSS serait en mesure de frapper dès 1954[36]. En collaboration avec les États-Unis, il fut décidé en 1954 d'établir la ligne de détection du Moyen-Canada et en 1955, le système d'avertissement avancé[37]. En 1958, le système NORAD fut créé; il avait été préparé déjà à l'époque du gouvernement Saint-Laurent[38].

Le Canada se distancia des États-Unis à nouveau concernant l'Asie orientale. Lorsque la Chine continentale bombarda dès 1955 les îlots de Quémoy et Matsu et que les États-Unis ripostèrent en engageant les forces américaines dans la défense de Formose, Pearson refusa de prendre fait et cause pour des îles qui appartenaient à la Chine continentale. Il considérait que cette affaire était plutôt la continuation d'une guerre civile. En août 1958, à propos des mêmes îles, le Canada adopta la même attitude[39].

À l'égard de l'URSS, le Canada manifestait aussi une attitude plus souple. En octobre 1955, Lester B. Pearson fut le premier ministre des Affaires étrangères occidental à se rendre à Moscou depuis le début de la guerre froide. Son homologue soviétique, Molotov, qualifia le Canada de grande puissance. Krouchtchev et Pearson eurent une discussion controversée sur la question de savoir si l'OTAN était un bloc agressif ou une alliance défensive et si les États-Unis étaient impérialistes ou non. Pearson fut frappé de la mauvaise connaissance qu'avaient les Soviétiques de l'Occident[40]. L'écrasement de la révolution hongroise pour les troupes soviétiques, l'année suivante, allait refroidir les relations entre le Canada et l'URSS. Saint-Laurent adressait le 13 novembre 1956 une lettre d'indignation à Boulganine, et Pearson qualifia devant la Chambre des communes de «sauvage» l'action soviétique qui fut dénoncée aussi par le représentant canadien à l'Assemblée générale de l'ONU. Le Canada accueillit généreusement 33 000 réfugiés hongrois[41]. Le gouvernement Diefenbaker adopta une politique de dénonciation du colonialisme soviétique et en faveur du droit d'autodétermination des peuples allogènes de l'URSS, refroidissant davantage les relations.

Le Canada fut confronté à un autre problème des relations Est-Ouest. Lorsque les États-Unis décrétèrent en octobre 1960 un embargo commercial à l'égard de Cuba, le Canada maintint des relations commerciales normales malgré les pressions américaines. Lors de la crise des missiles d'octobre 1962, le gouvernement Diefenbaker favorisait un règlement du conflit par le truchement de l'ONU. Il n'apprécia pas l'action unilatérale du président Kennedy et, à l'heure décisive du conflit, attendit 40 heures avant de donner l'ordre aux forces canadiennes du NORAD de se mettre sur un pied d'alerte. Il n'avait pas apprécié d'avoir été placé devant le fait accompli et manifestait ainsi l'originalité de la politique étrangère canadienne dans les relations Est-Ouest[42].

LA DÉTENTE

À partir de 1963, les rapports Est-Ouest furent caractérisés par la détente en Europe. Pearson, devenu premier ministre, estima qu'il fallait développer les contacts les plus étroits possibles avec le monde communiste. Ainsi sera-t-il possible de négocier des solutions aux problèmes Est-Ouest, en faisant évoluer les perceptions des dirigeants communistes. Et un des moyens de contact par excellence est le commerce. Le Canada renouvela pour trois ans son traité de commerce avec l'URSS. Le blé en était la principale transaction. Il en allait de même avec la Tchécoslovaquie, la Bulgarie et la Pologne. Avec Cuba, au grand déplaisir de certains cercles américains, le Canada maintint également un commerce actif[43].

Cette politique d'ouverture à l'Est fut maintenue et amplifiée par le gouvernement Trudeau. Il est frappant de noter que, lors de la réunion ministérielle du Conseil de l'Atlantique Nord des 15 et 16 novembre 1968 à Bruxelles qui fut en large part consacrée à l'intervention de l'URSS et de ses alliés en Tchécoslovaquie, le ministre canadien des Affaires extérieures affirma qu'«il était essentiel que l'OTAN recherchât clairement toutes les occasions raisonnables pour reprendre le dialogue avec l'Union soviétique et pour faire ainsi progresser le règlement pacifique des questions pendantes en Europe»[44]. La révision de la politique étrangère canadienne, qui intervenait peu après, proclamait les mêmes objectifs:

> Le Canada insistera sur les actions qui peuvent résoudre les causes profondes de la tension en Europe, notamment le contrôle des armements et le désarmement. Il cherchera à faire engager des négociations sérieuses sur ces questions, partout où le lieu paraîtra propice et le temps venu, dans une conférence à une série de conférences sur la sécurité européenne[45].

La visite du premier ministre Trudeau en URSS du 17 au 28 mai 1971 consolidait l'ouverture à l'Est. Au cours de ce voyage, le premier ministre exprima la volonté du Canada de développer ses relations économiques et politiques avec l'URSS. Il signa un protocole de consultations entre les deux pays, qui portait sur les questions de politiques économique et culturelle, d'environnement et d'autres sujets bilatéraux ainsi que sur les questions internationales, les problèmes multilatéraux et tout autre sujet que les parties jugeraient utiles. Notamment, il était prévu que les deux États se consulteraient en cas de danger pour le maintien de la paix[46]. Notons que ce protocole n'a pas été beaucoup appliqué et est presque tombé en désuétude.

À la réunion ministérielle de l'OTAN de juin 1971, le ministre des Affaires extérieures insista pour qu'on ne mette pas en doute la volonté de l'URSS de négocier. M. Trudeau alla jusqu'à dire à l'époque que le règlement de la question de Berlin n'était pas un préalable à l'ouverture d'une Conférence sur la sécurité et la coopération en Europe[47]. Le Canada fut donc satisfait de l'ouverture des pourparlers préparatoires de la conférence d'Helsinki en novembre 1972. Il commença aussi sa participation aux négociations sur la réduction mutuelle et équilibrée des forces en Europe (MBFR) qui débutèrent à Vienne le 31 janvier 1973, mais qui s'enlisèrent immédiatement.

À Helsinki, le Canada a pu faire valoir ses objectifs. Dans sa première déclaration, l'ambassadeur du Canada en Finlande, M.E.A. Côté, qui avait rappelé les liens ancestraux qui rattachent les Canadiens à l'ensemble de l'Europe, insista sur l'importance que le Canada accorde au développement des échanges commerciaux, économiques, scientifiques, technologiques et culturels avec l'Europe tout entière. Il souligna le fait que les pourparlers d'Helsinki faisaient partie d'un ensemble de négociations pour diminuer les tensions, renforcer la sécurité, promouvoir la coopération et «augmenter le respect de la liberté et de l'intégrité des individus et des pays». Il tint aussi à rappeler que le Canada avait depuis longtemps proposé des pourparlers pour préparer la conférence. Il insista aussi sur une préparation soigneuse de la conférence, pour éviter qu'elle se résume en «de grandes envolées oratoires vides de sens». Au contraire, des mesures précises, même modestes, susceptibles de réaliser de véritables progrès en matière de sécurité et de coopération, devraient être réalisées.

Après avoir ensuite décrit la marche à suivre des pourparlers (établissement d'un ordre du jour clair, organisation et règles de fonctionnement de la conférence, fixation de la date et du lieu de celle-ci), l'ambassadeur Côté présenta les propositions canadiennes. Dans le domaine de la sécurité, deux points étaient avancés par le Canada. Premièrement, sur les principes directeurs régissant les relations entre États, il fallait éviter que le principe interdisant de modifier les frontières par la force aboutisse à reconnaître *de jure* des frontières permanentes en Europe. Notons que cette position canadienne tendait à protéger la politique de la République fédérale d'Allemagne qui ne veut pas que les frontières orientales de fait soient consacrées par le droit international, alors que seul un traité de paix fixera ces frontières. D'autre part, le Canada, dont de nombreux ressortissants viennent des pays baltes, ne voulait pas que les annexions soviétiques de la Deuxième Guerre mondiale soient également consacrées par le droit. Cette politique allait directement à l'encontre des objectifs que l'URSS poursuivait à la conférence. Toujours dans le domaine de la sécurité, le Canada proposait l'institution de préavis sur les déplacements militaires ainsi que des missions d'observations lors des manœuvres militaires. D'une manière générale, les positions du Canada en matière de sécurité s'inscrivaient dans la stratégie de l'OTAN à la conférence et n'avaient donc pas une grande originalité.

Le Canada insista tout particulièrement sur la coopération, qu'il considérait comme aussi importante que la sécurité proprement dite. C'est là une position qui correspond aux grandes orientations de la politique étrangère canadienne adoptées en 1970. En considérant les positions détaillées, la volonté de mise en œuvre de ces grandes orientations apparaît encore plus clairement. Le Canada proposait, en effet, que la conférence complète les efforts des Nations Unies pour la protection et l'amélioration de l'environnement. Elle devait aussi mettre au point les moyens d'augmenter et d'étendre les bienfaits dus aux progrès de la science et de la technologie. Sur le plan du commerce et des paiements, la préoccupation qu'éprouvait le Canada à l'idée de se trouver isolé face à de grands ensembles économiques était évidente. Le Canada réclamait de la conférence une réduction des barrières douanières et une élimination des obstacles au commerce, suivant les principes du GATT. Il faut noter que, sur ce point, le Canada rejoignait les objectifs des pays de l'Est et s'éloignait de la position des membres de la Communauté européenne, ses alliés dans l'OTAN. D'autre part, le Canada voulait que les pays sous-développés bénéficient de cette libéralisation des échanges Est-Ouest.

Le Canada accordait une importance toute particulière à la circulation des personnes. Il est certainement le pays qui insista le plus sur cet aspect de la coopération Est-Ouest. Il voulait que les obstacles qui entravaient ces déplacements soient progressivement supprimés. L'ambassadeur Côté attira notamment l'attention sur le sort des familles dont les membres sont en partie à l'Ouest et en partie à l'Est. Le Canada pensait à ses nombreux citoyens originaires de pays de l'Est qui désiraient faire venir définitivement au Canada des proches habitants des pays de l'Est, ou avoir la possibilité d'échanger des visites avec eux sans problème. Enfin, le Canada désirait une intensification des échanges culturels au sens large.

Incontestablement, dans les deuxième (janvier-février), troisième (février-avril) et quatrième (avril-juin) phases des pourparlers, la délégation canadienne fut particulièrement active. Des divers points à l'ordre du jour divisé en quatre «corbeilles», où furent symboliquement versées les questions relatives respectivement à la sécurité, aux problèmes économiques, aux échanges humains et culturels et aux mécanismes organisationnels, le Canada concentra surtout son action sur les échanges humains.

En février, l'ambassadeur Côté s'employa à réaffirmer publiquement en réunion plénière la position du Canada sur les échanges humains. Après s'être félicité que contacts humains, culture et information soient placés dans une corbeille séparée de celle des questions économiques, il ne cacha pas les divergences concernant les contacts entre les êtres humains, que certains pays cherchaient surtout à restreindre. Il est parfaitement évident que ses allusions visaient les pays de l'Est à plusieurs titres. En effet, ceux-ci auraient préféré grouper questions économiques, culturelles et humaines dans le même panier pour diminuer l'impact des échanges humains. D'une manière générale, l'URSS et ses alliés mettaient l'accent d'abord sur la conservation du statu quo frontalier, question qui relève de la sécurité. Venaient ensuite les problèmes économiques; les échanges culturels formels étaient relégués au troisième rang, tandis qu'ils s'efforçaient d'empêcher la libre circulation des personnes.

C'est dire que le Canada avait un ordre de priorité presque inverse des pays du pacte de Varsovie. L'ambassadeur Côté ne s'était pas fait faute d'opposer à la conception de certains pays qui assignent un rôle primordial à l'État dans les relations humaines et culturelles internationales, la position canadienne qui met l'accent sur la jouissance la plus complète possible par l'être humain «de sa liberté de pensée, de mouvement et d'action dans ses relations avec les autres hommes de la Terre». L'ambassadeur canadien réaffirma avec vigueur l'importance que le Canada attache à la réunion des familles dont les membres sont séparés, les uns à l'Est, les autres à l'Ouest. Il conclua son intervention en soulignant que, pour assurer la sécurité collective, il fallait éliminer les sentiments d'insécurité que créent la séparation et les obstacles aux liens familiaux et amicaux.

Au cours de la troisième phase des pourparlers préliminaires, qui s'est déroulée du 26 février au 6 avril 1973 et qui a traité en séances de travail du détail de l'ordre du jour, le Canada s'employa très activement à faire admettre son point de vue sur la réunion des familles, tant permanente que par des visites mutuelles. Les pays de l'OTAN et les neutres étaient convaincus d'avance de cette position: il s'agissait de vaincre les réticences des pays de l'Est. Seuls des entretiens personnels avec les ambassadeurs de l'Est, à commencer par M. Zorine de l'URSS, pouvaient éventuellement amener un assouplissement de leur point de vue. C'est ce à quoi le Canada s'employa. Les pays de l'Est préféraient que la question de la réunion des familles soit réglée sur le plan bilatéral, mais il était aisé de leur rétorquer que les accords bilatéraux entre l'Allemagne fédérale d'une part, et l'URSS, la Pologne et l'Allemagne de l'Est d'autre part, ne satisfaisaient pas entièrement le désir de sécurité des pays de l'Est. La consécration multinationale des arrangements bilatéraux en matière de sécurité était pour eux une garantie indispensable. Le Canada voulait la pareille pour les échanges humains et plus spécialement en ce qui avait trait à la réunion des familles.

C'est très probablement ce désir d'aboutir sur le plan de la sécurité qui a servi d'aiguillon afin d'obliger l'URSS et ses alliés à faire des concessions au début de la quatrième phase des pourparlers. Lors de la première réunion, le 25 avril, le délégué canadien était revenu à la charge sur l'importance que le Canada accorde aux contacts humains. Il insistait pour que le groupe de travail s'attaque avec résolution au problème afin qu'à la conférence, on discute sérieusement de la question de la réunion des familles séparées et des mesures qui permettraient aux citoyens des divers pays de se mieux connaître. Cependant, il tendait habilement la perche aux représentants de l'Est en soulignant que ces contacts devaient avoir lieu «dans le cadre des lois des divers pays», un point sur lequel les Soviétiques et leurs alliés sont particulièrement sensibles. Le lendemain, l'ambassadeur Zorine indiqua pour la première fois que l'URSS considérait que les contacts humains devaient être développés. La partie était gagnée sur le principe et le Canada fit ensuite preuve d'une souplesse plus grande que certains de ses alliés dans la discussion des détails de la partie de l'ordre du jour consacrée aux contacts humains[48].

Lors de la première phase de la conférence d'Helsinki, M. Sharp, ministre des Affaires extérieures, présenta la position canadienne dans sa déclaration d'ouverture. Il tira d'abord les leçons des pourparlers préparatoires. La première d'entre elles était que le succès des négociations ne serait assuré que par des conversations sérieuses et détaillées assorties d'un esprit d'accommodement plutôt que de confrontation. En deuxième lieu, il ne fallait pas fixer un délai artificiel. En troisième lieu enfin, les négociations ne devaient pas être isolées, mais devaient faire partie d'un processus général qui incluait d'autres négociations multilatérales comme les SALT. En ce qui concernait directement le Canada, M. Sharp déclara que son pays avait un intérêt quant aux principes qui régissent les relations entre ces États, puisque la sécurité canadienne et la sécurité européenne étaient interdépendantes. Il se déclarait d'accord avec les autres ministres des Affaires étrangères que l'usage ou que la menace de l'usage de la force devait être complètement banni. Un corollaire de ce principe était que les frontières nationales devaient être inviolables, quoique rien n'empêchait leur ajustement pacifique. Le ministre réitérait la position canadienne selon laquelle la conférence devait prendre en considération les négociations commerciales multilatérales et les discussions sur la réforme monétaire qui avaient lieu ailleurs, en évitant de dédoubler les institutions existantes.

Puis, il insistait sur la nécessité d'accroître les contrats entre les personnes et de résoudre les problèmes humains. Le Canada pensait que les membres d'une même famille ne devaient pas rester séparés et que les citoyens de pays différents devaient pouvoir se marier librement. Si des cas spécifiques devaient être réglés sur une base bilatérale, il insistait cependant pour l'énoncé de principes et l'adoption de mesures concrètes sur les familles qui amélioreraient les relations interétatiques. Pour le Canada, la liberté de mouvement était une question de la plus haute importance, «la pierre de touche du succès de la conférence». Un progrès dans la suppression des barrières empêchant le mouvement des personnes et la circulation de l'information créeraient la compréhension et la confiance mutuelles nécessaires pour une sécurité et une coopération durables.

Le Canada restait ouvert quant à l'avenir. Lors des négociations, il serait facile de juger si l'établissement d'un organisme se justifiait. Toutefois, celui-ci ne devrait pas dédoubler les institutions existantes et assurer une participation pleine et entière au Canada et aux États-Unis. Il souligna la nouveauté du processus de négociation par consensus.

> La détente implique non la suppression des différences entre systèmes et idéologies, mais leur acceptation mutuelle et l'ajustement des intérêts pour une plus grande coopération, le mouvement plus libre et des communications plus ouvertes aussi bien entre les peuples que les États.

Le 5 juillet, M. Sharp soumit à la conférence cinq propositions canadiennes pour faciliter les mouvements et contacts entre les personnes. Il s'agissait premièrement de la libéralisation des procédures de sortie des individus et de leur famille ainsi que de l'octroi des passeports. Ensuite, les familles devaient être rapidement réunies, les contacts familiaux autorisés et les mariages de ressortissants de différents pays permis. Les restrictions quant à la validité des passeports, aux allocations de voyage et à la disposition de la propriété devaient être levées. Les zones interdites, mis à part les régions de sécurité militaire, devaient être ouvertes. L'accès à leurs services diplomatiques devait être enfin assuré aux visiteurs d'autres États[49].

LA DÉTENTE EN QUESTION

À partir de l'automne 1973, les questions Nord-Sud prirent de plus en plus d'importance. Dans le tiers-monde, on assista à un affrontement Est-Ouest. C'est d'abord vers l'Afrique que se tournèrent les regards. L'indépendance de l'Angola commença par une guerre civile où Est et Ouest, avec la Chine à ses côtés, s'affrontèrent par groupes politiques angolais interposés. Cuba envoya des troupes en Angola pour aider le gouvernement du MPLA que les maquisards de l'UNITA, soutenus militairement par l'Afrique du Sud, menaçaient. Pierre E. Trudeau en discuta avec Fidel Castro lors de sa visite à Cuba en janvier 1976 dans une conversation où chacun chercha à convaincre l'autre. Il est à noter que le Canada consolidait alors ses relations avec Cuba même si les États-Unis ne le voyaient pas d'un bon œil.

L'occupation de l'Afghanistan par l'URSS provoqua l'indignation du Canada. Elle fut fermement condamnée par le premier ministre Clark le 4 janvier 1980. Le Canada ne reconnut pas le nouveau régime afghan, annula deux projets d'aide à ce pays d'une valeur de 3,1 millions de dollars et envoya une lettre au président Brejnev, l'exhortant à retirer ses troupes d'Afghanistan. En outre, le Canada restreindrait ses ventes de blé à l'URSS, boycotterait les Jeux olympiques de Moscou, supprimerait ou limiterait les visites en URSS de ministres, hauts-fonctionnaires et personnalités scientifiques et culturelles, romprait les négociations pour un accord consulaire et supprimerait le vol hebdomadaire supplémentaire d'été d'Aeroflot. M. Clark pousserait également au transfert des Jeux olympiques sur un autre site. Le ministre des Affaires étrangères, madame MacDonald, dénoncerait de son côté l'URSS en déclarant que son action menace la paix et a pour objectif les pays pétroliers du Moyen-Orient. Le ministre de la Défense nationale, M. McKinson, annoncerait que le Canada serait prêt à envoyer un bataillon au Moyen-Orient sous commandement de l'OTAN, si la situation l'exigeait. Lorsque Sakharov fut exilé de Moscou pour avoir protesté contre l'invasion soviétique de l'Afghanistan, madame MacDonald condamna cet acte et demanda à l'URSS de l'annuler.

Au Conseil de sécurité des Nations Unies, le représentant permanent du Canada, M. Barton, déclara le 7 janvier que l'invasion soviétique d'un pays indépendant était une violation grossière de la Charte et du droit international. De plus, cette action constituait un renversement du processus de décolonisation. Il rappela qu'un ministre soviétique des Affaires étrangères avait dit 50 ans plus tôt que la paix était indivisible. La détente était indivisible: elle ne pouvait fleurir dans une partie du monde, tandis qu'elle était foulée au pied dans une autre. Le Canada doutait des engagements soviétiques en faveur de la détente. L'invasion soviétique avait exacerbé une situation régionale déjà complexe et difficile et constituait un danger majeur pour les nations et peuples de la région. Le système entier de relations entre l'URSS et les autres pays était miné. Le Canada exhortait le Conseil de condamner l'URSS et d'exiger le retrait de toutes les forces soviétiques. Le Conseil de sécurité condamnait, par 13 voix sur 15, l'URSS qui opposait son veto. L'affaire était portée devant l'Assemblée générale, à laquelle, le 11 janvier, M. Barton expliquait que celle-ci était rassemblée parce que l'URSS avait empêché par son veto le Conseil de sécurité d'exercer ses responsabilités. La grave brèche à la paix internationale que constituait l'invasion et l'occupation d'un petit pays non aligné ne devait pas être ignoré. L'URSS avait envoyé en Afghanistan 100 000 hommes, plus que le total des forces armées canadiennes. Elle menaçait les autres pays non alignés de la région. La communauté mondiale devait condamner l'URSS pour sa claire violation des principes fondamentaux de la Charte et exiger le retrait immédiat de toutes les troupes soviétiques de l'Afghanistan. L'URSS ne devait pas être laissée impunie de son action et ses relations avec les autres pays devaient en souffrir. Le Canada soutenait chaleureusement la résolution condamnant l'URSS, qui fut adoptée par 104 voix contre 18, et 18 abstentions[50].

Les relations Est-Ouest se tendaient et le Canada, le 7 février, renvoyait un membre de la section commerciale de l'ambassade soviétique en représailles à l'expulsion, le 31 janvier, de l'attaché militaire canadien à Moscou. Le 9 février, madame MacDonald s'adressait à une réunion du Comité canadien pour les nations européennes captives et déclarait que le Canada avait été outragé par l'invasion de l'Afghanistan. De son côté, la *Pravda* accusait le Canada de soutenir sans réserve le président Carter et se réjouissait ensuite de la défaite électorale des Conservateurs[51].

Le nouveau gouvernement Trudeau, qui réaffirmait immédiatement le rôle du Canada comme pont entre l'Est et l'Ouest, faisait un pas en arrière et reconsidérait la question du boycott des Jeux olympiques[52]. Ce n'est que le 22 avril que le ministre des Affaires extérieures, M. MacGuigan, annonça que le Canada avait finalement décidé de le maintenir. Cette décision intervenait après que 33 pays eurent préalablement annoncé qu'ils soutenaient le boycott[53].

Dans les premiers mois de la conférence, le Canada s'opposa à une conférence de désarmement proposée par l'Union soviétique et la France, puisqu'on lui refusait une réunion sur les droits de l'homme[54]. La conférence de Madrid, après avoir traîné en longueur et subi des suspensions, finit par accoucher d'un document final, dans lequel il était prévu qu'«à l'invitation du gouvernement du Canada», se tiendrait «une réunion d'experts des États participants sur les questions relatives au respect, dans leurs États, des droits de l'homme et des libertés fondamentales, sous tous leurs aspects, tels qu'énoncés dans l'Acte final» d'Helsinki. Le document final prévoyait aussi la tenue, dès 1984, d'une conférence sur le désarmement en Europe. Enfin, la prochaine Conférence sur la sécurité et la coopération en Europe se tiendrait à Vienne en 1986[55]. Dans son intervention à la session ministérielle qui clôturait la conférence de Madrid, le ministre canadien d'État (Relations extérieures), Jean-Luc Pépin, se félicitait de ses modestes résultats, mais soulignait aussi la «tragédie» que revêtait «la destruction d'un Boeing 747 de la société Korean Airlines le 31 août [...] par des chasseurs soviétiques [...]»[56].

En effet, après l'invasion de l'Afghanistan (1979) et l'imposition de mesures militaires en Pologne (1981), l'affaire du Boeing de la Korean Airlines venait alourdir le climat des relations Est-Ouest. Or, le premier ministre Trudeau – comme nous l'avons vu – avait, en mars 1980, peu après son retour au gouvernement, tempéré la position canadienne vis-à-vis de la question de l'Afghanistan et réaffirmé le rôle du Canada comme pont entre l'Est et l'Ouest. De même, sur la question polonaise, M. Trudeau avait eu une réaction très modérée, allant jusqu'à dire que l'imposition des mesures militaires avait évité la guerre civile et que l'URSS n'était pas impliquée dans ces événements. Le premier ministre était avant tout préoccupé que:

> la rhétorique des allégations et des condamnations, jointes à l'imposition de sanctions économiques, ne mène qu'à la destruction irrévocable des restes de la détente et engendre une nouvelle guerre froide[57].

Dans l'affaire du Boeing de la Korean Airlines, c'est tout d'abord M. Pépin, agissant en tant que premier ministre intérimaire, qui, le 1er septembre 1983, convoqua le chargé d'affaires soviétique et exigea «une explication complète des raisons de cette attaque non provoquée[58]. Le lendemain, le secrétaire d'État aux Affaires extérieures, M. MacEachen, déplora cette «tragédie» et souligna «l'incertitude et l'appréhension» qu'elle faisait naître quant aux relations Est-Ouest. Le 5 septembre, en plus des excuses et des compensations pour les familles des dix Canadiens qui avaient péri dans la destruction de l'avion, M. MacEachen annonça que le Canada suspendait pour 60 jours le droit d'atterrissage des avions soviétiques[59]. Toutefois, à la fin de septembre, M. Trudeau répéta à plusieurs reprises que l'avion coréen avait été abattu par «accident». Interrogé le 4 octobre à la Chambre des communes qui avait, quant à elle, condamné à l'unanimité la destruction de l'avion, M. Trudeau déclara qu'en effet, «c'est par accident que le pilote coréen survola le territoire soviétique [...]. Ainsi, un accident se produisit». Il ajouta qu'il fallait cesser de crier et amorcer un dialogue, car «le monde est au bord du désastre et de la guerre atomique»[60].

La préoccupation qu'exprimait le premier ministre était alors au centre de ses réflexions et consultations. Il avait rencontré le secrétaire général de l'ONU le 1er octobre[61] et pris conseil d'un certain nombre de personnalités, notamment l'ancien secrétaire à la Défense des États-Unis, M. McNamara[62]. Déjà, au printemps 1982, il avait exprimé, dans un discours à l'Université Notre-Dame, son inquiétude face au piétinement des négociations soviéto-américaines sur le contrôle des armements et, lors de la deuxième session de l'Assemblée générale des Nations Unies sur le désarmement, le désir «passionné» des Canadiens d'un succès de ces négociations quant aux forces nucléaires intermédiaires. Il avait en outre, à cette même session, plaidé pour un accord interdisant le déploiement de toute arme dans l'espace. Un an plus tard, fin mai 1983, au Sommet des Sept à Williamsburg, il avait fait insérer dans le communiqué final la promesse «de déployer toutes nos ressources politiques pour réduire le danger de guerre». M. Trudeau avait pris très au sérieux la stratégie des deux voies décidées à la fin 1979 par l'OTAN pour faire face à l'installation des fusées SS'20 soviétiques. Si l'une des voies consistait à déployer des fusées *Pershings* et *Cruise*, ce déploiement était conditionné par l'échec de la deuxième voie: les pourparlers avec l'URSS. Très loyal à l'égard de la première voie, puisque allant jusqu'à accepter en juin 1983 le test des missiles *Cruise* sur sol canadien, il n'en était que plus résolu à pousser la deuxième et s'inquiétait de la voir aboutir à une impasse et plus généralement de la tension Est-Ouest[63].

Le 27 octobre 1983, M. Trudeau lança, dans un discours prononcé à l'Université de Guelph, une initiative pour la paix. Cette initiative était toute personnelle – on le lui reprocha. Elle était le fruit de deux motivations: cette profonde inquiétude pour la paix – qui était ancienne, comme en témoignent ses prises de position contre l'arme nucléaire dès 1963[64] – et la conviction qu'il devait agir pour la paix alors qu'il était encore au pouvoir et non, comme d'autres, après s'être retiré. D'emblée dans son allocution à Guelph, il exprimait ses sentiments:

Je vous avouerai sans détour que je suis profondément troublé par le climat d'acrimonie et d'incertitude qui règne à l'heure actuelle, par l'état alarmant des relations Est-Ouest.

Après avoir fait un état de cette situation de tension, il annonçait qu'il allait soumettre à plusieurs dirigeants d'États ses «recommandations pour l'élaboration d'une stratégie de rétablissement de la confiance politique». Cette stratégie comportait plusieurs aspects:

- mettre sur pied une structure cohérente propre à susciter la confiance politique et économique;
- détourner les superpuissances de leurs préoccupations militaires pour s'engager dans un dialogue régulier et productif;
- amener les cinq États dotés d'armes nucléaires à entamer des négociations destinées à fixer des limites globales à leurs arsenaux nucléaires stratégiques;
- améliorer la sécurité en Europe en relevant le seuil nucléaire et en redonnant en même temps une dynamique politique aux négociations sur la réduction mutuelle et équilibrée des forces, à Vienne, pour les tirer de leur stagnation;
- prévenir la prolifération des armes nucléaires dans les autres États[65].

Pour mettre en œuvre ces propositions que M. Trudeau qualifiait de «troisième voie, celle qui dit qu'il faut injecter la volonté politique», il effectuait un rapide voyage en Europe, le menant successivement à Paris, Bruxelles, La Haye, Rome, Bonn et Londres. Les chefs de gouvernements et d'États européens lui accordaient leur soutien et, rendant compte de son voyage dans un discours prononcé à Montréal le 13 novembre, il était amené à préciser sa stratégie en quatre «éléments»:

- créer en 1985 «une tribune pour la négociation des limites globales à fixer aux arsenaux des cinq États nucléaires»;
- «renforcer le Traité sur la non-prolifération»;
- équilibrer les forces classiques grâce aux «négociations sur la réduction mutuelle et équilibrée des forces qui se déroulent à Vienne», ainsi que la conférence de Stockholm «sur les mesures de confiance et de sécurité et sur le désarmement en Europe», qu'il faut tenir «à un haut niveau»;
- conclure «une entente pour interdire l'essai et le déploiement de systèmes anti-satellites à haute altitude»[66].

Ce message, le premier ministre allait le porter dès le 18 novembre au Japon et au Bangladesh, puis à la Conférence du Commonwealth à New Dehli, dont il obtenait l'appui, et enfin à Pékin. À la mi-décembre, il était à Washington pour rencontrer le président Reagan, qui lui donnait son «encouragement». Début janvier 1984, il faisait visite au secrétaire général de l'ONU à New York et recevait à la mi-janvier le premier ministre de la Chine qui accordait un appui modéré à son initiative. À la fin de janvier, M. Trudeau se rendait en Tchécoslovaquie où il recevait un accueil chaleureux, puis participait au European Management Forum à Daves et rencontrait le ministre suisse des Affaires étrangères. Il obtenait ensuite l'appui de M. Honecker en Allemagne de l'Est et de M. Ceaucescu en Roumanie. Enfin, couronnant son initiative, il rencontra à la mi-février, lors des funérailles d'Andropov, son successeur Tchernenko, qui l'encouragea à continuer.

Mais l'initiative touchait à sa fin. Même si, à la veille de son retrait de la vie publique, M. Trudeau écrivit encore à la mi-mai à M. Reagan et M. Tchernenko pour les inciter à négocier la réduction des armements nucléaires, il est certain qu'en février le gros de l'effort avait été accompli. Il est évident que M. Trudeau fut loin d'atteindre tous les objectifs de son initiative. Toutefois, il réussit à faire relancer les MFBR par les membres de l'OTAN, qui arrivèrent à Vienne avec des propositions concrètes. De plus, la conférence de Stockholm commença à un haut niveau comme il l'avait suggéré, en l'occurrence par la présence des ministères des Affaires étrangères. Enfin, la contribution la plus importante de M. Trudeau fut certainement d'avoir été le premier chef de gouvernement à percevoir la nécessité de renouer le dialogue Est-Ouest et d'avoir eu le courage de le dire publiquement et d'entreprendre des démarches à la fois rapides et spectaculaires[67]. M. Trudeau terminait ainsi sa carrière sur un paradoxe: après avoir préconisé à son arrivée au pouvoir une politique étrangère réaliste, prolongement à l'extérieur des intérêts intérieurs, il concluait, comme son prédécesseur Pearson l'avait toujours pratiqué, sur un rôle de médiateur et d'«apaiseur» de conflits.

NOTES

1. John W. Holmes, *Canada and the Search for World Order 1943-1957*, Toronto, University of Toronto Press, 1979, p. 170-171.

2. *Ibidem*, p. 234-237.

3. *Ibidem*, p. 249.

4. James Eayrs, *In Defence of Canada*, Tome III: *Peacemaking and Deterrence*, Toronto, University of Toronto Press, 1972, p. 320-321.

5. *Ibidem*, p. 324-325.

6. *Ibidem*, p. 218.

7. *Ibidem*, p. 319-332.

8. *Ibidem*, p. 331-333.

9. *Ibidem*, p. 333-334.

10. *Ibidem*, p. 176 et 334-335.

11. *Ibidem*, p. 177-178.

12. *Ibidem*, p. 178-182.

13. Robert A. Spencer, *Canada in World Affairs: From UN to Nato 1946-1949*, Toronto, Oxford University Press, 1979, p. 124-142.

   John W. Holmes et Jean-René Laroche, «Le Canada et la guerre froide», dans *Le Canada et le Québec sur la scène internationale*, édité par Paul Painchaud, Québec, CQRI, 1977, p. 279-281.

   James Eayrs, *op. cit.*, p. 285-295.

14. James Eayrs, *op. cit.*, p. 339-343, 347-349 et 355-356.

15. Don Page et Dun Munton, «Canadian Images of the Cold War 1946-47», *International Journal*, vol. XXXII, n° 3, été 1977, p. 577-604.

16. James Eayrs, *op. cit.*, p. 3-128. Robert A. Spencer, *op. cit.*, p. 243-282. R.A. Mackay, *Canadian Foreign Policy 1945-1954: Selected Speeches and Documents*, Toronto, McClelland and Stewart, 1971, p. 95-97. John Holmes et Jean-René Laroche, *op. cit.*, p. 281-283. Wilfrid F. Knapp, *A History of War and Peace 1939-1945*, Londres, Oxford University Press, 1967, p. 136-140.

17. «Traité de l'Atlantique Nord (Washington, le 4 avril 1949)», dans *Traités et documents diplomatiques*, édité par Paul Reuter et André Gros, Paris, PUF, 1960, p. 153.

18. James Eayrs, *op. cit.*, p. 38-51.

19. Denis Stairs, *The Diplomacy of Constraint: Canada, the Korean War and the United States*, Toronto, University of Toronto Press, 1974, p. 29.

20. *Ibidem*, p. 3-28.

21. *Ibidem*, p. 41.

22. *Ibidem*, p. 69.

23. *Ibidem*, p. 70.

24. *Ibidem*, p. 77-79.

25. *Ibidem*, p.88-90.

26. *Ibidem*, p. 96-97.

27. *Ibidem*, p. 136-137.

28. *Ibidem*, p. 148-149.

29. *Ibidem*, p. 151-153.

30. *Ibidem*, p. 154-178.

31. *Ibidem*, p. 223-226.

32. *Ibidem*, p. 227-278.

33. *Ibidem*, p. 291-293.

34. Wilfrid F. Knapp, *op. cit.*, p. 274.

35. James Eayrs, *In Defence of Canada:* tome IV: *Growing Up Allied*, *op. cit.*, p. 210-222.

36. James Eayrs, *In Defence of Canada:* tome III: *Peace Making and Deterrence*, *op. cit.*, p. 359.

37. *Ibidem*, p. 370-372.

38. Albert Legault, «Trente ans de politique de défense canadienne», dans *Le Canada et le Québec sur la scène internationale*, *op. cit.*, p. 113-115.

39. John W. Holmes et Jean-René Laroche, *op. cit.*, p. 289-291. James Eayrs, *Canada in World Affairs: October 1955 to June 1957*, Toronto, Oxford University Press, 1959, p. 79-84.

40. André Donneur, «Le système paneuropéen», dans *Le Canada et le Québec sur la scène internationale*, *op. cit.*, p. 335-336. James Eayrs, *Canada in World Affairs: October 1955 to June 1957*, *op. cit.*, p. 24-31.

41. James Eayrs, *Canada in World Affairs: October 1955 to June 1957*, *op. cit.*, p.42-49.

42. John W. Holmes et Jean-René Laroche, *op. cit.*, p. 291-293.

43. Charlotte S.M. Girard, *Canada in World Affairs*, vol. XIII: *1963-1965*, Toronto, Canadian Institute of International Affairs, 1980, p. 131-136.

44. Cité dans le *Monthly Report on Canadian External Relations*, vol. VII, n° 11, novembre 1968, p. 124.

45. Mitchell Sharp, éd., *Politique étrangère au service des Canadiens*, Information Canada, 1970, p. 26.

46. *International Canada*, vol. 2, n° 5, mai 1977, p. 111-117.

47. *International Canada*, vol. 2, n° 6, juin 1971, p. 141-142.

48. André Donneur, «Le Canada et la sécurité européenne», dans *La sécurité européenne dans les années 1970-1980*, Québec, CQRI, 1973, p. 161-165.

49. *International Canada*, vol. 4, n°s 7-8, juillet-août 1973, p. 203-204.

50. *International Canada*, vol. 11, n° 1, janvier 1980, p. 1-4.

51. *International Canada*, vol. 11, n° 2, février 1980, p. 35.

52. *International Canada*, vol. 11, n° 3, mars 1980, p. 49.

53. *International Canada*, vol. 11, n° 4, avril 1980, p. 70.

54. *International Canada*, vol. 12, n° 4, avril 1981, p. 90.

55. «Document final de la Conférence de Madrid sur la sécurité et la coopération en Europe», *Le Monde*, 9 septembre 1983; «International Canada», août-septembre 1983, dans *International Perspectives*, novembre-décembre 1983.

56. Jean-Luc Pépin, «L'affaire de la Korean Airlines à la Conférence sur la sécurité et la coopération en Europe», *Déclarations et Discours*, 83/15, 7 septembre 1983.

57. Harald van Riekhoff, «The Desirability of a Graduated Increase of International Pressure», dans Adam Bromke *et al.*, *Le Canada face à la crise polonaise*, Toronto, Institut canadien des affaires internationales, 1982, p. 18-19.

58. «International Canada», août-septembre 1983, dans *International Perspectives*, novembre-décembre 1983.

59. *Ibidem*.

60. «International Canada», octobre-novembre 1983, dans *International Perspectives*, janvier-février 1984.

61. «International Canada», août-septembre 1983, *op. cit.*

62. Harald van Riekhoff et John Sigler, «The Trudeau Peace Initiative: The Politics of Reversing the Arms Race», dans *Canada Among Nations, 1984: A Time of Transition*, édité par Brian W. Tomlin et Maureen Molot, Toronto, Lorimer, 1985, p.52.

63. *Ibidem*, p. 53-55.

64. John Kirton, «Trudeau and the Diplomacy of Peace», *International Perspectives*, juillet-août 1984, p. 3.

65. Pierre E. Trudeau, «Réflexions sur la paix et la sécurité», *Déclarations et Discours*, n°s 83/18, 27 octobre 1983.

66. Pierre E. Trudeau, «Une initiative globale propre à améliorer les perspectives de paix», *Déclarations et Discours*, n°s 83/20, 13 novembre 1983.

67. Harald van Riekhoff and John Sigler, *op. cit.*, p. 67.

BIBLIOGRAPHIE

BERG, Eugène. *Chronologie internationale 1945-1977,* Paris, PUF, 1979.

BROMKE, Adam *et al. Le Canada face à la crise polonaise,* Toronto, Institut canadien des affaires internationales, 1982, 52 p.

CANADA. Ministère des Affaires extérieures, Rapports annuels 1968-1984.

CARLE, François. «Les pourparlers exploratoires d'Helsinki», *Études internationales,* vol. IV, n° 3, septembre 1973, p. 297-361 et vol. IV, n° 4, décembre 1973, p. 502-551.

Déclarations et Discours. 1975-1984.

DONNEUR, André. «Le Canada et la sécurité européenne», dans *La sécurité européenne dans les années 1970-1980,* Québec, CQRI, 1973, p. 153-167.

DONNEUR, André. «Le système pan-européen», *Le Canada et le Québec sur la scène internationale,* édité par Paul Painchaud, Québec/Montréal, CQRI/PUQ, 1977, p. 329-346.

EAYRS, James. *Canada in World Affairs, October 1955 to June 1957.* Toronto, Oxford University Press, 1959.

EAYRS, James. *In Defence of Canada,* vol. III: *Peacemaking and Deterrence,* Toronto, University of Toronto Press, 1972.

EAYRS, James. *In Defence of Canada,* vol. IV: *Growing Up Allied,* Toronto, University of Toronto Press, 1980.

GIRARD, Charlotte S.M. *Canada in World Affairs,* vol. XIII: *1963-1965,* Toronto, Canadian Institute of International Affairs, 1980.

HOLMES, John W. *The Shaping of Peace: Canada and the Search for World Order,* vol. I et II, Toronto, University of Toronto Press, 1979 et 1982.

HOLMES, John W. et LAROCHE, Jean-René. «Le Canada et la guerre froide», *Le Canada et le Québec sur la scène internationale,* édité par Paul Painchaud, Québec/Montréal, CQRI/PUQ, 1977, p. 275-302.

International Canada. 1971-1984.

KIRTON, John. «Trudeau and the Diplomacy of Peace», *International Perspectives,* juillet-août 1982, p. 3-5.

KNAPP, Wilfrid F. *A History of War and Peace 1939-1965,* Londres, Oxford University Press, 1967.

KNAPP, Wilfrid F. «The Cold War Revisited», *International Journal,* vol. XXIII, n° 3, été 1968, p. 344-356.

LEGAULT, Albert. «Trente ans de politique de défense canadienne», *Le Canada et le Québec sur la scène internationale,* édité par Paul Painchaud, Québec/Montréal, CQRI/PUQ, 1977.

PAGE, Donald. «Canada and European Detente», *Foremost Nation: Canadian Foreign Policy and a Changing World,* édité par Norman Hillmer et Garth Stevenson, Toronto, McClelland and Stewart, 1977.

PAGE, Donald et MUNTON, Donald. «Canadian Images of the Cold War 1946-1947», *International Journal,* vol. XXXII, n° 3, été 1977, p. 577-604.

RIEKHOFF, Harald van et SIGLER, John. «The Trudeau Peace Initiative: The Politics of Reversing the Arms Race», dans *Canada Among Nations, 1984: A Time of Transition,* édité par Brian W. Tomlin et Maureen Molot, Toronto, Lorimer, 1985, p. 50-69.

SHARP, Mitchell, éd. *Politique étrangère au service des Canadiens,* Ottawa, Information Canada, 1970.

SKILLING, H. Gordon. «CSCE in Madrid», *Problems of Communism,* vol. XXX, n° 4, juillet-août 1981, p. 1-16.

SPENCER, Robert A. *Canada in World Affairs: From UN to NATO, 1946-1949,* Toronto, Oxford University Press, 1959.

STAIRS, Dennis. *The Diplomacy of Constraint: Canada, the Korean War and the United States,* Toronto, University of Toronto Press, 1974.

Traités et documents diplomatiques. Paris, PUF, 1960.

ZORGBIBE, Charles. *Le monde depuis 1945,* Paris, PUF, 1980.

6

Canadian Policies on North-South Relations

Bernard Wood
North-South Institute

It is, in which terms, anachronistic to attempt to trace and assess Canadian policies on North-South relations over the entire period since 1945. The North-South axis of international relations only began to be defined as an arena of Canadian foreign policy in the mid-1960s, becoming important only in the mid-1970s[1]. Bearing in mind this reservation, a discussion of «North-South relations», in a volume which covers in detail so many of the constituent relationships, offers an unusual opportunity to trace the roots, the linkages and the enduring significance of the North-South axis. Canada began the postwar period with minimal interests and roles in the developing countries of Asia, Africa and Latin America but came in latter decades to play a central part in the North-South diplomatic dialogue. For these reasons, it is important here to follow the evolution of the international debate, weaving Canada's part into the picture where justified, rather than attempting to build the picture around Canadian policies and actions.

The terms «North» and «South» have become widely accepted shorthand for the groups of «industrialized» and «developing» countries respectively. While there is both geographical and political imprecision in the terms, they have been accepted terminology since they were first used at the 1975 Paris Conference on International Economic Cooperation, the first meetings to be christened the «North-South dialogue».

DECOLONIZATION AND THE COLD WAR

Historically, Canada is one of the industrialized countries which has been *least* linked to the developing countries of Asia, Africa and Latin America. Most of the Western industrialized countries have in this century shared with developing countries the intense and ambivalent relationship of colonialism. Others assumed, in different regions, a *de facto* political and economic overlordship which approximated colonialism in many respects. Canada, like Australia and New Zealand, entered the century if not still a colony, at least with no aspirations to be an international colonizer. Indeed, the base and structure of the Canadian economy and society were such as to extend its colonial role of resource supplier, first to the former metropolitan power, and later, to the burgeoning United States economy.

In 1945, as Canada emerged strengthened politically and economically from World War II, Latin America and the still-colonized regions of Africa and Asia figured little in Canadian foreign policy. Direct trade was very small – although the long-standing historical link with the West Indies was still significant –, and political and other linkages were largely channelled, through the British connection, to what were to become the Commonwealth countries. Meanwhile, because of the war-weakened state of most European nations, Canada loomed disproportionately large in the North Atlantic community and in the fledging organizations of the United Nations and Bretton Woods institutions. These arenas offered major scope and challenge for pursuing Canadian interests and influence.

The great postwar spasms of decolonization touched Canada less than they did the former colonizers and probably less than they touched the United States, with its growing world responsibilities and its historical anti-colonialist sentiment. Canadian opinion and policy were sometimes torn, both on the issues raised by decolonization and between conflicting West European and American responses. The Canadian responses were several, and only infrequently were they a major influence on the course of world events. For example, Canadian participation was significant in legitimizing and building the Colombo Plan as a new vehicle of development aid to Commonwealth Asian countries. As a nation that strongly supported the United Nations system, Canada logically supported the admission and participation of many newly-independent states. Finally, the Suez Crisis in 1956 drew forth a special new mediatory role for Canadian diplomacy, carried on through successive peacekeeping involvements in different parts of the Third World.

From the time that the Cold War set in the late 1940s, and for the following fifteen years, the instruments of both Western and Eastern foreign policy in the developing countries – aid programs, investment, scholarships, exchange schemes and, on occasion, military aid and intervention – all took on a distinctly competitive aspect. A key objective with respect to Third World countries was the promotion of alignment or sympathy with one Cold War «camp» and its denial to the other.

While most of these elements (including limited military assistance) were to be found in Canadian policies towards the Third World, the Cold War perspective was never so strong as to preclude Canadian openness to «non-alignment» and a range of more or less independent positions on the part of developing countries. It is possible that this openness was initially linked to Canada's special relationship with India under Nehru, one of the principal architects of non-alignment. In the early 1960s, a further test case for Canadian policy was presented by the inter-American boycott of revolutionary Cuba, a boycott which Canada refused to join. In other festering issues in the Third World where East-West conflict has been a factor, for example, the struggles in postcolonial Indo-China and in Southern Africa, the Canadian reactions have been mixed. Membership on the tripartite Indo-China Truce Commission led on occasion to a staunch Canadian defence of Western interests and sometimes to more independent conciliatory initiatives. In Southern African affairs, too, the record allowed for an important role in securing the withdrawal of the racist South African regime from the Commonwealth, a very cautious approach to pressure for change in Rhodesia (now Zimbabwe) and Namibia and, more recently, membership on the Western Contact Group for Namibia.

On the economic front, meanwhile, selective beachheads of Canadian-based private investment in the Caribbean and parts of Latin America were being strengthened and extended. The locations of such investment were also diversified, extending to new areas from the South Pacific to sub-Saharan Africa. Traditional interests in banking and utilities were matched by new activities in various resource sectors and in a few manufacturing industries, such as farm machinery. At the same time, some of the oldest investments, particularly in Latin American utilities, were being taken over by the governments and nationals of host countries. Other non-official linkages, such as the historically-strong Canadian missionary presence in many developing countries, were maintained and paralleled by the growth of non-governmental organizations (NGOs) such as the Canadian University Services Overseas (CUSO).

Probably the most visible of Canada's linkages with the Third World during the 1960s and 1970s, and the most debated[2], was its program of aid or official development assistance. While the evolution, growth and diffusion of Canadian aid are traced in detail in a separate chapter of this volume, it is important to underline here that this program has substantially shaped, and on occasion limited, the overall Canadian approach to North-South policy, as indeed it has with most of the other industrialized countries.

The official and public overemphasis on the importance of aid, despite its limited real role as an instrument of development, was understandable. Official aid allocations have been the only significant government expenditures explicitly directed to relations with developing countries, and the aid agency (since 1968 the Canadian International Development Agency, or CIDA) has been the only arm of Government whose principal, indeed exclusive, task has been to work on these relationships.

During the period under review, there was a strong tendency among Western nations to view the central problem of developing countries as one of some «missing factor» (for example, capital, skills, technology or infrastructure). Similarly, the role that industrialized countries saw for themselves was one of helping to supply that factor.

Thus, public and parliamentary discussion of North-South issues tended to focus on information about new Canadian aid involvements in different developing regions and countries and Canada's attempts to meet the accepted international targets for aid in relation to the Gross National Product of donor countries. The aid program was equated with Canada's policy towards developing countries and only occasionally did the emphasis shift to peacekeeping involvements or political issues (*e.g.*, with respect to relations with Cuba, Southern African controversies, concern over human rights or foreign investment disputes).

For their part, policy makers saw the aid program as their principal instrument for protecting and enhancing Canadian interests and projecting Canadian values in different parts of the developing world. However, the development of different regional focuses was often less the result of strategic priority-setting than of a broad diplomatic concern to secure some Canadian «presence» in each region. Thus, the focus widened steadily, from the early subscription to the Colombo Plan for Commonwealth Asian countries, to special assistance for the more familiar countries of the Commonwealth Caribbean and the newly-independent countries of Commonwealth Africa. One conscious and deliberate shift, made in response to domestic concern over reflecting Canada's Francophone character and containing some of the international linkages being sought by successive Québec governments, was the rapid movement into Francophone African countries, most notably with the Chevrier Mission in 1967. Finally, the desire to establish commercial and other contacts with certain other countries (notably in Southeast Asia and Latin America), previously downplayed in Canadian foreign policy, eventually led to their inclusion as targets of Canadian policy abroad.

EARLY NORTH-SOUTH DEBATE

Thus, while the regional emphasis in Canadian policy in the Third World was broadly sensitive to Canadian political and commercial interests, it was not tightly concentrated or targeted in accordance with those interests. At the international level, however, it is possible to trace a more coherent set of Canadian reactions to the growing demands from the developing countries as a group for changes in the international economic order.

It was in the mid-1960s that the grievances of developing countries about their position in the international economy, and their proposals for change, began to take clear shape. Analyses of the dependency of Third World countries vis-à-vis the countries of the industrialized world – and of the remedies required – were first developed through the UN Economic Commission for Latin America (ECLA). They were then carried over into the UN Conference on Trade and Development (UNCTAD), which became in 1964 a *de facto* permanent UN organization.

From the start, UNCTAD was viewed by the governments of developing countries as «their» organization, and many other governments, including Canada's, shared this appraisal. The Bretton Woods institutions and the General Agreement on Tariffs and Trade (GATT) had been inherited from an era in which there were fewer independent developing countries and where international decision-making was mainly responsive to the vastly superior economic and financial power of the Western industrialized countries. UNCTAD, reflecting more of the one-flag/one-vote style of the UN General Assembly, was far more receptive to the preoccupations of its new majority – the Third World. This was reflected in its agendas and debates, in its studies and in its staffing. Successive UNCTAD conferences, and the committee and secretariat work that took place in between, concentrated on the set of issues that would later be crystallized in the developing countries' demand for a «new international economic order». These were the instability and relative weakness of primary product trade; the need for expanded and preferential market access for developing countries; and controls over transnational investment, shipping, technology communications and human resource flows.

Throughout the 1964-1974 period, most Western governments were basically distrustful (and frequently disdainful) of UNCTAD's analysis and debates, and their participation in the organization's activities was approached as a kind of «damage-limitation» exercise. Since UNCTAD lacked authoritative jurisdiction over most of the policy areas it dealt with, there was little fear that it could critically impair Western interests as long as its resolutions could be kept at a declaratory level and the more ambitious experiments resisted. A further irritant, from the perspective of Western nations, was the extent to which the Soviet Union and its allies, with little constructive stake or intent in the underlying issues, courted the favour of Third World nations by joining them in excoriating Western countries' shortcomings and supporting Third World proposals.

Because of UNCTAD's lack of jurisdiction, its perceived bias towards Third World viewpoints, and the general assumption that those viewpoints were of marginal importance in the international economy, Western governments made practically no effort to contribute alternative viewpoints or suggestions to help meet the special problems of developing countries. Thus, for example, there was a decade-long debate before the US and Canada implemented a modest «Generalized System of Preferences» for manufactured and semi-manufactured products from developing countries. The schemes finally adopted, like those of other granting countries, were so minimal in their scope and hedged in by exemptions that they proved to be of little value.

Throughout these years, it was increasingly recognized by specialists and decision-makers around the world that securing increased benefits from trade and investment would be far more important for developing countries than any conceivable amounts of official development assistance. This was recognized in the Pearson Commission report, prepared by the former Canadian Prime Minister for the World Bank, and was endorsed in a report of the first Parliamentary Subcommittee on International Development Assistance (1970). Significantly, this policy issue was largely sidestepped in the Government's own foreign policy review, *Foreign Policy for Canadians* (1970), the reason being that the allocation of increasing aid budgets would be less painful for the Canadian Government, than would, for example, the opening up of Canadian markets to competitive Third World goods.

Furthermore, the policy instruments required to assist developing countries' trade or monetary situations were predominantly in the hands of departments of Government which traditionally acted for domestic interests or in close concert with the governments of other industrialized countries. It would clearly have been a radical shift for them to give major weight to the developmental interests of Third World countries in their work, and they did not. Furthermore, after some early supportive interest in the «non-aid» issues of relations with developing countries, the «development community» in Canada soon became frustrated by the lack of action and the seemingly abstract level of much of the discussion. Canadian church-people and other representatives of non-governmental organizations would still rally, well into the 1970s, in support of UNCTAD conferences, but their main energies seemed to shift to human rights issues and to domestic questions.

Without very forceful prodding at home and facing an unappealing «no-win» situation in UNCTAD and other fora where developing countries aired their grievances, the general Canadian policy became one of jockeying among the range of «Western» responses to the Third World. While policy-makers assumed that Canada should strive to be as open-minded and forthcoming as possible in response to Third World demands, there was little or no expectation that Canada would find itself, together with the Scandinavian countries, at the forefront of Western generosity and responsiveness. In fact, it was a tacit, and sometimes explicit, article of faith that Canada could not, and should not, deviate too far from the position of the dominant (and often most conservative) OECD members – the United States, West Germany and Japan[3]. Canada's credibility, it was reasoned, together with its presumably benign influence on the key Western powers, hinged on attributes such as moderation, «realism» and gradualism.

In spite of the apparent disavowal of some of Canada's leading postwar multilateralism suggested by the foreign policy review of 1970, a responsible and responsive approach to international (and especially UN) organizations remained a significant touchstone of Canadian policy. To the surprise of most participants as well as most observers, the Commonwealth emerged as a special and important cross-cutting caucus of the international community. It was one of few fora where a smaller network of leaders from both the Western and Third World voting blocs at the UN met informally and in an environment where they were compelled to try to comprehend each other's preoccupations and reactions. For historical reasons, Canada was often thrust into playing a key «bridging» role on behalf of the old «White Commonwealth». Inevitably, expectations that Canada would continue in this role were to carry over into North-South debates in the wider UN fora.

The recognition of the developing countries' demands as a significant arena of policy focus for Western governments first came in the mid-1970s. The vehicle for change was the Organization of Petroleum Exporting Countries (OPEC) and its dramatically successful campaign to increase its members' revenues from petroleum exports and to use their collective economic power to achieve international political leverage. The oil weapon, used most directly in the oil boycott, struck at the economic jugular of the industrialized countries, precipitating domestic and international political crises.

In tacit recompense for Third World support of the Arab members' anti-Israel positions, and perhaps in anticipation of immunity from Third World criticism for its oil price increases, OPEC immediately lent its new power to the longsidelined agenda of the «Group of 77» developing countries. A special session of the UN General Assembly (the sixth such session since its establishment) was convened in April 1974, and provided the occasion for some of the most bitter generalized confrontation ever witnessed in the world body. A Seventh Special Session, also on international economic cooperation, was called in the following year and, although slightly less acrimonious, it ended with no concrete agreement on action either to attack the development problems of Third World countries, or to address the concerns of Western countries regarding the supply and affordability of oil. the developing countries' coalition was now equipped with resolutions endorsing (with a number of Western reservations) a declaration and program of action for the establishment of the «New International Economic Order» – a complex program of economic, structural and institutional change that captured the full set of the developing countries' demands. The prospects for Western action on the program were minimal, however, without the inclusion of oil discussions, discussions that the OPEC bloc adamantly resisted.

Although the Seventh Special Session had seen some effective small group activity (with important Canadian involvement) to assist the plenary in making progress, a number of Western governments expressed a strong concern that the UN forum itself was an obstacle. The result of this concern, the Paris Conference on International Economic Cooperation (CIEC), informally called the «North-South dialogue», brought together, at the invitation of the Government of France, 27 governments: 19 from the «South» and eight «Northern» industrialized countries. One country from each group was called upon to co-chair, with Canada being selected to represent the North, and Venezuela the South. In each case the selection criteria included having sufficient weight and skill for credibility, and sufficient moderation vis-à-vis the concerns of the other group to encourage a spirit of compromise and possible agreement.

With formal representation at the ministerial level and intensive work carried on at senior official levels for nearly two years, CIEC was an important experiment for the international community, and a major responsibility for the co-chairing governments. However, not very far into the process it became apparent that the more restricted participation at CIEC was not going to eliminate the most serious problems of North-South negotiation as encountered in the United Nations. The conference in fact exhibited some special difficulties of its own.

For the developing countries, three continuing problems emerged. First, the 19 participating countries had no effective mandate to negotiate for those which were not present, and the latter were actively concerned that the «insiders» not go too far. A second, and related, problem was that of setting priorities among the different issues to be negotiated, while still maintaining the interest and commitment of all: among the Third World participants, the predominant issues included market access, primary commodity trade, debt relief and increased aid. These concerns, however, did not have equal priority among all of the participants. The third difficulty was that, apart from moral suasion, the only negotiating «chips» held by the Group of 77 were in fact in the hands of the OPEC countries, and they soon showed themselves as unwilling or unable to open up the issues of oil pricing or supply for serious North-South discussion – thus reducing the Northern interest in negotiating other questions.

In any case, Northern responsiveness was on the wane. Having weathered the initial shocks of the oil boycott and the first rounds of price increases, Northern governments were generally somewhat more confident about the future. They were also beginning to see that the dependence of OPEC countries on the West for healthy markets for their exports and for stable investment opportunities represented some significant mutual interests that would limit OPEC's bellicosity.

In such a situation, where the ardour of the two sets of participants had cooled, the co-chairs were in a particularly difficult position. They retained a responsibility for trying to achieve a successful conclusion, but basically lacked the means to do so. As the conference moved towards its inevitably disappointing conclusion in mids-1977, the Canadian Government felt impelled to contribute to a major round of official debt write-offs for the poorest countries, a gesture joined by the other «progressive» and «moderate» Western donors. Finally, in a pattern that was already familiar, the only front on which the Western group could fully agree, in order to try to salvage the Conference from complete failure, was in the area of aid. A special fund of $1 billion for the countries hardest-hit by the recent crises was the eleventh-hour outcome.

The Canadian Government team emerged from the CIEC process especially frustrated and disillusioned. So, to one extent or another, did most other participants; an important experiment in shifting the setting and style of North-South discussions had failed, and a pattern of stalemate had been confirmed. Only a few governments – those which had always believed, or had come to believe, that a change in the *status quo* would damage their interests – could greet the result with equanimity.

COMMODITY TRADE – A TEST CASE FOR DIALOGUE

When it became clear that neither the Special Sessions nor CIEC were going to yield across-the-board advances on the Group of 77's agenda for reform, the

Group's strategists decided to focus in a concerted way on one broad area – that of primary commodity trade, the mainstay of a good number of Third World economies. Their campaign for change was embodied in the Integrated Program for Commodities, launched under UNCTAD auspices. This program aimed, through a series of ambitious measures affecting 18 «priority» commodities, to stabilize and increase prices through a «Common Fund» and to help producing countries to extend and diversify the economic benefits derived from these resources. For much of the following three years, the Integrated Program was the central focus of the North-South dialogue[4].

The new debates about primary commodity trade placed the Canadian Government in some peculiar situations. Like most of the *developing* countries, Canada was heavily dependent on primary products for its exports earnings, although not to the same extent[5]. Again, like Third World governments, Canadians in the producing sectors had long believed that they were victims of disruptive boom-and-bust cycles and the price and earnings instability that they brought. Canada shared with many developing countries the aspiration to capture a larger share of the value-added in upgrading and processing raw materials prior to export.

Despite the fact of these shared experiences and concerns, Canada's primary identification was with the Western industrialized countries. As a group these countries embraced a «consumer» perspective in response to the Integrated Program proposals. Most Western governments also objected to the Program because of their expectation that it would introduce a massive degree of intervention and thus, in their view, inefficiencies, into international commodity markets. Since implementing the proposals would also require substantial financial contributions and guarantees, Western resistance was doubly strong. Private sector producing and processing firms in Canada and other Western nations were concerned that the Program would hamper their freedom of action.

Since governments like Canada's are heavily dependent on the information and advice emanating from such firms (many of which are integrated transnationals with a range of consumer and producer interests), the national position articulated in international negotiations is a complex amalgam of public and private, domestic and foreign interests. In executing these various balancing acts then, Canada was unable to exercise any particular leadership, or even sustain its «bridging» role in the negotiations on commodities. By the latter years of the 1970s, the program had been whittled down to a pale shadow of the original, with some of its initial proponents becoming disgruntled critics and refusing (like Canada) to ratify the limited agreement. So ended the first test case of the New International Economic Order.

STALEMATE-BREAKING

Towards the end of the decade, two major new thrusts were undertaken in an effort to break the deepening state of stalemate in North-South relations. The first, promoted by World Bank President Robert MacNamara, was the convening of an Independent Commission on International Development Issues, chaired by former West German Chancellor Willy Brandt. The Brandt Commission, established a decade after the similar Commission chaired by Lester B. Pearson, was to attempt to cut across the sterile agendas and the now-fixed positions of governments. Its compo-

136

sition of mainly elder statesmen from both North and South was intended to provide new political insight and impetus. The Commission worked for two years, finally reporting in early 1980[6]. Canada, while not an original sponsor of the Commission idea, was an early supporter. Joe Morris, an elder statesman of the Canadian labor movement, served as the Canadian member of the group.

Some representatives of the Group of 77 remained skeptical of the non-governmental and Bank-sponsored Brandt Commission, as they had been of CIEC. Frustrated by the emasculation of the Integrated Program negotiations in Geneva and the shelving of their other demands, they began a new campaign, centered at the United Nations in New York, to force a new series of «global negotiations» – global both in the sense of being comprehensive and integrated in their subject matter, and in their direct involvement of all member-states of the United Nations family.

The arguments between North and South about the desirability, feasibility and appropriate mandate of such new negotiations were to become the dominant diplomatic touchstone of progress on North-South relations for three years to come. The points of difference were hoary and predictable ones. Developing countries have insisted on the new negotiations going beyond the limits set by such bodies as the International Monetary Fund (IMF) and the General Agreement on Tariffs and Trade (GATT) whose clubbish competence has been jealously protected by the industrialized countries. The latter, meanwhile, have been insistent on bringing world energy discussion prominently into the negotiations – a demand generally resisted and obstructed by OPEC nations with at least tacit support from other Third World nations. Thus, a fundamental standoff persisted, in spite of the publication of the conciliatory, and in some countries influential pleas of the Brandt Commission for a new «political will» to recognize and act upon the urgent mutual interest of North and South in speeding Third World development. The prospects for negotiations seemed darkened by the election of the Reagan Administration in the United States – an administration whose major representatives initially made it a matter of pride that they had little knowledge of or interest in the economic problems or proposals of developing countries.

Canada, meanwhile, under both Progressive Conservative and Liberal Governments[7], had been playing an active role (with some of the other liberal «like-minded» Western nations), in trying to keep the dialogue alive and to make it more constructive. A new impetus came with the return of Pierre E. Trudeau's Liberal Government in 1980, and the coincidence that 1981 would see Canada hosting the Western Economic Summit.

Operating on a somewhat qualified mandate from the previous summit held in Venice, the Canadian Government as host and organizer began an extensive effort, internationally and domestically, to ensure that North-South issues would be, for the first time, a major focus of these top-level Western meetings.

To help lay the groundwork at home, a special parliamentary task force on North-South relations[8] was struck, and the Canadian Government committed itself to restore growth to the aid program which had been cut back under both Liberal and Conservative regimes. Internationally, the work involved close consultation with other summit countries (including prime ministerial visits to most of their leaders) to maintain prominence and substance for the agenda item on North-South relations. Preparations for the Western summit, to be held at Montebello, were carried out in parallel with the Mexican and Austrian leaders' efforts to try to convene an unprecedented North-South summit, one of the special deadlock-breaking efforts suggested by the Brandt Commission. Preparations for both the Montebello and North-South summits were thrown into some disarray by the US election and the succeeding organizational period. These uncertainties were further exacerbated by the serious wounding of President Reagan in an assassination attempt.

Nonetheless, Prime Minister Trudeau incorporated many other capitals into his travel plans, combining discussion of possible initiatives for consideration at Montebello with persuasion to make sure that the wider North-South summit would take place and be well-attended and productive. The latter summit, originally proposed to precede Montebello, was moved back to Autumn 1981, and the locale set in Cancun, Mexico. Thus, the North-South discussion at Montebello took on more of the character of a pre-Cancun caucus of key Western countries. The key initiatives before Western leaders were: special concerted measures to grapple with the ominous debt and payments problems of developing countries; the proposal for the creation of a special «energy affiliate» attached to an organization like the World Bank to help oil-importing developing countries find domestic energy supplies; and, finally, proposals for new terms under which the «New Global Negotiations» might be agreed upon and launched.

The Canadian Government, with special support from the newly-elected Mitterand Government of France, was instrumental in achieving a generally positive statement on Global Negotiations, but little progress was realized on other North-South fronts. Canada remained sufficiently central to the follow-up process that it was a foregone conclusion that it would be called upon to step in to co-chair at Cancun when the Austrian Chancellor proved unable to participate. The Cancun Summit was a remarkable event, but one whose results fell short of the many expectations that had been held for it. Prime Minister Trudeau, the Canadian Co-Chairman, drawing on his unique experience as a participant in multiple Commonwealth Heads of Government meetings, was able to make a special contribution to some extraordinary informal exchanges of views among the 25 leaders present. The most important test of the meeting's success, however, came to be seen as the amount of progress that could be made towards starting Global Negotiations. Persistent divisions, and dubious commitment by some countries of both the North and the South, however, meant that no substantial progress was made either during Cancun or follow-up process. Canadian officials continued to serve as central actors in subsequent efforts to pick up the enterprise, but the high-profile «year of the summits» was over, and the deadlock in the diplomatic dialogue remained.

NORTH-SOUTH RELATIONS IN FOREIGN AND DOMESTIC POLICY

The Realities of Interdependence

To trace the history of North-South «pre-negotiations» at the international level, and the extremely limited tangible results which appear to have been achieved, seems almost to invite dismissal of the significance of the whole arena. It also allows for some questioning of the special investment (if mainly a diplomatic investment) made by Canada in this arena at certain key stages.

To place the history of diplomatic debate and effort in some context, however, it is important to focus at the same time on the substance of economic and political trends. Throughout the history of the postwar era, it is possible to chart an inexorable underlying increase in the importance of developing countries on the world stage. This growing importance is multidimensional – political, strategic, economic, demographical, cultural – and inconstant, with different regions and countries rising or falling on one or another scale. Unquestionably, however, government, business, banking and labour communities, informational, educational and cultural institutions in Northern countries now must all focus much more of their attention on developing countries than in the past. As with other international relationships these growing links have both positive and negative aspects for both parties, but that fact in no way diminishes their importance.

This evolution of the Third World is both part of and a reflection of increasing polycentrism in the international system, although only China (which sometimes claims Third World standing) can yet lay claim to be a global power centre on many indices. Nearly every region of the Third World, however, now includes unmistakable regional powers which command respect and, for many purposes, limit the influence of even the superpowers. The accession to greater absolute and relative power by some Third World countries, of course, can sometimes give them a greater stake in some elements of the *status quo* under which they have achieved such progress. This tendency leads many to question whether the vocal Third World coalition for change in fact has substance, given the divergent interests and stakes of its different members, particularly some of the most powerful.

Perception, Ideology and Reality in North-South Debate

The roles of perceptions or misperceptions and ideology must be analysed to arrive at any understanding of the gap between the frustrated diplomatic dialogue on the one hand and the realities of growing North-South interdependence on the other[9]. For the major part of the period under review, most of the governments of Western industrialized countries have perceived their relations with developing countries to be of secondary or tertiary importance. Except when embroiled in some particular crisis situation (*e.g.,* in the Middle East, Cuba, Rhodesia, Afghanistan or Iran), Western countries have tended to assume that their vital interests lay in relations with each other or with their Eastern adversaries. Even when Third World crises were viewed as important, it was frequently because of the perceived linkages to these other axes.

Intermittent crises, most notably the full emergence of OPEC power, were not enough to shift or widen the dominant focuses of Western foreign policies on a durable basis. Meanwhile, however, developing countries and particularly the «newly-industrialized countries» (NICs), were assuming more and more economic importance, as trade customers and competitors and as borrowers. In hard bilateral bargaining, the NICs attempted to maintain market access against new non-tariff barriers, while in United Nations fora the Southern trade campaign was ostensibly focused on primary commodity problems and a demand for special tariff preferences. While most developing countries, in a forum like CIEC, pressed for measures of generalized debt relief to ease their situation, some of the most powerful forcefully downplayed this prospect for fear of jeopardizing in any way their commercial creditworthiness. Finally, even the majority of OPEC nations which had pioneered «commodity power» and committed that power to the achievement of the goals of the new international economic order were soon seen to have acquired a major stake in the new *status quo* and to be defending it accordingly.

Thus, the sweeping campaign for change by developing countries, while still impressively widely-based, was not deep-rooted enough to withstand the strains of competing interests and priorities when real negotiations approached[10]. Yet for most of the coalition there was no choice but to strive to maintain the perceived common front at the highest level possible. That level included general agreement on the list of changes demanded in the NIEO and subscription to its broad underlying ideology. That ideology hinged on national independence and sovereignty, resource control and deliberate international actions in various areas to remove the economic and technological disadvantages chronically suffered by developing countries. These principles, together with the impetus to secure decisive power for developing countries in international decision-making, were the constant touchstone of Third World statements and joint positions, however imperfectly they reflected some of the interests of certain coalition members. These divergencies, however, have only infrequently been forced into the open because the Group of 77 encountered such extreme resistance to testing, or even seriously negotiating, its proposals.

A major source of this resistance was the North's own common screen of ideological assumptions, assumptions which its member-governments have brought to the bargaining table with equal persistence. Principal among these has been the belief that Third World proposals would introduce heavy-handed and damaging governmental and intergovernmental intervention into international economic relations.

Since developing countries have necessarily been the *demandeurs* in this bargaining, Northern positions have logically been somewhat more responsive or reactive. In fact, this reactiveness has been almost absolute. Because the proposals for change have constituted an attack on the *status quo* (which Western governments, at least until recent times, believed to have served their countries well), there has also been a distinct defensiveness and resistance built into most Western reactions. As with the Southern coalition, it may be that Northern ideological positions (and technical arguments) have served principally to justify and rationalize positions based on perceived interests.

On both the Northern and Southern sides of the debate, these broad ideological stands have generally overridden not only diverse real interests but also conflicting practices at both the national and international levels. Thus, most Western governments derided the feasibility and desirability of cooperative action to stabilize and improve the prices of primary products in international trade, while practically all of them have elaborate systems of supply control and price maintenance for their domestic agricultural sectors. Further, both American and Canadian governments have long collaborated, as major wheat-exporting nations, to achieve similar international objectives in that area. Different forms of cartelization in other fields (*e.g.,* uranium) are far from unknown.

It is tempting, in this light, to take these inconsistences between national postures and practices in both North and South as evidence of hypocrisy, and therefore to discount much of the dialogue process as a sham. In fact, the phenomenon deserves, and has recently begun to receive, some deeper examination. In 1980, an international group of concerned economists assembled in Norway to examine in depth the relationships between economic theory and North-South negotiations. In his introduction to the volume reporting on those discussions, Gerald K. Helleiner suggests some important factors in these gaps:

> Once in the difficult world of policy formation [...] students of economics are prone to forget all the qualifications and assumptions, and frequently apply instead the simplest and crudest versions of the models they were taught, using, as they would put it, only «the basic principles»[11].

He goes on, focusing on Western countries, to indicate how much more serious the gap is likely to be at the international level, since «In domestic economic policy, the power of the crude underlying model to influence policy-makers has been tempered by the exigencies of politics...». In the light of these problems, and many related ones, he arrives at the following conclusion:

> Northerners often genuinely believe that logical and factual errors abound in the details of Southern proposals and that some of their proposals could therefore be prejudicial to development or inequitable in their distribution of benefits; but it would not and does not matter if they thought that their arguments were faultless. *By now neither side believes what the other says. The mutual credibility of ostensibly intellectual arguments in North-South debates has been severely impaired*[12].(Emphasis added.)

Failing intellectual persuasion then, the advocates of either major position must rely either on more direct pressure, if they can muster it, or the force of events to lead to a re-examination of the positions themselves and their intellectual and ideological underpinnings. At the beginning of the 1980s, it was becoming apparent that the collective Third World capacity for effective direct pressure as earlier exercised by OPEC was not improving. However, it also appeared that the force of events, particularly the growing importance of the developing countries' unstable debt on the one hand and their market potential on the other, might finally lead to serious Northern initiatives, if not to greater acceptance of the developing countries' original proposals.

The Canadian Government, although it has clearly shown more openness and flexibility than most (perhaps because of some of its own experience with mixed enterprise and «development» problems), has not been able to extricate itself from the common Western ideological framework. Because expressions of the opposing framework have been at least as firm, opportunities for alternative pragmatic initiatives have been very limited. The vigorous and committed Canadian advocacy of the energy affiliate scheme to assist oil-importing developing countries was one promising example which ran afoul of some powerful misperceptions in the United States and lukewarm reactions among some OPEC member-governements.

Canada appears to have unusual scope and openness but it also finds that when some of the debates become specific enough to draw in domestic interest groups (for example firms and industry representatives on commodity stabilization issues), there are powerful reassertions of the prevailing ideological catechism which must be heeded. Thus, «non-intervention» will be invoked to protect the freedom of operation of firms even when markets may be far from competitive or when these same interests under other circumstances (as in the Law of the Sea provisions on seabed mining control) actively call for government intervention on their behalf.

NOTES

1. A useful comparative analysis of the historical, current and prospective linkages between nine industrialized countries and the South is to be found in Robert Cassen *et al.* (eds.), *Rich Country Interests in Third World Development,* Washington, D.C.: Croom Helm Ltd., 1982. Readers of the present volume may be especially interested in the chapter 3 of *«Canada and Third World Development: Testing Mutual Interest»,* by Bernard Wood.

2. A possible exception was the changing pattern of immigration flows, which saw a substantial shift in favour of Third World nationals.

3. Canadian ministers and officials have sometimes been quite candid about their strategy of attempting to exert leverage over the major Western countries (see references in *North-South Encounter,* Ottawa, North-South Institute, 1977, p. 39. Further valuable materials on the dialogue and on Canadian policy were assembled in Canada, Department of External Affairs, *The North-South Dialogue: Some Basic Documents,* February, 1977.

4. See Robert L. Rothstein, *Global Bargaining,* Princeton, N.J., Princeton University Press, 1979, p. 39-166 for a detailed interpretive account.

5. Such products accounted for some 50 % of Canadian export receipts in comparison with an average of roughly 80 % for the developing countries.

6. Independent Commission on International Development Issues, *North-South: A Programme for Survival,* Cambridge, Mass., MIT Press, 1980.

7. Because of the very short tenure of the Conservative Government, it is of course difficult to make definitive assessments of its directions. However, in spite of the problems caused by the Jerusalem embassy issue, and a sometimes misplaced emphasis on «Cold War» and «Free Enterprise» rhetoric in international discussions, the basic Canadian role and positions did not shift markedly.

8. See Canada, House of Commons, Parliamentary Task Force on North-South Relations *Report,* Ottawa, Supply and Services, 1980, and North-South Institute, *North-South Relations 1980-85,* Ottawa, North-South Institute, 1980. The latter document is the report of a study commissioned by the Parliamentary Task Force.

9. Relatively few practitioners or analysts now place very much weight on institutional deficiencies themselves, but see them as being shaped by political and ideological problems.

10. Some Western governments had long seen, in this diversity of interests among developing countries, a vulnerability to be exploited. While the Canadian Government as well has had its advocates of a deliberate strategy of «differentiation», there has also been a positive and respectful recognition of the important community of interests among developing countries. This was clearly articulated by Prime Minister Trudeau in the House of Commons on June 15, 1981. See *Debates.* First Session, Thirty-Second Parliament, 124 (211), p. 10596.

11. Gerald K. Helleiner, ed., *For Good or Evil: Economic Theory and North-South Negotiations,* Toronto, University of Toronto Press, 1982, p. 4.

12. *Ibidem,* p. 6.

BIBLIOGRAPHY

BIGGS, Margaret A. *The Challenge: Adjust or Protect*. Ottawa, North-South Institute, 1980.

CANADA. Canadian International Development Agency. *Annual Report,* Various.

CANADA. Department of External Affairs. *Foreign Policy for Canadians,* Ottawa, Queen's Printer, 1970.

CANADA. Department of External Affairs. *The New Economic Order, Selected Documents,* Ottawa, May 1975.

CANADA. Department of External Affairs. *The North-South Dialogue, Some Basic Documents*. February, 1977.

CANADA. House of Commons. Parliamentary Task Force on North-South Relations, *Report,* Ottawa, Supply and Services, 1980.

CASSEN, Robert *et al. Rich Country Interests in Third World Development*. Washington, D.C., Croom Helm, 1982.

COMMISSION ON INTERNATIONAL DEVELOPMENT. *Partners in Development,* Report of the Commission on International Development, Lester B. Pearson, Chairman, New York, Praeger, 1969.

HELLEINER, Gerald K., editor. *For Good or Evil: Economic Theory and North-South Negotiations,* Toronto, University of Toronto Press, 1982.

INDEPENDANT COMMISSION ON INTERNATIONAL DEVELOPMENT ISSUES. *North-South: A Program for Survival,* Cambridge, Mass, MIT Press, 1980.

JENKINS, Glenn P. *Costs and Consequences of the New Protectionism: The Case of Canada's Clothing Industry,* 2nd edition (revised), Ottawa, North-South Institute, 1985.

NORTH-SOUTH INSTITUTE. *North-South Encounter, The Third World and Canadian Performance,* Ottawa, 1977.

NORTH-SOUTH INSTITUTE. *North-South Relations/1980-85*. A discussion paper prepared for the Special Committee of the House of Commons on North-South Relations, Ottawa, November, 1980.

ROTHSTEIN, Robert L. *Global Bargaining*. Princeton, N.J., Princeton University Press, 1979.

UNITED NATIONS GENERAL ASSEMBLY. *Declaration of the Establishment of a New International Economic Order,* [A/RES/3201 (S-VI)], May 9, 1974.

UNITED NATIONS GENERAL ASSEMBLY. *Programme of Action on the Establishment of a New International Economic Order,* [A/RES/3202 (S-VI)], May 16, 1974.

UNITED NATIONS CONFERENCE ON TRADE AND DEVELOPMENT. Fourth Session, *The Integrated Programme for Commodities,* [TD/RES/93 (IV)], June 16, 1976.

WOOD, Bernard. «Canada and Third World Development: Testing Mutual Interest», *in* Robert Cassen *et al., Rich Country Interests in Third World Development*.

7

Canada in the World Economic Order

Duncan Cameron
University of Ottawa

INTRODUCTION

The transition from a liberal economic order, which was dominant for much of the period since 1945, to the emerging global economy of the 1980s provides the context for Canadian foreign policy responses to developments within the world economy. During the period of economic shortages and reconstruction from 1945 until 1958, the liberal order served as an ideal to the attained. Liberal institutions were developed but states had to follow restrictive policies due to the economic difficulties. The era of relative prosperity and favorable conditions for international trade from 1958 to 1968 permitted a fuller flowering of economic liberalism. By the 1970s, the foundations of the liberal order were weakened. States increasingly had to deal with international economic disorder and the emergence of a global economy. And the liberal order was being directly challenged by the Third World. In the 1980s, states had to come to terms with a transnational development of economic forces that tended to make the liberal order obsolete.

The liberal order can be understood as relations among autonomous states that have agreed to progressively dismantle barriers to international trade in goods and services. By providing national producers with access to a world market for exports, the liberal order encouraged an international division of labour. The growth of world trade was accompanied by international movements of capital for investment purposes and international lending, which served to finance trade imbalances. It was generally assumed by proponents of the order, including Canada, that the liberal international economy led to increased understanding among nations and that international security was enhanced by the steadily progressing standard of living which it promised to participants.

Canada is often cited as the typical example of an open economy in that a large share of production is sold abroad and imports represent an important share of consumption. But Canadian external trade, rather than being spread indifferently throughout the world economy, has been historically limited to certain markets. Successively, France, Great Britain and the US have been principal trading partners. Though by 1986 Canada exported roughly 30 % of Gross Domestic Product (GDP), about 75 % of exports were sold in the US and Canada's participation in the world economy was in large measure accounted for by the relationship with its continental neighbour. The level of Canada's international trade and the disproportionate importance of the US market have influenced Canadian negotiators in their approach to international economic questions[1].

The problem to be considered is how Canadian foreign policy adjusted to an evolving world economic order. In a general way, the policies adopted were a part of Canada's overall foreign policy stance; that is to say its position as a wealthy industrialized member of NATO, which though committed to acting as a middle power within the UN, established its foreign policy priorities within the context of relations with the other western liberal democracies. Yet in a particular sense it is Canada's place within the world economy which determined the limits to Canadian foreign policy and provided it with objectives. Not only were policies shaped by perceptions of Canada's place in the world: Canadian interests and capacities were assessed using the world economic order as a principal reference point.

An economic order contains elements of power, ideology, and structure. It has a discernable form and thus can be understood by policy-makers. As efforts are made by states to control and influence the order, a hierarchy develops, within which individual states are constrained by the position they occupy at any given moment[2]. For policy-makers, the world economy is a changing context to which they must adjust but which simultaneously sets limits on their power to influence change. The way in which they approach this adjustment entails an articulation of policy, which in so far as it attempts to give a meaningful basis for action, is presented in the form of ideology, that is to say a coherent expression of ends and means[3]. The context to which they adjust can be described as a structure: foreign policy is preoccupied by the question of structural evolution and change.

Part I

Power and Hierarchy Within the World Economic Order

CANADA AND THE LIBERAL ORDER

Canadian foreign policy-makers approach international economic relations globally through multilateral institutions and bilaterally through consultation with other nations. In the period of postwar reconstruction, Canadians played an important role in the negotiation of multilateral arrangements which were to serve as the pillars of the liberal order, GATT (General Agreement on Tariffs and Trade), the IMF (International Monetary Fund) and the World Bank. It was expected that Canadians would benefit from access to world markets and that an international division of labour would allow for purchases abroad on favorable terms. It was believed that multilateral agreements would provide the basis for a general prosperity, essential to peace in the world, and harmony at home.

Yet at the close of World War II, the position of Canada within the world economy was ambiguous. On the one hand Canada emerged from the war a prosperous nation whose relative economic standing in the world had increased considerably. On the other hand Canada's international trade was in jeopardy due to the impoverishment of its European trading partners, particularly Great Britain, and a trading deficit with the US. The problem was to resolve the apparent contradiction between Canada's new found influence in world affairs and the serious external financial difficulties.

For Canadian policy-makers, the importance of sales to the US was clear from the outset [4]. Indeed the strength of the Canadian economy after nearly seven years of war could be attributed to offshore American purchases in Canada throughout the period of hostilities. Canada had markets to supply in postwar Europe but in order to service them was obliged to provide credit. In this respect Canadian aid was perhaps overgenerous, amounting to about one-third of American assistance[5]. At the same time, Canada was short of foreign exchange with which to pay for American imports, and until 1950 was forced to practice comprehensive foreign exchange controls.

Though Canadian policy-makers believed that the surest method for assuring Canada's future prosperity was through free trade at the world level, and participated in agreements that required all participants to offer equal trade concessions to each other, financing the trade deficit with the US was the immediate problem. To this end, secret negotiations for free trade agreements were undertaken with Washington in 1947 but in the end were abandoned for political reasons. Prime Minister Mackenzie King decided that political support within Canada was insufficient to carry such an undertaking through to its conclusion. The dollar gap was eventually closed by borrowing in the US capital market, and encouraging the US to think of Canada as a reliable supplier of raw materials, as well as by acception US investment in Canada. As a result of these policies, the Canadian economy became increasingly integrated into a North American market for goods, services, money, and capital[6].

Canada's relative standing in the world entitled it to act on questions of global concern. But maintaining good relations with the US required that Canada proceed carefully when it found itself in disagreement with the US on multilateral questions. The task facing Canadian negotiators was somewhat simplified in that Canada shared US views about the general nature of the liberal order. But Canadians were concerned with developing an institutional framework within which political representation would reflect the contributions made by Canada and other middle powers. The wartime experience as a junior ally motivated Canadian diplomats to seek a policy stance appropriate to exercising national independence while recognizing the necessity of international cooperation.

To this end, Canada promoted the «functional» principle of international organization[7]. In Canada's view, problems of international relations could be best managed by apportioning them according to functional concern to international institutions where experts whould meet together, and questions could be dealt with on their merits. Political representation should take into account both the nature of the problems under discussion and the capacity of states to contribute to their resolution. In this fashion, Canada could be expected to play an important role where Canadian economic interests were involved and where Canada would be called upon to supply resources. For example, as a food exporter, Canada provided the site (Québec) and the Chairman (Lester B. Pearson) for the founding conference of the FAO (Food and Agriculture Organization).

Canadian support for the functional principle was related to Canada's global foreign policy concerns. «Quiet diplomacy», a policy of close bilateral consultation with the US, was envisaged in order to enhance Canadian influence in Washington at a time when US foreign policy action was likely to be decisive in international negotiations[8]. It was considered that Canada could indirectly influence world affairs by raising international questions of concern to Canada privately with the US. Not incidently, smoother bilateral relations between the two countries, would be developed at the same time.

So long as Canada and the US shared a similar foreign policy orientation, functionalism and quiet diplomacy could be complimentary policies. The first would ensure Canadian independence, the second would magnify Canadian influence. The desire to establish the basic for prosperity in the world economy through multilateral institutions was a principal concern of Canadian policy-makers. The key role of the US in the elaboration of the postwar order was recognized in Canada's support for US leadership.

MULTILATERAL PAYMENTS AND EXCHANGE

The liberal international order represented a «consensus» established among the industrialized nations about the nature of international economic relations. It developed under conditions of American hegemony where other industrialized states were prepared to acquiesce in US leadership – perhaps because they saw little alternative. Though the Soviet Union was present at the Bretton Woods negotiations where the IMF and World Bank were created, it did not participate in these institutions and neither did the Eastern European nations which came under Soviet influence. The process of decolonization eventually resulted in a great number of newly independent Third World states joining the IMF and the World Bank, and the institutions which characterized the liberal order expanded to encompass most of the non-communist world. Even the communist nations had to come to terms with the «rules of the game» established by the postwar consensus and reflected in the practices and GATT, the IMF, and the World Bank.

Underlying the liberal order was a belief in the capacity of markets to provide for efficient production of goods and services. States were assumed to pursue national goals of full employment, price stability, and external equilibrium; but the expansionary benefits of international trade were to be made available equally to all states. Though production naturally took place within nations, they were expected to accept the primacy of international trade. Measures to restrict international commerce were to be proscribed; initiatives to increase the mobility of traded goods were to be encouraged. Economic expansion was to be assured by a regime of freely convertible currencies, that is to say by the absence of restrictions on the use of currencies for the current account transactions of international commerce. Under the rules of GATT, nations were expected to offer to all GATT signatories equal access to their domestic markets. The «most favoured nation» clause required that nations extend to all nations the trade concessions (principally low tariffs) they offered to any one nation. Non-discrimination between national production and exports from other nations was an important feature of the liberal trading regime.

The multilateral trading agreement reflected the desire of the US to see the breakup of the former colonial system whereby Great Britain and France in particular were seen to have excluded other nations from colonial markets. By opening up markets on an equal basis it was believed that efficient production would flourish and all would benefit. The industrialized nations would compete in each others' markets as well as in the markets of Asia, Africa, and Latin America. In order for multilateral trade to expand it was necessary to have an agreed mechanism for its financing.

The Bretton Woods agreement set out the framework within which the world monetary system developed. It provided for means of adjusting trade imbalances as they appeared in the accounts of individual nations and suggested to national policy-makers measures they could take to ensure that national difficulties would not interfere with trade expansion. Under the Articles of Agreement of the IMF, nations were expected to eliminate exchange restrictions (maintain freely convertible currencies), in order to qualify for IMF balance of payments loans.

In the event that imbalances appeared in the external accounts of IMF members, they could draw upon the resources of the IMF, provided that the imbalance was considered temporary. If the imbalance was considered fundamental, it was expected that the nation would adjust the exchange rate of its currency (devalue or revalue). The role of the IMF was then to ensure that nations could stabilize their exchange rates around an agreed parity without recourse to restrictive or discriminatory measures. To this end, the IMF accepted deposits from its members and these pooled resources could then be lent out to nations suffering from a trade deficit. Ultimately of course the loans were subject to conditions laid down by the lender, and since contributions to the IMF were made on the basis of quotas in the Fund based on economic strength, the largest and richest nations provided the majority of the resources and had the greatest influence over their management[9].

Generally speaking, the sum of all trade balances for the world taken as a whole is necessarily zero. That is to say one nation's surplus represents another nation's deficit. If the nations in surplus, who are accumulating funds on the foreign exchange market as a result of the surplus, agree to relend them to the deficit nations, there should be no problem in financing the expansion of international trade. However, since it is likely that some nations find themselves with either persistent deficits or surpluses, it is necessary to provide for an adjustment mechanism; so that no one nation be consistently in the position of providing credit to others, or conversely, of receiving unlimited credit from the surplus nations.

Under Bretton Woods, it was the adjustment mechanism of currency parity changes which was emphasized in combination with a modest exchange stabilization fund represented by the resources of the IMF. Each nation was to declare a par value for its currency in terms of gold. In practice, since the US authorities had unilaterally committed themselves to convert dollar balances held abroad into gold, and since the US dollar was itself tied to gold at a fixed price: a decision to establish a par value for a currency was really a decision to establish its exchange rate vis-à-vis the dollar. Nations maintained currency convertibility, at a fixed rate, by intervening in the foreign exchange market to sell dollars from national reserves when a deficit appeared in international transactions or to buy dollars, and accumulate reserves in the event of a surplus. Since overseas holdings of dollars were convertible into gold, the international monetary system was often considered as being based on a «gold exchange standard». Only the US was prepared to exchange gold for dollars. Thus, they were at the centre of the system.

The stability of the Bretton Woods system was to be assured by the workings of the price system. With respect to flows of goods and services between nations, it was assumed that by changing the price of the national currency (the exchange rate), relative prices of traded goods would adjust to restore equilibrium. Any nation facing a deficit could devalue, rendering exports more attractive and imports more costly, and the imbalance could be made to disappear quasi-automatically through the operation of the price mechanism in the international market place. At the same time it was believed that flows of funds for investment could be controlled through the use of variations in interest rates.

The external adjustment mechanism proved faulty in two important respects. Firstly, it was difficult to identify a fundamental disequilibrium which required exchange rate adjustment and distinguish it from a temporary imbalance which could be financed from reserves, «offshore» borrowing, or by IMF loans. Secondly, the mechanism itself proved to be asymmetrical in that countries in deficit were under pressure to devalue – given that their stock of foreign exchange was limited – but nations in surplus were often unwilling to revalue – preferring to build up their reserves by accumulating foreign exchange[10].

It was apparent as well that an asymmetry existed between the US and other nations[11]. American deficits were financed automatically by the accumulation of dollars by the rest of the world. Although other nations had to adjust payments imbalances, the Americans could simply allow others to increase their holdings of American currency. In the period from 1945 until 1958 when the dollar was in short supply, and thus world liquidity inadequate to finance the expansion of international trade, American deficits were looked upon favourably as contributing to prosperity. US deficits allowed European nations to progressively eliminate restrictions on trade. By 1968, it was considered that American deficits were too large and that excess liquidity creation through the dollar outflow was causing international inflation.

The pressures on the US external accounts caused by the Vietnam War expenditures, overseas military commitments, investment abroad, and domestic inflation (the «great society» programmes were being financed without tax increases) led to a continued deterioration of its balance of payments. In August 1971, President Nixon announced the closing of the gold window, the devaluation of the dollar with respect to gold, and an import surtax. The end of the liberal international order, as characterized by the Bretton Woods regime, came when states were unwilling to stabilize their currencies around fixed parity, and adopted the nationalist alternative of «floating» exchange rates. The fixed rate regime had failed because in part the international mechanism to adjust trade imbalance was inadequate. In particular, the American authorities were limited to domestic adjustments in order to reduce external imbalance, and for political reasons were unwilling to undertake the deflationary policies (raising taxes, cutting spending) necessary to eliminate the balance of payments deficit. Under the Bretton Woods system, there was really no international adjustment mechanism available to the US. But the US could use the international monetary privileges available to it, because of the role of the US dollar as a reserve currency, to advance their foreign policy objectives, through overseas spending, lending, and investment. By adopting floating rates, certain European nations were signaling not only their unwillingness to maintain a system whereby US deficits required them to purchase US dollars in the foreign exchange market (in order that exchange rates remain fixed), but also a desire to disassociate themselves from the US policies which led to the dollar outflow. The breakdown of the Bretton Woods regime reflected a decline in American hegemony. The US could no longer impose its leadership internationally.

INTERNATIONAL CAPITAL FLOWS AND MULTILATERALISM

An account of the Bretton Woods system as a multilateral payments and exchange regime tends to obscure the role played by international capital flows and their importance to the health of world economy. It was evident in the postwar period that only an outflow of funds from the US would allow other industrialized nations to progressively dismantle barriers to international trade. In fact, European nations were able to declare free convertibility for their currencies only by 1958, fourteen years after Bretton Woods. In the interim period the European Payments Union (EPU) had allowed them to husband their scarce foreign exchange, and sales to the US, plus capital inflows, permitted the accumulation of the exchange reserves necessary to underwrite convertibility[12].

The outflow of capital from the US was in part related to its key role within the NATO alliance for collective security and its global military commitments. This role, created in anticipation of covert and overt Soviet expansionism, was also an important consideration in the decision to provide Marshall Plan funds bilaterally to Europe; as well as to promote economic reconstruction through World Bank lending.

As prosperity returned to Europe, American private investment became an important feature of the economic landscape. American corporations were quick to understand the potential for expansion within the emerging European Community (EC). Rather than rely on the traditional pattern of exports to overseas markets, American-based corporations were prepared to invest in manufacturing capacity within other industrialized countries and produce locally. The economic integration among the members of the EC served to attract American investment as free trade among participating states made servicing an expanding market by implanting US subsidiary operations in Europe an attractive possibility. By 1970 the value of American production abroad was four times greater than that represented by US exports.

The international activities of national business enterprises led to increased movements of private investment capital. By transferring technology and accumulated expertise from the national base in order to produce for regional markets, a number of firms were able to integrate their activities across national boundaries. The creation of these Transnational Enterprises (TNEs) was a principal feature of the 1960s. Operating on a world scale, outside the control of any one government, TNEs were an unintended consequence of the era of economic prosperity. The growth of industrial production was accompanied by increased demand for consumer goods and efficient national producers were able to extend their activities and take dominant positions within world markets. Though the majority of TNEs had American ownership, eventually all of the industrialized countries had entrants into the field of transnational production[13].

The international flow of private investment took on a new dimension with the creation of the Euromarkets for money and capital. As a result of the dollars flowing out of the US through the balance of payments deficit, dollar balances were accumulated abroad. Since US banks were limited in the amount of interest they could pay on deposits, and since demand for dollar was strong, it was profitable for non-American banks[14] to bid for dollar deposits and make dollar-denominated loans. The Eurodollar market for bonds and securities, as well as short-term finance, became an important alternative source of operating capital for TNEs. The market developed because national restrictions on banking made the operation of Eurobanking outside national control attractive. American banks opened European subsidiary operations and became major operators in the Euromarket for US funds. So long as banks were prepared to pay competitive rates on US dollar deposits held abroad, and borrowers were eager for US funds because of economic expansion, quick and substantial profits could be made in the Eurodollar markets[15].

The effect of the process was to accelerate the outflow of dollars and weaken national control over capital movements. The growth of this offshore market for funds was spectacular. From modest beginnings in the early 1960s, the size of the Euro-markets by 1980 was equivalent to the amount of money in circulation in the US! When the market for dollars weakened in the latter part of the 1960s, the Euromarkets for other currencies developed.

The amount of outstanding dollars «over-hanging» foreign exchange markets was one reason for the inability of states to re-introduce fixed exchanged rates in the 1970s. During the same period, that part of the international monetary system, based on official transactions between governments, became less significant; and the importance of transactions in the private system based on the Euromarkets increased. Many governments found it convenient to borrow in the Euromarket in order to finance current account deficits.

The integration of national capital markets implied by the Euromarkets meant that individual interest rate policies were less effective in influencing capital movements. The interdependence of the industrialized economies became widely recognized by the late 1960s and serious doubt was cast on the ability of individual states to undertake domestic policy adjustment without international coordination of national economic policy[16].

Part II

The Breakdown in Consensus

The factors which led to the erosion of the liberal order included disagreement between the US and the EC (plus Japan) over the management of the world economy, a challenge by the Third World to the «rules of the game» implied by the order, and the appearance of massive trade imbalances due to the operation of the OPEC cartel. The liberal ideology – the free play of market forces leading to international harmony – was under attack.

POLICY DISAGREEMENT BETWEEN THE US AND THE EC

The disagreement between Europe and the US had to do with the effects of the dollar outflow which by the early 1970s had reached flood proportions. West Germany and Japan had accumulated great amounts of US dollars in their reserves as they intervened in the market to maintain fixed exchange rates. Despite successive revaluations of the German mark, Japanese yen and Swiss franc, the dollar outflow and the process of purchasing American dollars with national currencies continued. Europeans argued that the process was inflationary. The counterpart of the dollar purchases, the selling of national currencies, increased the supply of domestic money and created inflation. In effect, it was argued that the US exported inflation to Europe through their balance of payments deficit[17]. To compound the problem, some Europeans held their exchange reserves in the form of US Treasury Bills and thus were financing the US national budget deficit which itself was considered to be a principal cause of the balance of payments deficit! Rather than continue to accumulate dollars, the Europeans chose to float their currencies. They argued that the US should combat domestic inflation which was flowing out to the rest of the world economy by practicing deflationary policies. Successive US governments were largely unwilling to cut national spending, for fear of creating unemployment, reducing military capacity, and losing electoral support from constituencies dependent on government support.

For their part, the US argued that European nations should open up their markets to exports from abroad. The US authorities suggested that the EC and Japan were both practicing «protectionism», favouring national producers over free trade, and that only more international competition would reduce price inflation and allow for growth within the world economy.

Multilateral trade negotiations were undertaken in the 1960s (Kennedy Round) and the 1970s (Tokyo Round) with a view to reducing tariff barriers to international trade. In the latter talks it became clear that despite liberal ideology, non-tariff barriers to commerce had become an important part of national and regional policies; and that they were especially difficult to dismantle multilaterally.

Discussions on a reform of the international monetary system took place in the early 1970s[18]. The balance of power between the industrialized nations was such that neither the US nor the EC were able to impose a solution on the other. Though it had been agreed in the late 1960s to introduce Special Drawing Rights (SDRs) through the IMF to serve as an international monetary unit, it was not possible to agree on a mechanism to replace the Gold Exchange standard. The SDR, while useful as a unit of account, did not emerge as a serious alternative to other reserve assets. Nations continued to hold dollars and gold as reserves while diversifying into other strong currencies. Ultimately, the negotiations failed and the multilateral system of payments was left in place without an agreed international adjustment mechanism. The national policy alternative of allowing floating exchange rates to adjust current account imbalances was to be relied upon. In the meantime, it was becoming increasingly clear that international economic conditions had worsened and that no measures for international concertation were capable of attracting support. Americans pointed out that Europeans were not paying their share of defence requirements. Since US deficits were in part attributable to European unwillingness to protect themselves militarily, the Europeans should bear the burden of adjustment[19].

The dilemma for both sides to the dispute was that neither could practice their favoured policies without cooperation from the other. In 1975, the major industrial countries began meeting at regular intervals[20]. The «economic summits» were designed to promote public confidence that international misunderstanding would not lead to international depression. But despite various attempts to fine-tune national macro-economic policies in an harmonious fashion, the traditional instruments of monetary, fiscal, and exchange rate policy appeared ineffective in the face of international economic disorder and the emerging global economy characterized by TNEs.

THE THIRD WORLD CHALLENGES THE LIBERAL ORDER

The first comprehensive challenge to the liberal ideology as embodied in the postwar arrangements for managing the international economy came from the Third World states at the first UNCTAD conference held in Geneva in 1964. At this occasion, the coalition of Third World states, known as the «Group of 77», came into being, and the arguments they put forward, later to be refined as proposals for a New International Economic Order (NIEO), constitute both the initiation of the so-called North-South dialogue, and a comprehensive critique of the liberal order[21]. Briefly stated, the position of the Group of 77 contained three elements[22]. Firstly, a secular deterioration of the terms of trade for Third World countries was identified. Given that for the most part exports of Less Developed Countries (LDCs) consist of primary products, and that prices of these commodities fluctuate unevenly on international markets, export revenues vary greatly from year to year, and overall, a declining trend is identified. At the same time imports, which largely consist of manufactured goods from the industrialized countries, when taken as a whole, show a pronounced tendency to increase in cost over time. The combination of falling export revenues and rising import prices creates a structural trade deficit which must be financed.

Secondly, it follows from the analysis of trade flows that Third World countries could greatly benefit from measures to stabilize commodity prices. The Group of 77 suggested that producer and consumer nations come together and form a «Common Fund» to regulate commodity prices by controlling directly the supply and demand for widely traded Third World primary products. Prices would be managed through recourse to market sharing by exporters, and by the creation of «buffer stocks» to be financed jointly by consumers and producers, but with the industrialized importers paying the lion's share. This proposal represents the replacement of the market mechanism by an international planning authority. As such it has been criticized by the industrialized world which is unwilling to accept a comprehensive project whereby the major commodities would be linked together and the consumers would absorb both the increased commodity prices and the cost of financing the scheme. Notwithstanding this opposition to measures which contradict the principles of the liberal economy, the industrialized nations have agreed to a very limited version of the Common Fund proposal and in the past have supported limited compensation for commodity exporters through IMF lending.

Thirdly, the Group of 77 argued that the rules of the game of international trade do not provide access to international markets on a non-discriminatory basis as is suggested by proponents of the liberal order; rather, the effect on Third World countries is to condemn them to a position of structural inferiority characterized by unequal access to finance for purposes of economic development. Given the balance of payments deficits of LDCs, they are forced to choose between three unacceptable alternatives. They can reduce manufactured imports, needed to carry out development plans; they can borrow abroad to finance the deficit, though capacity to repay is limited; or they can abandon economic planning and allow market forces to determine their economic future. The Third World has rejected these alternatives. LDCs have called for a Generalized Special Preference (GSP) to be accorded for their exports in the markets of the industrialized countries. They have suggested that a net creation of international liquidity for development purposes be undertaken through the IMF by linking the allocation of SDRs to the balance of payments needs of LDCs (the «link» proposal). And they have insisted that the rules of market practice be modified in order to introduce considerations of equity in relations between unequals, democratic authority in decision-making in international forums, and redistribution of income between rich and poor nations[23].

Taken together, these proposals which make up the NIEO project would drastically, change the international liberal order. The industrialized world has been reluctant to accept the modification of international markets for commodities, goods and finance this implies. Yet within international forums, the Group of 77, which now counts among its number some 125 members, has a voting majority. The power of the industrialized nations to resist the NIEO resides in their role as major contributors to UN agencies. And they have been willing to wield a financial veto.

In the past, the industrialized countries used the functionalism characteristic of the liberal order to divide up the subjects under discussion and assign them to the competent body (food to the FAO, labour to the ILO, trade to GATT, etc.). The Group of 77 called for Global Negotiations so that all issues would be taken together comprehensively (a «holistic» approach) and debated within the UN. The industrialized nations have managed to separate the financial institutions (IMF, World Bank), where voting is weighted according to financial contributions, from other forums where a one nation, one vote, procedure is followed; and has argued that financial agencies, are executive agencies, while others are not. This strategy has been accompanied by stalling tactics and attempts to belittle the importance of the UN as a forum for discussing the world economy. North-South questions have been the subject of special conferences held outside the UN in an effort to overcome the negative effects of the confrontation over the NIEO. As the economic circumstances of the Third World taken as a whole worsened, and as international economic conditions deteriorated, the appearance of the OPEC (Organization of Petroleum Exporting Countries) nations as a new power centre within the world economy took on a particular importance.

OPEC AND THE WORLD TRADING SYSTEM

The decision taken by the OPEC nations to increase the price of petroleum by 400 % in 1973-1974 called into question the dominance of the industrialized countries within the international order. The effect of the pricing decision, and of subsequent price increases in 1979, was to create a new distribution of purchasing power within the world economy and to alter the structures underlying the multilateral payments and exchange regime[24].

OPEC pricing policies changed the terms of trade between oil importers and oil exporters. Price increases in manufactured goods had historically outstripped increases in the price of the non-renewable petroleum resources. OPEC arranged to peg oil prices at a level which would account for inflation in industrialized countries and provide compensation for past policies of «cheap oil». The argument used by OPEC was to suggest that the optimum price for oil should be equal to the cost of substituting other energy resources for petroleum. Rather than equating oil prices with either the cost of producing oil (plus a profit margin) or allowing it to be determined by the forces of supply and demand on the international marketplace, OPEC argued that as a producers association, it had the responsibility for assuring that a fair return be assured to the owners of a diminishing resource, even if this meant modifying the market mechanism.

In the 1970s, as a result of higher oil prices, the oil exporters taken as a whole accumulated great purchasing power which made them a major market for imports of all sorts. In addition, certain OPEC members built up enormous surpluses in international trade as a result of the disparity between their revenues and their capacity to absorb imports. Oil importers suffered unequally as a consequence of more expensive petroleum.

The non-oil LDCs had experienced persistent deficits in their balance of payments since independence and their situation deteriorated seriously as a result of higher costs for petroleum. The non-oil industrialized countries were forced to increase their exports in order to finance the higher oil costs and competition in world export markets increased substantially. The problem for the world trading community was how to adjust the imbalances in trade associated with the persistent surpluses accruing to OPEC.

OPEC countries acquired liquid assets in excess of spending requirements which they placed with the Euromarkets, or in the financial markets of the US and to some extent other industrialized countries. Private bankers were then led to extend loans to oil importers and non-OPEC oil producers. The Third World countries were unable to meet their oil bills through increased exports. Some LDCs had their payments imbalance financed by the commercial banks which make up the Euromarkets. But for less credit-worthy nations, the only option was to reduce oil imports. It quickly became apparent that the recycling of petro-dollars to nations in deficit was a delicate process and that the international monetary system was increasingly subject to stress as a result. By the time of the world recession of 1981-1982, individual states such as Poland, Mexico, Brazil and Argentina, were over-burdened with debt.

Though it is desirable and necessary to ensure finance will flow from surplus to deficit nations, the debt crisis of the 1980s showed that it is by no means clear that private markets alone can provide the solution to structural problems. In the absence of an internationally agreed mechanism for «global adjustment» of petro-deficits, the pressure on states to adopt protectionist policies was very great. As states came to terms with the modification of international trading patterns induced by OPEC price increases and accentuated by international indebtedness, the liberal order was weakened. By for a time reducing the dominant position of the industrial exporters within the world economy, OPEC has heightened Third World dissatisfactions with liberal trading rules and increased protectionist tendencies, always present below the surface, in the West. Though the world recession and the growth in importance of non-OPEC oil production both served to reduce the power of OPEC, the continued importance of private bank financing of trade imbalances, as opposed to Bretton Woods style international adjustment, led to an important expansion of interest rate sensitive flows of money across the world economy.

ORDER AND DISORDER IN THE WORLD ECONOMY

A significant development within the world economy was, on the part of some states, to advance regional solutions. The EC has succeeded in introducing a European Monetary System (EMS); including provision for pooling national reserves;

and the introduction of a unit of account, the ECU (European Currency Unit); as well as procedures for limiting exchange rate variations within the Community through agreement on market intervention policies. The effect has been to insulate intra-Community trade from disturbances caused by the effects of fluctuations in the value of the US dollar on European exchange rates. As well, the stage is now set for the ECU to rival the dollar as a reserve currency. The EMS has allowed European nations to pursue common policies, but did not allow them to escape the impact of «stagflation», the combination of high unemployment and high inflation that preceded the world recession of 1981-1982.

Other regional integration schemes in Latin America, the Caribbean, Africa and Asia have been even less successful. But with stalemate being characteristic of North-South relations, the possibilities inherent in South-South forms of cooperation were subject to increased attention.

The position of the Soviet Union and the other Comecon states within the world economy has changed considerably since the period of the early Cold War. East-West trade represented an attractive alternative to western industrial economies during the period of slow growth that began in the 1970s, and it appeared that the Comecon countries accepted the necessity of increased economic relations with the West for the sake of their own economic development. Indeed by the late 1970s, it seemed that Eastern Europe was increasingly a part of the world economy. Comecon countries participated in joint ventures with TNEs, borrowed on the Euro-markets, and exported consumer goods to the West. Soviet exports of natural gas and petroleum allowed Western Europe to reduce its dependence on OPEC and permitted the Soviet Union to finance imports of western technology. Cooperation between TNEs and Comecon state enterprises even extended to joint projects in Third World countries. As elsewhere in the world economy, commodity and goods trade between states was overshadowed by the implications of direct investment abroad for production, marketing and finance, all of which brought about more collaboration between firms across national boundaries. Increased participation in the global economy was now seen as complimentary to regional integration within Comecon[25].

Throughout the 1970s and into the 1980s, the ongoing transformation of the world economy served to erode the basis of the liberal order. The international economy of states trading with each other at arms length, so to speak, was being transformed into a global economy where intra-firm trade across national jurisdictions became increasingly important. The liberal international economy allowed for both a measure of national autonomy in policy-making and agreement on policies of inter-national cooperation. International institutions reflected agreement on the limits of national policy and acceptance of rules governing practices in relations among na-tions. As the global economy emerged under the aegis of TNEs, and as a world market for finance, in the form of the Euromarkets, took shape, states reacted to their increas-ing lack of control over global developments, not by acting in concert to establish new «rules of the game», but by striving to protect their national economies from the effects of the transnationalization of economic activity.

The liberal order was predicated on the existence of an international economy composed of national states who had agreed to allow reciprocal access to each others' markets. With the development of transnational production, finance and marketing, the old order had ceased to be as important. Transnational markets had replaced national markets. Yet despite the transformation of the liberal international economy, no new consensus as to policies that should be adopted for the global economy emerged to attract support from states. In the absence of agreement, states resorted to protectionist polices, and this tendency was accentuated by inflation and stagnation within the world economy.

Part III

Canada Responds to Structural Evolution in the World Economic Order

The Canadian economic policies, which require a foreign policy expression, can be characterized as the desire to ensure that productive capacity within Canada is adequate to provide growth in employment and revenue; the concern that within a global economy, Canadian policy must account for the dominant role played by TNEs; and the belief that in order for Canada to maintain a viable presence within the world economy, effective national instruments must be available to the Canadian State.

FROM KEYNES TO NEO-MERCANTILISM

In the postwar world, the industrialized countries were persuaded by the social chaos of the 1930s, and the thinkng of John Maynard Keynes to attach a high priority to eliminating unemployment. This was to be accomplished by public spending, in times of economic weakness, to restore business profitability and simultaneously ensure that economic growth would provide jobs for all who were willing and able to work. Through the stimulation of effective demand for goods and services, government spending would act as the auxiliary motor for an economy dependent on private business enterprises operating in the market[26]. Canada was in the first rank of those nations which accented the commitment to Keynesian full employment policies[27].

Within the global economy, the movement of capital internationally creates a new international division of labour[28]. Rather than production taking place within the national territory of the state and flows of goods and services between states accounting for the significant international aspect of economic policy – as was the case in the international economy; the global economy has as its principal feature the transnationalization of production. The state, rather than controlling national production through Keynesian public spending policies, is more often in the position of reacting to the effects of the transnationalization of production by TNEs.

International investment capital has moved from high-wage countries to low-wage countries in order to produce goods which are then sold to the high-wage countries. The export of capital from the industrialized countries to the Third World has contributed to the emergence of the NICs (Newly-Industrializing Countries) as productive capacity in labour intensive industry is transferred from Europe and North America to countries such as South Korea, Taiwan, Brazil, India and Hong Kong. The movement of investment capital within the industrialized world has continued to increase in importance throughout the postwar period and greatly overshadows the flow from North to South. The result is the progressive inter-linking of the industrialized economies through the establishment of branch-plant operations by TNEs and the acceleration of intra-firm transfers of goods, services, technology, and capital. It is highly difficult to apply economic policy designed for a world of independent national production to a global economy dominated by a network of TNEs which account for 50 % of world production[29]. Rather than simply seeking to dismantle tariff barriers to trade amongst nations, economic policy must account for the power of TNEs to shift productive capacity and replace international trade by intra-firm trade. Most states have attempted to formulate some policies to influence the decisions of TNEs directly. To overcome the deficiencies of Keynesian policies of demand management many countries resort to neo-mercantilism.

The old mercantilism had as its goal the accumulation of wealth in the form of gold. It was believed that through the surplus in international exchange, one could accumulate the precious metal; the amount of which measured the wealth of the nation. The classical liberalism of Adam Smith and David Ricardo suggested that on the contrary the wealth of nations was to be advanced by lowering the cost of economic transactions through national specialization and increased international trade. It was deemed that nations should pursue those economic activities for which they possessed an international comparative advantage. Gains from trade would be maximized when low-cost national production was exchanged for low-cost production from other countries. Their thinking provided the basis for justifying the liberal international order.

The new mercantilism measures national wealth not in gold but rather in productive capacity[30]. The goal of neo-mercantilist nations is to increase the amount of employment and profits within their national territory, and to do so, they rely on measures familiar to the old mercantilism; such as protectionism in the form of tariffs, trade quotas, and other subsidies to national producers. In addition, the new mercantilism provides measures more suitable to the age of the transnational corporation: research and development grants, regional development subsidies, export credit assistance, «voluntary» import quotas; and incentives to increase the productivity of labour, including pensions, social welfare, education and training; as well as subsidized energy, transport, communications and a range of scientific services, in order to enable domestic capital to compete with international capital.

Yet, despite the range of services designed to increase production within the national economic space, tensions have developed between the neo-mercantilist state and TNEs. The new international division of labour means that in the case of TNEs head office management functions such as finance, marketing, research and development, stay in the «country of origin» while the actual manufacturing process and its attendant administration takes place in NICs and other industrialized countries. In order to influence decisions taken by the industrial corporations, states attempt to provide advantages for companies which produce for the local market within the national territory. Branch-plant operations were a familiar development in the postwar period. More recently, the tendency is for the production of world products where the parts may be built separately in different countries and assembly may take place in several locations. While efforts were made at the UN and elsewhere to impose a «code of conduct» on TNEs, nothing concrete was achieved internationally.

Canada was perhaps the first State in which the signs of developing global economy appeared. The arrival of American-based TNEs began in earnest in the

1950s and continued through the 1960s. State policy-making in a context where a large share of production was undertaken by foreign-owned enterprises was experienced in Canada on a scale which, although not to be duplicated elsewhere, provided evidence of some of the difficulties which most states would encounter. The transnationalization of the Canadian economy had important implications for Canada's position within the world economy.

CONFRONTING THE GLOBAL ECONOMY

The presence in Canada of an extraordinary number of foreign TNEs has had an inhibiting effect on the development of a manufacturing export sector and has limited Canada's role as centre for product development and indeed scientific research[31]. The Canadian balance of payments reflects the presence of TNEs and the trends identified in its evolution explain some of the responses of the Canadian State as attempts are made to come to grips with Canada's position with respect to the world economy.

The TNEs in Canada represent a stock of foreign investment which regularly emits profits to head offices, and dividends to shareholders abroad. Interest on foreign borrowings adds to this outflow of «invisible» items as recorded in the balance of payments. In addition, foreign-owned firms transfer money out of the country in the form of management fees, licensing arrangements, patents, and other costs associated with the operations of a foreign subsidiary. At the same time, the opportunity cost of foregone secondary effects from financial services, advertising, marketing, research and development, which in the case of a TNE are normally centralized at head office, are considerable for the Canadian economy. The dominance of foreign-owned corporations within Canada then explains the large, persistent, and growing invisibles deficit on current account of the balance of payments[32].

In order to offset the outflow of funds in this fashion, one alternative is to set up a corresponding inflow from the activities of Canadian TNEs. The short-term charge to the balance of payments of the capital outflows necessary to develop a larger Canadian presence abroad is considerable. However in general, if well placed, the investments will over time create an inflow on the current account as profits, interest and dividends flow back to Canada. After being a capital importer throughout its history, Canada has recently become a capital exporter[33].

In order for Canadian TNEs to be able to compete in the world market, they first need a strong base. Given the small Canadian market and the historically high costs of production in Canada due to tariffs, high wages, large transport costs, distance from world markets, and climate, the necessary base for expansion abroad can only be provided through the formation of very large operations within Canada. This point was made by the Royal Commission on Corporate Concentration[34]. The commissioners pointed out that rather than being exclusively concerned about the costs of large-scale organizations in the Canadian marketplace one should look to their competitiveness in international activities.

It has been argued that the adoption of a free trade arrangement with the US would provide Canadian enterprise with the large market necessary for their emergence as world-scale operations. This policy option, which has been supported by the

C.D. Howe Institute, the Economic Council of Canada and a Canadian Senate committee, the Macdonald Royal Commission, and embraced by the Mulroney Government, has in fact been very nearly achieved through the various negotiations both multilateral and bilateral of the past 20 years. As a result of the Tokyo Round, nearly 80 % of Canada's exports will go duty-free to the US.

In the modern world economy, non-tariff barriers (NTBs) to trade have grown in importance and states have attempted to promote directly the international expansion of domestic industry through the adoption of industrial strategies. State participation and direction of economic activity (statism) is a characteristic of the global economy[35]. In the context of free trade talks with the US, NTBs are an item of concern to both sides. Indeed one of the principal objections to free trade comes from those Canadian groups who would like to see Canada adopt an industrial strategy and fear that by eliminating some so-called NTBs, Canada would at the same time forsake the industrial strategy option[36].

INDUSTRY AND STATE IN CANADA

In Canada, a number of state mechanisms have been put into place to assist industry. The Export Development Corporation (EDC) has a mandate to promote sales abroad through the provision of supplier credits. All major trading nations have similar organizations and international competition is fierce. Interest rates are often cut in order to win contracts. The result is that exporters are directly subsidized by the state. The EDC has the futher mandate of insuring investment abroad against expropriation or other political interference. It is hoped that this will encourage Canadian business interests to expand their activities to the third markets where the industrialized nations compete so actively.

The Canadian International Development Agency (CIDA), while originally designed to assist selected developing countries to meet their basic needs as well as to promote economic development, has more recently stressed commercial motives. It is expected that projects abroad financed through CIDA will have a spin-off effect in rendering Canadian corporations more knowledgeable about prospects in the Third World, and that ultimately customers for aid will become commercial customers. Again other countries do likewise. It is interesting to note that, though the US have been lukewarm if not hostile to Third World aspirations, Canadian foreign policy has exhibited great concern with North-South issues.

Given the high level of export competition among developed economies in each others' markets, it has become clear that sales to non-industrialized countries represent an important alternative to traditional markets. Canadian exports to Third World countries were equal to only 8 % of total exports for the period 1966-1975, and a desire to improve this performance may explain increased attention to Third World questions by successive Liberal governments.

In its major review of foreign policy in 1968-1969, the first Trudeau Government gave as the first objective of Canadian foreign policy the promotion of Canadian economic development. In particular, the paper on Canadian-US relations, which appeared after the initial studies, dealt directly with the importance of initiating closer relations with Western Europe and Japan in order to counterbalance American influence over Canadian economic life and provide alternative outlets for economic development. When it came to giving concrete expression to this policy, it was decided to negotiate a contractual link with the European Community. This implied that for Canadian corporations to penetrate the European market, closer links with the Canadian State would be necessary. In the event, the efforts to pursue this «Third Option» floundered because of the inability of government and business in Canada to find ways of working together to build links to Europe.

In order to expand Canadian commercial relations with the OPEC nations, Japan and the NICs, it would also be necessary to deal with them on a state-to-state basis. Greater understanding of the future direction of state policy in other countries is necessary in order to identify Canadian trade and investment prospects. The world economy in the post-Bretton Woods era is characterized by statisms and Canadian policies are subject to the same influences which have increased state direction and participation in economic life elsewhere[37]. However resurgent economic liberalism in Canada, as evidenced in the final report of the Macdonald Commission, blocked efforts to adopt the sort of industrial policies needed to deal with economies which relied more on state direction than market forces in economic policy.

CANADIAN FOREIGN POLICY AND ECONOMIC DEVELOPMENT

After World War II, Canada was anxious to establish a political position commensurate with its economic strength. The policy adopted was functionalism; the environment in which it was practiced was multilateral. This policy was not adopted for ethical or moral reasons. It corresponded to attempts to establish a framework within which Canada's prosperity could be assured.

It was perhaps natural to assume that Canadian relations with the rest of the world would flourish within the multilateral context. In fact, throughout the period under review, the importance of trade, financial and industrial ties with the US increased as a percentage of general commercial relations with the rest of the world. Multilateralism did not serve to diversify Canadian external relations. The degree of vulnerability of the Canadian economy to events within the US became a great cause for concern. It was considered that in order for Canada to have a solid base for economic development, ties with other economies had to be strengthened. The policy of the Third Option was adopted to signify Canada's concern to diversify its external economic relations and reduce its dependence on the US market for exports and investment capital, but in fact, if anything, Canadian dependence on the US increased despite the Third Option policy.

Under the Liberals, Canadian foreign policy towards the world economy turned in the 1970s towards national interest and bilateralism rather than the functionalism and multilateralism of the immediate postwar period. The reasons for this change in emphasis are to be found in the general concern for Canada's economic development prospects.

The response of Ottawa to growing tensions between the provinces and the Federal Government was to asser the legitimacy of the Central Government as an agent of what it perceived to be the principal concern of the Canadian electorate – economic development. Rather than accede to requests for greater provincial autonomy, the federal authorities argued that international conditions required a strong Central Government to exercise leadership to promote economic development across the country. In the absence of federal leadership, the Trudeau Liberals argued, only the wealthy provinces would be able to make their way in the world economy of the 1980s.

In concrete terms, this meant that the Federal Government used those powers available to it under the Constitution. One of its advantages in any contest with the provinces was its responsibility for external relations including powers over international exchange. While not blocking provincial representation abroad, federal authorities attempted to establish the principle that any further decentralization of Canadian federalism would weaken efforts to promote international trade and commerce. The Department of External Affairs asserted its position within the federal bureaucracy as a «central agency»: one capable of coordinating the international policies of the Canadian State. As a part of a major re-organization of economic departments, External acquired the trade policy and administration branch of the old Department of Industry, Trade and Commerce.

By the early 1980s, the Liberals were arguing that if Canadian prospects for economic development were to be enhanced, means had to be found to protect Canada from the negative effects of developments abroad. One way of achieving this was to improve Canadian relations with those states with the potential to become important markets for Canadian exports. Among the countries mentioned for fa-voured relations were Mexico, Venezuela, Brazil, Algeria, Saudi Arabia and South Ko-rea[38]. At a time when protectionism characterized the attitude of the EC, the US and Japan, the oil-producing nations promised to be lucrative outlets for Canadian busi-ness. The list of candidates for improved bilateral relations include nations which have enjoyed close ties with the US, and it was expected that like Canada, they would be interested in diversifying their external relations. However, the bilateralism policy was overwhelmed by the world recession which saw many of the target countries expe-rience severe economic difficulties.

In the absence of an international regime to regulate the global economy, and indeed where a sharp divergence of views existed between North and South as to the future of the world order, the Liberals chose to advocate – within the industrialized group of nations – the view that interdependence of North and South required greater efforts by the North to assure that the South has the means of becoming a full par-ticipant in international trade. This implied that concessions be made so that a measure of economic growth in the South would enable the North to expand produc-tion through sales to the South. It also implied that the North be willing to adjust its own productive apparatus in order to allow increased imports from the South in sectors where the South could be competitive. It is not apparent that the Canadian argument has had much effect either on its summit partners or on Canadian industry. At the very least, the Canadian contribution to the North-South dialogue promised improved bilateral relations with prospective trading partners in the South.

Ultimately, a policy of neo-mercantilism within the world economy could not be expected to provide the states which adhered to its much concrete benefit. the «sauve qui peut» mentality engendered by the absence of an internationally accept-able regime for managing the world economy had been seen before; and the evidence of its effects is clear enough to those willing to remember the 1930s.

International economic disorder requires concessions from the strong, not from the weak. Faced with the continued determination of the major countries to act in their own interest, regardless of the consequences for others, Canada was undoubtedly concerned for its own vulnerability. And if the neo-mercantilism of Canadian foreign policy was not particularly noble, it was accompanied by efforts to achieve international concertation to deal with international problems, though these efforts were unlikely to succeed so long as Canada and other industrialized nations resisted political and economic transformation.

The election of the Conservatives provided for a major shift in Canadian policy towards the world economy. The new government agreed in March of 1985 to undertake a study of the possibilities of reaching a trade agreement with the US. In September 1985, the free trade initiative was announced to Parliament. Though the Conservatives had also indicated great interest in multilateral trade talks, the bilateral agreement with the US had a high priority among government initiatives. Indeed, in some respects, assuring Canadian access to the US market became the major policy thrust of the Mulroney Government.

In a sense, Canadian policy towards the world economy had come full circle. Canada was back to the economic liberalism of the postwar period in its attempts to promote economic development through the extension of Canadian markets to include those abroad. As in 1947, this meant a trade pact with the US. But this time, the negotiations would be undertaken with the full knowledge of the Canadian electorate. The political risks of dealing with the world economic order in this way are more visible than usual because of the historical precedents of conflict over free trade with the US. However, it remains that Canada's place in *the* world economy is a fundamental aspect – perhaps *the* fundamental aspect – of its foreign relations.

NOTES

1. A good general study of Canada's international trade is: B.W. Wilkinson, *Canada in a Changing World Economy*, Montréal, C.D. Howe Research Institute, 1980. See as well: John A. Stovel, *Canada in the World Economy*, Cambridge, Mass., Harvard University Press, 1967.

2. Robert W. Cox, «The Crisis of World Order and the Problem of International Organization in the 1980s», *International Journal*, Vol. 35, No. 2, Spring, 1980.

3. Ideology is one of the controversial terms in social sciences. Many policy studies avoid it. However, any attempt to assign meaning to activities involves an ideology. In the policy-making context, an ideology justifies, directs and gives meaningful content to objectives and the choice of means to attain them. See the discussion in Joyce Oldham, Appleby, *Economic Thought and Ideology in Seventeenth-Century England*, Princeton, Princeton University Press, 1978, and Louis Dumont, *From Mandeville to Marx* (The Genesis and Triumph of Economic Ideology), Chicago, Chicago University Press, 1977.

4. R.D. Cuff and J.L. Granatstein, *American Dollars – Canadian Prosperity* (Canadian American Economic Relations 1945-1950), Toronto, Samuel-Stevens, 1978.

5. On the imbalance between Canadian and US efforts, see: A.F.W. Plumptre, *Three Decades of Decision* (Canada and the World Monetary System, 1944-75), Toronto, McClelland and Stewart, 1977.

6. Maureen Appel Molot and Glen Williams, «A Political Economy of Continentalism», in Michael S. Whittington and Glen Williams (eds.), *Canadian Politics in the 1980s*, Toronto, Methuen, 1981.

7. An account of «functionalism» is given by John W. Holmes, *The Shaping of Peace*, Vol. 1, Toronto, University of Toronto Press, 1979.

8. The clearest statement on quiet diplomacy remains: Peyton Lyon, «Quiet Diplomacy Revisited», in Stephen Clarkson (ed.), *An Independent Foreign Policy For Canada?*, Toronto, McClelland and Stewart, 1968.

9. Marcello de Cecco, «Origins of the Postwar Payments System», *Cambridge Journal of Economics*, Vol. 3, No. 1, March, 1979.

10. Duncan Cameron, «The Reform of International Money», *International Journal*, Vol. XXXIV, No. 1, Winter, 1978-1979.

11. Robert Triffin, *Gold and the Dollar Crisis*, New Haven, Yale University Press, 1960. His views were prophetic.

12. Robert Triffin, *Europe and the Money Muddle*, New Haven and London, Yale University Press, 1957.

13. *Les Multinationales*, Les Cahiers français, La Documentation française, Paris, No. 190, March-April, 1979.

14. Fred Hirsch, *Money International*, London, Penguin, 1969. Supreme irony, the Soviet-controlled Moscow Narodny Bank was an initiator of the Euro-dollar market. The Soviet Union sold gold in the Zurich market to pay for imports of western wheat; the proceeds of the sale were payed in dollars. Soviet officials were nervous about depositing dollars with a US bank, fearing that these assets could be frozen or confiscated by the US Government, they opened US dollar accounts in the Moscow Narodny Bank, and it was discovered that these dollars could be lent to others, earn interest and that profits were high while risks were low. Not only did the Soviet Union contribute to capitalist banking practice, in 1968, by selling gold when the US dollar was under pressure, they helped to stabilize the dollar price of gold, and thus the gold exchange standard!

15. Paul Einzig, *The Euro-Dollar System*, London, Macmillan, 1964.

16. Harry Johnson, «Problems of Stabilization Policy in an Integrated World Economy», appearing in his *Further Essays in Monetary Economics*, London, Allen and Unwin, 1972.

17. François Perroux et al., *Inflation, dollar, euro-dollar*, Paris, Gallimard, 1971.

18. Duncan Cameron, *Le système monétaire international en voie de réforme*, Ottawa, Éditions de l'Université d'Ottawa, 1977.

19. Henry Brandon, *The Retreat of American Power*, New York, Doubleday, 1975.

20. The first summit was convened by the President of France. The US, Japan, UK and West Germany were the countries present. The second summit, hosted by the US, added Canada and Italy to the number of summit countries. Canada hosted the seventh meeting in July 1981 (Ottawa-Montebello). The EC has been represented at these meetings by the President of the European Commission.

21. Robert W. Cox, «Ideologies and the New International Economic Order: Reflections on Some Recent Literature», *International Organization*, Vol. 33, Spring, 1979.

22. Ervin Laszlo et al., *The Objectives of the New International Economic Order*, New York, Pergamon Press, 1978. A comprehensive account of Third World proposals to modify the existing order is provided.

23. For a sympathetic account of the Third World position, see: Willy Brandt (for the independent commission on international development issues), *North-South: a Programme for Survival*, London, Pan Books, 1980.

24. Zuhayr Mikdashi, «Oil Pricing and OPEC Surpluses: Some Reflections», *International Affairs*, Vol. 57, No. 3, Summer, 1981.

25. A. Koves, «Socialist Economy and World Economy», *Acta Œconomica*, Vol. 21, No. 4, 1978.

26. The clearest statement on this subject is perhaps James Meade, «The Keynesian Revolution», in Milo Keynes (ed.), *Essays on Joan Maynard Keynes*, Cambridge, Cambridge University Press, 1975.

27. On the relevancy of Keynesian thinking today, see Don Patinkin and J. Clark Leith (eds), *Keynes, Cambridge and the General Theory*, London, Macmillan, 1977.

28. See Duncan Cameron and François Houle (eds.), *Canada and the New International Division of Labour*, Ottawa, University of Ottawa Press, 1985, and Jurgen Heinrichs, «The Impact of the New International Division of Labour on the Patterns of Transfer of Technology and the Related Social Costs», *Millennium: Journal of International Studies*, Vol. 8, No. 3.

29. Perhaps the most important publication on the subject of TNEs is Charles-Albert Michalet, *Le Capitalisme mondial*, Paris, Presses universitaires de France, 1976.

30. Joan Robinson, «The New Mercantilism», in her *Contributions to Modern Economics*, New York, Academic Press, 1978.

31. John N.H. Britton and James M. Gilmour, *The Weakest Link* (A Technological Perspective on Canadian Industrial Underdevelopment), Ottawa, Science Council of Canada, 1978.

32. Duncan Cameron, «Public Credit and Private Profit: The Politics of the Canadian Current Account Deficit», *Our Generation*, Vol. 14, No. 3, Winter, 1981.

33. I.A. Litvak and C.J. Maule, «Canadian Outward Investment: Impact and Policy», *Journal of World Trade Law*, Vol. 14, No. 4, July-August, 1980.

34. Sometimes called the Bryce report; *The Report of the Royal Commission on Corporate Concentration*, Ottawa, 1978.

35. Jeanne Kirk Laux, «Global Interdependence and State intervention», in B. W. Tomlin (ed.), *Canada's Foreign Policy: Analysis and Trends*, Toronto, Metheun, 1978.

36. See Daniel Drache and Duncan Cameron (eds.), *The OTHER Macdonald Report*, Toronto, James Lorimer and Co., 1985.

37. André Blais and Philippe Faucher, «La politique industrielle dans les économies capitalistes avancées», *Revue canadienne de science politique*, Vol. XIV:1, March, 1981.

38. Allan Gotlieb and Jeremy Kinsman, «Reviving the Third Option», *International Perspectives*, January-February, 1981.

8

Le Canada et les Nations Unies

Guy Gosselin
Université Laval

Que l'on se situe parmi les Canadiens bien informés de la politique du pays ou parmi les autres, on sait fort probablement que des militaires canadiens sont à garder la paix quelque part à l'étranger, non pas au service du Canada mais à celui des Nations Unies. On sait peut-être que c'est Lester B. Pearson qui est à l'origine de cette utilisation des militaires par l'ONU et que c'est cette initiative qui lui a valu le prix Nobel de la paix. Certains savent encore que le Canada est membre de plusieurs organisations internationales. D'autres, enfin, observent qu'il est souvent fait référence aux organisations internationales dans la politique étrangère du Canada. Dans l'un ou l'autre cas, on présume que les organisations internationales revêtent de l'importance pour le Canada. Qu'en est-il exactement?

Ce chapitre tentera de décrire la place qu'occupent les organisations inter-nationales, spécialement les Nations Unies, dans la politique étrangère canadienne, et d'identifier les principaux facteurs qui déterminent cette place. Plus précisément, nous dégagerons les grandes lignes de la politique adoptée par le Canada à l'égard des organisations internationales en suivant l'évolution de cette politique à travers les thèmes qui l'ont caractérisée depuis 1945. D'autre part, nous ferons état des déter-minants et des paramètres proposés par divers auteurs pour expliquer les tendances et les variations de la politique canadienne.

TENDANCES ET VARIATIONS

La politique envers les organisations internationales s'insère évidemment dans l'ensemble de la politique étrangère tout en présentant certaines caractéris-tiques qui permettent de la retracer dans cet ensemble. Afin de décrire la place qu'occupent les organisations internationales dans la politique étrangère canadi-enne, nous rappellerons les grands thèmes qui ont marqué cette politique, con-sidérée à la fois dans son ensemble et relativement aux organisations internationales. Ces grands thèmes seront présentés dans une perspective évolutive qui distinguera les quatre périodes que constituent les gouvernements qui se sont succédé à Ottawa de 1945 à 1984[1]. Certains thèmes sont propres à une période, tandis que d'autres apparaissent constants.

1945-1957: Un internationalisme fonctionnaliste

La première période, qui s'étend à peu près de 1945 à 1957, est marquée par Louis Saint-Laurent et Lester B. Pearson. Elle a débuté par le rejet de l'isolationnisme de l'avant-guerre et par une option nette en faveur de l'internationalisme. Ce dernier, qui sera une constante de la politique étrangère canadienne, a privilégié la voie multilatérale, perçue comme une excellente façon d'assurer l'indépendance du pays par rapport au Royaume-Uni et aux États-Unis et d'avoir une politique étrangère distincte. L'appui aux organisations internationales est ainsi devenu l'un des principes fondamentaux de la politique canadienne. On a relevé encore dans la politique étrangère canadienne une forte tendance idéaliste que l'on a parfois appelée altruiste ou volontariste et qui désigne une préoccupation continue de contribuer à l'instauration d'un ordre international souhaitable. Mais on y a dénoté en même temps un pragmatisme aussi fort qui a poussé vers la recherche de solutions pratiques aux problèmes internationaux ainsi que vers des attitudes de prudence, de patience, de compromis et de flexibilité. Alors que le pragmatisme peut s'identifier à l'héritage britannique, l'idéalisme apparaît comme étant un trait caractéristique du Nord-Américain.

C'est ainsi que, vers la fin de la guerre et immédiatement après, le Canada a poursuivi une politique d'appui actif aux organisations internationales, spécialement celles des Nations Unies. Il a souvent joué un rôle important lors de la création de ces organisations et est devenu membre de toutes celles qui furent établies. Il a développé et tenté d'appliquer alors une théorie fonctionnaliste selon laquelle chaque pays devrait avoir des responsabilités adaptées à ses capacités particulières. Dans le cas du Canada, l'application de la théorie fonctionnaliste a tendu à privilégier les activités non politiques, car c'était là surtout que se trouvaient les capacités particulières du pays. De même, les Nations Unies devenaient la pierre angulaire des relations internationales du Canada parce qu'elles offraient les meilleures possibilités d'avoir une politique étrangère indépendante et distincte. Enfin, la reconstruction des pays dévastés par la guerre constituait à ce moment pour le Canada une tâche importante et immédiate non seulement pour certaines agences provisoires, mais également pour les organismes permanents.

Très tôt cependant, de grandes désillusions ont été ressenties face à l'ONU. Celles-ci provenaient d'une part de la guerre froide qui s'installait et, d'autre part, du fonctionnement de certaines organisations. Le Canada n'en maintenait pas moins une participation active, mais il privilégiait certains aspects. Ainsi, dans le secteur des activités politiques, les gouvernants canadiens exprimaient de plus en plus souvent en 1947 et en 1948 leur insatisfaction à l'égard de l'ONU dont l'utilité se heurtait à la fin de la coopération entre les grandes puissances et à leur opposition grandissante. C'est ce qu'illustraient, par exemple, la doctrine Truman de 1947, qui visait à l'endiguement de l'URSS, et le blocus de Berlin de 1948, imposé par l'URSS. Cette expression d'insatisfaction s'accompagnait de plus en plus nettement d'une volonté de suppléer l'ONU par une organisation régionale de sécurité dans l'Atlantique Nord. Le Canada se retrouvait ainsi parmi les initiateurs de l'OTAN à l'établissement de laquelle il a pris une part active.

Toutefois, la création de l'OTAN et le grand intérêt qu'y portait le Canada ne semblaient pas affecter l'appui accordé à l'ONU. On notait les limites imposées à l'ONU par la guerre froide, mais on affirmait encore qu'elle constituait la pierre angulaire de la politique étrangère canadienne et on soulignait que son utilité comme lieu de rencontre et instrument de médiation n'en était que plus grande. La conception que se faisait le Canada du rôle de l'ONU est alors bien décrite par Lester B. Pearson devant l'Assemblée générale de l'ONU en septembre 1949[2]. Ce que disait

Pearson du Conseil de sécurité valait pour l'ensemble de l'ONU. Il soutenait que le Conseil ne devrait pas prendre l'initiative d'actions qu'il n'était pas en mesure de réaliser avec ses propres ressources, qu'il devrait laisser le règlement des problèmes politiques autant que possible à ceux qui sont directement concernés, et qu'il devrait concentrer son attention sur l'arrêt des hostilités et des troubles où qu'ils surgissent.

Cette politique se caractérisait donc par son aspect pratique. On mettait l'accent sur la conciliation plutôt que sur l'intervention, sur la persuasion plutôt que sur la coercition. C'était d'ailleurs ce qui guidait le Canada dans ses interventions, comme l'illustrent les questions du Cachemire, de l'Indonésie et de la Palestine dont l'ONU était alors saisie[3].

La participation active du Canada au secteur politique de l'ONU s'est manifestée sans doute le mieux en matière de désarmement et de contrôle de l'énergie atomique[4]. Dès le début, le Canada s'est trouvé au cœur des efforts visant à mettre sur pied un système de contrôle de l'énergie atomique en raison de sa participation aux recherches ayant conduit à la mise au point de la bombe atomique pendant la guerre et en raison des importantes quantités d'uranium qu'il possédait. C'est pourquoi le 15 novembre 1945, le premier ministre Mackenzie King du Canada s'est joint au président Truman des États-Unis et au premier ministre Attlee de la Grande-Bretagne pour demander, dans une déclaration commune, la création d'une Commission des Nations Unies pour le contrôle de l'énergie atomique et pour assurer l'usage pacifique de l'atome. Dès le mois de janvier 1946, l'Assemblée générale de l'ONU a créé une Commission de l'énergie atomique dont le Canada était nommé membre permanent. Le Canada, qui siégeait au Conseil de sécurité à ce moment, a été désigné en février 1947 parmi les onze membres de la nouvelle Commission des armements conventionnels. Par la suite, en janvier 1952, lorsque l'Assemblée générale a établi la Commission du désarmement avec le mandat de traiter à la fois des armes atomiques et des armes conventionnelles, le Canada y a obtenu un siège permanent. De nouveau, en 1955, le Canada a déployé une grande activité lors de la création de l'Agence internationale de l'énergie atomique (AIEA). La politique du Canada en ce domaine visait d'une part à lier la recherche du désarmement et le maintien de la sécurité; c'est pourquoi on s'est attaché d'une façon particulière aux questions de l'inspection et du contrôle. D'autre part, la politique canadienne cherchait à assurer que l'énergie atomique serve à des fins pacifiques.

C'est encore pendant cette période que s'est produite l'affaire de Corée[5]. Le Canada a apporté un appui immédiat aux premières actions de l'ONU qui prenaient la forme de résolutions du Conseil de sécurité dès les 25 et 27 juin 1950. Dans un premier temps, le Conseil a demandé la cessation des hostilités et le retrait des forces militaires. Dans un second temps, il a recommandé aux membres de l'ONU de fournir les forces requises pour repousser les attaquants et restaurer la paix. Des troupes canadiennes ont été effectivement envoyées en Corée sous le drapeau des Nations Unies. À l'Assemblée générale qui s'est réunie en septembre 1950, Lester B. Pearson a expliqué que le gouvernement canadien estimait que l'affaire de Corée correspondait au type de situation pour laquelle les membres de l'ONU étaient appelés à se préparer par l'article 43 de la Charte. Aussi le Canada a-t-il décidé, ajoutait-il, de constituer une force spéciale qui serait utilisée non seulement en Corée mais aussi en d'autres occasions similaires, conformément à la Charte.

Les circonstances dans lesquelles l'ONU est intervenue dans les événements de la Corée ont également amené les États-Unis à chercher un moyen de contourner la paralysie du Conseil de sécurité, provoquée par l'usage du veto. Ce moyen a été fourni par la résolution de l'Assemblée générale du 3 novembre 1950, dite «Union pour le maintien de la paix», en vertu de laquelle l'Assemblée peut, sans se substituer au Conseil, prendre la relève de ce dernier dans les cas où il est incapable de jouer son rôle dans la préservation de la paix. Le Canada fut l'un des sept parrains de cette résolution qui a pour effet de renforcer le rôle de l'Assemblée générale en matière de paix et de sécurité.

À titre de dernier exemple de participation active du Canada aux travaux de l'ONU pendant cette première période, mentionnons l'affaire de Suez à l'automne 1956. Dans cette affaire où le Canada s'est illustré par l'intermédiaire de Lester B. Pearson, il est intéressant de noter que l'ONU a pu intervenir parce que l'Assemblée générale a pris la relève du Conseil de sécurité en vertu de la résolution «Union pour le maintien de la paix», et que la force de maintien de la paix qui a caractérisé l'intervention de l'ONU représente une interprétation originale de la notion de forces armées contenue dans la Charte et à laquelle le Canada s'était référé en 1950.

Le Canada a en effet pris l'initiative de proposer la constitution d'une Force internationale d'urgence des Nations Unies, chargée d'assurer et de surveiller la cessation des hostilités. Cette force n'était pas une force combattante mais une force de police et elle accomplissait son rôle avec l'assentiment des nations intéressées. Cette initiative a valu non seulement le prix Nobel de la paix à Lester B. Pearson, mais elle a également créé un précédent à partir duquel d'autres forces de maintien de la paix furent mises sur pied. Le Canada a ainsi contribué au développement d'une capacité d'action nouvelle de l'ONU qui n'était pas prévue par la Charte, mais qui est maintenant bien implantée dans la pratique des Nations Unies. C'est ainsi que des forces de maintien de la paix ont été envoyées au Congo en 1960, à Chypre en 1964, de nouveau au Moyen-Orient à la suite de la guerre de 1973, ainsi qu'au Liban en 1978. Le Canada a participé ou continue à participer à chacune de ces forces, fidèle à la fois à son rôle d'initiateur majeur en cette matière et à la théorie fonctionnelle qu'il a défendue dès l'origine de l'ONU.

Des désillusions sont apparues aussi pendant cette période dans le secteur des activités non politiques. Le Canada y a tôt mis l'accent sur la praticabilité et sur la coordination afin de limiter les projets trop ambitieux d'organisations comme l'UNESCO et l'OMS et afin d'arrêter la multiplication des organismes et la duplication des activités. Il a cherché également à améliorer le fonctionnement et l'efficacité des diverses institutions. Il s'est trouvé par exemple parmi ceux qui ont amené le Conseil économique et social de l'ONU à adopter en 1950 une série de critères destinés à la sélection de priorités par les institutions spécialisées des Nations Unies[6].

L'enthousiasme du début avait voilé jusqu'à un certain point le fait que le Canada n'entretenait pas un intérêt égal envers toutes les institutions spécialisées. L'évolution de ces dernières, comme nous venons de l'esquisser, a contribué à éclaircir la sélectivité que la politique canadienne a appliquée à ces organisations. Cette sélectivité s'est fondée en premier lieu sur les intérêts du pays qui sont d'abord d'ordre économique et, en second lieu, sur un ensemble de valeurs au sein desquelles les choses concrètes et pratiques occupent la position la plus élevée et les choses intellectuelles ou abstraites, la position la plus basse. En conséquence, la politique canadienne a favorisé par exemple le GATT, ou les questions monétaires, mais pas l'UNESCO, ou la question des droits de l'homme[7]. On en trouve encore une illustration dans les votes du Canada à l'Assemblée générale des Nations Unies.

A.J. Miller[8], qui a analysé ces votes pour les années 1946 à 1966, observe que deux périodes apparaissent nettement à propos des questions sociales et culturelles. D'une part, la deuxième session en 1947 marque le début d'un affaiblissement considérable de l'appui du Canada aux questions sociales et culturelles. D'autre part, la quatorzième session en 1959 indique un changement de politique évident et le commencement d'une période d'appui relativement élevé aux mêmes questions. Par ailleurs, observe-t-il encore, alors que le Canada vote avec la majorité en 1946, il vote à l'inverse à partir de 1947 et de nouveau avec la majorité après 1959.

1957-1963: Un internationalisme idéaliste

La deuxième période, 1957-1963, est celle pendant laquelle le Parti conservateur a formé le gouvernement sous la direction de John Diefenbaker. Elle se caractérise par un certain nombre d'inconsistances qui témoignent à la fois de la méfiance entretenue par Diefenbaker envers la bureaucratie fédérale et du contrôle personnel qu'il a voulu conserver sur la politique étrangère ainsi que du choix qu'il a fait de nommer des ministres des Affaires extérieures inexpérimentés. Cependant, l'option internationaliste s'est maintenue et la tendance idéaliste s'est accentuée, comme l'illustrent particulièrement les initiatives qu'ont prises dans le cadre des Nations Unies le premier ministre Diefenbaker et le ministre Green.

Le ministre des Affaires extérieures, H.C. Green, a soutenu fermement les Nations Unies et il a fait du désarmement son thème favori. Aussi le Canada a-t-il poursuivi une participation active aux efforts reliés à cette question. Lorsque, par exemple, le groupe soviétique s'est retiré du Comité des Dix sur le désarmement à la suite d'une aggravation de la tension entre l'Est et l'Ouest dramatisée par l'incident de l'avion U-2, le Canada a pris des initiatives pour faciliter la reprise des négociations au cours de la session de l'Assemblée générale de l'automne 1960. À l'automne 1961, l'Assemblée générale a élargi le Comité des Dix en y ajoutant huit nouveaux membres pour représenter les principales régions géographiques du monde, reprenant ainsi une suggestion faite par le Canada pour aider à la reprise des négociations sur le désarmement. De même en 1961 et en 1962, le Canada a déployé une grande activité à l'ONU lorsque l'URSS a repris les essais d'armes nucléaires dans l'atmosphère et qu'une vive inquiétude a surgi devant l'augmentation des retombées radioactives. Les initiatives canadiennes se sont alors dirigées vers l'interdiction des essais d'armes nucléaires et vers l'étude des effets des radiations ionisantes[9].

D'un autre côté, la croisade contre le colonialisme soviétique qu'a menée le premier ministre Diefenbaker illustre bien la tendance idéaliste de la politique canadienne pendant cette période. C'est à l'Assemblée générale de 1960 que Diefenbaker s'est engagé vraiment dans cette croisade. À ce moment, 17 anciens territoires coloniaux qui venaient d'accéder à l'indépendance ont fait leur entrée aux Nations Unies. La question du colonialisme était en conséquence l'objet d'une grande partie des délibérations et, en particulier, d'une résolution sur l'octroi de l'indépendance aux peuples et aux pays coloniaux qui demeuraient encore nombreux. Pour leur part, les Soviétiques, par la bouche même de Khrouchtchev qui assistait à la session de l'Assemblée générale, utilisaient ces débats pour dénoncer les pays occidentaux. Diefenbaker, qui était aussi présent à New York, a répondu à Khrouchtchev en qualifiant la domination exercée par l'Union soviétique en Europe orientale comme une forme de colonialisme qu'il fallait supprimer.

Par la suite, le Canada a continué à attirer l'attention sur l'impérialisme soviétique et à soutenir que les principes énoncés dans la Charte de l'ONU et dans la résolution de 1960 devraient être d'application universelle. Ainsi, à l'Assemblée générale de 1962, le représentant canadien a attaqué durement l'URSS en rappelant l'expansion du régime colonial soviétique depuis 1939 et en formulant le vœu que l'ONU examine avec soin la situation régnant au sein de l'empire soviétique, particulièrement le déni des droits de l'homme et des libertés fondamentales[10].

En relation aux problèmes de colonialisme et de décolonisation, signalons encore que c'est en 1960 que l'ONU est appelée à intervenir au Congo et que le Canada a aussitôt accepté de prendre une part importante à la fois dans la force de maintien de la paix et dans les opérations d'assistance civile. La participation canadienne s'est maintenue pendant toute la durée de cette intervention, jusqu'en 1964.

Enfin, l'année 1960 fut également celle où Diefenbaker a proposé la création d'une banque alimentaire qui permettrait de distribuer des excédents alimentaires dans les régions qui en nécessiteraient le plus. Il a en effet invité les Nations Unies à s'unir pour contribuer à la solution à l'échelle mondiale du problème que posait l'alimentation de millions d'humains continuellement affamés. Rappelant que plusieurs pays avaient une production alimentaire insuffisante, il a soutenu qu'il fallait d'abord les nourrir aux périodes de disette et ensuite les aider à relever leur propre production. Il précisa toutefois qu'il incombait à l'ONU d'assumer cette tâche plutôt qu'aux pays possédant des excédents. C'est pourquoi il a proposé «la création d'une banque alimentaire qui assurerait la fourniture de ravitaillement aux États membres par l'intermédiaire des Nations Unies»[11]. L'Assemblée générale a finalement adopté une résolution demandant la création d'une telle banque. Cette dernière a été mise sur pied l'année suivante à titre d'essai, sous le nom de Programme alimentaire mondial (PAM). Le PAM est devenu un programme permanent le 1er janvier 1963 et, depuis cette date, il a presque toujours recueilli la plus large part des contributions[12] du Canada aux programmes d'assistance des Nations Unies.

L'accentuation de la tendance idéaliste notée pendant le gouvernement Diefenbaker semblait indiquer un renouveau de la politique canadienne envers les Nations Unies à la suite des désillusions exprimées au cours des années précédentes. Ce renouveau était sans doute amorcé par le grand succès remporté par Pearson lors du règlement de l'affaire de Suez en 1956 et il s'est poursuivi avec le nouveau gouvernement l'année suivante. Mais dès 1960, les Nations Unies subissaient d'importants changements en raison de l'arrivée massive de nouveaux États indépendants et de l'ampleur et de l'urgence de leurs besoins.

1963-1968: Un internationalisme formaliste

C'est dans ce contexte qu'a débuté la troisième période en 1963, alors que le Parti libéral formait de nouveau le gouvernement après un intermède conservateur. Cette fois, Pearson est premier ministre et il le demeurera jusqu'en 1968. Il a maintenu bien sûr les orientations qu'il avait tant contribué à imprimer à la politique étrangère. Mais cette période en fut une de transition parce que le rôle international que jouait le Canada est devenu de plus en plus difficile en raison des changements importants qui survenaient dans le monde. Sans compter qu'au même moment, le Canada connaissait des problèmes internes graves qui affectaient l'unité nationale tandis que les responsables de la politique étrangère canadienne faisaient face non seulement à un accroissement de l'ampleur et de l'intensité des demandes d'origine domestique, mais aussi à une prolifération des canaux d'expression de ces demandes[13]. Cette situation a conduit le Canada à développer ce que Thomas A. Hockin[14] a appelé une approche fédéraliste. Cette approche est une variante de la tendance volontariste et constitue une transposition au niveau international des tactiques de maintien ou de préservation de la viabilité de l'organisation et de courtage auxquelles Pearson avait alors recours pour traiter les problèmes internes du pays. Cependant, cela résultait en une sorte d'évasion dans des attitudes tactiques et dans des procédures qui faisait oublier ou laissait beaucoup d'ambiguïté autour des questions fondamentales comme les finalités de l'organisation. Aussi un sentiment d'insatisfaction envers la politique étrangère canadienne s'est-il progressivement développé.

Quant aux Nations Unies, la satisfaction des besoins exprimés par les nouveaux États indépendants généralement démunis les occupait à des tâches concrètes et pratiques qui cadraient bien avec les conceptions canadiennes. Mais d'autre part, «puisqu'ils [comptaient] parmi les membres les plus riches des Nations Unies, les Canadiens [développaient] une certaine nervosité face à l'exercice de la contrainte par les organes de l'ONU»[15] qui étaient dominés par une nouvelle majorité. La nervosité canadienne résultait également de la tendance manifestée par la nouvelle majorité à «politiser» les questions traitées par les organes «non politiques» des Nations Unies. Cette tendance se heurtait à la tendance inverse du Canada à réserver les questions politiques aux organes proprement politiques afin que les travaux des organes techniques ou fonctionnels se fassent dans les meilleures conditions. La théorie fonctionnaliste défendue par le Canada dès l'origine de l'ONU l'amenait en effet à valoriser les organes techniques plutôt que politiques, car c'était là que se trouvait la plus grande part des intérêts canadiens et que pouvaient être les mieux utilisées les capacités canadiennes.

Cependant, cette période s'est ouverte par une initiative qui concentrait l'attention sur un thème cher au Canada, celui des forces de maintien de la paix[16]. Dans son discours à l'Assemblée générale à l'automne 1963, Pearson a traité longuement de cette question et il a proposé de créer un petit groupe de planification composé d'experts militaires qui apporteraient l'assistance et le conseil dont le Secrétaire général avait besoin pour organiser des opérations de maintien de la paix d'urgence. Contribuant lui-même à la mise en œuvre de cette suggestion, le Canada a convoqué une rencontre internationale sur le sujet. Celle-ci s'est tenue à Ottawa en novembre 1964 et a réuni des experts militaires de 23 pays qui ont concentré leurs discussions sur les aspects techniques des opérations de maintien de la paix, les aspects politiques ayant été spécifiquement exclus. Au même moment, dans un livre blanc sur la défense, le gouvernement canadien soulignait la grande importance qu'il accordait au maintien de la paix et à l'intégration des politiques étrangère et de défense en incluant le maintien de la paix dans la liste des tâches assignées aux forces armées.

Entretemps, des hostilités armées ont éclaté entre les communautés grecque et turque de Chypre et le Conseil de sécurité a recommandé, en mars 1964, l'envoi d'une force de maintien de la paix sur l'île. Les négociations nécessaires à la mise sur pied de cette force se sont révélées particulièrement longues et difficiles. Le Canada s'est montré d'abord hésitant et a posé des conditions; la force devait contribuer à réaliser la paix et sa durée devait être limitée. De plus, le Canada voulait approuver le choix du médiateur chargé de trouver une solution. Cette hésitation et ces conditions furent associées au fait que pour la première fois, le rôle du Canada dans ces opérations soulevait des critiques au pays.

Néanmoins, le Canada a été le premier à répondre à l'invitation du Secrétaire général et il s'est engagé à payer les coûts de ses troupes pendant les trois premiers mois en raison de l'urgence de la situation. Aussitôt, Paul Martin s'est activé pour convaincre d'autres pays de contribuer à la force. Il semble bien que sans ces initiatives canadiennes, l'opération de Chypre n'aurait sans doute pas pu être lancée. Mais une fois déployée, elle ne paraît plus devoir s'arrêter, contrairement à la position défendue par le Canada. Comme le rappelait Pearson à la Chambre des communes trois ans plus tard, le Canada avait clairement établi que le but de la force envoyée à Chypre était de maintenir la paix pendant le déroulement des négociations politiques. En l'absence de telles négociations, la force perdait sa raison d'être. La force et le contingent canadiens n'avaient pas encore quitté Chypre en 1986 même si, de temps à autre, le Canada exprimait sa déception devant l'impasse des négociations et laissait planer la menace du retrait de son contingent[17].

Par ailleurs, la difficulté qu'a éprouvée l'ONU à organiser une force de maintien de la paix pour Chypre résultait des problèmes engendrés par les forces de paix existantes. Ces problèmes se sont manifestés concrètement au plan financier, mais ils étaient fondamentalement d'ordre constitutionnel. C'est en effet pour assurer le contrôle exclusif du Conseil de sécurité sur ces forces que l'URSS et la France refusaient de contribuer au financement de la FUNU et de l'ONUC[18]. Ce refus a conduit l'ONU à une crise financière, puis à une crise politique.

Le Canada s'est efforcé de trouver une solution à la crise, d'abord au sein du Groupe de travail des 21 établi à cette fin par l'Assemblée générale, puis au cours de la session spéciale de l'Assemblée générale de mai 1963 œuvrant sur la base d'un rapport du Groupe de travail. C'est à l'Assemblée générale de l'automne 1964 qu'a éclaté la crise politique, alors que l'URSS et la France se sont vu menacées par une application de l'article 19 de la Charte de l'ONU qui les priverait de leur droit de vote en raison du retard dans le paiement de leur contribution aux dépenses de l'Organisation. Le Canada, qui soutenait fortement les forces de paix et qui payait plus que sa part des coûts, a tenté d'amener les deux pays à contribuer aux dépenses sans provoquer de confrontation directe et de protéger l'autorité de l'Assemblée générale tout en respectant celle du Conseil de sécurité.

La crise politique s'est finalement dénouée et l'Assemblée générale a établi un nouveau comité, dit Comité des 33, ayant mandat d'entreprendre une étude d'ensemble des opérations de maintien de la paix. Le Canada a été désigné membre de ce comité et il y a participé activement tout en annonçant qu'il verserait une contribution spéciale de quatre millions de dollars dans le but de résoudre la crise financière. En dépit d'initiatives comme celles-ci, le Comité des 33 poursuit toujours ses travaux en 1986, sans être parvenu à des solutions acceptables au plus grand nombre.

L'enthousiasme canadien à l'égard des forces de maintien de la paix devait finalement se transformer en frustration en mai 1967. Le Secrétaire général de l'ONU a alors accepté, contrairement à l'avis du Canada, la demande de retrait de la force de paix du territoire égyptien formulée par Nasser le 17 mai. Ce dernier a ensuite dénoncé les «machinations» et les «parti pris» de Pearson et a exigé le retrait du contingent canadien dans les 48 heures. L'un des principaux rôles du Canada sur la scène internationale était ainsi remis en cause.

D'autres changements sont venus encore affecter le rôle du Canada pendant cette période[19]. Le premier se rapporte à la représentation de la Chine à l'ONU. Dans ce cas, le Canada s'est adapté rapidement en souhaitant la représentation de la Chine communiste au Conseil de sécurité et des «deux Chine» à l'Assemblée générale. Cette adaptation s'est manifestée en 1966 par l'abstention du Canada, pour la première fois en seize ans, lors du vote sur une résolution demandant de remplacer Taiwan par Pékin[20]. Les autres changements se sont situés principalement en Afrique et ont placé le Canada dans des situations difficiles au moment où il siégeait au Conseil de sécurité pendant les années 1967-1968.

La question du Sud-Ouest africain, maintenant désigné sous le nom de Namibie, a connu un développement important en 1966 alors que l'Assemblée générale a déclaré que le mandat de l'Afrique du Sud était terminé et que le Sud-Ouest africain relevait désormais directement de l'ONU. Le Canada a appuyé cette décision mais il s'est abstenu l'année suivante lorsque l'Assemblée générale a créé le Conseil des Nations Unies pour le Sud-Ouest africain, dont la tâche était d'administrer le territoire et d'assurer le retrait de l'Afrique du Sud. Refusant même d'être désigné membre de ce conseil, le Canada a soutenu que la tâche assignée au Conseil était irréalisable parce qu'elle ne reconnaissait pas la réalité d'une présence sud-africaine solidement ancrée dans le territoire. En prenant des dispositions comme celles-ci, le Canada est apparu aux Africains comme un État prêt à déplorer le racisme et le colonialisme au niveau des principes, mais plutôt disposé à s'abstenir quant vient le moment d'agir.

Le même type de problèmes surgit à propos de la Rhodésie, dont le gouvernement contrôlé par la minorité blanche du pays a déclaré unilatéralement son indépendance en novembre 1965 face au refus de la Grande-Bretagne d'accorder l'indépendance en l'absence d'un gouvernement par la majorité. Le Canada a condamné ce geste unilatéral et imposé à la Rhodésie certaines sanctions décidées dans le cadre du Commonwealth et recommandées par le Conseil de sécurité. Ce dernier a ensuite rendu les sanctions économiques obligatoires en 1966 et il les a élargies en 1968. Le Canada a cherché à se conformer à ces sanctions, mais il n'a pas appuyé les résolutions habituellement soumises à l'Assemblée générale au sujet de la situation politique et des sanctions.

La décolonisation soulève par ailleurs un problème plus fondamental et à plus long terme que la simple accession à l'indépendance. C'est celui du développement, particulièrement au plan économique, des nouveaux États. À cette fin, l'aide des pays très développés apparaît nécessaire. Sans atteindre la proportion de 1 % du produit national brut (PNB) que l'ONU a souvent suggérée, les montants que le Canada a versés à l'aide au développement se sont accrus considérablement au cours des années 60. De façon générale, les formes et le caractère de l'aide canadienne se sont diversifiés. L'assistance multilatérale s'est accrue, particulièrement par les programmes des Nations Unies, et elle se montait aux environs de 20 % du total en 1969. Au sein de la communauté internationale, le Canada était considéré comme l'un des plus fervents défenseurs des programmes d'aide multilatéraux. C'est sans doute pour cette raison que Lester B. Pearson, après sa retraite du gouvernement, a été appelé par la Banque internationale pour la reconstruction et le développement à présider une commission internationale d'étude des problèmes du développement[21].

Finalement, il faut signaler la conclusion dans le cadre de l'ONU de deux traités en matière de désarmement et de contrôle des armements. Activement engagé d'une part dans les négociations du traité de 1967 interdisant la mise en orbite d'armes de destruction massive et d'autre part dans celles du Traité de non-prolifération de 1968, le Canada y a adhéré dès leur adoption par les Nations Unies.

1968-1984: Un internationalisme réaliste

Lester B. Pearson s'est retiré en 1968 et Pierre E. Trudeau lui a succédé à la tête du Parti libéral et du gouvernement. Ce fut le début de la quatrième période parce que Trudeau, en réponse à une insatisfaction croissante envers la politique étrangère, a amorcé aussitôt une révision complète et approfondie de cette politique. La révision a abouti à la publication en 1970 d'un livre blanc en six fascicules, intitulé *Politique étrangère au service des Canadiens.* Le livre blanc a produit certains changements mais qui ne furent pas aussi considérables qu'on semblait le prévoir. On a parlé de l'accent nationaliste que Trudeau a donné à la politique étrangère en lui assignant les mêmes objectifs que la politique interne, mais avec mission de les réaliser dans le milieu international. En réalité, l'orientation internationaliste est demeurée alors que l'aspect volontariste simplement altruiste a diminué pour laisser une plus grande place aux intérêts nationaux. Ceux-ci d'ailleurs ont toujours été présents dans la politique étrangère qui les a constamment servis, et la plus grande place qui leur fut faite à ce moment-là n'était en quelque sorte qu'une place plus évidente. Cette mise en évidence était rendue d'autant plus nécessaire par le développement des relations internationales des provinces canadiennes que le Québec illustrait de façon spectaculaire.

Les changements qui ont affecté l'ONU depuis le début des années 60 ont graduellement provoqué, comme on l'a indiqué, un désenchantement des États occidentaux envers cette organisation. Pour le Canada en particulier, c'était une part importante de sa politique étrangère qui était remise en cause. Si le livre blanc de 1970 se situait dans ce courant[22], il n'en conservait pas moins le postulat d'un appui actif aux organisations internationales. Cet appui était cependant tempéré par une attitude plus réaliste et un souci plus marqué des intérêts nationaux. «L'adhésion aux organisations internationales, énonçait en effet le livre blanc, n'est pas une fin en soi, et le Canada devra toujours s'efforcer de vérifier leur utilité et leur efficacité[23].» Le livre blanc réservait par contre un fascicule complet aux Nations Unies dans lequel on indiquait la façon dont les objectifs assignés à la politique étrangère seraient poursuivis au sein de cette organisation.

Une analyse des objectifs énoncés par le gouvernement canadien dans une sélection de discours officiels entre 1968 et 1980 montre bien l'importance qu'ont continué à revêtir les Nations Unies pour le Canada. L'ONU est demeurée d'abord un lieu privilégié d'exercice de la diplomatie canadienne. Quand on comptabilise en effet les lieux où furent exprimés les objectifs relevés, on observe que 56,5 % le furent au Canada, 23,3 % à l'ONU et les autres en des endroits très divers. Deuxièmement, l'ONU a encore été l'objet d'une attention importante. Si l'on considère les cibles visées par les objectifs, on découvre que le plus grand nombre est indéterminé

(27,3 %) et que parmi les autres, l'ONU se situe au premier rang (10,7 %). Enfin, quand on classe les objectifs énoncés par catégorie, on retrouve au premier rang (11,2 %) la catégorie «renforcer les organisations internationales en matière de paix et de sécurité», et au sixième rang (4,9 %), la catégorie «renforcer les organisations internationales d'aide au développement»[24].

Conservant de l'importance pour le Canada mais largement transformée, l'ONU rendait nécessaires des ajustements dans la politique canadienne. C'est ce à quoi s'est attaché le gouvernement Trudeau en cherchant à réduire l'accent mis sur les rôles d'intermédiaire *(helpful fixer)* et de gardien de la paix et à œuvrer davantage au contrôle des armements et à l'aide au développement. Se fondant sur plusieurs indices, Peyton V. Lyon et Brian W. Tomlin soutiennent cependant que, en dépit d'une baisse évidente de l'enthousiasme canadien pour les Nations Unies, le Canada est demeuré l'un des défenseurs les plus consciencieux de l'ONU et de ses agences. Le nombre considérable de résolutions parrainées par le Canada témoigne en particulier de son intérêt constant pour l'activité politique de l'Assemblée générale[25]. Les conditions d'exercice du rôle de médiateur dans la situation nouvelle de la fin des années 60 et des années 70 sont cependant bien illustrées par les problèmes de l'Afrique australe[26].

Si la position du Canada à l'égard de la Rhodésie est apparue assez ferme et assez claire particulièrement à partir de 1975, les choses ne furent pas aussi simples à propos de l'Afrique du Sud et de la Namibie (ancien Sud-Ouest africain). Comme le montrait bien le livre blanc de 1970 et surtout le «livre noir» qui lui donna la réplique, il n'était pas facile de «concilier les objectifs du Canada en Afrique australe»[27]. Le commerce canadien avec l'Afrique du Sud et les investissements canadiens dans ce pays ont été et sont demeurés considérables. Ils rendaient en conséquence très ambiguës les positions canadiennes condamnant le racisme et appuyant la décolonisation de la Namibie.

Le Canada a l'habitude de respecter les résolutions du Conseil de sécurité et il a mis l'embargo sur l'exportation de matériel militaire et de pièces détachées vers l'Afrique du Sud. Mais en 1974 et par la suite, il s'est opposé à la tentative d'exclure l'Afrique du Sud de l'ONU et même à sa suspension, au nom du principe de l'universalité de l'ONU qu'il a toujours défendu[28] et en vue de maintenir la communication en situation de conflit.

Par ailleurs, alors qu'il siégeait au Conseil de sécurité en 1977-1978, le Canada a été amené à s'engager davantage dans la recherche d'une solution à ces problèmes. Face à une offensive des pays africains du Conseil de sécurité au début de 1977 relativement à l'Afrique australe, les membres occidentaux du Conseil (États-Unis, Grande-Bretagne, France, République fédérale d'Allemagne et Canada) se sont réunis au siège de la mission canadienne afin de se concerter. Cette concertation a abouti en novembre 1977 à l'approbation unanime par le Conseil d'un embargo obligatoire sur les armes à destination de l'Afrique du Sud. C'était la première fois de son histoire que l'ONU décidait de telles sanctions contre l'un de ses membres[29]. Pour sa part, en décembre 1977, le gouvernement canadien annonçait le retrait d'Afrique du Sud de ses représentants commerciaux ainsi que la suspension de l'aide à l'exportation. Si l'objectif de ces mesures n'était pas de décourager le commerce avec l'Afrique du Sud mais seulement d'en cesser la promotion par le gouvernement, elles avaient au moins l'avantage de mettre fin à la double politique du discours et de l'action.

C'est encore l'Afrique du Sud que met en cause la décolonisation de la Namibie. Là aussi la position canadienne a évolué lentement et difficilement. Depuis la déclaration de l'Assemblée générale en 1966 à l'effet que le mandat de l'Afrique du Sud était terminé et que la Namibie relevait désormais directement de l'ONU[30], le Canada a tenté de donner suite aux résolutions de l'Assemblée générale, mais dans la mesure où il jugeait qu'il s'agissait de tentatives réalistes de solution au problème. Il a rejeté en particulier les appels à la lutte armée et aux mesures de coercition prévues au chapitre VII de la Charte de l'ONU.

Un nouveau pas a été franchi en juillet 1971 lorsque, conformément à une résolution du Conseil de sécurité de l'année précédente, le Canada a déclaré à l'Afrique du Sud qu'il ne reconnaissait pas son autorité en Namibie. Et en 1977, dans un deuxième volet de leur concertation, les cinq membres occidentaux du Conseil de sécurité ont décidé d'utiliser leur influence de principaux partenaires commerciaux de l'Afrique du Sud pour tenter de persuader le gouvernement sud-africain d'accepter un plan conforme aux directives établies par le Conseil de sécurité, qui permettrait la tenue à brève échéance d'élections libres en Namibie en vue de l'indépendance. Pour mener les négociations à ce sujet, les Cinq ont formé un Groupe de contact constitué des représentants adjoints des cinq délégations. Le Groupe de contact a progressé d'espoirs en déceptions pendant les deux années suivant sa constitution. Le Canada en est demeuré membre après la fin de son mandat au Conseil de sécurité. En 1986, la composition et le bilan du Groupe de contact n'avaient pas changé!

Comme pour le rôle de médiateur, l'évolution de la situation internationale et celle de l'ONU semblaient peu favorables au rôle de gardien de la paix au début des années 70. Le livre blanc le reconnaissait clairement en observant que les grandes puissances avaient tendance à traiter directement l'une avec l'autre pour contrôler les conflits et que le genre de conflit auquel il fallait de plus en plus s'attendre ne se prêterait pas facilement à l'intervention des Nations Unies[31]. De plus, il apparaissait que les pays du tiers monde accepteraient moins facilement qu'auparavant la présence sur leur territoire de troupes provenant de pays blancs, riches et alignés. Enfin, le gouvernement canadien lui-même posait des conditions à sa participation à des forces de maintien de la paix, particulièrement depuis la mésaventure de la FUNU en 1967[32]: la force devait contribuer au règlement du conflit; elle devait être responsable devant une autorité politique ayant le pouvoir d'en superviser le mandat; elle devait avoir un mandat clair; elle devait être acceptée par les parties au conflit; et elle devait être financée d'une façon claire et équitable. Tirant la conclusion qui semblait s'imposer, le livre blanc sur *La défense dans les années 70,* publié en 1971, plaçait le maintien de la paix en quatrième et dernière position parmi les tâches assignées aux Forces canadiennes[33]. Par rapport au livre blanc sur la défense de 1964[34], ce changement est apparu comme une réduction de l'importance du maintien de la paix et comme une illustration du nouveau classement des priorités nationales.

En pratique, le maintien de la paix a continué à être une activité importante pour le Canada. Ce dernier a maintenu ses troupes à Chypre malgré ce qu'il avait affirmé. Il a participé à la FUNU II, qui a opéré de 1973 à 1979 et à la FNUOD, qui a été installée en 1974 au Golan. Il a également contribué à la FINUL, œuvrant au Liban mais, dans ce cas-ci, pour une courte période de six mois en 1978. Le Canada est ainsi demeuré le plus gros contributeur de troupes aux opérations de maintien de la paix. Le dernier discours du Trône du gouvernement dirigé par Pierre E. Trudeau annonçait enfin en décembre 1983 une «attention renouvelée» à la contribution canadienne aux opérations de maintien de la paix des Nations Unies[35].

Le maintien de la paix ne cesse donc pas d'être privilégié par le Canada. Bien que exercé d'une façon plus prudente et plus réaliste qu'auparavant, ce rôle semble encore avantageux et compense peut-être partiellement celui de médiateur. En effet, «le Canada considère depuis toujours que la participation aux opérations de maintien de la paix des Nations Unies présuppose une attitude impartiale à l'égard des parties aux conflits et que le degré d'objectivité nécessaire à cette fin rend impossible une participation active aux efforts de règlement»[36].

À la différence des domaines précédents, le gouvernement Trudeau entendait être plus actif en matière de désarmement[37]. Le livre blanc de 1970 affirmait d'ailleurs la haute priorité que le Canada devait assigner aux efforts pour freiner la course aux armements. Il précisait aussi que «le Canada ne devrait pas se contenter de laisser aux grandes puissances nucléaires l'exclusivité de déterminer le rythme du progrès en matière de contrôle des armements». Cette «approche activiste» a effectivement caractérisé cette période, comme ce fut le cas pendant celle du gouvernement Diefenbaker[38].

Les efforts canadiens ont porté prioritairement sur la limitation et la réduction des armes nucléaires. De manière spécifique, le Canada s'est intéressé à l'interdiction totale de tous les essais d'armes nucléaires. À cette fin, il a apporté une contribution importante à la solution technique du problème de la vérification reliée aux essais souterrains grâce aux travaux de ses séismologues. Il a également cherché à renforcer et à étayer le système existant de non-prolifération nucléaire. Sa contribution en cette matière a aussi été importante parce qu'il est lui-même un des principaux producteurs et exportateurs de matériaux et d'équipement nucléaires. Les conditions dont il a assorti ses ventes d'uranium et de réacteurs CANDU à des fins de production d'électricité sont parmi les plus strictes qui soient et lui ont fait perdre certains avantages commerciaux. L'orientation internationaliste et volontariste l'a emporté ici sur l'intérêt national.

Cette tendance s'est manifestée encore lors des deux sessions spéciales de l'Assemblée générale sur le désarmement en 1978 et 1982. Le premier ministre Trudeau, qui avait jusque-là refusé d'apparaître à la tribune des Nations Unies, s'y est présenté pour la première fois au cours de la première session spéciale. Il a proposé une stratégie d'asphyxie destinée à couper la course aux armements de «tout ce qui l'alimente». De nouveau présent au moment de la seconde session spéciale, il a réitéré sa stratégie d'asphyxie en y ajoutant un volet de stabilisation des armements par la réduction des armements nucléaires existants et l'établissement d'un équilibre à des niveaux moins élevés. Les diplomates canadiens furent aussi actifs lors de ces sessions puisque l'un des trois groupes de concertation, qui étaient réunis au moment de la première session spéciale, et au Comité préparatoire de la deuxième session spéciale, était désigné «Groupe Barton». Ce groupe, réunissant des pays occidentaux et quelques autres, a emprunté le nom de William Barton, alors représentant permanent du Canada aux Nations Unies, qui fut le premier à le convoquer.

Entretemps, peu après la première session spéciale, le gouvernement canadien assumerait de nouveau le poste de conseiller en matière de désarmement et de contrôle des armements, qui avait existé dans le gouvernement Diefenbaker.

En 1980, ce poste se transformait en un poste permanent d'ambassadeur pour le désarmement.

Enfin, indice ultime de l'intérêt particulier manifesté par Pierre E. Trudeau à l'égard du désarmement, celui-ci entreprenait au cours des derniers mois dans sa fonction de premier ministre une mission de paix à travers le monde. Cette mission de paix visait spécifiquement le rétablissement du dialogue Est-Ouest et la limitation des armements nucléaires en général. Conduite à l'automne 1983 et à l'hiver 1984, la mission de paix de Pierre E. Trudeau comportait une rencontre avec le Secrétaire général de l'ONU dont il sollicitait aussi l'assistance[39].

De même que le désarmement, l'aide au développement devait être l'objet d'une attention privilégiée de la part du gouvernement Trudeau[40]. C'était un fascicule complet qui lui était consacré dans le livre blanc de 1970 et c'était dans ce domaine, soutient Peter Dobell, que le gouvernement Trudeau avait choisi de faire son principal effort international[41]. Au cours de cette période, les montants de l'aide publique au développement n'ont pas augmenté au rythme annoncé, et encore en 1980, à la onzième session extraordinaire de l'Assemblée générale, le Canada affirmait de nouveau vouloir accroître son aide à 0,5 % du PNB dans un effort pour atteindre l'objectif de 0,7 % d'ici la fin de la décennie.

D'autre part, la proportion de l'aide multilatérale, incluant les institutions financières et l'aide alimentaire et dont la plus grande part va aux Nations Unies, représentait 41 % du total en 1980-1981, soit le double de ce qu'elle était en 1969. Mais comme les bénéficiaires des fonds versés à des programmes multilatéraux ne sont pas tenus de les dépenser au Canada, les efforts visant à les accroître se heurtent en général à une vive opposition politique intérieure, surtout en période de récession économique. Et au sein même des Nations Unies, le Canada, comme les autres pays industrialisés, préfère généralement concentrer son aide multilatérale au développement à la Banque mondiale où les donneurs sont en mesure d'exercer un plus grand contrôle sur les déboursements que ce n'est le cas au PNUD[42].

Au début des années 70, mécontents des piètres résultats obtenus au moyen des programmes d'assistance, les pays du tiers monde ont commencé à revendiquer la refonte complète du système économique international afin de mieux l'adapter à leurs besoins. Ces nouvelles revendications sont désignées sous l'expression «nouvel ordre économique international» (NOEI), et elles ont été l'objet entre autres des sixième et septième sessions extraordinaires de l'Assemblée générale en 1974 et 1975. En 1974, le gouvernement canadien annonça que sa contribution à l'aide au développement ne se limiterait pas à une augmentation du volume, mais que des mesures touchant les relations économiques du Canada avec les pays en voie de développement seraient réexaminées. Ces mesures ont été précisées dans un document publié en 1975 sous le titre *Canada – Stratégie de coopération au développement international 1975-1980.*

Cependant, les réalisations ne furent pas conformes aux déclarations. L'aide publique au développement a diminué par rapport au PNB. La protection de certaines industries canadiennes a conduit à la réduction de l'accès au marché canadien de produits manufacturés des pays en développement. La réponse du Canada (comme celle d'autres pays développés) à certaines réformes souhaitées, tel le programme intégré des produits de base mis au point par la CNUCED[43], a démontré peu d'empressement. En somme, comme l'écrivait James P. Sewell, la réponse du Canada au NOEI peut être qualifiée de prudente, de lente, de distraite[44].

Les négociations sur le droit de la mer offrent une autre illustration de la politique canadienne relative au NOEI. L'intérêt du Canada en cette matière a été avivé à la fin des années 60 par certaines menaces aux intérêts économiques et environnementaux canadiens dans les régions côtières, et en particulier dans l'Arctique. Pour y faire face, le Canada a étendu unilatéralement en 1970 la zone de contrôle de la pollution dans l'Arctique à 100 milles et, afin de se soustraire à une contestation juridique, il a suspendu son acceptation de la juridiction de la Cour internationale de justice pour les différends relatifs à la pollution des côtes. En 1977, il a de nouveau unilatéralement élargi sa zone de contrôle des pêches à 200 milles.

Profitant d'une convergence d'intérêts sur plusieurs questions importantes avec d'autres pays côtiers et des pays en développement, le Canada a joué un rôle actif à la Troisième Conférence des Nations Unies sur le droit de la mer qui s'est tenue de 1973 à 1982[45]. Ses objectifs étaient de conférer une légitimité internationale à ses gestes unilatéraux et de protéger ses intérêts environnementaux et économiques[46].

Finalement, le Canada a obtenu un très grand succès dans la réalisation de ses objectifs[47]. Mais, comme le notent Peyton V. Lyon et Brian W. Tomlin[48], l'influence exceptionnelle du Canada dans les négociations sur le droit de la mer a favorisé les demandes des pays riches aux dépens des pays pauvres. Ces négociations peuvent être considérées comme la plus grande opération d'accaparement de territoire de l'histoire, avec le Canada en tête. Cela est difficile à concilier avec les déclarations canadiennes favorables à un nouvel ordre économique international et à un partage plus équitable des ressources dans la perspective d'un «patrimoine commun de l'humanité». L'intérêt national semble bien dominer ici la tendance internationaliste idéaliste.

Le gouvernement Trudeau parut revenir à son point de départ en ce qui concerne les organisations internationales lorsque le ministre des Affaires extérieures a annoncé, en janvier 1981, «une nouvelle politique de bilatéralisme pour le Canada»[49] dont l'objet apparent était d'accroître l'importance du bilatéralisme par rapport au multilatéralisme qui avait particulièrement marqué la politique étrangère jusqu'alors. Notant le besoin pour le Canada de définir des priorités et de concentrer ses ressources, l'ambassadeur canadien aux Nations Unies commentait ainsi la nouvelle politique: «La nécessité d'établir un dialogue plus intime avec ces États clés [que vise la politique de bilatéralisme] et, grâce à eux, d'exercer une plus grande influence sur les groupements régionaux et internationaux dont ils sont membres, illustre la nette complémentarité qui existe entre la promotion de nos intérêts sur les plans bilatéral et multilatéral[50].» Était-ce la fin d'un certain idéalisme altruiste ou une manifestation de la place plus évidente faite aux intérêts nationaux? La seconde hypothèse semble confirmée par la réorganisation administrative qui fut annoncée en janvier 1982 et qui visait à amener le ministre des Affaires extérieures à privilégier les objectifs commerciaux dans la conduite de la politique étrangère canadienne[51]. Toutefois, ces développements n'ont pas empêché le premier ministre Trudeau, quelques mois plus tard (juin 1982), de reprendre ses efforts en vue du contrôle des armements et du désarmement[52].

Dans l'une de ses dernières déclarations, en mars 1984, le gouvernement Trudeau confirmait le soutien actif du Canada au système des Nations Unies au moment où le multilatéralisme traversait une crise importante. Par la voix du Secrétaire d'État aux Affaires extérieures, il rappelait certains avantages importants qu'en retirait le Canada avant de noter les «sources de désillusion» les plus évidentes que sont devenus l'UNESCO et le Conseil de sécurité. Affirmant la nécessité de renforcer de manière pratique les institutions existantes, le Secrétaire d'État aux Affaires extérieures réclamait d'un côté l'amélioration des relations entre les superpuissances dans le cadre de rencontres privées aux Nations Unies et, de l'autre, une nouvelle maturité à la fois de la part des pays du tiers monde en reconnaissant et acceptant la responsabilité qui va de pair avec leur supériorité numérique et de la part des pays développés, qui fournissent la plus grande partie des fonds, en admettant les objectifs légitimes de la majorité[53].

ÉPILOGUE: LE GOUVERNEMENT MULRONEY

Le Parti libéral perdait les élections de septembre 1984 alors que le Parti conservateur formait le gouvernement sous la direction de Brian Mulroney. Ce gouvernement entra en fonction au moment où la crise du multilatéralisme était très forte. Dans le cas des Nations Unies, l'Organisation était très peu utilisée, elle se trouvait plutôt paralysée et les États-Unis considéraient l'option du retrait, option qu'ils choisirent par ailleurs relativement à l'UNESCO.

Dans son premier grand discours de politique étrangère, le Secrétaire d'État aux Affaires extérieures a affirmé devant l'Assemblée générale des Nations Unies la continuité des objectifs poursuivis par le Canada. Il a même ajouté que son gouvernement jouerait un rôle plus actif que les précédents au sein de l'ONU et de ses institutions. Prônant le renforcement des Nations Unies, il a réclamé en particulier une plus grande marge d'initiative et d'indépendance pour le Secrétaire général et une dépolitisation des débats[54]. Quelques semaines plus tard, le gouvernement annonçait une révision de la politique étrangère du Canada, révision qui était présentée non pas comme une remise en cause de questions fondamentales comme la participation à l'ONU, mais comme un exercice concentré sur les questions économiques. Le gouvernement indiquait en même temps son intention de privilégier les relations avec les États-Unis. Enfin, au terme de la session d'automne de l'Assemblée générale, le Canada estimait qu'il était temps «de lancer une campagne concertée pour la défense et le renforcement des Nations Unies» à l'occasion du quarantième anniversaire de l'Organisation[55].

En mai 1985, le gouvernement publiait un livre vert qui devait servir de base au processus de révision de la politique étrangère. Le livre vert visait à illustrer les importants changements survenus dans le monde et à soulever des questions. Parmi ces changements, il notait une crise de confiance dans les institutions internationales en raison principalement de difficultés d'adaptation au changement, de la rivalité entre les superpuissances, de l'apparition de nouveaux États et de leurs immenses besoins ainsi que de la politisation des questions économiques et sociales, notamment à l'UNESCO. Se servant de l'UNESCO comme d'un cas type, le livre vert ouvrait explicitement l'option entre la réforme et le retrait[56]. Ces réflexions créèrent de l'incertitude malgré les déclarations antérieures parce que le gouvernement a fait du rapprochement avec les États-Unis la première priorité de sa politique étrangère à un moment où ceux-ci n'ont jamais été aussi hostiles envers les Nations Unies.

Par contre, à la fin de juin 1985, le Canada se joignait à l'Argentine, l'Autriche, la Jordanie, la Malaisie, le Sénégal, la Suède et la Tanzanie pour lancer, à l'occasion du quarantième anniversaire de la signature de la Charte des Nations Unies, un appel commun à renforcer l'Organisation[57]. Mais traitant elle aussi essentiellement de réformes, la ministre des Relations extérieures affirmait d'abord devant la Conférence générale de l'UNESCO en octobre 1985 l'intention du Canada de revoir sa position au sein de l'Organisation. Les résultats de la Conférence ayant été conformes aux vœux du Canada, la ministre indiquait ensuite en novembre que le Canada resterait au sein de l'UNESCO pour y poursuivre les réformes souhaitées[58]. Cette décision eut pour effet de rendre clair un aspect important de la politique étrangère du nouveau gouvernement qui, au cours de sa première année en fonction, apparaissait hésitant dans une situation internationale particulièrement difficile pour les Nations Unies. La révision en cours de la politique étrangère confirmera probablement ces orientations si la crise du multilatéralisme se résorbe.

Déterminants et paramètres

De Saint-Laurent et Pearson à Trudeau, on a observé une constante, l'internationalisme multilatéral, qui apparaît comme une caractéristique principale de la politique étrangère canadienne. Cet internationalisme s'explique conjoncturellement par la décision de renoncer à l'isolationnalisme antérieur, prise à la fin de la Deuxième Guerre mondiale, et par la présence à des postes clés de deux internationalistes convaincus, Louis Saint-Laurent et Lester B. Pearson. Le choix du multilatéralisme tient essentiellement au fait que le Canada se trouve, au plan international, dans la situation d'un pays sans région. Récemment indépendant d'une Grande-Bretagne dont l'influence est encore sensible, le Canada émerge de la guerre avec un voisin unique, les États-Unis, qui a le statut de principale puissance mondiale. La recherche d'une plus grande indépendance de la Grande-Bretagne et la crainte du continentalisme ont ouvert la voie du multilatéralisme qui offrait les meilleures perspectives d'une politique étrangère distincte. Ces facteurs n'ont pas changé, ni leur effet sur la politique étrangère canadienne[59].

Une communauté de valeurs a de plus facilité l'orientation multilatérale du Canada, du moins en ce qui concerne les organisations internationales qui présentaient un intérêt particulier pour lui. La petite élite ayant la responsabilité de la politique canadienne, explique Garth Stevenson, était dès le début prédisposée par idéologie et antécédents à apprécier les Nations Unies que l'on considérait assez justement comme une expression concrète du libéralisme anglo-américain et de la prédominance anglo-américaine dans les affaires mondiales. Aussi a-t-on posé qu'il y avait conformité entre les objectifs du Canada et ceux attribués à l'ONU, qui, par définition, étaient ceux de l'humanité en général[60]. Si cette conformité a débouché parfois sur un certain idéalisme, elle a amené les dirigeants canadiens à assimiler le plus souvent les intérêts du Canada et ceux de l'humanité sous le couvert du fonctionnalisme[61].

La poursuite des intérêts canadiens dans un cadre multilatéral a reposé dès l'origine sur la constatation que le Canada y disposait de certains avantages reliés à ses antécédents, son statut, ses capacités et sa réputation. L'ambassadeur canadien aux Nations Unies décrivait en 1981 ces atouts de la façon suivante: «L'influence que nous pouvons exercer est fonction de nos positions multilatérales et bilatérales sur les questions politiques et économiques, de l'orientation et des opérations de notre programme d'aide, de la personnalité, des intérêts et de la réputation de nos dirigeants politiques ainsi que de la compétence de nos représentants. Et l'Organisation des Nations Unies est l'instance où ces facteurs et ces interrelations ont le plus d'importance[62]. »

Les intérêts canadiens en cause ont pris des formes très diverses au cours des années, comme l'ont illustré les pages précédentes. Ils se résument dans la poursuite d'une politique étrangère distincte. Sans l'ONU, l'OTAN ou le Commonwealth, soutient John W. Holmes, «un pays comme le Canada se retrouverait sans grand pouvoir sur son destin». Il affirme même à propos des Nations Unies que le Canada a trouvé là un but dans la vie[63]. Le Canada y a sûrement recherché un statut, une image et un cadre dans lesquels il se sentirait moins isolé et où il pourrait trouver des appuis sur les questions affectant ses intérêts.

Cela s'est traduit dans un comportement marqué par le pragmatisme plutôt que par une approche doctrinaire. Cette caractéristique émane de la culture politique canadienne qui, autant en politique interne qu'en politique étrangère, favorise les compromis pragmatiques de préférence à des solutions imposées. Aussi le comportement habituel du Canada dans les organisations internationales a-t-il été de réagir utilement aux initiatives des autres et non pas de prendre lui-même les devants. La revue de la politique étrangère canadienne conduite par le gouvernement Trudeau s'est révélée critique de cette tendance «réactive», mais cette dernière avait sans doute facilité l'adaptation au changement. Étroitement associé au pragmatisme se trouve également le fonctionnalisme dont le Canada s'est fait le champion précoce et assidu. Excellent couvert des intérêts canadiens, le fonctionnalisme a encore orienté les activités du Canada vers les secteurs où se situaient ses intérêts et où ses capacités lui offraient les meilleures possibilités d'action. Les pages précédentes ont apporté des exemples de ces secteurs et des institutions spécialisées ainsi privilégiées[64].

D'autre part, «c'est notre image en tant que bon citoyen international, écrit John W. Holmes, plutôt que les obligations formelles de notre adhésion qui, règle générale, gouverne nos actions à l'ONU». Cette image a conduit le gouvernement canadien, particulièrement sous la direction de Pearson, à donner souvent la priorité à la préservation des institutions aux dépens d'autres considérations. C'est ce que Thomas A. Hockin a appelé une approche fédéraliste. Trudeau lui-même s'est préoccupé de la bonne image du Canada en concevant ce dernier, selon l'expression de Michael Tucker, comme un État mentor qui prend des initiatives au nom de la communauté mondiale[65].

Qu'ont apporté en fin de compte ces 40 années de participation aux institutions des Nations Unies? En deux mots, elles ont produit des bénéfices nettement supérieurs aux coûts assumés. Les résultats d'une enquête menée en 1975 par Peyton V. Lyon et Brian W. Tomlin révèlent que 87 % des responsables canadiens de la politique étrangère et 94 % de l'élite étrangère (non canadienne) interrogés s'accordent pour dire que l'activité du Canada dans les affaires mondiales se distingue par ses efforts pour soutenir les organisations internationales[66]. D'autre part, une série d'études faites sous la direction de Robert Cox et Harold Jacobson et touchant plusieurs institutions spécialisées des Nations Unies a montré que le Canada avait eu une plus grande influence dans diverses organisations internationales qu'en dehors de celles-ci[67]. Ces études venaient d'ailleurs confirmer une étude antérieure de Chadwick Alger, axée sur l'Assemblée générale et sur un cas limité[68].

Enfin, comme le note bien James P. Sewell, la participation du Canada aux organisations internationales s'est caractérisée à différents moments par la prédominance de soucis opposés. Pendant que se formaient les organisations internationales, les Canadiens se sont inquiétés de ce que trop peu pourrait être demandé de leur pays et de ce qu'une trop petite place pourrait lui être réservée dans ces organismes. À d'autres moments, ils se sont inquiétés de ce que l'on pourrait requérir trop de leur pays. Ce souci a prédominé dans les années 60 alors que l'influence canadienne s'est amoindrie en raison de la remontée de l'Europe, de la multitude de nouvelles adhésions aux Nations Unies et de la dépréciation des sièges des conseils exécutifs par la large expansion de leur nombre[69]. Dans les années 80, ce souci apparaît de nouveau très présent alors que certains auteurs disent du Canada qu'il est devenu une puissance principale[70].

NOTES

1. Un aperçu des orientations du nouveau gouvernement formé par le Parti conservateur en 1984 servira d'épilogue à cette première partie. Par contre, il ne sera pas traité de façon particulière du très bref gouvernement conservateur qui a été en fonction de juin 1979 à février 1980.

2. Cité dans Frederic H. Soward et Edgar McInnis, *Canada and the United Nations*, New York, Manhattan Publishing Co., 1956, p. 101.

3. *Ibidem*, p. 101-113.

4. *Ibidem*, p. 114-123.

5. *Ibidem*, p. 124-136.

6. *Ibidem*, p. 186.

7. Le Canada a toujours été réservé sur ces questions, au début par manque d'intérêt et par méfiance, et par la suite pour des raisons constitutionnelles. Toutefois, il a adhéré en 1976, après consultation des provinces, aux deux pactes et au Protocole facultatif sur les droits de l'homme mis au point par les Nations Unies et entrés en vigueur en 1976.

8. Anthony J. Miller, *Functionalism and Foreign Policy*, An Analysis of Canadian Voting Behaviour in the General Assembly of the United Nations, 1946-1966, McGill University, thèse de doctorat, 1971, p. 189 et 241.

9. Voir la publication du ministère des Affaires extérieures, intitulée *Le Canada et les Nations Unies*, pour les années 1960 à 1962. Pour une perspective critique de l'initiative canadienne relative aux radiations, voir Peter C. Dobell, *Canada's Search for New Roles*, Toronto, Oxford University Press, 1972, p. 144.

10. *Ibidem*, et Peyton V. Lyon, *The Policy Question. A Critical Appraisal of Canada's Role in World Affairs*, Toronto, McClelland and Stewart, 1963, p. 116.

11. Canada, ministère des Affaires extérieures, *Le Canada et les Nations Unies 1960*, Ottawa, Imprimeur de la Reine, 1962, p. 39.

12. Les contributions au PAM comprennent les apports en espèces et en nature. Voir Canada, ministère des Affaires extérieures, *Apport financier du Canada aux Nations Unies*, Ottawa, ministère des Approvisionnements et Services, 1979 (Documents, n° 21).

13. Cette période marque le début d'un long et difficile processus de révision constitutionnelle. À propos des demandes d'origine domestique, voir Denis Stairs, «Publics and Policy-Makers: the Domestic Environment of Canada's Foreign Policy Community», *International Journal*, 26(1), hiver 1970-1971, p. 221-248.

14. Thomas A. Hockin *et al.*, *The Canadian Condominium*, Domestic Issues and External Policy, Toronto, McClelland and Stewart, 1972, p. 141, et «Federalist Style in International Politics», *An Independent Foreign Policy for Canada?*, éd. par Stephen Clarkson, Toronto, McClelland and Stewart, 1968, p. 119-129.

15. John W. Holmes, «Les institutions internationales et la politique extérieure», *Études internationales*, vol. 1, n° 2, juin 1970, p. 29.

16. Sur les aspects de la question des forces de maintien de la paix abordés ici, voir en particulier Alastair Taylor, David Cox et J.L. Granatstein, *Peacekeeping. International Challenge and Canadian Response*, Toronto, The Canadian Institute of International Affairs, 1968, 211 p., et la *Canadian Annual Review of Politics and Public Affairs*, publiée sous la direction de John Saywell, University of Toronto Press.

17. Voir, par exemple, *Canadian Annual Review of Politics and Public Affairs 1983*, éditée par R.B. Byers, Toronto, University of Toronto Press, 1985, p. 181.

18. Force d'urgence des Nations Unies (au Moyen-Orient), et Opération des Nations Unies au Congo.

19. Voir la *Canadian Annual Review of Politics and Public Affairs* publiée sous la direction de John Saywell, University of Toronto Press, et Canada, ministère des Affaires extérieures, *Canada et Nations Unies 1945-1975*, Ottawa, ministère des Approvisionnements et Services, 1976.

20. À la suite de la reconnaissance de la République populaire de Chine en 1970, le Canada a voté en faveur de l'attribution du siège de la Chine à Pékin.

21. Lester B. Pearson, *Partners in Development: Report of the Commission on International Development*, New York, Praeger, 1969.

22. Voir, par exemple, Margaret Doxey, «Canada's International Connections: the Canadian Foreign Policy Review in Review», *The Year Book of World Affairs*, 1978, p. 43-63.

23. *Politique étrangère au service des Canadiens*, fascicule général, p. 29.

24. *Les politiques étrangères régionales du Canada: éléments et matériaux*, sous la direction de Gérard Hervouet, Québec, Centre québécois de relations internationales et Presses de l'Université Laval, 1983, p. 23-50. Les discours analysés sont ceux de la série *Déclarations et Discours*, publiée par le ministère des Affaires extérieures.

25. Peyton V. Lyon et Brian W. Tomlin, *Canada as an International Actor*, Toronto, Macmillan of Canada, Canadian Controversies Series, 1979, p. 169. Voir aussi Peyton V. Lyon, «Le Canada aux Nations Unies», *Perspectives internationales*, nᵒˢ 1-2, 1985, p. 42-52.

26. Voir sur cette question: Michael Tucker, *Canadian Foreign Policy Contemporary Issues and Themes*, Toronto, McGraw-Hill Ryerson, 1980, p. 113-116; W.M. Dobell, «United Nations: Sea Law, Peacekeeping and Southern Africa», *International Journal*, 33(2), printemps 1978, p. 420-423; W.H. Barton, «Un mandat au Conseil de sécurité», *Perspectives internationales*, mai-juin-juillet-août 1979, p. 13-14; Canada, ministère des Affaires extérieures, *Canada et Nations Unies 1945-1975*, Ottawa, ministère des Approvisionnements et Services, 1976, p. 96-107.

27. *Politique étrangère au service des Canadiens*, fascicule sur les Nations Unies, p. 17-20. Garth Legge *et al.*, «The Black Paper: an Alternative Policy for Canada Towards Southern Africa», *Behind the Headlines*, vol. 30, nᵒˢ 1-2, septembre 1970, 18 p.

28. La défense de ce principe s'est manifestée d'une manière particulièrement éclatante en 1955 lorsqu'une initiative canadienne mit fin à une impasse qui durait depuis quelques années et que seize nouveaux membres furent admis à l'ONU (Voir Robert W. Reford, «Le Canada et les Nations Unies», *Le Canada et le Québec sur la scène internationale*, sous la direction de Paul Painchaud, Québec et Montréal, Centre québécois de relations internationales et Presses de l'Université du Québec, 1979, p. 427-430.

29. Les premières sanctions obligatoires furent décidées contre la Rhodésie en 1966, mais celle-ci n'était pas membre de l'ONU.

30. Voir *supra*.

31. *Politique étrangère au service des Canadiens*, fascicule sur les Nations Unies, p. 7 et 16.

32. Voir *supra*.

33. *La défense dans les années 70*, Ottawa, Information Canada, 1971, p. 18. Le maintien de la paix venait à la suite de la défense du Canada, de celle de l'Amérique du Nord et de la participation à l'OTAN.

34. Voir *supra*.

35. *Canadian Annuel Review of Politics and Public Affairs 1983*, p. 182.

36. *Où vont les Nations Unies?*, document de discussion préparé par le ministère des Affaires extérieures, avril 1977, p. 8.

37. Cette section s'inspire des sources suivantes: *Politique étrangère au service des Canadiens*, fascicule général, p. 38-39 et fascicule sur les Nations Unies, p. 14-15; *Canada and the United Nations in a Changing World*, Ottawa, United Nations Association in Canada, 1977, p. 109-112; *Le Canada et UNSSOD II*, document préparé par Robert W. Reford pour le ministère des Affaires extérieures, 30 septembre 1981; ministère des Affaires extérieures, *Déclarations et Discours*, nᵒ 82/10, «La poussée technologique alimente la course aux armements».

38. Cette catégorisation est tirée de Michael Tucker, «Canada and Arms Control: Perspectives and Trends», *International Journal*, 36(3), Summer 1981, p. 635-656.

39. Hélène Galarneau, «Chronique des relations extérieures du Canada et du Québec», *Études internationales*, vol. XV, nᵒ 1, mars 1984, p. 176-177 et *ibidem*, vol. XV, nᵒ 2, juin 1984, p. 366-367.

40. Les données utilisées dans cette section sont tirées des sources suivantes: *Canada Nord-Sud 1977-1978. Le défi Nord-Sud: le Tiers Monde et les réalisations du Canada*, Ottawa, Institut Nord-Sud, 1977, p. 129; *Les Canadiens dans le Tiers Monde. Revue annuelle de l'ACDI 1980-1981. Annexe statistique*, Ottawa, ministère des Approvisionnements et Services, 1982; *Canada et Nations Unies 1945-1975*, p. 129-152; *Canada and the United Nations in a Changing World*, p. 72-88; A.L.C. de Mestral et L.H.J. Legault, «Multilateral Negotiation – Canada and the Law of the Sea Conference», *International Journal*, 35(1), hiver 1979-1980, p. 47-69; Lyon et Tomlin, *Canada as an International Actor*, p. 163-189; Tucker, *Canadian Foreign Policy: Contemporary Issues and Themes*, p. 175-196.

41. *Politique étrangère au service des Canadiens*, fascicule sur le développement international, Peter C. Dobell, *Canada's Search for New Roles*, p. 136.

42. Programme des Nations Unies pour le développement.

43. Conférence des Nations Unies sur le commerce et le développement.

44. James P. Sewell, «Canada and the Functional Agencies: the NIEO's Challenge, Trudeau's Response», *International Journal*, 33(2), printemps 1978, p. 347.

45. Lors de la session finale de la conférence tenue en Jamaïque en décembre 1982, 117 États, dont le Canada, ont signé la Convention des Nations Unies sur le droit de la mer qui avait été élaborée par la conférence. Cette conférence sur le droit de la mer se situe parmi une série de conférences qui ont été convoquées par les Nations Unies depuis le début des années 70 sur des thèmes divers, dont l'environnement et les établissements humains, l'eau, la population, l'alimentation, les femmes.

46. Les intérêts économiques recouvrent surtout les pêcheries et les ressources minières sous-marines, particulièrement le nickel, dont le Canada est le principal exportateur mondial.

47. Robert E. Hage, «The Third United Nations Conference on the Law of the Sea: a Canadian Retrospective», *Behind the Headlines*, vol. 40, n° 5, 1983, 27 p.

48. Lyon et Tomlin, *Canada as an International Actor*, p. 180-181.

49. Canada, ministère des Affaires extérieures, *Déclarations et Discours*, n° 81/2, «Approche bilatérale de la politique étrangère du Canada».

50. Michel Dupuy, «Quelques réflexions sur l'ONU», *Bulletin* (Association canadienne pour les Nations Unies), 7(3), automne 1981, p. 3.

51. À cette fin, on transférait au ministère des Affaires extérieures les fonctions commerciales du ministère de l'Industrie et du Commerce ainsi que la responsabilité de la Société pour l'expansion des exportations et la Corporation commerciale canadienne. De plus, trois ministres allaient diriger le ministère transformé: le Secrétaire d'État aux Affaires extérieures, le ministre d'État au Commerce international et le ministre des Relations extérieures (voir Hélène Galarneau, «Chronique des relations extérieures du Canada et du Québec», *Études internationales*, vol. 13, n° 2, juin 1982, p. 323.

52. Voir *supra*.

53. Canada, ministère des Affaires extérieures, *Déclarations et Discours*, n° 84/3, «Les Nations Unies – Une perspective canadienne».

54. *Idem*, n° 84/6, «La paix et le désarmement seront la préoccupation majeure de la politique étrangère canadienne». Hélène Galarneau, «Chronique des relations extérieures du Canada et du Québec», *Études internationales*, vol. 15, n° 4, décembre 1984, p. 889.

55. Hélène Galarneau, «Chronique des relations extérieures du Canada et du Québec», *Études internationales*, vol. 16, n° 1, mars 1985, p. 115-116 et 122-123.

56. Joe Clark, Secrétaire d'État aux Affaires extérieures, *Compétitivité et sécurité: orientations pour les relations extérieures du Canada*, Ottawa, Approvisionnements et Services Canada, 1985, p. 2 et 45.

57. Hélène Galarneau, «Chronique des relations extérieures du Canada et du Québec», *Études internationales*, vol. 16, n° 3, septembre 1985, p. 615-616.

58. *Idem*, vol. 17, n° 1, mars 1986, p. 132-133.

59. John W. Holmes, «Les institutions internationales et la politique extérieure», p. 20-40. Michael Tucker, *Canadian Foreign Policy: Contemporary Issues and Themes*, p. 1-22. Cependant, Lyon et Tomlin concluent que l'activité publique (parrainage de résolution et vote) du Canada à l'Assemblée générale des Nations Unies ne démontre pas que celui-ci a utilisé son appartenance à l'ONU pour établir son identité et manifester son indépendance des États-Unis (Lyon et Tomlin, *Canada as an International Actor*, p. 169-178).

60. Garth Stevenson, «Canada in the United Nations», *A Foremost Nation: Canadian Foreign Policy and a Changing World*, éd. par Norman Hillmer et Garth Stevenson, Toronto, McClelland and Stewart, 1977, p. 151.

61. A.J. Miller, «The Functional Principle in Canada's External Relations», *International Journal*, 35(2), printemps 1980, p. 328; Michael Tucker, *Canadian Foreign Policy: Contemporary Issues and Themes*, p. 6.

62. Michel Dupuy, «Quelques réflexions sur l'ONU», p. 3.

63. John W. Holmes, «Le Canada et les Nations Unies: hier et aujourd'hui», *Bulletin* (Association canadienne pour les Nations Unies), 7(4), hiver 1981-1982, p. 10; *Idem*, «Canada's Role in International Organizations», *The Canadian Banker*, 74(1), printemps 1967, p. 119.

64. John W. Holmes, «Canada's Role in International Organizations», p. 120; *Idem*, «Les institutions internationales et la politique extérieure», p. 24; Michael Tucker, *Canadian Foreign Policy: Contemporary Issues and Themes*, p. 3; James P. Sewell, «Canada and the Functional Agencies: the NIEO's Challenge, Trudeau's Response», p. 339-349.

65. John W. Holmes, «Les institutions internationales et la politique étrangère», p. 28; *Idem*, «Le Canada et les Nations Unies: hier et aujourd'hui», p. 10. Thomas A. Hockin, «Federalist Style in International Politics»; Michael Tucker, *Canadian Foreign Policy: Contemporary Issues and Themes*, p. 10.

66. Lyon et Tomlin, *Canada as an International Actor*, p. 163; voir aussi Peyton Lyon, «Le Canada aux Nations Unies», *Perspectives internationales*, n°ˢ 1-2, 1985, p. 42-52.

67. Robert W. Cox, Harold K. Jacobson *et al.*, *The Anatomy of Influence Decision-Making in International Organization*, New Haven, Yale University Press, 1973, p. 410.

68. Chadwick, F. Alger, «Interaction and Negotiation in a Committee of the United Nations General Assembly», *International Politics and Foreign Policy*, éd. par James N. Rosenau, New York, Free Press, 1969, p. 483-497.

69. James P. Sewell, «Canada and the Functional Agencies: the NIEO's Challenge, Trudeau's Response», p. 354-355.

70. Voir surtout David Dewitt et John Kirton, *Canada as a Principal Power*, Toronto, John Wiley and Sons, 1983.

BIBLIOGRAPHIE

On peut obtenir un bon aperçu de la place des organisations internationales dans la politique étrangère canadienne en consultant les ouvrages suivants:

Canada in World Affairs. Cette série est publiée par le Canadian Institute of International Affairs et couvre, en plusieurs volumes, la période d'après-guerre jusqu'aux années 70.

CANADA. Ministère des Affaires extérieures. *Politique étrangère au service des Canadiens,* Ottawa, Imprimeur de la Reine, 1970, fascicule général.

CLARK, Joe, Secrétaire d'État aux Affaires extérieures. *Compétitivité et sécurité: orientations pour les relations extérieures du Canada,* Ottawa, ministère des Approvisionnements et Services, 1985, 47 p.

DOBELL, Peter C. *Canada's Search for New Roles.* Foreign Policy in the Trudeau Era, Toronto, Oxford University Press, 1972, VI-161 p.

DOXEY, Margaret. «Canada's International Connections: the Canadian Foreign Policy Review in Review», *The Year Book of World Affairs,* 1978, p. 43-63.

HAWES, Michael K. *Principal Power, Middle Power, or Satellite?* Competing Perspectives in the Study of Canadian Foreign Policy, Toronto, Canadian Institute of Strategic Studies, 1984, 52 p., York Strategic Studies.

HOCKIN, Thomas, A. «Federalist Style in International Politics», *An Independent Foreign Policy for Canada?,* éd. par Stephen Clarkson, Toronto, McClelland and Stewart, 1968, p. 119-129.

HOCKIN, Thomas A. *et al. The Canadian Condominium.* Domestic Issues and External Policy, Toronto, McClelland and Stewart, 1972, 176 p.

HOCKIN, Thomas A. «Foreign Affairs: Canada Abroad as a Measure of Canada at Home», *Approaches to Canadian Politics,* éd. par John H. Redekop, Scarborough, Prentice-Hall of Canada Ltd, 1978, p. 83-102.

HOLMES, John W. «Canada's Role in International Organizations», *The Canadian Banker,* vol. 74, n° 1, printemps 1967, p. 115-130.

HOLMES, John W. «Les institutions internationales et la politique extérieure», *Études internationales,* vol. 1, n° 2, juin 1970, p. 20-40.

HOLMES, John W. *The Shaping of Peace: Canada and the Search for World Order 1943-1957,* Toronto, University of Toronto Press, volume I, 1979, 349 p. et volume II, 1982, 443 p.

ICHIKAWA, Akita. «The *'*Helpful Fixer'*»*: Canada's Persistent International Image», *Behind the Headlines,* vol. 37, n° 3, 1979.

LYON, Peyton V. et TOMLIN, Brian W. *Canada as an International Actor,* Toronto, Macmillan of Canada, 1979, xiii – 209 p.

MILLER, A.J. «The Functional Principle in Canada's External Relations», *International Journal,* vol. 35, n° 2, Printemps 1980, p. 309-328.

TUCKER, Michael. *Canadian Foreign Policy: Contemporary Issues and Themes,* Scarborough, McGraw-Hill Ryerson Ltd, 1980, xii – 244 p.

Pour les grandes lignes de la politique canadienne envers les Nations Unies, on peut se référer aux ouvrages suivants:

Canada in World Affairs. Chaque volume de cette série déjà citée traite de la politique canadienne à l'égard des Nations Unies.

BARTON, W.H. «Un mandat au Conseil de sécurité», *Perspectives internationales,* mai-juin-juillet-août 1979, p. 11-16.

Canada and Peacekeeping: Prospects for the Future. éd. par R.B. Byers et Michael Slack, Toronto, Canadian Institute of Strategic Studies, 1984, 56 p.

Canada and the United Nations in a Changing World. Report of a Conference, Winnipeg, 12-14 May 1977, Ottawa, United Nations Association in Canada, 1977, 146 p.

CANADA. Ministère des Affaires extérieures. *Canada et Nations Unies 1945-1975,* Ottawa, ministère des Approvisionnements et Services, 1976, xv – 207 p.

CANADA. Ministère des Affaires extérieures. *Le Canada et les Nations Unies,* publication annuelle de 1947 à 1966.

CANADA. Ministère des Affaires extérieures. *Le Canada et UNSSOD II,* document préparé par Robert Reford pour le ministère des Affaires extérieures, 30 septembre 1981, 26 p.

CANADA. Ministère des Affaires extérieures. *Où vont les Nations Unies?,* document de discussion préparé par le ministère des Affaires extérieures, avril 1977, iii – 46 p.

CANADA. Ministère des Affaires extérieures. *Politique étrangère au service des Canadiens,* Ottawa, Imprimeur de la Reine, 1970, fascicule sur les Nations Unies.

DOBELL, W.M. «United Nations: Sea Law, Peacekeeping, and Southern Africa», *International Journal,* vol. 33, n° 2, printemps 1978, p. 415-424.

DUPUY, Michel. «Quelques réflexions sur l'ONU», *Bulletin* (Association canadienne pour les Nations Unies), vol. 7, n° 3, automne 1981, p. 1-4.

HAGE, Robert E. «The Third United Nations Conference on the Law of the Sea: A Canadian Retrospective», *Behind the Headlines*, vol. 40, n° 5, 1983, 27 p.

HOLMES, John W. *The Shaping of Peace: Canada and the Search for World Order 1943-1957*, Toronto, University of Toronto Press, volume I, 1979, 349 p. et volume II, 1982, 443 p.

HOLMES, John W. «Le Canada et les Nations Unies: hier et aujourd'hui», *Bulletin* (Association canadienne pour les Nations Unies), vol. 7, n° 4, hiver 1981-1982, p. 7-11.

IGNATIEFF, George. «Le Conseil de sécurité: un baril de poudre», *Perspectives internationales*, septembre-octobre 1976, p. 7-12.

JACOMY-MILLETTE, Annemarie. «Analyse du vote canadien à l'Assemblée générale», *Perspectives internationales*, septembre-octobre 1976, p. 23-28.

LYON, Peyton V. et TOMLIN, Brian W. *Canada as an International Actor*, Toronto, Macmillan of Canada, 1979, p. 9-34 et 163-189.

LYON, Peyton V. «Le Canada aux Nations Unies», *Perspectives internationales*, n°ˢ 1-2, 1985, p. 42-52.

MILLER, Anthony J. *Functionalism and Foreign Policy*, An Analysis of Canadian voting behaviour in the General Assembly of the United Nations, 1946-1966, McGill University, Ph.D. Thesis, 1971, 447 p.

REFORD, Robert W. «Le Canada et les Nations Unies», *Le Canada et le Québec sur la scène internationale*, sous la direction de Paul Painchaud, Québec et Montréal, Centre québécois de relations internationales et Presses de l'Université du Québec, 1977, p. 421-438.

SEWELL, James P. «Canada and the Functional Agencies: the NIEO's Challenge, Trudeau's Response», *International Journal*, vol. 35, n° 2, printemps 1978, p. 339-356.

SOWARD, Frederic H. et MCINNIS, Edgar. *Canada and the United Nations*, New York, Manhattan Publishing Co., 1956, 284 p.

STEVENSON, Garth. «Canada in the United Nations», *A Foremost Nation: Canadian Foreign Policy and a Changing World*, éd. par Norman Hillmer et Garth Stevenson, Toronto, McClelland and Stewart, 1977, p. 150-177.

TAYLOR, Alastair, COX, David et GRANATSTEIN, J.L. *Peacekeeping*, International Challenge and Canadian Response, Toronto, Canadian Institute of International Affairs, 1968, 211 p.

TOMLIN, Brian W. «Polarization and Alignment in the General Assembly: the Effects of World Cleavages on Canadian Foreign Policy Behaviour», *Canada's Foreign Policy: Analysis and Trends*, éd. par Brian W. Tomlin, Toronto, Methuen, 1977, p. 51-68.

TUCKER, Michael. *Canadian Foreign Policy: Contemporary Issues and Themes*, Scarborough, McGraw-Hill Ryerson Ltd, 1980, p. 107-125 et 181-188.

TUCKER, Michael. «Canada and Arms Control: Perspectives and Trends», *International Journal*, vol. 36, n° 3, été 1981, p. 635-656.

Comme source d'information courante et pour de brèves analyses, on se reportera à:

CANADA. Ministère des Affaires extérieures. *Apport financier du Canada aux Nations Unies*, Ottawa, ministère des Approvisionnements et Services (série Documents, n° 21). Cette publication est mise à jour régulièrement.

CANADA. Ministère des Affaires extérieures. *Rapport annuel*, Ottawa, ministère des Approvisionnements et Services.

Canadian Annuel Review of Politics and Public Affairs. Cette série est publiée par la University of Toronto Press.

«Chronique des relations extérieures du Canada et du Québec», *Études internationales*.

Perspectives internationales. Cette publication périodique contient de temps à autre de brèves analyses de divers aspects des activités des Nations Unies.

Une bibliographie complète est contenue dans:

A Reading Guide to Canada in World Affairs 1945-1971, compiled by Lawrence Motiuk and Madeline Grant, Toronto, Canadian Institute of International Affairs, 1972, xii – 313 p.

A Bibliography of Works on Canadian Foreign Relations 1945-1970, compiled by Donald M. Page, Toronto, Canadian Institute of International Affairs, 1973, xiv – 442 p.

A Bibliography of Works on Canadian Foreign Relations 1971-1975, compiled by Donald M. Page, Toronto, Canadian Institute of International Affairs, 1977, xiv – 300 p.

A Bibliography of Works on Canadian Foreign Relations 1976-1980, compiled by Jane R. Barrett and Jane Beaumont, Toronto, Canadian Institute of International Affairs, 1982, xii – 306 p.

9

Canada and the Commonwealth 1945-1980*

Margaret Doxey
Trent University

> *The Commonwealth [...] is a voluntary*
> *association of independent sovereign*
> *states [...] consulting and cooperating*
> *in the common interests of their peoples*
> *and in the promotion of international*
> *understanding and world peace.*
>
> Declaration of Commonwealth Principles, 1971.

> *[The Commonwealth] is certainly*
> *a ruminant, not a carnivore, in the*
> *international jungle.*
>
> Martin WIGHT

INTRODUCTION

The Commonwealth, the oldest and probably the strangest international association to which Canada has belonged, is no longer a dominant connection. In the period with which this study is concerned, membership of other organizations, particularly the United Nations and NATO, took precedence in Canadian foreign policy considerations and the Commonwealth became less salient. That it has not only survived to the 1980s but continues to have practical relevance for its members reflects a remarkable capacity for adaptation to changing circumstances. In fact, Commonwealth structure, norms and activities have been so transformed over the past 35 years that it is no exageration to write of a metamorphosis. While its imperial past provides a link to its contemporary form, British hegemony steadily dwindled and finally vanished – although like the grin of the Cheshire cat, the illusion lingered for some time – and egalitarianism and decentralization now characterize the modern Commonwealth which exists more for the benefit of newer members than older ones.

In this process of evolution, Canada has consistently played an important role: in the 19th and early 20th centuries leading the march to Dominion status; in the post-World War II period shaping the «new» Commonwealth and often helping to hold it together; in participating actively in the functional cooperation which has become a valuable aspect of contemporary Commonwealth relations. But Canada's relationship with the postwar Commonwealth is not only a slice of Commonwealth

* I am grateful to John W. Holmes for helpful comments on a draft of this chapter.

history; it also sheds light on the attitudes and perceptions of the makers of Canadian foreign policy and in a number of ways, helps to define its characteristic purposes and style. In historical perspective, the Commonwealth for Canada was not just part of the whole jigsaw puzzle of external relations; it was part of the «edge», the border which set the shape of the whole. In recent years, it has still represented a set of pieces without which the picture would be incomplete[1].

It would be true to say that Canadian and South African pressure for independent and equal status – the «retreat from imperial unity»[2] which was formalized in the Statute of Westminster – made it possible for Canada and the other Dominions to have a foreign policy of their own and their example provided a model for the further expansion of the Commonwealth on a basis of independence for its members. In 1945, there were seven members of the Commonwealth: Britain at the centre, the four Dominions (Australia, Canada, New Zealand and South Africa), plus Eire («a Dominion with a difference»[3]) and Newfoundland which was to join Canada in 1949. The «Empire» encompassed a very large number of territories and dependencies at varying stages of progress towards self-government, with India clearly in the vanguard of the group. Eire (now Ireland) and South Africa left the Commonwealth in 1949 and 1961 respectively, but membership was to grow by leaps and bounds until by 1980 it had reached a total of 44 independent states, with only a small number of dependent territories still under British administration. A quarter of the world's population is now encompassed by the Commonwealth. It is global in scope, exhibiting an immense diversity of race, religion, language, culture ideology and constitutional arrangement; within it, Third World states constitute an overwhelming majority and the twelve African members make up a significant subgrouping. Like Canada, most members have non-Commonwealth connections which are more important than those provided by the Commonwealth.

Expanding membership and a changing world inevitably brought new emphases. Defence and trade, which were the preoccupations of the interwar period[4], have now been relegated to history as Commonwealth issues and there is no longer any question of a common Commonwealth citizenship (although there are still some residual privileges)[5]. The postwar Commonwealth has been chiefly concerned with decolonization, with multiracialism and the end of white minority rule in Africa, and with the economic needs of the newer members. In these respects, it has mirrored some of the world's most pressing problems, although the absence of superpowers spared it the dominant strategic and ideological issues of East-West relations.

This «new» Commonwealth developed substantive norms of egalitarianism, non-intervention and non-discrimination which were eventually set out in 1971 in a Declaration of Principles; it also changed its style of operation. In 1944, the first of a series of Prime Ministers' meetings (now called Heads of Government meetings) broke with the tradition set by prewar Imperial Conferences. Procedural norms of informality, confidentiality, no voting, and no discussion of internal affairs of members without their specific consent or of disputes between members unless both consented, became a hallmark of Commonwealth conferences, with communication facilitated by the use of English as a working language.

The establishment of a Commonwealth Secretariat in 1965 brought a structural transformation. It was obvious that the planned merger of the British Foreign Office and Commonwealth Relations Office (accomplished in 1968) marked the end of an era in Whitehall, and indeed the time had passed when any British Government department – even one charged only with this function – could act as a Commonwealth office. The new Secretariat, financed by contributions from all members and staffed by personnel from all parts of the Commonwealth strengthened the image of the association as egalitarian, representative, less British. The symbolic status of the British monarch as «Head of the Commonwealth» recalls the former hierarchical pattern, and it is probably true that there are denser links between Britain and many other members (particularly the former Dominions) than between those members themselves, but the Commonwealth can no longer be described as a rimless wheel with Britain at the hub of radiating spokes. The contemporary metaphor would more appropriately be a cobweb of links, perhaps with the Secretariat performing some of the functions of a benevolent spider.

The contemporary Commonwealth operates at several levels. At the political level, it is a limited membership intergovernmental organization with no specific Commonwealth goals, but rather a general concern for maintaining open lines of communication and consultation on matters of common interest. Heads of government meet every two years and senior ministers and senior officials from departments such as Finance, Health, Education and Law also meet at regular intervals to discuss issues which are by no means confined to the Commonwealth in scope. On a second, practical level, the Commonwealth sponsors a broad range of functional activities, coordinated and fostered by the Secretariat. These Commonwealth programmes and services, which are particularly valuable for newer and smaller members, are also extended to Britain's remaining dependencies. The Commonwealth as a whole thus provides a framework for a network of programmes of action in technical assistance, education, health, and other welfare fields, and many of these links are reinforced by non-governmental bodies which make up the third, or «unofficial» level of Commonwealth relations[6]. Some of these bodies are old-established, like the Commonwealth Parliamentary Association (1911) and the Association of Commonwealth Universities (1913); others like the Commonwealth Foundation (1966) are of more recent vintage; all help to keep the idea of Commonwealth alive in a meaningful way at a person-to-person level[7].

In the context of Canada's membership of the Commonwealth, there are two major themes which should be addressed. One concerns the contribution made by Canada to the evolution of Commonwealth structure, norms and activities over the past 35 years; the other relates to the implications of membership for Canada and, in particular, whether there have been significant benefits or costs[8].

It may be useful initially to give a brief overview of the whole period and 1945 offers a convenient point of departure. World War II was clearly a watershed in international history, although to some extent for the Commonwealth, as for the world in general, the war years served to accelerate changes which were already manifesting themselves, particularly the rise to world power status of the United States and the Soviet Union and the decline of salt-water empires. In the history of the Commonwealth since 1945, certain achievements stand out, but there have also been periods of high tension when the fragility of Commonwealth bonds was clearly revealed and doubts about its future widely shared. From an overall Commonwealth perspective, one can identify the first decade after 1945 as crucial both in terms of structural change and the initiation of new kinds of economic cooperation particularly relevant to new members, while the next ten years served to consolidate the multiracial character of the association with the admission of nine African states and the withdrawal of South Africa. In the second postwar decade, however, Britain subjected the association to severe strain by her Suez venture in 1956 and five years later, there was further controversy when she made her first application to join the European Economic Community. The establishment of the Secretariat in 1965 helped the Commonwealth to weather the very heavy storms of the mid and late 1960s over Southern Africa, particularly those associated with Rhodesia's illegal and Unilateral Declaration of Independence (UDI). In the 1970s, there were further crises in Asia and in Cyprus, and there was still tension over South Africa and Rhodesia, but generally an improved atmosphere from 1971 onwards. The final emergence of Zimbabwe as an independent state with majority rule and a democratically elected government in 1980 was a triumph for Commonwealth diplomacy, but the 1970s proved the value of Commonwealth connections in many other ways. A significant expansion of programmes of practical utility, with the Commonwealth Fund for Technical Cooperation (CFTC) a major success story, marked this decade, and there were also some valuable Commonwealth initiatives in the context of Third World proposals for a new international economic order. The value of the Commonwealth as a forum for discussion which spanned the North-South chasm and the opportunities it provided for constructive dialogue in smaller groups than at the United Nations or UNCTAD came to be generally appreciated.

One can say perhaps that the early postwar years saw the conversion of the Commonwealth into a viable, late 20th-century association: a model of and for political decolonization. But from the outset, and assuming greater importance as the process of gaining political independence came to an end, was the need to give attention to the economic and social development of the former dependencies, now able to articulate their demands in concert as equal partners in international bodies. The Commonwealth, as a former empire which had to justify its survival in a new form, necessarily took up these challenges.

1945-1955: THE BIRTH OF THE «NEW» COMMONWEALTH

While Canadian governments in the interwar period had been concerned to achieve full Dominion status and were resolutely opposed to ideas of imperial federation and to binding external commitments (particularly defence commitments), post-World War II attitudes were imbued with a new philosophy of participatory internationalism, building for peace in conjunction with other democracies and particularly the United States and Britain[9]. The former was now the undisputed leader of the Western world. But formal commitments were to be in the context of the United Nations and (later) NATO; there was no disposition in Ottawa to integrate the Commonwealth. That the Canadian Government remained highly sensitive to any suggestion of a «Commonwealth foreign policy», or a «single Commonwealth voice» in world affairs, was made abundantly clear by Mackenzie King in reaction to the speech made by Lord Halifax in Toronto in January 1944, proposing the Commonwealth and Empire as a power grouping in its own right[10]. The Commonwealth was seen by Mackenzie King as the aggregate of its separate parts and not as any kind of bloc, especially not one which might vie with the new world organization[11]. But neither King nor Louis St. Laurent, who was to succeed him as Prime Minister in 1948, questioned the value of the association as a forum for consultation and as a purveyor of common ideals and principles to which Canada naturally belonged. This was the Canadian concept of the Commonwealth, which John W. Holmes notes came to prevail over the British concept[12]. It had not been shared by Australia prior to World War II[13], but it found favour with the Labour Government in Canberra in the mid-1940s and this gave it added strength.

It is true that in the immediate postwar period, the Commonwealth as it was or as it appeared to be – for it has always defied precise definition[14] – loomed much larger for Canada as a point of reference for its place in the international system than it does today. If not for defence, then to a certain extent for trade; in close relations with the Commonwealth Relations Office (as the Dominions Office was renamed in 1947); and generally in the cozy atmosphere of the «old» Commonwealth club. The Commonwealth framework was a kind of family network in which Canada could speak and be heard as a young member who had come of age. For English-speaking Canadians, there were still strong sentimental ties with Britain although the Commonwealth had no comparable appeal for French Canada. But for Canadian foreign policy, the United States was inevitably a sharper point of reference. Institutionally, the Commonwealth was subsumed in and by the United Nations and it was destined to continue shrinking in political and economic importance. In Canada, the Citizenship Act of 1946, which defined a Canadian citizen with the overall category of British subjects, the dropping of the term «Dominion» in 1947, and the abolition of appeals to the Privy Council in 1949, reaffirmed the independence and separateness of Canada from Britain. Commonwealth relations were already an aspect of *foreign* policy, although still a special aspect at this stage.

Canada as a nation had come to a new prominence in the immediate postwar period as a result of its contribution to the war effort, its economic strength which stood in sharp contrast to the shattered European economies, and its close links with both the United States and Britain. It is interesting to recall that the first Commonwealth recipient of Canadian help to meet severe economic problems was not what would now be termed a Third World country but Britain itself. Canada, like Australia, was a «middle power» and the Australian and Canadian governments took the lead in discussions preceding the establishment of the United Nations and in other forums in seeking to limit the hegemony of the great powers and at the same time to establish a role for «middle powers». This heightened stature for Canada was translated into action by an enlarged and vigorous Department of External Affairs, led by an exceptionally capable team. Lester B. Pearson, as Deputy Minister from 1946 to 1948 with Norman Robertson and Hume Wrong, and others such as Escott Reid and Dana Wilgress, shaped Canadian foreign policy for the postwar world in a pragmatic and imaginative way. John W. Holmes, who had joined External Affairs in 1943 and who shared the perceptions and attitudes of members of this group, has noted that in some respects they were well out in front of the Government in their thinking, although in no danger of being repudiated[15]. When St. Laurent became Prime Minister in 1948, Pearson became Secretary of State for External Affairs, and his close relations with his former colleagues in the Department of External Affairs obviously made for harmony of effort. These men shared a liberal-internationalist outlook; they believed in cooperative efforts through international institutions as the most promising way to preserve the peace which had been so dearly won and to handle postwar problems; they saw Canada as both able and required to play an active role in world affairs. The functional principle, that representation in international bodies should be directly linked to members' contributions to their work, was an article of faith in their credo. In the Commonwealth context, Canada could obviously exert considerable influence, even if hopes of a substantial role in the UN were to be disappointed. And the Commonwealth's flexibility, historical evolution and appropriateness for the pursuit of common goals commended it as worthy of conservation. At the time, the Westminster system of Parliamentary democracy was seen as the model for present and future Commonwealth partners.

The years following 1945, which brought not only problems of postwar reconstruction but the onset of the Cold War and disillusion with the United Nations, were to be crucial for the survival of the Commonwealth. Independence for India, Pakistan, Ceylon (now Sri Lanka) and Burma brought the first three into the Commonwealth as full members in 1948 of their own volition and to a warm welcome from the older members, particularly Canada. Following the admission of these Asian countries came the Declaration of London in 1949. This was a landmark in the history of the Commonwealth in that it provided a formula for the acceptance of republics as members alongside monarchies, with all acknowledging the monarch (not the crown) as a symbol of their free association and as such, the «Head of the Commonwealth»[16]. Individual countries could still choose to owe allegiance to the Crown (as did Canada), but no issue of sovereignty was raised for republics; henceforth Commonwealth membership carried no constitutional or quasi-constitutional trappings. The London formula made it possible for India to remain a member; it also made possible the transformation of the Commonwealth into a multiracial body which could accommodate all types of political systems. This «new» Commonwealth owed much to the Canadian concept of its potential[17]. Moreover, the Canadian Government at the time was active in support of change. Mackenzie King appears to have played some part at the 1948 Prime Ministers' Conference in reassuring the Asian Prime Ministers that they should remain in the Commonwealth[18]; indeed Gordon Walker, who was Parliamentary Under-Secretary for Commonwealth Relations in the British Labour Government of the day, notes that their continued membership was taken for granted[19]. At the conference hurriedly convened in the following April to discuss the republican issue, Lester B. Pearson represented the new Prime Minister, St. Laurent, and took an active role in diplomacy and in drafting[20]. Later that year, on a visit to Ottawa, the Indian Prime Minister, Pandit Nehru, paid tribute to Canada as a «pioneer in the evolution of the Commonwealth of absolutely independent members»[21]. Canada's role in welcoming the Asian members and helping to loosen constitutional requirements so that they could comfortably remain members was critical for the survival of the Commonwealth; it also led to a very close relationship between Ottawa and New Delhi over the next decade which was helpful in preserving communications and developing new links[22]. India's non-aligned posture, which was resented in the United States and Britain, provided an important strand in Commonwealth development; the association could not become an adjunct to the anticommunist bloc led by the United States.

At the level of political consultation, the Commonwealth formed a subgroup within the United Nations, and there were close contacts between delegations in New York. John W. Holmes notes that the «Commonwealth as a group was an active force during the UN's first decade[23]. A Security Council non-permanent seat went to a Commonwealth member in this period, and Canada served from 1948 to 1949. Traditions of cooperation with Britain and the sharing of information by the Commonwealth Relations Office helped to cement the links. There was regular consultation during the Korean War, in which a Commonwealth Division saw service, made up of units from Britain, Canada, Australia, New Zealand and South Africa and an Indian medical unit, and Commonwealth members shared concern over the extension of the war in Korea and over US policy towards Asia. India was able to act as a channel for communication with Peking during these years.

On the international economic front, the inauguration of the Colombo Plan in 1950 focused attention on the urgent need of these new Asian members for development assistance and pointed the way towards an important role for the «new» Commonwealth. In Ottawa, economic cooperation was seen as an important and integral part of the search for peace. From the beginning, Canada had laid stress on economic and social aspects of the work of the United Nations – John W. Holmes notes that «[...] they were in theory the Canadian priority[24]» – and also tried hard to give NATO an effective economic arm. At the Commonwealth Foreign Ministers' meeting in Colombo in January 1950, initiatives from Australia and Ceylon brought to the fore the economic problems faced by Asian countries and a Consultative Committee for South and Southeast Asia was set up to consider measures which would be taken to help them. This committee reported in September with detailed plans for aid and development for Ceylon, India, Pakistan, Malaya, Singapore, North Borneo and Sarawak[25]. The Colombo Plan provided a new framework for cooperation and assistance in a variety of forms; it reassured the Asian members of the Commonwealth that their needs were recognized and encouraged cooperation between them. The Plan was open-ended and not restricted to Commonwealth members. The United States became a member at the end of the year and thereafter took the lead in contributions: in the first decade, US aid amounted to 85 % of the total ($5 660 millions of a total of $6 500 millions).

The Colombo Plan thus fulfilled the Canadian philosophy of making Commonwealth effort part of a wider effort and emphasizing the non-exclusive character of the association, although it has to be admitted that Canadian support was given rather grudgingly. At Colombo, Pearson noted the burden of heavy Canadian commitment elsewhere and Canada's initial contribution of $25 000 was approved by Cabinet with some reluctance[26]. Support for the Plan, and for the Expanded Programme of Technical Assistance set up by the United Nations in 1949, led to the establishment in Ottawa of the International Economic and Technical Cooperation Division of the Department of Trade and Commerce; in 1960, an External Aid Office was set up which became a government Department and was renamed the Canadian International Development Agency (CIDA) in 1968.

1956-1964: YEARS OF HEAVY STRAIN

If the first postwar decade had shown how Commonwealth membership, norms and activities could be successfully adapted to changed circumstances, the second was to put the association under very heavy strain, partly because of British policies and partly because the new African members brought racial questions to the fore, challenging assumptions and prejudices in a manner which had not previously characterized Commonwealth dialogue.

A major international crisis erupted in 1956 with the Egyptian nationalization of the Suez Canal and the subsequent Anglo-French military operation. There is no doubt that this nearly wrecked the Commonwealth: Pearson reported in the House of Commons in November that it was not only «badly and dangerously split», but «at one stage, after the fighting on land began, it was on the verge of dissolution»[27]. Britain's Conservative Government, headed by Prime Minister Anthony Eden, had apparently assumed – wrongly as it turned out – that the Commonwealth and the United States would automatically support its foreign policy, or if they did not, that criticism would be muted. United States' opposition to the Suez venture and pressure to end it are well documented; and although Australia, New Zealand and South Africa chose not to make an issue of Britain's complete disregard for the principle of prior consultation – which had been seen as a Commonwealth tradition – and did not publicly censure her action, the Asian Commonwealth members were outraged and there was much talk of leaving the Commonwealth in protest[28]. The Canadian Government was also shocked by the Anglo-French venture, which flouted UN principles of non-intervention and peaceful settlement, but was anxious above all, to defuse the crisis, thereby healing the breach between Britain and the United States – Canada's two major allies – and also the divisions within the Commonwealth[29]. It should be recorded, however, that the Opposition was sympathetic to the British position and as Pearson notes, the Conservatives reproached the Liberal Government for «deserting our two mother countries»[30]. Canada's opposition to British policy prevented the Commonwealth from being split on racial lines in this crisis and gave encouragement to the governments of India and Ceylon who saw long term advantages in the Commonwealth connection and did not necessarily want to quit in a huff over Suez. They could point to Canada as sharing their view (and also, of course, to the strong opposition to government policy voiced in Britain itself). In putting Canadian policy into practice at the United Nations, Pearson displayed his remarkable diplomatic skills and was later awarded the Nobel Peace Prize for his efforts. In collaboration with the UN Secretary-General, Dag Hammarskjold, he brought forward the plan for a UN Emergency Force which served effectively to replace the British and French forces in Egypt without total loss of face for these two powers.

The Suez crisis was handled at and through the United Nations, but the Commonwealth group provided a basis for dialogue and negotiations. John W. Holmes, who as Assistant Under Secretary in the Department of External Affairs accompanied Pearson to New York, recalls that even at the height of the crisis «contacts of the frankest, and in their own way, the most sympathetic kind were maintained between British and Canadian leaders [...]» while the British and Americans «were barely speaking to each other»[31]. He notes, however, that Commonwealth unity at the UN was never quite the same again[32].

In the Suez crisis, Canada enhanced its role and status both at the UN and in the Commonwealth and this may have been its high-water mark of «middle-powerism» and mediation. There is, however, a persistent element in Canadian foreign policy which seeks to conserve rather than to disrupt; thus for Canada on this and other occasions, holding the Commonwealth together took precedence over temporary and particular advantage. Perhaps this attitude has reflected the need to keep Canada itself together, despite its disparate parts, as well as a sense of the virtues of compromise; in any event, it was important for the postwar development of the Commonwealth[33].

The next serious issue to bring a crisis in Commonwealth relations was the vigorous challenge to South Africa's apartheid policy introduced by the new African members. Independence for British, French and Belgian colonies in Africa transformed the United Nations and the Commonwealth in the 1960s: Ghana was the first to achieve nationhood in 1967; by 1965, Nigeria, Sierra Leone, Tanganyika and Zanzibar (later united as Tanzania), Uganda, Kenya, Zambia and Malawi had all joined both organizations. The British Government under Harold Macmillan, who succeeded Eden after the Suez fiasco, was now anxious to shed the burden of empire in Africa as rapidly as possible, and the process rapidly gathered momentum.

The new African states were not comfortable with South Africa as a partner in international bodies and their views were shared by Asian countries and by the new states in the Caribbean area who also joined the Commonwealth in the early 1960s. Basic principles of non-discrimination and racial equality were directly flouted by the official apartheid system upheld by the South African Government. At the outset, however, it is doubtful if driving South Africa out of the Commonwealth was an immediate goal. Certainly the older members, Britain, Australia and Canada were quite opposed to such action; the record shows that they were anxious for compromise and would have welcomed some concession from the South African Government which would have avoided an open breach. Harold Macmillan records in his memoirs that «until the end of the unhappy controversy [he] was determined to make every effort to keep South Africa in the Commonwealth»[34].

Ironically, within the Commonwealth, the formula designed to accommodate India's continued membership in 1949 was now the machanism for testing South Africa's continued acceptability to its fellow members. The occasion for Commonwealth discussion of South Africa's racial policies was provided by the South African application to remain in the Commonwealth after becoming a republic. At the United Nations, of course, questions of the treatment of Indians in South Africa, the status of South-West Africa (Namibia) and the policy of apartheid had been on the agenda of the General Assembly since 1947, and as UN membership expanded, the strength of hostility to South Africa, and calls for sanctions against it grew apace. Western countries found themselves pressed hard on moral principles and the Commonwealth could not possibly have remained immune from controversy on these issues. At the Prime Ministers' meeting in May 1960, it was agreed that permission would be needed for South Africa to remain in the Commonwealth if it became a republic. Harold Macmillan had publicly warned the South African Government of its growing isolation within the Commonwealth in his «Wind of Change» speech in Cape Town in January; the Sharpeville incident in March exacerbated anti-South African feeling and it was clear that no automatic acceptance of South Africa as a republic was likely. In Canada, the Conservative Party had been returned to power with a small majority in 1957, converted to a very large one in 1958; thus, Diefenbaker now represented Canada at Prime Ministers' meetings. Like the Liberal Government, however, the Conservative Government was anxious to preserve the Commonwealth as a whole and it placed heavy emphasis on the Commonwealth connection. At the UN, Canada had taken a prohuman rights position but had not voted to condemn South Africa. The next decade was to see a change in that condemnation would become open, although sanctions would continue to be opposed. But both Liberal and Conservative governments believed in dialogue, in trying to move South Africa by discussion and persuasion[35]. Diefenbaker himself was well known for his commitment to human rights in Canada and he gave advance warning to the British Prime Minister that Canada could not «be counted upon to support South Africa's readmission to the Commonwealth» unless there were «significant changes» in its racial policies[36]. This prompted Macmillan to fear that Canada's position «might well be decisive if expressed when the Conference took place»[37]. Pressed by the African and Asian members, it was difficult for Diefenbaker not to take a firm stand and at the 1961 Prime Ministers' Meeting, he came out in support of Nigeria and India on the need for South Africa to make some concessions and for a statement in the final communique that racial equality was at the heart of the Commonwealth[38]. In the face of what became a consensus position on these issues, the South African Prime Minister elected to withdraw his country's application and South Africa left the Commonwealth on becoming a republic in May 1961. In this forced withdrawal, Canada was at least a catalyst and perhaps something of a leader in forming collective will. It had certainly contributed once again to the survival of the Commonwealth; if the South African membership question had not been resolved at this time, the association could not have continued to attract support from Third World members. Not only would the form and style of high level meetings have made it impossible for leaders from South Africa to meet with their African and Asian counterparts in friendly intimacy, but without racial equality at the hub, the Commonwealth wheel could not continue to turn.

Following South Africa's withdrawal, the Commonwealth was insulated to a degree from the continuing furore over apartheid and was able to get on with other business, but it remained a focus of controversy for issues of white minority rule in Africa. These are discussed later in this chapter. Meanwhile, the anti-apartheid campaign continued at the UN alongside the drive to free Namibia. In fact, the existence of the UN has been in many ways as crucial to the survival of the Commonwealth as the changes which the association itself has undergone. It has provided an alternative and comprehensive forum where highly contentious issues could be discussed and a more appropriate launching pad for peacekeeping initiatives. Suez (already discussed), Kashmir (a bone of violent contention between India and Pakistan), Rhodesia (to be discussed in the next section), are all examples of crises which could be handled effectively (or ineffectively) at the UN level, leaving the Commonwealth to some extent on the sidelines. From this point of view, the Canadian concept of the Commonwealth as *one* of a set of relationships, complementing each other, but with different functions, has proved workable and useful.

To conclude this brief survey of the Commonwealth's second postwar decade, it is necessary to pay some attention to broader questions of economic cooperation. Mention should be made of the 1958 Commonwealth Trade and Economic Conference in Montréal. Called on Canadian initiative and advertised as specifically trade-oriented, its achievements were modest, mainly in the realm of assistance. Britain introduced interest-free Commonwealth Assistance Loans; Canada proposed a Commonwealth scholarship scheme which has helped many students to obtain education and training which would otherwise not have been available to them. But there were no major outcomes, and in the circumstances of the declining importance of intra-Commonwealth trade relative to the dynamic growth of Western Europe (particularly Germany) and Japan, it was not likely that the Montréal conference could produce significant new directions[39]. Of more crucial importance was the decision of the British Government in 1961 to reverse earlier policy and apply for membership of the European Economic Community (EEC). While Britain's abandonment of political leadership within the Commonwealth was quite welcome to most members, this apparent subordination of the Commonwealth to new European connections was not, particularly if it meant a loss of economic advantage for them.

Britain as a member of the EEC would be inside the Common External Tariff wall and subject to the protective Common Agricultural Policy: hitherto duty-free or low-duty imports from Commonwealth countries would have to face new barriers and new competition, and there was understandable concern on the part of many Commonwealth members, particularly well founded in the case of New Zealand and the Asian countries, about the implications of Britain's membership for their export trade.

Commonwealth preference, which would obviously be doomed if Britain joined the EEC, dated from the Imperial Economic Conference held in Ottawa in 1932 to seek means of offsetting the worst effects of the Depression. In a series of bilateral trade agreements with other Commonwealth countries, Britain generally exempted their imports from duty in return for Commonwealth preference on her manufactured goods. But the system was always untidy: for instance, the exodus of Burma, Ireland and South Africa from the Commonwealth did not end their privileges. Moreover the Depression and the war, which had served to knit the Commonwealth temporarily together as an economic and financial grouping, were succeeded by circumstances which were distinctly disintegrative. Britain, as leader of the Commonwealth and banker for the Sterling Area – of which Canada was never a member – was afflicted with serious economic problems throughout the postwar period and although for political reasons British governments tended to emphasize the Commonwealth connection in their pronouncements in the 1940s and 1950s, the rhetoric masked the reality which was that economic as well as defence links within the Commonwealth were steadily eroding. The United States was hostile to the Commonwealth as a trading bloc and to Commonwealth preference and was keen for Britain to join the movement for a united Western Europe; the General Agreement on Tariffs and Trade (GATT) had brought general reductions in tariff levels and diminished the value of Commonwealth preference; the developing countries had particular needs which, in the 1960s, were to take the form of demands for preferential access to the markets of developed countries as well as for development assistance. Why then were there howls of protest from Commonwealth countries, including Canada, when Britain first applied to join the EEC? Commonwealth opposition was expressed in intensely hostile terms at a meeting of the Commonwealth Economic Consultative Council held in Accra in September 1961. Harold Macmillan attributed the strained atmosphere largely to «the Canadian representatives whose opposition to our move towards Europe was marked and even acrimonious»[40], but Australia and New Zealand, and the new Commonwealth countries were all extremely upset, and although Britain attempted to reduce tension by consultation and allay anxiety by pledges to safeguard Commonwealth interests, the communique issued after the Commonwealth Prime Ministers' meeting a year later was not of the usual bland type, thus indicating continuing strain[41].

Anglo-Canadian relations were at a low ebb over this period. Diefenbaker had been largely responsible for the convening of the Prime Ministers' meeting and was outspoken in his opposition to the British move. Macmillan records that he led a «broadside attack» on the first day[42].

Canadian nervousness over British entry stemmed from fears of a serious setback to Canadian exports, of which about 10 % were covered by Commonwealth preference, and also of weakening the counterweight to the United States embodied in the Commonwealth connection. British membership of the EEC would consolidate a giant economic community, with well-developed institutions and commitments to further economic and political integration, in which Canada would have no part and no privileges[43]. The Diefenbaker Government had made clear its desire to strengthen links with Britain and the Commonwealth from the outset, although the goal remained largely aspirational in the absence of any clear strategy for realizing it and indeed the trends of the times were unfavourable. In 1957, Diefenbaker had announced a plan to divert 15 % of Canadian trade from the United States to Britain, but if the aim was laudable, the figure was arbitrary and the means of achieving it elusive. Following the Commonwealth Finance Ministers' meeting in Québec in September of that year, Britain proposed an Anglo-Canadian free trade area, to be phased in over a fifteen-year period, but the proposal fell flat in Ottawa, and the only move made in this field over the next two years was the introduction of some Canadian tariff changes which were to Britain's disadvantage. Some British resentment resulted and perhaps a tendency to discount Diefenbaker's rhetoric. The 1958 Trade Conference has already been noted.

Diefenbaker's concern about trade and Britain's membership of the EEC were by no means misplaced, although a leading Canadian economist, Harry Johnson, commented at the time that emphasis should have been put on the overall challenge posed by the growth of Europe, not on the questions of British membership and Commonwealth preferences which diverted attention to a «relatively minor part of the total problem»[44]. It is true that Commonwealth preferences were not vital (although they were much more important for New Zealand than for Canada); nor were the Commonwealth and the EEC mutually exclusive alternatives for Britain. But Britain's turn to Europe which had political as well as economic connotations heavily underscored the changing character of the Commonwealth. The former leader of the Commonwealth, who at one time or another had been the power responsible for all other members, was now an applicant for membership of a powerful economic and political grouping which she had earlier disdained, in the hope, clearly expressed, that it could provide a remedy for the chronic ills which beset the British economy. It is true that there was considerable opposition in Britain to the new link with Europe, but British respect for the idea of «Commonwealth» was probably undermined by the negative attitude of other Commonwealth countries. Both Australia and Canada made heavy use of Commonwealth symbols and conventions in their campaigns to restrain Britain from joining, and this was resented[45]. Diefenbaker personally became extremely unpopular in British official circles.

Dislike for the Commonwealth in Britain, which had already been engendered by criticism expressed at the time of Suez and by the departure of South Africa, was thus reinforced during this period when Commonwealth countries seemed to want Britain to make the Commonwealth connection more central to its foreign policy than it was to theirs. The use of the Commonwealth framework to put pressure on Britain was to be repeated in more sustained form over Rhodesia: in this case, pressure came from African states, it was related directly to an unquestioned constitutional responsibility, and was backed by a moral principle[46]. Joining the EEC was a policy decision of a different kind, and even if British membership of the Community was more consequential for the Commonwealth than, for instance, African states' membership of the Organization of African Unity (OAU), the Commonwealth bond could not possibly be restrictive of membership of other associations. What was now made clear, was the rather nebulous character of the Commonwealth bond. Perhaps the British application to join the European Community marked the end of any semblance of a *British* Commonwealth, acknowledged or unacknowledged. Henceforth, the Commonwealth was mainly relevant for discussion of and action on North-South issues whether political, concerning decolonization or Southern African problems, or economic, concerning development assistance and the demands in the 1970s for a New International Economic Order (NIEO).

As for British membership of the EEC, De Gaulle's veto in January 1963 settled the matter for the time being, and when Britain reapplied in 1966, Commonwealth oppostion was much more muted. The signal given in 1961 had precipitated adjustment of perceptions and trade reorientation and no doubt further accelerated the decline of the Commonwealth as a trading system. In Canada, the Liberals were returned to power in 1963 and were less concerned to reduce trade and investment links with the United States which had been growing apace. By 1966, Nigeria had concluded an association agreement with the EEC – an option rejected by most Third World Commonwealth countries in 1962 as demeaning – and Protocol 22 of the Treaty of Accession eventually signed in 1971, made provision for African, Caribbean and Pacific Commonwealth countries to become associated with the Community through the renegotiation of the Yaoundé Agreement which gave former French and Belgian African colonies free access to the Common Market and eligibility for assistance from the European Development Fund[47]. Asian Commonwealth countries were to be covered by the Community's General System of Preference, and there were special provisions for New Zealand dairy products and for Commonwealth sugar; otherwise Commonwealth preference was to be phased out by Britain over the five-year transition period. There were, as expected, no concessions for Canada.

1965-1971: TURBULENCE AND PROGRESS

There was to be continuing turbulence in the Commonwealth during the years 1965-1971[48]. There had been antagonism between India and Pakistan since partition and continuing dissension over Kashmir; in 1965-1966 and again in 1970-1971, war erupted on the subcontinent. The second war was to end in 1972 with the breakup of Pakistan and its departure from the Commonwealth, coinciding with the admission of the independent state of Bangladesh (formerly East Pakistan). There was also a prolonged civil war in Nigeria and throughout the period, there was high tension over Rhodesia. All this intra-Commonwealth turmoil could well have proved too much to sustain and the previous decade of controversy had indeed brought a sharp reaction from the comfortable assumptions of the early postwar period. It had become common in Britain in both popular and scholarly writing to find statements that the Commonwealth had either died, or was about to die[49]. Internal racial tensions stemming from heavy immigration from the Caribbean and Asia in earlier years were becoming obvious and, as noted above, public opinion in Britain had become indifferent or even hostile to the Commonwealth, which was seen as a burden[50].

There are probably two main reasons why the Commonwealth did not actually break up during this period. The first is that no member would have gained any great advantage by leaving; indeed for the African countries, there would have been a forfeiture of opportunities to put additional pressure on Britain over Rhodesia and South Africa. The framework was useful for reinforcing norms important to them at minimal cost. Secondly, there was the timely establishment of the Secretariat by the 1965 Prime Ministers' meeting. A central bureau had been suggested by Australia on occasions prior to World War II and vigorously opposed by Canada and South Africa as likely to reinforce anglo-centricity. In 1964 however, a Secretariat was proposed by the newer members as a means of shifting the focus away from Britain and providing a specifically «Commonwealth» core to the association. Arnold Smith, a senior Canadian diplomat who was to be elected as the first Commonwealth Secretary-General, records that leaders from Ghana, Nigeria, Trinidad and Uganda all advocated a Secretariat, though each emphasized different advantages[51]. Support for the proposal entailed a shift in traditional attitudes in Ottawa; Paul Martin, Minister for External Affairs, described it as an «unwelcome development». There was concern, however, that Canada should not adopt a «negative posture»[52] and Pearson was able to join Britain and the other old Commonwealth countries in approving the new body provided it did not arrogate executive functions. In fact a flexible, typically «Commonwealth» set of guidelines allowed the Secretariat to establish itself within a very short space of time as a credible Commonwealth institution[53]. Besides servicing Commonwealth meetings, the Secretariat provided a convenient mechanism for coordinating and extending the functional activities which were becoming an increasingly important aspect of the Commonwealth. The flexible guidelines also allowed the Secretary-General to establish a Commonwealth role for himself: gaining the confidence of heads of government, exercising quiet diplomacy, giving discreet leadership, smoothing over differences, diffusing tension over the whole association. Arnold Smith rose admirably to these challenges.

Smith notes that the first year of the Secretariat's existence was «largely conditioned» by the Rhodesian crisis[54], although it was also faced with the Indo-Pakistani War. But Southern African issues have consistently been priority items on the Commonwealth agenda. The Smith regime in Salisbury declared independence for Rhodesia in November 1965, defying British warnings of penalties which would follow, and the issue was discussed at a stormy Heads of Government meeting in Lagos in January 1966, the first (and so far the only) conference called to deal with a single political issue, and at a further extremely difficult meeting in London in September. The differences of opinion were between the British (Labour) Government, headed by Harold Wilson and holding a bare Parliamentary majority, and the African Commonwealth countries. The British Government was anxious to end the illegal rebellion in Rhodesia and was prepared to withold independence until there was proof of significant advancement for the African population which would lead to majority rule[55]. But it was not prepared to employ more than diplomatic and economic pressures to bring this about. The African states, on the other hand, wanted Britain to use force. Their demands (and accusations) were put very bluntly and at great length at the two meetings in 1966. Harold Wilson describes the second conference as a «nightmare» and gives a graphic account of the African leaders' use of caucus techniques and breach of conventions of confidentiality by press statements which threatened not only the informal character of these high-level meetings, but their continuation[56]. He records that Lester B. Pearson's diplomatic and drafting skills were once again in demand, but it seems clear that the decisive factor in bringing the conference to an end on a note of consensus was the African group's realization that they were in danger of pushing Britain too far. Arnold Smith recalls advising African leaders against leaving the Commonwealth over the Rhodesian question and although Ghana and Tanzania broke diplomatic relations with Britain they did not take this decisive step. Zambia, too, was on the brink of leaving in 1966[57]. Following the September conference, Britain tried once more to negotiate with the Smith regime in Rhodesia and then, with Commonwealth agreement, took the matter to the UN Security Council which imposed mandatory sanctions in December 1966.

Henceforth the main locus of international pressure was the UN, but as Rhodesia remained a British constitutional responsibility, the African Commonwealth countries continued to monitor Britain's relationship with the Smith regime. Fortunately for the Commonwealth, however, the techniques employed in London in September 1966 were not to be repeated, and in the final resolution of the Rhodesian problem, the Commonwealth provided useful mechanisms for handling the transitional period before independence. These are noted in the next section. The 1969 Heads of Government meeting, according to Harold Wilson, was «by far the most successful ever held». Canada was represented by Pierre E. Trudeau, who had publicly expressed doubts about the value of the Commonwealth before leaving for London, but apparently changed his mind in the course of the meeting. He made a positive contribution to the discussions and two years later, at another stormy Heads of Government meeting in Singapore, he played an important role in reconciling divergent points of view, thereby carrying on the tradition of his predecessor. At Singapore, the new British Prime Minister, Edward Heath, came under heavy pressure to abandon his Government's plan to sell arms to South Africa despite a Security Council arms embargo against South Africa which had been recommended in 1964[58].

The Singapore meeting was also responsible for a Commonwealth Declaration of Principles – a useful codification of what the Commonwealth stood for – and for the establishment of the Commonwealth Fund for Technical Cooperation (CFTC) which was to be a Commonwealth success story in the 1970s. Established originally as an independent unit within the Secretariat with initial finance of $1 million (£400 000), the CFTC dealt with personnel who could provide technical expertise in developing Commonwealth countries, particularly in studying and assessing projects and needs and in export market development. It has also sponsored training courses in technical and vocational skills in developing countries for students from other developing countries, and has a small resident team of experts who can be sent to cope with urgent problems.

The first Managing Director of the Fund was a Canadian, George Kidd, and Canada has been a major contributor to the Fund from the beginning, consistently supplying about 30 % of its total budget. All members of the Fund contribute on a voluntary basis, and thus a truly multilateral agency has been established, blurring the rigid lines between donor and recipient which have been an unattractive feature of many international aid projects and agencies. The CFTC proved to be a model of efficiency; in a modest, pragmatic and speedy manner it met local needs and where possible used local skills[59].

1972-1980: CALMER WATERS

After Singapore, which was a very low point in Commonwealth affairs, the association moved into somewhat calmer waters. It seemed that the new Commonwealth, with its possibilities and limitations, had come to be accepted and was not in imminent danger of collapse. Its basic norms of multiracialism and cooperation were set firm, as was its character as a loose set of relationships with regular dialogue at ministerial levels. There were still unresolved problems: Rhodesia did not finally become independent as Zimbabwe until early 1980; Pakistan left in dudgeon over Bangladesh's admission in 1972; Cyprus, a Commonwealth member, was dismembered by Turkey with no forceful Commonwealth reaction in 1974; the Amin regime in Uganda brought calls for ostracism and condemnation (finally achieved in 1977); sports boycotts against South Africa continued to provoke controversy. But the Secretariat was able to play a useful mediatory role on many questions and there were also some practical achievements.

A sustained Commonwealth success story has been in the functional field. The CFTC was able to expand its work as contributions increased year by year; in addition, the Secretariat added divisions concerned with youth affairs and legal affairs to meet new needs. It also set up regional health offices in East and West Africa and in the Caribbean. The Secretary-General and his staff were able to give considerable help to Commonwealth African, Caribbean and Pacific (ACP) countries who, in terms of Britain's accession to the EEC, were eligible for association when the Yaoundé agreement was renegotiated. The new Lomé agreement, signed in 1974, represented gains for developing countries; the existing associates and the new associables held together as a bargaining team, drawing on the resources of the Secretariat[60].

The 1973 Ottawa Heads of Government meeting, hosted by Pierre E. Trudeau, was widely regarded as being very successful. It was carefully prepared by the Secretariat and Canadian officials; the format was designed to exclude long, set speeches and a weekend retreat of complete privacy and informality gave visiting leaders a chance to have «off-the-record» discussions.

Arnold Smith ended a decade of service as Commonwealth Secretary-General in 1975 and his successor, Shridath Ramphal, carried on where Smith left off, stressing that the Commonwealth did not exist to serve its members but the world as a whole. This non-exclusive principle which was first enunciated in the Colombo Plan in 1950, has had many applications, including Commonwealth help for Mozambique when it applied sanctions against Rhodesia and the extension of the work of regional health offices in Africa to neighbouring non-Commonwealth countries. There were also useful Commonwealth initiatives in the context of the dialogue over a New International Economic Order (NIEO) in the mid-1970s. For instance, a group of experts chaired by Alister McIntyre, Secretary-General of the Commonwealth Caribbean Community, was appointed by the 1975 Heads of Government meeting to make proposals on bridging the North-South gap and their interim report was made available to the Seventh Special Session of the UN General Assembly. The Final Report was published in 1977 and there have also been reports on *The Common Fund*, on *Cooperation for Accelerating Industrialization* and on *Constraints to Economic Growth*[61]. And on occasions, Commonwealth meetings can establish a common position which can be carried forward to other forums and serve, in Secretary-General Ramphal's words, as a catalyst in consensus forming.

The major political achievement in this period was the constitutional settlement of the Rhodesian question to which the 1979 Lusaka Heads of Government meeting contributed significantly, persuading the new British Prime Minister, Margaret Thatcher, that certain parameters should be observed and that the unilateral lifting of sanctions and recognition of the «internal settlement» in Rhodesia would be disastrous. Canada was represented at this meeting by Joe Clark, the Conservatives having been returned to power with a minority government in May 1979, and it was the Australian Prime Minister who appears to have been particularly influential as well as Commonwealth Secretary-General Ramphal[62]. There was no doubt that all Commonwealth governments were united in their desire for a settlement which would be legitimate inside and outside Rhodesia and bring to an end the tragic civil war and the international sanctions which were proving so damaging not only for Rhodesians but also for their immediate neighbours. The Lancaster House Conference between the British Government, the Rhodesian regime and the Patriotic Front followed this Commonwealth meeting and succeeded in producing agreement on a ceasefire, elections under a new constitution, and independence for the new State, Zimbabwe. In the final months before independence, Rhodesia reverted to colonial status. A Commonwealth force of 1 500 men monitored the ceasefire arrangements and a Commonwealth Observer Group monitored the organization and conduct of the elections. Gordon Fairweather was the Canadian member of an eleven-men team drawn from different parts of the Commonwealth which was able to report that, given the extraordinary circumstances in which the elections were held, in the immediate aftermath of a bitter civil war with rival armies still carrying arms, the elections were acceptable as giving an adequate opportunity for informed choices to be made[63].

At least until the 1980s, then, the Commonwealth has survived as an active group of states who have either found it worth belonging to or not worth leaving[64]. Since World War II, new states and new international institutions have proliferated. The drive for institutions has come from the search for security and order through formal organizations; efforts to integrate economies for greater prosperity; the need to tackle environmental and economic problems in concert, particularly the problems of the developing world; and the advantages of building coalitions to muster collective political will and to use institutions as pressure groups and standard-setters. The Commonwealth is obviously useful for some of these aims and its informality, flexibility and pragmatism have allowed it to respond rapidly to new developments. The fact that it emerged from an empire made it inevitable that decolonization and the problems which it left in its wake would be its main agenda and its value to the newer members is clear in these terms. The Canadian contribution to the evolution of the Commonwealth has been identified in broad outline. But what contribution does the Commonwealth make to Canada?

CANADA AND THE COMMONWEALTH:
A COST-BENEFIT APPROACH

The cost to Canada of Commonwealth membership is obviously minimal in financial terms. Although Canada is the second largest contributor to the Secretariat's regular budget, giving 17,8 % compared with Britain's 30 % and Australia's 9,9 %, the annual subscription is very small. In 1980-1981, for instance, it amounted to $1,3 million. Canada is also a major contributor to the Commonwealth Fund for Technical Cooperation (CFTC) and the Commonwealth Youth Programme, but this forms a very small part of the overall Canadian contribution to multilateral bodies and programmes. In 1979-1980, for instance, multilateral aid (excluding aid to non-governmental organizations but including food aid) was $500,5 million, or 41 % of total official development assistance, and of this $10,3 million, or 2 %, went to Commonwealth and Francophone programmes. Contributions to the CFTC of $8,8 million and to Francophone programmes of $1,44 million can be compared with $217,6 million disbursed to UN agencies and other international organizations.

Canada has also made a major contribution in personnel to the Secretariat, the CFTC and other Commonwealth programmes but if these individuals were lost to Canada for that time, there was also a gain from their participation in international affairs. For ten years, Arnold Smith, a diplomat in the Pearsonian mould, was at the helm of the Secretariat and gave it a form and style characteristic of Canadian internationalism at its best. But there are no other costs. Commonwealth membership does not restrict membership of other bodies and imposes no obligations in terms of security, defence, or peacekeeping, and no burdensome economic ties. Moreover, obligations to support Commonwealth norms have not borne particularly heavily on Canada; Canadians supported decolonization and like other rich countries, Canada has accepted a responsibility for improving the lot of the developing world. For all Western countries, there are moral questions relating to apartheid and racial discrimination which are likely to be raised in all international forums and in this regard, Commonwealth membership does not place any additional burden on Canada. Mandatory sanctions against Rhodesia were imposed by the United Nations Security Council which is authorized to require such action of its members; Commonwealth sanctions could only be applied on a voluntary basis.

On the other side of the «balance sheet», the benefits for Canada of Commonwealth membership are modest, but have certainly exceeded the costs. They are to be categorized mainly in terms of communication and participation, status and role, and they have accrued to the country as a whole and to its leaders. Membership of the Commonwealth has given Canada many points of contact in Asia and Africa which would not otherwise have been easy to develop. Canada has always eschewed too close an embrace from the United States which could suffocate it, and having no regional group to adhere to and with Britain no longer a «counterweight», it must look for other ways to diversify its international connections. While not the most significant of international groupings, the Commonwealth does offer an opportunity to cultivate direct relations with countries in all parts of the world on a basis of some shared experience and principles. It facilitates multilateral political dialogue and in fact Commonwealth-style heads of government meetings have become a model for other «summits», where leaders can exchange views in relative informality. Direct communication with their counterparts enables leaders to establish personal contacts and gain a better understanding of each other's problems[65]. The «links of affinity» which bound Canada to Britain and to some extent to the other old Dominions are now weaker, although they have not entirely disappeared; «links of convenience» are still strong enough to make membership worthwhile[66].

One can judge too that Canadian support for the idea of a Francophone community reflects a sense in Ottawa that the Commonwealth is not only valuable per se but as a model for the widening and deepening of Canada's external relationships, particularly with Third World countries. The non-exclusive, egalitarian and practical nature of the Commonwealth connection provides encouragement for the idea of a Francophone counterpart; a dual emphasis which makes a great deal of sense in terms of Canada's two founding cultures[67].

The Commonwealth, together with La Francophonie, also provides a useful framework for the disbursement of bilateral as well as multilateral aid. In 1979-1980, 23 % of official bilateral development assistance went to Commonwealth Africa, and

25 % to Francophone Africa, while 21 % went to Commonwealth Asian countries and 5 % to the Commonwealth Caribbean.

In role terms, Britain's loss of primacy has provided opportunities for other members, particularly Canada, to give leadership at certain times and on certain issues[68]. Canada's strong position on Commonwealth membership questions, its help both in preserving the association in times of crisis and in developing its potential by supporting the programmes of functional cooperation coordinated by the Secretariat, have all been noted in this chapter. These roles have sharpened Canada's external profile. And for government leaders, a distinctive international role is generally welcome, particularly if it can be exercised at summit meetings. It confers prestige at home and abroad and ensures media coverage. It has been suggested that the Canadian Prime Minister «exerts more of a direct foreign policy influence in his Commonwealth negotiations than in any other area of foreign policy with the possible exception of summit meetings»[69]; if this is true, it goes a long way towards explaining Trudeau's speedy conversion to the value of the Commonwealth.

What the Commonwealth does not offer – and what Canada would not favour – is a coalition for political action against others. Commonwealth observer status at the UN since 1974 is mainly a function of its role in facilitating dialogue over the NIEO; representation for places on UN bodies is handled regionally and there is no question of the Commonwealth forming a voting bloc at the UN. Once Britain ceased to be the leader, the Commonwealth became leaderless; given its multitude of internal divisions, it cannot hope to function as a pressure group for change in the wider world, although it can and should facilitate discussion and compromise. Internally, pressures have mainly been *on* Britain from the Third World majority; recently (1981) they have been directed at New Zealand. If this tendency is pushed too far, whether on sports boycotts or other issues, the Commonwealth's days could be numbered.

The contemporary Commonwealth, with considerable Canadian input, has succeeded in completely revamping a set of imperial connections to create an acceptable framework first for decolonization and subsequently for continuing consultation and cooperation on the basis of a certain level of shared experience and interest and a substantial measure of assistance for the newer and smaller members. As an association bridging the North-South gap, it obviously has a special value and although its future is uncertain, it may continue to surprise us. What would be surprising would be any move in Canada to leave it. John W. Holmes' comment that the Commonwealth «has been more than appears to the public eye»[70] is worth pondering.

NOTES

1. The scant references to the Commonwealth in the 1970 White Paper *Foreign Policy for Canadians* could have been taken to indicate that the pieces of the jigsaw were becoming fewer and fewer. In fact, the White Paper reflected the new Prime Minister's initial lack of interest in the Commonwealth which was soon to be reversed and the 1970s were to prove the value of the Commonwealth connection in a number of ways.

2. Alexander Brady, «Canada and the Commonwealth», *International Journal,* Vol. IV, 3, Summer 1949, p. 196.

3. J.D.B. Miller, *Britain and the Old Dominions,* London, Chatto & Windus, 1966, p. 146.

4. *Cf.* H.V. Hodson (ed.), *The British Commonwealth and the Future* (Proceedings of the Second Unoffocial Conference on British Commonwealth Relations, Sydney, 3-17 September 1938), London, Oxford University Press, 1939, where it is recorded that matters «most commonly discussed» were defence, foreign policy and the role of the Commonwealth as a group in world affairs, trade among the members, the future of the «C» class Mandates and migration.

5. For instance, in Ontario where British subjects (who are not Canadian citizens) still enjoy the right to vote in Provincial elections. The Canadian Citizenship Act of 1946 marked a new trend by defining citizens in terms of specific Canadian nationality while continuing to recognize citizens of other Commonwealth countries as British subjects (*i.e.* non-aliens). But the crucial change has come with Britain's progressive elimination of free entry for Commonwealth migrants. The British Immigration Act of 1962 sounded the death knell of the «common citizenship» ideal.

6. See *Commonwealth Non-Governmental Organizations,* Commonwealth Secretariat Information Leaflet, February 1980; *Summary Report on the Dalhousie Conference: The Commonwealth and Non-Governmental Organizations,* Dalhousie University, 25-29 October 1976 (mimeog.); *Choix: Francophonie et Commonwealth,* Centre québécois de relations internationales, 1978, Ch. 5.

7. See, for instance, *The First Ten Years: 1966-76,* Fifth Report of the Commonwealth Foundation, London, 1976.

8. For detailed studies of postwar Commonwealth history, see the bibliographical essay by J.D.B. Miller, «Commonwealth Studies», in Roger Morgan (ed.), T*he Study of International Affairs,* London, Oxford University Press for the Royal Institute of International Affairs, 1972, p. 136-155 and also Miller's own extensive and scholarly work on the Commonwealth, particularly his *Survey of Commonwealth Affairs, Problems of Expansion and Attrition 1953-1969,* London, Oxford University Press for the Royal Institute of International Affairs, 1974. In *Stitches in Time: the Commonwealth in World Politics,* Toronto, General Publishing, 1981, Arnold Smith gives a personal account of the years 1965-1975 when he was the (first) Commonwealth Secretary-General.

9. John W. Holmes gives a full account of these new dimensions of official thought and action in *The Shaping of Peace: Canada and the Search for World Order 1943-1957,* Vol. 1, Toronto, University of Toronto Press, 1979.

10. See R.A. Mackay (ed.), *Canadian Foreign Policy 1945-1954: Selected Speeches and Documents,* Toronto, McClelland and Stewart, 1971, p. 346-353.

11. Nicholas Mansergh, writing in 1948, suggested that the Canadian approach to the Commonwealth was «[...] too easily disposed perhaps to place international and Commonwealth cooperation in a false antithesis [...]», *The Commonwealth and the Nations: Studies in British Commonwealth Relations,* London, Royal Institute of International Affairs, 1948, p. 73. But at the time a sense of antithesis may have been useful.

12. *The Better Part of Valour: Essays on Canadian Diplomacy,* Toronto, McClelland and Stewart, 1970, p. 109; see also Mansergh, *op. cit.,* Chapter III, «Dominion Conceptions of the Commonwealth».

13. Patrick Gordon Walker notes that the Canadian and Australian concepts were actually in conflict prior to World War I. *The Commonwealth,* London, Secker and Warburg, Mercury Books, 1965, p. 92.

14. Hedley Bull, writing in the late 1950s, suggested that too close an examination of the Commonwealth might explode the myth and accelerate the process of disintegration. «What is the Commonwealth?», *World Politics,* Vol. XI, N° 4, 1959, p. 587.

15. *The Shaping of Peace,* p. 297.

16. The text of the Declaration which was issued as a final communique after the meeting is in N. Mansergh, *Documents and Speeches on British Commonwealth Affairs 1931-1952,* London, Oxford University Press for the Royal Institute of International Affairs, 1953, p. 846-847.

17. See Gordon Walker, *op. cit.,* p. 33.

18. Robert A. Spencer, *Canada in World Affairs: From UN to NATO, 1946-1949,* Toronto, Oxford University Press, 1967, p. 398-399.

19. *The Commonwealth,* p. 137.

20. See John A. Munro and Alex I. Inglis (eds.), *Mike: the Memoirs of the Rt. Hon. Lester B. Pearson, 1948-1957*, Toronto, University of Toronto Press, 1973, p. 107-117; Lester B. Pearson, *The Commonwealth 1970* (Smuts Memorial Lecture), Cambridge University Press, 1971, p. 15-24.

21. Noted in Spencer, *Canada in World Affairs*, p. 402. See also M.S. Rajan, «Relations between the Old and the New Members» in W.B. Hamilton *et al.* (eds.), *A Decade of the Commonwealth 1955-1964*, Durham, N.C., Duke University Press, 1966. He notes that Canada showed «great understanding and accommodation on questions affecting the new nations» (p. 152).

22. See for instance M.S. Rajan, «The Indo-Canadian Entente», *International Journal*, Vol. XVII, N° 4, Autumn 1962, p. 358-384.

23. «The Commonwealth and the United Nations», *A Decade of the Commonwealth*, p. 350.

24. *The Shaping of Peace*, p. 269.

25. Douglas Le Pan, who travelled from Ottawa to attend the meeting of senior officials held simultaneously in Colombo to discuss sterling area problems, gives a first-hand account of the proceedings of the Foreign Ministers' Conference and the subsequent very contentious follow-up meeting in Sydney in September of the same year in *Bright Glass of Memory: A Set of Four Memoirs*, Toronto, McGraw Hill Ryerson, 1979.

26. Le Pan, *Bright Glass of Memory*, particularly p. 190, 218-219.

27. Cited in Mansergh, *Documents and Speeches on Commonwealth Affairs, 1952-1962*, London, Oxford University Press for the Royal Institute of International Affairs, 1963, p. 515.

28. *Ibidem*, p. 517-534.

29. It seems that Prime Minister St. Laurent first read of the Anglo-French «ultimatum» to Egypt and Israel in an Ottawa newspaper and some of Pearson's celebrated diplomacy was exerted to moderate his reaction. See Dale Thomson, *Louis St. Laurent, Canadian*, Toronto, Macmillan, 1967, p. 462.

30. *Mike: Memoirs [...] 1948-1957*, p. 273. James Eayrs examines Canadian reactions to the Suez crisis in his *Canada in World Affairs: October 1955 to June 1957*, Toronto, Oxford University Press, 1959, p. 182-193.

31. «The Relationship in Alliance and World Affairs» in John Sloan Dickey (ed.), *The United States and Canada*, Englewood Cliffs, N.J., Prentice Hall, 1964, p. 112. See also Terence Robertson, *The Inside Story of the Suez Conspiracy*, McClelland and Stewart, 1964, who in addition to documenting Pearson's skill in handling the UN debate over UNEF notes that «the Ottawa bridge was virtually the only means of communication between Washington and its belligerent allies» (p. 202).

32. *A Decade of the Commonwealth*, p. 354.

33. J.D.B. Miller notes that in the Suez crisis, among old Commonwealth members, «only Canada seemed worried about the effect of British actions upon the survival of general Commonwealth goodwill», *Britain and the Old Dominions*, p. 253-254.

34. *Pointing the Way: 1959-1961*, London, Macmillan, 1972, p. 292.

35. See Diefenbaker's own comments, cited by Frank Hayes in «South Africa's Departure from the Commonwealth», *The International History Review*, Vol. II, N° 3, July 1980, p. 463, n. 26.

36. *Pointing the Way*, p. 293.

37. *Ibidem*, p. 294.

38. See Hayes, *loc. cit.*, especially p. 473, 476; Peter Harnetty, «Canada, South Africa and the Commonwealth», *Journal of Commonwealth Political Studies*, Vol. II, November, 1963, p. 33-43.

39. See Trevor Lloyd, *Canada in World Affairs: 1957-1959*, Toronto, Oxford University Press, p. 183-188.

40. *At the End of the Day: 1961-1963*, London, Macmillan, 1973, p. 29. See also Denis Austin in P. Uri (ed.), *From Commonwealth to Common Market*, Harmondsworth, Penguin Books, 1968, p. 167.

41. It referred to «many different viewpoints» and «many uncertainties» and to «anxieties expressed by Commonwealth governments about the possible effects of British membership of the EEC». Text in Mansergh, *Documents and Speeches 1952-1962*, p. 656-660.

42. *At the End of the Day*, p. 132.

43. These issues are well set out by Peyton V. Lyon in *Canada in World Affairs: 1961-1963*, Toronto, Oxford University Press, 1968, Chapter 8.

44. *Canada, the Commonwealth and the Common Market* (Report of the 1962 Summer Institute, Mount Allison University), McGill University Press, 1962, p. 106.

45. This point is developed further by J.D.B. Miller in *Britain and the Old Dominions*, where the attitudes of Australia, Canada and New Zealand are characterized as «old-fashioned» (p. 268-270).

46. See Margaret Doxey, «Strategies in Multilateral Diplomacy: The Commonwealth, Southern Africa and the NIEO», *International Journal*, Vol. XXXV, No. 2, Spring 1980, p. 329-356.

47. The (second) Yaoundé Convention was due to expire on 31 January 1975.

48. From 1965 onwards, the Commonwealth's ups and downs and the work of the Secretariat are clearly recorded in the biennial *Reports* of the Commonwealth Secretary-General, published by the Commonwealth Secretariat in London. Arnold Smith's memoir, *Stitches in Time*, is noted in n. 8 above.

49. *Cf.* Hedley Bull, «What is the Commonwealth?». In April 1964, an article in the London *Times,* attributed to Enoch Powell, characterized the Commonwealth as «a gigantic farce»; in 1970, Max Beloff wrote to the *Times* asking «Does Britain Need the Commonwealth?» and concluded it did not.

50. J.D.B. Miller notes that «Commonwealth» became «almost a dirty word in Britain». «Britain and the Commonwealth», *South Atlantic Quarterly*, Vol. LXIX, No.2, 1970, p. 196.

51. *Stitches in Time*, p. 4-5.

52. *Ibidem,* p. 8.

53. The Agreed Memorandum establishing the Secretariat was published after the 1965 Prime Ministers' meeting as Cmnd. 2713, London, July 1965.

54. First *Report* of the Commonwealth Secretary-General, 1966, p. 5.

55. The Six Principles which Britain required to be satisfied before independence would be granted to Rhodesia were set out in *Rhodesia: Documents Relating to Proposals for a Settlement, 1966,* Cmnd. 3171, London, 1966, p. 3.

56. Harold Wilson, *The Labour Government 1964-1970: A Personal Record,* London, Weidenfeld & Nicolson and Michael Joseph, 1971, p. 276-287.

57. *Stitches in Time,* p. 31-32.

58. Once again, Tanzania and also India and Nigeria contemplated withdrawal and Arnold Smith recalls talk of «expelling» Britain from the Commonwealth. *Stitches in Time,* p. 213-214.

59. For a detailed account of the CFTC, see *Commonwealth Skills for Commonwealth Needs,* Commonwealth Secretariat, 1981. the CFTC is noteworthy for keeping administrative overheads to a low 12 %, compared with the 30 % typical of other multilateral aid agencies.

60. This process is described in some detail by Smith in *Stitches in Time,* p. 183 ff. But it can also be argued that these arrangements had a divisive effect within the Commonwealth, creating two «classes» of developing countries, the associated and the non-associated. See *The Commonwealth and Development,* London, Overseas Development Institute, 1976.

61. These have all been published by the Commonwealth Secretariat.

62. But see Patrick Keatley's report on the Lusaka Conference in the *Guardian Weekly,* 19 August 1979. He notes that Clark volunteered «for mediator, a job he did superbly».

63. The Final Report of the Commonwealth Observer Group, *Southern Rhodesia Elections,* February,1980, was sent to Heads of Government in August 1980, and was published by the Commonwealth Secretariat.

64. It is interesting that Pakistan, which was over-hasty in leaving, has expressed interest in renewed membership on several occasions.

65. Trudeau wrote on the advantages of frank and informal dialogue at Commonwealth summit meetings in «The Commonwealth after Ottawa: Looking to the Future», *The Round Table,* No. 253, January 1974.

66. The terms are Patrick Gordon Walker's.

67. Arnold Smith notes that initial concern in Ottawa over the possible utilization of L'Agence de coopération culturelle et technique for the furtherance of France's political goals gave way to a more positive approach and describes his own cordial relations and useful contacts with Jean-Marc Léger, the first Secretary-General of L'Agence. See *Stitches in Time,* p. 178-182.

68. *Cf.* Peyton V. Lyon and Brian W. Tomlin, *Canada as an International Actor,* Toronto, Macmillan, 1979, Ch. 2.

69. Peter Boehm, «Canada and the Modern Commonwealth: the approaches of Lester Pearson and Pierre Trudeau», *Bulletin of Canadian Studies,* Vol. III, No. 1, June 1979, p. 23.

70. *A Decade of the Commonwealth,* p. 365.

BIBLIOGRAPHY

BALL, M. Margaret. *The «open» Commonwealth.* Durham, N.C., Duke University Press, 1971.

DOXEY, Margaret. «The Commonwealth, in the 1970s», *The Year Book of World Affairs,* 1973, Vol. 27, p. 90-109.

EAYRS, James. *The Commonwealth and Suez: A Documentary Survey,* London, Oxford University Press, 1964.

GLAZEBROOK, G. de T. and BRADY, Alexander. «Canada and the Commonwealth», *Round Table,* No. 240, November 1970, p. 557-566.

GROOM, A.J.R. and TAYLOR, Paul (eds.). *The Commonwealth in the 1980s,* London, Macmillan, 1984.

HAMILTON, W.B. *et al.* (eds.) *A Decade of the Commonwealth 1954-1964,* Durham, N.C., Duke University Press, 1966.

HARNETTY, Peter. «Canada, South Africa and the Commonwealth», *Journal of Commonwealth Political Studies,* Vol. II, November 1963, p. 33-43.

HAYES, Frank. «South Africa's Departure From The Commonwealth 1960-61», *The International History Review,* Vol. 2, No 3, July 1980, p. 453-484.

HOLMES, John W. *The Shaping of Peace: Canada in the Search for World Order 1943-1957,* 2 vols., Toronto, University of Toronto Press, 1979, 1982.

HOLMES, John W. «A Canadian's Commonwealth: Realism out of Rhetoric», *Round Table,* No. 56, October 1966, p. 335-347.

RAJAN, M.S. «The Indo-Canadian Entente», *International Journal,* Vol. XVII, N° 4, Autumn 1962, p. 358-384.

SMITH, Arnold (with Clyde Sanger). *Stitches in Time: The Commonwealth in World Politics,* Don Mills, Ontario, General Publishing, 1981

See also the *Canada in World Affairs* series published by the Canadian Institute of International Affairs, Toronto, and the *Survey of British Commonwealth Affairs* series published by the Royal Institute of International Affairs, London.

10

La Francophonie et la politique étrangère du Canada

Gilles Lalande *

INTRODUCTION

Si facile à appréhender lorsqu'on s'en tient au sens commun du terme, la Francophonie soutient difficilement la comparaison avec le Commonwealth quand on la considère en tant qu'élément de la politique étrangère du Canada. Le Commonwealth a été, oserait-on dire, porté sur les fonts baptismaux de la politique extérieure du Canada alors que la Francophonie, cette «entreprise ardente et ambiguë»[1], toujours en voie de construction au sens institutionnel du terme, n'est venue que tardivement à constituer un élément sectoriel identifiable de la politique étrangère canadienne. Alors que le Commonwealth est un rassemblement de pays qui ont tous été à l'origine des colonies britanniques et qui, au moment de leur accession à l'indépendance, ont volontairement choisi pour la plupart d'adhérer à une communauté de nations dont le caractère premier est d'être essentiellement politique, la Francophonie quant à elle regroupe des pays dont le français, à des degrés infiniment divers, est le seul véritable trait commun, et qui, n'ayant commencé à prendre forme qu'à partir des années 60, correspond beaucoup plus à une tentative nouvelle d'organisation et de développement des relations multilatérales entre nations dont la conviction ou la motivation francophone, c'est le moins qu'on puisse dire, est loin d'être la même.

Cette différence si nette entre ce qui, d'une part, inspire la construction de la Francophonie et ce qui, d'autre part, sous-tend la remarquable association qu'est devenu au fil des années le Commonwealth, n'est pas sans soulever une série d'interrogations auxquelles nous tenterons de répondre dans ce chapitre. Ces questions sont les suivantes: pourquoi et comment le Canada a-t-il été amené à s'intéresser à la mise en place d'une communauté internationale des pays francophones? Quels ont été au Canada les acteurs qui ont joué un rôle significatif dans l'organisation d'une telle communauté? Quels ont été les objectifs poursuivis à cet égard par les uns et les autres et quelle sorte de dynamique a résulté de leur action respective? Enfin, quelle place occupait la Francophonie dans la politique extérieure du Canada au moment où a pris fin le régime Trudeau en juin 1984? À ces questions qui visent toutes à faire voir ce qu'a été la contribution du Canada à la Francophonie, nous ajouterons celle de savoir si la Francophonie a eu un impact sur la conduite de la politique étrangère du Canada. Mais posons-nous auparavant la question préalable: pourquoi la Francophonie?

---

* L'auteur est décédé au moment de la publication de cet ouvrage. Il fut directeur du Département de science politique de l'Université de Montréal; il fut également vice-président de l'ACDI et ambassadeur du Canada en Afrique.

Les origines de la Francophonie au plan international

Il nous faut en premier lieu reconnaître que la Francophonie, au sens de communauté internationale de pays francophones, a été recherchée d'abord par des Africains d'expression française, au premier rang desquels figurent Léopold Senghor du Sénégal, Habib Bourguiba de Tunisie et Hamani Diori du Niger. Lancée en 1955 par le premier, alors que celui-ci était encore Secrétaire d'État dans le gouvernement français, l'idée de la Francophonie a été reprise en 1965 par le président Bourguiba qui l'a traduite à sa façon en préconisant l'établissement d'un «Commonwealth francophone», ou d'une communauté francophone dont l'objectif serait de renforcer les liens, les échanges et la coopération entre pays où la langue française occupe une place importante, et où la population se réclame en tout ou en partie de la culture française. Ce qui en tout cas ne fait aucun doute, c'est que dès l'origine, la Francophonie s'articulera à partir de la conception que s'en font certains dirigeants d'États de l'Afrique noire française et des pays du Maghreb, conception qui finira par être acceptée par les gouvernements successifs de l'ancienne puissance coloniale qu'est la France.

Cette Francophonie, dont on ne savait pas encore quelle forme institutionnelle elle allait prendre, existait pourtant déjà en germe dans plusieurs organisations africaines régionales, dont le Conseil de l'entente qui, dès 1959, réunissait quatre États d'Afrique francophone: la Côte d'Ivoire, le Dahomey, le Niger et la Haute-Volta, auxquels se sont joints le Togo en 1966, l'Union africaine et malgache (mise sur pied en 1961), l'Organisation africaine et malgache de coopération économique (OAMCE), qui devint en 1965 l'Organisation africaine et malgache (OCAM). Elle se traduisait également dans les nombreuses conférences tenues à partir de 1960 entre les ministres africains et malgaches de l'Éducation et ceux des Finances.

Ce sont à vrai dire les assises tenues par l'OCAM à Tananarive en juin 1966 qui consacrèrent l'existence officielle d'une première communauté régionale se définissant comme étant formée de pays francophones. À la suite de cette réunion, le président Diori du Niger soumit le 16 septembre 1966 au général de Gaulle, au nom de l'OCAM, un avant-projet d'organisation de la Francophonie qui, ayant défini celle-ci comme «une communauté spirituelle de nations qui emploient le français, que celui-ci soit langue nationale, langue officielle ou langue d'usage», comprenait trois cercles concentriques dont le principal, le plus restreint, regroupait la France et les États africains et malgache, et le plus étendu allait jusqu'à englober l'ensemble des pays entièrement ou partiellement de langue française. Ainsi ce projet préfigurait-il ce qui allait devenir dans le temps une Francophonie à deux vitesses, ou mieux encore une Francophonie à deux paliers, à savoir une Francophonie postcoloniale, plus intime, ostensiblement axée sur une région unique, l'Afrique, et aujourd'hui traduite par le Sommet annuel franco-africain, puis une autre, plus universelle et forcément plus relâchée, incarnée depuis 1970 par l'Agence de coopération culturelle et technique, dont sont aujourd'hui membres des pays aussi différents que le Canada, la Belgique, la Suisse, Haïti et le Viêt-nam.

Malgré l'extrême réserve gardée pour des raisons évidentes par la France à l'égard de toute forme d'organisation de relations multilatérales entre pays d'expression française, la proposition de l'OCMA évoqua de la part des autorités françaises dès le 8 novembre 1966 une réaction officielle dite «sympathique et de plus en plus positive». Et le 26 janvier 1967, se déclarant prêt au nom de la France à aborder l'étape des contacts multilatéraux, Jean de Broglie, Secrétaire d'État aux Affaires étrangères, rappela fort opportunément que l'organisation de la Francophonie, à cause de son envergure, ne pouvait pas être seulement l'œuvre des gouvernements. C'était reconnaître l'action indispensable et le rôle précurseur sur le plan de l'organisation d'une kyrielle d'organisations privées ou non gouvernementales, dont entre autres l'Association des universités partiellement ou entièrement de langue française (AUPELF), fondée en 1961, dont le premier secrétaire général, Jean-Marc Léger, avait antérieurement défini la responsabilité commune de tous les pays francophones envers la langue française, l'Institut international de droit des pays de langue française (IDEF), créé en 1964, et l'Association internationale des parlementaires de langue française (AIPLF), mise sur pied en 1967. Prêchant l'exemple, le gouvernement français allait lui-même créer par décret le 31 mars 1966 le Haut-Comité pour la défense et l'expansion de la langue française, puis susciter la fondation en janvier 1967 de l'Association de solidarité francophone dont la raison d'être demeure de favoriser les contacts et les relations entre personnalités, organismes et gouvernements de pays qui font une large utilisation de la langue française.

Aux appels précoces et appuyés des premiers promoteurs africains en faveur d'une Francophonie internationale, et au ralliement subséquent, au demeurant relativement timide des Français, allait correspondre l'appui enthousiaste et empressé des Canadiens, et plus particulièrement des Québécois, qui pour des raisons historiques, démo-linguistiques et politiques, reconnaîtront à leur tour qu'il leur était indispensable de promouvoir la construction d'une communauté internationale des pays francophones.

Les fondements de la Francophonie au Canada

Le caractère partiellement francophone du Canada, est-il besoin de le rappeler, tient à ses origines historiques. De langue française dès sa découverte, le Canada ne comptait pas moins de six millions de francophones sur une population totale de 25 millions en 1981. Cette masse de parlants français constitue à vrai dire la raison d'être de la Francophonie canadienne qui, étant isolée et terriblement minoritaire à l'échelle nord-américaine, ne pouvait que bénéficier de l'organisation et du développement d'une Francophonie internationale. Or, il faut souligner que cette population francophone se concentre en grande partie au Québec, où vivent près de 85 % de la population canadienne de langue maternelle française, et que l'ensemble des Canadiens de langue française bénéficient sur le plan politique, en raison du système fédéral de gouvernement, de deux niveaux de gouvernement à travers lesquels les francophones peuvent exprimer leurs aspirations en matière de francophonie. Il s'agit du gouvernement fédéral qui, selon la Constitution, a la responsabilité de la conduite de la politique étrangère et des gouvernements des provinces, particulièrement celles où vivent des francophones, qui eux ont juridiction sur d'autres matières ayant le plus souvent des prolongements dans le champ des relations internationales.

Ce qui pourrait paraître dans les circonstances, du moins jusqu'au début des années 60, comme un extraordinaire manque d'intérêt tant de la part du gouvernement du Canada que de celui du Québec à l'égard de la Francophonie hors frontières, s'explique par deux causes principales. La première tient, semble-t-il, à l'évolution constitutionnelle du pays, qui a résulté dans le maintien de relations privilégiées entre le Canada et le Royaume-Uni, et qui s'est traduite à la fin de la Deuxième Guerre mondiale par l'attribution d'un caractère hautement prioritaire aux relations du Canada avec les pays du Commonwealth. La deuxième est due à ce que d'aucuns ont décrit comme l'isolement du Canada français jusqu'à la fin des années 50 et qui, on s'en serait douté, a réduit à sa plus simple expression l'attention que les Canadiens d'expression française estimaient devoir porter aux relations de leurs gouvernements avec celui de la France. À ces deux raisons s'en ajoute une troisième, à savoir la place prépondérante qu'occupaient durant la période qui a suivi la guerre de 39-45 le Royaume-uni et les États-Unis dans le commerce extérieur du Canada.

Les événements qui allaient se produire au Québec à partir de 1959 se chargèrent de remettre en question l'ensemble de cette situation. Sous la Révolution tranquille des années 60, le gouvernement du Québec entama le processus du développement accéléré de ses relations avec la France. Des hommes politiques québécois avancèrent de leur propre chef auprès des autorités françaises l'idée d'une communauté culturelle des peuples de langue française. Enfin, une campagne de presse menée à la fin de 1960 et au début de 1961 par Jean-Marc Léger du journal *Le Devoir* allait aider à convaincre le gouvernement conservateur de l'époque, celui du premier ministre Diefenbaker, de la nécessité d'amorcer un programme d'aide en faveur des États africains d'expression française. Cette campagne devait aussi contribuer à faire avancer l'idée que la création de relations étroites avec le monde francophone était essentielle à l'épanouissement du fait français au Canada et à l'affirmation de l'identité culturelle du Québec.

Ainsi, l'éveil du gouvernement fédéral aux préoccupations de la population francophone du pays, l'activité du gouvernement du Québec en faveur de liens privilégiés avec la France, l'arrivée d'un premier ministre francophone, Pierre E. Trudeau, à la tête de l'administration fédérale en 1968, et l'incrustation conséquente dans l'administration fédérale de ce qui a été appelé le *French power,* conjuguées aux pressions exercées sur la France à partir du début des années 60, par des États africains francophones, voilà autant d'éléments qui, par leur addition ou leur convergence, contribueront à enclencher le processus menant à l'institutionnalisation et au développement d'une communauté internationale de pays francophones. En somme, le souci d'établir cette Francophonie répondait à un double, sinon à un triple besoin. D'une part, dès les débuts des années 60, les nouveaux États africains francophones cherchaient à recréer à leur avantage les liens qu'ils avaient eus jusque-là avec la France. D'autre part, des hommes politiques canadiens, tant au niveau du gouvernement fédéral qu'à celui du gouvernement québécois, plus ou moins conscients de cette conjoncture historique et réalisant que l'avenir de leur pays et celui de l'une de ses parties, le Québec, exigeaient le renforcement du caractère francophone des institutions et réclamaient de part et d'autre leur participation à la construction de la Francophonie. C'est là la réponse la plus plausible à donner à notre question préalable: pourquoi la Francophonie?

LA PÉRIODE PRÉINSTITUTIONNELLE

Les relations entre la France et le Canada de 1940 à 1959

Comme nous l'avons laissé entendre précédemment, les relations entre la France et le Canada, voire les relations entre la France et le Canada français, n'ont pas toujours été ce qu'elles sont devenues grâce à la Francophonie internationale. En fait, jusqu'à la Deuxième Guerre mondiale, il ne fait aucun doute que les rapports de tous genres existant entre les deux pays étaient très limités[2]. On peut même dire que jusque vers les années 60, les relations de gouvernement à gouvernement entre le Canada et la France sont demeurées plus formelles que substantielles. Les gouvernements en cause se conduisaient, semble-t-il, comme si leur pays appartenait à des univers différents. En France, on attendra jusqu'en 1961 avant qu'on ne commence à reconnaître l'entité distincte qu'est le Québec et, par ricochet, le potentiel du Canada français. Au Canada, le gouvernement de l'immédiat après-guerre, dirigé jusqu'en 1948 par Mackenzie King, aura été trop carrément absorbé par des problèmes de politique intérieure[3] pour concevoir l'idée même d'une Francophonie à l'échelle internationale. Dans une déclaration de politique étrangère du 4 septembre 1946 qu'il jugeait pourtant importante, le premier titulaire du portefeuille des Affaires extérieures dans le gouvernement canadien, Louis Saint-Laurent, ne trouva mieux à dire des relations entre le Canada et la France que «nous n'avons jamais oublié que la France est l'une des sources fondamentales de notre vie culturelle».

Et pourtant, des liens étaient nés au cours des années 40 de la participation du Canada, au côté de la France, à la Deuxième Guerre mondiale et plus spécifiquement du rôle joué par les soldats canadiens dans la libération de la France, comme en témoignent les deux séjours du général de Gaulle au Canada en juillet 1944, comme président du Comité français de libération nationale, et en août 1945, comme président du gouvernement provisoire de la France. Subséquemment, durant la période de l'après-guerre, on avait assisté à un accroissement marqué des échanges culturels entre les deux pays. Des liens s'étaient créés rapidement entre les radio télévisions française et canadienne. Un accord avait été signé en 1950 prévoyant l'inauguration d'un premier service aérien entre Montréal et Paris. Et les chefs d'État ou de gouvernement des deux pays échangèrent moultes visites: Mackenzie King se rendit en France à l'occasion de sa participation à la Conférence de Paris de 1946, le premier ministre Louis Saint-Laurent fit une visite officielle en France en janvier 1951, le président Vincent Auriol vint au Canada en avril 1951, et le premier ministre Pierre Mendès France fut accueilli à Ottawa en novembre 1954. Enfin, le premier ministre John Diefenbaker effectua une visite officielle à Paris en novembre 1958.

Par ailleurs, sur le plan politique ou diplomatique, le rapprochement entre les deux pays a certes été moins soutenu et, par conséquent, moins réussi. Si, par exemple, le Canada n'hésita pas à appuyer une proposition française visant à faire du français l'une des cinq langues officielles de l'Organisation des Nations Unies, on s'explique mal ce qui amena le représentant du Canada à la Première Conférence de l'Organisation des Nations Unies pour l'alimentation et l'agriculture, qui s'est tenue dans la ville de Québec en octobre 1945, à s'abstenir devant une proposition identique cherchant à donner au français, au même titre que l'anglais, le statut de langue de travail à cette conférence[4]. Puissance moyenne à l'époque, le Canada suivit bien entendu de près le rôle que joua la France dans le processus menant à l'intégration économique de l'Europe occidentale, de même que les positions successives qu'adopta le gouvernement français face aux luttes d'émancipation coloniale en Asie et en Afrique au cours des années 50. Mais rien ne permet d'affirmer que les dirigeants des deux pays partageaient sur ces questions, et sur bien d'autres, des points de vue communs, voire même convergents. Aux yeux des autorités françaises, les prises de position du Canada étaient vraisemblablement perçues comme étant trop proches de celles de ses partenaires traditionnels, la Grande-Bretagne et les États-Unis. Vu de la France, le caractère en partie francophone du Canada n'était pas encore vraiment perceptible. Le gouvernement canadien, quant à lui, ne regrettait que trop l'instabilité politique du gouvernement français sous la IVᵉ République. Les rapports annuels du ministère des Affaires extérieures de 1946 à 1954 attestent d'ailleurs de façon éloquente du peu d'intérêt que le Canada témoignait à la France à cette époque. Bien sûr, les difficultés que connut cette dernière dans la décolonisation des pays de la zone d'influence française retinrent l'attention du gouvernement canadien à partir de 1955. Et, dès 1956, une mission canadienne d'exploration, formée de fonctionnaires, fut dépêchée au Maroc et en Tunisie[5]. Mais il n'en reste pas moins que la politique française d'indépendance nationale préconisée par le général de Gaulle depuis son retour au pouvoir en 1958 laissait un goût amer au gouvernement canadien. Bref, le Canada prenait peu à peu conscience au cours de ces années des problèmes qu'allait bientôt poser l'émergence de nouveaux pays indépendants issus de l'Empire colonial français. La France du général de Gaulle commençait, pour sa part, à deviner les aspirations des francophones du Canada. Bref, tout était maintenant en place pour le grand tournant des années 60.

Le tournant du début des années 60

La décolonisation du début des années 60 a probablement été l'élément qui a déterminé l'intérêt du Canada à la Francophonie. Au niveau du gouvernement canadien, déjà préoccupé à l'époque par l'évolution parallèle que connaissait le Commonwealth, on prit d'abord acte de l'admission aux Nations Unies, le 20 septembre 1960, d'une quinzaine d'États francophones nouvellement indépendants et on délégua dès la fin de l'année l'ambassadeur du Canada à Paris en tournée de reconnaissance à travers l'Afrique francophone dans le but d'y apprécier la situation. Au niveau de l'opinion publique, principalement celle du Canada français, des voix au début isolées se firent entendre dès 1960 pour inciter les gouvernements canadien et québécois à s'intéresser à la création de relations étroites avec le monde francophone. Ainsi, à la suite d'une campagne de presse menée dans *Le Devoir* à la fin de 1960 et au début de 1961, le gouvernement canadien décida de créer en avril 1961 un programme d'aide à l'Afrique francophone qui se voulait le pendant du programme d'assistance technique établi en 1960 en faveur des États africains membres du Commonwealth. Si modeste qu'il ait été à l'origine, ce «programme d'aide à l'enseignement en Afrique francophone» n'en constituait pas moins la réponse du gouvernement canadien à ceux qui soutenaient que la politique étrangère du Canada devait tenir compte des aspirations de sa population francophone.

C'est l'établissement de relations diplomatiques entre le Canada et les États de l'Afrique francophone qui traduit cependant le mieux ce tournant que le gouvernement canadien venait de prendre. Dans un premier temps, soit entre 1962 et 1964, les gouvernements d'une majorité des nouveaux États francophones d'Afrique désignèrent les uns après les autres leur représentant officiel auprès des autorités canadiennes. Deux d'entre eux, le Cameroun et le Zaïre, ouvrirent même des missions diplomatiques à Ottawa dès 1962. Pour sa part, ayant déjà accrédité en 1961 son ambassadeur en Suisse et son ambassadeur en Yougoslavie respectivement auprès du gouvernement de la Tunisie et du gouvernement de l'Algérie, le Canada ouvrit en 1962 une ambassade au Cameroun avec accréditation multiple au Gabon, au Tchad, en République centre-africaine et au Congo-Brazzaville, et il procéda presque simultanément à l'accréditation de ses chefs de mission au Ghana et au

Nigéria, le premier auprès de la Côte d'Ivoire, de la Haute-Volta, de la Guinée et du Togo, et le second auprès du Sénégal, du Niger et du Dahomey. On accrédita aussi auprès du gouvernement du Maroc l'ambassadeur du Canada en Espagne au cours de la même année. Poursuivant ce mouvement de pendule, les gouvernements du Cameroun et du Zaïre élevèrent à leur tour en 1965 leur mission à Ottawa au rang d'ambassade. L'intérêt croissant manifesté par le Canada aux États africains franco-phones devenait dorénavant réciproque. Deux autres gestes en témoignent: le premier a été une initiative quelque peu intempestive prise le 20 février 1962 par le Niger, proposant au gouvernement canadien de conclure avec lui un traité d'amitié et d'assistance technique; le second fut la décision du gouvernement canadien d'augmenter le budget du programme d'aide à l'enseignement en Afrique franco-phone, qui passa, durant l'année fiscale 1964-1965, de 300 000 $ à 4 000 000 $.

Mais les choses n'étaient pas sans bouger dans le champ des relations entre le Canada et la France. Il y eut d'abord la visite officielle qu'effectua au Canada du 19 au 22 avril 1960 le chef de l'État français, le général de Gaulle, puis celle du minis-tre d'État français à la Culture, André Malraux, du 7 au 15 octobre 1963. Il y eut surtout celle du premier ministre du Canada, Lester B. Pearson, qui au cours de sa visite officielle à Paris, du 15 au 17 janvier 1964, chercha à signifier clairement aux autorités françaises son intention d'étendre et d'intensifier les relations entre le Canada et la France. On peut raisonnablement croire que le premier ministre du Canada s'efforça au cours de cette visite de convaincre les autorités françaises de la sincérité des intentions canadiennes en évoquant notamment la conclusion encore récente d'un accord de coopération cinématographique, signé en octobre 1963, et de l'accord sur des échanges d'information scientifique entre le Conseil canadien de recherches pour la défense et le Conseil français de l'inspection des fabrications d'armement, signé en mai 1962. Mais on imagine facilement que le premier ministre du Canada pouvait aussi être mû, au cours de ces entretiens, par les appréhensions que son gouvernement éprouvait à ce moment-là devant la vague nationaliste qui s'était emparée du Québec francophone en juin 1960 et qui avait rapidement amené le gou-vernement du Québec, comme nous le verrons plus loin, à faire valoir son droit à entretenir des relations directes et privilégiées avec la France. Quant aux autorités françaises, on sait que la prestation de leur interlocuteur les laissa plutôt sceptiques[6], bien que le général de Gaulle tint à rassurer le gouvernement canadien en déclarant à cette occasion que dans la solidarité «particulière et naturelle» entre la France et le Canada français, il ne saurait y avoir rien qui doive contrarier les heureuses relations entre la République française et «votre État fédéral»[7].

Si ambigus qu'aient pu paraître aux dirigeants canadiens ces propos du chef de l'État français, ils n'en rappelaient sans doute pas moins au premier ministre du Canada le souvenir encore récent d'événements qui étaient les signes avant-coureurs d'une remise en question par le Québec de la pratique canadienne en matière de relations internationales. Le premier de ces événements avait été l'ouverture d'une maison du Québec à Paris dont l'inauguration, le 5 octobre 1961, avait marqué le début d'une ère au cours de laquelle le gouvernement français ne se fera pas scrupule d'aider le Québec à obtenir une personnalité internationale. Le deuxième a été un échange de notes entre le gouvernement canadien et le gouverne-ment français concernant l'admission d'élèves canadiens et québécois à l'École nationale d'administration, à la suite des discussions conduites par le ministère de la Jeunesse du Québec et l'ambassade de France à Ottawa en vue de conclure des accords de coopération culturelle. Enfin, le troisième a été l'entente signée en décembre 1963 par le ministère de l'Éducation du Québec et le président de l'ASTEF qui permettait l'organisation de stages en France de Québécois dans les domaines économique, scientifique et technique et qui, avec l'autorisation du gouvernement canadien, établissait une première commission mixte de coopération franco-québécoise. Si l'on ne pouvait encore parler en ce début de l'année 1964 de rivalité déclarée entre Québec et Ottawa, la question se posait cependant de savoir si le gouvernement canadien faisait suffisamment sur le plan de la francophonie et, dans le cas d'une réponse négative, si la poussée du Québec en vue d'établir des liens directs avec la France ne risquait pas d'avoir de sérieuses répercussions sur la conduite de la politique étrangère du Canada.

Dans un mémoire du 27 juillet 1963[8] qu'il adressait à Paul Martin, le ministre canadien des Affaires étrangères, le Sous-secrétaire d'État aux Affaires extérieures, Norman Robertson, se chargea de répondre à ces questions à la lumière d'une série d'articles qui venaient de paraître dans *Le Devoir*, sous le titre «Le Québec dans le monde francophone». Apparemment inquiet des conséquences que ne manquerait pas d'avoir, selon lui, dans le champ des relations internationales, la campagne en cours au Québec en faveur de l'autonomie provinciale, monsieur Robertson y reconnaissait la nécessité pour le gouvernement canadien: 1. de promouvoir l'utilisation du français dans l'administration fédérale, notamment au sein du ministère des Affaires extérieures et du Bureau de l'aide extérieure; 2. d'accroître la représentation diplomatique du Canada dans les pays de langue française; et 3. d'augmenter substantiellement les montants de l'aide canadienne aux pays de langue française. Tout en se gardant d'évoquer l'hypothèse de la formation d'une communauté internationale entre pays francophones, et *a fortiori* celle de la contribution que le Canada aurait à y apporter, il avançait néanmoins pour la première fois l'idée que le Canada devrait tendre vers un équilibre entre ses relations avec les pays francophones et ses relations avec les pays du Commonwealth. Monsieur Robertson recommandait notamment non seulement que le Canada se rapproche de la France, mais que le gouvernement canadien étende sa coopération avec le gouvernement français bien au-delà du champ des relations culturelles. Le premier ministre, avançait-il, se devait d'effectuer une visite officielle en France à la première occasion. En somme, ce que le Sous-secrétaire d'État aux Affaires extérieures préconisait dans son mémoire, c'est que le Canada commence effectivement à se donner une politique cohérente à l'égard du monde francophone.

Il est aussi important de noter que le sens de ce mémoire correspondait en tous points à la réorientation fondamentale que le gouvernement canadien venait de prendre sur le plan intérieur en instituant une commission royale d'enquête – la Commission royale d'enquête sur le bilinguisme et le biculturalisme – chargée de lui faire des recommandations en vue de promouvoir le bilinguisme – donc une plus grande utilisation du français – dans les institutions du Parlement et du gouvernement du Canada, et d'assurer une plus grande place aux francophones au sein de l'administration fédérale. Mais il est non moins intéressant de souligner que ce mémoire reconnaissait, de façon implicite il est vrai, qu'il y avait nécessairement, voire inévitablement, une étroite corrélation en matière de francophonie entre la politique extérieure et la politique intérieure.

Or on sait que le gouvernement canadien ne tarda pas à accepter les conclusions et les recommandations de ce mémoire. À vrai dire, à partir de ce moment-là, on ne mit plus en doute la nécessité d'aller de l'avant et d'agir rapidement dans l'appui à donner à la Francophonie. On annonça d'ailleurs dès le mois d'avril 1964 la création d'un nouveau programme d'échanges culturels avec trois pays européens de langue française, la France, la Belgique et la Suisse. On décida également d'ouvrir à Marseille un premier consulat général du Canada en France. On donna instruction, à l'intérieur du ministère des Affaires extérieures, de chercher à approfondir le champ des relations du Canada avec les pays de l'Afrique francophone. On se prépara enfin à amorcer une campagne, tant à l'intérieur qu'à l'extérieur du pays, qui ferait ouvertement état des intentions du gouvernement canadien de développer et d'approfondir ses relations avec les pays francophones. Bref, on était sur le point d'entrer dans la période qu'on peut désigner comme la période de l'engagement progressif du Canada dans le monde francophone.

L'engagement du Canada dans le monde francophone de 1965 à 1969

Si le début des années 60 avait imprimé un premier élan aux relations internationales du Canada en direction des pays francophones, la période qui va de 1965 à 1969 sera celle de l'engagement progressif du Canada dans le monde francophone. Cette période sera d'abord celle du renforcement et de l'accentuation des relations entre le Canada et la France. Ce sera aussi celle de la multiplication des contacts avec les autres pays francophones, celle de l'intensification des consultations avec leurs représentants, et celle de l'augmentation et de la diversification des programmes d'aide du Canada aux pays africains francophones. Mais le souvenir le plus aigu que l'on gardera peut-être de ces années sera celui du défi posé aux autorités canadiennes par le gouvernement du Québec qui, avec la complicité du gouvernement français, s'appliqua à traiter d'égal à égal avec les gouvernements des pays francophones, ce qui amena le gouvernement canadien à vouloir clarifier les règles de la conduite des affaires étrangères du Canada et à préciser les conditions qu'il allait poser au développement de ses relations avec les pays francophones et à sa participation éventuelle à l'organisation d'une communauté internationale des pays francophones.

L'objectif du renforcement et de l'accentuation des relations avec la France apparut au grand jour au début de l'année 1965. Dès le 27 février 1965, le gouvernement du Québec signa en effet à Paris, avec le gouvernement français, une entente qui portait sur un programme d'échanges et de coopération entre le Québec et la France dans le domaine de l'éducation. Cette entente visait plus précisément à encourager l'échange de chercheurs, en particulier dans les domaines de la science et de la médecine, mais aussi de professeurs, d'étudiants et de spécialistes en éducation physique et en éducation populaire. Elle prévoyait l'établissement d'une commission permanente franco-québécoise pour en assurer la mise en œuvre. Comme cette entente internationale était la première que signait le Québec, les autorités canadiennes exigèrent et obtinrent des autorités françaises qu'elle fut sanctionnée le même jour par un échange de lettres entre le ministère des Affaires extérieures et l'ambassade de France à Ottawa, permettant au gouvernement fédéral d'établir qu'il était le seul pouvant agir au nom du Canada dans le domaine des affaires étrangères. Le gouvernement fédéral fit par ailleurs entendre le 26 mars 1965, par la voix du ministre canadien officieusement chargé des relations avec les pays francophones, Jean-Luc Pépin, le message, pour le moins présomptueux à l'époque, que le secteur des relations avec la France constituait l'un des quatre piliers de la politique étrangère du Canada. Et durant les mois de mars et avril 1966, le premier ministre du Canada et le président de la République française échangèrent entre eux des lettres qui passaient en revue les progrès accomplis dans les relations bilatérales depuis la visite de Pearson en France en janvier 1964.

Voulant prouver tout le sérieux de ses intentions et encadrer une fois pour toutes les initiatives qu'il anticipait de la part du gouvernement du Québec sur le plan international, le gouvernement canadien conclut le 17 novembre 1965 avec le gouvernement français un premier accord culturel qui visait à permettre au Québec ou, le cas échéant, aux autres provinces canadiennes, de conclure des ententes avec la France dans les domaines de la culture, de l'éducation et des sujets qui leur sont connexes. Cet accord-cadre reconnaissait la nécessité dans chaque cas de procéder à un échange de lettres entre le gouvernement canadien et le gouvernement français établissant, soit que ces ententes étaient conclues dans le cadre de cet accord culturel général, soit qu'elles bénéficiaient de l'assentiment du gouvernement canadien. Cet accord-cadre prévoyait aussi, bien entendu, la mise sur pied d'une commission permanente franco-canadienne qui, lors de sa première réunion à Ottawa à la fin novembre, entreprit une étude générale portant sur les relations économiques, financières et commerciales entre les deux pays. Quelques jours à peine après la conclusion de l'accord-cadre culturel France-Canada, des représentants du gouvernement québécois et du gouvernement français signèrent à Québec, le 24 novembre, une entente de coopération culturelle entre la France et le Québec. D'autre part, au cours de l'année 1965, le gouvernement canadien ouvrit à Bordeaux un second consulat général en France, dans le but entre autres d'encourager les milieux universitaires français à s'intéresser aux études canadiennes. Il contribua également à la création d'une association qui allait réunir des parlementaires canadiens et des parlementaires français. Enfin, il porta à 1 000 000 $, soit une multiplication par quatre, le montant des crédits qui étaient consacrés au programme d'échanges culturels avec les pays européens de langue française.

Cette activité débordante dans les relations entre le Canada et la France se poursuivit au cours de l'année 1966. L'Association interparlementaire France-Canada, par exemple, tint sa première réunion à Paris en avril. Par ailleurs, le gouvernement canadien affecta durant la même année une subvention d'un demi-million de dollars à des travaux d'agrandissement de la Maison des étudiants canadiens à la Cité universitaire de Paris, qui porta ainsi sa capacité d'accueil de 70 à 125 étudiants. Et en juin, une mission composée de représentants canadiens de divers secteurs de l'activité économique fit une visite en France. Mais en 1966, il y eut surtout la visite officielle qu'effectua du 28 au 30 septembre au Canada M. Couve de Murville, le ministre français des Affaires étrangères[9], et celle en France, du 16 au 20 novembre 1966, du sous-ministre des Affaires extérieures du Canada, Marcel Cadieux. La visite de Couve de Murville faisait suite à la visite du premier ministre Pearson et du ministre des Affaires extérieures du Canada en janvier 1964 à Paris. La partie de cette visite qui se déroula à Ottawa permit au ministre des Affaires extérieures du Canada, Paul Martin, de réitérer que le gouvernement canadien souhaitait intensifier sa coopération avec la France, notamment dans les secteurs considérés comme les plus difficiles, soit ceux du commerce, des investissements et du partage des connaissances technologiques. Celui-ci profita de l'occasion pour faire aussi mention des difficultés qu'éprouvait le Canada sur le terrain dans la mise en œuvre de ses programmes d'aide aux pays africains francophones. Il indiqua même que le gouvernement était prêt à examiner la possibilité de coordonner ses efforts avec ceux de la France dans le domaine de l'aide à ces pays. Le ministre français des Affaires étrangères déclara pour sa part qu'il souhaitait également voir s'accroître les relations bilatérales entre les deux pays, mais il laissa entendre que, pour ce qui est de la France, ce vœu était en grande partie inspiré par la vitalité du fait français au Canada. À propos de la question générale de la francophonie, Paul Martin indiqua que le gouvernement canadien était en principe favorable à une plus large coopération entre pays francophones, mais il ne manqua pas de faire valoir à son interlocuteur qu'il faudrait cependant qu'on respecte les impératifs de la situation constitutionnelle canadienne. Tout en maintenant la position dite de sympathie et de prudence du gouvernement français à l'endroit de la Francophonie, Couve de Murville n'en établit pas moins que la France restait disposée à tenir compte des initiatives qui pourraient être prises à cet égard par les représentants des autres pays francophones, y compris ceux du Canada. À Québec, où il se rendit par la suite, avec l'assentiment du gouvernement canadien, Couve de Murville évita bien entendu tout ce qui aurait pu irriter les susceptibilités déjà vives des autorités fédérales en regard des contacts directs entre le gouvernement québécois et le gouvernement français.

La visite en France du Sous-secrétaire d'État aux Affaires extérieures offrit une autre occasion à un représentant du gouvernement canadien de passer en revue, avec les autorités françaises, les questions de la Francophonie[10]. En plus de rappeler que l'intérêt porté par le Canada au développement d'une communauté francophone ne ferait que s'accroître si la France et les autres pays francophones respectaient la situation constitutionnelle canadienne, Marcel Cadieux fit valoir qu'il était dans l'intérêt de tous que le mouvement fut bien lancé. Une certaine coordination des efforts lui paraissait également souhaitable en matière d'aide à l'Afrique francophone. Il invoqua par ailleurs le fait que le gouvernement canadien n'avait pas reçu d'invitation à participer au colloque que se proposait de tenir à Lomé en janvier 1967 l'Institut international de droit des pays d'expression française pour illustrer le besoin d'une meilleure concertation entre tous les pays francophones.

On assista par ailleurs en 1966 au rapprochement du Canada avec certains pays africains francophones. Le Canada décida, par exemple, d'ouvrir deux nouvelles ambassades en Afrique francophone, l'une au Sénégal, l'autre en Tunisie, deux pays qui, avec le Cameroun, furent désignés au cours de l'année 1966 comme pays de concentration de l'aide canadienne. D'autre part, les crédits de l'aide à l'Afrique francophone furent portés au niveau de 12 millions de dollars au cours de l'année financière 1966-1967. Alors que cette aide avait jusque-là été affectée au domaine de l'assistance technique et de l'éducation, l'idée commença alors à s'imposer qu'il faudrait bientôt l'étendre aux domaines de l'agriculture, de la santé publique, des transports, des communications et des infrastructures, sans négliger bien entendu le secteur alimentaire chaque fois que le besoin s'en ferait sentir. Pour ce qui est des contacts personnels entre dirigeants canadiens et africains, il faut surtout signaler la visite qu'effectua du 19 au 27 septembre au Canada le président Senghor du Sénégal[11]. Cette visite, la première visite officielle au Canada d'un chef d'État de l'Afrique francophone, permit au président Senghor de poser le problème général de la participation canadienne au développement du Sénégal et lui offrit l'occasion de discuter, tant au niveau fédéral qu'au niveau provincial, de la francophonie en général et du projet particulier de communauté francophone que venait alors d'avancer l'OCAM pour fins de consultation. Le communiqué de presse qui fut émis au terme du séjour à Ottawa du président Senghor fait effectivement état d'une coopération plus étendue entre les deux pays et de personnel canadien mis à la disposition du gouvernement sénégalais. Il évoque, par ailleurs, le besoin d'accroître les liens et les échanges entre les pays de langue et de culture françaises «par des moyens s'inscrivant dans un cadre large, équilibré, tenant compte des problèmes particuliers de tous les pays qui, à un titre ou l'autre, sont de la Francophonie». Cette dernière précision, on l'imagine facilement, visait à rappeler la compétence exclusive du gouvernement fédéral dans le domaine des affaires étrangères. Quant à la partie de la visite qui se déroula au Québec, elle permit au président Senghor d'entendre le point de vue du premier ministre Daniel Johnson sur la participation du Québec à la Francophonie et, plus particulièrement, de prendre connaissance de l'intention du gouvernement du Québec de convoquer une conférence des ministres de l'Éducation et de la Culture des pays francophones, et du désir du Québec de conclure un accord culturel avec le Sénégal. Comme on pouvait s'y attendre, le gouvernement canadien apporta sans tarder au gouvernement sénégalais, par voie diplomatique, les mises au point jugées nécessaires dans les circonstances.

Le gouvernement canadien indiqua de diverses autres façons en 1966 son intérêt à participer à la Francophonie. Aux Nations Unies, le Canada se joignit au groupe des pays francophones désireux de faire campagne pour obtenir une meilleure place du français au sein de l'organisation internationale. Au pays, le gouvernement canadien annonça qu'il allait dorénavant accorder une subvention de 50 000 $ par année à l'AUPELF et verser une contribution annuelle de 100 000 $ au Fonds international de coopération universitaire (FICU), dont l'objectif principal est de promouvoir le développement des universités du tiers monde francophone. Une étude qui tentait d'analyser les avantages que comporterait l'adhésion éventuelle du Canada à une communauté internationale des pays francophones fut conduite au ministère des Affaires extérieures. Il reste qu'on n'avait pas encore jugé utile en 1966 de créer, au sein de ce ministère, une direction ayant la responsabilité principale de suivre de près les relations avec les pays francophones. Et que, comme devait le révéler une étude commanditée par la Commission royale d'enquête sur le bilinguisme et le biculturalisme, l'emploi du français comme langue de travail dans l'administration centrale de ce ministère en 1965 était toujours extrêmement bas[12]. Mais c'est surtout vers les pays africains francophones que se portaient à la fin de l'année 1966 les regards inquiets.

La question de la participation canadienne au colloque de l'Institut international de droit des pays d'expression française (IDEF) tenu à Lomé, au Togo, du 18 au 25 janvier 1967, illustre bien la préoccupation essentielle du gouvernement canadien en matière de francophonie à la fin de l'année 1966, qui était que «lorsqu'il s'agit de participation gouvernementale à des activités internationales, dans quelque domaine que ce soit, c'est au gouvernement fédéral que la question relève en premier lieu»[13]. Cette préoccupation était particulièrement vive, sinon prédominante chez Marcel Cadieux, Sous-secrétaire d'État aux Affaires extérieures, qui est celui qui orchestra une série de manœuvres qui aboutiront à l'admission d'un représentant du gouvernement canadien en tant que membre du Comité de parrainage de l'IDEF, au même titre que le représentant du gouvernement du Québec, et à l'obtention pour ce représentant, le ministre de la Justice du Canada, d'une invitation à participer au colloque de Lomé. Or c'est Pierre E. Trudeau, alors secrétaire parlementaire du premier ministre, qui représenta le ministre de la Justice à ce colloque et qui, à la demande du ministère des Affaires extérieures, se rendit par la suite au Cameroun, en Côte d'Ivoire, au Sénégal et en Tunisie à des fins de consultation. La mission ainsi confiée à monsieur Trudeau visait essentiellement trois objectifs: 1. dissiper la confusion qui semblait exister parmi les responsables de l'IDEF et ceux de quelques pays francophones indépendants quant aux responsabilités respectives du gouvernement fédéral et des gouvernements des provinces dans le domaine des affaires étrangères; 2. explorer la conception que se font de la Francophonie les leaders africains et réaffirmer l'intérêt que le Canada porte lui-même à la Francophonie; et 3. confirmer l'intention du Canada de continuer à développer ses relations avec l'Afrique francophone.

M. Trudeau mit effectivement ses interlocuteurs au fait des «subtilités» de la situation constitutionnelle au Canada. Il établit notamment que le gouvernement fédéral était en fait le seul qui fut habilité à parler au nom de tous les Canadiens et que, par conséquent, le Canada ne pourrait envisager sa participation à la Francophonie que sous le parrainage de l'État central. Il confirma du même coup que le Canada voulait participer à toutes les réunions internationales où sera discutée l'organisation de la Francophonie et informa tous ceux qu'il rencontra de la procédure à suivre, en vertu de la Constitution du Canada, pour s'assurer d'une participation canadienne à des conférences intergouvernementales. À Yaoundé, Trudeau obtint plus spécifiquement du secrétaire exécutif de l'Organisation de coordination pour la lutte contre les grandes endémies l'engagement qu'il se mettra à l'avenir en contact avec les «officiels» canadiens par l'intermédiaire du ministère des Affaires extérieures. À Dakar, il s'assura auprès du président Senghor que le gouvernement canadien serait invité à participer à la conférence alors envisagée des ministres de l'Éducation des pays francophones chargée par l'OCAM de lancer la Francophonie. Enfin, à Paris, au cours de son dernier arrêt sur la voie du retour, Trudeau réitéra aux autorités françaises l'intérêt du gouvernement canadien à participer à la Francophonie qu'il présenta comme une occasion d'équilibrer l'anglophonie, c'est-à-dire son appartenance au Commonwealth et sa proximité des États-Unis, de même que la volonté des autorités fédérales de jouer pleinement leur rôle dans l'organisation de la Francophonie. Bien que convaincu que la Francophonie avait encore un long chemin à parcourir avant de devenir une institution structurée, Trudeau se montra néanmoins d'avis, à l'issue de son voyage, que l'activité prévisible, et notamment le nombre de rencontres internationales à venir dans le monde francophone, commandait au gouvernement canadien de se donner une politique en matière de Francophonie. Il importait d'abord, selon lui, de compléter de toute urgence les études en cours dans l'administration fédérale sur la situation constitutionnelle et les affaires extérieures. Il reconnaissait, d'autre part, que le pouvoir fédéral dans le domaine des affaires extérieures ne saurait être sérieusement menacé par celui des provinces, et plus particulièrement par le Québec, «si nous accomplissons notre tâche». Il ajoutait enfin que, pour accomplir sa tâche, le gouvernement fédéral devra nécessairement y consacrer plus de temps et plus d'argent. Trudeau recommanda en conséquence qu'une nouvelle direction soit établie au ministère des Affaires extérieures pour mieux suivre le développement des relations entre les pays francophones. Dans un mémoire adressé le 24 février 1967 à la Direction du personnel, qui s'inspirait visiblement de cette recommandation, le Sous-secrétaire d'État aux Affaires extérieures proposait une augmentation des effectifs dans les directions chargées des différents aspects de la francophonie, reconnaissant ainsi la nécessité de prendre des mesures immédiates pour faire face aux tâches nouvelles qu'entraînait déjà le phénomène de la francophonie.

Le gouvernement canadien se crut par ailleurs obligé, au début de 1967, de réagir à l'initiative prise en France en novembre 1966 de créer, sous le patronage d'honneur du Secrétaire d'État français aux Affaires étrangères, l'Association de solidarité francophone (ASF), dont deux des principaux objectifs étaient de coordonner l'action des associations internationales existantes, par exemple l'AUPELF et l'IDEF, et d'aider à l'organisation du monde francophone. Redoutant que cette nouvelle association dite privée donne au gouvernement français un puissant levier de commande sur la Francophonie, et jugeant que cette initiative risquait de créer des difficultés à la participation du Canada à la construction de la Francophonie, le gouvernement canadien choisit en effet cette occasion pour faire connaître comment, pour sa part, il envisageait l'élaboration de rapports multilatéraux au sein de la Francophonie[14]. Cette mise au point prit la forme d'un important discours que Paul Martin, ministre des Affaires extérieures, prononça le 11 mars 1967 devant la chambre de commerce des Jeunes de Montréal, dans lequel il rappela d'abord que la politique internationale du Canada visait à donner «pleine expression au caractère bilingue et biculturel de notre pays», puis montra jusqu'où le gouvernement canadien était prêt à aller pour stimuler le développement de la francophonie. Martin déclara en effet que dans le but d'assurer à la francophonie un développement efficace et cohérent, le gouvernement canadien venait de soumettre aux gouvernements des pays francophones un projet de création d'un organisme international de caractère essentiellement privé, dont l'appellation pourrait être, dit-il, l'Association internationale de solidarité francophone et qui, par sa fonction, serait un instrument majeur de la mise en œuvre de la coopération culturelle «entre pays francophones pleinement autonomes et indépendants». Il est permis de croire que le gouvernement canadien entendait rappeler par le biais de ce discours qu'il souhaitait vraiment être consulté sur tout ce qui a trait au développement de la Francophonie. Il reste que le projet de création d'une association internationale de solidarité francophone n'évoqua que peu d'appuis de la part des dirigeants africains et très peu d'écho dans les pays francophones d'Europe. Quant à la condition préalable, celle de la création d'une association canadienne de solidarité francophone, elle resta aussi sans lendemain.

Le Canada se rallia par contre beaucoup plus facilement à la suggestion avancée à plusieurs reprises dans des milieux africains, et encouragée par les autorités françaises, de mettre sur pied une Association internationale des parlementaires de langue française, qui fut effectivement créée à Luxembourg le 17 mai 1967 avec la participation active de membres du Parlement canadien. Au plan des relations bilatérales, cette année fut également fertile. Du côté fédéral, il y eut la tenue d'une réunion de la Commission culturelle franco-canadienne et d'une autre du Comité France-Canada du commerce et des relations économiques, de même que diverses prises de contacts entre la société d'État connue sous le nom d'Énergie atomique du Canada Ltée et la Commission française de l'énergie atomique, et une visite en France d'une mission scientifique canadienne. Un premier accord culturel inspiré de l'accord-cadre France-Canada fut signé en mai 1967 entre le Canada et la Belgique. Du côté québécois, après une visite du premier ministre Daniel Johnson à Paris en mai 1967, la décision fut prise d'étendre les projets existants d'échanges culturels et techniques entre la France et le Québec à la confrontation des expériences pédagogiques respectives de la France et du Québec dans le cadre d'un Centre franco-québécois de développement pédagogique. Un échange de lettres entre le général de Gaulle et le premier ministre Daniel Johnson prépara par ailleurs la voie à l'établissement d'un organisme commun et permanent qui devait être l'équivalent d'un Secrétariat général de la coopération, à la tenue de réunions ministérielles à caractère régulier, et à la formation d'une sous-commission chargée de proposer la création d'un mécanisme approprié à des échanges de jeunes entre le Québec et la France, le futur Office franco-québécois pour la jeunesse. Au cours de la même année, le gouvernement français accorda à son consulat général à Québec un statut spécial qui lui assurait un accès direct au gouvernement québécois. Quant aux relations bilatérales avec les autres pays francophones, on profita de la tenue de l'Exposition universelle de Montréal (Expo 67) pour y accueillir au moins treize chefs d'État ou de gouvernement de pays africains francophones avec lesquels les dirigeants canadiens et québécois purent s'entretenir, soit de relations bilatérales, soit du projet de communauté francophone et des conditions de sa réalisation. L'exception à cette règle fut, bien entendu, la visite à Montréal du général de Gaulle et l'incident du discours du 24 juillet, dit du balcon de l'hôtel de ville, qui tout en jetant un froid sur les relations entre le Canada et la France, ne modifia pas en profondeur le cours des événements, comme en témoigne un communiqué du 2 novembre du ministère des Armées de France faisant état du renforcement de la coopération militaire franco-canadienne.

Au-delà de tous ces développements, le ministère des Affaires extérieures annonça enfin en septembre 1967 sa décision de créer une Direction des relations entre pays francophones dont le mandat serait: 1. de coordonner la politique à suivre à l'égard de la Francophonie; 2. d'étudier les relations entre pays francophones; et 3. de suivre l'activité des organisations internationales du point de vue de la Francophonie, et une Direction de la coordination chargée, pour sa part, de la responsabilité de suivre les aspects internationaux des relations fédérales-provinciales et en particulier les activités internationales des provinces, dont bien sûr celles du Québec. Le 1er décembre 1967, le premier ministre Pearson adressait une lettre au premier ministre Daniel Johnson, soulevant précisément l'intérêt manifesté par le Québec à participer à des conférences internationales.

On comprit mieux le sens de la démarche de Pearson, en tant que chef de la diplomatie canadienne, lorsque le Québec fut invité seul par le gouvernement du Gabon à participer à la Conférence des ministres de l'Éducation nationale de la France et des quatorze États d'expression française et de Madagascar (CONFEMEN), tenue à Libreville en février 1968. En plus d'avoir été irrité par le fait que le premier ministre du Québec avait fait mine d'ignorer sa lettre du 1er décembre 1967, et plus encore celle du 8 mars 1968 qui en était le complément, ce qui inquiétait vraisemblablement davantage le premier ministre Pearson, c'est que la CONFEMEN avait été chargée en 1967, par les chefs d'État de l'OCAM, d'étudier les modalités d'organisation de la Francophonie. Pour paraître conséquent avec le message qu'il avait jusque-là laissé entendre au plus grand nombre possible de ses partenaires, à savoir que l'organisation de la Francophonie ne saurait se réaliser sans qu'il soit lui-même consulté, le gouvernement canadien prit aussitôt la décision de suspendre l'établissement de ses relations diplomatiques avec le Gabon. Et pour rendre sa position encore plus claire, le gouvernement canadien fit remettre au gouvernement français par l'ambassade du Canada à Paris une note verbale sur l'incident du Gabon. D'autre part, sur le plan intérieur, le gouvernement canadien poursuivit ses contacts avec le gouvernement du Québec en vue de conclure avec lui des arrangements qui «permettraient à la province de Québec de participer pleinement au développement de la Francophonie et d'être représentée dans les discussions relatives à son élaboration, d'une façon qui soit compatible avec l'existence d'un Canada souverain et indépendant». On mena aussi rapidement à terme les études déjà en cours au ministère des Affaires extérieures, qui prirent éventuellement la forme de livres blancs publiés durant l'année 1968 sous les titres *Le fédéralisme et les conférences internationales sur l'éducation* et *Le fédéralisme et les relations internationales*. Ces deux livres blancs définissaient en réalité les règles générales que le gouvernement fédéral se proposait de suivre dans la conduite de la politique étrangère et celles qu'il entendait appliquer quant à la représentation du Canada auprès des organisations internationales, et quant à la participation des provinces aux conférences internationales, y compris celles portant sur des sujets dits de juridiction exclusivement provinciale comme l'éducation et, évidemment, celles qui pourraient aussi se tenir entre les seuls États francophones. On peut raisonnablement estimer que ces deux livres blancs n'auraient pas vu le jour si le gouvernement du Québec n'avait pas, au cours des années, poussé aussi loin la thèse du prolongement international de ses compétences internes, ou si la Francophonie ne lui en avait pas offert le prétexte. On pourrait même avancer ici l'hypothèse que la Francophonie a été la cause réelle de cette clarification des règles de conduite de la politique étrangère du Canada ou, en d'autres mots, que la Francophonie a sûrement eu un impact sur la diplomatie canadienne. Ces règles fédérales n'allaient bien entendu ne gêner en rien la poursuite du mouvement général déjà largement amorcé d'élargissement et d'approfondissement des relations directes entre le Québec et la France. Mais on peut cependant être certain qu'elles joueront à plein lorsque le Québec voudra se rapprocher davantage des autres États francophones, ou lorsque le moment viendra de mettre en place ou d'institutionnaliser une Francophonie intergouvernementale à caractère international. Il est vrai que beaucoup restait encore à faire avant d'en arriver là.

Préoccupé à la fois par certaines séquelles de la visite en juillet 1967 du général de Gaulle au Canada et ce qui lui apparaissait comme le piétinement de son programme d'assistance aux pays francophones, le gouvernement canadien décida en février 1968 de confier à un ancien ministre sénior francophone, Lionel Chevrier, le soin de conduire une mission extraordinaire de coopération économique en Afrique – la mission Chevrier –, dont le mandat était de lui faire des recommandations sur l'orientation, le contenu et l'expansion du programme canadien d'aide à l'Afrique francophone. Cette mission, qui débuta à Paris et qui se poursuivit du 14 février au 25 mars 1968 dans sept États francophones, à savoir le Maroc, l'Algérie, la Tunisie, le Cameroun, la Côte d'Ivoire, le Niger et le Sénégal, avait incontestablement un caractère exceptionnel dans la mesure où elle était investie du pouvoir d'engager financièrement les autorités canadiennes dans des projets agréés sur place avec les représentants des gouvernements des pays visités. La mission Chevrier eut à vrai dire plusieurs effets bénéfiques sur les relations canado-africaines. D'une part, elle accrut substantiellement – de 40 millions de dollars pour la période 1968-1973 – le budget du programme canadien d'aide à l'Afrique francophone. Elle assura en outre une plus grande diversification aux activités canadiennes de coopération dans cette région du monde, ajoutant aux programmes traditionnels d'assistance technique des projets d'assistance-équipement dans des domaines aussi variés que l'agriculture, la santé physique, les ressources naturelles et les infrastructures, qui répondaient dans plus de la moitié des cas à la définition de projets dits intégrés. Pour la première fois, des prêts de l'ordre de 21 millions de dollars furent consentis par les autorités canadiennes à des pays francophones. D'autre part, la mission Chevrier eut des résultats extrêmement positifs sur le plan politique. Elle permit entre autres d'apporter aux pays africains une preuve tangible du sérieux de l'intérêt que portait le gouvernement canadien à l'Afrique francophone. Elle contribua aussi à mieux faire apprécier dans les pays visités la compétence que se réclamait le gouvernement canadien dans la conduite des affaires internationales. À l'inverse, elle permit aux membres de la mission Chevrier de prendre connaissance de l'omniprésence française en Afrique, ce qui conduisit à une bien meilleure compréhension de la part des autorités canadiennes du rôle de premier plan que jouait la France dans le développement de la plupart des pays de l'Afrique francophone. Bref, la mission Chevrier a donné au gouvernement canadien, à un moment critique de l'histoire des relations du Canada avec le monde francophone, la crédibilité qui lui manquait. D'aucuns apprécièrent mieux à partir de là la contribution que le gouvernement canadien pouvait effectivement apporter à l'organisation de la Francophonie.

À la suite des représentations qu'il avait faites au moment de la conférence tenue en 1968 à Libreville des ministres de l'Éducation des pays francophones (CONFEMEN), le gouvernement canadien reçut une invitation pour participer à la réunion de janvier 1969 du même groupe à Kinshasa (Zaïre). Conformément aux règles mises de l'avant dans son livre blanc sur les conférences internationales sur l'éducation, le gouvernement canadien profita de l'occasion pour y faire accepter le principe d'une seule délégation canadienne qui comprenait, en l'occurrence, outre des représentants du gouvernement fédéral, des représentants des quatre provinces canadiennes participantes, à savoir le Québec, le Nouveau-Brunswick, l'Ontario et le Manitoba, de même que pour en établir les modalités de fonctionnement. Ainsi la conférence de Kinshasa fut-elle témoin de l'adoption de la formule qui devait effectivement régir la participation canadienne aux instances de la Francophonie.

À l'invitation du président de l'OCAM, alors président de la République du Niger, qui mettait en application la résolution adoptée en janvier 1968 par les chefs d'État de l'OCAM envisageant la création d'une conférence annuelle des chefs d'État francophones, et par conséquent d'une Francophonie institutionnalisée, une délégation canadienne, formée cette fois des seuls représentants du gouvernement fédéral et du gouvernement du Québec, participa à la Conférence des États francophones à Niamey, capitale du Niger, du 17 au 20 février 1969. Cette conférence, qui devait ouvrir la voie à l'émergence d'une communauté internationale des pays francophones, déboucha sur l'adoption d'une résolution qui, d'une part, endossait le principe de la création d'une agence ou d'un office de coopération culturelle et technique entre pays francophones, et qui, d'autre part, acceptait la mise sur pied d'un Secrétariat exécutif provisoire chargé de préparer les statuts d'une telle organisation et d'élaborer un programme de coopération multilatérale dans le domaine de l'éducation et de la culture. S'il est vrai que cette conférence donna lieu à de sérieux tiraillements entre les représentants du Québec et du Canada à l'intérieur de la délégation canadienne, elle n'en permit pas moins au gouvernement canadien de se mériter une place de choix dans l'organisation de la communauté des pays francophones. D'entrée de jeu, le Canada offrit en effet de participer au financement du Secrétariat provisoire, dont la direction fut confiée à un Canadien d'expression française, Jean-Marc Léger, Secrétaire général de l'AUPELF, qui était celui qui, au Canada, avait le plus milité jusque-là en faveur de l'établissement de relations étroites avec le monde francophone.

Au terme de cette période qui marqua l'engagement progressif du Canada dans la Francophonie, il nous faut constater que la politique étrangère du Canada était alors bien proche d'atteindre son but: assurer la mise en place d'une coopération multilatérale institutionnalisée entre pays francophones, garantissant le respect des prérogatives de l'État fédéral dans le domaine des affaires étrangères. Du point de vue du gouvernement canadien, il importait en effet que l'agence ou l'office dont la création était prévue par la conférence de Niamey réponde d'abord aux critères d'une organisation internationale de type classique: une organisation formée d'États souverains et indépendants.

LA PÉRIODE INSTITUTIONNELLE

La période qui va de 1970 jusqu'à nos jours, ou plus précisément jusqu'au 22 juin 1985 pour les fins de cette étude, sera définie comme la phase proprement institutionnelle de la coopération multilatérale entre pays francophones. L'élément principal de cette période sera l'Agence de coopération culturelle et technique (ACCT), née à Niamey en 1970, qui est à la fois une organisation internationale de type classique et la seule expression à ce jour d'une communauté véritablement internationale des pays francophones. Nous traiterons donc ici en priorité de cette organisation. Nous aborderons dans le reste de ce chapitre tout ce qui, du point de vue de la politique étrangère, a trait aux autres relations bilatérales et multilatérales entre le Canada et les pays francophones, notamment celles qui s'inscrivent dans le cadre des conférences ministérielles entre pays francophones et des programmes canadiens de coopération internationale, puis nous rendrons compte des relations bilatérales entre le Canada et la Belgique, d'une part, entre le Canada et la France, d'autre part, et enfin des relations qui naissent de l'intérêt que des Canadiens et des Québécois portent aux organisations internationales non gouvernementales francophones.

Le Canada et l'Agence de coopération culturelle et technique

Le gouvernement canadien n'a pu que se féliciter de la tenue au Niger, du 16 au 20 mars 1970, de la deuxième conférence de Niamey dont les travaux aboutirent à la mise sur pied de la première organisation internationale à caractère universel entre pays francophones, l'Agence de coopération culturelle et technique. Fidèle à une déclaration du président de la délégation canadienne à la première conférence de Niamey, Gérard Pelletier, à l'effet qu'une participation à la Francophonie correspondait à un besoin vital «pour tous ces francophones de chez nous», le gouvernement canadien prit soin d'inclure dans la délégation canadienne à cette conférence des représentants de quatre provinces canadiennes, le Québec, le Nouveau-Brunswick, l'Ontario et le Manitoba qui furent, avec les représentants du gouvernement fédéral, cosignataires de la convention portant création de cette nouvelle organisation internationale.

L'Agence de coopération culturelle et technique (ACCT) a souvent été désignée par le gouvernement canadien comme la clef de voûte des organisations internationales francophones. Si en vertu de sa charte, l'ACCT a pour fin essentielle l'affirmation et le développement entre ses membres d'une coopération multilatérale dans les domaines ressortissant à l'éducation, à la culture, aux sciences et aux techniques, elle a d'abord été, du point de vue canadien, l'instrument qui aura permis d'associer formellement le gouvernement fédéral et le gouvernement des provinces, et au premier chef celui du Québec, à une action commune de politique étrangère à l'endroit des pays francophones. Cette action conjointe, dont on peut penser que la formule a été progressivement mise au point au cours de la ronde de consultations qu'a eues au début de 1970 le secrétaire général par intérim, notamment avec les autorités canadiennes et québécoises, trouve son point d'appui dans l'article 3.3 de la Charte de l'ACCT. Cet article, en effet, après avoir évoqué le principe du respect absolu de la souveraineté des États, stipule que «tout gouvernement peut être admis comme gouvernement participant aux institutions, aux activités et aux programmes de l'Agence, sous réserve de l'approbation de l'État membre (en l'occurrence le Canada) dont relève le territoire sur lequel le gouvernement participant concerné exerce son autorité et selon les modalités convenues entre ce gouvernement et celui de l'État membre». Or il se trouve que de telles modalités furent convenues et consignées dans une entente signée le 1er octobre 1971 entre le gouvernement du Canada et le gouvernement du Québec, qui prévoit entre autres les conditions de la présence et de la participation de représentants du Québec aux institutions, aux conférences et aux réunions officielles de l'Agence, qui détermine la quote-part du gouvernement du Québec aux frais de fonctionnement du Secrétariat de l'Agence, et qui anticipe que le Québec pourra contribuer au financement des programmes de celle-ci. Pour des raisons qui tiennent à la logique de la position constitutionnelle du gouvernement fédéral, un accord similaire fut signé avec le gouvernement du Nouveau-Brunswick en décembre 1977.

Il ne fait aucun doute que les arrangements qui ont conduit à partir de 1971 à la contribution du Québec à l'ACCT en tant que gouvernement participant équivalaient dans un certain sens à un règlement du contentieux qui, au cours des années, avait opposé, d'une part, le gouvernement canadien au gouvernement français et, d'autre part, le gouvernement canadien au gouvernement de certains pays francophones d'Afrique, au sujet de l'action internationale du Québec. Il n'en fallait pas plus pour que le Canada accepte de jouer, au cours de la phase de démarrage, le rôle de pays-moteur ou de locomotive de l'ACCT. Qu'un Québécois, par surcroît citoyen canadien, Jean-Marc Léger, ait été de 1970 à 1974 Secrétaire général de l'organisation ne pouvait que contribuer à stimuler dans ce sens le gouvernement canadien et le gouvernement québécois. La deuxième conférence générale de l'Agence fut de ce fait, peut-on croire, tenue au Canada en octobre 1971. Mais le geste le plus significatif fut la décision prise dès le départ par le Canada d'accepter de prendre à son compte 35 % du budget total de l'Agence. En 1985, cette contribution était répartie entre le gouvernement fédéral (31,13 %), le gouvernement du Québec (2,94 %) et le gouvernement du Nouveau-Brunswick (0,29 %). Bien que deuxième en importance après celle de la France, qui est de l'ordre de 45 %, ce niveau relativement élevé de contribution a assuré un rôle clé au Canada à l'intérieur de l'ACCT. Au fil des années, plusieurs Canadiens y ont occupé des postes clés, soit à titre d'adjoint au Secrétaire général, de directeur général, de directeur de programme, de conseiller, ou de chef de Cabinet du Secrétaire général. D'autre part, en plus d'être associé à l'élaboration, sinon à l'exécution de la plupart des programmes, le Canada a pu contribuer de façon particulière à la création par l'ACCT en 1972 de l'École internationale de Bordeaux, principalement vouée à la formation des cadres de la fonction publique des pays membres, qui est l'une des réalisations de premier plan de l'Agence. Toutefois, en vue d'assurer un meilleur équilibre entre le volet culturel favorisé par la France et le volet scientifique, économique et technique favorisé par l'ensemble des pays africains, le Canada s'est surtout fait le promoteur à la quatrième conférence générale de l'Agence, tenue à l'Île Maurice en 1975, d'un Programme spécial de développement (PSD), qui a effectivement donné un second souffle à l'organisation. Inspiré d'un programme du Commonwealth connu sous le nom de Commonwealth Fund for Technical Cooperation (CFTC), le Programme spécial de développement a débuté ses opérations en 1977. Il a pour fonction principale de permettre la réalisation de projets à caractère ponctuel jugés par les parties comme ayant un effet multiplicateur et qui s'inscrivent dans le cadre des plans de développement des pays membres, habituellement les pays dits les moins avancés. Compte tenu du fait que le Canada a été depuis le début le premier bailleur de fonds de ce programme, qui est alimenté uniquement par des contributions volontaires des États membres – la contribution canadienne atteignait 77 % du budget du PSD en 1984 –, la direction du PSD a toujours été confiée jusqu'à maintenant à un citoyen canadien.

L'Agence de coopération culturelle et technique a été durant quelques années un lieu de rencontres ministérielles sectorielles entre ses pays membres. La première de ces rencontres réunit à Luxembourg en 1977 les ministres de la Science et de la Technologie. La deuxième regroupa à Paris en septembre 1980 les ministres de la Justice et en mars 1981, les ministres de l'Agriculture. Puis, ce fut le tour des ministres de la Culture de se réunir en septembre 1981 à Cotonou.

L'ACCT n'a pas pour autant su répondre à tous les espoirs que le Canada avait fondés en elle. La première, sinon la plus grande source d'insatisfaction, a été l'administration déficiente de cette organisation, à laquelle le Canada a lui-même inconsciemment contribué en s'employant activement à faire élire en 1981 un secrétaire général, François Orvono-Nguema, qui s'est révélé par la suite manifestement incapable d'assurer une gestion valable. En réalité, ni les efforts combinés du Canada, de la Belgique et de la France, qui sont ses trois principaux bailleurs de fond, n'ont réussi à ce jour à empêcher que les frais de fonctionnement n'absorbent près de 50 % du budget total de l'Agence. Or, malgré sa frustration, le Canada paraît avoir toujours refusé d'adopter des attitudes d'affrontement à l'intérieur de l'ACCT, même lorsqu'il s'est agi de la remise en cause du principe de la collégialité au sein du secrétariat général, pourtant inscrite dans la Charte, et qui avait entraîné à la fin des années 70 de sérieuses difficultés de fonctionnement et des tiraillements extrêmes à l'intérieur de l'organisation. Envers et contre tout, pourrait-on dire, le Canada est resté obstinément positif à l'égard de l'Agence. La meilleure illustration de ce comportement aura été la proposition avancée par le Québec en septembre 1985 de créer au bénéfice des pays membres de l'ACCT une Fondation internationale de la Francophonie dont l'objectif serait d'obtenir des milieux d'affaires de nouvelles ressources financières pouvant aider à développer les programmes de l'Agence.

On pourrait avancer sans risque de se tromper que la conception que se fait le Canada de l'ACCT en est une qui correspond essentiellement à celle de la majorité des États membres, dont la plupart comme on le sait sont des pays en voie de développement, à savoir une institution d'aide multilatérale axée d'abord sur le développement des pays francophones. Du point de vue du gouvernement canadien, cette conception permet de considérer les programmes de l'ACCT comme une sorte de prolongement du volet francophone des programmes d'aide bilatérale et multilatérale de l'ACDI. Du point de vue du gouvernement du Québec, cette conception fait de l'ACCT l'instrument qui légitimise une action du Québec sur le plan de la politique étrangère et qui favorise l'établissement de relations concrètes, positives et réciproques entre le Québec et les pays francophones. On peut pratiquement en dire autant de la participation des représentants des autres provinces aux conférences techniques des ministres des pays d'expression française.

Le Canada et les conférences ministérielles entre pays francophones

C'est depuis la réunion de janvier 1969 à Kinshasa au Zaïre que le Canada participe officiellement à la Conférence des ministres de l'Éducation nationale des pays francophones (CONFEMEN). On se rappellera que c'est à l'occasion de cette réunion, qui suivait celle de 1968 à Libreville – où s'était produite l'affaire du Gabon –, que le gouvernement canadien avait fait accepter un mode de représentation conforme aux énoncés de son livre blanc sur la participation du Canada aux conférences internationales sur l'éducation. Or, comme l'éducation, selon la constitution canadienne, est du ressort des provinces, le gouvernement du Canada et celui des provinces durent convenir d'abord entre eux d'arrangements particuliers régissant la composition et le fonctionnement de la délégation canadienne à cette conférence. L'esprit de ces arrangements sera d'ailleurs sanctionné quelques années plus tard par l'ensemble des membres de la CONFEMEN. Le Canada participe également à la Conférence des ministres de la Jeunesse et des Sports (CONFEJES) des pays d'expression française, régie par un protocole d'accord signé à Kigali en août 1975. Comme pour la CONFEMEN, la délégation canadienne aux réunions comprend, outre des délégués du gouvernement fédéral, des représentants du Québec, du Nouveau-Brunswick, de l'Ontario et du Manitoba, et son mode de fonctionnement est plus ou moins le même. En règle générale, la délégation canadienne y est présidée par un ministre de l'une des provinces participantes.

La participation canadienne à la Conférence des ministres de l'Éducation nationale (CONFEMEN) et à la Conférence des ministres de la Jeunesse et des Sports (CONFEJES) des pays d'expression française se traduit par une contribution financière au budget de fonctionnement de leur secrétariat exécutif permanent (STP), dont le siège est à Dakar, qui est de l'ordre de 35 %, et par une participation aux programmes d'activités de ces deux organisations. Ainsi, pour l'année 1985-1986, il est prévu que la contribution canadienne à ces programmes sera de 700 000 $ dans le cas de la CONFEJES et de 110 000 $ dans le cas de la CONFEMEN. Mais au-delà de cet appui financier, la participation canadienne aux activités de ces organisations permet aux spécialistes et aux experts des provinces canadiennes et des pays participants de mettre en commun leurs connaissances et de tirer profit de leurs expériences respectives. Les réunions de la CONFEMEN et de la CONFEJES sont particulièrement utiles aux pays en voie de développement sur le plan technique. Elles offrent par ailleurs aux membres de la délégation canadienne de nombreuses occasions de se familiariser avec les milieux africains et d'établir avec leurs vis-à-vis des liens qui sont le fondement même des relations internationales culturelles et techniques.

L'aide canadienne au développement des pays d'Afrique francophone et de Haïti

Afrique francophone

Déjà avantagée par la mission Chevrier de 1968, l'aide canadienne à l'Afrique francophone a bénéficié particulièrement durant les années 1970 de l'augmentation considérable des budgets consacrés à l'aide publique au développement et, de façon générale, du renouvellement de l'approche canadienne en matière d'aide accordant la priorité aux pays les plus pauvres et mettant notamment l'accent sur le secteur agricole[15]. Ainsi, les décaissements de l'aide bilatérale du Canada aux pays d'Afrique francophone passèrent de 29,7 en 1970-1971 à 104,99 millions de dollars en 1975-1976 et les déboursés, dans le seul secteur agricole, augmentèrent de 1974-1975 à 1975-1976 de 10,5 à 23,5 millions. Comme seize des 36 pays désignés par l'Organisation des Nations Unies comme «pays les moins avancés» sont en Afrique francophone, plusieurs d'entre eux profitèrent de l'annulation par le Canada au cours de la même période des dettes contractées au titre de prêts au développement et de l'engagement que le Canada soit le premier à prendre à la conférence tenue à Paris au printemps de 1977 (dialogue Nord-Sud) de transformer en subvention toute son aide aux pays les moins développés. En 1983-1984, l'aide canadienne à l'Afrique francophone avait atteint 137,56 millions de dollars, soit 20 % du total du programme de l'aide bilatérale, et les secteurs prioritaires de cette aide étaient l'agriculture, la forêt et les pêcheries, l'énergie et le développement des ressources.

À l'heure actuelle, le Canada accorde son aide à pratiquement tous les pays de l'Afrique francophone. Dans neuf de ces pays, le Sénégal, le Zaïre, le Rwanda, le Cameroun, le Niger, le Mali, le Burkina Faso (Haute-Volta), la Côte d'Ivoire et la Guinée, qui sont désignés comme pays de concentration, l'ACDI y poursuit un programme pluriannuel de coopération. Dans les 18 autres, elle fournit une aide alimentaire et une assistance technique, industrielle et institutionnelle variée. Par des projets comme la fourniture d'équipement ferroviaire en Tunisie, le renforcement du réseau ferroviaire Abidjan-Niger, l'aménagement des installations portuaires de Douala (Cameroun), la commercialisation de la pêche artisanale au Sénégal, la ligne d'électrification de Kossou-Daloa, l'aménagement du fleuve Sénégal, le réseau panafricain de télécommunications (PANAFTEL), et le projet de développement rural de Kaarta (Mali), le Canada contribue effectivement à doter les pays de l'Afrique francophone d'infrastructures indispensables à leur développement. Au plan des ressources humaines, l'accent de l'aide bilatérale canadienne a été régulièrement mis sur des projets d'appui institutionnel, comme la construction et l'aménagement de l'Université nationale du Rwanda dont la direction a été confiée au départ à un Québécois, le R.P. Georges-Henri Lévesque, de l'École polytechnique de Thiès (Sénégal), du lycée de Bonabéri (Cameroun), du Centre universitaire des sciences de la santé (Cameroun) et du Centre de formation hôtelière (Côte d'Ivoire). Plus récemment, le lancement d'un programme énergétique canadien en Afrique a permis à la corporation Petro-Canada d'intervenir en Gambie, au Maroc et au Sénégal en vue du développement de sources d'énergie nouvelles et renouvelables, et à la Société Géomines de Montréal de s'engager dans la réalisation d'un projet d'assistance en recherche minière au Niger. Le Canada a de même acheminé au fil des années par des voies bilatérales une aide alimentaire destinée à des réfugiés, aux victimes de cataclysmes et à des populations d'Afrique francophone particulièrement défavorisées. Enfin, le Canada a constamment greffé à la plupart de ses projets d'aide un programme d'assistance technique, soit par le biais de coopérants canadiens travaillant à la préparation d'une relève africaine, soit par le truchement de boursiers et de stagiaires africains au Canada, et surtout au Québec. Par exemple, au 1er janvier 1976, l'Afrique francophone accueillait 419 coopérants canadiens, dont 290 dans le secteur de l'éducation, et 756 étudiants et stagiaires de pays francophones d'Afrique poursuivaient leur formation au Canada ou dans des pays tiers grâce à des bourses de l'ACDI[16]. Au niveau multilatéral, le Canada est membre depuis 1976 du Comité inter-États pour la lutte contre la sécheresse au Sahel et du Club des amis du Sahel.

L'aide canadienne au développement de l'Afrique francophone passe également par d'innombrables organisations non gouvernementales et par des organisations ou associations internationales bénéficiant de l'appui du gouvernement du Québec et de l'ACDI. Dans la première catégorie, et pour nous en tenir aux seules dernières années, il y a entre autres le Groupe Opération Haute-Volta de Québec, qui participe au financement d'un programme de développement rural intégré, la Fédération des caisses populaires Desjardins, qui s'est impliquée dans la mise en œuvre d'un projet de développement de coopératives d'épargne et de crédit au Burkina Faso, au Togo, au Cameroun et au Zaïre, le Conseil de la coopérative du Québec (CCQ) et la Société de coopération pour le développement international (SOCODEVI), qui, ayant hérité en 1984 des activités du Service international de la CCQ, travaille à la réalisation de programmes de formation de coopérateurs au Burundi, au Burkina Faso et en Haïti.

Haïti

Une aide canadienne est en effet aussi accordée à Haïti, autre pays de concentration, avec lequel fut signé en 1973 un accord général de coopération bilatérale qui visait à appuyer les plans de développement de ce pays touchant particulièrement aux secteurs de l'agriculture, de l'énergie et de l'éducation. À la fin de l'année 1980-1981, l'ACDI avait injecté pas moins de 41,3 millions de dollars dans des projets bilatéraux en Haïti. Comme en Afrique francophone, l'ACDI participe au financement en Haïti de nombreux projets conduits par des organisations non gouvernementales (ONG), notamment le Conseil de la coopération du Québec, la Fondation Témoignage Fraternité, Care du Canada, le Plan de parrainage du Canada, l'Organisation catholique canadienne pour le développement et la paix et diverses autres congrégations religieuses.

Le Canada participe au développement des pays d'Afrique francophone et de Haïti en contribuant également aux activités des institutions financières internationales, dont la Banque internationale pour la reconstruction et le développement (BIRD), l'Association internationale de développement (AID), la Société financière internationale (SFI), le Fonds africain de développement (FAfd) dont le Canada est l'un des principaux pays membres donateurs depuis sa création en 1972, la Banque africaine de développement (BAfD), dont il est l'un des membres non régionaux avec 3,2 % du capital souscrit en 1984 et la Banque interaméricaine de développement (BID). Il verse en outre des contributions aux programmes généraux de coopération technique des Nations Unies, dont le Programme des Nations Unies pour le développement (PNUD), le Fonds des Nations Unies pour l'enfance (UNICEF), dont les programmes s'adressent aux populations les plus vulnérables du tiers monde, le

Programme alimentaire mondial (PAM), qui constitue l'une des principales formes de l'intervention canadienne en faveur des plus démunis, et le Fonds international de développement agricole (FIDA).

Les autres relations bilatérales

Les Pays d'Afrique francophone

L'augmentation considérable des programmes canadiens d'aide à l'Afrique francophone depuis la fin des années 60 explique en bonne partie pourquoi le Canada et les pays d'Afrique francophone ont poursuivi l'établissement et le développement de leurs relations diplomatiques au cours de cette période. Le Canada a, pour sa part, ouvert plusieurs ambassades en Afrique francophone durant les années 70: en Côte d'Ivoire en 1970, en Algérie en 1971, au Maroc en 1974, au Gabon en 1981. Des bureaux d'ambassade furent ouverts par la suite, aux fins des programmes d'aide, en Haute-Volta, au Niger et en Guinée. Les pays africains en firent autant au Canada en ouvrant les uns après les autres une ambassade à Ottawa: l'Algérie en 1968, la Tunisie en 1969, le Rwanda en 1970, le Niger et le Gabon en 1971, le Maroc et le Dahomey (Bénin) en 1972, la Côte d'Ivoire et la Haute-Volta en 1973. Des visites ministérielles s'ensuivirent de part et d'autre, nombreuses et répétées de la part des pays africains, plus rares ou plus sélectives, souvent exceptionnelles, de la part du Canada. Ainsi, c'est en juillet 1979 qu'eut lieu la première visite en Afrique franco-phone d'un premier ministre canadien, Joe Clark, qui en réalité fit simplement escale durant deux jours au Cameroun en route pour une réunion des chefs de gouverne-ment des pays du Commonwealth.

Par ailleurs, plusieurs commissions mixtes ou commissions bilatérales furent établies durant la même période entre le Canada et les pays de l'Afrique fran-cophone dans le but de promouvoir leurs relations dans tous les domaines d'intérêt mutuel. Ainsi, pour ce qui est des commissions mixtes: en 1969 avec la Tunisie, en 1979 avec le Cameroun et avec la Côte d'Ivoire; puis avec l'Algérie en 1980, avec le Gabon en 1981 et avec le Maroc en 1982. Et quant aux commissions bilatérales: en 1972 avec le Rwanda et le Niger, puis avec le Mali en 1977, avec la Haute-Volta (Burkina Faso) en 1979, avec le Sénégal et le Zaïre en 1981, et avec la Guinée en 1982. Ces commissions, qui se réunissent normalement tous les deux ans, passent en revue les relations générales, commerciales et financières, le cas échéant, et les divers programmes d'échanges ou de coopération entre les pays concernés.

De façon générale, les relations économiques, commerciales et financières entre le Canada et la plupart sinon tous les pays d'Afrique francophone sont liées aux programmes canadiens d'aide publique au développement. La fourniture de biens et de services canadiens tiennent le plus souvent aux critères des politiques canadien-nes de «l'aide liée» (au moins 80 % de l'aide bilatérale excluant les coûts de transport) et du «contenu canadien» qui s'applique à l'ensemble des biens et services de chaque projet d'aide. Les programmes d'aide à l'Afrique francophone sont le plus souvent financés par l'ACDI ou cofinancés par l'ACDI et d'autres organismes, cana-diens comme la Société pour l'expansion des exportations (SEE), ou internationaux comme la Banque mondiale, la Banque africaine de développement, le Fonds africain de développement ou les Fonds arabes/OPEP.

Le Canada accorde le traitement de la nation la plus favorisée aux pays d'Afrique francophone, qui bénéficient également du système canadien de préférences généralisées. Le Canada n'a cependant signé aucun accord commercial bilatéral avec ces pays qui, comme le Maroc, la Tunisie, le Cameroun ou le Gabon offrent les perspectives les plus intéressantes, ou même l'Algérie qui absorbe près du tiers (près de 500 millions de dollars) des exportations canadiennes vers l'Afrique. Il est vrai cependant que les sociétés canadiennes actives dans ces pays profitent de diverses lignes de crédit parallèles SEE/ACDI et de programmes de coopération industrielle. Malgré les progrès réalisés au cours des dernières années, la présence économique canadienne en Afrique francophone demeure, comme dans le reste de l'Afrique, bien modeste. Les principaux secteurs canadiens d'activités sont ceux des communications, de l'énergie, des mines, des forêts et de l'agriculture. Comme on pouvait s'y attendre, la balance commerciale y est partout favorable au Canada.

Belgique

Bien qu'établies depuis 1939, les relations diplomatiques entre le Canada et la Belgique connurent un renforcement, à vrai dire, en avril 1973 avec l'accréditation d'un ambassadeur canadien à plein temps auprès du gouvernement belge. Déjà en 1971, les deux pays avaient signé un Accord de coopération scientifique, industriel et technologique. Sur le plan des échanges commerciaux, le Canada et la Belgique semblaient se diriger en 1985 vers un équilibre de leur balance commerciale. De 1982 à 1984, les exportations belges vers le Canada ont connu une remontée spectaculaire, passant de 263 à 446 millions de dollars. Durant la même période, les exportations canadiennes vers la Belgique ont chuté de 773 à 674 millions de dollars.

Par ailleurs, les échanges culturels s'accrurent considérablement durant la décennie 70. Le Canada ouvrit en 1974 un Centre culturel et d'information à Bruxelles. La Commission mixte Canada-Belgique formée en vertu de l'accord culturel de 1967 tint sa première réunion en décembre 1975. En 1972, une entente fut conclue entre le gouvernement canadien et le gouvernement québécois, établissant une sous-commission belgo-québécoise à l'intérieur de la Commission mixte Canada-Belgique. Au cours de la même année, le Québec procéda à l'ouverture à Bruxelles d'un bureau économique qui est devenu en 1973 une délégation générale du Québec en Belgique. En 1977, la Radiotélévision belge conclut un accord avec Radio-Québec au sujet d'un programme d'échanges. En mars 1978, la Société de développement industriel du Québec (SDI) et l'Office de promotion industrielle de Belgique (OPI) signèrent une convention de coopération visant à favoriser des échanges d'information et mettant sur pied un groupe de travail conjoint. En 1980, une déclaration commune fut signée entre le gouvernement du Québec et l'exécutif régional wallon, définissant un ensemble d'actions communes dans le domaine des exportations canadiennes. En 1984, avec un total de 701 millions de dollars, soit à peine plus que le montant des exportations canadiennes vers la Belgique, le Canada n'occupait que 1,4 % du marché d'importation français. Dans l'autre sens, les exportations françaises vers le Canada étaient, la même année, de l'ordre de 1,2 milliards de dollars, dont plus de 50 % avait comme destination le Québec. À la fin de 1984, les investissements français directs au Canada atteignaient 1,25 milliards de dollars, soit 1,5 % de la valeur comptable de tous les investissements étrangers au Canada. En sens inverse, les investissements canadiens en France étaient en 1984 de l'ordre de 300 millions de dollars. D'autre part, le problème des droits de pêche de la France dans le golfe Saint-Laurent et autour des îles de Saint-Pierre et Miquelon n'était toujours pas résolu.

Le gouvernement français a par ailleurs graduellement redécouvert durant les années 70 les communautés franco-canadiennes hors-Québec. Il a par exemple déplacé son consulat de Halifax à Moncton pour se rapprocher des francophones de l'Est du Canada et accroître les échanges avec les Acadiens. Il a développé et renforcé ses contacts avec les Franco-Manitobains à travers le consulat français de Winnipeg. Mais c'est cependant avec le Québec que la France a intensifié ses relations au cours des années, par le Québec au point d'en arriver à des rapports privilégiés et uniques en leur genre.

Pour nous en tenir à la seule période récente, plusieurs ententes furent signées entre la France et le Québec: en 1979, une entente de réciprocité en matière de sécurité sociale; en 1980, une entente créant un Centre de promotion des coopérations technologiques et industrielles avec une section à Paris et une section au Québec; en 1982, quatre accords relatif aux biotechnologies, à l'informatique, à la télématique et à la normalisation du contrôle et de la qualité des produits industriels; et en 1983, un accord de coopération en matière de télédistribution et de câblodistribution. Parmi les organismes de coopération franco-québécoise, l'Office franco-québécois pour la jeunesse soutient depuis 17 ans des échanges de jeunes et des projets conçus pour contribuer au rapprochement du Québec et de la France et au développement de cette coopération bilatérale. Une Commission permanente franco-québécoise se charge de la coordination et de la mise en œuvre de l'ensemble des programmes de coopération entre la France et le Québec. Au niveau des rapports politiques, les premiers ministres français et québécois se rencontrent dorénavant régulièrement, en principe sur une base annuelle, une année en France et l'autre au Québec. En fait, on ne compte pas moins de 19 visites ministérielles entre la France et le Québec au cours de la seule année 1984.

Les organisations internationales non gouvernementales francophones

Les organisations internationales non gouvernementales francophones, dont on compte aujourd'hui une trentaine, représentent une autre des formes institutionnelles des relations multilatérales entre pays francophones. Or il n'est pas sans intérêt de remarquer que si les premières de ces organisations sont toutes nées au Canada, ou plus précisément au Québec, ce sont elles, dans leur ensemble, qui ont contribué à faire prendre conscience tant au niveau de l'opinion publique qu'à celui des gouvernements et des administrations publiques de la nécessité d'entreprendre une action en vue de l'organisation d'une communauté internationale des pays francophones. Du point de vue de l'action internationale du Canada et du Québec, rappelons brièvement celles de ces organisations ou associations à la fondation desquelles des Canadiens ou des Québécois ont joué un rôle déterminant, à savoir l'Union internationale des journalistes et de la presse de langue française (UIJPLF), fondée en 1952 sur l'initiative d'un journaliste canadien-français, Dostaler O'Leary, qui a été la première organisation internationale non gouvernementale francophone, l'Association des universités partiellement ou entièrement de langue française, fondée à Montréal en 1961 à l'initiative de Jean-Marc Léger, qui bénéficie depuis ses débuts de la part du gouvernement du Québec, et à partir de 1966 de la part du gouvernement canadien, de subventions budgétaires annuelles, et son Fonds international de coopération universitaire (FICU), créé en 1966, qui a pour objet principal la promotion du développement des universités du tiers monde, et qui reçoit également des gouvernements du Canada et du Québec des contributions annuelles, le Conseil international de la langue française (CILF), fondé en 1967 à l'occasion de la Deuxième Biennale de la langue française tenue à Québec et la Fédération internationale des professeurs de français (FIPF) fondée subséquemment en 1969, le Conseil international des radiotélévisions d'expression française (CIRTEF), fondé à Montréal en juin 1968, à la suite du Colloque international des radiotélévisions d'expression française, tenu à Montréal en juin 1977, avec le concours notamment du ministère des Affaires extérieures du Canada et du ministère des Affaires intergouvernementales du Québec, l'Association internationale des parlementaires de langue française (AIPLF), qui comprend depuis 1975 une section canadienne, une section québécoise et une section du Nouveau-Brunswick, toutes autonomes, l'Association mondiale des médecins francophones (AMMF), fondée en octobre 1973 à Ottawa sous l'impulsion de l'Association des médecins de langue française du Canada, l'Association internationale des maires francophones, fondée à Québec en mai 1979, et le Richelieu international, qui est l'émanation de la Société Richelieu, elle-même incorporée à Ottawa en 1944. Rappelons également que la plupart de ces organisations ont été ou sont aujourd'hui membres du Conseil consultatif de l'Agence de coopération culturelle et technique (ACCT), apportant ainsi à la coopération francophone intergouvernementale le soutien d'une francophonie au niveau des individus et des institutions du secteur privé ou semi-privé, dont le rôle est essentiel à la vitalité et au dynamisme de la communauté des pays francophones.

CONCLUSION

Force est de constater, au terme de cette étude, que les pays francophones occupent dorénavant une place relativement importante dans les relations internationales du Canada et du Québec. On pourrait même soutenir qu'en juin 1985, à la fin du régime Trudeau, la francophonie était effectivement devenue l'une des dimensions non négligeables de la politique étrangère du Canada. Il nous reste cependant à établir, en guise de conclusion, si l'engagement du gouvernement du Canada et du gouvernement du Québec dans la francophonie internationale repose sur des bases vraiment solides, si cet engagement se traduit par des politiques précises et quelque peu articulées, et enfin comment cet engagement, en ce qui concerne le gouvernement canadien, se compare au niveau des moyens mis en œuvre et des actions qui en découlent à l'engagement correspondant du Canada dans l'anglophonie, ou plus précisément dans le Commonwealth. Pour répondre à ces interrogations, il nous faudra maintenir, dans la mesure du possible, une distinction entre l'engagement du gouvernement fédéral et l'engagement du gouvernement du Québec. Il nous faudra aussi bien sûr distinguer ce qui, dans la Francophonie, s'adresse d'une part aux pays en voie de développement, les pays francophones s'entend, et ce qui concerne d'autre part les pays européens francophones, et plus particulièrement la France.

En ce qui a trait aux pays francophones en voie de développement, l'engagement du Canada, et accessoirement celui du Québec, tant sur le plan bilatéral que multilatéral, nous paraît évident, et par conséquent peu contestable, en ce qu'il répond à un problème majeur et durable de notre temps – celui du sous-développement économique des pays de l'Afrique francophone et de Haïti –, et qu'il s'inscrit dans le cadre d'une politique cohérente et globale d'aide au développement, qui prévoit que l'aide à fournir aux pays les moins avancés sera équivalente à 0,15 % du PNB du Canada, que 80 % de l'aide bilatérale du Canada sera affectée aux pays à faible revenu, et que de 20 à 21 % du programme d'aide bilatérale canadienne sera accordée à l'Afrique francophone. Ainsi, la participation du Canada, du Québec et du Nouveau-Brunswick à l'Agence de coopération culturelle et technique, et plus encore leur soutien au Programme spécial de développement (PSD), de même que l'appui du Canada et du Québec aux conférences ministérielles des pays francophones, la CONFEMEN et la CONFEJES, sont parfaitement compatibles avec l'orientation générale de la politique canadienne d'aide au développement. L'opinion publique canadienne souscrit d'ailleurs à cette politique et appuie l'engagement du Canada de contribuer au développement des pays francophones d'Afrique et d'Amérique. Pour le Canada, le champ de l'aide publique au développement occupe à vrai dire pratiquement tout l'espace économique de la Francophonie.

Il faut par ailleurs noter que si, à des fins de planification, la proportion de l'aide bilatérale du Canada à l'Afrique francophone (20 % en 1983-1984) est à peu près équivalente à celle de l'Afrique anglophone (22 % en 1983-1984), il existe toujours un profond écart en 1985-1986 entre le total des contributions que le Canada prévoit verser aux instances de la Francophonie (ACCT, PSD, AUPELF, CONFEJES, CONFEMEN, CAMES, Fonds 672, CILF, BLF et CIEFDC), qui est égal à 7 836 833 $, et le total des montants à verser aux institutions du Commonwealth (Commonwealth Secretariat, CFTC, Commonwealth Foundation, Commonwealth Youth Programme, Commonwealth Scholarship and Fellowship Plan, Commonwealth Science Council, Commonwealth Air Transport Council, Commonwealth Legal Advisory Service, Commonwealth Forestry Institute, Commonwealth Association of Task Administrators, Commonwealth Agricultural Bureau et Commonwealth War Graves Commission), qui est de 29 903 756 $. La raison de cet écart tient vraisemblablement à la fois de l'organisation tardive de la Francophonie, au degré de moindre développement des institutions francophones internationales, et à leur plus faible cohésion par rapport à celles du Commonwealth. L'ACCT, notamment, pour les raisons que nous savons, n'a pas su prendre en quinze ans d'existence son plein essor, et sa croissance reste à l'heure actuelle toujours problématique. On pourrait aussi croire que le volet culturel de l'ACCT, qui a clairement la faveur de la France, occupe peut-être une trop grande place dans les programmes de cette organisation par rapport au volet technique (PSD), qui est celui que veut en réalité privilégier le Canada.

Pour ce qui est de l'autre aspect majeur de l'engagement du Canada dans la Francophonie, à savoir celui des relations bilatérales avec la France, il convient en premier lieu de constater l'accroissement constant mais encore modeste des rapports entre le gouvernement canadien et le gouvernement français d'une part, et l'intensification remarquable au cours des années des relations entre le gouvernement du Québec et le gouvernement français. On pourrait certes tenter de savoir si des obstacles structurels et l'appartenance de la France et du Canada à des zones monétaires différentes ne sont pas les causes principales de la faiblesse des liens économiques entre les deux pays. On pourrait aussi chercher à établir si la détermination du gouvernement canadien de se rapprocher de la France n'a pas surtout été motivée, du moins au départ, par un souci de contenir ou d'encadrer les efforts du Québec en vue d'acquérir une personnalité internationale. Ou tenter d'établir si les succès du Québec à développer des relations directes et privilégiées avec la France n'a pas été ce qui a subséquemment aiguillonné le gouvernement canadien à suivre, à rattraper, voire à déborder le Québec à cet égard[17]. On pourrait par ailleurs vouloir aussi se poser la question à savoir si ce qui a motivé les gouvernements successifs du Québec à traiter directement avec le gouvernement français était vraiment «une recherche d'une compétence plus vaste en vue d'affirmer l'identité du Québec»[18], ou si en d'autres termes, «c'est pour le résoudre [le problème de l'identité culturelle] qu'il a développé ses échanges dans le cadre de la Francophonie»[19]. Mais tenons-nous en plutôt à la question principale que nous avons posée au début de ce chapitre: y a-t-il une politique canadienne, ou une politique québécoise à l'égard de la Franco-phonie ou à l'égard de la France?

S'il faut en croire l'ancien ambassadeur du Canada en France, Gérard Pelletier, «le Canada ne s'est jamais donné une politique d'ensemble à la fois prévisionnelle, cohérente et articulée à l'égard de la France»[20]. La raison en serait que, tant au niveau de l'opinion publique canadienne qu'à celui de l'administration fédérale, selon monsieur Pelletier, «nos perceptions, notre degré de connaissance, nos évaluations et nos priorités varient de façon aberrante», ou selon le professeur Paul Painchaud de l'Université Laval, les élites qui composent le système de politique étrangère du Canada «appartiennent à un réseau d'intérêts et entretiennent des perceptions vis-à-vis de la vie internationale où la France ne peut avoir qu'un rôle secondaire». À vrai dire, le gouvernement canadien paraît s'être satisfait jusqu'à maintenant de considérer la dualité linguistique canadienne comme toute la raison d'être et la justification de son engagement en faveur de la Francophonie. Il en découlerait essentiellement sous lui la double obligation de projeter à l'étranger l'image d'un pays bilingue et d'établir un plus juste équilibre entre sa politique à l'égard des pays francophones et sa politique à l'égard des pays du Commonwealth. Or il est encore loin d'être certain que le ministère des Affaires extérieures sera un jour en mesure de laisser entrevoir le visage en partie francophone du Canada à l'étranger[21]. Si l'on ajoute à ces faiblesses le caractère embryonnaire des consulta-tions politiques, des échanges économiques et des relations culturelles entre Otta-wa et Paris, on mesure le côté fragile et aléatoire de la politique du Canada à l'égard de la France et, par voie d'extension, à l'égard de la francophonie internationale.

À l'opposé, pour le Québec, dont on a pu dire que «son seul point d'appui extérieur, sa raison d'être devant l'histoire, c'est la France»[22], nous nous devons de noter qu'il s'est donné en juin 1985, à la suite d'une longue gestation, un énoncé de politique de relations internationales dont un des volets, portant sur la francophonie, précise au niveau des objectifs: l'élargissement de la communauté d'intérêts entre États francophones, la promotion de l'utilisation du français comme outil de dévelop-pement, la participation aux institutions francophones internationales, le développe-ment de la coopération bilatérale avec les pays francophones, notamment ceux de l'Afrique, et l'appui à des organisations non gouvernementales francophones, et un autre volet, portant sur la France, souligne entre autres la priorité à accorder à la coopération scientifique et technologique, à la coopération industrielle, aux investis-sements et aux procédés de transfert technologique, au développement du dialogue entre les instances politiques et à la nécessité de mieux articuler les instances de planification de la coopération[23]. Fort de l'appui de l'opinion publique du Québec à la Charte de la langue française, qui décrète que le français est la langue officielle du Québec, et soutenu par l'utilisation commune et généralisée du français au niveau de son administration publique, l'engagement du Québec en faveur de la franco-phonie paraît donc à la fois fondé, valable et durable. Si comme l'a écrit le professeur André Donneur de l'UQAM au sujet des relations franco-canadiennes, «il est indéni-

able que le pivot de ces relations est le Québec»[24], on peut sans doute tirer la conclusion qu'au lieu de lui nuire, l'engagement du gouvernement du Québec dans la
francophonie s'additionne à celui du gouvernement canadien, donc renforce considérablement la dimension francophone des relations internationales et de la politique étrangère du Canada.

NOTES

1. Jean-Marc Léger, «L'entreprise ardente et ambiguë de la francophonie», *Perspectives internationales*, novembre-décembre 1975, p. 35-42.

2. Renée Lescop: «En fait, les rapports entre les deux pays demeurent très limités: pas de représentation diplomatique de haut niveau, des échanges commerciaux pratiquement nuls et des relations culturelles relativement importantes mais canalisées par l'Église catholique et dans l'ensemble très élitistes. Rien en somme qui rapproche l'un de l'autre les deux pays», *Le pari québécois du général de Gaulle*, Boréal Express, 1981, p. 9.

3. Jean Chapdelaine: «Le souci, quasi exclusif, de Mackenzie King, en matière internationale, était d'empêcher que l'extérieur ne compliquât sa gouverne des affaires canadiennes [...]», «Esquisse d'une politique extérieure d'un Québec souverain: genèse et prospective», *Études internationales*, vol. VIII, n° 2, juin 1977, p. 342-355.

4. André Patry, *Le Québec dans le monde*, Leméac, 1980, p. 21.

5. Paul Gérin-Lajoie, «Le Canada et le Sud francophone», *Allocution à la 6ᵉ Conférence annuelle de l'Association des études prospectives*, tenue à Montréal le 2 octobre 1981.

6. Couve de Murville: «Lui-même [Pearson] apparemment étranger aux milieux francophones du Québec, et ne parlant pas français, n'était sans doute pas porté à se pencher sur des problèmes fort éloignés de ses préoccupations habituelles», «Pearson et la France», *International Journal*, vol. XXIX, n° 1, hiver, 1973-1974, p. 24-32.

7. André Patry, *ibidem*, p. 59.

8. Norman Robertson, *Memorandum for the Minister: Provincial Autonomy and External Relations*, ministère des Affaires extérieures, dossier 2727-AD-40, n° 8, 27 juillet 1963.

9. Canada, ministère des Affaires extérieures – dossier 20-FR-9, vol. 1 et 2; *Sujets d'entretiens: visite de M. Couve de Murville*, 20-30 septembre 1966, dossier 17-FR-1966/1A, et *Bulletin des affaires extérieures*, 1966, vol. XVIII, p. 505-507.

10. Canada, ministère des Affaires extérieures, dossier 20-1-2-FR: *Canadian Foreign Policy Trends and Relations – France*, vol. IV et dossier 26-1: *Francophonie – Orientation et développement*, vol. 4.

11. Canada, ministère des Affaires extérieures, dossier 17-SEN-1966/1A: *Visit of President Senghor of Sénégal*, Briefing Book et dossiers 20-SEN-9, 20-1-2-SEN, vol. 1, 22-15-5-SEN, et 26-1, vol. 2.

12. Gilles Lalande, «Le ministère des Affaires extérieures et la dualité culturelle», étude n° 3, *Commission royale d'enquête sur le bilinguisme et le biculturalisme*, Ottawa, 1969, 217 p.

13. Canada, ministère des Affaires extérieures, dossiers 20-CDA-9-AFR, vol. 1, 26-6-*IDEF*, vol. 1 et 26-1, vol. 3 et 4.

14. Canada, ministère des Affaires extérieures, dossier 26-6-ASF: *Francophonie: Association de solidarité francophone*; dossier 26-1, vol. 3: *Francophonie: orientation et développement*.

15. Agence canadienne de développement international, *Stratégie de coopération au développement international 1975-1980*.

16. Agence canadienne de développement international, *Le Canada et la coopération au développement*, rapport annuel 1975-1976, p. 40.

17. Jean Chapdelaine, *ibidem*, p. 354.

18. Louis Sabourin, «L'action internationale du Québec – Expression et recherche de compétence», *Perspectives internationales*, mars-avril 1977, p. 3-8.

19. Claude Morin, «La politique extérieure du Québec», *Études internationales*, vol. IX, n° 2, juin 1978, p. 286.

20. Gérard Pelletier, La dépêche d'adieu de l'ambassadeur du Canada en France de 1975 à 1981, *Le Devoir*, 12 septembre 1981.

21. Rapport de vérification linguistique: ministère des Affaires extérieures – missions à l'étranger et bureau des passeports, *Commissariat aux langues officielles*, Ottawa, décembre 1983, 45 p.

22. Gérard Bergeron, *Le Canada français après deux siècles de patience*, Éditions du Seuil, Paris, 281 p.

23. Québec, ministère des Relations internationales, *Le Québec dans le monde: énoncé de politique de relations internationales – synthèse*, Québec, juin 1985.

24. André P. Donneur, «Les relations franco-canadiennes: bilan et perspectives», *Politique étrangère*, vol. 38, n° 2, 1973, p. 197.

BIBLIOGRAPHIE

Bibliographie

CARTIGNY, Sylvie. Bibliographie sur la francophonie, *Études internationales*, vol. V, n° 2, juin 1974, p. 399-427.

DONNEUR, André P. *Politique étrangère canadienne: bibliographie, 1972-1975, 1976-1977, 1978-1981*, Montréal, UQAM.

PAINCHAUD, Paul. *Francophonie: bibliographie, 1960-1969*, Québec, Centre québécois des relations internationales.

Ouvrages

MORIN, Claude. *L'Art de l'impossible – La diplomatie québécoise depuis 1960*, Montréal, Boréal-Express, 1987, 470 p.

PATRY, André. *Le Québec dans le monde*, Montréal, Leméac, 1980, 168 p.

VINANT, Jean. *De Jacques Cartier à Péchiney*, Paris et Montréal, Chotard et Associés/Québec-Amérique, 390 p.

Articles de revues

COUVE DE MURVILLE, Maurice. «Pearson et la France», *International Journal*, vol. XXIX, n° 1, hiver 1973-1974, p. 24-32.

DE GOUMOIS, Michel. «Le Canada et la francophonie», *Études internationales*, vol. V, n° 2, juin 1974, p. 355-366.

DONNEUR, André P. «Les relations franco-canadiennes: bilan et perspectives», *Politique étrangère*, vol. 28, n° 2, 1973, p. 179-200.

FONTAINE, André. La France et le Québec, *Études internationales*, vol. VIII, n° 2, juin 1977, p. 393-402.

LALANDE, Gilles. «Hypothèses et interrogations», *Espoir*, n° 12, octobre 1975, p. 47-53.

LÉGER, Jean-Marc. «Testament d'un Francophone», *Jeune Afrique*, 3 novembre 1973.

MORIN, Claude. «La politique extérieure du Québec», *Études internationales*, vol. IX, n° 2, juin 1978, p. 281-289.

PAINCHAUD, Paul. «Les relations du Canada, de la France et du Québec», *Perspectives internationales*, janvier-février 1975, p. 6-11.

SABOURIN, Louis. «Ottawa, Québec dans l'Agence: une coopération à inventer», *Perspectives internationales*, janvier-février 1972, p. 18-24.

SABOURIN, Louis. «La coopération entre pays francophones dans une perspective globale», *Études internationales*, vol. V, n° 2, juin 1974, p. 195-207.

SABOURIN, Louis. «L'action internationale du Québec, Expression et recherche de compétence», *Perspective internationales*, mars-avril 1977, p. 3-8.

TRUDEAU, Pierre Elliott. «Double allégeance du Canada: Francophonie et Commonwealth», *Politique internationale*, n° 2, 1978-1979, p. 33-42.

«Le Canada et l'Afrique», *Marchés tropicaux et méditerranéens*, n° 2058, numéro spécial (2e édition), 19 avril 1985, p. 917-982.

Documents non publiés

MALONE, M. *La francophonie 1965-1972*, Paris, thèse de doctorat de recherche, 372 p.

Rapport Beaulieu sur *Le Canada et la francophonie:* série d'études préparées de 1974 à 1979 sous la direction de M. Paul Beaulieu, ministère des Affaires extérieures, Ottawa.

Les systèmes régionaux   The Regional Systems

11

Les relations canado-américaines

Louis Balthazar
Université Laval

Les États-Unis, seul véritable voisin du Canada, occupent une telle place dans la politique étrangère du Canada que cette politique parvient difficilement à se définir sans référence à la politique américaine. On pourrait même dire que la présence énorme des États-Unis dans les préoccupations canadiennes constitue une sorte d'écran entre le Canada et le monde.

En fait, c'est toute l'histoire du Canada qui est conditionnée par les États-Unis. Le Canada moderne est issu de la révolution américaine, dont il est une sorte de sous-produit. L'Amérique du Nord britannique est née d'une volonté de distanciation par rapport à la république américaine et c'est dans l'intégration aux États-Unis qu'elle perd sa raison d'être. Entre ces deux extrêmes, le Canada cherche péniblement sa voie comme nation autonome.

La relation canado-américaine n'est donc pas une relation parmi les autres à l'intérieur de la politique étrangère du Canada. Elle est au cœur même de la question de l'identité canadienne. Il est difficile, sinon impossible, d'envisager quelque dimension importante de la vie canadienne sans se référer à nos relations avec les États-Unis.

Il est important de noter que ces relations sont d'une fréquence et d'une intensité sans pareilles. Les relations transnationales, c'est-à-dire toutes les transactions d'un pays à l'autre qui échappent au contrôle des gouvernements, sont si nombreuses et variées que les relations officielles entre les deux pays ne constituent que la pointe de l'iceberg d'une réalité extrêmement complexe.

Il sera surtout question de cette pointe dans les lignes qui suivent, mais il ne faudrait jamais oublier la réalité sociale qui sous-tend et façonne les relations politiques.

Après avoir passé en revue l'évolution des relations canado-américaines depuis la dernière guerre mondiale, nous relèverons quelques caractéristiques fondamentales de ces relations pour ensuite traiter de leurs structures institutionnelles. Trois questions considérées comme prioritaires dans le dossier canado-américain feront l'objet de la dernière partie de ce chapitre.

HISTOIRE RÉCENTE

Si l'histoire du Canada est marquée par une volonté de maintenir en Amérique du Nord un mode de vie distinct de celui des États-Unis, il faut dire aussi que les Canadiens ont souvent lorgné avec envie du côté de leur puissant voisin. Si John MacDonald a proclamé et mis en œuvre la *National Policy*, le courant d'ouverture aux États-Unis n'en est pas disparu pour autant. Le Parti libéral s'est identifié jusqu'à 1968 comme proaméricain, faisant contre-partie aux positions impérialistes ou plus axées sur la politique britannique chez les Conservateurs. Il est symptomatique que le Parti libéral soit demeuré au pouvoir pour la majeure partie du XXᵉ siècle.

C'est le premier ministre libéral Mackenzie King qui a présidé à l'amenuisement du lien britannique et au renforcement de l'amitié canado-américaine. En 1938, au président F.D. Roosevelt qui s'engageait à défendre le Canada au besoin, King répondait que les Canadiens veilleraient à ce que jamais leur pays soit utilisé comme base d'une agression contre les États-Unis.

Ces déclarations d'intention sont sanctionnées par les accords d'Ogdensburg (1940) qui établissent la Commission mixte de la défense des deux pays (Joint Board of Defence) en vue de «considérer de façon globale la défense de la moitié nord de l'hémisphère occidental». L'année suivante (1941) à Hyde Park, les États-Unis et le Canada mettent en commun leur production de défense. Paradoxalement, c'est au moment même où, pour la dernière fois, le Canada s'engage à combattre aux côtés de la Grande-Bretagne, que s'amorce l'intégration militaire et économique du Canada aux États-Unis.

Dès après la guerre, Washington continue de traiter le Canada comme un allié privilégié. Le programme de reconstruction européenne, dit «plan Marshall», permet aux Européens d'acheter des produits canadiens avec les dollars américains dont ils sont bénéficiaires. Cela contribue à renflouer les réserves canadiennes[1].

De plus, en novembre 1947, à l'occasion de pourparlers américano-canadiens sur la libéralisation des échanges économiques, au-delà des accords internationaux sur les tarifs (GATT), les Américains proposent l'établissement d'une union douanière entre les deux pays, sans obligation quant à un tarif commun vers l'extérieur. On prévoit une période de transition de cinq ans pour permettre aux entreprises canadiennes de s'ajuster. Les négociateurs canadiens accueillent la proposition avec enthousiasme. Mais le premier ministre Mackenzie King, craignant d'être accusé de trahison à l'endroit de la Grande-Bretagne ou d'avoir vendu le pays aux États-Unis, opposera son refus[2].

Le processus d'intégration économique se poursuit tout de même. À la faveur de la prospérité d'après-guerre, le commerce entre les deux pays s'accroît et les investissements américains affluent vers le Canada. Le gouvernement de Louis Saint-Laurent, inspiré par le ministre de l'Industrie et du Commerce, C.D. Howe, se montre très accueillant et libéral quant à ces investissements.

L'intégration n'est pas moins forte sur le plan militaire. Dans l'esprit d'Ogdensburg et dans l'atmosphère de la guerre froide qui s'intensifie, les Américains sont très préoccupés par la défense de l'espace aérien du Canada. Des lignes de radar sont installées aux frais des deux gouvernements et bientôt, dans la perspective d'une menace de bombardiers soviétiques venant du nord, on projette de donner un cadre explicite à la défense du continent.

Le gouvernement Diefenbaker, pourtant fort méfiant à l'endroit des États-Unis, hérite de ce dossier et s'empresse de signer les accords de NORAD (North American Air Defence Command) qui instituent un commandement conjoint de la défense aérienne, avec des quartiers généraux à Colorado Springs, aux États-Unis. Durant toute la durée du mandat conservateur (1957-1963), la question de la participation canadienne à la défense de l'Amérique du Nord sera un objet de débat, de tensions et d'hésitation au sein du gouvernement Diefenbaker. Après avoir abandonné le projet, déjà avancé et générateur d'emplois, de la construction de l'avion supersonique *Arrow*, les Conservateurs se rabattent sur les missiles Bomarc, de fabrication américaine. Mais face à une forte opposition de la population, ils ne se résoudront jamais à rendre ces missiles efficaces en les équipant d'ogives nucléaires, comme il avait été prévu. Quand les Libéraux, arrivés au pouvoir en 1963, accepteront d'honorer l'engagement, les missiles seront démodés. Plutôt que de recevoir leurs têtes nucléaires, ils seront démantelés.

Ces hésitations, ajoutées à la personnalité de Diefenbaker qui ne se gênait pas pour tonner contre la domination américaine, ont profondément déplu à Washington. John F. Kennedy, irrité par certaines indiscrétions et la tiédeur du premier ministre au moment de la crise des fusées de Cuba, en vint à exprimer le souhait que le gouvernement conservateur soit défait. Cela n'a pas peu contribué à la chute de Diefenbaker et à son amertume quant à ce qu'il a appelé l'ingérence indue des Américains dans la politique canadienne.

On peut dire de John Diefenbaker qu'il est le dernier véritable leader tory du Canada. Avec lui s'éteint une tradition qui, depuis MacDonald, avait fait du Parti conservateur canadien le porteur des aspirations les plus probritanniques, le gardien de la fidélité à l'Empire, puis au Commonwealth. C'est selon cet esprit que Diefenbaker avait proposé, dès son arrivée au pouvoir, une diversification du commerce canadien des États-Unis vers la Grande-Bretagne. La proposition est demeurée lettre morte, et pour cause. La vocation économique du Canada était déjà trop bien dessinée et la Grande-Bretagne, elle-même loin d'accueillir cette nouvelle orientation, s'affairait à poser sa candidature à la communauté européenne, au grand déplaisir du premier ministre canadien. L'ère britannique du Canada était désormais révolue. Les Conservateurs canadiens en prirent conscience et leur révolution de palais a porté plus que sur le leadership d'un homme en particulier: le parti devait opérer un revirement idéologique. Il allait passer de la tradition «tory» à la tendance néo-conservatrice nord-américaine.

Quant au Parti libéral, de retour au pouvoir en 1963, il réinstaura bientôt le climat d'amitié canado-américaine entretenu durant les années d'après-guerre. Avec Lester B. Pearson, l'ancien ambassadeur aux États-Unis, l'ancien Secrétaire d'État aux Affaires extérieures, c'est un diplomate bien vu à Washington qui prend la direction du gouvernement canadien. Avec lui, la «diplomatie tranquille» reprend ses droits. Les deux gouvernements doivent éviter de se heurter et les Canadiens auront tout à gagner en faisant valoir leurs griefs le plus discrètement possible[3].

C'est le triomphe de ce qu'on appelle la «relation privilégiée» entre les deux pays. À trois reprises, le Canada obtient un traitement de faveur de Washington: il est exempté de mesures américaines visant à réduire le déficit de la balance des paiements avec des pays exportateurs[4].

Mais déjà on aperçoit des failles dans l'édifice de la bonne entente canado-américaine. L'engagement américain au Viêt-nam apparaît de plus en plus répréhensible à la population canadienne. Le premier ministre Pearson, en avril 1965, prononce un discours à l'Université Temple de Philadelphie, dans lequel il propose la suspension temporaire des bombardements américains au Viêt-nam du Nord. Cette intervention provoque la colère du président Johnson, qui ne se gêne pas pour semoncer le premier ministre canadien.

De plus, le ministre des Finances dans le Cabinet Pearson, Walter Gordon, est l'un des premiers instigateurs de ce qu'on appellera plus tard le «nationalisme canadien». Il dénonce la trop grande part des capitaux américains dans l'économie canadienne et commande la tenue d'une enquête sur la structure de l'investissement étranger au Canada. Le rapport Watkins, déposé en 1968, recommande la création d'agences gouvernementales visant à contrôler les investissements. De plus en plus, au sein des élites canadiennes, il existe un malaise quant à l'état de dépendance dans lequel se trouve le Canada par rapport aux États-Unis.

Tout est en place pour le grand revirement de 1968. Le Parti conservateur avait opéré sa petite révolution. En 1967, il s'était donné un nouveau chef et une nouvelle image nord-américaine. L'antiaméricanisme ne serait plus de mise au sein de ce parti. Le Parti libéral, de son côté, allait devenir peu à peu le parti du nationalisme canadien. Avec Pierre E. Trudeau comme chef du gouvernement, la politique étrangère du Canada cherche à se définir davantage en termes d'intérêts nationaux concrets plutôt qu'en fonction d'un rôle international très largement conçu: participation aux organismes multilatéraux de maintien de la paix et autres. Le livre blanc publié en 1970 place la protection de la souveraineté et le bien-être économique parmi les priorités de la nouvelle politique [5].

Cela ne satisfait pas les nationalistes qui reprochent au document de ne comporter aucune section particulière sur les États-Unis. Le premier ministre demande alors au ministre des Affaires extérieures d'examiner différentes options quant à l'orientation de la politique canadienne à l'endroit des États-Unis. Le groupe d'analyse politique du ministère se met à l'œuvre et produit un document au printemps 1972. Mitchell Sharp, alors ministre des Affaires extérieures, signe le document qui paraîtra à l'automne de la même année dans un numéro spécial de la revue du ministère, *Perspectives internationales*[6].

Entre-temps, le président Nixon était venu à la rescousse des nationalistes canadiens; à tel point qu'on a pu interpréter la politique canadienne comme une simple réaction aux nouvelles orientations des États-Unis. En août 1971, Washington impose une surtaxe de 10 % à toutes les importations, dans le but de rétablir l'équilibre de la balance des paiements. Ottawa cherche à obtenir une exemption comme dans les années passées. Peine perdue. Le président Nixon lui-même vient à Ottawa pour y énoncer sa doctrine: «[...] il est temps, dit-il, que les Canadiens et les Américains oublient la rhétorique sentimentale du passé et reconnaissent – qu'ils ont chacun une identité propre – que des différences marquées les séparent [...][7]»

Ces déclarations donnaient pour ainsi dire le feu vert aux politiques canadiennes fondées sur l'intérêt national. L'article de Sharp, «Relations canado-américaines: choix pour l'avenir», annonçait en octobre 1972 un choix arrêté sur la troisième de trois options envisagées face aux «forces d'attraction continentale», c'est-à-dire «une stratégie générale à long terme visant à développer et à raffermir notre économie et les autres aspects de notre vie nationale et, ce faisant, réduire la vulnérabilité actuelle du Canada»[8]. La première option était le *statu quo*, la seconde, une intégration plus étroite.

Cette «troisième option» devint la politique officielle du Canada pour une période d'environ cinq ans. Comme telle, cette politique ne se voulait pas antiaméricaine; elle ne se voulait pas non plus protectionniste. Mais certaines de ses applications n'eurent pas la chance d'être agréées à Washington. Par exemple, le gouvernement canadien, à la suite des recommandations du rapport Gray déposé en 1972, mit sur pied en 1974 une agence d'examen des investissements étrangers (en anglais FIRA, Foreign Investment Review Agency) qui avait pour but de contrôler les investissements et de s'assurer que leurs retombées seraient bienfaisantes pour la population canadienne. De plus, après le choc pétrolier de 1973, le gouvernement canadien entreprit de réduire les exportations de pétrole vers les États-Unis et de hausser le prix du gaz naturel. Mentionnons aussi des politiques canadiennes en matière de fiscalité, comme la non-déductibilité des dépenses publicitaires dans des revues américaines distribuées au Canada comme *Time* et sur les ondes des stations de télévision américaines situées en bordure de la frontière canadienne. Tout cela provoquait une hostilité de plus en plus grande aux États-Unis. L'ambassadeur américain, William Porter, au moment où il quittait son poste à la fin de 1975, parlait d'une détérioration grave des relations.

La politique de «troisième option» devait cependant s'éteindre en douce à compter de 1976. En même temps, le climat des relations canado-américaines s'était grandement amélioré. Un certain nombre de facteurs ont contribué à ce changement.

D'abord, la fureur des réactions américaines a bientôt incité Ottawa à chercher des accommodements. À la faveur d'une bonne relation personnelle entre le premier ministre Trudeau et les présidents Ford et Carter, des échanges accrus entre fonctionnaires ont amené les deux parties à se comprendre davantage. Les Américains ont mieux accepté la politique énergétique canadienne et les Canadiens se sont mis à interpréter la troisième option dans un sens exclusivement positif. Cette politique, conçue pour réduire la vulnérabilité du Canada à l'égard de son voisin du Sud, était désormais interprétée comme ne s'adressant pas aux États-Unis mais plutôt à l'Europe et au Japon. Il s'agissait d'abord d'accentuer les relations commerciales avec les partenaires d'outre-mer et non plus d'atténuer les échanges avec les Américains.

Cet effort de diversion n'a cependant pas été suivi des résultats escomptés. En dépit de tournées répétées du premier ministre dans les capitales européennes et de la signature d'un «accord contractuel» avec les communautés européennes, rien de significatif n'est apparu quant à la progression des échanges commerciaux avec les pays d'Europe. Le Japon continuait de s'intéresser presque exclusivement aux matières premières du Canada.

Au pays même, l'arrivée au pouvoir du Parti québécois dans la province de Québec signalait une crise constitutionnelle. Le nouveau gouvernement québécois, sans avoir reçu de mandat quant à son projet souverainiste, promettait cependant la tenue d'un référendum sur la souveraineté du Québec et manifestait beaucoup de détermination dans l'atteinte de l'objectif. C'était assez pour créer un état de panique à travers le Canada et de même aux États-Unis, dans les milieux où l'on s'intéressait aux affaires canadiennes. Comme les Américains n'entretenaient pas plus de sympathie pour le projet de sécession que les Canadiens anglophones eux-mêmes, la menace québécoise eut l'effet de rapprocher les représentants des deux gouvernements et les deux populations. À Washington, on n'osait plus critiquer Ottawa de crainte de gêner les efforts du gouvernement central pour consolider l'unité du pays. À Ottawa, par contre, toutes les énergies étaient concentrées sur l'objectif d'unification, qui s'adressait non seulement au Québec mais aussi à des provinces jalouses de leur autonomie, comme l'Alberta. Le gouvernement canadien ne se sentait pas en très bonne posture pour proclamer sa souveraineté à l'endroit des États-Unis.

La «troisième option» semblait bien morte et enterrée. Au surplus, en mai 1979, le Parti conservateur était porté au pouvoir à Ottawa avec une plate-forme qui annonçait une politique plus favorable à l'entreprise privée, plus ouverte aux États-Unis. Mais les Conservateurs, minoritaires, furent bientôt défaits à la Chambre des communes et d'autres élections à l'hiver 1980 ramenaient les Libéraux au gouvernement. Trudeau réussit à faire battre l'idée de souveraineté québécoise au référendum de mai 1980 et, fort de sa victoire, amorça immédiatement le processus de rapatriement de la Constitution qui allait intensifier le contrôle du gouvernement central sur le pays. Les négociations avec les provinces furent ardues et pénibles, mais déjà le premier ministre canadien se sentait prêt à faire face à nouveau aux États-Unis.

Dès sa réélection, il s'engageait à donner plus de force à l'Agence d'examen des investissements. Le concepteur de cette agence, Herb Gray, était nommé ministre de l'Industrie et du Commerce. De plus, à l'automne 1980, à l'occasion de la présentation du budget, on annonçait un nouveau programme énergétique national comprenant des mesures assez draconiennes en vue de canadianiser l'entreprise de production d'énergie et d'assurer au gouvernement central un meilleur contrôle sur ces importantes activités. En corollaire de ce programme, des accords allaient être conclus, l'année suivante, entre Ottawa et la province récalcitrante d'Alberta concernant les prix de l'énergie exportée et la distribution des profits. Le programme énergétique touchait directement un certain nombre d'entreprises américaines en leur prescrivant des impôts plus élevés qu'à leurs concurrents canadiens: plus le contrôle canadien d'une firme était élevé, plus l'impôt était réduit. Il frappait aussi toutes les entreprises engagées dans l'exploration pétrolière sur les terres de la Couronne d'une clause dite «*black-in*», qui donnait automatiquement au gouvernement fédéral une part de 25 % sur des revenus provenant de toute nouvelle découverte d'énergie.

Il n'en fallait pas plus pour ameuter les milieux financiers américains. Il faut ajouter à cela l'élection d'un des gouvernements les plus nationalistes du siècle à Washington et une agressivité nouvelle de la part des investisseurs canadiens aux États-Unis. Les gens d'affaires américains qui criaient à la discrimination, qui accusaient le gouvernement canadien de dirigisme éhonté, de socialisme et de nationalisme étroit, trouvaient désormais une oreille favorable au sein d'un gouvernement voué à défendre les intérêts de l'entreprise privée et à redonner aux États-Unis leur image de puissance et de suprématie universelle.

Le président Reagan effectua une visite de courtoisie à Ottawa en mars 1981. Son message n'était pas particulièrement hostile, mais il ne contribuait en rien à améliorer les relations. Bien au contraire, il annonçait, juste avant sa visite à Ottawa, son intention de révoquer un traité sur les pêches dans l'Atlantique conclu en 1979 et qui traînait toujours au Sénat en vue de sa ratification. Il laissait son Secrétaire d'État et son représentant au Commerce extérieur adresser des notes menaçantes, sinon injurieuses, au gouvernement canadien.

Encore une fois, devant la tempête, Ottawa cherchait des accommodements. La clause *black-in* fut modifiée pour introduire des compensations. On renonça à renforcer les mécanismes de l'Agence d'examen des investissements. Les Américains, de leur côté, avaient parlé beaucoup de ripostes éventuelles, mais rien ne s'est produit.

À travers ces nouvelles manifestations de nationalisme canadien, on pouvait entrevoir une sorte de résurrection de la «troisième option» sous la forme de ce qu'on a appelé le «bilatéralisme»[9]. Cette fois-ci, la diversification du commerce extérieur devait s'opérer en direction de nouveaux partenaires parmi les pays du tiers monde en forte croissance: Brésil, Mexique, Vénézuela, Algérie, Arabie saoudite, Corée du Sud et autres. En dépit d'un net progrès du commerce canadien avec ces pays, le «bilatéralisme» ne connut guère plus de succès que les tentatives précédentes, du moins quant à la diversification. En 1983, 72,9 % des exportations canadiennes allaient vers les États-Unis et 71,6 % des importations en provenaient, une augmentation du pourcentage par rapport aux années précédentes.

Malgré la crise de 1981, les États-Unis demeuraient toujours le partenaire privilégié du Canada à la fin du dernier mandat de Pierre Elliot Trudeau. Mais l'accession du gouvernement conservateur de Brian Mulroney a signalé une nette reprise de l'amitié canado-américaine. La plupart des politiques dites nationalistes furent renversées. Et la visite du président Reagan à Québec en mars 1985 se déroula dans l'euphorie. Plusieurs dossiers demeuraient sans résolution mais l'ouverture du Canada aux États-Unis était plus grande que jamais. La crise était complètement résorbée.

Ainsi, les relations canado-américaines se sont poursuivies, depuis la Deuxième Guerre mondiale, selon des cycles plus ou moins longs de détente et de tension. Jusqu'en 1957, tout allait pour le mieux. Sous Diefenbaker, les relations se sont envenimées. De 1963 à 1968, à part quelques orages, on revenait au beau fixe. À mesure que les positions de Trudeau et de Nixon se confirmaient au cours des années 70, c'était à nouveau l'affrontement, suivi d'une trêve entre 1976 et 1980. La crise éclata en 1981 pour faire suite à une lente résorption jusqu'à la grande détente de l'automne 1984. Les facteurs qui ont fait évoluer ce jeu de pendule apparaîtront mieux à la lumière des caractéristiques très particulières des relations entre le Canada et les États-Unis.

LES PARAMÈTRES DE LA RELATION

Les Américains se sont souvent laissé aller à traiter le Canada comme une partie de leur territoire. En 1958, un rapport du Comité des affaires étrangères de la Chambre des représentants déclarait ce qui suit: «Canadian and United States' interdependence demands a new category of relationship. Canada does not stand in a position towards us of a ˮforeignˮ country. En 1965, le président Johnson disait à son tour: «Canada is such a close neighbor that we always have plenty of problems there. They are kind of like problems in the hometown[10].» De telles attitudes ont eu pour effet d'offenser les élites canadiennes préoccupées de défendre et de préserver la souveraineté du Canada. De temps à autre, des auteurs américains ont protesté contre cette complaisance et ont insisté pour que leur gouvernement situe sa politique à l'intention du Canada dans un contexte international[11].

Le modèle «intérieur»

Pourtant, même s'il est à conseiller aux diplomates américains d'être toujours respectueux de la souveraineté canadienne, plusieurs raisons peuvent inciter l'analyste à adopter un modèle de relations «intérieures» ou «domestiques» pour éclairer les relations canado-américaines. En effet, le modèle international classique apparaît souvent inadéquat pour rendre compte de ces relations qui, au dire de tous, sont tout à fait uniques.

De façon générale et sommaire, on pourrait dégager trois éléments qui caractérisent les relations internationales et les différencient des relations à l'intérieur d'un même État. D'abord, la possibilité – parfois menaçante et prochaine, parfois très latente et presque oubliée – de l'utilisation de la force comme règlement des conflits. C'est ce que l'on appelle l'état de guerre international et qui correspond à la souveraineté des forces militaires des divers États. Même les États les plus pacifiques entretiennent des armées. En deuxième lieu, l'hétérogénéité des cultures, des mentalités, des langages. D'un État à l'autre, on ne s'exprime pas de la même façon, on perçoit le monde différemment, on ne privilégie pas les mêmes valeurs. Cette hétérogénéité culturelle rend particulièrement délicates les négociations internationales. C'est l'art de la diplomatie que de surmonter ces difficultés. Enfin, toutes les relations entre États souverains sont caractérisées par l'absence d'une autorité suprême capable de réglementer les rapports et de faire appliquer ces réglementations. En d'autres termes, il n'y a pas de véritable pouvoir international. Il arrive que des États acceptent de se soumettre à des organismes internationaux comme la Cour internationale de justice, mais celle-ci n'a ni l'autorité ni les moyens de convoquer les États et de leur imposer des sanctions contre leur gré.

Si l'on tente d'appliquer ces trois normes aux relations canado-américaines, il semble bien que seule la troisième corresponde à la réalité, bien qu'il arrive que le Canada et les États-Unis, plus souvent que d'autres couples d'États, acceptent de soumettre leurs litiges à un organisme international. La deuxième norme s'applique plutôt mal en raison de la quasi-similarité des cultures américaine et canadienne-anglaise. Des auteurs se sont employés à démontrer les différences culturelles et sociétales entre le Canada et les États-Unis[12]. Mais toutes ces distinctions s'évanouissent devant l'incapacité de la plupart des observateurs de différencier concrètement un Canadien de langue anglaise d'un Américain. Un Canadien de Calgary est-il plus différent d'un Américain de Minneapolis que ne l'est un Américain de Louisiane? Reste la spécificité culturelle des Canadiens français, surtout des Québécois. Mais le moins qu'on puisse dire est que ces derniers n'ont pas donné le ton à la politique canadienne à l'endroit des États-Unis, et les Québécois s'affirment de plus en plus comme des Nord-Américains. Enfin, il n'est pas facile d'appliquer la notion d'«état de guerre» à la frontière non défendue, quand on prend conscience du fait que, depuis 1940, Washington considère, pour des fins de défense, le territoire canadien comme si c'était le sien propre[13].

En conséquence, à bien des égards, les relations canado-américaines doivent être dissociées des relations bilatérales de type classique et considérées comme des relations de politique intérieure. Ce qui ne signifie pas que ces relations ne sont pas conflictuelles. Bien au contraire, les conflits qui éclatent à l'intérieur d'une même entité sociale sont souvent plus intenses que des conflits internationaux avec cette différence notable, toutefois, qu'ils se situent, à moins d'une guerre civile, dans une zone où les consensus ne sont pas disparus.

De plus en plus, l'Amérique du Nord est une grande unité sociologique. Le Canada peut toujours conserver sa souveraineté politique et la défendre; les Américains eux-mêmes n'auront pas intérêt à battre en brèche cette souveraineté[14]. L'intégration économique, culturelle et militaire du Canada aux États-Unis ne s'en poursuivra pas moins de façon quasi irrémédiable. Ce qu'on appelle le continentalisme peut être considéré, selon les termes de John W. Holmes, comme une «force de la nature» que les institutions canado-américaines cherchent à contrôler, à régulariser pour que le Canada conserve une place qui lui est propre[15].

Examinons un peu les données évidentes. Sur le plan économique, le Canada est désormais inextricablement lié aux États-Unis. Les efforts pour diminuer la proportion des échanges commerciaux avec le voisin du Sud ont notablement failli, comme on l'a vu plus haut. En 1983, les Américains investissaient 57 milliards de dollars canadiens au Canada, soit la très grande majorité des investissements étrangers au Canada, et environ 20 % des investissements américains hors des États-Unis. Les Canadiens, de leur côté, injectaient 25 milliards de dollars aux États-Unis[16], une somme énorme pour un pays de la taille du Canada. Les États-Unis et le Canada sont l'un pour l'autre, et de loin, le partenaire économique le plus important. Il n'existe pas deux pays dont les économies sont plus liées.

C'est peut-être sur le plan culturel que l'intégration est la plus avancée. Le gouvernement canadien, par l'intermédiaire du Conseil de la radiodiffusion et de la télédiffusion canadiennes (CRTC), peut bien faire la promotion du produit culturel indigène en imposant un contenu canadien aux stations de télévision et de radio. La grande majorité de la population préfère encore les émissions américaines aux canadiennes. On a pu passer des lois pour restreindre indirectement les activités de magazines américains au Canada. Un magazine comme *Time*, qui a dû abandonner son édition soi-disant canadienne, conserve toujours un tirage très fort au Canada. L'édition qui circule depuis Toronto est la copie conforme de celle qui est produite aux États-Unis, mais la publicité qui y est incluse est presque entièrement canadienne. Les Canadiens lisent en grande majorité des livres publiés aux États-Unis. Ils voient surtout des films américains. Ils assistent à des compétitions sportives organisées dans un cadre américain. Ils passent souvent leurs vacances aux États-Unis où ils voyagent fréquemment. Plus de 70 millions de personnes traversent chaque année la frontière américaine. Enfin, très souvent, l'ascension dans la carrière, pour un Canadien de langue anglaise, se poursuit aux États-Unis.

Quant à l'intégration militaire, elle était déjà annoncée dans les accords de 1940 et de 1941, formalisée dans la participation du Canada à l'OTAN dès sa création en 1949, dans les accords de NORAD de 1958, dans les accords de partage de la production de défense de 1959. En pratique, que les Canadiens le veuillent ou non, et en fait ils le veulent bien le plus souvent, la défense du continent nord-américain est une et indivisible.

Ce phénomène d'intégration est encore accentué par le fait que la population canadienne, nonobstant l'immense territoire du pays, est distribuée en très grande majorité sur une bande qui s'étend le long de la frontière américaine. La plupart des Canadiens vivent à moins de 100 kilomètres des États-Unis. Il n'est donc pas étonnant qu'ils se sentent souvent plus près de la population américaine avoisinante que de celle de régions plus éloignées du Canada. Vancouver vit à l'heure de Seattle beaucoup plus qu'à celle de Toronto. Les Montréalais partagent probablement plus de valeurs avec New York qu'avec Saskatoon.

D'ailleurs, et c'est là une dimension extrêmement importante des relations canado-américaines, dans la plupart des dossiers qui constituent le contentieux entre les deux pays, les appuis aux gouvernements canadien et américain ont tendance à se distribuer des deux côtés de la frontière. Il existe souvent un grand nombre de Canadiens pour critiquer leur gouvernement et appuyer le point de vue américain et beaucoup d'Américains pour soutenir une politique canadienne. Par exemple, ce sont des écologistes américains qui ont parfois éveillé l'attention des Canadiens à la détérioration de l'environnement. Des gens d'affaires canadiens ont, à l'occasion, été aussi critiques que leurs homologues américains des interventions d'Ottawa dans l'économie. Il est important de ne pas confondre Ottawa et le Canada, ni Washington et les États-Unis. En fait, on pourrait probablement démontrer que les divergences d'opinion sont souvent plus fortes entre le Secrétariat d'État et des groupes de pression des États du Nord qu'entre les diplomates américains et canadiens.

Perspectives différentes

En dépit de tout ce qui précède, le Canada demeure un pays souverain. Il existe des intérêts canadiens différents des intérêts américains et la politique canadienne est conçue fort différemment de la politique américaine. On peut regrouper toutes ces différences essentiellement sous deux chefs: le Canada a été organisé et développé selon un modèle britannique; même si la Grande-Bretagne n'est plus présente à la politique canadienne, les traditions britanniques le sont toujours. Le Canada est à la fois plus petit, moins développé et moins unifié que les États-Unis. Il n'existe pas encore au Canada un véritable «mythe national» qui se comparerait avec celui des États-Unis.

Ces deux facteurs ont contribué à façonner le caractère qui apparaît comme le plus distinctif du Canada quand on le compare à son voisin: une tendance beaucoup plus accusée à l'intervention gouvernementale. Cette tendance est à l'origine de la plupart des malentendus entre Canadiens et Américains, au cours des dernières années. La population canadienne accepte volontiers qu'une compagnie aérienne, un réseau de télévision et de radio ou une compagnie pétrolière soient entre les mains du gouvernement. Vus avec des yeux américains, ces phénomènes apparaissent comme une forme de socialisme. Les Américains n'acceptent pas que leur gouvernement intervienne dans l'économie sauf pour éliminer des entraves à la libre entreprise, comme on l'a fait avec les lois antitrusts par exemple. Mais pour les Canadiens, habitués à vivre dans des institutions d'origine britannique, il apparaît tout naturel que le gouvernement se soit arrogé une fonction de redistribution de la richesse, comme c'est le cas en Europe.

Il s'est trouvé beaucoup de Canadiens, cependant, pour manifester une certaine tiédeur à l'endroit du modèle européen. La tradition britannique, à elle seule, ne suffit pas à expliquer pourquoi les Canadiens n'ont pas copié plus volontiers la façon de faire américaine. Il faut invoquer aussi la faiblesse numérique de la population et sa grande dispersion. Dès le début de la Confédération canadienne, il apparaissait évident que le gouvernement allait jouer un rôle important dans la construction d'un chemin de fer pancanadien. Seul le gouvernement pouvait plus tard bâtir un réseau radiophonique à travers le pays et, plus récemment, canadianiser l'entreprise énergétique.

On pourrait même aller jusqu'à dire que les Américains eux-mêmes ont favorisé une certaine intervention gouvernementale dans l'économie quand, après 1787, il s'agissait de bâtir un pays, d'unifier des États divers et de consolider une force économique. Si leur pays était encore aujourd'hui aussi peu peuplé et aussi divers que le Canada, ne seraient-ils pas plus enclins à accepter l'intervention gouvernementale?

Un autre trait qui oppose souvent le Canada aux États-Unis est une plus grande préoccupation canadienne pour l'équilibre mondial, la répartition des richesses, les problèmes du tiers monde, la paix. Les Canadiens sont moins portés que les Américains à favoriser l'usage de la force. Ils sont moins hostiles aux régimes d'inspiration marxiste ou socialiste que ne le sont généralement les Américains.

Il n'est pas sûr que ces généralisations s'appliquent très bien aux populations en général. Il existe sûrement beaucoup de Canadiens plus anticommunistes que bien des Américains. Mais il est certain que les prises de position des gouvernements canadiens sont tantôt plus modérées, tantôt plus idéalistes que celles des gouvernements américains. Cela relève-t-il d'un trait fondamental de la vie politique canadienne? Ou n'est-ce pas là encore un effet direct de la taille de l'importance du pays? Les États-Unis sont une superpuissance et leurs comportements sont ceux d'une superpuissance avec toute l'arrogance qu'entraînent cette situation et le rôle qui l'accompagne. Le Canada, une puissance moyenne, peut se permettre de regarder les choses avec plus de sérénité. Si les rôles étaient inversés, les comportements ne seraient-ils pas différents? En tous cas, on peut noter que des Américains émigrés au Canada s'adaptent très vite aux positions canadiennes. Il n'apparaît pas non plus que les Canadiens vivant aux États-Unis soient plus pacifistes que leurs concitoyens.

Enfin, on peut citer la présence d'une importante population francophone au Canada pour distinguer ce pays du *melting-pot* américain. Il est vrai que le caractère biculturel de la politique étrangère du Canada peut la différencier de celle des États-Unis. Mais, outre que ce caractère ne se soit manifesté que récemment, il n'est pas encore très frappant dans la relation canado-américaine. Les quelques francophones qui ont été actifs dans les affaires américaines ces dernières années, se comptent sur les doigts de la main. Il faudrait voir aussi s'ils se sont comportés suivant un style différent de celui de leurs collègues anglophones.

Une relation asymétrique

Quoi qu'il en soit, il est indéniable que les relations canado-américaines sont marquées par l'*asymétrie*. Toute analyse sérieuse de ces relations se doit de tenir compte de cette importante caractéristique. Charles F. Doran a fort bien rendu compte de cette asymétrie en notant que les Américains on tendance à voir le Canada comme une partie de leurs préoccupations mondiales tandis que, pour les Canadiens, la politique étrangère, c'est d'abord les relations avec les États-Unis[17]. Les relations canado-américaines vues de Washington sont des questions mineures, d'ordre régional, des préoccupations bien particulières de quelques groupes dispersés: les propriétaires de stations de télévision de Buffalo, les pêcheurs de la Nouvelle-Angleterre, quelques financiers de New York ou de Chicago. Vues d'Ottawa, les relations canado-américaines sont des questions d'envergure nationale où il y va de la souveraineté du Canada, de sa santé économique, de la préservation de grands espaces naturels. Il est bien inévitable que des perspectives aussi différentes provoquent parfois des malentendus et des tensions. Doran note encore que Washington a tendance à demeurer enfermé dans une perspective politico-stratégique, étant donné ses responsabilités mondiales. Ottawa, pour sa part, se confine souvent à la dimension commerciale de la relation avec les États-Unis, en raison de la proportion si importante de ses échanges commerciaux avec les États-Unis et du commerce extérieur par rapport à son produit national brut. Les deux partenaires devraient pourtant se concentrer davantage, poursuit Doran, sur la dimension psycho-culturelle de la relation et prendre conscience des perceptions différentes de l'interlocuteur.

Cette asymétrie, ces différences de perspective et d'orientation rendent bien compte, croyons-nous, des flambées fréquentes du nationalisme canadien. Vivre à côté d'une grande puissance, c'est déjà suffisant pour créer un mouvement nationaliste. Mais en raison de l'importance du modèle de politique intérieure souligné plus haut, en raison de l'existence d'un «nous» nord-américain, ce nationalisme semble voué à ne jamais dépasser un certain seuil au-delà duquel il abolirait la conscience continentaliste toujours vivante. Ce sentiment de solidarité nord-américaine s'est manifesté dans des structures, des institutions dont la fonction est de canaliser, de discipliner cette «force de la nature» continentale, pour reprendre l'expression de John W. Holmes.

STRUCTURES INSTITUTIONNELLES

Il n'existe pas deux États au monde capables de communiquer entre eux aussi rapidement, aussi efficacement, et d'en arriver à d'heureux compromis, que les États-Unis et le Canada. Mais on commet une erreur de perspective quand on cite les institutions canado-américaines comme un modèle de relations bilatérales. C'est bien plutôt en raison de la mentalité continentale et d'un processus d'intégration toujours à l'œuvre, au moins de façon latente, que ces institutions fonctionnent bien.

Les contacts sont tellement nombreux entre représentants officiels ou semi-officiels des deux gouvernements qu'il serait difficile et fastidieux de retracer tous les canaux dans lesquels ils se poursuivent. Étant donné la proximité des deux pays et la facilité des transactions entre Canadiens et Américains, on communique énormément d'un pays à l'autre à de multiples niveaux.

C'est probablement en raison de ces multiples communications de plusieurs branches des deux gouvernements que, pendant longtemps, la diplomatie officielle entre les deux pays était réduite à sa plus simple expression. Ce n'est qu'en 1973, à la suite du lancement de la politique de la «troisième option», que la direction des États-Unis, au ministère des Affaires extérieures, s'est vue confier des tâches importantes: établir une vision d'ensemble des relations canado-américaines, coordonner tout ce qui s'y rattache et offrir des suggestions sur toute question impliquant les États-Unis. Cette direction fut bientôt promue au rang de bureau, puis réorganisée en 1983 en dépendance directe d'un sous-ministre adjoint à la direction des États-Unis. «Le sous-ministre adjoint est chargé de tous les domaines des relations économiques et d'investissement, des questions d'ordre social et juridique, ainsi que de la défense[18].» En contrepartie, à Washington, ce n'est que depuis récemment qu'il existe au département d'État un Bureau des affaires européennes et canadiennes (autrefois Bureau des affaires européennes) et un Sous-secrétaire d'État adjoint aux Affaires canadiennes.

La réorganisation récente du ministère des Affaires extérieures contribue à en faire le canal privilégié de la politique à l'endroit des États-Unis. Il n'est pas sûr que tout passe par ce canal mais l'inclusion du commerce extérieur dans la structure du triumvirat (affaires extérieures, générales, politique et commerce) permet au ministre principal, le Secrétaire d'État aux Affaires extérieures, de mieux contrôler l'ensemble de la relation. Ce contrôle est souvent soumis à celui du bureau du premier ministre. Des leaders comme Trudeau et Mulroney sont soucieux de conférer leur marque propre aux relations avec les États-Unis.

Afin d'éviter le plus possible les malentendus, de s'informer mutuellement des politiques et de passer en revue l'ensemble des problèmes, les deux secrétaires d'État responsables de la politique étrangère ont convenu, en octobre 1982, de se rencontrer quatre fois par année.

En plus de ces relations officielles par l'intermédiaire des ministères attitrés et des fréquentes transactions entre ministères spécialisés (Commerce, Finances, Agriculture, Énergie, etc.) sous le contrôle plus ou moins efficace du «*State Department*» et des Affaires extérieures, un nombre impressionnant d'organismes conjoints ont été créés pour traiter de différentes questions.

La plus illustre de ces organismes est sans doute la Commission mixte internationale sur les eaux frontalières. Depuis sa création en 1909 à l'issue du Traité sur les eaux frontalières, elle a toujours fonctionné, hors du circuit diplomatique, selon un véritable esprit continental. Il semble bien que les représentants des deux États en aient presque oublié souvent qu'ils représentaient un État et aient conçu leur rôle avant tout au niveau du développement de l'Amérique du Nord. C'est à cette commission qu'on doit la canalisation du Saint-Laurent et des études sur la pollution des cours d'eaux frontaliers et sur le niveau de l'eau dans les Grands Lacs. Ses fonctions sont d'ordre judiciaire et d'investigation; elle est considérée comme un véritable tribunal international, un organisme quasi indépendant des pressions politiques. On a souvent souhaité, de part et d'autre de la frontière, que la juridiction de cette commission soit étendue à d'autres matières ou que d'autres commissions de ce genre soient créées. Mais on craint également que des contentieux d'ordre politique, s'ils étaient soumis à la Commission mixte, ne viennent brouiller les eaux limpides de cet organisme qui a bien fonctionné dans la mesure où les dossiers qu'il traitait pouvaient être dépolitisés.

La Commission internationale sur les frontières, avec une juridiction moins étendue, n'a pas fonctionné moins efficacement. Créée en 1925, elle a le mandat d'assurer des inspections régulières des frontières et de voir à ce que les lignes de démarcation demeurent toujours claires et bien signalées.

Il existe aussi trois commissions bilatérales traitant des pêcheries, une éternelle source de conflits entre les deux États, sans compter cinq commissions multilatérales auxquelles participent le Canada et les États-Unis.

L'intégration est fort avancée dans le domaine de la défense, comme nous l'avons souligné plus haut. Dès 1940, à la suite des accords d'Ogdensburg, fut créée la Commission mixte permanente de la défense (Permanent Joint Board on Defence). Cet organisme comprend une section pour chaque État, avec représentants des forces armées et des Affaires extérieures. Le rôle de cette commission consiste essentiellement à discuter des nécessités de la défense en relation avec les grandes orientations politiques des deux États. Il s'agit d'un organisme assez simple ayant un pouvoir de recommandation dans les seuls cas où l'unanimité a été atteinte.

En 1958, dans la foulée de NORAD, on a créé un Comité ministériel sur la défense commune dont les membres étaient les Secrétaires d'État à la Défense et au Trésor pour les États-Unis; et les ministres canadiens des Affaires extérieures, de la Défense et des Finances. Ce comité n'a été que très rarement convoqué mais cette structure pourrait être utile en cas de crise.

Un autre comité ministériel fut mis sur pied en 1953 sur les affaires économiques et commerciales. Ce comité, au rôle mal défini, n'a été réuni, comme le précédent, qu'en de rares occasions. Il a tout de même joué un rôle très important en établissant les bases du pacte canado-américain sur l'automobile et en commanditant une étude sur l'ensemble des relations entre les deux États sous la présidence conjointe de deux anciens ambassadeurs américain et canadien. Le rapport Merchant-Heeney parut en 1965 et fut favorablement accueilli dans les milieux politiques et économiques des deux pays[19].

Enfin, le Groupe parlementaire canado-américain[20] est un organisme dont on dit ironiquement que son rôle est plutôt social que politique. Établi en 1959, il comprend habituellement 24 députés du Parlement canadien et 24 membres du Congrès américain choisis en fonction de leur intérêt dans les affaires canado-américaines. Même si l'influence réelle de ce groupe n'est pas facile à déterminer, il demeure que ses rencontres annuelles sont toujours susceptibles de faire progresser certaines idées et d'influer éventuellement sur les législations.

Il est à noter que tous ces organismes plus ou moins efficaces ont été créés avant 1970. Ils sont probablement typiques de l'époque de la «diplomatie tranquille» et des relations privilégiées. Ils reflètent une certaine dépolitisation des problèmes qui prévalaient à cette époque (exception faite de l'intervalle Diefenbaker). Ils n'ont pas tous perdu de leur opportunité durant les quinze dernières années de relations plus troublées, car d'innombrables questions continuaient d'être traitées sereinement, loin des tribunes politiques.

Mais la tendance des dernières années n'a pas été de créer de nouvelles structures formelles pour faire face aux nouveaux problèmes. On s'en est remis davantage à des comités particuliers portant sur une question précise ou même à des rencontres improvisées, sinon à des conversations téléphoniques. Certains experts ont réclamé que des structures plus fermes soient mises sur pied pour régulariser les relations. Il n'est pas sûr toutefois que la solution aux problèmes réside dans les structures. Ces dernières demeureront caduques si la volonté politique est absente et peut-être ne seront-elles plus nécessaires si, de part et d'autre, on a établi des objectifs de coopération à long terme.

On a encore proposé récemment la création d'un cadre de bonne entente visant à réduire les effets délétères des actions unilatérales de part et d'autre. Il ne s'agit pas cette fois d'une structure formelle, mais de l'acceptation mutuelle d'un ensemble de normes devant guider les politiques réciproques. On donne en exemple une meilleure attention aux motivations et priorités de l'autre gouvernement, un effort pour atteindre ses objectifs tout en minimisant les coûts pour le partenaire, un meilleur processus de consultations et un engagement à traiter chaque question à son mérite sans utiliser une question pour riposter à une politique dans un autre domaine (*linkage*)[21].

Il faut enfin mentionner des structures affectant les deux États à des niveaux sous-étatiques ou superétatiques. De plus en plus, des relations sont engagées entre États américains et provinces canadiennes. Des accords sont conclus, des structures de coopération sont créées, comme par exemple la Conférence des États de la Nouvelle-Angleterre et des provinces de l'Est du Canada. En principe, ces organisations sont supervisées par les gouvernements fédéraux des deux pays. Mais la dynamique engagée peut amener les gouvernements centraux à perdre des initiatives et à subir des influences des autres niveaux de gouvernement.

Par contre, le climat de solidarité qui prévaut entre les États-Unis et le Canada entraîne parfois les deux États à recourir à l'autorité internationale pour pallier l'absence d'autorité nord-américaine. Par exemple, on a eu recours récemment à la Cour internationale de justice pour régler le problème des pêcheries le long des côtes atlantiques. On a aussi invoqué le recours du GATT et de l'OCDE (Organisation de la coopération et de développement économique). Il n'est pas impossible que ces organisations internationales, à défaut d'institutions proprement canado-américaines, jouent un rôle plus important dans l'avenir des relations entre les États-Unis et le Canada.

Ce sont là les plus importantes des structures formelles qui régissent les relations canado-américaines. Elles ne doivent pas faire oublier que ces relations sont également influencées par la multitude des relations transnationales et non formelles qui échappent le plus souvent au contrôle des gouvernements.

Une telle situation et une frontière aussi poreuse ne peuvent que donner lieu à d'innombrables problèmes et parfois à de sérieux conflits. Voyons de plus près quelques-unes des questions parmi les plus susceptibles de demeurer à l'ordre du jour durant les prochaines années.

TROIS QUESTIONS PRIORITAIRES

Parmi toutes les questions qui ont fait l'objet des préoccupations canadiennes dans les relations avec les États-Unis, on peut en retenir trois qui continueront longtemps d'occuper une place centrale à cause de leur importance et de l'ampleur de leurs conséquences. Ce sont les échanges commerciaux, la défense de l'espace aérien et la protection de l'environnement.

Échanges commerciaux[22]

Les échanges commerciaux entre le Canada et les États-Unis sont les plus intenses qui existent entre deux pays. Ils ont dépassé les 150 milliards de dollars canadiens en 1985. On sait que plus de 70 % des exportations canadiennes vont aux États-Unis et que cette proportion a plutôt tendance à augmenter qu'à diminuer. En 1983, par exemple, le taux de croissance des exportations canadiennes était de 15 % vers les États-Unis et de 7,6 % vers les autres pays. De plus, ce sont les exportations dirigées vers les États-Unis qui sont les plus susceptibles de générer des emplois et de faire progresser l'économie canadienne. Autrement dit, ce sont les entreprises les plus dynamiques qui exportent aux États-Unis. En 1983, des 33,4 milliards de dollars de produits finis non comestibles exportés par le Canada, 29,4 milliards de dollars l'étaient vers les États-Unis, représentant 89 %[23]. C'est donc un truisme de dire que le marché américain est d'une importance vitale pour l'économie canadienne, surtout si l'on considère que le Canada est essentiellement un pays exportateur; c'est-à-dire que les Canadiens ont besoin, plus que d'autres, de vendre à l'étranger, pour développer leur industrie.

Ce qui apparaît moins évident, c'est l'importance du marché canadien pour les États-Unis. Les chiffres sont pourtant clairs. En 1983, les Américains exportaient au Canada pour 43,8 milliards de dollars, c'est-à-dire 22 % de toutes leurs exportations, soit deux fois plus qu'au Japon, leur deuxième partenaire commercial et plus qu'aux dix pays de la Communauté européenne réunis. Les importations venant du Canada se chiffraient à 21 %[24]. Il est bien vrai que ces proportions ne rendent pas les États-Unis aussi dépendants du Canada que les Canadiens ne le sont des Américains. Mais le Canada n'en représente pas moins pour son voisin le plus important marché extérieur.

Tous s'accordent donc, parmi les observateurs canadiens, pour réagir à une situation qui rend l'entreprise prisonnière des volontés américaines, soit parce que cette entreprise est contrôlée par des citoyens américains, soit parce qu'elle est constamment menacée par des mesures protectionnistes aux États-Unis. Quand, par exemple, à la faveur d'une conjoncture favorable, comme un dollar canadien fortement déprécié, l'entreprise canadienne a opéré une percée assez importante sur le marché américain pour concurrencer l'entreprise américaine, des voix se sont élevées aux États-Unis pour proposer des mesures dilatoires à l'endroit des produits canadiens. Des Américains ont accusé le gouvernement canadien d'intervenir trop fréquemment dans le processus du marché en accordant des subventions aux entreprises exportatrices. De leur côté, les législateurs américains ont eu recours à ce qu'on appelle des *mirror legislations,* c'est-à-dire des lois destinées à contrer les avantages jugés indus des exportateurs canadiens. On a imposé des «droits compensatoires» aux marchandises canadiennes. On a introduit des législations de type «*Buy America*», imposant un certain taux de fabrication américaine pour un produit donné.

Devant ces pratiques, les nationalistes canadiens ont proposé de réduire la vulnérabilité de l'entreprise canadienne en la rendant plus autosuffisante et en poursuivant une politique industrielle vigoureuse sous l'égide du gouvernement fédéral. Les tenants du libre-échange, de leur côté, ont proposé une libéralisation qui devait interdire toute mesure protectionniste, y compris les barrières non tarifaires et qui aurait ainsi assuré à l'entreprise canadienne une ouverture totale sur les marchés américains.

Bien que les nationalistes aient obtenu un certain succès auprès du gouvernement Trudeau, surtout entre 1972 et 1976 et de 1980 à 1983, la libéralisation des échanges entre le Canada et les États-Unis s'est sans cesse poursuivie. D'abord, le libre-échange existe depuis longtemps dans deux secteurs importants. Le Pacte de l'automobile, signé en 1965, a toujours été considéré comme bienfaisant pour l'économie canadienne. Même si les déboires de l'entreprise américaine de fabrication d'automobiles ont contribué à accentuer le déficit de la balance canadienne dans ce secteur, il reste que les exportations les plus lucratives pour le Canada se sont toujours situées dans ce domaine.

De plus, l'accord de 1959 de partage de la production de défense permet aux Canadiens de vendre en franchise aux États-Unis du matériel militaire, comme il ouvre le marché canadien aux producteurs américains dans le domaine de la défense. Ici aussi le Canada est déficitaire, en raison surtout des achats d'avions de chasse et autres matériaux onéreux. Mais en 1983, 250 entreprises canadiennes, œuvrant dans l'électronique, l'aérospatiale, le génie maritime, les véhicules de combat, l'armement et les articles de ravitaillement, bénéficiaient de cette ouverture de marché[25].

De plus, les accords conclus au sein du GATT ont fait qu'en 1987, 80 % des échanges commerciaux entre le Canada et les États-Unis étaient tout à fait libres et 90 % n'étaient pas affectés de tarifs supérieurs à 5 %. Cette situation a amené les avocats du libre-échange à faire remarquer qu'un accord global ne serait pas très révolutionnaire.

On a cherché, au cours de l'année 1984, à conclure des accords sectoriels. Mais on s'est buté à toutes sortes d'obstacles. Il est rare qu'Américains et Canadiens se soient accordés pour voir des avantages mutuels dans un secteur particulier, chaque partie favorisant le libre-échange dans le secteur où elle a plus de chance d'enregistrer des surplus. Il devait être plus simple et plus prometteur, semble-t-il, de viser un accord global pour ensuite négocier des exceptions dans certains domaines, comme par exemple dans le secteur de la production culturelle, pour des raisons évidentes du côté canadien. Les défenseurs d'un accord global ont fait valoir de nombreux avantages dont bénéficierait l'entreprise canadienne. Elle devait être amenée, disait-on, à se développer selon ses composantes les plus dynamiques, à croître en raison du vaste marché nord-américain et à réaliser par là des économies d'échelle. Par opposition à la menace toujours présente du protectionnisme américain, les exportations devaient se faire en toute sécurité, sans craindre une intervention extérieure au marché. La croissance des entreprises exportatrices devait entraîner sans doute la création de nombreux emplois bien rémunérés, ce qui compenserait, assurait-on, les pertes d'emploi engendrées par la fermeture d'entreprises non concurrentielles. Le libre-échange pourrait même contribuer à canadianiser davantage l'entreprise puisque les multinationales américaines n'auraient plus avantage à s'installer au Canada pour échapper aux barrières tarifaires tandis que les Canadiens, de leur côté, perdraient beaucoup d'intérêt à investir aux États-Unis puisqu'ils pourraient atteindre le marché américain à partir d'une base canadienne. Enfin, le consommateur canadien, n'ayant plus à faire les frais du protectionnisme, verrait son niveau de vie s'améliorer[26].

Mais les adversaires du libre-échange ont fait valoir que ces avantages seraient annulés par les effets néfastes et anarchiques de la libéralisation. D'abord, un accord global devait entraîner une perturbation profonde de la structure industrielle du Canada. Quantité d'entreprises, ne pouvant supporter l'énorme concurrence de voisins plus riches et mieux organisés, se verront forcer de fermer leurs portes et de provoquer un chômage qui ne sera que très lentement compensé par la croissance des entreprises qui réussiront à se tailler une place dans le grand marché. On craint aussi que le libre-échange, entraînant un ajustement des politiques fiscales canadiennes à celles des États-Unis, ne permette pas au Canada de maintenir des politiques sociales dont les Canadiens sont fiers. De plus, une politique industrielle canadienne deviendra impensable. Ce sera la perte inévitable de l'autonomie du Canada en matières économique, culturelle et politique.

On répondait à ces craintes, dans l'autre camp, en faisant valoir les bienfaits du libre-échange ailleurs dans le monde, en dissociant l'autonomie politique et culturelle (qui est encore forte en Europe, par exemple) de l'autonomie économique. Mais le Canada est-il comparable à un pays européen?

Le débat, qui n'est pas récent, se poursuivra probablement longtemps, même si l'accord est conclu, car les résultats n'apparaissent pas très clairement. Un argument qui fait réfléchir toutefois: le Canada était, avant 1989, le seul pays industrialisé, à part l'Australie, à ne pas avoir un accès direct à un marché de 100 millions de population.

Quoi qu'il en soit du bien-fondé du libre-échange ou d'une politique industrielle autonome, il demeure inévitable que l'économie canadienne soit fortement liée à celle des États-Unis et que les deux pays forment, à toute fin pratique, une seule zone économique, comme ils constituent d'ailleurs une seule zone dans le domaine de la défense, surtout celui de la défense aérienne.

La défense aérienne du continent

C'est là un fait trop souvent oublié: depuis Ogdensburg, mais surtout depuis l'apparition des armes nucléaires aux États-Unis, puis en Union soviétique, les systèmes de défense américain et canadien sont fortement intégrés; plus précisément, le système de défense américain porte sur le territoire canadien autant que sur le territoire américain. Les Européens peuvent toujours se demander si vraiment les États-Unis se porteront, en toute occasion, à la défense de l'Europe. Les Canadiens n'ont pas à se poser cette question. Car, quelle que soit la politique du Canada à l'endroit des États-Unis (même si d'aventure le Canada allait se proclamer neutre) et quelles que soient les dispositions des dirigeants américains à l'endroit du Canada, Washington défendra le territoire canadien. C'est là ce qu'on a appelé la «garantie involontaire» qui découle de la position stratégique du Canada par rapport aux États-Unis et à leurs adversaires éventuels, les Soviétiques. Cette garantie est devenue plus claire encore avec le Traité de non-prolifération nucléaire signé en 1968 par le Canada et les États-Unis avec beaucoup d'autres États. En vertu de ce traité, Washington s'engage à assurer à ses alliés non nucléarisés une protection adéquate et Ottawa s'en remet à Washington pour que soit assuré le nécessaire équilibre nucléaire. C'est encore ce qu'on a appelé, pour le Canada, le *free ride* (le «transport gratuit»), c'est-à-dire la protection assurée du parapluie nucléaire américain. Voilà la réalité quasi immuable de la situation stratégique du Canada et de sa sécurité. L'intégration militaire (surtout en matière de défense aérienne et nucléaire) est une donnée indépendante d'Ogdensburg, de l'OTAN, de NORAD et d'autres accords formels.

De cette réalité, on peut tirer deux types de conséquences: la première, qui n'a jamais été totalement celle du gouvernement canadien bien qu'il s'en soit parfois inspiré, c'est d'adopter l'attitude japonaise. Puisque, de toute façon, les Américains se sont engagés à nous protéger et qu'il est de leur intérêt de le faire, nous aurions bien tort de maintenir un arsenal militaire dispendieux. Utilisons plutôt nos ressources à d'autres fins plus utiles et plus rentables[27]; l'autre consiste à faire oublier la dépendance canadienne en contribuant à la défense de l'Amérique du Nord, en accroissant notre sentiment d'autonomie par la participation volontaire la plus grande possible au système qui nous est imposé. C'est la politique officielle du gouvernement canadien[28].

C'est ainsi que le Canada s'est fait le champion de l'Alliance atlantique et de son organisation, créée en 1949. L'OTAN représentait, pour les diplomates canadiens, une sorte de contrepoids à la dépendance américaine car elle incluait le Canada dans un système multilatéral où la présence américaine était inévitablement moins lourde. Mais il faut bien reconnaître que, le plus souvent, quant il y a eu division entre les Européens et Washington, c'est du côté de ce dernier que le Canada s'est rangé. Et il arrive que l'adhésion ferme du Canada à la stratégie de l'OTAN renforce sa dépendance bilatérale, comme, par exemple, dans le cas des essais du missile *Cruise* en sol canadien[29].

NORAD, le partage de la production de défense, l'établissement et la modernisation des systèmes d'alertes sont d'autres façons d'institutionnaliser, de canaliser l'intégration militaire. Au moment de la création de NORAD, la stratégie de dissuasion nucléaire des Américains portait essentiellement sur les bombardiers dont la route passait par l'espace aérien du Canada. Le Canada était donc un élément essentiel de la stratégie américaine. Plus tard, avec la multiplication des missiles balistiques et l'apparition des sous-marins porteurs de missiles, le Canada perdait de son importance dans l'équilibre de la terreur. Si la stratégie devait à nouveau être bouleversée et s'appuyer sur des systèmes défensifs de type ABM ou sur l'utilisation de l'espace, comme c'est le cas avec l'Initiative de défense stratégique (IDS) dite «guerre des étoiles», le Canada pourrait à nouveau être un objet particulier d'attention de la part de Washington. Déjà, l'utilisation de missiles volant à faible altitude, comme le *Cruise*, a donné une importance nouvelle au Canada.

L'opinion publique canadienne est très préoccupée par ce qui est perçu comme une trop grande dépendance du Canada à l'égard du système de défense américain et des politiques militaristes jugées dangereuses du gouvernement Reagan. Ainsi, de forts courants plus ou moins pacifistes se sont opposés aux essais de missiles *Cruise* en Alberta, puis à la participation canadienne à l'IDS.

Face à ces courants d'opinion, il est important de rappeler l'irrémédiable inclusion du Canada dans la zone de défense américaine. Les pacifistes ont le droit de s'attrister de cette situation mais ils doivent bien se résigner à ne pouvoir la changer. Ainsi, en raison même de cette situation, il serait étonnant que nous puissions, en cas de crise, garder intacte notre virginité nucléaire. On peut souhaiter que le Canada ne soit jamais «nucléarisé» en permanence, mais il est difficile de penser que des armes nucléaires ne seront jamais utilisées par des Américains en territoire canadien. C'est là ce que rappelait le Secrétaire américain à la Défense, Caspar Weinburger, lors de la visite du président Reagan à Québec, en mars 1985. La remarque était pour le moins mal placée et imprudente, mais il serait bien étonnant qu'elle ne corresponde pas à des visées réelles.

D'autre part, si le Canada est partie intégrante d'un tout américain, il ne lui est pas interdit, à l'intérieur de ce tout, d'adopter une position critique quant à certaines politiques jugées peu heureuses. Le premier ministre Pearson s'est joint à plusieurs personnalités américaines en 1965 pour condamner les bombardements au Viêt-nam du Nord. Pourquoi ne serait-il pas permis aux Canadiens de rejeter, par exemple, la politique de l'IDS du président Reagan, comme l'ont fait plusieurs experts aux États-Unis, la majorité des Démocrates et un nombre croissant de Républicains? Comme le fait remarquer Albert Legault, du point de vue de l'intérêt canadien, il est mieux de tenter d'influer sur le système de l'intérieur que de s'y opposer de l'extérieur[30]. De toute façon, le Canada n'a guère d'autres choix.

Pluies acides

Le choix du Canada est encore plus limité en ce qui a trait à la protection de l'environnement. S'il est à peu près impossible de changer le cours de nos échanges commerciaux ou de la stratégie américaine, il est strictement et physiquement impensable de modifier l'orientation des vents et d'empêcher que des émissions polluantes venant du Nord des États-Unis affectent le Canada.

Déjà, le Traité sur les eaux frontalières de 1909 et la création de la Commission mixte internationale manifestaient une prise de conscience de l'interdépendance des deux États en matière d'environnement et de conservation. Mais c'est plutôt récemment, notamment au cours des années 70, qu'on a sonné l'alarme. Au départ et en principe, les Américains ont fait preuve d'autant de préoccupation et de bonnes intentions quant à la nécessité de s'attaquer au problème de la pollution des cours d'eau. En 1972, sous la présidence de Richard Nixon, un accord voyait le jour sur la qualité des eaux des Grands Lacs. En 1978, sous Carter, l'accord était renégocié et les mesures prises pour combattre la pollution de ces étendues d'eau commune se faisaient plus incisives. Le problème de la pollution des Grands Lacs n'est pas réglé, loin de là. Mais il a cédé la place, dans les priorités canadiennes, au problème des pluies acides.

Il s'agit essentiellement d'émissions d'anhydride sulfureux (SO_2) et d'oxyde d'azote (NO_x) provenant, entre autres, de la combustion du charbon dans les centrales thermiques non pourvues de dispositifs antipollution. Ces émissions peuvent voyager sur de grandes distances, transportées par les vents, et se mêler aux précipitations en leur imposant un taux d'acidité beaucoup plus élevé que la normale. Cette acidité est susceptible de détruire des espèces de poissons, de contaminer les eaux, d'affecter considérablement les arbres des forêts et même d'endommager des édifices.

Paradoxalement, ce sont des groupes de pression américains qui ont, les premiers, placé cette question à l'ordre du jour. En 1978, ces groupes ont alerté le Congrès américain des dangers que pourraient faire subir à l'environnement américain des installations comme les centrales productrices d'électricité d'Atikokan, au Nord-Ouest de l'Ontario et de Poplar River, au sud de la Saskatchewan. Des membres du Congrès américain ont alors demandé au département d'État de négocier un accord avec le Canada sur la qualité de l'air. Le Canada a bien accueilli la proposition et un groupe bilatéral de consultations sur les recherches fut créé, et déposa un rapport en 1979. Ce rapport révélait, entre autres choses, que les États-Unis produisaient de trois à quatre fois plus d'émissions polluantes que le Canada.

En août 1980, un mémorandum déclaratif d'intention est signé. Le Canada et les États-Unis s'entendent en vue d'élaborer un accord de coopération sur la réduction des polluants atmosphériques de part et d'autre de la frontière. Des négociations officielles ont commencé en juin 1981 et se sont poursuivies en 1982. Le Canada a annoncé, en février 1982, qu'il était prêt à réduire de 50 % les émissions d'anhydride sulfureux dans l'Est du Canada avant 1990, à condition que les États-Unis en fassent autant. Les Américains n'ont pas accepté la proposition canadienne, la jugeant prématurée.

En fait, le bouleversement qu'a imposé l'administration Reagan à la bureaucratie américaine a profondément affecté l'organisation et la stratégie concernant les questions touchant l'environnement. Ces questions étaient désormais considérées comme très secondaires. La priorité était plutôt accordée aux besoins de l'entreprise. Des représentants de l'industrie du charbon, par exemple, ont trouvé des oreilles réceptives à Washington. Les positions d'Ottawa et de Washington allaient désormais être plus éloignées que jamais les unes des autres.

La question devenait fortement politisée. Pour Washington, l'intérêt majeur consistait à protéger l'industrie, en particulier dans des États menacés comme la Pennsylvanie et l'Ohio (grandes sources d'émissions d'anhydride sulfureux), à ne pas lui imposer des coûts trop considérables. Il est vrai que les pluies acides ont imposé des dommages aux États-Unis mais, comme les vents ont tendance à voyager vers le nord-est, ce sont les provinces centrales du Canada, surtout le Québec, qui ont souffert davantage du phénomène. Pour le Canada, les pluies acides sont donc un véritable fléau qui pourrait signifier, avec le temps, des pertes de revenus énormes au chapitre du tourisme, des pêcheries et de l'exploitation forestière.

Précisément parce que la question est politisée, personne ne songe à la remettre entre les mains de l'auguste Commission mixte internationale. Il ne semble pas non plus que les données scientifiques joueront un rôle déterminant. Même si la science devient de plus en plus importante dans les relations internationales, elle ne vient pas à bout d'une opposition politique déterminée[31]. Restent les pressions politiques. Devant les fins de non-recevoir de l'administration Reagan qui invoquait l'insuffisance des recherches en dépit d'une évidence qui en avait persuadé plusieurs aux États-Unis, les responsables canadiens ont entrepris une véritable campagne auprès de divers groupes de pression américains. On n'a pas raté une occasion de s'adresser à des congrès d'associations vouées à la préservation de l'environnement. Il semble bien qu'un accord finira par être signé. La question est de savoir jusqu'à quel point les Américains voudront imposer des obligations à leurs industries.

Nouvelles orientations

La nature des actions de la diplomatie canadienne sur cette question des pluies acides est un bon exemple d'une nouvelle orientation de la politique canadienne envers les États-Unis. Les diplomates canadiens ont découvert l'importance du Congrès et des groupes de pression en matière de relations canado-américaines. Ce n'est pas du département d'État que naissent les problèmes et les conflits. En général, dans les milieux de l'administration à Washington, on trouve des gens qui sont fort sensibles aux préoccupations des Canadiens. Ce sont plutôt des groupes de personnes des régions frontalières ou des gens d'affaires possédant des intérêts au Canada qui réagiront parfois violemment aux politiques canadiennes et qui porteront leur amertume ou leur hostilité jusqu'au Congrès. D'où l'importance pour les représentants canadiens de s'adresser directement à ces groupes ou, au moins, de s'appliquer à faire connaître le point de vue canadien à des membres clés du Congrès.

Voilà donc les diplomates canadiens en train de constituer un lobby. Sans doute ne sont-ils pas les seuls à agir ainsi à Washington. Japonais, Arabes, Israéliens, Coréens et autres sont aussi très actifs. Mais la facilité avec laquelle les représentants canadiens circulent dans tous les milieux aux États-Unis n'illustre-t-elle pas encore la pertinence du modèle «intérieur» déjà énoncé?

Il en va de même, pour une bonne part, du côté américain. Ses représentants ont découvert la politique provinciale au Canada. Sans jamais accepter de traiter officiellement avec les gouvernements des provinces canadiennes, Washington demeure très attentive aux mouvements des capitales provinciales, en particulier Edmonton et Québec. On a dit du consulat général de Québec, par exemple, qu'il jouait un rôle politique non officiel de contact direct avec le gouvernement québécois.

Récemment – et qu'on mesure la distance parcourue depuis le rapport Merchant-Heeney de 1965 –, deux ambassadeurs, Paul H. Robinson, Jr. à Ottawa et Allan Gotlieb à Washington, n'ont pas fait un mystère de la dimension politique de leurs actions et de ce qu'on a appelé une diplomatie ouverte. L'ambassadeur américain déclarait:

> Diplomacy among friends should not only follow usual diplomatic channels but should also include an open discussion of common concerns between a diplomat and the host country. If this open diplomacy is carried out in a straightforward manner, it can usefully contribute to public debate[32].

Son homologue canadien confessait, pour sa part:

> J'ai voulu mettre l'accent sur une diplomatie ouverte, et je crois que j'ai eu raison de le faire. Cette dimension me paraît importante pour le Canada et pour nos relations avec les États-Unis en ce moment en particulier [...] Notre action envers le Congrès, c'est d'expliquer la position du Canada lorsqu'un projet de loi a des répercussions chez nous[33].

Ces deux citations résument bien les relations canado-américaines. Ce sont toujours des relations privilégiées, non pas qu'elles soient exemptes de conflits et de tensions, mais en ce que Américains et Canadiens traversent le plus allègrement du monde, pour le meilleur ou pour le pire, cette frontière non défendue. Des intérêts américains s'opposeront, parfois durement, à des intérêts canadiens. Les gouvernements pourront être amenés à soutenir des positions antagonistes en raison de ces intérêts. Les populations elles-mêmes pourront être amenées à manifester un certain nationalisme. Tout cela n'empêchera pas la réalité profonde d'une sorte de consensus nord-américain de faire son chemin et d'avoir raison, en définitive, de toutes les oppositions. Qu'on le veuille ou non, le destin du Canada est irrémédiablement lié à celui des États-Unis. Si les Canadiens veulent contester la politique américaine, c'est souvent avec des Américains qu'ils y parviendront le mieux.

NOTES

1. J.L. Granatstein, «Cooperation and Conflict: The Course of Canadian-American Relations since 1945», in Charles F. Doran and John H. Sigler (éd.), *Canada and The United States, Enduring Friendship, Persistent Stress,* Englewood Cliffs, N.J., Prentice-Hall, 1985, p. 47-48.

2. *Ibidem,* p. 48-50.

3. Voir le rapport Merchant-Heeney publié en 1965 et qui porte la signature d'un ancien ambassadeur américain à Ottawa (Livingston Merchant) et d'un ancien ambassadeur canadien à Washington (Arnold Heeney): *Principles for Partnership,* Ottawa, 1965.

4. Il s'agit de «Interest Equalization Tax» (juillet 1963), «Voluntary Cooperation Program» (décembre 1965) et «Mandatory Direct Investments Guidelines» (janvier 1968).

5. *Politique étrangère au service des Canadiens,* Ottawa, Information Canada, 1970.

6. «Relations canado-américaines: Choix pour l'avenir», *Perspectives internationales,* automne 1972.

7. Cité par Alex I. Inglis, «Les relations canado-américaines sous un jour nouveau», *Perspectives internationales,* mars-avril 1975, p. 4.

8. *Perspectives internationales,* automne 1972, p. 16.

9. Voir Jeremy Kinsman et Allan Gotlieb, «Reviving the Third Option», *International Perspectives,* janvier-février 1981, p. 2-18. Voir aussi le discours du Secrétaire d'État aux Affaires extérieures, Mark MacGuigan, à Toronto, le 22 janvier 1981.

10. Ces deux dernières citations sont tirées de Roger F. Swanson, *Intergovernmental Perspectives on the Canada-US Relationship,* New York, New York University Press, 1978, p. 1.

11. Voir, entre autres, l'ouvrage remarquable de Charles F. Doran, *Forgotten Partnership, US - Canada Relations Today,* Baltimore, The Johns Hopkins University Press, 1984. Voir aussi les déclarations du président Nixon lui-même lors de sa visite au Canada en 1971: citées plus haut.

12. Voir Seymour Martin Lipset, «Canada and the United States: The Cultural Dimension», in Doran et Sigler (éd.), *Canada and the United States [...],* p. 109-160.

13. «Qu'on le veuille ou non [...] le Canada fait sociologiquement partie de l'espace américain [...] De ce point de vue, les rapports de pouvoir du gouvernement d'Ottawa face à Washington apparaissent de plus en plus, toutes proportions gardées, comme ceux du Québec face à Ottawa.» Paul Painchaud, «La méthode Mulroney dans les relations canado-américaines», *Le Devoir,* 11 mars 1985, p. 7.

14. Il existe un certain nombre d'avantages que Washington peut retirer de la souveraineté politique du Canada. Personne aux États-Unis n'envisage sérieusement une éventuelle annexion du Canada à la république. Voir Louis Balthazar, «Les relations canado-américaines: nationalisme et continentalisme», *Études internationales,* vol. XIV, n° 1, mars 1983, p. 23-37.

15. John W. Holmes, *Life with Uncle, The Canadian-American Relationship,* Toronto, University of Toronto Press, 1981, p. 43.

16. Canada, ministère des Affaires extérieures, *Rapport annuel 1983-1984,* Ottawa, 1985, p. 23.

17. *Op. cit.*

18. Canada, ministère des Affaires extérieures, *Rapport annuel 1983-1984,* p. 20.

19. Voir note 3.

20. Voir Matthew J. Abrams, *The Canada-United States Interparliamentary Group,* Ottawa, Parliamentary Center for Foreign Affairs and Foreign Trade, Canadian Institute for International Affairs, 1973.

21. David Leyton-Brown, *Weathering the Storm: Canadian-US Relations, 1980-1983,* Toronto et Washington, Canadian-American Committee, C.D. Howe Institute, National Planning Association, 1985, p. 79-82.

22. Rappelons que le présent chapitre a été rédigé avant que débutent les négociations qui ont abouti au traité de libre-échange entre les États-Unis et le Canada. Les arguments soulevés ici n'en conservent pas moins toute leur pertinence.

23. Canada, ministère des Affaires extérieures, *Rapport annuel 1983-1984,* p. 22 et 59.

24. Richard G. Lipsey et Murray G. Smith, *Taking the Initiative: Canada's Trade Options in a Turbulent World,* Toronto, C.D. Howe Institute, 1985, p. 82.

25. *Le Devoir,* 6 décembre 1984, p. 16.

26. Pour un plaidoyer intelligent et bien documenté, voir Richard G. Lipsey et Murray G. Smith, *op. cit.*

27. James Eayrs faisait, en 1969, un plaidoyer en ce sens devant le Comité permanent des affaires extérieures et de la défense nationale de la Chambre des communes. Voir *Behind the Headlines,* Canadian Institute of International Affairs, vol. XXVIII, n°s 1-2, avril 1969. Ce plaidoyer a été partiellement entendu par le gouvernement Trudeau qui réduisait par la suite de moitié la contribution canadienne à l'OTAN.

28. Voir Stephen Clarkson, *Canada and the Reagan Challenge,* Toronto, James Lorimer, 1982, p. 251-252.

29. *Ibidem*, p. 251 et 281.

30. Charles F. Doran et John H. Sigler (éd.), *op. cit.*, p. 165.

31. Don Munton, «Acid rain – silver clouds can have black linings», *International Perspectives*, janvier-février 1981, p. 9.

32. Paul H. Robinson, Jr., «Fortifying the ties that bind», *Maclean's*, 23 août 1982.

33. Allan Gotlieb, cité par Sylviane Tramier, *Le Devoir*, 1ᵉʳ novembre 1982, p. 14.

12

Les relations du Canada avec les communautés européennes: un processus de diversification

Panayotis Soldatos
Université de Montréal

Les relations du Canada avec les communautés européennes, essentiellement amorcées avec l'accord Canada-EURATOM de 1959, mais surtout développées dans les années 70, comportent un certain nombre de traits spécifiques qu'il convient d'esquisser ici en guise d'introduction, pour que l'on puisse y trouver les paramètres essentiels de ce *partnership* transatlantique.

1. Certains éléments de *discontinuité* et d'*arythmie* caractérisent ces relations. Quoique amorcées dès 1959-1960, lors de la signature d'un traité de coopération nucléaire avec l'EURATOM (1959) et l'accréditation simultanée auprès des communautés de l'ambassadeur canadien en Belgique (1960), elles n'ont connu leur développement *multidimensionnel institutionnalisé* que dans les années 70, grâce à la nouvelle politique de diversification internationale du gouvernement Trudeau (1970 et 1972) et les mécanismes de l'*Accord-cadre de coopération commerciale et économique* avec les communautés européennes, établis en 1976[1].

En effet, le Canada, depuis la création des communautés européennes dans les années 50, et jusqu'au développement d'une «option Europe» dans les années 70, avait, tant au niveau de ses élites qu'à celui de sa population, une attitude qui évoluait entre l'indifférence et l'*attention sélective*, en passant même par des phases d'*inquiétude,* voire d'irritation, à propos, par exemple de la politique agricole commune, des politiques dans le domaine de la pêche ou de celles sur l'uranium ou, encore, des candidatures britanniques à l'admission[2]. Les incertitudes entourant la naissance des communautés, leurs premières étapes et leurs finalités ultérieures (oppositions britanniques, politiques gaullistes, incertitude quant à l'avenir du protectionnisme régional, objectifs politiques insuffisamment circonscrits, processus incertain de *spill-over* intégratif, etc.) ont contribué grandement à cette attitude canadienne.

2. Ces relations entre le Canada et les communautés européennes se situent dans le *prolongement naturel des rapports bilatéraux* que le Canada avait avant l'avènement de l'Europe communautaire, avec chacun des pays concernés, entre autres, et en particulier, avec le Royaume-Uni; il s'agit de rapports bilatéraux que l'accord-cadre de 1976 a voulu préserver, dans certains champs, par une disposition précise. En effet, on y prévoit que, «sans préjudice des dispositions applicables en la matière, des traités instituant les communautés, le présent accord ainsi que toute action entreprise dans son cadre laisseront entièrement intactes les compétences des États membres des communautés d'entreprendre des actions bilatérales avec le Canada dans le domaine de la coopération économique et de conclure, le cas échéant, de nouveaux accords de coopération économique avec le Canada»[3].

3. Le processus de contacts et de *négociations* (1972-1976), précédant la signature de l'accord-cadre d'institutionnalisation des relations du Canada avec les communautés, révèle un ensemble d'incertitudes et d'ambiguïtés sous-tendant et, jusqu'à un certain point, hypothéquant ces relations: le contenu vague et peu innovateur, par rapport aux règles du GATT, de certaines propositions canadiennes en vue d'un accord avec les communautés ainsi que certaines divergences d'objectifs y afférant (le Canada étant à la recherche de nouveaux marchés pour ses produits industriels, surtout finis, les communautés étant attirées par le potentiel de ressources naturelles du Canada) sont, notamment, parmi les éléments explicatifs des difficultés de ce dialogue canado-européen de la première moitié des années 70, du caractère fort général de l'accord-cadre conclu en 1976, et des contours encore vagues de ce rapprochement[4].

4. Loin d'être un acte isolé, l'institutionnalisation des relations entre le Canada et les communautés européennes s'inscrit dans la dynamique plus générale de la politique canadienne de *diversification* des relations extérieures du pays: l'ouverture du Canada vers l'Europe communautaire a été sous-tendue par la volonté du gouvernement canadien de faire de cette relation une pièce maîtresse de son dessein global de diversification, y recherchant un certain contrepoids aux relations canado-américaines[5].

Aussi n'est-il pas possible de saisir les dimensions essentielles des relations étudiées ici sans les replacer dans le cadre plus vaste des orientations canadiennes de diversification de la fin des années 60 et, surtout, de la décennie qui suivit. L'«option communautés européennes» fut, en effet, le *hard core* d'une politique de *diversification sélective*, basée sur une approche *régionale* et *bimultilatérale*[6].

Cette brève esquisse introductive des principales caractéristiques de la relation nous suggère déjà un plan pour son étude qui comporte les niveaux d'analyse suivants: une présentation synthétique de la politique canadienne de diversification, dont l'actualisation entraîna, dans le cadre de l'«option Europe», un accord-cadre et un schéma institutionnel d'interaction avec les communautés; une démarche explicative de cette ouverture canadienne vers l'Europe communautaire; une esquisse de contenu essentiel des relations Canada-communautés européennes dans la perspective dudit accord-cadre de 1976, en y insistant sur le processus de sa négociation et en proposant, par ailleurs, un inventaire globalisant des réalisations de cet accord et de l'ensemble de la coopération Canada-communautés; un essai d'évaluation critique de ce processus de coopération, en insistant, d'une part, sur les difficultés d'une telle démarche d'évaluation et, d'autre part, sur les facteurs qui ont eu un impact restrictif sur cette relation canado-européenne; des considérations finales permettant d'aborder la question du devenir de la relation, compte tenu, notamment, de certains changements dans l'orientation internationale du Canada depuis 1983 ainsi que de l'évolution de la réalité communautaire durant la présente décennie.

LES COMMUNAUTÉS EUROPÉENNES, PIERRE ANGULAIRE DANS LE PARI CANADIEN DE DIVERSIFICATION

L'orientation canadienne de diversification et son actualisation par une politique de rapprochement avec les communautés européennes

1. La *diversification*, comme concept général de relations extérieures, se référant souvent, mais pas exclusivement[7], au champ des relations économiques, correspond à une *philosophie de politique étrangère: celle qui suggère l'utilité d'assurer à un système étatique un large éventail de partenaires et une gamme de relations étendues et approfondies, d'un point de vue quantitatif (volume des relations) et qualitatif (types et domaines précis de relations), l'affranchissant ainsi, à des degrés divers, d'une relation extérieure exclusive, souvent de dépendance.* L'ampleur souhaitable (en termes d'affranchissement) de l'éventail des partenaires et des relations dépendra, dans chaque cas concret, de certaines variables ne pouvant pas être envisagées *in abstracto* (vulnérabilités et éléments de puissance internes et externes du système étatique concerné; structures internes en général; structure de l'environnement international; contexte géopolitique; etc.). C'est ainsi, par exemple, que certains pays, plus vulnérables sur le plan interne (niveau économique, politique, militaire ou culturel) et avec des voisins puissants, auront peut-être besoin d'une plus grande diversification dans leurs relations extérieures par rapport à des pays plus forts qui, malgré l'absence de diversification, pourraient maintenir des liens d'interdépendance plutôt que de dépendance.

   Pareille philosophie de diversification peut devenir, si elle est acceptée par les décideurs, une *orientation* et une *option de politique étrangère* et conduire, dès lors, à des *politiques* et à des *mesures concrètes d'actualisation* d'un dessein de diversification[8].

2. Dans le contexte canadien, la notion de diversification, dans son acception la plus fondamentale d'une *réaction aux pressions de l'environnement externe par la recherche de nouvelles relations de substitution ou de contrepoids,* apparaît avec une impressionnante régularité dans le discours et les comportements d'actualisation des décideurs canadiens, certaines de ces manifestations étant même antérieures à la Confédération: l'instauration, en 1849, du libre-échange réciproque entre les colonies canadiennes et la conclusion, en 1854, du Traité de réciprocité avec les

États-Unis représentent une réaction de diversification de l'Amérique du Nord britannique, recherchant des *liens de substitution partielle* (trouver de nouvelles relations pouvant se substituer, ne fût-ce que partiellement, à celles que l'on perdait alors du côté des rapports avec la Grande-Bretagne); vient, ensuite, et après la fin du Traité de réciprocité, la longue période du *jeu triangulaire de diversification* de nos relations économiques extérieures avec la Grande-Bretagne et les États-Unis, jeu compromis, en termes d'équilibre, par la diminution constante de l'importance de nos relations avec la Grande-Bretagne au profit de la courbe ascendante des relations canado-américaines, qui vont devenir prédominantes dans l'entre-deux-guerres[9]; il y a, enfin, le «sursaut» plus contemporain de diversification dans la politique étrangère du Canada, manifesté d'abord par J. Diefenbaker en 1957, cherchant une diversification en direction du Royaume-Uni[10], mais développé surtout par Pierre E. Trudeau, à la faveur de ses orientations de politique internationale de la fin des années 60 et de la décennie 70[11].

En effet, c'est dès 1968[12] que P. E. Trudeau utilisa le thème de diversification, et celui-ci a été, depuis lors, souvent repris durant la période 1968-1972. Le rapport du groupe STAFEUR (1969) et le livre blanc (1970) sur la *Politique extérieure au service des Canadiens* (livret sur l'Europe) s'y réfèrent également, considérant que le Canada, tout en maintenant ses relations étroites et spéciales avec les États-Unis, devrait poursuivre des objectifs de diversification, notamment dans ses rapports avec l'Europe. Ceci dit, c'est en 1972 que cette politique se précisa par le lancement de la «troisième option», c'est-à-dire par l'annonce d'une politique établissant que «le Canada peut adopter une stratégie générale, à long terme, visant à développer et à raffermir son économie et les autres aspects de sa vie nationale et, ce faisant, réduire la vulnérabilité actuelle du Canada»[13]. La réduction d'une vulnérabilité multidimensionnelle – attribuée, en grande partie, aux relations trop «concentrées» avec les États-Unis et aux problèmes, non sans relation de causalité, de *nation-building* que connaissait le Canada – constituait une option prioritaire, qui n'était troisième que par rapport à deux autres, à ne pas suivre: celle du maintien, plus ou moins, de l'état «actuel» des relations avec les États-Unis (première option) et celle de la recherche délibérée d'une intégration plus grande avec les États-Unis (deuxième option)[14]. Ce fut donc en réaction au *continentalisme spontané* (première option) ou *délibéré* (deuxième option) que l'on cherchera alors de nouveaux partenaires de diversification.

3. Ceci dit, les communautés européennes ne furent initialement que l'un des nombreux destinataires de la politique canadienne de diversification d'alors, la «troisième option» comportant, dans sa version de 1972, une orientation *mondialiste*[15].

À cette orientation succéda, progressivement, un rétrécissement de l'éventail de nos partenaires cibles: l'amorce d'un dialogue canado-européen, exploratoire d'un accord de coopération institutionnalisée avec les communautés européennes, et le *discours de Winnipeg*, de 1975, du secrétaire d'État aux Affaires extérieures d'alors, A. MacEachen[16], lançant l'«option Japon» et l'«option Europe», ont fait des communautés européennes un partenaire privilégié dans le processus de diversification de nos relations extérieures. C'est ainsi que, en 1976, on a abouti à la signature de l'accord-cadre avec les communautés, assurant un cadre institutionnalisé à nos politiques de diversification vers l'Europe communautaire.

Les tableaux 1 et 2 schématisent cette articulation reliant le trinôme «politique étrangère canadienne – diversification – option communautés européennes».

Les déterminants de l'«option communautés européennes» du gouvernement canadien

Il convient de s'interroger ici sur les raisons de ce «crescendo» de diversification vers l'Europe, développé dans les années 70, surtout si l'on considère que le Canada, depuis la création des communautés européennes, entre 1951 et 1957, a eu, tant au niveau de ses élites qu'à celui de sa population, une attitude fort différente de celle du rapprochement étroit, voire institutionnalisé, manifestée par l'accord-cadre. Car, en effet, cette attitude passée évoluait entre l'indifférence du départ et l'attention sélective, en connaissant également des périodes d'«irritants» dans la relation[17].

La réponse à cette question sur les déterminants de la «troisième option» et de son *hard core*, l'«option communautés européennes», comporte un faisceau de variables explicatives que nous esquissons, ci-après, dans une énumération sélective plutôt qu'exhaustive.

1. Les deux principaux éléments explicatifs d'ordre *conjoncturel.*.

   - Il y a d'abord la surtaxe de Nixon, de 1971, qui a révélé aux décideurs canadiens notre vulnérabilité face aux États-Unis: on a constaté que lorsque ceux-ci deviennent protectionnistes sans nous exempter de leurs mesures, ils nous affectent de façon profonde vu l'interdépendance asymétrique, voire la dépendance qui caractérise nos relations et nos structures économiques dans ce contexte de rapport continentaliste canado-américain;
   - Ensuite, il y a eu la nouvelle politique euratlantique de Nixon (on parla même à l'époque de *doctrine Nixon*) qui incitait ses alliés, dans une perspective de nouveau pacte atlantique, à conduire de façon plus autonome leurs affaires, comme consécration d'une maturité plus grande et vu le besoin pour eux de raffermir leur économie et d'accroître leur contribution à la défense du monde occidental[18].

2. Sur le plan régional (Amérique du Nord), la *pénétration structurelle* croissante de l'économie canadienne par les forces économiques américaines faisait prendre conscience, au niveau des élites et de la population canadienne, de certains dangers liés à notre dépendance face aux États-Unis.

3. Dans une perspective *internationale* plus vaste, diverses autres évolutions, souvent structurelles, amenèrent cette nouvelle option.

   - Dans les années 70, l'Europe communautaire se consolidait et s'élargissait, connaissant aussi des phénomènes d'*externalisation*[19], c'est-à-dire un développement de son réseau de communications internationales qui répondait, entre autres, aux souhaits des pays tiers de conclure des accords de coopération avec ce nouveau bloc dynamique de l'économie internationale;

- Il y a eu, aussi, le fait que la Grande-Bretagne y prenait sa place et que le Canada risquait ainsi de perdre son contrepoids traditionnel et de se retrouver en marge de cette nouvelle structuration dans le système économique international, tombant dans un continentalisme irréversible;

- Compte tenu de l'*évolution de l'économie mondiale*, on a senti au Canada le besoin d'accentuer l'internationalisation du capital canadien[20] par une présence active sur de nouveaux marchés de produits, de capital et de technologie, par un rôle économique international plus agressif qui porte la concurrence et la coopération sur de nouveaux terrains, en dehors de celui de l'Amérique du Nord, déjà largement exploré. C'est pourquoi, d'ailleurs, cette politique de diversification vers les communautés européennes n'a pas été conçue comme une option antiaméricaine, d'éloignement des États-Unis, mais plutôt comme une option dynamique d'élargissement des cadres et du volume de nos relations économiques par une présence plus grande au sein de l'Économie-monde et d'un système international en voie de multipolarisation.

4. Au niveau des *facteurs internes,* le besoin de prendre en main les relations avec l'Europe des Neuf, occupant ainsi le terrain devant un Québec de plus en plus intéressé à l'Europe communautaire et à ses membres francophones, le souhait d'actualiser les objectifs du livre blanc de 1970 sur la politique étrangère (notamment l'objectif de croissance économique), la pression de certains milieux qui voyaient dans le rapprochement avec la communauté la garantie du maintien de nos engagements au sein de l'OTAN, engagements quelque peu ébranlés par la décision de 1969[21], ont constitué autant de raisons d'ordre interne ayant pu sous-tendre l'«option communautés européennes».

Mû par toutes ces considérations, le gouvernement canadien lança sa «troisième option», souhaitant son actualisation, par rapport à l'Europe communautaire, par l'établissement d'un accord qui jette les bases d'un dialogue et d'une coopération institutionnalisés, continus, systématiques, approfondis et élargis. Tout cela n'a toutefois pas été sans péripéties, et l'accord-cadre de 1976 n'a été que l'aboutissement d'un processus incertain et arythmique de négociation et de dialogue avec les Neuf, processus qui, en dehors de ses aspects de routine procédurale, comporte d'importants éléments de fond à ne pas négliger dans la démarche de description et d'explication du devenir et de prédiction de l'avenir de nos relations avec les communautés européennes.

LES RELATIONS CANADA-COMMUNAUTÉS EUROPÉENNES DANS LA PERSPECTIVE DE L'ACCORD-CADRE DE 1976

Le processus d'une longue négociation débouchant sur l'accord-cadre

Une importante initiative d'actualisation de la troisième option, même si la corrélation à ce propos n'a pas toujours été explicite, fut l'amorce de négociations entre le Canada et les communautés européennes. Précédé par un appel des chefs d'État ou de gouvernement des pays membres des communautés européennes, en faveur d'un dialogue constructif avec le Canada, ce processus de négociation a été amorcé, en 1972, par la présentation d'un premier aide-mémoire canadien; il fut intensifié en 1974, à la suite de la présentation d'un second aide-mémoire du Canada, et complété, après diverses arythmies dans les pourparlers, par la signature, en 1976, d'un accord-cadre entre les deux parties[22].

Sans vouloir reconstituer ici ce processus de négociations qui a connu des pauses et arythmies et que la littérature spécialisée a déjà explicité avec précision[23], nous nous limitons à tracer succinctement les contours des pourparlers, leurs principales orientations et leurs obstacles de base.

L'approche initiale du Canada, au niveau des négociations, s'est caractérisée par des démarches floues et incertaines quant au contenu d'un éventuel accord. Quoique intéressé à l'établissement d'un cadre de consultation institutionnalisée, à la libéralisation et la promotion de nos échanges ainsi qu'à un cadre général de coopération économique, notamment dans le domaine industriel, le gouvernement canadien n'a pas cru devoir présenter, dès le départ, des propositions de contenu suffisamment explicites, indiquant avec précision les dispositions d'un accord spécifique de coopération avec les communautés européennes. Pour l'essentiel, dans le premier aide-mémoire de 1972, il s'agissait d'une proposition de reprise de certaines dispositions du GATT dans le domaine de la libéralisation des échanges et le cadre d'une coopération commerciale, tandis que, par la suite, au moment du second aide-mémoire et des négociations afférentes, certaines précisions au niveau de la coopération économique ont été données, mais sans toujours offrir un contenu de traité assez spécifique.

D'autre part, il y a eu plusieurs autres obstacles de négociations, dus, notamment, à la question de l'éventuel impact des pourparlers sur les attitudes des États-Unis, aux réticences britanniques et françaises de voir les communautés conclure un accord qui déborderait le strict cadre commercial, aux objections du Danemark, souhaitant un accès non discriminatoire aux ressources naturelles canadiennes et s'opposant, de ce fait, aux politiques canadiennes de fixation des prix du pétrole et du gaz[24].

Un accord a toutefois été signé en juillet 1976, d'une durée indéterminée et avec des caractéristiques qui vont au-delà du domaine commercial, s'agissant d'un accord de coopération commerciale mais aussi économique. Ses principaux volets d'engagements sont les suivants: traitement de la nation la plus favorisée; diversification et libéralisation accrues des échanges; maintien et développement de conditions de libre concurrence; accès aux ressources et leur transformation ultérieure; promotion d'un développement socio-économique et régional; coopération industrielle, notamment par des *joints ventures* sur l'espace des deux partenaires ou dans les pays tiers, par un échange dans le domaine technologique et scientifique et par une coopération constante de rapprochement; accroissement des investissements mutuellement avantageux; institutionnalisation de cette coopération grâce à l'établissement d'un comité mixte de coopération, dont les sous-comités et les groupes de travail furent appelés à jouer un rôle moteur dans l'encadrement d'un dialogue périodique mais systématique et institutionnalisé, qui aborde les grandes questions en suspens au niveau des parties contractantes, mais qui porte aussi sur l'évolution générale des économies concernées, sur celle du système international ainsi que sur les champs potentiels de développement de cette coopération. Et sans éliminer le cadre de la coopération bilatérale entre le Canada et les pays membres des communautés[25], on instaure en plus un dialogue direct avec les autorités communautaires.

Absence de grande originalité, pragmatisme, vue sur l'avenir, pari sur certaines complémentarités entre les deux partenaires[26], voilà les traits dominants d'un accord qui n'a pas pour but le changement radical de la relation canado-européenne mais qui vise plutôt à l'encadrer de façon continue et, si possible, diversifiée. On ne serait pas éloigné de la réalité si l'on disait que l'accord-cadre a été un accord sur des arrière-pensées (les uns pensant surtout aux matières premières, les autres surtout aux produits finis), un acte de formulation solennelle de réalités de coopération existantes, un acte de foi en l'avenir de la coopération canado-européenne.

Essai d'un inventaire globalisant des réalisations de l'accord-cadre et de l'ensemble de la coopération Canada-communautés européennes

Il est fort malaisé de tenter un inventaire des résultats de cette coopération, dans la mesure où les politiques qui la sous-tendent et les instruments de leur actualisation sont nombreux et diversifiés. En effet, la relation Canada-communautés européennes est, comme expression d'une orientation de diversification, principalement sous-tendue par diverses actions et notamment la «troisième option», comportant une «option communautés européennes», mais incluant aussi, directement ou indirectement, un train de mesures internes de raffermissement de l'économie canadienne (voyez, par exemple, l'institution de AEIE/FIRA, le processus de «canadianisation» dans le domaine énergétique, la «staticisation» (*Staticization*), c'est-à-dire l'intervention accrue, directe, de l'État dans la vie économique du pays, etc.); l'accord-cadre Canada-communautés européennes; les accords avec l'EURATOM[27]; les ententes de coopération en matière environnementale; le dialogue avec les communautés en dehors de l'accord-cadre (contacts semi-annuels, contacts inter-parlementaires, etc.); le faisceau des relations bilatérales avec les pays membres de la communauté; l'ensemble des relations transnationales, attribuées ou non à l'accord.

Ceci dit, nous pouvons tenter ici une esquisse globalisante de cette coopération avec les communautés européennes, en prenant l'accord-cadre comme toile de fond[28].

1. Sur le plan *commercial*, qui représente un secteur bien précis et fondamental de cette coopération, les résultats incitent à une évaluation à deux faces.

Sur le plan positif, on peut signaler l'augmentation en *valeur*, presque constante, de nos importations en provenance de la communauté, entre 1976 et 1984, tandis que nos exportations, en valeur toujours, ont été plus fluctuantes, ayant connu une première période de courbe ascendante, pour diminuer, dans les années 80, avec toutefois quelques signes d'amélioration en 1984 (figure 1). Cela dit, une certaine prudence s'impose lors de la lecture de ces données, et ceci pour trois raisons: on doit tenir compte des fluctuations monétaires; l'importance d'un nombre limité de grands secteurs de commerce fait que ces derniers peuvent avoir une grande influence sur les fluctuations du commerce global; il en va de même de l'aspect «gonflé» des données statistiques, dû à certains contrats ou à certains produits importants[29]. Il faut enfin préciser que des ajustements saisonniers modifient légèrement de telles données dans diverses sources statistiques.

Le côté le moins encourageant pour le développement de ces relations commerciales nous est donné par les données statistiques sur le *pourcentage* des échanges du Canada avec les communautés européennes, depuis 1976, dans le commerce global du Canada. Ainsi que l'indique la figure 2, nos importations (en pourcentage) des communautés européennes ont peu évolué, avec même des périodes de tendance à la baisse, tandis que nos exportations (en pourcentage) vers les communautés européennes ont connu, dans les années 80, une chute considérable. Par ailleurs, la structure des exportations canadiennes vers les communautés reste dominée par les matières premières et les produits semi-finis. Enfin, des irritants dans les dossiers de la pêche, de l'agriculture, de l'uranium et de certains produits forestiers (le papier en particulier) freinent le «déblocage» décisif de nos relations commerciales avec les communautés[30]. Enfin, la progression très rapide du commerce canadien avec les États-Unis (dépassant, en 1984, la barre de 75 % au niveau de nos exportations vers les États-Unis) accroît cette asymétrie dans le commerce extérieur du Canada (figure 3).

2. Au niveau de la *coopération industrielle*, la difficulté de conclure certains grands accords de diversification, dans le domaine notamment de l'aéronautique et des *joints ventures*, ainsi que le rythme fort lent des consultations pour le développement sectoriel de cette coopération (par les groupes de travail existant par secteurs) laissent sceptiques ceux qui ont cru à des «déblocages» substantiels en cette matière et qui ne se satisfont pas du stade exploratoire de la relation, ou de l'échange d'informations et de la coopération limitée.

À propos de cette coopération, en effet, et en se référant aux groupes de travail constitués, on devrait mentionner les secteurs des métaux et des minéraux, parmi les plus actifs, tandis qu'un groupe de travail sur le transport urbain a laissé apparaître quelques aspects prometteurs de coopération. En revanche, dans le secteur des produits forestiers, on note certaines difficultés dues, entre autres, aux secteurs des pâtes et papier. Quant aux secteurs de l'aéronautique et des télécommunications, les groupes de travail créés n'ont pas pu répondre aux espoirs des deux partenaires[31].

3. Dans le domaine de *l'investissement,* certaines politiques et stratégies européennes d'investissement ne furent pas toujours orientées dans le sens souhaité par le Canada (place importante, dans certaines périodes, de l'investissement indirect et de celui dans le secteur des services; préférence, dans certains cas, pour des acquisitions européennes d'entreprises (au Canada) sous contrôle canadien plutôt qu'étranger; etc.[32]; par ailleurs, l'AEIE/FIRA n'a pas été un instrument favorisant l'inves-tissement européen; l'attrait, enfin, des États-Unis comme espace éco-nomique d'investissement européen (dû, entre autres, aux politiques américaines de taux d'intérêt), combiné aux faiblesses de la structure de l'économie canadienne ainsi qu'à la chute des prix du pétrole, n'a pas aidé au développement des flux d'investissements escomptés.

4. Dans le domaine des *acteurs,* la firme multinationale, canadienne ou filiale américaine, souvent enfermée dans une structure nord-américaine de division internationale du travail, ne s'est pas suffisamment ouverte vers l'Europe communautaire. Les petites et moyennes entreprises, par ailleurs, n'ont pas été assez conscientisées, ni pu manifester assez d'«entrepreneurship»[33] pour une présence plus active en Europe, même si (comme d'ailleurs certaines grandes firmes) elles se sont insérées au processus de socialisation (information, missions, etc.) offert par les pouvoirs publics dans le cadre de la promotion des objectifs de l'accord de 1976.

5. Quant à la *consultation* entre les deux parties et aux *mécanismes* de l'accord-cadre, il s'agit là d'un schéma qui permet le maintien d'un dialogue continu. Cela dit, certaines critiques, à propos du caractère limité des résultats de ce cadre de dialogue, ont été formulées, portant, entre autres, sur la lourdeur du processus ou la participation limitée de certaines provinces, et nuancent ainsi l'évaluation positive. En effet, le niveau d'information assez bas sur l'accord-cadre au sein des élites gouvernementales et socio-économiques de la plupart des provinces, la concertation fédérale-provinciale insuffisante en matière de participation aux mécanismes et travaux de l'accord-cadre, les ressources limitées affectées par certaines provinces (en dehors de l'Ontario et du Québec, participants actifs des mécanismes de l'accord-cadre) à la «machinerie» de l'accord, limitent les possibilités de fonctionnement réussi de ce cadre de coopération institutionnalisée Canada-communautés européennes[34].

La question de l'évaluation critique du processus de coopération Canada-communautés européennes

Les difficultés d'une évaluation des réalisation de diversification vers les communautés européennes

Parmi les principales difficultés d'une telle évaluation, dont certaines sont d'ordre méthodologique, nous pouvons mentionner les suivantes:

a) l'imprécision de l'option de diversification lorsqu'il s'agit de cerner les dimensions quantitatives et qualitatives de l'affranchissement à obtenir et de la dépendance à accepter dans les relations canado-américaines (des interprétations d'objectifs «maximalistes» et «minimalistes» en ont découlé, avec des bilans tantôt négatifs et tantôt positifs, en fonction du contenu que l'on veut donner à la politique de diversification);

b) le caractère à long terme de l'option de diversification, qui permet d'atténuer la portée des critiques de ceux qui s'impatientent pour souligner l'échec de cette politique d'ouverture vers les communautés européennes;

c) la difficulté d'attribuer, de façon directe, à une intervention gouvernementale d'actualisation de la «troisième option» toutes les actions et tous les résultats en matière de diversification, l'établissement d'une causalité devenant, en effet, une tâche hasardeuse;

d) l'ampleur et la variété des politiques de «troisième option», qui consistent en un faisceau complexe de politiques internes et extérieures que l'on ne peut pas toujours classer facilement sous le signe de l'option de diversification;

e) l'incertitude quant aux motifs réels de la «troisième option» et à la volonté politique pour sa réalisation. Car, à côté des défenseurs des objectifs de l'option et de ceux qui s'y opposent, il y a tous ceux qui n'y voient pas une politique crédible de diversification, vu les ambiguïtés déjà évoquées de l'option, certaines motivations de politique interne, voire électoralistes, et l'idée d'un expédient face au nationalisme économique de certains milieux du Canada anglais et aux pressions protectionnistes des États-Unis.

Ceci dit à propos des paramètres limitatifs d'une telle évaluation, nous pouvons identifier, ci-après, plusieurs catégories de facteurs, ayant eu un impact restrictif sur cette relation de coopération Canada-communautés européennes.

Les facteurs restrictifs de la Coopération Canada-communautés européennes

1. Au *niveau interne*, on note plusieurs servitudes.

- La fragmentation politique et économique au Canada a empêché une politique cohérente de diversification et d'ouverture vers les communautés européennes qui soit appuyée sur une stratégie économique (commerciale, industrielle, technologique, etc.) cohérente et nationale. À ce propos, il y a la fragmentation au niveau fédéral, entre institutions fédérales (fragmentation horizontale ou fonctionnelle) et la fragmentation entre le gouvernement fédéral et les provinces (fragmentation verticale ou territoriale); il s'agit d'une fragmentation politique et administrative, vu les deux niveaux de gouvernement, et d'une fragmentation économique[35], due aux différences de structures économiques des diverses provinces et régions du Canada qui sous-tendent des politiques divergentes face à la question de la diversification et de l'«option Europe»[36].

  Au niveau de la fragmentation horizontale, on remarque que la troisième option étant, en majeure partie, identifiée comme une politique du ministère des Affaires extérieures, diverses autres institutions publiques (notamment l'ancien ministère de l'Industrie et du

Commerce) n'ont pas mis beaucoup d'ardeur à la tâche de diversification et d'ouverture vers l'Europe communautaire et n'ont pas suffisamment développé des politiques économiques d'appoint pour le succès de l'option[37].

Quant à la fragmentation verticale, il convient de mentionner que certaines des provinces ont été et restent moins tournées vers les communautés européennes, compte tenu de facteurs géographiques, culturels et économiques. Aussi, elles ne s'attellent pas toutes à l'œuvre de diversification avec le même degré de motivation et d'efficacité.

- Le débat constitutionnel canadien a détourné l'attention des gouvernants de certains processus d'innovation en politique étrangère, tels que celui du rapprochement avec les communautés.
- Les élites politiques[38] et économiques canadiennes n'ont pas toujours voulu, pour des raisons structurelles, idéologiques ou perceptuelles[39], se consacrer systématiquement à des tâches de coopération avec les communautés européennes.
- Le nationalisme économique des divers segments de l'opinion publique canadienne a régressé, surtout à partir de la seconde moitié des années 70, la crise socio-économique y contribuant grandement[40]. Dès lors, la philosophie de contrepoids communautaire a subi un recul certain.
- La crise socio-économique au Canada a découragé le dynamisme d'un «entrepreneurship» et d'un «marketing» innovateurs à la recherche de nouveaux marchés en Europe, la voie continentaliste des relations canado-américaines déjà tracée apparaissant, dès lors, plus facile que les bouleversements de réorientations diversifiées vers les communautés (ceci surtout au niveau des PME)[41]. À cela s'ajoute la compétitivité limitée de nos produits finis sur les marchés européens.
- L'État canadien, aussi interventionniste qu'il soit, n'a pas su (volonté politique insuffisante, moyens économiques limités, carences institutionnelles et de politiques, etc.) aiguillonner suffisamment le secteur privé dans la voie de la diversification vers l'Europe communautaire, laissant, par là même, apparaître les limites du rôle de l'État dans la réorientation d'une politique économique internationale.

2. Sur le *plan régional* (Amérique du Nord), la dépendance structurelle de l'économie canadienne («interaction verticale» et «lien féodal», selon la terminologie de J. Galtung) et notamment la concentration de commerce, la propriété et le contrôle américains dans l'économie du Canada, un certain type de dépendance des filiales américaines au Canada de leur société mère, renforcée par la législation américaine en matière d'extraterritorialité, le continentalisme transrégional (relations entre États américains et provinces) sont autant d'hypothèques ayant compromis le succès de la diversification vers l'Europe communautaire.

Par ailleurs, le protectionnisme américain incite les gouvernements canadiens à des politiques continentalistes plutôt qu'à des contrepoids européens.

3. Au *niveau international global,* on note plusieurs obstacles.

- La crise économique, qui a également affecté les communautés européennes, a réduit le dynamisme et donc l'importance de ce partenaire du Canada.
- Dans le cas des communautés européennes, un certain désintéressement de Bruxelles (lié, entre autres, à un certain désenchantement devant les hésitations de nos politiques de diversification, des eurocrates de Bruxelles et de certains milieux économiques européens ainsi qu'à des préoccupations internes de construction européenne) et le maintien, au sein des communautés, de politiques économiques fragmentées dans plusieurs domaines (politiques industrielles, politiques énergétiques, etc.) ont diminué l'efficacité du cadre bimultilatéral de l'accord de 1976.
- Certaines stratégies européennes d'investissement au Canada, déjà mentionnées, n'ont pas favorisé nos politiques de diversification[42].
- Des «irritants» provenant de certaines politiques communautaires (comme ils proviennent, du reste, de certaines politiques canadiennes) sont à signaler.
- Le processus de libéralisation tarifaire, décidé au sein du GATT pour la présente décennie, nous conduit, en partie, vers le continentalisme de la deuxième option (renforcement des échanges avec les États-Unis et développement de projets continentalistes de libre-échange).

CONSIDÉRATIONS FINALES

Au terme de cette étude sur les origines, le contenu et le devenir de la relation Canada-communautés européennes, il convient, croyons-nous, de consacrer nos considérations finales à un effort de réflexion visant à appréhender les contours essentiels de l'avenir de la relation. Cet avenir sera sans doute sous-tendu par de nombreuses variables, dont celles ayant trait à l'évolution de l'orientation de la politique étrangère canadienne, aux développements dans le processus d'intégration européenne et aux mutations du système international.

1. Pour ce qui est du Canada et de sa politique étrangère, nous assistons, durant les années 80, à un processus de reconsidération de la réalité de nos relations extérieures, imposé par une multitude de facteurs, dont on espère relever ici les plus déterminants.

La politique de «troisième option», avec sa composante de diversification, a manifesté, durant la décennie 80, des signes d'essoufflement, plus marqués dans le cas des relations Canada-communautés européennes[43]: la dose insuffisante de volonté politique des gouvernents, le degré limité de coopération rencontré au niveau du secteur privé et aussi au sein de certaines élites provinciales, l'incapacité de concevoir et d'exécuter de façon cohérente un projet de restructuration industrielle, combinée aux pressions d'une crise socio-économique sérieuse, le dynamisme de reprise de l'économie américaine et une volonté, chez nos voisins, de s'attaquer de façon résolue (moyennant même des mesures protectionnistes) à leurs problèmes de commerce extérieur, les phénomènes de crise socio-économique au sein des communautés européennes et les difficultés dans la relance du processus d'intégration européenne, l'ascension, sur la scène économique internationale, de la région du Pacifique, sont des éléments explicatifs de ce besoin canadien de revoir le dossier de sa politique étrangère.

C'est ainsi que le gouvernement libéral a proposé, en 1983[44], une nouvelle politique commerciale pour les années 80, affirmant, dans ce que nous qualifions de «quatrième option», la compatibilité entre le continentalisme (deuxième option) et la diversification (troisième option), et faisant du premier le tremplin pour la seconde. Quant au gouvernement conservateur, il a accentué cette approche, en recherchant, plutôt qu'un libre-échange sectoriel, un libre-échange général[45].

2. Du côté des communautés européennes, les défis de réorientation, dans les années 80, sont également de taille, affectant ainsi la «disponibilité», vis-à-vis du Canada, des années 70: on y trouve notamment la nécessité de «digérer» les effets des deux derniers élargissements (vers la Grèce, d'abord, vers le Portugal et l'Espagne par la suite), le besoin de revoir en profondeur le dossier agricole, l'impératif du parachèvement du marché intérieur et de la construction de l'Europe technologique, les soucis des contentieux commerciaux avec les États-Unis et avec le Japon.

Dans cette perspective, la portée du rapprochement canado-européen «se relativise» et les communautés ne lui consacrent pas des énergies renouvelées. Ceci d'autant plus que les velléités «continentalistes» du gouvernement canadien laissent l'Europe quelque peu sceptique face à l'avenir de la politique canadienne de diversification.

3. Il y a enfin l'évolution du système international qui suggère aussi aux dirigeants canadiens un réexamen de leurs orientations extérieures.

La Nouvelle Division internationale du travail impose au Canada des restructurations économiques qu'il ne semble pas encore en mesure de réaliser (difficultés objectives, problèmes de volonté politique et d'efficacité de ses politiques économiques, etc.) par un recours à une politique industrielle, pancanadienne et cohérente. Aussi la tentation de faire appel à des politiques commerciales, telles que celles qui sous-tendent le projet de libre-échange canado-américain, est-elle grande. L'espoir de pouvoir se servir du libre-échange comme tremplin pour une diversification (diversification, toutefois, du système régional canado-américain plutôt que du système canadien) est également présent, tandis que, par ailleurs, les incertitudes européennes et l'endettement du tiers monde limitent le potentiel des partenaires canadiens de cette restructuration.

On pourrait donc conclure en disant que la diversification canadienne vers l'Europe communautaire et ses pays membres est un choix politique, culturel et économique, hypothéqué par la géographie et par l'économie, régionale et continentalisée, du sous-continent américain. Ceci amène les autorités canadiennes à réaliser qu'elles n'ont pas toujours les moyens de leurs politiques, surtout dans une période où l'État a du mal à déployer un dirigisme économique à l'intérieur et à s'insérer efficacement dans le processus de mutations du système international de cette fin de siècle.

Figure 1
Le commerce Canada – communautés européennes

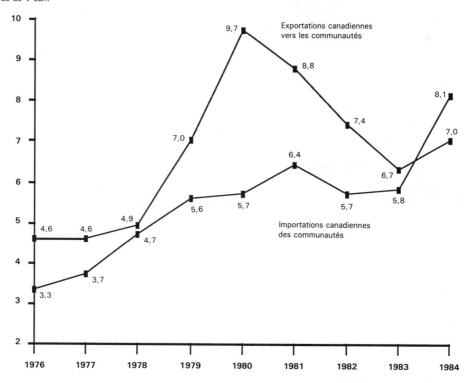

Milliards de $ can.

Source: *EUROPE,* magazine de la délégation de la Commission des communautés
européennes à Ottawa, printemps 1985 (par R. Buschardt Christensen).

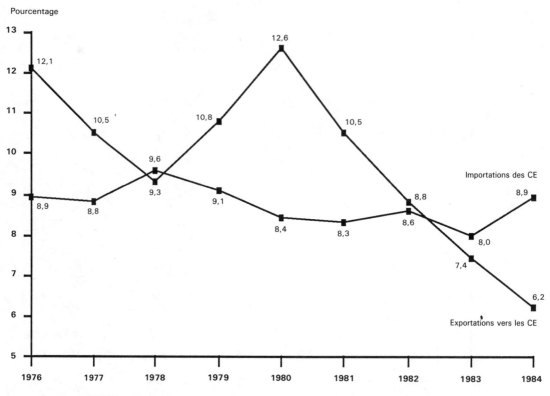

Figure 2
Le pourcentage du commerce avec les communautés européennes
dans le commerce extérieur du Canada

Pourcentage

13 ┬ 12,6

12,1

10,5   10,8   10,5

9,6   9,3

8,9   8,8   9,1   8,4   8,3   8,6   8,8   8,9

8,0   7,4   6,2

Importations des CE

Exportations vers les CE

1976   1977   1978   1979   1980   1981   1982   1983   1984

Source: *EUROPE, loc. cit.*

Figure 3
Le commerce extérieur du Canada

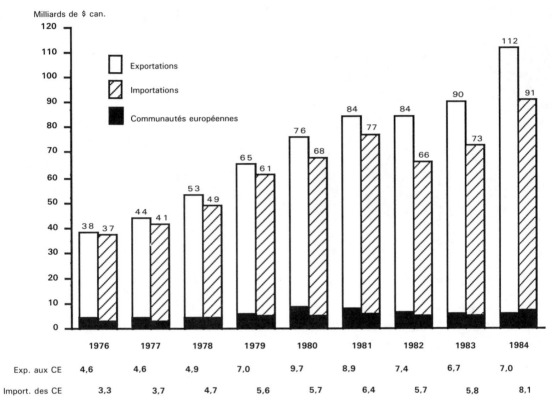

	1976	1977	1978	1979	1980	1981	1982	1983	1984
Exp. aux CE	4,6	4,6	4,9	7,0	9,7	8,9	7,4	6,7	7,0
Import. des CE	3,3	3,7	4,7	5,6	5,7	6,4	5,7	5,8	8,1

Source: *EUROPE, loc. cit.*

TABLEAU 1

Schématisation des principales composantes du processus canadien de diversification vers les communautés européennes

Environnement explicatif	Les acceptations de la diversification	Éléments d'une philosophie de politique étrangère, à la base de l'orientation de diversification vers les communautés européennes	Grandes finalités nationales (1970)*	Grands objectifs nationaux (1970)*	Option de politique reliée à la diversification (1972)
" environnement interne (politique, stratégico-militaire, économique, culturel) • environnement externe (politique, stratégico-militaire, économique, culturel) • régional international global • sous-continent américain	• philosophie de politique étrangère • orientation et option fondamentale de politique étrangère • politiques d'actualisation d'une option de diversification	• réalisme intériorisé • déterminisme économique • déterminisme socio-culturel et politique • vision d'un monde bi-multipolaire fonctionnel • fédéralisme diplomatique	• le Canada devra maintenir en toute sécurité son indépendance politique • le Canada et tous les Canadiens devront jouir d'une prospérité générale et croissante • tous les Canadiens devront trouver dans leur vie et dans leurs rapports avec les autres peuples des valeurs à conserver et à enrichir	• stimuler la croissance économique du Canada • promouvoir la justice sociale • enrichir la qualité de vie • préserver la souveraineté et l'indépendance du Canada • travailler à la paix et à la sécurité • maintenir l'harmonie du milieu naturel	• le Canada peut adopter une stratégie générale, à long terme, visant à développer et à raffermir son économie et les autres aspects de sa vie nationale et ce faisant, réduire la vulnérabilité actuelle du Canada (dite troisième option)**
			* Formulation du «livre blanc» de 1970	* Formulation du «livre blanc» de 1970	** Formulation du Document de 1972

Source: Department of External Affairs.

(*) Négligeable.

TABLEAU 2

De la troisième option à l'«option communautés européennes»

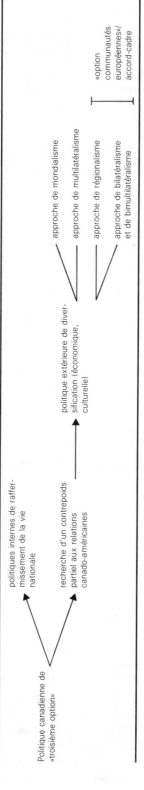

NOTES

1. Accord entre le Canada et les communautés européennes, signé à Ottawa le 6 juillet 1976 et entré en vigueur le 1er octobre 1976 (accord avec la Communauté économique européenne et avec l'EURATOM, suivi, en juillet toujours, d'un protocole de coopération avec la Communauté européenne du charbon et de l'acier). L'appellation «cadre» s'explique par le caractère général de l'accord et non pas son objectif de permettre, par sa conclusion, à l'État canadien et aux institutions communautaires de fournir aux divers secteurs des deux partenaires, et en particulier au secteur privé, l'encadrement nécessaire pour le développement d'autres initiatives et actions de coopération.

2. Voir sur ces aspects: E. Mahant, «Canada and the European Community: The First Twenty Years», dans *Journal of European Integration*, 1981, n° 3, p. 263-279; T. Cohn, «Canada and the European Economic Community's Common Agricultural Policy: The issue of Trade in Cheese», *Journal of European Integration*, 1978, n° 2, p. 125-142; L.A. Fisher, «Common Agricultural Policy of the EC: Its Impact on Canadian Agriculture», *Journal of European Integration*, 1979, n° 1, p. 29-50.

3. Accord-cadre de 1976, article III, 4.

4. Ch. Pentland, Linkage Politics: Canada's Contract and the Development of the European Community's External Relations, *International Journal*, 1977, n° 2, p. 207-232, relate avec pertinence et précision ces négociations. Voir aussi les développements et la rubrique «Chronologie» de l'ouvrage *Les relations extérieures de la communauté européenne: le cas particulier du Canada*, Montréal, CEDE, Actes des colloques du CEDE, 1976.

   Pour une bibliographie plus générale sur les relations Canada-communautés, nous jugeons utile de signaler au lecteur une bibliographie sélective sur le sujet, élaborée par D. Roseman (European Communities/Canada Relations: A Selected Bibliography, 1976-1981) et parue dans la *Revue d'intégration européenne*, 1981, n° 3, p. 327-334.

5. Parmi les termes utilisés à ce propos dans la littérature de langue anglaise comme synonymes de *contrepoids*, nous signalons les concepts de «partial counterweight», de «balancing the weight», de «countervailing influence». Voir, au sujet de cette conceptualisation: M.B. Dolan, «Western Europe as Counterweight: An Analysis of Canadian-European Foreign Policy Behaviour in the Post-War Era», dans B. Tomlin, ed., *Canada's Foreign Policy: Analysis and Trends*, Methuen, Toronto, 1978, surtout p. 19 et 27-29; H. Von Riekhoff, «The Third Option in Canadian Foreign Policy», in B. Tomlin, ed., *Ibidem*, p. 89.

6. Après une première approche de diversification «tous azimuts», c'est-à-dire mondialiste, s'intéressant à l'ensemble des régions et des États du système international (approche contenue dans le document dit de «troisième option», de 1972, M. Sharp (préface), «Relations canado-américaines: Choix pour l'avenir», *Perspectives internationales*, automne 1972), le Canada commença à identifier des régions et des partenaires cibles, dont les communautés européennes. Par ailleurs, l'accord-cadre de 1976 a établi un cadre institutionnel de relation à caractère bimultilatéral, le Canada entrant en dialogue bilatéral de coopération institutionnalisée avec une communauté d'États.

7. On peut parler (et ce fut le cas canadien) de diversification culturelle, politique, etc.

8. Pour une conceptualisation du terme de *diversification*, voir nos deux études: «Les données fondamentales du devenir de la politique étrangère canadienne», dans *Études internationales* (numéro spécial codirigé par A. Donneur et P. Soldatos), 1983, n° 1, p. 5-22, et notre chapitre «Quinze ans de politique étrangère canadienne», dans G. Gosselin (sous la dir. de), *La politique étrangère du Canada: approches bilatérale et régionale*, Québec, Université Laval et CQRI, 1984, p. 203-259.

9. Sur ces antécédents historiques et le jeu triangulaire d'équilibre du Canada, voir R. Tremblay, La politique commerciale et le développement du Canada, dans P. Painchaud, éd., *Le Canada et le Québec sur la scène internationale*, Québec, 1977, surtout p. 182-192. Cette étude nous a fourni de forts utiles éléments d'information sur le sujet. Sur les antécédents de la «troisième option», voir le mémoire de maîtrise de G. Beaulieu que nous avons dirigé sur *Les servitudes structurelles de la Troisième Option de la politique extérieure du Canada* (étude non publiée, Université de Montréal, 1981).

10. Nous dirigeons présentement un mémoire de maîtrise de P. Brisson portant, justement, sur la politique de diversification de Diefenbaker, politique qui a très peu retenu l'attention des spécialistes de la question.

11. Sur les idées de diversification de P.E. Trudeau, voir E. Mahant, *loc. cit.*, p. 269-270.

12. E. Mahant, *loc cit.*, p. 169-271, souligne cette «antériorité» (lancement, par P. E. Trudeau, de l'idée d'une politique étrangère canadienne de diversification déjà en 1968, et non pas en 1970).

13. «Relations canado-américaines», *loc cit.*, p. 3.

14. *Ibidem*.

15. Voir *supra*, note 6.

16. Discours prononcé à Winnipeg, le 23 janvier 1975, devant la section locale de l'Institut canadien des affaires internationales.

17. Sur cette évolution des attitudes et comportements canadiens à l'égard des communautés européennes, voir E. Mahant, *loc. cit.*, p. 263-279, ainsi que ses autres études afférentes, mentionnées dans la note n° 1 de son article. Voir aussi J. Lasvergnas-Gremy (en collaboration), *L'Europe vue du Canada* (résultats d'un sondage), Montréal, Centre de sondage et Centre d'études et de documentation européennes de l'Université de Montréal, 1976.

18. Le président Nixon avait à l'époque souligné, dans un discours devant la Chambre des communes, qu'«aucun pays qui se respecte ne peut ou ne devrait adopter pour postulat qu'il sera toujours économiquement tributaire d'une autre nation» (cité dans «Relations canado-américaines: Choix pour l'avenir», *loc. cit.*, p. 22).

19. Ce concept néo-fonctionnaliste (voir J.S. Nye, *Peace in Parts: Integration and Conflict in Regional Organization*, Boston, Little, Brown and Company, 1971, p. 91-92, et sa référence au travail de Ph. Schmitter, sur cette même question, *Ibidem*, p. 93, note 73) a été repris, développé et appliqué au cas des relations extérieures des communautés européennes dans le contexte transatlantique par Ch. Pentland, «L'évolution de la politique étrangère de la communauté européenne: le contexte transatlantique», *Études internationales,* numéro spécial (sous la dir. de P. Soldatos) sur les relations extérieures des communautés européennes, 1978, n° 1, surtout p. 111-118.

20. Sur cet objectif de la «troisième option», peu souligné dans la littérature spécialisée, voir l'étude de R. Hudon, *Nationalisme et économie mondiale: politiques des années soixante-dix au Canada*, communication à la Conférence annuelle de l'Association d'études politiques des provinces atlantiques, Moncton, octobre 1981 (étude se référant à l'analyse plus vaste d'une thèse de doctorat de l'auteur). Des éléments de cette interprétation sont repris dans la contribution de R. Hudon dans G. Gosselin (sous la dir. de), *op. cit.*

21. Nous nous reportons ici à la décision de réduire les forces canadiennes stationnées en Europe.

22. Pour cette tranche événementielle sur les contacts canado-européens durant cette période, voir le tableau de synthèse de E. Mahant, *loc cit.* p. 276-277, et les informations additionnelles du même texte.

23. Sur ces négociations, voir Ch. Pentland, Linkage Politics, *loc cit.* (voir aussi *supra*, note 4).

24. Voir sur les positions des États membres, Ch. Pentland, *loc. cit.* surtout p. 217-231.

25. Voir *supra*, note 3.

26. Sur ces complémentarités, voir M. Torrelli et K. Valaskakis, «Le Canada et la communauté économique européenne», dans P. Painchaud, dir., *Le Canada et le Québec sur la scène internationale, op. cit.*, surtout p. 354-359.

27. Sur ces accords avec l'EURATOM, voir R. Boardman, «Canadian Resources and the Contractual Link: The Case of Uranium», *Journal of European Integration,* 1981, n° 3, p. 299-325; J.W. Galbraith, «Les relations entre le Canada et l'EURATOM», *Ibidem,* 1981, n° 1, p. 53-78.

28. Pour un bilan plus circonstancié de ces réalisations, voir l'ouvrage dont nous sommes le coauteur, R. Boardman *et al., L'Accord-cadre Canada-communautés européennes/The Canada-European Communities Framework Agreement*, Montréal, Conseil canadien des affaires européennes, 1984.

29. En ce sens, voir R. Boardman *et al., op. cit.,* p. 19.

30. Pour plus de détails sur ce volet commercial, voir R. Boardman *et al., op. cit.,* p. 19-21.

31. Pour plus de détails sur le fonctionnement et les travaux de ces groupes ainsi que sur leur impact en matière de coopération industrielle, voir R. Boardman *et al., op. cit.,* p. 21-23.

32. Voir à ce sujet l'étude de M. Azoulay, *L'Accord-cadre et la coopération économique entre le Canada et les communautés européennes: évaluation des résultats,* Montréal, CEDE, note de recherche n° 3, 1979, p. 27-48.

33. Sur cet aspect d'«entrepreneurship» et sur les potentialités plus générales d'une coopération économique Canada-communautés européennes, voir K. Valaskakis, «L'Option Europe: une vue du long terme», *L'Actualité économique,* oct.-déc. 1976, p. 539-554.

34. Sur le point de vue des provinces face à l'accord-cadre et à ses mécanismes de coopération, voir R. Boardman *et al., op. cit.,* p. 27-52 et les recommandations de réforme formulées aux p. 61-65.

35. Sur cette question, voir J. Bérard, *Continentalisme et fragmentation économique au Canada*, mémoire de maîtrise, Département de science politique, Université de Montréal, 1983 (sous notre direction).

36. Sur cette question de fragmentation, voir parmi nos diverses études: notre article dans *Études internationales, loc. cit. (supra,* note 8); notre chapitre sur la fragmentation dans des États fédéraux, «The Explanatory Framework», dans H. Michelmann and P. Soldatos, *Federalism and International Relations: The Role of Subnational Units*, Oxford, Oxford University Press.

37. Sur les attitudes des divers secteurs de l'appareil gouvernemental et bureaucratique vis-à-vis de la politique de «troisième option», voir R.B. Byers *et al.*, «The Canadian International Image Study», dans *International Journal*, 1977, n° 3.

38. Voir notamment R.B. Byers *et al., loc. cit.*

39. Sur les attitudes de ces élites, voir G. Beaulieu, *op. cit.*, surtout p. 159 et s. Voir aussi Chambre de commerce du Canada, *Mémoire sur les investissements étrangers dans le contexte d'une stratégie industrielle pour le Canada*, 1973, ainsi que les témoignages d'hommes d'affaires devant le Comité sénatorial permanent des affaires étrangères chargé de l'étude des relations Canada-États-Unis (voir les conclusions de ses travaux publiées dans les volumes I-1975, II-1978 et III-1982).

40. Voir notamment le sondage CROP de mai 1982, dont certaines données sont citées par L. Bissonnette, *La vocation tardive: perception des milieux politiques québécois à l'égard des États-Unis*, communication à un colloque du CQRI et de la «World Peace Foundation», Harvard University, septembre 1982.

41. Et pourtant, on pourrait remplacer une partie significative de nos importations de produits industriels en provenance des États-Unis par des produits européens de même niveau technologique. Voir à ce propos J.-E. Denis et E. Lindekens, «Perspectives de coopération industrielle dans le contexte de l'Accord-cadre entre le Canada et les communautés euro-péennes», *Revue d'intégration européenne*, 1978, n° 2, p. 107-124.

42. Sur ces stratégies, voir M. Azoulay, «L'Accord-cadre et les nouvelles orientations des investissements des communautés européennes au Canada», *Revue d'intégration européenne*, 1980, n° 2.

43. La diversification vers le Japon a permis, par exemple, pour la seule année 1984, une augmentation de nos exportations (en dollars canadiens) de 19 %; par ailleurs, certains résultats positifs de diversification commerciale et d'investissement sont aussi à signaler dans nos relations avec l'Asie. Ceci dit, il s'agit d'une diversification qui ne réussit pas à modifier le profil de notre structure de commerce extérieur, dans la mesure, par exemple, où, pour la même année 1984, les exportations canadiennes vers les États-Unis ont augmenté (en dollars canadiens et par rapport à l'année 1983) de plus de 28 %.

44. Voir le document gouvernemental *La politique commerciale du Canada pour les années 80*, Ottawa, 1983.

45. Sur cette évolution de la politique extérieure canadienne (dans une voie continentaliste), voir nos études: «Free Trade Continentalism in Canada-US Relations: Theorization on the Political Dimensions and Outline of an Institutional Framework», dans J.J. Quinn (ed.), *The International Legal Environment*, Toronto, University of Toronto Press, 1986 (il s'agit du vol. 52 des études publiées dans le cadre des travaux de recherche de la Commission royale sur l'Union économique et les perspectives de développement du Canada), p. 115-191; *Continentalism Revisited*, étude présentée à un séminaire de l'*University Consortium for Research on North America*, Harvard University, mars 1985.

13

Canada's Relations with the USSR and Eastern Europe

Adam Bromke
McMaster University

Canadian-Soviet relations acquired mutual significance only in the 1940s. In the interwar period, Canada's foreign policy independent of Britain was but nascent, while the USSR struggled with internal problems, emerging as a world power only during World War II. But with the bipolarization of international politics between the United States and the Soviet Union in the postwar years, relations with Moscow became one of Ottawa's major concerns. And with the dawn of the nuclear age, and the rise of long-range bombers and intercontinental missiles, Canada – due to its strategic location between the two superpowers – found itself at the very centre of global confrontation.

EARLY ENCOUNTERS[1]

The first direct contacts between Canadian and Russian governments date back to World War I. These were, however, mainly confined to the purchases in Canada of war materiel for Russia and ended in 1922 when the Western powers finally withdrew recognition from the representatives of the Imperial Government. In 1918-1919, small contingents of Canadian troops participated in the Allied intervention in Northern Russia and in Siberia. In the early 1920s, the Canadians offered modest aid to the famine-stricken Russian population, and particularly to the children.

In the interwar period, Canada paid little attention to the Soviet Union. Russia was far away and inward-looking – striving to recover from the devastating effects of World War I and the civil war, and then engaged in difficult internal industrialization. There was no sizeable Russian community in Canada; and most of Canadian-Ukrainians originated from Eastern Galicia, which had been part of Austria before being made part of Poland after World War I. Ottawa's attitude towards the USSR remained under strong London influence and its diplomatic relations with Moscow were basically handled through the British Foreign Office. As Canada's external relations gradually emerged from Britain's guardianship, however, it began increasingly to coordinate its policies – in the spirit of North American continentalism – with those of the United States.

Two issues, one negative and one positive, came to dominate Canada's bilateral relations with the Soviet Union. On the one hand the great majority of

Canadians were opposed to the Bolsheviks' ideology and their efforts to promote proletarian revolutions throughout the world; only among small groups at the extreme left did communism find some supporters. The French Canadians, still strongly under the influence of a conservative Catholic church, were alienated by the Bolsheviks' repudiation of religion: while in English-speaking Canada the industrialists, especially after the Winnipeg General Strike in 1919, were afraid of the communists' fomenting of labour unrest. The «Red Scare» was probably exaggerated, but close ties between the Communist Party of Canada (formed in 1921) and the Comintern did little to dispel it. The party never commanded much influence in the country, though during the depression years it did its best to exploit dissatisfaction among the workers. On the other hand, however, Canada was interested in developing trade relations with the USSR. The potentially vast Soviet market attested all their opposition to communism notwithstanding, to many Canadian industralists.

Throughout the 1920s and even into the early 1930s, thus, Canada's policy towards the Soviet Union oscillated between the two above tendencies. Decisions were often made on an *ad hoc* basis – reflecting various crosscurrents of external and domestic pressures – without being integrated into any systematic policy framework. In 1921, taking note of an Anglo-Soviet Trade agreement, Canada extended *de facto* recognition to the Soviet regime and in 1924, again following the British example, made it *de jure.* A Soviet trade mission was established in Montréal and Canadian trade representatives were attached to the British mission in Moscow. In 1927, however, once more in accordance to a British lead, diplomatic relations were abruptly broken off. In 1931, in response to alleged dumping practices by the USSR, Canada imposed an embargo on Soviet goods. The Soviet Union reciprocated and a small-scale economic war between the two countries ensued.

With Hitler's rise in Germany in 1933, a broader community of interests between the two countries emerged for the first time. It coincided, moreover, with the long-delayed establishment of diplomatic relations between the USSR and the USA. In 1934, Canada joined the other countries in inviting the Soviet Union into the League of Nations. In the summer of 1936, the Canadian Minister of Trade visited Russia and in the fall, commercial relations between the two countries were restored. Yet, until World War II trade between them remained insignificant. The USSR's signing of a non-aggression treaty with Nazi Germany in August 1939 and their joint military action against Poland the next month, followed by the Soviet attack against Finland in November, led to a new deterioration in Canadian-Soviet relations[2]. The Soviet Union was classified among Canada's wartime enemies and all trade with it came to a halt. The Communist Party of Canada, which supported the Molotov-Ribbentrop Pact, was formally banned in May 1940 as threatening to the country's war effort.

Hitler's attack in June 1941, however, pushed the USSR into an alliance with the Western democracies, and Canadian-Soviet relations underwent a major improvement. In February 1942 an agreement to exchange diplomatic representatives was signed in London and in the same month the Soviet consulate was opened in Halifax. In October, a Soviet legation was established in Ottawa, and in March 1943, a Canadian representative, Dana L. Wilgress, arrived in Kuibyshev (to which the diplomatic corps had been temporarily evacuated from still-threatened Moscow). The next year, the two legations were raised to the rank of embassies.

During the war Canada assisted the USSR both directly and by extending credits. In 1942, the Canadian icebreaker *C.G.S. Montcalm* was donated to the Soviets. Under the Mutual Aid arrangements, a total of $159 million of Canadian arms and war provisions was supplied to the Soviet Union. The attitudes of Canadians towards the USSR also underwent a major change. The struggle of the Red Army and of the Soviet people against the German invaders was widely praised by the Canadian mass media. In 1941, 91 % of Canadians favoured aid to the Soviet Union. In 1942, the private Canadian Aid to Russia Fund was started and raised $14 million before the war was over. Canadian cities were «twinned» with Soviet ones – for example, Toronto with Stalingrad. The main groups remaining uneasy about the improvement in Canadian-Soviet relations were the immigrants from Eastern Europe, increasingly apprehensive about Soviet designs to introduce communism in their native lands.

Immediately after the end of the war, however, relations between Canada and the Soviet Union once again plunged into eclipse. In September 1945, Igor Gouzenko, a cypher clerk at the Soviet Embassy in Ottawa, revealed the existence of an extensive Soviet espionage network in Canada. The Canadian public was angered by the USSR's evident duplicity in spying inside a country from which it was receiving substantial sympathy and aid. Prime Minister Mackenzie King was stunned, he could not believe that the Soviet Union would do something like this, and he even contemplated going to Moscow to clear the matter personally with Stalin; but he was wisely advised against it. In February 1946, fourteen persons were arrested and formally charged with spying for the USSR. The affair was serious: both ambassadors were withdrawn and replaced by chargés. Canadian-Soviet relations, thus, were the first to be chilled by that political climate soon to be know as the Cold War.

THE COLD WAR

It was during the late stages of World War II – when it became apparent that after the defeat of Germany and Japan the USSR would emerge as a major world power – that the Canadians made a serious intellectual effort to look into the future of relations between the two countries. An important role in shaping the opinions of the Canadian Government in this regard was played by the reports sent from the USSR by Dana L. Wilgress, and later on by his two successors: John W. Holmes and Robert A.D. Ford. Wilgress was a Canadian diplomat with long experience in Soviet affairs. He had been a Canadian Trade Commissioner in Vladisvostok in 1919, then a Canadian Trade Representative in Moscow in the 1920s, and he accompanied the Trade Minister to the USSR in 1936. His first-hand knowledge of the country made him a perceptive observer of the Soviet scene. Even after his return home in 1947 he continued to exert an important influence over the course of Canadian-Soviet relations.

In his reports, Wilgress revealed a considerable capacity for *Realpolitik*. He pointed out that under Stalin, communism was becoming increasingly integrated with the traditional Russian nationalism, but he saw in this a source of strength rather than of weakness for the system. He anticipated no major changes in the USSR and certainly no early collapse of communism. Wilgress was under no illusion as to Soviet expansionist tendencies, particularly in Eastern Europe, which he regarded as virtually lost to the West. At the same time he did not believe that in pursuing its expansionist goals the USSR would risk a war with the Western powers. He warned against adopting shallow stereotypes in dealing with Moscow. «The Western world, he wrote in 1945, is living in dread that the Soviet Union is out to spread communism throughout the world. Do they ever stop to think that the Soviet Union is also living in dread that the Western world is out to restore capitalism in the Soviet Union? If we could succeed in removing these two obsessions, cooperation between the Soviet Union and the Western world would become operative without the friction now so obvious[3].» To achieve this he advocated for the West neither appeasement nor aggravation of conflict, but rather a middle course: a firm, but flexible stand vis-à-vis the USSR. Wilgress, thus, was an early proponent of what 20 years later became NATO's official «two-track» doctrine.

In 1947, another prominent Canadian diplomat, Escott M. Reid, prepared a comprehensive report on the future of American-Soviet relations and their implications for Canada. Like Wilgress, Reid did not believe that a war with the USSR was imminent, but he advocated that in order to protect its position the West had to maintain its strength. Particularly interesting were Reid's recommendations for Canada in such a context. He, of course, assumed that Canada would be a part of the Western alliance and that the United States would play a key role in it. Canada's influence in world affairs then would be primarily exerted, he argued, through its participation in the intra-alliance councils. The effectiveness of his policy would depend on the intensity of East-West confrontation. The more intense the conflict the greater would be Ottawa's dependence on Washington; and, conversely, with any reduction of East-West tensions Canada's international role would be enhanced. In essence, Reid suggested that Canada's main target should be to moderate the United States' policy towards the Soviet Union. «If we play our cards right, he wrote, we can exert an influence in Washington out of proportion to the relative importance of our strength... The game would be difficult, the issues would be delicate, but with skill we can play it successfully[4].»

The Canadian diplomats tried to put Wilgress' and Reid's recommendations into practice. Even at the founding United Nations' conference in San Francisco in the spring of 1945, Pearson attempted to mitigate American-Soviet confrontation, though with little success. Soon however the Gouzenko affair poisoned Canadian-Soviet relations. Wilgress and his successors found the climate in Moscow distinctly hostile, so much so that in 1949 the possibility of actually closing the Canadian mission was contemplated. Meanwhile, the Cold War between the United States and the Soviet Union grew in intensity. Moscow proceeded with systematic communization of Eastern Europe and in 1947, Washington responded with the policy of containment of the USSR. Early in 1948 a communist coup in Czechoslovakia took place, followed by the Soviet blockade of West Berlin. In April 1949, NATO was formed.

Entry into the Atlantic alliance was a natural thing for Canada. It fitted into the ideological predilections of the overwhelming majority of the Canadians by now aggravated by the Gouzenko affair. It provided an effective defensive shield not only over North America, but also for Western Europe, whose freedom Canadians traditionally regarded as essential to their security. It also enabled Canada to preserve close bonds with Britain, France and, above all, the United States. Multiple contacts between Ottawa and Washington developed during the war and now strengthened by the common concern over the defence of the North American continent, placed Canada in a special relationship with the United States. In the late 1940s and still during the 1950s, Canada's influence upon its Southern neighbour did indeed exceed the country's actual strength. With Western Europe and Japan still recovering from war wounds, Canada – economically and even militarily – was one of the major United States' allies. During the climax of the Cold War, however, there were fewer opportunities for Canada to pursue its other foreign policy goal, namely, to moderate East-West tensions. In a world tightly polarized between the two antagonistic superpowers there was little room for middle-power diplomacy. The St. Laurent Government, thus, had little choice but to concentrate upon strengthening the Western alliance. Canada willingly did so, both diplomatically and militarily; it also made a significant contribution to the conduct of the Korean War.

The death of Stalin in 1953 led to easing the Cold War. The conflict in Korea was terminated and the East-West diplomatic dialogue was resumed, culminating in the Geneva summit in 1955. A memorandum on the ramifications of the Geneva meeting for Canada was prepared by the Department of External Affairs. It basically followed the Wilgress-Reid line of reasoning: «[...] if the Americans believe a real danger of attack [from the USSR] across Canada remains, there will be pressure on us to accept the United States bases and troops in the North and *ipso facto* pressure on our sovereignty. If, therefore, one of our aims is to retain and strengthen our independence of the United States, it follows that we can best accomplish this in a world where the danger of war is diminished. Thus the two basic Canadian aims – security vis-à-vis the USSR, and the maintenance of our national independence – coincide at the present time in a policy to exploit the present Soviet willingness to establish more peaceful and normal relations between the two power blocs[5].»

The new international climate, then, offered opportunities for improvement of Canada's relations with the USSR. In 1953, a Soviet ambassador arrived in Ottawa and the next year, a Canadian ambassador was again sent to Moscow. Soon contacts at the ministerial level were established: in July 1955, the Canadian Fisheries' Minister attended a meeting of the International Whaling Commission in Moscow and in August, the acting Soviet Minister of Agriculture toured Canada. In October, the Secretary of State for Canadian External Affairs, Lester B. Pearson, visited Moscow – the first among NATO's foreign ministers to do so. After meeting with Kaganovich in Moscow he held talks with Khrushchev and Bulganin in the Crimea. An important result of Pearson's trip was the conclusion in January 1956 of a three-year Canadian-Soviet agreement under which the two countries accorded each other «Most Favoured Nation» status and the USSR agreed to purchase $60 to $75 million worth of wheat annually. But the Soviet invasion of Hungary later on in the year led to renewed East-West tensions. Canada condemned the USSR's action and received some 20 000 Hungarian refugees.

With Khrushchev's visit to the United States in 1959 the momentum in East-West relations once more picked up, although it was still to be interrupted by recurring crises – the U-2 incident, a new flare-up in Berlin, and the Cuban missile confrontation. Meanwhile, the Liberal Government in Canada was replaced in 1957 by a Progressive Conservative once. The new Prime Minister, John G. Diefenbaker, was more strongly motivated in opposing communism than his predecessors and he also paid more attention to cultivating the votes of Canadians of Eastern European background. In December 1960 in the UN General Assembly, he strongly denounced violations of human rights in the USSR and the Soviet domination over Eastern Europe. Yet, despite all his rhetoric, Canadian-Soviet relations continued to be expanded in the Diefenbaker years. In 1960 and again in 1963, new trade agreements were signed, the latter providing for the Soviet purchase of $500 million worth of grain in Canada. In 1959 an exchange agreement between the National Research Council and the Soviet Academy of Sciences was concluded.

With the 1960s, Ottawa's influence in Washington declined markedly. As Western Europe and Japan recovered from war ruin (and the European Common Market arose), the United States paid more attention to them, and advent of intercontinental ballistic missiles meant joint American-Canadian defence of the North against Soviet bombers became less important. Also, as the years went by, the special relationship between the two countries largely wore off. Close personal contacts established during the war between government officials still continued in the St. Laurent-Eisenhower days; but then – as younger people came to the fore in both countries – they largely lapsed. Relations between the Diefenbaker and the Kennedy governments were visibly strained. And after the return to power in Canada of the Liberals under Pearson's leadership in 1963, the United States involvement in Vietnam had a further dampening effect upon Canadian-American relations. In fact, both the Government in Ottawa and a large segment of the Canadian population, although their criticism was tempered by an awareness of the Johnson administration's extreme sensitivity over this issue, were openly critical of the American action.

In contrast, in the mid-1960s, Canadian-Soviet bilateral relations continued to expand. In July 1966, Soviet First Deputy Premier Dimitry Poliansky visited Canada; and in November Canadian External Affairs' Secretary Paul Martin went to the USSR. One result of his visit was the opening of the Soviet consulate in Montréal. In the same year the trade pact was renewed and substantial Soviet purchases of Canadian grain continued. An air transport agreement providing for regular service between Moscow and Montréal was concluded. Cooperation in the exploration of the North was launched. And in 1964, an exchange agreement between the University of Toronto and Moscow State University was signed.

On a broader international plan Canada persisted in its efforts to mitigate East-West tensions. In his first speech to NATO as Prime Minister, Pearson urged Canada's allies to avoid confrontationist policies and instead to try «[...] to solve political problems, one by one, stage by stage, if not on the basis of confidence and cooperation, at least on that of mutual toleration based on a common interest in survival[6].» Canada welcomed the Harmel Report of 1967 which committed NATO to a «two-track» course (so reminiscent of the Wilgress' recommendations) by simultaneously preserving the Alliance's strength and seeking reduction of tensions with the Communist bloc. During the exchanges between Poliansky and Martin, both governments confirmed their desire to improve the political climate in Europe. The Warsaw Pact invasion of Czechoslovakia in 1968, however, once again interrupted the progress of East-West détente. Canada condemned the communist states' action and in the following years admitted many refugees from Czechoslovakia.

THE RISE OF DÉTENTE

When the Czechoslovak crisis receded into history, Canadian-Soviet relations once more picked up momentum to reach, in the first half of the 1970s, a hitherto unprecendented level of cooperation. Various factors contributed to this development. First of all, the new expansion of relations between Ottawa and Moscow was a part of a general movement in East-West relations from the Cold War to détente. Above all, American-Soviet relations were undergoing substantial improvement. In 1969, negotiations between the two superpowers to restrict nuclear race were started, resulting in the 1972 SALT I agreement. In 1972-1974, American and Soviet leaders regularly exchanged visits which were marked not only by a spirit of cooperation, but even by some cordiality. Simultaneously West Germany launched its *Ostpolitik,* expanding relations with the USSR and the Eastern European countries in a move that also helped to defuse the perennial Berlin issue. In 1969, the communist states put forward a proposal to hold a Conference on Security and Cooperation in Europe with both the United States and Canada as full-fledged participants. The Conference began in 1973, culminating in the signing of the Final Act in Helsinki in July 1975. In 1973, the Mutual Balanced Force Reductions Talks – aimed to reduce the level of conventional forces in Central Europe – started in Vienna, with Canada as one of the participants on the Western side.

In 1968, Pearson resigned and Pierre Elliot Trudeau took over as the new Prime Minister. Trudeau was acutely aware of Canada's diminishing role in the changing postwar world. He wanted to reduce some Canadian commitments abroad, including those to NATO, and instead to focus on those aspects of external relations which were of a direct benefit, especially in trade, to the country. In contrast to the St. Laurent-Pearson internationalist approach, Trudeau's foreign policy was distincly more nationalistic[7]. This, however, coincided with similar trends south of the border. The «Nixon doctrine», unveiled in 1969, stressed the need to reduce some of the United States' global commitments and intended to pass some of these burdens over to its allies. The objectives of the two countries, thus, were largely incompatible. Washington's «economic shocks» of 1971 galvanized Ottawa into responding with the «Third Option» in 1973, aimed at reducing Canada's economic dependence on the United States by expanding its trade with other countries. The climate of Canadian-American relations deteriorated markedly.

In the new international context, some of Trudeau's critics on the extreme right charged that Canada's efforts to improve relations with the USSR amounted to a movement away from the alliance with the United States. There was no substance to those allegations. The hierarchy of Canadian objectives remained basically unchanged. The Trudeau Government, like all its predecessors, was acutely aware that the country's security is best served by a close alignment with its Southern neighbour, and it was under no illusion that expanded trade with the Soviet Union could ever replace its intimate economic ties with the United States. If anything, Ottawa still adhered to Reid's prescription that good relations with Washington provided additional leverage in Moscow. Canada's reduction of its NATO contingent was largely symbolic and its representatives in the intra-allied councils, in fact, continued to be as active as ever. In the more propitious international climate, they not only worked to strengthen the Atlantic alliance, but also seized the opportunity to advance East-West détente. Canada's traditional «two-track» policy underwent no essential change in the Trudeau years.

In the 1970s, Canadian-Soviet relations were expanded very considerably. In October 1969, Soviet Foreign Minister Andrei Gromyko visited Ottawa to hold talks on both bilateral and multilateral problems. In May 1971, Prime Minister Trudeau went for an eleven-day official visit to the USSR. On that occasion the Protocol on

Consultations was signed, providing for regular exchange of opinions on matters of mutual concern to the two governments. Summing up his trip, Trudeau restated the traditional Canadian attitude towards the USSR: «I harbour no naive belief, he said, that as a result of this protocol our two countries will find themselves suddenly in a relationship which will reflect nothing but sweetness and tender feelings. [...] there remain many fundamental differences between us: differences relating to deep-seated concerns springing from historic, geographic, ideological, economic, social and military factors. But surely, the only way to resolve these differences and eliminate these concerns is by increased contact and effort at understanding[8].»

In October 1971, Soviet Premier Alexei Kosygin made a return visit to Ottawa. On that occasion the Canada-USSR Exchange Agreement was signed. It established a mixed commission to meet every two years «to promote scientific technical, cultural, academic and sports exchanges». In the remainder of the 1970s, exchanges between the two countries at a ministerial level were also frequent. In 1972 and again in 1975, the Soviet First Deputy Premier visited Canada. In 1973, Canadian External Affairs Secretary Mitchell W. Sharp went to Moscow and in 1975 Gromyko again came to Ottawa. In 1972 the trade agreement was renewed for five years, followed by a long-term agreement which established a Mixed Commission to oversee the progress of economic and scientific cooperation. Substantial Soviet purchases of Canadian grain continued. In December 1975, a Joint Fisheries Consultative Committee was established and by 1977, the thorny issue of Soviet fishing in Canadian waters was satisfactorily resolved.

There was also considerable progress in the scientific and cultural realms. 1971 saw the signing of an Agreement on Cooperation in the Industrial Application of Science and Technology. Cooperation in the exploration of Northern territories also proceeded apace. In 1972, a Canadian-Soviet hockey series was launched, and in the next year a general agreement to promote exchanges in sports was concluded. In 1974, cooperation between the Canadian Broadcasting Corporation and the Soviet State Committee for Broadcasting and Television was established. In 1973, the Stratford Theatre and the NCA Orchestra performed in the USSR and in 1977, some Group of Seven's paintings were displayed at the Hermitage in Leningrad. Meanwhile, academic exchanges continued – both under the umbrella of a general agreement and between individual universities. At the First World Congress for Soviet and East European Studies, held in Banff in 1974, the head of the Soviet delegation, Academician A.L. Narochnitsky, symbolically sat next to the Secretary of State for External Affairs, Allan MacEachen.

Canadian-Soviet cooperation extended to various international forums. The two foreign ministers held regular talks at the UN General Assembly sessions in New York as well as at the CSCE Conference in Helsinki. At the CSCE negotiations in Geneva, Canada and Denmark were the NATO caucus members given special responsibility for promoting family reunification. In response to the urgings of the Canadians of Eastern European background, this matter was pressed vigorously by the Canadian delegates. Many of the Canadian proposals became part of the Final Act. The Canadian representatives also contributed to the elaboration of the Confidence Building Measures. The Canadians' ability to find suitable compromises, acceptable to all, won praise from the Soviet side[9].

THE DECLINE OF DÉTENTE

By the second half of the 1970s, East-West détente declined markedly. The SALT II negotiations dragged on and the MBFR talks became stalemated. Meanwhile, the Soviet Union pressed on with armaments – notably by introducing new, more powerful intercontinental missiles and the medium-range SS-20s in Europe. The expansion of its navy and air force enhanced the USSR's capability to project its power into distant parts of the world. Its African ventures, and especially the introduction of Cuban troops to support the radical regimes in Angola and Ethiopia, cooled off the political atmosphere between the two superpowers. In fact there was such disillusionment with détente in the United States that when President Fort took over in 1974, he even banned official use of the term. Under President Carter, American-Soviet relations improved with the Vienna summit meeting and the signing of the SALT II treaty in 1979, but after the Soviet invasion of Afghanistan at the end of the year, plummeted to a new low. The American administration came out with strong reprisals: economic relations with the USSR, including a grain embargo, were imposed, a boycott of the Olympic Games in Moscow was declared, and, most seriously, the SALT II Treaty was withdrawn from consideration by the Senate.

During the decline of détente, the Trudeau Government stayed on course, maintaining a moderate stance towards the USSR – closer to those of France and West Germany than to that of the United States. But there were reasons for disenchantment with Moscow in Ottawa too. During the heyday of détente, when American-Soviet relations were good, the USSR tended to downplay the importance of its ties with Ottawa. It is difficult to assess how far this Soviet attitude may have influenced Trudeau's views, but by the mid-1970s his interest in East-West relations had visibly declined. He rarely addressed himself publicly to those issues and instead paid more attention to the North-South problems[10].

There were other bilateral problems. In economic relations, Canadian businessmen found dealing with the Soviet bureaucrats tedious and in scientific and cultural relations, Canadian scholars often felt that the Soviet exploited the exchanges to their unilateral advantage. Then early in 1978, a new Soviet espionage ring was discovered. Both sides did their best to prevent its exploding into another Gouzenko affair, but it was serious enough to merit the cancellation of a planned visit by the Canadian Secretary of State to Moscow, and to postpone the meeting of a mixed commission. Canada was also frustrated by the lack of progress in the MBFR negotiations and the Soviets' persistent ignoring of the human rights' provisions of the Helsinki Final Act. The Canadian representatives criticized the Soviet conduct at the CSCE Review Conference in Belgrade in 1977-1978, at which no progress was made beyond an agreement that another meeting be held in Madrid in 1980.

There were also some domestic reasons for Canada's declining interest in East-West relations. With the rise of a new generation with no memories of World War II or the Cold War, the urgency to preserve détente was blunted. Young Canadians became preoccupied with domestic problems, above all, with the Québec issue and the declining economy. The Trudeau Government did little to reverse this trend – the Prime Minister and his fast-changing External Affairs Secretaries rarely elucidated the complexities of East-West relations for the benefit of the public. As a result, there was a widespread conviction that there was little that Canada could do to stem the adverse tide in the international sphere. The disillusionment with détente also spilled over into Canada from the United States through the American mass media, with various Canadian newspapers critical of the Trudeau Government eagerly following suit. It would be an exaggeration to say that their foreign policy led to the defeat of the Liberals in 1979 – for external relations here rarely played a major role in Canadian elections – but the Liberals' foreign policy was no longer a plus for them.

The short-lived Progressive Conservative Government was more stringent in its anti-communist rhetoric, but initially continued to follow the traditional Canadian «two-track» line in East-West relations. In December 1979, Canada duly endorsed the NATO decision to install, in response to the Soviet SS-20s, *Pershing II* and *Cruise* missiles in Western Europe. Upon the signing of the SALT II treaty in June 1979, Prime Minister Joe Clark sent letters of congratulations to Presidents Carter and Brezhnev. In the fall, the new External Affairs Secretary, Flora MacDonald, had a businesslike session with Gromyko in New York, where arrangements were made for her to visit Moscow. In 1980, Canadian trade with the USSR amounted to $1 535 million in exports and $59 million in imports – the difference affecting the Soviets' ongoing substantial purchases of Canadian grain. Following the Soviet invasion of Afghanistan, however, there was an abrupt change. Ottawa sided firmly with Washington in condemning Moscow. Canada's response was similar to that of the hardline American allies: Britain and Australia; while Canada stood in contrast to France and West Germany which adopted a softer stand. Ottawa showed its displeasure with the Soviet action by sharply curtailing cultural exchanges as well as trade, including the grain sales, and by declaring its intention to boycott the Moscow Olympics. In January 1980, three more Soviet diplomats were charged with espionage and expelled from the country.

Upon the Liberals' return to power in February 1980, the more moderate, Canadian stance was resumed. In his victory speech, Trudeau presented a comprehensive agenda of the outstanding East-West issues, implying that as a senior NATO statesman, he was ready to assist in resolving them. After some hesitation Canada went ahead with the boycott of Olympic Games in Moscow, but the grain embargo was lifted. In 1981, Canadian exports to the USSR increased to $1 865 million and imports to $77 million.

During the Polish crisis, Canada displayed a good deal of circumspection, insisting all along that it should be resolved by the Poles themselves, without any outside intervention. Canadian sympathies – those of the public as well as the government – were clearly on the «Solidarity» side, but Ottawa did not want the situation in Poland to explode into still another East-West crisis. When martial law was introduced in Poland in December 1981, Trudeau sighed a relief that at least a Soviet invasion was averted. The Canadian representatives at the CSCE Review Conference in Madrid condemned the curtailment of civil rights in Poland, but they sided with the Western Europeans against the Americans in opposing a move to terminate the Conference over the Polish issue[11].

Meanwhile, with the ascendancy to power in Washington of the Reagan administration, American-Soviet relations went from bad to worse. The President and his close associates repeatedly indulged in strong anti-communist rhetoric. The SALT II treaty was not reintroduced into the Senate, and the two new sets of arms control negotiations in Geneva – covering the strategic weapons and the medium-range missiles in Europe – made little progress. At the same time, the United States went ahead with massive new armaments. Washington continued to insist upon a

Soviet withdrawal from Afghanistan, and after the introduction of martial law in Poland, it imposed punitive sanctions against both that country and the USSR. And in the Third World, the Reagan administration tended to view local conflicts primarily in terms of its global rivalry with the Soviet Union. In Central America, it threw its support to the forces opposing the radical Sandinistas' regime in Nicaragua and the leftist revolutionaries in El Salvador. With the change of the governments in France and West Germany, which both led to tougher stances vis-à-vis the USSR, there was a shift in Western Europe closer to the American position. By 1983, then, Canada remained virtually the sole major NATO member still committed to preserving 1970"s style East-West détente.

Under Reagan, Canadian-American relations also deteriorated. There were long-standing frictions over fisheries, acid rain and a number of other bilateral issues. Even more important was an ideological dispute over the role of the State in the economy. The Liberal Government was reelected in 1980, having promised to reduce foreign investments and to Canadianize the oil industry. When the Reagan administration came to power in 1981, it embarked on a vigorous effort to protect the American interests in Canada threatened by these initiatives and, at times resorting to less than subtle pressure; it managed to have the initiatives modified by the Canadian Government.

There were also marked differences between the two governments over several international issues. The Canadians were none too happy over the demise of SALT II treaty and continued to advocate nuclear arms control measures. In contrast to the United States, Canada's sanctions against Poland were largely symbolic. Ottawa also took a more detached view of the revolutionary movements in the Third World – seeing them not as instigated from outside, but as primarily stemming from local economic and social inequalities. At a meeting to review the assistance to the developing countries, held in Cancun, in Mexico, in 1981, Prime Minister Trudeau and President Reagan clearly did not see eye to eye. Despite persistent efforts on both sides to patch up their disputes, and even to preserve a façade of cordiality, the special relationship between Ottawa and Washington was no longer there.

In the early 1980s, there also appeared growing concern over the United States' foreign policy among the Canadian public. This time, the perennial presence of the American media in Canada worked in the opposite direction: while watching on television Mr. Reagan's bellicose statements towards the USSR, many Canadians were clearly not impressed. In a pool undertaken in 1982, asking who posed the main threat to the world peace, 51 % of the respondents named the Soviet Union, but 21 % named the United States[12].

In the same year, a strong peace movement emerged in Canada, opposed to the testing of American *Cruise* missile in Alberta. Despite widespread protest – as ever, giving first priority to its obligations in NATO, and also in order not to further strain its relations with Washington – ,Ottawa agreed to testing[13].

Meanwhile, the Canadian Government kept its lines of communication to the USSR open. In September 1982, External Affairs Secretary MacEachen met with Gromyko in New York. In November, Prime Minister Trudeau personally attended Brezhnev's funeral. While in Moscow he held talks with Premier Nicolai Tikhonov, although (surprisingly, in view of Trudeau's status as a senior NATO statesman) not with Andropov. Soon afterwards a Canadian delegation, headed by the Deputy

Minister of External Affairs, arrived in Moscow for a comprehensive review of relations with the USSR – the first since the Soviet invasion of Afghanistan. Canadian-Soviet relations appeared one more to be on the mend.

In the latter part of 1983, American-Soviet relations plunged again. When the Korean Airliner 747 was shot down in September, the chill between Washington and Moscow became immediate and pervasive. And in December, when the first American *Pershing II* and *Cruise* missiles were installed in Western Europe, the Societs walked out of the Geneva nuclear arms control talks. Relations between the two superpowers began to resemble those of the worst years of the Cold War.

Ottawa's reaction to the Korean Airliner incident (with ten Canadians among the 269 civilians dead) was also sharp. It was unanimously condemned in the House of Commons and Aeroflot flights to Montréal were suspended for 60 days. MacEachen also demanded compensation from the Soviet Government to the families of Canadian victims. Yet, in a subsequent parliamentary debate, the Prime Minister showed considerable restraint – he clearly did not want this incident to wreck Canada-USSR relations.

The deteriorating international climate, moreover, jolted Trudeau into action. In a speech at the University of Guelph on October 26, he announced the launching of his «peace mission» of travel to various capitals in the world to try to bring the nuclear powers to the negotiating table. And, indeed, before resigning as Prime Minister in June, he saw the leaders of several countries promoting the stabilization of both nuclear and conventional armaments at a lower level.

Internationally, Trudeau did not accomplish much[14]. He was received politely in London, Paris and Peking (now Beijing), but was told that before the minor nuclear powers would be ready to join in the negotiations, the example should be set by the two superpowers. In Washington, Trudeau's initiative was unmistakably dismissed by Reagan, while some American officials even derided it. And in Moscow, Trudeau did not fare much better. With Andropov in his dying throes, the Canadian Prime Minister's visit was interminably delayed. Eventually, Trudeau made it to Moscow for the occasion of Andropov's funeral and presented his proposals to the new Soviet leader, Konstantin Chernenko. Yet, with the apparent fiasco of Trudeau's preceding visit to Washington, the Soviets also did not take him seriously. The failure of Trudeau's endeavors clearly indicated the limits on Canada's major role in East-West relations.

Yet, Trudeau's diplomatic swan song was not all in vain. The Prime Minister's efforts to promote peace internationally evoked generally favorable response at home. They were praised by the media and supported by the opposition parties in Parliament. Evidently, the Canadians were still faithful to the «two-track» approach in East-West relations[15]. And, significantly, among the Trudeau's eloquent admirers was the former Prime Minister, Joe Clark, who in September 1984, was to take charge of Canada's foreign policy as Secretary of State for External Affairs.

EARLY RELATIONS WITH EASTERN EUROPE[16]

Canada's relations with various Eastern European countries, notably Poland and Czechoslovakia, date back to the interwar period; yet, as in the case of the USSR, they acquired importance only during World War II. In the Cold War era, except for relations with Yugoslavia, they became virtually dormant. It was only during the 1960s, when several Eastern European states assumed a more independent stance from the USSR, that Ottawa started to pay more attention to them.

In a way, close contacts with the Eastern European middle powers, like Poland or Yugoslavia, were more natural for Canada than contacts with the USSR. Yet, since they were of little intrinsic value (except trade) to Ottawa, they were placed within a broad context of Canada's strategic priorities. Canada, thus, was primarily interested in those Eastern Europeans countries which could make a valid contribution to East-West détente. This particularly benefited those states which – like Canada vis-à-vis the United States – followed a relatively independent course from the USSR, but at the same time, paradoxically, preserved close contacts with it.

An additional factor in Canadian policy towards Eastern Europe was the pressure from those Canadians who originated from that region. Naturally enough, those people strove to induce the Canadian Government to adopt a tougher stance vis-à-vis the USSR, which since World War II had dominated their homelands. In 1956, the Hungarians, in 1968 the Czechs and the Slovaks, and in 1980-1981 the Poles, wanted Canada to uphold their countries' right to independence. The Canadian politicans, of course, readily agreed with this principle and, if only to gain potential votes, often spoke of it with conviction. Yet, they remained painfully aware that they were not in a position to enforce it in practice and they were not prepared, in the name of it, to sacrifice Canada's immediate interests. The example of Wilgress, who during World War II advised the Poles, in order to salvage whatever still could be salvaged of Poland's independence, to reach a compromise with the Russians, was not forgotten in the Department of External Affairs. As a result, the only issue on which the Canadian Government consistently and vigorously responded, in line with pressure from the Eastern European groups, was the revification of families.

It would be a mistake, however, to attribute this course in Canada's foreign policy merely to selfish national interests. The External Affairs officials – who were often more on the top of actual developments in the area than were those who had left it years before as refugees – were convinced that the most effective way to reduce the Eastern European dependence on the USSR, like Canada on the United States, was through relaxation of East-West tensions. The Canadians, however, resented this comparison's being drawn overtly, stressing that their cooperation with the United States had been voluntary, while the Eastern Europeans' with the USSR had been forced. While this was undoubtedly true, the fact nevertheless remained that both the Canadians and the Eastern Europeans had vested interests in reducing the rigid bipolarization of the world between the two superpowers and in advancing détente. And it was on that basis that Canada's relations with Eastern Europe were primarily developed.

Historically, Canada's relations with Eastern Europe progressed in stages somewhat similar to those with Russia. Since most countries in that region obtained independence after World War I, simultaneously with Canada's emergence from British tutelage, they became its partners only in the interwar period. The only exception was Poland, with which first official contacts were actually established during the war. When a Polish army was formed by the Polish National Committee in Paris, to fight on the French side in 1917, Canada provided transit for Poles from the United States to join its ranks. In the interwar period, consular and modest trading relations were maintained between Canada and Poland[17]. There were no Canadian diplomats in Warsaw – Canadian interests there being represented by the British – but in view of the already substantial, and through the interwar years steadily rising, presence of the Polish community in Canada, a Polish consulate in Montréal was opened in 1919. Canada's relations with Czechoslovakia go back to 1928 when the Convention on Commerce was signed – the Czechoslovak consulate in Montréal was established in 1936.

It was over Germany's attack on Poland in 1939 that Canada, following the British and French example, entered into World War II. Once again Canada provided training facilities for the Polish forces in France and, then, in Britain. Canadians and Poles fought side by side in Italy, and then in France and Germany; in fact, a Polish Armored Division was part of the Canadian Army and shared in its victorious march all the way from Normandy to the North Sea. In 1940, the Polish art treasures, which had been evacuated from the country after the German attack, were stored in Ottawa. During the war, Canada also established formal diplomatic relations with those Eastern European countries represented by governments-in-exile in London: Poland, Czechoslovakia and Yugoslavia. The Canadian representative at large was Brigadier General Georges Vanier, and when he left with the Gaulle for Algiers, representation was left in the hands of chargés. At the end of the war, however, Canada shifted its recognition to the communist-dominated governments in Poland and Yugoslavia; only in the case of Czechoslovakia, where President Benes returned to Prague in 1945, and then in 1948 sanctioned the communist takeover, was continuity in diplomatic relations preserved.

With the rise of the Cold War, Canada's relations with Soviet-dominated Eastern Europe virtually froze. Diplomatic relations with Poland and Czechoslovakia were maintained, and in 1946, relations with Hungary were established (a Hungarian consulate in Montréal was opened in the same year), they were kept at a minimum level. Trade was virtually non-existent and the Canadian and Eastern European representatives at the United Nations, reflecting their participation in the opposing blocs, took often different positions. The only exception was Yugoslavia which in the late 1940s broke with the Soviet Union and assumed an independent stance in international affairs. In 1951, the Canadian legation in Belgrade and the Yugoslav legation in Ottawa were raised to embassy status. Subsequently, Yugoslavia also opened consulates in Toronto and Vancouver.

It was only after the improvement in Canadian-Soviet relations in the mid-1950s that Canada's relations with the Eastern European communist states were expanded too. Following the internal liberalization in Poland upon Wladyslaw Gomulka's coming to power in 1956, Canada's contacts with that country picked up momentum A regular service was launched between Montréal and Gdynia by the Polish liner *Batory*. Canadian-Polish relations, however, were complicated by the «cause célèbre» of the Polish art treasures, some of which were handed over at the end of the war by the Polish Government-in-exile into the custody of Premier Duplessis of Québec, who stubbornly refused to return them to the Communist Polish Government. With the death of Duplessis in 1959, the treasures were eventually returned to the Royal Castle in Cracow[18]. In the early 1960s, the Polish and the Czechoslovak legations in Ottawa, and the Canadian legations in Warsaw and Prague, were raised to embassy status.

Meanwhile, as liberalization progressed in Hungary, in 1965 Canada's ambassador to Prague was also accredited to Budapest. In 1970, Hungary opened another consulate in Toronto. Both countries installed resident ambassadors in 1975. In the mid-1960s, when Czechoslovakia began to thaw internally, Canada's relations with that country also underwent a marked improvement. At Expo 67, an impressive Czechoslovak pavilion was constructed and was visited by President Antonin Novotny. At the same time various government, cultural and sports exchanges were intensified. They continued during the Prague Spring in 1968, but after the Warsaw Pact invasion of Czechoslovakia in August, and especially after the fall from power of Alexander Dubcek in the spring of 1969, they once more declined. Some 15 000 Czech and Slovak refugees, escaping the rigors of the strict communist system reimposed at home, were admitted to Canada. At the same time, Canada's relations with Poland and Hungary – who participated in the Warsaw Pact invasion of Czechoslovakia – distinctly cooled off.

In the 1960s, Canada entered into direct contact with other Eastern European countries. In 1966, diplomatic relations were established with Bulgaria. The first Bulgarian ambassador arrived in Ottawa in 1965. Since Bulgaria followed the USSR very closely in its foreign policy, it was of little intrinsic interest to Canada; as a result, no Canadian embassy was opened there, but the Canadian ambassador to Belgrade was accorded dual accreditation to Sofia. Romania, which since the early 1960s followed a course largely independent of the Soviet Union, was a different case. Canada and Romania entered into diplomatic relations in 1967. The first Romanian ambassador arrived in Ottawa in 1970, and the Canadian embassy in Bucharest was opened in 1977; meanwhile, a Romanian consulate was established in Montréal. Finally, after relations between the two Germanies were normalized in 1972, Canada also recognized the German Democratic Republic, although full diplomatic relations were established only in 1975 when non-resident ambassadors – the Canadian in Warsaw and the East German in Washington – were exchanged. Thus, by the 1970s, Canada had ties with all the Eastern European states (except the still intransigeantly Stalinist Albania) and was ready to try its «two-track» policy towards the East in this region too.

POLITICAL RELATIONS WITH EASTERN EUROPE

The rise of East-West détente greatly intensified Canada's relations with Eastern Europe. The communist states there bacame Canada's partners in the CSCE and the MBFR negotiations, requiring much political consultation. Opportunities to develop other bilateral relations: trade, scientific and cultural contacts, and exchanges in sports, also appeared. In the improved political climate, the resolution of the thorny issue of family reunification was somewhat facilitated.

In the political realm Yugoslavia, as a non-aligned communist country with close ties to the East as much as to the Third World, was of special interest to Canada. Relations between the two countries were given new impetus by the visit to Canada of President Josip Tito in 1971. Subsequently, there were frequent ministerial exchanges including a visit to Ottawa by the Yugoslav Secretary for Foreign Affairs in 1975, and a visit by Canadian Secretary of State for External Affairs, Don C. Jamieson, to Belgrade in 1977. Yugoslav special interests at the CSCE in the Confidence Building Measures were shared by Canada. In May 1980, Governor-General Edward Schreyer led the Canadian delegation to the funeral of President Tito; and in June 1982, Prime Minister Trudeau made an official visit to Yugoslavia.

In 1970, Gomulka was replaced as the First Secretary of the Polish Communist Party by Edward Gierek. Under the new leader, Poland, while maintaining close ties with the USSR, substantially expanded its relations with the West, including Canada. In 1975, Canadian External Affairs Secretary MacEachen visited Warsaw, and the next year the Polish foreign minister came to Ottawa. Several other ministerial and parliamentary exchanges also took place in the 1970s and there were regular political consultations between the two foreign ministries' officials over international problems of mutual interest, especially the CSCE and the MBFR. Trudeau was invited to visit Poland, but with the political crisis under way in that country in 1980, the invitation was not followed up.

With the imposition of martial law in Poland in December 1981, Canada adopted a relatively moderate posture – in striking contrast to the United States. Prime Minister Trudeau, of course, expressed regret over the curtailment of the Poles' civil rights, but he characterized the Polish military rule as a lesser evil than a Soviet intervention. Normal diplomatic relations between the two countries were maintained. Immigration rules were eased to admit into Canada several thousands of Polish refugees and the Canadian Governement contributed to the humanitarian aid to Poland, sponsored by the Polish-Canadian Congress. On July 22, 1983, on a Polish national day – which was also the occasion for lifting martial law – the Canadian Governor-General, in a message to the Polish Head of State, expressed the wish that the Poles would achieve national reconciliation. Gradually, high-level political contacts were restored with MacEachen meeting the Polish Foreign Minister, Stefan Olszowski, in New York in September 1983, and again in Stockholm in January 1984.

Canadian-Hungarian relations improved at a slower, but steadier pace. In 1981, Secretary of State for External Affairs, Mark R. MacGuigan, visited Budapest and held talks there with Communist Party Secretary Janos Kadar; while the next year the Hungarian foreign minister paid a visit to Ottawa. These contacts were supplemented by several other ministerial exchanges. During the 1970s, Canada's relations with Romania also progressed. In 1970 and in 1971, the Canadian and Romanian foreign ministers exchanged visits. In July 1975, on the occasion of signing the CSCE Final Act, Prime Minister Trudeau held talks with President Nicolae Ceausescu in Helsinki. And in 1982, the Governor-General paid a state visit to Romania.

After the Soviet invasion of Czechoslovakia and the suppression of liberal reforms there, Canadian-Czechoslovak relations were maintained in a low key. There were no exchanges of foreign ministers' visits, and few Canadian ministers visited Czechoslovakia. However, regular consultations between the Foreign Ministry officials, mainly on the CSCE, were maintained. In 1978, Prime Minister Trudeau met the Czechoslovak Foreign Minister in New York; the next year, External Affairs Secretary

Flora MacDonald also held talks with him there. And during his «peace mission», Trudeau included Prague in his itenerary and conferred there with President Gustav Husak.

In relations with Bulgaria, so far no high-level exchanges have taken place, with the major attention being given to developing economic ties. There, important contacts with the German Democratic Republic. Political consultations between Foreign Ministry officials, however, have been held regularly since 1977 and in 1981, the two foreign ministers held talks in New York. And early in 1984, Prime Minister Trudeau visited East Berlin to present his peace proposals to the East German leader Erich Honecker.

TRADING WITH EASTERN EUROPE

Trade with Eastern Europe in 1981 amounted to $558 million in exports and $247 in imports (see table at the end of this chapter).

In terms of country-by-country breakdown, Poland was Canada's most important trading partner. As an importer of Canadian grain it was second only to the Soviet Union. There were problems, however, in the Canadian-Polish trade. Despite substantial Polish exports, which consisted chiefly of textiles, footwear and apparel, there remained a serious trade imbalance between the two countries in favor of Canada. The bulk of Polish imports consisted of grain: the only other major transaction being purchases of pulp and paper equipment for the mill in Kwidzyn. The Poles' efforts to interest the Canadians in purchasing Polish ships or mining equipment have not been successful. Furthermore, in view of Poland's massive hard currency indedness (in the case of Canada amounting close to $1 billion), by 1982, there was evident reluctance on the part of the Canadian Government to extend it additional credits to facilitate continued purchases of grain. Thus, Canadian exports to Poland declined from $345 million in 1980 to $49 million in 1983.

Czechoslovakia was Canada's second most important trading partner in Eastern Europe. In the period 1970-1978 the balance of trade was substantially in Czechoslovakia's favor, but with the award of the Ruzemberok pulp mill to a Canadian firm, the situation improved by 1979. The other Canadian exports: oil seeds, hides and skins, asbestos fibre, etc., however did not amount to very much, and, consequently, the prospects for continued trading at the level of the early 1980s did not appear to be good.

Canada-Yugoslavia trade also expanded, although – especially since both countries are interested in diversifying their export markets – it has not reached its potential. Canada has traditionally enjoyed a trade advantage – its major exports were wood pulp, iron ore, asbestos, motor vehicles and aircraft engines and parts; while its imports from Yugoslavia were leather, footwear, furniture and machine tools. Unfortunately, however, Yugoslavia's economic difficulties, which led it in 1980 to severely restrict hard currency imports, dampened the prospects for any increase of trade between the two countries.

The growth of Canada's trading relations with Romania was due largely to the nuclear cooperation programme. For Canada, the sale of CANDU reactor to that country was the first in Eastern Europe, and for Romania, the establishing of a nuclear station in Cernavoda represented «the project of the century». Unfortunately, a serious liquidity crisis in Romania, and the Canadian Export Development Corporation's consequent suspension of disbursement of funds under the loan agreement, slowed down the completion of the Cernavoda project. Commercial relations with Hungary were expanded too, although they remained far below their potential. Hungarian exports consisted chiefly of clothing, while they imported valves for nuclear plants, grain elevators and grinding equipment – the Canadian producers often winning tenders in that country over stiff Western European competition.

Bilateral trade between Canada and Bulgaria remained modest. Canadian exports were mainly fish, dried peas, zinc concentrates and asbestos; while the imports from Bulgaria were machine tools, clothing, food and beverages. There was, however, mutual awareness of further trading opportunities and, consequently, in the early 1980s, more aggressive Canadian exploration of the Bulgarian market was undertaken. Canada and the German Democratic Republic, when they entered into bilateral relations, were both interested in establishing commercial ties. An initial trade agreement was concluded between the two countries in 1981.

Side by side with the expansion of trade, Canada regularized various other economic and social aspects of its relations with the Eastern European countries. Outstanding Canadian claims were settled. Fisheries' treaties were negotiated, and cooperation in agriculture was developed. Health and veterinary agreements were signed. In 1970, air services were launched – in 1970 between Montréal and Prague via the Czechoslavak airline, and in 1976 between Mirabelle and Warsaw via the Polish. Step by step, an infrastructure was developed, reflecting the efforts of governments on both sides to bring Canada and Eastern Europe closer together.

SCIENTIFIC, CULTURAL AND PERSONAL CONTACTS
WITH EASTERN EUROPE

Unlike the USSR, Canada was reluctant to enter into formal scientific and cultural agreements with individual Eastern European countries. The Canadian Government did not believe that the size of those countries, complicated by the variety of their languages, merited sufficient interest on the part of the Canadian scholarly and artistic community to sustain regular exchanges. The Canadian Government did not ignore such contacts, however, on the contrary, it offered sponsorship of many initiatives and supported others undertaken by private institutions. It was, however, on an *ad hoc* basis.

Scientific and cultural cooperation was complicated by the political vagaries in the different Eastern European countries. Generally, a more liberal internal climate there would lead to an expansion of contacts with the West, including Canada; and, vice versa, an internal political tightening would be adverse to such efforts. With Yugoslavia, there were no political obstacles; but the Yugoslavs – with their widespread contacts East, West and South – showed no special interest in Canada. Throughout the 1970s, the closest contacts were maintained with Poland, but after the political eruption there in 1980, they have declined. Cooperation with Hungary was expanded in the second half of the 1970s and continued uninterrupted into the early 1980s. In the case of Czechoslovakia, despite a cool political climate, a respectable level of artistic and sports exchanges was preserved. There were fewer contacts in this domain with Romania and Bulgaria, and relations with the GDR are sill at an early stage.

On the Canadian side, exchanges with Eastern Europe have been supported by the government Awards Programme as well as by the Canada Council and its successors. Funding has been limited, but many academics and graduate students have benefited. On the Eastern European side, where all the reasearch institutions and the universities are government-controlled – funds come from the public purse and in recent years have been adversely affected by shortages of the hard currencies. In addition, the National Research Council has carried out exchanges with the Academies of Sciences and the Canadian Broadcasting Corporation has developed cooperation with some of the radio and television networks in Eastern Europe.

Individual Canadian universities also financed many scholarly contacts and research projects, although in the second half of the 1970s, when their funds became more scarce, their level of support declined. Some regular exchanges have nevertheless been carried on. The University of Warsaw, for example, has had an ongoing exchange with several universities in Canada; Carleton University has signed an agreement with the Hungarian Cultural Institute; and in the early 1970s, McMaster University organized special summer programmes for its graduate students at the University of Lubljana and the University of Budapest. There have been joint meetings of Canadian academics with Polish sociologists and Hungarian economists. Scholars from several Eastern European countries participated in the First International Congress in Soviet and East European Studies held in Banff, Alberta, in 1974.

The Canadian Institute of International Affairs held regular round tables – allowing for informal discussions of current international and bilateral issues by knowlegeable individuals – since 1968 with the Poles, and since 1974 with the Hungarians, there was also one such meeting in 1969 (arranged before the suppression of the Prague Spring) with the Czechoslovaks. In the spring of 1973, a special issue of the *Canadian Slavonic Papers* was devoted to Poland, including several articles by noted Polish scholars. In return in 1978, a book on contemporary Canada, authored mostly by the Canadians, was published by the Polish Institute of International Affairs[19]. The University of Budapest has introduced a course in Canadian studies and plans are under way to do the same at the University of Debrecen.

In the performing arts, numerous Polish musical and theatrical groups have toured Canada (often gearing their programmes to Polish-Canadian audiences) and prominent Polish theatrical figures have been invited by Canadian theatre companies. In 1971, the Moravian folk dance ensemble and in 1972, the Dukla Ukrainian Dance Company performed in various Canadian cities, while in 1971, the Théâtre du Nouveau Monde visited Prague and in 1977, the McGill Chamber Orchestra played in Ostrava. There have been several exchanges of musical ensembles and concert musicians with Hungary, too. Polish, Czechoslovak and Hungarian films have been displayed in Canada.

In 1974, the exhibition «Understanding through Culture» was opened at the Czechoslovak Pavilion at Man and His World in Montréal. In 1981, an exhibition of works by Tom Forrestal won acclaim in Hungary and the next year, an exhibition of contemporary Canadian tapestries, as well as «Paysages du Canada», evoked a similar response. Soon afterwards, an exhibition of Hungarian sculpture toured Canada. Contacts with Eastern Europe in sports have also been expanded. Since

1972, there have been ongoing exchanges of hockey teams with Czechoslovakia; while exchanges of athletic teams with East Germany were, in fact, one of the first areas of bilateral cooperation between the two countries.

Canada has become home to many immigrants from Eastern Europe. The Polish-Canadian community is over 300 000 strong and there are more than 150 000 Canadians of Yugoslav origin. There are also substantial groups of Hungarians, Czechs, Slovaks, Romanians and others. Many of these people still maintain close links with their homelands. The liner *Batory* has carried many Polish-Canadians, and their families and friends from Poland, between Montréal and Gdynia. In the second half of the 1970s, approximately 30 000 Canadians – the great majority of them of Polish extraction – had visited Poland annually. There has been similar traffic with Yugoslavia and Hungary, where entry by foreigners poses no major problems.

The Canadian Government has been sensitive to those personal needs of its citizens and, both within the framework of the CSCE and in bilateral contacts with the Eastern European states, has tried to foster the granting of visas and the extension of proper consular protection to them. Especially in the post-Helsinki period, there has been considerable progress over those matters, although there have been some continuing irritants too. The issue of divided families has been particularly acute with Czechoslovakia, where in 1977 the so-called «Directive 58» was promulgated, demanding that all those who had left the country illegally regularize their status with the Czechoslovak authorities. In October 1980, a series of consular negotiations was started to find a solution to this problem satisfactory to the Canadians of the Czech and Slovak background.

Many Canadians of Eastern European origin left their homeland precisely because they disliked the communist system there. Their ethnic organizations often retain a distincly anti-communist profile and they have tried to pressure the Canadian Government to take a stronger stand in upholding the rights of the Eastern European nations to freedom and independence. These activities by the Polish, Croat or other emigrants in Canada, in turn, have been irritants to the communist governments at home. In opposing them, however, the communists at times have confused the official position of the Canadian Government and the activities of what are basically private associations which under Canadian democratic system are free to express whatever political views they may hold. The Canadian leaders, of course, have been quite sympathetic towards the Eastern Europeans' aspirations for freedom, which has been manifested by Canada's warming up its relations with the different communist regimes whenever they revealed some liberalizing tendencies. Yet, Ottawa generally has not let itself be swayed by the pressure from the ethnic groups from its traditional «two-track» policy towards the USSR and the communist states in Eastern Europe. The Canadian officials, moreover, have tended to believe that closer personal contacts with the region can be most effectively advanced in a climate of détente.

In the 1970s and the early 1980s, thus, Canada's cooperation with various Eastern European countries has been very considerably increased – largely overcoming the barriers erected during the Cold War. These manifold personal exchanges contribute to the better understanding of Eastern Europe in Canada and vice versa, and provide a solid foundation for continuing a more relaxed political climate between them.

Canadian trade with Eastern Europe
($ millions)

	EXPORTS			IMPORTS		
	1979	1980	% Increase (Decrease)	1979	1980	% Increase (Decrease)
Albania	0,1	0,1	—	—	0,9	—
Bulgaria	9,3	5,1	(45,3)	6,3	4,7	(25,8)
Czechoslovakia	35,2	126,9	260,3	67,5	63,3	(6,2)
German Democratic Republic	35,9	9,9	(72,3)	9,8	9,6	(1,6)
Hungary	14,1	10,6	(24,6)	31,2	25,8	(17,3)
Poland	261,6	345,5	32,1	82,8	72,1	(12,9)
Romania	32,2	21,4	(33,6)	39,5	37,8	(4,3)
USSR	763,0	1 534,9	101,2	64,1	59,3	(7,5)
Yugoslavia	52,7	68,7	30,4	25,8	33,0	27,8
Total	1 204,0	2 123,2	76,3	327,0	306,4	(6,3)

Source: Department of External Affairs.

NOTES

1. The most comprehensive treatment of early Canada-USSR relations is presented by Aloysius Balawyder, *Canadian-Soviet Relations Between the World Wars*, Toronto, University of Toronto Press, 1972; for the years 1919-1927, see also James Eayrs, *Northern Approaches*, Toronto, University of Toronto Press, 1961.

2. Relations since the outbreak of World War II are dealt with in considerable detail in Aloysius Balawyder (ed.), *Canadian-Soviet Relations, 1939-1980*, Oakville, Ontario, Mosaic Press, 1981. The book includes a particularly valuable chronology of Canadian-Soviet relations prepared by the Department of External Affairs. Much of the information presented in the first part of this chapter is derived from this volume.

3. Quoted by Donald Page, «Getting to Know the Russians – 1943-1948», *ibidem*, p. 25-26.

4. Quoted by Larry D. Collins, «Canadian-Soviet Relations During the Cold War», *ibidem*, p. 46.

5. *Ibidem*, p. 52-53.

6. Quoted by Donald Page, «Détente: High Hopes and Disappointing Realities», *ibidem*, p. 61.

7. The new Canadian foreign policy was unveiled in June 1970 in the Government paper: *Foreign Policy for Canadians*.

8. «A Canadian Leader Looks at the Soviet Union», a Statement by Prime Minister Pierre Elliot Trudeau in the House of Commons, May 28, 1971, Information Division, Department of External Affairs (Mimeographed), p. 3.

9. Page, op. *cit.*, p. 72; for an excellent review of Canada's role in promoting East-West détente, see also: Donald Page, «Canada and European Détente», in Norman Hiller and Garth Stevenson (eds.), *A Foremost Nation, Canadian Foreign Policy in the Changing World*, Toronto, McClelland and Stewart, 1977, p. 37-62.

10. Valuable information about the Canadians' self-image in international affairs is contained in Peyton V. Lyon and Brian W. Tomlin, *Canada as International Actor*, Toronto, Macmillan of Canada, 1979.

11. For Canada's attitude towards the developments in Poland in the early 1980s, see: Adam Bromke et *al.*, *Canada's Response to the Polish Crisis*, Toronto, Canadian Institute of International Affairs, 1982. More detailed discussion of this topic is included in the section dealing with Canadian-Polish relations.

12. Don Munton and Michael Slack, «Canadian attitudes on disarmament», *International Perspectives*, Ottawa, July-August 1982, p. 12.

13. See Franklyn Griffiths, «Canada's role in START talks offstage but vital», T*he Globe and Mail*, January 28, 1983; and Adam Bromke, «Looking beyond the Cruise debate», *The Globe and Mail*, March 25, 1983.

14. For the accounts of Trudeau's «peace mission», see: Adam Bromke and Kim R. Nossal, «Trudeau rides the 'third rail'», and Michael Tucker, «Trudeau and the politics of peace», *International Perspectives*, May-June 1984, p. 3-10; also John Kirton, «Trudeau and the diplomacy of peace», *International Perspectives*, July-August 1984, p. 3-5.

15. For a comprehensive assessment of Trudeau's era in Canadian foreign policy, see: Adam Bromke and Kim R. Nossal, «Tensions in Canadian Foreign Policy», *Foreign Affairs*, Vol. 62, No. 2, Winter 1983-1984, p. 335-353.

16. The factual information on Canada's relations with Eastern Europe comes from material prepared by the Eastern European Division, Department of External Affairs. The author wishes to express his sincere thanks to one and all of the members of the Division who found time to do it.

17. For a comprehensive treatment of Canadian-Polish relations, see: Aloysius Balawyder, The *Maple Leaf and the White Eagle*, Boulder, Colorado, East European Monographs, 1980; see also Adam Bromke, «Unique chance for cooperation in second century of relationship», *International Perspectives*, March-April 1975.

18. See A. Balawyder, The *Odyssey of the Polish Treasures*, Antigonish, N. S., St. Francis Xavier University Press, 1978.

19. Michal Dobroczynski and Roman March (eds.), W*spolczesna Kanada*, Warsaw, Polish Institute of International Affairs, 1978.

14

Le Canada et l'Asie orientale[*]

Gérard Hervouet
Université Laval

Ce n'est qu'à la fin de la Deuxième Guerre mondiale que le Canada découvrit véritablement sa façade maritime sur le Pacifique et qu'il prit conscience de la nécessité et des avantages d'oser se détourner quelque peu d'une vocation historique atlantique. L'océan Pacifique, perçu traditionnellement comme un rempart dans la conscience collective canadienne, évoquait plus la protection qu'il n'invitait à la communication. Au-delà se trouvait le mystère des territoires où seuls se risquaient les missionnaires et les commerçants aventureux.

La poussée vers l'Ouest canadien, sa mise en valeur et la construction du chemin de fer transcontinental amenèrent une population asiatique – Japonais et Chinois surtout – qui fut très tôt victime d'une ségrégation dont le souvenir demeure encore vivant. Déjà, cependant, des liens non négligeables avaient été noués avec le Japon. En 1929, le Canada y ouvrait une de ses premières ambassades, mais ce ne fut toutefois qu'après la fin du deuxième conflit mondial que le gouvernement d'Ottawa entreprit de donner plus d'ampleur à sa présence dans cette région que l'on appelait encore l'Extrême-Orient.

De 1945 à la période actuelle, la diplomatie canadienne dans la région peut s'analyser en trois phases distinctes. Chacune d'elles constitue tout autant une illustration des politiques asiatiques du Canada que de sa politique étrangère en général. Dans un premier temps, longue période qui s'étendit jusqu'en 1968, le Canada assuma dans le Pacifique des rôles qui lui paraissaient être conformes à ses obligations de membre des Nations Unies, membre du Commonwealth et allié des États-Unis. L'Asie était alors une région où plus qu'ailleurs les conflits réels alimentaient cette guerre «froide» entre les deux grandes puissances. Le Canada fut alors, à plusieurs reprises, pris dans la tourmente d'antagonismes qui lui étaient étrangers mais auxquels il ne pouvait demeurer indifférent. Sollicité, et finalement peut-être satisfait de l'être, le Canada entendait remplir une «mission» conforme à ses idéaux. Que cette mission fût en Asie, seuls les événements imposèrent la région car le Canada n'y avait en aucune façon défini une vocation particulière.

---

[*] Ce chapitre s'inspire de l'ouvrage *Le Canada face à l'Asie de l'Est*, Montréal, Nouvelle Optique, 1981, dont il reproduit de larges extraits.

À partir de 1968, le nouveau gouvernement fédéral entendait désormais définir une attitude nouvelle envers l'Asie orientale. Sans renier véritablement les rôles de médiateur qu'on lui faisait jouer, le Canada souhaitait se mettre dans une position de plus grande autonomie afin d'échapper aux contraintes de la région et à celles plus précises des États-Unis. Avec une grande détermination, on formula une politique dont les objectifs visaient essentiellement à la poursuite des intérêts nationaux canadiens les plus immédiatement tangibles.

Après 1975, de multiples événements régionaux mais aussi une réorientation interne des priorités canadiennes firent que l'on entreprit de réévaluer ce qui avait été accompli depuis 1968. Avec encore plus de réalisme, il convenait de préciser davantage les cibles privilégiées tout en étudiant avec soin la place que pouvait tenir le Canada dans l'avenir de la région la plus prospère, la plus dynamique et actuellement la plus stable du système international. C'est donc dans la succession de ces trois phases qu'on reconstituera analytiquement le cheminement de la politique canadienne en Asie de l'Est[1] depuis 1945.

LES ANNÉES D'ILLUSIONS ET DE CONVICTIONS

Sur le théâtre d'opération de la guerre du Pacifique, la présence canadienne fut modeste. En 1941 cependant, le Canada dépêcha deux bataillons pour renforcer la garnison britannique de Hong Kong. Ce premier engagement dans la Deuxième Guerre mondiale fut éphémère puisque peu de temps après leur arrivée, les soldats canadiens subirent l'assaut des troupes japonaises. Les pertes furent lourdes et les survivants vécurent une longue captivité dans les camps japonais[2]. En Birmanie et dans les îles aléoutiennes, le Canada avait également envoyé quelques militaires mais leur présence demeura symbolique puisque l'essentiel de l'effort fut déployé sur le front européen.

La fin des hostilités avec le Japon mit un terme aux préparatifs d'un engagement canadien plus appuyé dans la guerre du Pacifique. Le Canada ne fut pas convié à l'occupation du territoire japonais, mais il participa activement aux travaux de la Far Eastern Commission et de l'Inter-Allied Trade Board. Le littoral sur l'océan Pacifique obligeait le gouvernement d'Ottawa à ne pas demeurer indifférent à la réinsertion du Japon dans la communauté internationale, mais aussi dans ses rapports bilatéraux avec le Canada.

Dans le climat de l'après-guerre qui invitait à se consacrer davantage aux problèmes internes qu'à la politique étrangère, on ne peut s'étonner que l'Asie ne devînt plus une région prioritaire dans l'attention du gouvernement. Très rapidement cependant, l'antagonisme entre les deux blocs idéologiques, entre les deux grands vainqueurs de la Deuxième Guerre mondiale, accentua la tension des rapports Est-Ouest. Dans ce contexte de froides hostilités, le Canada articula sa politique extérieure autour de trois convictions: la première était de s'en tenir et de respecter ses obligations comme membre des Nations Unies, la deuxième visait à tout mettre en œuvre pour établir un véritable système de sécurité collective, et la troisième était de faire échec à l'expansion du communisme dans le monde. Comme investi d'une mission, sollicité par les autres États, pris au piège de ses convictions et peut-être de ses illusions, le Canada se retrouva dans des situations qui outrepassaient, à n'en pas douter, ses volontés et ses intérêts.

Cinq ans après la fin de la Deuxième Guerre mondiale, les soldats canadiens allaient se retrouver sur le champ de bataille: celui de la Corée. Lorsque le 25 juin 1950 la nouvelle du franchissement du 38e parallèle par les troupes nord-coréennes parvint à Ottawa, le gouvernement fédéral soutint immédiatement la position américaine en précisant cependant que l'action qu'il convenait d'entreprendre devait être conforme aux obligations de la Charte des Nations Unies. La justification auprès de l'opinion publique de l'engagement du Canada fut malaisée. Le 7 août 1950, dans un discours radiodiffusé, le premier ministre Saint-Laurent évoquait la nécessité pour le Canada de ne pas se dérober dans ses engagements au sein des Nations Unies: «Afin d'éviter une nouvelle guerre mondiale, disait-il, le Canada doit soutenir l'action des Nations Unies.» Et, rassurant, il précisait que cette entreprise en Corée «n'est pas la guerre mais une action de police destinée à prévenir la guerre en décourageant l'agression»[3].

Aux côtés des États-Unis, le Canada dépêcha 8 000 hommes de troupe, deux destroyers et un escadron d'avions de transport. Convaincu que l'intervention des États-Unis était justifiée, le gouvernement canadien apportait à ses voisins un soutien non négligeable. Toutefois, comme le précise John W. Holmes, «sans l'intervention tardive de l'ONU, le Canada n'aurait, sans aucun doute, participé activement aux opérations militaires»[4].

Le problème coréen fut toutefois l'occasion qui permit au gouvernement d'Ottawa de mesurer les divergences de vues qui existaient avec le gouvernement américain à propos des questions de sécurité dans le Pacifique et en Asie. Ces divergences apparurent tout au long des diverses phases de la question coréenne. Avant que n'éclatent les hostilités, le Canada, qui participait aux travaux de la commission intérimaire ayant pour but l'unification éventuelle de la Corée et le retrait des forces d'occupation, avait déjà eu l'occasion de s'exposer à certaines propositions américaines[5]. Des différences de point de vue purent être notées tout au long du conflit et perdurèrent. En 1954, par exemple, au moment de la première crise à propos des îles Quemoy et Matsu, le gouvernement d'Ottawa laissa entendre que ces îles appartenaient effectivement à la Chine populaire et qu'elles ne représentaient pas une menace à la sécurité du bloc occidental et plus particulièrement à celle des États-Unis[6].

De toute évidence, ces oppositions aux politiques asiatiques du grand voisin du Sud traduisaient bien l'intention de ne pas devoir être impliqué trop ouvertement dans des problèmes qui n'étaient pas évalués par le gouvernement canadien comme des menaces susceptibles de porter atteinte à la sécurité ou aux intérêts du Canada dans la région.

En 1954 encore, lorsque fut conclu à Manille le 8 septembre l'Organisation du traité pour l'Asie du Sud-Est (OTASE)[7], le Canada ne fut pas invité à participer mais il ne fit rien également pour l'être. Non seulement doutait-on de l'efficacité du pacte, mais encore l'on mesurait de façon rationnelle les avantages à ne pas être membre. Enfin, le Canada venait d'être appelé par les accords de Genève à participer aux commissions de contrôle et de supervision en Indochine. L'obligation d'objectivité fut dès lors l'argument décisif pour refuser toute appartenance à la nouvelle alliance militaire[8]. Il apparaissait de plus en plus enfin que les engagements canadiens risquaient d'être disproportionnés par rapport à ses capacités réelles; petit pays, le Canada ne pouvait assumer à la fois des responsabilités militaires en Europe et en Asie. D'ailleurs, très vite, les vocations du Canada étaient apparues dans le continent asiatique.

Associé très étroitement au plan de Colombo, le Canada préférait ne pas venir contrarier, par son adhésion à l'OTASE, des pays comme l'Inde et l'Indonésie qui avaient dénoncé en termes non équivoques la conclusion du traité. Il n'était enfin pas évident que les États-Unis eussent été très favorables à un accroissement du nombre de pays non asiatiques au sein de la nouvelle alliance[9]. Le débat tourna au court lorsque le Canada accepta de participer à la Commission internationale de contrôle en Indochine.

Cette double participation du Canada au plan de Colombo, puis à la Commission internationale de contrôle en Indochine, achevait de souligner la vocation que l'on voulait donner à la politique extérieure canadienne. L'assistance économique et la participation aux opérations du maintien de la paix furent désormais les deux grands axes autour desquels allaient s'articuler les objectifs des divers gouvernements d'Ottawa.

Dans le même temps où le Canada intervenait militairement en Corée, il s'associait à la Grande-Bretagne, à l'Australie, à la Nouvelle-Zélande, à l'Inde, au Pakistan et à Ceylan (Sri Lanka) pour établir le plan de Colombo dont l'objectif était d'assurer la stabilité et le progrès des États constitués à partir d'anciens territoires britanniques en Asie du Sud et en Asie du Sud-Est. Opposés dans leurs moyens, ces deux types d'intervention visaient cependant un objectif identique, à savoir l'endiguement du communisme en Asie. Le 22 février 1950, le Secrétaire d'État aux Affaires extérieures, Lester B. Pearson, exprimait cet objectif dès son retour de la Conférence de Colombo. Constatant que le centre de gravité du système international s'était déplacé vers l'Asie, Pearson expliquait en chambre qu'il appartenait au monde libre de déployer ses efforts pour prouver que c'était bien le monde occidental, et non la Russie, qui prônait la libération nationale ainsi que le progrès social et économique[10]. Un mois auparavant, John Diefenbaker avait, pour sa part, constaté que «50 millions de dollars par an constituaient une assurance bon marché contre le communisme en Asie».

Cette candeur dans la franchise illustrait bien une stratégie de développement qui trouvait ses fondements dans la rivalité idéologique exacerbée de l'époque. Pendant de longues années, le plan de Colombo fut le seul programme d'aide bilatérale du Canada. Jusqu'en 1969-1970, le programme allait absorber la moitié des sommes consacrées à l'aide internationale par le gouvernement d'Ottawa[11].

Combinant l'aide en capitaux à l'assistance technique, mais également par la fourniture de surplus de matières premières, le Canada apporta un concours efficace à la construction des complexes hydro-électriques de Warsak et Shadiwal au Pakistan, ainsi qu'à la construction d'un réacteur atomique en Inde[12]. D'autres projets furent amorcés sur le fleuve Mekong, des transferts de cuivre, de blé, d'aluminium et d'amiante furent également effectués. L'Inde, le Pakistan et Ceylan devinrent les principaux récipiendaires de l'aide bilatérale canadienne. Les pays de l'Asie du Sud-Est, fortement négligés, ne reçurent qu'à peu près 5 % des sommes allouées[13]. En 1969-1970, par exemple, sur les 124,8 millions de dollars consacrés au plan de Colombo, il fut attribué 114,5 millions aux pays de l'Asie du Sud.

La rencontre entre le Canada et l'Asie du Sud-Est ne se fit pas véritablement par l'intermédiaire du Commonwealth; elle intervint surtout par la participation canadienne aux côtés de l'Inde et de la Pologne, aux commissions internationales de contrôle et de supervision au Viêt-nam, au Laos et au Cambodge.

En assurant pendant près de 20 ans une présence en Indochine, le Canada fit l'expérience des réalités fort complexes de l'Asie du Sud-Est. Frustré par un rôle assez ambigu et par la tâche ingrate d'avoir à contrôler une paix qui n'était définie que par ses violations permanentes, le Canada subit alors les désillusions amères d'une conjoncture régionale outrepassant ses possibilités.

Le Canada n'avait en aucune façon recherché cette participation. Conséquence semble-t-il d'une suggestion du gouvernement indien à laquelle le premier ministre chinois Zhou Enlai aurait donné son accord, la proposition prit le gouvernement d'Ottawa par surprise. C'est sans empressement et avec un scepticisme doublé de certaines illusions que le Canada accepta les responsabilités qui découlaient des accords de la Conférence de Genève en 1954.

Par sa désignation, le Canada était appelé à jouer bon gré mal gré le rôle d'«occidental» dans la commission tripartite. Responsable devant la Conférence de Genève, la délégation canadienne s'était engagée à présenter ses rappoprts avec honnêteté et dans la mesure du possible avec objectivité. La contradiction entre la position et la fonction allait placer le Canada dans une situation délicate par rapport aux États-Unis. Comme le soulignent John W. Holmes et Jean-René Laroche: «Il y a plusieurs façons de présenter la position du gouvernement vis-à-vis de la guerre au Viêt-nam. L'une d'entre elles fait ressortir la similitude des points de vue entre Ottawa et Washington. Une autre interprétation accuse le gouvernement canadien de s'être fait le complice de Washington, en lui vendant des armes que les forces américaines ont utilisées au Viêt-nam et en lui fournissant des données acquises lors des travaux de la Commission[14].»

Il est vrai que le gouvernement d'Ottawa n'osa jamais aller trop loin dans sa critique de la politique américaine au Viêt-nam. En 1965, dans un rapport minoritaire de la Commission, la délégation canadienne indiquait clairement que le gouvernement d'Hanoi était bien le responsable des actes d'agression contre le Viêt-nam du Sud. Ce rapport donnait encore une fois l'impression d'un soutien canadien aux États-Unis. Pourtant, le gouvernement d'Ottawa était en désaccord sur le fond avec l'intervention de plus en plus évidente des États-Unis à tel point, comme le remarque G. Lalande, qu'en «avril 1965, de passage aux États-Unis, monsieur Lester B. Pearson, premier ministre du Canada, encourut le déplaisir du président Johnson pour avoir invité publiquement les États-Unis à cesser "au moment opportun" leurs bombardements aériens contre le Nord-Viêt-nam»[15].

L'expérience indochinoise fut en fin de compte assez pénible pour le Canada. Tiraillée entre plusieurs intérêts, confrontée sur le terrain à des problèmes trouvant le plus souvent leurs origines au plus profond de l'histoire des peuples de l'Asie du Sud-Est, cette participation laisse une marque indélébile sur les perceptions canadiennes de la région. Ceci paraît d'autant plus vrai qu'en 1972, 1 300 militaires et un agent sur trois du ministère des Affaires extérieures avait servi en Indochine[16].

À partir de 1963, une autre situation conflictuelle en Asie du Sud-Est entraîna encore le gouvernement canadien à faire des choix susceptibles de perturber l'amorce d'une politique dans la région. À l'occasion, en effet, du conflit entre l'Indonésie et la jeune fédération de Malaysia, le Canada dut prendre parti pour cette dernière. Les causes du conflit légitimaient cette position mais l'appartenance de la Malaysia au Commonwealth achevait de l'expliquer. Aux côtés de la Grande-Bretagne, de l'Australie et de la Nouvelle-Zélande, sans être toutefois autant impliqué que ces derniers, le gouvernement d'Ottawa s'engagea à fournir un matériel militaire léger, à entraîner des troupes malaysiennes et à augmenter ses crédits de façon à permettre à la Malaysia de faire l'achat d'avions canadiens d'entraînement et de transport.

Cherchant à ménager l'avenir des rapports entre le Canada et l'Indonésie, pays le plus important de la région, le gouvernement adopta une politique assez réaliste qui lui permit de continuer son aide sous forme de blé et de farine tout en suspendant en 1965 la vente de douze avions «otter» après que l'Indonésie eût utilisé trois appareils semblables – fournis dans le cadre du plan de Colombo – contre la Malaysia[17].

Il n'est pas inutile de rappeler ici que le Canada s'était déjà gagné la sympathie de l'Indonésie à l'époque où celle-ci luttait contre la Hollande pour son indépendance. En 1948, comme membre du Conseil de sécurité, le Canada avait su trouver la formule qui avait mis fin à l'«action de police» hollandaise. Et, lorsque l'Indonésie obtint son indépendance en décembre 1949, le gouvernement d'Ottawa reconnut immédiatement le nouvel État[18].

Si l'on fait bien sûr exception de la situation particulière en Asie du Sud-Est et de l'engagement en Corée, c'est en Asie de l'Est que l'on pouvait entrevoir des possibilités d'action plus en rapport avec les aspirations réelles du Canada. Signataire du traité de paix de 1951 avec le Japon, le Canada allait d'emblée situer ses rapports avec ce pays au plan commercial. Les séquelles de la guerre mais aussi celles des flambées de racisme à l'endroit des immigrants asiatiques, et particulièrement japonais, qu'avait connues l'Ouest canadien[19], s'estompèrent graduellement et le gouvernement d'Ottawa put en 1954 conclure un accord de commerce avec le Japon.

Aux termes de cette entente, le Japon se voyait octroyé la clause de la nation la plus favorisée mais le Canada s'était toutefois réservé le droit d'imposer des tarifs particuliers sur l'importation de produits japonais pouvant concurrencer dangereusement leurs équivalents canadiens. Déjà à l'époque, le gouvernement d'Ottawa allait s'employer à mettre en place les systèmes de restrictions volontaires des exportations japonaises. Dès la signature de l'accord, on n'avait pas manqué de pressentir les rapports difficiles qui pourraient à l'avenir s'établir entre deux pays concurrents, tous deux dépendants de leur commerce extérieur. En 1954, le ministre de l'Industrie et du Commerce, C.D. Howe, exprimait en ces termes cette inquiétude prémonitoire: «J'espère cependant que le commerce entre le Canada et le Japon évoluera sans que cela ne crée de graves problèmes pour l'industrie canadienne...[20]»

La croissance rapide des échanges, dont la balance fut toujours favorable au Canada, entraîna en 1961 la création du Comité ministériel consultatif Canada-Japon qui devait depuis se réunir deux fois par an. En peu de temps, le Japon allait devenir, au début des années 70, le deuxième partenaire commercial du Canada. En 1953, le volume total des échanges entre les deux pays était de 133 millions de dollars, et en 1969, il franchira le milliard.

Alors que les relations canado-japonaises empruntaient des avenues sans surprise, les rapports avec la Chine allaient connaître, dès la prise du pouvoir par le Parti communiste chinois, des lendemains plus amers.

De 1949 à 1970, la question de la reconnaissance diplomatique de la Chine constituera l'un des problèmes les plus épineux de la politique étrangère canadienne.

Elle fut à la fois le symbole et l'illustration de l'incapacité du Canada à prendre des décisions pouvant contrarier Washington. En outre, quelles que fussent au début des années 50 les interventions des dirigeants canadiens, ceux-ci ne pouvaient être suivis par une opinion publique fortement conditionnée par la guerre froide et l'anticommunisme.

À la fin de l'année 1949, puis en janvier 1950, le Secrétaire d'État aux Affaires extérieures, Lester B. Pearson, avait très certainement été gagné par l'idée de suivre l'exemple britannique. À la conférence inaugurant le plan de Colombo en janvier 1950, le premier ministre de l'Inde, Nehru, avait en effet invité les États participants à reconnaître le gouvernement de Pékin. La réaction du premier ministre Saint-Laurent fut à l'époque très positive. Prudemment toutefois, afin de ne pas diviser l'opinion publique canadienne sur une question qu'il considérait comme non prioritaire, mais aussi afin d'éviter d'être en contradiction avec la diplomatie américaine, le Cabinet libéral opta pour l'attentisme et l'observation de l'expérience britannique.

Le déclenchement des hostilités en Corée qui survint quelques mois plus tard, puis l'engagement des «volontaires chinois» dans le conflit, balayèrent rapidement tous les projets éventuellement envisagés. L'hostilité de l'opinion publique canadienne à l'endroit de la Chine était telle qu'en 1954, elle contraignit le premier ministre Saint-Laurent à revenir sur des propos favorables à la reconnaissance diplomatique qu'il avait tenus lors d'un voyage en Asie[21].

Ce fut paradoxalement au début des années 60 que le gouvernement conservateur de Diefenbaker posa les premiers jalons d'un rapprochement entre les deux États. En fait, les avantages commerciaux et les possibilités qu'offrait le marché chinois l'emportèrent sur les convictions idéologiques les plus fermes. C'est ainsi que l'on vit Diefenbaker se montrer beaucoup plus favorable au commerce avec la Chine lorsque cette dernière passa la commande de blé la plus importante que le Canada n'ait jamais reçue[22].

Les ventes de blé canadien firent beaucoup pour transformer l'état d'esprit des milieux les plus conservateurs, elles furent impuissantes cependant à faire aboutir le processus de rapprochement qui était amorcé et, chaque année aux Nations Unies, le Canada exprimait un vote défavorable à la résolution concernant l'admission de la Chine dans l'Organisation internationale. En 1968, la détermination du premier ministre Pierre E. Trudeau et sa volonté de faire en sorte de n'être plus un simple spectateur sur la scène asiatique, allaient entraîner le Canada vers un rapprochement avec la Chine. L'initiative allait s'inscrire dans une conjoncture favorable. La Chine réévaluait en effet son isolement dans le système international, et les États-Unis, affectés par les tourments du Viêt-nam, n'étaient pas en mesure de contrarier des politiques qui pouvaient éventuellement leur être favorables.

L'ÉPOQUE DE LA DÉTERMINATION

En 1968, l'arrivée au pouvoir du premier ministre Trudeau fit dévier la politique étrangère canadienne de la trajectoire qu'elle avait adoptée depuis 1945. Les nouvelles politiques extérieures canadiennes se voulurent alors conformes aux impératifs de l'environnement international et donc en rupture avec les habitudes d'antan. «La situation mondiale du Canada est aujourd'hui bien différente de ce qu'elle était après la guerre», déclarait le premier ministre; désormais, ajoutait-il, «le réalisme devrait être le mot d'ordre de nos visées internationales». Il s'agissait dès lors d'entreprendre une vaste révision des objectifs de la politique étrangère canadienne et de faire «[...] plus de bien en réussissant bien ce que nous *savons* être en mesure d'accomplir, qu'en prétendant être capables de faire des choses qui dépassent clairement nos possibilités nationales[23].»

Ainsi, comme le soulignera plusieurs fois par la suite le Secrétaire d'État aux Affaires extérieures, Mitchell Sharp, le Canada devait redevenir cette «puissance moyenne dans un monde en évolution»[24]. Le temps du Canada «missionnaire» était révolu, désormais le «réalisme» évoquerait beaucoup plus la promotion des intérêts économiques du Canada à l'extérieur que sa propension à se faire l'artisan et le défenseur d'un système de sécurité collective de plus en plus contesté.

Les objectifs

Dès l'amorce de cette orientation nouvelle qui trouvera son achèvement en 1972 avec la politique de «troisième option», l'Asie, incluse dans l'englobant vocable du Pacifique, eut une place privilégiée. En 1970, le livre blanc sur la politique étrangère canadienne notera, dans sa brochure sur le Pacifique, que cette région possède des ressources immenses et variées et qu'elle «offre de belles possibilités d'augmenter les échanges économiques et commerciaux. Ce potentiel se développera non seulement dans la mesure où, grâce à des efforts concertés, nous pourrons répondre aux besoins du marché dans cette région, mais aussi dans la mesure où il s'y établira un climat propice à la stabilité et à la paix»[25].

D'emblée, les priorités étaient annoncées et les nécessités de stimuler la croissance économique se situèrent dans la logique de ce «réalisme» qui assujettissait les politiques à suivre aux nécessités internes de l'économie canadienne.

Depuis 1965, en effet, l'on pouvait constater une croissance assez spectaculaire des échanges avec la région du Pacifique comprise dans son acception la plus large. On notait par exemple que la valeur des exportations canadiennes avait doublé entre 1965 et 1971, pour passer de 699 millions à 1,4 milliard de dollars. La croissance de la valeur des importations avait encore été supérieure à cela puisque de 406 millions de dollars en 1965, elle atteignait 1,2 milliard en 1971. La ventilation des échanges par pays indiquait une croissance très nette avec chacun d'entre eux tout en mettant en relief surtout le développement assez exceptionnel des transactions commerciales avec le Japon, Taiwan et la Corée du Sud.

Le Canada souhaitait donc profiter davantage encore de cette conjoncture favorable et, par la négociation bilatérale et multilatérale, l'on entendait œuvrer en identifiant de façon aussi plus précise la nécessité d'amener le Japon à éliminer les obstacles restreignant l'exportation des produits canadiens manufacturés. La promotion des transports et du tourisme et enfin l'encouragement aux investissements constituaient les autres volets de la détermination canadienne à pénétrer le marché asiatique. L'énoncé d'un ensemble de moyens parachevait les objectifs du gouvernement.

Les objectifs, par ailleurs, du programme d'aide au développement en Extrême-Orient étaient également en tous points conformes au contenu du chapitre sur le développement international. Dans une formulation plus concrète, l'Asie du Sud-Est, et en particulier l'Indonésie, devenaient les cibles privilégiées de l'aide canadienne. L'aide au redressement de l'Indochine, une fois la paix revenue, était également envisagée. Tant sur le plan bilatéral que dans sa participation financière à des organisations régionales, telles la Commission économique de l'Asie et de l'Extrême-Orient ou encore la Banque asiatique de développement, on précisait que «le souci du développement et les considérations d'ordre humanitaire continuent de présider à l'élaboration de la politique d'aide du gouvernement canadien»[26]. Quelques lignes plus loin cependant cet altruisme de conviction était pondéré par le lien nettement formulé entre l'aide et les «chances commerciales» des manufacturiers canadiens.

Les conditions de la paix et de la stabilité dans la région étaient évoquées en termes de prérequis aux autres objectifs. Tout en s'en tenant au postulat maintes fois évoqué, selon lequel le Canada ne détenait pas les capacités d'affirmer autrement que sur le plan commercial sa présence en Asie, on retenait essentiellement de la nouvelle orientation que le gouvernement fédéral investissait toute sa détermination dans l'établissement de liens diplomatiques avec la Chine.

Cet objectif, manifestation la plus spectaculaire de la volonté canadienne d'indépendance, se légitimait officiellement au premier chef par l'importance «[...] pour la paix et la stabilité du monde de mettre terme [sic] à l'isolement de la Chine», et par l'espoir de promouvoir ainsi «des rapports plus constructifs entre la Chine et la communauté mondiale»[27].

Dans la logique d'une orientation dûment inscrite dans le livre blanc sur la politique étrangère canadienne, l'enrichissement de la qualité de la vie devait «ajouter une autre dimension aux politiques de croissance économique et de réformes sociales»[28]. À propos du Pacifique, ce souci se manifestait par quelques paragraphes coiffés de l'intitulé «Compréhension mutuelle accrue». Situés entre les objectifs de l'aide au développement et ceux visant à la paix et à la sécurité, trois types d'actions étaient énoncés. Il s'agissait tout d'abord de projeter l'image du Canada à l'étranger, puis d'«aider les Canadiens à comprendre les rapides transformations sociales qui ont cours dans les pays du Pacifique en voie de développement, à en bénéficier et à y contribuer d'une façon constructive»[29] et, enfin, d'organiser des échanges culturels et scientifiques. Pour chacun de ces objectifs, quelques initiatives possibles étaient suggérées.

Les objectifs qu'exprimait le Canada dans le vaste espace du Pacifique reflétaient donc fidèlement l'orientation générale de la politique étrangère canadienne. Reproductions en sous-catégories d'une panoplie de vastes aspirations, aucun d'entre eux n'était altéré par les spécificités de la région, à laquelle ils s'adressaient. En d'autres termes, si les cibles suffisaient à différencier les objectifs, leur portée, leur nature profonde, puisaient à une source commune d'inspiration, celle des grandes options définies dans le livre blanc.

La reconnaissance diplomatique de la Chine

Bien avant l'annonce à la Chambre des communes, le 13 octobre 1970, de l'établissement de relations diplomatiques avec la Chine, les pourparlers entamés dès le mois de février 1969 dans la capitale suédoise par les deux parties avaient fait l'objet de commentaires dubitatifs ou convaincus. Pour de nombreux observateurs, il fut difficile d'admettre que le Canada ait pu délibérément entreprendre ces négociations sans avoir reçu l'aval de Washington; pour d'autres c'était le gouvernement chinois qui «octroyait» au gouvernement d'Ottawa le privilège de le reconnaître[30]. Ces deux types de commentaires extrêmes n'étaient pas sans fondement mais ils devaient être considérablement atténués et nuancés. Ils devaient surtout être remis à leur juste place en considérant que l'initiative fut dès son origine essentiellement canadienne et qu'elle se situait dans le prolongement d'une volonté clairement et à maintes reprises exprimée par le nouveau premier ministre, Pierre E. Trudeau.

Peu de temps après son élection, ce dernier avait d'ailleurs déclaré sans ambiguïté son intention «d'examiner notre politique à l'égard de la Chine dans le contexte de l'intérêt nouveau porté aux affaires du Pacifique en général. Notre objectif sera de reconnaître le gouvernement de la République populaire de Chine aussitôt que possible et de permettre à ce gouvernement d'occuper le siège de la Chine aux Nations Unies, sans oublier qu'il y a un gouvernement distinct à Taiwan»[31]. Le rôle personnel du premier ministre fut considérable puisqu'il intervint constamment dans ce dossier[32].

Contrairement à des convictions bien ancrées, le gouvernement américain ne protesta pas vraiment et n'intervint pas auprès du gouvernement d'Ottawa. En fait, pendant tout le déroulement des négociations, le Canada tint Washington informé des discussions, ce qui était le moyen le plus sûr de désamorcer toute velléité d'ingérence. Si l'on fait exception de quelques protestations sporadiques, l'opinion publique canadienne était favorable à l'initiative du gouvernement fédéral. Les milieux d'affaires poussaient à la reconnaissance du gouvernement de Pékin et l'Ouest canadien, pourtant fort conservateur, n'avait aucune objection à envisager l'occasion d'accroître encore ses ventes de blé à la Chine.

Les incertitudes et les appréhensions des représentants canadiens en Suède s'estompèrent assez rapidement devant les réactions assez favorables de leurs homologues chinois. Il n'y eut pas de négociations sur l'opportunité de négocier[33]. On nota divers éléments qui expliquèrent l'attitude conciliante de la Chine. Parmi ceux-ci, la volonté clairement exprimée à maintes reprises du Canada d'aboutir, l'augmentation des échanges commerciaux entre les deux pays ainsi que l'absence d'ambassade canadienne à Taiwan furent sans nul doute importants. Ce qui paraît toutefois plus déterminant fut la conjoncture et la situation canadienne par rapport aux États-Unis.

Les relations sino-soviétiques, fortement détériorées en 1969, imposaient à la Chine une réorientation de sa politique étrangère. De façon plus concrète, il devenait souhaitable d'opérer pour la Chine un rapprochement avec les États-Unis. À Washington, la politique étrangère du président Nixon et de son conseiller Kissinger allait arriver aux mêmes conclusions. À l'époque cependant où s'amorcèrent les négociations avec le Canada, rien ne laissait présager l'accélération du rapprochement sino-américain et tout laissait croire, surtout au gouvernement chinois, que le Canada constituerait le tremplin le plus adéquat pour amorcer graduellement de nouveaux rapports avec Washington.

Jusqu'au 13 octobre 1970, il fallut 21 séances de négociations pour aboutir. Comme il fallait s'y attendre, la question de Taiwan occupa, aux dires d'un participant, 95 % des discussions. Il n'était plus question pour le Canada de pratiquer «une politique des deux Chines»; il était par ailleurs exclu d'endosser totalement la position chinoise. En fait, l'attitude canadienne à l'endroit de Taiwan consistait à faire preuve d'une indifférence calculée et à convaincre ses interlocuteurs qu'il n'y avait pas de politique canadienne envers Formose. Outre les questions commerciales, le règlement des contentieux hérités du passé, comme l'ambassade canadienne à Nankin ou encore les compensations réclamées par Ottawa après l'arrêt en 1951 des paiements du gouvernement chinois à la Ming Sung Industrial Company Limited of Montreal, furent avec le traitement des diplomates et la position canadienne dans l'admission de la Chine aux Nations Unies, quelques-uns des principaux sujets abordés. L'intervention directe de Sharp, Secrétaire aux Affaires extérieures, eut un impact dans la négociation et Trudeau lui accorda plus tard tout le crédit pour la formule décisive à propos de Taiwan, formule selon laquelle le Canada «prenait note de la position chinoise sur ce point».

Le 13 octobre 1970, alors que l'opinion publique canadienne était surtout mobilisée par «les événements» d'octobre au Québec, Sharp lisait à la Chambre des communes le communiqué en quatre points auquel avaient abouti les deux parties:

1. Le gouvernement de la République populaire de Chine et le gouvernement du Canada, conformément aux principes du respect mutuel de la souveraineté et de l'intégrité territoriale, de la non-intervention dans les affaires internes l'un de l'autre, ainsi que de l'égalité et de la réciprocité des avantages, ont décidé d'accorder mutuellement la reconnaissance et d'établir des relations diplomatiques à compter du 13 octobre 1970.

2. Le gouvernement chinois réaffirme que Taiwan est une partie inaliénable du territoire de la République populaire de Chine. Le gouvernement canadien prend note de cette position du gouvernement chinois.

3. Le gouvernement du Canada reconnaît le gouvernement de la République populaire de Chine comme étant le seul gouvernement légal de la Chine.

4. Les gouvernements chinois et canadien sont convenus d'échanger des ambassadeurs dans les six prochains mois et de fournir toute l'aide nécessaire à l'établissement de missions diplomatiques dans leurs capitales respectives ainsi qu'à l'exercice des fonctions de ces missions, dans le respect de l'égalité, de la réciprocité des avantages et de l'usage international[34].

Alors que la Chine s'était assurée que la position canadienne aux Nations Unies serait désormais conforme à la seule reconnaissance du gouvernement de Pékin, elle fut vivement contrariée en constatant que trois semaines après la date de la création du comité conjoint, le Canada avait exprimé un vote qui considérait la question chinoise comme «importante». Or, en fonction de l'article 18 de la Charte, une majorité des deux tiers des membres était alors requise et cela rendait donc plus difficile l'admission de la Chine aux Nations Unies. Il fallut aux diplomates canadiens beaucoup de talent pour convaincre le gouvernement chinois que la Chine était aussi «importante» avant qu'après la reconnaissance diplomatique! En automne 1971, cependant, le Canada ne considéra plus que la question chinoise était «importante» et vota par la suite en faveur de la résolution «albanaise», demandant l'admission de la Chine aux Nations Unies.

Le retrait des commissions internationales de contrôle et de surveillance en Indochine

Dès 1963, l'intérêt du gouvernement d'Ottawa s'était également tourné vers l'Asie du Sud-Est mais surtout dans les pays périphériques à l'Indochine, aux régimes non communistes et au potentiel économique déjà fortement mis en valeur. Les multiples voyages du premier ministre dans ces États, l'ouverture de consulats et bureaux commerciaux puis la mise en place des structures d'échanges économiques indispensables préfiguraient le déploiement d'un vaste projet canadien dans cette région.

Les événements pénibles qui se déroulaient alors dans la péninsule indochinoise apportaient une fausse note dans la mise en œuvre du processus amorcé. Engagé, nous l'avons déjà vu, dans les trois commissions internationales de surveillance et de contrôle (CISC) au Viêt-nam, au Laos et au Cambodge depuis 1954, le Canada avait à maintes reprises exprimé son scepticisme à propos de l'efficacité de ces institutions.

Dès le début de son mandat, le nouveau premier ministre libéral avait clairement énoncé, lors des conférences de presse tenues pendant sa tournée du Pacifique en 1970, sa volonté de mettre fin à ces missions impossibles, ou du moins de réévaluer en fonction de ses propres critères tout nouvel engagement canadien. Pourtant, vers la fin de l'année 1972, alors qu'un accord de cessez-le-feu parut possible au Viêt-nam, le Canada apprit que les États-Unis et la République démocratique du Viêt-nam avaient convenu d'une nouvelle Commission internationale de contrôle et de surveillance composée de la Hongrie, de l'Indonésie, de la Pologne et... du Canada.

L'accord de cessez-le-feu n'eut pas lieu au moins d'octobre, ce qui permit au gouvernement d'Ottawa, en période électorale, de pouvoir différer sa décision. Le 27 janvier 1973, l'accord fut signé et le Canada comme prévu était appelé à devenir membre de la Commission aux côtés des trois autres participants déjà mentionnés. Une fois encore, un peu malgré lui, le gouvernement fédéral se retrouvait impliqué dans un rôle qu'il n'avait pas vraiment souhaité[35]. Le Canada acceptait toutefois, après avoir posé un certain nombre de conditions, de s'engager pour une période initiale de 60 jours et dépêchait un contingent de 290 militaires et civils au Viêt-nam.

Au mois de février, le gouvernement d'Ottawa reconnaissait celui de la République du Viêt-nam, ce qui «revenait à accorder effectivement un statut égal aux gouvernements des deux Viêt-nams et devait faciliter la tâche de la délégation canadienne à la CICS»[36]. Le mois suivant, le Secrétaire d'État aux Affaires extérieures se rendait en Indochine et rencontrait les autorités des gouvernements de Saigon, Vientiane et Hanoi. À son retour, devant le Comité permanent de la Chambre sur les affaires extérieures et la défense nationale, Sharp affirmait que malgré tous les efforts déployés par la délégation canadienne, la CICS n'accomplissait pas les tâches qui lui avaient été confiées aux termes de l'accord de cessez-le-feu. Il s'était produit des milliers d'incidents, dont certaines opérations de grande envergure[37].

Afin que la «structure fragile» de la paix au Viêt-nam ne fût point trop ébranlée par le retrait du Canada, il fut décidé d'une prolongation additionnelle de 60 jours au sein de la CICS. Au terme du nouveau délai, le 29 mai 1973, Sharp annonçait que le Canada se retirait de la Commission.

À l'issue de son engagement, le gouvernement d'Ottawa mit en relief le fait que sa brève participation avait au moins permis de procéder, dans des conditions convenables, à l'échange des prisonniers[38]. On nota plus tard que le Canada s'était senti fort mal placé pour refuser aux États-Unis un engagement conforme aux désirs maintes fois exprimés de voir le gouvernement américain se retirer du Viêt-nam. On remarqua encore que le gouvernement d'Ottawa avait peut-être aussi craint que le grand voisin puisse user de représailles économiques à son endroit[39].

Envers les deux autres pays d'Indochine, le Laos et le Cambodge, les intérêts du Canada s'étaient limités essentiellement à la nécessité pour le gouvernement d'Ottawa de projeter sur cette Asie francophone son propre caractère biculturel. Au Cambodge, le Canada avait là aussi fait l'expérience d'une participation à une commission de contrôle impuissante à entreprendre quelque enquête que ce soit. En 1969, le 4 décembre, le prince Sihanouk demandait à la Commission de s'ajourner *sine die* à partir du 31 décembre de la même année.

Lors de l'entrée des troupes américaines et sud-vietnamiennes sur le territoire cambodgien en 1970, le gouvernement d'Ottawa, par l'intermédiaire de son Secrétaire d'État aux Affaires extérieures, fit à la Chambre des communes un rapport-synthèse sur le rôle que le Canada avait joué dans ce pays. À propos des événements en cours, Sharp déclara: «Je veux qu'on sache bien que le Canada n'a pas été informé à l'avance des décisions des États-Unis. Nous n'en avons eu aucune connaissance préalable et, bien entendu, il n'y avait aucune raison pour qu'on nous ait prévenus[40].»

Les intérêts et l'attitude canadienne à l'endroit du Laos furent à peu près semblables, et, lorsque le 15 juin 1974, la délégation du Canada se retira, une page lourde de 20 années de participation canadienne en Indochine était tournée. À la même date, le Laos et le Canada convinrent d'établir des relations diplomatiques et de procéder à l'échange d'ambassadeurs.

L'Asie orientale: marché pour les exportations canadiennes

Après la reconnaissance diplomatique de la Chine, le retrait canadien des commissions de contrôle et de surveillance en Indochine marqua une rupture significative dans la politique étrangère du gouvernement fédéral. En Asie de l'Est, comme en d'autres régions, on entendait rentabiliser la présence canadienne et les «missionnaires commerciaux», tout comme ceux de l'ACDI, allaient devoir désormais se substituer aux troupes canadiennes.

Dans la formulation encore hésitante de la troisième option, il était d'ores et déjà acquis que le Japon constituerait la clé de voûte orientale de la nouvelle politique extérieure du Canada. Dès l'accession au pouvoir du gouvernement libéral, le Japon avait à ce titre fait l'objet d'une attention particulière et, en ce début de mandat, le gouvernement de Trudeau entendait diversifier davantage la gamme des rapports bilatéraux demeurés trop exclusivement commerciaux.

Malgré des efforts dans le domaine des échanges culturels et de la coopération politique au sein d'organisations internationales, les initiatives économiques furent de loin les plus significatives. C'est ainsi par exemple qu'au moins de janvier 1972, Jean-Luc Pépin, alors ministre de l'Industrie et du Commerce, se rendit à Tokyo à la tête de la plus importante mission économique jamais envoyée par le Canada à l'étranger. Ce geste, comme de nombreux autres, fut l'occasion de mesurer les difficultés, à première vue paradoxales, d'un commerce prospère, toujours excédentaire en faveur du Canada, mais fortement déséquilibré dans la composition des produits échangés.

Ainsi en 1973, le Japon devenait le deuxième partenaire commercial du Canada. L'excédent du commerce canadien avec le Japon avait atteint le sommet des 800 millions de dollars. Les exportations avaient augmenté de 87 % pour atteindre 1,811 million et les importations avaient diminué de 5,5 % pour s'établir à 1,011 million de dollars. De 1968 à 1973, le taux de croissance annuel moyen des exportations canadiennes vers le Japon avait été de 23,84 %. En contrepartie, le taux de croissance annuel des importations se situait à 23,15 %. La lecture de la composition des échanges montrait en revanche que les produits finis constituaient plus de 95 % des importations canadiennes alors que les exportations en ce domaine ne parvenaient pas à se situer au-delà de 20 %.

En fait, à l'époque comme aujourd'hui, le Canada demeure essentiellement pour le Japon un fournisseur de matières premières industrielles mais aussi de produits agricoles, comme le blé, le colza, l'orge et la viande de porc. En contrepartie, le Japon importe 93 % des exportations canadiennes de charbon et 75 % du minerai et des concentrés de cuivre. Il est aussi le plus gros client du Canada pour l'achat de minerai de plomb et ses concentrés ainsi que pour le molybdène; il se classe au deuxième rang des importations pour la pâte de bois, le zinc et l'aluminium. Malgré une augmentation substantielle chaque année du volume total des échanges ainsi qu'une balance commerciale qui est largement favorable au Canada, le commerce japonais ne représente depuis plusieurs années que 5 % du volume commercial canadien. Même si l'inflation constitue le facteur qui explique le plus cette stagnation, il convient toutefois de mentionner l'incapacité du Canada à accroître les exportations de produits finis et semi-finis.

Ainsi, en dépit de toutes les réunions conjointes par le truchement de comités ou de commissions, les missions commerciales, les rencontres des premiers ministres et des ministres des Affaires étrangères ou de l'Industrie et du Commerce, il apparaît simplement, à la lumière des statistiques, que de 1970 à 1977, le pourcentage de la vente des produits finis par rapport aux exportations totales annuelles est passé de 2,5 à 1,9 % alors que celui des matières brutes non comestibles s'élevait encore de 50,1 % en 1970 à 52,5 % en 1977. En revanche, le pourcentage que représentent les produits finis dans les importations en provenance du Japon est passé de 66,7 % en 1970 à 74,9 % en 1977.

Au début des années 70, la Chine devint l'autre grand partenaire asiatique du Canada. Avec prudence et réalisme, on s'était employé à éviter les engouements et la fascination exercés par le marché chinois sur l'Occident. Pourtant, deux semaines après la reconnaissance diplomatique, le Canada négociait avec la Chine ce qui était à l'époque le plus gros contrat de vente de blé. Dès lors, il fut permis de croire qu'il était possible de faire mieux et plus vite encore. Les initiatives furent nombreuses, les efforts considérables et constants et plusieurs observateurs estimaient qu'il était possible, pour un temps, d'aller au-delà des attentes issues de ce rapprochement sino-canadien. En fait, le Canada n'eut pas vraiment le temps de bénéficier de l'avantage qu'il avait acquis. Le rapprochement sino-américain qui survint très tôt, puis l'inclination de la Chine à se tourner vers le Japon et l'Europe occidentale, placèrent rapidement le Canada en situation concurrentielle. Il apparut ainsi clairement qu'il convenait de composer avec le rythme imposé par la diplomatie chinoise.

En 1970, la simple lecture du bilan commercial annuel des échanges avec la Chine montrait un déséquilibre impressionnant entre les exportations et les importations avec une balance extrêmement favorable au Canada. Phénomène encore plus intéressant, on pouvait constater, de 1961 jusqu'à 1969, que l'importance des ventes de céréales par rapport à l'ensemble des exportations canadiennes à destination de la Chine s'était toujours établie à plus de 96 %, ce pourcentage étant même de 99,9 % pour certaines années.

À partir de la reconnaissance diplomatique, les deux parties s'employèrent à résoudre ces déséquilibres en permettant un accroissement assez significatif des importations de marchandises chinoises au Canada. En dépit des efforts entrepris, les fonctionnaires du ministère de l'Industrie et du Commerce estimèrent qu'il était encore possible d'accroître les exportations canadiennes.

Ces convictions ne furent pas illusoires puisque la part des exportations de céréales diminua progressivement à partir de 1971, avec une exception conjoncturelle en 1975. En contrepartie, le Canada allait vendre plus d'aluminium, de nickel, de produits forestiers, de potasse, de matériel de télécommunication et d'équipement ferroviaire.

Le premier ministre Trudeau allait parachever les initiatives entreprises en effectuant au mois d'octobre 1973 la première visite officielle d'un chef de gouvernement canadien en Chine. La chaleur des contacts avec les principaux dirigeants chinois, mais surtout les résultats obtenus, firent de ce voyage un grand succès pour le prestige personnel du premier ministre, mais aussi pour la diplomatie canadienne.

À l'issue des entretiens qu'il eut avec le premier ministre Zhou Enlai et le président Mao Ze-dong, le premier ministre canadien annonçait que d'importants accords ou arrangements bilatéraux avaient été conclus dans les secteurs du commerce, des affaires consulaires et des programmes d'échanges bilatéraux. L'accord commercial prévoyait l'échange du traitement de la nation la plus favorisée – article 1 – et la mise sur pied du Comité mixte du commerce – article 8. Ce comité s'est réuni par la suite annuellement depuis 1973.

Ailleurs en Asie de l'Est, d'autres pays firent l'objet d'une attention nouvelle. L'ouverture par exemple de l'ambassade canadienne en Corée du Sud en 1973 marqua le point de départ des rapports économiques extrêmement prospères entre les deux pays. De 1962 à 1973, les exportations canadiennes avaient augmenté de près de 97 % et le dynamisme de l'économie coréenne en faisait désormais un pays cible pour les investisseurs et gens d'affaires canadiens. En Asie du Sud-Est, l'instabilité politique, la méconnaissance et la distance constituaient quelques-uns des facteurs expliquant le peu d'intérêt du Canada pour cette région.

Au début des années 70, les objectifs de la stratégie gouvernementale la désignait tout naturellement comme cible complémentaire à l'effort entrepris vers le Pacifique. Dans le réseau des interactions croissantes du Canada avec les pays de l'Asie du Sud-Est, le commerce devint le principal foyer de convergence de toutes les initiatives. Les échanges commerciaux, négligeables dans les années 60, allaient atteindre, lors de la décennie suivante, des niveaux un peu moins insignifiants.

Les efforts portèrent essentiellement vers les pays aux économies à forte croissance. Les liens du Commonwealth privilégièrent aussi la Malaysia et Singapour, mais c'est sur le potentiel considérable de l'économie indonésienne que se fondèrent les espoirs du Canada. Les richesses minières et les besoins d'infrastructure de ce pays attirèrent les investisseurs canadiens, en particulier l'International Nickel of Canada (INCO). En outre, de nombreux programmes d'aide, administrés par l'ACDI et fortement liés à la pénétration économique du Canada, furent à l'époque mis en place en Indonésie mais aussi en Thaïlande et aux Philippines.

LE TEMPS DE LA RÉÉVALUATION

Dans les premières années qui suivirent la révision de la politique étrangère, le déploiement des activités canadiennes visant à affirmer la vocation «pacifique» du pays fut placé sous le signe de l'imagination et de l'initiative. Les relations nouvelles avec la Chine et une attention plus particulière accordée au Japon pouvaient en témoigner. Un observateur japonais confirmait récemment ce dynamisme canadien au début de la décennie; il concluait par ailleurs que c'était le Japon qui était alors demeuré passif[41]. Cette détermination, cet engouement d'une première époque allaient cependant trouver rapidement leurs limites. Le premier ministre lui-même, inspirateur d'une vision nouvelle qui devait faire reculer les horizons du Canada, s'employa alors à démontrer qu'il ne convenait pas d'outrepasser des objectifs mesurés à l'aune des contraintes de la politique intérieure.

Ainsi dans un deuxième temps, l'élan initial s'affaiblit faute d'impulsions nouvelles. Beaucoup plus que les déconvenues enregistrées dans des rapports délicats avec des partenaires difficiles, beaucoup plus que les impératifs d'un environnement international asiatique caractérisé par les conflits, ce furent des contraintes extérieures à la région qui expliquèrent l'essoufflement de la politique canadienne en Asie de l'Est.

En effet, à partir de l'énoncé formel de la politique de «troisième option» en 1972, beaucoup fut dit et fait pour démontrer qu'il ne s'agissait en aucune façon de remettre en cause les rapports privilégiés avec les États-Unis. En d'autres termes, le Canada s'employait avec énergie à tempérer sa propre audace en reconnaissant à de multiples occasions, comme il l'avait toujours fait, «[...] que pour la réalisation de chacun des aspects de notre politique étrangère, nous devons tenir compte des objectifs, des initiatives et des activités de la politique étrangère des États-Unis»[42].

Affirmant à maintes reprises l'importance qu'il convenait désormais d'accorder au Pacifique, on s'empressait aussi de souligner qu'aucune autre région du monde ne serait lésée et plus particulièrement l'Europe qui, en fin de compte, retint, considérablement plus que l'Asie, l'attention du Canada.

Par ailleurs, et parce que le Canada ne voulait pas exagérer l'étendue de son influence sur «le cours des événements mondiaux»[43], l'essentiel des actions en Asie de l'Est avait été récupéré ou identifié prioritairement à la recherche de nouveaux marchés commerciaux. La fuite devant toute autre responsabilité dans la région – en particulier dans le domaine de la sécurité – allait contribuer à provoquer un flou dans la désignation des intérêts canadiens en Asie de l'Est.

Il serait cependant inexact de vouloir minimiser l'impact des transformations régionales sur les politiques du Canada en Asie de l'Est. Les années 1975-1976 furent en effet fertiles en changements et les modifications apportées aux structures politiques des trois pays de la péninsule indochinoise, ainsi que les conséquences de la mort du président Mao Ze-dong en Chine au mois de septembre 1976, ne manquèrent pas d'affecter la politique canadienne dans la région. D'une façon générale, on peut dire que les rapports du Canada avec l'Asie de l'Est ont marqué le pas jusqu'en 1978; à partir de cette date, les intérêts de l'Ouest canadien, associés à une conjoncture économique difficile, ont incité tout à la fois le gouvernement fédéral et les milieux d'affaires à se tourner davantage vers l'océan Pacifique.

S'adapter aux changements

Les événements de 1975 en Indochine affectèrent assez peu les positions canadiennes. Lorsque les «Khmers rouges» capturèrent, le 25 avril, la capitale Phnom Penh et renversèrent le régime du général Lon Nol, le Canada reconnut le nouveau gouvernement du Kampuchea sans qu'il fût nécessaire d'établir avec lui des relations diplomatiques.

Au Viêt-nam, le personnel de l'ambassade canadienne à Saigon fut évacué puis, le 25 juin, il fut décidé d'établir de nouveaux liens diplomatiques avec le gouvernement provisoire de la République du Viêt-nam du Sud. Avant que les bureaux ne fussent réouverts, l'unification du Viêt-nam fut achevée l'année suivante et le Canada n'eut pas à reconnaître officiellement le nouvel État puisque ses relations avec lui furent «jugées être la continuation de celles déjà établies avec les anciens gouvernements des Viêt-nams du Nord et du Sud[44].

Au Laos, l'arrivée au pouvoir au mois d'août 1975 du Pathet Lao ne modifia pas l'attitude du Canada, qui maintint avec le nouveau régime les relations qu'il avait avec l'ancien. L'ambassadeur canadien en Thaïlande demeura accrédité auprès du gouvernement de Vientiane.

En réalité, tous ces liens avec les pays de la péninsule indochinoise demeuraient assez symboliques. Il importait de maintenir ouverts les canaux de communications; mais dans les faits, le Canada ne portait désormais plus son attention sur cette région où allait perdurer une instabilité et des événements que l'on préférait ignorer. Il fallut en 1979 la fuite massive de ceux que l'on surnomma les «*boat people*» pour que l'on se souvint à nouveau des peuples de la péninsule indochinoise.

Se détournant désormais des pays trop instables, c'est vers les pays non communistes de l'Asie du Sud-Est qu'allait se concentrer l'attention principale des dirigeants canadiens. La situation en Indochine affectait les cinq pays de l'ASEAN et la perception des menaces nouvelles allait faire revivre une Association qui, depuis 1967, était demeurée assez inactive. Pour le Canada, soucieux d'accroître sa présence après des pays de l'Association, il importait dès lors d'avoir envers l'Indochine une politique conforme aux positions de l'ASEAN. Dans la perspective des intérêts canadiens, les changements rapides qui affectèrent la Chine en 1976 eurent beaucoup plus de conséquences.

Au début du mois de septembre 1976, la disparition pourtant anticipée de Mao Ze-dong entraîna la Chine dans l'incertitude d'une chaude lutte pour le pouvoir. Pendant tout l'intermède qui s'étendit depuis «l'écrasement de la bande des quatre» en octobre 1976 jusqu'au retour du vice-premier ministre Deng Xiaoping, lors du onzième congrès du Parti communiste chinois en août 1977, les relations sino-canadiennes subirent les effets des changements graduels qui s'opéraient en Chine.

De l'automne 1976 au printemps 1977, il n'y eut pas d'échanges significatifs entre les deux pays. Le 13 octobre 1976, qui marquait le sixième anniversaire des relations diplomatiques entre le Canada et la Chine, seule une brève cérémonie souligna cette occasion et l'on procéda à un échange de notes pour reconduire l'accord de commerce de 1973[45].

Puis, à partir du printemps 1977, ce fut sous le signe de la culture que s'amorça une lente reprise. Les orchestres canadiens croisèrent les ballets de Shanghai et les visites ministérielles se succédèrent. Ces prises de contact laissaient entrevoir une nouvelle société, celle qui promettait les «quatre modernisations» à sa population, celle qui désormais semblait ne plus répugner à ouvrir son territoire aux biens et services des pays étrangers. C'est ainsi que la multiplicité des activités, des rencontres et des initiatives traduisit fort bien cette fébrilité des milieux d'affaires mais également du gouvernement fédéral à ne pas se laisser distancer dans la course au «marché chinois».

De la même façon que l'avait auparavant fait le Japon, la Grande-Bretagne et la France, le Canada ouvrait en 1979 à la Chine, par l'intermédiaire de la Société pour l'expansion des exportations, une ligne de crédit de 2 milliards de dollars. Destinée à faciliter l'achat de biens et de services auprès de fournisseurs canadiens au cours des trois prochaines années, cette facilité de crédit, la plus importante jamais accordée à un autre pays que le gouvernement d'Ottawa, allait être assortie d'un accord commercial.

L'accord fut en fait un renouvellement de celui de 1976 auquel fut adjoint un protocole par lequel les deux pays s'engageaient à accroître les échanges commerciaux et la coopération économique de façon substantielle. L'entente était intervenue à l'occasion de la visite à Ottawa de Li Qiang, ministre chinois du Commerce extérieur. Robert de Cotret, alors ministre du Commerce dans le Cabinet conservateur, précisait que le Canada avait décidé d'appliquer à la Chine à partir du mois de janvier 1980 la clause de la nation la plus favorisée, «ce qui conduira à une baisse de 33 à 20 % des tarifs sur toutes les marchandises chinoises entrant au pays»[46].

Le tableau des échanges commerciaux avec la Chine depuis 1965 constitue l'indicateur le plus éloquent des problèmes rencontrés – voir le tableau 1, présenté en fin de chapitre. Parmi les particularités les plus saisissantes apparaît d'emblée le déséquilibre constant de cette balance commerciale. Malgré un accroissement du volume des exportations chinoises ces dernières années, le solde des échanges demeure très confortablement favorable au Canada. Le pourcentage des ventes de blé constitue l'explication la plus évidente de ce déséquilibre. On remarque toutefois que les efforts visant à diversifier les exportations canadiennes ont commencé à porter fruit puisque ce pourcentage a été ramené graduellement à moins de 60 % ces trois dernières années. On doit également noter que depuis 1972, le pourcentage des produits finis dans le total des exportations canadiennes est passé de 0,2 à 2,05 % en 1984. Il reste que la difficulté première réside dans le déséquilibre des échanges et surtout dans la nature des produits commercés. Lorsque l'on analyse la ventilation des exportations chinoises vers le Canada, on remarque très vite que les textiles représentent pour la Chine la contrepartie évidente de ce que sont les ventes de blé pour le Canada. Or, comme les industries textiles canadiennes demeurent particulièrement protégées par l'imposition de quotas et de tarifs douaniers et que le gouvernement canadien ne semble pas disposé à atténuer le protectionnisme en ce domaine, on se trouve en présence d'un obstacle qui nuit considérablement aux efforts pour accroître encore les ventes canadiennes en Chine tout en contrariant beaucoup, à n'en pas douter, le gouvernement chinois.

Le Canada face à l'Asie prospère

Depuis quelques années, plusieurs pays de l'Asie orientale se sont distingués par les performances exceptionnelles de leurs économies. Certains d'entre eux, comme la Corée du Sud, Taiwan ou Singapour – pour ne citer que ceux là – figurent au nombre des partenaires privilégiés par le Canada dans cette région du monde. La constitution de cette nouvelle clientèle a, en revanche, obligé le marché canadien à s'ouvrir aux produits manufacturés exportés par ces pays.

Malgré des politiques douanières protectionnistes, notamment dans les secteurs des textiles ou du cuir, le Canada n'a pas d'autre choix que celui de composer pour les années à venir avec les effets de plus en plus marqués de la croissance de ces économies. Il n'en reste pas moins que, dans cette Asie prospère, le Japon tient toujours une place obligée puisque la valeur totale du commerce entre les deux pays dépasse annuellement les 8 milliards de dollars, ce qui depuis 1973 le place au deuxième rang des partenaires commerciaux du Canada.

Depuis 1976, le gouvernement fédéral s'est employé à consolider ses rapports avec le Japon. En cette même année en effet, le premier ministre Trudeau effectuait une visite officielle au Japon dont l'objet essentiel allait être la signature d'un «accord-cadre de coopération économique». On s'était employé à parachever la logique de la troisième option en définissant un accord qui ressemblait au «lien contractuel» avec la Communauté économique européenne.

Les dispositions de cet accord-cadre se divisent en trois grandes catégories: le développement du commerce, le développement de la coopération économique et les arrangements en vue de consultations. Le directeur général du Bureau des affaires de l'Asie et du Pacifique au ministère des Affaires extérieures, R.L. Rogers, soulignait en 1977 que la disposition relative au développement de la coopération économique était l'élément clé du document. Cette disposition, déclarait-il,

> invite en effet les deux parties à encourager et à faciliter:
>
> • la coopération entre leurs industries respectives, par exemple dans le cadre d'entreprises de coparticipation;
>
> • la coopération en matière de mise en valeur et de mise en marché des ressources et des produits transformés et manufacturés (y compris des produits finis perfectionnés);
>
> • une plus grande stabilité en matière de production et d'approvisionnement des produits agricoles;
>
> • l'accroissement d'investissements avantageux pour les deux parties[47].

Malgré cet accord, les nombreuses visites ministérielles et les énoncés de bonnes intentions, les rapports économiques entre les deux pays demeurent contrariés par des incompatibilités inhérentes à la structure de leurs économies respectives. Ainsi, le Canada est considéré par le Japon à la fois comme une source de matière première sécuritaire et comme un marché ouvert à ses produits manufacturés.

En dépit d'une balance commerciale demeurée jusqu'en 1980 largement excédentaire, le gouvernement fédéral a manifesté à plusieurs reprises son mécontentement à l'endroit de ce déséquilibre dans la composition des échanges. Le Canada est demeuré – comme il l'a toujours été – le fournisseur du Japon en matières premières industrielles mais aussi en produits agricoles. Le Japon importe 93 % des exportations canadiennes de charbon et 75 % du minerai et des concentrés de cuivre. Il est aussi le plus gros client du Canada pour l'achat de minerai de plomb et ses concentrés ainsi que pour le molybdène; il se classe au deuxième rang des importations pour la pâte de bois, le zinc et l'aluminium.

Comme l'indiquent les statistiques les plus récentes dans la composition des exportations canadiennes vers le Japon, le Canada ne parvient pas à augmenter sensiblement la part des produits finis dans le total de ses ventes: ce pourcentage était de 3 % en 1970, et il est actuellement de l'ordre de 6 %.

À plusieurs reprises, le gouvernement fédéral a manifesté son mécontentement à l'endroit de ce déséquilibre dans la composition des échanges puisqu'en contrepartie, le Canada est essentiellement importateur de produits finis japonais. Le différend à propos des importations massives d'automobiles japonaises demeure l'un des épisodes illustrant une fois encore ce contraste dans le profil des produits échangés par les deux pays. Ce contentieux qui perdure est également entretenu par les difficultés des milieux d'affaires canadiens à pénétrer le marché japonais ou encore le non-aboutissement de la vente d'un réacteur nucléaire CANDU[48].

Malgré ces problèmes inhérents à la structure des échanges commerciaux, il serait abusif d'envisager une détérioration des rapports entre les deux pays. Aucune des parties ne peut en effet se permettre de prendre à l'endroit de l'autre des mesures excessives. Pour les Japonais, le Canada est un pays stable, grand fournisseur de matières premières indispensables à son économie, alors que pour les Canadiens, pour l'Ouest canadien et surtout pour la Colombie-Britannique, le Japon est l'investisseur indispensable pour l'exploitation des mines de charbon et pour le gaz naturel.

Depuis 1977, année pendant laquelle fut institué le «dialogue» Canada-ASEAN, mais plus particulièrement depuis 1979 lorsque le Secrétaire d'État MacGuigan fut invité aux réunions annuelles des ministres des Affaires étrangères des cinq pays membres, l'Association des pays de l'Asie du Sud-Est a fait l'objet d'une attention toute particulière dans la politique étrangère canadienne. De nombreux facteurs expliquent la lenteur du Canada à reconnaître une association dont les membres possèdent des richesses naturelles considérables, un marché de 240 millions d'habitants et une croissance inégalée dans le monde. Aucun n'est véritablement convaincant et seule l'inexpérience et le goût de la facilité expliquent le retard enregistré dans la mise en place de politiques adéquates.

Depuis quatre ans, on a souhaité rattraper le temps perdu puisque le commerce total du Canada avec l'Association a été marqué par une croissance assez spectaculaire. Depuis 1980, les échanges totaux dépassent, comme l'atteste le tableau 3, le milliard de dollars.

Dans le rapprochement avec l'ASEAN, l'accord de coopération économique conclu entre le Canada et les cinq membres de l'Association, le 25 septembre 1981, a constitué une étape importante. Aux termes de cet accord, les rapports futurs devront se concentrer sur trois secteurs: la coopération industrielle, la coopération commerciale et la coopération au développement. Les parties contractantes ont également convenu de créer une commission consultative conjointe pour promouvoir et examiner les diverses activités de la coopération envisagée. Avec son programme industriel établi depuis 1978, l'ACDI constitue l'institution privilégiée pour inciter les entreprises canadiennes à s'intéresser à l'Asie du Sud-Est et l'ASEAN a jusqu'à maintenant bénéficié, plus que toute autre région du monde, de ce programme.

En quête d'une approche régionale

Au mois de juillet 1980, par des propos tenus à Hong Kong, MacGuigan, ministre des Affaires extérieures, esquissait les principes d'une relance de la politique canadienne dans la région: «Pendant la prochaine décennie, le Canada devra affronter un grand défi international, celui de s'adapter à cette nouvelle ère du Pacifique. Nous voulons participer à cette expérience excitante, contribuer au développement de la région et en partager les avantages. Notre ultime objectif serait la création d'une communauté de nations plus stables et plus prospères dans la région du Pacifique [...] Entre-temps, nous devons cultiver et développer les relations bilatérales qui sont le fondement du concept. À cette fin, le Canada entend donner un nouvel élan à ses relations politiques et économiques avec les pays de la région asiatique du Pacifique[49].»

Le ministre convenait qu'il s'agissait là d'un défi. Défi, car malgré tout ce qui avait été entrepris depuis dix ans, force était de reconnaître que l'on butait sur un obstacle psychologique important s'exprimant, comme l'écrivait le professeur Saywell, par une mentalité collective tournée davantage vers le Sud et le Nord de l'Atlantique[50]. La solution, comme l'indiquait MacGuigan, exigeait «une bonne dose d'énergie créative», et elle consistait aussi à faire comprendre aux Canadiens que leur pays était une nation du Pacifique afin que ceux-ci puissent appuyer les initiatives gouvernementales.

Cette prise de conscience renouvelée de l'importance de l'Asie s'appuyait en tout premier lieu, on ne peut en douter, sur des considérations économiques. À l'époque, comme encore, la croissance annuelle du PNB de tous les pays de l'Asie de l'Est n'avait pas manqué d'étonner les économistes occidentaux. En 1978 par exemple, elle était de 13 % pour la Corée du Sud, de 12,8 % pour Taiwan, 10 % pour la Chine, 8,3 % pour Hong Kong et se situait entre 6 et 8 % pour les pays de l'Asie du Sud-Est, à l'exception des États de la péninsule indochinoise[51]. Il convenait dès lors pour le gouvernement fédéral d'orienter davantage la stratégie commerciale du Canada vers l'Asie orientale d'autant plus que la part de celle-ci dans le commerce international s'était accrue de façon évidente. De 1961 à 1976, par exemple, elle était passée de 4,86 % à 9,36 %.

Ce qui paraît nouveau dans la mise en place simultanée d'une approche canadienne à la fois multilatérale et bilatérale est aussi la prise de conscience des rapports d'interdépendance qui caractérisent les États de la région. Les liens complexes entre les économies de la région, l'omniprésence du Japon, les particularités propres aux milieux d'affaires asiatiques et la nécessité de mieux évaluer les conséquences de politiques trop exclusivement bilatérales, constituent quelques éléments d'une expertise régionale qui n'existait pas autrefois.

Cette prise de conscience s'est par ailleurs manifestée dans plusieurs autres secteurs que ceux de l'économie. Ainsi, dans le domaine de l'aide canadienne, traditionnellement très liée à la politique commerciale, on a senti dès 1975 le besoin de reformuler une stratégie plus régionale. À cet effet, la nouvelle «stratégie de coopération au développement industriel» de l'ACDI énonçait dans son point 10 que: «Le Canada encouragera et suscitera une approche régionale aux problèmes du développement en aidant les institutions régionales auxquelles participent plusieurs pays, en développant et en appuyant les projets de développement mis en œuvre par des groupes de pays[52].»

En Asie du Sud-Est depuis 1970, l'aide canadienne s'était trop exclusivement concentrée sur l'Indonésie, pays cible, dont le choix permettait de combiner de façon évidente la promotion des investissements canadiens dans le pays et l'assistance au développement. À l'époque, l'Indonésie fut d'ailleurs largement citée dans les controverses multiples à propos de l'aide canadienne.

Depuis 1975, les priorités s'étant quelque peu modifiées, de nouvelles séries de projets mettent davantage l'accent sur le développement rural et l'aide agricole. Le développement social retient beaucoup plus l'attention et l'on favorise actuellement une utilisation renouvelée de l'assistance technique. Il ne s'agit plus comme auparavant d'apporter une aide de nature générale au secteur de l'éducation, mais plutôt d'intégrer étroitement la formation technique aux projets d'aide de manière à assurer la relève locale nécessaire et à permettre la poursuite autonome des projets pendant des années[53].

Sur le plan de la régionalisation de l'aide, on remarque par ailleurs une pratique, trop peu répandue encore, permettant de financer par des fonds bilatéraux des projets qui profitent non pas à un seul pays, mais à toute une région. C'est notamment le cas de l'aide apportée dans les années 70 par le Canada à l'Institut asiatique de développement à Bangkok, qui a permis de donner une formation spécialisée à des ingénieurs de différentes nationalités. Un nouveau programme identique a été établi pour les années 1980; il devrait contribuer à la formation de 200 personnes originaires de divers pays de l'Asie du Sud-Est.

Outre sa participation au développement régional par l'entremise de la Banque asiatique de développement, c'est aussi dans le cadre du dialogue avec l'ASEAN que le Canada finance des projets régionaux. Ainsi en 1981, deux projets ont été élaborés avec l'Association. Le premier de ces projets est la création d'un centre d'ensemencement forestier en Thaïlande pour former des techniciens en foresterie et alimenter les stocks de semence d'essences tropicales. Le second projet vise à fournir une assistance technique pour permettre à chacun des pays de l'ASEAN de se doter de compétences en techniques de conservation des produits de la pêche.

La prise en compte de l'interdépendance des rapports régionaux ne peut ni omettre les conséquences des gestes posés ni ceux qui exigent l'appréhension du futur dans la région. La première de ces deux exigences apparut clairement lors des politiques du Canada à l'endroit du Viêt-nam dès 1978 mais surtout à l'endroit de celui des réfugiés de la péninsule indochinoise[54]. L'accueil assez spectaculaire et surprenant réservé par la société canadienne à ceux que l'on appela les «réfugiés de la mer» eut des répercussions dans toute l'Asie orientale. Au-delà de la signification humanitaire, le geste fut aussi perçu comme la volonté canadienne de s'impliquer davantage dans une région jusque-là fort négligée. Sur le plan politique, l'attitude du gouvernement d'Ottawa à l'endroit du Viêt-nam ne fut pas étrangère à l'amélioration évidente des rapports avec l'ASEAN ou à la consolidation des relations sino-canadiennes.

Dans un deuxième temps, face au futur de la région, le Canada, bien que sceptique, n'est pas demeuré indifférent aux propositions d'une «Communauté du Pacifique». Toujours à l'état de projet, la formule japonaise de «Communauté du Pacifique» se comprendrait davantage comme l'indicateur d'une volonté d'opérer des changements qu'en propositions concrètes précisant dès maintenant les contours d'un aménagement nouveau. Pour certains, il s'agirait là d'une zone de libre-échange, tandis que pour d'autres, ce serait une union douanière ou encore une aire de coopération, d'échange et de compréhension mutuelle accrue. Certains détracteurs l'imaginent aussi comme un arrangement nouveau par lequel pourrait s'exercer la domination de l'économie japonaise.

Même si le concept demeure flou, le gouvernement d'Ottawa, par les propos de son Secrétaire d'État aux Affaires extérieures, a déjà indiqué son attitude face au concept de «Communauté du Pacifique». MacGuigan soulignait en effet que cette communauté serait vraisemblablement «une entreprise unique sur le plan humain, peut-être davantage un mariage informel et multiforme d'associations et de liens qu'une organisation intergouvernementale rigide où différents groupes participeront à des activités différentes»[55]. Quoi qu'il arrive, ajoutait le ministre, «le Canada compte être présent à toutes les étapes du développement de ce concept. Nous restons prudents face à l'adhésion et à l'organisation de la future Communauté du Pacifique ainsi qu'aux éventuelles responsabilités économiques et autres de cette dernière»[56].

De ces hésitations en fin de compte entre une approche bilatérale et la conception d'une action élargie au plan régional, on retiendra surtout l'évaluation qui fut faite du meilleur intérêt pour formuler une stratégie commerciale canadienne particulièrement rigoureuse.

Ainsi, en 1980, le gouvernement soulignait l'importance qu'il accordait aux performances de l'exportation dans un document intitulé *Une stratégie canadienne des exportations pour les années 1980*. Le document faisait appel à une plus grande collaboration entre les partenaires fédéraux et provinciaux et ceux des secteurs public et privé pour atteindre l'objectif de l'accroissement des exportations. On précisait à ce propos qu'il conviendrait notamment de «[...] concentrer et coordonner tous les programmes et politiques du gouvernement fédéral ayant une incidence sur les exportations, dans les plans du développement des marchés visant des régions et pays sélectionnés pour leur fort potentiel du point de vue des exportations canadiennes»[57].

La mise en œuvre de cette stratégie se fit en concertation étroite avec les milieux d'affaires et plus particulièrement pour la région Asie-Pacifique, plusieurs groupes de pression furent très actifs dans leurs interventions auprès du gouvernement. On citera ainsi, par exemple, le Comité canadien du Conseil économique du bassin du Pacifique, représentant plus d'une centaine d'affaires canadiennes, et qui, en raison de son réseau de contact au sein des gouvernements fédéral et provinciaux, est très efficace. On mentionnera également le Conseil Canada-Philippines, le Conseil des affaires Canada-Corée, le Conseil commercial Canada-Chine et le Comité de coopération d'affaires Canada-Japon[58].

Le début des années 80 a donc marqué l'amorce d'une détermination nouvelle du gouvernement fédéral d'appuyer son action pour susciter un effort national dans l'exportation des produits canadiens. On identifia des secteurs prioritaires déterminés en fonction de ces critères: «la capacité réelle ou potentielle de créer des emplois et de contribuer à la croissance économique du Canada; la possibilité de retirer des avantages importants pour la société canadienne en retour de l'aide financière apportée par le gouvernement aux initiatives d'exportations[59]». De la même façon furent désignés des pays prioritaires selon les quatre critères suivants: leur potentiel pour les exportations des secteurs prioritaires, leur potentiel global pour les exportations de produits canadiens, la taille de leur marché et le rythme de croissance de leur marché[60]. C'est ainsi que pour l'Asie-Pacifique, on identifia le Japon, l'Australie, Hong Kong, la Corée du Sud et les cinq pays de l'ASEAN.

La mise en pratique des politiques nouvelles trouva plus de crédibilité encore lorsque fut annoncé en février 1982, par le premier ministre Trudeau, le transfert des activités commerciales du ministère de l'Industrie et du Commerce à celui des Affaires extérieures. Cette réorganisation particulièrement exigeante pour la fonction publique fédérale visait à faire en sorte que le Canada parle d'une «seule voix à l'extérieur» et plaçait les politiques d'exportation au premier rang des priorités de la politique étrangère du pays[61].

Le changement de gouvernement survenu au mois de septembre 1985 n'a en aucune façon modifié les priorités commerciales canadiennes. Plus sensibles encore peut-être que les Libéraux à la promotion des produits de l'Ouest canadien dans la région de l'Asie-Pacifique, les Conservateurs ont renforcé les priorités initiales. Les visites ministérielles et missions commerciales attestent de l'étroite imbrication et de l'appui des milieux d'affaires canadiens aux initiatives gouvernementales dans la région.

On retiendra enfin les propos très clairs du ministre du Commerce extérieur, James Kelleher, qui dès octobre 1985, déclarait: «Mon gouvernement lance actuellement une grande initiative commerciale dans la région de l'Asie et du Pacifique. Pour le présent exercice, nous avons décidé d'engager 6,5 millions de dollars supplémentaires pour grossir notre représentation commerciale dans les pays en bordure du Pacifique. Nous ouvrons à Osaka un consulat général qui sera fortement axé sur le commerce et sur l'acquisition de technologies. Nous envoyons quatre autres délégués commerciaux en Chine et nous ouvrirons un consulat à Shanghai avant la fin de l'année. Nous avons aussi commencé à préparer une vingtaine de projets spéciaux pour toute la région de l'Asie et du Pacifique, et nous nous penchons sur les mérites de plusieurs autres, dont certaines en Corée[62].»

CONCLUSION

Le Canada n'est jamais réellement parvenu à assumer la vocation «pacifique» que lui impose sa géographie. À diverses époques, comme en diverses occasions, seuls des facteurs parfois étrangers à sa volonté ont conduit la société canadienne à se tourner vers cette région du monde. Comme on l'a souvent remarqué, le Canada, «puissance régionale sans région», n'a jamais osé faire des choix géographiques et s'il avait souhaité le faire, peut-être n'aurait-il pas choisi l'Asie.

Depuis 1945, le défi constant que doit relever le gouvernement fédéral est celui de convaincre la population canadienne que le Pacifique est important. Depuis quelques années, et par nécessité, l'économie canadienne et plus précisément les milieux d'affaires ont mieux répondu aux initiatives gouvernementales, mais les gains actuels demeurent encore très fragiles.

Après être intervenu en Asie beaucoup plus en raison des principes qu'il défendait que de l'intérêt qu'il portait à cette région, le Canada a mieux défini par la suite sa politique. Ce ne furent plus les obligations de la Charte des Nations Unies, ni les liens du Commonwealth ou la guerre froide qui inspirèrent ses actions, mais bien plutôt un schéma, une sorte de plan directeur où l'Asie orientale devenait l'un de ces pôles retenus pour détourner quelque peu la société canadienne de l'attraction des États-Unis. D'une façon générale, le bilan des dernières années d'actions entreprises en Asie de l'Est paraît ainsi conforme aux grandes orientations définies vers la fin des années 60. Dans une conception de la politique étrangère considérée comme le prolongement des politiques internes, chaque initiative fut inscrite à l'intérieur des six grandes orientations retenues en 1970[63]. Parmi celles-ci, la première était de façon évidente la plus concrète et l'on ne peut ainsi s'étonner que la priorité fût accordée à la promotion de la croissance économique. En Asie de l'Est, l'essentiel des actions canadiennes peut être répertorié sous cette rubrique. La conformité au schéma général ne fut cependant pas synonyme de succès et les objectifs commerciaux prématurés de la troisième option ne furent pas atteints, du moins dans leurs dimensions initialement fixées.

Dès leur formulation, ces grandes orientations parurent trop floues; paradoxalement, elles semblaient affirmer plus clairement ce que le Canada ne désirait plus être, qu'elles n'indiquaient ce qu'il aspirait à devenir. En Asie de l'Est, ces grands objectifs invitaient à fuir les réalités conflictuelles pour ne considérer et retenir que les éléments les plus rentables. Cette attitude traduisait une volonté d'indépendance et le désir de ne plus se retrouver impliqué dans des rôles et des situations imposés par la conjoncture ou par les États-Unis. Dans le même temps, pour se réconcilier avec le réalisme, on souhaitait se limiter à une vocation marchande que l'on croyait plus conforme aux possibilités du Canada.

Comme ce schéma, trop vite plaqué à toutes les régions du monde, ne correspondait pas aux réalités changeantes de l'Asie de l'Est, il fallut réévaluer les politiques définies. Dans cette troisième phase qui est amorcée, le réalisme et les contraintes de l'économie canadienne se sont substituées aux grands schémas. L'avenir des relations avec l'Asie orientale dépendra désormais du succès de chacune des provinces et des entreprises canadiennes à prendre la relève des initiatives gouvernementales.

TABLEAU 1
Commerce du Canada avec la Chine
(en millions $ can.)

Année	Exportations	Blé en % dans les exportations	Importations	Balance
1965	105	104/99 %	15	+ 90
1972	261	234/90 %	48	+ 213
1978	503	347/69 %	95	+ 408
1979	592	411/69 %	167	+ 425
1980	866,4	527,4/61 %	154,9	+ 711,5
1981	1 005	687/68,4 %	220	+ 785
1982	1 227,9	736/59,9 %	203	+ 1 024,2
1983	1 607,2	916/56,9 %	245,8	+ 1 361,4
1984	1 272,1	602/47,3 %	333,5	+ 938,6

Source: Ministère des Affaires extérieures – Ottawa.

TABLEAU 2
Commerce du Canada avec le Japon
(en millions $ can.)

	1981	1982	1983	1984	1985
Exportations vers le Japon	4 485	4 571	4 728	5 629	5 745
Importations depuis le Japon	4 039	3 527	4 409	5 711	6 118
Balance	446	1 044	319	− 82	− 368

Source: Cabinet du premier ministre, 1986.
Voyage de M. Mulroney en Asie.

TABLEAU 3
Commerce du Canada avec les cinq pays de l'ASEAN
(en millions $ can.)

Année / Pays	1971 Exp.	Imp.	Bal.	1979 Exp.	Imp.	Bal.	1980 Exp.	Imp.	Bal.	1983 Exp.	Imp.	Bal.	1984 Exp.	Imp.	Bal.	1985 Exp.	Imp.	Bal.
Indonésie	10,1	1,0	+9,1	62,6	42,1	+20,5	212,9	28,9	+184,0	209,8	40,0	+169,8	290,4	71,9	+218,5	257,6	81,8	+175,8
Malaysia	15,6	26,8	−11,2	65,3	96,3	−31,0	93,0	83,3	+9,7	114,0	115,5	−1,5	187,7	167,9	+19,8	204,3	146,0	+58,3
Philippines	39,8	6,2	+33,6	84,4	78,3	+6,4	107,8	101,4	+6,4	76,8	88,2	−11,4	56,7	117,3	−60,6	45,7	109,0	−63,3
Singapour	9,6	18,4	−8,8	116,8	164,0	−49,2	198,1	149,5	+48,6	126,7	168,4	−41,7	143,0	214,2	−71,2	106,3	210,4	−104,1
Thaïlande	13,2	3,0	+10,2	87,2	31,7	+55,5	141,6	24,6	+117,0	146,4	60,5	+85,9	116,8	103,3	+13,5	126,9	108,6	+18,3
Total	88,3	55,4	+32,9	414,6	412,4	+2,4	753,4	387,7	+365,7	673,7	472,6	+201,1	794,6	674,6	+120,0	740,8	655,8	+85,0

Source: Ministère des Affaires extérieures, Ottawa, et *Reportage Canada*, vol. 2, n° 6, 19 mars 1986.

NOTES

1. L'Asie est géographiquement l'adjonction de l'Asie du Nord-Est et de l'Asie du Sud-Est.

2. Voir J. Arthur Lower, *Canada on the Pacific Rim*, Toronto, McGraw-Hill Ryerson, 1975, p. 111.

3. R.A. Mackay, éd., *Canadian Foreign Policy 1945-1954. Selected Speeches and Documents*, Toronto, McClelland and Stewart, 1970, p. 302.

4. John W. Holmes et Jean-René Laroche, «Le Canada et la guerre froide», dans Paul Painchaud (éd.), *Le Canada et le Québec sur la scène internationale*, Québec, CQRI, 1977, p. 284.

5. *Ibidem*, p. 275-302. Voir aussi Denis Stairs, *The Diplomacy of Constraint: Canada, the Korean War and the United States*, Toronto, University of Toronto Press, 1974.

6. J.W. Holmes et J.-R. Laroche, *op. cit.*, p. 291.

7. Les pays signataires étaient: l'Australie, les États-Unis, la France, la Nouvelle-Zélande, le Pakistan, les Philippines, le Royaume-Uni et la Thaïlande.

8. John W. Holmes, *The Better Part of Valour: Essays on Canadian Diplomacy*, Toronto, McClelland and Stewart, 1970, p. 196.

9. Voir, sur cette question de l'OTASE, James Eayrs, *Canada in World Affairs,* octobre 1955-juin1955, Toronto, Oxford University Press, 1965, p. 84-87.

10. Keith Spicer, «Clubmanship Upstaged: Canada's Twenty Years in the Colombo Plan», *International Journal*, vol. XXV, n° 1, hiver 1969-1970, p. 25.

11. *Ibidem*, p. 24.

12. Voir Trevor Lloyd, *Canada in World Affairs, 1957-1959*, Toronto, Oxford University Press, 1968, p. 199-200; également Richard Preston, *Canada in World Affairs, 1959-1961*, Toronto, Oxford University Press, 1965, p. 227-228.

13. Lorne J. Kavic, «Canada and the Security of Southeast Asia», dans Mark W. Zacher et R. Stephen Milne, éd., *Conflict and Stability in Southeast Asia*, New York, Anchor Books, 1974, p. 401.

14. J.W. Holmes et J.-R. Laroche, *op. cit.*, p. 294.

15. G. Lalande, «Le Canada et le Pacifique», *Le Canada et le Québec sur la scène internationale, op.cit.*, p. 365.

16. Paul Bridle, «Canada and the International Commissions in Indochina, 1954-1972», *Conflict and Stability in Southeast Asia, op. cit.*, p. 407-450.

17. Voir à ce propos Lorne Kavic, «Canada and the Security of Southeast Asia», *Conflict and Stability in Southeast Asia, op. cit.*, p. 396-398 et Edward D. Greathed, «Canada and the Asian World», *International Journal*, vol. XX, n° 3, été 1965, p. 369.

18. D.H. Gardner, *Canadian Interests and Policies in the Far East since World War II*, Toronto, Canadian Institute of International Affairs, 1950, p. 12.

19. On consultera sur ce sujet l'ouvrage de H.F. Angus, *Canada and the Far East, 1940-1953*, Toronto, University of Toronto Press, 1953.

20. R.A. Mackay, *op. cit.*, p. 291.

21. D.C. Thomson et R.F. Swanson, *Canada Foreign Policy: Options and Perspectives*, Toronto, McGraw Hill-Ryerson, 1971, p. 112.

22. *Ibidem*, p. 113.

23. Pierre Elliott Trudeau, «Le Canada dans le monde», 29 mai 1968, *Déclarations et Discours*, ministère des Affaires extérieures, Ottawa, n° 68/17.

24. Mitchell Sharp, «Le Canada, puissance moyenne dans un monde en évolution», *Déclaration et Discours*, ministère des Affaires extérieures, Ottawa, n° 69/16.

25. *Politique étrangère au service des Canadiens, le Pacifique*, Ottawa, ministère des Affaires extérieures, p. 24.

26. *Ibidem*, p. 20.

27. *Ibidem*, p. 24.

28. *Politique étrangère au service des Canadiens*, brochure principale, p. 16.

29. *Politique étrangère au service des Canadiens, le Pacifique, op. cit.*, p. 22.

30. Cette dernière attitude fut notamment celle de l'ancien premier ministre Diefenbaker; voir sur ce point F.Q. Quo et Akira Ichikawa, «Sino-Canadian relations: A new Chapter», *Asian Survey*, mai 1972, vol. XII, n° 5, p. 392.

31. *Déclarations et Discours*, ministère des Affaires extérieures, Ottawa, n° 68/17, p. 5.

32. Voir sur ce point la confirmation par Trudeau lui-même dans John D. Harbron: «Canada Recognized China: The Trudeau Round 1968-1973». *Behind the headlines*, octobre 1974, Vol. XXII, n° 5, Toronto, Canadian Institute of International Affairs.

33. Voir Maureen Appel Molot, «Canada's Relations with China since 1968», dans Norman Hillmer et Garth Stevenson, éd., *A Foremost Nation: Canadian Foreign Policy and a Changing World*, Toronto, McClelland et Stewart, 1977, p. 230-267.

34. *Déclarations et Discours,* Ottawa, ministère des Affaires extérieures, n° 70/19, 1970.

35. Kim Richard Nossal, «Retreat, Retraction and Reconstruction: Canada and Indochina in the Post-Hostilities Period», dans Gordon P. Means, éd., *The Past in Southeast Asia's Present,* Ottawa, Canadian Society for Southeast Asian Studies, 1977, p. 173.

36. M. Sharp, *Vietnam: Participation à la Commission internationale de contrôle telle qu'envisagée par le Canada,* Ottawa, ministère des Affaires extérieures, mai 1973, p. 19.

37. *Ibidem,* p. 25.

38. Ivan L. Head, «Canada's Pacific Perspective», *Pacific Community,* vol. 6, oct. 1966, n° 1, p. 13.

39. Voir David Van Praagh, «Canada and Southeast Asia», dans Peyton V. Lyon and Tareq Y. Ismael, *Canada and the Third World,* Toronto, MacMillan, 1976, p. 318.

40. M. Sharp, «Le Cambodge», *Déclarations et Discours,* n° 70/8, 1ᵉʳ mai 1970, p. 3.

41. Okuma Tadayuki, «Passive Japan – Active Canada», *International Journal,* vol. XXXIII, n° 2, printemps 1978, p. 443-448.

42. M. Sharp, «Le Canada, puissance moyenne dans un monde en évolution», *op. cit.,* p. 1.

43. Voir P.E. Trudeau, «Le Canada dans le monde», *op. cit.,* p. 7.

44. *Revue Annuelle,* ministère des Affaires extérieures, Ottawa, 1976, p. 14.

45. Ministère des Affaires extérieures, *Communiqué,* n° 109, 13 octobre 1976.

46. *La Presse,* 20 octobre 1979.

47. «Le Canada et les pays de la région du Pacifique», *Déclarations et Discours,* Ottawa, ministère des Affaires extérieures, n° 77/7, p. 2-3.

48. On pourra consulter sur ces points particuliers Frank Landgon, «Problems of Canada-Japan Economic Diplomacy in the 1960s and 1970s: The Third Option», A paper for the conference, *Canadian Perspectives on Economic Relations with Japan,* Toronto, mai 1979; également du même auteur: «Canada's Struggle for Entrée to Japan», *Canadian Public Policy,* hiver 1976.

49. MacGuigan, «Le Canada renforce ses liens avec la région du Pacifique», *Discours,* 2 juillet 1980, p. 4.

50. William Saywell, «Pierre and the Pacific: A Post-Mortem», *International Journal,* vol. XXXIII, n° 2, printemps 1978, p. 414.

51. Anthony C. Albrecht, «American Economic Policy in East Asia», dans Arthur S. Hoffman, *Japan and Pacific Basin,* The Atlantic Papers, n° 40, Atlantic Institute for International Affairs, p. 23.

52. ACDI, *Stratégie de Coopération au développement international 1975-1980,* Ottawa, sept. 1975, p. 32.

53. ACDI, «Aide canadienne en Asie», Miméo, p. 4.

54. La question de l'accueil des réfugiés indochinois a volontairement été omise dans cette étude; voir à ce propos notre chapitre dans *Le Canada face à l'Asie de l'Est,* p. 137-162. Ou encore Elliot L. Tepper, éd., *Southeast Asian Exodus: From Tradition to Resettlement,* Ottawa, Canadian Asian Studies Association, 1981.

55. M. MacGuigan, Allocution prononcée lors du «Symposium Canada-Japon» Discours, Toronto, 14 octobre 1980, p. 18.

56. *Ibidem, p. 18.*

57. Canada, *Une stratégie canadienne des exportations,* Industrie et Commerce, novembre 1980, p. 1.

58. Voir *Le commerce du Canada avec les pays en développement de la région Asie-Pacifique,* septembre 1983, Ottawa, Institut Nord-Sud, p. 9.

59. *Une étude de la politique commerciale canadienne,* Ottawa, ministère des Affaires extérieures, 1983, p. 193.

60. *Ibidem,* p. 193.

61. On consultera à ce sujet le très bon article de Robert Boardman: «The Foreign Services and the Organization of the Foreign Policy Community: Views from Canada and Abroad», dans Denis Stairs et Gilbert Winham (éd.), *Selected Problems in Formulating Foreign Economic Policy,* Toronto, University of Toronto Press, 1985, p. 59-103.

62. James Kelleher, *Discours,* Ottawa, ministère des Relations extérieures, n° 85/5h, p. 1.

63. Pour mémoire, ces orientations étaient ainsi définies: «En principe, la politique nationale du Canada dans son ensemble cherche à: stimuler sa croissance économique; préserver sa souveraineté et son indépendance; travailler à la paix et à la sécurité; y promouvoir la justice sociale; y enrichir la qualité de la vie; maintenir l'harmonie du milieu naturel. *Politique étrangère au service des Canadiens,* Ottawa, ministère des Affaires extérieures, 1970, p. 14.

15

Canadian Relations with South Asia

W.M. Dobell
University of Western Ontario

INTRODUCTION

«The main avenue of approach for Canada to the problems of Asia has been by way of the Indian subcontinent[1].» So wrote the principal exponent of Canadian foreign policy of the 1950s. Within the subcontinent, central to Canada's relations with South Asia since World War II has been the Canadian-Indian relationship. Given the Indo-Pakistani rivalry that has prevailed ever since their separate creation out of British India in 1947, Canadian-Pakistani relations have always been conducted against a backdrop of potentially adverse reaction from New Delhi. Canadian-Bangladeshi relations have enjoyed a bare decade of existence, little of it significant except in a development assistance context. As the eighth most populous state in the world, Bangladesh became the recipient of resident Canadian accreditation. Yet as the poorest of highly populated nations, Bangladesh lacks political influence and economic purchasing power. With Canada's immigration officers resident in New Delhi and commercial officers in Bangkok, the High Commission in Dacca represents a tactical response to the trauma of the nation's birth and an ongoing recognition of the humanitarian impulse as one factor in Canada's development assistance.

Off the Southern coast of India lies the island of Sri Lanka, know pre-1972 as Ceylon. With a population slightly over half that of Canada, Canadian-Sri Lanka relations have rarely been important to either party. During some of the period 1956 to 1977, the island was under nonaligned, left-wing leadership, whereas the United States experienced conservative, alliance-prone administrations. Particularly in 1957, these antipodal perceptions could have led to the abandonment of the modernization of Colombo's airport, had not Canada stepped in. This was the largest and most visible Canadian involvement for 20 years, be eclipsed in time by the Mahaweli irrigation and power project, in which Canada became a prominent contributor.

On the northern fringe of the subcontinent lie the Himalyan border states. Most prominent of these is Nepal, which has a population of comparable size to Sri Lanka's but a foreign policy of undeviating discretion. During the 1950s and 1960s, Canada occasionally showed mild concern that the road network being constructed by the People's Republic of China might integrate Nepal unduly with its Northern neighbour. It was not a concern that Nepal would forfeit its independence, since that status was a somewhat nominal one. Rather it was a question of which much larger neighbour would exert the most influence in Katmandu. During the 1970s, it was most certainly India. Canada has at no time been more than an observer of events in Nepal, and, with accreditation through its High Commission in New Delhi, a non-resident one at that.

Canada has no relations with Bhutan, an almost impenetrable nation of a million people whose quasi-independence derives from that very inaccessibility. Since 1949, Bhutan has agreed by treaty to be guided by the Government of India in regards to its foreign policy, as it had been previously guided by that of Great Britain. Canada may communicate with Bhutan through New Delhi, but has virtually no occasion to do so. Sikkim lies between Nepal and Bhutan, and, more significantly, astride the major pass or invasion route linking China and India. With a mere quarter of Bhutan's population, its significance had been exclusively strategic. British India controlled its defence and foreign policy for 60 years, as did India in the third quarter of this century. A holiday there for a Canadian External Affairs Minister, which Lester B. Pearson enjoyed in 1955, was an administrative matter to be cleared through Delhi. Sikkim was absorbed as a state of the Indian Union in 1975, presumably in the hope of exerting a more effective control of its defence. Reporting of this event in Canadian newspapers was extremely slight. However imperative the action may, or may not, have been to the national interest of India, the decision was not characterized in Ottawa as pertinent to that of Canada. No official congratulations or regrets were dispatched to mark the occasion.

To the east of the subcontinent is situated Burma, another residual state of British India. The Burmese independence movement of World War II was directed both against Japan's wartime ascendancy and Britain's anticipated re-ascendancy. Totally isolated from potentially persuasive intermediaries like Canadian official representatives, the Burmese resistance regime took a premature decision to sever all links with the existing Commonwealth. With the British imperial link to South Asia severed, Burma has drifted back to its natural geographic status as a South-East Asian nation. Lacking Commonwealth membership, Burma has received a modicum less Canadian development assistance than might otherwise have been the case, though the aid would still have been slight. Canada's minor and somewhat ambivalent relationship to Burma has been reflected in accreditation from Kuala Lumpur prior to Bangladesh's independence, and political representation from Dacca — with commercial, development and immigration liaison from Bangkok – since that time.

On the Western border of the subcontinent are located Iran and Afghanistan. The former lies to the west of the mountains which separate South Asia and the Middle East, and has always been regarded by Canada as a Middle Eastern nation. Afghanistan, however, straddles the mountains that divide Pakistan from the Middle East and Russia from South Asia. Its population overlaps with that of its three neighbours, Pakistan, Iran and Russia. Its traditional role has been that of the buffer state, a Switzerland in Asia, though subject to much more recent encroachments. To Ottawa, Canadian-Afghanistani relations have comprised an extension of Canadian-Pakistani relations, conducted through Canadian missions at Karachi and Islamabad, Pakistan's successive capitals. Were this not the case, non-resident accreditation could have been maintained from, say, New Delhi, since Indian-Afghanistani relations have not been marked by as much friction as Pakistani-Afghanistani relations.

The Russian involvement in Afghanistan in December 1979 was not regarded by the Canadian Government as the product of a genuine invitation to intervene[2]. Canada has been sensitive to the burden placed on Pakistan by the increasing millions of Afghanistani refugees, to the risk of a great power war spreading to South Asia, and to the setback to détente resulting from Soviet behaviour. It wished to see Russian troops withdrawn, without having any illustions that an anti-Soviet Government would be allowed to take its place. Finland in the late 1940s and Austria in the mid-1950s acceded to international agreements that reduced Soviet involvement in their affairs, but commited them to follow policies that the Soviet Union did not categorize as hostile. Adaptation of such a formula, sometimes called neutralization, was advocated within the Department of External Affairs in Ottawa. There was little Canada could do beyond marketing the idea discretely in receptive capitals closer to the area and with more powerful voices. The European Community proved to be the most responsive group, and British Foreign Secretary Lord Carrington, with whom the concept came to be identified, its most convinced exponent.

Having briefly described the essence of Canada's relations with countries on the periphery of the subcontinent, it is time to turn in greater depth to the examination of Canada's relations with India and Pakistan, the rivals of the subcontinent. The larger and more powerful of these two is India, the more so after Pakistan's loss of its eastern wing in December 1971, so particular emphasis will be placed on the Canadian-Indian dimension. The first-time frame to consider is that of the 1940s and 1950s, the early years of independence following the British departure and the division of British India.

THE EARLY YEARS

Prior to 1947, what became the Congress Party of India was a mass-pressure group oriented to securing British withdrawal from the subcontinent. As early as 1942, Prime Minister Mackenzie King (1935-1948) saw encouraging parallels between Jawaharlal Nehru, the Congress leader, and King's grandfather, William Lyon Mackenzie[3]. The two were perceived by King as pathmakers in the cause of self-government. Congress reflected the Hindu predominance of most of the area, but not Hindu religious beliefs. Devotion to the preservation of the unity of India transcended, within Congress, the disparities of denominational faiths. Opposed both to the unity of India, and to what it perceived as a veneer of secularism within Congress, stood the Muslim League. The League was dedicated to the establishment of an overwhelmingly Muslim and theocratic state, involving of necessity the transfer of millions of people. Pakistan would comprise two distinct Muslim-majority areas, an eastern and a western wing, separated by a thousand-mile rump of India. The decision to accede to this Muslim League demand was an exclusively British decision. Canada's huge 1947 loan to Britain was extended to help avert British bankruptcy, and Britain's withdrawal from Empire in India was welcomed by Canada as a reduction in Britain's economic liabilities and as a response to the aspiration for independence. The dual form of self-determination, however, was not subject to Canadian approval. That was no doubt just as well, since Canadian policy-makers were not anxious to share responsibility for the breakup of another nation[4].

The first decade of independence coincided with the St. Laurent Government (1948-1957) in Canada, and there was early rapport between the Canadian Prime Minister and his Indian and Pakistani counterparts. L.B. Pearson was almost an *alter ego* of St. Laurent in these dealings, the trust each having in the other's judgment and integrity being remarkably complete. A lifetime spent in the Canadian political environment had attuned each to accept without question the secular role of the state, an approach perfectly consistent with St. Laurent's devout Catholicism and Pearson's Methodist parson parentage. The intellectual secularism of Nehru, who became Indian Prime Minister and External Affairs Minister, held instant appeal to the two Canadian leaders as the soundest approach to the governing of a hetero- geneous people of immense cultural diversity. More unexpected to the Canadians, an efficient and non-ideological approach to government marked the short-lived prime ministership of Pakistan's Liaquat Ali Khan. Following his tragic assassination, only one other Pakistani Prime Minister up to the military coup d'état of 1958 enjoyed the considered respect of Canadian leaders. This was H.S. Suhrawardy, a strong- minded Bengali whose announced belief that the direction of the Chinese People's Republic's policies could be more constructively channelled within the United Na- tions than outside it reflected the private views of St. Laurent and Pearson.

A forum in which personal relations were rather important was the Common- wealth Conference. In 1947 it was far from clear that the white British Common- wealth would evolve into the multiracial Commonwealth of Nations. The British were open-minded, but not forcefully committed. As the senior ex-colony, Canada was in a pivotal position. Had Canada opted for maintaining the Commonwealth as a club for members of primarily British extraction, Australia and New Zealand would have offered no resistance. South Africa was in its last year of a United Party Government that professed to a form of partnership with its Hindu and Muslim subjects of British Indian origin, but neither it nor its following government was enthusiastic about a coloured Commonwealth. Broadening of the basis of the Commonwealth took place in two stages. The first was the agreement to permit non-White membership, repre- sented in the change of nomenclature to Commonwealth of Nations. The second followed a year later with the agreement to permit republics to be members, the sovereign becoming the symbol of the Commonwealth but not necessarily the monarch of each member state. The entry of India, Pakistan and Ceylon was the con- sequence of the first decision. The desire of India and, by reflex action, Pakistan to become republics was the impetus for the second. Nehru was very conscious that the attitude of St. Laurent and Pearson had been crucial to the principle of adapting the Commonwealth to accomodate subcontinent membership, and to its further adaption with respect to the head of state. In his first visit to Ottawa as head of government, Nehru paid a gracious public tribute to the role of his hosts in orches- trating these events. The Pakistani External Affairs Minister played a minor but positive role in refining the final formula. Krishna Menon, sometime Indian Ambas- sador, High Commissioner and Minister of Defence, credited his own influence as paramount in the transformation of the Commonwealth. While there is no disputing that Menon consistently conveyed a pronounced impression, it must also be record- ed that the influence he had on people and events was not always the influence he intended. The key Indian statesman in determining that the Commonwealth might indeed possess the requisite resilience to warrant Indian membership was his mentor, Prime Minister Nehru[5]. In the rituals of diplomatic etiquette in India, Cana- dians were not above a generous acknowledgement of that contribution.

It was at a Commonwealth Conference held in Colombo, Ceylon in 1950 that the Canadian Development Assistance Programme was first launched[6]. Significant was the early South Asian focus of the programme, and the proportion of aid distributed between the three subcontinent recipients. The concentration on South Asia has steadily diminished over the next 30 years, despite the concentration there of so much of the world's direst poverty and densest population[7]. The 350 million Indians living in absolute poverty outnumber the entire population of Black Africa. On a per capita basis, nevertheless, South Asia's starting advantage did not last very long. Less populated Caribbean and African countries came to receive relatively more Canadian assistance in relation to their less desperate needs, just as within South Asia tiny Ceylon was allocated more aid per capita than Pakistan, and highly populated India obtained proportionately the least. India began receiving development assistance from Canada in 1952 of $15 million, Pakistan some $8 millions and Ceylon about $2 million. Compared to a 1980 total programme of a billion dollars, the sums of the early 1950s smack of tokenism. Yet the principles established for South Asia at that time of extending greater per capita assistance to countries whose aid could have a more measureable impact, and greater overall but lower proportional assistance to impoverished mass population nations, have continued to be operative throughout much of the succeeding period.

Until the further Commonwealth additions of the late 1950s, South Asia provided the only coloured members. All three behaved constructively within the conference milieu and proved by example that the experiment was successful. In cooperation with Canada, their advice to Britain was to avoid undue caution about the extention of independence to colonial people. They were not particularly aware of why Canada had sought the creation of the North Atlantic Treaty, but explanations had more credibility coming from a sympathetic source than, say, from the British Prime Minister of 1951-1955, Winston Churchill, whom they saw as an imperialist who had sought to perpetuate British rules in India. Escott Reid had been Acting Under Secretary of State for External Affairs in 1948 when NATO was negotiated, and was High Commissioner to India in 1952-1957. His relations with Nehru were perhaps the closest any ambassador or high commissioner has had with an Indian Prime Minister in over three decades. Reid shared his own Prime Minister's and Nehru's sense of moral outrage at the Anglo-French intervention in Egypt over the Suez crisis of 1956, and this made it possible to convince Nehru that Pearson was working to extract Anglo-French forces from Egypt rather than as their agent and defender. Reid was also instructed to brief Nehru on the nearly simultaneous Russian invasion of Hungary, about which Nehru was neither as interested nor as informed as he was concerning Britain and Egypt. The feat of persuading Nehru to issue a belated condemnation of the Hungarian invasion required leaking to him a telegram from Canada's United Nations mission which exposed Krishna Menon's factual and interpretative mistakes in handling the Hungarian issue at the UN[8]. Despite Reid's view that India could influence the USSR, the condemnation had no impact on Soviet policy. Some Canadians overestimated India's influence, as Pearson thought Indians were prone to do about Canada.

Had the Canadian and Indian governments not played such an active and swiftly-executed role in defusing the Suez crisis, the Commonwealth could well have disintegrated[9]. The Australians and New Zealanders were ranked in support of British intervention, with the three South Asian members opposed. The Muslim population of Pakistan identified with the Muslim population of Egypt and with its renowned

President, Gamal Abdul Nasser. An undiscriminating anti-Western emotion was unleashed over Suez, and Prime Minister Suhrawardy was not in control of it. Prolongation of the crisis would have prejudiced Canadian-Pakistani relations, even though sympathy and understanding prevailed at the official level. The Canadian and Pakistani governments were never unsynchronized over their perceptions of the Russian action in Hungary. Pakistan had joined the Baghdad Pact or Central Treaty Organization (CENTO) the year before, a treaty implicitly directed against the Soviet Union, and intelligence on Russian activities was readily available through this channel. Pakistan did condemn the Soviet invasion without Canadian prompting, but it was difficult for the populace to understand at a time when Russia was hotly articulating popular support of Nasser in defence of Egypt.

Canadian-South Asian cooperation occurred as well in New York within the United Nations. Until the membership explosion of the 1960s, there was a non-permanent Commonwealth seat on the Security Council, which India and Pakistan occupied in succession to Canada, and a Commonwealth caucusing group. Such groups, being informal and non-institutionalized, could discuss matters of which the UN was not officially seized. Canada and the South Asian nations were in general agreement on their perceptions regarding the recognition of the People's Republic of China, the Korean War, the French struggle in Indochina, the Suez crisis and ultimately the Hungarian invasion. Similar perceptions did not always lead to parallel voting behaviour on colonial and racial questions, as Canada was much more sensitive to possible embarrassment of its NATO allies than was India[10]. Canada was not above sympathizing with India's outlook but voting in a tactically different way. This occurred on occasion during the Korean War. Unlike the United States, Canada accepted the credibility of the warning from the Indian embassy in the People's Republic of China that extension of the UN offensive up to the Yalu River would spark Chinese intervention. Its voting record, nevertheless, was broadly supportive of American leadership of the UN operations[11]. There was thus less symmetry in certain Canadian and Indian voting patterns pre-1956 than thereafter, although in general Canadian-Indian amity was at its height during the St. Laurent years.

India was regarded by Canada in the 1950s as China's window on the world. India's approaches to China had been well received, not rebuffed like Britain's. India had conveyed accurately China's warning on the limited theatre of the Korean War. China had ceased to rely on its Soviet ally. India and China shared an intense aversion to the South-East Asia Treaty Organization (SEATO) of 1954 as a Western intrusion into Asian affairs, rather than the Pakistani defence that it was not directed against China. While remaining officially silent on the merits of SEATO and CENTO, Canada was understanding of India's interpretation. Pearson considered Indian criticisms as overdone, but sympathized with the Indian approach to China as a potentially more fruitful way of influencing Chinese foreign policy than that chosen by American Secretary of State Foster Dulles. When the Afro-Asian Movement was launched at Bandung in 1955, Canada regarded Nehru as the key figure of the conference and India as pivotal power. Although some regarded Nehru as patronizing towards Chinese Premier Chou En-lai, Canada saw the rationale as welcoming China as an Asian power and encouraging its outside contacts rather than rebuffing it as a Communist power and limiting it to Soviet Bloc contacts.

In the late 1940s and 1950s, Canada could see India as a major power in Asia, perhaps for a while the major power of Asia. India escaped almost untouched from

World War II, even accumulating Sterling balances from its remunerative contribution to the war effort. China, however, had been racked throughout much of the 1930s and 1940s by Japanese occupation and civil war. In the Afro-Asian Movement, the world's second most populous state seemed more influential than the first. Conversely, India understood Canada to be third power within NATO, as it had been the third Western power at the close of World War II. Both powers were internationalist, enjoyed clear stature within the Commonwealth and the UN, and dealt with each other as if they respected that stature. Each accepted the other as sympathetic, powerful in its own right, and a prime conduit to larger interests. As long as these conditions held, they formed a sound basis for an effective relationship.

THE TRANSITION

These conditions did not hold, for they were not static. In the 1960s, both powers had to adapt to a developing environment. Despite the wishes of Britain, Australia and New Zealand, South Africa was not invited to remain in the Commonwealth when it became a Republic. Canada voted with the South Asian powers on this essentially African issue, but thereafter the increasingly numerous African members led rather than followed Canada and India on colonial and racial issues. The UN Security Council's Commonwealth seat was dropped in 1965, and the Commonwealth members thereafter ceased to caucus regularly together. India and Canada found themselves relegated to separate coloured and Caucasian groups. The influx of French-speaking nations meant that English was no longer the only lingua franca of Afro-Asian meetings, and the English-trained South Asian politicians and diplomats lost their easy ascendancy over conference communications. The recovery of Western European nations from their prolonged penalty of wartime destruction reduced Canada to an offshore power in a Western European and other group at UN conferences, and to a middling role in a more Eurocentric NATO.

Canada continued its internationalist role, but on a diminished scale. Diefenbaker, that most political of Prime Ministers, weighed every suggested move abroad in terms of its likely domestic impact. Pearson, that most international of Prime Ministers, found himself preoccupied with domestic events. This was partly due to the expensive social programmes launched in the mid-1960s, partly due to the strains Québec's Quiet Revolution was beginning to place on Confederation, and partly due to the adversarial rivalry of Pearson and Diefenbaker in the minority government Parliaments of 1962-1968. Temperamentally the two men were poles apart, and their appreciation of South Asian leaders varied enormously. Pearson became privately more critical of the sometimes aloof and now aging Nehru, who was to remain Prime Minister until his death in 1964. Yet Pearson continued to respect Nehru's alert, reflective mind and broad grasp of affairs. Diefenbaker found it easier to deal with the simpler, unequivocal and direct Ayub Khan, President of Pakistan from 1958 to 1969. Both Canadian Prime Ministers found West Pakistanis to be franker and more straightforward than Indians, an inference that may have been caused by the dominance of the British-trained administrative and military elite in Pakistan as opposed to the indigenous populist tradition of Indian political leaders.

Nehru and Ayub Khan had little more in common than the two Canadian leaders, but their mutual indifference was less distracting than the Canadians' mutual antipathy. The 1960s started on a hopeful note with the resolution, thanks to World Bank intervention and financial support, of the disposition between the two countries of the waters of the Indus River and its tributaries for purposes of irrigation, electric power generation and water control. The settlement of this frontier problem was intended to be followed by rectification of boundary disagreements and other differences between India and Pakistan. It was not to be. Having signed boundary treaties with Pakistan, Burma and Nepal, China sought a border settlement with India that reflected the traditional Chinese-Indian frontier more closely than that which resulted from the British advances of the late 19th century. When the Indians refused to budge from the maximum claims of the British India period, the Chinese in 1962 marched to within 30 miles of the Assan plain, camped there until they had established the point that they were unassailable, and quietly departed.

The Chinese venture was an exercise in humiliation, and a conspicuously successful one. Canadian newspapers, like those in many other countries, were full of stories of Indian retreats. There was more sympathy for the Indian army than for the Defence Minister who was perceived as having reduced it to this state, the ubiquitous Krishna Menon. Labelled at fault for excessive promotion of personally loyal officers and insufficient funding of the armed forces, Menon retired in disgrace, one of the best known and least loved of India's international spokesmen. There was more sympathy for his long time protector, although Nehru recovered neither his health nor his reputation after the Chinese invasion.

Canadians were overwhelmingly critical of the Chinese Government[12]. The construction of a Chinese road right through the Himalayan Ladakh section of Kashmir was cited as an example of galling provocation. English-Canadian editorial writers saw no reason to regard a frontier that India had inherited from the British as other than an established and equitable boundary. The Department of External Affairs and a few politicians, however, were aware that Victorian Britain's Himalyan policy had been expansionist. Beyond this core, expertise on Himalayan frontiers was a rare and esoteric concern[13]. The popular Canadian impression, derived in some measure from the well-publicized and virtually unanimous viewpoint of the American administration, Congress and US media, was that the Chinese were guilty of unprovoked aggression. After 1962, concern in Ottawa over causal factors wanned. What remained was the conviction that the most important and powerful country in Asia was not India.

India's mortification was observed with almost morbid fascination from Pakistan. The need to patch up relations in silent response to India's military superiority suddenly appeared based on an obsolete premise. The major source of discord between the two powers had always been Jammu and Kashmir, the former princely state in the Northwest of the subcontinent. In 1948, Pakistan expected the accession of Kashmir as a Muslim majority area, despatching irregulars to induce the desired result. The Hindu ruler telephoned New Delhi for military support, was advised that this would be forthcoming promptly upon his accession to India, and accordingly accepted the Indian terms. Regular forces from both sides rushed in, Pakistan seizing the Muslim Northern and Western parts and India the larger portion to the east. A cease-fire was eventually achieved in 1949, but neither accepted a *de jure* division of the state. A United Nations Military Observer Group in India and Pakistan (UNMOGIP) was thereafter maintained in Kashmir, always including a handful of Canadian troops as the largest contingent. It was a minor case of Canadian involvement in South Asia, and one that would not have occurred but for Pearson's commitment to the Commonwealth and to the United Nations. It might not ever have been necessary, had the Canadian willingness to see the state divided been more readily acceptable in Delhi and Karachi, the disposition of the prized valley of Kashmir being determined by plebiscite or internationalized by joint agreement.

After the Sino-Indian War tension in Kashmir seemed to increase, and by 1964, there were 17 Canadians in UNMOGIP, including a Caribou aircraft and its crew. This was not expected to be a deterrent to the build-up towards hostilities, merely a means of keeping track of its more obvious manifestations. War broke out between India and Pakistan in 1965, first over a sandbar in the Indian Ocean that was of such obvious unimportance that the psychological nature of the conflict was at once transparent. Then in the autumn it spread to the fertile Punjab area, and there was a renewal of the 1948 struggle over the control of Kashmir. Again there was no clear victor, but that in itself gave substance to Pakistan's claim to be treated as the equal of India. A United Nations India-Pakistan Observer Mission (UNIPOM) was established under a Canadian Major-General, involving 112 Canadians and five RCAF aircrafts. Its responsibilities were outside of Kashmir, and within six months it could be disbanded. The political conciliation of the 1965 war was not picked up by a Canadian, but by the Soviet Premier at Tashkent in January 1966, a reflection of the much increased influence of Russia in South Asia. It was successful in winding up the war, though the strain was fatal to Nehru's successor as India's Prime Minister. With Shastri's death at Tashkent, Nehru's daughter, Indira Gandhi, became Prime Minister.

India's embittered relations with Pakistan and China were to a slight degree contributary to a transformation of the Afro-Asian Movement into a Nonaligned Movement. In 1961, along with President Tito of Yugoslavia and Nasser, Nehru launched the new movement at Belgrade. Since Pakistan was a member of SEATO and CENTO and China was still technically allied to Russia, these powers were excluded from the first Nonaligned Conference. When China saw the consequences of using political rather than racial criteria for membership, it sought to convene another conference to Bandung in 1964 to rival the second Nonaligned Conference being held in Cairo. It failed, and nonaligned conferences have flourished instead, albeit with an increasingly loose definition of nonalignment. The advantage for India of the Nonaligned over the Afro-Asian Movement was temporary. This was because the demise of SEATO and CENTO brought Pakistan into the Nonaligned Movement, and because the Indian Prime Minister, while still a figure of some prominence in a conference of 25 in 1961, was by 1978 almost unnoticed in a crowd of 88 nations at the Nonaligned Summit Conference in Havana. From a Canadian perspective, India was no longer the operative actor.

One aspect of Canadian-South Asian relations that did not become significant until the 1960s was immigration to Canada from the subcontinent. Prior to South Asian independence, immigration from South Asia had been unimportant. This was untrue of 1906 to 1908, when entrepreneurial Canadian steamship companies generated nearly 5 000 passengers for themselves without consultation with any level of government in Canada, without any thought to the possible unreceptivity of white Canadians, and without warnings to the immigrants regarding the degression in progress in much of Canada. This business venture was socially disastrous, and led to a near ban on South Asian immigration for 40 years. The relaxation at the time of independence discussions was politically motivated, for the Canadian Government was disturbed by the Burmese precedent of forsaking the Commonwealth and was busily promoting Commonwealth membership. The immigration flow gradually increased. Yet, until a year after new regulations were introduced in 1962, the total merely grew from dozens to hundreds. Then for about a dozen years immigration from South Asia was in the thousands and mounting. By the mid-1970s, the South Asian population of Canada was over a hundred thousand, since which time the growth has been slowed by Canadian unemployment and a more cautious immigration act.

South Asian (or East Indian) Canadians are thus under 0,5 % of the Canadian population, too small a number to have much impact on Canadian foreign policy unless they were concentrated and united. This they are not. Although three-quarters of them live in Ontario and British Columbia, they are dispersed between different towns and between different residential areas of the larger cities. They represent different ethnic, religious and linguistic traditions both between and within South Asian countries. Those who have reached Canada after residence in Britain or Uganda have a tenuous link with the subcontinent, and South Asian governments seldom recognize any residual rights or citizenship claims. Many have come to Canada in search of different business practices and living standards, and this attitude places priority on quiet acceptance over publicized lobbying. Their educational and technical training might have led to charges that Canada had induced a brain drain, but unemployment among the intelligentsia, particularly in India, has undermined this criticism.

Some correlation has been noted between Canadian trade and immigration[14], which raises the question of whether more trade and immigration offices in South Asia would have transformed the relationship. Too much should not be made of such a correlation. The United States had long been Canada's principal trading partner. Yet despite the numerous Canadian Government offices in the United States, emigration has been prompted more by variables like the Vietnam War protest movement. Japanese-Canadian trade developed a tremendous growth momentum in the 1960s and 1970s, yet the Japanese have never shown the slightest interest in emigrating to Canada. Trade and immigration offices have been limited to the Indian and Pakistani capitals in South Asia, with little impetus towards extension. Many more immigrants to Canada could have been secured through a network of immigration offices, particularly if assisted passage had been offered, but that is to look at means rather than ends. The thrust of Canadian immigration policy of the mid and late 1970s has been on improved absorption rather than on increased inflow. The other end of the correlation, the trade picture, has always been limited by the potential market for each other's goods and the vast transportation distances. The largest items in Canadian export figures have usually involved either development assistance or export guarantees. Changes in trade figures over 35 years have reflected increases in the respective gross national products and inflationary factors, but at no time has there been evidence of dramatic growth and a basis for a significant and sustained trading relationship.

Canadian-Indian relations were marred during the 1960s by differing interpretations over the proper handling of responsibilities in the International Control Commission (ICC) for Vietnam. This was a peacekeeping unit established in 1954 by the Geneva Conference that finalized the departure of the French from Indochina. Britain and Russia, rather than the United Nations, had convened the conference. The military observer group that was despatched to South-East Asia was expected to complete its work within two years, report on the impartiality of elections, and disband. India was early picked for the role of neutral chairman, and Poland for that of the power sympathetic to the Vietnamese Communists. Canada was not the expected choice for participant nation sympathetic to the French; reportedly the suggestion came from India[15]. The ICC did in fact work well during its expected life, but the envisaged elections did not take place in 1956 or thereafter, so its work was protracted indefinitely. Although assassinations of South Vietnamese officials were stepped up in the late 1950s, the Commission did not face serious problems until the scale of fighting was intensified in the early to mid-1960s. This time the Americans assumed the former French role of military and economic backer of South Vietnam. It was not a situation that the ICC had been established to handle, and it was incapable of doing so properly.

Canadian-Indian differences within the Commission developed over how the other was responding to the new circumstances. To India, it appeard as if Canada found it more difficult to be independent when the United States was involved, becoming somewhat of an apologist for the American-backed South Vietnam regime. To Canada, it seemed as if India was more interested in majority resolutions than in fairness; since the Poles invariably supported the Communist side, this meant India did less than justice to the opposing side. Canada resented a situation in which it was forced to present the South Vietnamese case, whether or not it agreed with it, just to get it on the record. Canada regarded Poland as the Communist explanator and justifier. It picked up its eventual role of South Vietnamese explanator reluctantly, tardily, unenthusiastically, and legalistically. Considering that it followed its outlining of the South Vietnamese case with criticisms of South Vietnamese actions where required, Canada insisted that its distinction between being an explanator and an apologist was perfectly clear. Although unstated, implicit in the Canadian position was the view that failure to appreciate the distinction was either simplistic or tendencious. It did not help the Canadian Government when some intelligent Canadian journalists failed to accept this distinction and criticized Canada for being the Americans' spokesman within the Commission[16]. That brought the Indian interpretation of Canadian actions into Canadian domestic politics and made it an alternative Canadian viewpoint. It was not an outcome for which the Indian Government could really be held responsible, but it did nothing to improve government-to-government relations.

During the 18-year life of the ICC between 1954 and 1972, scores of Canadian diplomats and military officers served tours in Indochina, some two or three tours. A few also had occasion to serve in New Delhi at the High Commission, many of whom moved on to more senior positions within External Affairs and National Defence. Very few came to admire Indian officialdom more as a result. It is probable that, beyond the veneer of common British political and bureaucratic training, there remain fundamental cultural differences concealed by the easy use of the same former imperial language. Alternatively, traditional diplomats and military officers may not be the most suitable of Canadians for dealing with Indian temperaments and thought processes. Somehow or other a corps of the Canadian bureaucratic elite embarked on the 1950s minimizing differences in Indian approaches and perspectives and emerged a generation later exaggerating them. The experience of the first ICC in Vietnam was prejudicial to amicable Canadian-Indian understanding[17]. When the second and much briefer ICC was formed in 1973 to observe the American departure from Vietnam, the one lure that the United States was confident would attract Canadian participation was reconstitution of the Commission in such a way as to exclude India.

THE CURRENT PHASE

In the beginning of the 1970s, India was too preoccupied with events in the subcontinent to worry very much about its image in Canada. Its big concern in 1970 and 1971 was in regard to Pakistan. After a dozen years of virtual military government, the Pakistani ruling council held Parliamentary elections in 1970 with the object of restoring civilian government. The leader of the largest West Pakistani political party, Ali Bhutto, had been acting as a self-appointed Leader of the Official Opposition, clamouring for popular elections. Like Bhutto, the Pakistani military rulers were West Pakistanis, moderately well informed of political under-currents in West Pakistan but unaware of how little they understood the linguistically and culturally distinct Bengalis of East Pakistan. They expected some sort of West Pakistani-led coalition to emerge, including an element of East Pakistani support. They did not want the latter to comprise Mujibur Ali Rahman's Party, which they regarded as separatist.

From their perspective, the worst happened. In the more populated eastern wing of Pakistan, Mujibur won the popular vote in a landslide and all but two of the eastern wing's seats in the Parliament. With or without some coalition support from the western wing, Mujibur was in a position to dominate Parliament with a very comfortable majority, and reverse what his supporters regarded as the long-standing discrimination against their wing. That depended on Parliament being allowed to meet, and Mujibur being permitted to become head of government. The West Pakistanis decided that there was too much risk involved, and that the army should be used to suppress the latent separatism. The immediate result of the application of force was terror, stigmatized by the *Montréal Star* on June 18, 1971, as genocide. It was followed by a much more clearly focused and imperative urge towards separatism among the Bengalis, and an exodus of East Pakistanis into Eastern India in refuge from the Pakistani army estimated by an official Canadian mission at 9,6 million. The Canadian High Commissioners to India and Pakistan jointly cabled their recommendation that the welfare of the refugees should be Canada's first concern[18]. India was prepared to tolerate and feed the endless influx of refugees for weeks, not years, and informed Canada and other nations through diplomatic channels that it would not accept the situation for long. India had quickly responded to the virtual civil war in Pakistan by assisting the Bengali guerrillas with military equipment, and the diplomatic warnings implied more direct Indian military intervention would follow unless other powers pressured Pakistan into reversing its policy. Canada attempted to discuss curtailment of its development assistance to Pakistan as a lever in this direction[19], but was disinclined to overdo such a questionable threat when American policy was directed to securing a strong and united Pakistan.

Canadian policy was similar to that of other Western countries: sympathy to the refugees on their plight, gratitude to India for its mass hospitality, and limited humanitarian assistance by way of concrete action. It was a diplomatic way of indicating that India would have to look after the cause of the problem itself, and India grasped the message. It signed a friendship treaty with Russia in August 1971 which was universally interpreted as a warning to China not to come to Pakistan's assistance while India moved against the Pakistan army in East Pakistan. Then Mrs. Gandhi embarked on a speaking tour of Western Europe and North America to publicize the immensity of the enforced migration and the scale of human suffering. Although there were the necessary formalities of meetings with government leaders as well, policy changes were not expected. Nor were they obtained. As late as December 6, Canadian External Affairs Minister Sharp was still publicly counselling patience. The trip constituted an appeal over the heads of governments for the sympathy of western publics, and for later understanding that whatever might have to be done had been unavoidable. That accomplished, Mrs. Gandhi returned to India and authorized the carefully-planned logistical operation to begin. It was an outstanding success. By Christmas, the Pakistan army in East Pakistan had to surrender, and in the new year a new country, Bangladesh, under a government indebted to India, came into being.

India's success had a stimulating effect on Canadian public awareness of India, and a depressing effect on Indian public appreciation of Canada. Canada claimed an official impartiality was required by its involvement in UNMOGIP, an even-handedness that Indians found totally misplaced in the face of genocide[20]. Official relations were strained for other reasons as well, and some critics viewed the Indian action as aggression. However, the humanitarian explanation for the moves had been skilfully prepared, the swiftness and efficiency of the operation was technically extremely impressive for an unevenly developed country, and it was all over before opponents could mobilize against it. Mujibur appeared to be a colourful and kindly leader, and his people deserving of a chance to run their own affairs. Canadian-Pakistani relations were satisfactory, but the Pakistani image was of an insensitive, unimaginative and clumsy regime. Militarily it was to Pakistan's advantage to fight India in the West of the subcontinent, not in the East, yet its military rulers were responsible for transferring much of the army to that part of Pakistan where they could be least effective against India should the Indian army be ordered into action. Canadian respect for India's achievement was due in no small measure to the political, military and public relations mistakes of Pakistan.

The 1971 war left India supreme in South Asia. India had recovered remarkably from its 1962 defeat at the hands of China. Given time and a great deal of Western economic and military help, Pakistan might recover to the point of becoming a credible military rival to India. For the balance of the 1970s, however, India was relatively secure from serious challenge from that quarter. It was more concerned with its military capability relative to its Northern neighbour, China. China had detonated a nuclear device in 1964. Since the early 1950s, Canada had been aiding the Indian atomic research programme. The greatest crisis in Canadian-Indian relations was to arise from the Indian decision to follow China along the path of nuclear proliferation[21].

Indian interest in atomic power dated from the beginning of its independence. The Atomic Energy Commission was created in 1948, and thereafter worked closely with the Prime Minister. Nehru explained to the Indian Lower House on May 10, 1954, that there was a risk industrially-advanced countries might exert their authority to restrict the use of atomic energy at some stage, since it did not appear to them necessary. Their needs were not the same as those of developing nations with limited energy resources, he argued, and for India atomic energy was far more important than it was for developed countries. The idea of international control and inspection was a potentially discriminatory tool of great powers, and India would not accept controls that worked to its disadvantage. The following year when India was seeking a nuclear reactor for power generation, it approached the one non-great power possessing nuclear technology, Canada, and offered its pledge that it would use the reactor purely for peaceful purposes. Between Commonwealth partners, it was claimed, a word was as good as a bond. The request was not entirely unexpected. As early as 1947, Canada had supplied India with a ton of crude uranium oxide in the hope of future access to India's plentiful thorium, already recognized as an alternative ingredient to uranium in atomic power production. Why Commonwealth membership should have been put forward as a substitute for international control and a talisman of good intentions is quite another matter. Ottawa and New Delhi both understood, for example, that Pakistan's reasons for joining SEATO and CENTO at that time were incompatible with trust and confidence in India, reasons that were hardly negated by common membership in the Commonwealth.

Safeguards at that time were unsufficiently important to be made mandatory, but important enough that the attempt to obtain them was pressed far enough to determine that insistence would nullify the deal. No other country had an exportable atomic power plant at that moment, but refusal to supply the research reactor would have ended a promising supplier relationship. The United States favoured proceeding with the agreement, supplying the heavy water itself. The reactor seemed a good visible symbol of Western assistance to counter-balance high-profile Russian projects, and was to become the most prominent example of Canadian-Indian cooperation. The cost was incorporated into Colombo Plan assistance, and the fledgling Canadian atomic energy industry received an immediate $7,5 million in contracts. This was crucial to keeping the Canadian skills together, developing manufacturing experience, ironing out structural defects, and building export sales. Canadian technological assistance was undeniably critical to this stage of India's nuclear development, but it was also a turning point in a Canadian programme that had to expand or be terminated. It was only in 1961 that a Special Committee of the Canadian House of Commons under a Progressive Conservative Government became concerned over the agreement, and that concern sprang from delays and cost overruns rather than from deficient safeguards. Another thirteen years passed before plutonium from the research reactor fueled India's first nuclear test.

The nuclear reactors sales of the 1960s were neither as controversial at the time nor thereafter. The reactors erected in Rajasthan were both subject to inspection by the International Atomic Energy Agency (IAEA), which was not in operation at the time of the research reactor agreement. They were contracted as a result of competitive negotiation, and were tied to purchase in Canada and hard loans to a significant degree. Outside of Canada they were regarded more as commercial sales than as development assistance. It could not be argued that, had Canada not made the sales, India could not have obtained the reactors from elsewhere. Without the research reactor agreement, however, Canada probably would not have been the preferred supplier for the Rajasthan reactors. With that working background, India believed Canada best suited to enhancing Indian training, developing Indian nuclear self-reliance, and permitting Indian participation in final design engineering and construction.

The Chinese atomic detonation of 1964 provoked tremendous discussion within the Indian Government, but Shastri opposed mass diversion of scarce resources to nuclear development. Mrs. Gandhi accepted this view at the time, but after the Chinese hydrogen bomb detonation of 1966, she swung over as Prime Minister to the argument that atomic power would ultimately reduce India's fuel bills. That may have been a domestic policy rationalization to a reactive foreign policy, but her May 1967 statement that ministers might have to take a nuclear decision at any moment was considerably less ambiguous. The Nuclear Non-Proliferation Treaty took effect in 1970, which India objected to as freezing the existing nuclear hierarchy, discriminatory in its inspection provision, and leaving non-nuclear states dependent on security assurances from nuclear powers which the latter might not honour. Mrs. Gandhi admitted to the Indian Upper House on August 27, 1970, that defence needs were foremost when development of nuclear energy was considered, and submitted to the Nonaligned Summit a fortnight later that staging nuclear explosions was the right of nonaligned nations. Canada, which had been monitoring deliberations in India closely, was not in doubt over the trend of Indian policy.

What the Canadian Government was endeavouring to do in 1970 and 1971, including Trudeau personally in encounters with Mrs. Gandhi, was to turn the clock back. India appeared likely to be the first country receiving development assistance to detonate a nuclear device, and Canada was uncomfortable with the prospect of appearing as the short-sighted Samaritan. Canada renewed its requests that output from the original research reactor be placed under IAEA inspection, and took to interpreting the agreement as if that commitment already existed. Mrs. Gandhi declined to accept a unilateral understanding of the intent of the agreement, and implied that the question of a peaceful nuclear explosion was hypothetical. After the Nuclear Non-Proliferation Treaty, Canadian policy had accepted a distinction between great power ability to conduct peaceful and military nuclear explosions, and abnegation on the part of others. India had not, but posed a distinction between peaceful and military purpose detonations which Canada had come to reject. Mrs. Gandhi's suggestion that a peaceful nuclear explosion was hypothetical was an implication that the decision whether and when to conduct a detonation was exclusively India's. Nevertheless, the rebuff, together with the pledge made at the time of the research reactor agreement, were later held up in Canada as examples of India's betrayal of trust. In India, on the other hand, Canadian inferences appeared as preparatory steps in the building of the case of an aggrieved party.

The nuclear explosion of May 1974 was predictably interpreted, within India and virtually everywhere else, as prompted by military rather than by peaceful goals. China's head-start was a public explanation, but disenchantment with the Western powers' paltry response to the East Pakistan refugee problem was a private one. Nuclear self-reliance appeared to India dictated by its predicament in the autumn of 1971; its validity appeared confirmed by India's triumph that winter. Although two and a half years elapsed between the third Indian-Pakistani War and the Indian nuclear experiment, nothing transpired in the intervening period to indicate that India had altered its policy. The delay was technical, not political, and when India was ready, the test took place. Sharp's reaction was one of controlled anger, the attitude of a man who had been let down. Only the moment of detonation should have proved a surprise to his department, whereas Indians were quite unprepared for the extreme Canadian reaction[22].

Canada promptly cancelled planned discussions on existing commercial loans. The talks were subsequently held and loans re-scheduled, but there was no recognition that Indian needs were exceptional and assistance should be special. Sharp did not consider that the development of a nuclear industry could be convincingly related to the provision of cheap energy. Indian policy therefore had to be related to big power aspirations, hardly a reason for Canadian philanthropy. Food and agricultural aid were not interrupted, since they could be viewed as humanitarian assistance. Nuclear supply contracts were suspended, and in May 1976 terminated. India did not suggest that this was contract breaking, although the Canadian case for termination was based on a Canadian interpretation of agreements and exchanges which India had never entirely accepted. The effect of ending agreements was to de-control those reactors on which a control agreement had been established. Subsequent Indian compliance with international safeguards owed nothing therefore to Canadian leverage[23]. The Canadian decision of May 1976 is not easily explained in terms of either its nuclear non-prolifaction policy or of improving Canadian-Indian relations. Public opinion polls indicated that the Government was experiencing unpopularity in the country, however, and the Conservative Opposition was berating the Government on the issue in Parliament. Sharp was House Leader, having exchanged portfolios with the Liberals' specialist on Parliamentary control, Allan MacEachen. It was a situation conducive to the suppression of an emotive but little-understood foreign policy issue in the interest of a more tractable House of Commons. For better or worse, after May 1976, Canadian-Indian relations were a dormant issue in Canadian politics[24].

The Pakistani perspective on India's nuclear breakthrough was comparable in value and emotion to that in Canada, but far more intense. Canada and Pakistan viewed Russia and China as North Asian rivals and India and Pakistan as South Asian rivals. Neither saw Asia through Indian eyes as a continent of two traditional rivals, China and India, with Pakistan an aberration on India's flank. Where Canada and Pakistan differed in their appreciation, it was in Canada seeing India as pretentious in aspiring to rival China, whereas Pakistan continued to interpret Indian policy as if the Pakistani-Indian relationship was India's primary and dominant concern. Canadian-Pakistani atomic energy policy has reflected Pakistan's perception of reality, and has thus attempted to copy Canadian-Indian atomic energy policy.

When India approached Canada for a nuclear reactor in 1955, Pakistan predicted that it would install 1 077 MW of nuclear capacity by 1975[25]. This was far from a firm plan, for by 1975 Pakistan possessed only one power reactor, a 137 MW heavy water reactor acquired from Canada. It was in operation by 1975 using US-supplied heavy water, firm negotiations only dating from 1965. In addition, Pakistan had a very small medical and agricultural research reactor, acquired from the United States, which was in operation in 1965. The overseas training programme for Pakistanis did get started in the 1950s, including nuclear-related scientific training in Canada analogous to that supplied to Indians, but Pakistan started from a weaker scientific base than India. Pakistan's nuclear contingency plan appears to date from 1964. This was in the context of Indian vulnerability as exposed by China in 1962, China's detonation in 1964, and the inference from statements and actions of various alarmed Indian authorities that India would seek to become a nuclear power. It was followed by the second Indian-Pakistani War, and by the first of many public warnings by Bhutto that Pakistan would eat grass if necessary to obtain nuclear parity with India.

Bhutto was Prime Minister at the time of the 1974 Indian atomic test, an event he categorized as nuclear blackmail of Pakistan. One month before, work had begun on a Pakistani fuel fabrication plant designed to make 20 tons of uranium rods per annum. It was started with Canadian technical and financial assistance, and was expected to be operational in 1978. In reaction against the South Asian race towards nuclear proliferation, however, Canada withdrew from the commitment. Pakistan persevered on the nuclear path, planning in 1975 for the installation of a 600-MW reactor in 1980, a prediction that was not fulfilled. However, in March 1976, France signed an agreement with Pakistan to supply a nuclear reprocessing facility. This was not another remote planning target, but an entirely feasible international deal. It was reminiscent of Indian completion in June 1964 of a plutonium separation plant designed and built to process the spent fuel from the Canadian research reactor. According to India's interpretation, spent fuel was a national ingredient, the raw material for a separation plant, and not subject to IAEA control. Canada had ensured that the power reactor at Karachi was subject to IAEA safeguards, and no technically-advanced nation had at the time seemed disposed to circumvent the safeguards by providing a nuclear processing facility. Canada protested the French sales agreement of 1976. As bilateral relations were strained over restrictions, Canada was imposing on proposed uranium sales to France, however, the French Government dismissed these further demands as typical of Canadian rigidity and high-handedness in atomic energy matters. Canada then sought a Pakistani commitment not to process spent fuel from the Canadian reactor at Karachi in the proposed French reprocessing facility. As both nations know perfectly well that expensive plants are not purchased to be kept idle, the Canadian request was politely ignored. In 1978, the French withdrew from the agreement, probably less due to Canadian than to American pressure, plus a realization that the Pakistani market was not important enough to it to justify all the criticism it was receiving.

With the reprocessing route closed for the foreseeable future, Pakistan was left with two options. The first was to persevere with the idea of a nuclear free zone in South Asia. This would subject India to IAEA control of its reprocessing, if India could be somehow forced to agree, and remove India's advantage over Pakistan. This option has Canada's endorsement and has been pursued by General Zia Ul-Haq, who displaced Bhutto in 1977. It has not, needless to say, made any progress in India. This has left Pakistan with a second option, pursued clandestinely since 1977 parallel to the first, of purchasing centrifuge plant components for an enrichment plant. No components have apparently been purchased in Canada, and Pakistan denies that an enrichment plant is operational or planned, so Canadian-Pakistani relations have not yet become embittered by this furtive option. Insofar as it is directed towards nuclear proliferation, it is, of course, contrary to Canadian policy. Ironically, this Pakistani option was embarked on during that unique period of Indian experience since independence when Congress was out of office, March 1977 to January 1980, and Prime Minister Desai was pursuing a strong anti-proliferation policy.

There was disappointment in Ottawa at this second South Asian deviation from Canada's chosen path of non-proliferation, but exemplary political leadership was not something Canada had come to expect of Pakistan. From the late 1960s to the early 1980s, Pakistan was led by two autocratic and narrowly-based military regimes separated by an intelligent and popularly elected, but demagogic and manipulative, government under Bhutto. India was another matter. Roughly during the Nehru period, there had been a Canadian-Indian accord at the government level.

Press coverage of the other in each country, though limited, was generally favourable. The North American news agencies described India as the world's largest democracy whenever general elections were held. For some concerned Canadians, the bloom had faded by the mid-1960s. India's reputation suffered from the Sino-Indian War, the acrimony over peacekeeping in Vietnam, the construction of the plutonium separation plant, and the gratuitous 1965 Indo-Pakistani War. For Indophilis, it lasted a decade longer. The nuclear test and the dictatorial period of 1975-1977, known in India as «Emergency Rule», marked the end of what had once seemed a special relationship. India's place was not really taken by any other Asian power, although in press coverage it was replaced by China. As the first of the second wave of powers to recognize the People's Republic of China and prepare its seating in the United Nations, Canada could call on a measure of Chinese goodwill and gratitude. After a generation of isolation, Canadian politicians, officials, businessmen and wealthy tourists descended on China during the course of the 1970s. It was regarded as the major Asian power, and one more resistant to Russian pressure and influence than India. Yet for Canada the Chinese connection was not a relationship of unguarded friendship, and the trading dimension experienced limited growth.

Trade with India continues, at a modest level, to be Canada's strongest continuing link with New Delhi. After a period of zero growth accompanying the cool relations of the mid-1970s, Canadian-Indian trade moved slowly forward in the period 1978-1980 to around a quarter of a billion dollars of Canadian exports annually and under $100 million of imports into Canada from India. Five good harvests in India reduced the once major item of Canadian wheat exports, but newsprint, pulp and paper, rapeseed oil, potash, asbestos, coking coal and aluminum continued to be needed. India sold Canada jute, engineering castings, tea, coffee, spices, nuts, leather, precious stones, jewelry (gold, silver and enameled), oriental rugs, cotton blouses, and cotton and rayon blend woven fabrics. Values of these diversified commodities were lower than for Canada's more concentrated range of items. Leather, blouses and fabrics would have featured more prominently had they not often been categorized by Canadian Customs as footwear and textiles, the importation of which was being restricted by the Canadian Government. India sought to have hand-loomed fabrics and products made from them classified as handicrafts, which would exempt them from quotas. This particularized Canadian protectionism represented a 1977 exception to its 1974 implementation of the Generalized Preference Scheme endorsed at successive meetings of the United Nations Conference on Trade and Development. South Asian nations were not the only ones subjected to quotas and «voluntary» export restraints in the interest of one-industry Québec and Ontario towns, and Third World interest groups in Canada argued that access to Canadian markets was necessary for balanced trade and subsequent expansion of Canadian exports[26].

The Canadian Government's reservation regarding the nature of Canadian-Indian trade was concerned instead with the low percentage of manufactured and high technology items amongst the export total. This was the consequence of import substitution through encouragement of domestic manufacturing. It was a disappointment to Canada, but not one to which it could object much in principle. Both countries have been hewers of wood and drawers of water; both have sought to favour domestic over foreign manufacturers. The same can be said of the general rule that foreign direct investment in Indian enterprises is limited to a maximum of 40 % of equity. Although an exception might be drawn for the 1979-1980 Clark Government, the Trudeau Governments that established the Canada Development Corporation and the Foreign Investment Review Agency were not free to criticize the foreign investment policies of foreign nations other than in instances of limited and specific application.

To the extent that it can afford it, India would like to upgrade its hydroelectric generation, communications, transportation, and metal and mineral development. Canadian engineers, consultants and manufacturers are suited to this work. European Community and Japanese companies bidding on Indian contracts, however, have longer and therefore cheaper production runs, shorter and therefore quicker transportation routes, and broader and therefore sounder governmental financial guarantees. Canada discussed a joint venture in aeronautical development in a mission to India in 1979, and Indian officials in Canada in 1980 discussed joint collaboration of Indian heavy electrical generators combined with Canadian turbines. Each envisaged the other as a basic market from which to expand into third country markets. Joint ventures must start from such tenuous initiatives, recognizing that more often than not they fail to reach fruition. Joint commissions, however, are more often chimeras conjured up by governements anxious to create an impression of activity when there is little of substance to offer. The 1979 agreement in principle to form a Canadian-Indian joint commission to increase trade and economic cooperation between the two countries is perhaps another example of an agreement almost forgotten by those responsible for its framing.

Canadian-Indian trade is not a big enough item to feature in global trade figures, and is usually buried in Canadian-Asian trade statistics. Indian imports into Canada are a negligible percentage of Canadian imports, and a total embargo would have no impact outside of a very few Indian fabric shops in Canada. Indian imports from Canada are some 2 % of India's total imports. Though not a high percentage, it is much larger than the Indian percentage input into Canadian import statistics. This is less due to the two-and-a-half times larger figure for the Indian imports from Canada than to a much more nearly comparable gross national product than one would expect from the immense population disparity, and to the much smaller percentage of Indian GNP involved in international trade. The growth rates of the Canadian and Indian economies in the 1970s were a pale reflexion of their spurts in the 1950s. The improvement in Canadian export figures to India in the period 1978-1980 was thus an encouraging sign. They were not based on an increase in Canadian development assistance, but on export sales. Half of Canadian exports to India were based on trade, not aid. As a contribution to the trade diversification (or Third Option) policy of the early 1970s, the change was scarcely worth mentioning. But with the ending of a political partnership, the stabilizing of migration and development assistance patterns, and governments losing office in both countries because of their inability to cope with grave crises, any favourable sign was to be welcome. It was the one slender but encouraging sign at the beginning of the 1980s that there was room for forward anticipation of a developing relationship in place of backward recrimination and fading nostalgia.

CONCLUSION

The attempt to examine Canada's relationship with the Indian subcontinent over a three to four-decade period has required selectivity of subject matter as well as of approach. Selectivity of subject has involved more emphasis on Canada's relationship with India than with Pakistan, and little or no attention to nations dotting the fringes of the subcontinent. Selectivity of subject matter has also required discussion only of those areas of cooperation or of discord that required the attention of the respective political leaders and officials over a sustained period. Selectivity of approach has involved some reflexion in advance as to whether posing hypotheses on a few topics for fuller testing would permit of as comprehensive an assessment of the Canadian-South Asian relationship as would be possible, using a more chronological approach. The conclusion that the former alternative would not permit of as comprehensive an assessment of Canadian-South Asian relationships determined that the latter, more chronological method, would suit best. The choice of organization through three rough time frames has permitted concentration on a topic during the period when its positive or negative effects on the relationship were most pronounced. Comparing the relationship as a whole at the end of the period with what it was at the beginning, it is clear that there has been a considerable transformation.

Before the subcontinent's independence, British India had no foreign policy apart from that determined for it by the British Government, and Canadian foreign policy barely stretched beyond North America and Western Europe. By 1947, however, Britain was exhausted from over-commitment and beginning its long retreat, whereas Canada and the subcontinent emerged from World War II wealthier, more developed and more internationalist. Both saw the colonial aspiration towards independence as the wave of the future, chanced to be in positions to influence that trend, and cooperated to that end. Although Canada was careful to consult with the other South Asian nations, the influence of India was more prominent in diplomatic exchanges. The Commonwealth and the United Nations were avenues for the application of the common commitment to more broadly-based international organizations, the former from Caucasian to multiracial, the latter from Eurocentric to universalist. Yet the very expansion to which they contributed diluted their influence, and well before 1980 each had lost that intangible authority derived from appearing to speak for a group of powers.

Although it was possible to rationalize inconsistencies, the Afro-Asian Movement's colour consciousness was philosophically divergent from the Commonwealth's multiracialism. The strategic particularism of NATO was also the product of a different intellectual response to international tensions than the universalism of the United Nations. The Afro-Asian Movement could be presented as the response of former colonies to the divisiveness of imperialist forces. NATO could be justified as the reply of Western nations to the divisiveness of the Iron Curtain. Sceptics on both sides, however, could view the other organization as adversarial and divisive. One reason why Canada saw the Afro-Asian Movement as potentially useful in the 1950s, and India managed to tolerate NATO, is that each imagined the other as a key actor in the suspect organization. Each nation valued the other as a prime conduit to larger interests, a possible educator, an ally at a foreign court. This is not the same as a treaty ally, for such a Canadian-Indian relationship never existed. The introduction of treaty alliance to the subcontinent via Pakistan was indeed responsible for diverting Indian impetus from the Afro-Asian to the Nonaligned Movement, qualifying in the process its adherence to the cause of universality. The anti-Pakistani aspect of the maneuvering, combined with a continued reluctance to permit a plebiscite in Kashmir, registered as a visible Indian descent from the pedestal of international principle to the bazaar of competitive interests. Canada, meanwhile during the course of the 1960s, lost its own influence in NATO, and could not plausibly represent the interests of another group.

Canada's early prominence in South Asian development assistance was timely, but was increasingly eclipsed by great power aid. As a contribution to South Asian economies, it was always marginal. As a percentage of Canadian assistance, it has steadily decreased as the global allocation has risen far faster than the South Asian allotment. Some have argued that development assistance to South Asia should be further reduced, since the recipient area is too vast to yield any impact. The peacekeeping experience with India in Indochina, launched in an atmosphere of mutual trust, deteriorated after two promising years to providing an embittered political socialization to the many affected diplomats and soldiers from which they have never recovered. The peacekeeping in Kashmir was intended to be temporary, but has proved interminable though limited. The 1971 war left India more ascendant than at any time during the subcontinent's independence, which might have been expected to restore Canadian confidence in India's power and influence after the nadir of the 1962 Sino-Indian War. It did not have that effect. The working relationship with Canada had deteriorated too much by that time, and India's leadership was not accepted outside of her immediate environs.

The nuclear research reactor was both a product of Canadian trust and a symbol of Canadian-Indian amity for a few years after its installation. But India's construction of a plutonium reprocessing plant in 1964 raised doubts over whether the trust had not been misplaced, and the 1974 nuclear test confirmed that India was preparing for the military application of atomic power. The Canadian Government reacted much more adversely than it would have to a government from which it had expected less. The detonation cut right across the Canadian Government's non-proliferation policy. This, together with the accumulated disappointments over the slide from the zenith of Canadian-Indian relations, produced an embittered spilling over upon public opinion of an embarrassment that the Government might ordinarily have been expected to contain. It approximated the timing of a movement within the Canadian Government to restrict immigration in the face of rising unemployment. The unsympathetic attitude towards India occasioned by the nuclear test and its reception in Canada hardly boded for making an exception of immigrants from India.

By the time Trudeau and Mrs. Gandhi were returned to power early in 1980, the only indicator that appeared to be slightly positive was the trade one. After several years without real growth in commercial exchanges between the two nations, the trade figures began to move up again in 1978. It was far from a dramatic change, and could be followed by stagnation if others proved more competitive or both became more protectionist. At least commercial sales had risen to the point of equalling donor assistance. From the Indian perspective, their sales to Canada were absolutely lower than their imports from Canada, and a lower (even insignificant) percentage of Canadian imports. A five-year extension of the Canadian restrictions on textile and clothing imports was not expected to help Indian exports in the first half of the 1980s. Inter-flow of investment capital, joint ventures and joint commissions were avenues to be explored in the future more than roads crossed in the past.

If one considers the correct and routine Canadian-South Asian relationship of 1980, the surprising aspect is not that it was not more substantive but that the question should have to be posed. Why should Canada enjoy one of its most extensive and fruitful relationships with a subcontinent on the other side of the world composed of very different races, religions, colours, cultures, educational levels and indigenous languages, and with a standard of living so vastly different as almost to be that of another planet? The elaboration of a common British heritage becomes very tenuous if traced to pre-Victorian times. Canada was a land of British settlement more than of conquest, whereas the Indian Empire was almost exclusively the fruit of conquest. The English language is established deep in Canada, shallow in the subcontinent. To some extent, the structure of institutions in India and Sri Lanka are western and democratic, but the experience has been short and ignores differences in processes in nations where high literacy levels are limited to the very few.

The independence of the subcontinent was followed by a decade of close accord, particularly between Canada and India. The imprecise but suggestive phrase of a special relationship, also at time used to describe the Canadian-American and Canadian-British relationship, was even applied to Canadian-Indian relations. The long-term basis of such a special relationship did not exist. Europe, Russia and China were suffering from the ravages of war when the Canadian-Indian accord was at its peak. Two-thirds of the independent nations of the world were still colonies, unable to represent their own interests on the world stage. The Indian subcontinent was granted a head-start rather than an extended priority in the Canadian development assistance programme. Such factors were transient, and the natural evolution of time restored the relationship to a lesser dimension. The special rapport with India, like the golden age of Canadian foreign policy elsewhere, was the product of a special time and circumstance. It is unlikely to occur again.

NOTES

1. L.B. Pearson, «The Development of Canadian Foreign Policy», *Foreign Affairs*, Vol. 30, No. 1, October 1951, p. 17-30.

2. Statement delivered by Ambassador Barton in the Security Council on January 7, 1980. Ambassador Ford in Moscow emphasized that the Soviets were prepared to do anything to protect their interests in a neighbouring state. See R.A.D. Ford, «La perception canadienne des relations Est-Ouest», *Politique Internationale*, Vol. 12, Summer 1981, p. 217-224. The Progressive Conservative External Affairs critic, who had been a member of the inner Cabinet in 1979-1980, was reported to have interjected in an altercation with the Minister that «the Afghanistan Government invited the Soviets to go in there» (*Globe & Mail*, May 22, 1982). This claim, however, is not to be found in the published version of Hansard for May 21, 1982.

3. J.K. Hilliker, «The British Columbia Franchise and Canadian Relations with India in Wartime, 1939-1945», *BC Studies*, No. 46, Summer 1980, p. 50.

4. J.W. Holmes, *The Shaping of Peace*, Vol. 2, Toronto, University of Toronto Press, 1982, p. 169.

5. M. Brecher, «India's Decision to Remain in the Commonwealth», *Journal of Commonwealth & Comparative Politics*, Vol. XII, No. 1, March 1974, p. 62-90; A.K. Banerji, «The Nehru-Menon Legacy That Still Survives», *Round Table*, No. 284, October 1981, p. 346-352.

6. D. LePan, *Bright Glass of Memory*, Toronto, McGraw-Hill Ryerson, 1979, Ch. 4.

7. For advocacy of increased assistance to South Asia, see Brecher, «The Continuing Challenge of International Development: A Canadian Perspective», *Queen's Quarterly*, Vol. 82, Autumn 1975, p. 323-343. For a contrasting viewpoint, see T.H. Cohn, «Politics in the World Bank Group: The Question of Loans to the Asian Giants», *International Organization*, Vol. 28, No. 3, Summer 1974, p. 561-571.

8. E. Reid, *Envoy to Nehru*, Delhi, Oxford University Press, 1981, Ch. 11.

9. P. Gordon Walker, *The Commonwealth*, London, Secker & Warburg, 1962, p. 321.

10. T.F. Keating and T.A. Keenleyside, «Voting Patterns as a Measure of Foreign Policy Independence», *International Perspectives*, May 1980, p. 21-26.

11. D. Stairs, *The Diplomacy of Constraint*, Toronto, University of Toronto Press, 1974.

12. P.V. Lyon, *Canada in World Affairs, 1961-1963*, Toronto, Oxford University Press, 1968, p. 487-490.

13. For example, W.M. Dobell, «Ramifications of the China-Pakistan Border Treaty», *Pacific Affairs*, Vol. 37, No. 3, Fall 1964, p. 283-295.

14. D.M. Indra, «Changes in Canadian Immigration Patterns over the Past Decade with Special Reference to Asia», in K.V. Ujimoto and G. Hirabashi (eds.), *Minorities and Multiculturalism: Asians in Canada*, Toronto, Butterworth, 1980, Ch. 11.

15. M. Brecher, *India and World Politics: Krishna Menon's View of the World*, London, Oxford University Press, 1968, p. 49.

16. For example, C. Taylor, *Snow Job*, Toronto, Anansi, 1974 and D. Van Praagh, «Canada and Southeast Asia», in P.V. Lyon and T.Y. Ismael (eds), *Canada and the Third World*, Toronto, Macmillan, p. 307-342. Alternative viewpoints are presented in P. Bridle, «Canada and the International Commissions in Indochina, 1954-1972», in M.W. Zacher and R.S. Milne (eds.), *Conflict and Stability in Southeast Asia*, New York, Ancor Press, 1974, p. 407-450 and W.M. Dobell, «A 'Sow's Ear' in Vietnam», *International Journal*, Vol. 29, No. 3, Summer 1974, p. 356-392.

17. For the view that this factor was insufficiently appreciated in India, see R.C. Thakur, «Change and Continuity in Canadian Foreign Policy», *India Quarterly*, Vol. 33, October 1974, p. 414.

18. A. Smith, *Stitches in Time*, Don Mills, General Publishing, 1981, p. 135.

19. P.V. Lyon, «Introduction» in Lyon and Ismael (eds.), *Canada and the Third World, op. cit.*, p. XI.

20. S. Clarkson, «Just What is Canada Accomplishing in India?», *Saturday Night*, October 1972, p. 15-17.

21. The Canada-India nuclear issue is covered in L. Beaton and J. Maddox, *The Spread of Nuclear Weapons*, London, Chatto & Winders, 1962, Ch. 8; B. Morrison and D.M. Page, «India's Option: the Nuclear Route to Achieve Goal as a World Power», *International Perspectives*, July 1974, p. 23-28; R.S. Anderson and B.M. Morrison, «Power from Power: A New Scenario Emerges for India's Scientists», *Science Forum*, Vol. 7, No. 6, December 1974, p. 10-13; G. Bindon and S. Mukerji, «How Canada's and India's Nuclear Roles Have Been Sadly Misrepresented», *Science Forum*, February 1977, p. 3-7; A. Kapur, *India's Nuclear Option*, New York, Praeger, 1976, Ch. 5; A. Kapur, «The Canada-India Nuclear Negotiations», *The World Today*, August 1978, p. 311-320; Robin Ranger,

Arms and Politics 1958-1978, Toronto, Macmillan, 1979, Ch. 16; and E.W. Lefever, *Nuclear Arms in the Third World,* Washington, D.C., Brookings, 1979, Ch. 2.

22. For the Indian counter-reaction, see M.S. Rajan, «India: A Case of Power Without Force», *International Journal,* Vol. 30, No. 2, Spring 1975, p. 299-325; R. Thapar, «Canada's Transition», *International Journal,* Vol. 33, No. 2, Spring 1978, p. 437-443.

23. India-US negotiations in the wake of Canada's action are outlined in J.S. Nye, Jr., «Nuclear Policy: Nuclear Fuel Exports to India», *Department of State Bulletin,* July 1978, p. 45-47.

24. One scholar who interviewed the executive officers of over 30 Canadian associations and companies in the spring of 1974 found that, within Asia, the area of greatest present interest to them was India. See. B. Morrison, «Canada and South Asia», in Lyon and Ismael (eds.), *Canada and the Third World, op. cit.,* p. 42-57. Presumably the linguistic factor had prolonged an interest that might otherwise have been transferred to Japan or China.

25. The Canada-Pakistan nuclear issue is covered in part in Z. Khalilzad, «Pakistan and the Bomb», *Survival,* Vol. 21, No. 6, November 1979, p. 244-249; B.M. Kaushik and O.N. Mehrotra, *Pakistan's Nuclear Bomb,* New Delhi, Sopan Publishing, 1980; and S. Weissman and H. Krosney, *The Islamic Bomb,* New York, Time Books, 1981.

26. Publications of the North-South Institute are notable in this regard. It is also true of select publications of the Economic Council of Canada, *e.g., For A Common Future* (1978), and V. Corbo and O. Hawrylyshyn, *Canada's Trade Relations with Developing Countries* (1980).

BIBLIOGRAPHY

BINDON, G. and MUKERJU, S. «How Canada's and India's Nuclear Roles have been Sadly Misrepresented», *Science Forum*, February 1977, p. 3-7.

HARNETTY, P. «Canada's Asian Policy: The Case of Pakistan», *South Asian Review*, Vol. 3, No. 2, January 1970, p. 117-129.

KAPUR, A. «The Canada-India Nuclear Negotiations», *The World Today*, August 1978, p. 311-320.

MORRISON, B. «Canada and South Asia», in P.V. Lyon and T.Y. Ismael (eds.), *Canada and the Third World*, Toronto, Macmillan, 1976, p. 1-59.

RAJAN, M.S. «The Indo-Canadian Entente», *International Journal*, Vol. 17, No. 4, Autumn 1962, p. 358-384.

REID, E. *Envoy to Nehru*, Delhi, Oxford University Press, 1981.

THOMSON, D.C. «India and Canada: A Decade of Cooperation 1947-1957», *International Studies*, Delhi, Vol. 9, No. 4, April 1968.

16

Canadian Policy
in the Middle East

Janice Stein
University of Toronto

INTRODUCTION

Canadian foreign policy towards the Middle East is a mirror in which we can see ourselves. A look in the mirror illuminates not only changes in the tone and substance of our policy in a region of endemic conflict, but also the more general dynamics which affect the form, content, and direction of Canadian foreign policy across a wide variety of issues. This look at Canadian policy in the Middle East suggests that in the last decade, new and powerful industrial and financial interests at home have gradually become important in shaping policy towards that troubled part of the world. As we enter the 1980s the impact of these powerful groups, working closely with senior mandarins in key ministries, is now visible to the naked eye: public policy has been privatized and internationalism domesticated.

This rather controversial interpretation of Canadian policy towards the Middle East does not represent a scholarly consensus. On the contrary, there is little agreement on the dynamics of Canadian policy in the region or on its substance and analysts write from quite different perspectives. The most widely accepted interpretation, a central tradition within Canadian scholarship, emphasizes the commitment to peacekeeping, mediation, and problem-solving which is characteristically and uniquely Canadian. Indeed, policy in the Middle East is part and parcel of a broader Canadian emphasis on a civilized and restrained approach to the solution of international disputes. Ottawa traditionally has excelled in the art of the possible and this pragmatic and functional approach to accommodation has shaped the tone and substance of Canadian policy not only in the Middle East but in the United Nations and NATO as well. Canada has been the quintessential peacemaker among its allies and peacekeeper in the Middle East.

A second interpretation challenges this portrait of a benevolent and helpful neutrality. Canada, the argument goes, is neither neutral nor even-handed but parochial and partisan in its approach to the Middle East: parochial in its ignorance of Middle Eastern history and culture, and partisan in its sympathy with Israel[1]. Those who consider Canada's policy unbalanced pay careful attention to the nuances and shadings of terminology and actively urge a reorientation of Canadian policy in the region.

A third approach looks not to ethnic lobbies at home but rather to Canada's perennial preoccupation with the behemoth to the South. Seeking to distinguish itself from its powerful neighbour, to establish its own identity, this smaller member of the North-Atlantic alliance looks to Western Europe for company and, indeed, at times for shelter. Some who have looked closely at Canadian policy towards the Middle East, especially as it is enunciated at the United Nations, suggest that Canada actively seeks the company of Europeans in determining its policy positions[2]. To understand the nuances of Canadian policy towards the Middle East, we must first look at policy in Europe.

A fourth approach, the one that animates this paper, challenges the heavy emphasis on mediation, peacekeeping, partisan politics, or bloc voting as the core of Canadian policy in the Middle East. It points rather to the enlarged network of bilateral relationships, the new institutional arrangements put in place to accommodate commercial transactions, the expansion of trade with the Middle East in the last several years, and most important, the emergence of powerful financial and industrial interests with a stake in these new economic transactions and interactions[3]. Policy no longer responds principally to the needs of the international community but largely to the dictates of national interest defined in economic terms. It is the political economy of foreign policy which is now critical to an understanding of the main-springs of Canadian policy in the Middle East. Canada may have been a «helpful fixer» 25 years ago, but now it seeks to be an efficient entrepreneur.

These approaches are not mutually exclusive, of course, at every point in the argument. In part, the differences are time-bound: Canadian policy may have been firmly anchored in the international community in the postwar years but in the harsh-er, more competitive environment of the 1980s, a policy that promotes peacekeeping and peacemaking may be a luxury that Canadian leaders feel they can no longer afford. The approaches do differ, however, in the weight they attach to the interna-tional and domestic determinants of Canadian policy. Insofar as these differences in time, context and dynamics are important, Canadian policy in the Middle East reflects in microcosm more general changes in the thrust of Canadian foreign policy as a whole. A look at Canadian policy in the region in the last 30 years should capture these changes and allow some evaluation of these different analytical perspectives.

1947-1967: CANADA AS «HELPFUL FIXER»

The early years

Canada first became directly involved with the Middle East when Britain renounced its responsibilities as a mandatory power in Palestine in 1947 and turned to the United Nations. In the immediate postwar period, the United Nations was a central building block of Canadian policy. It was not surprising, therefore, that in April 1947, Lester B. Pearson, then Under Secretary of State for External Affairs, headed the Canadian delegation to a special session of the General Assembly and was elected chairman of the Assembly's committee to study the Palestine question. One month later, the committee was replaced by the United Nations Special Committee on Palestine (UNSCOP) with Canada as one of its eleven members. The Canadian representative on the Committee, Justice Ivan C. Rand, drafted the majority report recommending partition of Palestine into Arab and Jewish states and an internationalized Jerusalem. Ottawa considered partition to be the best among four difficult and unattractive alternatives; it was the logical and fair solution given mutually irreconcilable claims[4]. It also promised to prevent division between the United States and the United Kingdom, Canada's two most important allies, at a time when Cold War in Europe loomed on the horizon. Canada's first involvement in the Middle East emphasized conflict resolution between the parties, the consistent theme of policy in the next decade.

Canada also suggested that the Security Council implement partition under the provisions of the United Nations Charter which deal with international peace and security[5]. Again, this recommendation was consistent with the broad parameters of Canadian foreign policy: in a regional dispute which threatened great power relationships and international peace, the United Nations must provide an alternative to confrontation and war. Canada had long urged the formation of an international peacekeeping force under the auspices of the United Nations which could guarantee international security under the Charter.

By the spring of 1948, it was apparent that the compromise embodied in the partition resolution would fail. Although division of Palestine was unacceptable to the Arab states, Britain nevertheless withdrew its forces unexpectedly early. On May 14, 1948, Israel declared its independence and the following day, the armies of five neighbouring Arab states invaded the newly-established State. The United Nations – and Canada – confronted a major threat to international peace.

In the autumn of 1948, a new government took office in Ottawa with Louis St. Laurent as Prime Minister and Lester B. Pearson as the new Secretary of State for External Affairs. During the summer, Canada had voted for the resolution of July15, designating the situation as an immediate threat to world peace and actively urged a cease-fire and a truce between the warring parties[6]. Pearson insisted, however, that a cease-fire in the absence of an effort to resolve the issues underlying the conflict was insufficient. At the meeting of the General Assembly that autumn, Canada cosponsored a resolution calling for a negotiated armistice and the nomination of a mediator, as well as the creation of a commission to facilitate the resolution of the conflict[7]. That same November, Israel's application for admission to the United Nations confronted Canada with a dilemma: although the United States and the Soviet Union supported the application, Britain opposed membership. In a precursor to many such votes three decades later, caught between its allies, Canada abstained and did not grant Israel *de facto* recognition until December 24, 1949[8]. Ottawa concentrated its efforts on reducing both conflicts: the military struggle between Israel and its Arab neighbours and the diplomatic dispute between Britain and the United States. In Europe, the Cold War had heated up and Atlantic solidarity was the overwhelming imperative.

The escalating tension between East and West dominated the agenda of Canada's policy-makers who devoted correspondingly less attention to the ongoing conflict in the Middle East in the next few years. After the armistice negotiations of 1949, Canada did initiate and participate in several attempts to set in motion a process of conflict resolution. In 1950, Pearson was one of the sponsors of an eight-member United Nations resolution calling for direct negotiations between Israel and the Arab states and again, in 1952, in the *Ad Hoc* Political Committee, Canada supported a resolution proposing direct negotiations[9]. Although both resolutions failed to win the necessary two-thirds majority, Canada was successful in modifying the resolution which enabled the Conciliation Commission to continue its mandate.

During the same period, Canada initiated its first bilateral relationships within the Middle East. In a balanced expansion of diplomatic representation, Canada opened embassies in Cairo and Tel Aviv in 1954 and in Beirut in 1955. However, the ambassador to Israel was also accredited to Greece and, indeed, was resident in Athens, while the ambassador to Lebanon was based in Cairo with the legation in Beirut under the supervision of a chargé d'affaires. A commercial Secretary, attached to the embassy in Cairo, acted as trade commission for Egypt, the Sudan, Cyprus, Aden, Ethiopia, Saudi Arabia and Yemen. His counterpart in Athens was responsible for Greece, Turkey and Israel, while a third Secretary in Beirut looked after commercial interests in Lebanon, Syria, Iraq, Jordan, and the Gulf states. The scope of Canada's bilateral relationships within the Middle East was marginal within the broader context of Canada's foreign policy; in 1955, Canadian diplomats were accredited to 47 different capitals in every major region of the world.

Canada's military involvement in the Middle East was also extremely limited. Ottawa did receive requests for military equipment from two of the major participants in the conflict, but Pearson made it clear that Canada would sell only «defensive» equipment to the confrontation states. Israel had received $1 332 110 worth of defensive hardware, principally anti-aircraft guns and munitions, while Egypt obtained 15 Harvard training planes and spare parts valued at $770 825[10]. In early 1956, however, Israel attempted to arrange the purchase of 24-36 F-86 Sabre jet fighters from Ottawa. Under the Tripartite Agreement of 1950, Britain, France and the United States had embargoed military equipment to the major parties to the conflict, but the embargo was emasculated by the Czech, really Soviet, arms agreement with Egypt and Syria in September 1955. Replying to the request, Prime Minister St. Laurent explained that Canada was not prepared to restore the military balance without joint action by the other Western powers; this was especially so since Canadian interests were so much more limited than the other allies[11]. At American urging, an export permit was eventually approved in September 1956 but revoked one month later at the beginning of the Suez crisis. Canada would not reconsider its policy on arms exports for two decades.

At the United Nations, on the contrary, the Canadian profile on Middle Eastern issues remained high. A Canadian, General Kennedy, was appointed Director of the United Nations Relief and Works Agency (UNRWA) in 1950 and in 1954, General Burns, a colleague, became Head of the United Nations Truce Supervision Organization (UNTSO) which monitored the armistice lines. Pearson continued to urge mutual concessions by both parties: while he recognized that some readjustment of boundaries between Israel and neighbouring Arab states was necessary, he believed that each Arab state must recognize the legitimacy of Israel within the Middle East and that Israel must compensate the Palestinians for their loss of land and home[12].

An examination of Canadian policy in these early years illustrates the basic characteristics of Ottawa's policy in the region. First and foremost, multilateral activity dwarfed bilateral relationships. Indeed, in the postwar period, Canadian policy in the Middle East can almost be explained as a function of Ottawa's policy at the United Nations. Canada emphasized the imperative of international involvement in regional conflict deescalation and the urgency of negotiation between the parties if further hostilities were to be avoided. These two focal points were the basis of Canadian policy at the United Nations for the next two decades.

Second, necessary and complementary to Canada's policy in the United Nations was a policy of «even-handedness» in the Middle East. A partisan position on the issues of the Arab-Israel conflict was neither consistent with Canada's support for mediation and conciliation on the international level nor required by the scope of Canadian interests within the region. Canada approached the Middle East almost exclusively as a conciliator: the Arab-Israel conflict was the most salient issue, an issue which demanded a capacity to promote constructive solutions. A one-sided commitment would impair Canada's future usefulness as a problem-solver at the United Nations.

Finally, Canada's support of the United Nations complemented a second major policy objective, that of containing conflict between the Western allies. Both Britain and the United States were vitally important to Canada's economic growth and security. Before World War II, Britain was still the most important reference point of Canadian policy, but after the war, increasingly the United States occupied the attention of Canadian policy-makers and, indeed, became the preeminent object of concern. Disagreement between these two major allies created uncomfortable choices for Canadian leaders. When Britain and the United States differed, for example, on appropriate solutions for the Middle East from 1947 to 1949, Canada attempted not only to mediate the conflict between the disputants in the Middle East but, equally important, to resolve the difference between its allies.

In these early years, the evidence overwhelmingly supports the first interpretation of Canadian policy in the Middle East as a «helpful fixer» and problem solver. The commitment to conciliation, the reiteration of the determinants of a fair and equitable solution, preclude much of the charges of partisanship. This is not to suggest that domestic groups did not lobby actively to influence the direction of Canadian policy; they most certainly did. When recognition of Israel was under consideration in 1948, for example, the United Zionist Council of Canada struggled vigorously to promote early recognition. It did not succeed, however, and the competing effort by the Canadian Arab Friendship League was poorly organized and inconsequential. Activity did not translate into influence and Canadian policy responded to international rather than domestic imperatives[13]. Finally, the bilateral dimension of Canadian policy was conspicuous by its absence. Trade with the Middle East amounted to no more than 0,5 % of Canada's total trade, military sales were inconsequential, and diplomatic representation was marginal. Canada saw the Middle East through the prism of the world community, and the crisis diplomacy of the coming decade would reinforce these parameters of policy.

Crisis diplomacy: 1956-1967

The Middle East once again captured the attention of the world when, after long and fruitless negotiations, President Nasser nationalized the Suez Canal on July 26, 1956. Although Canada had no share in the ownership of the Canal, it was threatened by the possibility of a rift between Britain, a principal shareholder, and the United States, a strong opponent of the use of force to reclaim the international waterway. A complicating factor, moreover, was the Soviet penetration of the Middle East through its supply of arms to Egypt and Syria. In the context of the Cold War, the consequences of a split among the Western allies were even more serious and the Canadian policy concentrated on mediating the dispute between the allies. In a letter written to the Canadian High Commissioner in London during the long summer before the crisis exploded, Pearson, then Secretary of State for External Affairs, explained the premises of the Canadian policy:

> It is clear that every possible effort must be made to prevent a chain of developments which would result in an Anglo-French military force being exerted against Egypt in a way which would split the Commonwealth, weaken the Anglo-American alliance, and have general consequences which would benefit nobody but Moscow[14].

Policy-makers in Ottawa were well aware of the increasing gap between their **two** closest allies as negotiations to settle the dispute with Egypt stalemated throughout the summer and early autumn. Canada supported the convocation of a conference of those states whose interests were directly affected by the nationalization of the Canal. Although Canada was not a participant, on August 30, Pearson added Ottawa's weight to the majority report of the conference: as a trading nation, Canada was firmly committed to the principle of the free and unrestricted use of the waterway[15]. At the same time, through private diplomacy, Canada informed Britain that the use of force would be unacceptable to members of the Commonwealth and to the international community[16]. The basic principles of Canadian policy were already clear in this early phase of the crisis: rejection of a use of force as inconsistent with the obligations of members of the United Nations; freedom of passage through international waterways; the importance of a negotiated settlement on terms acceptable to all the major parties; and the avoidance of a disruptive and harmful split within the Western community.

Canada did not receive advance warning of Israel's attack across the armistice lines and the British and French ultimatum to the belligerents, an ultimatum which was to serve as the pretext for invasion. Immediately, however, the Government expressed its regrets at the use of force and began to consider appropriate measures of deescalation[17]. At the first Cabinet meeting in Ottawa after the invasion, the prospect of an international peacekeeping force was raised. After the meeting, Pearson flew directly to New York to participate in the debate at the United Nations and, in the vote on the American-sponsored resolution for an immediate cease-fire, abstained[18] Pearson's policy position was consistent: he opposed a cease-fire resolution which made no provision for enforcement and settlement procedures, arguing that such a resolution would at best be meaningless and at worst expose the inability of the United Nations to contribute constructively towards the resolution of the dispute. He similarly opposed resolutions which branded one or another participant as aggressors; such resolutions, he insisted, would contribute nothing to the process of settlement and could, on the contrary, impede progress[19].

The abstention by the Canadian delegation recorded Ottawa's position of balance not only between the great powers but also between the regional belligerents. While Pearson unequivocally condemned Israel's resort to force, he acknowledged that the *feda'yeen* raids and border incidents, compounded by the escalating arms race between Egypt and Israel, had fatally undermined the fragile armistice that had existed within the region. A return to the *status quo ante*, Pearson argued, would not contribute to the maintenance of international peace and security[20].

While negotiations were ongoing at the United Nations in New York, Ottawa initiated consultations with London and Washington to ensure that the proposed peacekeeping force would be acceptable. Without great power consent, the project-ed force would be stillborn as it had been since Pearson first made the proposal in 1948. That same day, Pearson consulted with the Secretary-General, who remained skeptical about the possibility of an international force and then flew to Ottawa to brief his colleagues[21]. The following day, assured of Cabinet support, Pearson retur-ned to the United Nations to mobilize support from other delegations. In order to ensure passage of the Canadian resolution, he agreed to support a cease-fire reso-lution, sponsored by India and other members of the Third World, which exerted con-siderable pressure on Britain, France and Israel. In return, India agreed to vote for the Canadian resolution to create a United Nations force. Pearson had succeeded in averting a major split within the Commonwealth[22].

The Canadian resolution was adopted early on the morning of November 4, with Britain, France, Egypt and all members of the Soviet bloc abstaining. The reso-lution proposed that the General Assembly request the Secretary-General to submit a plan within 48 hours for the establishment, with the consent of the parties concern-ed, of a United Nations Emergency Force[23]. An informal planning group of Canada, India, Colombia and Norway, meeting on the same day, decided to recommend the establishment of a United Nations command under General Burns, the chief of UNTSO. Once the General Assembly approved the report, the commitments of contributing countries could be increased.

The Secretary-General, by now convinced of the merits of Pearson's propo-sal, presented his first report twelve hours later. The report was approved by the Assembly but, ominously, Egypt abstained. Its acquiescence was critical to the success of UNEF, for the resolution explicitly established the necessity of the con-sent of the parties concerned. The newly-appointed ambassador to Cairo, the only Canadian envoy then resident in the Middle East, arranged an extraordinary meeting with Nasser to urge Egyptian acceptance of UNEF troops. On November 5, Egypt cabled the Secretary-General announcing acceptance of the force; the terms «con-sent» and «acceptance» were subsequently to become objects of great controversy.

The following day, Prime Minister St. Laurent announced that Canada would contribute a self-contained battalion to the fledging force[24]. President Nasser, however, objected to the participation of Canadian ground forces in UNEF, arguing that Canadians in uniform might be mistaken for British troops. In reply, Pearson rejected the principle that any government, even the host country, could determine the composition of UNEF. He argued that Egypt's consent to the stationing of UNEF was necessary, but, once established, the composition of the force was to be deter-mined by the appropriate United Nations authority. Pearson was also explicit on the mandate of UNEF: «If their [the Government of Egypt] position is that they at any time could decide that the United Nations force had finished its work and should leave, that, I think would be quite intolerable[25]. » Pearson expected that UNEF would remain in the area until its task was complete, a determination that only the United Nations could make.

In an effort to break the impasse over the composition of the force, the Secretary-General met with Egypt's Foreign Minister in Cairo. In a joint statement they agreed that «at the present time» Canada could usefully contribute air support in transport of troops from Italy and, at the same time, General Burns, the commander of the new force, advised the Secretary-General and the Government of Canada that a contribution of air transport and administrative personnel would be more immediately useful than the infantry which other countries were providing. On this basis, Canada agreed to changes in the forces it would commit to UNEF. Despite the controversy by the end of 1956, Canada had made a significant contribution to the international force: of some 5 000 men, 1 100 were Canadians.

Once UNEF was in place, Canada continued to try to find an acceptable basis for disengagement between Israel and Egypt. Although British and French forces were withdrawing, thereby reducing the possibility of a divisive split within the Western alliance, Israel's forces were still in the Gaza Strip and at Sharm el-Sheikh, awaiting international guarantees of security from guerilla incursions and naval blockade of the southern port of Eilat. At the United Nations, non-aligned states were pressing for sanctions to compel Israel's withdrawal. Tension ran high.

Pearson opposed any resolution calling for sanctions as impractical and ineffective and urged that detailed arrangements to follow the withdrawal be made explicit in advance. Arguing that the conditions which initially provoked military action should not be recreated, he recommended that UN forces be used to provide security within the region to reduce the possibility of military clashes and a cycle of violence. Pearson proposed that Israel and Egypt pledge to observe scrupulously the provisions of the 1949 armistice agreement that UNEF be deployed along the armistice line; that the Assembly affirm the right of free passage through the Straits of Tiran; that UNEF follow Israel's withdrawal from Sharm el-Sheikh and station forces at the tip of the Sinai peninsula; and that UNEF administer the Gaza Strip. He refrained from formally introducing this last point only when he realized that it stood no chance of obtaining the required two-thirds majority in the Assembly[26]. The adoption of the Canadian resolution was an eloquent testimony to Pearson's creativity in conflict management. The arrangements put in place in March of 1957 made a significant contribution to the stabilization of the Arab-Israel conflict: the eleven years that followed were the longest period of freedom from war in contemporary Arab-Israel relations.

Canada's extraordinary diplomacy built heavily on past policy. During the Suez crisis, Ottawa did have a very limited number of personnel in the field, but the major focus of policy continued to be the United Nations; the preferred channel of action remained multilateral. The deployment of UNEF, consisting exclusively of «middle» powers, introduced local stability by separating the belligerents. At least in part it met Canada's objective of conflict deescalation.

Canada also continued to pursue an even-handed policy within the region as a necessary complement to its role at the United Nations. It is true that Canada became more explicit than in the past on the minimum security arrangements prerequisite to a process of negotiation and settlement. This insistence on appropriate security along the borders would certainly displease Arab governments unwilling to recognize the existence of Israel within the Middle East. It is also true that the Suez crisis provoked a flurry of activity and interest by a wide variety of domestic groups. The Public Relations Committee, the lobbying arm of the Canadian Zionists, and the Canadian-Arab Friendship League had been active throughout 1956 in the debate on the proposed arms sales to Israel and Egypt. When the Suez crisis exploded, however, pro-British and anti-American opinion, a strong component of Canadian political culture, deluged ministers, members of Parliament, and newspapers with critical comment[27]. But the substance of Canada's position was little affected by the heightened passions within the country. Canada's support of international law on navigation rights, opposition to the use of force, and emphasis on the urgency of negotiation were long-standing policy commitments. There is little support for charges of partisanship.

Finally, Canada was again uniquely successful in containing conflict among the Western allies. The probability of Anglo-American division was even higher in 1956 than in 1947-1949 and the consequences of such a split, should it occur, were even more serious: not only would Canada face unpleasant choices, but Commonwealth and Western unity would be fractured. Canada did attach overriding importance to Anglo-American friendship.

Partly because of a unique interplay of international factors and partly because of the stewardship of an unusually talented Secretary of State for External Affairs, Canada was able to make an extraordinary contribution to the management of an acute conflict within a region of endemic violence. The Western alliance was badly divided; the Soviet Union was preoccupied with a revolution in Hungary; and Canada seized the opportunity to work with the «great» and the «middle» powers at the United Nations. 1956 was the highwater mark of Canada's exercise of the art of the possible. Policy was quintessentially internationalist.

Lester B. Pearson was Prime Minister of Canada when a new crisis erupted in the Middle East in the spring of 1967. After a series of guerilla raids from Syria into Israel and threats by Israel to retaliate President Nasser, responding to Syrian and Soviet pressure, demanded the withdrawal of UNEF forces from the Israel-Egypt border so that Egyptian troops could come to the assistance of Syria. In New York, the Secretary-General, after informal consultation with the American and Canadian ambassadors to the United Nations, acceded to the Egyptian request and ordered the withdrawal of the force. Within 48 hours, the intricate and laboriously-elaborated security arrangements of 1956 were disrupted.

The Canadian Government was dismayed. Pearson had contended ten years earlier that Egypt, once having agreed to the presence of United Nations forces, could determine neither their composition nor their date of termination[28]. Paul Martin, the Minister for External affairs, flew to New York even before the Secretary-General agreed to the Egyptian request to urge that no precipitous action be taken and that he could consult the Advisory Committee of UNEF. After U Thant agreed to remove the peacekeeping force, Canada joined the United States and Britain in requesting a meeting and then asked that the General Assembly convene to override the Secretary-General's assent to withdrawal. These intense efforts to preserve a United Nations presence as a buffer to hostilities met with no success.

On May 23, President Nasser announced the closure of the Straits of Tiran to Israel's shipping. Since Israel had repeatedly declared the closure of the Straits to be a *casus belli*, the likelihood of hostilities loomed large. Canada, with Denmark, insisted on a meeting of the Security Council to discuss the grave deterioration of security arrangements in the Middle East. The Council met twice on May 24, but adjourned with no action.

The focus of those attempting to deescalate the conflict shifted from a restoration of a United Nations presence to the lifting of the blockade. On May 25, President Johnson visited Ottawa and the Prime Minister agreed to participate, if necessary, in an international maritime effort to reopen the Straits. Canada would not, however, assume the leadership of such an effort. Pearson, reporting to the House of Commons on his meeting with the President, explained that the two leaders were «in complete agreement on the importance of maintaining the right of access of innocent passage through the Gulf of Aqaba and everything possible should be done through the United Nations to remove the danger»[29]. The Security Council, however, seemed incapable of action: Canada supported Egypt's demand for a continuous weekend meeting but the other delegates were opposed and the Council adjourned again until May 29.

In the ensuing days, Canadian support for an international maritime action to lift the blockade began to erode. In a television appearance on May 30, the Prime Minister proposed the emplacement of United Nations' troops on both sides of the border and suggested that Israel make some compromise concerning its right of passage through the Straits[30]. Ominously, however, Egyptian troops had begun to move into the Sinai in significant numbers. While Israel's attention shifted from the withdrawal of UNEF to a projected international maritime force and then to the presence of 100 000 Egyptian troops on the frontier, the maritime nations retreated from the prospect of an international naval force and began to discuss a common declaration. On June 1, Prime Minister Wilson, still a proponent of the naval task force, urged Ottawa to contribute two destroyers; this, he insisted, was the only alternative to unilateral military action by Israel to break the blockade. Pearson would not make such a commitment and insisted that the United Nations would first have to consider the proposal[31]. Israel's ambassador in Ottawa requested clarification of the Government's position and was told that Canada was not prepared to join an international naval task force[32]. On June 5, Israel's air and ground forces attacked across the armistice lines.

As soon as the fighting began, domestic lobbies and pressure groups sprang into action. The Canada-Israel Committee, now the official representative of the Jewish community in Canada on matters relating to Israel, organized demonstrations of support which cut across religious, ethnic and linguistic communities. The Canadian-Arab Friendship League, although active in support of Arab governments, had neither the public nor the private resources to compete with those in support of Israel. The task was made even more difficult by the public sympathy with Israel's predicament in the three weeks before the outbreak of war. The mail to the Prime Minister was overwhelmingly supportive of Israel's position as was almost all the daily press across the country in its editorial comment[33]. The opposition that did exist tended to concentrate among senior officials of the Department of External Affairs who anticipated a strong and negative Egyptian reaction to Canadian policy, a reaction which could jeopardize Canada's peacekeeping mission[34]. Generally, however, Canadian policy did not excite much domestic controversy: there was a fit between public attitudes and official policy.

In the long debate that ensued at the United Nations after the fighting stopped, Canada reiterated its traditional insistence that censure of the parties to the dispute made long-term solutions more difficult. At the emergency meeting of the General Assembly, Canada's ambassador again argued that a long-term solution must address all aspects of the conflict: the territorial integrity of all states; the right of innocent passage; a solution to the problem of the Palestinian refugees; and the preservation of the rights of religious interests in Jerusalem. And, as in 1956, a withdrawal of Israel's forces could not precede but must be related to the other basic issues in dispute[35]. For precisely these reasons, Canada strongly opposed Israel's unilateral annexation of East Jerusalem immediately after the war, a measure which precluded the open-ended bargaining essential to an equitable settlement. In November, members of the Security Council finally agreed on Resolution 242, which incorporated this multifaceted and interlinked strategy: withdrawal from territories captured during the war, respect for the territorial integrity and political independence of all states within the region, the right of innocent passage and freedom of navigation, and a solution to the problem of the refugees. Resolution 242 would serve as the benchmark of Canadian policy during the coming decade.

While the substance of Canadian policy differed little in 1967 from that of a decade earlier, the effectiveness of that policy was markedly different. This difference in impact cannot be attributed to any change in Canada's position on the issues that animated the Arab-Israel conflict. Canada's refusal to identify and label an aggressor, its support of the United Nations as the appropriate forum of debate and mediation, its rejection of a use of force, its prescription for effective peacekeeping and peacemaking, all date from 1948. Indeed, these policies had by now become quintessentially «Canadian» in the public mind.

International conditions, however, were markedly different. Most important, the role of intermediary between a fractious Britain and the United States had rapidly become superfluous. The British had cultivated their own «special relationship» with the United States and needed no intermediary; the positions of the two powers were closely coordinated in the crisis of May-June 1967 and in the ensuing months of debate. Second, acute conflict between the two superpowers, both heavily engaged in the Middle East, paralyzed the United Nations, Canada's traditional focus of attention and forum of action. Conditions in the international system were no longer conducive to creative «middle powersmanship».

Even if Canadian policy was marginal in its impact, it was nevertheless very much within the tradition of the helpful mediator. The allegation that Canada abandoned its traditional even-handedness in its opposition to the withdrawal of UNEF simply does not stand up to the evidence. Opposition to the Egyptian demand stemmed not from domestic lobbying – the time between Egypt's request and the Secretary-General's acquiescence was far too short to permit any lobbying – but rather from an almost reflexive support of the United Nations. There was a convergence of interest between those lobbying actively on behalf of Israel and Canadian opposition to the emasculation of the United Nations as a peacekeeper. This was the last time, however, that Canadian policy-makers would respond almost exclusively to the needs of the international community. A new order was on the horizon.

1968-1973: THE TRUDEAU YEARS AND THE OCTOBER WAR

The disappointing experience with UNEF was only one element in the decision by the new Government of Pierre E. Trudeau to undertake a far-reaching review of Canadian foreign policy in 1968. The Prime Minister wanted a reexamination of Canadian policy towards its powerful neighbour and an analysis of the relationship between military and foreign policy. He also expressed grave reservations about Canada's traditional role as an «honest broker» and peacekeeper. Trudeau argued that Canadians had overestimated their importance in the international community and, in so doing, they had dissipated their energy and diminished their usable influence. The Prime Minister wanted tighter linkage between domestic and foreign policy.

The completion of the review signaled a major change in the tone, if not in the substance, of Canadian foreign policy: the good samaritan was to be replaced by the maximization of national interest. The new emphasis on interests, economic growth, and the creation of alternatives to dependence on the American economy and policy left little scope for international activism in regions of limited concern like the Middle East. Indeed, the review contained no paper on Canadian policy towards the Middle East. Only in North Africa, where the new leaders in Ottawa saw a direct link to a growing Francophone presence in foreign policy did Canada move to strengthen its economic and political relationships. Generally, however, as the Minister for External Affairs acknowledged, Canada did not single out the Middle East in any way for special treatment[36]. The reduced emphasis on the United Nations further margin-alized the Middle East as an appropriate arena of foreign policy action. Canada adhered to the basics of Resolution 242 and willingly ceded to the four major powers – the United States, the Soviet Union, Britain and France – the formidable task of mediating the Arab-Israel conflict. This policy of low profile was a luxury that Canada could no longer afford, however, when the October War erupted in 1973 and forced the Arab-Israel conflict back to the top of the international agenda.

Multiple Canadian interests were directly engaged within three weeks of the outbreak of war. Canada's allies – the United States and Europe – were once again in disarray in the face of an urgent and continuing threat to international peace and security. And despite Canada's special relationship with the United States, Washington did not consult with Ottawa before instituting a global military alert which could affect Canada directly. To ameliorate the serious threat to international security, Canada was once again invited to participate in a United Nations peacekeeping force between Egypt and Israel. At home, Canadian objectives of growth and development were jeopardized by the possible curtailment of assured supplies of oil. In 1973, conditions in the international system were not dissimilar from those in 1956 but this time, domestic interests were closely related to the source of international tension.

In the first official statement of policy after the outbreak of war, the Secretary of State for External Affairs, Mitchell Sharp, reaffirmed Canada's support of Resolution 242 and condemned the use of force and the violation of the cease-fire:

> Canada has supported Resolution 242 since its adoption in 1967. Our adherence has been total but strictly limited to the terms of the resolution itself and we have always refused to add anything to it or subtract anything from it or draw implications from it that were not immediately apparent from the wording[37].

In urging support of United Nations, resolutions and the necessity of negotiation between the parties, this first statement reflected traditional Canadian even-handedness. This position was to undergo considerable change during the next several years, change which was not simply incremental adjustment to an evolving international environment but rather a substantial reorientation of Canadian policy which reflected new priorities and new perspectives.

THE TRUDEAU YEARS AND THE CLARK INTERLUDE: THE DOMESTICATION OF FOREIGN POLICY

The years following the October War witnessed the culmination of basic changes in Canada's approach to the management of the Arab-Israel conflict. Policy no longer centered on the United Nations as the appropriate forum for conflict management, but looked rather to the great powers to mediate the explosive conflict. Second, Canada altered its views on the appropriate modalities of conflict management and on the relationship among the basic components of a settlement. Third, Canada changed its approach to and policy towards the Palestinians. And finally, and most important, Ottawa attempted to reduce the significance of the Arab-Israel conflict in its Middle Eastern policy and to expand its bilateral economic and trading relationships in the region. To avoid controversy at home and maximize its economic interests abroad, Canada attempted to bypass the conflict. In its foreign policy, Canada moved from «high» to «low» politics. These changes in Canadian policy towards the Middle East were of a piece and reflected fundamental forces at work in the formulation and implementation of Canadian foreign policy as a whole. We look first at the changes in policy and then at the constellation of factors which explain these shifts in Canadian policy towards the Middle East.

The marked lack of enthusiasm in Canada's response to the demand to participate in a second United Nations peacekeeping force in the Sinai reflected a change in the general direction of Canadian foreign policy. Canada's disappointment in UNEF I was not an isolated experience: in 1972, Ottawa reluctantly participated in the ICCS in Vietnam and quickly withdrew after six months. In 1973, the Government recognized that a clear threat to international peace and security did exist and, consequently, agreed to participate in UNEF II, but insisted on progress towards a political settlement, supervision by the United Nations, and the consent of all the parties, especially the host State, to the deployment of the force[38]. After the second disengagement agreement between Egypt and Israel in September 1975, Ottawa indicated its satisfaction with the rate of political progress towards a settlement and extended its participation in UNEF and UNDOF, the force stationed on the Golan Heights between Israel and Syria. Even then, however, there was substantial opposition from the Department of Defence and when the United Nations decided to commit a peacekeeping force to Lebanon in 1978, Defence officials strongly opposed an open-ended commitment to UNIFIL. They were unhappy about the force's terms of reference, its command structure and logistics, the difficulties of interposition between irregular and conventional forces, and the demands on Canada's limited military resources[39]. After considerable discussion among the Prime Minister, the Secretary of State for External Affairs and the Minister of Defence, Ottawa agreed to participate for only six months. This was the first United Nations force in the Middle East which did not include a significant Canadian contingent. Four years later, when an international force was required in conformity with the Egypt-Israel peace treaty, Canada again hesitated. To avoid an anticipated Soviet veto, a veto expected because of Soviet opposition to the Camp David accords, the United States undertook to organize an international force outside the framework of the United Nations. Although almost all of the principal powers in Western Europe agreed to participate, Ottawa did not. Foreign policy in the 1980s differed substantially from policy under Lester B. Pearson.

In this last decade, the reluctance to commit forces to international peace-keeping grew out of several factors. Canadian leaders were increasingly skeptical of the contribution peacekeeping made to the resolution of conflict. When he was Secretary of State for External Affairs, MacEachen speculated that peacekeeping tended to perpetuate rather than ameliorate acute international conflict, by permitting the parties to avoid indefinitely the critical issues in dispute[40]. More to the point, Canada's military manpower was overextended. Consistent with Trudeau's focus on national priorities rather than international concerns, by the mid-1970s, defence planners began to pay more attention to the protection of Canadian sovereignty in the North and the patrol of Canada's coastline. In a period of relative decline in defence spending, the commitment of specialized personnel abroad seriously depleted the manpower available for these new tasks. Finally, the new Canadian leadership saw little benefit from continuing participation in peacekeeping forces. Canada received no credit from its NATO allies for its troop contributions nor was it privy to extraordinary intelligence information from the United States. At times, moreover, Canadian forces might well be exposed to danger in the theatre of conflict[41]. By the 1980s, Canadian political and military leaders were no longer enamored of peacekeeping in the international community. Their objectives were less ambitious – and their perspectives narrower.

The change in Canadian attitudes towards peacekeeping was not the only difference in Canadian policy towards the United Nations. For almost three decades the United Nations had been the cornerstone of Canadian foreign policy, but this too began to change. After the October War and the accompanying oil embargo, the international redistribution of wealth and political power which followed affected the functioning of the General Assembly and many of the specialized agencies. Many resolutions put before the Assembly were controversial, polemical in tone and unbalanced in substance. Much of the time of the Assembly in the years immediately following the October War was spent in debate on the Middle East and Canada frequently found the debate to be one-sided and injurious to processes of conflict resolution[42]. A well-known case in point was approval by the Assembly at its meeting in 1974 of a resolution which, inter alia, equated Zionism with racism[43]. These kinds of actions provoked controversy within Canada and reduced support both among the public and the policy-making community for the United Nations and its affiliated agencies. For the rest of the decade, Ottawa discussed the Middle East and many other urgent issues on the international agenda outside the auspices of the United Nations. This retreat from almost reflexive support of the United Nations, the premier international organization, demarcated a fundamental reorientation of Canadian policy, a turn from internationalism to nationalism in foreign policy.

This change in Canadian policy towards the United Nations was related to a second component of Middle East policy, policy towards the Palestinians. In the years which followed the October War, Arab participants in the conflict expanded the arena and shifted the emphasis of the dispute. Although a solution to the Palestinian problem had always been important, it became the overwhelming focus of attention in international meetings. Particularly at the United Nations, Arab members insisted that the Palestinian question be treated as a national and political issue, not as a refugee question. Partly because Canada had to vote so frequently on resolutions put before the Assembly, it had little choice but to consider carefully its policy both on the status and on the representation of the Palestinian people in the wider context of the Arab-Israel dispute.

Within a month of the October War, the Minister of External Affairs first spoke explicitly of the need for some representation of the Palestinian people in the negotiations that were to begin[44]. A year later, when the Minister spoke to the General Assembly, he referred to the collective interests of the Palestinian people[45]. Although Canada no longer considered the Palestinian problem an exclusively humanitarian issue, support for the legitimate aspirations of the Palestinians was conditional on their recognition of the existence of Israel and its right to survive[46]. The emphasis was on the mutuality of obligations which would make political compromise possible between the two peoples. Addressing the same forum two years later, the Canadian representative took policy one step further when he spoke of the need for «an appropriate structure for their [Palestinian] political self-expression, within a suitable territorial framework[47]». Canadian leaders refused to specify appropriate or «suitable» territorial boundaries; indeed, they considered such specification an inappropriate interference in negotiations that must ensue directly between the parties to the conflict. In a display of linguistic acrobatics, however, Canada did argue in 1977 that the future of the Palestinian people was a central element in the Middle East conflict and that an enduring solution must provide « [...] a territorial foundation for political self-expression by the Palestinian people consistent with the principle of self-determination»[48]. This formulation would become the leitmotiv of Canadian policy. By the end of the decade, policy had evolved from sympathy with the humanitarian needs of the Palestinians as refugees to recognition of their collective interests and the imperative of a solution to the conflict. Ottawa insisted throughout, however, that a political solution must encompass the right of Israel to recognition and survival as well as the collective interests of the Palestinian people. It was precisely on this point that Canadian leaders expressed strong reservations about the intentions of the Palestine Liberation Organization, the premier representative of the Palestinians internationally.

Canadian leaders were skeptical of the willingness of the PLO, led by Yasser Arafat, to recognize the legitimacy of Israel within the Middle East. They could find little in his public or private statements which testified to movement from the pro fessed, maximalist objective of destruction of the Jewish state and its replacement by a secular, democratic Government. Ottawa was unwilling, consequently, to pronounce formally on the issue of the appropriate representation of the Palestinians in the negotiating process. It was unwilling to do so formally because it considered representation as a matter properly determined solely by the parties themselves. If Palestinian representation were to advance the prospects of a negotiated settlement moreover, the representatives must be acceptable to all the principal parties. In practice, Canada viewed the policies of it as unhelpful to the peace process and explained that unless it were prepared to accept Resolution 242 and the legitimacy of Israel, Canada could not envisage its participation in the negotiating process[49]. At most, a reevaluation of Canadian policy towards the conflict recommended a broadening of contacts with the PLO to encourage «moderation and realism and [...] open acceptance of the legitimacy of the State of Israel»[50]. In considering the representation of the Palestinian people, an issue quite distinct from their status, the criterion of Canadian policy was the encouragement of constructive participation in negotiation.

Canada's new policy towards the Palestinians, with its nuances, reservations and ambiguities, had its baptism of fire in the domestic arena even before it was fully formulated. This too was a harbinger of things to come. Canada had invited the Crimes Congress, a UN conference to meet in Toronto in 1975 and a second conference on human habitation to Vancouver in 1976. Ottawa issued both these invitations before the General Assembly accorded official observer status to the PLO and consequently extended to the PLO an invitation to participate in both meetings. This signaled the beginning of a major politicization of the foreign policy process as domestic groups organized to bar entry of the PLO into Canada. A broad coalition of political forces including opposition political parties, provincial Premiers and municipal leaders, government officials, civil libertarians, and, of course, the Canada-Israel Committee argued that Canadian law and traditional opposition to terrorism precluded admission of members of a terrorist organization. The influential *Globe and Mail* disagreed, as did the Canadian-Arab Federation, who favoured the admission of the PLO. The *Globe and Mail* argued that Canada's even-handed policy in the Middle East and support of the United Nations were at issue.

Caught in the cross-fire, the Government decided to «postpone» the Crimes Congress but to proceed with the meeting in Vancouver and to admit members of the PLO who were not known terrorists by special ministerial permit. Unfortunately, Government policy satisfied no one and clarified nothing; the logic of the compromise was difficult to understand. Although policy-makers had anticipated that the principal costs of the postponement would be international, paradoxically the major costs were domestic. The PLO had threatened reprisals, but Canadian policy towards the PLO proved to be no barrier to subsequent improvement of economic and commercial relationships with major Arab governments[51]. At home, however, the foreign policy professionals disapproved strongly of the penetration of their sphere of competence by domestic interest groups. Their protest was in vain. By the end of the decade, if not before, the politicization of Canadian policy towards the Middle Fast was the norm rather than the exception. The Arab-Israel conflict had become a domestic political issue which mobilized powerful groups who competed to modify the tone and substance of every dimension of Canadian foreign policy in the Middle East.

The third component of policy to undergo change was Canada's attitude towards strategies and procedures of conflict resolution. Long an advocate of direct negotiation and balanced compromise, Canada considered Resolution 242 a measured and carefully-negotiated package which, in all its parts, was the appropriate framework for resolution of the conflict. Within a few months of the October War, however, the new policy towards the Palestinians compromised Canadian support for the integrity of Resolution 242 as the basis of a comprehensive settlement. More to the point was the change in the American strategy of conflict management. Immediately after the war, Secretary of State Kissinger opted for a partial, incremental approach whose objective was a reduction in the probability of renewed warfare and its attendent dislocations and dilemmas. Very much preoccupied with the possible rather than the desirable, American diplomacy succeeded in disengaging the military forces of the combatants and engineered a series of agreements between Egypt and Israel, the two most forthcoming participants in the negotiating process. When President Carter assumed office he experimented briefly with a comprehensive settlement but the attempt so frustrated Egypt that Sadat launched his unilateral initiative which culminated in the Camp David accords and the peace treaty between Egypt and Israel in March of 1979. The agreements were comprehensive – all outstanding bilateral issues between the two signatories were resolved – and partial – in their creation of a loosely defined framework for further open-ended negotiation with the other participants who had not yet joined the process. It was a signal moment in the long and tortured history of the Arab-Israel conflict.

Canada was strongly supportive of Camp David and the ensuing treaty. Officials in Ottawa considered the treaty to be the most significant development in the 30-year history of the conflict[52]. Fully cognizant of strong Arab opposition to the treaty, especially that of the PLO who was given no formal role in the projected series of negotiations, Canada was careful to add that a comprehensive peace treaty between all Arab participants in the conflict and Israel was essential if peace were to be permanent and stable. Ottawa insisted nevertheless that the settlement between Egypt and Israel was a valuable first step and deserving of international support. Even after almost a year of frustrating deadlock in the negotiations on Palestinian autonomy, a special report prepared for the new Conservative Government reaffirmed the importance of ongoing negotiations between the parties: Arab opposition to Camp David, it concluded, must go beyond general statements to concrete alternatives[53].

To provide the best possible climate for negotiation, Canada opposed any unilateral change in the status of the territories while negotiations were pending. Prime Minister Trudeau repeatedly expressed his objection to Israel's establishment of settlements on the West Bank of the Jordan. On the other hand, Canada did not share the attitude of its European allies who, in a declaration issued in Venice in June 1980, recommended unconditionally that the PLO be «associated» with ongoing negotiations[54]. The declaration no longer made explicit reference to a mutuality of obligation which would require PLO recognition of Israel within the context of a broader settlement. In its analysis of the peacemaking process, Canada placed as much emphasis on reciprocal obligation and on the evolutionary component of the negotiating process as on the substantive content of the agreement.

The undertaking in 1979 by a new Conservative Government to move Canada's embassy from Tel Aviv to Jerusalem was especially surprising given the caution and precision of past policy. Although the initiative was aborted – Canada's embassy remains in Tel Aviv – it exemplifies both the manipulation by a hungry opposition of Middle East policy as an electoral issue and the unprecedented intervention by powerful interest groups in the foreign policy process. This single incident dramatizes the domestication of internationalism, a domestication which now shapes Canadian policy.

Following the visit of Israel's Prime Minister to Canada in the autumn of 1978, the Leader of the Opposition, anticipating a close contest and electoral gain in constituencies with substantial numbers of Jewish voters, promised in the heat of the election campaign in the spring of 1979 to move Canada's embassy. The pledge was given on the advice of non-Jewish Tory counsellors rather than at the behest of the organized Jewish lobby, but a surprised Jewish community was undoubtedly delighted[55]. As a recent investigation of the politics of the decision concluded, the Clark pledge «was less a case of an interest group exercising pressure on a political party than a political party using an interest group for electoral gain»[56]. Nevertheless, Canadian policy in the Middle East had openly become a partisan political issue in the domestic arena.

The Department of External Affairs was strongly opposed, of course, and in a paper authored jointly with the Privy Council, urged the Government not to proceed with their election commitment[57]. Prime Minister Clark was unmoved. Indeed, he insisted that the mandarinate in Ottawa, a group long subject to Liberal authority, would have to comply with the wishes of the Conservative Government. Opposition was not restricted only, however, to senior civil servants. Abroad, the Arab Monetary Fund threatened to withdraw its assets from Canadian banks and other financial institutions, but the Fund had less than a million dollars on deposit[58]. Iraq warned of an oil embargo, but only 0,005 % of Canadian oil came directly from Iraq. More relevant was the prospect of a loss of jobs by Canadians working directly or indirectly on contract in the Arab world. In particular, Bell Telephone of Canada had negotiated a contract of over $2 billion to provide communications technology and services to Saudi Arabia, but only 500-600 personnel were involved. Indeed, following Clark's announcement, only $4,5 millions in contracts were cancelled[59] and although External Affairs and Industry, Trade and Commerce acknowledged that these economic losses were inconsequential, they argued that the losses were harbingers of much more serious and damaging sanctions to come if Canada persisted in moving its embassy. Arab governments objected not only from abroad but urged their representatives in Ottawa to protest to the new government. Arab ambassadors met with a sympathetic Minister for External Affairs who promised serious consideration of their views. Finally, President Carter voiced his opposition to Prime Minister Clark when they met in Tokyo for the annual economic summit.

Even more important than pressure from abroad were the powerful domestic groups who moved forcefully into the political arena[60]. Three important sectors of the Canadian corporate community were especially active: oil importing companies with American multinational parents; Canadian banks and financial institutions, particularly the Royal Bank, the largest bank in Canada; and manufacturers with large export contracts pending or in force in the Middle East – Bell Canada, ATCO International, Canadair, de Havilland, Westinghouse – as well as large engineering firms with major projects in Arab countries, such as Lavalin of Montréal[61]. The principal business and trade association lobbies – the Canadian Manufacturers Association, the Canadian Federation of Independent Businesses, and especially the Canadian Export Association – were extraordinarily active as well and met with senior civil servants, members of the Cabinet, and with the Prime Minister[62]. Experienced in the representation of their interests to political and bureaucratic elites, these corporate and financial interests had easy access to senior civil servants and political leaders. The ethnic lobbies – the well-organized Canada-Israel Committee and the much less effective Canadian-Arab Federation – could not compete with the powerful array of domestic corporate actors who drew a direct linkage between Canadian policy in the Middle East and corporate profits.

Five months later, in October, the Prime Minister announced the postponement of any action pending a specially-commissioned investigatory report by Robert

Stanfield, the immediate past Leader of the Conservative Party. Not surprisingly, in February 1980, Stanfield recommended against movement of Canada's embassy[63]. Although the policy initiative was itself both ill-advised and unhelpful, the unprecedented activity by a powerful corporate lobby testified to the shifting basis of Canadian policy. Canada no longer responded to international dictates, irrespective of how these were interpreted, but rather to the demands of a financial and business lobby who viewed the Middle East principally as an arena of commercial opportunity and profit and treated the Government as their handmaiden.

The new premises of Canadian policy were evident long before the Jerusalem embroglio. As early as February 1976, when the Cabinet approved its first comprehensive policy towards the Middle East, it called for «close and mutually beneficial bilateral with all states of the area, outside the context of any regional disputes or problems, and with particular emphasis on trade and economic cooperation»[64]. Confronted with increasingly expensive oil imports and lured by the prospect of trade opportunities, Canada decided to try to encapsulate the Arab-Israel conflict and base its foreign policy not on multilateral institutions but on bilateral relations with the major governments of the Middle East. In the 1960s, in an effort both to preempt an independent Québec initiative and to strengthen the Francophone component of its foreign policy, Canada deepened its economic and cultural relationships with the French-speaking countries of the Maghreb. Ottawa established a Joint Economic Committee with Tunisia in 1968 and in 1973, Canada concluded a bilateral agreement with Algeria for a $100-million line of credit funded chiefly by the Export Development Corporation and by Canada's chartered banks[65].

Responding to quite different imperatives in the next decade, Canada drew on multiple resources to enlarge the scope of its bilateral economic and commercial relations in the core of the Middle East. Although such an expansion was under consideration for a long time, immediately after the October War in 1973 the Department of External Affairs announced the establishment of an embassy in Saudi Arabia. The following year, Canada established diplomatic relations with Bahrain, Qatar, Oman and the United Arab Emirates, and opened an embassy in Iraq. The commitment of scarce diplomatic personnel was visible testimony to the new importance of direct relationships between Canada and the governments of the Middle East.

In an effort to increase economic opportunity and commercial profits, Canada also moved to formalize and institutionalize bilateral economic activity. In addition to the Canada-Tunisia Mixed Committee in place, Ottawa established a Canada-Iran Joint Commission in 1975, a Canada-Saudi Arabia Joint Committee and a Canada-Israel Joint Committee, both in 1976, and a Canada-Algeria Joint Commission in 1978. In 1979, the Minister of Agriculture and his counterpart in Israel created a Canada-Israel Joint Agricultural Committee to exchange scientific and technical information and to develop joint agricultural research programs. The Government also adopted a less restrictive policy towards military exports and, in a procedural change with obvious implications, invited a representative of Industry, Trade and Commerce to participate in reviewing arms applications. And in 1982, in a major change of policy, Ottawa announced its intention to sell a CANDU nuclear reactor to Egypt.

The intensification of bilateral economic interaction between the governments of the Middle East and the Federal Government in Ottawa has been complemented by parallel activity at the provincial and transnational levels. The Québec

Government has been especially active in creating the Québec-Palestine Committee and in working through the international service arm of the Conseil de la coopération de Québec. Montréal-based labor movements also have established close contacts with Palestinian leaders. Illustrative also is the effort now under way in Ontario by a leading polytechnical institute, in collaboration with the Provincial Government, to develop a telecommunications institute in Jordan through a consortium of public and private firms. Member of the Ontario Government have also travelled in the Middle East to promote the purchase of Ontario goods and services. In the private sector, large engineering and industrial firms have signed export contracts with Middle Eastern governments through the assistance of Ottawa's Export Development Corporation.

This considerable expenditure of diplomatic and political resources has generated somewhat disappointing results. Trade between the Middle East and Canada has grown, but sharp asymmetries have developed. In 1970, Canada imported $1 043 350 while a decade later, it bought over $3 billion worth of products from the Middle East; of this total, crude petroleum accounted for 97 %[66]. Exports did not grow commensurately: in 1970, Canada sent products worth $124 million to the Middle East and a decade later exported goods and services just over a billion dollars[67]. At least two issues are relevant here. First, trade with the Middle East remains marginal as a proportion of Canadian trade generally. By 1980, the countries of the Middle East still accounted for only 4 % of Canada's global trade. Second, the expansion of trade that has occurred has been imbalanced and not in Canada's favour. Although Canada does have a favourable balance of trade with those Middle Eastern countries who are not oil exporters, the imbalance in Canada's economic interaction with OPEC exceeds any surplus that is generated in exchange with other members of the Middle East. Canada's trading relationship with Saudi Arabia dramatized these unfavourable terms. In 1980, Canada imported $2 450 789 000 worth of oil, but exported only $310 million worth of goods and services, ranging from prefabricated houses and automobiles to aircrafts[68]. Even though these figures are disappointing to a beleaguered Canadian economy, they are less resonant politically given Canada's favourable energy profile in comparison to those of other developed, industrialized economies. They need not constrain Canadian foreign policy.

If aggregate trade figures suggest that Canadian policy towards the Middle East should be less constrained than that of much of the energy-hungry industrialized world, powerful groups within Canada have specific interests which they seek to maximize through the foreign policy process. Some of the largest Canadian banks and industrial firms have important investments at stake in the oil economies and seek to safeguard and promote these interests with Ottawa's assistance. The economic groups which lobbied strenuously and openly against the projected move of Canada's embassy were not doing so for the first time. Increasingly over the last decade, engineering and manufacturing firms and banking interests have sought to tighten the link between private economic benefit and national policy abroad. In the mid-1970s, for example, when the Trudeau Government was considering the enactment of anti-boycott legislation, a broad coalition of political, ethnic, religious and educational interests opposed discrimination against Canadian citizens in the international market. The Canadian Association of Statutory Human Rights Agencies, the Canadian Labour Congress, the Ontario Federation of Labour, the Canada-Israel Committee, the Canadian Council of Churches, influential members of the Canadian academic and legal community, and much of the national press came out strongly in favour of federal legislation which would prohibit the issuance of certificates of religious affiliation to Canadian citizens seeking to work or trade with the Arab world. Arrayed in opposition to any federal initiative were most of Canada's large banks, the Canadian Manufacturer's Association, the Canadian Export Association, the Association of Construction Engineers of Canada, major corporations such as ATCO, Canadian Bechtel, Canadian Westinghouse, SMC Engineers, ethnic groups such as the Canadian-Arab Federation, the religious Council of Muslim Communities, and most of the senior officials in Industry, Trade and Commerce, and External Affairs. It is not surprising that an alliance of business, banking and bureaucrats won easily against religious and ethnic groups[69]. Even on a foreign policy issue directly affecting Canadian citizens, Middle Eastern policy has become increasingly privatized.

THE DOMESTICATION OF INTERNATIONALISM

The last decade has witnessed a fundamental shift in the tone, the substance, and the sources of Canadian foreign policy in the Middle East. In the early years, Canada demonstrated its extraordinary capacity as peacekeeper and conciliator, a capacity which sprang naturally from a commitment to peaceful resolution of international disputes and a deep aversion to the use of force. Canadian leaders believed profoundly in the importance of the United Nations as the alternative to international anarchy and struggled to stretch its capacity to mediate effectively. In the Middle East, Canada succeeded in designing innovative arrangements for international peacekeeping and a balanced policy which emphasized the urgency of an equitable solution to the bitter conflict between Isrealis and Arabs. Responding largely to the needs of the international community, an extraordinary group of statesmen almost inadvertently created a special role for Canada which was apparent in policy towards the Middle East. This period of creativity in the decade after the war was the highwater mark of Canadian internationalism.

Under the leadership of Pierre E. Trudeau, policy began almost imperceptibly to change. The new emphasis on maximization of national interest, at least in policy towards the Middle East, became the maximization of economic interest. Policy no longer focused on creative conflict management, on international peacekeeping, or even on the contribution Canada could make to a rapidly evolving Middle Fast. On the contrary, Canada's leaders acknowledged explicitly that they wished to bypass the Arab-Israel conflict and establish bilateral relationships with the governments of the Middle East; the emphasis was on economic and commercial exchanges. Although Canada could not ignore the conflict, by the 1980s, public policy had been privatized and internationalism domesticated. Why?

Several different hypotheses profess to explain this shift in Canadian foreign policy, a shift which may be general rather than particular to the Middle East. Perhaps this shift in policy was the logical corollary of the effort to distance Canada from the United States, a struggle by a «mouse» to escape the embrace of an «elephant». The foreign policy review of the Trudeau Government culminated in the identification of a third option in Canadian-American relations, the cultivation of Canada's economic, political and cultural relations with other Western allies to counterbalance the heavy American domination of Canada's economy and society. Can we explain the shift in Middle East policy as an attempt to distinguish Canadian from American policy and associate it more closely with that of Europe[70]? Although the evidence is somewhat inconsistent, generally it does not support this interpretation.

Some officials of the Department of External Affairs have suggested that they felt the need to distinguish Canadian policy from that of a superpower with major interests, responsibilities and commitments[71]. But while Allan MacEachen, Minister from July 1974 to September 1976, at times expressed interest in closer identification with the European community at the United Nations[72], his successor, Don Jamieson, disagreed, insisting that if Canada did find itself in agreement with the United States on an issue of Middle Eastern policy, Canada was not necessarily «in the wrong pew»[73]. Inspection of Canada's voting record at the United Nations from 1974 to 1979 shows that on the majority of the resolutions dealing with the Middle East, Canada voted along with most of the EEC and the United States. When the US and the EEC disagreed, Canada voted more frequently with the EEC in 1975 and 1976, but associated itself more frequently with the US in the last two years[74]. The explanation of the search for «good company» does not stand up to the evidence.

A second interpretation looks as well to the international community and posits that changes in the international environment diminished rivalry between the two superpowers, the emergence of new centers of power in the Third World, the decline of the United Nations – have limited the opportunities for an active Canadian diplomacy. The high profile Canada had in 1956 was an artifact of unique international conditions which no longer hold. It is, of course, undeniable that the international environment has changed profoundly in the last two decades, creating new constraints and new opportunities. But despite far-reaching change in the perspective and functioning of the United Nations, its forces are widely deployed as truce supervisory personnel and peacekeepers; the need has not diminished even if the execution has become more difficult. It seems somewhat premature as well to conclude that the two superpowers have transcended their rivalry, or even that they are better able to manage their conflict. On the contrary, analysts write of the «new Cold War» as the critical problem of the 1980s. Nor are friction and misunderstanding between the United States and the Western allies, on Middle Eastern as well as on other policy issues, unusual. Although much has changed, much remains to challenge a foreign policy that is internationalist in outlook.

If we cannot trace the reorientation in Canadian foreign policy to changes in the structure and functioning of the international community, we must look closer to home. At least two variants of a domestic explanation merit attention. The first suggests that Canadian policy in the Middle East is a function of partisan politics, of ethnic lobbies that shape, constrain, and indeed imbalance Canadian policy in that part of the world. Here, analysts look particularly to the Jewish lobby, well-organized and long-active in trying to influence policy towards the Middle East[75]. Precisely because the Jewish lobby has been so consistently active throughout the last three decades, however, the argument does not withstand the evidence. Since 1948, in one institutional form or another, the Jewish community has lobbied the Canadian Government on issues pertaining to the Arab-Israel conflict. It was not less active, less well-organized, or less adequately financed in the last several years than it was a decade ago. If anything, the record shows increasing professionalization and institutionalization. Yet the lobby was unable to prevent policy outcomes it regarded as undesirable: Canada did not move its embassy, it did permit members of the PLO to participate in an international conference in Vancouver, and it did not enact even modest anti-boycott legislation, that was a long-standing priority of the Canadian Jewish community. The evidence cannot support the argument that the Jewish lobby dictated Canadian policy in the Middle East.

A far more convincing explanation looks to the emergence of new and powerful groups who pursue specific interests in the Middle East and see Canadian policy as a vehicle to promote and protect these interests. The corporate lobby, especially the large financial institutions and high-technology manufacturers, have broad and easy access to senior officials and members of the Government. Long accustomed to representing their interests at home to the political elite, they bring to bear expertise and political capital when they lobby the Government on foreign policy issues. The linkage they draw between private profit and policy towards the Middle East encourages an active, efficient and successful lobbying effort. The entrance of a new kind of player into the foreign policy arena is an important component in the change of tone and substance of Canadian policy towards the Middle East. This privatization of public policy, the emergence of a strong corporate-financial lobby on foreign policy issues, is an important component of the domestication of internationalism. In the next decade, it may extend well beyond Canadian policy towards the Middle East.

NOTES

1. See Tareq Ismael, «Canada and the Middle East», *Behind the Headlines*, Toronto, The Canadian Institute of International Affairs, 1973, and «Canada and the Middle East», in Peyton V. Lyon and Tareq Ismael, eds., *Canada and the Third World*, Toronto, Macmillan, 1976. See also Paul Noble, «Where Angels Fear to Tread, Canada and the Status of the Palestinians, 1967-1980», unpublished paper, 1981.

2. Laurence Grossman, «The Shifting Canadian Vote on Mideast Questions at the UN», *International Perspectives*, Ottawa, Department of External Affairs, May-June 1978, p. 9-13.

3. An embryonic version of this argument is developed in my «La politique étrangère du Canada au Moyen-Orient: stimulus et réponse», in Paul Painchaud, ed., *Le Canada et le Québec sur la scène internationale*, Montréal, Presses de l'Université du Québec, 1977, p. 379-420. Trends that were barely apparent in the mid-1970s are, of course, much clearer now. David Dewitt and John Kirton look at the same data but see these trends somewhat differently as part of a larger process of «complex neo-realism». See their «Canadian Foreign Policy Towards the Middle East, 1947-1980: International, Domestic, and Governmental Determinants», unpublished paper, 1981, forthcoming in *Canada in a Changing Global Environment*, New York, John Wiley & Sons.

4. See John Munro and Alex Inglis, eds. *Mike, The Memoirs of the Right Honourable Lester B. Pearson*, Vol. II, 1948-1952, Toronto, University of Toronto Press, 1973, p. 214.

5. See Donald Creighton, *The Forked Road, Canada 1939-1957*, Toronto, McClelland and Stewart, 1976, p. 152.

6. *Mike, op. cit.*, p. 216.

7. *Ibidem.*

8. *Ibidem*, p. 216-217.

9. *Ibidem*, p. 217-218.

10. See Donald C. Masters, *Canada in World Affairs, 1953-1955*, Toronto, Oxford University Press, 1959, Chapter VI.

11. *Mike, op. cit.*, p. 219-220.

12. See *House of Commons Debates, Hansard*, February 1 1956, p. 777. See also *Mike, op. cit.*, p. 217.

13. Dewitt and Kirton, *op. cit.*, p. 15-19, 39.

14. Cited in Robert Reford, *Canada and Three Crises*, Toronto, Canadian Institute of International Affairs, Contemporaty Series, No. 42, 1968, p. 88.

15. See *Hansard*, 1 August 1956, p. 6787 and *Mike, op. cit.*, p. 288.

16. *Mike, op. cit.*, p. 230.

17. *Ibidem*, p. 233-237.

18. *Ibidem*, p. 245 and James Eayrs, *Canada and World Affairs, October 1955 to June 1957*, Toronto, Oxford University Press, 1959, p. 258.

19. *Mike, op. cit.*, p. 247.

20. *Ibidem.*

21. *Ibidem*, p. 247-249.

22. *Ibidem*, p. 251-252 and Eayrs, *op. cit.*, p. 262.

23. *Mike, op. cit.*, p. 254 and Eayrs, *op. cit.*, p. 263.

24. *Mike, op. cit.*, p. 258 and 261.

25. *Hansard*, Reply to a Question in the House of Commons, 7 November 1956, p. 61-62.

26. *Mike, op. cit.*, p. 272.

27. See Dewitt and Kirton, *op. cit.*, p. 32.

28. See *Hansard*, 7 November 1956, p. 61-62.

29. See *Hansard*, Vol. I, 1967, p. 601-602.

30. *Montréal Star*, 31 May 1967.

31. *Hansard*, Vol. I, 1967, p. 520-521.

32. Benjamin Geist, «The Six-Day War: A Study in the Setting and Process of Foreign Policy Decision-Making Under Crisis Conditions», unpublished doctoral dissertation, Jerusalem, The Hebrew University of Jerusalem, 1974, p. 227.

33. Dewitt and Kirton, *op. cit.*, p. 57.

34. *Ibidem*, p. 59.

35. See *General Assembly Official Records* (GAOR), Fifth Emergency Special Session, Plenary, 1548th meeting, p. 4. Canada's Ambassador, George Ignatieff, explained that the several draft resolutions under consideration suffered «from the basic defect that the withdrawal of Israeli forces, vital as it is, is not related to the other basic issues involved, which, in our view, are essential to any enduring settlement». See his address to the General Assembly, 3 July 1967, UNDOC A/PV/1546, p. 16.

36. In reply to a question in the Commons a few months before the October War, the Minister explained: «I can make the general answer that we have not singled out the Middle East in any way for special treatment.» See Canada, House of Commons, *Committee on External Affairs and National Defence*, Minutes of Proceedings and Evidence, 5 May 1973.

37. Mitchell Sharp, Address to the House of Commons, 16 October 1973, Ottawa, Department of External Affairs, Information Division, p. 1.

38. Mitchell Sharp, «Canada and the European Community», *Statements and Speeches*, Ottawa, Department of External Affairs, Information Division, 73/29.

39. Interview of senior official in the Department of Defence, May 1979.

40. Allan J. MacEachen, Address to the Twenty-Ninth Session of the General Assembly, *Statements and Speeches*, Ottawa, Department of External Affairs, Information Division, 25 September 1974, p. 6.

41. Interview, member of the Department of External Affairs, September 1975.

42. See the text of the report prepared by R.L. Stanfield, the Special Representative of the Government of Canada and the Ambassador-at-Large, submitted to the Government of Canada on 20 February 1980, p. 14. Hereafter this document is referred to as the Stanfield Report.

43. See GAOR, 1974 annual meeting, Resolution 3379.

44. See *Hansard*, November 27, 1973, p. 8174.

45. Allan J. MacEachen, «Address to the United Nations General Assembly on the Palestinian Issue», November 20, 1974, *Statements and Speeches*, Ottawa, Department of External Affairs, Information Division, 74/16.

46. *Ibidem*.

47. R. Stanbury, Statement by the Canadian Delegation at the United Nations, December 6, 1976, Press Release 49, p. 2.

48. M. Fernand Leblanc, Parliamentary Secretary to the Minister for External Affairs, «Canada and the United Nations' Resolutions Concerning Israel and the Middle East», *Statements and Speeches* 77/12, Ottawa, Department of External Affairs, Information Division, 1977.

49. Interview, official of the Department of External Affairs, January 1980.

50. See the Stanfield Report, *op. cit.*, p. 10.

51. Mohammed Nashashibi, Secretary-General of the Executive Committee of the PLO, said that the PLO had called on Arab governments «[...] to take the necessary measures in reply for the Canadian Government's support of the Zionist enemy». See the *Toronto Star*, 23 July 1975. George Hajjar of the Canadian-Arab Federation said on 24 July that he had warned Canadian officials that a refusal to seat the PLO at the Crimes Congress could lead to trade reprisals by Arab governments. See *The Montréal Star*, 25 July 1975. No reprisals were taken against Canada, however, by any Arab government.

52. Interview, Department of External Affairs, December 1979.

53. Stanfield Report, *op. cit.*, p. 8.

54. The text of the Venice Declaration is reprinted in full in *The New York Times*, 14 June 1980.

55. Two studies recently completed examine the political processes which provoked and aborted the Clark Government's decision to move Canada's embassy from Tel Aviv to Jerusalem. See George Takach, «Clark and the Jerusalem Embassy Affair: Initiative and Constraint in Canadian Foreign Policy», unpublished masters thesis, School of International Affairs, Carleton University, 1980, and Howard Adelman, «Clark and the Canadian Embassy in Israel», *Middle East Focus* 2, March 1980, p. 6-18. See Takach, p. 104.

56. Takach, *op. cit.*, p. 28.

57. *Ibidem*, p. 45.

58. Adelman, *loc. cit.*, p. 17.

59. Cancelled were a $4,2 million lumber sale, a $350 000 poultry contract with Iraq, and a $60 000 student exchange with Saudi Arabia. See Takach, *op. cit.*, p. 57.

60. Adelman, *loc. cit.*, p. 18.

61. Takach, *loc. cit.*, p. 78.

62. *Ibidem*, p. 79-80, p. 96.

63. Stanfield Report, *op. cit.*, p. 14.

64. «Memorandum to the Cabinet, the Arab Boycott of Israel», p. 8, cited in Dewitt and Kirton, *op. cit.*, p. 66.

65. L.A. Delvoie, «Growth in Economic Relations of Canada and the Arab World», *International Perspectives*, November-December 1976, p. 29-33, p. 30, and Antoine Ayoub, «How Should Canada Approach the Many Faces of the Maghreb?», *International Perspectives*, May-June 1972, p. 36-40.

66. See *Imports, Merchandise Trade*, Ottawa, Statistics Canada, Catalogue 65-203, 1972, 1980.

67. See *Exports, Merchandise Trade*, Ottawa, Statistics Canada, Catalogue 202, 1972, 1974, 1977, 1980.

68. *Ibidem*.

69. The definitive study is a recently-completed doctoral dissertation at Brandeis University by Howard Stanislawski, «Elites, Domestic Interest Groups, and International Interests in the Canadian Foreign Policy Decision-Making Process: the Arab Economic Boycott of Canadians and Canadian Companies Doing Business with Israel», 1981. See p. 404.

70. See Grossman, *loc. cit.*, for a statement of this argument.

71. Interview with an official of the Department of External Affairs, cited by Noble, *loc. cit.*, p. 77.

72. Noble, *loc. cit.*, p. 89.

73. Testimony by Mr. Jamieson to the Committee on External Affairs and National Defence, *loc. cit.*, November 29, 1977, p. 15.

74. The United States and a majority of the EEC voted differently on approximately half the resolutions pertaining to the Middle East: two of five resolutions in 1975, six of eleven in 1976, four of ten in 1977, seven of fourteen in 1978, and three of nine in 1979. When they disagreed, Canada voted with the EEC on all resolutions in 1975 and 1976, divided its votes evenly in 1977, and voted with the United States on four of the seven controversial resolutions in 1978 and on two of the three resolutions in 1979. For a more detailed discussion, see our «Alice in Wonderland, the North-Atlantic Alliance and the Arab-Israel Dispute», in Steven L. Spiegel, ed., *The Middle East and the Western Alliance*, London, Allen and Unwin, 1982.

75. See Noble, *loc. cit.*, and Ismael, *op. cit.*

17

Les relations du Canada avec l'Amérique latine et les Caraïbes

Gordon Mace
Université Laval

Au moment de l'intervention des États-Unis en république Dominicaine, en 1965, il y avait peu à relater à propos des relations qu'entretenait le Canada avec l'Amérique latine, d'une part, et les Caraïbes, de l'autre. Outre la question de l'adhésion éventuelle mais sans cesse repoussée à l'OEA[1], on avait guère à se mettre sous la dent sauf peut-être le cas de Cuba et la réaction subséquente du Canada dont on se servait à qui mieux mieux pour cautionner une politique étrangère prétendument indépendante.

Plus de quinze ans ont passé et les rapports entre le Canada et l'Amérique latine ont bien changé. Aujourd'hui, cette région est devenue, avec l'Asie, l'une des plus importantes dans le cadre de la politique étrangère canadienne. Elle a même constitué une région prioritaire pour la réalisation de la stratégie de «troisième option» adoptée par le gouvernement fédéral dès 1972[2].

Ce n'est évidemment pas le cas pour les Caraïbes, où la position relative du Canada a décliné constamment depuis le début du siècle. Cependant, comme nous le verrons, les Caraïbes demeurent une région privilégiée pour la politique étrangère canadienne, et ceci pour un certain nombre de raisons.

Il s'est donc produit une mutation profonde dans les rapports du Canada avec les pays du Sud du continent américain depuis environ une vingtaine d'années. Nous nous proposons, dans le cadre de ce chapitre, d'examiner attentivement les traits caractéristiques de cette mutation et d'en soumettre une interprétation. Pour y arriver, il nous faudra remonter jusqu'au milieu du siècle précédent, en établissant une périodisation appropriée, et avoir toujours le souci, pour chaque période historique donnée, de bien saisir la nature de l'articulation d'un pays comme le Canada avec le système d'économie-monde[3].

La démonstration, en effet, ne vaudra, pour chacune des périodes, que si nous sommes en mesure d'analyser avec exactitude la situation du Canada au sein du système mondial. Car c'est à la lumière de cet examen que nous pourrons rendre compte des rapports entretenus par le Canada avec l'Amérique latine et les Caraïbes tout en présentant l'analyse la plus cohérente possible du comportement canadien envers ces régions et de la mutation dont nous avons parlé précédemment.

DEUX PÉRIPHÉRIES QUI S'IGNORENT (1850-1939)

C'est un fait connu qu'il existait, dès le XVIIᵉ siècle, un lien commercial entre les possessions britanniques du Nord de l'Amérique et celles des Antilles. La Grande-Bretagne, à la différence de la France et de l'Espagne, encourageait en effet le développement de relations commerciales entre ses colonies et c'est ainsi que déjà à cette époque, les Terre-Neuviens livraient de la morue aux colons européens des Caraïbes tandis que cette dernière région approvisionnait en sucre les futures provinces de l'Atlantique⁴. Ces quelques contacts sont à l'origine d'une relation commerciale qui s'est poursuivie sans arrêt jusqu'à aujourd'hui, à l'exception de la période 1793-1808, où les marchands de la Nouvelle-Angleterre avaient remplacé ceux des Maritimes dans le commerce avec les Antilles. Cependant, les quelques liens commerciaux qu'il entretenait alors avec les possessions anglaises des Caraïbes avaient une importance toute limitée par rapport au développement économique du Canada ainsi qu'en regard des quelques relations que le pays maintenait à l'époque avec l'extérieur.

Car jusqu'au statut de Westminster, en effet, le Canada demeurait, sur le plan du droit international, une colonie britannique. C'est donc dire que Londres contrôlera les relations extérieures du pays pratiquement jusqu'à la veille de la Deuxième Guerre mondiale et que tous les contacts formels ou informels avec l'étranger se feront par l'entremise du Foreign Office britannique. Le Canada, bien sûr, obtiendra le gouvernement responsable dès la deuxième moitié du XIXᵉ siècle mais l'autonomie interne nouvellement acquise et les stratégies de développement économique des gouvernements d'alors, comme la *National Policy* de Macdonald de 1879, auront peu de conséquences sur la nature de l'articulation de l'économie canadienne avec l'ensemble du système mondial à ce moment.

C'est qu'en effet, dès son incorporation au système global à partir du début du XVIIᵉ siècle et jusqu'aux années 40, le Canada, tout comme les autres colonies européennes d'Afrique, d'Asie et d'Amérique⁵, a été appelé à jouer le rôle de périphérie du système mondial. Pays politiquement dominé jusqu'en 1940 par les métropoles européennes qu'étaient Paris et Londres, le Canada, sur le plan économique, s'est ainsi vu imposer les fonctions essentielles de marché d'écoulement pour les surplus de produits manufacturés anglais et américains ainsi que de source d'approvisionnement en matières premières nécessaires au fonctionnement de l'économie britannique⁶.

Cette situation perdura tout au long du XIXᵉ siècle et jusqu'au milieu du XXᵉ siècle. Toutefois, un transfert de métropole allait s'opérer progressivement puisque les États-Unis remplaceraient peu à peu la Grande-Bretagne à titre de puissance économique dominante du Canada. En effet, le Canada, sur le plan commercial, est demeuré principalement lié à la Grande-Bretagne jusque dans les années 1840 où Londres adopta la pratique du libre commerce et mit fin, par conséquent, aux préférences impériales qui avaient donné jusque-là aux colonies britanniques un accès privilégié au marché anglais. Ce tournant décisif dans la politique commerciale anglaise obligea les colonies à s'adapter rapidement à la nouvelle situation. La première réaction des colonies britanniques d'Amérique du Nord fut d'instaurer, dès 1849, un libre-échange réciproque entre elles pour les échanges de produits naturels. La seconde consista à opérer un rapprochement avec les États-Unis, lequel rapprochement se concrétisa par la signature, en 1854, d'un Traité de réciprocité qui englobait la majorité des échanges de produits naturels, mais laissait de côté les échanges de produits manufacturés[7].

L'impossibilité de renouveler le Traité de réciprocité en 1866 contribua à l'adoption par le gouvernement canadien, à la fin des années 1870, d'une politique commerciale protectionniste et axée sur l'autosuffisance. Toutefois, cette politique n'était point en mesure de contrebalancer l'attrait bien réel du marché américain et, dans une moindre mesure, du marché britannique. À preuve, les ententes commerciales bilatérales conclues avec le gouvernement de Washington à partir de 1935 et le tarif préférentiel britannique adopté par le gouvernement canadien en 1898 et complété, la même année, par le rétablissement des préférences impériales britanniques transformées, en 1932, en préférences du Commonwealth. De telle sorte qu'entre 1867 et 1910, le Canada fera plus de 85 % de son commerce extérieur avec les États-Unis et la Grande-Bretagne, tandis qu'aujourd'hui encore, près de 70 % des échanges canadiens avec l'étranger se font avec les États-Unis[8].

La situation ne sera guère différente sur le plan des investissements étrangers puisqu'en effet, dès 1900, 85 % des investissements[9] faits au Canada proviennent de Grande-Bretagne, alors que 12 % viennent des États-Unis. Par ailleurs, le déplacement vers les États-Unis avait débuté dès 1926 puisqu'à cette date, la part de ce pays dans les investissements faits au Canada était de 53 % par rapport à 44 % pour la Grande-Bretagne. Et à partir de 1950, la part des États-Unis ne descendra guère en bas de 75 %[10]. Qui plus est, il y a lieu de souligner la nature essentiellement différente des investissements américains faits au Canada par rapport à ceux venus d'ailleurs. Les seconds en effet consistaient surtout en des investissements de portefeuille tandis que les premiers étaient le fait d'implantations de filiales d'entreprises étrangères avec ce que tout cela pouvait représenter d'influence et de pressions sur les politiques gouvernementales étant donné l'attitude positive des gouvernements canadiens face aux investissements étrangers et l'inexistence quasi totale de contrôles à leur égard.

Cela étant, on est mieux en mesure de comprendre l'étroitesse de la marge de manœuvre des décideurs canadiens sur le plan interne, bien sûr, mais principalement dans le domaine des relations extérieures. On comprendra surtout qu'il n'y avait à peu près aucun stimulant pour amener les autorités politiques canadiennes à s'intéresser, sur une base permanente, aux pays du Sud de l'hémisphère américain. Dominé politiquement, à tout le moins dans le domaine des relations extérieures, par la métropole britannique jusque dans les années 30 et très dépendant, sur le plan économique, de son puissant voisin américain, le Canada, de 1850 à 1939, n'avait à peu près aucune autonomie sur le plan externe. Tout contribuait, dans les domaines politique, économique et culturel, à orienter l'action extérieure du Canada, d'une manière quasi exclusive, dans une double direction: d'une part vers les États-Unis et, d'autre part, vers la Grande-Bretagne et le reste de l'Europe. C'était à l'époque, et c'est encore aujourd'hui, une des données de base avec lesquelles doivent composer les pays de ce qu'on est convenu d'appeler la périphérie du système mondial.

Il n'y a donc guère eu de contacts officiels entre le Canada et l'Amérique latine entre 1850 et 1939, à l'exception de deux missions qui furent envoyées là-bas. La première quitta le Canada en décembre 1865 pour se rendre d'abord à Londres où on lui précisa que son rôle consistait essentiellement à échanger de l'information et non à conclure des ententes. Cette prérogative appartenait au gouvernement canadien par l'entremise des autorités britanniques. Composée de représentants de chacune des provinces, la mission canadienne visita successivement le Brésil, Porto Rico, Cuba et Haïti[11].

Le moment choisi pour cette première mission est tout à fait révélateur du comportement canadien envers l'Amérique latine puisqu'on y voit déjà le rôle que sera appelé à jouer la région dans l'effort de diversification commerciale du Canada et dans la tentative de ce pays d'accroître sa marge de manœuvre face aux États-Unis. En effet, la seule raison d'être de la mission de 1866 consistait à rechercher des débouchés commerciaux pour les produits canadiens qui ne pourraient plus être expédiés aux États-Unis dans l'éventualité du non-renouvellement du Traité de réciprocité de 1854. Car il y a tout lieu de penser que si l'on avait reconduit ce traité, les Latino-Américains auraient attendu bien longtemps avant de recevoir la visite de dignitaires canadiens.

À tout événement, cette mission ne donna à peu près aucun résultat et le rapport rédigé par les envoyés canadiens fut vite remisé. La mission de 1930, d'abord organisée par l'Association canadienne des manufacturiers et chapeautée sur le tard par une représentation ministérielle, connut le même sort[12].

Voilà à quoi se résume l'intérêt officiel porté par le Canada à l'Amérique latine avant 1940. Le seul autre point par rapport auquel le gouvernement canadien aurait pu avoir à se prononcer concerne sa participation à l'Union panaméricaine. Toutefois, aucune attention sérieuse ne sera portée à ce problème avant le début de la Deuxième Guerre mondiale.

Sur le plan des relations gouvernementales toujours, la situation sera différente en ce qui concerne les Caraïbes à cause de l'appartenance commune du Canada et de la majorité des îles des Antilles à l'empire britannique. Dès avant 1900, en effet, existait une longue tradition de liens commerciaux entre les deux régions eu égard au fait que la métropole considérait plus économique, étant donné les distances et la complémentarité de certaines productions, d'encourager le commerce entre ces colonies plutôt que de tout centraliser à Londres.

Et ce sont ces relations commerciales qui fourniront l'occasion des premiers liens officiels entre les deux régions. Le commerce du Canada avec les Caraïbes n'a pourtant jamais constitué une part significative de nos échanges avec l'extérieur[13], mais ce commerce était jugé suffisamment important, au début des années 1900, pour qu'on lui adjoigne un cadre juridique. C'est à cela que serviront les ententes commerciales négociées en 1912, 1920 et 1925.

Parmi celles-ci, l'entente de 1925 est la plus importante puisqu'elle servira de cadre juridique aux échanges commerciaux entre les deux régions jusqu'en 1966. L'accord consistait essentiellement en des concessions tarifaires préférentielles que s'accordait chacun des partenaires et prévoyait l'établissement d'un système de transport maritime avec financement conjoint[14]. Cependant, bien qu'il ait été nécessaire de fournir un cadre juridique aux échanges commerciaux existants et à venir, on ne peut pas dire que les accords du début du siècle aient contribué à une augmentation des échanges entre les deux régions. Ainsi que nous le verrons, ces échanges ont plutôt diminué et ceci à un point tel qu'on en est venu à ne plus considérer comme indispensable la flotte de transport prévue dans le cadre de l'accord de 1925. Celle-ci fut définitivement mise au rancart en 1958.

Cela dit, si les liens officiels entre le Canada et les pays de l'hémisphère sud du continent ont été a peu près inexistants jusqu'en 1940, il n'en a pas été de même des autres types de relations qui ont contribué à assurer une présence canadienne dans la région dès le XVIIIe siècle. Ces relations non gouvernementales ont été essentiellement le fait de deux groupes d'individus: les missionnaires et les hommes d'affaires.

Ce sont d'abord des missionnaires de foi protestante qui se sont établis dans les Antilles et en Amérique latine au cours de la deuxième moitié du XVIIIe siècle. Les missionnaires catholiques se sont intéressés plus tardivement à la région. Mais dans l'un et l'autre cas, les modes d'intervention ont été les mêmes, la transmission de la foi se faisant par le biais de l'éducation et de l'organisation communautaire. Toutefois, on ne saurait affirmer que cette présence religieuse ait eu une influence déterminante sur le développement des relations du Canada avec la région puisque les missionnaires représentaient moins le Canada que leur Église respective[15].

Cela ne sera pas tout à fait le cas des hommes d'affaires qui, eux, seront clairement identifiés à leur pays d'origine et s'efforceront d'impliquer le gouvernement canadien dans la région afin d'y mousser les relations d'affaires. Des relations qui, sur le plan strictement commercial, nous l'avons dit, ne constitueront jamais, avant 1960, une part importante du commerce extérieur canadien mais qui se développeront néanmoins de façon suivie.

Tout au long de cette première période des relations entre le Canada et les pays de l'hémisphère sud du continent, le commerce canadien avec l'Amérique latine ne dépassera guère 3 % de notre commerce total. À ce moment, les principaux partenaires commerciaux du Canada dans la région étaient l'Argentine, le Brésil, le Mexique, la Colombie, le Vénézuela et le Pérou et l'essentiel du commerce consistait en un échange de matières premières principalement. Le Canada exportait déjà quelques produits manufacturés mais ces derniers formaient une part minimum de nos exportations vers la région[16]. La situation sera sensiblement la même pour le commerce canadien avec les Caraïbes où nos principaux partenaires étaient alors la Jamaïque, Trinidad et Tobago, la Guyane et la Barbade[17].

Sur le plan des flux de capitaux, par ailleurs, le Canada a déjà, en 1925, une présence appréciable dans les Caraïbes ainsi que dans certains pays d'Amérique latine. Les principaux secteurs d'investissements à l'époque sont les banques, l'assurance, les services publics et, dans une moindre mesure, les mines et le secteur manufacturier. Le secteur où l'implantation canadienne a été la plus ancienne en même temps que la plus névralgique a certainement été celui des banques. La première banque canadienne à ouvrir une succursale dans la région a été la Banque de Nouvelle-Écosse avec un premier établissement en Jamaïque en 1889. La Banque Royale commençait ses opérations dix ans plus tard à Cuba, suivie des autres grandes banques canadiennes. L'expansion s'est poursuivie jusqu'à la fin des années 30 alors que les banques canadiennes possédaient plusieurs succursales dans presque toutes les îles des Antilles et dans la majeure partie des pays d'Amérique latine. La présence, déjà massive pour l'époque, des banques canadiennes dans la région permettait à ces dernières d'avoir un impact non négligeable sur la vie économique et politique des pays concernés[18] en plus d'ouvrir la voie à une expansion économique canadienne plus large.

Le secteur des assurances, pour sa part, n'était pas en reste avec l'arrivée dans la région, peu après les banques, d'entreprises comme la Sun Life, la Dominion Life et autres. La présence de ces compagnies était aussi diversifiée que celle des banques et l'on estimait à 168 millions de dollars les avoirs de ces entreprises en Amérique latine et dans les Caraïbes en 1946[19]. Ce montant d'argent n'était pas, bien sûr, uniquement le fait de l'assurance proprement dite mais englobait aussi les achats ou prises de participation de ces entreprises dans d'autres secteurs à partir des gains réalisés dans l'assurance. Cela étant, l'on est mieux à même de saisir l'influence déterminante que pouvaient avoir ces entreprises dans la vie économique et politique de certains pays, en particulier dans les Caraïbes.

Dans le secteur des services publics, les investissements directs venant du Canada se concentraient surtout dans les domaines du transport urbain et de l'électricité avec, comme principaux exemples connus, la Brazilian Traction et la Mexican Light and Power Company. Ce réseau était complété par des investissements alors moins importants dans les secteurs du pétrole, des mines, du transport ainsi que dans le secteur manufacturier (Massey-Harris, Hiram-Walker, etc.)[20].

Ainsi donc, tout au long de cette première période des relations du Canada avec l'Amérique latine et les Caraïbes, nous observons deux régions qui sont, l'une et l'autre, des périphéries du système d'économie-monde. La fonction de chacune consiste à servir de source d'approvisionnement en matières premières pour les métropoles européennes d'abord et les États-Unis ensuite ainsi que de marché pour l'écoulement des surplus de capitaux et de produits manufacturés des puissances du Centre. Cet état de choses, nécessaire à la dynamique même du système mondial, a résulté en un minimum de contacts politiques et commerciaux entre le Canada et les pays de l'hémisphère sud du continent américain puisque les flux des uns et des autres étaient orientés, pour l'essentiel, vers les États-Unis et l'Europe de l'Ouest. La seule exception à ce *pattern*, et elle est importante, vient des flux de capitaux et des investissements directs à l'étranger. L'expansion canadienne, dans ce domaine, en Amérique latine et dans les Caraïbes est le résultat de l'arrivée à la maturité économique du secteur bancaire canadien, le premier à y parvenir. Et ce phénomène aura une double signification. Sur le plan du système global, il contribuera à favoriser le changement de statut du Canada, faisant passer celui-ci du statut de périphérie à celui de semi-périphérie[21]. D'autre part, sur le plan des relations avec l'Amérique latine et les Caraïbes, il assurera la base de la présence canadienne dans la région et préparera le terrain pour une expansion économique à venir.

UNE OUVERTURE POLITIQUE PRUDENTE (1940-1967)

Au moment où l'Europe s'embrasait à nouveau à la suite de l'expansionnisme allemand, le Canada n'était déjà plus le pays périphérique qu'il avait été au cours des premières décennies de ce siècle. L'économie canadienne s'était en effet profondément transformée alors que le mouvement d'industrialisation, amorcé dans les années 1860, donnait maintenant des résultats tangibles. Au sortir de la guerre de 39-45, le Canada n'était surpassé que par les États-Unis en termes de production manufacturière per capita[22] alors que, par la suite, le secteur de la fabrication ne constituera jamais moins que 25 %[23] du produit national brut canadien.

En 50 ans, le Canada avait donc développé une base industrielle significative qui, en conjonction avec l'expansion de son secteur bancaire, lui assurait une présence importante sur la scène économique mondiale. Et la position du pays est améliorée encore plus dans les 20 années qui ont suivi la fin de la Deuxième Guerre mondiale à cause d'une croissance économique remarquable due, pour une grande part, à l'effet d'entraînement de l'économie américaine.

À cette transformation des structures de l'économie canadienne, prérequis indispensable à un changement du statut du Canada au sein du système mondial, a correspondu une métamorphose importante du système global qui n'a pas été non plus sans influencer le rôle que fut appelé à jouer le Canada au cours des années 50 et 60. Au sortir de la guerre, en effet, les États-Unis et le Canada étaient pratiquement les deux seuls pays industrialisés à voir leur territoire épargné par les hostilités. Ce qui a permis au pays, pendant que les autres se consacraient à la reconstruction, d'occuper sur la scène mondiale un espace tout à fait disproportionné par rapport à son potentiel économique et militaire.

Semi-périphérie selon tous les critères, le Canada n'en jouera pas moins le rôle de puissance occupant le vide laissé momentanément par les anciennes métropoles dévastées par la guerre. Et c'est à cette étape de son évolution que correspondra, tout naturellement, la période d'internationalisme dans la politique étrangère canadienne. Tout naturellement, avons-nous écrit, parce qu'il s'agira là du seul véritable moment dans l'histoire du Canada où, sur le plan externe, les dirigeants canadiens pourront penser avoir les moyens de leur politique. Mais tout naturellement aussi parce que la nouvelle transformation du système mondial, rejetant encore plus le Canada à l'ombre de son voisin immédiat, obligera déjà les décideurs canadiens à rechercher les moyens d'élargir leur marge de manœuvre. Et historiquement, sur le plan externe, l'internationalisme servira d'instrument premier à cet égard.

Cependant, comme nous le verrons, le statut artificiel de nouvelle puissance octroyé au Canada ainsi que le choix qui s'ensuivit de la voie multilatérale n'auront pas un effet positif en ce qui concerne les relations du Canada avec l'Amérique latine et les Caraïbes. La région était encore de trop peu d'importance pour susciter un intérêt suivi de la part d'un pays appelé à une présence et à un rôle «mondiaux».

C'est par conséquent avec une certaine réticence qu'au départ le gouvernement canadien envisagea l'ouverture de relations diplomatiques formelles avec les pays d'Amérique latine. Il aura en effet fallu plusieurs mois, voire plusieurs années, de sollicitations de la part de différents pays pour que le Canada daigne ouvrir quelques ambassades dans la région.

Mais il est vrai que le problème n'était pas simple puisque perdurait, d'une part, la confusion quant à savoir si les pays étrangers devaient s'adresser directement au gouvernement canadien ou alors emprunter le canal du Foreign Office britannique. Du point de vue canadien, d'autre part, se posait le problème délicat de la localisation des ambassades à créer. Car la rareté de ressources, en argent et en personnel compétent, ne permettait guère d'ouvrir plus de quelques ambassades et il convenait de ménager les susceptibilités des gouvernements de pays qui n'apparaissaient pas sur la liste des priorités canadiennes[24].

Le gouvernement canadien s'est donc laissé courtiser pendant un certain temps sans réagir, mais le début des hostilités sur le continent européen allait amener un changement d'attitude de sa part. Le conflit européen, en effet, devait, pour un temps, fermer ce marché traditionnel à la production canadienne et, par voie de conséquence, obliger le gouvernement à rechercher des marchés de remplacement. C'est là la raison principale du bref sursaut d'intérêt que l'on constate, au début des années 40, de la part du Canada face à l'Amérique latine. Ce qui constitue d'ailleurs une constante de la politique étrangère du Canada envers la région. Qu'il s'agisse de 1866, de 1940 ou du début des années 70, le Canada abordera toujours l'Amérique latine, au départ, soit comme marché de remplacement pour ses exportations, ou encore comme instrument géographique pour sa diversification commerciale et économique.

Cela dit, le Canada réagit à la situation en envoyant d'abord une mission commerciale, dirigée par le ministre de l'Industrie et du Commerce de l'époque, James McKinnon. La mission de 1940-1941[25] visita plusieurs pays d'Amérique latine et des Caraïbes et des accords commerciaux furent conclus avec certains d'entre eux. Toutefois, la mission et les accords n'ont pas amené une augmentation substantielle des échanges commerciaux.

Puis, vinrent les relations diplomatiques formelles avec l'ouverture des ambassades canadiennes à Rio de Janeiro et Buenos Aires à l'automne 1941. Ces deux capitales avaient été choisies essentiellement, ainsi que l'avait déclaré le Sous-secrétaire d'État aux Affaires Extérieures de l'époque, parce que le Brésil était le chef de file des pays de la région maintenant des relations commerciales importantes avec les États-Unis tandis que l'Argentine était le principal partenaire culturel et commercial de l'Europe en Amérique latine. Le sous-ministre Skelton considérait de plus que les autres pays latino-américains importants pour le Canada étaient, dans l'ordre, le Chili, le Mexique et Cuba[26]. Le gouvernement canadien dut d'ailleurs répondre favorablement, dès l'année suivante, aux représentations chiliennes en faveur de l'établissement de relations diplomatiques en grande partie à cause de pressions du gouvernement américain qui voyait là un geste susceptible de favoriser la défense de l'hémisphère américain en éloignant le Chili des puissances de l'Axe[27]. Deux ans plus tard, l'ouverture d'ambassades canadiennes à Lima et à Mexico suivit. La situation était quelque peu compliquée en ce qui concernait le Mexique, car la nationalisation des entreprises pétrolières, par le gouvernement de Cardenas en 1938, avait entraîné la rupture des relations diplomatiques entre ce pays et la Grande-Bretagne alors que cette dernière, appuyée par les États-Unis et la France, organisait un boycott mondial du pétrole mexicain. Néanmoins, certains hauts fonctionnaires canadiens considéraient qu'il fallait une présence du Commonwealth à Mexico et ce facteur contribua sans doute à la décision canadienne de procéder à l'établissement de relations diplomatiques avec le Mexique en 1944[28].

Le Canada élargira son réseau diplomatique avec les pays d'Amérique du Sud jusqu'en 1953, mais, dès la guerre terminée, l'intérêt du gouvernement canadien pour la région s'affaiblira à nouveau sauf peut-être en ce qui concerne les relations commerciales. La nouvelle situation internationale, du fait des conséquences de la guerre, permettra au Canada de se voir octroyé un rôle que les dirigeants canadiens n'auraient jamais pensé pouvoir jouer auparavant. Consacré artificiellement grande puissance, le Canada reviendra, pour la majeure partie des années 50, à ses relations traditionnelles avec les États-Unis et les pays européens et orientera sa politique étrangère dans le sens d'un internationalisme qui l'amènera, sous l'impulsion de Lester B. Pearson et d'autres, à jouer un rôle important dans la mise sur pied du système des Nations-Unies ainsi que dans le fonctionnement des agences multilatérales au détriment de relations qu'il aurait pu approfondir avec l'Amérique latine et les Caraïbes[29].

Cette attitude des dirigeants canadiens prévaudra jusqu'à la fin des années 50 où des modifications au paysage politique des Antilles obligeront le nouveau gouvernement Diefenbaker à réorienter l'attention du Canada vers les Caraïbes et l'Amérique latine. Le phénomène qui eut sans contredit le plus d'impact à cet égard fut la révolution cubaine de 1958 et l'adoption, quelques années plus tard, d'une stratégie de développement socialiste par le gouvernement Castro.

L'épisode cubain et les événements qui s'y rattachèrent, en particulier l'embargo américain et le refus canadien de rompre ses relations diplomatiques et commerciales avec La Havane, eurent deux conséquences immédiates pour le Canada. Ils permirent d'abord au Canada d'occuper la place laissée vacante par les États-Unis à Cuba avec l'espoir d'améliorer nos relations commerciales et économiques avec ce pays et ils serviront surtout de prétexte à l'une des rares affirmations d'indépendance d'Ottawa face à Washington sur le plan de la politique étrangère[30].

De façon plus large aussi, les événements de Cuba suscitèrent un regain d'intérêt de la part de l'ensemble de la population canadienne face à l'Amérique latine et aux Caraïbes. Regain d'intérêt également chez le personnel politique et au sein de la diplomatie canadienne avec la visite à Ottawa du président mexicain Lopez Mateos et de d'autres hommes politiques latino-américains pendant que, de son côté, le premier ministre Diefenbaker se rendait au Mexique.

C'est donc dans un climat favorable que put agir le nouveau ministre des Affaires extérieures, Howard Green, intéressé depuis longtemps par les relations internationales et décidé à se faire le promoteur d'une intensification des relations du Canada avec les pays du sud de l'hémisphère. C'est lui, en effet, qui mit sur pied, au ministère des Affaires extérieures, une division distincte pour les affaires d'Amérique latine. Et c'est au cours de son mandat également que le Canada devint membre de la Commission économique pour l'Amérique latine (CEPAL) et entreprit d'établir les premières relations diplomatiques avec l'Amérique centrale[31].

Cela dit, les événements du début des années 60 fourniront aussi l'occasion de reprendre la discussion à propos d'un vieux problème pour lequel on n'avait pas encore trouvé de solution. Il s'agit du problème de la participation canadienne au système interaméricain qui s'était posé dès la naissance même de l'Union panaméricaine. À cette époque, en effet, les États-Unis et les pays latino-américains étaient tous favorables à une participation canadienne à l'Union panaméricaine[32], mais le gouvernement canadien, lui, n'était guère intéressé. Car le problème se posait déjà pour le Canada d'avoir à participer à un organisme dominé par les États-Unis avec le risque de prises de position de sa part pouvant indisposer soit les républiques américaines, soit encore le gouvernement de Washington qui aurait pu alors réagir par des gestes au niveau bilatéral. La position canadienne face au système interaméricain a toujours été d'éviter de se voir placé entre l'arbre et l'écorce. Et cette position dénote une tendance profonde de la politique étrangère canadienne face à l'Amérique latine qui a généralement consisté à minimiser les gestes politiques afin de ne pas mettre en danger les relations d'affaires considérées comme la principale raison d'être de la présence canadienne dans la région[33].

Le seul moment où le Canada est venu près d'opérer un revirement à sa politique fut en 1941 où le gouvernement King s'aventura à penser qu'une présence officielle du pays à l'Union panaméricaine serait de nature à aider les États-Unis à convaincre les pays neutres d'Amérique latine de joindre le camp des alliés. Cependant, l'initiative fut loin de plaire au gouvernement américain et le département d'État avisa l'ambassadeur canadien à Washington qu'il n'y avait aucun moyen de permettre au Canada de joindre l'Union. Le prétexte officiel invoqué par Washington était la charte même de l'Union panaméricaine mais en réalité le gouvernement américain craignait que le Canada ne serve que de paravent à une présence britannique, jugée néfaste, au sein de l'Union[34]. Et lorsque, 20 ans plus tard, le gouvernement de Washington deviendra favorable à une participation canadienne à l'Organisation des États américains, pour des raisons essentiellement financières, le Canada, lui, sera revenu à sa politique de non-participation. La seule concession d'Ottawa aux demandes américaines consistera alors à déléguer un observateur à l'OEA à partir de novembre 1965[35].

Mais à la fin des années 50, il n'y avait pas que dans les pays d'Amérique latine, et surtout à Cuba, que cela bougeait. Le paysage politique des Caraïbes anglophones commençait lui aussi à se transformer avec la mise sur pied, dès janvier 1958, de la Fédération des Antilles du Commonwealth[36]. C'était là une façon pour la Grande-Bretagne de se dégager progressivement de la région en tant que puissance métropolitaine. Et aux yeux des autorités britanniques, la Fédération constituait le meilleur moyen de permettre à la région d'accéder à la souveraineté politique.

L'initiative reçut dès le départ un accueil favorable de la part du Canada et le gouvernement Diefenbaker ne tarda pas à instaurer un programme spécial d'appui à la région. Le gouvernement canadien accepta de débourser, sur une période de cinq ans, une somme de dix millions de dollars qui devrait être consacrée à l'amélioration du système d'éducation et à la bonification de l'infrastructure portuaire. Une partie des montants alloués devait aussi être utilisée pour la mise en service de deux bateaux destinés à satisfaire les besoins en communication de la Fédération[37]. L'aide canadienne aux Caraïbes anglophones devenait aussi le premier programme d'envergure à être instauré en dehors du plan de Colombo.

Malgré cela, la Fédération ne fut point en mesure de franchir avec succès les obstacles qui se dressaient sur sa route et l'expérience prit fin quatre ans plus tard. Les îles les plus viables, d'un point de vue économique, proclamèrent progressivement leur indépendance politique et le Canada n'hésita pas à établir des relations diplomatiques avec chacune d'elles[38].

En dépit, cependant, des nouvelles relations politiques et malgré l'extension importante du réseau bancaire canadien dans la région, les relations commerciales entre le Canada et les Antilles n'allaient point cesser de se détériorer. En effet, en 1963, la nature des biens échangés entre les deux régions n'avait, à toutes fins pratiques, à peu près pas varié par rapport à ce qu'elle était au début du siècle. Qui plus est, la part canadienne dans le commerce extérieur de la région était en constante régression pour la très grande majorité des pays concernés en même temps que les achats canadiens dans la région augmentaient dans une proportion beaucoup moindre que ceux faits au Canada par les pays des Caraïbes[39]. À cette dernière constatation s'ajoutait le fait d'une détérioration constante des termes de l'échange au détriment de la zone antillaise à un point tel que, pour la seule année 1961, l'on constate une perte de 20 millions de dollars à ce chapitre pour la région dans son commerce avec le Canada[40]. Et ce n'est pas les nouvelles sommes consacrées au programme d'aide, en 1964-1966, qui allaient atténuer les critiques formulées de plus en plus nettement par les dirigeants politiques de la région puisque les revenus tirés par l'Alcan, à partir de l'exploitation de la bauxite en Guyane et en Jamaïque, dépassaient à eux seuls la moyenne annuelle d'aide canadienne accordée à la région de 1958 à 1966.

Le Canada ne pouvait donc plus éviter le moment d'une réévaluation de ses relations avec la région et la conférence d'Ottawa de 1966 allait en fournir l'occasion. La conférence réunit, au Canada, le premier ministre Pearson et les chefs d'État des Antilles du Commonwealth. Plusieurs sujets furent abordés dans le cadre de la conférence et les éléments suivants résument les principaux points d'entente: un protocole commercial fut tout d'abord adopté en remplacement de l'accord de 1925. Il s'agissait essentiellement d'améliorations touchant les marges préférentielles accordées par le Canada aux pays des Caraïbes et concernant les barrières non tarifaires ainsi qu'un accès éventuel privilégié sur le marché canadien pour les fruits et le rhum antillais. L'élément principal du protocole concernait naturellement le sucre, auquel le gouvernement canadien accordait une nouvelle marge préférentielle supérieure à ce qui existait auparavant. Les pays antillais, pour leur part, s'engageaient à tenter de maintenir la position existante du Canada sur leurs marchés pour certains produits dont la farine, le blé et la morue tandis que les deux parties s'entendaient pour étudier les possibilités de créer une zone de libre-échange entre elles. Sur le plan de l'aide, le Canada s'engageait à accroître le nombre de projets dans la région, à contribuer aux coûts locaux de ces projets et à mener une étude de faisabilité quant à la mise en place éventuelle d'une banque régionale de développement. Des mesures furent aussi adoptées dans les domaines de l'immigration et du tourisme tandis que le Canada proposa la signature de traités évitant la double imposition afin de favoriser un accroissement des investissements canadiens dans la région. Finalement, on accepta la mise sur pied du Comité économique et commercial Canada-Caraïbes qui devait servir de principal mécanisme de consultation à venir entre les participants[41].

Il n'y a pas eu de conséquences véritables à la conférence de 1966 et, de l'avis des principaux observateurs, la rencontre n'a pas constitué un point tournant dans les relations économiques et commerciales du Canada avec la région. Tout au plus s'entendait-on pour constater qu'il ne pouvait s'agir là que d'un premier pas à l'intérieur d'une démarche plus substantielle[42] qui, malheureusement, n'a pas eu de suite. Comme nous le verrons, des événements nouveaux modifieront le cours des choses et les Antilles du Commonwealth perdront encore de leur importance pour le Canada sur le plan économique et commercial.

Ce qui ne fut pas le cas pour l'Amérique latine. Car si la part de la région dans notre commerce extérieur ne s'appréacia guère au cours de la période que nous étudions, il reste néanmoins que les échanges du Canada avec ces pays ont augmenté de plus de 200 % de 1959 à 1970[43]. À ce moment, les principaux partenaires commerciaux du Canada dans la région demeuraient l'Argentine, le Brésil, le Vénézuela, le Mexique et Cuba. Le Canada y exportait surtout des pièces d'automobile et de l'équipement d'aviation, du papier, du blé et de l'aluminium ainsi que de la machinerie diverse. Nous importions, en retour, principalement du pétrole brut et raffiné, du café, des fruits et légumes ainsi que du textile[44].

Il y avait donc un progrès certain dans nos échanges commerciaux avec l'Amérique latine depuis le début des années 60 mais ce progrès n'était pas suffisant pour permettre à la région d'améliorer sa part relative à l'intérieur du commerce canadien avec l'étranger. Qui plus est, les investissements privés canadiens en Amérique latine n'augmentaient que faiblement d'une année à l'autre alors que les entreprises-conseils s'établissaient de plus en plus dans la région.

Ces différents éléments, tantôt positifs tantôt négatifs, rendaient difficile, par conséquent, une appréciation exacte de l'importance économique que pouvait avoir, à l'époque, l'Amérique latine pour le Canada. C'est pourquoi, malgré la décision importante du gouvernement canadien de mettre sur pied, en 1964, un programme d'aide dans le cadre de la Banque interaméricaine de développement, l'on conclut qu'il y avait à ce moment un manque d'intérêt de la part du Canada pour l'Amérique latine et ceci durant la majeure partie des années 60[45].

Il est vrai que l'Amérique latine et les Caraïbes n'ont pas constitué une région de première importance dans la politique étrangère canadienne de 1945 à 1968. Le Canada était naturellement plus préoccupé à cette époque par son rôle au sein des Nations Unies ainsi que par ses liens traditionnels avec les États-Unis et l'Europe. Mais les transformations du système mondial à partir du début des années 60 allaient affecter la position canadienne à l'intérieur de ce système. Et il n'est sans doute pas exagéré de penser que déjà les dirigeants canadiens commençaient à mesurer les effets de la nouvelle situation et à comprendre l'importance que pouvait avoir l'Amérique latine dans la stratégie canadienne d'adaptation aux transformations structurelles existantes et à venir.

LA ZONE PRIVILÉGIÉE POUR LA STRATÉGIE CANADIENNE DE DIVERSIFICATION (1968-1984)

Dès le milieu des années 60, la situation s'était modifiée d'une façon qui n'était pas nécessairement à l'avantage du Canada. Sur le plan mondial, certains pays européens de même que le Japon étaient redevenus de grandes puissances ramenant en cela le Canada à son rôle plus normal de «la plus grande des petites puissances». Simultanément s'étaient développées les expériences d'intégration économique, en Europe, en Afrique et en Amérique latine, dont l'objectif de construction de marchés régionaux protégés risquaient, en limitant l'accès à ces marchés des produits canadiens, de poser des obstacles sérieux à l'expansion des relations commerciales du Canada. Le phénomène pouvait avoir des conséquences néfastes à la fois pour le développement même de l'économie canadienne de même que sur la marge de manœuvre du Canada face aux États-Unis puisqu'il y avait menace de voir le pays de plus en plus confiné à l'Amérique du Nord pour le gros de ses échanges économiques. Enfin, se profilait déjà le problème de la domination des entreprises transnationales dont le comportement agressif risquait d'empêcher toute expansion du capital canadien sur les marchés internationaux.

À ces transformations structurelles sur le plan mondial correspondait, sur le plan interne, un accroissement de la domination des entreprises américaines, en

particulier dans le domaine des ressources naturelles et dans le secteur manu
rier. Cette «économie de succursales», comme on a qualifié l'économie canadi
pouvait avoir, plus que d'autres formes de domination économique, des conséquences importantes eu égard au contrôle et à l'orientation même de l'économie canadienne[46].

Le Canada se retrouvait donc dans une situation précaire au milieu des
années 60. Précarité qui allait être accentuée quelques années plus tard par l'émergence de nouvelles puissances régionales, comme le Brésil et l'Iran, et par l'arrivée,
sur la scène économique mondiale, de ce qu'on allait appeler par la suite les «nouveaux pays industrialisés». Deux phénomènes qui risquaient, là aussi, de menacer
la position canadienne dans le domaine des échanges internationaux. À quoi s'ajou-
terait une initiative qui, avec les mesures Nixon d'août 1971, briserait en quelque
sorte la «relation spéciale» unissant le Canada aux États-Unis. Ces mesures, qui
plaçaient le Canada sur le même pied que les autres pays du point de vue de l'accès
au marché américain, mettaient ainsi fin à un avantage qui avait permis en quelque
sorte de contrebalancer l'effet négatif de la présence massive des filiales d'entreprises américaines au Canada, à tout le moins aux yeux des dirigeants canadiens.

Tous ces événements traçaient les contours d'une situation qui faisait
apparaître la précarité du statut du Canada au sein du système mondial. Le pays allait-
il redevenir un État-satellite ou prendrait-il les moyens afin de préserver son rôle de
semi-périphérie et la marge de manœuvre qui allaient de pair? L'idée d'une reprise
en main et d'un contrôle national accru de l'économie avait déjà commencé à faire
son chemin au Canada avec certaines politiques du ministre libéral Walter Gordon[47]
ainsi qu'avec l'expression de demandes en faveur de l'adoption d'une nouvelle
«politique nationale» au milieu des années 60. Mais c'est l'arrivée au pouvoir du
gouvernement Trudeau qui fournira l'occasion et le prétexte de la mise en place des
instruments nécessaires à cette fin.

La nouvelle situation internationale, ainsi que l'arrivée à maturité du capitalisme canadien[48], obligeait en effet le gouvernement à adopter une stratégie d'adaptation aux transformations structurelles du système mondial de même qu'au changement des politiques américaines face au Canada. La stratégie, qualifiée par la suite
de «troisième option», impliquait à la fois une politique de diversification des échanges et une politique de restructuration de l'économie canadienne qui passait par
l'adoption d'une stratégie industrielle.

Mais on ne pouvait compter uniquement sur l'entreprise privée pour réussir
la stratégie d'adaptation envisagée. Car le fonctionnement même du système
mondial exige de la part d'un pays semi-périphérique, en plus de tirer tout le profit
possible de son rôle de tampon politique et économique entre les pays du centre et
ceux de la périphérie, qu'il renforce le rôle de l'État à titre d'intervenant économique
étant donné l'incapacité de ses entreprises nationales à manipuler à leur profit les
règles d'un système dont le fonctionnement profite d'abord aux monopoles des pays
dominants. Ce renforcement de l'État implique naturellement une remise en question de certaines règles de conduite du libéralisme classique.

C'est ce qui s'est produit dans une certaine mesure au Canada à partir de
1968 où l'on assista à un renforcement des structures d'État ainsi qu'au renforcement et à la mise sur pied d'instruments d'intervention économique. Aucun instrument et aucune structure n'échappa à l'examen. C'est ainsi qu'au plan de l'aide

publique au développement, le gouvernement Trudeau créa, dès 1968, l'Agence canadienne de développement international (ACDI)[49] à partir des structures de l'ancien Bureau d'aide à l'étranger tandis qu'il fit voter, deux ans plus tard, la loi instituant le Centre de recherche pour le développement international (CRDI). On a déjà montré ailleurs le rôle de l'aide publique au développement du triple point de vue de l'amélioration de l'image du pays à l'étranger, de l'augmentation des échanges commerciaux ainsi que du renforcement des investissements canadiens dans le tiers monde[50]. La création, en 1971, de la Division de l'industrie et des affaires au sein de l'ACDI et le fonctionnement de la Division depuis lors constituent des témoignages éloquents à l'égard de ce dernier point.

Dans le domaine plus spécifique du commerce et des investissements, le gouvernement modifia les statuts de la Corporation commerciale du Canada et il transforma, dès 1969, la Société d'assurances-crédits à l'exportation en société pour l'expansion des exportations. Il ne s'agissait pas que d'un changement de nom de l'organisme puisque ses fonctions furent aussi élargies dans le sens d'un appui additionnel à la fois aux exportations et aux investissements. Enfin, et dans le même ordre d'idées, on opéra, deux ans plus tard, une transformation des structures du ministère de l'Industrie et du Commerce avec la mise sur pied de la Division de la promotion des marchés d'exportations et de la Division du développement de l'industrie de la défense.

Il s'établit par la suite une concertation entre la SEE, le ministère de l'Industrie et du Commerce ainsi que la Division de la coopération industrielle de l'ACDI. Les agents diplomatiques, pour leur part, furent appelés à approfondir l'aspect économique de leur tâche et le tout fut complété par la réorganisation récente du ministère des Affaires extérieures dont le rôle consistera dorénavant à piloter et à coordonner l'expansion économique du Canada sur les marchés étrangers[51].

La stratégie de troisième option[52], annoncée en 1972 par le ministre Sharp, devait donner son sens et poser les balises pour la diversification et la restructuration à venir. Mais quelles régions seraient privilégiées pour l'application de cette stratégie? Il semble que les dirigeants canadiens aient accordé à l'Amérique latine un rôle prioritaire à cet égard.

La première manifestation substantielle d'intérêt de la part du nouveau gouvernement Trudeau pour l'Amérique latine a consisté en l'envoi d'une mission dans la région dès l'automne 1968. Ce fut la plus importante mission officielle canadienne à visiter l'Amérique latine tant du point de vue du nombre de pays parcourus que du point de vue du personnel politique et administratif impliqué. En effet, pas moins de cinq ministres et plus de 30 conseillers politiques et fonctionnaires participaient à la mission canadienne. Celle-ci séjourna un mois dans la région et ses principaux objectifs étaient de se familiariser avec les développements récents qui s'étaient produits dans la région, d'étudier les bénéfices pouvant résulter de relations plus étroites entre le Canada et l'Amérique latine, d'amorcer des contacts directs avec les dirigeants politiques et économiques des pays visités ainsi que de faire mieux connaître le Canada dans la région et accroître l'intérêt des Canadiens pour l'Amérique latine. Cependant, il semble bien que l'aspect commercial des relations du Canada avec la région constitua la préoccupation principale de la mission canadienne.

Par ailleurs, la mission de 1968 était aussi extrêmement importante eu égard à la tâche qu'on lui avait confiée d'assembler une information devant être utilisée dans le cadre du processus de révision de la politique étrangère qui avait été demandé, dès son arrivée au pouvoir, par le nouveau chef du gouvernement canadien. C'est pourquoi, à son retour au pays, la mission soumit un *Rapport préliminaire* dans lequel elle notait, entre autres conclusions, l'importance croissante de l'Amérique latine dans les affaires internationales de même qu'elle rappelait la nécessité de ne point perdre de vue l'hétérogénéité de la région[53].

La mission du ministre Sharp en Amérique latine subira donc un sort différent des missions précédentes dans la région puisque son rapport, plutôt que de s'empoussiérer sur une tablette, servira effectivement dans le cadre du processus de révision de la politique étrangère qui aboutit, en 1970, à la présentation du livre blanc. D'ailleurs, le livre blanc ne constituera, pour l'essentiel, qu'une version abrégée du *Rapport préliminaire* soumis un an auparavant.

Pour certains, le livre blanc de 1970 était, dans toute l'histoire du ministère des Affaires extérieures, la première manifestation de l'élaboration d'une politique globale face à l'Amérique latine[54]. Essentiellement, le document traçait trois orientations possibles pour la politique étrangère canadienne face à la région:

[...] poursuivre essentiellement la politique actuelle: on développerait le commerce et les investissements, on augmenterait légèrement les activités d'assistance au développement, mais on laisserait les relations politiques, culturelles et scientifiques évoluer suivant les circonstances;

[...] d'élargir et d'approfondir à dessein nos relations avec l'Amérique latine, non seulement sur le plan économique mais encore sur le plan politique, de même que dans les domaines culturel, éducatif [...] Cette dernière solution pourrait être mise en œuvre de deux manières [...] opter pour une attitude totalement multilatérale; [...] demander à devenir membre à part entière de l'OEA;

[...] renforcer de façon systématique les liens de toute nature qui nous unissent à l'Amérique latine [...] sans pour autant devenir membre de l'OEA[55].

C'est naturellement la troisième solution qu'adopta le gouvernement[56]. Une solution qui rejetait l'adhésion à l'OEA à cause des possibles implications éventuelles sur les relations canado-américaines ainsi que sur la marge de manœuvre de la politique étrangère canadienne face aux États-Unis. Mais une solution qui minimisait également, sans qu'on le dise ouvertement, les initiatives politiques canadiennes dans les affaires du sous-continent. Ainsi, le Canada demeurait fidèle à son attitude passée consistant à ne pas trop s'impliquer politiquement afin d'éviter que certains gestes politiques n'entravent les relations économiques du pays avec la région. Néanmoins, le livre blanc de 1970 traduisait une véritable volonté gouvernementale d'accroître singulièrement la présence canadienne en Amérique latine.

Par ailleurs, et fait assez surprenant étant donné la conférence de 1966 ainsi que les événements récents de Trinidad et Tobago[57], le livre blanc ne consacrait aucun fascicule à la région des Caraïbes et n'abordait à peu près pas le sujet. C'est qu'en effet, la visite tumultueuse du gouverneur général à Trinidad et Tobago, en février 1969, avait incité le Sénat canadien à entreprendre immédiatement une analyse globale des relations du Canada avec les Antilles du Commonwealth. Et comme les résultats de l'analyse furent publiés à peu près en même temps que parut le livre blanc, on pouvait penser qu'il traduisait, jusque dans une certaine mesure, la position du gouvernement face à la politique canadienne envers les Caraïbes.

Le rapport du Sénat fut jugé, par plusieurs observateurs, comme une contribution extrêmement valable à l'étude des relations canado-antillaises[58]. Après avoir noté les changements importants survenus dans la région au cours des années 60 et leurs effets pas toujours positifs sur le plan des relations canado-antillaises, le rapport du Sénat insistait d'abord sur la nécessité pour le Canada d'accorder une priorité plus grande à la région et d'adopter à son égard une politique cohérente. Le gouvernement canadien devrait dorénavant développer ses relations avec la région sur une base multilatérale qui exigeait des consultations suivies plutôt que des décisions unilatérales teintées d'un certain paternalisme. Néanmoins, il convenait de respecter en même temps le caractère distinct et les aspirations diverses des pays composant la région. Il serait aussi approprié pour le gouvernement canadien d'adopter un comportement appuyant les transformations sociales dans la région de manière à éviter le plus possible les critiques ou jugements hostiles de la part de certains secteurs d'ici ou de là-bas face à la politique canadienne. Enfin, et de manière un peu surprenante, le rapport du Sénat recommandait au gouvernement de demeurer prêt à répondre à des propositions lui venant de la région concernant des liens économiques, voire une association politique entre le Canada et certains pays de la région[59].

En plus de ces recommandations d'ordre général, le rapport du Sénat proposait aussi un certain nombre de mesures spécifiques dans des domaines aussi variés que le tourisme, l'immigration, l'aide et le commerce. Des mesures que le gouvernement canadien, de l'avis du Sénat ainsi que de plusieurs intervenants, se devait de mettre en application s'il voulait demeurer un interlocuteur privilégié face à une région où sa marge de manœuvre, en politique étrangère, était certainement plus considérable qu'ailleurs. Car, comme le remarquera plus tard un observateur:

> Canada has no colonial past and ranks third, behind the United States and Britain, as a metropolitan economic center for the Commonwealth Caribbean. If Ottawa, therefore, is unable to maintain a close and constructive relationship with the States of the Commonwealth Caribbean, doubts arise concerning the efficacy of more general Canadian responses to present changes in the structure of the international system[60].

C'est pourquoi le gouvernement canadien avait déjà posé des gestes et continuait d'agir dans le sens des propositions formulées par le comité du Sénat. L'action la plus consistante du Canada à cet égard fut dans le domaine de l'aide publique au développement. De 1969 à 1972, en effet, le Canada fournit 20 % de l'aide totale accordée aux Antilles du Commonwealth par les pays de l'OCDE. Il devenait ainsi le deuxième contributeur le plus important après la Grande-Bretagne[61]. Sur le plan de l'aide bilatérale, le gouvernement canadien doubla pratiquement sa contribution de 1968 à 1973 alors que ces sommes furent utilisées principalement dans les secteurs de l'infrastructure portuaire et aéroportuaire, du tourisme, de l'agriculture, de l'éducation et de l'approvisionnement en eau. On accorda surtout des prêts à faible taux d'intérêt aux pays les plus développés comme la Jamaïque, la Guyane et Trinidad tandis qu'une assistance sous forme de dons fut consentie aux régions moins développées de Belize et des Îles-du-Vent et Sous-le-Vent[62].

Sur le plan multilatéral, d'autre part, l'action canadienne utilisa principalement le canal de la Banque interaméricaine de développement dont deviendront membres, à la fin des années 60, les principaux États indépendants des Caraïbes. Au milieu des années 70, la BID avait déjà prêté près de 100 millions de dollars à la Jamaïque, à la Barbade et à Trinidad, essentiellement pour des projets d'infrastructure[63].

En plus d'utiliser ces canaux traditionnels, le Canada innova quelque peu en appuyant dès le départ les efforts des pays des Caraïbes en faveur de l'intégration régionale. Cet appui, il est vrai, avait commencé avec l'octroi d'une aide financière à la Fédération des Caraïbes en 1958 mais il deviendra beaucoup plus substantiel à partir de 1969. C'est à ce moment, en effet, que le Canada deviendra l'un des deux seuls membres non régionaux (l'autre étant la Grande-Bretagne) de la Banque de développement des Caraïbes chargée d'appuyer essentiellement des projets de portée régionale. Par ce biais, le gouvernement canadien continuera naturellement à fournir son appui à l'Université des Indes occidentales mais il contribuera surtout à des organismes comme le Fonds spécial de développement ainsi que le Fonds agricole[64].

Ce comportement illustre le fait que la politique canadienne face à la région ne se faisait déjà plus à la pièce. Certaines idées maîtresses guidaient déjà l'action du Canada face aux Antilles du Commonwealth et l'une d'elles consistait à favoriser le régionalisme économique, voire politique, comme instrument principal pour assurer la croissance économique et la stabilité de l'ensemble de la région. Un régionalisme économique auquel le Canada, s'il le voulait, pouvait être associé étroitement avec les dividendes commerciaux et économiques qui pouvaient en résulter pour lui.

La politique d'aide pouvait naturellement devenir un instrument privilégié à cet égard mais elle ne se développa point sans anicroches. Car en plus des projets qui ne connurent pas une fin heureuse, la proportion importante de l'aide canadienne liée fit en sorte, à cause de l'obligation d'acheter au Canada avec tous les frais additionnels que cela comportait, que les pays de la région ne retiraient pas tous les bénéfices possibles de la contribution canadienne. D'autant plus que l'effort du Canada ne fut pas des plus soutenus puisque la part des Caraïbes du Commonwealth dans la répartition régionale des déboursés d'aide bilatérale canadienne passa de 7,2 % en 1970-1971 à 4,3 % en 1974-1975[65]. Enfin, la collaboration, un peu trop suivie aux yeux de certains, entre la Division de la coopération industrielle de l'ACDI d'une part et, de l'autre, la Société pour l'expansion des exportations et le ministère de l'Industrie et du Commerce, prêtait de plus en plus le flanc à la critique. Une des fonctions de l'aide consistait-elle, en effet, à favoriser un accroissement des ventes et des investissements canadiens dans la région?

Car le gouvernement canadien n'utilisait pas que la politique d'aide pour accroître sa présence. Il se servait aussi abondamment de la Société pour l'expansion des exportations dans sa double fonction de promotion des exportations et d'encouragement à l'investissement. La SEE remplit cette dernière fonction par le biais de son programme d'assurance-investissement[66] qui accordait, encore en 1975, une place privilégiée aux Caraïbes. En effet, 28 % des assurances contractées par la SEE à partir du début du programme, en 1971 et jusqu'en 1974, concernaient les Caraïbes du Commonwealth[67].

Et pourtant, malgré cet effort, la position du Canada dans les Caraïbes était menacée au milieu des années 70. La proportion d'aide bilatérale allouée à la région, nous l'avons vu, avait diminué essentiellement pour des impératifs de redistribution géographique. Les investissements canadiens demeuraient, pour leur part, importants. En effet, plus de 260 entreprises canadiennes avaient investi au-delà de 510 millions de dollars dans la région au début des années 70. Les principaux secteurs de concentration étaient le tourisme, l'assurance, l'industrie de la bauxite ainsi que les banques[68]. Dans ce dernier secteur, les données révèlent que les grandes banques canadiennes contrôlaient totalement le système bancaire de la région. En effet, il y avait déjà, à la fin de 1971, un nombre impressionnant de succursales de grandes banques canadiennes dans plusieurs pays des Antilles du Commonwealth[69]. Et les activités de ces banques n'étaient contrôlées en aucune façon par le gouvernement canadien alors que les législations adoptées par certains pays des Caraïbes n'avaient qu'un effet minime du fait de l'absence de concertation régionale[70]. Malgré tout, ici encore la position du Canada dans la région d'affaiblissait. Car la part des Caraïbes dans les investissements du Canada dans le tiers monde de 46,2 % qu'elle était en 1965, diminuera à 35 % en 1975 pour atteindre finalement 26,6 % deux ans plus tard[71].

Enfin, et c'était aussi un aspect alarmant pour le gouvernement canadien, la position commerciale du Canada dans la région se détériorait elle aussi gravement. Avant la guerre de 1939, en effet, les Caraïbes faisaient près de 25 % de leurs ventes à l'étranger au Canada et s'accaparaient environ 20 % de nos exportations, tandis que les chiffres respectifs pour le milieu des années 60 n'étaient plus que de 13 et 8 %[72]. Et nous avons vu que, par la suite, la conférence de 1966 n'avait pas réussi à modifier la situation. C'est ainsi que pour la période 1970-1980, les exportations canadiennes vers les Caraïbes du Commonwealth n'augmenteront que de 132 % par rapport à des augmentations de plus de 500 % pour l'Amérique latine et de 522 % pour l'ensemble des ventes canadiennes à l'étranger. La situation sera identique sur le plan des importations puisque celles en provenance des Caraïbes anglophones n'augmenteront que de 94 % par rapport à une hausse de 522 % pour l'Amérique latine et près de 400 % pour l'ensemble des achats canadiens à l'étranger[73].

Toutes ces données, et d'autres, traduisaient une situation qui n'était pas la plus favorable possible dans le cadre des relations entre le Canada et les Caraïbes du Commonwealth. Mais l'événement le plus inquiétant pour le Canada fut la signature, par les pays des Caraïbes, de l'accord de Lomé de 1975 qui garantissait à ces pays l'accès au marché européen ainsi que l'écoulement, dans des conditions meilleures que l'ancien Commonwealth Sugar Agreement, des exportations de sucre antillais. Ce fut là en quelque sorte un catalyseur majeur de la réaction canadienne. Car l'accord de Lomé, liant sur le plan commercial les Caraïbes à la CEE, diminuait l'importance du Canada dans la stratégie de diversification commerciale des pays antillais; avec toutes les conséquences que cela pouvait entraîner quant à la présence canadienne dans la région tant sur le plan des investissements que sur le plan plus largement politique, sans oublier la dimension purement stratégique que les crises pétrolières de 1973 et de 1979 allaient ramener au premier plan. Car la réorientation subséquente des achats pétroliers canadiens vers le Vénézuela d'abord et le Mexique ensuite accentuait en effet l'importance stratégique de la région pour le Canada.

Le gouvernement se devait donc de réagir, mais cette réaction ne fut pas immédiate. Elle survint quelques années plus tard alors que le Canada décida de participer plus activement, tant sur le plan politique qu'économique, au développement de la région. Cette participation prit tout d'abord la forme d'un engagement canadien au sein du Groupe des Caraïbes, créé en 1978. L'objectif essentiel du Groupe consistait à favoriser une coordination informelle entre les pays antillais et les membres non régionaux afin d'assurer le développement économique le plus rationnel et le plus efficace possible. Il convient aussi d'inscrire dans cette perspective l'Accord de coopération commerciale et économique entre le Canada et le Caricom[74], conclu en janvier 1979. Cet accord, le premier du genre à être signé par le Caricom, remplace dans les faits l'accord de 1925 et vise à fournir un cadre général appelé à régir les relations futures du Canada avec la région. Il comporte, entre autres, un protocole de coopération industrielle et il traduit, de l'aveu même du ministre canadien signataire, monsieur Jamieson, une volonté politique ferme de la part du Canada à s'impliquer plus activement dans la région[75]. Par ailleurs, la base régionale sur laquelle, selon le ministre, repose la coopération du Canada avec le Caricom, annonce déjà la politique régionale qu'adoptera le gouvernement canadien face à la région deux ans plus tard.

Une autre réaction canadienne a consisté pour le gouvernement à mettre en branle un processus de révision de la politique étrangère canadienne face aux Caraïbes du Commonwealth, dont les résultats furent soumis et discutés par le Cabinet fédéral au cours de l'année 1980. Cette réflexion permit au gouvernement d'annoncer deux décisions importantes quant à l'avenir des relations canado-antillaises et quant à l'attitude canadienne pour maintenir ou renforcer sa position. La première décision: faire des Caraïbes du Commonwealth une région prioritaire non seulement du point de vue de la politique d'aide mais aussi dans l'ensemble de la politique étrangère canadienne. La deuxième: adopter une approche politique régionale face à cette région[76]. Selon le ministre MacGuigan, c'était la première fois dans l'histoire de la politique étrangère canadienne que le gouvernement adoptait une telle politique régionale qui «tourne principalement autour de la coopération économique [...] mais prévoit également un renforcement des liens politiques et sociaux»[77].

Le Canada a donc choisi de réagir à un affaiblissement de sa performance économique dans les Caraïbes du Commonwealth par une intensification de ses relations politiques et économiques en particulier sur le plan régional. Pour certains, l'option fondamentale de la politique étrangère canadienne face à la région consiste à choisir entre une attitude et un comportement indépendants ou une participation subordonnée à la position américaine[78]. À cet égard, l'attitude canadienne face au plan des Caraïbes[79], proposé par le président Carter en novembre 1979 et repris et aménagé par l'administration républicaine depuis, pourra être déterminante. Jusqu'ici, le plan n'a suscité que des commentaires mitigés. Certains lui reprochent d'être une initiative mal planifiée[80] tandis que d'autres l'accusent de constituer purement et simplement une tentative de faire de la Jamaïque du nouveau premier ministre Seaga une vitrine du libéralisme économique proposé à l'ensemble de la région[81]. Le Canada s'est jusqu'à maintenant montré très prudent face à ce plan, allant même jusqu'à manifester son hostilité à une utilisation idéologique face à certains pays de la région. Reste à voir ce qui se produira dans le proche avenir. Il n'y a pas de doute, en tout cas, que les Caraïbes du Commonwealth demeurent une région importante pour le Canada non seulement sur le plan stratégique, mais aussi, et plus fondamentalement, quant au statut de semi-périphérie que le Canada cherche à maintenir au sein du système mondial.

Cela dit, nous avons mentionné précédemment que le livre blanc de 1970 constituait une manifestation de la volonté politique du gouvernement canadien d'accroître ses relations avec l'Amérique latine et même d'en faire une région prioritaire pour l'application de la troisième option. Il nous reste maintenant à préciser quels instruments ont été utilisés à cette fin de même qu'à apprécier les résultats obtenus.

D'abord, les intentions du livre blanc n'ont pas tardé à se traduire en gestes concrets. La première mesure d'importance fut sans contredit la création, dès 1971, du Bureau pour les affaires de l'hémisphère occidentale avec une Division de l'Amérique latine. Si l'on voulait en effet développer la politique étrangère canadienne face à l'Amérique latine, il fallait au moins un instrument approprié pour en assurer une coordination efficace. Puis le Canada entreprit, peu après, de poser certains gestes afin de démontrer aux Latino-Américains son intérêt réel pour la région. C'est ainsi qu'en 1972, il demanda et obtint le statut d'observateur permanent à l'OEA. La même année, il deviendra membre de l'Institut interaméricain de la santé. Et en 1972 toujours, il deviendra membre de la Banque interaméricaine de développement, ce qui constituera un geste stratégique puisque, comme le remarque un observateur, le Canada se trouvera ainsi placé au cœur de la prise de décision économique en ce qui concerne le développement de l'Amérique latine[82]. Ce qui ne sera pas sans importance eu égard à l'intérêt accordé par le Canada au commerce, à l'aide et aux investissements dans ses relations avec la région. Enfin, le gouvernement canadien ne manquera pas d'utiliser un ensemble d'instruments dans le domaine de l'aide, du commerce, des investissements ainsi que dans le secteur politique proprement dit.

Le Canada a utilisé sa politique d'aide à l'Amérique latine en procédant essentiellement par le biais de quatre canaux. Sur le plan multilatéral, il est bien évident que les organismes internationaux comme le groupe de la Banque mondiale, où le Canada est présent, accordent une part parfois importante de leurs fonds à l'Amérique latine. Mais le gouvernement canadien a plutôt choisi de fournir des fonds par le biais de la Banque interaméricaine de développement à laquelle il avait contribué pour plus d'un milliard de dollars à la fin de 1981[83]. Le choix de la BID comme canal principal d'aide multilatérale s'explique aisément si l'on tient compte qu'il s'agit là d'un lieu stratégique pour la circulation d'informations économiques concernant l'Amérique latine et aussi parce que l'apport canadien peut être plus facilement identifié, et donc apprécié, par les pays de la région.

Le deuxième canal utilisé par le gouvernement canadien passe par les organisations non gouvernementales pour lesquelles l'ACDI souscrit un financement appréciable pour la réalisation de nombreux projets locaux. De façon générale, l'aide fournie par ces organismes est celle qui est la mieux perçue de la part des bénéficiaires qui considèrent les projets mieux adaptés à leurs besoins. Enfin, l'aide canadienne passe aussi par les ambassades qui peuvent chacune consacrer jusqu'à 200 000 $ par année au financement de projets modestes certes mais néanmoins utiles pour l'image du Canada dans les pays concernés[84].

Malgré tout, la forme d'aide la plus significative demeure l'aide bilatérale. C'est en effet celle-là que le gouvernement peut le mieux contrôler et qu'il peut faire servir parfois à des objectifs de politique étrangère. À cet égard, il convient de noter que si la proportion d'aide bilatérale canadienne accordée à l'Amérique latine demeure nettement inférieure à celle fournie à l'Afrique et à l'Asie, il n'en reste pas moins que cette proportion a presque doublé depuis dix ans, passant de 3,4 % en 1970-1971 à 5,8 % en 1979-1980. Depuis le milieu des années 70, l'Amérique latine est devenue la troisième région en importance du point de vue de l'aide bilatérale canadienne, dépassant les Caraïbes du Commonwealth[85]. Mais le point vraiment essentiel de l'aide bilatérale envers l'Amérique latine concerne la Division de la coopération industrielle de l'ACDI qui joue un rôle non négligeable du point de vue de la promotion des exportations de produits manufacturés canadiens ainsi que de celui du développement des entreprises-conseils[86]. Il apparaît en effet que l'Amérique latine a été et demeure une région cible autant pour la Division de la coopération industrielle que pour la Division de l'industrie et des affaires qui l'a précédée[87]. C'est donc dire que l'Amérique latine constitue une zone privilégiée dans la stratégie canadienne qui utilise certains secteurs de l'ACDI pour mousser les ventes de produits finis canadiens.

L'encouragement aux investissements directs à l'étranger est un autre domaine d'action du gouvernement canadien afin d'accroître sa présence en Amérique latine. Un encouragement qui a pris essentiellement deux formes. La première fut de laisser une liberté d'action complète aux entreprises canadiennes présentes sur les marchés internationaux en ne soumettant leurs activités à aucun contrôle gouvernemental et en adoptant une attitude réservée face aux propositions d'établir un code de conduite pour les entreprises transnationales. La deuxième méthode, plus interventionniste, a été de mettre sur pied, dans le cadre de la SEE, un programme d'assurance-investissement offert principalement aux entreprises canadiennes présentes dans le tiers monde. Le programme vise surtout à permettre aux entreprises canadiennes de maintenir une position concurrentielle face aux entreprises des autres pays industrialisés profitant d'avantages similaires de même qu'à favoriser la croissance industrielle au Canada et dans les pays hôtes. La valeur des investissements assurés n'a cessé de croître depuis 1974 et l'Amérique latine occupe la première place quant à la localisation géographique de ceux-ci. C'est ainsi qu'en 1978, par exemple, la région s'appropriait environ 30 % des investissements assurés par rapport à 26 % pour le Moyen-Orient et moins de 10 % partout ailleurs, sauf en Afrique de l'Ouest[88]. C'est encore une fois souligner l'importance de l'Amérique latine dans ce secteur de l'action gouvernementale canadienne.

Mais il est un secteur où le gouvernement du Canada intervient encore plus: celui du commerce, ou plus précisément des exportations. Le ministère de l'Industrie et du Commerce joue naturellement un rôle important à cet égard avec des programmes comme la promotion des marchés d'exportation et le développement de l'industrie de la défense en plus de l'action continue des agents commerciaux présents dans chacune des ambassades canadiennes. Mais c'est encore la SEE qui constitue l'instrument d'action le plus révélateur de l'attitude et des intentions gouvernementales. Au seul chapitre du financement à l'exportation[89], l'Amérique latine a devancé, pour la période 1971-1980, toutes les régions du monde à l'exception de l'Asie avec plus de 2,5 milliards de dollars mis à sa disposition[90]. Parmi les principaux pays bénéficiaires de la région, on note le Mexique (1,1 milliard de dollars), l'Argentine (427 millions), Panama (268 millions), le Brésil (265), le Pérou (149) et le Vénézuela (121 millions de dollars).

Sur le plan du commerce, le gouvernement canadien n'a pas négligé d'appuyer un organisme qui a pris de plus en plus d'importance quant au renforcement des échanges économiques entre le Canada et l'Amérique latine. Que ce soit par des subventions du ministère des Affaires extérieures, du ministère de l'Industrie et du Commerce ou encore de l'ACDI, le gouvernement a fourni un appui constant à la CALA (Canadian Association for Latin America), un regroupement d'hommes d'affaires intéressés à des contacts suivis avec l'Amérique latine. La CALA, créée en 1969 à l'instigation de la Brascan[91], voulait contribuer à l'amélioration des contacts entre les hommes d'affaires du Canada et de la région par la mise sur pied de comités mixtes ainsi que par l'organisation de séminaires et de conférences annuelles. La philosophie de l'organisme était que le Canada ne développe ses échanges commerciaux avec l'Amérique latine que s'il augmente au départ ses investissements dans la région[92]. L'organisme, dont le nombre de membres est passé de 62 en 1970 à 141 en 1977, est devenu un acteur important non seulement dans l'accroissement des contacts entre hommes d'affaires mais aussi à titre de groupe de pression au niveau de l'élaboration de la politique canadienne face à l'Amérique latine. Ce qu'attestent les échanges d'information et les contacts de plus en plus fréquents entre la CALA et plusieurs organismes gouvernementaux[93].

Enfin, le quatrième canal d'intervention gouvernementale pour accroître la présence canadienne an Amérique latine fut le secteur politique proprement dit. En plus de la mise sur pied de nombreux comités mixtes et de la signature d'accords multiples, le gouvernement a particulièrement mis à profit le mécanisme des missions et des visites. Depuis la mission Sharp de 1968, plusieurs ministres du gouvernement ont en effet dirigé de nombreuses missions commerciales et autres dans différents pays d'Amérique latine. Et le premier ministre lui-même a apporté son concours en visitant la région en particulier en 1976 et en 1979[94]. En fait, de 1973 à 1977, l'Amérique latine (principalement le Mexique, le Brésil, le Vénézuela et Cuba) a reçu 25 missions canadiennes et elle fut la région à recevoir le plus fort pourcentage de visites de 1968 à 1980, à l'exception de l'Europe de l'Ouest[95].

Ce qui précède montre jusqu'à quel point la dernière décennie a été la plus active dans l'histoire des relations du Canada avec l'Amérique latine depuis les années 1895-1905[96]. Cela montre aussi à quel point le gouvernement n'a pas lésiné sur les moyens de concrétiser les vœux exprimés dans le livre blanc de 1970 et d'accroître la présence canadienne en Amérique latine. Il reste maintenant à nous tourner vers les résultats obtenus au prix de ces efforts afin d'apprécier jusqu'à quel point l'Amérique latine a servi, comme nous l'avons suggéré précédemment, de zone principale d'application pour la stratégie de troisième option.

Les résultats les plus significatifs de l'action canadienne en Amérique latine concernent le commerce et les investissements directs. Pour ce qui est des exportations canadiennes, on aura tôt fait de remarquer que la part de l'Amérique latine n'a guère varié depuis le début des années 60 puisqu'elle s'est maintenue, depuis lors, autour de 4,5 %[97]. C'est à partir de ce chiffre uniquement que l'on n'hésite pas, le plus souvent, à minimiser l'importance de l'Amérique latine dans le commerce extérieur canadien et en même temps à remettre en question les progrès canadiens dans la région sur ce plan.

Pourtant, une lecture attentive des séries statistiques révèle des faits intéressants et prometteurs pour le futur du commerce canadien avec cette région. C'est ainsi, par exemple, que l'on remarque, pour l'année 1980, que l'Amérique latine détient le premier rang parmi les régions du tiers monde pour ce qui est du volume des exportations canadiennes[98]. Qui plus est, et c'est encore plus révélateur, au cours de la période 1971-1975, plus de 63 % des exportations canadiennes vers l'Amérique latine sont le fait de produits manufacturés (le total le plus élevé de toutes les régions du monde) tandis que la région, à elle seule, s'accapare, de 1966 à 1975, plus de 50 % des exportations canadiennes de produits manufacturés dans le tiers monde[99]. On est en mesure, par conséquent, d'apprécier le rôle crucial de l'Amérique latine à titre de marché pour l'écoulement de produits manufacturés canadiens.

Les statistiques sont encore plus probantes en ce qui concerne les investissements directs du Canada à l'étranger. À cet égard, il convient d'abord de remarquer que le taux d'augmentation annuel des investissements directs nets du secteur privé canadien a été de près de 30 % de 1970 à 1976, classant ainsi le Canada au deuxième rang des pays de l'OCDE derrière la Belgique[100]. Par ailleurs, une proportion sans cesse croissante de ces investissements est allée vers le tiers monde alors que la part des investissements canadiens dans les pays sous-développés a atteint 24 % en 1976[101]. Enfin, il importe de noter que les investissements du Canada à l'étranger ne sont plus principalement le fait de filiales d'entreprises étrangères établies au pays. C'est ainsi qu'en 1974, 85 % directs du Canada dans le tiers monde furent des investissements sous contrôle canadien[102], ce qui traduit bien la maturation du capitalisme canadien.

Encore une fois, l'Amérique latine joue un rôle important en ce domaine et plus encore, peut-être, qu'en ce qui a trait aux exportations. En effet, de 1970 à 1977, la région a reçu plus de 50 % de tous les investissements canadiens dirigés vers le tiers monde[103]. Bien sûr, plus de la moitié des investissements canadiens en Amérique latine sont concentrés au Brésil, mais il reste que les entreprises canadiennes ont maintenant des filiales dans tous les pays de la région dont les principaux demeurent le Brésil, l'Argentine, le Mexique, Panama et le Vénézuela. Il est intéressant de constater enfin que les investissements canadiens dans la région sont concentrés essentiellement dans le secteur des mines, de l'alimentation, des services de même que dans le secteur manufacturier[104].

C'est donc dire que l'Amérique latine a occupé, depuis la fin des années 60 et continuera à occuper une position stratégique dans les relations extérieures du Canada tant sur le plan commercial que dans le domaine des investissements. Et ce ne sont pas là, malgré ce qu'on pourrait penser, des éléments mineurs de la politique étrangère canadienne. Car, comme le rappelait Thomas Bata, les investissements précèdent généralement le commerce et contribuent à le développer. Le commerce à son tour (et plus particulièrement les exportations) contribue à la croissance économique[105], qui elle-même permet d'améliorer la marge de manœuvre du Canada en politique étrangère. C'est en ce sens, par conséquent, que l'Amérique latine a plus que toute autre région du tiers monde, joué un rôle important dans la stratégie canadienne de troisième option.

Cela dit, il n'y a pas que la tentative d'utilisation coordonnée de certains instruments de politique étrangère qui a caractérisé l'action canadienne face à l'Amérique latine depuis 1968. Il y a aussi la méthode qui a changé. Bien sûr, le Canada n'a jamais véritablement utilisé une approche multilatérale dans ses relations avec l'Amérique latine comme ce fut le cas au niveau de l'ensemble de sa politique étrangère de l'après-guerre et jusqu'à la fin des années 60. Mais est-ce à dire que le Canada n'a pas introduit une dimension régionale dans ses relations avec l'Amérique latine ainsi que l'affirmait le ministre MacGuigan en mars 1980[106]? Et qu'en est-il véritablement de «l'approche bilatérale» qu'il annonçait un an plus tard[107]?

Il est important, croyons-nous, d'éviter la confusion entre les termes «multilatéral», «bilatéral» et «régional». Une politique multilatérale aurait consisté pour le Canada à développer ses relations avec l'Amérique latine en utilisant le canal privilégié de l'OEA ou plus largement le système interaméricain, ou encore en procédant par le biais de l'ALALC ou du SELA par exemple. Il est tout à fait manifeste que ce n'est pas là la voie que le gouvernement canadien a décidé de suivre depuis 1945. Par ailleurs, la politique bilatérale, dont certains n'hésitent pas à prétendre qu'elle constitue depuis toujours la politique officielle canadienne envers l'Amérique latine[108], implique que l'on oriente ses relations avec chacun des pays pris séparément et sans trop tenir compte, généralement, de ce qui se produit chez le voisin. Ce qui n'a pas été, depuis 1970 au moins, la politique canadienne face à l'Amérique latine. Enfin, une politique régionale est celle où un pays développe ses relations avec une région géographique donnée (l'Amérique latine, par exemple) en la considérant dans son ensemble, en tenant compte de la stratification du pouvoir politique, économique et militaire qu'on y retrouve et en étant conscient des relations de dépendance et de domination qui peuvent exister entre les pays de cette région. Une telle politique implique naturellement des relations privilégiées avec les États dominants mais aussi une action bilatérale envers les autres pays, conditionnée cependant par les relations privilégiées entretenues avec les acteurs dominants et compte tenu des intérêts que nous y avons.

Par conséquent, l'approche globale que demandent, dans leur rapport de 1981, Dosman, North et Rocha[109] et la nouvelle approche de «bilatéralisme concentré» amorcée par le ministre MacGuigan en janvier de la même année[110] constituent, en fait, deux versions d'une seule et même politique qui paraît avoir été appliquée depuis 1970. Il nous semble en effet que le gouvernement canadien, depuis l'arrivée au pouvoir du gouvernement Trudeau, a tenté essentiellement d'esquisser et de mettre en application une politique régionale face à l'Amérique latine.

Car les données, dont nous avons fait état jusqu'ici, confirment que le Canada, depuis les années 60, oriente ses relations essentiellement vers les trois «puissances régionales»[111] que sont le Brésil, le Mexique et le Vénézuela. Le Brésil parce qu'il domine le Cône Sud, le Mexique à cause de l'influence qu'il exerce en Amérique centrale[112] et le Vénézuela pour son rôle dominant dans les Andes et dans les Caraïbes. Par conséquent, la décision prise en 1981 par le Cabinet fédéral (sur la base de rapports encore confidentiels) d'établir un choix de pays de concentration vers lesquels le Canada orientera dorénavant ses relations[113] ne fait qu'entériner, en ce qui concerne l'Amérique latine, une situation qui paraît exister depuis déjà plus de dix ans.

Mais la politique régionale n'implique pas seulement l'établissement de relations privilégiées avec des puissances régionales. Elle suppose aussi l'articulation des relations avec les autres pays de la région en fonction de ces relations privilégiées. Et c'est ce que semble aussi avoir fait le Canada en Amérique latine, comme en fait foi la réaction canadienne aux événements qui se sont produits au Chili à partir de 1970. Il y a tout lieu de penser en effet que le gouvernement canadien a usé de deux poids, deux mesures dans ses relations avec le Chili sous Allende et sous Pinochet. On fait régulièrement état, bien sûr, du refus canadien de faire servir la BID dans le cadre des représailles américaines face aux nationalisations du gouvernement Allende en 1973[114], mais on feint d'ignorer la diminution des relations politiques et économiques du Canada avec ce gouvernement alors que, pourtant, elles sont redevenues au beau fixe avec le gouvernement Pinochet[115]. Ce comportement canadien doit-il être mis en relation avec l'attitude des autorités brésiliennes face au Chili d'Allende de même qu'avec les intérêts canadiens au Brésil? Plusieurs raisons donnent à y penser et devront cependant être vérifiées dans le cadre d'analyses plus approfondies[116]. Il n'en demeure pas moins que de nombreux indices tendent à indiquer que, non seulement dans le Cône Sud mais ailleurs en Amérique latine, le Canada a posé et pose encore des gestes qui orientent sa politique dans le sens d'une approche régionale.

CONCLUSION

Tout au long de ce travail, nous nous sommes efforcé de faire ressortir ce qui nous est apparu comme les traits fondamentaux du comportement canadien dans l'histoire des relations du Canada avec l'Amérique latine et les Caraïbes. Ce qui frappe le plus l'observateur à ce sujet, c'est comment l'action du Canada face à l'Amérique latine a été en quelque sorte conditionnée par le statut du Canada au sein du système mondial. En effet, le gouvernement canadien n'a véritablement commencé à s'intéresser à l'Amérique latine qu'à la fin des années 60 alors que des transformations structurelles au sein du système mondial ont commencé à menacer le statut de pays semi-périphérique du Canada. Ce n'est qu'à ce moment que l'on s'est tourné vers l'Amérique latine pour s'en servir comme une sorte d'instrument, ainsi qu'on avait déjà tenté de le faire en 1866 et en 1940, afin de diversifier ses relations économiques dans le but d'accroître sa marge de manœuvre en politique étrangère et de s'adapter aux transformations du système. L'action canadienne envers les Antilles anglophones fut, à cet égard, de nature différente à cause de la «relation spéciale» qui unit jusqu'à récemment le Canada à cette région étant donné leur appartenance commune au Commonwealth.

Cette différence de nature dans les relations du Canada avec l'une et l'autre régions est le deuxième point qui retient l'attention. Car l'effritement de la «relation spéciale» dont nous venons de parler ainsi que la dégradation des relations économiques entre le Canada et les Caraïbes ont obligé le gouvernement canadien à s'engager de plus en plus sur la voie d'une intervention politique qui a amené les autorités fédérales à adopter une approche globale par le biais de laquelle le Canada a promis de soutenir les efforts du Caricom dans l'espoir d'un rétablissement de sa position économique dans la région. À l'inverse, cependant, l'intervention politique du Canada en Amérique latine fut toujours maintenue au minimum et a constamment été subordonnée aux impératifs commerciaux et plus largement économiques.

Malgré tout, l'Amérique latine a continué à jouer un rôle des plus stratégiques dans la politique canadienne de troisième option. Et c'est en partie afin de réaliser l'objectif de diversification qu'implique la troisième option que le gouvernement canadien a semblé avoir incorporé une dimension régionale à sa vision et à son comportement face à l'Amérique latine. Dimension régionale qui l'a amené à privilégier le Brésil, le Mexique et le Vénézuela dans ses relations avec la région mais qui l'a obligé aussi à orienter son action vers les autres pays d'Amérique latine en fonction de ses liens avec les puissances régionales.

Cela dit, il faut bien constater que les relations du Canada avec l'Amérique latine et les Caraïbes ont connu un creux ces dernières années. Depuis 1982, en effet, on remarque un affaiblissement des relations commerciales et économiques qu'explique, bien entendu, la récente crise économique internationale qui a obligé chaque pays à se tourner vers lui-même pour éviter le pire et tenter de protéger les acquis.

Pour le moment, les dirigeants canadiens semblent plus préoccupés par l'avenir de nos relations avec les États-Unis. Mais avec ou sans libre-échange, le Canada ne pourra pas se permettre de ne pas être présent dans chacune des grandes régions du monde.

Il faudra donc réactiver les relations avec l'Amérique latine et les Caraïbes. Des thèmes importants continueront, bien sûr, de retenir l'attention, tels l'énergie et le pétrole, la prolifération des armes, les problèmes financiers et économiques ainsi que les questions de sécurité et de stabilité dans le Cône Sud, dans les Caraïbes et en Amérique centrale[117].

C'est dans cette dernière région, d'ailleurs, où la diplomatie canadienne est apparue la plus active ces dernières années sans toutefois qu'il en résulte une politique parfaitement claire et cohérente. Ce qui se comprend dans la mesure où le gouvernement canadien y marche un peu sur une corde raide, étant donné que toute prise de position tranchée, dans un sens ou dans l'autre, ne sera pas sans conséquence pour l'avenir de la politique canadienne en Amérique latine aussi bien que pour les relations à venir entre le Canada et les États-Unis. C'est sans doute ce qui explique l'attitude de prudence de la fin du régime Trudeau bien que soit apparu, lors des derniers mois de ce gouvernement, un net rapprochement entre les positions canadiennes et celles des pays membres du Groupe de Contadora.

Tout compte fait, il y a tout lieu de penser, cependant, que l'attitude canadienne face à ces problèmes, de même que par rapport à d'autres qui ne manqueront pas de surgir, continuera à être évaluée et, dans une bonne mesure, conditionnée par ce fait fondamental de l'importance nouvelle de la région dans la stratégie canadienne d'adaptation aux transformations structurelles du système mondial.

NOTES

1. L'Organisation des États américains, groupant l'ensemble des républiques américaines, a été créée en 1948. Elle a pris la relève de la défunte Union panaméricaine mise sur pied, elle aussi, à l'instigation des États-Unis.

2. Le document qui lança la troisième option est un texte du ministre des Affaires extérieures d'alors, Mitchell Sharp, paru dans la revue *Perspectives Internationales*. Voir M. Sharp, «Canada-US Relations: Options for the Future», *International Perspectives*, automne 1972.

3. Sur les analyses faites à partir de la perspective du système mondial, voir, entre autres, I. Wallerstein, *The Modern World-System*, New York, Academic Press, 1976. Voir aussi du même auteur *The Capitalist World-Economy*, Cambridge/Paris, Cambridge University Press/Éditions de la Maison des Sciences de l'Homme, 1979, ainsi que *The Modern World-System II*, New York, Academic Press, 1980. Dans le domaine plus spécifique des études sur la politique étrangère, voir Ch.W. Kegley, Jr. et P. McGowan, eds, *The Political Economy of Foreign Policy Behavior*, vol. 6, Beverly Hills, Sage International Yearbook of Foreign Policy Studies, Sage Publications, 1981.

4. R. Pomfret, *The Economic Development of Canada*, Toronto, Methuen, 1981, p. 14.

5. Ceci vaut également pour les pays latino-américains ayant acquis l'indépendance politique dans les années 1810-1820. Voir sur ce point S. Stein et B. Stein, *L'Héritage colonial de l'Amérique latine*, Paris, Maspero, 1974 ainsi que G. Martinière, *Les Amériques latines, une histoire économique*, Paris, Presses universitaires de Grenoble, 1978.

6. C'est ainsi que l'utilité économique du Canada pour l'ensemble du système mondial s'est d'abord traduite par la fourniture de poissons, de fourrures et de bois, et ensuite par l'approvisionnement en matières premières plus diversifiées. Ce qui, naturellement, n'a pas été sans conséquences majeures pour l'ensemble du développement économique canadien. Voir à cet égard Pomfret, *op. cit.*, chap. 2 et 5 en particulier.

7. Sur ce point, voir R. Tremblay, «La politique commerciale et le développement du Canada», dans P. Painchaud, éd., *Le Canada et le Québec sur la scène internationale*, Québec/Montréal, CQRI/Presses de l'Université du Québec, 1977, p. 182 et s.

8. Chiffres de Statistique Canada compilés par R. Tremblay. *Ibidem*, p. 187.

9. Comprenant les investissements directs de l'étranger ainsi que les investissements de portefeuille.

10. Chiffres tirés de Pomfret, *op. cit.*, p. 62.

11. La mission s'était en fait scindée en deux à son arrivée dans les Caraïbes, le premier groupe visitant le Brésil tandis que le second demeurait dans les Antilles.

12. Sur le sujet, voir J.C.M. Ogelsby, *Gringos From the Far North*, Toronto, Macmillan, 1976, chap. I.

13. La part des Caraïbes dans le commerce extérieur canadien n'a jamais dépassé 2 %, selon Levitt et McIntyre. Voir K. Levitt et A. McIntyre, *Canada-West Indies Economic Relations*, Montréal, Center for Developing Area Studies, McGill University, 1967, p. 13.

14. *Ibidem*, p. 14 et s.

15. C'est du moins l'opinion de Ogelsby. Sur ce sujet que nous ne pouvons malheureusement traiter en plus d'un paragraphe, voir Ogelsby, *op. cit.*, chap. 8 à 11. Pour les Caraïbes, voir Robert Chodos, *The Caribbean Connection*, Toronto, James Lorimer and Co., 1977, chap. 12.

16. Sur cette période du commerce canadien avec l'Amérique latine, voir A.L. Neal, «Canada's Trade Ties with Latin America», *Canadian Geographical Journal*, vol. XXXI, n° 2, août 1945, p. 79-95.

17. Voir Levitt et McIntyre, *op. cit.*, chap. 2.

18. R.J. Alexander et W. Singer, «Canadian Investments in Latin America», *Inter-American Economic Affairs*, vol. IV, n° 4, printemps 1951, p. 73-82. Ces derniers, reprenant les chiffres de McKay et Rogers, estimaient à 200 millions de dollars les investissements canadiens en Amérique latine en 1948.

19. *Ibidem*, p. 78.

20. Voir sur l'ensemble de ce sujet Levitt et McIntyre, *op. cit.*, p. 24-27, Ogelsby, *op. cit.*, chap. IV ainsi que *ibidem*, p. 73-82.

21. Pour une définition de ce terme, voir les références indiquées à la note 3.

22. Pomfret, *op. cit.*, p. 122.

23. Le chiffre est de 50 % si l'on inclut la production manufacturière dans les secteurs de l'énergie, de la construction et des mines.

24. Sur le sujet, voir D.R. Murray, «Canada's First Diplomatic Missions in Latin America», *Journal of Interamerican Studies and World Affairs*, vol. 16, n° 2, mai 1974, p. 154 et s. ainsi que Ogelsby, *op. cit.*, chap. 2.

25. La mission quitta le Canada en décembre 1940 mais dut revenir assez rapidement à la suite de problèmes de santé éprouvés par le ministre. Elle repartit pour un périple plus long à l'automne 1941.

26. Murray, *loc. cit.*, p. 161-162.

27. J.C.M. Ogelsby, «Canada and Latin America», dans P.V. Lyon et T.Y. Ismael, éd., *Canada and the Third World*, Toronto, Macmillan, 1976, p. 169.

28. Murray, *loc. cit.*, p. 168-169.

29. La mission commerciale de 1953, sous la direction du ministre C.D. Howe, ne dérogera guère au *pattern* des missions précédentes en ce qu'elle ne suscitera que peu de retombées commerciales.

30. Ogelsby, «Canada and Latin America», *op. cit.*, p. 178.

31. Les relations diplomatiques du Canada avec cette sous-région seront complétées avec l'ouverture de l'ambassade canadienne au Costa-Rica en 1964.

32. On se rappellera l'épisode du siège laissé vacant en prévision du moment prochain, pensait-on, où le Canada se joindrait à l'organisme.

33. En réponse à une question sur la position canadienne face à un *membership* éventuel du Canada au sein de l'Union panaméricaine, le sous-ministre Skelton avait énoncé, en avril 1940, ce qui allait être l'attitude officieuse d'Ottawa pour les années à venir: «The one general statement that might perhaps be made [...] is that *we refrain carefully from becoming involved in any political commitment.*» Cité dans Ogelsby, *Gringos* [...], p. 50. Nous soulignons. L'analyse des événements montre que cet énoncé était valable pour l'ensemble des problèmes politiques en Amérique latine et que rien ne permet de constater un changement véritable de politique à cet égard depuis lors.

34. *Ibidem*, p. 49 et s.

35. Sur ce sujet de la participation canadienne au système interaméricain, voir Ogelsby, *Canada* [...], p. 174 et s. Voir aussi, entre autres, J.I.P. Humphrey, *The Inter-American System: A Canadian View*, Toronto, Macmillan, 1942, M. Roussin, *Le Canada et le système interaméricain*, Ottawa, Éd. de l'Université d'Ottawa, 1959 et J.D. Harbron, *Canada and the Organization of American States*, Montréal, Private Planning Association, 1963.

36. Qui comprenait alors la Jamaïque, Trinidad et Tobago, la Barbade, Antigua, St. Kitts-Nevis, Montserrat, Grenade, la Dominique, Sainte-Lucie et Saint-Vincent.

37. H. MacQuarrie, «Canada and the Caribbean», dans Lyon et Ismael, *op. cit.*, p. 211.

38. Avec la Jamaïque ainsi que Trinidad et Tobago en 1963 et avec la Guyanne en 1964. Des liens officiels seront aussi établis avec Haïti dès 1963 et par la suite avec la Barbade en 1973.

39. Levitt et McIntyre, *op. cit.*, p. 15 et s.

40. H. Brewster, «Canada and the West Indies: Some Issues in International Economic Relations», *Journal of Canadian Studies*, 11, août 1967, p. 28.

41. Sur le sujet, voir Macquarrie, *op. cit.*, p. 212 ainsi que Levitt et McIntyre, *op. cit.*, p. 27-30.

42. Levitt et McIntyre, *ibidem*, p. 125.

43. C.I. Bradford, Jr. et C. Pestieau, *Canada and Latin America: The Potential for Partnership*, Montréal, Private Planning Association et Canadian Association for Latin America, 1971, p. xv et 87.

44. *Ibidem*, p. 84 et s.

45. Voir, entre autres, Ogelsby, *Gringos* [...], *op. cit.*, p. 62.

46. La période couverte par cette étude se termine au moment de la victoire du gouvernement conservateur au Canada en septembre 1984.

47. Voir à ce sujet K. Levitt, *La Capitulation tranquille*, Montréal, Réédition Québec, 1972. Les filiales d'entreprises étrangères ont un impact plus considérable sur différents secteurs de l'économie que d'autres formes d'investissements étrangers et rendent plus difficile, de ce fait, le contrôle gouvernemental sur l'économie d'un pays.

48. Voir D. Godfrey et M. Watkins, éd., *Gordon to Watkins to You*, Toronto, New Press, 1970, p. 9 et s.

49. Sur ce point particulier et sur ses conséquences quant à la restructuration de l'économie canadienne et à la nécessaire mise en place de nouveaux instruments d'intervention économique de l'État canadien, voir P. Resnick, *The Maturing of Canadian Capitalism*, texte soumis à la réunion annuelle de l'Association canadienne de science politique de juin 1982, miméo. Voir aussi R. Hudon, *De la gérance de l'intégration continentale au redéploiement de l'économie canadienne*, thèse de doctorat non publiée. Queen's University, 1981.

50. Budget d'au-delà d'un milliard de dollars annuellement dans les années 1970.

51. Voir en particulier R. Clarke et R. Swift, éd., *Ties That Bind: Canada and the Third World*, Toronto, Between the Lines, 1982 ainsi que R. Carty et V. Smith, *Perpetuating Poverty*, Toronto, Between the Lines, 1981.

52. *Le Devoir*, 12 janvier 1982.

53. La stratégie de troisième option favorisait au départ la CEE et le Japon comme cibles privilégiées pour la réalisation de la politique de diversification. À partir du milieu des années 70, cependant, il apparut que l'Amérique latine, l'Asie et l'ensemble des pays semi-industrialisés plus particulièrement constituaient des cibles plus indiquées.

54. Sur la mission de 1968, voir Ogelsby, *Gringos* [...], *op. cit.*, p. 30-36.

55. J.J. Guy, «Canada and Latin America», *The World Today*, XXXII, octobre 1976, p. 377. Ailleurs, le même auteur défend l'idée que le gouvernement canadien a modifié fondamentalement sa politique étrangère depuis 1968. À une politique d'adoption par préservation aurait succédé depuis lors une politique d'adoption par promotion dans le cadre de laquelle l'Amérique latine serait appelée à jouer un rôle important comme marché alternatif à l'Europe de l'Ouest et au Commonwealth pour l'écoulement des exportations canadiennes. Voir J.J. Guy, *Canada's External Relations with Latin America: environment, process and prospects,* thèse de doctorat non publiée, St-Louis University, 1975.

56. *Politique étrangère au service des Canadiens, l'Amérique latine,* Ottawa, Imprimeur de la Reine, 1970, p. 21. Voir aussi Ogelsby, «Canada and Latin America», *op. cit.,* p. 182-183.

57. Répondant en cela à certaines suggestions, dont celle de ne pas adhérer à l'OEA, faites par des coopérants et missionnaires oblats canadiens. Voir *Mémoire sur la politique extérieure du Canada envers l'Amérique latine,* Montréal, s.l., 1970.

58. L'arrestation et le passage en jugement d'étudiants de Trinidad et Tobago à la suite de la destruction de l'ordinateur principal de l'Université Sir George Williams de Montréal en 1968 fut en partie responsable de la réception hostile que reçut, en février 1969, le gouverneur général du Canada lors de son passage à Port-of-Spain. Les mêmes événements servirent en partie de prétextes aux émeutes qui eurent lieu un an plus tard dans la capitale alors que furent saccagées les vitrines de banques et de commerces canadiens actifs dans ce pays.

59. MacQuarrie, *op. cit.,* p. 225.

60. Voir *Senate Report of the Standing Committee on Foreign Affairs of the Senate of Canada on Canada-Caribbean Relations,* Ottawa, Imprimeur de la Reine, p. 19. Voir aussi *ibidem,* p. 226 et s.

61. G.R. Berry, «The West Indies in Canadian External Relations: Present Trends and Future Prospects», *Canadian Public Policy*, vol. III, nº 1, hiver 1977, p. 51.

62. *Ibidem,* p. 57.

63. Sur l'aide canadienne aux Caraïbes anglophones, voir *ibidem,* p. 57-59, Chodos, *op. cit.,* chap. 11, ainsi que R.R. Paragg, «Canadian Aid in the Commonwealth Caribbean: Neo-Colonialism or Development?», *Canadian Public Policy,* vol. III, nº 4, automne 1980, p. 628-641.

64. Chodos, *ibidem,* p. 196.

65. K. Levitt, «La politique Caraïbes du Canada, rapport au Sous-comité du Comité permanent des affaires extérieures et de la défense nationale», dans Sous-comité du Comité permanent des affaires extérieures et de la défense nationale, *Les relations du Canada avec l'Amérique latine et les Antilles,* fascicule nº 22, Ottawa, Imprimeur de la Reine, 1982, p. 697.

66. Une entreprise canadienne investissant dans le tiers monde peut se prévaloir de cette assurance qui lui accorde des compensations en cas de guerre, révolution et insurrection mais aussi dans les cas d'expropriation ainsi que dans les cas de non-convertibilité de devise à la suite des décisions gouvernementales de pays hôtes.

67. Chodos, *op. cit.,* p. 193.

68. Berry, *op. cit.,* p. 54-57.

69. Ainsi, il y avait à ce moment trois succursales à Antigua, 24 aux Bahamas, seize à la Barbade, six à Grenade, 43 à la Jamaïque et 31 à Trinidad. Il s'agissait dans tous les cas de succursales de quatre banques canadiennes seulement: la Banque de Nouvelle-Écosse, la Banque Royale, la Banque canadienne impériale de commerce ainsi que la Banque de Montréal. Voir D.J. Baum, *The Banks of Canada in the Commonwealth Caribbean,* New York, Praeger, 1974, p. 25.

70. *Ibidem,* p. 32. Il est vrai qu'en contrepartie, le gouvernement canadien refusera, à part quelques représentations verbales, d'intervenir au profit d'entreprises canadiennes nationalisées ou connaissant des difficultés avec certains gouvernements locaux. Le cas de la nationalisation de l'Alcan en Guyane en 1971 est à cet égard illustratif. Sur ce point voir Chodos, *loc. cit.,* chap. 8, Berry, *loc. cit.,* p. 55 ainsi que I.A. Litvak, et C.J. Maule, «Forced Divestment in the Caribbean», *International Journal,* vol. XXXII, nº 3, été 1977, p. 501-532.

71. Levitt, *op. cit.*, p. 694.

72. Berry, *loc. cit.*, p. 51.

73. Levitt, *op. cit.*, p. 685-686.

74. Il s'agit du Marché commun des Caraïbes, groupant les États anglophones de la région avec la Guyane, qui fut mis sur pied en 1974 comme solution de remplacement au Carifta, la Caribbean Free Trade Association.

75. Voir «Le Canada et le Caricom», *Déclarations et Discours*, n° 79/2, Ottawa, ministère des Affaires extérieures, 1979, p. 2.

76. Les décisions furent annoncées par le ministre MacGuigan à la réunion du Comité Canada-Caricom qui se réunit à Kingston en janvier 1981. Voir «Intensification des relations entre le Canada et les Caraïbes du Commonwealth», *Déclarations et Discours*, n° 81/1, Ottawa, ministère des Affaires extérieures, 1981.

77. *Ibidem*, p. 4.

78. Levitt, *op. cit.*, p. 436.

79. Il s'agit d'un plan d'aide élaboré par le gouvernement de Washington pour l'ensemble des Antilles et de l'Amérique centrale. Les États-Unis veulent y associer le Canada, le Mexique et le Vénézuela à titre de donateurs.

80. Comité permanent des affaires extérieures et de la défense nationale, *Les relations du Canada avec l'Amérique latine et les Antilles*, rapport au Parlement, fascicule n° 48, Ottawa, Imprimeur de la Reine, 1981, p. 48:8.

81. Levitt, *op. cit.*, p. 480 et s.

82. J.C.M. Ogelsby, «Latin America», *International Journal*, vol. XXXIII, n° 2, printemps 1978, p. 403.

83. Berry, *op. cit.*, p. 110.

84. «Canadian Investment, Trade and Aid in Latin America», *LAWG Letter*, vol. VII, n°s 1/2, mai-août 1981, p. 38.

85. Levitt, *op. cit.*, p. 697.

86. Voir à cet égard J.H. Adams, *Liaison Dangereuse: Promotion des Exportations et Aide au Développement*, Ottawa, Institut Nord-Sud, 1980, p. 22 et s.

87. «Canadian Investment [...]», *loc cit.*, p. 38.

88. I.A. Litvak et C.J. Maule, *The Canadian Multinational*, Toronto, Butterworths, 1981, p. 97. À noter que les chiffres, tirés du rapport annuel de la SEE pour 1978, isolent l'Amérique du Sud (20,8 %) mais regroupent l'Amérique centrale avec les Caraïbes et les États-Unis (19,1 %). Puisque les investissements canadiens dans ce dernier pays n'ont pas, de façon générale, à être assurés, on peut en déduire une proportion d'environ 10 % pour l'Amérique centrale comprenant le Mexique.

89. Comprenant les lignes de crédits et les garanties de prêts.

90. Ce chiffre et ceux qui suivent sont tirés d'un projet de recherche portant sur l'analyse des politiques étrangères régionales du Canada dont un premier rapport d'étape fut publié en 1983. Voir G. Hervouet (sous la direction de), *Les politiques étrangères régionales du Canada: éléments et matériaux*, Québec, Centre québécois des relations internationales et Presses de l'Université Laval. Il convient par ailleurs de nuancer l'affirmation qui vient d'être faite en notant que 2,3 des 3 milliards de dollars mis à la disposition de l'Asie sont allés à la Chine uniquement. La situation est la même pour l'Afrique où l'Algérie a accaparé 2 milliards de dollars sur les 2,3 milliards réservés pour cette région. La situation en ce qui concerne l'Amérique latine est caractérisée, comme nous le verrons, par un meilleur équilibre.

91. Dont le président d'alors, Robert Winters, était auparavant ministre de l'Industrie et du Commerce.

92. Ce que semble croire aussi le gouvernement canadien. Cette philosophie de la CALA est bien exprimée dans le discours de l'ancien président de l'organisme, Thomas Bata, dans *The America's in the 80s, Proceedings*, Canadian Association-Latin America and Caribbean, avril 1979. Sur l'attitude et le comportement que doivent avoir, d'après la CALA, les gouvernements des pays du tiers monde désireux d'obtenir des investissements étrangers, voir le discours du président Bata dans *Canada and Latin America, The Implementation of the Partnership, Proceedings*, Canadian Association for Latin America, janvier 1976, p. 15.

93. Sur le rôle et les activités de la CALA, voir «Canadian Investment [...]», *loc. cit.*, p. 28, J.C.M. Ogelsby, «A Trudeau Decade, Canadian-Latin American Relations 1968-1978», *Journal of Interamerican Studies and World Affairs*, vol. 21, n° 2, mai 1979, p. 197-198 ainsi que J. Harbron, «Pour l'intégration du Canada à la Communauté des Amériques», *Perspectives Internationales*, mai-juin 1974, p. 35.

94. En 1976, le premier ministre visitait le Mexique, le Vénézuela et Cuba tandis qu'en 1979, il se rendait au Brésil et au Mexique.

95. Chiffres tirés du projet sur l'*Analyse des politiques régionales du Canada* (PERC).

96. Ogelsby, «A Trudeau Decade [...]», *loc. cit.*, p. 214.

97. Chiffre tiré du projet PERC.

430

98. «Canadian Investment [...]», *loc. cit.*, p. 25 et 27. Elle dépasse même l'Asie si l'on en excepte le Japon.

99. V. Corbo et O. Havrylyshyn, *Les Relations commerciales entre le Canada et les pays en développement*, Ottawa, Approvisionnements et Services, 1980, p. 7-11. Si l'on tient compte, par ailleurs, du stade de fabrication, c'est plus de 60 % des produits finis exportés par le Canada vers le tiers monde qui vont en Amérique latine.

100. J.H. Adams, «L'Investissement transnational au niveau tiers-mondial: perspectives canadiennes», *L'enjeu canadien ou le développement du tiers monde dans les années 80,* Ottawa, Institut Nord-Sud, 1980, p. 127.

101. *Ibidem,* p. 125.

102. S. Langdon, *La présence des sociétés canadiennes dans le tiers monde,* Ottawa, Approvisionnements et Services, 1980, p. 13.

103. «Canadian Investment [...]», *loc. cit.,* p. 6. En 1977, les chiffres étaient de 52,1 % pour l'Amérique latine, 26,6 % pour les Caraïbes (en déclin), 19 % pour l'Asie (en progression) et 2,3 % pour l'Afrique (en progression par rapport à 1975 mais en déclin par rapport à 1970).

104. *Ibidem,* p. 7.

105. Il convient de rappeler ici que le commerce extérieur compte pour 25 % du produit national brut du Canada. Ce pourcentage est l'un des plus élevés de l'ensemble des pays de l'OCDE.

106. M. MacGuigan, «Le Canada et l'Amérique latine – Hier, aujourd'hui et demain», *Déclarations et Discours,* nº 80/4, Ottawa, ministère des Affaires extérieures, 1980, p. 2. Le ministre parlait même d'une «politique régionale».

107. M. MacGuigan, «Approche bilatérale de la politique étrangère du Canada», *Déclarations et Discours,* nº 81/2, Ottawa, ministère des Affaires extérieures, 1980, p. 2 et s.

108. Voir, entre autres, E. Dosman, L. North et C. Bocha, «Le Canada et l'Amérique latine, nouveaux modèles de développement», *Les relations du Canada avec l'Amérique latine et les Antilles, op. cit.,* p. 333 et 352.

109. *Ibidem,* p. 378.

110. M. McGuigan, «Approche bilatérale [...]», *loc. cit.,* p. 3.

111. C'est le terme qu'utilise le Comité permanent des affaires extérieures et de la défense nationale dans son rapport d'étape de décembre 1981. Voir *Les relations du Canada avec l'Amérique latine et les Antilles,* rapport au Parlement, *op. cit.,* p. 7.

112. À noter que le gouvernement canadien a fait du Mexique son instrument privilégié de pénétration en Amérique latine, tandis que ce dernier pays vient de choisir le Canada comme un des cinq pays avec lesquels il désire intensifier ses relations.

113. Voir McGuigan, «Approche bilatérale [...]», *loc. cit.,* p. 5, ainsi que J. Cahill, «Canada Seeks New Friends for the 1980s», *Toronto Star,* 18 avril 1981.

114. Ogelsby, «A Trudeau Decade [...]», *loc. cit.,* p. 193.

115. Voir «Worlds Apart, Economic Relations and Human Rights – Canada – Chile», *LANG Letter,* vol. V, nᵒˢ 4/5, mai-juin 1978, p. 1-36 et «Worlds Apart Update – Canadian Trade With Chile, 1973-1978», *LANG Letter,* vol. VI, nº I, juin 1979, p. 1-27.

116. L'auteur travaille actuellement à ce type d'analyse dans le cadre du projet PERC.

117. Voir sur ce point H.P. Klepak et G.K. Vachon, *A Strategic and Economic Analysis of Canadian National Interests in Latin America,* Ottawa, ministère de la Défense nationale, ORAE Extra-Mural Paper No. 2, mars 1978, ainsi que D. Murray, «Trading for Latin American Oil», *International Perspectives,* nov.-déc. 1980, p. 28-30.

BIBLIOGRAPHIE

BRADFORD, C.I., Jr., et PESTIEAU, C. *Canada and Latin America: The Potential for Partnership,* Montréal, Private Planning Association et Canadian Association for Latin America, 1971.

«Canadian Investment, Trade and Aid in Latin America», *LANG LETTER,* vol. VII, n°ˢ 1-2, mai-août 1981, p. 1-40.

CANADA. Sous-comité du Comité permanent des affaires extérieures et de la défense nationale. *Les relations du Canada avec l'Amérique latine et les Antilles,* différents fascicules, Ottawa, Imprimeur de la Reine, 1981-1982.

DONNEUR, A. «La pénétration économique en Amérique latine», *Études internationales,* vol. XIV, n° 1, mars 1983, p. 83-102.

DOSMAN, E.J. *Latin America and the Caribbean: the Strategic Framework – A Canadian Perspective,* Ottawa, ministère de la Défense nationale, ORAE Extra-mural paper No. 31, 1984.

GUY, J.J. «Canada and Latin America», *The World Today,* vol. XXXII, octobre 1976, p. 376-386.

KLEPAK, H.P. et VACHON, G.K. *A Strategic and Economic Analysis of Canadian National Interest in Latin America,* Ottawa, ministère de la Défense nationale, ORAE Extra-mural paper No. 2, 1978.

MURRAY, D.R. «The Bilateral Road: Canada and Latin America in the 1980s», *International Journal,* vol. 37, n° 1, hiver 1981-1982, p. 108-131.

OGELSBY, J.C.M. *Gringos from the Far North,* Toronto, Macmillan, 1976.

OGELSBY, J.C.M. «A Trudeau Decade, Canadian-Latin American Relations 1968-1978», *Journal of Interamerican Studies and World Affairs,* vol. 21, n° 2, mai 1979, p. 187-205.

18

Le Canada et l'Afrique

Bernard Charles
Université de Montréal

«L'Afrique à sauver! L'Afrique à changer!» Notre imaginaire collectif demeure, bien que les points d'ancrage se soient modifiés. Autrefois, il fallait sauver son âme. Ne fallait-il pas la convertir et l'arracher aux ténèbres du paganisme? Aujourd'hui, c'est de la faim et du sous-développement qu'il faut la tirer. N'est-ce pas en Afrique que se comptent 26 des 36 «pays les moins avancés» de la planète[1]? Les images et les représentations projetées par les médias nous évoquent les calamités naturelles, les aberrations de certains régimes politiques ou les multiples facettes d'un sous-développement accablant. Au mieux, elles provoquent d'extraordinaires mouvements de générosité populaire mobilisée pour des mesures d'urgence. Elles ne vont pas jusqu'à remettre fondamentalement en cause nos relations avec l'Afrique, qu'il s'agisse de la mise en place d'un nouvel ordre économique mondial ou de s'attaquer aux causes profondes du sous-développement en assumant nos responsabilités propres.

Avant la Deuxième Guerre mondiale, les gouvernements canadiens ignoraient pratiquement l'Afrique. Ils avaient sans doute de bonnes excuses car, sur la scène internationale, elle n'avait pas d'existence par elle-même. On ne pouvait compter que quelques États indépendants (Éthiopie, Égypte et Libéria) ou dotés d'une autonomie plus ou moins grande comme l'Union sud-africaine et la Rhodésie du Sud. De plus, le Canada était demeuré à l'écart de toute conquête coloniale en Afrique. Seule une partie de l'opinion publique se trouvait périodiquement sensibilisée par les nombreux missionnaires, catholiques et protestants, travaillant en terres de mission: leurs récits, leurs lettres, leurs campagnes de prédications pour susciter aides et vocations entretenaient une certaine connaissance de l'Afrique et de ses problèmes.

Après 1945, le Canada va se trouver confronté aux problèmes de la décolonisation dans le cadre de l'Organisation des Nations Unies puis de ses relations avec les nouveaux États indépendants d'Afrique: six entre 1950 et 1959, 18 en 1960, quatorze entre 1961 et 1969, et onze entre 1974 et 1981. Dans le même temps il lui faudra établir des relations diplomatiques, mettre en place une administration spécialisée, définir et gérer sa politique d'«aide» à l'égard des pays en voie de développement et singulièrement de l'Afrique. Soucieux de jouer son rôle sur la scène internationale, fut-il celui de «l'une des plus grandes parmi les petites puissances»[2], il ne pourra éviter de se prononcer sur les problèmes africains. Ce faisant, il n'aura garde d'oublier ses intérêts politiques, culturels et commerciaux. Comme pour tout État, politiques intérieure et extérieure s'imbriqueront en interagissant sous les pressions de groupes de toute espèce: gouvernements central et provinciaux, fonctionnaires et entreprises, églises et autres organisations non gouvernementales (ONG)... sans parler des gouvernements étrangers, qu'ils soient africains ou non.

PLACE DE L'AFRIQUE

L'Afrique, cependant, il faut bien le constater, ne va prendre que tardivement et progressivement une place dans la politique étrangère canadienne. Elle n'apparaît pas ou peu, si ce n'est sous forme de grandes généralisations, dans les tentatives faites périodiquement par le gouvernement central pour conceptualiser et planifier sa politique étrangère comme en 1970 le livre blanc sur la *Politique étrangère au service des Canadiens* ou en 1975, la *Stratégie de coopération au développement* ou enfin, en 1985, le livre vert sur la *Compétitivité et sécurité: orientations pour les relations extérieures du Canada.*

C'est bien plutôt à travers les déclarations gouvernementales, les prises de position dans les organisations internationales (telles l'ONU, le Commonwealth ou la Francophonie) et de manière spécifique dans les décisions de l'Agence canadienne de développement international (ACDI) ou à travers certaines actions ponctuelles des ONG qu'on peut retrouver les grandes lignes de la politique canadienne à l'égard de l'Afrique. Les débats à la Chambre des communes ou à son Comité permanent sur les relations extérieures et la défense nationale sont également, mais au gré des circonstances, l'un des lieux privilégiés pour la saisir. Enfin, on ne saurait méconnaître les éléments de politique étrangère mis en œuvre par les provinces dont, au premier rang se trouve sans doute le Québec.

Une analyse systématique du contenu des *Déclarations et Discours* publiés par le ministère des Affaires extérieures entre 1968 et 1979 permet de se faire une idée assez précise de la place réservée à l'Afrique. Elle n'est visée que dans 7 % des cas, à égalité il est vrai avec l'Asie ou l'Europe de l'Ouest, avec des variations très importantes comme en 1968 (guerre civile au Nigéria) et 1977 (participation du Canada au groupe de contact du Conseil de sécurité sur la Namibie)[3]. La justice sociale et la question des droits de l'homme y constituent l'essentiel du discours. D'autres coups de sonde pourraient être faits à propos des débats aux Communes. Ainsi, de 1964 à 1966, il n'y eut qu'un nombre infime d'interventions consacrées à l'Afrique (moins d'une vingtaine). Par contre en 1968, on peut en répertorier plus de 80 dont 66 consacrées au Nigéria et 17 à la Rhodésie. Pour la période des années 1980-1986, on recenserait sans doute un nombre plus important d'interventions officielles portant sur l'Afrique, à la suite des situations d'urgence causées par la famine.

Si l'Afrique en général et tel autre pays africain ne figurent que de manière conjoncturelle dans les présentations de la politique étrangère canadienne, il n'en va pas de même dans les structures ministérielles, dans les relations diplomatiques et dans l'«aide» canadienne aux pays en voie de développement surtout depuis 1970. On doit à ce sujet souligner une très grande continuité par-delà les chefs de gouvernements et les ministres successifs en charge de la politique étrangère, par-delà les clivages des parties politiques.

À plusieurs reprises, des modifications de structure ont été opérées au sein des ministères pour tenir compte d'une plus grande place à reconnaître à l'Afrique. Si assez tôt une division du Commonwealth fut mise en place aux Affaires extérieures, une division de l'Afrique et du Moyen-Orient y sera ensuite créée. À partir de 1967 s'y adjoindra une division des relations avec les pays francophones, puis en 1968, une division de l'aide et du développement. Une nouvelle réorganisation interviendra en 1971 avec la mise en place d'un Bureau des affaires d'Afrique et du

Moyen-orient, subdivisé en trois divisions, notamment Affaires d'Afrique anglophone et Affaires d'Afrique francophone et du Maghreb. Dans la plupart des autres structures, comme à l'ACDI qui relève toujours des Affaires extérieures, on distinguera également les «deux Afriques». D'autres ministères et organismes s'y intéressent bien sûr, pour une part de leurs activités, comme les ministères du Commerce extérieur et de l'Expansion industrielle ou la Société pour l'expansion des exportations[4], la Corporation commerciale canadienne[5], etc. On assiste, au fil des années et sous les variations d'appellation, à une complexité et une multiplicité croissantes des organes publics concernés entièrement ou partiellement par les questions africaines. On comprendra qu'il n'est pas toujours aisé d'assurer harmonisation et cohérence dans les politiques gouvernementales, d'autant plus que toutes ces structures gèrent un nombre assez considérable de programmes.

Le chiffre élevé des fonctionnaires affectés aux questions africaines au ministère des Affaires extérieures et dans ses postes diplomatiques ainsi qu'à l'ACDI et dans d'autres ministères, tout comme l'importance des fonds budgétaires attribués, constituent d'autres signes non équivoques de l'intérêt accru porté à l'Afrique. Des quelques dizaines d'individus sans grande formation africaniste en 1960, on est passé à plusieurs centaines vingt ans plus tard. Leur compétence, professionnelle et académique, est assez largement reconnue, les universités contribuant à leur formation depuis les années 1965. À ceux-là s'ajoutent les nombreux coopérants revenus au pays après avoir œuvré en Afrique sous l'égide de l'ACDI ou au sein de l'une des fort nombreuses organisations non gouvernementales (entre 400 et 500 à s'intéresser à l'Afrique et aux pays sous-développés!). Il n'est pas jusqu'au monde des affaires et des entreprises qui ne comptent désormais ces spécialistes.

Quelques exemples? En 1984, près de 700 personnes, dont un tiers de Canadiens travaillaient dans les postes diplomatiques en Afrique, tandis que l'ACDI fournissait, au titre de ses divers programmes, 370 experts. Les dépenses budgétaires de l'ACDI dans le cadre des programmes bilatéraux consacrés à ce continent ont aussi passé de 18 millions de dollars en 1961-1965 à près de 400 millions de 1984-1985, ce qui représente 44 % de l'aide totale bilatérale canadienne[6]. S'y ajoute la part de l'Afrique dans l'assistance de pays à pays et dans l'assistance multilatérale. De ce point de vue, comme le constatait, déjà en 1970, le premier ministre d'alors: «L'Afrique demeure une priorité[7].»

LES RELATIONS DIPLOMATIQUES

La mise en place du réseau diplomatique canadien s'est effectuée assez lentement. Jusqu'en 1940, le Canada n'était représenté en Afrique que dans deux pays, l'Union sud-africaine et l'Égypte, par des commissions commerciales installées respectivement en 1902 et 1930. Les premières ambassades seront créées dans ces deux mêmes pays en 1940 et 1954. Suivront par la suite celles du Ghana (1957), du Nigéria (1960), de Tanzanie, du Cameroun et du Congo-Kinshasa (1962). Il faut attendre ensuite 1966 pour voir celles d'Éthiopie, du Sénégal et de la Tunisie. Les autres s'échelonneront au fil des ans.

En 1981, il y avait 17 ambassades pour 48 pays avec lesquels le Canada entretenait des relations officielles, un certain nombre d'ambassadeurs se trouvant accrédités dans plusieurs pays. Leur installation a obéi à des considérations de géopolitique. Chaque région géographique fut d'abord pourvue d'un ambassadeur résidant, la priorité ayant été donnée aux pays membres du Commonwealth avec une exception, celle du Congo-Kinshasa[8]. Dès 1960 y fut installé un consulat général (érigé en ambassade en 1962). Ceci s'explique par la participation du Canada aux forces de l'ONU opérant dans le pays. Dans le cas de l'Éthiopie, son rôle au sein de l'Organisation de l'unité africaine fut sans doute un facteur déterminant à l'époque. La mise en place du réseau ne fut pas concomitante pour la plupart des pays francophones à leur accession à l'indépendance. Désormais, la liste des postes d'ambassadeurs résidants concorde, pour l'essentiel[9], avec la liste des États africains classés selon l'importance de leur commerce avec le Canada.

De la sorte se trouve constitué un important noyau qui permet au Canada d'être régulièrement informé sur ce qui se passe en Afrique ou sur tout ce qui la concerne. À cet égard, il n'y a plus aucune commune mesure avec la situation à laquelle faisait face le gouvernement dans les années 60. Les communications se trouvent encore décuplées par la fréquence des missions envoyées de plus en plus fréquemment en Afrique ou venues de ce continent ainsi que des visites officielles de chefs d'État ou de premiers ministres. Dès 1958, K. Nkrumah, premier ministre du Ghana, était invité à Ottawa par son homologue canadien, J. Diefenbaker. Viendront par la suite l'empereur d'Éthiopie en 1963, le chef d'État du Sénégal, L.S. Senghor, et celui de Zambie, K. Kaunda, en 1966; puis en 1967-1969, ceux du Cameroun, du Niger, du Ghana, d'Éthiopie, de Tunisie, de Tanzanie, etc. Au total, ce sont 18 visites au plus haut niveau de 1958 à 1971 et une dizaine de 1975 à 1985.

Par contre, les Africains ne furent guère payés de retour puisque, chose surprenante, ce ne sera qu'en juillet-août 1979 qu'un premier ministre canadien, en l'occurrence Joe Clark, fera une tournée en Afrique à l'occasion d'une réunion des premiers ministres du Commonwealth tenue à Lusaka en Zambie. De même, ce ne fut qu'en mars 1971 qu'un Secrétaire d'État aux Affaires extérieures se rendit dans plusieurs États africains. La fréquence des déplacements au plus haut niveau (premier ministre ou Secrétaire d'État) ne s'est guère améliorée depuis. La signification largement symbolique de tels voyages ne devrait pas cependant être mésestimée à une époque où les «rencontres au sommet» sont l'un des moyens privilégiés de la diplomatie. La multiplicité des échanges de missions au niveau ministériel ou à celui des hauts-fonctionnaires ne saurait y suppléer dans la mesure où le premier ministre se réserve habituellement le dernier mot et les décisions importantes en politique étrangère.

Nous ne pensons pas non plus que les grands rassemblements de premiers ministres et de chefs d'État, comme ceux du Commonwealth, puissent constituer des substituts. Ils ont leurs fonctions propres, entre autres celle de permettre des échanges collectifs conduisant, dans certains cas, à des décisions ou à des prises de position, parfois sur le plus petit commun dénominateur. On peut retenir comme exemple la 10e réunion tenue à Londres en mars 1961. Les premiers ministres y affirmèrent catégoriquement que dans une «association de pays de races multiples il n'y aurait aucune distinction de race ou de couleur», pour reprendre les termes de Diefenbaker. L'Union sud-africaine retira alors sa demande de continuer à en faire partie. On sait d'ailleurs que ce premier ministre canadien y joua un rôle de premier plan malgré les réticences et objections de la plupart de ses ministres[10].

Que ce soit lors de telles réunions organisées régulièrement tous les deux ans ou à celles des autres organismes du Commonwealth (ministres de l'Éducation, des Finances, etc.) ou encore, depuis 1969, de la Francophonie (conférences des ministres de l'Éducation, de l'Agence de coopération culturelle et technique, etc. auxquelles s'ajoutent depuis peu les «sommets francophones»), sans compter les voies diplomatiques ordinaires, les interventions de groupes de toute sorte, les médias, etc., le gouvernement a toutes les possibilités de fort bien connaître les points de vue africains pour déterminer et mener sa politique étrangère.

Comme tout État, le Canada s'est préoccupé d'établir avec ses partenaires le cadre juridique de ses relations en négociant et en signant traités, accords et conventions qui définissent ses obligations. Ces actes sont également un assez bon indicateur pour apprécier la variété et l'intensité des liens ainsi que leur nature avec l'étranger. Nous devons cependant nous contenter de quelques indications, ne disposant pas en particulier de données comparatives pour apprécier la spécificité des constatations faites à propos des liens juridiques noués avec l'Afrique.

Les plus anciens accords furent signés avec l'Union sud-africaine dès 1928, entre autres un accord de commerce en 1932. Ce dernier fut périodiquement reconduit et modifié jusqu'à son abrogation en juillet 1979 par le Canada, enfin soucieux de traduire par des actes concrets sa condamnation de l'apartheid. Les seuls autres accords signés avant les années 60 le furent avec l'Égypte (1952) et la Fédération Rhodésie-Nyassaland (1955) pour régir les relations commerciales.

La décennie 1961-1970 verra la conclusion d'accords d'assistance technique au sujet de la formation par le Canada de militaires africains. Ils interviennent avec les seuls États membres du Commonwealth (Ghana, Nigéria, Tanzanie et Ouganda). Une exception: l'Accord de coopération économique et technique avec le Cameroun en septembre 1970. En fait, c'est à partir de 1970 que l'établissement de liens juridiques, au sens du ministère des Affaires extérieures, sera systématiquement poursuivi. On peut relever ainsi la signature d'une trentaine d'accords et conventions avec une quinzaine d'États africains. Ils concernent le commerce avec l'Algérie et la Tunisie; la coopération au développement avec le Congo, la Haute-Volta, le Zaïre et le Soudan; la protection des investissements canadiens[11] et la fiscalité[12]. Depuis 1980, ces types d'accords se multiplient: 27 en quatre ans, dont onze de coopération au développement. Quelques États se sont ajoutés sur la liste antérieure comme la Côte d'Ivoire, la Zambie, le Zimbabwe et le Mali. L'intensification des relations devrait se traduire par une augmentation et une plus grande diversification de ces accords.

Un tel tableau devrait cependant comporter deux autres volets pour fournir une vue plus complète et précise de la situation. Divers ministères, des organismes publics et des sociétés de la couronne concluent un nombre considérable d'ententes entraînant des engagements, même si ceux-ci ne pèsent pas du même poids juridique en regard du droit international et ne sont pas homologués comme tels. Mentionnons plus particulièrement la multitude d'ententes souscrites par l'ACDI avec 42 États africains recevant de l'aide. Il y a enfin le volet des relations entretenues par des gouvernements provinciaux, au premier rang desquels se trouve sans doute celui du Québec. Ce dernier a réussi à se tailler une place originale en Afrique, après bien des difficultés avec Ottawa. Sous la forme d'échanges de lettres, d'ententes, de procès-verbaux de réunion, le gouvernement québécois a aménagé ses relations avec 22 États francophones dans son champ de compétences propres: l'éducation et la coopération culturelle[13].

LES RELATIONS COMMERCIALES

L'un des secteurs d'activités les plus importants entre États est bien sûr celui des relations commerciales. Avec l'Afrique, ces relations se sont développées fort tardivement, à l'exception de celles avec l'Union sud-africaine et l'Égypte. Malgré un accroissement considérable à partir des années 80, le commerce global (exportations + importations) avec ce continent n'atteint qu'un faible pourcentage du commerce canadien: il oscille entre 0,8 et 1,8 %, bon an mal an, pour la période 1960-1985. La modestie des échanges place l'Afrique au tout dernier rang, bien après l'Asie et l'Amérique latine[14]. D'importantes fluctuations caractérisent le commerce. En 1961, il se chiffrait à moins de 150 millions de dollars. Dix ans plus tard, il ne se montait encore qu'à 324 millions. En 1985, il atteignait presque les 2 500 millions de dollars[15]. On peut constater également que le commerce cumulé pour la période 1981-1985 dépasse largement, avec ses 12 milliards de dollars, le commerce cumulé des 20 années précédentes. L'ouverture réalisée dans la période récente est donc impressionnante.

Les sept pays retenus (dans le tableau présenté en fin de chapitre, sous le titre «Commerce du Canada avec l'Afrique (en millions $ can.)») et classés par ordre décroissant sont ceux dont le commerce cumulé sur les cinq dernières années (1981 à 1985) dépassent les 470 millions de dollars. Pour neuf autres États, les résultats s'échelonnent pour la même période de 200 à 100 millions de dollars. À lui seul, le «Groupe des Sept» constitue, pour chacune des quatre années repères du tableau, environ 85 % du commerce, sauf en 1975 (70 %). Ce sont donc les partenaires commerciaux les plus importants. L'Afrique du Nord est pour le Canada son plus grand marché africain.

Toutefois, autre caractéristique, les relations commerciales du Canada avec l'Afrique soulèvent des difficultés qui pourraient devenir préoccupantes. La balance commerciale est constamment positive, et de beaucoup pour le Canada depuis 1977, celui-ci vendant plus qu'il n'achète. L'excédent cumulé en sa faveur dépasse les 6 milliards de dollars! Il atteint près de 2 milliards envers le «Groupe des Sept» pour les cinq dernières années, dont 900 millions de dollars à l'égard de l'Égypte et 680 millions de dollars avec l'Algérie. Le Canada ne pourra plus esquiver longtemps le problème de l'ouverture de ses frontières aux produits africains, même sans tenir compte du cas spécial de l'Afrique du Sud. Seuls quelques rares États africains, fournisseurs de matières premières, comme la Guinée (bauxite) et le Nigéria et le Gabon (pétrole), ont une balance habituellement excédentaire avec le Canada depuis cinq ans ou plus. Le succès de la percée du Canada, en Algérie plus particulièrement[16], ne pourra aller sans contrepartie!

Quant à la composition des échanges, signalons seulement que le Canada exportait surtout des biens d'équipement (entre 50 et 60 %), des produits agricoles et alimentaires (entre 25 et 40 %) ainsi que des matières brutes (15 %) selon l'analyse des statistiques des dernières années. Il importait dans la même période des matières brutes (pétrole et minerais, de 65 à 75 %), des produits agricoles et alimentaires (de 15 à 20 %) et des produits finis (de 10 à 15 %). Il faut noter enfin que les importations ont été profondément modifiées à partir de 1981[17].

L'«AIDE» CANADIENNE

Lorsque les puissances occidentales eurent à redéfinir leurs relations avec l'Afrique au début des années 60, les mots clés furent «aide et coopération». Prenant conscience de leurs responsabilités envers les pays en voie de développement, commençant à mesurer l'écart toujours croissant qui se creusait entre leur propre niveau de vie et celui de ces pays, elles entendaient désormais tenir compte des énormes besoins de ceux-ci en en faisant un axe de leur politique étrangère. Pour sa part, l'ONU lança successivement deux «décennies du développement» en 1960 et en 1970. Elle fixa aux pays nantis des objectifs à atteindre pour concrétiser leur solidarité: ils étaient appelés à verser une aide globale se montant à 1 % de leur produit national brut. Elle reprit aussi à son compte la suggestion faite par la commission Pearson, qui préconisait que l'aide publique atteigne 0,7 % à partir de 1975.

Le Canada a fait siennes de telles préoccupations et objectifs tout en précisant périodiquement qu'il n'était pas en mesure d'atteindre les objectifs d'aide définis ni de prévoir un calendrier strict pour leur réalisation. Il s'était pourtant engagé relativement tôt dans une politique d'aide avec le lancement en 1951 du plan de Colombo à destination de l'Asie. Mais c'est surtout avec la création en 1960 d'un bureau de l'aide extérieure qu'ont vraiment démarré les programmes d'aide à l'Afrique. Ce bureau fut chargé en effet de gérer, en plus du plan de Colombo, un programme spécial d'aide à l'Afrique. En quelques années, l'aide deviendra un instrument majeur utilisé par le Canada dans ses relations avec l'Afrique, surtout à partir des années 1966-1968: nomination de M. Strong, puis transformation du bureau en ACDI. La venue de P. Gérin-Lajoie, l'attribution d'un budget de 400 millions de dollars et l'installation d'une bureaucratie importante avec 600 employés traduisent la «montée en puissance» du nouvel organisme. La part réservée à l'Afrique ira croissante avec les années, passant de 6 % de l'aide bilatérale totale à plus de 40 % depuis 1978.

Les responsables ambitionnaient de donner aux programmes canadiens une spécificité propre qui les distinguerait de ceux mis en œuvre par les anciennes puissances coloniales comme la France, la Grande-Bretagne et la Belgique ou par les supergrands États-Unis et Union soviétique. Force est de reconnaître qu'avec le temps, l'originalité s'est estompée largement, s'agissant des caractéristiques générales. Les mêmes questions et critiques surgiront, donnant lieu périodiquement à des tentatives de redéfinition et à des réorientations: l'aide doit-elle continuer à être liée? conjonction aide et commerce? caractère humanitaire? concentration ou saupoudrage géographique? priorité à donner aux pays les plus pauvres? faut-il tenir compte de la nature dictatoriale de certains régimes politiques et du non-respect des droits de l'homme?...

Le livre blanc de 1970 précise que l'aide doit «favoriser la croissance et l'évolution des régimes sociaux, éducatifs, industriels, commerciaux et administratifs des pays en voie de développement». Pas moins que cela! Comment traduire un objectif aussi général à travers tous les programmes mis en œuvre dans 42 pays, pour se limiter à ceux de l'Afrique? Par contre, la condition politique est claire: refléter la nature biculturelle du Canada. En 1978, on procède à un réexamen. Désormais, l'accent devra être mis de plus en plus sur les pays à revenus moyens ou élevés et non plus sur les plus pauvres. S'agit-il d'une «révision déchirante» dont serait victime l'Afrique, qui comprend à elle seule 19 pays sur 33 classés alors parmi les plus pauvres de la planète?

En 1979, on veut bien encore «continuer à faire la charité avec l'aide alimentaire mais pour le reste, il faut le plus de retombées possibles pour le Canada»[18]. C'était faire bon marché de toutes les études qui démontraient que 70 à 80 % de l'aide revenaient au Canada. L'année suivante, un groupe de travail parlementaire demande instamment l'instauration d'une politique nouvelle: «l'aide ne doit viser qu'à aider»! Il voudrait aussi qu'elle soit concentrée sur les pays et les citoyens les plus pauvres. Quatre ans plus tard enfin, en avril 1984, le gouvernement entendra lier l'aide et les échanges, car «le Canada est un pays commerçant». Les études effectuées en 1976[19] par le Conseil du Trésor ou par le Conseil économique en 1978[20] et préconisant un déliement graduel de l'aide selon certaines modalités étaient-elles donc dénuées de toute valeur?

Un rôle plus important sera dévolu aux organisations non gouvernementales dans la réalisation des projets d'aide sur fonds publics car leur degré d'efficacité peut être grand et elles sont plus proches des populations. Quant au montant global que doit atteindre l'aide, l'objectif (0,7 % du PNB) est à nouveau reporté, cette fois-ci à l'an 2000, ou presque[21]!

Il ne saurait être question d'établir en quelques paragraphes un véritable bilan des réalisations échelonnées sur 25 ans. Aussi nous contenterons-nous d'en dégager quelques points saillants. De 1960 à 1985, c'est une masse globale de 6,2 milliards de dollars sur les 15 milliards d'aide bilatérale «de gouvernement à gouvernement» qui a concerné l'Afrique. Elle a bien sûr été répartie progressivement. Durant la première décennie 1961-1970, la part attribuée à l'Afrique passe de 6 à 21 %. De 1971 à 1977, elle s'établit en moyenne à 37 %. Désormais, elle dépasse les 42 %.

Quels en furent les bénéficiaires pendant ce quart de siècle? Tout d'abord, trois pays du Commonwealth: Tanzanie (368 millions de dollars) Kenya (228 millions de dollars) et Ghana (216 millions de dollars). Viennent ensuite trois pays francophones: Cameroun et Tunisie avec 183 millions de dollars, et Sénégal qui reçoit 150 millions de dollars. La liste se continue avec, en ordre décroissant, la Zambie (144 millions de dollars), l'Égypte (137 millions de dollars), le Niger (130 millions de dollars), le Zaïre (125 millions de dollars), le Nigéria (120 millions de dollars), le Malawi (119 millions de dollars), la Côte d'Ivoire (105 millions de dollars), le Rwanda (99 millions de dollars), l'Algérie (96 millions de dollars) et le Mali (94 millions de dollars). Les autres pays s'échelonnent du Burkina (78 millions de dollars) à la République centrafricaine avec 2 millions de dollars.

Si pendant très longtemps les pays du Commonwealth obtinrent la part la plus importante, la règle fut posée dans les années 1975 de répartir l'aide à peu près également entre les «deux Afriques», anglophone et francophone[22]. Les autres critères devant présider tant aux décisions d'inscription sur la liste des pays admissibles à recevoir l'aide canadienne qu'à celles d'attribution de l'aide laissent une large latitude aux divers décideurs, qu'ils soient de l'ACDI ou du gouvernement, ainsi qu'au facteur politique.

La liste d'admissibilité comporte cinq catégories: les pays de concentration pouvant faire l'objet d'engagements importants et à long terme (15 «anglophones»: Kenya, Tanzanie, Zimbabwe, Ghana, etc.; neuf «francophones»: Cameroun, Sénégal, Zaïre, pays du Sahel, etc.), pays où une présence canadienne significative est nécessaire pour des raisons politiques et commerciales mais qui ne peuvent recevoir une aide à long terme (huit «anglophones»: Nigéria, Ouganda, Soudan, etc.; cinq «francophones»: Algérie, Tunisie, Maroc, Gabon, Togo). Les trois autres catégories concernent les pays pouvant recevoir des aides ponctuelles (aide alimentaire d'urgence, par exemple) comme la Somalie et l'Angola ou ceux qui sont «non bénéficiaires» comme Mayotte ou «non admissibles» comme la Libye[23].

28 pays dans les deux premières catégories, c'est dire que les critères d'attribution devraient peser d'un grand poids. Malheureusement, ils sont d'application malaisée car ils portent aussi bien sur la situation du pays concerné (besoins, niveau d'engagement dans le développement, respect des droits de l'homme) que sur les intérêts canadiens (qualité des relations avec Ottawa, comportement régional et international, etc.) et les circonstances exceptionnelles (périodes de reconstruction ou de bouleversements politiques). Finalement et compte tenu de tous ces critères, il faut concentrer l'aide sur les pays les plus démunis et ceux où le revenu est le plus faible! Le problème n'est pas simple à résoudre. Il est d'ailleurs le même pour tous les autres pays «donateurs» et on ne sait si le Canada trouve les meilleures solutions. Les critiques sont inévitables, les justifications jamais satisfaisantes ou suffisantes, le jeu des intérêts et des pressions toujours présent.

Constatons qu'au regard de la concentration de l'aide sur les pays les plus démunis, il ne semble pas y avoir de corrélation entre le classement selon le PNB par habitant (indicateur classique du sous-développement) et le classement selon le volume d'aide reçue (aide bilatérale de gouvernement à gouvernement) pour chacune des deux Afriques durant la période 1975-1985. Il faut ajouter cependant que sur les 16 pays ayant reçu l'aide la plus importante durant cette décennie, six sont classés parmi les plus démunis, dont la Tanzanie. De plus, le Nigéria ne reçoit pratiquement plus d'aide du Canada depuis 1979.

D'autres aspects seraient à retenir, notamment ceux des autres formes d'aide (multilatérale, humanitaire, etc.), de l'efficacité de l'aide par rapport au développement des pays receveurs. Il importe cependant de se demander si les décisions en matière d'aide ne demeurent pas en deçà de ce qui serait possible en prenant davantage en considération l'opinion publique canadienne. La population a réagi en effet avec une vigueur inattendue face aux situations tragiques créées en Afrique par la sécheresse et la famine en 1984-1985: «500 000 Canadiens ont versé plus de 50 millions de dollars en dons à des organismes volontaires[24].»

PRISES DE POSITION SUR LES PROBLÈMES AFRICAINS

La politique du Canada à l'égard de l'Afrique ne se limite pas à établir des relations diplomatiques et commerciales, ni à réaliser des programmes d'aide. Elle consiste également à prendre position, voire à intervenir de manière concrète, sur les problèmes auxquels ce continent est confronté. Bon gré, mal gré, le Canada est amené à se prononcer sur la scène internationale à l'ONU, comme membre de celle-ci et à certaines périodes du Conseil de sécurité; ou sur des scènes régionales lors des réunions du Commonwealth et de la Francophonie; ou sur la scène nationale lorsqu'il est interrogé aux Communes ou par l'opinion publique sur les problèmes d'actualité et sur sa politique extérieure.

Dans ce domaine aussi, on peut se demander si le gouvernement ne se trouve pas souvent en arrière de l'opinion publique et s'il ne table pas trop sur les réactions supposées de la fameuse «majorité silencieuse». Très ferme sur certains principes: respect scrupuleux du droit international tel qu'il est en vigueur, non-ingé-rence dans les affaires des autres États, rejet quasi absolu de la violence comme moyen de règlement des litiges internationaux ou nationaux, solidarité maximale avec ses alliés occidentaux. Il risque trop souvent avec ces derniers de contribuer à maintenir indéfiniment un statu quo intolérable à ceux qui en sont victimes et que lui-même condamne. Ceci dit, il est bien évident que le Canada n'a jamais eu en main les clés permettant de dénouer les situations africaines. Sans être majeur, son rôle n'en est pas pour autant négligeable. Dans certaines circonstances, comme en mars 1961, il fut l'un des acteurs déterminants du retrait de l'Union sud-africaine du Commonwealth.

Très tôt, le Canada dut se prononcer sur les problèmes de décolonisation de l'Afrique. Il l'a fait principalement dans le cadre des Nations Unies. D'entrée de jeu, pourrait-on dire, il est pris dans un dilemme à propos de l'Égypte qui abroge unilaté-ralement le traité anglo-égyptien de 1936 et va nationaliser le canal de Suez en 1951. Il reconnaît le «désir naturel et justifiable des États qui ont subi pendant longtemps l'intervention étrangère d'affirmer leur droit de diriger eux-mêmes leurs affaires intérieures». D'un autre côté, il juge essentiel qu'aucun geste ne soit posé pour modifier par la force le régime actuel (défense du canal par la Grande-Bretagne). On sait que les événements en décideront autrement. Il n'est pas aventureux de penser que le Canada, en l'occurrence, était aussi fort soucieux de sauvegarder les intérêts occidentaux.

C'est au cours de ces mêmes années 1946-1951 que le Canada commence à être aux prises avec les épineuses questions de l'apartheid en Union sud-africaine (dénommée plus tard Afrique du Sud) et du Sud-Ouest africain (ou Namibie). Il y a donc plus de 40 ans! Chaque année désormais, ces questions reviendront à l'ordre du jour de l'ONU. Il serait fastidieux de relever toutes les déclarations faites inlassa-blement pour condamner l'immoralité du régime installé en Afrique du Sud au mépris des droits les plus élémentaires de l'écrasante majorité noire ou plus fondamentale-ment encore de la personne humaine. Les variations de style et de condamnation dépendront de la personnalité des représentants appelés à exprimer la position du Canada.

Mais tout aussi inlassablement sera affirmé le refus d'appliquer quelque sanction que ce soit. Il se prononcera régulièrement contre l'expulsion de l'Afrique du Sud en tant que membre de l'ONU (par exemple en 1961, en 1972 et en 1974), et cela au nom du principe de l'universalité des Nations Unies. Il rejettera le plus longtemps possible toute forme de sanction économique car comme il le dira en 1962, il doute de leur opportunité dans une conjoncture ne présentant «ni agression de l'extérieur ni question de paix ou de guerre». De plus, des sanctions risqueraient de gêner surtout la population de couleur. On le voit, l'argument n'est pas d'aujour-d'hui! En 1969, l'Assemblée générale de l'ONU votait une résolution demandant aux États de n'offrir aucune aide au Portugal, à la Rhodésie et à l'Afrique du Sud. Le Canada s'abstint, considérant les conditions comme irréalisables et que certaines idées contenues dans la résolution étaient erronées.

À d'autres occasions (en 1970), il s'abstiendra également à propos des actions à entreprendre car c'est au Conseil de sécurité qu'il appartient de décider des mesures à prendre. Il adoptera la même attitude chaque fois que les pays occiden-taux se verront reprocher d'entretenir d'importantes relations économiques avec l'Afrique du Sud, comme en 1976. L'année suivante encore, le délégué du Canada au Conseil de sécurité se prononcera pour le maintien des liens commerciaux avec tous les pays, même avec ceux avec lesquels le Canada est en profond désaccord sauf si le Conseil de sécurité a décrété qu'il s'agit d'une menace à la paix internationale. Ceci ne risque guère de se produire, vu les positions des États-Unis, de la France et de la Grande-Bretagne ainsi que leur droit de veto.

La position canadienne connaîtra malgré tout une lente évolution, d'une part sous la pression de plus en plus forte de la communauté internationale et celle des autres membres du Commonwealth, ceux de la ligne de front en particulier (Zambie, Tanzanie puis Zimbabwe), et d'autre part sous les pressions accentuées de l'opinion publique canadienne. Les positions de plus en plus intransigeantes et agressives de l'Afrique du Sud ne laisseront d'ailleurs pas grand choix au gouvernement. Ainsi, à la suite du Conseil de sécurité, il interdira en 1963 toute exportation de matériel militaire puis de tout matériel pouvant servir à la mise en œuvre de l'apartheid. En 1970, le premier ministre Pierre E. Trudeau ira même jusqu'à exprimer ses «sérieuses appréhensions» à la suite de la décision de la Grande-Bretagne de reprendre ses ventes d'armes à l'Afrique du Sud.

Finalement, le Canada reconnaîtra à partir de 1973, lors de la réunion du Commonwealth, «la légitimité de la lutte pour le respect intégral des droits de l'homme et pour l'autodétermination». Puis en décembre 1977, c'est enfin la remise en cause de ses relations économiques, de manière extrêmement prudente il est vrai: fermeture de deux consulats sur trois et suppression des mesures encourageant les échanges commerciaux, création d'un code d'éthique à l'intention des entreprises travaillant avec l'Afrique du Sud. Deux ans plus tard, il abroge son accord commercial de 1932 mais se refuse toujours, malgré les pressions, à faire obstacle aux relations économiques (échanges, investissements). Les premières mesures ayant une certaine portée interviendront seulement en 1985 avec la déclaration du Secrétaire d'État, Joe Clark, à Baie-Comeau: embargo plus strict sur les livraisons aux organismes de répression sud-africains (ordinateurs), suppression de l'aide fournie par la SEE aux exportateurs canadiens...

Devant une telle politique, louvoyante à souhait si ce n'est dissimulatrice[25], comment ne pas partager le jugement sévère porté par les chefs d'État africains pressant le Canada de prendre enfin des mesures en conformité avec ses condamnations morales, ou celui porté maintes fois par les porte-paroles de groupes africains ou canadiens, dont la Conférence des évêques?

L'affaire sud-africaine n'est pas le seul exemple d'une politique péchant par une prudence excessive et n'excluant pas les contradictions au nom du réalisme. Au sujet de la Rhodésie du Sud qui avait proclamé unilatéralement son indépendance au profit de sa minorité blanche, le Canada adoptera des positions plus nettes en reconnaissant, dès 1966, la nécessité de sanctions économiques fortes pour contraindre le régime de I. Smith. Il se trouvait conforté dans cette politique par le Commonwealth, le Conseil de sécurité, les États-Unis et la Grande-Bretagne. Le Canada a toujours été préoccupé de concerter ses positions avec ces deux partenaires. Il est peu d'exemples où il se soit dissocié de leurs positions.

La Namibie en est un. Tous les efforts seront faits par le Canada, au sein en particulier du Groupe de contact formé lors de sa participation au Conseil de sécurité, pour trouver un dénouement satisfaisant à l'accession à l'indépendance de ce territoire occupé illégalement par l'Afrique du Sud depuis 1955. Le Canada se refusera cependant toujours à apporter la moindre aide aux mouvements nationalistes, autre que vaguement symbolique et humanitaire pour ne pas paraître cautionner le recours à la violence, quelle que soit la légitimité de l'objectif, hautement affirmé par lui. Le problème n'est toujours pas réglé en 1987, mais le Canada n'acceptera pas de lier l'accession à l'indépendance de la Namibie au retrait des troupes cubaines opérant en Angola, comme le font les États-Unis et l'Afrique du Sud.

Indépendance de la Namibie, accession des Noirs à la dignité des droits de l'homme et à l'exercice du pouvoir politique avec la dislocation du régime de l'apartheid en Afrique du Sud, contribution à un réel développement des populations des États africains, tels sont les domaines dans lesquels le Canada doit contribuer à œuvrer s'il veut jouer un rôle à sa mesure en Afrique. Il y faut une volonté politique déterminée, en prise avec l'opinion publique qui paraît pousser fortement en ce sens.

Commerce du Canada avec l'Afrique
(en millions $ can.)

	1970	1975	1980	1985
Commerce total	324	932	1 676	2 483
dont:				
Afrique du Sud	150	330	552	381
Algérie	19	103	405	654
Égypte	38	7	140	223
Nigéria	53	120	144	300
Libye	3	60	72	133
Maroc	6	21	78	184
Tunisie	7	10	59	180

NOTES

1. Selon la classification des Nations Unies: produit national brut par habitant inférieur à 400 dollars en 1984.

2. P.E. Trudeau, interview au journal Le Monde, 21 février 1970.

3. «Les objectifs dans le discours de la politique étrangère», dans G. Gosselin (éd.), *Les politiques étrangères régionales du Canada*, CQRI, Québec, 1983.

4. Société de la couronne qui a conclu des accords financiers (prêts, assurances, garanties) concernant l'Afrique pour près de 2,5 milliards de dollars en 1983.

5. Celle-ci aura un volume de ventes de 40 millions de dollars en Afrique sur un total de 626 millions en 1983-1984.

6. Assistance de gouvernement à gouvernement. L'aide publique totale au développement (2,1 milliards de dollars) se ventilait de la manière suivante: de gouvernement à gouvernement = 875, de pays à pays = 534, assistance multilatérale = 691 millions de dollars.

7. P.E. Trudeau, interview au journal *Le Monde*, 21 février 1970.

8. Devenu par la suite le Zaïre.

9. Exception notoire: la Libye.

10. Selon les procès-verbaux du conseil des ministres. M. Arseneault: «Le Cabinet Diefenbaker était partagé sur l'expulsion de l'Afrique du Sud du Commonwealth.» Journal *Le Devoir*, 4 mars 1986.

11. Ainsi que leur garantie par la SEE (Libéria, Maroc, Gambie, Ghana, Guinée, Malawi, Cameroun et Rwanda).

12. Conventions pour éviter la double imposition en matière d'impôts et prévenir l'évasion fiscale (Maroc, Libéria).

13. Sur ce point, lire autre autres «Le Québec et l'Afrique sub-saharienne», dans G. Hervouet et H. Galarneau (éd.), *Présence internationale du Québec, chronique des années 1978-83*, CQRI, Québec, 1984.

14. L. Freeman, «L'ouverture sur le marché africain: le Canada et l'Afrique dans les années 80», *Études internationales*, vol. XIV, n° 1, mars 1983.

15. Données de *Statistique Canada*. Commerce total: exportations + importations.

16. De 30 millions de dollars en 1971, les échanges ont passé à 650 millions en 1985.

17. B. Reysset, «Les échanges commerciaux entre le Canada et l'Afrique», dans *Marchés tropicaux et méditerranéens*, n° 2058, 19 avril 1985 (numéro spécial «Le Canada et l'Afrique», 1984-1985).

18. Interview du ministre responsable de l'ACDI à *La Presse*, 21 novembre 1979.

19. Conseil du Trésor, *Les effets économiques d'un déliement de l'aide bilatérale canadienne*, 1976.

20. Conseil économique du Canada, *Pour un commun avenir. Une étude des relations entre le Canada et les pays en développement*, Hull, 1978.

21. Déclaration du ministre des Finances, 8 novembre 1984.

22. Certains pays sont classés dans l'une ou l'autre de ces deux catégories pour des raisons de commodité administrative et de proximité géographique: Éthiopie et Mozambique dans la première, Gambie et Guinée-Bissau dans la seconde.

23. Voir *Marchés tropicaux et méditerranéens*, *loc. cit.*

24. Déclaration de Mᵐᵉ M. Vézina, ministre d'État aux Relations extérieures et chargée de l'ACDI, 21 février 1985.

25. Collusion entre la Space Research Corporation et la Corporation sud-africaine pour le développement des armements en 1976-1977. Voir L. Freeman, *loc. cit.*

19

Canada as a Circumpolar Nation

Erik Solem
Keith Greenaway
Department of National Defence

INTRODUCTION

According to a recent, relevant, and by now quite frequently quoted Government document, Canada is an Arctic nation[1]. The «Green Paper» on Canada's future international relations, although intended – as all or most «green papers» seem to have been – as an «aid» to public review and as such a «discussion paper», the most recent one is nevertheless quite specific on this point. The North holds a distinct place in our nationhood and sense of identity, it states[2]. Canadians view the North as «special» and themselves as special because of this fact.

It is, we submit, in reality somewhat debatable whether or not Canada *is* an Arctic nation, it probably is not if past collective behaviour and our ordering of priorities is anything to go by. The present paper will argue that we, as a nation, have been if not remiss, certainly curiously absent-minded in this particular respect. That Canada is a *curcumpolar* nation is, however, beyond the slightest shadow of doubt and an inescapable fact of life, dictated by the geographical and geostrategic environment within which we live.

As far as the evolution of a Canadian foreign policy which takes cognizance and reacts to this fact is concerned, there have been ebbs and tides. Two observations stand out: first, Canada seems to go through cycles with respect to its concern for the North, and these appear to run in intervals of some seven to nine years each; secondly, foreign policy development and formulation with respect to Arctic matters – as with much else – seems to have been, at least until very recently, largely *reactive*. To explore if and why this has been so, and to what extent it is related to governmental decision-making in general will be the purpose of this paper.

However, it is also – or should be – fairly clear that at the present juncture we may well find ourselves in a situation where the concurrence of forces and determinants is such that we are able to get a closer grip on – or control over – our destiny as far as being a circumpolar country is concerned. This also will be explored further.

The present chapter examines the evolution of Canada as a circumpolar nation, it is firmly assumed that we *are* one due to inescapable geographical realities, mentioned above, while looking at how we have responded – or perhaps failed to respond – to this fact. Several levels of analysis are needed for this task, as they interact and interpenetrate each other and help bring about national stimulus-response behaviour. Do we *conceive* of ourselves as a circumpolar country? If so, when is this felt more strongly, for what reasons and how does this particular form, or subset, of «national identity» express itself? Does it come about as a result of internal pressures, external events or – more likely perhaps – as a combination of both forces? As foreign policy is most frequently little more than the extension of national policy, or somewhat like war perhaps, politics by other means, it is of no trouble at all that more than one level of analysis must be adopted.

Furthermore, there are several dimensions to this problem, if that is what it is. The most important of those would be the geographical/cultural, and institutional/political dimensions. Both of these contribute to, shape and determine foreign policy. Of overriding concern and importance is of course the question of national security and general national well-being. No government which wishes to stay in power more than spasmodically can afford to ignore such concerns. Underlying all of this is the need for, and central importance of, properly identifying and articulating one's national role and purpose. This, we submit, is perhaps the most important general determinant in all policy-making involving a nation.

THE GEOGRAPHICAL/CULTURAL DIMENSION

Geography shapes nations, it gives them advantages as well as disadvantages or at least, vulnerabilities. The last part of this statement may require some explanation. It is possible that a country can be so well endowed from nature's side that it simply forgets or ignores the fact that many or most countries do *not* possess such privileges and advantages as ample space, good resources, free access to water and so on. Or, the particular country in question may be so arranged geographically that it spans waste areas with great temperature or even climatic difference, resulting in very uneven distribution of its population. Despite modern, relatively sophisticated metropolitan areas where very large portions of the population resides (as in Canada), big areas may be relatively uninhabited, very sparsely populated and – hence – vulnerable from the point of view of penetration. Whether such penetration (or «development», which may be the case) is desirable or not is of course open to question. More about this later on.

We have used «the North» in the context of Canada as a circumpolar state, and it frequently means different things to different people. Since the vast majority of Canadians live along a relatively narrow strip of territory running East-West along the furthermost Southern part of the country, many of them will almost invariably think of anything north of them as «the North»[3]. Howerver, the North could also more specifically be defined by such political criteria as Yukon, the Northwest Territories, or north of 60 degrees north latitude. In one sense, «the North» has no landform or other environmental uniformity, since it varies in terms of mountains, hills and plains, some of which are forested, others not, some of which are tundra and, again, others are bare rock. Arctic *as well as* subarctic climates can be found in our North and also, uniquely, a frozen ocean environment.

During summer there is, as most of us may know, a long period of daylight throughout the North. However, due to sea ice, the heating is restricted and warm temperatures are rare. In the Northeast Arctic, there is no summer as we know it. The same does not apply to the large land mass of Northwestern Canada where warm summers occur. The winters, however, are long, cold and dark. A severe and continuous cold makes it very costly and difficult to operate and maintain machinery and equipment. This, however, also applies to large areas of the South from time to time during the depth of winter.

There is extremely little precipitation in the North, although some regional difference may be observed across this vast expanse of land. The central Canadian Arctic as opposed to much of the Arctic USSR is really a cold «desert». Another environmental feature is the permafrost, which creates problems and difficulties with constructing buildings, laying of pipelines and so on. Furthermore, the surface – if consisting of unconsolidated materials – can become a soggy, spongy mass-making overland travel by foot or vehicles very difficult indeed[4].

As far as vegetation goes, the Northeastern Arctic is treeless, while the Northwestern subarctic has some forested areas. There are fewer animals in the Northeast than Northwest, creating quite different conditions for the dwellers of those areas. As Robinson reminds us, the past adoptions of the Inuit in an Arctic climate and treeless tundra has had to be different from those of the Indians and Europeans of the subarctic. Past generations, Eskimos, depending mainly on animal resources in the sea for food or clothing, tended to live along the coastline, whereas Indians in the North lived much like other Indians in Southern Canada before the Europeans arrived. These factors are also determinants in the creation of political culture, and should for that reason not be overlooked.

A brief word about sea ice. This environmental phenomenon does not exist in Southern Canada to any degree. It also makes it very arduous, if not impossible, to navigate in sea areas for most of the year. Whereas the Hudson Bay and Strait are navigable for three months (or less) per year, the channels west of Lancaster Sound are normally ice-free for only one month annually. In the far Northwestern Arctic, these channels virtually *never* break up.

If the North is defined as the political area of Yukon and the Northwest Territories, as suggested above, it would constitute a land area of roughly 4 000 000 square kilometers, comprising some 40 % of Canada's total land mass. This does not include the several thousand square kilometers of water between the Arctic Islands, nor the rather vaguely defined pie-shaped wedge of ice-covered Arctic Ocean shown on certain Canadian maps extending to the geographical North Pole[5].

Another useful observation, perhaps, is the fact that the North is the only Canadian region with a larger native population than non-native. This population, also, is scanty, although its birth rate proportionally speaking outpaces anything to the South in Canada[6]. However, the local Indian and Inuit population have had their traditional way of life profoundly affected by developments taking place elsewhere in Canada, especially in the post-World War II period. It is perhaps not exaggerated to state that some of these changes have been as abrupt and serious as those experienced by Indians in Southern Canada more than a century ago.

Whereas in the Yukon some 60 % of the population reside in Whitehorse, its capital, in the Northwest Territories most inhabitants are fairly widely scattered. Two-thirds of the population live in seven settlements in the Mackenzie Valley, whereas Yellowknife, the capital, is the only relatively large community, with some 9 500 persons in 1981[7].

In summary, it must be stated that from a strictly speaking *geographical* point of view, we are faced with formidable obstacles in our North. Compared to neighbouring circumpolar countries such as the USSR and the Scandinavian states, it becomes evident that much more of our North than theirs is Arctic. The Soviet North for example is to a much large extent subarctic. In may ways the Soviets are more favourably endowed with respect to their North from a geological and climatic point of view. They are also, perhaps partly for this reason, more advanced in some Arctic-related activities[8].

THE INSTITUTIONAL/POLITICAL DIMENSION

To carry the comparison with the USSR a bit further, as is the Soviet Union so is Canada like the United States, a federal state. However, unlike the USSR, we have no single administrative unit – such as the Russian Federation (RSFSR) – extending from West to East throughout the Northern part of that country[9]. Four of Canada's provinces have an Arctic seacoast, and seven of them have at least some subarctic territory. However, north of the 60th parallel it is the Federal Government which is responsible for the overall administration of the nearly 4 million square kilometers with a population of less than 70 000 Indians, Metis, Inuit and «Southerners».

To carry the comparison further, it should be noted that the Scandinavian countries, including Iceland, are all unitary states with, at various degrees, centralized control which simplifies both the institutional and political dimensions of policy-making. The one possible exception to this is Denmark, with the current home rule policy for Greenland, with possible future implications for Canada.

A thesis which is expressed, and has been hinted at earlier in this chapter, is that success can – and often does – bring failure. A note of explanation may be needed. Because so much of what goes on in the North has been looked at primarily through «national» lenses, and because so much has reflected – or even mirrored Canadian political reality elsewhere, *i.e.* with a relatively «weak» centre –, certain aspects of our North have developed very slowly. Our preoccupation with province-building the East-West development of the country has dominated the Canadian scene, both economically and politically over the years. Only recently (in the last two or three decades) have we seen a more or less continuous thrust in the northward development of Canada. From the «foreign policy» point of view this is by now quite evident. Just in case it still is not – and despite a rather large literature to the contrary[10], some select examples or «flash points» for illustration may be in order.

Prior to World War II, Canada's national interest in the North expressed itself spasmodically. By and large, our claims to the North were based on a series of explorations undertaken by British seamen and some explorers over a period of some 400 years. These explorations, which formed the basis of British claims, were later transferred to Canada in part in 1870 along with all the land claims of the Hudson's Bay Company[11].

Some ten years later, Britain transferred sovereignty over its remaining claims in the North to Canada, the lands in question consisting of the Arctic archipelago. It seems that Britain has moved primarily to counter US commercial pressures in Baffin Island, as in 1874 requests had been received for permission to establish a whaling station as well as a mining operation on the island, and Britain was afraid that further US penetration could follow[12].

However, for a variety of reasons, there was little Canadian interest in taking control of the territory in question. Our country was facing a depression in industry, and several awkward questions remained, such as: where exactly *were* the boundaries; and how should the territory be transferred – by imperial order or by a separate Act of Parliament? Eventually, by 1878, a resolution was introduced in the House of Commons recommending acceptance of the British offer[13]. In this context, it is worth noticing that first, this resolution was carried far from unanimously, and secondly, the overriding concern seems to have been that if Canada did *not* take control, the US would, and this option should clearly be avoided. Additionally, it was assumed that the territory would cost next to nothing to administer until Canada was ready to settle and exploit it. Granatstein refers, correctly, to the resolution as «inglorious but practical»[14], and it says a great deal of what was to become Canada's approach to its circumpolar territories in times to come.

Canada did not rush to assert its newly acquired sovereignty. In fact, an order in council as late as 1882 had recommended that no steps be taken with the view of legislating for the good government of the country «until some influx of population or other circumstances shall occur to make such provision more imperative than it would at the present seem to be»[15]. As is by now known, there was no external challenge or threat to Canada's claim to its North up to that point. Had another power wished to exert itself in this region, it probably could have done so with impunity. As Morris Zaslow noted, what needs were there to challenge Canada's claims as long as the region was completely open to all comers, and no effort was made to obstruct activities there[16]? In fact, it was not until 1895-1897 that the Canadian Government even bothered to draw boundaries on the map to subdivide its North into administrative districts[17].

By 1897, however, pressures were mounting for Canada to exert more and effective control of its circumpolar regions. This time, the pressures for action were «informal» in origin, as they related to horror stories of rape and pillage by, largely, American whalers, and the gradual destruction of Eskimo communities. Several official missions were sent north and efforts made to explore how Canada's North could be more effectively tied to the rest of the country. Again, questions of costs were raised and debated before it was finally agreed upon, albeit somewhat hesitatingly, that yes, we could and should afford the necessary costs of supervision and control.

The fact that some of these objections were made to what now seems self-evident, namely Canada exerting its own sovereignty in the North, is in itself an indication of how strongly felt the principle of a «scorched ice»[18] policy was with regards to our Arctic, although problems involving «sovereignty» continued unabated for some time, especially with regards to the US. Various explorers exerted themselves forcefully, and in the process made «claims» for their mother countries[19]. However, by the end of the 1920s, Canada's claims in the North were relatively well established and by 1933, V.K. Johnston could write with some confidence that «Canada's sovereignty was clear»[20].

It must be stated, however, that *still* no effort to develop the Canadian North by the Government had seen the light of day. Not even the discovery of oil at Norman

Wells, N.W.T., after World War I and the successful establishment of an operating well in 1920 had changed this, and the Government's efforts to aid its Eskimos and Indians were minimal[21]. This Canadian position was eloquently summed up by the explorer Vilhjalmur Stefansson in 1939 when he stated that «Canada is less interested in her Arctic domain than most people suppose, [...] [and] has no immediate need for her Arctic regions»[22]. The Canadian-born American Arctic explorer had given us a very insightful assessment not only of Canada's perceived «needs» for her circumpolar territories, but also the dominating mode of thought in the country.

The Canadian North has in fact not profited from any deliberate policy of self-sufficiency, let alone foresight. For example, resource development has been left largely to private enterprise, where the primary concern has been – as may have been expected – one of high costs vs. Northern development in general. Until World War II, activities related to sovereignty in the North consisted almost entirely of RCMP patrols, Eastern Arctic patrols and the establishment of a number of outposts. Until this point in time, the strategic significance of the Canadian Arctic, which rests on economic and political as well as military considerations, was seen as minimal[23].

IMPACT OF WORLD WAR II

World War II woke us up, at least for the moment. With the Ogdensburg Agreement, signed by Mackenzie King and Roosevelt in August 1940, came the establishment of a Permanent Joint Board of Defence. Following Japan's entry into the war, US concerns for Alaska increased leading, in short, to the construction of the Alaska Highway, the Canol Project[24], the Northwest Staging Route to Alaska and on to the USSR with its airfields, as well several weather stations throughout the Arctic. Under a Canadian-US agreement, airfields were built by the Americans at Goose Bay, Fort Chimo and Frobisher; and in 1942, the Crimson air route was established with the construction of air bases at The Pas, Churchill and Coral Harbour. Whereas the North's development was speeded up, the new American presence created problems as well. The need for the Alaska Highway was seen by some, including Prime Minister MacKenzie King, perhaps correctly, as a US excuse to increase its influence in Canada, as well as part of a policy of Western hegemony, both of which he strongly opposed. But how to do it? At the end of 1942, there were nearly 15 000 Americans in the Canadian North, and our measures to protect and enhance sovereignty had made Mackenzie King appalled[25]. It was not until May 1943 that the Government finally appointed a Special Commissioner for Defence Projects in the Northwest, instructing him secretly that his duties were to ensure:

> that the natural resources of the area shall be utilized to provide the maximum benefit to the Canadian people and to ensure that no commitments are to be made and no situation allowed to develop as a result of which the full Canadian control of the area would be in any way prejudicial or endangered[26].

By the middle of 1942, some important changes had taken place in the balance of sea-power in the Western Pacific. The battles of the Coral Sea and Midway had shifted the balance in favour of the US, whose strategic planning in the Pacific theatre from then on became mainly concerned with Japan. More specifically, this strategy concentrated on the penetration of the Japanese defensive perimeter as well as the development of military operations against the Japanese homeland[27]. However,

Alaska remained a point of some sensitivity until 1944, when Japan was expelled from the Aleutians.

The purpose of the Canol project, mentioned earlier, was to try to develop a source of petroleum products closer to Alaska than the continental US. Additional explorations had been carried out at Norman Wells, with the drilling of new wells, and the construction of a refinery and several pipelines. However, unlike the Alcan Highway and the Northwest Staging Route, discussed above, the Canol project itself made little contribution to the Canadian North. As local demand was found to be insufficient for economic production and transport costs to more distant markets deemed to be excessively high, operations were closed down in mid-1945[28].

In retrospect, as Sutherland argues, it seems that the US fears for Alaska had been somewhat exaggerated. Very likely a significant factor had been the desire to obtain a secure line of communications to Alaska as a long-term requirement of US defence. Also, there may have been a need to initiate vigorous action at a time when American military power was still being mobilized[29]. However, before the end of World War II, US interest in the area had declined so much so that in 1944, proposals were made for Canada to take over responsibility for the Alcan Highway, and the Crimson route bases were abandoned. By 1946, this proposal had been implemented. «The war and the aeroplane have driven home to Canadians the importance of their Northland, in strategy, in resources and in communications», Lester B. Pearson wrote in July 1946[30]. He went on stating that the earth is still round and that the shortest route between important places lie over the North Pole.

A NEW ERA

The three decades following World War II witnessed a greater degree of the «rounding out» of Canada than seen during the previous century. Although the major developmental thrust continued in an East-West direction within Canada, much more attention was directed northwards.

The thrust northwards covered the full range of nation-building, albeit with some gaps. For convenience this era is divided into the following fields for discussion: Defence; Sovereignty; Scientific Investigation and Inventory Taking; and Institutional Developments. As could be expected, there was much interaction between activities in these fields which caused new stresses and strains domestically and internationally.

Defence

World War II had, quite obviously, brought US and Canada closer together in many respects, particularly concerning continental defence. It had also formalized a series of relationships, working agreements and understandings which had, so far, remained informal. In many ways, these were seen as positive developments.

The early postwar period found us concerned with a potential rather than an actual threat. This potential threat consisted of long-range bombers with nuclear weapons capable of reaching North American cities as well as military or industrial installations. A varient of the potential threat towards North America foresaw the possibility of airborne troops being dislodged in the North American Arctic. Whereas in 1945 the former threat did not exist, it was nevertheless foreseen that it might develop.

With respect to the potential threat of airborne invasion, several defence-oriented programmes were undertaken by Canada, alone or jointly with the US, to acquire the ability to implement northern operations by the Canadian Army and/or the Royal Canadian Air Force, to carry out cold-weather operations involving specialized activities, and to carry out military activities including research and development which could contribute to the development and exploitation of Canada's Northern regions[31].

Whereas the army had resumed responsibility for the Northwest Highway system, the RCAF took over the airfields of the Northwest Staging Route. Furthermore, an Arctic test and development station was set up at Fort Churchill, and the army as well as the RCAF initiated northern training exercises. Several research and development projects, including work on vehicles, clothing and auxiliary equipment for northern operations saw the light of day. Later on, the Royal Canadian Navy constructed the large icebreaker HMCS *Labrador*[32].

The general approach towards defence of the North had been to cooperate with the natural elements of terrain and climate rather than to try to overcome them. «To conquer Nature one must follow her» would be a somewhat «noble» or idealized summing up of this type of policy. However, other reasons and motives played a role as well, and not all of them equally valiant or well thought out.

Yet as time progressed, the Canadian military presence in the North decreased. Operations and facilities were transferred to civilian agencies, and activities of purely National Defence character became sporadic and transient. Military activities were practically all related to continental defence arrangements.

Between 1945 and 1950, political developments moved dramatically on the international level, peaking with the signature of the North Atlantic Treaty in April 1949. An early sign of the growing imminence of a military threat was the appearance of the first Tu-4, a Soviet copy of the B-29 plane in May 49, and in August of the following year the first USSR nuclear detonation took place[33].

The outbreak of the Korean War in June 1950 had several significant results, some of them beneficial to defence spending and preparedness. For one thing, the US defence budget increased by 400 %. As Southerland shows, during the 1950s, there was not one but a series of genuinely revolutionary changes in military technology and strategic thinking. These changes involved thermonuclear weapons, longer-ranged and higher-performance aircraft, aerial refueling and long-range missiles[34]. Within the decade, the US and Canada had invested some $50 billion in continental air defence. The changes in the technology of this branch of defence alone had been staggering. Anti-aircraft guns were superseded by missiles, profound changes had taken place in the areas of fighter armour and performance, higher-performance radars, as well as the automation of the ground environment[35]. Whether or not the technological breakthroughs necessitated increased resources being spent on defence, or vice versa, the net result was further development and refinement in strategic thinking.

Canada was, to a large extent due to its lesser stature and limited resources, compared to its Southern superpower neighbour, playing a secondary role. From a military point of view, however, her Northern regions could offer both additional warning against an approaching USSR bomber threat, as well as defence in depth. As Sutherland argues, by extending the air defence system northwards, bombers could be engaged prior to reaching their target and, almost equally important, by extending the area of radar coverage the risk of saturation of the defences could be reduced. Furthermore, by locating strike aircraft or refueling aircraft on northern bases, the range and speed of response of the strike forces could be improved[36].

The overall planning for the Northern American air defence system, involved attempts to dispel major sources of uncertainty by technological investigation (technology forecasting), solidly-based military strategic analysis and war gaming. As such it was a major, but not always well known, ingredient and determinant in Canadian-American relations throughout the early postwar period.

Tangible results of such analysis were the North American Air Defence Command (NORAD), equipping the Canadian forces with similar weapons and the three great radar lines constructed in Canada in the 1950s. By 1951, Canada and the US had agreed to construct the Pinetree line, which was a radar belt located in Southern Canada and in the Northern United States[37]. By 1954, the Mid-Canada Line was constructed, following the 55th parallel and – in that same year – the construction of the Distant Early Warning (DEW) line along the 70th parallel took place. Although the Mid-Canada Line was phased out and changes made to the Pinetree and DEW Lines, the system with its interceptor aircraft continued to protect the US deterrent force from attach by aircraft and air or sea-launched *Cruise* missiles.

The technological and political development of the early post-World War II period tended to speed up and intensify the Western Worlds' concern for security. Canada shared this concern and sought protection through its commitments to NATO and NORAD. Thus Canada entered an era when its military effort was almost totally devoted to alliance activities. The nature of these contributions, as some argue, have not always adequately protected or taken into account national interests. The acceptance of the current location of the DEW Line roughly along 70° N and well inside Canada's northern perimeter is a case in point[38].

Sovereignty

Mackenzie King, partially for very good reasons, was worried about the Americans as a potential threat to our sovereighty in the North, but there was also the USSR to think about. The problem of a possible US-USSR confrontation in the North had been a subject of study and analysis from 1944 onward. One conclusion reached was that a greater US interest in Canadian defence after the war would follow for geostrategic reasons as Canada was, as it were, the meat in the sandwich between these two superpowers, lying as it did directly on the overland route between the US and the Soviet Union, and – as the Americans saw it – on the most probable route of approach to North America.

As Granatstein has argued, both new technology and traditional «sovereignty» were tested by the construction of the DEW Line. Whereas the former went quite well, the latter was less-successfully handled.

The official announcement of the DEW Line project had noted, in November 1954, that:

> Experience has shown that projects of this nature can be carried out most effectively by vesting responsibility for all phases of the work of construction and installation in a single authority – it has been agreed that although both Canada and the United States will participate in the project, responsibility for the work of construction and installation should be vested in the United States[39].

The DEW Line itself, at the peak of construction, had employed some 4 140 persons with a payroll of nearly $33 million[40]. The total cost of the DEW Line would eventually reach $600 million. However, as Sutherland observed, through this agreement Canada had managed to secure what the US, up to now, had assiduously tried to avoid, *i.e.*, the explicit recognition of Canadian claims to sovereignty in its Far North, particularly pertaining to land[41].

Controversies connected with the DEW Line had also raised concerns about Canada's sovereignty in the North generally. Whereas Prime Minister Pearson has stated in 1946 that Canada's territory included not only her Northland but also the islands and frozen seas north of the mainland between the meridians and its east and west boundaries extended to the North Pole[42], some ten years later a different view was expressed from an official level, only subsequently to be rendered an alternate interpretation[43]. This was, as is well known by now, the beginning of a long period of debate and discussion, much of it curiously cyclical in nature, some of it confused and confusing bearing on the, as yet, – at least from a practical point of view – relatively ill-defined concept of sovereignty.

With the commencement of transpolar flying on a regular basis, Canada took steps to protect the sovereignty of its air space. In the late 1950s, Canada introduced a Flight Information Service for intercontinental flights. The Goose Bay Air Control Centre (ACC) served the area east of 70° W and the islands beyond 72° N. For the region south of 72° N and west of 70° W flight information was provided by the Edmonton ACC. In 1968, the Edmonton ACC assumed responsibility for flight information for the Arctic Islands north of 72° N.

In April 1970, Canada through the International Civil Aviation Organization (ICAO) began providing an area control service for the Canadian Sector of the Arctic Ocean extending from the Archipelago to the North Pole between 60° W and 141° W, for flights at 29 000 feet and above. More recently the Northern domestic airspace has been subdivided into two control areas, the Northern Control Area occupying the region south of 72° N and the Arctic Control Area extending from 72° N to the Pole[44].

It is largely accepted that no nation can really assume that it has control and jurisdiction over its aerospace unless it has the capability of controlling and identifying air traffic within that zone. In other words, the sovereignty of its air space is not secure without an airspace control system although there may be some small gaps in the Canadian system south of roughly 72° N. The Northern detection limit of the DEW Line – the large area to the north encompassed by the Arctic Control Area – is completely void of any means if detecting or identifying aircraft penetrating that air space. Yet we have declared internationally responsibility for providing a control service within this region.

Concern about sovereignty in Canada's Northwest regions gradually turned from land to sea. This change of focus, as Gordon W. Smith observes in his meticulous studies, took place almost imperceptibly. There were, as he puts it, a number of «snowflakes in the wind» indicating the trends to come; such as the treaty between Great Britain (on behalf of Trinidad) and Venezuela (1942) concerning the submarine areas of the Gulf of Paria; US President Truman's proclamations regarding the continental shelf and fisheries (1945); the International Court of Justice landmark judgement in the Anglo-Norwegian fisheries dispute (1951); and subsequent Law of the Sea Conferences (1958, 1960)[45]. Of a more directly physical nature were the US Plans – some of which now implemented – to sail through the Northwest Passage, US naval exercises in Northern waters as well as submarine voyages to the North Pole, across the Arctic Ocean and through the Northwest Passage and, finally, US and USSR drifts on ice islands and ice floes, some of which entered the Canadian sector[46].

Practical issues had forced themselves to the forefront since the US had initiated icebreaker programs and – in 1958 – sent its nuclear-power submarine *Nautilus* under the polar icecap. The latter was taken as a clear challenge to claims of sovereignty held by the USSR as well as Canada. Further complication, form a Canadian point of view, was added when US international lawyers started to argue that the Arctic ice constituted international territory[47].

Arguments about these matters continued, and doubt remained for some time. Attempts by the Government of Lester B. Pearson to enclose the Arctic channels of Canada's internal waters in the early 1960s resulted in sharp reactions from the US, which led Canada to drop its plans. According to some students of international law, this was an unfortunate development as it henceforth limited Canada to a three-mile territorial waters concept with, possibly, historic bays, «a three-plus nine-mile fisheries zone, introduced in 1964, and a tentative claim for treating old, semi-permanent ice between some islands as if it were a land bridge»[48]. However, by April 1970, the then Canadian Minister of External Affairs had been on the record, stating flatly that Canada had always regarded the waters between the islands of the Arctic archipelago as belonging to Canada[49]. Shortly thereafter the Canadian Government extended its territorial waters to twelve miles, in the process securing control over the normal entrances and exits of the Northwest Passage.

However, as was to be pointed out by several experts subsequently, Canada's rights were far from absolute. According to Donat Pharand, for example, Canada could not bar the innocent passage of foreign vessels, or even foreign warships[50]. He has subsequently argued, privately as well as in public, for Canada adapting a policy of strategic use of Arctic antipollution legislation combined with *inter alia* increased ice-breaking capability[51].

Technological breakthroughs, as well as questions of resource development tended to, again, bring attention to Canada's role as a Northern state[52]. A variety of resources, such as copper, gold, silver, asbestos, tungsten, lead-zink and gas are available in ample supply as is (probably) petroleum, although the current glut on the international market acts as a serious obstacle for further development. This glut is in the final analysis artificial in the sense that 1. oil is in finite supply, and 2. mankind will only run out of it *once*[53]. At any rate, Canadian control of its claimed territories would seem to be vital for this and other reasons. However, the lack of concern and, as Granatstein puts it, almost automatic acquiescence to American requests since 1942 have eaten away some of our rights[54]. For sovereignty, properly and practically-defined presupposes, in fact it requires some back-up work, preparations and (ideally) foresight. Sovereignty has to be *exercised,* and that means more than simply making declaratory statements.

The long, drawn-out discussions of the postwar years had failed to produce much action in the North, of the type designed to safeguard, protect and further Canada's sovereignty claims as for example the Northern Sovereignty Crisis 1968-1970 and subsequent developments showed clearly[55]. Dosman, for example, in his 1976 article, gives a vivid account of the general lack of preparation, ad-hockery and administrative confusion which seemed to reign at External Affairs during much of this period[56]. Legal complexities and general lack of *action* did not make matters easier for Canada. As it is known, the US decided to put the *SS Manhattan,* with an accompanying vessel, through the Northwest Passage. As of November 1968, no official request for permission from the Canadian Government had been received. Whereas the US was simply acting as a Great Power might be expected to, in the process it challenged Canadian sovereignty beyond the three-mile territorial sea.

The chain of events which followed, discussed in considerable detail by, among others, Dosman[57], may be seen either as a «success story» for crisis foreign policy-making under seemingly great pressure, or – as the above author seems to imply strongly, and possibly correctly – an example of the absence of necessary foresight in decision-making. There is no doubt that the various maneuvers undertaken managed to get us «off the hook», at least in terms of appearance, which by itself is perhaps no minor matter in such an important case involving a superpower and otherwise friendly next-door neighbour with whom we have much in common and much to protect. But is it, by itself enough, and will this type of ad-hockery be sufficient to safely see us through future events (or crises) like this one?

The unwillingness to draw baselines had permitted the North to remain the last area where Canadian sovereign territorial integrity could be questioned and challenged. As had been the case in the past, timidity won out, and Canadian subservience to Washington remained the order of the day. This does not mean to say that Canada did not *express* its concern, as several important speeches were made in Parliament and elsewhere. The proposed antipollution act, for example, was levied as a weapon of defence of Canada's Northern territorial interests by the then Prime Minister Trudeau in April 1970. Canada should want to protect itself against «grave threats towards the environment», a right it had in common with other coastal states. From the point of view of international law, also, this made eminent sense. However, laws, in order to remain guarantees, have to be backed up by appropriate enforcement capabilities. And, as is by now quite well known, in the realm of international law *per se,* this is often a difficult point. Laws by themselves, and in particular international laws, *without* any such capability will, at best, be high-sounding declarations, at worst they are simply scraps of paper. Had Canada pursued a policy of vigorous Northern activities including, say – as was argued by some – expanded ice-breaking capacities, it may have been easier to rest our case on antipollution legislative measures, for example, although it is doubtful that in the long run this alone would suffice. Such, however, was not the case, and not to be for some time.

Things were even a bit worse than that. If the fragile nature of the Northern environment was intended to be used as the «backdrop» for sovereignty claims involving antipollution laws, then – clearly – a well-established expertise on Arctic matters, *i.e.* solid, scientific research would be needed.

The threat of environmental damage in the North did, however, turn out to be quite a useful working hypothesis, which generated not only sympathy in Parliament and elsewhere, but also led to a fair amount of activity, albeit much of it of a primarily bureaucratic nature, i.e. meetings, discussions groups, task forces, panels, elaborative and travelling committees and the like with little to show for practical, technical and security-related results pertaining to «sovereignty». Whereas a series of functional approaches on these, as on other, matters should not be scoffed at – they nevertheless would seem to call for additional work.

The sharp confrontation with the US with regards to Northern sovereignty in 1968-1970 was probably unavoidable at any rate. Much of it seems to have been based on the more practical and basic driving forces of the need – perceived or de facto – for resources in general and energy sources in particular. In part, therefore, when it became clear that the oil companies preferred pipelines to tankers as far as the transport of Alaska oil to Southern markets were concerned, much of the steam went out of the debate[58]. This, in turn, provided Canada with a «breathing spell», which it seems in retrospect could have been better used than was to be the case. The question of military security has been downplayed somewhat in this paper, as it is discussed more fully elsewhere[59]. Of course, this does not mean that it remains of secondary importance.

In the summer of 1985, the US coast guard put the icebreaker *Polar Sea* through the Northwest Passage, without asking prior permission from the Canadian Government. As in 1969, with the voyage of the *Manhattan*, this caused considerable anxiety in Canada. The deficiencies in backing up Canada's claim to sovereignty was, again, highlighted[60]. The events also caused pressure to build up fairly quickly this time around, leading to the need for a government statement in the House of Commons, detailing some very important measures which it intended to undertake. These included drawing straight baselines around the archipelago to delineate Canada's claims, the removal of the 1970 reservation to the jurisdiction of the International Court of Justice[61], increased aerial surveillance, naval activities in the Eastern Arctic waters, as well as the construction of a class-8 polar icebreaker[62]. *In toto*, if carried out fully, these measures represent the biggest step taken forward by any Canadian Government to protect, safeguard and further our Arctic interest and to make it clear to anyone that we consider ourselves to be a circumpolar nation.

There was, however, one negative impact of all of this, a sort of fly in the ointment. Whereas the North American alliance remained the centerpiece of postwar Canadian defence policy in the postwar period, Canada's concerns for sovereignty by now had started to make themselves feel more strongly in some circles. In part this was a natural development for any nation coming of age, in part – as we shall see – there were some extraordinary aversions to US presence and influence. Throughout this period, in fact until now, the concept of sovereignty had been fairly poorly defined in terms other than legal ones. That is to say, we have largely failed to properly decompartmentalize sovereignty as a useful strategic concept, i.e. in terms of distinctive differences pertaining to its meanings for, say, land, sea and air, to say nothing of its utility for industrial or cultural or indeed overall strategic purposes.

Scientific Investigation and Inventory Taking

The era of geographical exploration and general surveying came to a close during the early postwar years, and Northern Canada entered a period of intensive scientific investigation and inventory taking. Initially, the Defence Research Board, and more recently the Polar Continental Shelf Project, played a major role in the range of scientific activities with considerable potential and long-term utility for Canada.

In retrospect, the period of «government by science» in the North, seems to have been a high point in Canada's coming to grips with its role as a circumpolar nation. What was understood quite well, and is worth noting for the future, is that to invest heavily in scientific investigation may be one of the cheapest yet most effective means of demonstrating sovereignty[63]. In the process, much useful and important work had been undertaken.

It is conservatively estimated that during three decades of scientific investigation, the Federal Government spent well over a third of a billion dollars on scientific activities in the two territories. In the fiscal year 1975-1976, over $42 million was devoted to science in the North; during a 10-year period (1974-1984), over $157 million were spent on research programs and studies by the Federal Government alone[64]. In addition, many millions were spent by industry and universities. The need to establish scientific facilities in the Canadian North was realized in the late 1950s, and during the next 30 years, a number of permanent and temporary research centres and stations were located across the North by government and universities.

The plethora of scientific activities, often appearing to lack coordination and direction, created much discussion in and out of government over the need for a Northern science framework and a mechanism for focusing federally-sponsored science on the government's Northern objectives. Although this concern was often expressed during the 1970s, such a framework and mechanism still remains elusive. Nevertheless, as a result of a federally-sponsored seminar attended by scientists from industry, universities and government on «Science and the North» in 1972, «Guidelines for Scientific Activities in Northern Canada» were prepared and published. The guidelines, the first to be enunciated in such detail, provided useful direction for the scientific community for almost a decade.

Interest in Northern resources increased in the late 1950s. Mineral and gas discoveries, and the large oil discovery at Prudhoe Bay, Alaska, in 1968, triggered off a major resource «inventory taking» exercise in Northern Canada. The delineation of hydrocarbon deposits attracted the most attention and effort, and several billions of dollars were spent over the next two decades by industry; a great deal of the effort was financed through Federal Government incentive programs[65].

Concern over the potential adverse impact of oil and gas development on the environment and other resources resulted in a wide range of studies and investigations which have contributed to a better understanding of the renewable resources of the North.

The massive amount of scientific, technical and other data acquired on the North during this era is unparalleled in Canadian history; the accumulation is still going on albeit at a slower pace. To what extent Canada will benefit domestically and internationally from this knowledge is difficult to say. It is possibly too early to voice an opinion. Internationally, it has drawn the attention of scientists and industry, but the impact on the socio-economic development of the region has been marginal to date. In 1968, O.M. Solandt, then Chairman of the Science Council of Canada, when appearing before a US science committee, stated «Canada should be the free world's leading expert on the social and technical problems of life in cold climates»[66]. The scientific and technical resource base developed during the post-World War II era, could go a long way towards achieving this goal if built upon and effectively utilized.

Institutional Developments

As we have seen, and for administrative reasons, the area is divided into two «territories», the Yukon and the Northwest Territories with, respectively, 536 000 and 3 366 000 square kilometers. The Federal Government provides roughly two-thirds of the annual costs in the Territories, and in all matters regarding natural resources (except game) it maintains complete and exclusive authority. Furthermore, it is also responsible for Indian and Eskimo (now Inuit) affairs[67].

However, matters do not stop here. Each territory has a regional administration which, to some extent, mirrors that of the provinces although naturally down-scaled. Matters are, as we shall see, further complicated somewhat due to the fact that some 30 or more departments and agencies of the Federal Government are involved in a variety of activities pertaining to the North, such as taxation, transport, health and welfare, protection and security, police work, and environmental concerns. Presiding over this bureaucratic maze, in theory if not always in practice, is the Minister of Indian Affairs and Northern Development. Whereas this arrangement is not neat administratively it has proven to be reasonable up to now[68]. We will argue that in the light of recent developments and seen in the context of the future evolution of the international system, especially in terms of long-term strategy and security issues, it may behove us to try to optimize and improve existing arrangements, wherever possible, and to look to new ones where needed.

For example, in 1972, the Minister of Indian and Northern Affairs, charged with coordination of the whole, enunciated the following seven objectives according to which government policies concerning the North should be implemented[69]:

a) The achievement of a higher standard of living, quality of life and equality of opportunity for all Northern residents;

b) The maintenance and improvement of the Northern environment with due allowance for economic and social development;

c) The systematic encouragement of viable economic development, within selected regions of the North;

d) The enablement of Northern Canada to contribute to the social and cultural development of the country as a whole;

e) The aiding in the evolution of local self-government in the North;

f) The maintenance of sovereignty and security of Canada in the North;

g) The development of leisure and recreational opportunities in the North for the benefit of all.

What is quite remarkable is that the question of «sovereignty and security» here is in sixth place, just ahead of «leisure and recreational opportunities for the benefit of all». We have here, we will submit, possibly the kernel of why it is that, up

to now at any rate, Canada's concerns for its role as a circumpolar nation internationally has been somewhat spasmodic and possible less than that expected of it as a
Northern nation. Whereas the above list of objectives did not constitute an ordering
of priorities per se, nevertheless the sixth position may reflect the limited attention
the government of the day played on sovereignty and security in the North. However,
the report itself is possibly the most complete statement of national objectives and
strategies enunciated by any government to this date.

As there have been quite remarkable changes in the way of life and status
of the Northern native people, so have concerns for their well-being been publicly
expressed and safeguarded. Several examples come to mind, such as educational
reforms initiated in the late 1940s, much improved health services, aid to the emerging cooperative movements, and governmental assistance to Indian and Eskimo
organizations for a variety of purposes[70].

Additionally, the very genuine concern for putting more importance on the
needs of the people in the North than on resource development per se is of course
admirable and quite in character with the Canadian spirit. For when the first mining
developments in Canada were started, there had been no consultation whatsoever
with the native people[71]. At this stage of the game no such undertaking, let alone
preliminary investigations such as seismic exploration for oil, for example, can be
carried out without consultation by the Northern residents liable to be affected.

In recent years, we have witnessed dramatic discussions concerning possible future routes for oil and gas transportation, should they materialize, both in the
form of shipping or pipelines. A mass of documentation exists, as does an intricate
web of administrative consultative machinery. The concern for the North is genuine,
its internal manifestations are evident enough and reflect – by and large – the political
culture of Canada.

THE FUTURE

The East-West development of the country will continue to dominate the
Canadian scene domestically and internationally, but the Northern dimension has
been established and will play a role in future affairs; albeit with varying degrees of
attention depending upon the ebb and flow in resource development and tensions
in the circumpolar region.

It is important to note, however, that the three major socio-political variables
which will influence and shape the strategic future of Canada's Arctic are technology
and weapons developments, economic and resource developments, and demographic and related changes, including sovereignty pressures. Furthermore, it is the interaction of these three major variables which is most likely to produce the most
important impacts on Canada's Arctic regions. And it is by controlling, and possibly
manipulating some of these variables that Canadian national aims can best be achieved.

For once, Canada now seems poised on taking the necessary steps for fully
asserting the legitimacy of its claims in the High Arctic, and its role as a circumpolar
nation. This presupposes both a strong civilian as well as a certain military presence,
which may be easier said than done, due to various – largely geographical and climatic

– factors already discussed. From the point of view of national will, purpose and direction there is little doubt that these measures deserve to be undertaken. What is needed more than anything else, it seems, is a strategically balanced approach towards Canada's Arctic regions. This balanced approach means that attention must also be focused on the linkages between the military-strategic environment and the prospects for political change and development in the North[72]. As most of the necessary analysis has been already carried out, the next step would be to get on with their implementation.

More specifically, areas of public concern will likely include sovereignty matters involving not only defence but industrial/commercial agreements, demographics and opportunities for international cooperation in Arctic research and institution building with our circumpolar neighbours. In almost all these areas of activities, pressures are likely to be put on us. For the reasons stated above, it is in our very best long-term interest that we now concentrate on the reconciliation of our international commitments with our own national security and sovereignty concerns.

NOTES

1. See *Competitiveness and Security: Directions for Canada's International Relations,* presented by the Right Honourable Joe Clark, Secretary of State for External Affairs, Ottawa, 1985, Supply and Services Canada, Cat. No. E2-110/1985, p. 1.

2. *Ibidem,* p. 1.

3. See *Concepts and Themes in the Regional Geography of Canada* by J. Lewis Robinson, Vancouver, Talon Books, 1984.

4. *Ibidem.*

5. *Ibidem.*

6. The population of Yukon increased from 5 000 in 1941 to 23 000 in 1981. Whereas this is an impressive *percentage* increase, indicating that demographic trends are on the increase in the North, the *numerical* increase of some 18 000 persons within a 40-year period is less than the annual increase in larger Canadian cities. While the population of the Northwest Territories doubled within the 20-year period 1961 to 1981, its *total* population of 46 000 was only equivalent to that of an average size Canadian city. See also *Ibidem.,* on which some of the subsequent sections are based.

7. *Ibidem.*

8. See James R. Gibson, «The Geographical Context: Canadian-Soviet Comparisons», *Strategy and the Arctic,* by R.B. Byers and Michael Slack (eds), The Polaris Papers, 4, the Canadian Institute of Strategic Studies, 1986.

9. For a good comparison, see Trevor Lloyd, «Canadian Policies in the North», *The Arctic Circle: Aspects of the North From The Circumpolar Nations,* by William C. Wonders (ed), Longman, Canada, 1976 and J.R. Gibson, *loc. cit.*

10. See, for example, Trevor Lloyd, «Some International Aspects of Arctic Canada», *International Journal,* 25, Autumn 1970; Maxwell Cohen, «The Arctic and the National Interest», *International Journal,* 26, Winter 1970-1971; *Northward Looking: A Strategy and a Science Policy for Northern Development,* The Science Council of Canada, 1977; Morris Zaslow (ed.), *A Century of Canada's Arctic Islands: 1880-1980,* Ottawa, The Royal Society of Canada, 1981; Lincoln P. Bloomfield, «The Arctic: Last Unmanaged Frontier», *Foreign Affairs,* 60, Fall 1981; Douglas Johnston (ed.), *Arctic Ocean Isssues in the 1980s,* Honolulu, Law of the Sea Institute, University of Hawaii, 1982; John Kirton, «Beyond Bilateralism: United States-Canadian Cooperation in the Arctic», *United States Arctic Interests, The 1980s and 1990s,* by William E. Westermeyer and Kurt M. Schusterich (eds.), New York, Berlin, Heidelberg, Tokyo, Springer Verlag, 1986, and – in general – the bibliographical list of the present paper.

11. A very useful, meticulous, and detailed account of this process may be found in Gordon W. Smith, «The Transfer of Arctic Territories from Great Britain to Canada in 1880, and some Related Matters, as Seen in Official Correspondence», *Arctic,* 14, No. 1, March 1961, and *Canada's Arctic Archipelago: 100 Years of Canadian Jurisdiction,* by Gordon W. Smith, Ottawa, Northern Affairs Program, Indian and Northern Affairs, Canada, 1980.

12. See, for example, J.L. Granatstein, «A Fit of Absence of Mind: Canada's National Interest in the North to 1968», *The Arctic in Question,* by E.J. Dosman (ed), Oxford University Press, 1976, on which some of the subsequent sections are based, and Smith, *loc. cit.*

13. Both Gordon W. Smith and J.L. Granatstein have produced detailed accounts of this period. Their writings referenced here should be read concurrently as they supplement each other, yet offer somewhat different interpretation in one or two cases regarding possible motives of the political actors involved.

14. Granatstein, *op. cit.*

15. See Morris Zaslow, *The Opening of the Canadian North 1870-1917,* Toronto, 1971, as quoted in Granatstein, *op. cit.*

16. *Ibidem.*

17. See Granatstein, *op. cit.*

18. This term was applied by, *inter alia,* Lester B. Pearson when referring to Canada's defence of its North in an article the *Toronto Globe and Mail* of November 27, 1948.

19. The US and Denmark were two cases in point.

20. See V.K. Johnston, «Canada's Title to the Arctic Islands», in *Canadian Historical Review,* XIV, March 1933.

21. Granatstein, *op. cit.*

22. See Vilhjalmur Stefansson, «The American Far North», *Foreign Affairs,* Vol. 28, April 1939, and Granatstein, *op. cit.*

23. See George Lindsey, «The Strategic Environment of the Arctic», and Erik Solem, «Energy, Technology and Strategy in the Arctic», *Strategy and the Arctic* by R.B. Byers and Michael Slack (eds.), Toronto, The Polaris Papers, 4, The Canadian Institute of Strategic Studies, 1986.

24. An oil-distribution system based on the oil field at Norman Wells, N.W.T., the purpose of which was to develop a source of petroleum products closer to the Alaskan theatre than the continental United States.

25. Granatstein, *op. cit.*

26. Department of External Affairs, External Affairs Records, file 52-B(s), Memo, March 30, 1943 and MacDonald's note «On Developments in North-Western Canada»: April 6, 1943; King Diary, 1939-1945, Ottawa, 1970, as quoted in Granatstein, *op. cit.*

27. See R.J. Sutherland, «The Strategic Significance of the Canadian Arctic», in *the Arctic Frontier*, by R. St. J. Macdonald (ed.), Toronto, University of Toronto Press, 1970.

28. See S.W. Dziuban, «US Army in World War II, Special Studies – Military Relations Between the United States and Canada, 1939-1945», Office of the Chief of Military History, Washington; Department of the Army, 1959, as quoted in R.J. Sutherland, *op. cit.*

29. *Ibidem.*

30. Lester B. Pearson, «Canada Looks 'Down North', *Foreign Affairs*, July 1946.

31. See also Sutherland, *op. cit.*, on these points.

32. Sutherland, *op. cit.*

33. *Ibidem.*

34. *Ibidem.*

35. *Ibidem.*

36. Sutherland discusses these developments in great detail, as well as the number of existing alternatives for each case. For example, with respect to warning, options included large radars capable of providing height and track information, simpler equipment as well as airborne radars. For «defence in depth», two major alternatives existed; either to extend northwards the system of radars and airfields, or to construct a long-range aircraft with integral radar capable of operating beyond the area of continuous radar cover. Concerning strike forces, the options were even more complex, including several combinations of aircraft, bases, and operating policies.

37. For which the Americans picked up two-thirds of the cost.

38. C.E. Beattie and K.R. Greenaway, «Offering up Canada's North», *Northern Perspectives*, Vol. 14, No. 4, 1986; and Alasdair MacLaren, «Canada Needs to Reconcile Foreign and Defence Policies», *International Perspectives*, March-April 1977.

39. R.A. MacKay, *Canadian Foreign Policy 1945-1954*, Selected Speeches and Documents, Toronto 1971, quoted in Granatstein, *op. cit.*

40. See K.J. Rea, *The Political Economy of the Canadian North*, Toronto, 1968, and Granatstein, op. c*it.*

41. See Sutherland, *op. cit.*

42. Lester B. Pearson, *op. cit.*

43. In 1956, the Hon. Jean Lesage stated in the House of Commons that Canada had never subscribed to the sector theory in application to the ice, and that it was content with sovereignty covering the Arctic Islands, not over the sea, be it open or frozen. This statement was contradicted a few months later by Prime Minister St. Laurent who stated that the Arctic waters were Canadian territorial waters. See Granatstein, *op. cit.*, and also House of Commons, *Debates*, August 3, 1956 (p. 6955).

44. Keith R. Greenaway and Moira Dunbar, «Aviation in the Arctic Islands»: *A Century of Canada's Arctic Islands: 1880-1980,* by Morris Zaslow (ed.), The Royal Society of Canada, 1981.

45. Gordon W. Smith, *loc. cit.*

46. *Ibidem;* see also E.J. Dosman (ed.), *The Arctic in Question*, Toronto, Oxford University Press, 1976.

47. Granatstein, *op. cit.*

48. According to Maxwell Cohen, as quoted in Granatstein, *op. cit.*

49. See *Statements and Speeches* 70/5, statement in Parliament, April 16, 1970 by Secretary of State for External Affairs, the Hon. Mitchell Sharp.

50. Donat Pharand, «Innocent Passage in the Arctic», *Canadian Yearbook of International Law,* 1968.

51. Private communication.

52. See, for example, «Energy, Technology and Strategy the Arctic», in *Strategy and the Arctic*, by R.B. Byers and Michael Slack (eds.), The Polaris Papers, 4, Toronto, The Canadian Institute of Strategic Studies, 1986.

53. See «Strategic Implications of Resource Policy», *Energy Resources and Centre-Periphery Relations,* by F.C. Engelmann and R.R. Gilsdorf (eds.), University of Alberta Press, 1981; «Energy and Changing Strategic Aspects of Canada's Arctic Regions», *Canadian Defence Quarterly,* 11, Winter 1981-1982, and (with Antony F.G. Scanlan), «Oil and Natural Gas as Factors in Strategic Policy and Action: A Long-Term View», *Global Resources and International Conflict,* by Arthur H. Westing (ed.), A SIPRI-UNEP Study, Oxford-New York, Oxford University Press, 1986.

54. Granatstein, op. *cit.*

55. See, for example, E.J. Dosman, «The Northern Sovereignty Crisis 1968-1970», in his *The Arctic in Question, op. cit.*

56. *Ibidem.*

57. *Ibidem.*

58. *Ibidem.*

59. See Sutherland, Lindsey, Gellner and Solem, *op. cit.*, as well as in particular B. Gen (Ret.), in C.E. Beattie and B. Gen (Ret.), K.R. Greenaway (Ret.), «Offering Up Canada's North», *Northern Perspectives,* Vol. 14, No. 4, September-October 1986; G.R. Lindsey, «Defence in the North» and Erik Solem, «Should Canada Have a Long-Term Strategy for the Arctic?», The *Arctic: A Vital Strategic Region for the Great Powers?,* Centre québécois de relations internationales, October 1986.

60. See «The Question of Sovereignty», *Northern Perspectives,* Vol. 14, No. 4, September-October 1986, and Chapter 10, «A Northern Dimension for Canada's Foreign Policy», *Independence and Internationalism,* Report by the Special Joint Committee on Canada's International Relations, Ottawa, 1986.

61. In response to the 1969 voyage of the *Manhattan,* Parliament had passed the Arctic Waters Pollution Prevention Act, proclaiming a 100-mile pollution prevention zone in the area. This legal concept was entirely new, and the Government at that time had decided that the new law might not stand up to a challenge in the International Court of Justice. Hence, to protect the new Canadian position, the Government had entered a reservation as to the competence of the Court. The removal of the reservation was made possible due to the developments in Arctic environmental law achieved at the Law of the Sea Conference, as quoted in «The Question of Sovereignty», loc. *cit.*

62. *Ibidem.*

63. See G. Hattersley-Smith, *North of Latitude Eighty,* Defence Research Board of Canada, 1974; and C. Marino, *Polar Shelf: The Saga of Canada's Arctic Scientists,* N.C. Press Ltd., 1986.

64. See *Inventory of Federal Northern Science Projects, 1975-1976,* Ministry of State for Science, 1977; and *Ten Years of Northern Research in Canada 1974-1984,* Vol. 1, Indian Affairs and Northern Development, 1985.

65. See *Arctic Systems,* Proceedings of a conference held by the NATO Special Panel on Systems Science, Plenum Press, 1977; *Canada's North Today,* Indian Affairs and Northern Development, 1978; *Unter the Beaufort,* Indian Affairs and Northern Development, 1980; *Energy Update,* Energy, Mines and Resources, 1981; *Financial Post,* January 9, 1982; and *Panarctic Briefing Notes* for Heads of Missions' Northern Tour, 1983.

66. See O.M. Solandt, *The Utilization of Scientific and Technical Resources in Canada,* presented to the Committee on Science and Astronautics, US House of Representatives, 1968.

67. See T. Lloyd, *op. cit.*

68. *Ibidem.*

69. *Canada's North 1970-1980:* Statement of the Government of Canada on Northern Development in the 1970s. Presented to the Standing Committee on Indian Affairs and Northern Development by the Honourable Jean Chrétien, Minister of Indian Affairs and Northern Development, Ottawa, March 28, 1972; Information Canada, 1972. See also T. Lloyd, *op. cit.*

70. Trevor Lloyd discusses some of these initiatives at length; *op. cit.*

71. For example, oil at Norman Wells in the 1920s, radium at Great Bear Lake in 1936 and – two years later – gold at Yellowknife. See also Lloyd, *op. cit.*

72. See *Strategy and the Arctic, op. cit.*

BIBLIOGRAPHY

BACH, H.C. and TAAGHOLT. *Greenland and the Arctic Region: Resources and Security Policy*, Copenhagen, 1982.

BEATTIE, C.E. and GREENAWAY, K.R. «Offering Up Canada's North, *Northern Perspectives*, Vol. 14, No. 4, Ottawa, CARC, September-October 1986, 1986.

BEAUCHAMP, Ken. «International Issues in Arctic Waters», *Northern Perspectives*, Ottawa, CARC, December 1983, No. 2, 1983.

BYERS, R.B. and SLACK, Michael (eds). *Strategy and the Arctic*, The Polaris Papers, 4, The Canadian Institute of Strategic Studies, 1986.

DOSMAN, E.J. (ed.) *The Arctic in Question*, Oxford University Press, 1976.

DOSMAN, E.J. «The Northern Sovereignty Crisis 1968-1970», *The Arctic in Question*, by E.J. Dosman (ed.), Oxford University Press, 1976.

DUNBAR, Moira and GREENAWAY, K.R. *Arctic Canada from the Air*, Defence Research Board, Canada, 1956.

DYSON, John. *The Hot Arctic*, Boston-Toronto, Little, Brown & Company, 1979.

GELLNER, JOHN. «The Military Task: Sovereignty and the Security, Surveillance and Control in the Far North», *The Arctic in Question*, by E.J. Dosman (ed.), Oxford University Press, 1976.

GELLNER, John. «The Arctic and the Strategic Forcefield», *Strategy and The Arctic* by R.B. Byers and K. Michael Slack (eds.), The Polaris Papers, CISS, 1986.

GRANATSTEIN, J.L. «A Fit of Absence of Mind: Canada's National Interest in the North in 1968», The *Arctic in Question*, by E.J. Dosman (ed.), Oxford University Press, 1976.

GREENAWAY, Keith and DUNBAR, Moira. «Aviation in the Arctic Islands», A *Century of Canada's Arctic Islands: 1880-1980*, by Morris Zaslow (ed.), The Royal Society of Canada, 1981.

GRIFFITHS, Franklyn. «Canadian Sovereignty and Arctic International Relations», *The Arctic in Question*, by E.J. Dosman (ed.), Oxford University Press, 1976.

GRIFFITHS, Franklyn. «A Northern Foreign Policy», *Wellesley Papers*, 7/1979, Canadian Institute of International Affairs, 1979.

HATTERSLEY-SMITH, G. *North of Latitude Eighty*, Defence Research Board, Canada, 1974.

HOCKIN, T.A. and BRENNAN, P.A. «Canada's Arctic and its Strategic Importance», *The Arctic in Question*, by E.J. Dosman (ed.). Oxford University Press, 1976.

LINDSEY, G.R. «Strategic Aspects of the Polar Regions», *Behind in the Headlines*, 34, No. 6, 1977.

LINDSEY, G.R. «The Strategic Environment of the Arctic», *Strategy and the Arctic* by R.B. Byers and Michael Slack (ed.), Polaris Papers 4, CISS, 1986.

LLOYD, Trevor. «Frontier of Destiny – The Canadian Arctic», *Beyond the Headlines*, CIIA, 1946.

MACDONALD, R. St. J. (ed). *The Arctic Frontier*, Toronto, University of Toronto Press, 1966.

PEARSON, L.B. «Canada Looks Down North», *Foreign Affairs*, XXIV, July 1946.

PHARAND, Donat. *The Law of the Sea of the Arctic*, Ottawa, 1973.

PULLEN, T.C. «Arctic Marine Transportation: A View from the Bridge», *Northern Perspectives*, No. 2, December 1983, Ottawa, CARC, 1983.

PULLEN, T.C. «That Polar Icebreaker», *Northern Perspectives*, Vol. 14, No. 44, September-October 1986, Ottawa, CARC, 1986.

PURVER, Ron. «The Strategic Importance of the Arctic Region», *Strategy and The Arctic*, by R.B. BYERS and Michael Slack (eds.), Polaris Papers 4, CISS, 1986.

PURVER, Ron. «The Prospects for Arms Control in the Arctic», *Strategy and The Arctic*, by R.B. Byers and Michael Slack (eds.), Polaris Papers 4, Canadian Institute of Strategic Studies, 1986.

SCANLAN, A.F.G. «Resource Endowment and Exploitation», *Northern Waters: Resources and Security Issues*, RIIA, London, Chatham House, 1986.

SMITH, Gordon. «The Transfer of Arctic Territories from Great Britain to Canada in 1880, and Some Related Matters, as Seen in Official Correspondence», *Arctic*, Vol. 14, No. 1, March 1961.

SMITH, Gordon. «Sovereignty in the North: The Canadian Aspect of an International Problem», *The Arctic, Frontier*, by R. St. J., Macdonald, Toronto, 1966.

SMITH, Gordon. «Canada's Arctic Archipelago: 100 Years of Canadian Jurisdiction», Northern Affairs Program, Indian and Northern Affairs, Canada, Ottawa, 1980.

SOLEM, Erik. «Strategic Implications of Resource Policy», *Energy, Resources and Centre – Periphery Relations* by F.D. Engelmann and R.R. Gilsforf, (eds.), University of Alberta Press, 1981.

SOLEM, Erik. «Energy and Changing Strategic Aspects of Canada's Arctic Regions», *Canadian Defence Quarterly*, 11, Winter 1981-1982.

SOLEM, Erik. «Energy, Technology and Strategy in the Arctic», *Strategy and the Arctic,* by R.B. Byers and Michael Slack (eds.), The Polaris Papers 4, The Canadian Institute of Strategic Studies, 1986.

SOLEM, Erik. «Should Canada have a Long-Term Strategy for the Arctic?», T*he Arctic: A Vital Strategic Region for the Great Powers?»,* Centre québécois des relations internationales, 1986.

SUTHERLAND, R.J. «The Strategic Significance of the Canadian Arctic», *The Arctic Frontier,* by R. St. J. Macdonald, Toronto, 1966.

WESTERMEYER, William E. and SCHUSTERICH, Kurt M. «United States' Arctic Interests the 1980s and 1990s», New York-Berlin, Springer Verlag, 1986.

YOUNG, Oran. «The Age of the Arctic Region», *Foreign Policy,* Winter 1985-1986.

YOUNG, Oran. «The Militarization of the Arctic, Political Consequences and Prospects for Arms Control», Paper presented for the Conference on «Sovereignty, Security and the Arctic» at York University, Toronto, May 8-9, 1986.

YOUNG, Oran and OSHERENKO, Gail. «Arctic Resource Conflicts: Sources and Solutions», *United States Arctic Interests, The 1980s and 1990s,* by W.E. Westermeyer and K.M. Shusterich (eds.), New York-Berlin, Springer Verlag, 1986.

ORVIK, Nils. N*orthern Development: Northern Security,* Kingston, Centre for International Relations, Queen's University, 1983.

QUATRIÈME PARTIE   PART FOUR

Les politiques sectorielles   *The Sectorial Policies*

20

La politique de défense canadienne

Michel Fortman
Université de Montréal

Une politique de défense, en temps de paix, lorsqu'elle n'est pas simplement ignorée, suscite invariablement les controverses les plus passionnées, et celle du Canada apparemment ne fait pas exception à la règle. Il existe cependant une opinion que partagent la grande majorité des observateurs de cette politique: celle-ci est très mal en point. Comme le notait en juin 1986 le rapport Hockin-Simard dans ses conclusions: «À l'heure actuelle, les forces armées canadiennes n'ont pas les moyens de s'acquitter des multiples tâches qui leur sont confiées. Elles doivent se débrouiller avec un personnel trop réduit et un équipement désuet.» Par conséquent, «le gouvernement doit réduire cet écart entre nos engagements et nos possibilités pour éviter qu'il en résulte des conséquences désastreuses»[1].

Cette situation n'est pas nouvelle, et des déclarations similaires émaillent toute notre histoire d'après-guerre. La plupart des pays occidentaux ont eu, eux aussi, leur part de problèmes en matière de défense, mais il est tout de même remarquable qu'un pays si éloigné des zones de tensions internationales ait autant de mal à s'orienter en matière de sécurité. Les raisons les plus souvent citées pour expliquer cet état de choses sont bien connues, mais leur importance justifie qu'on les cite ici.

Le Canada, tout d'abord, n'est pas menacé directement du fait de sa situation géographique et des liens traditionnels qui l'unissent à son voisin du Sud. Une défense de type conventionnel n'est donc pas nécessaire pour assurer sa protection. Une telle défense serait impensable, compte tenu de l'immensité de notre territoire et de la modestie relative de nos ressources. En d'autres mots, nous n'avons pas besoin et nous ne pourrions d'ailleurs pas maintenir un équilibre militaire spécifique pour contrebalancer, par exemple, les divisions ou la flotte des USA. Notre situation est donc très différente de celle des pays européens qui, précisément, doivent maintenir un tel équilibre face au pacte de Varsovie.

Paradoxalement, depuis l'ouverture de l'ère nucléaire, le Canada subit une menace de destruction totale, mais celle-ci est largement indépendante de la volonté politique et des décisions que pourrait prendre l'État canadien. Une guerre nucléaire éventuelle entre l'URSS et les USA, dans ce sens, ne dépendrait que marginalement de nos choix, mais garantirait, par contre, notre destruction. La situation canadienne est donc délicate. Nous n'avons pas directement besoin d'une armée, mais notre survie dépend de nos efforts en faveur de la paix. Ceci soulève immédiatement la question de la neutralité ou du non-alignement qui nous offrirait la possibilité de contribuer à la détente Est-Ouest tout en gardant nos distances vis-à-vis des super-puissances. Toutefois, ceci ne tient pas compte d'un autre trait fondamental de la sécurité canadienne: l'indivisibilité de la défense du continent nord-américain. Notre territoire constitue, dans le contexte nucléaire, un élément indissociable de la défense américaine. Des attaques soviétiques dirigées contre les USA pourraient ainsi avoir pour point de passage notre espace aérien ou notre espace maritime. La défense du Canada est donc vitale pour Washington, et ceci donne aux États-Unis un droit de regard direct sur notre politique. Cette influence est renforcée encore par les liens économiques étroits qui unissent nos deux pays et qui offrent aux Américains de multiples moyens de pression sur le Canada. En conséquence, comme l'a noté John W. Holmes: «Dans l'après-guerre, la politique étrangère qui a fait du Canada un allié occidental a été virtuellement déterminée par un certain nombre de réalités: la structure bipolaire rigide du système international de l'époque, les données géographiques, les alliances et les liens historiques du Canada avec l'Angleterre, la structure politique et économique canadienne... Toute autre orientation de cette politique vers la neutralité ou vers une alliance avec l'URSS aurait buté sur ces réalités[2].»

Dans l'ensemble, le Canada constitue donc, en matière de sécurité comme sur le plan économique, un système pénétré qui est largement condamné à subir les pressions diverses et changeantes que lui vaut son statut d'allié occidental. *Bref, le grand problème du Canada, en termes de sécurité, n'est pas d'être un pays sans défense, mais un pays sans sa propre défense.*

Il est clair, en effet, que le gouvernement et le public canadien ne considéreront pas sans scepticisme un ensemble de contraintes et d'exigences qui, après tout, sont dictées par des circonstances fluctuantes et complexes sur lesquelles le Canada n'a que peu de prise. Et, cependant, ni le gouvernement ni le public canadien n'ont vraiment le choix de s'isoler du système dans lequel le Canada se trouve inséré. Il est donc tout à fait logique que la politique de défense canadienne fasse l'objet d'un mécontentement chronique et ce que l'on appelle l'antimilitarisme des Canadiens n'est probablement pas étranger au fait que l'armée symbolise une politique qui n'est pas tout à fait la nôtre.

Le poids des contraintes que subit le Canada en matière de défense a toutefois masqué une question importante: quelle marge de liberté nous laisse le système de sécurité occidental? Existe-t-il des orientations politiques qui nous permettent d'exprimer notre indépendance tout en respectant le cadre du système international dans lequel nous sommes intégrés?

Dans le but de répondre à cette question, nous tenterons de faire le bilan de 40 ans de politique de défense canadienne. La tâche est probablement ambitieuse, mais nécessaire vu l'absence d'études systématiques sur la question. Notre objectif est donc moins de présenter une analyse globale qu'un essai historique qui résume et synthétise les diverses périodes de notre politique de défense d'après-guerre. Toutefois, cet essai n'est que partiel: pour être plus concis, nous en excluons volontairement les opérations de maintien de la paix, la politique de contrôle des armements ainsi que les opérations de maintien de l'ordre au Québec en 1970. Nous avons découpé historiquement le texte en quatre sections qui correspondent en général au mandat des principaux gouvernements canadiens, de 1945 à 1980. La première, couvrant les gouvernements Mackenzie King et Saint-Laurent, va de 1945 à 1957; la deuxième porte sur le gouvernement conservateur de 1956 à 1963, la troisième fait le bilan du gouvernement Pearson et la dernière, allant de 1968 à 1980, trace les grandes lignes de la politique militaire du gouvernement Trudeau.

Compte tenu des questions qui orientent notre synthèse historique, nous ne nous encombrerons pas d'un appareil théorique qui ne serait pas pertinent ici. Nous porterons une attention particulière aux décisions successives qui ont orienté la politique de défense canadienne et au style de leadership qui a caractérisé les différents gouvernements. Dans cette perspective, l'hypothèse qui sous-tend notre étude est que, contrairement à l'opinion commune, le Canada détient une marge de manœuvre appréciable en matière de défense. Cependant, la complexité de la situation canadienne dans le domaine exige à la fois une capacité de réflexion peu commune, des choix clairs et une grande unité d'action à long terme. Le fil conducteur de notre historique pourrait donc se résumer à une question: un gouvernement canadien de l'après-guerre a-t-il au moins partiellement satisfait à ces exigences?

Partie I

Vent d'est, vent d'ouest

La politique de défense canadienne,
de la démobilisation à la fin
du gouvernement Saint-Laurent
1945-1957

L'ADIEU AUX ARMES

Pour le Canada, comme pour l'ensemble des pays alliés, 1945 représente la victoire, l'aboutissement d'un effort économique et militaire massif qui pour certains a duré plus de cinq ans. Le Canada, quant à lui, ayant entamé les hostilités avec une armée de moins de 10 000 hommes, dispose en 1945 d'une force qui fait de lui la quatrième puissance militaire du monde[3]. Sa flotte de guerre, avec 939 vaisseaux, est la troisième après celle des États-Unis et de l'Angleterre. En fait, le Canada peut à plus d'un titre considérer sa contribution à la victoire comme remarquable, autant sur le plan humain que sur le plan économique. Plus de 730 000 Canadiens se sont ainsi engagés dans les forces armées et 42 000 d'entres eux ont perdu la vie sur les divers théâtres d'opération. L'armée de terre, à elle seule, représente en 1945, avec ses cinq divisions, une charge financière de 1,5 milliard de dollars, soit 44 fois le budget de la défense canadienne de 1938-1939. De plus, en 1939 et 1945, le Canada a distribué plus de 70 % de sa production de guerre aux alliés, méritant ainsi le titre d'arsenal des démocraties. Sans contribution directe de la part des Américains, il fournit, à partir de 1943, 2,5 milliards de dollars en aide mutuelle aux pays européens ravagés par la guerre, la Grande-Bretagne recevant une aide supplémentaire d'un milliard en 1945. Pour un pays dont la population était à l'époque de 11 millions d'habitants et le produit national de 11,8 milliards de dollars, ceci représente une charge très lourde. Spécifiquement, le coût de la guerre pour le Canada s'élève à 18 milliards dont 10 viendront s'ajouter à la dette publique.

L'année 1945, si elle symbolise la victoire pour le Canada, est aussi une année de décision en ce qui a trait à sa politique de défense. À quels besoins devait répondre l'armée? Qui était l'ennemi d'après-guerre? Quels seraient les objectifs de la politique de sécurité canadienne? Quel prix le Canada était-il prêt à payer pour sa défense? Telles étaient quelques-unes des questions auxquelles les décideurs politiques avaient à répondre.

La logique de la politique, cependant, ne répond pas toujours aux exigences de la raison. Dans ce cas précis, il apparaît clairement que les décisions sur lesquelles a reposé la réorientation de la politique de défense canadienne d'après-guerre ont été prises à l'aveuglette, sur la base de deux critères prioritaires: démobilisation et économie[4]. En l'espace de deux ans, le budget de la défense passe ainsi de 3 milliards à 195 millions (1947) et les forces canadiennes sont réduites, dès 1945, à 36 000 hommes. James Eayrs l'a noté à propos du budget de 1946: «Une réflexion [stratégique] est indispensable pour pouvoir justifier l'existence d'une armée de façon logique, mais ce type de considération n'a peu ou pas influencé la planification de la défense canadienne d'après-guerre. Le budget de cette année est la résultante d'une lutte qui a opposé les ambitions des chefs d'état-major et la volonté d'économie draconienne du gouvernement. Chaque budget est plus ou moins le produit d'une telle lutte, mais celle-ci suit en général une analyse de la stratégie. Le budget de la défense canadienne pour l'année 1946, quant à lui, ne fut accompagné d'aucun énoncé de principe, si ce n'est que l'avenir était flou[5].»

En fait, il faudra attendre le 9 juillet 1947 pour que B. Claxton, ministre de la Défense, annonce les objectifs de la politique de défense canadienne, pour la première fois depuis la Deuxième Guerre mondiale. Ceux-ci étaient:

- de défendre le Canada contre l'agression;
- d'assister le pouvoir civil dans la tâche du maintien de l'ordre;
- de se charger de toute mission que le Canada pourrait volontairement entreprendre en coopération avec ses alliés ou dans le cadre d'une action collective des Nations Unies[6].

En pratique, cependant, ces objectifs étaient bien peu convaincants: aucune agression directe ne menaçait le Canada, aucun soulèvement n'était prévisible et la nature des missions de sécurité collective restait indéfinie. En fait, durant cette période l'armée, était simplement conçue comme l'école de formation professionnelle de la réserve, qui constituerait en cas de nécessité le noyau des forces canadiennes[7]. Il n'est donc probablement pas excessif de dire que le Canada n'a pas réellement eu de politique de défense de 1945 jusqu'en 1948. Ceci s'explique, dans une large mesure, par la personnalité et les opinions du premier ministre. Mackenzie King qui, en effet, dirige les destinées canadiennes depuis 1935 et domine la scène politique depuis la fin de la Première Guerre mondiale, n'est guère connu pour son amour pour la chose militaire. Guidé par sa méfiance des grandes puissances, de la Grande-Bretagne en particulier, et par sa tendance à l'isolationnisme, il perçoit l'armée canadienne comme l'instrument ou le catalyseur par lequel le Canada peut se trouver entraîné dans de coûteuses aventures militaires. Plus que tout autre, Mackenzie King est aussi extrêmement conscient des dommages politiques qu'a occasionnés la conscription au Parti libéral. Comme l'a souligné V. Massey: «Il semble avoir considéré les forces armées comme un mal nécessaire et toute suggestion de les employer était rarement discutée jusqu'au dernier moment[8].»

Il n'est donc pas étonnant que le principe d'économie ait tenu lieu de politique militaire au Canada jusqu'à la démission de King, le 15 novembre 1948. Comme il le disait lui-même en 1946: «Ce dont nous avons besoin maintenant est de revenir aux principes libéraux traditionnels qui sont l'économie, la baisse des impôts et l'antimilitarisme[9].»

Il était erroné, cependant, de faire reposer l'entière responsabilité de la situation sur les épaules du premier ministre. Le climat de la période, après cinq ans de guerre, se prêtait mal à un effort militaire d'envergure et comme le notait un observateur: «Le grand problème de ce gouvernement n'est pas de décider quelle doit être la dimension des forces armées, le grand problème de ce gouvernement est de susciter un certain intérêt pour l'armée... alors que tout le monde veut en sortir[10].»

ILLUSIONS OU DÉSILLUSIONS: LES MIRAGES DE LA SÉCURITÉ COLLECTIVE

L'absence de politique de défense ne signifie pas l'absence d'une politique de sécurité. Et l'on peut raisonnablement avancer que, de 1945 à 1950, le Canada a donné la priorité à la première en espérant qu'elle permettrait de définir la seconde[11].

Plus précisément, c'est à cette époque que se forme, au sein de l'élite politique fédérale, un noyau de diplomates de très fort calibre qui marqueront la politique de sécurité jusqu'à la fin des années 60. Ceux-ci, au nombre desquels figurent Louis Saint-Laurent, Lester B. Pearson, John W. Holmes, Georges Ignatieff et Escott Reid, pourraient être qualifiés d'internationalistes[12]. Pour eux, la sécurité canadienne est étroitement liée à celle de la communauté mondiale. À leurs yeux, l'organisation des Nations Unies, en 1945, offrait la possibilité unique de créer un système de sécurité collective au sein duquel le Canada pourrait contribuer à la paix et s'assurer un statut de puissance moyenne. Ce que l'on entendait à l'époque par sécurité collective était, comme l'a noté J.W. Holmes, une coalition mondiale, un front commun international, détenant le pouvoir militaire d'imposer des sanctions aux États qui useraient de la force pour promouvoir leur politique. L'ONU, en quelque sorte, était perçue comme le berceau naturel d'un tel système dans la mesure où elle pouvait être dotée de l'autorité et de la force militaire nécessaires[13].

Il est possible de considérer, a posteriori, qu'une telle vision des choses était utopique et naïve. Il ne faut cependant pas assimiler ce mouvement d'idées à une illusion passagère, rapidement dissipée par les réalités de la guerre froide et de l'équilibre bipolaire. La lecture des mémoires des différents acteurs canadiens de l'époque confirme, en effet, la sincérité fondamentale de leur entreprise, ainsi que leur volonté têtue de prouver que les conflits et les crises pouvaient être réglés autrement que par la force[14]. L'action canadienne, au sein des Nations Unies, fondera une tradition diplomatique qui, quoiqu'étant d'ambition modeste, n'en portera pas moins des fruits très honorables. Au sein de la Commission de l'énergie atomique, par exemple, puis au Conseil de sécurité, le Canada, par l'entremise du général MacNaughton, défendra les causes conjointes du désarmement et de la paix, et contribuera, dans une large mesure, à la résolution de crises telles que celles du Cachemir (1947) ou de l'Indonésie (1948)[15]. Cette politique se poursuivra avec vigueur à partir de 1949. En effet: «Étant donné la foi de monsieur Saint-Laurent dans le concept de sécurité collective, son accession à la tête du gouvernement et l'arrivée de Lester B. Pearson aux Affaires extérieures marqueront un tournant dans les relations du Canada avec le monde extérieur. Pour la première fois, une véritable vocation apparaît dans notre politique étrangère, une conviction selon laquelle le Canada, en tant que puissance moyenne disposant d'un pouvoir économique honorable et d'un prestige international, avait à la fois l'obligation et la capacité d'agir pour apporter des solutions pacifiques à des problèmes difficiles[16].»

C'est au cours de cette période, qui connaîtra son apogée en 1956 lors de la crise de Suez[17], que le Canada acquerra la réputation d'«honnête courtier», et c'est probablement à juste titre que l'on a appelé ces années l'«âge d'or» de la diplomatie canadienne.

Une politique de sécurité, surtout lorsqu'elle se veut internationaliste, ne peut se substituer à une politique de défense si elle ignore les réalités de la géographie et de la stratégie, et en ce début de guerre froide, le Canada ne pourra échapper à cette réalité. Celle-ci lui sera imposée par les nécessités de la défense continentale et par la logique même du principe de sécurité collective.

LA DÉFENSE CONTINENTALE: D'OGDENSBURG À COLORADO SPRINGS

Il est toujours un peu ironique de se rappeler, dans le contexte de la défense canadienne, que les plans opérationnels de l'état-major comportent, jusqu'en 1938, un scénario désignant les États-Unis comme notre principal ennemi[18].

En 1945, cependant, les choses avaient bien évolué. Dès 1936, en effet, le président Roosevelt avait déclaré: «Nous entretenons d'excellentes relations de bon voisinage avec nos voisins immédiats [...] nous pouvons et nous entendons défendre notre territoire mais aussi ses approches[19].»

En 1938, à Woodbridge, Mackenzie King lui rétorquait: «En raison de nos relations de bon voisinage, nous avons aussi des obligations et, entre autres, celle de protéger notre pays de toute attaque et celle de veiller à ce que ses forces ennemies ne puissent, en franchissant le sol canadien, atteindre les États-Unis par voie de terre, par mer ou par les airs[20].»

Les deux pays se promettaient donc une protection mutuelle. Le Canada s'engageait à assurer sa propre protection afin d'assurer celle de son voisin et ce dernier lui garantissait son aide, même dans les cas où le Canada ne pourrait veiller à sa propre sécurité. En d'autres termes, le Canada reconnaissait implicitement aux États-Unis un droit de regard sur sa propre sécurité, celle-ci étant considérée comme extension naturelle de celle des USA.

La politique de rapprochement des deux pays, en matière de défense, évolua rapidement dès le déclenchement des hostilités en Europe. Le 18 août 1940, le président américain et le premier ministre canadien signaient la déclaration d'Ogdensburg qui réaffirmait les principes de la coopération et annonçait la création de la Commission mixte permanente de défense (Permanent Joint Board of Defence), composée de représentants des deux pays. Ceux-ci, dans les termes de la déclaration, entreprendraient «des études sur les problèmes ayant trait à la défense maritime, terrestre et aérienne, y compris ceux qui concernent le personnel et le matériel.

Elle [la Commission] s'intéresserait d'une façon générale à la défense de la moitié septentrionale de l'hémisphère occidental»[21].

Plus prosaïquement, la CMPD a pour tâche de dresser les plans opérationnels de la défense continentale et de répartir les responsabilités à cette fin. La CMPD rédigera donc respectivement le Joint Canadian-USA Basic Defence Plan (ABC-1), de septembre 1940 à mars 1941, puis son successeur (ABC-22) qui restera valide jusqu'à la fin de la guerre[22].

Dans l'ensemble, malgré quelques difficultés touchant au partage des responsabilités opérationnelles, le Canada arrivera à faire respecter ses droits, particulièrement au plan du commandement maritime[23].

La présence américaine au Canada s'accentue beaucoup de 1941 à 1945. Les USA acquièrent ainsi six bases à Terre-Neuve (janvier 1941), obtiennent un droit de passage sur la Northwest Staging Route allant vers l'Alaska et l'URSS, construisent la route de l'Alaska et installent plusieurs bases aériennes dans le Grand Nord (projet Crimson)[24]. De 1942 à 1943, le nombre d'Américains stationnés au Canada passe de 15 000 à 33 000, ce qui n'est pas sans poser certains problèmes car, comme le note un observateur de l'époque: «Les Américains sont arrivés et ont pris possession du territoire comme si le Canada était un pays sauvage habité par une race docile d'autochtones[25].» Ceci, bien sûr, n'était pas l'expression d'une politique officielle de la part des Américains, mais pouvait être considérée comme une indication des ambiguïtés futures que pouvait impliquer une défense conjointe. Celles-ci apparaissent dès 1944, lorsque le problème de la défense continentale d'après-guerre commence à se poser.

Pour le Canada, les termes du problème sont clairs[26]. Les deux océans ne fournissent plus la protection dont le continent jouissait avant la guerre; en fait, le Canada se trouve précisément sur la route d'une attaque aérienne directe, passant par le pôle. Il est donc logique de penser que la coopération de défense canado-américaine devra être poursuivie après 1945. De plus, malgré l'absence de menace immédiate de guerre générale, on ne peut s'attendre à ce que l'effort de défense américain retombe à son niveau d'avant-guerre. Le Canada devra donc assumer sa part dans cet effort, surtout en ce qui concerne la défense de son propre territoire. Si cet effort n'était pas entrepris, il faudrait en effet s'attendre à ce que les États-Unis se chargent eux-mêmes des tâches nécessaires, ce qui pourrait, bien sûr, affecter la souveraineté canadienne.

Sur la base de ces donnés, clairement exprimées et approuvées par le Cabinet le 19 juillet 1945, des négociations avec les États-Unis sont entreprises au sein de la CMPD à laquelle se joint, dès novembre, un nouveau groupe conjoint: le Comité de coopération militaire Canada-États-Unis (CANUS-MCC). La première tâche de ces organismes est de rédiger un nouveau plan de défense, l'ABC-22 étant maintenant dépassé. Le projet de plan (Basic Security Plan) est prêt dès le 5 juin 1946. Son contenu est inquiétant. Les auteurs prévoient en effet que dès 1950, l'URSS serait à même de lancer une attaque massive sur le continent à travers l'Arctique. Il est donc primordial que le Canada et les États-Unis prévoient une défense aérienne qui comporterait un système de radar, des bases météo, un système de communication ainsi que des bases aériennes dans l'Arctique. De plus, dès ce moment, une intégration partielle des commandements canado-américains est prévue[27].

D'emblée, la perspective d'installer un système massif de défense aérienne au Canada, une sorte de ligne Maginot, inquiète le gouvernement. Comme l'exprimera le premier ministre: «Le Canada ne pouvait tout simplement pas faire ce qui était nécessaire pour assurer sa protection[28].» En fait, l'idée même d'une menace aérienne totale ne convainc ni les diplomates ni même les militaires canadiens. Pour eux, une attaque directe n'est guère à craindre pour l'instant et la prudence est de règle[29]. Après de nouveaux pourparlers, les Américains acceptent de modifier leur évaluation de la menace, et les exigences concernant le déploiement d'avions de chasse dans le Grand Nord sont abandonnées. Le principe de la défense aérienne conjointe est pourtant approuvé ainsi que le Basic Security Plan[30], ce qui permettra plus tard au général Foulkes de déclarer à propos des accords NORAD: «La décision d'entreprendre une défense aérienne conjointe n'a pas été prise en 1958, mais en 1946[31].»

Un accord formel de défense entre les deux pays n'était cependant toujours pas réalisé. Compte tenu de la prudence canadienne, cet accord prit la forme d'une recommandation de la CMPD, déposée le 16 septembre 1946 et annoncée publiquement en février 1947[32]. La collaboration de défense avec les États-Unis serait poursuivie, mais de façon semi-formelle. L'accord, en ce sens, n'était ni un traité ni un pacte de défense et chaque pays pouvait se retirer s'il le jugeait nécessaire. Les éléments concrets de l'accord étaient modestes. On y annonçait que les deux pays:

- faciliteraient les échanges de personnel militaire;
- favoriseraient la coopération;
- échangeraient des observateurs lors des manœuvres ou de tests d'armement;
- favoriseraient la standardisation des armes, des équipements, de l'organisation et des méthodes de formation;
- s'accorderaient réciproquement le droit d'utiliser leurs bases aériennes et navales.

Finalement, le Canada et les USA affirmaient leur volonté de respecter mutuellement leur souveraineté dans le cadre de tout projet entrepris en commun[33].

À partir de cette date, les relations de défense entre les deux pays atteignent rapidement un rythme de croisière. Le Canada récupère ainsi le contrôle de la route de l'Alaska du Northwest Staging Route et du projet Crimson. Les États-Unis gardent cependant des droits de base spéciaux à Goose Bay (Labrador) et les conserveront jusqu'en 1973[34]. Par ailleurs, les Américains demeurent très présents dans le Grand Nord (Alert, Resolute). Ils obtiennent ainsi, dans les premiers mois de 1946, un droit de survol de l'Arctique afin de tester le système de navigation LORAN destiné pour leurs bombardiers. Cinq stations fixes de navigation seront installées au Canada, entre 1947 et 1950, dans le cadre de cette opération. Le Canada n'en récupérera la responsabilité complète qu'en 1972[35].

De façon plus inquiétante, compte tenu des nécessités de la stratégie nucléaire, Goose Bay devient un des éléments essentiels d'une éventuelle contre-attaque américaine sur l'URSS. Fin 1947, les bombardiers B-47 du SAC sont déjà stationnés à Goose Bay[36].

Dès cette période, on voit donc se dégager très nettement un scénario d'interaction dans les relations de défense entre les États-Unis et le Canada. Dans le cadre de ce schéma, l'influence du Pentagone, quoique discrète, repose premièrement sur sa propension à définir unilatéralement la nature de la menace et, deuxièmement, sur sa capacité presque illimitée d'entreprendre des projets techniquement et financièrement ambitieux. Face à cela, l'attitude canadienne vise principalement à limiter les élans américains, tout en préservant du mieux possible le caractère amical des échanges et en évitant de politiser les questions abordées. La position canadienne est donc fondamentalement réactive, mais il serait faux pourtant de se représenter le Canada comme l'éternelle victime d'une forme de néo-colonialisme militaire. Le cœur du problème, dans ce sens, réside moins au Pentagone que dans les réactions imprévisibles du Congrès ou de l'opinion publique américaine. En d'autres termes, le problème fondamental que pose dès cette époque la défense continentale, est non de faire face à la menace soviétique ni de répondre aux demandes de l'armée américaine, mais de rassurer le public américain en ce qui concerne la défense du Nord. Comme le note M. Pope: «Ce que nous avons à craindre est moins une action de l'ennemi qu'un manque de confiance des États-Unis quant à notre sécurité. Pour exprimer cela d'une autre façon, si nous en faisons assez pour satisfaire les USA, nous en aurons fait plus que ce qu'exigerait une analyse pondérée des risques militaires[37].»

Le réalisme de ces propos ne tardera pas à s'imposer au Canada. En août 1949, en effet, l'URSS fait exploser sa première bombe nucléaire, deux ans plus tôt que ne le prévoyaient les experts. La réaction américaine est immédiate. En décembre 1949, le gouvernement canadien est informé par Washington que les évaluations de la menace soviétique ont été modifiées. Selon les nouvelles prévisions, l'URSS disposerait en 1954 d'un stock de 150 armes nucléaires et des vecteurs nécessaires pour lancer une attaque d'envergure contre les USA[38]. Dès l'année suivante, le premier plan de défense aérienne conjointe est mis en place. Il définit des zones d'identification aériennes pour les deux pays et autorise les interceptions des deux côtés de la frontière. L'armée de l'air canadienne établit son quartier général à Saint-Hubert afin de contrôler les opérations de défense aérienne en territoire canadien.

Au plan des systèmes d'alerte, les États-Unis construisent 75 stations radar aux USA et en Alaska. Deux accords, l'un en 1951, l'autre en 1955, prolongent ce système au Canada; il formera ce qu'il est convenu d'appeler la Pine Tree Line qui longe le 50e parallèle. Elle sera complètement opérationnelle en 1955. Ces premiers échanges définissent les principes financiers sur lesquels se fonderont ultérieurement les accords de défense canado-américains. Dans ce cas, deux tiers des coûts en capital (300 millions) sont pris en charge par les USA; quant aux coûts de fonctionnement, le Canada se charge de financer onze stations et les États-Unis, 17[39]. Dans l'ensemble, l'opération n'aura guère coûté au Canada plus de 160 millions[40]. Il est d'ailleurs intéressant de noter que le Canada ne défrayera jamais plus de 12 % des coûts totaux de la défense continentale[41].

L'intérêt des Américains pour la question de la défense aérienne ne diminue pas pour autant après la conclusion de l'accord de la Pine Tree Line. En effet, dès 1951, le gouvernement américain confie au laboratoire Lincoln (MIT) l'étude du problème de la défense aérienne. Celui-ci, dans le cadre du projet Charles puis dans celui du Lincoln Summer Study Group (1952), contribuera à la définition d'un concept global de défense aérienne. Spécifiquement, il est envisagé de construire dans le Nord du Canada une ligne de radar permettant la détection avancée de toute incursion aérienne[42]. Dès le mois de décembre 1952, le Conseil national de sécurité annonce ainsi son intention de mettre au point un tel système et, à l'été 1953, la nécessité d'associer le Canada au projet est explicitement mentionnée dans un mémorandum de la Maison Blanche. «La réalisation d'un système d'alerte avancée dépend de la rapidité à obtenir la coopération du Canada; une approche à haut niveau pour convaincre le gouvernement canadien de l'urgence de la menace est donc nécessaire; les progrès relatifs à la défense continentale paraissent ralentis dans certains cas, faute de pouvoir dégager une évaluation commune de la menace, mais aussi du fait de diverses considérations internes politiques et économiques. L'accord du Canada ainsi que sa participation substantielle sont essentiels à la réalisation rapide de plusieurs programmes prioritaires[43].»

Le gouvernement canadien, ayant tant bien que mal résisté aux pressions américaines dans l'immédiat après-guerre, était – et à juste titre – extrêmement réticent à la perspective de se faire imposer un tel projet, et ceci autant pour des raisons techniques, politiques qu'économiques. Le plan américain prévoyait en effet un budget quinquennal de défense de l'ordre de 20 milliards et la construction de plus de 70 stations radar dans le Grand Nord[44]. Or, compte tenu de la politique de partage des responsabilités techniques et financières, ceci mettait le gouvernement devant un ensemble d'obligations lourdes d'implications politiques.

La résistance canadienne, cependant, n'eut guère de chance de s'exprimer. Le 12 août 1953, l'URSS faisait exploser sa première bombe à hydrogène. En octobre 1953, le gouvernement américain adoptait les conclusions du mémo NSC 162 qui décrivait la menace soviétique comme étant «totale» et annonçait conséquemment l'adoption d'une stratégie globale de défense aérienne[45]. Compte tenu du climat de panique qu'exprimait la presse américaine de l'époque, il était donc difficile pour le gouvernement canadien de résister plus avant.

L'esprit de défense l'avait emporté sur le désir d'économie. Mais était-ce réellement la menace soviétique qui avait été déterminante? B. Claxton, pour sa part, voyait dans les réactions de la presse américaine non pas un effet spontané, mais bien une campagne orchestrée par l'administration américaine: «Il n'est pas excessif de suggérer, disait-il, que la cause de ce flot de propagande n'est pas tant la peur d'une attaque soviétique que la crainte de voir les électeurs découvrir la vacuité des promesses du Parti républicain. Apparemment, l'administration [américaine] a pensé que la colère publique pourrait être noyée par une vague de peur nucléaire[46].»

Quoi qu'il en soit, le 26 novembre 1954, Claxton annonce au Parlement la construction d'une chaîne de radars dans le Grand Nord[47]. Elle serait constituée de quatre stations principales, employant 500 personnes, et de 71 stations automatiques; l'ensemble étant réparti le long du 70e parallèle. Les coûts (600 millions) seraient entièrement défrayés par les États-Unis. Le Canada, pour sa part, construirait à ses frais (210 millions) une barrière électronique de 98 stations le long du 55e parallèle. Celle-ci (la Mid-Canada Line) servirait à détecter – mais non à suivre – toute intrusion entre la future ligne DEW et la ligne Pine Tree. L'accord de la ligne DEW fut formalisé le 15 mai 1955 par un échange de notes entre les gouvernements canadien et américain.

Cet épisode est important à plus d'un titre. En effet, il préfigure l'orientation de la défense canadienne en matière continentale pour les 20 années à venir. Dans cette perspective, il faut réaliser que l'accord de la ligne DEW annonce déjà NORAD qui, à son apogée au début des années 60, représentera pour le Canada et les États-Unis un effort de très grande envergure dont la justification stratégique n'a jamais été établie. Le système de défense complet, en effet, inclura plus de 2 600 intercepteurs dont 200 CF-100 canadiens, 700 missiles Bomarc et Nike, plus de 460 radars divers, 68 centres de contrôle opérationnels ainsi qu'un ensemble d'éléments annexes, maritimes et aériens, l'ensemble occupant plus de 240 000 personnes[48]. Or, l'ironie de la chose est que la menace pour laquelle un tel système sera mis sur pied ne se matérialisera jamais. Techniquement et quantitativement, l'aviation lourde soviétique demeurera à des niveaux extrêmement modestes et le fameux «bomber gap» de 1956 restera un mythe[49]. Dans une large mesure, donc, un élément important de la défense canadienne devient, en ce début des années 50, l'otage du climat politique américain et des dynamismes qui le sous-tendent. Répétons encore qu'il ne s'agit pas de voir dans ces événements un plan machiavélique de Washington, mais bien une donnée de la situation géostratégique qui souligne à la fois les contraintes subies par les décideurs canadiens et le caractère illusoire des consultations politico-militaires entre les deux pays. Dans cette mesure, la décision prise à l'automne 1953 n'a été conjointe qu'en apparence: ce fut une décision purement américaine qui exigeait simplement l'assentiment d'Ottawa[50].

Le tableau des relations canado-américaines que nous venons de dresser ici ne serait pas complet s'il n'était fait mention des accords industriels de défense passés entre les deux pays. Ceux-ci constituent le contre-point économique des ententes purement militaires et, vu leur importance par la suite, ils ne sauraient être passés sous silence.

Les données initiales étaient simples. Compte tenu de l'inexistence d'une industrie de défense nationale et polyvalente, le Canada était et demeure toujours un importateur d'armement, particulièrement dans le domaine des systèmes lourds et complexes. Il est donc apparu rapidement nécessaire, dans le cadre de l'effort industriel exigé par la Deuxième Guerre mondiale, de rééquilibrer la balance des échanges canadiens sur la base d'ententes bilatérales avec notre principal fournisseur, les États-Unis. La négociation de ces accords suivit immédiatement la déclaration d'Ogdensburg et, dès le 20 avril 1941, ceux-ci furent entérinés par la déclaration de Hyde Park[51]. Celle-ci prévoyait la mise en place d'un système de troc entre le Canada et les États-Unis et contribua à éliminer, du côté américain, les barrières fiscales et administratives symbolisées par le fameux «Buy-American Act» de 1933. Cette entente, ainsi que les accords qui ont suivi, ont permis au gouvernement canadien de jeter les bases d'une industrie de défense prospère qui profita magnifiquement des contrats américains placés au Canada. De 1941 à 1945, en effet, les exportations canadiennes de matériel de guerre vers les USA s'élèvent à plus de 1,25 milliard de dollars[52]. La guerre constituait cependant une situation d'exception, et la fin des hostilités vit rapidement se reconstituer les barrières légales et réglementaires d'avant 1941. Les gouvernements tentèrent de poursuivre tant bien que mal leur politique de coopération. Un échange de notes, en mai 1945, puis un programme proposé en 1949 par la CMPD, recommandaient ainsi d'augmenter la base industrielle de défense américaine et de disperser la production militaire par l'intermédiaire de l'industrie canadienne. La nécessité de promouvoir la standardisation et d'équilibrer les échanges bilatéraux était soulignée.

Il faudra cependant attendre le début de la guerre de Corée pour que les USA acceptent d'inscrire ces principes dans la déclaration commune du 26 octobre 1950[53] qui souhaitait éliminer à nouveau les barrières tarifaires à l'importation d'armement. De son côté, le Canada crée, en 1951, la société d'État Construction de défense limitée (CDL) qui a pour mission de restaurer et de protéger la base industrielle de défense canadienne[54]. Pourtant, malgré quelques beaux succès dans le domaine de la construction aéronautique et des progrès notables dans le secteur de la standardisation[55], l'entente canado-américaine ne porte pas les fruits qu'on en attendait et l'on assiste, de 1950 à 1958, à une diminution progressive des contrats américains placés au Canada[56]. La valeur de ceux-ci tombe de 179 millions en 1951 à 35 millions en 1958 et il faudra attendre la fin des années 50 pour assister à un redressement sensible des échanges. L'importance de cet aspect des relations de défense entre Washington et Ottawa ne réside toutefois pas dans la dimension purement économique. Quels que soient les bénéfices pour le Canada d'une entente de partage de la production, les concessions que le gouvernement américain fait à l'industrie canadienne forment un élément supplémentaire d'un réseau d'influence politico-militaire dont le Canada subit les pressions discrètes. Comme le note J.W. Holmes: «À travers l'histoire du partage de la production, les USA se sont toujours plus intéressés aux aspects militaires [qu'aux aspects économiques]. Après la guerre, ils étaient anxieux d'acquérir la coopération canadienne en matière de défense continentale et l'aide qu'ils pouvaient apporter à l'économie canadienne représentait un prix modeste à payer. Ils pensaient avoir besoin des ressources canadiennes et désiraient mobiliser le continent. Les leaders politiques américains ainsi que les responsables du Pentagone étaient conscients de la susceptibilité canadienne en matière de souveraineté, particulièrement dans le domaine de la défense aérienne, et ils ont réalisé que le partage de la production était une façon habile d'amener le gouvernement canadien à faire sa part de façon économique[57].» C'est d'ailleurs dans cet esprit que l'on peut percevoir les avantages industriels qu'a pu retirer le Canada des accords de la Pine Tree Line et de la ligne DEW[58].

Ces ententes ont-elles eu un effet décisif sur notre politique de sécurité? L'accès partiel de notre industrie au marché américain a-t-il empêché le développement d'une orientation plus indépendante? Ceci semble probable, comme le note encore Holmes: «Il n'y a pas de doute, le Canada, en cherchant à satisfaire ses intérêts économiques légitimes, a mis en place lui-même un ensemble de contraintes sur sa liberté de mouvement en matière de politique extérieure; [ces contraintes] sont plus importantes que de simples pressions diplomatiques de la part de Washington, dans la mesure où elles impliqueraient des coûts politiques très graves pour tout gouvernement canadien qui remettrait en question l'économie de la défense.» Le poids de ces contraintes, d'ailleurs, se fera lourdement sentir au cours de la décennie suivante[59].

LA DÉFENSE ATLANTIQUE: DE WASHINGTON À LISBONNE

Si les premiers pas de la défense continentale font apparaître clairement le poids de l'influence américaine sur la politique canadienne, la question de la sécurité européenne définit d'emblée un système de relations plus complexes, caractérisé lui aussi par ses contraintes, mais offrant parallèlement un espace de liberté plus grand aux initiatives canadiennes.

Au plan des contraintes, il est important de noter qu'à la fin de la Deuxième Guerre mondiale, comme en 1918, le Canada n'avait aucune intention de prendre part au règlement des problèmes politico-militaires relatifs à la sécurité européenne[60]. Le manque d'intérêt personnel de Mackenzie King pour les questions européennes, l'absence du Canada des conférences de Potsdam et de Yalta ainsi que le retrait rapide des forces canadiennes d'Allemagne soulignent clairement ce fait. Ce n'était pas tant ces détails ni la menace soviétique qui intéressaient le Canada, mais plutôt la réalisation de la paix au sens large, et dans ce cadre, l'opinion qui prévalait à Ottawa au sujet de l'Union soviétique était marquée par la prudence et la modération. Comme le notait Pearson dans une analyse typiquement «kennanienne»: «L'URSS en Europe profiterait de toutes les possibilités d'expansion politique que lui offrirait la situation, mais respecterait scrupuleusement les limites concrètes que lui imposeraient les traités[61]. L'URSS [insistait à son tour l'ambassadeur canadien à Moscou] est désireuse d'éviter la guerre, ce qu'elle veut par-dessus tout c'est une longue période de paix au cours de laquelle elle pourrait reconstruire son économie[62].»

Les rouages de la guerre froide, cependant, étaient déjà en mouvement et, dès 1946, secoué par l'affaire Goujenko[63], le gouvernement canadien se ralliera peu à peu au courant d'opinion que symbolisent le discours de Fulton, la doctrine Truman et la résolution Vanderberg[64].

Curieusement, c'est dans cette période difficile que la diplomatie canadienne prouvera sa capacité d'initiative. Déçus, en effet, dès 1946, par l'incapacité de l'ONU de mettre en place un véritable système de sécurité international, certains diplomates canadiens avaient conçu l'idée de s'appuyer sur l'article 51 de la Charte des Nations Unies pour proposer la réalisation d'une alliance de défense occidentale. On passait ainsi d'un système de sécurité collective à un système de défense régional. Comme l'exprimait Escott Reid, le 13 août 1947: «Pour réduire la possibilité d'un conflit, le premier devoir des puissances occidentales est d'acquérir un avantage militaire décisif par rapport à l'URSS, et d'user de cet avantage pour contenir l'expansion de la puissance soviétique tout en évitant de provoquer une réaction désespérée de sa part[65].» C'est là la première mention officielle et publique d'un système occidental de défense en Europe. Le Canada venait d'ouvrir la route de l'Alliance atlantique. En septembre 1947, puis en avril 1948, le ministre des Affaires extérieures (Saint-Laurent) répétait cet appel à l'ONU, d'abord, puis au Parlement canadien, suscitant ainsi l'appui des USA et de la Grande-Bretagne[66]. L'initiative canadienne, notons-le, se fondait sur la philosophie internationaliste que nous avons mentionnée plus haut. Dans ce sens, la contribution prévue du Canada à l'Alliance était moins de nature militaire que politique. En fait, en encourageant la coopération multilatérale, le Canada poursuivait la tâche qu'il avait entreprise à l'ONU, visant, d'une part, à promouvoir son rôle de puissance moyenne et, d'autre part, à équilibrer ses relations de défense avec son puissant voisin. La participation du Canada aux discussions qui précédèrent et suivirent la création de l'Alliance fut donc discrète, circonscrite et précise.

En termes militaires, il n'était pas question de stationner un contingent canadien en Europe, mais bien de présenter les forces canadiennes comme une réserve stratégique disponible en cas de besoin. On jugeait essentiel de garantir l'engagement des États-Unis face à la sécurité européenne et d'inscrire, dans le cadre du traité, le principe de la coopération économique et politique au sein de l'Alliance. À ce titre, l'action canadienne fut décisive et ce dernier principe fut inscrit dans l'article 2 du traité que l'on surnomme communément l'«article canadien»[67].

La résistance du Canada à une participation militaire au sein de l'OTAN fut pourtant un combat d'arrière-garde. La guerre froide s'intensifiait avec la crise tchèque puis celle de Berlin[68], durant le printemps et l'été 1948. L'URSS devenait une puissance nucléaire, l'année suivante, et, en septembre 1949, les troupes communistes chinoises entraient dans Pékin; la menace se précisait. Au Canada, cependant, le ministre de la Défense annonçait encore en juin 1950 qu'il n'était pas prévu d'envoyer des soldats canadiens en Europe[69]. La contribution canadienne à l'OTAN s'était résumée jusque-là à fournir des équipements et des cours de formation militaire, et cela était estimé suffisant[70].

L'invasion coréenne, survenant quelques semaines plus tard, renversera complètement la position canadienne. Ainsi, en deux ans, le budget de la défense quadruplera, passant de 384,9 millions de dollars à 1,415 milliards de dollars en 1951[71]. Le 5 février 1951, après une dernière tentative pour freiner le mouvement, Claxton annonce au Parlement l'envoi prochain des troupes canadiennes en Europe et un programme de rééquipement massif: 100 vaisseaux pour la marine, 40 unités aériennes pour l'aviation et une division d'infanterie pour l'armée. Le 27e groupe de brigade (10 000 hommes) serait déployé en RFA et une division aérienne de douze escadrilles équipées de Sabre F-86 l'accompagnerait[72].

Le Canada venait encore une fois d'être engagé contre son gré dans un rôle qu'il n'avait ni voulu ni planifié.

Compte tenu des circonstances, cependant, le Canada fait très honorablement face à ses obligations[73]. En plus du groupe de brigade et de la division aérienne, en effet, le Canada met à la disposition des forces de l'ONU plus de 6 000 hommes intégrés à la division du Commonwealth. Des grandes quantités d'équipement sont fournies à la Belgique, la Hollande et l'Italie, et le programme d'aide canadienne à l'OTAN s'élève, de 1951 à 1958, à plus de $1,5 milliard, ce qui inclut l'achat d'équipement, le transfert de stocks d'armes, la formation et l'entraînement de pilotes alliés et la contribution aux infrastructures de l'Alliance. De plus, il faut souligner que la marine canadienne met, dès 1952, la totalité des ressources du commandement atlantique, soit une vingtaine de vaisseaux dont un porte-avions et une quarantaine d'avions, à la disposition de SACLANT. Elle reçoit d'ailleurs le commandement de la zone CANLANT (zone du Nord-Ouest atlantique) dont elle avait été responsable durant la Deuxième Guerre mondiale[74].

Dans l'ensemble, donc, si un bilan total est esquissé, le Canada a donné à l'OTAN, durant les huit années couvertes ici, plus d'argent et d'équipement qu'aucun des membres de l'Alliance, compte tenu de son produit national brut. Comme le souligne Gellner, si l'on inclut la contribution navale du Canada ainsi que les frais d'infrastructure, la moitié au moins du budget canadien de ces huit années, soit 13 milliards, peut être attribuée à l'OTAN[75].

Parallèlement, la contribution politique du Canada au dynamisme de l'Alliance ne doit pas être négligée. À ce sujet, il faut en particulier souligner le rôle de Lester B. Pearson dans la promotion de meilleurs mécanismes de consultation parmi les alliés. Pearson, en effet, percevait l'OTAN comme une communauté dont les buts dépassaient largement la défense de l'Europe. Comme il le disait lui-même: «Lorsque la tâche de l'OTAN était strictement militaire, les moyens d'assurer une défense contre l'agression pouvaient être définis en termes d'hommes et d'armes. Mais la force dont l'OTAN a besoin maintenant doit être tirée des attitudes collectives, de la consultation et de la coopération intergouvernementale[76].»

Les diplomates canadiens furent presque les seuls à voir dans l'OTAN l'instrument d'une association plus large qui s'inspirerait de l'esprit de l'article 2. Parmi les nombreuses initiatives entreprises dans ce sens, on peut signaler la fondation de l'Association parlementaire de l'OTAN, la mise sur pied du Comité de la communauté atlantique – présidé par Pearson – et le rapport des trois sages, de 1956, relatif à la consultation dans l'Alliance. Ce rapport soulignait, en particulier, la nécessité d'engager des discussions préliminaires avant que les positions individuelles des États membres de l'Alliance ne soient fixées. La politique suivie par l'OTAN devait être le fruit de décisions collectives, de façon à assurer, au minimum, que les actions entreprises individuellement par les alliés puissent être connues et discutées au préalable[77]. Les obstacles, quant à l'application de tels principes, étaient malheureusement nombreux. En particulier, les divergences d'intérêts des pays européens en matière de politique extérieure et les réticences américaines à l'idée de soumettre leurs projets politiques à la discussion rendaient illusoire le concept d'une politique atlantique commune. En novembre 1956, d'ailleurs, la crise de Suez, qui survenait au moment même où le rapport des trois sages était en cours de rédaction, montrait à quel point les divisions de l'Alliance étaient profondes. Il est remarquable pourtant de constater que c'est précisément à cette occasion que la politique canadienne s'est avérée la plus utile et la plus efficace, en grande partie grâce à l'intervention de Pearson. Comme le note McLin, en particulier, l'intervention canadienne pendant la crise de Suez constitue l'illustration la plus frappante du type de médiation que le rapport des trois sages cherchait à promouvoir[78].

Le rôle d'honnête courtier qu'a assuré le Canada durant cet épisode, quoique exemplaire, n'était pourtant pas une panacée aux maux de l'Alliance. Deux problèmes dont les ramifications se prolongent jusqu'à nos jours allaient en particulier rendre la position canadienne en Europe très inconfortable. Le premier est attaché à ce qu'on appelle les objectifs de Lisbonne, le second a trait à la stratégie nucléaire de l'Alliance.

Jusqu'en 1952, en effet, la politique canadienne en Europe s'était appuyée sur un large consensus au sein des divers partis politiques et dans l'opinion publique. Toutefois, en février 1952, une réunion du Conseil atlantique à Lisbonne brisera ce consensus en adoptant une série d'objectifs matériels hautement irréalisables. Il est décidé, à cette occasion, de déployer 50 divisions OTAN, fin 1952, et 96, en 1954. 25 divisions devaient être prêtes en tout temps sur le front central. En fait, seules 16 divisions seraient réellement déployées en 1957[79]. Compte tenu des efforts déjà accomplis et des maigres résultats obtenus au titre de l'article 2, de nombreuses critiques commencent donc à s'exprimer au Canada. Fondamentalement, l'expansion de la contribution militaire du Canada à l'OTAN n'était tout simplement pas envisageable. En conséquence, le gouvernement refusera d'accepter les recommandations du SHAPE concernant les forces canadiennes[80]. En pratique, au cours de la période subséquente, la contribution du Canada déclina de façon significative par rapport à celle des autres membres de l'Alliance. Ces derniers, en effet, étaient maintenant en mesure d'assumer les coûts croissants de leurs dépenses d'équipement alors que le budget canadien, quant à lui, plafonnait du fait des frais de fonctionnement disproportionnés créés par le besoin de soutenir un contingent à 5 000 kilomètres de ses bases[81]. Si l'on ajoute à cela l'importance croissante accordée à la menace aérienne en Amérique du Nord, à partir de 1953, le dilemme présenté à la politique canadienne devient évident.

Fallait-il d'abord satisfaire aux besoins de la défense européenne ou bien répondre en priorité aux exigences de celles du continent? Compte tenu des ressources limitées du Canada, un choix délicat s'imposait. La solution la plus simple était, bien sûr, de ramener les forces canadiennes en Amérique du Nord, mais ceci, pour des raisons évidentes, n'était pas acceptable pour les Européens. Un tel geste, en effet, ne préluderait-il pas à un désengagement américain? Cette solution n'était donc pas envisageable. La redéfinition du rôle des unités canadiennes en Europe était une autre possibilité. Le rapport annuel de la défense, en 1957, précisait ainsi que le concept de «forces collectives équilibrées», privilégié jusque-là, était rejeté au bénéfice d'une contribution canadienne plus spécialisée[82]. D'ailleurs, cette orientation correspondait aux décisions prises à l'OTAN en matière de stratégie nucléaire. En décembre 1957, en effet, un communiqué de l'Alliance annonçait que des charges nucléaires ainsi que des missiles à moyenne portée seraient déployés en Europe[83].

En fait, l'OTAN, suivant en cela la stratégie de représailles massives, venait d'adopter un plan de défense (MC-14/2) qui prévoyait l'emploi immédat et massif des armes nucléaires tactiques et stratégiques en cas d'agression du pacte de Varsovie[84]. Ceci répondait clairement à l'incapacité manifeste des Européens de satisfaire aux objectifs de Lisbonne. Pratiquement, on tentait ainsi de compenser les faiblesses militaires de l'Alliance en remplaçant la dissuasion conventionnelle par la dissuasion nucléaire.

Dans l'immédiat, le gouvernement canadien pouvait donc entrevoir une solution à son dilemme, dans la mesure où une tâche nucléaire pourrait lui permettre de structurer ses forces de façon plus économique. Cependant, la nucléarisation de l'OTAN – et des forces canadiennes – ouvrait une boîte de Pandore dont le gouvernement canadien n'était pas prêt de voir le fond. L'année 1957, dans ce sens, constituait pour le Canada le prélude d'une période de crise qui allait durer plus de six ans, et la question nucléaire allait occuper une position centrale dans ce contexte. La période que l'on appelle l'«âge d'or de la diplomatie canadienne» venait de s'achever et avec elle une certaine qualité de réflexion, une philosophie de l'action internationale allaient disparaître pendant quelques années. Certaines leçons stratégiques fondamentales seront oubliées et les diplomates canadiens auront à se rappeler, un peu trop tard, les paroles prophétiques de Pearson qui, en 1950, avait déclaré: «L'arme nucléaire est considérée universellement comme l'arme absolue. Elle devrait être traitée comme telle[85].»

Le naufrage

La politique de défense canadienne
durant la période Diefenbaker
1957-1963

À LA CROISÉE DES CHEMINS

En 1957, la politique de défense canadienne se trouve à un point charnière de son histoire. La situation internationale a progressivement évolué. La menace – réelle ou imaginée – d'une offensive soviétique directe en Europe s'est dissipée pour l'instant. La sécurité occidentale n'est plus seulement une question d'hommes et d'armes à tout prix, mais un enchevêtrement complexe de problèmes où les divergences politiques, les égoïsmes nationaux, les ambiguïtés stratégiques et les facteurs politiques internes jouent un rôle croissant.

En soi, le contexte international appelle donc un réexamen approfondi de la position canadienne, et cette exigence est encore accentuée par une série de facteurs et de considérations très spécifiques.

Si le but de la politique de sécurité canadienne durant ces douze années d'après-guerre a, en effet, été la recherche d'influence par le biais d'un ensemble d'ententes collectives, le coût de cette influence semble être devenu trop lourd pour un pays comme le Canada. Comme le notait R. Campney, successeur de B. Claxton, en 1956: «Le Canada a entrepris et soutenu un effort militaire qui est tout à fait excessif par rapport à son statut de puissance moyenne[86].»

La réorientation de cette politique présentait cependant un défi de taille qui exigeait un ensemble de décisions coûteuses à long terme, et il n'est pas certain que le gouvernement Saint-Laurent ait été en mesure de relever ce défi sans dommages. L'avantage considérable du gouvernement libéral est pourtant d'avoir accumulé une expérience considérable en matière de politique internationale et les relations exceptionnelles du premier ministre avec Pearson assurait, à tout le moins, que les décisions futures seraient prises par un leadership politique homogène[87]. Contre toute attente, cependant, les Conservateurs, dirigés par Diefenbaker, gagnent les élections de juin 1957 et reprennent le pouvoir après un hiatus de 22 ans.

Le Canada fera donc face à des choix politiques très difficiles, sous la direction d'un gouvernement totalement inexpérimenté en matière de politique extérieure et de politique de défense. Les conséquences de cette situation seront dramatiques.

En premier lieu, l'arrivée du nouveau gouvernement déréglera le système extrêmement délicat des rouages politico-bureaucratiques qui président à l'élaboration de la politique extérieure canadienne[88]. La confiance qui doit exister entre le leadership politique et les diplomates de carrière disparaît et fait place à la méfiance, à l'incertitude et à l'indécision. En outre, les canaux de communication qui relient les ministères entre eux et ces derniers au Cabinet se dissolvent, remettant ainsi en question l'intégration des différents éléments de la politique de sécurité. Mais plus encore, la personnalité du premier ministre aura un impact décisif sur les événements ultérieurs et aggravera encore, s'il est possible, les problèmes précédents. La plupart des sources s'accordent, en effet, pour dire que Diefenbaker, du fait de son indécision, de son entêtement et de sa façon très particulière d'aborder les problèmes, fut un facteur déterminant dans la débâcle de la politique de défense canadienne entre 1957 et 1963. Comme le note G. Ignatieff, par exemple: «Il n'était pas dans la nature de monsieur Diefenbaker de prendre des décisions claires... Il avait une tendance malheureuse à personnaliser les problèmes, à accuser ses conseillers de l'abandonner et, le cas échéant, à les monter les uns contre les autres[89].» De plus, compte tenu de l'importance des relations canado-américaines, un élément clé de la situation réside dans l'hostilité personnelle que le premier ministre manifestera à l'égard du nouveau président américain à partir de 1961[90]. Ceci, associé, semble-t-il, à une vague d'antiaméricanisme au Canada, accentuera encore les difficultés déjà considérables du nouveau gouvernement en matière de défense.

LES RÉCIFS: LA QUESTION DE NORAD

Le premier problème sur lequel va buter le gouvernement conservateur est l'accord NORAD. À la suite d'ententes déjà signées, le Pentagone projette de réunir les segments canadiens et américains de la défense aérienne du continent sous un même commandement. Ceci avait déjà été envisagé en 1953, mais les rivalités opposant les différents services concernés de la défense américaine avaient freiné le processus[91]. En mai 1956, finalement, un groupe de recherche conjoint (CANUS) avait été formé, et dans son rapport, remis en décembre de la même année, il recommandait la création d'un commandement binational[92]. Cette recommandation était acceptée, au début de l'année suivante, par les états-majors des deux pays et le principe fut entériné immédiatement par le Secrétaire américain de la Défense. En pratique, il ne restait qu'à obtenir l'assentiment du Cabinet canadien pour qu'un accord officiel puisse être conclu.

Contrairement aux apparences, le problème d'un commandement conjoint était loin d'être simple, même s'il constituait une mesure logique en termes militaires. Celui-ci mettait en effet une partie des forces canadiennes directement aux ordres du président américain, qui légalement est seul habilité à autoriser l'emploi des armes nucléaires faisant partie de l'arsenal de NORAD. La mise en alerte du système impliquait naturellement qu'une consultation intergouvernementale ait lieu, mais il était assez douteux que les contraintes militaires et techniques permettent une telle consultation en cas d'urgence. Ce problème avait d'ailleurs été soulevé dans des conversations antérieures de Pearson et J.F. Dulles[93]. Cette entente affaiblissait donc le contrôle du gouvernement canadien sur l'emploi des forces militaires nationales. Il était aussi risqué d'abandonner à l'autorité militaire un certain nombre d'initiatives opérationnelles qui auraient trouvé leur origine dans les plans d'emploi d'un état-major conjoint, largement dominé par les Américains. Il était significatif et inquiétant de constater que les forces aériennes des deux pays avaient établi une relation professionnelle probablement trop étroite pour être inoffensive[94]. La RCAF trouvait trop d'avantages aux échanges bilatéraux d'information technique et militaire pour ne pas être insensiblement amenée à accepter les principes d'une stratégie et d'une politique qui, en fait, n'étaient pas nécessairement celles du Canada. Comme le souligne McLin: «Un problème se pose lorsqu'un élément de l'armée canadienne adopte des opinions plus proches de son *alter ego* américain que de celles de son propre gouvernement[95]. »

La question de NORAD, répétons-le, était donc politiquement délicate et les Affaires extérieures n'avaient pas manqué de soulever le problème lors d'un premier examen du dossier, à l'hiver 1956[96]. Malheureusement, le Cabinet n'avait pu aborder le problème avant que ne commence la campagne électorale du printemps 1957. La question était donc encore en suspens à l'arrivée des Conservateurs au mois de juin. En principe, la procédure à suivre était assez simple: le dossier devait d'abord être examiné par le comité spécialisé du Cabinet, puis soumis à ce dernier, avant que l'annonce publique de l'accord soit transmise au Parlement aux fins éventuelles d'un débat. La signature de l'entente aurait suivi la décision du gouvernement et sa mise en application aurait pu avoir lieu immédiatement après. En pratique, cependant, la décision gouvernementale n'obéira à aucune de ces règles. Talonné par le chef d'état-major (le général Foulkes), le premier ministre prend sa décision le 24 juillet avant même que le Cabinet n'ait pu se réunir. Le 31 juillet, celui-ci est simplement mis devant le fait accompli, comme d'ailleurs le Parlement qui n'entamera réellement un débat sur la question que l'année suivante. Le gouvernement américain, quant à lui, avait donné son aval à NORAD le 11 avril et l'assentiment canadien lui fut transmis lors de la visite de J.F. Dulles à Ottawa, le 28 juillet. L'accord est annoncé publiquement à Washington le 19 août, et le 12 septembre 1957, le commandement intérimaire de NORAD devient opérationnel.

Le Canada venait ainsi de conclure l'un des accords les plus importants de l'après-guerre sans réflexion, sans analyse et sans débat. L'ambiguïté – pour ne pas dire la confusion intellectuelle – du gouvernement à l'égard de NORAD fut clairement mise en évidence un an plus tard lorsqu'aux questions des parlementaires concernant les liens de l'OTAN et de NORAD, il fut répondu que NORAD était un commandement intégré de l'OTAN, ce qui était totalement inexact[97]. La chose fut d'ailleurs clairement mise au point par nul autre que le Secrétaire général de l'Alliance[98].

L'incident NORAD n'était cependant pas terminé; il constituait le premier épisode d'une longue liste noire qui n'allait s'achever qu'en 1963.

LES RÉCIFS: LES ARMES DE NORAD ET CELLES DE L'OTAN

Parmi les dossiers chauds qui attendaient le gouvernement Diefenbaker, il s'en trouvait un qui marquerait pendant longtemps la mémoire politique des Canadiens. Le CF-105 Arrow, prévu dès 1950 pour remplacer le CF-100, était en effet une création et une réalisation essentiellement canadienne, et sa survie, en 1957, était sérieusement compromise[99].

L'Arrow, pour brosser rapidement son histoire, avait été conçu par la compagnie A.V. Roe. Commandé en 1954 à 600 exemplaires, il devait satisfaire aux besoins de la RCAF à la fois en Amérique du Nord et en Europe. Le développement de l'appareil n'avait cependant pas été sans problèmes. L'Arrow, d'abord, répondait à des exigences techniques et militaires propres au Canada et ne se présentait pas a priori comme un produit d'exportation. De plus, compte tenu de ses caractéristiques particulières et contrairement aux pratiques habituelles, le Canada dut se charger du développement de tous les éléments de l'appareil: la cellule (A.V. Roe), les deux réacteurs (Orenda Engines), le système de tir (RCA) et l'armement (Missile Velvet Glove). Ceci représentait un défi technique et financier hors du commun. En conséquence, après quatre années de développement, 60 modifications de design et plusieurs changements d'entrepreneurs, il n'est pas étonnant que le futur intercepteur de la RCAF ait constitué une charge financière très lourde pour le gouvernement. En fait, après la mise au point tardive d'un système comptable permettant d'évaluer les coûts globaux de l'Arrow, son prix unitaire fut estimé à plus de 10 millions de dollars, soit quinze fois celui du CF-100. Une analyse du ministère de la Défense, en 1958, évaluait d'ailleurs à 871 millions de dollars la somme nécessaire pour compléter le développement. Finalement, au moment même où l'Arrow entrerait en production (1960), il serait fort à craindre qu'il ne soit déjà dépassé. Dès 1957, en effet, les stratèges devaient compter sur l'apparition prochaine des missiles et la défense aérienne, de ce fait, perdait de son importance.

À l'été 1958, le moment de la décision était donc arrivé. L'état-major canadien esquissa plusieurs solutions pour sauver l'Arrow. Il était prévu, en particulier, de combiner l'achat d'un nombre réduit de CF-105 avec l'acquisition de missiles Bomarc et la construction de plusieurs sites de contrôle électronique SAGE, mais cette solution – pour être économiquement viable – impliquait l'achat par les USA d'un certain nombre d'Arrow pour équiper leurs unités au Labrador et à Terre-Neuve. Malgré les efforts renouvelés du ministre de la Défense, G. Pearkes, les Américains refusèrent cette solution. En fait, ils n'aiment pas l'Arrow, pour des raisons à la fois techniques et économiques. Si les Canadiens voulaient réellement leur avion, ils auraient donc à payer le plein prix.

Pour des raisons politiques et financières, la décision canadienne était donc prise d'avance. Mais les conséquences étaient graves, l'arrêt du projet allait en effet menacer l'emploi de plus de 25 000 Canadiens et occasionner des pénalités pour bris de contrat estimées à plus de 170 millions de dollars.

Le Cabinet, au mois d'août 1958, acceptait cependant les recommandations du Comité de défense. Le projet Arrow serait mis en attente jusqu'en mars 1959 pour permettre une révision d'ensemble du dossier et, pour l'instant, il était décidé de prolonger l'existence des CF-100 et d'acquérir le missile Bomarc. La décision fut annoncée le 23 septembre au Parlement. Il était clair que le CF-105 était condamné et que la rémission temporaire offerte par le processus de révision n'était qu'une tactique visant à rendre le choix moins douloureux. Ceci devint évident, en février 1959, lorsque le premier ministre annonça officiellement l'arrêt définitif du projet. La réaction publique fut dramatique; mais, contrairement à la perception commune, ce n'était pas la décision concernant l'Arrow qui était la plus importante. Comme l'a souligné Granatstein, le premier ministre, dans les circonstances, avait fait le bon choix, le seul possible. Mais une autre décision – masquée par le contexte dramatique de la situation – avait été prise et, comme l'a avoué D. Horkness: «Les conséquences de l'arrêt du projet Arrow avait occupé une telle place dans les préoccupations du Cabinet que la signification du Bomarc et l'acquisition subséquente des têtes nucléaires qui devaient l'équiper ne firent pas grande impression sur les ministres[100].»

Le missile sol-air Bomarc constituait un des éléments principaux du système de défense antiaérien de NORAD. Développé depuis 1950 par l'USAF, son rôle était d'intercepter les bombardiers soviétiques volant à basse altitude, et ceci à une distance d'environ 250 milles (400 km)[101]. Il existait en deux versions. Le Bomarc A, plus ancien, était un missile à carburant liquide efficace jusqu'à 60 000 pieds (2 km). Il pouvait transporter, au choix, une tête nucléaire ou un explosif conventionnel et ce détail s'avérera très important dans la suite des événements. Le Bomarc B, développé à partir de 1958 seulement, était à carburant solide, avait une portée supérieure avec 400 milles (640 km) et ne pouvait transporter qu'une tête nucléaire.

Vu leur portée relativement limitée par rapport aux chasseurs, les Bomarc devaient évidemment être déployés le plus au nord possible et donc éventuellement au Canada, ce qui avait été envisagé dès mai 1958. En fait, compte tenu de la puissance de la charge nucléaire (de 500 kt à 1 Mt), l'usage de missiles au-dessus du territoire américain était absolument exclu. L'installation du Bomarc à la frontière canado-américaine et au Canada constituait donc à la fois une solution techniquement et politiquement satisfaisante pour les Américains et une porte de sortie au cul-de-sac dans lequel se trouvaient les décideurs canadiens. Le Bomarc, dans ce sens, se présentait comme le complément du CF-100 et, en tant que tel, il évitait – ou à tout le moins retardait – la décision d'acheter un successeur de l'Arrow aux USA.

Deux problèmes fondamentaux, cependant, n'avaient pas été considérés par le gouvernement canadien. En premier lieu, le type de Bomarc qui allait être déployé au Canada était le modèle B, strictement nucléaire, et ceci, semble-t-il, n'avait pas été compris par le premier ministre qui continua plus tard à maintenir que le missile pouvait être équipé d'une tête conventionnelle[102]. En second lieu, les responsables canadiens n'avaient pas non plus saisi que le système Bomarc était d'ores et déjà l'enjeu d'une compétition très serrée entre l'armée américaine et l'USAF. L'armée, en effet, avait développé ses propres missiles, les Nike et les Hawk, et ceux-ci, compte tenu des fortes restrictions budgétaires, étaient maintenant les concurrents directs des Bomarc. En pratique, le Canada venait donc de choisir une arme qui risquait d'être éliminée au Congrès, avant même d'avoir été déployée ou même produite. Ce danger, d'ailleurs, devint évident lorsque les sept premiers tests du Bomarc B se révélèrent des échecs. Parallèlement, d'ailleurs, en mars 1960, l'armée de l'air américaine annonçait une révision du plan de la défense aérienne et précisait que le nombre des missiles Bomarc serait réduit en conséquence. De surcroît, en avril, le Congrès décidait de couper les fonds du programme de façon draconienne, l'éliminant pour ainsi dire du budget. Le gouvernement canadien voyait donc brutalement ses décisions remises en question et, même si l'on admet que le Canada ait été consulté à cette occasion, la dépendance de la défense canadienne face aux aléas de la politique américaine était à nouveau clairement mise en évidence.

Heureusement ou malheureusement, suivant le point de vue où l'on se place, les législateurs américains revinrent sur leur décision et, dès le mois de juin, après que le Bomarc ait réussi finalement son premier test, le président Eisenhower put annoncer au premier ministre canadien que les fonds nécessaires seraient alloués au programme.

L'image du leadership conservateur venait d'être sérieusement ternie et, pour la première fois, l'opposition libérale allait remettre en question le rôle canadien dans NORAD et soulever clairement le problème de la nucléarisation des forces canadiennes.

Le dossier NORAD, déjà très lourd, n'était pas encore clos. Le Bomarc, en effet, n'était qu'un complément à la défense aérienne et le choix d'un nouvel intercepteur s'imposait. De plus, dans le cadre de l'OTAN la question du rééquipement des forces canadiennes en Europe n'était pas résolue.

En ce qui concerne le nouvel intercepteur, la question était politiquement délicate, après la débâcle de l'Arrow, et le gouvernement remit la décision le plus longtemps possible. En fait, ce n'est que le 12 juin 1961, après plusieurs années de négociation, que le choix du CF-101 Voodoo est fait.

Le contrat conclu avec les USA est complexe, mais très favorable. Il prévoit en effet que:

- le Canada prendrait en charge le fonctionnement et les coûts afférents de seize stations de la ligne Pine Tree ainsi que les coûts de cinq autres stations dont le fonctionnement est d'ores et déjà assuré par des Canadiens;
- les États-Unis fourniraient gratuitement 66 CF-101 Voodoo à la RCAF;
- les États-Unis s'engageraient à acheter du Canada plus d'une centaine de F-104 fabriqués sous licence par Canadair, la valeur totale du contrat s'élevant à 200 millions de dollars.

Par ailleurs, la commande en question étant destinée à l'OTAN dans le cadre de l'aide mutuelle fournie par les USA, le Canada s'engageait à financer un quart de la valeur du contrat, soit 50 millions[103].

En somme, le Canada reprenait le contrôle sur une partie de la ligne Pine Tree, faisait l'acquisition avantageuse d'un nouvel intercepteur et se voyait octroyé un contrat important dont les bénéfices étaient multiples. La construction sous licence du F-104 permettait, en effet, d'envisager des exportations ultérieures et d'équiper éventuellement les forces canadiennes aériennes en Europe à un prix plus avantageux. En somme, le gouvernement canadien faisait une bonne affaire, lui permettant, à court terme, d'assurer la viabilité de son industrie aéronautique; mais en même temps, en choisissant le Voodoo qui devait, lui aussi, être équipé d'armes nucléaires, il s'engageait plus avant dans une mission militaire délicate dont les tenants et les aboutissants n'avaient pas été examinés.

Le F-104 Starfighter, que nous venons de mentionner, allait constituer un autre symbole de la nucléarisation du Canada. Après l'épisode que nous avons relaté à la dernière section, des pressions avaient été effectuées auprès du gouvernement canadien pour qu'une nouvelle mission aérienne soit assignée aux forces canadiennes en Europe. Celle-ci, désignée sous le nom de «Strike/Reconnaissance», impliquait que les avions canadiens, munis de charges nucléaires, effectuent des bombardements à l'arrière des forces soviétiques sur la base d'un plan d'opérations établi par l'OTAN. En juillet 1959, après la visite à Ottawa du général Norstadt, commandant des forces européennes de l'OTAN, la nouvelle mission est acceptée par le Cabinet, et le F-104 est choisi pour l'accomplir[104].

Les forces terrestres en Europe, conformément à la décision annoncée dès le 23 septembre 1958, seraient munies d'un missile sol-sol, lui aussi nucléaire: l'Honest John[105].

Le gouvernement conservateur, sur la base d'un ensemble de décisions précises et officielles, venait donc d'adopter, pour la défense canadienne, une stratégie essentiellement nuclaire, alors que son prédécesseur avait, dès la fin de la guerre, refusé sciemment de s'équiper d'une arme qu'il était en mesure de construire[106], mais qu'il jugeait trop dangereuse. Pour compléter ces décisions, il ne restait finalement qu'à obtenir les charges nucléaires elles-mêmes. Le décor était donc planté pour le dernier acte du drame.

LA TEMPÊTE: LE GOUVERNEMENT CONSERVATEUR ET LE DÉBAT NUCLÉAIRE

Au début des années 60, le dossier nucléaire n'était pas tellement neuf. Les premières demandes américaines concernant l'installation de charges nucléaires au Canada dataient, en effet, du mois de décembre 1957[107]. À cette date, le Pentagone avait exprimé le souhait de stocker à Goose Bay (Labrador) et à Harmon Field (Terre-Neuve), d'une part, des bombes destinées aux B-52 et, d'autre part, des missiles air-air MB-1 (Genie) pour deux unités de F-86 installées au Canada. Le gouvernement conservateur, quels que soient ses motifs, choisit de faire la sourde oreille[108].

Le président américain, ne prévoyant pas les difficultés qui allaient suivre, réitéra sa demande, envisageant même d'accorder le contrôle complet des têtes nucléaires au Canada, au cas où la RCAF manifesterait le désir d'en équiper ses propres forces[109]. Ceci, notons-le, aurait enfreint les dispositions de la loi MacMahon qui interdisait tout transfert d'autorité sur les armes nucléaires à un autre pays que les USA. Il s'agissait donc d'une concession importante que le gouvernement américain était prêt à faire pour s'assurer de la coopération du Canada.

Diefenbaker, pourtant, repoussa à nouveau l'offre américaine, mais n'exclut pas la possibilité d'équiper les forces canadiennes d'armes nucléaires, si la nécessité s'en faisait sentir.

C'est apparemment sur ces bases que des négociations furent entreprises au printemps 1959, dans le but de définir un accord-cadre dont les détails techniques seraient ultérieurement précisés au niveau des autorités militaires des deux pays.

Une entente-cadre offrait, en effet, la possibilité de réaliser rapidement un accord politique qui autrement aurait pu buter sur les multiples technicalités du dossier. Celui-ci s'était considérablement épaissi et comprenait au moins six éléments:

- les missiles MB-1 Genie destinés aux F-86 américains;
- les armes nucléaires anti-sous-marins destinées aux forces navales américaines et canadiennes à Argentia (T.-N.);
- les bombes destinées aux bombardiers du SAC;
- les têtes nucléaires des Bomarc;
- les missiles MB-1 destinés aux forces canadiennes;
- les têtes nucléaires des missiles Honest John et les bombes devant équiper les F-104 canadiens en Europe[110].

Vu la complexité évidente d'une entente formelle détaillée et minutieuse couvrant tous ces éléments, un accord-cadre s'imposait. Cette option, cependant, fut opiniâtrement rejetée par le ministre des Affaires extérieures, Howard Green. Celui-ci avait fait du contrôle des armements et, en particulier, de la non-prolifération, une croisade personnelle. Profitant des hésitations du premier ministre, mais aussi de la confiance que ce dernier lui témoignait, il mena dans les débats confus qui suivirent une lutte farouche pour s'opposer à la conclusion d'un accord qui aurait fait du Canada une puissance nucléaire[111].

D'après les témoignages de l'époque, l'attitude du ministre se fondait sur des convictions profondes et l'honnêteté de sa position ne peut être mise en doute[112]. Cependant, il faut bien constater que, vu des États-Unis, le blocage volontaire des négociations, à ce moment précis, rentrait en contradiction flagrante avec toutes les décisions prises jusque-là par le gouvernement conservateur. De plus, l'opposition systématique de Green à tout compromis provoqua un conflit majeur entre son ministère et celui de la Défense, ce qui accentua encore le climat d'incohérence dans lequel s'enfonçait progressivement le gouvernement conservateur. La suite des événements illustre fort bien ce constat. Le 22 septembre 1959, contre toute attente, le Cabinet donne son accord de principe à l'entreposage d'armes nucléaires à Goose Bay et à Harmon Field[113]. Cette décision est cependant liée à la réalisation d'une entente concernant le contrôle conjoint de ces armes, dont les termes se définissent de la façon suivante:

- le gouvernement canadien serait le seul à pouvoir autoriser l'emploi des armes entreposées sur son territoire;
- les charges stockées au Canada ne pourraient être transférées sans l'autorisation du gouvernement;
- une entente assurant la garde conjointe des charges déployées ou entreposées au Canada devra être réalisée[114].

À l'été 1960, les Américains ont accepté les conditions canadiennes, à la seule condition que les armes puissent être rapatriées aux États-Unis, le cas échéant. À l'automne, l'accord est donc prêt à être signé mais, surprise, en décembre, le Cabinet décide de retenir l'accord jusqu'à la conclusion de l'entente relative à l'équipement nucléaire des forces canadiennes[115]. De surcroît, le premier ministre mentionne en public le lien qui existe entre la décision canadienne et les progrès des négociations sur le désarmement[116]. Cette décision, en fait, pourrait être reportée pour favoriser ces dernières. Les négociations sont donc à nouveau bloquées et l'arrivée de John F. Kennedy à la présidence américaine n'arrangera guère les choses. C'est d'ailleurs au printemps de 1961 que les relations personnelles de deux chefs d'État s'enveniment, sous prétexte d'un incident anodin[117]. Les échanges continuent donc de piétiner pendant un an, sans perspective de déblocage.

LE NAUFRAGE: LA CRISE DE CUBA ET LA CHUTE DU GOUVERNEMENT CONSERVATEUR

Pour les Conservateurs, l'année 1962 ne s'annonce guère reluisante. La campagne électorale a ralenti l'activité gouvernementale et l'élection de juin décime la majorité conservatrice. En outre, le premier ministre se brise la cheville en juillet et sera immobilisé pendant plus d'un mois. Le Cabinet ne sera réorganisé que le 9 août. Comme le note Granatstein: «Le parti, le Cabinet et le pays étaient partis à la dérive sans gouvernail.» La conjoncture politique n'allait cependant pas épargner le premier ministre, et les événements de l'automne lui préparaient un choc brutal.

Le 14 octobre, en effet, un vol de reconnaissance au-dessus de Cuba détecte et photographie plusieurs sites de missiles en construction. Les engins s'avèrent être des missiles nucléaires à moyenne portée. Le 16 octobre, les photos sont présentées au président américain. La crise soviéto-américaine la plus importante de l'après-guerre est déclenchée.

Au Canada, cependant, les nouvelles de la crise n'atteignent le premier ministre que le 22 octobre. L'ambassadeur américain vient l'informer de la situation et lui remet le texte du discours que prononcera le président en soirée. Diefenbaker promet d'appuyer l'action américaine[118]. Le même jour, à la suite du message présidentiel, les forces américaines, y compris celles de NORAD, sont mises en état d'alerte avancée (DEFCON 3). Le premier ministre demeure cependant indécis, il a annoncé en Chambre l'envoi éventuel d'une mission d'observation à Cuba et va réunir le Cabinet le lendemain, mais les forces canadiennes restent l'arme au pied. Le ministre de la Défense, D. Harkness, conscient des obligations imposées par NORAD, fait de son mieux pour préparer une alerte militaire et en faciliter le déclenchement éventuel. Le 23 octobre au matin, le Cabinet se réunit et décide d'attendre les réactions des autres pays avant de s'aligner sur Washington. Harkness, outré par cette indécision, demande au chef d'état-major de mettre les forces canadiennes en alerte le plus discrètement possible. Mais le 24 octobre, trois jours après le début de la crise et au moment où commence le blocus de Cuba, le Cabinet refuse toujours de prendre une décision. Les États-Unis sont maintenant à l'échelon d'alerte le plus élevé avant la guerre ouverte: DEFCON 2. Ce ne sera qu'à ce moment que le premier ministre se laissera fléchir et autorisera une alerte officielle des forces canadiennes.

Quelle que soit l'évaluation ultérieure des événements, le gouvernement canadien, en dépit des accords passés avec les États-Unis, fit preuve d'une indécision coupable que les Américains n'oublieraient pas de sitôt. Une relation de confiance venait en ce sens d'être brisée, et l'on peut se demander si celle-ci a été rétablie depuis. Par ailleurs, l'attitude de Diefenbaker avait soulevé une tempête de critiques au Canada. L'opinion publique, en effet, appuyait l'action du président américain dans une proportion de 80 %[119]. Finalement, le Cabinet lui-même était au bord de la révolte et le leadership politique du premier ministre était sérieusement remis en question. La résonance de ces événements allait s'amplifier encore dans la crise qui allait suivre à l'hiver.

Le 30 octobre, le Cabinet, reprenant le dossier nucléaire et continuant son travail de Sisyphe, entérine un accord partiel concernant l'équipement nucléaire des forces canadiennes en Europe. L'armement des Bomarc et Voodoo bute cependant sur des technicalités. Malgré deux rencontres canado-américaines en novembre et en décembre, les négociations sont toujours au point mort et le premier ministre refusera, jusqu'au 23 février 1963, de signer un compromis difficilement mis sur pied par le Cabinet.

Les choses se précipitent toutefois. Le 3 janvier, le général Norstadt, au cours d'une conférence de presse houleuse, admet que le Canada ne fait pas face à ses responsabilités. Les chasseurs F-104 sont sur le point d'arriver en Europe et les forces canadiennes n'auront pas les armes nucléaires qui leur sont destinées[120].

Le 25 janvier, face à une vague montante de critiques, Diefenbaker prononce un discours confus qui assure la Chambre que le Canada respecterait ses engagements, mais qu'en attendant les décisions prochaines de l'OTAN et les résultats des pourparlers concernant le désarmement, le gouvernement reporte sa décision[121]. Ulcéré par l'attentisme du premier ministre et la confusion qui règne au Cabinet, le ministre Harkness donnera sa démission quelques jours plus tard[122].

Parallèlement, le 30 janvier, dans un communiqué sans doute unique dans les annales de la diplomatie, le Département d'état américain reprend, point par point, le discours du premier ministre en le contredisant systématiquement[123]:

- le Bomarc B n'a jamais été conçu pour transporter un explosif convention-nel;
- aucune entente n'a été conclue entre les États-Unis et le Canada pour équiper les forces canadiennes de missiles à tête nucléaire;
- des négociations sont en cours, mais le Canada n'a proposé aucune solu-tion pratique dans ce cadre;
- les accords de Nassau[124] ne remettent pas en question la mission nucléaire des forces canadiennes en Europe;
- l'équipement nucléaire du Canada ne constitue en aucun cas une proliféra-tion, étant donné que les charges seraient sous l'autorité unique des USA.

En somme, le gouvernement américain traite implicitement le chef d'État d'un pays ami de menteur. L'impact conjoint du communiqué et de la démission de Harkness est immédiat: le 5 février, le chef de l'opposition, Pearson, demande un vote de non-confiance, et celui-ci est appuyé par une requête identique du Parti créditiste. Les deux motions passent par une confortable majorité de 31 voix. C'était la deuxième fois qu'une telle chose se produisait au Canada depuis la Confédération, et la première motion, en 1926, n'avait obtenu qu'une voix de majorité...

Que deviendra le dossier nucléaire qui avait occasionné la chute du gouver-nement? Le post-scriptum est évocateur: le 22 avril 1963, un gouvernement libéral, sous la direction de Lester B. Pearson, est formé, et, après une rencontre au sommet de Kennedy et Pearson, les accords couvrant le transfert des charges nucléaires au Canada est signé le 16 août 1963[125]. Le Canada conservera un statut de puissance semi-nucléaire jusqu'en 1984.

Quelles sont les leçons à tirer de cette période de six années? Le bilan, en effet, n'est guère réjouissant: aucune réorientation organisée de la politique de défense n'a eu lieu; aucun des problèmes fondamentaux que nous avons signalés n'a été résolu; presque tous les éléments de la politique de défense ont fait l'objet d'erreurs de gestion ou de scandales; le consensus, qui a longtemps soutenu la position gouvernementale en matière de sécurité internationale, est en pièces, et des clivages profonds commencent à apparaître entre les positions des partis politiques au sujet de la défense canadienne[126]. De plus, les relations canado-américaines ont été soumises à dure épreuve et, ce qui est plus grave, les dernières crises de la période Diefenbaker ont montré le type de pressions directes et brutales que pouvait exercer notre puissant voisin. Dans ce sens, le *post mortem* de la période, rédigé par l'ambassadeur américain à Ottawa, est sans équivoque: «De toute façon, les résul-tats de la crise contiennent des leçons salutaires qui ne seront oubliées par aucun futur leader politique au Canada[127].»

Seul point positif du bilan: les accords de partage de la production en matière de défense ont reçu une impulsion décisive[128]. Une entente, signée le 30 décembre 1958, élimine un grand nombre d'obstacles qui interdisaient aux forces canadiennes l'accès au marché américain. Ce marché leur est maintenant ouvert en quasi-totalité. De 1959 à 1965, les contrats américains placés au Canada totalisent ainsi plus d'un milliard de dollars et la guerre du Viêt-nam continuera à favoriser l'équilibre des échanges en faveur du Canada jusqu'en 1971. Ceci doit-il être considéré comme un succès oublié de la politique conservatrice? Certainement, mais les contraintes qui l'accompagnent sont significatives. Comme le note, avec naïveté, un des créateurs canadiens du concept de partage de la production: «La résiliation de notre entente avec les USA serait désastreuse. Nous ne pouvons espérer que Washington continue à faire des choix difficiles comme, par exemple, nous accorder des avantages en matière commerciale, si nous refusons nous-mêmes de prendre les décisions politiques délicates qui s'imposent. Si nous ne voulons pas d'armes nucléaires, nous devons être prêts à accepter les conséquences. Cette année [1962], nous vendrons aux USA pour plus de 200 millions de dollars d'équipement dans le cadre du partage de la production. C'est cet échange qui forme la base sur laquelle se développera notre industrie de haute technologie. C'est cet avantage qui nous a permis d'étendre notre marché d'exportation à d'autres parties du monde. Mais, si nous perdons le marché américain, c'est la fin. La demande canadienne est tout simplement insuffisante pour permettre le développement d'une industrie de pointe[129].» Les fantômes évoqués précédemment par J.W. Holmes sont donc toujours présents.

Si nous avions à tirer une conclusion d'ensemble de cette période, celle-ci pourrait se formuler de la façon suivante: compte tenu de la complexité des problèmes de sécurité auxquels le Canada fait face et compte tenu surtout des lourdes contraintes que lui imposent sa dépendance face aux USA et son statut de puissance moyenne, la politique de défense canadienne ne supporte pas la médiocrité et l'incompétence, et la comparaison de l'époque Saint-Laurent avec celle que nous venons de relater est significative à cet égard.

Partie III

Nouveau cap

*La politique de défense canadienne
1963-1967*

LES LIBÉRAUX ET LE DÉBUT DU PROCESSUS DE RÉVISION

Lorsqu'il accède au pouvoir au printemps 1963, le gouvernement de Lester B. Pearson fait face à une situation internationale très différente de celle qui prévalait dans les années 50. Les pires années de la guerre froide et leur cortège de crises sont passés et une période de détente Est-Ouest est en train de s'ouvrir en Europe et entre les deux superpuissances. Le long processus, qui aboutira à la stabilisation formelle de la situation européenne en matière de sécurité et aux négociations SALT, est entamé. Par ailleurs, l'engagement américain au Viêt-nam va peu à peu détourner l'attention des décideurs de Washington des questions touchant à la défense continentale et à l'Alliance atlantique. NORAD, qui, en 1963, constitue un système de défense et d'alerte massif, entre dans une période de démantèlement progressif qui aboutira à sa mise en veilleuse presque complète dans les années 70. Il est vrai que l'on est passé à l'ère du missile intercontinental et que la défense aérienne n'a plus grande importance au plan stratégique.

La situation se prête donc fort bien à une révision importante de la politique de défense canadienne et c'est à cette tâche que s'attaque, dès l'été 1963, le nouveau gouvernement libéral. Les principes sur lesquels se fonde cette révision ont d'ores et déjà été soulignés au cours de la campagne électorale[130]. Les ressources du Canada sont limitées, une politique réaliste et à long terme doit être définie, et celle-ci doit tenir compte, en priorité, des types de besoins que le Canada pourra satisfaire dans la limite de ses moyens. Il n'est plus question, comme le dira Pearson, que l'armée se voie confiée des missions sans que les moyens appropriés lui soient accordés[131].

Par ailleurs, l'accent est mis sur les aspects industriels de la défense. On s'efforcera de choisir des missions militaires pour lesquelles l'industrie canadienne sera en mesure de fournir les équipements. La qualité de ces équipements devra être de premier ordre et le gouvernement s'engage à encourager l'industrie dans cette voie: «Nous devons, disait le premier ministre, harmoniser notre politique de défense et nos ressources industrielles[132].»

C'est donc une réflexion en profondeur qui s'annonce, et il est implicite que les engagements majeurs du Canada seront examinés à cette occasion. Dès l'été, la parution d'un nouveau livre blanc est annoncée. Elle sera précédée par un ensemble d'études ministérielles et accompagnée d'un débat public. À cette fin, le gouvernement crée un comité spécial bipartisan présidé par M. Sauvé. Ce forum, quelques années plus tard, acquerra un statut permanent sous le nom de Comité des affaires extérieures et de la défense nationale (SCEAND)[133].

Après une série de débats animés qui remettent en question l'appartenance du Canada à l'OTAN, le Comité déposera son rapport en décembre 1963. Son contenu n'est guère innovateur[134]. Malgré de nombreuses critiques, le rapport Sauvé recommande le maintien des engagements traditionnels et souligne, en particulier, l'importance de la contribution politique du Canada à l'Alliance. De plus, le rapport présente une lacune majeure et, comme le note Andres Brewin, il évite de prendre position en ce qui concerne la doctrine stratégique ou militaire qui doit sous-tendre l'effort canadien de défense[135]. Pendant ce temps, les études internes de la Défense nationale suivent leur cours et le livre blanc, rédigé en majeure partie par le ministre Hellyer lui-même, reçoit le feu vert du Cabinet le 25 mars 1964.

LE LIVRE BLANC DE 1964

Le texte du livre blanc présente un ensemble de qualités plutôt peu communes pour un exercice de ce genre: il est homogène, clair, et une série d'idées fortes s'en dégage nettement[136]. En ce qui concerne les forces de l'OTAN, le gouvernement projette simplement de rendre au contingent canadien son autonomie fonctionnelle. Le principe de la spécialisation avait en effet intégré les forces canadiennes à un système de défense qui, d'une part, rendait les unités nationales extrêmement dépendantes les unes des autres et, d'autre part, exigeait un entraînement spécifique pour la situation européenne. En d'autres termes, la structure militaire de l'OTAN était un carcan, et il était difficile de rajuster les missions et les besoins matériels des forces canadiennes tant que ceux-ci étaient dictés par les nécessités du déploiement global de l'Alliance. Par ailleurs, la spécialisation exigée par ce déploiement ne correspondait pas à la formation normalement offerte pour les besoins de la défense canadienne. Cette spécialisation, en fait, se juxtaposait à la formation militaire normale et alourdissait des coûts de fonctionnement déjà élevés. Il s'agissait, dans une perspective de rationalisation, de confier au contingent canadien en Europe des missions qui le rendraient plus indépendant des unités alliées et lui permettraient de se passer d'une partie d'équipement lourd et coûteux exigé par ses missions. On envisageait, en somme, de faire de la brigade et du groupe aérien une force souple, légère, mobile et autonome, plutôt qu'un élément spécialisé, intégré à une armée internationale, elle-même conçue dans la perspective d'une guerre terrestre classique et massive.

Dans cette perspective, le livre blanc annonce que le contingent canadien en Europe serait maintenu, mais sa mission serait peu à peu redéfinie. En premier lieu, les forces terrestres et aériennes seraient couplées, le groupe aérien abandonnerait progressivement son rôle nucléaire et aurait pour mission principale d'appuyer la brigade. Les CF-104 seraient remplacés par des avions appropriés. Les forces terrestres, quant à elles, conserveraient leurs fusées Honest John, mais celles-ci seraient munies d'une tête conventionnelle. La mobilité de la brigade serait renforcée, et on prévoyait acquérir des véhicules blindés de transport. De plus, la formation, au Canada, d'un bataillon mobile destiné à «l'Allied Mobile Force», était aussi annoncée.

Sur le plan de la défense continentale, le livre blanc souligne l'importance des responsabilités canadiennes. En particulier, il est fait mention des missions de surveillance du territoire et des côtes, du règlement des «incidents» en territoire canadien et de la défense de l'espace aérien national. En fait, il est clair, au niveau de l'OTAN et de la défense du continent, que l'intention sous-jacente du livre blanc est de redéfinir la politique de défense dans une perspective plus spécifiquement canadienne. La nécessité d'une coopération à long terme avec les États-Unis n'est pourtant pas ignorée, mais il est aussi prévu que l'importance de NORAD diminuerait progressivement. Les trois unités de CF-101 sont donc maintenues ainsi que les deux batteries de missiles Bomarc, mais le souhait d'abandonner la mission nucléaire est exprimé sans équivoque[137].

La réaction immédiate des milieux politiques et de l'opinion publique est très positive. Le ministre est félicité pour avoir enfin défini une orientation politique claire après six années de confusion. L'élément le plus remarqué du livre blanc ne concernait cependant ni l'OTAN ni NORAD, mais l'annonce d'une réorganisation globale des forces canadiennes. Celle-ci, qui, contrairement à ce que l'on a pu prétendre, est étroitement liée à la redéfinition de la politique de défense canadienne, constituera en effet un élément marquant et durable de la période.

LA RÉORGANISATION DE L'ARMÉE CANADIENNE

Il y avait certainement matière à critique dans l'organisation et le fonctionnement de l'armée canadienne en 1964[138], quoique ce constat puisse être aussi appliqué à bien d'autres pays. Le rapport Glassco, relatif à l'organisation gouvernementale, avait été explicite à ce sujet. La prolifération des comités et le désordre administratif avaient favorisé le retard et le gaspillage dans les programmes de développement militaires. L'échec de l'Arrow et l'abandon du Bobcat[139] illustrent en particulier cette affirmation. L'existence d'organismes spécialisés propres à chaque armée avait triplé les services de paie, de recrutement, d'information et de renseignements.

Chacun des trois chefs d'état-major avait accès direct au ministre, mais ni lui ni le président du Comité des chefs d'état-major n'avaient les moyens d'évaluer la légitimité des demandes budgétaires des services[140]. De plus, il n'y avait pas d'unité stratégique, pas d'unité de planification et aucun mécanisme permettant la définition de priorités en ce qui concernait les missions et les besoins matériels correspondants. «Il n'y avait, dira Paul Hellyer, aucun plan opérationnel cohérent; chaque service envisageait son propre scénario. Pour l'un, on prévoyait un spasme nucléaire de cinq jours; pour l'autre, une guerre longue et pour le troisième, une mobilisation prolongée[141].» En fait, l'armée canadienne souffrait d'un mal très commun: la sclérose organisationnelle de toute administration qui se retranche dans ses traditions pour survivre, faute d'une mission précise à remplir.

Paul Hellyer était l'homme de la situation. La réorganisation de la défense devint rapidement son grand dessein et, à l'instar de Green, il fit de sa vocation ministérielle une croisade personnelle, d'ailleurs couronnée de succès, ce qui le range, avec Claxton, au côté des meilleurs ministres de la Défense que le Canada ait produits.

La solution envisagée par lui n'était pas vraiment neuve: l'idée de mieux intégrer l'administration des forces canadiennes d'avant-guerre. Les mesures prises à cet égard avaient été timides et partielles. La création du poste de président du Comité d'état-major, en 1946, et la réunion des trois armées sous la direction d'un même ministre, à la même date, n'avaient été qu'un premier pas[142], ainsi, d'ailleurs, que l'intégration des services médicaux et religieux un peu plus tard.

Le projet envisagé par Hellyer était beaucoup plus ambitieux; il voulait, en effet, réunir les états-majors en un seul organisme interarmées, dirigé par un seul chef, et intégrer tous les services administratifs de l'armée, de la marine et de la RCAF. De plus, au niveau des commandements opérationnels, Hellyer prévoyait former un ensemble de commandements fonctionnels qui, chacun, réunirait les éléments nécessaires à leur mission. La division traditionnelle des armées de terre, air et mer était condamnée.

La première phase de la réorganisation fut entamée à l'été 1964. Le 16 juillet, la nouvelle Loi sur la défense nationale était adoptée sans problème par le Parlement, et la réorganisation de l'état-major était effectuée immédiatement. L'état-major était placé sous le commandement d'un chef unique, assisté par deux adjoints. Les chefs d'états-majors des trois armées étaient remplacés par cinq responsables, chacun dirigeant un service fonctionnel: personnel, logistique, génie, contrôle général et préparation opérationnelle (voir figure 1, présentée à la fin du chapitre).

Le 31 décembre 1964, la réorganisation se poursuit au niveau des services. Les trois branches du contrôle général sont intégrées ainsi que celles du personnel des services techniques, des relations publiques, de l'infrastructure et du génie. Fin 1965, les services de recrutement sont eux aussi réunis.

Parallèlement, le système de classification des emplois est simplifié. Il passe ainsi de 350 à 97 catégories. Le système de la paye est unifié et, le 1er avril, le système intégré de communication des forces canadiennes voit le jour. De façon presque surprenante, aucun problème majeur n'est apparu, aucune révolte n'a eu lieu[143].

Hellyer passe donc à la deuxième phase de la réforme, acceptée par le Cabinet le 29 mars 1965. Celle-ci implique une simplification de la structure des commandements, qui passent de onze à six. Leur description est importante car elle reste valide, dans ses grandes lignes, jusqu'à nos jours[144]. Elle résume aussi très clairement les fonctions essentielles de l'armée canadienne.

Le premier de ces éléments est le *commandement mobile* (*MOBCOM*)[145]. Il est composé de trois unités de la taille d'une brigade chacune. Deux de ces unités (le premier groupe de brigade canadien [GBC] de Calgary et le 5e GBC de Valcartier) sont destinées à renforcer le 4e GBC en Europe, et le personnel de ces brigades est en constante rotation entre le Canada et la RFA. La 3e unité, c'est-à-dire la «Special Service Force» à laquelle s'adjoindra le premier bataillon du «Royal Canadian Regiment», forme la base de brigade destinée à intervenir dans le Nord de l'Europe, sous les ordres du commandement mobile allié (Allied Mobile Command).

Chacune de ces brigades dispose, en théorie, des éléments qui font d'elle une unité multifonctionnelle et autonome. Ces éléments sont:

- trois bataillons d'infanterie;
- un régiment d'artillerie;
- un régiment de sapeurs-ingénieurs militaires;
- un bataillon de service;
- une unité (squadron) de transmission;
- une unité d'appui héliportée.

L'ensemble du commandement sera, par ailleurs, appuyé par un centre d'entraînement de combat (Gagetown) et un centre d'entraînement pour les troupes aéroportées (Edmonton). Le 10e Groupe aérien tactique, finalement, qui sera créé en 1968, aura pour mission d'appuyer la Special Service Force lors de son envoi éventuel en Europe. Il se composera de deux unités de CF-5, soit environ 24 avions.

Le deuxième élément de la structure, c'est-à-dire le commandement du transport aérien, ne nécessite pas de longs commentaires. Qu'il suffise de dire que sa mission principale et de seconder le commandement mobile en matière de transport. Il comprend, jusqu'en 1969, 24 C-130 Hercules et une quinzaine de Buffalos. Le contingent canadien en Europe n'est pas affecté par cette réforme et demeure un élément distinct.

Le troisième commandement est celui des forces maritimes. Ses responsabilités se divisent entre les côtes atlantique (MARCOM à Halifax) et pacifique (MARPAC à Esquimalt). Il est aussi chargé de la surveillance de la zone CANLANT dans l'Atlantique, sous le commandement de l'OTAN (SACLANT); en plus, il assure la surveillance maritime et côtière. Il dispose, à cet effet, d'avions spécialisés: les Argus et les Trackers.

Dans l'ensemble, le tableau 1 résume brièvement la répartition des forces du commandement maritime.

Le commandement de la défense aérienne, quant à lui, a principalement la charge des forces canadiennes de NORAD, soit en 1963-1967, les trois unités de CF-101 Voodoo (66 avions) et les deux batteries de Bomarc. Il a aussi la responsabilité des sites de la ligne Pine Tree. La Mid-Canada Line est supprimée en 1965.

Les deux derniers commandements, sur lesquels nous ne nous étendrons pas non plus, sont celui de l'entraînement et de la formation, et celui du matériel.

Comme on peut le constater, Hellyer venait, dans un temps record, de dépoussiérer l'organisation militaire canadienne, donnant ainsi aux structures de l'armée une précision fonctionnelle peu courante. Mais le programme ainsi entrepris ne visait pas – ou du moins pas seulement – à améliorer la qualité esthétique des organigrammes de la défense. Il était fondé, en effet, sur un plan d'économies draconiennes qui, lui-même, avait pour but de dégager les fonds nécessaires à un rééquipement militaire d'ensemble[146].

Dans cette perspective, dès 1963, Hellyer avait réduit la milice de 60 000 à 24 000 hommes et l'intégration des états-majors avait permis un dégraissage important. Les postes du quartier général, à Ottawa, avaient ainsi été coupés de 30 %. De plus, parallèlement à la réorganisation, le ministre avait fait admettre le principe d'une réduction de 20 % dans la catégorie «personnel de soutien», soit environ 10 000 postes. En fait, de 1963 à 1965, 26 300 personnes quittaient les forces canadiennes et un programme de retraite anticipée contribuait, avec succès, à ouvrir la voie à de nouvelles promotions.

L'opération permet dès la première année une économie de 144 millions et, dès 1966[147], la proportion du budget de la défense consacré aux équipements, qui était tombée de 42 % en 1954 à 13 % en 1964, remonte à 20 %. La réforme Hellyer est donc un succès[148].

Honorant ainsi ses promesses, le ministre peut donc réaliser un programme de rééquipement sans précédent, engageant sur cinq ans 1,5 milliard de dollars.

Dans le cadre de ce programme, le commandement mobile devait recevoir 115 Northorp F-5 pour la force d'intervention; 1 000 véhicules blindés d'infanterie étaient commandés pour les forces terrestres en général; 60 millions de dollars étaient consacrés à l'artillerie (Howitzer Pack 105 mm, M-109, Carl Gustav) et 48 millions de dollars à l'achat de plus de 3 000 camions. De plus, les chars Centurion équipant le 4e GBC en Europe seraient remplacés dès 1970. La force maritime, finalement, n'était pas oubliée et le porte-avions *Bonaventure* fut remis à neuf au coût de 18 millions de dollars). MARCOM recevrait aussi trois sous-marins de classe Obéron et quatre destroyers de type DDH 280[149].

LE BILAN DE LA PÉRIODE

Fondamentalement, la réforme Hellyer et le plan d'équipement n'étaient que les éléments d'une vaste opération d'assainissement qui annonçait seulement une redéfinition des objectifs de la défense canadienne. Les objectifs du livre blanc constituaient, en ce sens, la première esquisse d'une politique encore à venir. Dans cette perspective, il est significatif de souligner que la présence du Canada dans les grands débats internationaux de la période fut très discrète[150], particulièrement en ce qui concerne l'OTAN dont il n'est même pas fait mention dans le troisième volume des mémoires du premier ministre[151]. Ceci confirme le fait qu'à l'instar de Robert McNamara aux USA, P. Hellyer et Lester B. Pearson avaient compris qu'en matière de défense, l'organisation, la gestion et l'équipement ont tendance à dicter la rhétorique politique. La réorganisation et les économies effectuées par Hellyer permettaient donc de préparer un changement de politique qui ne se limiterait pas à un simple vernissage.

L'échange suivant, qui eut pour cadre une entrevue télévisée du ministre de la Défense, est significatif à cet égard:

M. TROYER: — Dans le passé, les ministres de la Défense se sont souvent réfugiés derrière nos engagements envers l'OTAN pour éviter d'exprimer leurs opinions à propos des changements que nous envisagions. Nous semblons avoir renversé cette situation et décidé d'opérer ouvertement ces changements, quitte à négocier plus tard avec l'Alliance. Ceci implique-t-il une plus grande indépendance du Canada face à l'OTAN?

M. HELLYER: — Dans une certaine mesure, c'est probablement exact. *Je pense qu'il s'agit d'une indication des missions futures que nous avons l'intention de négocier.*

M. TROYER: — Je pense que c'est la première fois que nous exprimons publiquement nos intentions de modifier notre rôle.

M. HELLYER: — Oui, je pense que c'est le cas[152].

Les intentions du ministre étaient donc claires et elles s'harmonisaient manifestement avec les points saillants du livre blanc. L'observateur ne peut cependant qu'imaginer la forme précise qu'auraient prise les futures missions de l'armée canadienne et la façon dont ces missions auraient été négociées. Un nouveau leadership politique allait, en effet, se substituer au gouvernement Pearson et une autre remise en question de la politique de sécurité canadienne allait suivre.

Une note finale est nécessaire pour compléter le tableau de cette brève période. Les œuvres du ministre de la Défense n'avaient pas été appréciées par tous. En poursuivant l'opération d'intégration des forces armées, Paul Hellyer avait, en effet, entrepris leur unification: les marins, les pilotes et les soldats de l'armée de terre seraient réunis en une seule entité (les forces canadiennes), ils auraient un seul uniforme, une seule échelle de grades et une seule politique de gestion de carrière. En somme, la quasi-totalité des traditions organisationnelles sur lesquelles se fonde l'identification spécifique du soldat à son armée devaient être supprimées, au détriment de ce que l'on appelle l'esprit de corps. Le militaire devait, en quelque sorte, être remplacé par un spécialiste anonyme pouvant passer d'un commandement à un autre, sans égard à son appartenance d'origine[153].

Compte tenu de l'attachement encore vigoureux de l'armée canadienne aux traditions britanniques, l'unification fut très mal reçue, et on peut avancer que l'entêtement du ministre à compléter son œuvre contribua à aigrir indiscutablement les rapports civils et militaires durant les années 1966-1968[154]. La Loi de l'unification (C-243) fut cependant imposée et mise en vigueur en février 1968.

De ce fait, Paul Hellyer, qui aurait pu être considéré par les militaires eux-mêmes comme le ministre de la Défense par excellence, fut jugé avant tout pour son arrogance, son manque de sensibilité, et même le travail considérable qu'il avait accompli dans le domaine de la gestion et du rééquipement fut minimisé, sinon tourné en dérision[155]. Comme le note Granatstein, en cherchant à unifier les forces canadiennes, le ministre avait oublié l'importance des loyautés traditionnelles de l'armée. «Celles-ci, en effet, sont essentielles pour des hommes dont le travail consiste à risquer leur vie pour leur pays; ils n'attendent pas, en temps de paix, des acclamations du public, mais leur substituent, par contre, une liturgie complexe à laquelle ils tiennent par-dessus tout[156].»

Le ministre venait en ce sens de démontrer, à ses dépens, les incompatibilités de la gestion et de l'art militaires.

Partie IV

La dérive

La politique de défense canadienne
durant la période Trudeau
1968-1979
1980-1984

LE CONTEXTE POLITIQUE EN 1968

À la fin de la période Pearson, les grands changements internationaux, qui s'annonçaient déjà en 1964, se traduisent maintenant dans les faits, et ceux-ci ont un impact direct sur la politique de défense canadienne.

Au plan de l'Alliance, par exemple, le rapport Harmel[157] vient d'inscrire la détente parmi les objectifs souhaitables de l'Organisation et les premières démarches, en vue de négocier une réduction des forces alliées en Europe, ont été entreprises auprès du pacte de Varsovie. En Allemagne, le chancelier Brandt s'engage sur la voie de l'*Ostpolitik* qui aboutira, quelques années plus tard, aux accords quadripartites de Berlin; et les pourparlers au sujet des armes stratégiques ont été entamés entre Washington et Moscou.

Dans une perspective plus large, le tiers monde, sortant de la période de décolonisation, apparaît comme un élément essentiel de la scène internationale des années 70, une scène qui promet d'être à la fois plus complexe, mais plus pacifique.

Paradoxalement, alors que les relations internationales semblent entrer dans une ère nouvelle, l'enlisement des États-Unis au Viêt-nam est perçu comme un anachronisme et suscite une vague montante de critiques, qui remettent en question le leadership américain en matière de sécurité et de politique étrangère.

Tous ces changements et leurs échos au niveau de l'opinion publique sont clairement perçus à Ottawa et, dès 1967, les déclarations des Affaires extérieures et les études de la Défense nationale reflètent ce sentiment général de mouvance. Lester B. Pearson lui-même, dans ses déclarations puis dans ses mémoires, se montre beaucoup plus critique à l'égard de l'OTAN et des USA qu'il ne l'a été. Il assiste d'ailleurs personnellement à la désagrégation du leadership américain dans les dernières années de la présidence Johnson, et ceci l'affectera visiblement beaucoup[158].

Toutefois, cette évolution ne favorise pas la révision de la politique de défense, longuement préparée depuis 1963. Les négociations envisagées par Paul Hellyer avec l'OTAN exigent, en effet, une période de stabilité autorisant des pourparlers calmes et pondérés. Or, au plan politique et militaire, la situation n'est guère propice.

En mars 1966, le gouvernement français retire ses forces de l'OTAN, provoquant une crise sans précédent. Plus discrètement, la Grande-Bretagne réduit les effectifs de son armée sur le Rhin de 77 000 à 46 000 hommes et, tout aussi discrètement, le Pentagone transfère 35 000 hommes de l'Europe au Viêt-nam[159]. Ces mesures n'ont pas manqué de susciter des velléités similaires de la part de la Belgique, du Danemark et de la Norvège. Finalement, le Sénat américain a entamé une longue offensive politique pour obtenir le retrait pur et simple des forces américaines d'Europe. Tous ces événements remettaient donc en question à la fois la structure militaire de l'Alliance et la politique de contrôle des armements en Europe. Pourquoi, en effet, l'URSS se soucierait-elle de négocier une réduction de ses propres forces si l'Alliance se désintégrait?

Il est donc évident, dans ce contexte, qu'une réorientation de la politique canadienne face à l'OTAN se présentait mal, et il aurait peut-être fallu se rappeler la devise de la diplomatie canadienne: «La prudence est la meilleure part du courage[160].»

En avril 1968, Pierre E. Trudeau remplace Lester B. Pearson à la tête du Parti libéral et, dans les mois qui suivent, une vague d'enthousiasme populaire le porte au pouvoir. Une ère nouvelle s'ouvre pour la politique canadienne.

LES PREMIERS PAS DU NOUVEAU GOUVERNEMENT

Contrairement aux pratiques traditionnelles, la nouvelle équipe libérale n'avait fait aucune promesse à l'électorat canadien en matière de sécurité et de défense. Le public n'avait d'ailleurs pas d'opinions passionnées sur la question et désirait seulement le statu quo[161].

Les premières déclarations officielles ne reflètent pas de changements révolutionnaires. Il est question de détente, de prospérité et d'ordre mondial, de nouvelle politique plus réaliste et plus efficace, mais aussi du respect des engagements passés; dans l'ensemble, les vaches sacrées de la défense canadienne ne semblent donc pas menacées[162].

Les mesures pratiques prises par le gouvernement sont cependant plus significatives. On annonce une coupure de 20 % des effectifs de la division aérienne en Europe ainsi que la fermeture de la base de Zweibrücken et le redéploiement des six escadrilles de la division, à Lahr et à Solingen. Le gouvernement reviendra sur sa décision en novembre, lors d'une réunion de l'OTAN, mais le geste est évocateur de ce qui allait suivre[163].

Parallèlement, le premier ministre annonce une révision complète de la politique étrangère canadienne et un processus complexe d'analyses, d'études et de débats est mis en branle[164].

Celui-ci est entamé, dès l'automne 1968, par une consultation discrète des milieux académiques spécialisés. Dans les mois qui suivent, quatre rapports relatifs à la défense sont rédigés. Les deux premiers sont respectivement celui du «Special Task Force on Relations with Europe (STAFFEUR)»[165] et le rapport conjoint Défense-Affaires extérieures[166]. Tous deux concluent également à la nécessité de respecter le statu quo.

Le troisième rapport, celui du Comité permanent des affaires extérieures et de la défense (SCEAND)[167], reflète un éventail d'opinions plus large, marquées par le radicalisme à la mode de l'époque, mais conclut, lui aussi, au besoin de maintenir notre contribution à l'OTAN.

Un consensus très clair était ainsi exprimé et il est significatif qu'un sondage Gallup de la même époque montrait qu'une majorité du public canadien était du même avis[168].

Le premier ministre, insatisfait de ces conclusions, demande à un groupe, dirigé par un membre de son bureau personnel (I. Head)[169], de rédiger un troisième rapport, plus conforme à ses objectifs. Ce groupe soumet le résultat de ses réflexions le 29 mars 1969. Il préconise la réduction du contingent européen à 3 000 hommes (une coupure des deux tiers), l'abandon du rôle nucléaire et le redéploiement des forces canadiennes. Ces conclusions seront adoptées par le gouvernement. Comme le confirme Thorardson: «En avril 1969, le premier ministre enleva à la fonction publique le pouvoir de définir les principes fondamentaux ainsi que les objectifs sur lesquels se fonderait la politique de défense. Alors que les décisions tactiques pourraient encore être prises par les fonctionnaires, ce serait maintenant au bureau du premier ministre que les choix stratégiques seraient faits[170].»

Dans une certaine mesure, cela était légitime, mais la centralisation des décisions peut favoriser une personnalisation excessive de la politique, au point que celle-ci perde contact avec la réalité. Les observateurs s'entendent pour dire que la philosophie et la formulation de la politique de défense, telle qu'elle s'exprimera dans les mois qui suivront, portent la marque personnelle du premier ministre. Il est par ailleurs admis que Trudeau donnait l'impression d'un intellect à la fois affirmé, brillant et complexe. Il est aussi évident que le leader libéral avait une conception très personnelle de la politique canadienne et des affaires internationales, et ses interventions, très remarquées dans le domaine du contrôle des armements, en sont la preuve[171].

On ne peut cependant que spéculer en ce qui concerne les motifs et la logique des décisions prises en 1969. Trudeau était-il un crypto-radical, un antimilitariste viscéral? A-t-il été influencé par le climat politique de la détente et l'ambiance pacifiste de la période? Voulait-il simplement clore au plus tôt le dossier de la défense canadienne afin de s'attaquer à celui de l'unité nationale? Ou bien avait-il sincèrement l'ambition de redéfinir, d'un seul coup, le corpus complet de la politique de sécurité canadienne? Ces questions, hélas! demeureront sans réponse tant que le principal intéressé ne se sera pas exprimé ou qu'on ne pourra examiner les documents internes de cette période. Les décisions de monsieur Trudeau doivent donc être évaluées, pour l'instant, sur la base des textes officiels de la période et de leurs conséquences pratiques.

LE «NEW LOOK» DE LA POLITIQUE DE DÉFENSE CANADIENNE ET LE LIVRE BLANC DE 1971

La présentation officielle de la nouvelle politique de défense canadienne a lieu le 3 avril, devant la presse[172]. Trois points en ressortent clairement: le Canada n'opterait pas pour le non-alignement; les alliances traditionnelles seraient respectées, mais le gouvernement canadien «avait l'intention, de concert avec ses alliés, de prendre les mesures préliminaires permettant la réduction planifiée et progressive des forces canadiennes en Europe»[173]. Finalement, la déclaration précise que les quatre objectifs de la défense seraient, par ordre d'importance:

- la surveillance du territoire et la protection de la souveraineté canadienne;
- la défense de l'Amérique du Nord;
- l'appui à l'OTAN;
- les opérations de maintien de la paix.

L'ordre de ces objectifs, notons-le, est inversé par rapport à celui qui prévalait auparavant. La volonté de désengagement en Europe est, elle aussi, nettement exprimée.

Le véritable exposé de la politique de défense ne se fait cependant que quelques jours plus tard, le 12 avril 1969, à Calgary[174]. À cette occasion, le premier ministre tient le raisonnement suivant: le but principal de la politique de défense canadienne est de servir l'intérêt national et, par extension, de contribuer à la paix mondiale. En effet, le Canada n'est pas seulement tourné vers l'Atlantique, mais aussi vers le Pacifique et l'Arctique. L'Europe a maintenant les moyens d'assurer sa défense et son unité en matière de sécurité ne dépend plus du Canada. Pour ce dernier, par ailleurs, la recherche de la paix prime sur celle de la sécurité européenne, et l'OTAN est une alliance trop orientée vers les questions militaires et pas suffisamment vers les questions politiques. Pour toutes ces raisons, l'Alliance n'est plus une priorité canadienne. La préoccupation première du Canada réside dans la protection de la souveraineté canadienne *dans toutes les dimensions du terme.*

Remarquons que le caractère un peu choquant de cette déclaration ne réside pas tant dans la substance même du passage que dans sa forme. Une révision de la position canadienne dans l'Alliance était en fait attendue et l'attention apportée à la sécurité du territoire canadien était la bienvenue. La hauteur presque gaullienne des propos, les remarques fondées, mais peu diplomatiques, à l'égard de l'Europe conféraient cependant aux déclarations de Trudeau une agressivité inutile sur laquelle on se perd en conjectures.

Dès le mois de septembre, le ministre de la Défense, Léo Cadieux, traduit la nouvelle politique dans les faits[175]. Le budget de la défense est gelé pour trois ans à son niveau actuel, soit 1,815 milliard de dollars. Le 4e GBC est redéployé à Lahr et à Solingen, dans le Sud de l'Allemagne près du Rhin, et les forces combinées du contingent canadien voient les effectifs réduits à 5 000 hommes, soit 2 800 pour la brigade et 2 200 pour les forces aériennes qui ne disposent plus maintenant que de trois groupes aériens, un pour la mission de reconnaissance et les deux autres pour l'appui tactique. Les unités canadiennes en Europe deviennent une sorte de force intérimaire et pour l'instant, gardent leur matériel actuel. Finalement, l'abandon du rôle nucléaire est officialisé et annoncé pour la période 1970-1972.

En terme de substance, le livre blanc de la défense de 1971 n'ajoute pas grand chose aux déclarations et aux décisions précédentes[176]. Il rappelle les priorités de 1969, affirme l'attachement du Canada à l'Alliance et précise que la contribution canadienne à l'OTAN se justifie simplement par des motifs politiques et des raisons de sécurité générale. Parmi les rares éléments notables, relevons l'annonce du retrait du char *Centurion* qui, en 1971, avait déjà 20 ans, et son remplacement par un véhicule blindé léger. Le livre blanc mentionne aussi le maintien de la contribution canadienne à la force mobile alliée. L'intégration de MARCOM à SACLANT est aussi respectée. Soulignons aussi la seule nouveauté: la mention discrète d'un rôle de maintien de l'ordre pour le commandement mobile, ce qui amène Granatstein à remarquer ironiquement que l'armée est devenue, aux yeux du premier ministre, une «gendarmerie en uniforme militaire» («*a glorified Gendarmerie nationale*»)[177].

Malgré l'ambiguïté des déclarations publiques concernant la révision de la politique de défense entre 1968 et 1971, il est nécessaire, dès maintenant, de faire un premier bilan et d'examiner surtout les postulats qui sous-tendent cette réorientation ainsi que les conditions de sa réalisation éventuelle.

La «nouvelle politique» de Trudeau se fonde, en fait, sur trois paris implicites ou explicites: la nature favorable d'un climat de détente en Europe, l'acceptabilité politique du retrait canadien ainsi que sa viabilité militaire, la possibilité de définir l'idée de souveraineté en termes concrets. Examinons chacun de ces éléments tour à tour.

En ce qui a trait à la détente, tout d'abord, il apparaît clairement qu'un retrait canadien était mal venu et que la stratégie de Trudeau ne s'harmonisait pas avec une politique de détente ou de contrôle des armements en Europe. En effet, l'OTAN, après les retraits français et britannique, avait plus que jamais besoin d'unité pour pouvoir négocier une réduction bilatérale des troupes, de part et d'autre du rideau de fer. Il était tout à fait mal venu, dès lors, de favoriser un mouvement de retrait unilatéral de la part des pays occidentaux, qui saperait, dès le départ, les bases de la négociation avec le pacte de Varsovie. Pour sa part, le gouvernement américain avait besoin, à Washington même, d'un soutien sans équivoque des membres de l'OTAN pour montrer au Sénat que les alliés présentaient un front politique et militaire uni en Europe et qu'en conséquence, la présence militaire américaine était nécessaire pour éviter que ce front ne se lézarde.

On peut d'ailleurs avancer que la stagnation des pourparlers MBFR, à Vienne, est en large mesure due à l'incohérence des politiques nationales des pays membres de l'OTAN au cours de ces premières années, et que le renouveau des tensions en Europe, après 1975, a pour origine l'échec d'une détente militaire parallèle à la détente politique qui se réalisait au sein de la CSCE. D'après les données disponibles à l'époque, un retrait canadien contrariait donc la détente et constituait une erreur politique qu'il était possible d'éviter.

Le retrait canadien était, par ailleurs, clairement inacceptable. Les Européens pouvaient considérer le geste du Canada comme une défection, et ceci pour plusieurs raisons. La réduction draconienne des effectifs canadiens présentait, d'abord, un coût économique important. Le vide laissé par la brigade dans le front de l'OTAN devait être comblé par une unité britannique. En fait, malgré son stationnement à Lahr, le contingent canadien disparaissait simplement du dispositif allié. Ensuite, le geste canadien faisait craindre en Europe l'adoption d'une mesure similaire par les Américains, ce qui aurait porté un coup mortel à l'Alliance. On peut d'ailleurs penser que les réactions très fortes des pays européens vis-à-vis du Canada étaient vraisemblablement dirigées indirectement vers les États-Unis.

De plus, le retrait du Canada accentuait encore la présence militaire allemande au sein du déploiement allié, ce qui pouvait inquiéter à la fois les Européens et les Soviétiques, compte tenu d'un contentieux historique encore très présent. Enfin, l'impact politique de la décision canadienne laissait présager une accentuation des divergences nationales au sein d'une alliance déjà secouée par plusieurs crises (le retrait de la France étant le cas le plus évident).

Il était donc clair et prévisible que la réaction européenne au retrait canadien serait extrêmement négative, surtout si une telle mesure n'était pas préparée par un ensemble de consultations discrètes. En fait, la réception que reçut l'annonce du retrait canadien au conseil de l'OTAN montrait clairement qu'une telle consultation n'avait pas eu lieu. Le chef de la délégation canadienne à l'OTAN rapporta d'ailleurs que l'annonce de la décision, au printemps 1969, donna lieu à une scène d'une rare intensité: «L'un des délégués fondit en larmes, l'autre accusa le gouvernement canadien d'avoir violé le principe de la sécurité collective et un troisième murmura sobrement que le Canada était un renégat[178].»

Il est donc manifeste que le choix canadien était inacceptable pour les membres de l'Alliance. La décision ignorait en effet de façon flagrante les conséquences politiques que le retrait militaire canadien aurait sur les relations du Canada avec les pays européens. M. Eustace le note, en ce sens: «Ce que Trudeau n'a pas saisi était l'importance du lien fondamental qui existait entre les relations politiques et militaires en Europe[179].» En d'autres termes, si le gouvernement canadien voulait, comme c'était le cas, développer ses liens économiques, politiques et commerciaux avec l'Europe, s'il voulait faire partie du «club européen», il devait montrer qu'il était un membre loyal de ce club, en matière de sécurité. Or, cet argument, que Pearson avait fort bien compris, n'avait visiblement pas trouvé grâce aux yeux de son successeur.

Pour ce qui est de la viabilité militaire maintenant, il était admis et recommandé depuis longtemps déjà que la réorganisation du contingent canadien en Europe s'imposait. J. Gellner, qui avait été en 1959 l'un des premiers critiques de la mission nucléaire, affirme: «D'un point de vue strictement militaire, le redéploiement – mais non la réduction – des forces canadiennes était parfaitement raisonnable[180].» Et rappelons-le, la réforme Hellyer constituait précisément un prélude à un tel redéploiement. La réduction imposée en 1969, par contre, n'avait guère de sens, car elle affaiblissait une force déjà limitée et ne permettait pas une économie financière considérable[181]. Mais ce qui était plus grave, la décision de 1969 ne précisait guère le sens militaire du redéploiement des forces canadiennes de l'OTAN. Celles-ci demeuraient un ensemble hétéroclite, chargé de missions très diverses et disposant d'un équipement insuffisant. L'idée centrale du livre blanc de 1964, à savoir la mise sur pied d'une force homogène, autonome et mobile semblait avoir été abandonnée ou, du moins, négligée. Autrement dit, la réduction et le redéploiement des forces canadiennes en Europe n'obéissaient ni à la logique militaire, ni même à la logique économique.

Tournons-nous finalement vers la notion de souveraineté. Ce concept, en effet, plus que la décision du retrait, légitimait la nouvelle politique de défense canadienne. Il permettait d'envisager, par exemple, une reprise en main des missions de sécurité concernant spécifiquement la protection du territoire et de l'espace (aérien et maritime) canadien. Dans cette perspective, les tâches à remplir ne manquaient pas et l'évolution du contexte stratégique, économique et international favorisait, dans une large mesure, une réflexion de fond sur le sujet. Après avoir consacré, pendant plus de 30 ans, la majeure partie de son budget de défense à la sécurité européenne et, dans une moindre mesure, à la défense aérienne du continent, le Canada pouvait maintenant tenter d'aborder certains problèmes affectant directement sa sécurité. La surveillance de l'Arctique et surtout le contrôle de son espace maritime posaient un ensemble de défis technologiques qu'il était nécessaire de relever. Mais ceci exigeait une définition précise du concept de souveraineté *dans toutes ses dimensions* et une analyse approfondie des possibilités et des contraintes que présentait une telle entreprise. La notion de souveraineté, en effet, n'a un sens que si elle a un contenu précis. Or, les déclarations et les textes politiques de l'époque sont remarquablement discrets à ce sujet. Comme l'a souligné Stewart: «Dans l'ensemble, la présentation de la nouvelle politique de défense contenait peu de propositions concrètes, l'analyse était souvent superficielle et les relations canado-américaines n'étaient même pas discutées[182].»

En fait, sans même tenir compte de l'ambiguïté de la structure d'objectifs élaborée pour le ministère de la Défense: «La protection de la souveraineté a été utilisée comme un concept parapluie destiné à masquer ce que l'on avait voulu ni analyser ni définir[183].»

Dans l'ensemble, donc, il est possible d'avancer que la nouvelle politique de défense s'appuyait sur une réflexion insuffisante, superficielle et lacunaire, et la suite des événements le prouvera.

LA PÉRIODE DES VACHES MAIGRES: L'IMPACT DE LA RÉVISION SUR LES FORCES CANADIENNES (1971-1975)

Les suites des mesures adoptées, en septembre 1969, n'ont pas tardé pas à se faire sentir. Leur impact est sensible au plan général du budget ainsi qu'à celui des différents commandements.

Pour ce qui est du global, tout d'abord, le gel du budget a diminué pendant trois ans le pouvoir d'achat du ministère de la Défense de 15 %. Les dépenses d'équipement de l'armée ont tombé de 16 % en 1967 à 9 % en 1972 (leur niveau le plus bas depuis la fin de la guerre).

En octobre 1973, une augmentation annuelle du budget de 7 % pour cinq ans est annoncée, mais, en 1974, un taux d'inflation de 10 % l'a déjà annulée.

Le 27 novembre 1975, à nouveau à l'occasion du Defence Structure Review, une nouvelle augmentation annuelle de 12 % est annoncée pour la période 1975-1980. Mais, là encore, des problèmes se posent. Les coûts relatifs au personnel ont augmenté de façon importante, en raison de l'indexation des salaires militaires sur ceux de la fonction publique (1972). Fin 1976, les coûts d'exploitation ont d'ailleurs atteint la proportion record de 84 % dans le budget de la défense (alors qu'aux États-Unis, ils ne représentent que 46 % du budget de la défense).

En janvier 1977, un nouvel effort est entrepris, le budget de la défense est indexé au coût de la vie, et l'on promet une augmentation de 12 % du budget d'équipement en termes réels. Des coupures à l'automne de la même année réduisent toutefois la croissance budgétaire à 2,8 %.

Pour l'ensemble de la période 1968-1980, alors que les dépenses gouvernementales ont passé de 10 milliards de dollars en 1969 à 45 milliards en 1978, les dépenses de défense ont augmenté de 1,8 à 4 milliards. Par rapport au produit national brut, le budget de défense est passé de 2,6 % (1968) à 1,6 % (1980) et la part des dépenses militaires dans le budget fédéral a chuté de 14 % (1970) à 8,7 % (1980)[184].

La décennie présente donc l'image d'une dégradation progressive des ressources financières de l'armée canadienne. Il faut bien sûr tenir compte des facteurs exogènes, comme les crises pétrolières de 1973 et 1979, et l'inflation qui ont contribué à accentuer l'impact des décisions politiques. Il est indubitable, cependant, que les problèmes mis en évidence par la situation budgétaire en matière de défense reflètent aussi des négligences graves et une grande réticence à faire face aux problèmes posés par la situation. Ceci est clairement mis en évidence par les problèmes spécifiques vécus par les différents commandements de l'armée canadienne.

La marine, d'abord, si l'on se réfère au tableau 1, représentait en 1968, avec 28 vaisseaux et 71 avions, une force respectable qui exigeait toutefois, au début des années 70, une réorganisation générale ainsi qu'un rééquipement approprié. La force maritime canadienne avait en effet été conçue dans les années 50 comme une flotte d'escorte, dans l'éventualité d'un scénario de conflit semblable à la Deuxième Guerre mondiale[185]. Dans le contexte d'une guerre nucléaire, cependant, le rôle de protection des voies maritimes atlantiques perdrait de son importance, du fait de la vulnérabilité des convois à une frappe nucléaire et de la brièveté éventuelle d'un tel conflit. Il était donc nécessaire d'examiner les possibilités d'une nouvelle mission pour les forces navales canadiennes. Celle-ci aurait pu être orientée vers la guerre anti-sous-marins, par exemple, ou bien vers une capacité plus grande de surveiller l'Arctique. Dans ce cadre, la question du remplacement des destroyers, qui pour la plupart avaient dépassé les trois quarts de leur existence utile (c'est-à-dire 20 ans), se posait avec acuité ainsi d'ailleurs que le problème des successeurs des avions de patrouilles Argus et Tracker.

En lieu et place d'une politique claire et des décisions attendues en matière d'équipement, la marine subit un démantèlement progressif et des coupures sévères de budget et d'effectifs[186].

Ainsi, le porte-avions *Bonaventure* est mis à la retraite en 1969, deux ans après avoir été remis à neuf. Il est cédé à un entrepreneur de Vancouver pour 850 000 dollars.

L'hydroglisseur *Bras d'Or*, pour lequel la marine avait investi près de 59 millions de dollars depuis 1961 en recherche et développement, est également remisé, ainsi que quatre destroyers d'escorte (1973).

Les forces de surveillance aériennes ne sont pas non plus épargnées, et la marine perdra, de 1969 à 1977, 18 avions sur 71. Dans l'ensemble, la situation de l'équipement naval est résumée par le tableau 2, qui reflète l'état de la flotte en 1978.

En dix ans, la flotte canadienne avait donc rétréci, malgré l'introduction des quatre nouveaux destroyers DDH 280, et notons qu'en 1986, les données du tableau sont toujours valables.

Les effectifs de la marine, par ailleurs, passent en 1974 à moins de 13 000 hommes (alors qu'ils étaient 17 000 six ans auparavant). En fait, le personnel naviguant ne comptait plus que 5 100 hommes, 100 de plus que n'en compte le porte-avions américain *USS Independence*. En 1977, la marine canadienne était dans un état déplorable et, comme le précisent un an plus tard les amiraux J.C. O'Brien et R.H. Lear: «La flotte de 1978 est plus proche de la ferraille que la plupart des gens ne le réalisent[187].»

En fait, dès 1975, le commandement maritime n'était plus à même d'assurer ses missions. Les opérations dites «de souveraineté» exigeaient en effet un minimum de 260 jours de navigation et deux vols de surveillance à longue distance par semaine; or, le commandement ne pouvait même pas fournir la moitié de ce service. De surcroît, compte tenu des coupures dans le budget de fonctionnement et du mauvais état de la flotte, la contribution canadienne à SACLANT avait baissé de 32 vaisseaux en 1964 à 8 navires en 1978. Et finalement, en juin 1976, la décision relative à l'achat d'un nouvel avion de patrouille (LRPA) n'avait toujours pas été prise.

La situation du commandement mobile n'était guère plus brillante[188]. Ses effectifs passaient ainsi de 26 000 hommes à 21 000, une coupure de près de 20 %. La milice, quant à elle, ne pouvait, en 1979, fournir que 3 000 hommes en cas d'urgence, alors que 15 000 réservistes étaient immédiatement disponibles en 1969.

Le programme d'équipement de Hellyer, de plus, s'était fait pour ainsi dire démanteler avant d'être appliqué. Les mille véhicules blindés de transport, achetés à 60 000 dollars l'unité, par exemple, furent remisés, faute d'emploi après la réduction du contingent européen. Les 115 CF-105, quant à eux, ne furent utilisés que pour l'entraînement des pilotes; 74 d'entre eux, à l'état neuf, furent simplement entreposés à Trenton et à North Bay. Et ceci fut décrit comme «le gaspillage le plus irresponsable des fonds publics que le Canada ait connu en temps de paix»[189].

Les forces canadiennes en Europe ainsi que celles de NORAD eurent, elles aussi, leur part de scandale. Il faut souligner en particulier le problème du char *Centurion*. Celui-ci, qui équipait le 4e GBC à Lahr, avait été acheté aux Britanniques en 1952. En 1970, il était donc d'ores et déjà obsolescent, sujet à des pannes fréquentes et dangereuses pour ceux qui le conduisaient. Le même type de problèmes se posait pour les véhicules blindés d'appui (M 113, Lynx, Ferrets) qui avaient dépassé la limite d'âge. La brigade elle-même ne disposait pas de l'ensemble des unités qui devaient, en principe, lui être allouées. Et finalement, les F-104 du groupe aérien devaient aussi être remplacés.

Les décisions urgentes qui s'imposaient, dès le début de la décennie, furent repoussées. Le remplacement du *Centurion*, par exemple, ne fut décidé qu'en octobre 1976 et l'achat du F-18, appelé à succéder au F-104, ne fut décidé qu'en 1980.

Les forces allouées à NORAD déclinèrent de la même façon que celles des commandements maritimes et mobiles. Les trois groupes de Voodoos, qui comptaient 66 avions en 1972, tombèrent à 36 en 1975[190].

Prenant un peu de recul par rapport à l'ensemble des faits que nous venons d'exposer et gardant à l'esprit qu'il ne s'agit que d'une photographie partielle de la situation, on peut donc avancer que la première moitié de la décennie représente probablement une des pires périodes vécues dans l'histoire de l'armée canadienne[191].

La politique gouvernementale avait déjà entamé un changement de cap qui, malheureusement, n'effacerait qu'en partie la négligence des cinq années précédentes.

LE DIFFICILE RÉALIGNEMENT DE LA POLITIQUE DE DÉFENSE CANADIENNE

En 1975, la position canadienne en matière de politique de défense évolue de façon significative. Une série de chocs inquiétants ont contribué à ce changement. En 1971, d'abord, les États-Unis, gênés par le déséquilibre de leur balance des paiements, annoncent le flottement de leur monnaie, ainsi que l'imposition d'une surtaxe de 10 % sur leurs importations. Le Canada, en tant que partenaire commercial principal des USA, est directement affecté par cette mesure qui annonce une longue période de récession.

En 1973, trois autres événements importants viennent aggraver la situation, l'embargo pétrolier, bien sûr, mais aussi l'entrée de la Grande-Bretagne dans le Marché commun ainsi que le lancement, par Kissinger, de «l'année de l'Europe». L'impact économique de la crise pétrolière est évident, mais l'intégration de l'Angleterre à la CEE suscite aussi des inquiétudes au Canada. Elle laisse craindre en effet que les liens politiques et économiques entre l'ancien dominion canadien et son ex-métropole seront sacrifiés sur l'autel de l'unité européenne. Le discours de l'année de l'Europe annonce de plus que les USA offriront leur appui à la CEE, s'attendant en contrepartie à un effort renouvelé de défense de la part des pays européens. Ceci semble signifier qu'une nouvelle entente atlantique est en train de se dessiner et que le Canada a de fortes chances de se trouver exclu de ce rapprochement[192].

Les milieux internationaux sont en effet convaincus que le Canada est destiné à graviter de plus en plus dans l'orbite américaine. Or, précisément, dans le cadre de la «troisième option», c'est ce que voulait éviter le gouvernement canadien. Pour des raisons politiques et économiques, le Canada change alors de cap, revenant progressivement sur les décisions de 1969. Et, dès le mois de décembre 1973, Sharp annonce: «Nous sommes arrivés à la conclusion qu'il n'y a pas d'alternative à l'Alliance. Sans elle, le monde serait un endroit très dangereux[193].»

Il n'est donc pas étonnant que, cette année-là, une première hausse du budget de la défense nationale soit annoncée ainsi qu'un programme de renouvellement et de modernisation. Comme nous l'avons montré plus haut, cette mesure ainsi que celles qui suivent furent cependant plus symboliques que réelles, en raison de la situation économique et des réticences gouvernementales. Le gouvernement semblait, en effet, décidé à attacher des conditions à toute concession qu'il ferait à l'Alliance et, comme l'exprimait le ministre de la Défense, J. Richardson: «Le Canada n'est pas dans l'OTAN pour des raisons économiques, mais nous voulons une part du gâteau comme tout le monde[194].»

En juin 1974, le gouvernement faisait un nouveau pas vers l'Europe en accueillant une session du Conseil de l'OTAN à Ottawa et, en novembre de la même année, un rapport dit de «révision de la structure de défense» (Defence Structure Review) était annoncé. Le débat et les opinions politiques exprimées demeurent cependant encore très confus et aucune décision majeure n'est prise en matière d'équipement ou en matière stratégique.

Mais parallèlement, une série de pressions très explicites sont exercées par les instances officielles de l'OTAN et par certains pays membres. Ces derniers précisent clairement que toute future réduction des forces canadiennes entraînerait de lourdes sanctions économiques pour le Canada. Le chancelier allemand,

Helmut Schmidt, suggère simplement à Trudeau de «remonter ses chaussettes militaires, s'il a l'intention d'obtenir des avantages commerciaux de la part de l'Europe»[195].

Plus rudement encore, le directeur de la planification militaire de l'OTAN, R. Braband, dit au délégué canadien: «Votre pays a beaucoup d'équipement obsolète. Nous sommes continuellement amenés à vous le rappeler; la RFA, la Grande-Bretagne et les USA introduisent progressivement des nouveaux équipements, mais votre pays a la réputation de toujours repousser ses décisions à plus tard[196].»

Ces pressions s'intensifient en 1975 avec la visite d'Alexander Haig, puis celle de J. Schlesinger, à Ottawa. Le Secrétaire général de l'OTAN, E. Luns, lui-même se met de la partie, en novembre, remarquant que le retard des décisions concernant le rééquipement des forces canadiennes «est devenu un souci majeur pour l'Alliance»[197].

Le 27 novembre 1975, enfin, les choses avancent avec la présentation au Parlement des résultats du rapport annoncé l'année précédente. Le gouvernement s'engage à dépenser, pendant les dix années à venir, 8,5 milliards de dollars en équipement. Mais il faudra encore attendre une année pour que soit annoncé l'achat du successeur du char *Centurion* en Europe et celui du nouvel avion de patrouille, le CP-140 Aurora (encore faut-il ajouter que ce dernier dossier constitue un cas flagrant de mauvaise gestion)[198]. Le 18 février 1977, par ailleurs, un contrat pour l'achat de 350 véhicules blindés est passé avec General Motors et, en décembre, la construction prochaine de six nouvelles frégates de patrouille pour le commandement maritime est annoncée ainsi qu'un programme de modernisation d'une partie des destroyers. Il ne reste qu'à décider du choix d'un nouveau chasseur destiné à remplacer à la fois les Voodoos et les CF-104. La décision sera prise en avril 1980, après le court épisode conservateur de 1979.

Dès 1978, cependant, la récession économique freine le développement des dépenses militaires et de certains programmes en cours et il s'avère rapidement que le Canada ne pourra respecter son engagement d'assurer une croissance réelle de 3 % de son budget militaire. Le ministre de la Défense nationale, B. Danson, se voit donc obligé, en janvier 1979, d'exprimer ses regrets à l'OTAN, tout en assurant les alliés que les programmes majeurs du Canada ne seraient pas affectés[199]. Les dernières années du gouvernement libéral illustrent donc, après les efforts tardifs de la période 1975-1977, un retour au statu quo antérieur et, comme le note Stewart: «La réalité était simplement que le Canada ne pouvait augmenter ses dépenses dans le cadre de son budget tant et aussi longtemps que ce dernier était utilisé pour payer les nouveaux équipements [dont on venait d'arrêter le choix][200].»

Le problème fondamental de la politique de défense canadienne, au début des années 80, ne se résume pas pourtant à une simple question de budget ou de matériel. La gravité de la situation réside plus dans l'incertitude relative aux objectifs de cette même situation. Si les priorités officielles de la défense n'ont pas varié, la substance des décisions, quant à elle, ne s'harmonise guère aux ambitions esquissées dans le livre blanc de 1971. La mission de souveraineté a tombé en désuétude, l'OTAN est redevenue la priorité matérielle de la défense et la protection aérienne du continent va ressortir de l'oubli grâce aux nouvelles orientations de la stratégie américaine. Faute d'avoir inscrit dans les faits les choix opérés entre 1969 et 1971, la Défense canadienne se retrouve à l'orée d'une nouvelle décennie sans gouverne précise, prête à se soumettre aux conditions fluctuantes de la météo stratégique internationale.

CONCLUSION

À l'issue de cet exposé, le lecteur comprendra qu'il nous est difficile de répondre aux questions posées dans l'introduction sans un certain engagement personnel. Il n'aura d'ailleurs échappé à personne qu'un certain nombre de jugements normatifs ont d'ores et déjà été formulés à propos des gouvernements et des acteurs qui ont marqué de leur empreinte la politique de défense canadienne d'après-guerre. Nous ne nous en cachons pas, et c'est d'ailleurs dans cette perspective que nous avons qualifié cette étude d'essai historique. Disons simplement en notre faveur que les qualités et les défauts de ceux qui ont eu la responsabilité de notre politique de défense sont suffisamment clairs pour assurer que nos opinions soient d'une part partagées, et d'autre part étayées par un nombre respectable de faits.

Mais pourquoi juger, demanderont certains, pourquoi ne pas se contenter simplement de connaître? À cela, W. Laqueur a apporté une excellente réponse: «La connaissance, si elle ne peut guider l'action, est un savoir stérile.» L'évaluation qualitative des performances politiques est, en ce sens, une partie intégrante de l'analyse politique.

Ceci dit, nous avons posé deux questions précises en entamant cette étude:

- Le Canada a-t-il une marge de liberté en matière de défense?
- Quelles sont les orientations politiques qui assureraient au Canada une mesure d'indépendance, tout en respectant les limites tracées par le système de sécurité auquel nous appartenons?

Considérant l'histoire de sa politique de sécurité, il est peut-être trop facile de tourner en dérision ce que nous avons appelé la marge de liberté du Canada en matière de défense. Compte tenu de la situation géopolitique décrite dans l'introduction, le Canada n'a pas le choix de l'abstention; il ne peut s'exclure de l'équation stratégique Est-Ouest. Il est donc, par définition, un élément du système de sécurité occidental, tant que les États-Unis auront les moyens et la volonté politique de garder le leadership de ce système et de lui conserver la forme qu'il a prise après 1945. Après tout, les réalistes se consoleront en disant qu'une *pax americana* vaut mieux que pas de paix du tout. Partant de là, il serait erroné de concevoir l'autonomie du Canada en matière de sécurité comme une forme de liberté gratuite, extérieure aux responsabilités collectives du Canada. Pourquoi, en effet, tenter de définir une indépendance dans l'absolu? Pourquoi dilapider des moyens d'influence, déjà rares, alors que c'est précisément face à nos alliés que nous avons à circonscrire une zone d'intérêt canadien?

L'expérience canadienne d'après-guerre, en matière de défense, souligne plutôt que c'est à l'intérieur de ses alliances que le Canada est en mesure de gagner son autonomie et de faire valoir sa souveraineté. La réalisation de ces objectifs repose cependant sur un devoir de loyauté et de compétence face aux États-Unis et aux membres de l'Alliance atlantique. La pise en charge de nos responsabilités en matière de défense collective précède, en quelque sorte, l'affirmation de nos droits. Précisons tout de suite que cette norme répond moins à une quelconque morale de l'action politique qu'à un simple souci pratique, à savoir: devancer les changements de la situation stratégique, contribuer à la définition concrète de ceux-ci avant qu'ils ne suscitent chez nos partenaires des orientations qui s'imposent à nous, sans tenir compte de nos intérêts.

Les conditions préalables d'une politique de défense réellement canadienne sont donc la prévision, la planification et la participation. Escott Reid a noté, en ce qui a trait aux relations canado-américaines: «En cas de guerre, nous n'aurons aucune liberté de choix dans les domaines jugés prioritaires par les États-Unis... En temps de paix [par contre], nous disposerons d'une autonomie d'action limitée, mais appréciable; nous pouvons critiquer la position américaine face à l'URSS. D'ailleurs, le fait que nous soyons avec les USA dans la même galère légitime ces critiques, surtout dans les circonstances où la politique américaine menace de nous envoyer par le fond. Si nous jouons bien nos atouts, nous pouvons exercer sur Washington une influence considérablement plus grande que ne nous le permettrait notre puissance militaire[201].»

En d'autres termes, le défi que présente la défense canadienne est d'inscrire nos analyses, nos préoccupations dans les calculs stratégiques de nos alliés et, au premier chef, dans ceux de notre voisin du Sud.

La recherche de l'influence demeurerait cependant une entreprise vaine, si la politique canadienne ne reflétait pas un engagement concret qui impose le respect à nos interlocuteurs, et c'est précisément à ce niveau que peuvent se rejoindre les exigences de la souveraineté et les impératifs de la sécurité collective. Il n'est pas besoin d'être Clausewitz pour comprendre qu'un certain nombre de tâches militaires, que les forces canadiennes seraient potentiellement en mesure d'effectuer, sont également importantes dans le cadre de la défense continentale, dans celui de l'Alliance et dans le cadre de la protection de notre propre souveraineté. La question est donc de savoir si le gouvernement canadien est en mesure de lever le voile d'incertitude qui a couvert la politique de défense canadienne depuis près deux décennies et d'orienter cette politique concrètement.

Les possibilités, comme nous venons de le dire, sont nombreuses: la rationalisation de notre déploiement en Europe attend toujours la suite des réformes entreprises par Hellyer dans les années 60; la modernisation de NORAD soulève à nouveau le problème de la surveillance aérienne dans l'Arctique et l'état de notre force navale rappelle, s'il en est besoin, que la souveraineté de notre espace maritime est mal assurée. Chacun de ces domaines offre au Canada la possibilité de renforcer sa crédibilité en tant qu'allié, d'affirmer son autonomie et de promouvoir son influence. L'absence d'une politique claire aura pour conséquence l'érosion d'une indépendance déjà bien limitée et la prise en main progressive de nos responsabilités de défense par d'autres que nous.

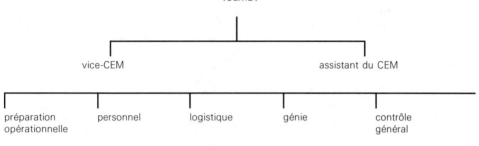

FIGURE 1
La réorganisation de l'état-major
des forces armées canadiennes (1964)

Chef de l'état-major de défense
(CEMD)

vice-CEM   assistant du CEM

préparation   personnel   logistique   génie   contrôle
opérationnelle   général

CEM fonctionnels

TABLEAU 1
Ordre de bataille de la flotte canadienne
(1968)

côte ouest	côte est
7 DDE (destroyers d'escorte)	1 porte-avions (HMCS Bonaventure)
1 sous-marin (HMCS Grilse)	9 DDH (destroyers porte-hélicoptères)
6 Argus	4 DDE (destroyers d'escorte)
	3 sous-marins de classe Obéron
	2 vaisseaux de soutien (HMCS Provider et Cape Scott)
	1 hydroglisseur
	26 Argus
	39 Trackers
Total	71 avions
	28 vaisseaux

TABLEAU 2
La flotte en 1978

	côtes	
	est	ouest
4 Tribal 280 DDH	4	
2 Annapolis DDH	2	
6 St-Laurent DDH	6	
4 Restigouche DDE		4
4 Mackenzie DDE		4
3 Obéron	3	
Total	15	8

NOTES

1. Rapport du Comité mixte spécial sur les relations extérieures du Canada, *Interdépendance et internationalisme*, juin 1986, Ottawa, p. 51-52.

2. John W. Holmes, *The Shaping of Peace*, vol. 2, 1982, p. 36. Toutes les citations qui suivent ont été traduites de l'anglais par l'auteur.

3. Pour ces données et celles qui suivent, nous avons consulté Brian Crane, *Canadian Defense Policy*, Toronto, Canadian Institute for International Affairs, 1964, p. 8-9; Melvin Conant, *The Long Polar Watch*, New York, Harpers & Brothers, 1964, p. 5; Brian Cuthbertson, *Canadian Military Interdependence in the Age of the Superpowers*, Don Mills, Ontario, Fitzhenry & Whiteside, 1977, p. 118; Vincent Massey (éd.), *The Canadian Military. A Profile*, Toronto, Copp Clark, 1972, p. 44; Desmond Morton, *A Military History of Canada*, Edmonton, Hurtig, 1985, p. 209.

4. À ce sujet, l'analyse la plus détaillée des faits est contenue dans James Eayrs, *The Defense of Canada: Peace Making and Deterrence*, Toronto, Toronto University Press, 1972, p. 75-136.

5. *Ibidem*, p. 77.

6. *Ibidem*, p. 95.

7. John W. Holmes, *op. cit.*, p. 9.

8. V. Massey, *op. cit.*, p. 40.

9. James Eayrs, *op. cit.*, p. 92.

10. *Ibidem*, p. 119.

11. Au sujet de cette période, nous disposons des mémoires de la plupart des acteurs ainsi que d'un ensemble d'études historiques approfondies. Voir, par exemple, John W. Holmes, *The Shaping of Peace* (2 volumes), Toronto, Toronto University Press, 1980-1982; George Ignatieff, *The Making of a Peace Monger*, Toronto, Toronto University Press, 1985; Lester B. Pearson, *Memoirs 1948-1957, The International Years*, Londres, Victor Gollancz, 1974; Escott Reid, *A Time of Fear and Hope*, Toronto, McClelland and Stewart, 1977; John Swettenham, *McNaughton*, Toronto, Ryerson Press, 1969.

12. Une définition précise des principes de cette école de pensée peut être trouvée dans Michael K. Howes, *Principal Power, Middle Power or Satellite: Competing Perspectives in the Study of Canadian Foreign Policy*, Toronto, Université York, 1984, p. 3-8; ainsi que dans J.W. Holmes (1982), *op. cit.*, p. 4-5.

13. J.W. Holmes (1982), *op. cit.*, p. 5.

14. Voir, en particulier, J.W. Holmes, *ibidem*, chap. 3 et 12.

15. Voir J. Swettenham, *op. cit.*, p. 109.

16. G. Ignatieff, *op. cit.*, p. 109.

17. Pour une analyse poussée des événements de Suez et du rôle canadien pour résoudre cette crise, voir T. Robertson, *Crises: The Inside Story of the Suez Conspiracy*, New York, Atheneum, 1965, ainsi que J.W. Holmes (1982), *op. cit.*, p. 348-370.

18. Voir James Eayrs, *In Defense of Canada: From the Great War to the Great Depression*, Toronto, Toronto University Press, 1964, p. 70-73.

19. Cité dans les *Procès-verbaux et témoignages du Comité permanent des affaires extérieures et de la défense nationale, ordre de renvoi relatif à NORAD*, Ottawa, Chambre des communes, 7 oct. 1985, fascicule 32, p. 32A:25.

20. *Ibidem*.

21. *Ibidem*, p. 32A:26.

22. B. Cuthbertson, *op. cit.*, p. 13-14.

23. *Ibidem*, p. 121-127.

24. *Ibidem*, p. 16-20.

25. J. Eayrs (1972), *op. cit.*, p. 349-350.

26. La perception canadienne de la situation est fort bien exposée dans le document intitulé *Report of the Advisory Committee on Post-Hostilities Problems, Post-War Canadian Defense Relationship with the United States: General Considerations*, Ottawa, département des Affaires extérieures – Archives, 23 janvier 1945, cité dans J. Eayrs, *ibidem*, p. 375-380.

27. À propos de cet épisode, voir B. Cuthbertson, *op. cit.*, p. 23-24 et J. Eayrs (1972), *op. cit.*, p. 338-339.

28. J. Eayrs, *op. cit.*, p. 339.

29. B. Cuthbertson, *op. cit.*, p. 25.

30. *Ibidem*, p. 26.

31. Charles Foulkes, *Canadian Defense Policy in the Nuclear Age*, Toronto, CIIA, Behind the Headlines (21), mai 1961, p. 5.

32. Ce sujet est traité dans J. Eayrs (1972), *op. cit.*, p. 347; John B. McLin, *Canada's Defense Policy 1957-1963*, Baltimore, Johns Hopkins University Press, 1963, p. 11 et J.W. Holmes (1982), *op. cit.*, p. 87.

33. J.B. McLin et J.W. Holmes, *ibidem*.

34. B. Cuthbertson, *op. cit.*, p. 28-29.

35. *Ibidem*, p. 29.

36. J. Eayrs (1972), *op. cit.*, p. 355.

37. *Ibidem*, p. 321.

38. B. Cuthbertson, *op. cit.*, p. 31.

39. *Ibidem*, p. 34.

40. Voir J. Swettenham, *op. cit.*, p. 200 et J. Eayrs (1982) *op. cit.*, p. 68.

41. B. Cuthbertson, *op. cit.*, p. 68.

42. Ces faits sont relatés dans J. Eayrs (1972), *op. cit.*, p. 360-364 et dans B. Cuthbertson, *op. cit.*, p. 37-39, ainsi que dans D. Cox, *Canada and NORAD 1958-1978: A Cautionary Perspective*, Ottawa, Aurora Papers, Canadian Center for Arms Control and Disarmament, 1985, p. 7.

43. *National Security Council Memorandum No. 159*, 22 juillet 1953, National Archives, Washington, D.C., p. 8, cité dans D. Cox, *op. cit.*, p. 8.

44. S. Huntington, *The Common Defense*, Columbia University Press, 1966, p. 334.

45. D. Cox, *op. cit.*, p. 8 et J. Eayrs (1972), *op. cit.*, p. 364.

46. J. Eayrs, *ibidem*, p. 365.

47. B. Cuthbertson, *op. cit.*, p. 40.

48. Voir Martin Shadwick, «North American Air Defense Modernisation», *Military Technology*, vol. 9, n° 9, 1985, p. 16.

49. Une des meilleures analyses à ce sujet figure dans John Prados, *The Soviet Estimates. US Intelligence Analysis and Soviet Strategic Forces*, Princeton, Princeton University Press, 1986, chap. 4; voir aussi N. Polmar, *Strategic Weapons. An Introduction*, New York, Crane Russak, 1982.

50. D. Cox, *op. cit.*, p. 9.

51. Sur l'histoire des origines des accords de production de défense, voir J.W. Holmes (1982), *op. cit.*, p. 88-97 et J.B. McLin, *op. cit.*, p. 173 et s., ainsi que Danford W. Middlemiss, *The Canadian-American Defense Production and Development Sharing Arrangements: A Canadian Perspective*, texte préparé pour la conférence «Ogdensburg 40», Toronto, Trinity College, Université de Toronto, juin 1980, p. 12-13.

52. J.B. McLin, *op. cit.*, p. 173.

53. *Ibidem*, p. 174.

54. D. Middlemiss, *loc. cit.*, p. 9.

55. J.B. McLin, *op. cit.*, p. 176-177.

56. M. Conant, *op. cit.*, p. 163.

57. J.W. Holmes, *op. cit.*, p. 284.

58. J.B. McLin, *op. cit.*, p. 178-179.

59. J.W. Holmes, *op. cit.*, p. 285.

60. Voir, à ce sujet, J. Eayrs (1964), *op. cit.*, chap. 1; J. Eayrs souligne dans ce texte les origines de l'attitude de MacKenzie King à l'égard de l'Europe; voir aussi J. Eayrs (1972), *op. cit.*, chap. 3 pour l'attitude de MacKenzie King dans l'immédiat après-guerre.

61. J. Eayrs, *In Defense of Canada. Growing Up Allied*, University of Toronto Press, Toronto, 1980, p. 5.

62. *Ibidem*, p. 6.

63. I. Gouzenko, un employé du chiffre de l'ambassade d'URSS à Ottawa, avait révélé, en septembre 1965, l'existence d'un réseau d'espionnage soviétique au Canada, et ceci avait beaucoup choqué le premier ministre; voir J.W. Holmes (1982), *op. cit.*, p. 24-29; J. Eayrs (1972), *op. cit.*, p. 319-320 et J. Sawatsky, *Gouzenko: The Untold Story*, Toronto, McMillan, 1984.

64. Pour un résumé succinct de ces événements essentiels, voir J. Gellner, *Canada and NATO*, Toronto, Ryerson Press, 1970, p. 1-15.

65. Cité dans J. Eayrs (1980), *op. cit.*, p. 17.

66. *Ibidem*, p. 19.

67. Pour une description de l'action canadienne pendant la période de gestation du traité, voir J. Eayrs (1980), *op. cit.*, chap. 2 et J.W. Holmes (1982), *op. cit.*, chap. 5.

68. Il est d'ailleurs remarquable et paradoxal que le Canada, à cette occasion, n'ait participé en rien au pont aérien destiné à soulager le blocus, *cf.* J. Eayrs (1980), *op. cit.*, p. 51.

69. Marilyn Eustace, *Canada's European Force (1964-1971), Canada's Commitment to Europe*, National Security Series No. 4, Center for International Relations, Kingston, Queen's University, 1982, p. 5.

70. J. Eayrs (1980), *op. cit.*, p. 195-198.

71. *Ibidem*, p. 192, et J. Conant, *op. cit.*, p. 163.

72. M. Eustace, *op. cit.*, et D. Morton, *op. cit.*, p. 237.

73. Les données suivantes sont tirées de J. Gellner, *op. cit.*, p. 20-22; J.B. McLin, *op. cit.*, p. 18-19; B. Crane, *op. cit.*, p. 23-25, M. Eustace, *op. cit.*, p. 5-7, J. Eayrs (1980), *op. cit.*, p. 220-277; B. Cuthbertson, *op. cit.*, p. 126 et J.W. Holmes (1982), *op. cit.*, p. 229-236.

74. B. Cuthbertson, *op. cit.*, p. 126.

75. J. Gellner, *op. cit.*, p. 28.

76. Lester B. Pearson, «International Cooperation and a new NATO», *Statements and Speeches*, 56/16, 3 juin 1956.

77. L'ensemble de la contribution canadienne en matière de consultation est discutée dans J.W. Holmes (1982), *op. cit.*, p. 244-248 et dans J.B. McLin, *op. cit.*, p. 21-24.

78. J.B. McLin, *op. cit.*, p. 23-24.

79. J. Eayrs (1980), *op. cit.*, p. 223-225.

80. *Ibidem*, p. 228-230.

81. M. Eustace, *op. cit.*, p. 8.

82. *Annual Report for 1957*, Ottawa, Canada DND, p. 5.

83. J. Gellner, *op. cit.*, p. 45.

84. John Steinbruner and Leon Sigal (éd.), *Alliance Security: NATO and the No-First-Use Question*, Washington, Brookings Institute, 1983, p. 8.

85. Cité dans J. Eayrs (1980), *op. cit.*, p. 151.

86. *Débats parlementaires* (1956), vol. 5, p. 5209.

87. À ce sujet, voir J. Eayrs (1972), *op. cit.*, p. 14-15.

88. G. Ignatieff (*op. cit.*, chap. 12) a relaté de façon saisissante la dégradation brutale des relations entre diplomates et politiciens, dans ses mémoires.

89. G. Ignatieff, *op. cit.*, p. 187-188.

90. Voir J.L. Granatstein, *Canada 1957-1967, The Years of Uncertainty and Innovation*, Toronto, McClelland and Stewart, 1985, p. 101-102.

91. Les rivalités entre l'armée américaine et l'URSS, au sujet de la défense aérienne, sont très bien traitées dans S. Huntington, *op. cit.*, chap. 25.

92. Au sujet de ce rapport et de la suite des événements relatés dans ce paragraphe, voir D. Cox, *op. cit.*, p. 14-15.

93. J. Eayrs (1980), *op. cit.*, p. 258.

94. D. Cox, *op. cit.*, p. 22-23.

95. McLin, *op. cit.*, p. 58.

96. D. Cox, *op. cit.*, p. 15.

97. *Ibidem*, p. 54.

98. *Débats parlementaires* (1958), vol. 1, p. 1004 (cité par Lester B. Pearson).

99. Les sources de la section qui suit sont principalement McLin, *op. cit.*, p. 61-83, ainsi que J. Granatstein, *op. cit.*, p. 105-109.

100. Cité dans Granatstein, *op. cit.*, p. 107-108.

101. Voir, au sujet du Bomarc, McLin, *op. cit.*, p. 84-100 et D. Cox, *op. cit.*, p. 23.

102. D. Cox, *op. cit.*, p. 23.

103. *Ibidem*, p. 23-26; B. Cuthbertson, *op. cit.*, p. 36 et J.B. McLin, *op. cit.*, p. 103-105.

104. Au sujet du F-104, voir J. Gellner, *op. cit.*, p. 55 et J.B. McLin, *op. cit.*, p. 114-120.

105. Au sujet des caractéristiques du Honest John, voir T.B. Cochran, W.H. Arkin, M.H. Hoenig, *US Nuclear Forces and Capabilities*, New York, Ballinger, 1984, p. 282-283.

106. Au sujet de la collaboration canadienne au projet Manhattan, voir J. Eayrs (1972), *op. cit.*, chap. 5.

107. J. Granatstein, *op. cit.*, p. 117.

108. D. Cox, *op. cit.*, p. 26.

109. *Ibidem*, p. 27.

110. *Ibidem*, p. 29.

111. Pour un portrait de H. Green, voir G. Ignatieff, *op. cit.*, p. 180, 190-201 et J. Granatstein, *op. cit.*, p. 118-119.

112. G. Ignatieff, dans ce sens, a clairement pris position pour Green; voir G. Ignatieff, *op. cit.*, p. 180.

113. Voir Bureau du conseil privé (BCP), archives; *Minutes du Cabinet*, 22 sept. 1959, doc. 70-11.

114. Voir D. Cox, *op. cit.*, p. 31.

115. BCP, archives, *Minutes du Cabinet*, 6 déc. 1960, doc. 70-22.

116. D. Cox, *op. cit.*, p. 32.

117. J.F. Kennedy, suivant les divers témoignages concernant l'incident, aurait oublié sur un divan une feuille d'instructions qui contenait des propos peu flatteurs à l'égard de monsieur Diefenbaker. Ce dernier aurait donc réagi très négativement à cela. Suivant les témoignages américains, il s'agirait d'un malentendu: le premier ministre aurait simplement mal interprété les notes, d'ailleurs manuscrites, oubliées par le président. Comme le dira Kennedy lui-même: «Je n'aurais pas pu le traiter de salaud (*SOB*), je ne savais pas à ce moment qu'il en était un.» Voir Theodore Sorensen, *Kennedy*, New York, Harper and Row, 1965, p. 575 et J. Granatstein, *op. cit.*, p. 112-113.

118. Voir Granatstein, *op. cit.*, p. 114-116.

119. *Ibidem*.

120. Voir le texte de la conférence dans J. Gellner, *op. cit.*, p. 65-66.

121. *Ibidem*, p. 70-72.

122. *Ibidem*, p. 73.

123. *Ibidem*, p. 74-75.

124. Les accords de Nassau entre la Grande-Bretagne et les États-Unis ont permis l'achat de sous-marins Polaris lance-missiles par les Britanniques. Voir *La stratégie*, C.-H. Favrod, Paris, 1975, p. 125.

125. Voir A. Legault, «Trente ans de politique de défense canadienne», dans P. Painchaud (éd.), *Le Canada et le Québec sur la scène internationale*, Québec, Presses de l'Université du Québec, 1977, p. 156.

126. Voir, à ce sujet, l'analyse de J.B. McLin, *op. cit.*, p. 151-156.

127. Yale University Archives, Walter Lippmann Papers, sec. III, vol. 59, file 351, Butterworth to Lippmann, 20 mai 1963, cité dans J. Granatstein, *op. cit.*, p. 138.

128. Pour les données qui suivent, voir J.B. McLin, *op. cit.*, p. 178-192 et D. Middlemiss, *op. cit.*, p. 14-24.

129. Cité dans Clive Baxter, «Now we Pay the Piper for Our Defense Tune», *Financial Post*, 1er décembre 1969.

130. Voir, à ce sujet, L.R. Stewart, *Canadian Defense Policy*, National Security Series, No. 1182, Center for International Relations, Kingston, 1982, p. 1-10 et M. Eustace, *op. cit.*, chap. 1; ainsi que J. Gellner, *op. cit.*, p. 77-78.

131. M. Eustace, *op. cit.*, p. 70.

132. *Débats parlementaires*, Chambre des communes, Ottawa (1962-1963), vol. III, p. 3124.

133. J.B. McLin, *op. cit.*, p. 193.

134. Pour les résumés des débats du comité Sauvé, voir M. Eustace, *op. cit.*, p. 23-36.

135. Andres Brewin, *Stand on Guard, The Search for a Canadian Defense Policy*, McClelland and Stewart, Toronto, 1965, p. 94.

136. Pour une analyse du livre blanc de 1964, voir M. Eustache, *op. cit.*, p. 37 et s. et A. Brewin, *op. cit.*, chap. 9.

137. L.R. Stewart (1982), *op. cit.*, p. 91.

138. Voir D. Morton, *op. cit.*, p. 249-250; l'ensemble du problème de la réorganisation est traité dans Vernon Kronenberg, *All Together Now: the Organisation of the Department of National Defense in Canada, 1964-1972* et dans W.H. Critchley, «Changes in Canada's Organisation of Defense, 1963-1983», dans R. Art, Y. Davis, S. Huntington, *Reorganizing America's Defense*, New York, Pergamon Brassey, 1985.

139. Le Bobcat, un véhicule blindé prévu pour les forces canadiennes, avait été abandonné en 1964 à la suite d'un développement de dix années. Voir J.B. McLin, *op. cit.*, p. 113-114.

140. J. Granatstein, *op. cit.*, p. 221-222.

141. *Ibidem.*

142. Voir J. Eayrs (1972), *op. cit.*, chap. 1, p. 107-119.

143. J. Granatstein, *op. cit.*, p. 227.

144. Ceci, toutefois, avec une modification importante: les commandements de la défense aérienne et du transport ont été réunis en 1975, intégrant les éléments aériens des commandements mobiles et maritimes. Voir W.H. Critchley, *op. cit.*, p. 147.

145. Pour une très bonne description de MOBCOM, voir Charles Cotton, «Canada», dans R.A. Gabriel, *Fighting Armies, NATO and the Warsaw Pact, A Combat Assessment*, Londres, Greewood Press, 1983, p. 43-62.

146. Les données précises du programme d'économie de Paul Hellyer sont contenues dans J. Granatstein, *op. cit.*, p. 228-229, J.B. McLin, *op. cit.*, p. 196 et J. Porter, *In Retreat, The Canadian Forces in the Trudeau Years*, Toronto, Deneau and Greenberg, 1979, p. 99.

147. J.B. McLin, *op. cit.*, p. 196.

148. *Ibidem*, note infrapaginale 13, le chiffre de 20 % n'est cependant pas admis par tous. Voir C. Gray, *Canadian Defense Priorities*, Clarke Irwin, 1972, p. 259.

149. J. Granatstein, *op. cit.*, p. 228; J. Porter, *op. cit.*, p. 93-94 et 105 et B. Cuthbertson, *op. cit.*, p. 129 et 134.

150. Voir M. Eustace, *op. cit.*, p. 42-45.

151. Voir J.A. Munro, A.I. Inglis, *Mike, The Memoirs of the Right Honorable Lester B. Pearson*, vol. 3, 1957-1968, University of Toronto Press, Toronto, 1975.

152. Cité dans J.B. McLin, *op. cit.*, p. 207-208; voir aussi M. Eustace, *op. cit.*, p. 42.

153. J. Granatstein, *op. cit.*, p. 233.

154. *Ibidem*, p. 233 et s. et D. Morton, *op. cit.*, p. 252 et s.

155. D. Morton, *op. cit.*, p. 254 et J. Granatstein, *op. cit.*, p. 231.

156. J. Granatstein, *op. cit.*, p. 241.

157. Voir *L'Alliance atlantique*, Service de l'information, Bruxelles, 1981, p. 314-316.

158. J.A. Munro, A.T. Inglis, *op. cit.*, p. 111 à 149 et S. Thorardson, *Trudeau and Foreign Policy*, Oxford University Press, 1977, p. 32-33.

159. M. Eustace, *op. cit.*, p. 5 et L. Hertzman, J.W. Warnock et T. Hockin, *Alliances and Illusions, Canada and the NATO-NORAD Question*, Edmonton, Hurtig, 1969, p. 114.

160. J. Eayrs (1972), *op. cit.*, p. 158.

161. B. Thorardson, *op. cit.*, p. 34.

162. Voir J. Gellner, *op. cit.*, p. 96 et L. Stewart (1982), *op. cit.*, p. 10 et 13-15.

163. Voir M. Eustace, *op. cit.*, p. 64.

164. Voir, au sujet de la révision, B. Thorardson, *op. cit.*, p. 121-137.

165. *Ibidem*, p. 135-136 et M. Eustace, *op. cit.*, p. 84.

166. *Op. cit.*, p. 136.

167. *Ibidem*, p. 127 et s.

168. M. Eustace, *op. cit.*, p. 91.

169. B. Thorardson, *op. cit.*, p. 91.

170. *Ibidem*, p. 163.

171. Particulièrement à la fin des années 70, voir L. Stewart (1982), *op. cit.*, p. 246-294 et M. Pearson *et al.*, «The World is Entitled to Ask Questions: the Trudeau Peace Initiative Reconsidered», *International Journal*, vol. 41, n° 1, hiver 1985-1986, p. 129-158 et R.B. Byers, «Trudeau's Peace Initiative», *The Canadian Strategic Review*, 1984, Toronto, CISS, 1985, p. 151-168.

172. L. Stewart (1982), *op. cit.*, p. 16 et M. Eustace, *op. cit.*, p. 93.

173. L. Stewart (1982), *ibidem*, p. 17.

174. Voir L. Stewart, *Canada's European Forces. A Defense Policy in Transition*, National Security Series, No. 5/80, Center for International Relations, Kingston, Queen's University, 1980, p. 3-4.

175. Voir L. Stewart (1982), *op. cit.*, p. 21-23.

176. *Ibidem*, p. 26 et *1971 White Paper on Defense*, Canada Department of National Defence, Queen's Printer, Ottawa, 1971.

177. Cité dans M. Eustace, *op. cit.*, p. 118.

178. P.C. Newman, «Killing Time in NATO», *Maclean's*, octobre 1972, cité dans M. Eustace, *op. cit.*, p. 107.

179. *Ibidem*, p. 110.

180. J. Gellner, *op. cit.*, p. 105.

181. M. Eustace, *op. cit.*, p. 114.

182. L. Stewart (1980), *op. cit.*, p. 8.

183. B. Cuthbertson, *op. cit.*, p. 139.

184. Les données précédentes sont tirées de J. Porter, *op. cit.*, p. 1-28.

185. B. Cuthbertson, *op. cit.*, chap. 4, 5 et 6.

186. Voir J. Porter, *op. cit.*, p. 29-88.

187. *Ibidem*, p. 67.

188. *Ibidem*, p. 89-138.

189. *Ibidem*, p. 103.

190. Voir *La défense aérienne du territoire canadien*, rapport du Comité spécial du Sénat sur la défense nationale, ministère des Approvisionnements et Services, 1985, p. 11.

191. L. Stewart (1980), *op. cit.*, p. 86.

192. *Ibidem*, p. 39-44.

193. *Ibidem*, p. 49.

194. *Ibidem*, p. 7.

195. Cité dans M. Eustace, *op. cit.*, p. 148.

196. Cité dans L. Stewart, *op. cit.*, p. 103.

197. *Ibidem*, p. 81.

198. L'histoire pitoyable de l'achat du CP-140 est magnifiquement relatée dans Michael Tucker, *Canadian Foreign Policy: Contemporary Issues and Themes*, Toronto, McGraw Hill/Ryerson, 1980, p. 143-174.

199. L. Stewart (1980), *op. cit.*, p. 133-134.

200. *Ibidem*, p. 146.

201. Cité dans J.W. Holmes (1982), *op. cit.*, p. 34.

BIBLIOGRAPHIE

Cette bibliographie contient exclusivement les titres qui nous ont été les plus utiles dans notre recherche

CRANE, Brian. *An Introduction to Canadian Defense Policy*, Toronto, CIIA, 1964.

CUTHBERTSON, Brian. *Canadian Military Interdependence in the Age of the Superpowers*, Don Mills, Fitzhenry and Whiteside, 1977.

EAYRS, James. *In Defence of Canada* (5 vol.), Toronto, University of Toronto Press, 1962-1983.

EUSTACE, Marilyn. *Canada's European Forces 1964-1971, Canada's Commitment to Europe*, Kingston, Center for International Relations, Queen's University, 1982.

GRAY, Colin. *Canadian Defense Priorities. A Question of Relevance*. Toronto, Clarke, Irwin and Company, 1972.

McLIN, J.B. *Canada's Changing Defense Policy, 1957-1963. The Problems of a Middle Power in an Alliance*, Baltimore, Johns Hopkins University Press, 1967.

MORTON, Desmond. *A Military History of Canada*, Edmonton, Hurtig, 1985.

PORTER, Gerald. *In Retreat. The Canadian Forces in the Trudeau Years*, Toronto, Deneau and Greenberg, 1979.

STEWART, Larry. *Canada's European Forces: 1971-1980. A Defense Policy in Transition*, Kingston, Queen's University, 1980.

STEWART, Larry. *Canadian Defense Policy, Selected Documents 1964-1981*, Center for International Relations, Kingston, Queen's University, 1982.

21

La politique commerciale

Claude Masson
Université Laval

Vers la fin de la Deuxième Guerre mondiale, un Canadien, à qui l'on demandait d'expliquer la différence entre le Parti libéral et le Parti conservateur en matière de politique commerciale, eut cette réponse amusante: «Les Libéraux sont contre toute hausse des tarifs et les Conservateurs, contre toute baisse[1].» Boutade, bien sûr. Qui montre bien, cependant, qu'en ce domaine comme dans beaucoup d'autres, le couloir que doit traverser la politique canadienne est étroit. La marge de manœuvre est réduite parce que le caractère de «petite économie ouverte» affiché par notre économie impose de lourdes contraintes. On s'explique ainsi le rapprochement entre les positions libérale et conservatrice, dont témoigne l'histoire de notre politique commerciale[2].

Le commerce international a toujours pesé lourd, en effet, dans l'histoire de la politique canadienne. La politique commerciale est ainsi devenue rapidement un des piliers soutenant la conception même de notre pays. On le verra plus loin, la problématique d'ensemble qui a inspiré la plupart des décisions et des gestes de nos gouvernements en cette matière a peu évolué au fil des années. L'analyse même la plus sommaire du tableau décrivant l'importance du commerce international canadien nous indique pourquoi il en a été ainsi.

On estime qu'en 1900, le Canada exportait déjà des marchandises pour une valeur de 156 millions de dollars et en importait pour 177 millions, enregistrant de la sorte un déficit de 21 millions à ce poste de sa balance des paiements. Les chiffres devenaient respectivement 281, 429 et −148 millions en 1910, 1 267, 1 429 et −162 millions de dollars en 1920 et, en 1947, deuxième année de l'après-guerre, 2 723, 2 535 et 188 millions de dollars (surplus).

Depuis la fin de la Deuxième Guerre mondiale, les exportations de biens et services ont toujours constitué entre le cinquième et le quart de la dépense nationale brute en dollars courants au Canada et il en a été à peu près de même des importations de biens et services. En 1984, par exemple, les exportations et les importations de biens et services ont même atteint, respectivement, 31 % et 30 % de la dépense nationale brute en dollars courants. Enfin, il ne faut pas oublier que bien au-delà de 50 % de la production des industries canadiennes productrices de biens[3] est couramment expédiée à l'étranger.

Ce sont certes là choses connues. Il faut toutefois les rappeler au moment d'aborder ce bref historique de la politique commerciale canadienne depuis 1945. Que l'on procède par une étude systématique de la problématique de la politique commerciale canadienne depuis la guerre ou, au contraire, que l'on présente le sujet comme une suite chronologique d'événements et, notamment, de participations à des accords internationaux, les préoccupations fondamentales du Canada ressortent nettement: ce sont celles d'un pays qui a tout à gagner d'un commerce international libéré du plus grand nombre possible d'entraves, par la voie, si possible, du multilatéralisme et ce, malgré des poussées périodiques de fièvre protectionniste sans doute normales.

Nous utiliserons cette double approche. Dans un premier temps, nous tenterons de dégager les principales composantes de la problématique d'ensemble de la politique commerciale canadienne. Celles-ci, on l'a déjà dit, ont eu un caractère de permanence remarquable.

En second lieu, nous rappellerons, en les commentant brièvement au besoin, les principaux jalons qui ont marqué la mise en place de la politique commerciale canadienne d'après-guerre. Enfin, en conclusion, nous jetterons un bref regard sur les défis posés à la politique commerciale au milieu des années 80.

Nous entendrons par politique commerciale l'ensemble des décisions de politique gouvernementale visant à modifier le volume ou la structure des échanges commerciaux d'un pays. Pour des raisons diverses, mais surtout parce que d'autres chapitres de cet ouvrage abordent ces sujets, nous laisserons de côté, sauf exception et en dépit de leur importance certaine, les échanges de services, les mouvements de capitaux et le commerce des produits énergétiques. Compte tenu, notamment, des liens étroits existant entre le commerce canadien et les politiques gouvernementales touchant les investissements étrangers, l'exclusion de ces dernières des propos qui suivent constitue sans doute une lacune, dont la justification tient toutefois à la nature même de cet ouvrage collectif.

PROBLÉMATIQUE D'ENSEMBLE

La formation du Canada en 1867 devait constituer une réponse au défi posé par la tâche gigantesque, alors perçue – et encore aujourd'hui? – comme urgente, de bâtir une économie dite «nationale» face au géant américain. En somme, il s'agissait de détourner une partie des échanges croissants Nord-Sud dans le sens Est-Ouest. Il s'agissait également de créer des liens entre des zones de peuplement très éloignées les unes des autres. Pour cela, on eut recours à une politique de construction de chemins de fer. Pour permettre l'industrialisation du Canada, on élabora une politique tarifaire d'allure plutôt protectionniste. Enfin, sachant que le Canada possédait d'énormes ressources naturelles, on vit dans celles-ci le moyen d'obtenir de l'étranger les biens et services qu'on était incapable ou qu'on estimait moins rentables de produire ici. Tout cela s'est réalisé grâce, en partie, au capital étranger, d'abord britannique, puis américain.

L'étude de la problématique fondamentale de la politique commerciale canadienne peut emprunter différentes voies. Il nous a paru utile, compte tenu de nos objectifs, de distinguer deux niveaux d'analyse: celui, d'abord, de la volonté politique telle qu'on peut la percevoir dans les écrits, discours ou prises de position officiels; celui, ensuite, du «vécu», de cet ensemble d'événements et de décisions concrètes, souvent prises d'ailleurs sous l'influence des pressions créées par l'état de la conjoncture intérieure ou extérieure.

Au premier niveau, la dimension principale à retenir est sans doute la permanence de l'idée ou de la volonté d'indépendance du Canada face à un voisin connaissant, à tous les égards, une forte croissance. Rappelons d'abord qu'un traité de réciprocité portant sur un vaste échantillon de matières premières a existé entre le Canada et les États-Unis de 1854 à 1866. Dénoncé alors par les États-Unis, il devint l'objet d'un certain nombre de tentatives infructueuses de négociation à partir de 1867. Ce résultat négatif conduisit en droite ligne à la politique nationale de 1879, carrément protectionniste et mise en place en pleine récession tout comme l'avait d'ailleurs été le tarif Cayley-Galt en 1858-1859 et le sera plus tard le tarif Bennett, en 1930-1931.

Le fait est que chaque fois que la question de l'opportunité d'un tel traité avec les États-Unis fut soulevée devant l'électorat canadien après 1867, les partisans de la réciprocité furent défaits: 1891 et 1911. Lors de l'élection de 1935, les deux partis en lice appuyaient l'idée, mais la venue de la guerre, entre autres, devait l'empêcher de suivre son chemin. Enfin, en 1947-1948, les pourparlers entrepris entre les deux gouvernements échouèrent avant même que le public ne soit informé du dossier[4].

Il n'est donc pas surprenant qu'au sortir de la guerre, le Canada soit devenu un des plus farouches partisans du concept de multilatéralisme en matière de politique commerciale et qu'il ait alors fortement appuyé la mise sur pied des institutions internationales ayant fait de cette orientation l'assise de leur fonctionnement. Pour le Canada, partenaire entretenant des liens commerciaux particulièrement étroits avec l'Angleterre d'abord, puis de plus en plus avec les États-Unis, le multilatéralisme devenait l'outil par excellence en vue du maintien d'une certaine indépendance nationale. La volonté exprimée par le gouvernement Diefenbaker à la fin des années 50 de modifier la structure des flux du commerce extérieur canadien devait déboucher sur un échec dont l'éclat témoignait de l'intérêt, pour le Canada, de continuer de s'associer aux initiatives mettant l'accent sur le multilatéralisme[5].

La seconde idée maîtresse qui se dégage de notre premier niveau d'analyse est la liaison que le Canada a progressivement établie à établir entre sa politique commerciale et ses tentatives d'élaboration d'une stratégie industrielle. L'approche dite «sectorielle» que le Canada a voulu promouvoir dans le passé, notamment lors des dernières négociations tenues dans le cadre du GATT, se situe carrément dans cette perspective. Nous aurons l'occasion d'y revenir ultérieurement.

La problématique est ici toute simple, pour ne pas dire banale. C'est celle que se donnent volontiers à peu près tous les pays, surtout en cette période de renaissance du protectionnisme. Reconnaissons cependant que les pays reconnus historiquement comme producteurs et exportateurs de matières premières s'y retrouvent particulièrement confortables. L'idée, exprimée tantôt en termes du concept de «grappe industrielle», tantôt en référence aux effets dits en «amont» ou en «aval», pour ne citer que ces exemples, vise essentiellement à faire en sorte que la part du commerce d'exportation attribuable aux produits finis ou semi-finis s'accroisse progressivement avec le passage du temps. Elle implique, en somme, une stratégie industrielle. Elle invite les gouvernants à «forcer la main», par divers moyens, aux avantages comparatifs. Elle a signifié, dans le cas du Canada, et ce dès la fin du siècle dernier, un choix de société: population relativement plus nombreuse (immigration, etc.), politique de protection de l'industrie secondaire – ce que d'aucuns ont appelé la «manufacturite» –, revenus réels relativement plus faibles – conséquence inévitable de ce qui précède – et enfin, volonté périodiquement manifestée par les gouvernements de privilégier l'approche sectorielle aux problèmes du développement économique et des déséquilibres régionaux.

Face à l'insatisfaction éprouvée à la lecture du bilan de ces multiples expériences de mise en place d'une stratégie industrielle, les Canadiens n'arrivent pas facilement à opter pour l'une ou l'autre des avenues qui s'ouvrent à eux. Le Canada doit-il, par exemple, tenter de conclure un pacte de libre-échange avec les États-Unis? ou encore, fidèle à son approche multilatérale, doit-il voir plus grand et laisser ses ambitions recouvrir d'autres territoires? ou enfin – et cette dernière éventualité n'épuise pas la liste des possibilités –, doit-il se contenter de rechercher de nouvelles ententes sectorielles de libre-échange, genre accords sur l'automobile, sur le matériel de défense ou sur la machinerie agricole?

Le défi est bien connu: il s'agit d'assurer un marché plus vaste aux entreprises canadiennes. À cet égard, le Canada connaît aujourd'hui les mêmes hésitations et se pose les mêmes questions que celles qui ont jalonné l'histoire de sa politique commerciale. À n'en pas douter, c'est sous cet angle qu'il faut voir le caractère permanent de la problématique sous-jacente à l'élaboration de la politique commerciale canadienne.

Mais il n'y a pas que la volonté des gouvernants ou les idées dont ils se font les promoteurs ou même seulement les interprètes. Il y a aussi le réel, les résultats concrets qui, notamment, jaillissent des pressions multiples exercées par la conjoncture interne ou externe.

C'est notre second niveau d'analyse. Une réalité crève les yeux: le commerce d'exportation du Canada est de plus en plus orienté vers les États-Unis et, si l'on fait abstraction du secteur de l'automobile, il continue d'en être un principalement d'exportation de matières premières et de produits semi-finis.

Les deux tableaux présentés en fin de chapitre illustrent bien la situation. Le tableau 1 nous indique, d'une part, le rapport des exportations canadiennes de marchandises vers les États-Unis aux exportations totales de marchandises pour quelques années de la période 1926-1983 et, d'autre part, le rapport de même nature compilé, cette fois, pour les importations canadiennes de marchandises en provenance des États-Unis.

Le tableau 2 montre, pour les principales catégories de produits transigés et pour un certain nombre d'années de la période 1955-1980, l'importance du marché américain pour les exportateurs canadiens de marchandises.

Le tableau 1 met d'abord en évidence la relative stabilité du rapport des importations en provenance des États-Unis aux importations totales de marchandises du Canada, de 1926 à 1983. Si l'on exclut, en effet, les années «spéciales» 1935, 1945 et même 1955, cette proportion s'est toujours située entre 65 et 72 %.

Il en va autrement du côté des exportations de marchandises. La part du marché américain dans celles-ci s'est fortement accrue depuis 1926: d'environ 40 % avant la guerre, elle passe à 56 % en 1960, 65 % en 1970 et 73 % en 1983. Cette hausse s'est faite en bonne partie au détriment des marchés du Royaume-Uni qui, par exemple, absorbaient environ 36 % de nos exportations en 1926, mais seulement 17 % en 1952.

Le tableau 2 fait ressortir le point suivant: ainsi que l'indiquent les deux dernières colonnes, deux catégories de produits ont vu leur importance relative diminuer fortement dans les exportations canadiennes de marchandises de 1955 à 1980: les produits de l'agriculture et de la pêche et les produits de la forêt. Ces deux catégories, on le remarquera, sont également celles pour lesquelles la part des exportations canadiennes se dirigeant vers les États-Unis a aussi fortement baissé de 1955 à 1980: de 30 % à 19 % pour les produits de l'agriculture et de la pêche et de 80 % à 63 % pour les produits de la forêt.

Par contre, la seule catégorie qui a montré un accroissement substantiel de sa part relative dans les exportations canadiennes entre 1955 et 1980 est celle des «autres articles manufacturés» (de 10 à 36 %). Or, c'est également celle pour laquelle la part du marché américain a connu la hausse la plus forte, soit de 56 % en 1955 à 76 % en 1980. Ce résultat, soulignons-le avant d'y revenir plus loin, est attribuable dans sa presque totalité aux effets de l'Accord canado-américain sur le commerce des véhicules automobiles et des pièces détachées.

Que conclure de notre second niveau d'analyse? Premièrement, il apparaît évident qu'en matière commerciale, tout au moins, l'intégration Canada-États-Unis est à se faire progressivement. À cet égard, les accords sectoriels de libre-échange, notamment le Pacte de l'automobile, peuvent être perçus comme des substituts imparfaits à un traité plus général de libre-échange et deviennent un «moyen» de bâtir un pont entre la volonté politique (notre premier niveau d'analyse) et des réalités économiques contraignantes (notre second niveau d'analyse).

Deuxièmement, cette intégration, bien qu'accélérée sans doute par l'entrée de la Grande-Bretagne dans le marché commun européen, n'a pas été causée par elle. Depuis longtemps déjà – et nous y reviendrons à l'occasion de notre rappel de la chronologie des événements –, le Canada et les États-Unis constituent des inter-locuteurs privilégiés l'un pour l'autre dans les rencontres internationales portant sur les politiques tarifaires et, de plus en plus depuis quelques années, non tarifaires. On l'a bien vu, par exemple, pendant les négociations dites du Tokyo Round, tenues sous les auspices du GATT.

Troisièmement, force est de constater que la participation du Canada aux échanges internationaux selon les dictées de ses avantages comparatifs demeure, même en longue période, un fait indéniable. Si l'on exclut les exportations de véhi-cules automobiles et de pièces détachées, les changements dans la structure du commerce d'exportation de marchandises du Canada de 1960 à 1980, bien qu'en-core significatifs, deviennent beaucoup moins prononcés. Ainsi, en incluant dans les calculs les exportations de véhicules automobiles et de pièces détachées, la part des trois premières catégories apparaissant au tableau 2 (produits de l'agriculture et de la pêche, produits de la forêt et métaux et minéraux) dans les exportations canadien-nes de marchandises passe de 86 % en 1960 à 58 % en 1980. En les excluant, elle diminue de 85 % à seulement 69 %.

Par conséquent, si les effets de l'accord de libre-échange sur l'automobile sont autant de signes de ce que pourrait devenir la structure industrielle du Canada une fois implanté un libre-échange généralisé entre le Canada et les États-Unis, cette entente sectorielle ne devient pas seulement un fait historique d'importance. Par les garanties qu'elle comporte pour le Canada, elle illustre en même temps les tiraille-ments qu'ont toujours connus les gouvernements canadiens au moment d'ouvrir le dossier des relations commerciales avec les États-Unis: comment, sans aller jus-qu'au libre-échange global, retirer le plus possible de ces relations sans pour autant

sacrifier l'essentiel, c'est-à-dire, surtout, des niveaux d'emploi et de production intéressants.

L'histoire de la politique commerciale du Canada depuis 1945 est en bonne
partie celle de ces tiraillements. Au moment où, en conséquence du Tokyo Round,
les barrières tarifaires entre le Canada et les États-Unis sont en voie d'être abaissées
progressivement à des niveaux presque négligeables, tout au moins dans le cas de
la plupart des marchandises, on comprend que le concept de multilatéralisme n'ap-
paraisse plus aussi net qu'au sortir de la guerre. La prise de conscience de l'importance des barrières non tarifaires n'est pas non plus étrangère à ces interrogations.
Et, par un curieux retour des choses, c'est en déposant une plainte contre le Canada
auprès du GATT, relativement à la politique canadienne de surveillance des investissements étrangers, que Washington espère pousser l'ensemble des pays vers de
nouveaux accords multilatéraux.

La chronologie des faits marquants de notre politique commerciale depuis
1945 devrait nous aider à mieux comprendre le cheminement vers ce point d'arrivée.

CHRONOLOGIE DES ÉVÉNEMENTS

Pour faire état de façon ordonnée des faits marquants de la période 1945-
1985, il nous faut découper le temps en un certain nombre de périodes. Le choix du
critère à retenir pour cette opération demeurant en bonne partie arbitraire, nous
avons divisé la période 1945-1948 en sept segments.

Avant 1945

Ces années sont, en principe, exclues de nos considérations. Elles ont
toutefois été marquées d'un certain nombre d'événements «porteurs de signes»
pour l'avenir. À cet égard, il nous semble nécessaire de souligner la mise au point d'un
traité commercial entre les États-Unis, la Grande-Bretagne et le Canada en 1938[6].
Cette entente, rendue inopérante à cause de la déclaration de la guerre en 1939,
demeure néanmoins importante en ce qu'elle laisse percevoir un esprit nouveau,
celui du multilatéralisme, qui allait s'implanter solidement après le conflit et aboutir
à la création du GATT.

Autre année importante: 1944. C'est l'accord sur la machinerie agricole. Le
Canada abolit les barrières tarifaires portant sur les accessoires et les machines
agricoles. En même temps, sous les pressions des milieux concernés au Canada, les
tarifs sur les engrais sont retirés. Ces décisions sont significatives: pour la première
fois, vraiment, l'approche sectorielle est mise à l'honneur dans la poursuite de la
politique commerciale canadienne.

1945-1950

C'est la période de la constitution du GATT. Le Canada, face au déclin de la
place de la Grande-Bretagne et à la montée de celle des États-Unis dans ses relations
commerciales, joue un rôle de premier plan dans la mise sur pied de cet organisme
(plus précisément de ces accords) qui fait du multilatéralisme son fondement.

Un bref retour sur le passé plus lointain s'impose ici. En 1897, le Canada avait établi unilatéralement un système de préférences impériales à l'avantage de la Grande-Bretagne. Cependant, c'est seulement en 1932, à l'occasion des Accords d'Ottawa, que ce dernier pays concède la réciprocité. Le Canada et la Grande-Bretagne se serrent alors les coudes face aux tarifs américains substantiels imposés en 1930 à la faveur de la crise économique.

Mais, à partir de 1935, il y a volte-face à Ottawa. On se tourne vers les États-Unis où, un an plus tôt, le Congrès a voté le Reciprocal Trade Agreements Act qui, faisant preuve d'un nouvel esprit en matière de politique commerciale, incorpore la clause de la nation la plus favorisée[7]. Le premier ministre King mènera à bonne fin des négociations commerciales avec les États-Unis en 1935[8].

Puis, dans l'après-guerre, l'important déséquilibre de la balance des paiements du Canada aura tendance à pousser le pays encore plus dans l'orbite des États-Unis. Conçue, en partie tout au moins, comme mesure défensive face à cette évolution, la promotion du multilatéralisme devient la pierre angulaire de la politique commerciale du Canada.

Le 21 août 1945, en effet, les États-Unis mettent fin au programme «Lend-Lease». Il en découle une crise d'importance majeure pour la balance des paiements du Canada, qui avait pourtant consenti, en mai 1946, un prêt de 1,250 millions de dollars à la Grande-Bretagne. L'année 1947 sera celle de la création du GATT mais aussi, paradoxalement, celle de la minute de vérité pour le Canada.

Le 5 juin 1947, annonce du plan Marshall pour la reconstruction de l'Europe. Il sera mis en opération le 2 avril 1948. Le 17 novembre 1947, le monde apprend la signature des accords de Genève sur le commerce international. Connus rapidement sous le sigle GATT, ils doivent demeurer en force jusqu'à l'adoption de la Charte de l'organisation internationale du commerce – The Havana Charter –, conçue pour administrer la Charte du commerce international alors en préparation – The Trade Charter.

Le Canada apporte son appui le plus total à ces nouvelles institutions et celui-ci ne se démentira pas, même lorsque le Congrès américain refusera d'adopter les lois nécessaires à leur mise sur pied. Mais en même temps, vers la fin de 1947, le Canada doit faire face à une crise majeure. Ses importations en provenance des États-Unis s'accroissent fortement et elles doivent, bien sûr, être payées comptant en devise américaine. Ses exportations, au contraire, même si elles sont également en forte progression, sont en bonne partie financées par les dons et les prêts du Canada à l'Europe. Le manque de dollars américains est alors perçu comme *le* problème de l'heure au Canada. Des restrictions diverses au commerce sont imposées, des tentatives sont faites pour exporter davantage vers les États-Unis ou, tout au moins, vers les pays capables de payer en dollars américains. On suppute de nouveau les avantages d'une éventuelle zone de libre-échange regroupant le Canada et les États-Unis. On dénonce avec amertume le caractère discriminatoire de la structure tarifaire américaine contre les produits finis en provenance du Canada et la façon dont les douaniers l'appliquent.

Le Canada, qui avait pourtant fixé la valeur du dollar canadien à un dollar américain le 5 juillet 1946, se voit contraint de recourir à des mesures d'urgence le 17 novembre 1947, face aux pertes substantielles de réserves qu'il a dû assumer. En même temps qu'il fait part de la signature des premiers accords du GATT, le gouvernement annonce en effet la mise sur pied d'un programme de contrôle des importations et de restrictions diverses visant à freiner l'utilisation de dollars américains (The Emergency Exchange Conservation Program)[9]. La conjoncture difficile force ainsi le Canada à recourir à un expédient de courte période entrant en contradiction flagrante avec sa politique à long terme favorisant une libéralisation du commerce dans un cadre de multilatéralisme.

Le système de préférences impériales de 1932 est évidemment touché par la signature des premiers accords du GATT. Celle-ci conduira le Canada et la Grande-Bretagne à renoncer, au moyen d'un échange de lettres, à toutes les marges de préférence mutuellement consenties. La voie est ainsi ouverte à des négociations touchant l'octroi de «nouvelles» préférences, mais à partir des principes retenus dans les accords de Genève: aucune préférence ne doit être consentie qui n'aurait pas préalablement existé et aucune préférence déjà accordée ne peut être relevée.

En 1948, d'autres négociations, de moindre importance, se déroulent à Annecy sous les auspices du GATT[10]. Le Canada et les États-Unis ne s'y affrontent pas directement. En 1948-1949, cependant, on vient près de conclure un accord de libre-échange impliquant le Canada et les États-Unis, à la suite des discussions entreprises dès la conclusion des premiers accords du GATT en 1947. Mais vers la fin des années 40 et le début des années 50, la politique commerciale ne soulève plus les passions au Canada: le pays est prospère, le monde souffre de graves pénuries, le réarmement accompagnant la guerre de Corée bat son plein, le dollar canadien a été dévalué.

1950-1955

Après les négociations peu spectaculaires de Torquay, tenues sous l'égide du GATT à l'hiver 1950-1951[11], la politique commerciale et, notamment, le rôle des tarifs au Canada reviennent au centre des préoccupations par le biais de la récession qui frappe le pays en 1953-1954. Pendant cette période, le Canada recourt pour la première fois à des accords de restriction volontaire des exportations avec le Japon et Hong Kong.

Mais ce qui domine ces cinq années est l'importante détérioration du climat de coopération et d'amitié qui s'était bâti entre le Canada et les États-Unis depuis une quinzaine d'années. Cette «crise de confiance» entre les deux partenaires est attribuable à la récession économique, mais aussi à l'installation à Washington, en 1953, d'une administration républicaine de tendance protectionniste. Les dossiers litigieux s'accumulent, comme autant de nuages à l'horizon: le Canada accuse les États-Unis de lui faire perdre des clients pour son blé en vendant le sien à des conditions très avantageuses sous l'empire de la loi P. L. 480; le gouvernement américain, dès 1953, impose des quotas sur l'importation des produits laitiers et, en 1954, procède de la même façon dans le cas de céréales comme l'orge et l'avoine. Le Canada se voit ainsi contraint de déposer des plaintes auprès du GATT au sujet de ces pratiques commerciales.

1955-1960

Il s'agit là d'incidents de parcours, aussi importants soient-ils. L'histoire des relations commerciales entre le Canada et les États-Unis permet d'en énumérer bon nombre d'autres, parfois encore plus graves. La tendance lourde, en effet, continue de faire sentir tout son poids et, lors des négociations du GATT à Genève en 1956, ainsi qu'il en avait d'ailleurs été lors de celles de Torquay en 1951, les accords canado-américains qui sont signés s'avèrent prioritaires pour les deux pays et constituent, de toute évidence, les principaux accords conclus à cette conférence. Ils intensifient les liens entre le Canada et les États-Unis peu de temps avant la naissance, le 1er janvier 1958, de la Communauté économique européenne.

En 1958, également, l'Accord canado-américain sur le partage de la production du matériel de défense (Defence Sharing Agreement) met les producteurs canadiens sur le même pied que les fabricants américains pour l'obtention de contrats d'approvisionnement touchant une gamme étendue de produits de nature militaire.

1960-1965

Le début des années 60 est marqué par deux événements. D'une part, Genève est à nouveau la scène, de 1960 à 1962, de négociations commerciales tenues sous les auspices du GATT. D'autre part, en 1962, le Canada fait face à une crise de confiance dans le monde vis-à-vis de sa monnaie et se voit contraint d'adopter un train de mesures d'urgence dont, notamment, une surtaxe à l'importation. Fort mal accueillies par les partenaires du Canada au sein du GATT[12], ces mesures peuvent être retirées somme toute assez rapidement à la faveur du rétablissement de la situation au pays.

Les négociations de 1960-1962 sont plutôt modestes. On se rend compte, surtout au Canada et aux États-Unis, que pour aller plus loin dans la voie d'une réduction multilatérale des barrières tarifaires, il faudra procéder à des ajustements structurels d'importance dans les industries touchées. Ce sentiment est accentué par l'ampleur de la récession qui touche entre autres l'Amérique du Nord au début des années 60 et le contexte n'est pas alors sans rappeler celui qui avait prévalu au début des années 50, et plus particulièrement en 1953.

En juillet 1961, le Royaume-Uni demande son admission au sein du marché commun européen. Cette décision soulève beaucoup d'émoi au Canada. D'aucuns craignent les conséquences d'un éventuel démantèlement du système des préférences du Commonwealth; d'autres redoutent surtout les conséquences touchant les exportations canadiennes de produits agricoles vers le Royaume-Uni. Mais, dans l'ensemble, on est avant tout consterné par l'appui américain à la décision du Royaume-Uni. C'est dans ce contexte, enfin, que le gouvernement Diefenbaker annonce son intention – pieuse, s'il n'en fut jamais une – de modifier les flux du commerce canadien à l'avantage de la Grande-Bretagne et au détriment des États-Unis. On pourra lire une appréciation de cette stratégie commerciale du Canada à l'aube des années 60[13].

Pendant ce temps, de nouvelles idées font leur apparition aux États-Unis en matière de politique commerciale. Elles aboutiront aux importantes négociations du GATT tenues à Genève de 1964 à 1967: le Kennedy Round.

1965-1970

Le Trade Expansion Act, voté par le Congrès en 1962, constituait, pour le gouvernement américain, une réponse à l'avènement réussi du marché commun européen, mais sans aller jusqu'à incorporer l'idée, chère à plusieurs Américains, d'un Atlantic Free Trade Area. Cette loi était importante pour le Canada à plusieurs égards, mais notamment à cause des pouvoirs qu'elle conférait au président des États-Unis pour la poursuite d'éventuelles négociations commerciales et de la méthode dite «linéaire» qu'elle mettait de l'avant pour en arriver à une réduction «équitable» des barrières douanières. C'est la possibilité d'y avoir recours avec succès qu'avaient démontrée et la Communauté économique européenne et l'Association européenne de libre-échange qui avait convaincu le Congrès américain de proposer cette méthode.

Le Canada, cependant, refusa cette approche, affirmant qu'elle ne tenait pas suffisamment compte de la structure particulière de l'industrie canadienne, notamment dans le secteur de la fabrication[14]. Il gagna son point. On s'entendit pour exiger de lui qu'il fût seulement disposé à consentir des avantages «de valeur équivalente» (en termes de flux commerciaux) en retour des bénéfices qu'il retirerait de l'application, par les autres pays, de la méthode «linéaire».

Le Canada devenait ainsi le pays commerçant le plus important à ne pas faire partie du «groupe linéaire» lors du Kennedy Round. Il fit cependant plusieurs concessions, mais l'impression est demeurée que le Canada s'en était finalement tiré à bon compte, peut-être même à trop bon compte, comme n'allaient pas manquer de lui rappeler plusieurs de ses partenaires au moment d'aborder le Tokyo Round quelques années plus tard[15].

Quoi qu'il en soit, le Kennedy Round devait s'avérer important pour le Canada à un autre point de vue. Ces négociations, en effet, marquaient la fin de la période d'après-guerre pendant laquelle l'attention avait été trop exclusivement braquée sur les barrières *tarifaires* affectant le commerce international. On allait dorénavant s'intéresser bien davantage aux obstacles non tarifaires[16].

La période 1965-1970 est également celle de l'avènement de l'accord canado-américain touchant l'industrie de l'automobile, plus important, selon certains, que le Kennedy Round lui-même[17]. Le concept de «contenu canadien», appelé à jouer un rôle fondamental dans cette entente, avait été élaboré dans le rapport de la commission d'enquête Bladen sur l'industrie automobile, au début des années 60. Au moment de la crise financière de 1962, par ailleurs, le Canada s'était engagé auprès du Fonds monétaire international et de ses principaux partenaires à prendre des mesures à long terme pour améliorer sa balance des paiements.

Ainsi, dès octobre 1962, le gouvernement conservateur décide d'accorder aux constructeurs canadiens une remise des tarifs payés sur l'importation des transmissions automatiques et de certains moteurs, à condition que ces achats à l'étranger soient contrebalancés par des exportations suffisantes de pièces d'automobile. En octobre 1963, le gouvernement libéral choisit de généraliser cette politique à presque toutes les pièces d'automobile. Cependant, ces mesures allant, semble-t-il, à l'encontre de certaines lois américaines et de l'esprit, sinon de la lettre, des accords du GATT, des négociations sont entreprises entre le Canada et les États-Unis. Elles aboutissent à l'Accord canado-américain sur l'automobile, annoncé le 15 janvier 1965[18].

Cette entente allait soulever un bon nombre de problèmes touchant l'interprétation de certaines de ses clauses. Mais il a eu un impact substantiel[19]. Ainsi, les importations en provenance des États-Unis comptaient pour 3 % en 1964 (mais pour 40 % en 1968) dans l'ensemble du marché canadien des véhicules produits en Amérique du Nord. Par ailleurs, 7 % de tous les véhicules produits au Canada en 1964 furent exportés, contre 60 % en 1968. Les chiffres sont donc éloquents: l'Accord canado-américain sur l'automobile a profondément modifié la structure de cette industrie en Amérique du Nord, et notamment au Canada. Mais, par les garanties qu'il comporte pour le Canada, il constitue en même temps une belle illustration des difficultés d'application de la politique commerciale dans une économie ouverte de dimension relativement petite.

Aujourd'hui, l'Accord canado-américain sur l'automobile demeure un fait d'importance, mais les événements des dernières années nous obligent à le considérer dans un contexte nouveau: hausse importante du prix de l'énergie, substitution de la petite et moyenne voiture au gros véhicule, invasion du marché nord-américain par l'industrie japonaise, incitation aux producteurs étrangers à venir s'installer aux États-Unis, arrivée sur la scène internationale de «nouveaux» producteurs, comme le Brésil. Bref, un ensemble d'éléments nous aidant à comprendre pourquoi, de part et d'autre de la frontière, une certaine volonté de renouveler l'accord à partir de fondements plus réalistes se manifeste périodiquement.

1970-1975

Peu de développements importants en matière de politique commerciale pendant cette période. Un événement majeur, cependant: le 14 septembre 1973, une déclaration des ministres du GATT, à Tokyo, lance la plus récente ronde de négociations en vue d'en arriver à de nouvelles réductions des barrières tarifaires sur une base multilatérale et, surtout, à des accords sur certaines barrières non tarifaires. Il s'agit du Tokyo Round.

1975-1985

Le Tokyo Round a duré jusqu'à juillet 1979. Pour le Canada, ces négociations devaient conduire aux principaux résultats suivants[20]: en premier lieu, un rapprochement considérable entre le Canada et les États-Unis en matière de relations commerciales. Éventuellement, en effet, 95 % des exportations canadiennes de produits industriels seront frappées de droits égaux ou inférieurs à 5 % à leur entrée aux États-Unis. 80 % ne feront face à aucun tarif. En revanche, 90 % des exportations américaines des mêmes produits à destination du Canada seront soumises à des tarifs égaux ou inférieurs à 5 %, et 65 % entreront en franchise.

En deuxième lieu, l'approche dite sectorielle[21] favorisée par le Canada pour le déroulement des négociations ne fut pas retenue. Troisièmement, un certain nombre d'accords portant sur des mesures restrictives de nature non tarifaire furent conclus. Le premier touche les subventions et les droits compensateurs – le récent dossier concernant l'exportation de matériel de transport en commun vers les États-Unis montre son importance pour le Canada –, le deuxième a trait aux marchés publics (politiques d'achats des gouvernements), un troisième s'intéresse aux problèmes soulevés par l'emploi de différentes méthodes d'évaluation en douane et un quatrième est lié aux obstacles techniques du commerce (normes et systèmes de certification).

La conclusion de ces accords marque un tournant important pour l'avenir des négociations commerciales multilatérales. Les obstacles non tarifaires sont maintenant devenus les outils préférés des gouvernements pour intervenir dans le commerce international. Ce fait indéniable définit les principaux paramètres que devra incorporer la politique commerciale canadienne dans l'avenir, surtout lorsqu'on se rappelle que le Tokyo Round a en même temps consacré, pour ainsi dire, des liaisons commerciales de plus en plus étroites entre le Canada et les États-Unis.

Enfin, dernier résultat d'importance du Tokyo Round pour le Canada: établissement du libre-échange en matière d'aéronautique civile. La place qu'occupe cette industrie au Canada fait de ce dernier un des principaux bénéficiaires de cette entente.

Paradoxalement, la forte récession du début des années 80 au Canada, comme ailleurs en Occident, devait relancer pour de bon les discussions sur le projet de libre-échange entre le Canada et les États-Unis. Vers la fin de 1985, le gouvernement du Canada faisait officiellement part aux autorités américaines de son désir d'avoir des négociations en vue d'en arriver à la conclusion d'un tel accord. Mis à part certains secteurs comme ceux de la culture et des institutions financières, cette entente serait la plus englobante possible.

On notera avec intérêt que cette prise de position officielle du gouvernement canadien suivait la parution du rapport de la Commission royale d'enquête sur l'union économique et les perspectives de développement du Canada, qui faisait précisément du projet de libre-échange avec les États-Unis la pierre d'assise de ses recommandations.

Il faut voir dans cette modification majeure de la politique commerciale canadienne la fin du rêve qui, en matière de commerce international, avait donné naissance à la théorie de la «troisième option». Pour le meilleur et pour le pire, la conjoncture internationale semble devoir rapprocher encore davantage le Canada et les États-Unis et on ne voit pas très bien quelle autre politique commerciale pourrait faire véritablement contrepoids aux lourdes tendances léguées par l'histoire et la géographie.

CONCLUSION

Constatons d'abord que ce bref historique de la politique commerciale canadienne depuis 1945 a laissé de côté des volets importants du dossier. Outre ceux mentionnés explicitement au début de ce chapitre, on aura remarqué que des sujets comme le commerce des produits agricoles, les accords internationaux sur les produits de base (le blé, par exemple), les rapports existant entre la politique canadienne d'aide aux pays en voie de développement et les exportations canadiennes et les positions canadiennes touchant les importations en provenance des pays à bas revenus n'ont pas été retenus. Des contraintes d'espace et, comme nous l'avons déjà indiqué, le caractère complémentaire des contributions à cet ouvrage collectif expliquent ces omissions.

En outre, il faut se rappeler que les produits agricoles échappent en grande partie aux règles du GATT. Le Canada et les États-Unis, par exemple, font tous deux usage d'un ensemble de barrières tarifaires et non tarifaires touchant ces produits. Des obstacles encore plus importants existent au sein de la CEE – ainsi, la politique agricole commune constitue un régime protectionniste s'étendant à la grandeur de l'Europe. Comme tous les autres pays, le Canada apporte son soutien à son industrie agricole. Il recourt, par exemple, aux offices de mise en marché. Les difficultés que soulèvent les relations fédérales-provinciales en cette matière sont indissociables du contexte international dans lequel le Canada opère et ne sauraient, en conséquence, être prises adéquatement en compte dans une présentation somme toute sommaire de l'histoire de la politique commerciale canadienne[22].

Que conclure? Faut-il, comme le prétend l'ex-principal négociateur canadien au Tokyo Round, reconnaître que, pour le Canada, la politique étrangère doit d'abord être la politique commerciale vis-à-vis des États-Unis, que l'accent dans cette politique commerciale doit être mis dorénavant sur les barrières non tarifaires et que, par conséquent, le Canada a raison d'entreprendre des discussions bilatérales avec son voisin sur ces divers sujets[23]? Compte tenu cependant de ses positions traditionnelles sur l'organisation du commerce dans le monde, comment le Canada pourra-t-il délaisser, même partiellement, l'approche multilatérale au profit de relations bilatérales plus nettement accentuées?

Voilà sans doute un des défis que doit relever la politique commerciale canadienne pendant la deuxième moitié des années 80 et, sans doute, dans un avenir encore plus lointain. Faudra-t-il pour autant aller jusqu'au libre-échange global avec les États-Unis? ou suffira-t-il de mettre au point de nouveaux accords de libre-échange dans des secteurs précis?

L'histoire montre, en tout cas, que l'aimant attirant le Canada et les États-Unis l'un vers l'autre a toujours été puissant. Au point, diront certains, que le Canada est inexorablement entraîné vers son voisin. S'il faut, d'ailleurs, en croire le Conseil économique du Canada[24], «[...] une réorientation équilibrée du commerce canadien, des États-Unis vers la CEE et le Japon, si elle n'altérait pas la composition récente des échanges, entraînerait des exportations nettes beaucoup plus importantes de produits tirés des ressources naturelles renouvelables et non renouvelables et des services fournis par le capital physique; en même temps, on augmenterait la création d'emplois pour les travailleurs ayant une instruction primaire, et on verrait un plus grand nombre de travailleurs ayant une formation secondaire ou universitaire remplacés par des importations concurrentielles». Est-ce là un scénario compatible avec d'autres positions non moins traditionnelles du Canada en ce qui a trait à la diversification et au renforcement de son économie?

Nous voici donc entraînés, par ce cheminement, vers la considération des grands objectifs de la politique commerciale du Canada dont nous faisions état dès le début: autonomie relative vis-à-vis des États-Unis, stratégie industrielle visant à dégager le pays d'une vocation «naturellement» trop centrée sur le primaire et la première transformation, le tout baigné dans un contexte de grande dépendance sur le commerce international. Rien n'a vraiment beaucoup changé depuis 1945 et peut-être même depuis 1867.

Mais il y a bien d'autres défis. Celui, par exemple, de la cohérence entre, d'une part, une volonté bien affichée de collaborer à la solution des immenses problèmes que rencontre le monde en voie de développement, notamment depuis le milieu des années 70, et, d'autre part, une politique commerciale à l'égard de ces pays qui ne se distingue souvent en rien de celle des autres États industrialisés.

On peut cependant voir un lien entre ces multiples défis. Au risque de répéter un lieu commun, comment conclure, sans souligner la vulnérabilité d'une économie industrialisée très ouverte sur l'extérieur mais possédant à peu près seule la caractéristique de ne pas être associée, au plan des échanges commerciaux, à un ensemble lui assurant l'accès à un vaste marché? Au milieu des années 80, le recours croissant aux barrières commerciales de nature non tarifaire – et donc moins facilement contrôlables – par des pays aux prises avec une opinion publique davantage portée vers le protectionnisme ne manque pas de rendre ce fait encore plus préoccupant.

TABLEAU 1
Importance relative des États-Unis dans le
commerce d'exportation et d'importation de
marchandises du Canada (1926-1980)

Année	Exportations vers les USA \ Exportations totales	Importations provenant des USA \ Importations totales
1926	0,36	0,66
1930	0,43	0,65
1935	0,36	0,57
1945	0,37	0,78
1948	0,49	0,67
1955	0,60	0,73
1960	0,56	0,67
1965	0,57	0,70
1970	0,65	0,71
1975	0,65	0,68
1980	0,63	0,70
1983	0,73	0,70

Sources: Données compilées à partir de la *Revue de la Banque du Canada* et de Banque du Canada/Bank of Canada, *Supplément/Statistical Summary*, diverses années.

TABLEAU 2
Importance relative des États-Unis
dans le commerce d'exportation de marchandises du Canada;
principales catégories de produits
et choix d'années pour la période 1955-1980

Catégorie	Exportations vers les USA			Exportations totales			% de la catégorie dans le total des exportations	
	1955	1960	1965	1970	1975	1980	1955	1980
Produits de l'agriculture et de la pêche	0,30	0,28	0,23	0,27	0,16	0,19	0,22	0,12
Produits de la forêt	0,80	0,79	0,76	0,69	0,66	0,63	0,35	0,17
Métaux et minéraux	0,60	0,52	0,58	0,53	0,67	0,66	0,29	0,29
Produits chimiques et engrais	0,47	0,39	0,54	0,59	0,71	0,56	0,04	0,05
Autres articles manufacturés	0,56	0,59	0,66	0,83	0,79	0,76	0,10	0,36
dont: véhicules automobiles et pièces détachées	n.d.	0,15	0,64	0,93	0,91	0,90	n.d.*	0,15

Sources: Données compilées à partir de la *Revue de la Banque du Canada* et de Banque du Canada/Bank of Canada, *Supplément/Statistical Summary*, diverses années.

(*) Négligeable.

NOTES

1. L'incident est raconté dans L.D. Wilgress, *Canada's Approach to Trade Negociations*, p. 1.

2. Ce rapprochement était de fait complété vers la fin des années 30-40.

3. L'agriculture, la pêche, l'exploitation forestière, le piégeage, les mines, la fabrication, la construction et les services d'utilité publique.

4. Notons que le Comité permanent des affaires étrangères du Sénat canadien a fortement endossé l'idée d'un libre-échange bilatéral avec les États-Unis dans un rapport datant de 1978. Voir *Comité sénatorial permanent des affaires étrangères*, juin 1978. Il est revenu à la charge avec force dans un deuxième rapport publié en 1982. Voir *ibidem*, mars 1982.

5. La proposition du gouvernement Diefenbaker visait à détourner environ 15 % du commerce canadien avec les États-Unis vers la Grande-Bretagne. «When the British Government suggested that the way to achieve this was to eliminate tariffs between the two countries (except on agricultural products), the Canadian reaction was one of 'shock and alarm'.» *The Times*, Londres, 5 octobre 1957.

6. L.D. Wilgress, *op cit.*, p. 11-13.

7. Cette clause, dont les États-Unis se feront alors les promoteurs, jouait *de facto* un rôle important dans leur politique commerciale depuis 1922.

8. L.D. Wilgress, *op. cit.*, p. 10.

9. J.D. Gibson, *Canada's Economy in a Changing World*, p. 5.

10. L.D. Wilgress, *op. cit.*, p. 18-20.

11. *Ibidem*.

12. Le Canada ne put même pas obtenir le «waiver» qu'il avait sollicité auprès de l'organisation internationale.

13. H.E. English, *Canada's International Economic Policy*, p. 158. C'est seulement en 1973 que la Grande-Bretagne a été finalement admise au sein de la CEE.

14. À ce sujet, on lira avec intérêt K.C. Mackenzie, *Tariff-Making and Trade Policy in the US and Canada*.

15. Voir, à ce sujet, J.R. Melvin et B.W. Wilkinson, *Protection effective dans l'économie canadienne*.

16. «One can now see that the Kennedy Round signaled the switch, in the United States and in Canada as well, from a commercial policy system centered on the published schedule of rates of duty to what one might call a system of 'contingent' protection.» R. de C. Grey, 1981, p. 13.

17. R. de C. Grey, *Trade Policy in the 1980s [...]*, p. 7.

18. Voir C.E. Beigie, *The Canada-US Automotive Agreement [...]*, pour un historique de cet accord et une évaluation de son fonctionnement pendant les premières années.

19. *Ibidem*, p. 4-5.

20. Voir *Le Comité sénatorial permanent des affaires étrangères*, 1978, 1982; R. de C. Grey, *op. cit.*

21. Pour le gouvernement canadien, une telle approche signifiait mener, «dans des secteurs soigneusement définis et choisis, une attaque complète contre tous les obstacles au commerce, surtout lorsqu'ils empêchent une plus grande transformation des ressources naturelles et l'augmentation de la valeur ajoutée dans le pays d'origine». *Commerce Canada*, février 1974, p. 39.

22. Voir, par exemple, K. Kock, *International Trade Policy and the GATT 1947-1967*, p. 285-286.

23. R. de C. Grey, *op. cit.*, p. 5 notamment. Voir aussi W. Diebold, Jr., *Financial Post*, 3 juillet 1982, p. 59.

24. *Conseil économique du Canada*, 1975, p. 26.

BIBLIOGRAPHIE

AXLINE, A., HYNDMAN, J.E., LYON, P.V. et MOLOT, M.A., eds. *Continental Community? Independence and Integration in North America*, Toronto, McClelland and Stewart, 1974.

BEIGIE, C.E. *The Canada-US Automotive Agreement: An Evaluation*, Montréal, Private Planning Association of Canada, 1970.

BRECHER, I. et REISMAN, S.S. *Les relations économiques canado-américaines*, Commission royale d'enquête sur les perspectives économiques du Canada, Ottawa, Imprimeur de la Reine, 1958.

CANADA. Comité sénatorial permanent des affaires étrangères. *Les relations Canada-États-Unis*, vol. II, *Les relations commerciales du Canada avec les États-Unis*, juin 1978.

CANADA. Comité sénatorial permanent des affaires étrangères. *Les relations Canada-États-Unis*, vol. III, *Les relations commerciales Canada-États-Unis*, mars 1982.

CANADA. *Propriété étrangère et structure de l'industrie canadienne*, Ottawa, Imprimeur de la Reine, 1968.

CANADA. *L'investissement étranger direct au Canada* (rapport Gray), Ottawa, Information Canada, 1972.

CANADA. *Rapport de la Commission royale d'enquête sur l'union économique et les perspectives de développement du Canada*, Toronto, University of Toronto Press, 1985.

CANADA. Ministère des Affaires extérieures. *Politique étrangère au service des Canadiens*, Ottawa, Information Canada, 1970.

CANADA. Ministère des Affaires extérieures. *La politique commerciale du Canada pour les années 1980*, document de travail, 1983.

CANADA. Ministère des Affaires extérieures. *Une étude de la politique commerciale canadienne*, document d'information, 1983.

CANADIAN PUBLIC POLICY. *Canada-United States Trade and Policy Issues:* Canadian Public Policy 8, octobre 1982.

CAVES, R.E. et HOLTON, R.H. *The Canadian Economy: Prospects and Retrospect*, Cambridge, Mass., Harvard University Press, 1961.

CONFERENCE PAPERS. *Canada and International Trade*, 2 vol., *Essays in International Economics*, Montréal, The Institute for Research on Public Policy, 1945.

CONSEIL ÉCONOMIQUE DU CANADA. *Au-delà des frontières. Une nouvelle stratégie commerciale pour le Canada*, 1975.

DALES, J.H. *The Protective Tariff in Canada's Development*, Toronto, University of Toronto Press, 1966.

D'CRUZ, J.R. and FLECK, J.D. *Canada can compete!*, Montréal, The Institute of Research on Public Policy, 1985.

DIEBOLD, W., Jr. «Canada in the world economy over ten years», *International Journal*, 33, printemps 1978, p. 432-437.

DORAN, C.F. *Economic Interdependence, Autonomy and Canadian-American Relations*, Montréal, Montréal Institute for Research on Public Policy, 1983.

EASTERBROOK, W.I. et AITKEN, H.G.J. *Canadian Economic History*, Toronto, Macmillan, 1975.

EASTMAN, H.C. et STYKOLT, S. *The Tariff and Competition in Canada*, Toronto, University of Toronto Press, 1967.

ENGLISH, H.E. *Canada's International Economic Policy*, dans Brewis, T.N., English, H.E., Scott, A. et Jewett, P.: Canadian Economic Policy, Revised edition, Toronto, MacMillan, 1965, p. 146-180.

GIBSON, J.D. *Canada's Economy in a Changing World*, Toronto, MacMillan, 1948, 380 p.

GREY, R. de C. *Trade Policy in the 1980s – An Agenda for Canadian-US Relations*, Policy Commentary No. 3, C.D. Howe Institute, 1981.

INSTITUT CANADIEN DES AFFAIRES INTERNATIONALES.

— *A Bibliography of Works on Canadian Foreign Relations 1945-1970* (compilée par D.M. Page).

— *A Bibliography of Works on Canadian Foreign Relations 1971-1975* (compilée par D.M. Page).

— *A Bibliography of Works on Canadian Foreign Relations 1976-1980* (compilée par J.R. Barrett et J. Beaumont).

KOCK, K. *International Trade Policy and the GATT 1947-1967*, Stockholm Economic Studies, New Series, XI, Stockholm, Almqvist et Wiksell, 1969.

LAZAR, F. *The new protectionism. Non-tariff barriers and their effects for Canada*, Toronto, J. Lorimer and Co., 1981.

LEA, S. *A Canada-US Free Trade Arrangement: Survey of Possible Characteristics*, Montréal, Private Planning Association of Canada, 1963.

LEA, S. *A Possible Plan for a Canada-US Free Trade Area*, Washington, Private Planning Association, 1965.

LEA, S. *Free Trade by Sectors*, Looking Ahead, Washington, National Planning Association, 1966.

LYON, Peyton V. *Le libre-échange canado-américain et l'indépendance du Canada*, Ottawa, Conseil économique du Canada, 1975.

MACKENZIE, K.C. *Tariff-Making and Trade Policy in the US and Canada*, Praeger Special Studies in International Economics and Development; F.A. Praeger, Publisher, 1968.

MELVIN, J.R. et WILKINSON, B.W. *Protection effective dans l'économie canadienne*, Ottawa, Conseil économique du Canada, étude n° 9, Imprimeur de la Reine, 1968.

MORICI, P. *Canada-United States Trade and Economic Interdependence*, Institut de recherche C.D. Howe et National Planning Association, 1980.

NAPPI, C. «Examen critique de quelques hypothèses sous-jacentes à la nouvelle politique commerciale suggérée par le Conseil économique du Canada», *L'Actualité économique*, vol. 52, n° 4, oct.-déc. 1976, p. 524-533.

ONTARIO ECONOMIC COUNCIL. *Developments Abroad and the Domestic Economy*, vol. 1, Toronto, 1980.

PESTIEAU, C. *The sector approach to trade negotiations: Canadian and US interests*, Montréal, Canadian Economic Policy Committee, 1976.

PROTHEROE, D.R. *Imports and Politics: Trade Decision Making in Canada*, Toronto, Institut de recherches politiques, 1980.

SAFARIAN, A.E. *Foreign Ownership of Canadian Industry*, Toronto, McGraw-Hill, 1966.

SÉGUIN-DULUDE, L. «Analyse de la politique commerciale canadienne: rétrospective et synthèse», *L'Actualité économique*, vol. 55, n° 3, 1979, p. 303-342.

STOVEL, J.A. *Canada in the World Economy*, Cambridge, Mass., Harvard University Press, 1959.

WILGRESS, L.D. *Canada's Approach to Trade Negociations*, Montréal, Private Planning Association of Canada, 1963, 68 p.

WILKINSON, B.W. *Canada in the changing world economy*, Montréal, C.D. Howe Research Institute, 1980.

WINHAM, G.R. «Bureaucratic politics and Canadian trade negotiations», *International Journal*, 34, hiver 1978-1979, p. 64-89.

WONNACOTT, R.J. *Tariff Policy*, dans Officer, L.H. et Smith, L.B., éd., *Canadian Economic Problems and Policies*, Toronto, McGraw-Hill, 1970, p. 126-142.

WONNACOTT, R.J. *Industrial Strategy: A Canadian Substitute for Trade Liberalization*, rapport de recherche n° 7409, London, Ontario, University of Western Ontario, 1974.

WONNACOTT, R.J. *Les options commerciales du Canada*, Ottawa, Conseil économique du Canada, 1975.

WONNACOTT, R.J. et P. *Free Trade between the United States and Canada, the Potential Economic Effects*, Cambridge, Mass., Harvard University Press, 1967.

WONNACOTT, R.J. et P. «Free Trade Between the US and Canada Fifteen Years Later», *Canadian Public Policy/Analyse de politiques*, 8, 1982, p. 412-427.

YOUNG, J.H. *La politique commerciale du Canada*, Commission royale d'enquête sur les perspectives économiques du Canada, Ottawa, Imprimeur de la Reine, 1958.

22

La dimension internationale de la politique monétaire canadienne

Roger Dehem
Université Laval

INTRODUCTION

Au terme de la Deuxième Guerre mondiale, la Banque du Canada n'avait encore que dix ans. Née dans le creuset de la grande dépression, agent du gouvernement dans la tourmente de la guerre, elle devait être le garant de la stabilité monétaire.

Le dollar canadien qui, dans l'entre-deux-guerres, n'avait pu maintenir sa parité fixe qu'entre juillet 1926 et septembre 1931, vit son prix officiel fixé à 0,90 $ US le 16 septembre 1939. À cette même date fut institué le Foreign Exchange Control Board, qui aurait à gérer le Fonds du change étranger, dont la création légale remontait au 5 juillet 1935. Ce Fonds était du ressort du gouvernement, alors que la Banque du Canada en avait l'administration.

À la suite de la détérioration rapide de la balance des paiements au début de la guerre, le gouvernement décréta, le 30 avril 1940, la réquisition des devises étrangères entre les mains de résidents canadiens, y compris l'encaisse de devises de la Banque du Canada. L'or détenu par cette dernière, soit 205,2 millions de dollars US, fut aussi transféré au Fonds du change étranger.

À partir de 1942, après l'entrée en guerre des États-Unis, la balance des paiements du Canada à l'égard de ce pays se redressa sensiblement, à tel point qu'au terme de 1945, la réserve officielle d'or et de devises fut quatre fois aussi élevée (1,508 millions) qu'elle ne l'avait été le 15 septembre 1939 (393,1 millions de dollars US). Cette augmentation avait toutefois été accompagnée d'une diminution du portefeuille canadien de titres américains et d'une augmentation de l'endettement à l'égard des États-Unis[1]. Au cours de cette même période, l'endettement canadien envers le Royaume-Uni diminua de 958 millions de dollars canadiens, et les actifs canadiens en Grande-Bretagne avaient augmenté de 1,531 millions, principalement à la suite du prêt de 700 millions accordé en 1942[2]. L'abondance de liquidités externes avait permis de révoquer certaines restrictions à l'octroi de devises, dès mai 1944.

LES PERSPECTIVES AU SEUIL DE L'APRÈS-GUERRE

Les souvenirs traumatisants de la grande dépression, l'expérience récente de l'économie de guerre et de son appareil administratif ainsi que les espoirs suscités par les projets de coopération internationale, notamment l'accord de Bretton Woods (1944), inspirèrent à la fois l'appréhension d'un retour de l'instabilité économique du passé et une confiance quelque peu téméraire de pouvoir mieux maîtriser l'évolution à venir.

En vertu des règles convenues à Bretton Woods, le régime des changes devrait dorénavant être maintenu stable. Ceci se révélera difficile, et même impossible à la longue. Les nouvelles idées keynésiennes devaient, en effet, imposer un style plus nationaliste ou égocentrique aux politiques monétaires, posant le problème de l'équilibre international en des termes nouveaux.

LES ÉTAPES DE L'ÉVOLUTION MONÉTAIRE AU CANADA DEPUIS 1945

De 1945 à 1950

La surabondance de liquidités engendrée par le financement de la guerre exerçait au Canada, comme ailleurs, de fortes pressions inflationnistes. Refoulées par des contrôles sur les prix et salaires jusqu'à l'été 1946, ces pressions devaient se manifester librement sur les marchés après l'abolition de ceux-ci. Aussi, pour en modérer la force, le gouvernement réévalua-t-il le dollar canadien, le 5 juillet 1946. La parité traditionnelle entre le dollar canadien et le dollar américain fut rétablie. Cette mesure fut une innovation qui étonna à l'époque. Elle devait être imitée par la Suède quelques jours plus tard. Alors qu'au cours de l'entre-deux-guerres la dévaluation avait été une opération fréquente, la réévaluation d'une monnaie n'avait jamais été envisagée.

Le 1er janvier 1947, une loi sur le contrôle des changes (Foreign Exchange Control Act) se substitua au décret de septembre 1939 et à la loi instituant le Fonds du change étranger de 1935, sans toutefois apporter de modifications majeures aux institutions en place.

Alors que l'équilibre de la balance des paiements du Canada avait été réalisé traditionnellement par la conversion des devises obtenues d'un excédent d'exportation vers l'Europe, de manière à régler le déficit envers les États-Unis, la situation d'après-guerre était caractérisée par l'inconvertibilité de la plupart des monnaies européennes. Les exportations canadiennes vers ces débouchés traditionnels ne pouvaient se faire que moyennant l'octroi de crédits. La Grande-Bretagne, notamment, avait bénéficié, en 1946, d'un crédit de 1,250 millions de dollars.

La nécessité de régler au comptant les importations provenant des États-Unis, alors que les exportations vers les autres pays étaient financées en partie par des crédits, entraîna un déclin rapide des avoirs officiels en or et devises. Après avoir atteint un maximum de 1,667 millions de dollars US en mai 1946, ils furent réduits à 461 millions le 17 décembre 1947[3]. Plutôt que de contracter la demande interne par une politique monétaire restrictive, qui aurait à la fois redressé la balance externe et contrecarré l'inflation, le gouvernement recourut, en novembre 1947, à des mesures de restriction des dépenses canadiennes aux États-Unis (Emergency Exchange Conservation Act). De sévères coupures furent faites dans les importations en provenance des États-Unis. Malgré le redressement de sa balance des paiements en 1948 et 1949, le Canada se laissa entraîner par la vague de dévaluations de septembre 1949. Le dollar canadien fut dévalué de 10 % le 20 septembre.

Cet ajustement de la parité fixe, que les autorités espéraient voir agir dans le sens de l'équilibre, ne fut pas plus définitif que les précédents. Au contraire, la conjoncture inflationniste qui se développa après le déclenchement de la guerre en Corée, en juin 1950, amena les spéculateurs à anticiper un nouvel ajustement de la valeur externe du dollar canadien. Un flux considérable de capitaux à court terme se plaça au Canada en vue de profiter d'une réévaluation éventuelle. Devant cette situation nouvelle et intolérable, le gouvernement réagit sagement en annonçant le 30 septembre que la valeur du dollar canadien serait déterminée par le marché à partir du 2 octobre. Cette décision, qui contrevenait aux engagements souscrits à Bretton Woods, en 1944, était présentée comme temporaire. Elle était cependant prémonitoire de développements futurs plus universels et durables.

De 1950 à 1962

Malgré la hausse du dollar canadien sur le marché des changes, le contrôle des changes ne fut relâché que progressivement, jusqu'à son abolition complète le 14 décembre 1951. Les capitaux à court terme qui avaient afflué massivement en 1950 en vue de gains spéculatifs ne refluèrent que partiellement et lentement vers l'étranger. Ils se muèrent en partie en placements à long terme. C'est à partir de 1950 que le Canada verra les placements étrangers à long terme prendre un nouvel essor, après une carence de plus de 20 ans. Leur flux annuel net passera de $608 millions en 1950 à $1,490 millions en 1956. Il y aura ensuite un certain déclin jusqu'en 1963. De 1953 à 1966, ces placements étrangers à long terme seront, en général, de l'ordre de grandeur du déficit de la balance courante. Après 1952 et jusqu'en 1966, les flux de capitaux à court terme garderont une faible ampleur. Après avoir été gonflée outremesure par la spéculation en 1950, l'encaisse officielle d'or et de devises demeurera relativement stable jusqu'en 1961.

La révélation de la période de flottement du dollar canadien fut la stabilité remarquable des changes. Le prix du dollar canadien évalua dans des limites relativement étroites autour d'une tendance ascendante jusqu'en 1957. Il toucha le pair avec le dollar américain le 22 janvier 1952, et fit prime ensuite. Celle-ci atteignit un maximum de 6 % au cours de l'été 1957.

Contrairement à la vision pessimiste du régime de changes flexibles, selon laquelle la spéculation y déstabiliserait le marché, l'expérience canadienne a montré que les flux de capitaux agissent dans le sens de la stabilisation. Les périodes de faiblesse du dollar canadien sont mises à profit par ceux qui anticipent un redressement des cours, tandis que les périodes où le dollar canadien est jugé anormalement cher sont marquées par un retrait de capitaux spéculatifs. Pour autant que les participants au marché des changes croient en l'existence d'une norme autour de laquelle les cotations fluctueront à court terme, celles-ci seront atténuées par la spéculation[4].

L'appréciation lente du dollar canadien au cours de la période 1950-1957 eut comme bienfait additionnel d'atténuer les pressions inflationnistes, alors que la croissance économique était rapide.

À la période d'évolution harmonieuse, de 1951 à 1957, devaient succéder cinq années de difficultés qui aboutiront à l'abandon du régime de changes flottants.

L'approche du faîte de la prospérité en 1956 et au début de 1957 devait naturellement accentuer les pressions inflationnistes et inciter les autorités à une politique monétaire plus restrictive. Ce fut le début d'une suite de manœuvres malhabiles et parfois incohérentes. En 1958, le gouvernement entreprit la conversion de plus de la moitié de la dette publique en un emprunt à long terme. Jusqu'au terme de l'opération, le 15 septembre 1958, la Banque du Canada procéda activement au soutien du marché et injecta des fonds à cet effet. Par la suite, elle retira ce qu'elle jugeait être de la monnaie excédentaire, et les taux de rendement des obligations se mirent à monter par rapport à ceux aux États-Unis. Ceci provoqua un influx de capitaux, maintenant le dollar canadien à un niveau élevé sur le marché des changes.

La conséquence de taux d'intérêt élevés et de la cherté du dollar canadien fut de déprimer l'activité économique au Canada. Les exportations étaient enrayées et les importations favorisées par le bas prix des devises étrangères, alors que les investissements étaient handicapés par les taux d'intérêt élevés et le marasme général.

La stratégie bien intentionnée – quoique malhabile – de la Banque du Canada en vue de réduire l'inflation se heurta à une opposition dans l'opinion publique. Le gouverneur James Coyne, précurseur du monétarisme à une époque keynésienne, fut forcé de démissionner, en juillet 1961. Impatient de corriger ses erreurs antérieures, le ministre des Finances essaya d'influencer le dollar canadien à la baisse par des déclarations publiques, une première fois le 20 juin 1960 et une deuxième fois en octobre de la même année. Cette façon de procéder ébranla la confiance dans la monnaie et provoqua une dépréciation sensible du dollar canadien sur le marché des changes. Le Fonds du change dut intervenir massivement au début de 1962. La réserve officielle baissa d'un demi-milliard entre la fin décembre 1961 et la fin mai 1962. Dans son désarroi, le gouvernement céda aux pressions du Fonds monétaire international et rétablit la parité fixe du dollar canadien au niveau de 92,5 cents des États-Unis, le 2 mai 1962. Ce retour à l'orthodoxie de Bretton Woods se révélera bientôt avoir été une erreur, et ne sera que transitoire.

De 1962 à 1970

Un marché soumis à la contrainte de prix fixe est naturellement sujet à des tensions, tantôt dans un sens, tantôt dans l'autre. La spéculation n'étant plus inhibée par le risque de perte, elle sera tentée d'anticiper tantôt la dévaluation, tantôt la réévaluation.

Dès le 24 juin 1962, le gouvernement dut imposer un programme d'austérité pour calmer la fièvre sur le marché des changes, alors que l'économie ne souffrait pas de surchauffe. Une taxe spéciale fut notamment imposée sur les importations dites «non essentielles», et des crédits furent sollicités du Fonds monétaire international, de sources officielles américaines et même de la Banque d'Angleterre. Tandis que la conjoncture du marché des changes se stabilisa et que les mesures exceptionnelles prises à cet effet purent être bientôt révoquées, le système demeura vulnérable à de nouvelles perturbations.

Le 18 juillet 1963, le gouvernement des États-Unis institua une taxe de péréquation des taux d'intérêt (Interest Equalization Tax) qui frapperait certaines formes d'exportation de capitaux à long terme. Très sensible à une telle mesure, le Canada négocia immédiatement son exemption de l'application de cette taxe aux nouvelles émissions de titres avec les États-Unis. Il ne l'obtint que moyennant l'engagement qu'il n'en profiterait pas pour augmenter sa propre réserve d'or et de devises. Les États-Unis étaient eux-mêmes aux prises avec un déséquilibre de leur balance de paiements. L'engagement canadien de ne pas augmenter les réserves officielles au-delà de leur niveau d'alors, soit 2,700 millions, était une assurance suffisante que l'objectif du gouvernement américain ne serait pas enfreint par le Canada. Mais cet engagement du Canada devait se révéler être une restriction significative à l'autonomie de la politique économique canadienne. Elle devait, en effet, empêcher les autorités canadiennes de pratiquer une politique suffisamment restrictive de l'inflation. Toute tentative de restreindre l'offre de crédit au Canada dans une mesure qui aurait relevé l'écart entre les taux d'intérêt canadiens et les taux américains aurait provoqué un afflux accru de capitaux et aurait augmenté les réserves de change au-delà de leur maximum convenu. La politique macro-économique du Canada s'était ainsi insensiblement alignée sur celle des États-Unis. C'était la conséquence inévitable de la fixité des taux de change. Le plafond des réserves de changes ne rendait le lien entre les deux économies que plus serré.

De nouvelles tensions se manifestèrent sur le marché des changes à la suite de la dévaluation de la livre sterling en novembre 1967. Le souvenir des liaisons historiques entre la livre et le dollar canadien suscita une spéculation à la baisse contre ce dernier. Comme le cours du change était inflexible, il fallut recourir à des mesures exceptionnelles pour pallier les sorties de devises. Les taux d'intérêt furent relevés, et des emprunts furent conclus auprès du Fonds monétaire international et de diverses banques centrales. Les restrictions américaines à l'exportation de capitaux au Canada furent entièrement levées et une entente plus souple entre les deux gouvernements devait dorénavant régir les transactions financières entre les deux pays.

Après l'alerte à la dévaluation et 1968, la balance canadienne des paiements se renforça sensiblement, principalement dans sa composante commerciale. Alors que la politique anti inflationniste du gouvernement en 1969 et au début de 1970 restreignit la demande d'importations, les exportations se maintinrent à des niveaux élevés, en raison de la haute conjoncture dans le reste du monde.

Une situation analogue à celle de 1950 réapparut. Le redressement de la balance courante et la volonté de combattre l'inflation suscitèrent la perspective d'une réévaluation de la monnaie. En régime de parités fixes, la spéculation pouvait anticiper une telle éventualité sans risque de perdre. La statistique révèle en effet un gonflement de l'entrée de capitaux à court terme et des réserves officielles au deuxième trimestre de 1970. Une telle spéculation plaça les autorités canadiennes dans une situation difficile. Alors qu'une spéculation contre la monnaie nationale peut être combattue par le recours à l'assistance extérieure, une spéculation à la hausse du dollar canadien force les autorités, en régime de changes fixes, à accumuler indéfiniment des devises étrangères. Ceci est sans doute techniquement possible, puisqu'il suffit que la Banque du Canada achète les bons du Trésor nécessaires à l'approvisionnement du Fonds des changes en monnaie canadienne. Mais comme il n'y a pas de limite naturelle à la spéculation en régime de changes fixes, le système est explosif. La solution innovée par le Canada en septembre 1950 devait s'imposer à nouveau. Le flottement du dollar canadien fut annoncé le 31 mai 1970 et entra en vigueur le 1er juin.

Cette mesure fut une fois de plus qualifiée de temporaire, et l'engagement fut pris envers le Fonds monétaire international (dont le Canada violait une seconde fois les statuts) de respecter à nouveau le principe des parités fixes, aussitôt que les circonstances le permettraient.

De 1970 à 1988

La décennie 1970 allait se révéler turbulente sur le plan économique. De nombreux déséquilibres latents précipitèrent une déstabilisation des prix, plus particulièrement du pétrole, et des cours des changes. Face à ces développements imprévus, les autorités gouvernementales manifestèrent un grand désarroi et réagirent de manières diverses, généralement peu coordonnées, aux circonstances nouvelles.

Plus encore que dans le passé, le Canada sera tiraillé par les métamorphoses de l'économie mondiale. Relativement favorisé par ses ressources énergétiques propres, le Canada aura à s'adapter aux transformations des relations entre les États-Unis, l'Europe et le Japon, tout en essayant de garder une certaine distance à l'égard de Washington.

Sur le plan de la politique monétaire, l'année 1975 marque un tournant dans les principes directeurs de la Banque du Canada. De 1962 à 1974, la gestion monétaire avait été du type keynésien, c'est-à-dire qu'elle visait avant tout à contrôler la disponibilité du crédit, les taux d'intérêt en particulier, de manière à stabiliser l'activité économique globale. Dans cette conception de la politique monétaire, l'évolution des prix à plus long terme est une préoccupation secondaire. On avait coutume d'expliquer l'inflation par des considérations ad hoc extrinsèques à la politique monétaire.

À partir de 1975, à la suite d'une réhabilitation de la théorie monétaire classique de l'inflation[5], la Banque du Canada s'est ralliée à la philosophie dite «monétariste». Celle-ci prescrit une régulation de la masse monétaire de manière à réduire progressivement le taux d'inflation. Cette règle, naturellement plus rigide que la pratique souple et opportuniste antérieure, aura des répercussions inattendues et pertubatrices sur le marché des changes.

Après la levée de son ancrage officiel, le 1er juin 1970, le dollar canadien s'apprécia, comme en octobre 1950. Cette réévaluation monta à 6 % en six mois. Par la suite, de 1971 à 1974, le dollar canadien fluctua dans un intervalle étroit à l'égard du dollar américain, en dépit des soubresauts majeurs auxquels était soumis le système monétaire international. Le dollar américain, déclaré inconvertible en or le 15 août 1971, avait été dévalué à deux reprises, en décembre 1971 et en février 1973. Lorsque le dollar des États-Unis fut dévalué de 10 % le 12 février 1973, son prix ne se déprécia temporairement que de 1 % en termes de dollars canadiens.

Au début 1971 jusqu'au printemps 1974, le prix du dollar canadien progressa de 0,98 $US à 1,04 $US. Ceci fut suivi d'un déclin jusqu'à 0,96 $US en août 1975. Sous l'effet d'une politique monétaire relativement restrictive au Canada, l'écart entre les taux d'intérêt canadiens et américains s'élargit, faisant remonter le dollar canadien jusque vers 1,03 $US en juin 1976.

Le dollar canadien se maintint ferme jusqu'au 15 novembre 1976. L'émotion causée par l'avènement d'un gouvernement indépendantiste au Québec provoqua un effondrement immédiat d'environ 6 % du dollar canadien. Le glissement se poursuivit en 1977, jusque vers les 0,90 $US. Cette faiblesse accusée et prolongée de la devise canadienne résulta du fait que, loin de contrecarrer les effets de l'incertitude politique, la Banque du Canada, désormais guidée par les indicateurs de la masse monétaire, laissa les taux d'intérêt canadiens s'abaisser, alors que les taux américains étaient à la hausse. L'écart considérable entre ces taux en 1976 se résorba presque entièrement dans le cours de 1977. La Banque du Canada, se contentant de régulariser la masse monétaire, se voyait désemparée devant l'évolution des taux d'intérêt et des cours du change. Elle intervint toutefois en puisant dans la réserve officielle de devises et en négociant une ouverture de crédit en dollars US auprès des banques à charte, le 27 octobre 1977. Ceci fut renforcé, à partir de 1978, par le recours à l'emprunt extérieur.

La crise du dollar canadien, amorcée en 1976, allait persister, pour des raisons diverses, jusqu'en 1986. La Banque du Canada eut la tâche ardue de naviguer dans une conjoncture externe mouvementée et un contexte politique interne plutôt défavorable. L'incertitude politique et économique au Québec de 1976 à 1980, le Programme énergétique canadien de 1980, le resserrement énergique de la politique monétaire américaine en 1980 et 1981 et l'explosion des déficits budgétaires aux États-Unis et au Canada ont soumis la Banque du Canada à de fortes pressions auxquelles elle eut le mérite de faire face sans renoncer à son objectif anti-inflationniste.

La volonté de vaincre la tendance inflationniste d'après-guerre amena la Banque à pratiquer une politique de type monétariste dès 1975. Cela consistait pour elle à se laisser guider par des agrégats monétaires. Toutefois, l'instabilité de la demande de monnaie et les innovations dans les modes de paiement compromirent le succès de cette initiative qui procédait de la meilleure intention. Cette stratégie fut abandonnée en 1982. Depuis lors, la Banque du Canada essaie de maîtriser l'évolution des cours du change en vue de réduire le taux d'inflation.

De 1983 à 1985, la baisse du dollar canadien par rapport à la monnaie américaine a pu se justifier par la forte appréciation de cette dernière relativement aux monnaies européenne et japonaise et aussi par la détérioration sensible des termes d'échange canadiens de 1984 à 1986. Le cours du dollar canadien atteignit son plus bas en février 1986, soit 0,69 $US. Depuis lors, le redressement des prix des matières premières exportées et un contexte politique interne plus serein ont permis une remontée significative de la monnaie canadienne. En 1987 et 1988, environ la moitié du terrain perdu depuis 1976 fut récupéré. L'amélioration des termes d'échange fit que cette revalorisation du dollar canadien n'enraya pas l'expansion de l'emploi, de la production et des profits d'entreprise. Elle contribua sensiblement à empêcher une recrudescence de l'inflation.

Le Traité canado-américain de libre-échange, en vigueur depuis le 1er janvier 1989, crée un contexte nouveau pour la politique monétaire canadienne. Bien que cet accord ne comporte pas d'engagement monétaire explicite, il ne fait pas de doute que son bon fonctionnement présuppose de la part du Canada une politique des changes qui n'enfreigne pas les normes de la compétitivité réelle. Toute tentative de la part des autorités canadiennes d'utiliser la Banque du Canada pour se donner des avantages anormaux dans la concurrence nord-américaine ne manquerait pas de susciter des griefs de la part de concurrents aux États-Unis. Cet accord pourrait donc constituer un rempart supplémentaire contre les forces, politiques ou autres, qui poussent à la dépréciation du dollar canadien. L'intégration monétaire entre les États-Unis et le Canada, effective depuis toujours, ne manquera pas de s'accentuer encore au cours des années à venir.

LE CANADA ET LE FONDS MONÉTAIRE INTERNATIONAL

La Deuxième Guerre mondiale engendra une institutionnalisation de la coopération internationale sur divers plans. Les relations monétaires ont fait l'objet de l'accord de Bretton Woods, en juillet 1944. Un code de règles fut convenu et un fonds fut créé afin d'aider les membres à s'y conformer. La norme première fut la stabilité des changes et la liberté des échanges[6].

Intermédiaire naturel entre le Royaume-Uni et les États-Unis, le Canada fut l'un des trois principaux négociateurs à Bretton Woods. Il soumit d'ailleurs ses propres propositions pour l'organisation d'une union monétaire internationale[7]. À cheval sur deux empires commerciaux et financiers, le Canada a un intérêt vital à la sauvegarde d'un ordre international libre et stable.

En 1961, le Canada participa aux Accords généraux d'emprunt entre le FMI et ses dix membres les plus riches. À ce titre, le Canada a pu occuper une place privilégiée dans les négociations relatives aux réformes du système qui se sont poursuivies depuis. Mais comment le Canada joua-t-il le jeu de Bretton Woods? Bien que membre influent du FMI, le Canada contrevint à la règle fondamentale souscrite à Bretton Woods, celle de la rigidité des changes, pendant de longues périodes. Il fut le premier à faire la preuve pratique de l'illusion fondamentale qui prévalut à Bretton Woods, celle du pouvoir effectif d'une institution administrative intergouvernementale sur la souveraineté des États.

Bien que la désagrégation de l'ordre institué à Bretton Woods ne devint manifeste qu'après le 15 août 1971, le FMI fut, dès ses débuts, confronté à une contestation implicite de ses statuts. Le premier pays membre qui tenta de démontrer l'inapplicabilité à son cas du principe de la parité fixe fut le Mexique en 1948. Il eut à faire face à une rigueur implacable de la part de la direction du Fonds[8].

Lorsque, le 19 septembre 1949, la Belgique sollicita l'autorisation du Fonds d'abandonner la parité fixe de sa monnaie et de laisser flotter celle-ci en attendant qu'une nouvelle parité puisse être établie, l'attitude du Fonds semblait s'être assouplie, bien que les statuts ne permissent pas une approbation. Ce fut le représentant du Canada (M. L. Rasminsky) qui eut, en l'occurrence, la position la plus intransigeante. Il exprima son inquiétude de voir que l'attitude des directeurs du Fonds avait changé à l'égard de changes fluctuants. La Belgique n'insista pas et fixa bientôt une nouvelle parité[9].

En septembre 1950, Rasminsky informa le FMI de la décision du gouvernement canadien de suspendre la parité du dollar canadien et de laisser flotter celui-ci sur le marché. L'afflux spéculatif de capitaux à court terme au Canada était tel que seul le flottement de la monnaie serait à même de l'endiguer. Malgré les objections de la direction du Fonds, liée par l'esprit et la lettre des Statuts, le gouvernement canadien fit prévaloir son point de vue, et cela pendant près de douze ans. Dans sa défense contre les objections renouvelées de la direction du FMI, le Canada tenta de démontrer la singularité de son problème: toute fixité de la parité créerait une situation instable qui donnerait lieu à des mouvements excessifs de capitaux à court terme, dans un sens ou dans l'autre. Par ailleurs, sous un régime de changes flexibles, la spéculation agit dans le sens de la stabilité. Comme le flottement du dollar canadien a permis l'élimination de toutes les restrictions aux transactions extérieures du Canada, l'objectif principal du FMI aurait été promu, d'autant plus qu'avec le passage du temps, le dollar canadien a fait preuve d'une stabilité remarquable par rapport au dollar américain.

Les difficultés de la politique économique canadienne à partir de 1958, ainsi que les répercussions sur le marché des changes, affaiblirent la position du Canada face aux objections institutionnelles du FMI à l'égard de la flexibilité des changes. Les autorités canadiennes cédèrent finalement le 2 mai 1962 en établissant une nouvelle parité.

Le retour du Canada à l'orthodoxie de Bretton Woods ne devait être que transitoire. Le 31 mai 1970, le gouvernement canadien annonça une nouvelle suspension de la parité de la monnaie. Ce fut le prélude à la désagrégation complète du système érigé à Bretton Woods. En mai 1971, le mark allemand et le florin des Pays-Bas ne purent être maintenus à leurs valeurs officielles. Le 15 août 1971, ce fut le dollar américain qui leva l'ancre. Les tentatives qui suivirent de restaurer le carcan des parités fixes firent toutes long feu, et le Fonds monétaire international ne put que s'en accommoder, malgré la rigueur de ses statuts.

CONCLUSION: LES LEÇONS DE L'EXPÉRIENCE CANADIENNE

1. La constante la plus remarquable qui se dégage de l'histoire monétaire canadienne depuis 1919 est la quasi-impossibilité pour le Canada d'adhérer à un régime de changes à parités fixes. Ceci fut la principale originalité du régime canadien jusqu'à ce que le flottement des monnaies ne se généralise, en 1973. À cet égard, l'expérience canadienne fut prémonitoire.

2. Du fait que le régime des parités fixes se soit révélé un carcan contre nature pour le Canada, il ne suit pas que le cours du dollar canadien doive fluctuer d'une manière erratique ou quelconque sur le marché des changes. Il est hautement significatif que les périodes de flottement aient été marquées d'une stabilité remarquable. Depuis 1976, ceci est devenu moins évident. Le fléchissement prononcé d'environ 20 % en deux ans, de 1976 à 1978, fut la conséquence d'une politique trop timorée de la Banque du Canada dans un contexte international instable et des circonstances politiques internes défavorables.

3. L'impossibilité du maintien prolongé d'une parité fixe à l'égard du dollar américain, ainsi que la tendance à maintenir une certaine stabilité en ter-

mes de cette monnaie en régime de flottement, découlent de deux caractéristiques propres de l'économie canadienne: son intégration de fait aux
marchés commerciaux et financiers des États-Unis et sa sujétion à un
pouvoir politique distinct qui se veut autonome. Cette volonté d'indépendance se manifeste sur différents plans, mais elle est restreinte par les
nécessités économiques, c'est-à-dire par le souci de réduire le coût de
cette autonomie. Lorsque l'orientation, ou la désorientation, des politiques
nationales, que ce soit sur le plan constitutionnel ou celui de l'énergie,
suscitent des réflexes défavorables dans le monde des affaires, au Canada
et à l'étranger, le marché des changes en est perturbé, et l'habileté tactique de l'autorité monétaire est mise à l'épreuve. En réduisant la marge de
manœuvre des autorités politiques dans le domaine économique, l'Accord
de libre-échange avec les États-Unis devrait contribuer à intégrer encore
davantage les marchés financiers et les politiques monétaires des deux
pays. Le dollar canadien devrait être ainsi mieux à l'abri de perturbations
politiques fortuites, et sa stabilité devrait être mieux assurée.

4. Au sein du Fonds monétaire international, le Canada, par nécessité ou
lucidité, montra maintes fois la voie à la solution raisonnable de problèmes
importants. Dès 1950, il parvint à faire accepter un régime particulier de
flexibilité relativement stable de sa politique des changes. Il anticipa ainsi
une évolution qui devint inéluctable à l'échelle du monde à partir de 1973.
Grâce au pragmatisme relativement éclairé dont il a longtemps fait preuve,
le Canada a fourni un exemple d'adaptation souple et judicieuse d'une
économie nationale à un contexte international de plus en plus intégré.

NOTES

1. Foreign Exchange Control Board, *Report to the Minister of Finance*, Ottawa, mars 1946, p. 20-21.

2. *Ibidem*, p. 30.

3. S.A. Shepherd, *Foreign Exchange and Foreign Trade in Canada*, 4ᵉ éd., Toronto, University of Toronto Press, 1923, p. 247.

4. R.E. Caves et G.L. Reuber, *Canadian Economic Policy and the Impact of International Capital Flows*, Toronto, University of Toronto Press, 1969, p. 76.

5. R. Dehem, «Living Beyond the Short Run», *The Canadian Journal of Economics*, VII, n° 4, 1974, p. 543-557.

6. Voir R. Dehem, *De l'étalon-sterling à l'étalon-dollar*, Paris, Calmann-Lévy, 1972, p. 139-153.

7. J.K. Horsefield, «Tentative Proposals of Canadian Experts for an International Exchange Union» (12 juillet 1943), *The International Monetary Fund, 1945-1965*, III, *Documents*, Washington, D.C., 1969, p. 103-118.

8. J.K. Horsefield et M.G. de Vries, *The International Monetary Fund, 1945-1965*, vol. II: *Analysis*, Washington, D.C., 1969, p. 153-154.

9. *Ibidem*, p. 155-156.

BIBLIOGRAPHIE

BANQUE DU CANADA. *Rapports annuels.*

CAVES, R.E. et REUBER, G.L. *Canadian Economic Policy and the Impact of International Capital Flows,* Toronto, University of Toronto Press, 1969.

CAVES, R.E. et REUVER, G.L. *Capital Transfers and Economic Policy: Canada, 1951-1962,* Cambridge, Mass., Harvard University Press, 1971.

COURCHENE, T.J. *Money, Inflation and the Bank of Canada,* Montréal, C.D. Howe Research Institute, 1976.

DEHEM, R. *De l'étalon-sterling à l'étalon-dollar,* Paris, Calmann-Lévy, 1972.

DEHEM, R. «Living Beyond the Short Run», *The Canadian Journal of Economics,* vol. VII, n° 4, 1974, p. 543-557.

FOREIGN EXCHANGE CONTROL BOARD. *Report to the Minister of Finance,* Ottawa, 1946.

HORSEFIELD, J.R. «Tentative Proposals of Canadian Experts for an International Exchange Union» (12 juillet 1943), *The International Monetary Fund, 1945-1965,* vol. III: *Documents,* Washington, D.C., 1969.

HORSEFIELD, J.R. et DE VRIES, M.G. *The International Monetary Fund, 1945-1965,* vol. II: *Analysis,* Washington, D.C., 1969.

SHEPHERD, S.A. *Foreign Exchange and Foreign Trade in Canada,* 4ᵉ éd., Toronto, University of Toronto Press, 1973.

STOKES, M.C. *The Bank of Canada,* Toronto, Macmillan, 1939.

WONNACOTT, P. *The Canadian Dollar, 1948-1962,* Toronto, University of Toronto Press, 1965.

WONNACOTT, P. *The Floating Canadian Dollar,* Washington, D.C., The American Enterprise Institute, 1972.

23

The Politics of Canadian Aid

Roger Ehrhardt
North-South Institute

INTRODUCTION

> *We think it is time to say simply that* aid is
> to aid. *Its purpose is to promote human
> and economic development and alleviate suffering*[1].

It may strike us as odd that the above words were penned, not in 1950 when Canada's aid program officially got underway, but 30 years thereafter, in 1980, by the seven members of the Parliamentary Task Force on North-South Relations. That these MPs felt compelled to write in such direct terms about the objectives of the aid program must tell us something about the program – that its purpose has not been solely to aid.

In fact, throughout its 35-year history, this program has, at various times and with varying degrees of intensity, been expected to serve four masters: development objectives, foreign policy objectives, economic objectives and domestic political objectives. Each set of objectives has left its mark on the program and each, in part because of the competing aims of the others, has not been well served. And this mingling of conflicting and complementary objectives has significantly influenced the program and its operations – the structure of the program and the regulations that govern it; the choice of channels through which aid is disbursed and the selection of countries which receive it; and the quantity and quality of the aid itself.

This article will attempt to illustrate the compromises that have been forced upon the aid program by these competing objectives and by those groups within and outside government who identify with each of them. In so doing it will examine the organizational setting of the program, its operations and its public information approach. But first, each of the aforementioned objectives will be discussed in greater detail.

Foreign Policy Objectives

Development assistance has always been perceived as just another tool in the foreign policy practitioner's kit and has thus been expected to contribute to foreign policy goals – whether they be the broad goals of perservering peace and security and generating goodwill towards Canada or more narrow ones such as establishing a Canadian «presence» in certain countries or showing our allies that Canada is willing to share in the «burden» of aiding the Third World.

The broad foreign policy goals are clearly consistent with an effective aid program based on development objectives, but the contribution of aid to peace or goodwill should not be overstated. First, while the prospects for peace would improve if gross disparities among nations were removed, the potential for conflict would still remain. And second, although an aid program can help set the tone of a relationship between countries, it is only one aspect, and in many cases a relatively minor one, of this relationship. Therefore, it can serve only to complement, or in some cases moderate, the images the Third World receives of Canada through other interactions[2].

The more narrow foreign policy goals, however, may conflict with development objectives. The desire to «establish a Canadian presence» throughout the world has led to an aid program with disbursements in over 90 countries, whereas a more concentrated effort would be more conducive to effective programming. And the wish to «burden share» has, at times, prompted an over-emphasis on the quantity of disbursements without the requisite attention being paid to their quality.

In sum, there is no trade-off required between broad long-term foreign policy objectives and development objectives, but when more specific foreign policy goals come to the fore, development goals may suffer.

Domestic Political Objectives

The key Canadian domestic political objective of the last two decades – the preservation of national unity – has been reflected in most actions by the government and has influenced many government programs, including the aid program. This program has been employed as a means of providing opportunity for French-speaking Canadians within the federal bureaucracy, of internationally reinforcing the bilingual nature of the country, and at the same time, of combatting the Québec Government's forays into foreign relations and reasserting the primacy of the Federal Government in this realm. One of the main consequences of this was an expansion of the aid program into Francophone Africa in the mid-1960s.

Other domestic political objectives can also affect the aid program. Like most government programs, it is subject to the political and economic climate of the country and to the government's response to this climate. For example, its budget presents an easy target for a government eager to show the populace that it is serious about cutting governement spending. On the other hand, aid is also a relatively non-controversial way (especially when compared to other measures such as decreasing tariff and non-tariff protection for Canadian textile, clothing and footwear manufacturers) for the government to illustrate its concern for the Third World. The result has been a push and pull on the aid budget and periods of expansion and contraction in the program.

Economic Objectives

In discussing economic objectives, it is important to distinguish between those that are immediate – the sale of Canadian goods and services – and those that are longer term – the development of export market potential. These two are not necessarily complementary; nor are their effects on the aid program identical.

A common justification for aid (and one that is endorsed by many Canadian Government officials and officials of other donor governments) is that it provides immediate returns to the donor's economy. Approximately 60 % of the aid funds disbursed by Canada are returned to it for goods and services purchased under the tying conditions of the program, thus increasing Canada's exports and leading to employment growth[3]. In effect, aid is an export and (indirectly) an employment subsidy.

Doubts have been raised about the effectiveness of using aid funds to meet these short-term economic objectives, especially when programs focused more clearly on subsidizing exports or on increasing employment already exist. Representing less than 0,5 % of Canada's GNP, the aid program obviously has limited resources to devote to the achievement of these goals. In addition, this emphasis on short-term gain may beget long-term pain. If goods and services supplied through the aid program are uncompetitive or if the follow-up and maintenance on them is poor, the reputation of all Canadian exporters may be tarnished – no future un*subsidized* sales are likely to follow. If, on the other hand, Canadian goods are competitive, Canadian firms will win their fair share of contracts, without tying their exports to aid funds[4]. Where subsidies to keep financing competitive are required, or where support to help identify markets is necessary, other instruments of government are available[5].

Canada's long-term export potential in the Third World depends mainly on the economic development of these countries and on the competitiveness and aggressiveness of Canadian exporters; it is not contingent upon aid tying. Hence, as was the case with foreign policy objectives, an effective development-oriented aid program is not inconsistent with economic objectives.

Development Objectives

Although the precise meaning of the term has changed with the evolution of development thinking over the years, development – whatever the popular definition of the day – has remained as a primary goal of the aid program. Much of the public support for the program has been based on this perceived goal of helping the poorest peoples of the world; continued support for it may be hinged on its ability to meet this goal.

What has been lacking in the attention given to this objective by the public is an appreciation of what the true developmental contribution of aid can be: its potential has been much overstated. For most developing countries, total aid flows pale in significance when compared to the domestic resources that can be harnessed for development; in these countries aid can only supplement domestic efforts[6]. Even in terms of the development input of donor countries, aid its marginal, since other actions by these countries – trade, migration, food and investment policies, for example – can have a far greater impact on the Third World.

Another commonly-held perception of aid (and of development itself) is that quick results are possible. But development is a complex and long-term process, so the contribution of aid to this process must be seen in the proper perspective and the proper time frame. Even in the poorest countries where aid funds can be critical to development[7], these funds can serve only to catalyze domestic development efforts. The ultimate achievements or lack thereof in these countries will still depend on their own efforts and on their non-aid interaction with the industrialized world.

In this section, an attempt has been made to place the aid program in its proper context; to illustrate how its potential contribution to any of the four sets of objectives thrust upon it is limited; and to show that emphasis on the development objectives – recognizing the long-term nature of this objective – is consistent with broad long-term political and economic objectives. The balance of the article will show how the interplay among the four objectives has forced trade-offs on the aid program that have detoured it from its development path.

CANADA'S AID PROGRAM: THE ORGANIZATION SETTING

From its earliest incarnation and through organizational changes that follow-ed, Canada's aid program has consistently been in an unenviable position within the federal bureaucracy, subordinate to three strong departments – External Affairs, Finance and Industry, and Trade and Commerce. Throughout the program's first decade – to 1960 – it was housed in the Department of Trade and Commerce, which guided its day-to-day administration, while its policies were constructed by an inter-departmental group chaired by External Affairs[8]. Other members of this group were Finance, Trade and Commerce and the Bank of Canada.

In 1960, the first major organizational shuffle occured – a change that signal-led recognition of the aid program as an integral part of foreign policy. An External Aid Office was created, with its head reporting directly to the Secretary of State for External Affairs, and a new interdepartmental group – the External Aid Board – was established to handle policy questions.

Since that date, the position of the aid program within the bureaucracy has changed relatively little. In 1968, a new body – the Canadian International Develop-ment Agency – was formed, but its President (whose status is equivalent to that of a Deputy Minister) still reports to the Minister of External Affairs and External still perceives itself as the «parent» Department.

The interdepartmental policy-making structure has also undergone little transformation. Names of the committees have changed, some committees have fallen out of favour, others risen in popularity, and the make-up of them has expanded to include many other actors, representing new and varied interests. Yet the basic trends established as early as 1950 remain. The policies guiding the aid program continue to be the subject of interdepartmental consultation and the lead depart-ments are, as before, External Affairs, Finance and Industry, and Trade and Com-merce. CIDA, without the status of a full department, has few chips with which to bargain in these interdepartmental negotiations. Thus, the policies that govern the aid program are not based solely, or even mainly, on development objectives – for which CIDA with its weak status is the spokesman, but on economic and political objectives – the interests represented by the three lead departments.

Moreover, while CIDA's influence in aid policy-making is slight, its impact on non-aid development policies is miniscule. These North-South issues, which despite the best efforts of the developing countries attracted little attention prior to 1974, are seen to fall outside the purview of CIDA. External Affairs views itself as representing the Third World perspective on these broader issues and both ITC and Finance see such matters as residing even more distinctly than aid questions within their policy realm.

Thus, we have a development agency (in name at least) whose mandate is essentially restricted to aid issues and whose power, even on these matters, is severly limited. One need look no farther than the *Strategy for International Development Cooperation 1975-1980* and the obvious differences between its «analysis» and «policies» sections to find an illustration of CIDA's limited influence. The former section of this interdepartmentally-prepared document gives considerable attention to non-aid issues in relations between the North and the South and presents a short but perceptive analysis of the development environment. By contrast, the «policies» section, in its 21 points, devotes most attention to aid policies, essentially ignoring the non-aid thrust of the «analysis». Apparently the senior departments, which were content to let CIDA take the lead in preparing the «analysis», dug in their heels when it came to the policies themselves. The result was a set of *aid* priorities which bore slight resemblance to the *development* analysis.

The position of CIDA within the bureaucracy is not only evident in policy decisions, it is also clear from the environment within which the Agency is forced to operate. Because the aid program must serve so many of the government's objectives, with no special consideration given to the difficulties associated with attempting to fulfill development objectives in countries miles from Canada's borders, it is expected to function within the same regulations imposed on other government operations. It is subject to Treasury Board financial controls and guidelines on evaluation, Public Service Commission regulations on employment, Department of Supply and Services procurement rules, and External Affairs foreign service control; it must submit to surveillance by the Auditor-General and the Comptroller-General; and its projects must be vetted through a lengthy selection process and finally submitted to the Secretary of State for External Affairs and the Treasury Board for approval[9].

These regulations, which have become more onerous in the latter part of the 1970s due to increased government emphasis on accountability and «value of money», have turned CIDA officials into form fillers, functioning with a government regulatory environment more suited to domestic than to international programs. In so doing, they have placed added pressures on CIDA officers – pressures which may limit the developmental effectiveness of the Agency. Moreover, these regulations also bring other departments – Supply and Services, for example – directly into aid projects without holding them as publicly accountable for their performance as is CIDA.

CANADA'S AID PROGRAM: OPERATIONS

Does CIDA's subordinate position with the bureaucracy and the push and pull exerted on it by other government departments have a significant impact on the direction and performance of the program? This section will address this question by examining Canada's program from a variety of criteria: its goals; the distribution of funds among aid channels; the selection of recipient countries and the allocation and concentration among them; planning and administration; the conditions attached to aid; and the quantity of aid.

Goals

The stated goals of the Canadian aid program have for the most part paralleled or followed the trends in development thinking in the industrialized countries. As the economic growth theory and the belief that the benefits of growth would «trickle down» to the poorest segments of the population fell into disfavor internationally and were replaced by concerns about the distribution of these benefits and by an emphasis on the basic human needs of the poorest (food, shelter, water, health, education), Canada followed suit. In the 1975-1980 Strategy, the focus on basic needs was clearly enunciated:

> The Canadian International Development Agency will focus its assistance to a greater extent on the most crucial aspects of development – food production and distribution; rural development; education and training; public health and demography; and shelter and energy[10].

Canada's stated intentions are basically beyond reproach and are consistent at least with the mainstream of Western development thinking. But how does the performance of the Agency compare to these intentions? Over the initial five-year period of the Strategy, the record was not good. As Table 1 illustrates at the end of this chapter, the commitments to these «crucial» sectors did not grow significantly during the latter part of the 1970s. In the period 1977-1980, the proportion of commitments to agriculture and rural development (including fertilizer) grew slightly from 12,2 to 14,6 %; those to education, health and social infrastructure fell from 7,8 to 5,1 %; and those to food aid remained relatively steady at just over 11 %[11]. Since 1980, however, there has been a considerable shift in expenditure. Aid to agriculture now accounts for close to one-third of Canadian bilateral aid disbursements.

Channels

Canadian aid is disbursed through three main channels – bilateral, multilateral and special programs; each with its own operational strengths and weaknesses. Bilateral or direct government-to-government aid, which goes to over 90 countries, is the most visible form of Canadian aid and the one that conforms most closely to Canadian developmental objectives. It is also subject to the plethora of regulations that govern governmental expenditure and is most susceptible to the influence of other Canadian economic and political objectives.

Canadian multilateral aid flows to a variety of multilateral institutions including, in order of the size of Canada's contribution: the International Development Association of the World Bank Group, the World Food Program (food aid), the Asian Development Bank, the United Nations Development Program, the Interamerican Development Bank and the African Development Bank, plus a host of other UN agencies, Commonwealth and Francophone institutions, and refugee and relief programs. These multilateral programs are generally free from the conditions (such as tied procurement) attached to bilateral aid and they also enable Canada to make a contribution in particular sectors (health and population, for example) in which Canadian expertise is quite scarce. However, the weighted voting structure in the World Bank and the regional development banks affords the major donors the opportunity to exert considerable control over their operations.

The much smaller special programs channel supports the efforts of Canadian and international non-governmental organizations (through the NGO and the International NGO divisions); encourages the involvement of Canadian cooperatives, unions and educational institutions (the Institutional Cooperation and Development Services Division); fosters private sector activity (the Industrial Cooperation Division); and, in conjunction with provincial governments, encourages activity in the agricultural sector (the Voluntary Agricultural Development Assistance Program). Of these, support to Canadian NGOs and institutions is most important – in 1983-1984, over $177 million were disbursed through these channels in part matching funds raised privately by the NGOs[12].

The Canadian NGOs involved in development activities have distinct advantages over other aid channels in that they are free from government regulations and can operate on a smaller, more personal scale. But few of them have the capability of disbursing large sums of aid money and are obviously subject to the internal pressures of their own organizations.

In a somewhat special category, since it operates separately from CIDA and in a considerably different fashion, is the International Development Research Centre (IDRC). Created in 1970 «to support research designed to adopt science and technology to the needs of developing countries»[13], this public corporation, which receives a grant from Parliament each year, administers its own efforts through an International Board of Governors. Despite its relatively small budget – total disbursements in 1983-1984 were $64 million, it has a widespread and positive reputation. And it has so far been relatively free from interference by other Canadian interests[14].

Because a good case can be made for the utility of each of these channels, the allocation of aid funds among them (and particularly between bilateral and multilateral which, with food aid, represent nearly 90 % of disbursements) becomes an important question for the Government, a question that has seldom been dealt with explicitly during the 35 years of the aid program's history.

Canada's earliest aid contributions, administered by the Department of Finance, were multilateral grant funds to United Nations specialized agencies. But bilateral programs soon became dominant, accounting for nearly 80 % of all appropriations during the period 1950 to March 31, 1964.

In this latter year, two important events took place that helped shape the aid program by bringing new attention to other aid channels. First, the Government gave its first substantial support to a non-governmental organization when it flew 150 CUSO volunteers abroad, and followed this up the next year by promising a financial grant to the same organization[15]. Second, Canada agreed to provide $19 million per year to the Interamerican Development Bank for loans to Latin American countries – subject to final Canadian approval and with procurement bidding restricted to Canadian suppliers of goods and services[16]. That this was done before a full bilateral program was established in Latin America was recognition that multilateral aid could also fulfill political and economic objectives.

From this point until 1975, each of the three channels through which Canadian aid is disbursed continued to expand as the program itself grew; there was no pre-planned mix of channels. In the 1975-1980 Strategy, however, a belated attempt was made to make the allocation process more rational.

In this document, the principle of «using a variety of means to transfer resources» was endorsed and percentage targets noted. Unfortunately, there has been so much confusion about the targets – whether certain categories do or do not include food aid, where the IDRC is to be grouped – that they proved almost meaningless. And while it is difficult to argue with the principle of diversity, no justification for the targets was given. Shortly thereafter, any meaning that may have resided in the targets was lost, as unspent allocations built up. To help reduce this backlog, more funds were allocated to the multilateral channel which grew considerably in 1976-1977, without any specific policy choices being made[17].

During the last years of the 1970s, however, the multilateral side of the program came under much pressure, both from «influence-minded» External Affairs officers who decried the anonymity of multilateral contributions, and from Industry, Trade and Commerce officials and the business interests they represent who felt that Canada was not getting an adequate return, in terms of the purchases of Canadian goods and services, on these contributions. Interdepartmentally, only Finance consistently backed multilateral institutions. Even in CIDA, the voices in support of multilateral efforts were few in number compared to those with a vested interest in bilateral activities. It therefore came as no surprise to most observers when, in early 1981, the Secretary of State for External Affairs announced Canada's new policy of giving greater emphasis to bilateral relations and included development assistance among the political instruments to be deployed to implement the policy[18]. The decision to make this shift was unfortunately based on purely economic and political consideration without any evaluation of the development effectiveness of either channel[19]. In the meantime, disbursements through the Special Programs Branch have grown steadily over 11 %, the IDRC share has remained relatively steady at 3 %, and an allocation of 4 % of ODA has been made to Petro Canada International Assistance Cooperation.

On balance, there are both positive and negative aspects to the allocation decisions that have been taken by Canada. On the plus side, innovative programs have been implemented through the Special Programs Branch and the IDRC (though combined they account for less that 15 % of total ODA disbursements), and Canada has been a substantial contributor to numerous multilateral organizations. On the minus side, political and economic objectives have often been predominant in decisions to alter the proportions being disbursed through each channel.

Countries[20]

From a program originally directed to the Commonwealth countries of Asia, the Canadian bilateral aid program has grown to one spread to all corners of the world. In 1983-1984, Canadian bilateral aid was disbursed to over 90 countries.

In the 1950s, the focus was the Commonwealth, with the Colombo Plan (1950), the Commonwealth Caribbean Special Assistance Program (1958), and the Special Commonwealth African Aid Program (1960). This Commonwealth specific vision was broadened to Latin America in 1964 when funds were allocated to the Interamerican Development Bank. But this region was not granted a full bilateral program until 1973 when ITC pressure to give greater support to middle-income countries won the day[21].

Of greater significance in the 1960s, was the growth in disbursements to Francophone Africa: from $300 000 in 1963-1964 to $4 million the following year, and, after the 1968 Chevrier Mission, from $12 million in 1967-1968 to $22,1 million the next year[22]. This foray into Francophone Africa is the most obvious and the most significant example of domestic political objectives permeating the aid program[23].

Canada's bilateral program is not as unconcentrated as it first appears, however. Disbursements to the 34 largest recipients, which each received over $5 million, and to the Sahel regional program, accounted for $563,9 million or 83 % of total government-to-government disbursements in 1983-1984 (see Table 3). Another 19 countries each received between $1 million and $5 million and the balance (50) received less than $1 million each. Thus, some concentration of effort does exist, but the far-flung nature of the program still must place a burden on the manpower of the Agency and on Canadian skills and expertise.

This clearly illustrates the trade-off between developmental and political objectives. Concern for the manageability of the program, and ultimately its effectiveness, should lead to a program concentrated in fewer countries. But the political need for a Canadian «presence» leads in the opposite direction, that is, to more countries. The upshot is that some 50 countries receive less than $1 million each – a sum more likely to fulfill political than developmental goals.

On other yardsticks of concentration, Canada measures up quite well. In 1983-1984, 37 % of government-to-government assistance went to the 36 least developed countries. Canada was also instrumental in achieving a 1981 consensus among the OECD donors to commit 0,15 % of GNP to the LLDCs.

Nevertheless, there are also some anomalies among the major recipients of Canadian aid which suggest that other than development objectives are at play. For example, middle-income countries such as Algeria, Tunisia, Thailand and Peru are in this group. And with the new policy of bilateralism, there is concern being expressed that more such countries will find their way into this group displacing poorer countries and thus reducing the percentage of funds going to the poorest. Burma has already been a casualty of this process.

Another example of the growing interest in the middle-income countries and an indication that this interest has spread to the Special Programs Branch is the very small, but rapidly growing, Industrial Cooperation Division of this Branch, which is attempting to marry the interests of Canadian private industry to those of the middle-income countries. This program entails a transfer of resources away from the poorest countries who need them most, but can offer few short-term business opportunities.

Planning and Administration

One of the features of the aid program that officials often point to proudly is its low administrative cost – about 5 % of the total budget. This has been achieved by a number of sacrifices that have not been without their costs in terms of the development performance of the Agency; indeed, they have been false savings. To keep administrative costs low, less that 100 of the more than 1 000 CIDA employees are posted abroad[24]; travel budgets are so limited that desk officers spend an average of eleven months in Hull to each one abroad; and a high disbursement/employee ratio is maintained.

The upshot is that those officers charged with the planning and administration of projects are often unable to remain fully knowledgeable about the recipient countries. They spend the bulk of their time in Hull and, due to the heavy administrative burden placed on them, have little time to devote to serious study of the recipients and their problems. Moreover, the few CIDA officers that are in the field have little input into the planning process; they tend to be inundated by the other duties they must fulfill[25].

As a result, most planning is carried out in Hull, with varying degrees of input from consultants who make reconnaissance field trips and from the host countries themselves. And there is a natural tendency to shy away from projets in the critical sectors noted above that generally require greater administrative care. Infrastructural projects, food, and commodity aid are more conducive to minimal administrative resources[26].

Until some modification is made to the present system to allow more CIDA officers to be posted to Canadian missions, or to enable more officers to be stationed abroad without being directly attached to the mission, or to facilitate the hiring of more locally-engaged staff by the mission, planning will not take place in the most appropriate venue – the recipient country – and the management of the program will suffer.

Conditionality

The main condition imposed on Canadian bilateral aid, a condition that has been with us almost as long as the program itself, is the tying of aid to the purchases of goods and services in Canada. Labelled a «red herring» by a former Secretary of State for External Affairs[27], tying was applied without exception until 1970; since then, CIDA has had the authority to untie up to 20 % of its bilateral disbursements[28].

Despite the opinion of the Secretary of State, aid tying has not been without its detractors. The main arguments against tying can be broken down into three categories: increased costs to recipients, distortions in emphasis within the program, and decreased flexibility to support local costs in the recipient countries.

Calculating or estimating the added costs to the recipients from aid tying is not a simple task, but most studies suggest that tying adds at least 20 % to the costs of projects[29]. Unfortunately, these studies are now quite dated and their results may not be applicable to the current economic situation. There is no reason to doubt, though, that procurement bidding restricted to the producers of only one country does not lead to the most efficient allocation of funds.

A more critical factor than the cost element is the distortion in the programs of donors caused by aid tying. Programs are skewed towards those sectors in which the donors are capable of producing goods and services for use in the program. And though some effort is made to match these capabilities with the needs of recipients, the tail is obviously wagging the dog. In part, this explains why Canada's disbursements have been high in infrastructure, in commodities and food aid, and low in agricultural production, public health, and education and training. These latter «crucial aspects or problems of development» require substantial amounts of untied funds; the former can often be nearly totally tied. (The relative shortage of Canadian expertise in tropical agriculture and health reinforces this tendency.)

Aid tying causes distortions within the recipient countries as well. It is generally easier to get donor approval for projects with donor sale potential than it is for projects with high local cost components[30]. And tied-aid projects tend to be import intensive, and ignore local production possibilities. Thus, recipient priorities are perverted.

The local costs associated with most projects can also present difficulties, especially for the poorest countries who may not have adequate resources to cover such costs if donors do not contribute to them. Breakdowns at the recipient end often result as equipment is poorly maintained, needed repairs are left undone and the necessary counterpart personnel are not kept in place. Donor reluctance to cover such costs, in part because of tying constraints, encourages poor maintenance and repair. Recipient countries prefer to defer maintenance and repair costs – for which they must pay – until the equipment is in such a poor state that it must be replaced – with some donor supplying it through tied aid funds.

The common arguments in support of the tying policy – voiced by the business community and their representatives – are that tying helps to build future export markets for Canada and that our aid funds should not be used to enrich the producers in other donor countries.

The former argument, essentially that «trade follows tied aid», seems to assume that uncompetitive export goods that must now be subsidized through the aid program will somehow magically become competitive at some future date when Third World countries – no longer reliant on aid – purchase what costs them least. In the meantime, Canada's commercial reputation in developing countries is «tied» to these uncompetitive exports[31].

The second line of reasoning seems to imply that Canada is a do-gooder among the donor group, that every other country accepts tying as a natural condition of aid. In fact, as Table 4 shows, Canada has one of the poorest records on this «quality criterion». Canada's attitude seems «mean-spirited», not «boy scoutish».

That the opposition to any further untying goes beyond this latter «why support other industrial countries' exporters» argument is best illustrated by the absolute failure of the Government to meet point 14 of the *Strategy* :

> The Government will liberalize the CIDA procurement regulations by immediately untying its bilateral development loans so that developing countries would be eligible to compete for contracts; it will consider untying to other donor countries in selected cases where this can demonstrably bring significant results to the development program[32].

It initially appeared that some progress would be made on this commitment[33], but in the face of concerns about the state of the Canadian economy and pressure from Canadian industry, from the Canadian Export Association, and from the Department of Industry, Trade and Commerce, the resolve to implement it disappeared[34]. In fact, by late 1977, even the President of CIDA was exhorting his colleagues to consider that Canadian economic conditions:

> require that CIDA strive to ensure that its activities maintain or generate employment and economic benefits in our own country[35].

By the end of 1977 it was obvious that even partial-untying would not occur; the Canadian export community had won its way. Yet within two years, the exporters were pressuring the Government for even more economic return from the aid program.

In the «trade-aid interface» section of the report of the Export Promotion Review Committee, the exporters lamented the «overly philanthropic giveaway approach to aid» taken by CIDA, recommended a reduction in the proportion of Canadian aid funds disbursed through multilateral channels, and called on CIDA to «set aside funds from the bilateral aid budget to enable it to engage in parallel financing with EDC when it is necessary to meet competition»[36]. Despite this self-serving attitude to the aid program, this report was highly regarded and influential in government circles, but criticized elsewhere[37].

Nevertheless, in 1984, the Government met one of the major goals of the Report by announcing the formation of an aid Trade Fund. This Fund, which is to be financed with up to one half of the proposed increases in Canadian development assistance up to 1990, will be used to provide revenues for mixed credit packages with the Export Development Corporation.

Aid tying has become so ingrained that it is now common to find personnel at all levels within CIDA who will defend the practice and few who will push programs with a high untied component[38]. Even the Parliamentary Task Force on North-South Relations, in its December 1980 report, was not able to match the *Strategy* commitment:

> Decisions concerning procurement of goods and services required for aid projects should be made by [CIDA] consistent with development assistance objective. While a significant portion should be procured in Canada, CIDA should be freed from any fixed percentage rule[39].

Canada has also imposed other conditions on the recipients of aid – to establish special committees, to restructure organizations, to set up new institutions, to alter price structures – but never with as much vigor as other bilateral donors or the World Bank. There have been suggestions, however, that Canada will take a more activist or interventionist role in the future.

From the Canadian perspective there may be some justification for such an approach since it is predicated on a concern for the effectiveness of the aid program; from the developing country perspective it is interference in domestic policy. It implies that donors know what is best for the recipients (a bold assumption considering the lack of CIDA personnel in these countries), and that development is a process of following instructions. Not only does it limit the «learning-by-doing process», but it can also impose inordinate burdens on the recipients who must attempt to meet the (sometimes conflicting) conditions put forward by a multitude of donors[40].

Aid Quantity

The Government of Canada has never been shy to affirm its support for the official United Nations target for development assistance of 0,7 % of GNP, but it has never set a specific date for attaining this goal, nor has it ever exhibited consistent movement towards it.

Canada's effort in terms of this aid/GNP standard peaked at 0,53 % in 1975-1976, the same year that the St*rategy* reaffirmed the Government's intention to reach the 0,7 % target[41].

Since then, as Table 5 shows, there has been a more or less steady back-sliding, highlighted by budget cuts in 1978-1979 and 1979-1980 and a virtual freeze in 1980-1981 vivid illustrations of the susceptibility of the program to domestic economic conditions and of the possible wanning of traditional public support for the aid effort. Many of the strongest supporters of aid were surprisingly silent during this period. The development-oriented segment of the public, many of whom have come to see the bilateral portion of the aid program as a messenger of commercial interest, may have no longer felt compelled to rise to its defence and those members of the public who harbour unrealistic expectations about the program – prompted in part by CIDA's public relations efforts – may have grown dissatisfied with the apparent lack of results. Whatever the reason, the base of support for the aid program seemed to have been weakened.

The September 1980 pledge by Canada to reach the 0,5 % level by 1985 and to make «best efforts» to attain 0,7 % by the end of the decade was a welcome reversal from the previous three years. Whether these targets will be achieved is an open question though. Support for the program has not been rebuilt and there is still much uncertainty caused by the blurring of aid objectives. As was exemplified by the record of the late 1970s, it takes very little to distract the Government from its aid targets.

CANADA'S AID PROGRAM: PUBLIC INFORMATION

As has been hinted at earlier, CIDA's public information program has not been successful at broadening public awareness and support for aid efforts. Indeed, CIDA's approach to public information can for the most part be characterized as public relations. Press releases on approved projects, annual reports (mainly descriptive and statistical), speeches by senior officials, and a variety of magazines (most short-lived) – all these constitute the major features of the public relations/information program.

Protected by a veil of secrecy (of which only a corner has been lifted by freedom of information legislation), the Agency (like all government departments) has chosen to make public few specific details of its operations, except on occasion to respond to direct criticism of certain projects. Seldom has it attempted to speak of development in long-range terms, to raise some of the difficulties faced by development efforts, or to point out the complex nature of the development process – in short to give the Canadian public a realistic view of what it can and should expect from aid efforts overseas. Only in the new defunt CIDA publication De*velopment Directions* (and there only occasionally) were questions raised about development, and alternative views encouraged and presented. If the Canadian public in general has unrealistic expectations of the aid program and little concrete knowledge about development issues, much of the blame must be shouldered by the Agency itself.

Another important missing ingredient of the information efforts of the Agency is self-criticism. Although this may be due in large part to the fact that until recently there was no formal evaluation system and, in the words of many CIDA officers, «no memory» within the Agency, there still has been a tendency to present the public with the good news only, for fear of tarnishing the Agency's reputation and of decreasing support for it. Thus, the public sees CIDA's mistakes only through the eyes of journalists or the Auditor-General. This has obviously contributed to lack of understanding of the high-risk nature of development expenditure.

Consistent with the muddling of objectives guiding the aid program, information activities have often been tailor-made for specific audiences or specific objectives. In one forum, CIDA or other government officials may defend the aid program in terms of its contribution to employment or short-term economic growth in Canada; in another, they may speak of the Agency's role in alleviating suffering in the Third World. To the high development expectations thrust on the Agency are thus added major domestic economic objectives; and the two blended together, to promote confusion instead of understanding.

One of CIDA's innovative information programs has been the public participation program within the NGO division, which supports groups throughout Canada who are attempting to build a greater public awareness of international development issues. Though relatively small in dollar terms, this program reaches diverse groups across the country – and through them a broad mix of the Canadian public.

In the late 1980s and the 1990s, it is likely that more attention will be given to keeping the Canadian public better informed on development matters. CIDA announced that 1 % of the official development assistance budget will be used to increase public awareness of these issues. The Public Affairs Branch in CIDA has been given a higher profile. And the past CIDA President, Margaret Catley-Carlson, took an aggressive approach to information activities.

CONCLUSION

In the best of circumstances, the planning and implementation of development programs in countries throughout the world – countries with very different needs, resources and skills – would be fraught with problems. (Experience suggests that the task is difficult enough within Canada's borders.) But the aid program does not operate in ideal circumstances; it must function within parameters established by those who do not necessarily give the development objectives of the aid program top billing, or perceive the need for any special dispensation for the difficulty of the development task. And the government Agency that is charged with administering the aid program is itself a weak sister in the bureaucracy, subordinate to more powerful federal departments and subject to the interests they represent.

In both its policies and its operations, therefore, the aid program is much influenced by other government departments and other governmental objectives. If we trace back many of the constraints that impair the program's effectiveness – the lack of field staff, the tying of aid funds, lengthy and cumbersome approval procedures, lack of flexibility in project implementation etc. –, we will find that they are the consequence of compromises that have been forced upon the program.

Although it must be acknowledged that a program which disburses over $1,8 billion of taxpayers money a year cannot operate independently of the Government's financial regulations, the cost to the program, and to development, of compliance with such regulations should be carefully examined. Do stringent controls on CIDA and on the programs it administers really lead to more value per taxpayers dollars? If the development objective of the aid program is valid, then perhaps it is time for the compromises to be forced on other interests and objectives, perhaps it is time to give aid a chance to show that it can aid.

TABLE 1
Canadian Bilateral Aid Commitments by Category (%)

Category	Calendar Year			
	1977	1978	1979	1980
Public Utilities*	28,0	29,8	43,4	11,3
Agriculture (includes rural development and fertilizer)	12,2	13,6	11,0	14,6
Education – Health – Social Infrastructure	7,8	4,7	6,6	5,1
Multisector	0,7	0,3	2,9	13,6
Unspecified	7,8	6,1	9,5	25,1
Other (public administration, tourism, industry, mining, construction)	6,2	4,3	4,6	5,4
Unallocable by sector				
Food aid	33,5**	9,8	11,3	11,6
Goods and services		4,0	2,9	2,8
Emergency and disaster relief	0,4	0,3	0,9	2,8
Debt reorganization	—	24,1	—	—
Other	3,4	3,0	6,9	7,7
Totals	100,0	100,0	100,0	100,0

* Consists of: power production and distribution, transportation, water supply and communication.

** Food aid and goods and services combined.

Sources: Derived from statistics supplied by CIDA to the OECD Development Assistance Centre.

TABLE 2
Canadian Official Development Assistance Disbursements by Program (%)

	1975-6	1976-7	1977-8	1978-9	1979-80	1980-1	1981-2	1982-3	1983-4
Bilateral (excluding food aid)	44,8	34,0	39,6	40,0	41,5	38,9	36,9	32,5	27,7
Multilateral (excluding food aid)	23,8	34,2	30,6	33,7	33,0	30,8	28,9	28,1	29,1
Bilateral food aid	13,2	15,5	13,3	8,0	6,5	5,6	7,9	8,4	9,7
Multilateral food aid	11,4	9,0	8,7	8,4	8,0	8,2	7,6	7,3	8,1
Non-governmental organizations	3,5	3,9	4,2	6,1	6,0	6,9	8,0	9,8	10,8
IDRC	3,2	3,0	3,3	3,0	3,0	3,0	3,1	3,2	3,5
* Other	0,2	0,2	0,3	0,8	2,0	6,6	7,6	9,7	8,8
Petro Canada International Assistance	—	—	—	—	—	—	—	1,0	2,3
	100,0	100,0	100,0	100,0	100,0	100,0	100,0	100,0	100,0

* **Note:** The increase in the «other» category commencing 1980-1981 is due mainly to the reporting of administrative costs as ODA. For the years 1980-1981 through 1983-1984 respectively, 4,8 %, 5,1 %, 5,2 % and 5,1 % of ODA.

Source: CIDA, *Canada and Development Cooperation: Annual Report*, various years.

TABLE 3
Largest Recipients of Canadian
Government to Government Aid
1983-1984
($ Millions)

Bangladesh	107,31	Egypt	11,59
Pakistan	50,79	Bolivia	10,24
India	39,47	Cameroon	9,08
Tanzania	30,05	Malouin	8,33
Algeria	24,46	Nepal	7,88
Indonesia	22,94	Nicaragua	7,15
Kenya	19,12	Niger	6,73
Jamaica	18,25	Haiti	6,52
Senegal	15,26	Thailand	6,44
Sahel Regional	15,12	Costa Rica	6,34
Zaire	15,07	Mali	6,10
Zambia	14,43	Tunezia	5,77
Sudan	12,91	Mozambique	5,65
Rwanda	12,28	Uganda	5,62
Ethiopia	12,26	Zimbabwe	5,30
Ghana	12,06	Buskino Faso	5,28
Sri Lanka	11,71	Botswamc	5,11
Peru	11,59		

Source: Statistics from CIDA, *Annual Report 1983-1984.*

TABLE 4
Tying Status of Total ODA*
1982-1983 Average

Countries	Percent Untied	Rank
Australia	70,2	6
Austria	31,3	15
Belgium	37,1	14
Canada	39,3	13
Denmark	69,0	7
Finland	82,5	1
France	45,5	11
Germany	73,6	5
Italy	N/A	N/A
Japan	74,4	3
Netherlands	61,8	8
New Zealand	57,3	10
Norway	79,1	2
Sweden	N/A	N/A
Switzerland	74,1	4
United Kingdom	43,1	12
United States	59,4	9
Total DAC	53,3	

* Includes both bilateral and multilateral disbursements.

Source: *OECD, Development Cooperation: Development Assistance Committee 1984 Review,* Paris, 1984, p. 196.

TABLE 5
Canadian Official Development Assistance
(Disbursements)

Fiscal Year	Amount in $ Millions	Percent of GNP
1970-1971	346,3	0,40
1971-1972	395,1	0,42
1972-1973	507,3	0,48
1973-1974	587,9	0,48
1974-1975	760,0	0,49
1975-1976	903,5	0,53
1976-1977	973,1	0,50
1977-1978	1 050,5	0,49
1978-1979	1 166,0	0,49
1979-1980	1 241,1	0,46
1980-1981	1 306,5	0,43
1981-1982	1 489,0	0,43
1982-1983	1 669,7	0,46
1983-1984	1 813,5	0,45

Sources: For years 1970-1971 — 1973-1974: *Minutes of Proceedings and Evidence of the Standing Committee on External Affairs and National Defence*, Issue 13 (April 13, 1977), Appendix, p. 33.

For years 1974-1975 on: *Minutes of Proceedings and Evidence of the Standing Committee on External Affairs and National Defence*, Issue 2 (May 6, 1980), Appendix, p. 9.

For years 1980-1981, 1983-1984, CIDA, *Annual Report*, various years.

TABLE 6
Official Development Assistance from Major Donor Countries
Calendar Year 1982

Donor Country	Total Disbursements	Rank in Terms of Total ODA	ODA/GNP Percentage	Rank in Terms of ODA/GNP
DAC Members	($US Millions)			
Australia	883	11	0,57	11
Austria	355	16	0,53	12
Belgium	501	15	0,60	10
Canada	1 197	9	0,42	14
Denmark	415	16	0,77	8
Finland	144	20	0,30	17
France	4 028	3	0,75	9
Germany	3 162	4	0,48	13
Italy	814	12	0,24	23
Japan	3 023	5	0,29	18-19
Netherlands	1 473	7	1,08	5
New Zealand	65	22	0,28	20
Norway	559	13	0,99	7
Sweden	987	10	1,02	6
Switzerland	252	17	0,25	22
United Kingdom	1 793	6	0,37	15
United States	8 202	1	0,27	21
OPEC Members				
Algeria	129	21	0,29	18-19
Iran	—	26	—	26
Iraq	—	25	—	26
Kuwait	1 295	8	4,86	1
Libya	43	24	0,18	24
Nigeria	58	23	0,08	25
Qatar	250	18	3,80*	2
Saudi Arabia	4 428	2	2,82	3
United Arab Emirates	563	14	2,06	4
Venezuela	216*	19	0,32*	16
Total	24 042			

* Estimate

Source: CIDA, *Canada and Development Cooperation: Annual Report 1983-1984.*

NOTES

1. Canada, House of Commons, Parliamentary Task Force on North-South Relations: *Report to the House of Commons on the Relations Between Developed and Developing Countries*, Ottawa, Supply and Services, 1980, p. 37.

2. For example, Canada's current positive image in the Third World is due more to the Prime Minister's efforts to promote the North-South dialogue, than to Canada's aid program.

3. It has been suggested that for each $1 million of CIDA funds disbursed, 120 man-years of work are created in Canada. See Peter C. Briant, Canada's *External Aid Program*, Montréal, The Canadian Trade Committee, Private Planning Association of Canada, 1965, p. 31. In May 1973, Paul Gérin-Lajoie, then President of CIDA, told the Montréal Board of Trade that CIDA was responsible for 48 000 man-years of work in 1973-1974. Cited in Clyde Sanger, «Canada and Development in the Third World», in Peyton V. Lyon and Tareq Ismael (eds.), *Canada and the Third World*, Toronto, Macmillan, 1976, p. 296.

4. For example, Canadian consulting firms have been particularly successful at winning World Bank contracts, and even Canadian equipment suppliers (or that small proportion and suppliers that enter bids) have been successful on 42 % of the procurement competitions they have entered. See Canada, Department of Industry, Trade and Commerce, «Notes for an Address by the Honourable Michael H. Wilson to the Canadian Manufacturers Association», Toronto, September 12, 1979.

5. Most obviously, through the Export Development Corporation and through various programs of the Department of External Affairs.

6. For the low income countries, net foreign resource inflows (official development assistance and commercial capital) represented 18 % of gross domestic investment in 1975. World Bank, *World Development Report, 1978*, Washington, The World Bank, 1978, p. 6.

7. In some of the least developed countries, foreign aid still finances the greatest portion of development expenditure.

8. Spicer suggests that this separation of policy-making and execution caused particular problems for the program during the decade. Keith Spicer, *A Samaritan State? External Aid in Canada's Foreign Policy*, Toronto, University of Toronto Press, 1966.

9. Until 1984, the President of CIDA had authority to approve projects only up to $250 000 and the Secretary of State for External Affairs had authority for projects which exceeded this amount. In addition, any project over $1 million (or $3 million in program countries) had to be submitted to the Treasury Board for final approval. In that year, dramatic revisions were made in these authorities. The new approval levels were: Area Vice-Presidents $8 million, President $10 million, Minister $15 million.

10. CIDA, *Strategy for International Development Cooperation 1975-1980*, Ottawa, Information Canada, 1975, p. 25.

11. Briant reports that bilateral grant allocations from 1950 to March 31, 1964, were dominated by power plants and transmission lines (29 %); metals and asbestos (21 %); wheat and flour (18 %); and locomotives and road transport (7 %). Agriculture including forestry, pesticides and fertilizers, represented just ove 4 %. Peter C. Briant, *op. cit.*, p. 30, Table 8.

12. This includes funds disbursed through the NGO and ICDS divisions.

13. International Development Research Centre, *Annual Report, 1979-1980*, Ottawa, 1980.

14. The IDRC has not been totally immune to pressures for greater Canadian content in its programming, however. The recent creation of the Cooperative Programs unit to link Canadian research institutes with similar institutes in the Third World attests to this.

15. Keith Spicer, *op. cit.*, p. 211.

16. J.E.M. Ogelsby, «Canada and Latin America», in Peyton V. Lyon and Tareq Ismael (eds.), *Canada and the Third World*, Toronto, Macmillan, 1976, p. 180.

17. North-South Institute, *Canada North-South 1977-1978*, Vol. 1: *Canada North-South Encounter: The Third World and Canadian Performance*, Ottawa, 1977, p. 113-124.

18. Canada, External Affairs, «Bilateral Approach to Foreign Policy», A Speech by the Honourable Mark MacGuigan, Secretary of State for External Affairs to the Empire Club of Canada, Toronto, Ontario, January 22, 1981, p. 4-5.

19. Interestingly, as Table 2 shows, the shift to bilateralism has not materialized. Multilateral aid has declined percentage – wise but so too has government-to-governement aid.

20. In this section, and the two following, the four area branches will be the main subject of the discussion as these three issues pertain most directly to them.

21. Sanger, *op. cit.*, p. 286.

22. The Chevrier Mission was sent to Africa by Prime Minister Lester B. Pearson to identify projects suitable for financing by Canada.

23. For a more detailed discussion see Gregory Armstrong, «From Colombo to CIDA: Aid Policies as a Reflection of Canadian Domestic Concerns», *International Perspectives,* March-April 1975, p. 44-48. To balance interests among various regions of the world, the Canadian Government has established a rough decision of bilateral aid: 40 % to Asia, 40 % to Anglophone Africa and Francophone Africa combined, and 20 % to the Americas.

24. There are also approximately 50 External Affairs officers abroad who have development responsibilities, and hundreds of Canadians serving on CIDA contracts in the Third World. The latter are usually not involved in projet planning – just project execution – and the experience they gain is not transferred back to the Agency when they return to Canada.

25. An aid official in Bangladesh told the members of the Parliamentary Task Force that his experience in Bangladesh, where three officers administer a program which disbursed over $65 million in 1979-1980, is «a bit like being at the bottom of a giant funnel». As quoted in Canada, House of Commons, Minutes of Proceedings and Evidence of the Special Committee on North-South Relations, Issue No. 29, April 21, 1981.

26. The importance of effective planning in rural development projects is thoroughly detailed in Uma·Lele, *The Design of Rural Development Projects: Lessons from Africa,* Baltimore, The Johns Hopkins University Press for the World Bank, 1979.

27. Canada, House of Commons, *Minutes of Proceedings and Evidence of the Standing Committee on External Affairs and National Defence,* Issue No. 40, April 21, 1981, p. 30.

28. This 20 % figure is applied on an aggregate basis for the Agency, then broken down by regional division so that individual projects or the sum of projects within any individual country do not have to fall in the 20 % range. This gives some added flexibility to the policy. In theory, at least, about 40 % of Canada's total aid disbursement is untied. This consists of all multilateral (except multilateral food aid), much of special programs, untied transport spending, and the 20 % of bilateral. But no accurate record of bilateral is kept, so the 40 % figure is just an estimate. Most observers suggest that in reality, less than 20 % of bilateral is untied.

29. See for example J.A. Pincus, «Costs and Benefits of Aid: An Empirical Analysis», Report for UNCTAD (TD/7Supp.10), October 26, 1967; J.N. Bhagwati, «The Tying of Aid», in S. Schiavo-Campo and H.W. Singer (eds.), *Perspectives of Economic Development,* Boston, Houghton Miffin Co., 1970; and Carl Hamilton, «On the Mixed Blessing of Tied Aid», T*he Bangladesh Development Studies,* Vol. 6, No. 4, August 1978, p. 461-474.

30. Those developing countries with skilled bureaucracies can mitigate both this and the added cost impact of tying. Knowing full well which donor country is most competitive in each sector, they can manage their project requests so as to get the best deal possible. Unfortunately, those countries which need aid the most are generally the least likely to be able to manage the donors in this way.

31. The Treasury Board could cast some light on the tying issue and on the arguments surrounding the potential impact of untying on Canadian industry by releasing to the public studies it once commissioned on the topic. These studies – proudly displaying their confidential stamp – are probably sitting on shelves, gathering dust.

32. CIDA, *Strategy for International Development Cooperation,* p. 32.

33. See for example «Ottawa working loose knot tying up foreign aid loans», *The Globe and Mail,* March 25, 1977.

34. Articles bemoaning the potential loss to Canadian industry appeared in numerous newspapers and the Committee on Development Aid of the Canadian Export Association made extensive presentations to the Government on the issue. See for example Canadian Export Association, *Export News Bulletin,* December 1976 and May 1977.

35. CIDA, «Directions for the Agency from now until 1980», December 1977, p. ii. Mr. Dupuy also commonly defended the aid program on the basis of its contribution to the Canadian economy.

36. The Export Promotion Review Committee was established in 1978 to make recommendations on how Canada might improve its export performance. Its final report, *Strengthening Canada Abroad* – commonly referred to as the «Hatch Report» after the Committee Chairman Roger Hatch – was released on November 30, 1979.

37. A critique of the Hatch Report and an explanation of the export credit war is found in: James H. Adams, *Oil and Water: Export Promotion and Development Assistance*, Ottawa, The North-South Institute, 1980.

38. This may in part be explained by the fact that CIDA does not closely monitor its untied funds so that individual officers must plan projects without knowing what proportion of tied funds may not yet be allocated. This seems to encourage timidity in untying, not excess demand for such funds.

It may also be explained by the internalizing of these interests by CIDA officers. In her perceptive study of the US Agency for International Development, Judith Tendler notes how the Agency comes to identify with the interests of those groups or departments that have tended to criticize the Agency, thus subverting development objectives. *Inside Foreign Aid*, Baltimore, The Johns Hopkins University Press, 1975, p. 30-35.

39. Canada, House of Commons, *Parliamentary Task Force on North-South Relations, Report to the House on the Relations Between Developed and Developing Countries*, Ottawa, Supply and Services, 1980, p. 40.

40. For discussion of some of the pressures placed on recipients, see Just Faaland (ed.), *Aid and Influence: The Case of Bangladesh*, Hong Kong, MacMillan Press Ltd., 1981. The last Chapter, «Aid and Dependence: Issues for Recipients», in G.K. Helleiner, *International Economic Disorder: Essays in North-South Relations*, Toronto, University of Toronto Press, 1981, A recent proponent of greater donor intervention is Gunnar Myrdal, «Relief Instead of Development Aid», *Inter-economics*, March-April 1981, p. 86-89.

41. CIDA, *Strategy*, p. 24.

BIBLIOGRAPHY

For an extensive listing of works on Canadian development assistance:

SEWARD, Shirley B. and JANSSEN, Helen. *Canadian Development Assistance: A selected Bibliography*, 1950-1977, Ottawa, International Development Research Centre in collaboration with the Norman Paterson School of International Affairs, Carleton University, 1978.

Other works include:

ADAMS, James H. Oil and Water: Export Promotion and Development Assistance, Ottawa, The North-South Institute, 1980.

BRADY, Philip H. «The Rubiks' Cube of Canadian International Development Cooperation in the 1980s,» *Canadian Journal of Development Studies*, vol. 5, No. 1, 1984, p. 129-139.

BRUNEAU, Thomas C. *et al. CIDA: The Organization of Canadian Overseas Assistance*, Working Paper No. 24, Centre for Developing-Area Studies, McGill University, 1978.

CANADA. House of Commons. *Parliamentary Task Force on North-South Relations: Report to the House of Commons on the Relations between Developed and Developing Countries*, Ottawa, Supply and Services, 1980.

CANADA. House of Commons. *Minutes of Proceedings and Evidence of the Special Committee on North-South Relations: The Fifth Report to the House*, Issue No. 29, April 21, 1981.

CARTY, Robert and SMITH, Virginia. *Perpetuating Poverty: The Political Economy of Canadian Foreign Aid*, Toronto, Between the Lines, 1982.

CHODAS, Robert. *The Caribbean Connection*, Toronto, James Lorimer and Co., p. 1977.

CIDA (Canadian International Development Agency). *A Report on Canadians' Attitudes toward Foreign Aid*, November 1980, Ottawa, May 1981.

DUDLEY, Leonard and MONTMARQUETTE, Claude. *The Supply of Canadian Foreign Aid: Explanation and Evaluation*, Ottawa, Economic Council of Canada, 1978.

ECONOMIC COUNCIL OF CANADA. *For a Common Future: A Study of Canada's Relations with Developing Countries*, Ottawa, Supply and Services, 1978.

EHRHARDT, Roger. *Canadian Development Assistance to Bangladesh*, Ottawa, The North-South Institute, 1983.

EHRHARDT, Roger *et al. Canadian Aid and the Environment*, Ottawa, The North-South Institute and the Institute for Resource and Environmental Studies, 1981.

ENGLISH, E. Philip. *Canadian Development Assistance to Haiti*, Ottawa, The North-South Institute, 1984.

FREEMAN, Linda. «Wheat and Rural Development in Tanzania», Paper presented to the Workshop on Development Policy, Centre for Development Projects, Dalhousie University, March 1980.

HELLEINER, G.K. *International Economic Disorder: Essay in North-South Relations*, Toronto, University of Toronto Press, 1981.

LADOUCEUR, Paul. «Canadian Aid to Africa: Perspectives and Problems», Conference on Canada and Africa: Sponsored by the United Nations Association in Canada, Mount Allison University, June 27-28, 1980 (mimeographed).

MASSE, Marcel. «The Third World: A Canadian Challenge», Speech to the Canadian Club, Toronto, April 6, 1981.

McALLISTER, R.I. *A Canadian Foreign Aid Case Study: Lessons and Issues from a Training Project in West Africa*, Centre for Development Projects, Dalhousie University, 1979.

MORRISON, David R. «Canada and International Development», *Journal of Canadian Studies*, Vol. 14, No. 4, Winter 1979-1980, p. 133-144.

NORTH-SOUTH INSTITUTE. *Canada North-South 1977-1978*, Vol. 1, *North-South Encounter: The Third World and Canadian Performance*, Ottawa, 1977.

NORTH-SOUTH INSTITUTE. *North-South Relations 1980-1985: Priorities for Canadian Policy*, a discussion paper prepared for the Special Committee of the House of Commons on North-South Relations, November, 1980.

NORTH-SOUTH INSTITUTE. *In the Canadian Interest? Third World Development in the 1980s,* Ottawa, 1980.

PARAGG, R.R. «Canadian Aid in the Caribbean: Neo-Colonialism or Development», *Canadian Public Policy,* Vol. VI, No. 4, Autumn 1980, p. 628-641.

ROCHE, Douglas. *What Development is All About,* Toronto, NC Press Ltd., 1979.

SCIENCE COUNCIL OF CANADA. *Food for the Poor: The Role of CIDA in Agricultural, Fisheries and Rural Development,* a discussion paper by Suteer A. Thomson, February 1980.

STEEVES, Jeffrey S. «The Canadian International Development Agency: The Policy Process and the Third World, 1968-1979», Workshop on Development Policy, Centre for Development Projects, Dalhousie University, March 1980.

Strengthening Canada Abroad, Final Report of the Export Promotion Review Committee, Chairman: Roger Hatch, November 30, 1979.

TAYLOR, Alan J. «CIDA in Disasters: A summary of the Agency's Policies, Procedures and Perceptions», Working Paper No. 2, Intertext, 1978.

TENDLER, Judith. *Inside Foreign Aid,* Baltimore, The Johns Hopkins University Press, 1975. Though this book deals with USAID, its perceptive analysis is still of relevance to Canadian development assistance.

WYSE, Peter. *Canadian Foreign Aid in the 1970s: An Organizational Audit,* Montréal, Centre for Developing Area Studes, 1983.

YOUNG, Roger. *Canadian Development Assistance to Tanzania,* Ottawa, The North-South Institute, 1983.

24

Les relations culturelles, scientifiques et techniques

Brigitte Schroeder-Gudehus
Université de Montréal

La culture, les sciences et la technologie occupent désormais l'avant-scène des théâtres diplomatiques. L'attention qu'on leur accorde est de fraîche date. Pendant longtemps et en dépit des traditions séculaires de relations culturelles et scientifiques au-delà des frontières, elles ne jouaient qu'un rôle négligeable dans l'activité des chancelleries et des postes diplomatiques. On peut certes identifier quelques exceptions: depuis la Great Exhibition of the Works of Industry of All Nations de Londres au milieu du siècle dernier, les gouvernements encourageaient leurs industriels et leurs artisans, leurs œuvres sociales, leurs institutions culturelles et éducatives à participer aux expositions universelles pour y témoigner de la richesse, de la compétence et du talent collectifs de la nation. Tout en célébrant le génie scientifique comme un fait culturel, on percevait déjà ses rapports étroits avec le développement industriel, la prospérité économique et la puissance militaire. Les ministères des Affaires étrangères intervenaient dans quelques domaines culturels particuliers: ainsi, certains pays européens veillaient à la survivance culturelle de leurs ressortissants émigrés outre-mer en les pourvoyant d'écoles; de même, la France se préoccupait de l'expansion du français comme langue internationale. L'encouragement officiel de relations universitaires – échanges de professeurs et accueil d'étudiants étrangers – se manifestait dès le début du siècle. L'enseignement supérieur devint rapidement un élément important des conventions culturelles qui connurent leur première grande vogue pendant l'entre-deux-guerres.

Notons que la conviction selon laquelle la patrie pouvait recueillir de substantiels avantages de son rayonnement culturel et scientifique était répandue surtout parmi les personnes qui exerçaient elles-mêmes des activités culturelles ou qui, de par leurs fonctions administratives, avaient pour mission d'en assurer le bien-être et l'épanouissement. Les milieux diplomatiques étaient généralement plus sceptiques. S'ils étaient conscients de l'importance du prestige culturel et des sympathies qu'il pouvait nourrir auprès d'élites étrangères influentes, ils se méfiaient en même temps d'activités internationales sur lesquelles ils n'avaient pas de contrôle, et ils détestaient voir leur travail perturbé par les initiatives parfois maladroites d'«ambassadeurs» improvisés. Si, *mutatis mutandis,* cette remarque s'applique encore à la situation actuelle, l'attitude des gouvernements a sans doute évolué. Cette évolution ne s'est pas seulement manifestée dans l'organisation de la fonction et des moyens qui y sont affectés, mais aussi sur le plan de la doctrine. Nous ne voulons pas dire par là que la place du culturel dans les relations internationales n'ait jamais fait l'objet jusque-là d'une réflexion systématique. Bien au contraire, aujourd'hui encore le discours officiel demeure tout imprégné d'anciennes références: re-lents de la mission civilisatrice, du cosmopolitisme des gens bien nés et de la con-fiance tout dix-neuviémiste dans les bienfaits d'une connaissance mutuelle des peuples.

Il y a un siècle, ces courants de pensée agitaient surtout des groupes de particuliers. Il serait difficile de prétendre qu'ils aient été absorbés aussitôt dans la pratique des politiques étrangères. L'endossement se fit graduellement; aujourd'hui et à de rares exceptions près, la coopération culturelle, scientifique et technique internationale est une composante indispensable de toute politique étrangère. La dimension politique d'opérations de nature scientifique ou technique assure à celles-ci une place de choix au nombre des instruments dont dispose la pratique diplomatique. Signaux de bonnes intentions et d'esprit de collaboration, certaines formules ont fini par s'imposer comme des règles de savoir-vivre entre États, de sorte qu'il est devenu difficile de rester à l'écart d'une organisation internationale ou d'hésiter à conclure un accord de coopération scientifique et technique avec un pays, sans que cette hésitation ne soit considérée comme un geste inamical. Néanmoins, l'inflation d'accords-cadres à la recherche de contenus a depuis quelque temps modéré l'enthousiasme pour cette formule de collaboration, encore que des négociateurs en mal d'entente continuent de voiler leurs insuccès par des gestes coopératifs dans les domaines scientifique et technique[1]. Quoiqu'il en soit, la pratique, même si elle est en déclin, illustre bien le potentiel symbolique des relations culturelles et scientifiques internationales.

Après la Deuxième Guerre mondiale, les problèmes internationaux appelant une intervention concertée se sont multipliés de façon spectaculaire. La plupart de ces problèmes étant liés d'une façon ou d'une autre aux répercussions de progrès dans les sciences et la technologie, les États se trouvent obligés d'appuyer leur action diplomatique sur des arguments scientifiques et techniques (on n'a qu'à penser au dossier des pluies acides qui pèse sur les relations canado-américaines). Sur le plan multilatéral, il est rare que les ententes, les programmes et les innombrables organisations et organismes internationaux créés depuis 30 ans n'aient pas un caractère au moins partiellement technique. S'il est vrai que le Canada participe à un nombre impressionnant d'entre eux, il faut accueillir avec prudence l'hypothèse selon laquelle cet engagement massif serait attribuable plus particulièrement aux traditions «fonctionnalistes» de la politique étrangère canadienne: il l'est sans doute autant à la force des choses. Comme dans d'autres pays, l'élargissement massif des responsabilités internationales de l'État a nécessité de réorganiser les instances d'élaboration et de mise en œuvre de la politique étrangère.

Le Canada a fait ses débuts de politique des relations culturelles et scientifiques internationales il n'y a qu'une vingtaine d'années. De dimensions plutôt modestes jusqu'au milieu des années 60[2], les engagements internationaux du Canada dans les domaines culturel, scientifique et technique ont pris un essor spectaculaire pendant l'époque qui coïncidait avec l'ère Trudeau. La prolifération d'accords et ententes internationaux s'accompagnait dès le début des années 70 d'efforts pour arriver à une coordination rationnelle de ces activités. Plafonnant depuis le début des années 80, les initiatives internationales du Canada dans les domaines culturel, scientifique et technique semblent de plus en plus obéir à des motifs d'ordre économique, conséquence à la fois de contraintes financières et, sans doute, d'une part de désillusion à l'endroit des «bénéfices intangibles».

L'arrivée tardive du Canada parmi les pays pratiquant la diplomatie culturelle n'a pas eu pour effet d'exonérer ses conceptions et pratiques des hypothèses et des ambiguïtés affectant les politiques culturelles extérieures des puissances qui les pratiquent depuis longtemps, ou de rendre limpide ce qui est, par définition, un mélange subtil mais trouble de générosité et de calcul. Quant au principe d'une «politique étrangère au service des Canadiens», c'est-à-dire d'une politique étrangère conçue comme un prolongement de la politique intérieure et en fonction des priorités de celle-ci, il soulève un certain nombre de problèmes sur lesquels nous aurons l'occasion de revenir. D'une manière générale, les thèmes principaux de la politique nationale énoncés par le gouvernement Trudeau (croissance économique, qualité de la vie, environnement, justice sociale, paix et sécurité internationales, souveraineté et indépendance) étaient définis de manière suffisamment globale pour justifier l'engagement du gouvernement fédéral dans toute une gamme d'activités culturelles, scientifiques et techniques sur le plan international. La question se complique quand on l'envisage sur le plan pratique. Sans même mentionner la compétition des ressorts à l'intérieur du gouvernement, il est évident que le gouvernement fédéral détient les moyens de rendre service, d'une manière très spécifique, aux professions culturelles et aux communautés scientifiques et technologiques nationales par le truchement d'opérations internationales dont ces milieux seraient nécessairement à la fois les instruments et les bénéficiaires. À ce niveau d'action concrète, quand il s'agit de choisir et d'arbitrer entre intérêts concurrents, le principe d'une politique étrangère subordonnée aux priorités de la politique nationale n'est pas d'un plus grand secours ici qu'il ne l'est dans d'autres domaines.

À mesure qu'un peu partout les politiques étrangères s'emparaient des relations culturelles, scientifiques et techniques, cette préoccupation trouvait graduellement son expression institutionnelle dans des unités administratives et des enveloppes budgétaires. Cependant, les motifs de la prise en charge de chacun de ces domaines se différenciaient progressivement, de sorte qu'il est difficile aujourd'hui de les traiter ensemble dans un seul chapitre. À la fois objets et instruments de la politique étrangère, la culture, la science et la technologie ne s'inscrivent pas nécessairement dans les mêmes stratégies, ne font pas appel aux mêmes clientèles et n'invoquent pas toujours des arguments semblables de légitimation sociale et politique. Il n'est pas possible, en dépit de leurs particularités, de tirer des lignes claires démarquant la «culture» de la «science», ce qui est «scientifique» de ce qui est «technique» et ce qui est «technique» de la «culture» au sens large[3]. Il y eut pendant longtemps unanimité pour considérer la science comme appartenant à la culture, et une perception superficielle s'obstine toujours à voir les techniques comme des applications de connaissances scientifiques. La science faisant œuvre de charnière, la séquence «culture-science-technologie» demeure ainsi sommairement plausible, bien qu'elle ne corresponde guère à la réalité. La culture, la science et la technologie sont, de plus, fréquemment mobilisées pour servir d'appui à des stratégies dont l'objectif se situe en dehors de leurs domaines propres, ce qui n'est pas sans poser des problèmes de gestion. Ceux qui sont responsables de cette gestion se trouvent aux prises non seulement avec les dynamiques propres à chacune de ces aires de création et de performance, mais également avec la nécessité d'articuler les priorités sectorielles formulées au plan national sur les objectifs de la politique étrangère. Les difficultés de concevoir et de mettre en œuvre, dans une perspective de politique étrangère, des interventions dans des domaines aussi variés que la culture, les sciences et la technique, se manifestent d'ailleurs par des tâtonnements sur le plan de l'organisation administrative, notamment par la redistribution, fréquente des fonctions parmi et à l'intérieur des ministères et par la tendance à abandonner certaines responsabilités de gestion à des organismes-relais parapublics ou privés.

Nous ne présenterons dans ce chapitre que certains aspects des relations culturelles, scientifiques et technologiques du Canada. L'extrême éparpillement des interventions dans les domaines tant du culturel que du scientifique et du technologique défie toute tentative de traitement compréhensif. Nous nous limiterons aux initiatives suscitées et encouragées par le gouvernement fédéral et dont le ministère des Affaires extérieures (MAE) assume entièrement ou partiellement la mise en œuvre ou la coordination. Nous ne traiterons pas des relations internationales des provinces[4] et des municipalités. Nous ne nous limiterons pas aux relations s'établissant dans le cadre formel d'accords intergouvernementaux ou d'organisations internationales; nous exclurons toutefois de nos observations le vaste réseau des relations transnationales d'individus et d'organismes privés – sans nous cacher par ailleurs que ce réseau, précisément, constitue un élément fondamental et à bien des égards la condition même de l'intervention étatique. Notre propos est d'esquisser une vue d'ensemble et non pas de présenter des inventaires. Nous essayerons de traiter la thématique de ce chapitre comme un tout, tant que cela est possible. Nous ne retiendrons des relations technologiques que celles dont le rapport avec la recherche scientifique est étroit et évident, excluant celles qui relèvent nettement des politiques commerciales[5]. Il ne nous échappe pas que cette démarcation est arbitraire, intellectuellement insatisfaisante et à la limite impossible. Nous l'introduisons afin que le texte ne déborde pas les dimensions qu'il est nécessaire de conserver à ce chapitre.

LES OBJECTIFS ET LES MOYENS

Fondamentalement, les États s'engagent dans des relations culturelles, scientifiques et techniques extérieures en raison des avantages qu'ils espèrent en retirer. Un des problèmes les plus difficiles que pose la gestion de ces relations réside dans la diversité des avantages escomptés.

La présence internationale et les représentations collectives

Quelle que soit la diversité des opérations, elles ont ceci de commun qu'elles manifestent toutes une présence en dehors des frontières nationales. Cette «visibilité» internationale est l'objectif fondamental des politiques culturelles extérieures. Le but n'est pas seulement d'être vu, cependant; il est aussi et surtout d'être perçu d'une certaine manière. À l'instar de beaucoup de pays, les programmes canadiens reflètent un effort entre autres de corriger une «image» considérée comme simpliste, façonnée par des souvenirs sélectifs d'une information surannée[6]. Les manifestations, sous les auspices du ministère des Affaires extérieures (MAE) voulant faire connaître le Canada au monde, réduisent ainsi à un minimum les compétitions de bûcherons ou les déploiements en grande tenue de la police montée. Les programmes de la diplomatie culturelle se veulent d'un autre ordre: représentation de troupes de ballet, de danseurs et de compagnies de théâtre; performances d'orchestres, récitals de solistes, tournées de compositeurs, de chanteurs, d'écrivains; expositions d'art, participation à des festivals de cinéma; invitations de journalistes et de critiques étrangers, afin qu'ils rendent compte, de retour chez eux, de la qualité de la culture canadienne.

Au Canada comme ailleurs, le concept de «culture» a connu une extension considérable. Quoiqu'une place avait toujours été accordée au folklore, la routine des diplomaties culturelles s'était orientée pendant longtemps principalement en fonction des représentations culturelles d'une certaine élite – la bourgeoisie cultivée. Actuellement, les programmes s'enrichissent de plus en plus de témoignages du genre de vie de l'ensemble des citoyens, tout en conservant bien entendu des éléments de la «haute culture». C'est ainsi que l'on entend mieux répondre aux besoins d'information et de loisirs des masses populaires. Le Canada n'y fait pas exception. Des expositions, des «semaines» ou «journées» canadiennes organisées dans de grandes villes étrangères se placent généralement dans cette perspective, au même titre d'ailleurs que les manifestations sportives[7]. L'inconvénient en est que les domaines du «culturel» s'en trouvent de plus en plus mal définis et que la politique culturelle extérieure, sous prétexte d'accroître et de diversifier la «visibilité» du Canada sur la scène internationale, s'en trouve empêchée de développer une stratégie plus sélective des opérations[8].

Parmi les manifestations de la culture canadienne, les sciences occupent une place particulière. Certes, depuis plusieurs années les programmes scientifiques ne relèvent plus du Bureau des relations culturelles internationales du MAE. Il répugne par ailleurs aux hommes de science de voir leurs activités et leurs performances évoquées en même temps que celles des corps de ballet et des chanteurs populaires. Quand au milieu des années 60 la politique étrangère canadienne commençait à s'intéresser à la coopération scientifique, la recherche canadienne était déjà pleinement intégrée aux réseaux internationaux de communication et de collaboration. Depuis la Deuxième Guerre mondiale, la réputation d'excellence des laboratoires du Conseil national de recherches n'était plus à faire. Les programmes internationaux d'échange de chercheurs ont sans doute contribué par la suite à étendre et à consolider cette réputation, mais c'est grâce à des distinctions plus spectaculaires – celles qui font les manchettes – que la réputation d'excellence ou de respectabilité scientifique du Canada s'est confirmée aux yeux du grand public: l'attribution du prix Nobel à Gerhard Herzberg en 1971 ou du prix Kalinga à Fernand Séguin en 1979.

Les efforts pour corriger l'image d'un Canada pourvoyeur de matières premières et de terrains d'activités de plein air se déploient avec une détermination particulière dans le domaine de la technologie de pointe. Nous ne nous référons pas ici à la promotion commerciale de produits déjà sur le marché, une tâche essentiellement du ressort des services commerciaux. Nous nous référons plutôt aux politiques visant à créer un climat de confiance dans la compétence technologique en général qui reste plus proche des préoccupations «d'image» et de présence internationale – même si en dernière analyse ce climat est recherché pour servir à la conquête de marchés. Il s'agit alors de faire connaître et reconnaître une haute performance dans le domaine de la technologie de pointe: l'énergie nucléaire, les télécommunications, l'hydro-électricité et l'exploration spatiale[9]. Les stratégies en ce sens vont de la conception de la participation dans des expositions universelles et internationales jusqu'aux efforts de la diplomatie canadienne de persuader les médias américains, lors du deuxième voyage de la navette spatiale à l'automne 1981, d'adopter le terme du «bras canadien» pour désigner le télémanipulateur développé au Conseil national de recherches.

Dans sa façon de présenter des témoignages d'une vie culturelle de haute qualité, riche et diversifiée, la diplomatie canadienne ne diffère guère de ce qui se pratique dans d'autres pays. C'est sur un plan plus «politique» qu'elle s'en différencie. Elle est portée, d'abord, par la volonté d'affirmer une *identité culturelle*, donc de démarquer la culture canadienne de la culture des États-Unis. Si la communauté de langue entre les États-Unis et une grande partie du Canada est généralement considérée comme un facteur positif pour les activités scientifiques et techniques, il en est autrement dans le domaine culturel, où elle prive le Canada d'un élément de démarcation en même temps que d'une barrière protectrice naturelle. Un trait de culture politique vient cependant à la rescousse de l'identité culturelle: à la différence d'un projet de «melting-pot», le gouvernement canadien proclame le principe d'une société bilingue et multiculturelle et s'empresse d'en faire connaître les mérites sur le plan international:

> Grâce à ses programmes d'information et d'affaires culturelles, peut-on lire dans la *Revue annuelle* du MAE de 1979, le ministère a sensibilisé davantage la communauté internationale au fait que le Canada est une société démocratique, bilingue, multiculturelle, richement dotée et *capable de résoudre positivement ses problèmes internes* (nous soulignons)[10].

Projetant une image de compétence et de maturité, le Canada se présente ainsi comme un partenaire digne de confiance.

C'est sans doute parce qu'il est à la fois convaincu de ce que l'expérience canadienne comporte des éléments exemplaires, et soucieux de rendre le Canada intelligible et sympathique aux élites étrangères, que le MAE encourage depuis la fin des années 60 la mise sur pied de programmes «d'Études canadiennes» aux États-Unis et en Europe et y apporte un soutien financier. L'idée, séduisante et ambitieuse, est d'offrir un enseignement universitaire de qualité, cohérent et continu sur les affaires canadiennes. Misant sur un intérêt suffisant et soutenu pour le Canada au niveau de l'enseignement supérieur des pays hôtes, on espère ainsi créer à l'étranger des noyaux de compétence dont la compréhension des problèmes et des intérêts légitimes du Canada s'étendra au-delà de «l'image» favorable[11].

L'éducation relevant de la juridiction provinciale, il est normal que le MAE ne se soit pas engagé massivement dans un domaine hérissé de conflits potentiels et que les échanges universitaires n'occupent pas ainsi dans la politique culturelle extérieure du Canada un créneau aussi important que celui qu'ils tiennent, par exemple, dans la politique française. Les opérations qui existent et dont la gestion est généralement déléguée à des organismes extérieurs au ministère procèdent cependant toutes de la même supposition, à savoir que des programmes d'études et d'échanges universitaires contribuent «à susciter et à entretenir un intérêt particulier pour le Canada parmi les personnes influentes à l'étranger»[12].

L'intérêt national bien compris

Parmi les avantages qu'un État compte retirer d'une politique des relations culturelles extérieures, l'*enrichissement collectif* en est incontestablement le plus librement admis. Cet enrichissement est de deux ordres: l'un qui se réalise selon «l'interfécondation» et en dehors de considérations économiques; l'autre, au contraire, qui se présente carrément suivant les marchés et l'écoulement de produits culturels.

L'hypothèse de l'interfécondation culturelle et scientifique transparaît dans le fait que les opérations culturelles internationales sont généralement conçues et mises en œuvre sur une base de réciprocité, que celle-ci se trouve ancrée dans un accord formel ou qu'elle repose sur les convenances. Dans le domaine scientifique, les relations internationales ont ceci de particulier qu'elles constituent les conditions mêmes du développement et de la vitalité d'activités scientifiques nationales[13]. Par conséquent, l'État se voit sommé de les promouvoir au même titre que la recherche elle-même. Communication et collaboration internationales s'imposent d'emblée, quand il s'agit de mettre en commun des résultats d'observations et de recherches (l'un des objectifs, par exemple, du Programme biologique international organisé par le Conseil international des unions scientifiques entre 1964 et 1974), de partager un équipement coûteux (comme le télescope franco-canadien à Hawaï) ou de s'adjoindre pour l'exécution d'un projet des spécialistes introuvables au Canada, ce qui n'est pas rare de se produire dans certains secteurs de la recherche de pointe. Rappelons enfin que les relations scientifiques internationales ne se développent pas uniquement dans le domaine de la recherche. Indépendamment des retombées escomptées au chapitre de «l'image» du Canada, les programmes d'échange institués dans l'enseignement supérieur permettent aux professeurs et aux étudiants d'obtenir des compléments d'expérience et de formation à l'étranger, et aux universités canadiennes d'enrichir leurs programmes grâce au concours de professeurs invités.

Des observations semblables s'appliquent, *mutatis mutandis,* aux domaines des arts et des lettres: l'accès à la scène internationale signifie pour les créateurs et les interprètes canadiens une extension de leur auditoire, donc une intensification des activités, un approfondissement de l'expérience professionnelle et, le cas échéant, la consécration. Même quand il s'agit d'opérations unilatérales – à plus forte raison alors dans le cas de programmes d'échange –, la mobilité internationale des œuvres et des interprètes provoque un contre-courant de contributions étrangères qui enrichissent et diversifient la vie culturelle canadienne: les trésors de l'Égypte, l'opéra de Pékin, le cinéma africain ou l'art italien. Est-il exact qu'à ce titre le Canada importe plus qu'il n'a à offrir à l'exportation? et que c'est dans ce fait qu'il faut chercher une des raisons de ce qu'on a appelé le «piteux état» de sa politique culturelle extérieure[14]? Poser la question d'une éventuelle asymétrie des échanges culturels en révèle à la fois la justesse et l'absurdité. Le cautionnement officiel de relations culturelles se définit certes en fonction d'avantages mutuels, mais ceux-ci ne se situent pas nécessairement sur le même terrain. Les relations culturelles représentent, en fait, un cas particulier de la «réciprocité diffuse» qui doit être prise en compte dans d'autres domaines de la politique étrangère[15].

L'accès des productions culturelles aux marchés internationaux ne se réduit pas à une question de consécration ou de prestige, mais constitue aussi un problème économique. Un marché national trop restreint risque de ne pas faire vivre ses écrivains et éditeurs, peintres, compositeurs et interprètes. Dans le cadre de ses programmes de promotion culturelle, le MAE intervient sous forme d'aide financière et logistique, facilitant les tournées, les expositions et les prises de contact avec des agences et des éditeurs. Les responsables de ces programmes ont cru pouvoir constater avec satisfaction qu'après une période initiale de performances subventionnées, un nombre toujours plus grand d'interprètes canadiens se produisent sur les scènes étrangères dans le cadre d'entreprises purement commerciales. La politique culturelle extérieure ne peut fournir qu'un concours d'appoint, cependant, pour remédier à la situation extrêmement précaire des industries culturelles canadiennes, menacées à l'extérieur et à l'intérieur des frontières par la concurrence (notamment des États-Unis). La santé de ces industries sur le plan national n'est pas du ressort du MAE. Il en va de la politique culturelle extérieure comme de la politique étrangère en général: «Une bonne politique intérieure est essentielle au succès des relations étrangères[16].»

Des considérations économiques interviennent également dans la gestion des relations scientifiques et techniques. L'objectif des politiques de coopération est non seulement d'accéder à des connaissances, de rattraper des retards technologiques ou simplement de réduire les coûts, mais aussi de créer des débouchés pour les produits. Les partenaires internationaux sont alors fréquemment recherchés pour partager à la fois le savoir et les marchés. Le fait que dans le domaine des technologies avancées, les industries canadiennes sont largement amarrées à une R-D étrangère, notamment américaine, crée une situation bien particulière. Les entreprises ne peuvent tirer profit de certaines positions de pointe qu'elles détiennent ni acquérir et faire fructifier de nouvelles technologies que dans la mesure où des arrangements coopératifs leur assurent l'accès à la fois à la dynamique générale du développement techno-scientifique et aux marchés. Recherche, développement, production et commercialisation se trouvent liés ainsi dans un faisceau d'obligations, de privilèges et de compensations internationales. Dans le domaine technologique, la politique étrangère intervient alors en prolongement d'options prises sur le plan national au sein de ministères, ou institutions à vocation technique et en association avec le secteur privé[17].

Au début des années 70, déjà, le Canada faisait partie de plus de 200 organisations internationales à caractère culturel, scientifique ou technique, dont un tiers était de nature intergouvernementale. Certaines œuvraient dans le domaine culturel, comme, en première place, l'UNESCO. La majorité des organisations intergouvernementales auxquelles le Canada adhère s'appliquent à résoudre des problèmes transnationaux d'ordre technique: la gestion des ressources naturelles, la protection du milieu, l'utilisation des espaces terrestres et extra-terrestres, etc. Cette coopération «fonctionnelle», loin de fournir un cadre idyllique à des manifestations de responsabilité collective et de solidarité, constitue au contraire un terrain où chaque pays membre veille au plus près à la sauvegarde de ses intérêts. De nombreuses organisations internationales – organisations spécialisées de l'ONU comme l'Organisation mondiale de météorologie ou l'Union internationale des télécommunications, et organisations régionales ou fonctionnelles comme l'Organisation de coopération et de développement économique (OCDE) ou l'Agence internationale de l'énergie atomique – ne constituent pas seulement des plaques tournantes de l'information, mais exercent des fonctions de coordination, de contrôle et de réglementation. La pertinence des positions nationales défendues est alors largement dépendante des compétences scientifiques et techniques que les gouvernements peuvent mobiliser pour saisir les enjeux et influencer les décisions dans un sens compatible avec l'intérêt national. La présence aux organisations ou réunions internationales fonctionnelles est indispensable pour un pays industrialisé. Pour que le Canada puisse concilier, en connaissance de cause, «ses intérêts fondamentaux avec les nécessités de la solidarité internationale»[18], cette participation requiert une collaboration étroite entre la diplomatie et les ministères à vocation technique.

LES PRIORITÉS POLITIQUES

À en croire le discours officiel, les programmes de relations culturelles et scientifiques internationales sont conçus pour servir d'appui aux objectifs de la politique étrangère. Le MAE, tout en reconnaissant que les programmes doivent tenir compte des priorités sur le plan national, fait valoir la nécessité de les adapter, «selon l'emplacement géographique, [aux] exigences de la politique étrangère»[19]. À première vue, cette adaptation semble relativement simple. «Dans la mesure où la politique étrangère est un prolongement des intérêts nationaux», peut-on lire dans un document du ministère, «il s'ensuit que les relations culturelles d'un pays avec les autres nations, tout en le rendant présent dans d'autres parties du monde, favorisent aussi son développement interne[20].» Nous venons d'esquisser dans la section précédente les principaux éléments de ce thème de l'enrichissement collectif. Le ministère des Affaires extérieures agit, en fait, dans beaucoup d'instances comme «fondé de pouvoir» des professionnels de la culture, utilisant sa présence sur la scène internationale pour leur faciliter l'accès à de nouveaux auditoires. C'est aussi par le truchement de sa contribution aux objectifs sectoriels que la diplomatie se déploie ici «au service des Canadiens».

Les problèmes se compliquent quand il s'agit d'objectifs reliés à la mission spécifique du MAE, à savoir la sauvegarde et le renforcement de la position canadienne au sein du système international. C'est dans la poursuite de ces objectifs que la diplomatie se saisit du terrain prétendument apolitique de la culture, des sciences et de la technique pour élargir sa marge de manœuvre. L'objectif des opérations n'est donc pas dans ce cas la promotion d'activités culturelles ou scientifiques. Au mieux, celle-ci est un objectif accessoire. Ce sont de ces fonctions plus spécifiquement politiques dont nous traiterons dans la prochaine section.

Des instruments de la diplomatie de détente

Si la culture et la science sont mobilisées à l'appui des politiques étrangères, elles le doivent en grande partie aux connotations d'universalisme et de progrès qui les accompagnent et à l'éthique dont explicitement ou implicitement elles se réclament. Il fallait donc s'attendre à ce qu'elles soient recherchées pour servir d'ornement à des opérations politiques, pour «ennoblir» des rapports dont l'objectif essentiel est qu'ils soient ou encore pour masquer l'absence, entre deux ou plusieurs États, d'accord sur tout autre terrain. Les relations culturelles et scientifiques s'imposent ainsi comme les méthodes par excellence de la diplomatie des bonnes causes: du préambule de l'Acte constitutif de l'UNESCO aux énoncés de l'Acte final de la conférence d'Helsinki, elles se voient assignées une fonction essentielle dans le maintien de la paix mondiale. L'humanisme universaliste qui a inspiré le concept de culture de l'UNESCO colore aussi celui dont se réclament généralement les politiques culturelles extérieures. L'imagination créatrice des peuples se voit ainsi investie d'une vocation transnationale et pacificatrice dont les tournées artistiques, les expositions itinérantes, les congrès scientifiques et des festivals de toutes sortes se font les témoins enthousiastes.

Internationale par définition, la coopération scientifique a été régulièrement mobilisée au service des politiques de détente. En 1959 déjà, un échange de lettres entre le Conseil national de recherches du Canada et l'Académie des sciences de l'URSS établissait un programme d'échanges limité à la recherche fondamentale. Interrompu en 1968 après l'invasion par l'Union soviétique de la Tchécoslovaquie, le programme fut repris à la suite d'une nouvelle entente signée en 1972 (renouvelée pour cinq ans en 1975). Entre-temps, la décision de mobiliser les relations scientifiques internationales au service d'objectifs politiques avait été prise au niveau du Cabinet. En janvier 1971, le Canada et l'Union soviétique signèrent un Accord sur les applications industrielles de la science et de la technologie et, au mois d'octobre suivant, un Accord général d'échanges dans les domaines de la culture, des sciences et de l'éducation. Ces accords englobaient alors les programmes mis sur pied auparavant, donc non seulement l'entente entre l'Académie des sciences et le Conseil national de recherches, mais aussi des ententes, par exemple, entre le Comité d'État à la science et à la technologie de l'URSS d'une part, et la Commission de l'énergie atomique du Canada (1964) et le ministère de l'Énergie, des Mines et des Ressources (1965) d'autre part. Le gouvernement canadien décida d'interrompre toute collaboration avec l'Union soviétique en 1980 au lendemain de la crise afghane. De nouvelles ententes sectorielles en 1981 (sur la coopération scientifique et technique agricole) et en 1984 (sur les échanges dans les sciences de l'Arctique) étaient les premiers pas vers une reprise des échanges qui aboutira sans doute au cours de l'année 1986 ou 1987[21].

Le Canada n'a pas conclu d'autres accords-cadres de coopération scientifique ou culturelle avec des pays du bloc socialiste, en dépit du désir que certains d'entre eux ont exprimé à cet égard. La collaboration scientifique entre le Canada et ces pays se fait par le truchement de programmes et projets spécifiques négociés de façon *ad hoc* entre organismes intéressés. Les mécanismes lourds et rigides des accords formels se sont révélés trop onéreux pour encourager l'extension de cette formule, l'accord avec l'Union soviétique causant à lui seul suffisamment de problèmes de rentabilité. Sur le plan de la substance – scientifique et technique – la coopération avec l'Union soviétique, largement unidirectionnelle, ne semble pas avoir apporté des bénéfices considérables aux partenaires canadiens[22]. L'analyse des coûts et des bénéfices de la coopération canado-soviétique est cependant compliquée à cause de l'asymétrie des motifs qui inspirent l'un et l'autre partenaires. Si le but de l'Union soviétique est avant tout d'obtenir l'accès à la science et à la technologie occidentales, les objectifs de la politique étrangère canadienne sont plus hétéroclites: favoriser un climat international de détente, tout en espérant introduire un élément d'ouverture, aussi minime soit-il, dans le système politique soviétique; créer et sauvegarder des possibilités de transactions commerciales, sans renoncer cependant à utiliser la suspension de la coopération comme signal de désapprobation... Même en concédant que dans les rapports Est-Ouest, la culture, les sciences et la technologie ont des fonctions essentiellement auxiliaires, l'évaluation de leur utilité demeurant un exercice délicat.

Des instruments de diversification des rapports internationaux

Si les rapports culturels, scientifiques et techniques avec l'Union soviétique constituent l'illustration la plus dramatique de stratégies d'appoint, ils ne sont pas la seule. Le contingent d'accords de coopération culturelle, scientifique et technique qui, durant une décennie – du milieu des années 60 au milieu des années 70 –, ont accompagné les efforts de diversification des relations extérieures canadiennes, en fournit une autre. Le gouvernement canadien avait certes conclu quelques ententes de coopération culturelle et scientifique au cours des années 50 et même avant (avec le Brésil en 1944 et l'Italie en 1954), mais c'est à partir de 1965 que le réseau des accords-cadres allait s'étendre de façon spectaculaire. Le Canada n'avait pas le monopole de cette formule[23], loin de là, mais elle semblait offrir à sa politique extérieure des moyens d'appui particulièrement appropriés aux stratégies de la «troisième option». Afin de réduire la part relative des relations technologiques, scientifiques et culturelles qu'un voisin omniprésent captait en les drainant vers le sud, les accords-cadres avec d'autres pays devaient inciter les Canadiens à aller chercher ailleurs qu'aux États-Unis leurs collaborateurs, leurs clientèles et la consécration de leur réputation.

Le premier accord-cadre de coopération culturelle avait été signé en 1965 avec la France, puis, après qu'un programme d'échange entre le Conseil national de recherches et le Quai d'Orsay fut mis sur pied en 1969, l'accord culturel fut précisé au chapitre des relations scientifiques. L'intention de stimuler la coopération avec la Belgique se trouva également concrétisée dans des accords-cadres, l'un portant sur la coopération culturelle (1967), l'autre sur la coopération scientifique, industrielle et technique (1971). L'accord conclu en 1971 avec la République fédérale d'Allemagne porte sur la coopération scientifique et technique (l'accord culturel date de 1975). Deux autres accords-cadres furent conclus en 1976: l'un avec le Japon, l'autre avec les Communautés européennes. Ces deux derniers ne réfèrent dans leur intitulé qu'à la coopération économique, mais incluent les domaines scientifique et technique (un accord-cadre de coopération scientifique et technique avec le Japon fut signé en mai 1986). Des initiatives furent prises en direction de la République populaire de Chine au début des années 70; on s'entendait sur des échanges scientifiques, mais il n'y eut pas d'accord-cadre. La même observation s'applique à l'Amérique latine. Parmi les pays nouvellement industrialisés, le Brésil est lié au Canada par un accord culturel (1944) et un accord de coopération scientifique et technique (1985). Avec les autres pays, les relations culturelles, scientifiques et techniques s'établissent par le truchement de projets et programmes spécifiques.

Les résultats des accords-cadres n'ont pas été concluants[24]. Il fallut se rendre à l'évidence que leur effet incitatif était faible. En l'absence d'institutions, de groupes ou de particuliers déterminés, de part et d'autre, à collaborer, les accords demeuraient des coques vides, encombrants et sources d'embarras. Les projets qui prirent effectivement forme dans le giron de ces accords se seraient probablement réalisés de toute manière par le truchement d'ententes plus spécifiques. Sans être totalement abandonnée – l'accord-cadre récent de coopération scientifique et technique avec le Japon en témoigne –, la formule a perdu de son attrait, s'étant révélée comme étant d'une efficacité nettement inférieure à celle des accords du «type III» (à savoir des ententes ponctuelles «en des domaines scientifiques ou techniques circonscrits, ou liés à des projets particuliers»; voir note 23). On a pu constater des répercussions significatives sur les flux commerciaux en direction et en provenance des pays partenaires, par exemple, ou une réorientation du réseau des rapports de coopération relatifs de transactions commerciales vers les pays partenaires aux accords. L'écrasante majorité des accords conclus par le Canada continuent de le lier aux États-Unis. Tout indique par ailleurs que ni l'Amérique latine, ni l'Afrique ou l'Europe socialiste ne se trouvent parmi les régions prioritaires de la politique actuelle des relations culturelles, scientifiques ou techniques; celle-ci semble plutôt se consolider en direction des États-Unis, de l'Europe occidentale et se développer en direction de l'Asie de l'Est.

Des instruments des politiques Nord-Sud

La politique canadienne à l'endroit des pays en voie de développement faisant l'objet d'un autre chapitre de cet ouvrage, il suffit d'en rappeler ici quelques points d'intersection avec les politiques culturelles, scientifiques et technologiques internationales. S'il est difficile de faire l'inventaire des éléments scientifiques et techniques des programmes de l'Agence canadienne de développement international (ACDI), il n'en est pas moins évident que le gouvernement attribue à la science et aux techniques un rôle moteur dans le processus de développement. Sa prise de position lors de la Conférence des Nations Unies sur la science et la technologie pour le développement (1979) en témoigne, comme sa participation au Groupe consultatif pour la recherche agricole internationale, l'orientation de ses contributions aux travaux de l'Organisation mondiale de la santé ou à l'UNESCO, et plus particulièrement l'initiative qu'il prit en 1970 en fondant le Centre de recherches pour le développement international à Ottawa.

Certains projets de l'ACDI, comme la mise sur pied, depuis le début des années 70, d'une école polytechnique à Thiès au Sénégal, sont des entreprises dont la portée à la fois technique, économique et culturelle est évidente. Cette implantation d'une institution d'enseignement supérieur technique prise en charge entièrement par une école canadienne, avait pour objectif précisément le transfert d'un modèle nord-américain de formation en génie. En dépit de tous les efforts pour adapter le contenu des enseignements aux besoins locaux, cette formation d'une élite technique s'accompagne nécessairement d'éléments d'acculturation aux normes professionnelles de l'institution parrainante. L'hypothèse selon laquelle cette formation à la canadienne créera chez les futurs ingénieurs l'habitude de faire appel non seulement aux méthodes mais également aux produits canadiens est tout à fait conforme aux objectifs généraux des politiques de coopération internationale[25].

Traditionnellement lié aux pays du Commonwealth et impliqué dans leurs politiques d'assistance et de coopération d'après-guerre, le Canada avait attendu les années 60 pour développer ses rapports avec le tiers monde francophone. Sur le plan culturel, ils culminaient dans la part décisive que le Canada prit dans la fondation, en 1970, de l'Agence de coopération culturelle et technique, organisation multilatérale à laquelle avaient adhéré entre-temps une trentaine d'États entièrement ou partiellement francophones. Cependant, cette entrée de la diplomatie en Afrique ne traduisait pas une évolution particulière de la conception canadienne du développement international. Elle était plutôt le prolongement, dans le domaine des politiques d'aide et de coopération, d'efforts de rapprochement avec l'humanité francophone et procédait du même dessein politique que les accords culturels conclus avec la France et la Belgique respectivement en 1965 et 1967. La fonction auxiliaire des rapports culturels, scientifiques et techniques s'articulait ici sur les préoccupations de politique interne.

Des instruments diplomatiques au service de l'unité nationale

Quand le gouvernement fédéral décida au cours des années 60 d'intervenir dans les relations culturelles et scientifiques qui semblaient spontanément s'orienter vers les États-Unis, l'Angleterre et le Commonwealth, en encourageant activement l'établissement de programmes d'échange avec certains pays du continent européen, le MAE n'hésita pas à s'expliquer. Ces programmes étaient établis parce qu'il importait d'avoir des relations privilégiées avec les pays d'origine de nombreux Canadiens. En 1968, les efforts en direction de la Francophonie furent justifiés de façon plus énergique: leur objectif était de «stimuler le bilinguisme et le biculturalisme sur le plan national en développant davantage les échanges de toutes sortes avec la France, la Belgique et la Suisse»[26]. Notons que le MAE contribuait déjà à ce moment au budget d'une organisation internationale non gouvernementale dont l'impulsion première était venue du Québec: l'Association des universités partiellement ou entièrement de langue française (AUPELF). Personne ne pouvait se tromper, un an après la visite du général de Gaulle au Québec, sur la véritable portée de ce déploiement d'initiatives à l'endroit des pays francophones. Il ne faut pas oublier que l'accord de coopération culturelle avec la France fut conclu en novembre 1965 avant tout pour absorber, dans la légalité constitutionnelle, l'accord intervenu en février entre le Québec et la France. Les rapports que le Québec entretenait avec la France[27] avaient commencé à inquiéter le gouvernement fédéral à mesure que la province se servait de sa juridiction exclusive en matière d'éducation pour fonder une capacité internationale. L'objectif de l'accord Canada-France était ainsi avant tout d'ordre constitutionnel, donc interne. Il s'agissait d'affirmer la juridiction exclusive du gouvernement fédéral sur le plan international. Pour prévenir des problèmes du même genre, le Canada signa l'accord-cadre avec la Belgique en 1967.

L'une et l'autre initiatives ne remportèrent qu'un succès médiocre. Tandis que les relations entre le Québec et la France se développaient activement, le MAE avait de la difficulté à donner aux accords-cadres un contenu significatif en dépit de l'établissement d'un Centre culturel à Paris. Les programmes et projets de recherche entrepris dans le cadre de l'entente entre le Conseil national de recherches et la France, conclue en 1969 et consolidée en 1973, ne semblent pas avoir confirmé son utilité: les partenaires étaient de l'avis que ces projets auraient été réalisés de toute manière[28].

Les relations avec la Belgique furent élargies en 1971, quand un accord-cadre de coopération scientifique et technique s'ajouta à l'accord culturel de 1967. L'un et l'autre ont entre-temps acquis une certaine notoriété. Ils sont évoqués chaque fois qu'il s'agit d'illustrer la stérilité de la formule des accords-cadres de coopération scientifique et technique. Opérations d'appui dans l'affrontement autour d'enjeux constitutionnels, ces initiatives de coopération se sont déployées avant tout sur un terrain symbolique. Leur impact est une diminution.

L'ORGANISATION ET LE FONCTIONNEMENT

Concurrence des objectifs, multiplicité des moyens, dispersion des compétences – il n'est pas surprenant que les relations culturelles, scientifiques et techniques internationales du Canada aient souvent offert le spectacle d'un grand remue-ménage plutôt que d'un déploiement de stratégies cohérentes. La difficulté d'instituer une organisation rationnelle et de formuler des principes directeurs clairs tient en partie de la nature même de la matière. Nous reprendrons à la fin du chapitre la discussion des problèmes qui en découlent. Nous nous bornerons ici à retracer les traits saillants de l'insertion institutionnelle.

L'organisation ministérielle et la représentation à l'étranger

La reconnaissance de la culture comme aire d'activité de la politique étrangère fut marquée en 1965 par la création d'une unité administrative chargée des affaires culturelles. En 1970, on en rescindait le domaine des sciences exactes et naturelles, les faisant passer sous la responsabilité de ce qui s'appelait alors la Direction des relations scientifiques et des problèmes de l'environnement. Une distinction était faite désormais entre les sciences au sens étroit d'une part, et la culture «proprement dite» de l'autre: les arts, les lettres et les activités relevant du «genre de vie». La création de la nouvelle unité et son insertion dans une des directions fonctionnelles du ministère n'enchantait ni la Division des affaires culturelles, ni les directions géographiques.

Établie dans sa forme actuelle en 1983, la Direction de la politique culturelle comporte trois sections: politique culturelle, relations universitaires et promotion artistique. Son mandat ne s'étend pas au-delà de l'élaboration de politiques dans ces domaines. Leur éventuelle mise en œuvre est du ressort des bureaux géographiques qui en évaluent l'opportunité à la lumière des priorités particulières établies d'une région à l'autre. Une grande partie des programmes financés par le budget modeste[29] est administrée par des organismes culturels comme le Conseil des Arts[30], le Conseil de recherches en sciences humaines[31] ou l'Association des universités et collèges du Canada[32]. La Direction des relations culturelles internationales collabore régulièrement avec d'autres services et institutions à caractère public (comme le ministère des Communications ou le Secrétariat d'État), parapublic (comme l'Office national du film) ou privé (comme l'Association des auteurs dramatiques canadiens). Il est question par ailleurs qu'elle se désaisisse encore davantage de ses activités de programme en les déléguant à des organismes culturels.

À l'extérieur du Canada, la représentation culturelle est assurée par des institutions de deux ordres: d'une part, les conseillers culturels d'ambassade dans pratiquement toutes les missions diplomatiques de quelque importance et, d'autre part, les centres culturels. Il avait presque été un point d'honneur pour ces centres de se distancer des ambassades et d'éviter tout soupçon d'être là en service commandé. Il semble qu'à l'avenir ils exerceront leurs activités beaucoup plus près de la diplomatie que ce n'était le cas jusqu'ici (notamment à Paris). Seulement trois des six centres actuels sont par ailleurs appelés à survivre, à savoir ceux de Londres, Rome et Paris. Les centres culturels canadiens de New York et de Tokyo renonceront à la diversité de l'offre culturelle pour se concentrer sur l'art contemporain, évoluant vers une prise en charge par le secteur privé[33].

Créée en 1970, l'unité chargée des questions scientifiques et techniques fut victime en 1977 d'une réorganisation de la Direction des questions économiques. Une partie des responsabilités de l'unité fut attribuée à d'autres sections du ministère et notamment aux bureaux géographiques, qui devenaient responsables de l'exécution des projets et programmes que la Division scientifique et technique leur soumettait. Au milieu des années 80, la Division des politiques relatives aux sciences, à la technologie et aux communications est une des trois directions du Bureau des relations en matière d'énergie, d'investissement et des sciences qui relèvent du sousministre du Commerce international et de la Coordination des relations économiques internationales. Ses tâches se résument à trois catégories principales: 1. la préparation et la mise en œuvre des rapports de coopération bilatérale; 2. la participation aux activités multilatérales; 3. la collecte, l'analyse et la diffusion d'informations. Cette dernière fonction a été précisée à l'automne 1985 par l'instauration du Programme d'acquisition de technologie étrangère (Technology Inflow Program), destiné aux industries canadiennes pour leur faciliter l'accès à des innovations technologiques étrangères[34].

Sur le plan extérieur, la gestion des affaires scientifiques et techniques internationales s'appuie sur un réseau de conseillers scientifiques dont six sont actuellement en fonction dans les ambassades du Canada à Washington, Londres, Bonn, Paris, Bruxelles et Tokyo, un septième étant accrédité auprès de l'Agence spatiale européenne à Paris. L'extension du système, prévue au milieu des années 70, ne s'est pas réalisée. Cependant, il a été renforcé à l'automne 1985 par l'affectation d'attachés technologiques (Technology Development Officers) aux ambassades canadiennes à Tokyo, Londres, Bonn et Stockholm et aux consulats généraux à Boston et Atlanta; la tâche de ces attachés – recrutés sur place – est évidemment de s'occuper plus particulièrement du Programme d'acquisition de technologie étrangère. À la différence des conseillers culturels qui sont des diplomates de carrière, les conseillers scientifiques sont généralement des ingénieurs de formation (de plus en plus rarement des scientifiques), détachés temporairement d'autres services gouvernementaux ou, parfois, recrutés dans les milieux universitaire ou industriel. Ils dépendent hiérarchiquement des bureaux géographiques du MAE, tout en assurant leur triple fonction (consultation, liaison et information) en collaboration étroite avec la Division des politiques relatives aux sciences, à la technologie et aux communications ainsi qu'avec les ministères à vocation technique, dont le ministère d'État aux Sciences et à la Technologie.

Les mécanismes de coordination

La nécessité de créer des structures administratives capables de prendre en charge les fonctions nouvelles n'était qu'une partie du défi que constituait l'acceptation de la culture, des sciences et de la technologie parmi les instruments de la politique internationale. L'autre défi surgissait de la nécessité de prendre en compte des relations internationales déjà existantes et les intérêts légitimes dont elles étaient l'expression. Au milieu des années 60, le MAE devait faire face à cet égard à un certain nombre de positions acquises.

Dès avant la Deuxième Guerre mondiale, le Conseil national de recherches du Canada (CNRC) avait assumé la représentation du Canada sur le plan international dans tout ce qui concernait la recherche. C'est par son intermédiaire que le Canada adhérait aux organisations scientifiques et techniques internationales. Il était un point d'appui important de la coopération scientifique interalliée et continuait de maintenir des représentants à Londres et à Washington même après la fin de la guerre. Comme toutes les académies des sciences, le CNRC avait un Bureau des relations internationales. Son «Comité permanent des relations extérieures» était pendant les années 60 la seule instance ayant un certain aperçu des rapports scientifiques et techniques que le Canada entretenait sur le plan international. C'est par son intermédiaire que le Canada collabora à des accords d'échange. À partir de 1969, le MAE participait au Comité permanent à titre d'observateur.

Le CNRC – dont la plupart des activités relevaient de toute manière du patrimoine commun de la recherche fondamentale – n'était pas la seule institution à être engagée dans la coopération internationale. Des ministères et des organismes à vocation technique n'avaient pas hésité à développer des relations internationales dans la mesure où celles-ci étaient nécessaires à l'accomplissement de leur mission: les ministères de l'Énergie, des Mines et Ressources, des Transports, de l'Agriculture, de la Santé et du Bien-Être et du Commerce pour en mentionner quelques-uns, et des organismes comme l'Énergie atomique du Canada. Ces administrations avaient par conséquent mis en place des infrastructures, créé des réseaux de communication et acquis de l'expérience, des compétences – bref, des traditions de relations internationales. Il était à craindre que tout effort de coordination ne soit interprété, de ce côté, comme une intolérable tentative d'ingérence.

C'est ce qui se produisit effectivement au début des années 70. Cependant, ce n'était pas le MAE qui s'attira, le premier, les foudres des administrations techniques. Celles-ci réagissaient d'abord contre l'enthousiasme coordinateur qui caractérisait le nouveau ministère d'État aux Sciences et à la Technologie (MEST) pendant les premières années de son existence. Ce ministère se mit en conflit, non seulement avec les ministères et organisations à vocation scientifique et technique, mais aussi avec le MAE. Le MEST interprétait en effet très largement le mandat qui lui était confié, aussi sur le plan international, et empiétait de cette façon sur les terrains notamment du MAE, mais aussi du ministère de l'Industrie et du Commerce dont le Bureau des sciences et de la technologie était, de la fin des années 60 jusqu'à sa disparition en 1977, en charge des aspects industriels des Accords de coopération scientifique et technique. Le MEST considérait, par exemple, le réseau des conseillers scientifiques comme relevant de sa seule compétence; il amorça aussi des contacts avec le Japon et la Chine sans s'inquiéter des observations d'opportunité que le MAE aurait pu contribuer à ce sujet. Comme l'observe une analyste de la question: «Sur le plan international, la création du MEST a eu pour effet de restreindre le potentiel de coordination du secteur public au lieu de la renforcer, comme prévu[35].»

Le MAE était habitué à ce que les relations internationales des ministères et organismes publics conduisent à des situations délicates. Son initiative d'établir le «Groupe des visites» était provoquée, par exemple, par l'indifférence caractéristique manifestée par certains milieux à l'endroit des problèmes de diplomatie et de sécurité liés aux échanges avec les pays de l'Est. Pour illustrer la situation, il suffit de rappeler que les accords-cadres (avec la France, la Belgique, l'URSS et l'Allemagne) – dont chacun mobilise la participation d'au moins une quinzaine de ministères et organismes publics (et parfois privés) – furent préparés et négociés en l'absence de toute structure permanente de planification et de coordination. Mais si le MAE était prêt à reconnaître que les activités scientifiques et techniques internationales souffraient d'un manque de coordination, il n'entendait pas abandonner au nouveau ministère d'État aux Sciences et à la Technologie le soin d'y remédier.

Quatre ans après la création du Comité interministériel des relations extérieures, fut mis sur pied, en 1975, un organisme de planification et de coordination plus spécialisé, le Comité interministériel des relations internationales scientifiques et techniques (CIRIST). C'est dans le cadre de ce comité dont le MAE assure la présidence que les ministères et organismes à vocation technique présentent, discutent et, le cas échéant, coordonnent leurs engagements et opérations internationaux. En rendant transparentes et accessibles à la discussion un grand éventail d'activités internationales, le CIRIST remplit une fonction importante dans la voie de la rationalisation des engagements internationaux du secteur public; il aurait été illusoire cependant de s'attendre à ce qu'il élimine par son existence même les conflits de priorité. Ceux-ci étaient endémiques depuis que la politique étrangère, le commerce extérieur et, pendant quelque temps, une politique scientifique euphorique avaient, chacun, intégré les relations scientifiques et techniques dans la panoplie de leurs stratégies promotionnelles. Au nom de l'intérêt du pays (ou de ses exportations ou de sa performance scientifique) et sans consultation préalable digne de ce nom, les ministères à vocation technique se trouvaient alors fréquemment invités à participer à des programmes se situant loin de leurs priorités, et ceci à même leur budget courant. En période de compression budgétaire, cette pratique conduisait nécessairement à des conflits. Le dilemme est cependant inévitable: en postulant que la politique étrangère, donc aussi la politique des relations scientifiques et techniques internationales, serve à renforcer les capacités de performances nationales, il fallait réserver aux représentants des ressorts scientifiques et techniques leur part d'autorité dans la définition des critères et dans la prise des décisions. En s'articulant ainsi sur les priorités des administrations et organismes fonctionnels, la politique des relations internationales scientifiques et techniques s'assurerait, certes, d'un consensus. Cependant, ce consensus ne serait obtenu, d'une part, que grâce à un désaveu implicite de toute volonté de mettre les sciences et techniques au service d'objectifs purement politiques; il entraînerait aussi, d'autre part, le risque d'un alignement sur les routines ministérielles et, partant, un danger d'immobilisme. En d'autres termes, si une politique canadienne des relations scientifiques et techniques internationales veut être autre chose que l'agrégat de programmes élaborés par les ministères et organismes fonctionnels, elle doit pouvoir s'appuyer sur une structure centrale ayant à sa disposition un budget. Un tel budget lui permettrait de financer ou de cofinancer des programmes ou des opérations jugés importants du point de vue de la politique étrangère et opportuns du point de vue scientifique et technique. Depuis 1984, la Division des sciences, de la technologie et des communications du MAE gère un fonds spécial dont l'importance est cependant trop réduite pour remplir le rôle du budget spécial que nous venons d'esquisser. Il est plutôt utilisé par le Programme d'acquisition de technologie étrangère à titre de «seed money» pour permettre de faire démarrer des projets dont le financement incomberait par la suite aux administrations intéressées.

Parallèlement à la mise en branle d'un processus permanent de planification et de coordination au sein du CIRIST, la répartition ministérielle des compétences en matière de relations scientifiques et techniques internationales commençait également à se clarifier. Le MAE et le MEST s'entendirent en 1976 sur une définition de leurs fonctions respectives. Depuis lors, le MAE assumait la responsabilité des relations bilatérales, prenant en charge la gestion des activités multilatérales à prédominance scientifique et technique, comme les relations avec le Comité scientifique de l'OTAN, le Commonwealth Science Council et, surtout, le Comité des politiques scientifiques et techniques de l'OCDE[36].

L'autorité du MAE a été confirmée en ce qui concerne la représentation scientifique à l'étranger. Les conseillers scientifiques sont dorénavant nommés par le MAE, sur proposition d'un comité de sélection dont le MEST est membre d'office. Amputé de ses fonctions subventionnaires, le CNRC continue d'exercer des responsabilités internationales (représentation du Canada auprès d'organisations internationales et à l'occasion de manifestations internationales; mise en œuvre d'échanges, de visites et de projets conjoints). Un représentant du CNRC siège au CIRIST et dans de nombreux sous-comités. Le Programme d'aide à la recherche industrielle du CNRC constitue un des points d'appui du Programme d'acquisition de technologie étrangère mentionné plus haut. Les programmes d'échange entre le Canada et la France, le Brésil, le Japon, la Tchécoslovaquie et l'URSS sont administrés par le Conseil national de recherches en sciences naturelles et génie. Finalement, l'intégration des services commerciaux internationaux au MAE au début des années 80 a minimisé les risques de double emploi entre le MAE et le ministère de l'Industrie et du Commerce.

Le CIRIST n'a pas d'équivalent dans le domaine des relations culturelles, quoiqu'il soit question d'y remédier. En attendant, la coordination procède à l'aide de comités consultatifs dont les fonctions comportent également l'intervention directe dans les opérations, notamment dans la sélection de projets et de candidats boursiers. Les institutions culturelles et les associations professionnelles participent d'ailleurs aussi, le cas échéant, à la gestion d'accords culturels en siégeant sur les commissions mixtes, par exemple. L'élaboration et la mise en œuvre de la politique des relations culturelles internationales procèdent enfin en collaboration avec le Comité consultatif fédéral-provincial en matière d'éducation. Sur le plan multilatéral, nous retenons le rôle particulier de la Commission canadienne de l'UNESCO. Relevant du Conseil des Arts, elle remplit une double fonction: elle veille à la mise en œuvre de programmes auxquels le Canada a décidé de participer et elle informe, par voie consultative, la politique canadienne. Ces activités se poursuivent de concert avec la délégation canadienne auprès de l'UNESCO, la Direction de la politique culturelle du MAE et par l'intermédiaire de comités interministériels fédéraux-provinciaux d'autres parties intéressées.

PROBLÈMES ET PERSPECTIVES

Les efforts n'ont pas manqué, ni sur le plan de la réflexion, ni sur le plan de l'organisation, pour doter le Canada d'une politique des relations internationales culturelles, scientifiques et techniques – travail sisyphien, à en juger par la procession d'études critiques et de projets de réformes que le sujet nourrit d'année en année. Si l'on tient à comparer la situation actuelle à la rhétorique qui avait entouré l'avènement officiel du culturel, scientifique et technique parmi les instruments de la politique étrangère, on risque, 20 ans après, de les trouver méconnaissables: les références d'antan au patrimoine de l'humanité, à la science au-dessus des frontières et à la technique au service des peuples démunis ont largement fait place au principe lapidaire des retombées économiques.

Une politique de relations culturelles ne peut être plus cohérente que ne le permettent les priorités des administrations impliquées et la sagesse des organismes relais[37]. Les affaires scientifiques, qui avaient réussi au seuil des années 70 à persuader le MAE qu'elles représentaient davantage que juste un volet des Affaires culturelles, ne se trouvent pas mieux loties finalement sur de nombreux points: à la remorque des secteurs économique et commercial, elles ne paient pas de mine; cantonnées dans des fonctions d'information et de consultation, elles n'aboutissent la mise en œuvre qu'à travers les rouages d'unités politiques.

Ce n'est pas qu'au Canada que la politique des relations internationales culturelles et scientifiques a quelque difficulté à trouver sa cohérence. Il est de bonne guerre que les promoteurs de cette politique dépeignent en couleurs luisantes la prise en compte de la compréhension intelligente et des moyens financiers dont elle bénéficie dans d'autres pays. L'exemple de la France jouit à cet égard, dans tous les pays et depuis tous les temps, de la faveur absolue des enthousiastes en quête de modèles[38]. Sans même aborder la question de savoir comment les choses se présentent quand elles sont vues de l'intérieur du Quai d'Orsay, il faut souligner que la France constitue un cas tout à fait unique en ce qui concerne le sens d'identité collective – politique et culturelle – de ses citoyens. Ce type d'identification culturelle, pour inévaluable qu'elle soit quand il s'agit de bâtir une politique étrangère, est un produit de l'histoire et ne s'obtient pas à coup d'exhortations. L'identité collective que le gouvernement fédéral s'efforce de forger autour d'un projet de société biculturelle et multiculturelle ne manque pas de fondement ni même d'attrait, mais elle prépare mal les citoyens à être mobilisés en ordre compact. La polarisation culturelle – notamment linguistique – propre au Canada permet aussi d'exprimer quelques doutes quant à la possibilité de confier l'ensemble de l'action culturelle internationale à un organisme modelé sur le British Council et d'en tirer les mêmes avantages.

Si ce problème est particulier au Canada, d'autres sont plus communs. Une des difficultés les plus intraitables auxquelles se heurtent toutes les politiques culturelles extérieures est l'évaluation objective de leurs effets. Le recensement des représentations des Grands Ballets canadiens, des personnes inscrites aux programmes d'études canadiennes ou ayant visité une exposition d'art inuit, le nombre de bourses attribuées, de visiteurs accueillis ou de livres distribués ne permet guère d'émettre des hypothèses sur l'évolution des représentations collectives ayant cours dans les publics destinataires, ni de conclure sur l'effet que ces représentations auront sur les habitudes de consommation ou sur les affinités politiques de ces publics[39]. À l'heure actuelle, «l'image» du Canada dans le monde rend sans doute davantage justice à la qualité de sa vie intellectuelle et artistique que cela n'était le cas il y a une vingtaine d'années. Encore faut-il se demander combien de cette amélioration est attribuable, en Europe en tout cas, aux efforts de la politique culturelle extérieure et combien à l'aisance intellectuelle avec laquelle, pendant des années, un premier ministre canadien évoluait sur la scène internationale. Il est peut-être temps de mettre en question l'axiome selon lequel le travail culturel est d'autant plus efficace qu'il échappe au soupçon du calcul politique. On pourrait essayer de renverser l'argument: la qualité culturelle d'un pays est d'autant plus convaincante et laisse une impression d'autant plus forte qu'elle s'exprime dans le comportement politique[40].

L'insistance actuelle sur les «retombées économiques» dans la planification et l'évaluation des programmes culturels; sur la nécessité de les réorienter en direction de pays avec lesquels le Canada compte intensifier ses relations commerciales et de les réduire dans les cas où ils ne servent qu'à des buts politiques, se double d'une détermination renouvelée d'intervenir à la défense des industries culturelles. De telles interventions relèvent du domaine des politiques commerciales, tant interne qu'extérieure et, entre autres, des fonctions du ministère des Communications[41]. Si, au MAE, les Affaires culturelles sont contraintes de se saisir du dossier des industries culturelles, c'est que les services commerciaux n'ont pas jusqu'ici fourni la preuve d'avoir la compétence et le flair nécessaires pour s'en occuper efficacement.

La carence des services commerciaux, quand il s'agit de promouvoir des produits d'une certaine complexité technique, a influencé également la fonction de la branche scientifique et technique du MAE. Le ministère ne fait qu'emboîter le pas ici à la conviction générale selon laquelle le niveau des activités scientifiques et techniques détermine le niveau de la prospérité économique. C'est en faisant valoir leur pertinence économique que les dossiers scientifiques avaient été passés sous la responsabilité de la branche économique du MAE en 1970. À mesure que les «retombées économiques» sont devenues le mot d'ordre, les conseillers scientifiques en poste à l'étranger ont également vu leurs mandats se transformer. Ils se trouvent davantage qu'auparavant chargés de veiller aux intérêts économiques et commerciaux dans le champ particulier de la technologie, à la rescousse d'un service commercial dont le personnel n'a généralement pas les connaissances requises pour appréhender les occasions du marché, ni l'habitude de s'occuper d'un secteur de production en transformation constante où des transactions se négocient souvent avant même que le produit fini n'attende les tablettes. Les conseillers scientifiques, de leur côté, doivent faire preuve d'un bon sens des affaires – une compétence qui ne figurait pas en tête de liste des compétences qui leur étaient demandées il y a 20 ans. Il est à suggérer que la polyvalence des agents – qu'il s'agisse d'un conseiller commercial averti des questions technologiques ou d'un conseiller scientifique averti des questions de mise en marché – ne soit plus confiée au hasard des heureuses coïncidences, mais fasse l'objet d'un projet de formation. La transformation du rôle des conseillers scientifiques dans un sens plus «économique» comporte évidemment des risques. Si personne ne voit plus dans un conseiller scientifique un chercheur en quête désintéressée de la connaissance, la fonction a néanmoins conservé quelques connotations de l'internationalisme propre à l'activité scientifique. À mesure qu'elle évolue vers des préoccupations strictement industrielles et commerciales, elle risque de perdre en crédibilité ce qu'elle gagne en efficacité.

La diversité des compétences requises pose ainsi des problèmes d'efficacité et d'autorité. Cette diversité se présente à l'intérieur, mais aussi à l'extérieur du MAE par rapport à son rôle de maître-d'œuvre de la politique internationale du Canada, où elle se double d'une diversité des objectifs poursuivis par chacun des acteurs. Nous y avons déjà fait allusion en évoquant le rôle parfois récalcitrant des ministères techniques dans la mise en œuvre d'accords généraux de coopération scientifique et technologique. L'opposition traditionnelle de ces ministères à la fonction d'écluse que le MAE revendique au nom de la cohérence de sa politique dans tous les domaines d'activité internationale, ne découle pas uniquement de préoccupations «territoriales». Les administrations techniques font valoir des réserves plus fondamentales, mettant en doute la sagesse de confier aux généralistes du MAE des responsabilités dans des domaines hautement spécialisés auxquels leur formation ne les a pas préparés et auxquels ils ne portent pas l'intérêt approprié. Envisagé d'une façon très terre à terre, le problème n'est pas insoluble: il devrait être possible d'attirer au Service extérieur des personnes ayant une formation scientifique ou technique; le système de la rotation entre affectations, parfaitement adapté à la logique d'une carrière de «généraliste» mais préjudiciable à la consolidation d'une compétence spécialisée, pourrait sans doute être aménagé. Ce n'est pas le processus d'élaboration et de mise en œuvre de la politique étrangère en matière scientifique et technique qui pose les problèmes les plus complexes, mais bien celui de l'autorité d'en définir les contenus.

Le MAE, à l'instar de ses homologues étrangers, revendique cette autorité en s'appuyant généralement sur deux arguments. Il fait valoir, en premier, que la conduite de la politique étrangère repose sur un savoir et un savoir-faire et constitue par conséquent une «discipline», une spécialisation au même titre que le génie nucléaire ou l'océanographie; il se fonde, ensuite, sur l'impératif de la cohérence de l'action internationale. L'affirmation selon laquelle cette cohérence serait compromise, si les moyens pour l'assurer ne se trouvaient pas entre les mains d'un ministère des Affaires étrangères, a été contestée; l'effet de la fragmentation qui en résulterait a été dédramatisé[42]. À un niveau plus théorique, on a fondé la compétence internationale d'un ministère technique sur le mandat de l'État relatif à la sécurité extérieure, en construisant le concept de la «sécurité environnementale internationale»[43]. La réorganisation du MAE au début des années 80 n'a pas suivi cette pente; elle traduisait au contraire un parti pris pour la coordination centralisée. Il n'en demeure pas moins que le MAE reste tributaire de services, d'institutions et de groupes qui sont seuls capables de donner corps aux relations internationales scientifiques et qui continueront d'agir en fonction de conceptions, d'intérêts et de besoins qui leur sont propres.

Le discours sur la politique des relations culturelles et scientifiques internationales s'exprime volontiers en termes de «troisième colonne», de «quatrième dimension de la politique extérieure» ou, un peu plus modestement, de «ciment» entre «les pierres de l'édifice des relations internationales»[44]. Seuls des esprits mesquins y verraient l'allusion à une fonction de bouche-trou. Sur le plan national, les conceptions d'une politique scientifique et technologique qui aurait été le maître d'œuvre de l'ensemble du développement économique ont fait place à une compréhension plus sectorielle de sa fonction. Nous en trouvons le reflet sur le plan de la politique étrangère.

NOTES

1. Comme titrait le magazine *Science* au sujet du sommet Reagan-Gorbatchev en novembre 1985: «A handful of scientific and cultural pacts substitute for progress on arms control in the superpowers' joint statement.» *Science*, vol. 230, 6 décembre 1985, p. 1142.

2. Les ententes internationales dans les domaines scientifique et technique se concentraient dans les secteurs de la recherche militaire, de l'énergie nucléaire et de l'exploration de l'espace.

3. La science a ceci de particulier, par exemple, qu'elle est, des trois aires d'activité, celle qui est la plus essentiellement internationale; en comparaison, les arts et les lettres sont plus étroitement liés aux collectivités qui les produisent. Les résultats de la recherche scientifique sont, à de rares exceptions près, ouverts et internationalement accessibles, tandis que les techniques (en plus du fait qu'elles sont souvent adaptées à des contextes géographiques et économiques particuliers) sont fréquemment des biens en possession de particuliers ou de groupes qui en déterminent l'utilisation. L'accessibilité des résultats de la recherche est un élément essentiel du processus de validation de l'activité scientifique et du système de la récompense: la reconnaissance d'une découverte, d'un chercheur et d'une communauté scientifique se renforce à mesure qu'elle s'internationalise. Il en résulte que les relations scientifiques internationales évoluent selon une dynamique propre qu'une politique étrangère doit prendre en compte.

4. Voir à ce sujet, entre autres, J. Maynard-Ghent, «The participation of provincial governments in international science and technology», *The American Review of Canadian Studies*, 10, printemps 1980, p. 48-62.

5. Nous ne traiterons pas des domaines particuliers de l'énergie atomique ni de la technologie spatiale ou militaire.

6. «On ne doit pas s'étonner», écrivait un observateur il y a quelques années, «que l'image du Canada à l'étranger soit vague, sinon totalement déformée. [...] Quelques-uns des vieux mythes 'des arpents de neige' persistent. [...] L'image du Canada se prête probablement à plus de déformations que celle de tout autre pays de calibre politique et économique comparable.» J.W. Graham, «Regain de vie des études canadiennes à l'étranger», *Perspectives internationales*, sept.-oct. 1976, p. 41-42. Le Canada n'est pas le seul pays à faire face à ce genre de problèmes. La Suisse, déterminée à s'insérer dans «la marche du monde en faisant connaître son apport», devait constater une situation de départ peu favorable: «[...] vantant la neutralité, l'honnê-teté, le sérieux des banques et des troupeaux montagnards, on a créé le sentiment que la littérature, le théâtre ou la peinture 'suisses' distillaient le même ennui.» *Éléments pour une politique culturelle en Suisse, Rapport de la Commission fédérale d'experts [...]*, Berne, 1975, p. 310.

7. Le MAE n'exerce dans le domaine des sports internationaux qu'une fonction consultative. Il apporte aussi, si l'événement l'exige, un certain soutien logistique (*Revue annuelle*, 1980, p. 72; 1981, p. 120; 1983-1984, p. 48).

8. Ainsi, une publication officieuse du MAE propose la définition suivante du «secteur culturel»: «Arts (musique, théâtre, opéra, mime, danse, peinture, sculpture, littérature, etc.); éducation (enseignement primaire et secondaire, formation technique et professionnelle, enseignement dispensé par les collèges communautaires et les universités, recherche, etc.); médias (édition, radio, télévision, cinéma, bibliothèque, archives, information, etc.); sciences (physique, chimie, génie, recherche en laboratoire, etc.); artisanat (tissage, céramique, soufflage du verre, fabrication de piqués, orfèvrerie, etc.); jeunesse (échange de jeunes, missions de travail, voyages d'études, etc.); loisirs (conditionnement physique, passe-temps, chasse, pêche, camping, jeux, parcs, réserves écologiques, etc.); sports (athlétisme, hockey sur glace, natation, football, crosse, gymnastique, etc.); coutumes et traditions (arts, artisanat, festivals, foires, traditions folkloriques, etc. des groupes ethniques.» D. Paul Schafer, *Les relations culturelles du Canada avec l'étranger*, Ottawa, MAE, mars 1979, p. 15.

9. «L'action la plus efficace pour le Canada», souligna le livre blanc sur la politique étrangère en 1970, «sera celle qui fera un usage judicieux des talents, de la compétence, des connaissances et de l'expérience des Canadiens dans certains domaines où ils excellent ou veulent exceller: l'agriculture, l'énergie nucléaire, les télécommunications, le commerce, l'aide au développement, les relevés géologiques, l'hydro-électricité, la fabrication d'avions légers [...].» *La politique étrangère au service des Canadiens*, Ottawa, Information Canada, 1970, p. 19.

10. Comité d'étude de la politique culturelle fédérale (Applebaum-Hébert), *Compte rendu des mémoires et des audiences publiques*, Ottawa, ministère des Communications, 1982, p. 4.

11. Les «Études canadiennes» ont connu un développement remarquable au cours des dernières années. En moins de dix ans, le nombre de cours et séminaires d'études canadiennes faisant partie des programmes

réguliers d'universités étrangères a passé d'environ 400 à 800; ces enseignements sont actuellement suivis aux États-Unis seulement par autant d'étudiants qu'il y en avait d'inscrits à ces cours dans le monde entier à la fin des années 70, à savoir à peu près 20 000. Le programme, qui bénéficie d'apports du secteur privé, est conçu sur le modèle des «*area studies*», mais ne se limite pas à l'enseignement; il inclut la recherche, les publications et l'activité d'«associations d'études canadiennes». Des programmes ou des chaires d'études canadiennes existent surtout aux États-Unis (le Center of Canadian Studies à la School of Advanced International Studies de la Johns Hopkins University à Washington étant sans doute le plus important), mais aussi notamment en Belgique, en France, en Angleterre, en Allemagne, en Union soviétique, en Inde, au Japon, en Thaïlande et en Australie (voir *International Directory of Canadian Studies,* Ottawa, 1986). Les revues annuelles du MAE rendent régulièrement compte de ce programme.

12. *Revue annuelle* du MAE, 1980, p. 73.

13. Les porte-parole de la communauté scientifique ne manquent pas d'y insister chaque fois que l'occasion se présente: voir, par exemple, l'allocution du président du Conseil national de recherches, Larkin Kerwin, lors de la réunion annuelle de l'Association américaine pour l'avancement des sciences, tenue à Toronto du 3 au 8 janvier 1981 (*Science,* 213 (4511), 4 septembre 1981, p. 1069-1072).

14. Brian Stock, «Canada's foreign policy vacuum: cultural affairs», *Canadian Forum,* mai 1973, p. 21; David W. Steedman, *Canadian cultural and academic relations abroad,* Ottawa, Humanities Research Council of Canada, 1977 (miméo), p. 5.

15. Voir Robert O. Keohane, «Reciprocity in international relations», *International Organization,* 40 (1), hiver 1986, p. 1-27.

16. *La politique étrangère au service des Canadiens, op. cit.,* p. 34.

17. Voir, pour plus de détail, J. Maynard-Ghent, *La participation du gouvernement canadien à l'activité scientifique et technique internationale,* Ottawa, Conseil des sciences du Canada, février 1981 (étude spéciale n° 44), p. 47-64 et *passim.*

18. *Le Canada, les sciences et la politique internationale,* Ottawa, Conseil des sciences du Canada, avril 1973, p. 30 (rapport n° 20).

19. «Mémoire sur les relations culturelles internationales», soumis par le ministère des Affaires extérieures (25 mars 1981) dans: Comité d'études sur la politique culturelle fédérale (Applebaum-Hébert), *Compte rendu des mémoires* [...], *op. cit.,* p. 10-11.

20. *Ibidem,* p. 2.

21. Nous renvoyons au rapports annuels du MAE pour l'inventaire des accords conclus depuis 20 ans et une description de leur contenu.

22. Pour le contexte économique des accords, voir I.A. Litvak et C.H. McMillan, «Intergovernmental cooperation agreements as a framework for East-West trade», dans C.H. McMillan, éd., *Changing Perspectives in East-West Commerce,* Lexington, Mass., 1974, p. 151-172.

23. Se bornant généralement à énoncer quelques lignes directrices et à mettre en place des mécanismes de consultation et de coordination, un accord-cadre est censé servir avant tout de catalyseur pour des programmes et projets de collaboration dans les domaines culturel, scientifique et technologique. La cheville-ouvrière en est une «commission mixte» bipartite qui se réunit à des intervalles réguliers, sélectionnant les projets et rendant compte de la marche des programmes.

J. Maynard-Ghent, dans son étude sur la participation du gouvernement canadien à l'activité scientifique et technique internationale (*op. cit.,* p. 32), établit une typologie fort utile des accords de coopération, en distinguant entre: accord généraux (accord-cadre) de coopération scientifique et technologique (type I); accords économiques ou culturels prévoyant une coopération scientifique ou technologique (type II); accords ponctuels dans des domaines scientifiques ou techniques circonscrits, ou liés à des projets particuliers (type III); accords généraux d'échanges ou de coopération entre organismes scientifiques déterminés (type IV). Les accords du type III, de loin les plus nombreux, incluent «toutes les conventions scientifiques et techniques du Canada avec les États-Unis, et plus des deux tiers des ententes conclues avec d'autres pays».

24. La meilleure analyse critique se trouve chez J. Maynard-Ghent, *La participation du gouvernement canadien* [...], *op. cit.,* p. 31-47, 82-86, 106-113, et sur la collaboration avec le Mexique, p. 72.

25. Rémi Tougas, «Thiès, P.Q.», *Le Devoir économique*, 2 (3), avril 1986, p. 39-44; voir aussi C. Davis et P. Laberge, «Le transfert de modèles d'enseignement supérieur technique du Québec au Sénégal: l'École polytechnique de Thiès», *Revue canadienne d'études africaines*, juillet-août 1986.

26. MAE, *Rapport annuel*, 1968, p. 46.

27. Un procès-verbal franco-québécois de 1964 avait conduit à un nombre considérable de programmes et de missions dans le domaine de l'éducation et de la formation technique. L'essor de la collaboration conduisit en 1967 à la création du ministère québécois des Affaires intergouvernementales. D'autres accords entre la France et le Québec furent signés par la suite.

28. Voir, par exemple, J. Maynard-Ghent, *La participation du gouvernement canadien [...], op. cit.*, p. 112-113. Il est évident que la *compétition* entre Ottawa et Québec finit par stimuler les rapports scientifiques entre le Canada et la France – ce qui n'était pas difficile, si l'on considère qu'entre 1961 et 1969, par exemple, le Conseil national de recherches avait attribué onze bourses de recherche (sur 1000) à des chercheurs français (150 étaient allées à des Indiens et 183 à des Japonais. *Ibidem*, p. 18-19.

29. Comme le soulignait récemment le rapport Nielson, le ministère dépense davantage au chapitre du protocole qu'à la promotion de la culture canadienne à l'étranger (Canada, Conseil privé, *Rapport du Comité chargé de l'examen des programmes*, Ottawa, 1985, p. 199). Le coût des programmes est d'environ 7 millions de dollars.

30. Par exemple, les programmes de bourses permettant à des artistes canadiens de séjourner à l'étranger et à des artistes étrangers de séjourner au Canada.

31. Par exemple, le programme de bourses du gouvernement du Canada pour ressortissants étrangers, l'échange de chercheurs avec la France, avec la République populaire de Chine et avec l'Union soviétique.

32. Par exemple, le programme de bourses offertes par d'autres pays à des ressortissants canadiens, ou le recrutement de candidats pour les programmes d'études canadiennes.

33. Et de se transformer en organisme sans but lucratif habilité à recevoir des subsides publiques.

34. Communiqué de presse du ministère des Affaires extérieures (n° 128) du 19 septembre 1985.

35. J. Maynard-Ghent, *La participation canadienne [...] op. cit.*, p. 24. Voir aussi, au sujet du MEST, P. Aucoin et R. French, *Knowledge, Power and Public Policy*, Ottawa, Conseil des sciences du Canada, novembre 1974.

36. La présidence de ce comité avait d'ailleurs été assurée entre 1978 et 1981 par le directeur de la Division internationale du MEST.

37. Notons que la Division des politiques culturelles du MAE ne traite pas de tous les dossiers culturels. Les affaires de l'UNESCO, par exemple, ne font pas partie de ses responsabilités, mais sont traitées par la Division des politiques relatives aux sciences, à la technologie et aux communications.

38. Voir, par exemple, A.E. Gottlieb, «La diplomatie culturelle: une question d'intérêt personnel», allocution prononcée devant l'Association des universités et collèges du Canada, le 12 novembre 1979 (Affaires extérieures, *Déclarations et discours*, n° 79/20).

39. Une évaluation des retombées financières a été récemment entreprise à l'endroit des Programmes d'études canadiennes. H. Babby, Canadian *Studies in the United States: A Survey of resources and expenditure*, Washington, D.C., Association for Canadian Studies in the US, 1985.

40. L'idée d'abandonner l'ordre de marche dispersée fait surface régulièrement depuis quelques années: il a été proposé d'intégrer les centres culturels aux services des ambassades; on a fait valoir aussi qu'un moyen de renforcer l'empreinte que le Canada laisserait sur les esprits serait de faire accompagner les visites à l'étranger du personnel politique par des manifestations culturelles.

41. Voir, par exemple, Francis Fox, *La culture et les communications, Éléments clés de l'avenir économique du Canada*, Ottawa, ministère des Communications, novembre 1983.

42. Voir, par exemple, S. Cohen, «En miettes? Fictions et faits du discours sur 'l'éclatement' de la politique extérieure», *Politique étrangère*, 51 (1), printemps 1986, p. 143-152.

43. *Propositions pour une politique internationale du ministère de l'Environnement*, Direction générale des affaires intergouvernementales, Environnement Canada, septembre 1983.

44. A.E. Gotlieb, «La diplomatie culturelle: une question d'intérêt personnel», *loc. cit.*, p. 2.

BIBLIOGRAPHIE

Relations culturelles

Les travaux analytiques sont rares à côté de nombreux inventaires et, surtout, d'ouvrages et d'articles tenant plus de l'essai ou du plaidoyer que de l'étude scientifique. On consultera avec prudence les études produites pour le compte d'institutions ou de groupes dont l'activité constitue habituellement la substance des relations culturelles internationales. Le meilleur texte récent est un document officiel:

RIGAUD, Jacques. *Les relations culturelles extérieures,* rapport remis au ministre des Affaires étrangères, Paris, La Documentation Française, septembre 1979.

Informé et incisif, un autre document officiel, quoiqu'en partie seulement consacré aux relations culturelles extérieures:

Éléments pour une politique culturelle en Suisse. Rapport de la Commission fédérale d'experts pour l'étude de questions concernant la politique culturelle suisse. Berne, 1975.

Les travaux anciens demeurent indispensables pour l'étude historique. Nous en citons, à titre d'exemple:

COOMBS, Philip H. *The Fourth Dimension of Foreign Policy,* publié pour le Council on Foreign Relations, New York, Evanston, 1964.

DOKA, Carl. *Les relations culturelles sur le plan international,* Neuchâtel, La Bâconnière, 1959.

DOLLOT, Louis. *Les relations culturelles internationales,* Paris, PUF, 1964. (Coll. «Que sais-je?»)

Pour la politique culturelle extérieure canadienne, on se référera à:

COOPER, Andrew F. (éd.) *Canadian Culture: The International Dimension.* Canadian Institute of International Affairs — Center on Foreign Policy and Federalism, Toronto-Waterloo, University of Waterloo/Wilfrid Laurier University, 1985.

PAINCHAUD, Paul. «La diplomatie culturelle du Canada: illusions et problèmes», *Perspectives internationales,* mai-juin 1977, p. 36-40.

Relations scientifiques et techniques

La littérature abonde en études de cas; elle est riche en travaux sur les implications de la coopération scientifique et technique internationale, mais lacunaire en ce qui concerne l'intégration des sciences et des techniques dans le processus de la politique étrangère. Le tour d'horizon le plus complet a été fait dans la collection d'études préparées pour la Chambre des Représentants par le Congressional Research Service de la Bibliothèque du Congrès des États-Unis:

Science, Technology and American Diplomacy. An Extended Study of the Interactions of Science and Technology with United States' Foreign Policy. 3 vol., Washington, D.C., USGPO, 1977, et dans cette collection notamment:

Science and Technology in the Department of State: Bringing Technical Content into Diplomatic Policy and Operations, Vol. 2, p. 1319-1504.

GREENWOOD, J.W. «The Science-Diplomat: A Hybrid Role in Foreign Affairs», *Science Forum*, février 1971, p. 14-18; et «The Science Attaché: Who He is and What He Does», *ibidem*, avril 1971, p. 21-25.

SKOLNIKOFF, Eugene B. *The International Imperatives of Technology. Technological Development and the International Political System*, Institute of International Studies, Berkeley, University of California, 1972. (Transformation du système international est traitée d'une façon systématique dans:)

DICKSON, David. *The New Politics of Science*, Chap. IV, New York, A. Knopf, 1984. (D'un point de vue critique à l'endroit de la politique américaine.)

Une approche historique et comparative est adoptée dans une présentation d'état des travaux (de 1976) par:

SCHROEDER-GUDEHUS, Brigitte. «Science, Technology and Foreign Policy», dans I. D. Spiegel-Roesing et de Solla Price, *Science, Technology and Society*, Londres et Beverly Hills, Sage Publications, 1977, p. 473-506; le même ouvrage contient une contribution d'E.B. Skolnikoff sur la coopération scientifique et technique internationale.

La plupart des études sur les rapports entre la coopération scientifique et technique et la politique étrangère ont été consacrées aux relations américano-soviétiques en traitant surtout du point de vue américain. Parmi les exceptions:

LUBRANO, Linda L. «National and international politics in US-USSR scientific cooperation», *Social Studies of Science*, 11 (4), novembre 1981, p. 451-480.

TOUSCOZ, Jean. *La coopération scientifique internationale*, Paris, Éditions techniques et économiques, 1973; il présente surtout le cadre juridique de la coopération.

COURTEIX, Simone. *Recherche scientifique et relations internationales: la pratique française*, Paris, Librairie générale de jurisprudence, 1972.

MAYNARD-GHENT, J. *La participation du gouvernement canadien à l'activité scientifique et technique internationale*, Ottawa, Conseil des sciences du Canada, 1981 (étude de documentation n° 44). (Politique de coopération scientifique et technique du Canada: excellente étude)

Cet ouvrage se limite aux relations bilatérales. Quelques années auparavant, les implications politiques de la participation du Canada aux affaires scientifiques internationales dans leur ensemble avaient fait l'objet d'une autre publication du Conseil des sciences: *Le Canada, les sciences et la politique internationale*, Ottawa, 1973 (rapport n° 20).

Les «sommes» et ébauches théoriques faisant encore défaut, on est réduit à suivre les études de cas et – source souvent oubliée mais riche – la partie éditoriale des grandes revues scientifiques (*Science, Nature, New Scientist, La Recherche,* etc.).

Il faut finalement signaler sans en fournir le détail les publications officielles des ministères et d'autres institutions publiques et parapubliques. L'imprécision étudiée des rapports annuels des ministères, et notamment du MAE, sont une source médiocre mais indispensable.

25

Canada and the Law of the Sea

David G. Haglund
Queen's University

INTRODUCTION

Recent discussion of the setting and process of Canadian foreign policy has focused on the relative utility of organizing devices. Whether they called them «paradigm», «theoretical frameworks», «models», «theories», or something else altogether, analysts of Canadian foreign policy during the past decade or so have made increasing use of such devices. This essay will be no exception to the trend, for it is our view that the work of political science proceeds poorly, if indeed it proceeds at all, in the absence of such useful constructs. In saying this, we are of course mindful that however useful, all such constructs are necessarily flawed, for the good reason that, as simplifying mechanisms employing unavoidably imprecise variables, they leave out – and must leave out – much of the reality they seek to elucidate. Let us then, at the outset, plead guilty to abusing reality in our treatment of Canada and the Law of the Sea in the post-World War II decades; for not only will we arbitrarily simplify objective reality, but in doing so we will be adopting one of the «simplest» of the simplifying concepts available to students of foreign policy, the idea of the «national interest»[1].

In what follows, we will also be implicitly utilizing the handy «black box», known as statist theory, to attempt to show how and why Canada has fairly consistently been able to achieve foreign-policy gains in the oceans issue-area during the 40 or so years since the end of World War II[2]. In addition, our analysis leads us to employ yet another helpful conceptual ordering device, that of Canada as a «principal power», for we shall attempt to show that insofar as ocean politics and Law of the Sea matters are concerned, images of Canada as either a peripheral or a middle power do not capture the true significance of Canadian geographic, political, and economic interests in the oceans, nor do they come close to accounting for the degree of skill with which those various interests have been articulated and defended by the Canadian «state»[3]. Though it may not be a leading actor in other issue-areas, it is clear that in the context of the Law of the Sea, Canada has been for much of the postwar period a major player with major stakes and assets.

At the most general level, Canadian foreign policy on the Law of the Sea can be characterized by two related tendencies during the post-World War II era: expansionism, and success. Since 1945, but especially since the 1960s, Canadian interests in ocean issues have increasingly been conceived by policy-makers in Ottawa as being preeminently those of a *coastal* state. This new conception marked a significant change from the pre-World War II era, when Canada consistently interpreted its interests to be those of a *maritime* state, and in this regard shared a common self-image with the major maritime powers, Great Britain and the United States. From the new conception of national interest has emerged a policy, namely to extend to the fullest degree consonant with international law – even if that meant, in some instances, creating international law – Canada's jurisdiction over the living and non-living resources of the continental shelf and the superjacent waters[4]. Additionally, Canadian ocean interests have been concerned with the furtherance of a non-material value, sovereignty, above all in the Arctic. In large measure, Canadian interests so conceived have been a function of geography: with frontage on three oceans and a margin area second only to that of the Soviet Union, and with neither the military/strategic nor the merchant-shipping interests of the maritime states, Canada it seems could scarcely have avoided being other than what it has become, a coastal state *par excellence*[5].

But to argue that interests are a «function of geography» is to run the risk of succumbing to the same kind of geographical determinism that plagued the study of «geopolitics» in the late 19th and early 20th centuries[6]. Clearly, Canada could not have become such a strong proponent of coastal states' rights if it did not have the physical attributes of a coastal state; but just as clearly, it requires more than geographical factors to explain satisfactorily the evolution of Canadian ocean policy in recent decades. Both Canadian expansionism and Canadian success in Law of the Sea issues stem from at least two non-geographical exogenous considerations: technology, and changes in the international political system. Technology has had a profound impact on Canadian ocean interests. Indeed, technology has forced the articulation of previously inchoate interests in such ocean matters as protection of the environment, management of the fisheries, and exploitation of seabed resources. And changes in the international political system have constituted the predisposing factor underlying many Canadian ocean initiatives since the 1960s, for in the past two decades Canada has been able to attain international legitimacy for many of its coastal state interests as a result of a shifting balance of power in multilateral fora away from the maritime states and towards the coastal states[7].

Since 1945, Canada has had several interests related to the sea, but for the purposes of this chapter, only the most important of those interests will be examined. They can be grouped into two sets of values: material and non-material values. In the category of material values are: 1. living resources of the continental shelf; 2. non-living resources of the continental shelf; and 3. non-living resources of the deep seabed. Put differently, material values comprise fisheries, offshore oil and gas, and deep-seabed minerals. The category of non-material values is practically synonymous with the issue of Arctic sovereignty, but it also touches on the preservation of the marine environment.

This chapter will consist in a review of the manner in which Canada's «objective» (or geographical) situation with regard to marine interests, under the stimulus of technological developments affecting certain important values, and abetted by a profound shift in the international organizational balance of power in favour of Canada and other coastal states, has led in the postwar decades to the development of an expansionist Canadian foreign policy in ocean issues – a policy that by the 1980s had succeeded in obtaining international recognition and therefore approval of most (but not all) of the country's major ocean interests. For the sake of imposing some sort of logical (albeit artificial) order to this review, chronological considerations will determine the sequence in which Canada's ocean interests are presented, beginning with the question of the fisheries.

LIVING RESOURCES OF THE CONTINENTAL SHELF

The fisheries represent the longest-standing Canadian ocean interest, dating back some 150 years prior to Canada's becoming an independent state[8]. Until the 1960s, fisheries issues had traditionally been bilateral ones involving the United States and Canada (and including, on Canada's behalf, Great Britain during the 18th and 19th centuries), and usually these centred on boundary or sovereignty issues, not on issues of actual resource depletion[9]. But starting in the initial post-World War II decade, and accelerating during the 1960s, there developed what for Canada became a very worrisome increase in the level of exploitation of East Coast stocks, particularly on the part of the technologically most advanced of the distant-water fishing nations. Among these, the Soviet Union was especially active off the East Coast: in the Georges Bank, one of the world's richest fishing grounds, the Soviet Union was harvesting some 40 % of the total catch by the early 1970s. In comparison, both the United States and Canada, who by the end of that decade would both claim jurisdiction over the entire Bank (as a result of their extension of fisheries jurisdiction to 200 miles) (One nautical mile: 1852 m)), were taking only 11 and 9 % of the catch respectively as recently as 1973[10].

From the Canadian perspective, there was on the East Coast a definite problem of maldistribution of resources. But there was another source of concern: it was feared that the level of exploitation might soon render some species of fish in dangerously short supply. In the long term, possible commercial extinction loomed[11]; while in the short term, declining harvests were having a serious effect on the economy of Atlantic Canada, a region in which fishing has a great economic impact. Beginning in 1968, total catch weights diminished in Atlantic Canada, primarily because of pressure put on stocks by the distant-water fishing fleets. Within a few years, catch weights had declined to levels that had not been seen since the early 1950s[12]. Although fishing accounts for about only 1 % of total employment in Canada, the majority of the 80 000 or so jobs in the fishing industry are located in the Atlantic provinces, where their economic significance is greatly magnified by the chronically weak economy of the region. As André-Louis Sanguin explains, there can be no question of the economic threat that foreign fishing posed to East Coast communities: «La logique de la position canadienne dans l'Atlantique du Nord-Ouest tient du fait que, pour 250 000 personnes des Maritimes, il n'y a pas d'autres sources de revenus que la pêche et qu'à Terre-Neuve, entre autres, 15 % de la main-d'œuvre travaille directement à la pêche et à son traitement[13].»

The «logic» of the Canadian position was the logic of protectionism and expansionism and at three Law of the Sea conferences since 1958, the Canadian delegations have sought to extend coastal state power[14]. As explained by Barbara Johnson, Canada's «policy can be characterized as *expansionist* throughout the period. This expansionism has not been directed against the United States. Instead, both countries have sought to exclude foreign distant-water fishing yet to accommodate each other»[15]. To be sure, what Canadian diplomats set out to achieve in 1958 was not at all what they were hoping to receive by 1977: in the earlier years, Canada was desirous of extending Canadian control over offshore fisheries in a rather circumscribed fashion, by extending the territorial sea to six miles, and adding an additional six-mile fishing zone beyond that[16]; in the latter year, Canada implemented legislation extending its exclusive control over offshore fisheries resources out to 200 nautical miles.

What was responsible for the changing order of magnitude of Canadian protectionist desires between 1958 and 1977? In the first place, as noted above, technology forced a reconsideration of the optimum limits that an effective fishing zone should have. In 1958 it was still not possible to discern future trends in the East Coast fishery; since there appeared to be ample stocks and relatively little danger of depletion, a narrower fishing zone was thought to be sufficient for the purposes of protection. By 1977, however, the situation had changed dramatically. Not only was the spectre of depleting resources in existence, but so too was the predisposing element for legitimizing extended coastal state jurisdiction. Thus, the second reason why Canada would go for a 200-mile fishing zone by the mid-1970s: it needed one, and it seemed quite apparent that, due to shifting international organizational realities, it could successfully claim one. Although it is true that Canada's claim to a 200-mile fishing zone was made unilaterally, it is nonetheless true the prevailing trend in international law was for increased coastal state control over offshore resources; hence the question of legitimacy that might otherwise attend a unilateral initiative of such nature was already answered by the time of implementation. Canada, in effect, *could* do what it *would* do, in the eyes of the international community[17].

The winning of jurisdiction over fisheries to a distance of 200 miles was undoubtedly a victory for Canadian foreign policy, but it was not a total victory. Canada sought, but did not get in UNCLOS III, exclusive management rights and preferential harvesting rights for coastal species *beyond* 200 miles, as well as exclusive rights for both management and harvesting of anadromous species (salmon) for the state of origin, even if the fish were taken in the open ocean. In addition, the implementation of the fishing zone, coupled with phase-out or phase-down agreements with distant-water fishing nations, and subsequently new bilateral treaties with some states, did lead to the reduction of tension between Canada and many of those states, but ironically at the cost of an increase in short-term tension from an unexpected quarter[18]. Up to 1977, both Canadian and American fishermen were more concerned with problems posed by distant-water fleets than by competition from each other. But once the former problem was mitigated by the introduction of the fishing zones, new problems arose of a bilateral nature: how to determine where one country's fishing zone ended and the other's began; and how to apportion the catch between Canadians and Americans in areas, like the Georges Bank, where each country had been fishing for centuries.

Canadian-American friction over the fisheries since 1977 could serve to illustrate F.S. Northedge's hypothesis that there is a «law of conservation of tension» in international relations (analogous to the law of the conservation of energy in the physical world), whereby «the reduction of tension in one area of the international system not only fails to prevent tension arising in another area, but may quite positively aggravate and encourage it»[19]. Canadian and American fishermen, content to imagine they shared a common interest so long as toghether they were taking only

20 % of the total catch (as they were in the early 1970s) from «their» Georges Bank, suddenly awoke to the realization after 1977 that now *they* were each other's biggest problem, not the distant-water fishing fleets.

Space permits only a cursory treatment of the current fisheries disputes between Canada and the United States[20]. The most important symbolic component of the dispute, of course, has been the failure of the United States to move the ratification of the East Coast Fisheries Agreement, calling for adjudication of the maritime boundary and cooperative management of the fisheries[21]. But there are other fishing disputes besides those on the East Coast; and on the Pacific Coast, questions of a different sort arose. There the major issue was not reciprocal access to a traditional fishing ground but rather a resolution of the salmon-interception problem. An important secondary issue was the Canadian-American difference of opinion on the question of jurisdiction over highly-migratory species like the albacore tuna: Canada claimed that the fishing zone confers jurisdiction over tuna; the United States disagreed. A short-lived «tuna war» was brought to a halt by a treaty giving each country's tuna fishermen access to fisheries of the other, as well as to specified ports in each country, where the landing of catches may occur[22]. This treaty aside, the dominant tendency on the West Coast seems to be, as Erik B. Wang has noted, for a «fence-building mentality» to take hold, resulting in a phasing out of reciprocal fishing rights for important stocks like halibut and ground-fish[23].

The East Coast Fishery Resources Agreement may have been withdrawn, but a companion Boundary Settlement Treaty did result in the boundary dispute in the Gulf of Maine being submitted to third-party arbitration. The refusal of the United States to ratify the fisheries agreement was widely seen in Canada as a betrayal of a commitment that, withal, was held to be fair to both sides. In the absence, however, of a resolution of the maritime boundary dispute, it was impossible really to determine the distribution of gain associated with the fishery resources treaty, for without clear agreement on the boundary, the question of trade-off became metaphysical: How can one «give something up» if one is not sure that one «owns» it to begin with? Suffice it to say in this context that while regional interests in the United States claimed to have gotten a «raw deal» from the Fishery Resources Agreement, there are at least a few observers in Canada who feel that *Canada* would have been the loser had the American Senate ratified[24].

The two countries did agree, in 1981, to send the question of the boundary between them in the Gulf of Maine to the International Court of Justice. In October 1984, a five-judge panel imposed, nearly two years after the submission of the case, a boundary settlement that was binding on each country. The settlement reflected the panel's view that neither the US claim nor the Canadian one adequately captured the most logical dividing line between the two states' conflicting economic zones. Still to be arranged, subsequent to the ICJ decision, was the negotiation of bilateral fisheries quotas.

In summary, Canada can be seen to have pursued with much (if not total) success an expansionary fisheries policy during the post-World War II decades. The result has been that by the early 1980s, Canada had beaten back the economic challenge of distant-water fishing, to find itself once again confronting its historical fisheries adversary, the United States. Whether Canadian interests are as well-served in the bilateral arena as they have been in the multilateral one remains unclear. But what does seem clear is that the success that was achieved in the latter arena is primarily owing not to any particular policy orientation of post-1968 Canadian governments, but rather to Canada's good fortune in having articulated a coastal state conception of ocean interests at precisely the moment when international trends in many issue-areas were moving against maritime states. In the words of Barbara Johnson, «while the Trudeau Government and its so-called nationalist foreign policy encouraged an aggressive Law of the Sea position, that policy was not initiated by the central political leadership. Canadian fishery policy during the last decade is the outcome of a dramatic shift in the international environment in favour of coastal state power and authority over the oceans[25].»

NON-LIVING RESOURCES OF THE CONTINENTAL SHELF

The fisheries may have represented the oldest, but they were far from being the only Canadian ocean interest in the post-World War II years. The non-living resources of the continental shelf constitute the second of the material values that Canadian ocean policy has sought to advance in recent years; and just as the emerging coastal state power bloc benefited Canadian fishery interests, so too did this emergence benefit Canadian interests in the mineral (essentially hydrocarbon) resources of the continental shelf. But the predisposing element of favourable international environment constituted only one part of the development of Canadian continental-shelf policy: it was a necessary, but not a sufficient condition. Technology was once again, as in the case of the fisheries, the motivating factor in Canadian policy-making.

The post-1945 years have witnessed an unprecedented, sustained, and ultimately triumphant challenge to the centuries-old regime that had previously governed the oceans and their exploitation. From the late 17th century until fairly recent, the Grotian doctrine of *Mare Liberum* constituted most of what was important about the law of the sea: narrow territorial seas of roughly three miles, beyond which lay the high seas open to the use of all. The Grotian concept rested upon the assumption that the seas were *res communis,* waters belonging to everyone, hence not to be appropriated by anyone. The opposing theoretical conception was of the oceans as *res nullius,* belonging to no one, hence subject to appropriation[26]. The striking feature of the past 35 years is the intensity with which the notion of *res communis* has been challenged by the competing idea of *res nullius.*

One of the ironies of the challenge is that it was the premier maritime power of the postwar period, the United States, that launched the scramble for the resources of the continental shelf. There had been, to be sure, pressure building (especially from Latin American states) before 1945 to extend jurisdiction over *living* resources substantially past the three-mile limit; but it was not until the Truman Proclamation of 1945 that any important claim was made to the mineral resources of the continental shelf beyond the territorial sea[27]. The Proclamation has been called «a landmark in seabed politics, [...] a conceptual breakthrough»[28], and rightly so, for it was not only the first claim made by a major maritime power to continental-shelf jurisdiction, but it also maintained that propinquity and not historical usage would determine a state's right to claim jurisdiction over the offshore seabed.

Canada was not a participant in the early *res-nullius* challenge, although it has been a major beneficiary of that challenge. As Barry Buzan has noted, «not until the late 1960s did Canada in any sense become a leader on this issue [...]»[29], but when it did begin to take a serious interest in the shelf, Canada did so for reasons identical to those of the United States: to gain exclusive access to the offshore oil lying outside the territorial sea. Technology in the case of the fisheries had presented a challenge of a negative sense, and had awakened in Canada a protectionist response; in the case of offshore oil, technology had created not so much a challenge as an opportunity, and had awakened in Canada an acquisitive response that some observers have considered highly inconsistent with the Trudeau Government's professed commitment to a more equitable international distribution of wealth[30].

The opportunity offered by technology to drill ever deeper in offshore areas coincided with the *need* for new domestic sources of oil to arrest the trend towards ever-growing oil imports into Eastern Canada; this was especially evident by the end of the 1970s[31]. The combination of technology and need made the continental shelf off the East Coast (and also in the Arctic) seem for a time an economically attractive, indeed necessary, adjunct to the Canadian landmass[32]. Accordingly, Canadian policy has in recent years been extremely expansionist, with the ultimate goal being to push Canadian jurisdiction over offshore mineral resources far out beyond the 200-mile limit of the emerging Exclusive Economic Zone[33]. This is considered necessary due to the great width of the continental shelf off the East Coast, where it extends to 265 miles. It is not just the shelf that Canada is claiming, but the entire margin, which off the Southeastern coast of Newfoundland reaches some 650 miles into the Atlantic[34]. Indeed, by the mid-1970s, Ottawa had already issued oil and gas exploration permits covering more than a million square miles, in some places as far as 400 miles offshore[35].

The issuance of permits itself constitutes one basis of the Canadian claim to the entire margin, but there are other bases to that claim with more of an international cachet. The most important of these is the 1958 Geneva Convention on the Continental Shelf, which established coastal state ownership of the shelf resources either to a depth of 200 meters or, beyond that depth, to the limit of resource exploitability – a limit that has advanced *pari passu* with the development of deep-water drilling technology. In addition, the Canadian claim rests on a 1969 World Court judgement involving a North Sea boundary dispute, in which the Court indicated that natural prolongation of territory must be given weight in support of a state's claim to the shelf. Canada also takes guidance from the way other states pursue maximalist claims over the shelf. The UN Convention on the Law of the Sea has attempted to resolve the problem of delimiting the continental shelf by merging the shelf and the margin in the following definition: «The continental shelf of a coastal state comprises the seabed and subsoil areas that extend beyond its territorial sea throughout the natural prolongation of its land territory to the outer edge of the continental margin, or to a distance of 200 nautical miles from the baselines from which the breadth of the territorial sea is measured where the outer edge of the continental margin does not extend up to that distance[36].» Of course, there still remains a delimitation problem, only this time it is the edge of the margin that must be determined (that is, for states like Canada, with shelves extending past 200 miles).

As with fisheries, so it has been with the non-living resources of the shelf (including the margin): Canada has achieved most (but not all) of what it has sought in the UN Law of the Sea process. Thus, if a comprehensive treaty does get ratified by the necessary 60 states, Canada will be accorded sovereign rights to the mineral resources up to the edge of the margin, subject, however, to an obligation to share resources that are exploited beyond 200 miles. The maximum sharing obligation ultimately will be 7 % of the value or volume (if sharing is in kind) of the yearly production of the resource[37]. In the unlikely event that the treaty fails to obtain necessary ratification, Canada would presumably have no sharing obligation, and could go on exploiting the offshore resources according to the «exploitability» criterion of the 1958 Convention[38]. In any case, Canada conceivably stands to benefit immensely (someday) from its offshore oil wealth, and since most of the oil and gas production will be coming from parts of the shelf not subject to the sharing provision, there is little likelihood of the sharing obligation becoming a drain on either federal or provincial revenues.

THE ISSUE OF ARCTIC WATERS

The third major, and in many ways the most important, ocean question to occupy Canadians in the postwar years has been the question of the status of Canadian claims to jurisdiction over Arctic waters. Primarily, this was and is a question of sovereignty, but it has also involved serious environmental concerns. Indeed, it was environmental concerns touched off by technological developments in the oil industry that reawakened Canadian interest in the somnolent Arctic-sovereignty issue during the late 1960s. Canada had for years assumed that the islands and the waters of the Arctic archipelago belonged to it, but the assumption was characterized by a certain degree of «casualness», which was born of a comforting knowledge that no other was disputing Canadian Northern claims[39].

The first, and, prior to the summer of 1985, only major challenge to Canadian sovereignty in the Arctic came in 1969, when Humble Oil Company of the United States, desirous of finding a commercially viable means of bringing Alaskan oil to the Eastern United States, sent the tanker *Manhattan* through the Northwest Passage, a strait that the United States considers to be an international passage, but which Canada argues is internal waters[40]. Here was exposed the core of the Arctic sovereignty problem: no one, least of all the United States, doubted that Canada was sovereign over the *islands* of the archipelago; the real question was whether Canada could claim sovereignty over the waters of the Arctic. Canada has long argued it could, first on the basis of the «sector theory» (which in effect would give Canada a pie-shaped slice of the area enclosed between 60 degrees west longitude to the east, and 141 degrees west longitude to the west), and more recently on the assumption that a coastal «archipelagic state» has the right to establish internal waters by drawing baselines (or closing lines) between the mainland and the various islands of the archipelago, thus effectively fencing off the entire chain of islands. Alternatively, Canada has advanced the claim that the Arctic constitutes internal Canadian waters because it consists of «historic waters», a category marked by not a little ambiguity[41].

Whatever the basis of the Canadian claim to the Arctic (including, it goes without saying, the Northwest Passage) as internal waters, the United States has consistently refused to recognize it. In the early 1960s, for instance, the Pearson Government attempted to press the archipelagic case for enclosing the Arctic waters, but Washington, fearful of Canada's setting a precedent for more bona fide archipelagic states like Indonesia and the Philippines, vigorously objected, forcing

Ottawa to withdraw its claim[42]. American concern over the Canadian Arctic-sovereignty claim focused, by the end of the 1960s, on two issues: the possible movement of Alaskan oil to East Coast markets via the Northwest Passage; and the more general problem of obstruction of navigation in international straits. Despite the construction of the Trans-Alaska Pipeline, which effectively laid to rest plans to move North Slope oil east through Arctic waters, the United States (and certain other maritime states) continued to view with extreme displeasure any Canadian attempt to make of the Arctic internal or even *territorial* waters. Were the Arctic recognized as Canadian internal waters by the international community, then of course foreign shipping, both military and commercial, would have no more «right» to be there than to be in any other Canadian internal waters, such as the Minas Basin. In internal waters, sovereignty is complete, and as E.J. Dosman has noted, «complete sovereignty in internal waters means that the national will can be imposed»[43]. But even though Canada has until recently restricted its claim only to the *incomplete* sovereign status known as territorial waters for the Northwest Passage (and other offshore areas in the Arctic)[44], the United States and some other maritime powers have continued to raise objections; for as international law now stands, «innocent passage» through territorial seas does not include submerged passage of submarines or any right of overflight[45].

Since it is quite apparent that the coastal state momentum in favour of a twelve-mile territorial sea is unlikely to be reversed, it follows that the entire Northwest Passage will be recognized (even by the United States) as Canadian territorial waters, with or without a comprehensive law of the sea treaty. But should the treaty be ratified, and should all or most of its provisions be recognized as binding on all states, then it is likely that the maritime powers will benefit from the creation of a new category to resolve the «innocent passage» dilemma. This new category, «transit passage», will allow vessels transiting international straits to do what they could do under «innocent passage», but it will also apply to submerged submarines as well as airplanes[46]. The status of the Canadian claim to the Arctic waters, thus, has become linked to the issue of passage through international straits[47]. The point is important, for if the Northwest Passage is considered an international strait (a matter on which there is no agreement at all between Canada and the maritime powers), then there can be no suspension of either the traditional right of innocent passage or its new jurisdictional cousin, transit passage. In other words, while territorial-waters status allows a coastal state to suspend, with cause, innocent passage, there is no such allowance for territorial waters that are also classified as international straits[48].

Recently, Ottawa has taken some dramatic steps to reiterate and defend the Canadian claim to the Northwest Passage and other straits in the Arctic archipelago as internal waters. In response to the transit of a US icebreaker, the *Polar Sea,* in the summer of 1985, made without permission being sought from Canada, the Mulroney Government has proposed the Canadian Laws Offshore Application Act. This proposed legislation was tabled on April 11 1986, at which time Justice Minister John Crosbie announced that «we are going to include in the boundaries of the Northwest Territories the Arctic archipelago and the islands and all the waters in between those islands [...] because of the historical use of those areas and the ice, and what lives under and on the ice»[49].

It can be argued that, *ceteris paribus,* the prospect of the Northwest Passage being considered an international strait would hinder any Canadian efforts to control pollution in the Arctic. As it turns out, however, all things are not equal in this matter, for two reasons. The first is that Canada has consistently and quite strenuously rejected the proposition that the Northwest Passage is an international strait. The status of the Northwest Passage remains at this writing ambiguous, with the Canadian position being that an international strait has to have been used historically for international navigation, something that Ottawa maintains has never been the case in the Arctic. Thus, until it can be determined – if, indeed, it *can* be – whether the Northwest Passage is or is not an international passage, the question of suspension of transit rights remains open. The second reason why Canadian antipollution efforts in the Arctic are unlikely to be challenged is that the unilateral measures adopted in the 1970 Arctic Waters Pollution Prevention Act have been given international approval in the UN Convention on the Law of the Sea. This is the famous «Arctic exception», an article giving coastal states certain rights in respect of pollution prevention in «ice-covered areas»[50].

The significance of this international sanctioning of Canada's unprecedented creation of an Arctic pollution control zone is that, for all practical purposes, Canada's limited sovereignty over the Arctic has been accepted by the international community. To be sure, the kind of complete sovereignty associated with internal-waters status is not now, and may never be, recognized by other states. But Canada's Arctic sovereignty concerns have undeniably been mingled with concerns over the Arctic environment; and to the extent that these latter concerns have resulted in the passage of strict antipollution measures, Canada can be said to have exercised a limited, or «functional», form of sovereignty in a successful manner[51]. The primary national interest in the Arctic, to repeat, was jurisdictional[52]; it was sovereignty, not the environment, that motivated Canadian policy-makers[53]. However, inasmuch as the effective establishment of sovereign status for the area was dependent upon international recognition of such status, for the moment a most unlikely outcome, Canada had no choice but to settle for a second-best, but still very good, solution to its Arctic problem[54].

That solution was to take international law into Canada's own hands and declare a 100-mile pollution control zone in Arctic waters north of 60 degrees north latitude[55]. The Arctic Waters Pollution Prevention Act and accompanying measures (such as the Government's announcement that it would not accept the compulsory jurisdiction of the International Court of Justice in this matter) constituted, as Peter Dobell has noted, a «unilateral action in breach of established international law»[56]. It also constituted something of a political «master-stroke»[57], for it allowed the Trudeau Government to defend an important national interest in the Arctic – an interest for which the Canadian public had been vociferously demanding protection – while at the same time it avoided the kind of confrontation with the maritime powers that a Canadian claim to complete rather than functional sovereignty in the Arctic would have occasioned. To be sure, the maritime powers (the United States in particular) objected to the imposition of the Arctic pollution control zone; but equally importantly, the maritime powers have, over the past decade, become reconciled to the idea that the zone is to be a permanent feature of the Arctic ocean regime, whether as a part of conventional international law with the ratification of the Law of the Sea Treaty, or as a part of customary international law without such ratification.

By the middle of the 1970s, the job of obtaining international recognition for Canada's Arctic pollution control initiatives had more or less been accomplished;

thereafter, the Canadian Government began to de-emphasize the environment as a priority Law of the Sea concern. Having been an early advocate of increased coastal state control over marine pollution, Canada was prepared to bow to the persistent maritime opposition that this particular issue awakened. On the environment issue, Canada after 1976 adopted what Barry Buzan has called a «spirit of reluctant realism», which has seen it acquiesce in «a compromise marine environment regime much weaker than that which it had originally advocated, though stronger than what had existed previously»[58]. But if on the related issues of Arctic waters and the marine environment Canada did not achieve the kind of near-total success that it obtained in the fisheries and the hydrocarbon resources of the continental shelf, it is still the case that it did achieve some important goals. Certainly, the goal of obtaining international recognition of the Arctic waters as internal Canadian waters has not yet been met; but it must be reiterated that Canada has solidified its claim to functional (or limited) sovereignty north of 60 with the international acceptance of the AWPPA and attendant measures. It may be that functional sovereignty will ultimately prove to have been a necessary stage in the gaining of complete sovereignty[59]. Whether it does or not, it remains that the country has done rather well for itself on yet another law of the sea issue.

NON-LIVING RESOURCES OF THE DEEP SEABED

The final major Canadian ocean interest under examination here was the most recent priority concern of Canadian delegations at UNCLOS III, and it is also the Law of the Sea issue about which it is most difficult to predict an ultimately successful outcome for Canadian interests. Canadian interest in the issue of deep-seabed mining is twofold: on the one hand, Canada is concerned that its domestic nickel mining industry, already feeling the effects of stern competition from foreign mining operations, might suffer real change if seabed nodule mining becomes economically feasible between now and the end of this century[60]; on the other hand, Canada has a vested interest in a successful conclusion of the UN Law of the Sea process, not specifically because of the seabed-mining issue, but because of its successes in other areas of the law of the sea[61]. Canada, in other words, wants at least a modicum of protection for its land-based nickel producers from a comprehensive Law of the Sea treaty; and it also wants to make sure that conflict over seabed mining does not put in jeopardy that comprehensive treaty, which offers Canada a wide range of benefits.

The main problem with the seabed-mining provisions of the treaty was that the United States and the developing countries were unable to come to an agreement over the method by which seabed minerals would be exploited, as well as over the division of the revenues from production. As things now stand, an International Seabed Authority will be created to conduct seabed mining. This UN agency will have as its operating entity something called «The Enterprise». The crux of the dispute between the United States (and some other advanced industrialized states) and the developing countries (the Group of 77) concerns the role of private mining corporations in the new regime: the United States wants enlarged opportunities for its mining companies to carry on business in those parts of the seabed not subject to any national jurisdiction, while the developing countries, in keeping with the premise that those parts of the seabed are the «common heritage of mankind», want the greatest possible involvement of The Enterprise[62]. No other single issue in the UN Law of the Sea process has generated as much debate as seabed mining, which as Victor Prescott has observed, became a contest between «two broad philosophies»[63].

But the debate was not solely «philosophical»; it also rested on a certain conception of material interest. This is particularly the case when one examines the position of the United States, the biggest stumbling block to quick passage of a comprehensive treaty, and the most conspicuous non-signatory. The seabed-mining provisions in the convention were seen by many in the United States to be antithetical to many of the ideological tenets of the Reagan administration. As one critic of the proposed seabed-mining regime tellingly put it, «a powerful new international cartel, operated under the United Nations and dominated by the world's socialist nations, would control the ocean bottom, demanding that private mining companies share their bounty [...] This treaty as it stands is an ideological surrender to Third World demands for a «new world economic order»»[64]. The disposition to link up the seabed-mining issue with the more general problem of a new international economic order indeed magnified, for many in the United States, the ideological stakes of the UNCLOS III process, but it would be a mistake to attribute American opposition to the convention solely to ideology.

Underlying American concerns – and of direct relevance to Canada – was the fear that the United States' position as a major importer of strategic minerals would become tenuous in the coming decades, primarily for geopolitical reasons. The United States, during the early 1980s, was worried that its increasing dependence upon certain mineral imports would make the country vulnerable to supply disruptions induced either by price or political considerations. Concern for raw-material supplies has been a recurring worry that has, at various times in this century, preoccupied American policy-makers[65]. The opinion of many at the start of this decade was that the coming 20 years would witness an acceleration in America's dependence upon mineral imports: America, it was thought, would be self-sufficient in only four minerals by 2000, after having been self-sufficient in 32 in the early 1970s[66]. Given that some of the minerals about which the United States considered itself to be most vulnerable were also minerals that might, or so it seemed at the time, someday be producible from the seabed, it is understandable that the seabed-mining issue should have had such salience in Washington.

For instance, in 1980, the United States was relying on imports for 98 % of the manganese it consumed, and 97 % of the cobalt. What made this reliance doubly worrisome was that the chief sources of these two minerals were felt to be unreliable, from a geopolitical standpoint: 82 % of American cobalt imports came from Zaire, and 72 % of imported manganese was supplied by South Africa and Gabon[67]. Both manganese and cobalt are present in the polymetallic nodules that are found in various parts of the deep seabed. The problem from the Canadian point of view is that so nickel is found in these «manganese» nodules (as well as copper, molybdenum, and vanadium). Since the United States is also a heavy importer of Canadian nickel (taking about 45 % of Canada's yearly production), it becomes evident that any large-scale American seabed mining – even if it were primarily intended to reduce American dependence upon imported cobalt and manganese – would have serious effects upon the land-based Canadian nickel industry.

The UN Convention will not result in an absence of seabed mining, but it will almost certainly lead to lower production levels than if there were no international regime for seabed mining, assuming of course such mining could be made economically feasible. Thus it is in Canada's interest to see that there is as little mining as the international environment will permit (and it should be noted in this context that the Group of 77 does, by and large, want production of seabed minerals – albeit production done under international auspices and shared in a way that reflects the «common-heritage-of-mankind» ethos). Canada would be best served in the medium term if there were no production of deep-seabed minerals; failing this, Canada looks favourably on any minimization of such production, and has been one of the beneficiaries of the struggle to impose production ceilings upon seabed mining[68].

The production ceiling will be determined by means of a complex formula, and it is really impossible at this stage to do more than guess at production levels for the 1990s[69]. Projections made only six or seven years ago assumed typically that the world demand for nickel, the variable upon which the ceilings are calculated, would grow at an annual rate of 3,5 % (using the years 1975 to 1984 as a base) and that nodule production would commence in 1988, and would be accounting for 32 % of world nickel demand by the year 2000[70]. This is by no means an insignificant figure, and if realizable it compels the conclusion that the convention's production ceilings would only be temporary protection at best for Canada's land-based nickel mining industry. However, what will really determine the amount of seabed mineral production under the treaty is not ceilings but market conditions: if such production is economic at 1990s' price levels for nickel and the other minerals contained in the nodules, then seabed mining will almost definitely take place on a significant scale. Whether the economic criterion can be met turns on the questions of future price levels and improvements in technology. While no one can say for sure what price and technology conditions will prevail in ten years' time, it is instructive that the economic potential of deep-seabed mining, once regarded by many as promising, is now seen to be extremely slight, at least for the rest of this century.

One thing does seem certain: if deep-seabed mining ultimately proves economic, there will eventually be a great deal of it taking place, whatever the future prospects of the convention are. What is uncertain is whether that mining would take place within an international regime and under conditions that would, temporarily at least, provide a breathing space for Canada's land-based nickel industry, or whether the United States, as the leader of a «Gang of Five» industrialized and technologically-advanced states (the others being Britain, France, Japan, and the Soviet Union) would continue to assert the *res-nullius* doctrine in this instance, and carve up the choicest seabed mineral sites between itself and the others. All that can be said at this juncture is that if a future US administration should bring itself to compromise on the seabed-mining provisions of the Convention (an open question at the moment), it will be in large measure because of a recognition that the US, like Canada, has much at stake in *other* parts of the treaty, especially (and here it is unlike Canada) in those dealing with the free navigation of the seas.

CONCLUSION

The above summaries have indicated both that Canadian ocean interests have been well-served and that those interests emerged principally as a result of the interplay between evolving technology and an improved political environment for the advancement of coastal state interests in general. In making such an assessment, one runs counter to another interpretation of Canadian ocean policy since 1968, namely that it was chiefly a function of the Trudeau foreign policy review of 1970, *Foreign Policy for Canadians,* which enjoined a greater attentiveness to the «national interest» as a guide to policy-making[71]. The purpose of this chapter has not been to slight the efforts of Canadian policy-makers and diplomats who have laboured on Law of the Sea issues, or to deny any influence to the Trudeau policy review. Obviously, they and it were important elements in the formulation of Canadian positions, but equally obviously, the conception of Canada as a coastal state had already developed by the mid-1960s, antedating Pierre E. Trudeau's attainment of power. That Trudeau and others were strong defenders of what they perceived to be the national interest does not detract from the conclusion of Barbara Johnson and Mark W. Zachar that «most other political leaders would have responded in the same way to the opportunities presented for furthering national oceans interests by the international political climate in the late 1960s and early 1970s»[72].

In a word, Canadian success in the creation and defence of its ocean policy stems from the fact that in this area of policy-making, the «national interest» seemed so limpid. Coupled with this clarity of perception was a decision-making apparatus that concentrated authority for ocean questions in one Department, External Affairs. To all intents and purposes, the «state» *was* External Affairs. Few countries could match the diplomatic effectiveness demonstrated by Canadian negotiators at various multilateral Law of the Sea sessions during the 1970s; the United States, for one, could not, in large measure because its Law of the Sea policy was to a significant extent the outcome of a clash of bureaucratic and domestic political interests clamoring for a variety of different policies[73]. In contrast to the Tower of Babel that was (and is) the American system of making foreign policy, Canada was able to articulate a coherent set of goals, and to defend them skillfully at various UNCLOS III sessions over the past thirteen year[74].

In this connection, it is worth suggesting that Canadian foreign policy in Law of the Sea matters disconfirms the applicability of the bureaucratic-politics model to this particular issue-area[75]. It may possibly be, as Denis Stairs has argued, that the bureaucratic-politics model is of less overall utility in the Canadian than in the American policy-making context[76]. But whether that is the case or not, it is arguable that based on the record of Canadian diplomacy on ocean issues, the rational-actor assumption implicit in «statist» paradigms provides a more effective medium for policy analysis[77]. That this should be so is simply another way of putting the point that policy-makers in Ottawa first developed a strong conception of Canada as a *coastal* state, then defended that coastal state set of interests born of the logic that inhered in Canada's geographical situation, and supported by a fortuitous shift in the international organizational balance of power away from the maritime interests.

NOTES

1. For an interesting discussion of the concept and its operationalization, see Donald E. Nuechterlein, *America Overcommitted: United States National Interest in the 1980s*, Lexington, University Press of Kentucky, 1985, chap. 1: «National Interest as a Basis of Foreign Policy Formulation».

2. Fundamental to any analysis of statist theory is Stephen D. Krasner, *Defending the National Interest: Raw Materials Investments and US Foreign Policy*, Princeton, Princeton University Press, 1978. The best recent application of statist conceptualizing to Canadian foreign policy-making is Kim Richard Nossal, *The Politics of Canadian Foreign Policy*, Scarborough, Prentice-Hall Canada, 1985.

3. The seminal work on this perspective remains David B. Dewitt and John J. Kirton, *Canada as a Principal Power: A Study in Foreign Policy and International Relations*, Toronto, John Wiley & Sons, 1983. A useful critique is Michael K. Hawes, *Principal Power, Middle Power, or Satellite?: Competing Perspectives in the Study of Canadian Foreign Policy*, Toronto, York Research Programme in Strategic Studies, 1984.

4. The continental shelf is but one part of the larger geological entity, the continental margin, which in turn is one of the two geographical divisions of the seabed, the other being the deep ocean floor. The margin constitutes roughly 15 % of the area of the seabed, and is divided into three conceptual parts: the continental *shelf*, held to be a natural extension of the land that inclines gradually towards greater depths; the continental *slope*, a discontinuity with the shelf that descends more steeply towards a great depth; and the continental *rise*, a sedimentary accumulation at the foot of the slope that gradually merges into the deep ocean floor. Barry Buzan, *Seabed Politics*, Praeger Special Studies in International Politics and Government, New York, Praeger, 1976, p. xiv.

5. «Like all other [Law of the Sea] Conference participants, Canada's objectives were largely determined by geography and economics.» Robert E. Hage, «The Third United Nations Conference on the Law of the Sea: A Canadian Retrospective», *Behind the Headlines*, July 1983, p. 2.

6. For a discussion of the postwar demise of geopolitics, see David G. Haglund, «La nouvelle géopolitique des minéraux: une étude sur l'évolution de l'impact international des minéraux stratégiques», *Études Internationales*, 13, September 1982, p. 445-471.

7. Barbara Johnson and Mark W. Zacher, «An Overview of Canadian Ocean Policy», *Canadian Foreign Policy and the Law of the Sea*, ed. Barbara Johnson and Mark W. Zacher, Vancouver, University of British Columbia Press, 1977, p. 363-364.

8. Interestingly, it was a fishery matter that marked an important stage in the development of Canadian constitutional status within the Commonwealth. In 1923, Canada signed a treaty entirely on its own for the first time. That treaty, concluded with the United States, regulated the Pacific halibut fishery. See. G. P. de T. Glazebrook, *A History of Canadian External Relations*, 2 vols., rev. ed., Toronto, McClelland and Stewart, 1966, Vol. 2, p. 69-70.

9. Except for the Canadian-American dispute over pelagic sealing in the Bering Sea, where the question of resource depletion was a central issue. See D. G. Paterson, «The North Pacific Seal Hunt, 1886-1910: Rights and Regulations», *Explorations in Economic History*, 14, April 1977, p. 97-119. Details of Canadian-British-American diplomatic wrangling over fisheries can be found in Donald C. Masters, *The Reciprocity Treaty of 1854*, Toronto, McClelland and Stewart, 1963, p. 20-25 and *passim*; Lester B. Shippee, *Canadian-American Relations, 1849-1874*, Carnegie Endowment for International Peace: The Relations of Canada and the United States, New Haven, Yale University Press, 1939, p. 161-187, 426-448; and Charles Callan Tansill, *Canadian-American Relations, 1875-1911*, Carnegie Endowment for International Peace: The Relations of Canada and the United States, New Haven, Yale University Press, 1943, p. 1-120, 267-295.

10. Erik B. Wang, «Canada-United States Fisheries and Maritime Boundary Negotiations: Diplomacy in Deep Water», *Behind the Headlines*, April 1981, p. 3.

11. Commercial extinction must be differentiated from outright physical extinction. If commercial stocks become too low as a result of excessive exploitation, fishing becomes uneconomic and ceases. Stocks then have a chance to recover, which leads to a rebirth of the fishing industry. Unless proper management techniques are applied to a fishery, the pattern recurs. Paul A. Driver, «International Fisheries», *The Maritime Dimension*, ed. R.P. Barston and Patricia Birnie, London, George Allen & Unwin, 1980, p. 43-44.

12. André-Louis Sanguin, «La zone canadienne des 200 milles dans l'Atlantique: un exemple de la nouvelle géographie politique des océans», *Études Internationales*, 11, June 1980, p. 242-243.

13. *Ibidem*, p. 242.

14. The First United Nations Conference on the Law of the Sea (UNCLOS I) was held in 1958, the second (UNCLOS II) in 1960, and the third (UNCLOS III) began in December 1973 and concluded in December 1982.

15. Barbara Johnson, «Canadian Foreign Policy and Fisheries», *Canadian Foreign Policy and the Law of the Sea*, p. 52. (Emphasis in original.)

16. In international law, the territorial sea is a band of water seaward of a state's internal waters and over which a state may claim all the rights associated with sovereignty, except that it must accord foreign ships a right of «innocent passage», which essentially means that transiting vessels must do so as expeditiously as possible, engaging neither in military exercises nor fishing. Today, more than 100 states (Canada included) claim a territorial sea of at least twelve miles, which is the distance recognized by Art. 3 of the UN Convention on the Law of the Sea.

17. «Politically, the claim to a 200-mile zone had been so legitimized by continuing sessions of the Law of the Sea Conference that the unilateral Canadian legislation of 1 January 1977 was implemented without resistance. This was in itself an enormous achievement.» Johnson, «Canadian Foreign Policy and Fisheries», p. 94. Art. 56 of the Convention accords to coastal states a 200-mile exclusive economic zone (EEZ).

18. Donald Barry, «The Canada-European Community Long-Term Fisheries Agreement: Internal Politics and Fisheries Diplomacy», *Journal of European Integration*, 9, Autumn 1985, p. 5-28.

19. F.S. Northedge, *The International Political System*, London, Faber & Faber, 1976, p. 274. For a discussion of bilateral fishing «tension», see Stephen Greene and Thomas Keating, «Domestic Factors and Canada-United States Fisheries Relations», *Canadian Journal of Political Science*, 13, December 1985, p. 731-750.

20. For a very good analysis of this complex set of problems, see Wang, «Canada-United States Fisheries and Maritime Boundary Negotiations».

21. Donald Barry, «The US Senate and the Collapse of the East Coast Fisheries Agreement», *Dalhousie Review*, 62, Autumn 1982, p. 495-503.

22. «Signature of a Canada/USA Pacific Coast Albacore Tuna Vessels and Port Privileges Agreement», Department of External Affairs, *Communiqué*, May 26, 1981.

23. Wang, «Canada-United States Fisheries and Maritime Boundary Negotiations», p. 17.

24. See, for this view, Hal Mills, «Georges Bank and the National Interest», *New Directions in Ocean Law, Policy and Management*, 1, February 1981, p. 4-5. According to Mils, «Canadians should breathe a collective sign of relief that the Agreement on East Coast Fishery Resources has not been ratified...»

25. Johnson, «Canadian Foreign Policy and Fisheries», p. 95.

26. For an elucidation of this distinction, see Buzan, *Seabed Politics*, p. 1. Also see F.V. Garcia Amador, *The Exploitation and Conservation of the Resources of the Sea*, Leyden, Neth., Sythoff, 1973; and Gerard J. Mangone, *The United Nations, International Law, and the Bed of the Seas*, Newark, University of Delaware Press, 1972.

27. Ann L. Hollick, «The Origins of 200-Mile Offshore Zones», *American Journal of International Law*, 71, July 1977, p. 494-500.

28. Buzan, *Seabed Politics*, p. 7-8.

29. Barry Buzan, «Canada and the Law of the Sea», *Ocean Development and International Law Journal*, 11, 1982, p. 160. Although some 40 states had made various kinds of unilateral claims to the continental shelf by the time of UNCLOS I in 1958, Canada was not among them.

30. See, for this view, Peyton V. Lyon and Brian W. Tomlin, *Canada as an International Actor*, Canadian Controversies Series, Toronto, Macmillan of Canada, 1979, p. 186: «One must conclude that Canada's performance in the Law of the Sea negotiations augurs ill for its response to the demands for fundamental changes that constitute the New International Economic Order. If Canada is so acquisitive concerning territory and resources that it got along without for many generations, what hope is there that it will agree to measures that would drastically alter existing structures to the advantage of the nations that must presently endure living conditions cruelly inferior to those of the industrialized North?»

31. Canadian reliance upon imported crude oil began to seem worrisome after the oil shock of 1978-1979. See David G. Haglund, «Canada and the International Politics of Oil: Latin American Source of Supply and Import Vulnerability in the 1980s», *Canadian Journal of Political Science*, 15, June 1982, p. 259-298. For offshore hydrocarbon exploitation in general, see Peter Odell, «Offshore Resources: Oil and Gas», *The Maritime Dimension*, p. 76-107.

32. Estimates of the size of potential reserves in Hibernia and nearby fields in the Atlantic Grand Banks varied widely, ranging from 1 to 10 billion barrels. The Newfoundland Government assumed some years ago that there were 1,8 billion barrels of proved reserves in offshore fields over which it was claiming jurisdiction. See Bob Williams *et al.*, «North American Arctic Report», *Oil and Gas Journal*, 25, June 1984, p. 55-77; David B. Brooks, «Black Gold Redrilled: Are the Economics of Beaufort Sea Oil Getting Better or Worse?», *Northern Perspectives*, 11, 3, 1984, p. 1-4; and John F. Helliwell, Mary E. MacGregor and André Plourde, «Changes in Canadian Energy Demand, Supply, and Policies, 1974-1986», *Natural Resources Journal*, 24, 1984, p. 297-324.

33. According to Art. 56 of the Convention, the coastal state has in the EEZ «sovereign rights for the purpose of exploring and exploiting, conserving and managing the natural resources, whether living or non-living, of the seabed and subsoil and the superjacent waters [...]»

34. Barry Buzan and Danford W. Middlemiss, «Canadian Foreign Policy and the Exploitation of the Seabed», *Canadian Foreign Policy and the Law of the Sea*, p. 3. Off the West Coast, the shelf averages only 20 miles in width, and the margin nowhere exceeds 120. In the Arctic, most of the margin lies within the 200-mile limit of the EEZ.

35. R.M. Logan, *Canada, the United States, and the Third Law of the Sea Conference*, Montréal, Canadian-American Committee, C.D. Howe Research Institute, 1974, p. 64.

36. Convention, Part VI, Art. 76, Sec. 1.

37. *Ibidem*, Art. 82, Secs. 1 and 2.

38. James H. Breen, «The 1982 Dispute Resolving Agreement: The First Step toward Unilateral Mining Outside of the Law of the Sea Convention», *Ocean Development and International Law*, 14, 2, 1984, p. 201-234.

39. J.L. Granatstein, «A Fit of Absence of Mind: Canada's National Interest in the North to 1968», *The Arctic in Question*, ed. E.J. Dosman, Toronto, Oxford University Press, 1976, p. 13.

40. Evan Browne, «Sovereignty Questions Remain after Century in the Arctic», *International Perspectives*, July-August 1980, p. 8; Donat Pharand, «The Legal Regime of the Arctic: Some Outstanding Issues», *International Journal*, 39, Autumn 1984, p. 742-799.

41. For a discussion of archipelagic and historic waters, see Donat Pharand, *The Law of the Sea of the Arctic (With Special Reference to Canada)*, Ottawa, University of Ottawa Press, 1973, p. 65-144.

42. E.J. Dosman, «The Northern Sovereignty Crisis, 1968-1970», *The Arctic in Question*, p. 35. This was not the first time that an American reaction to a Canadian initiative north of 60 degrees north latitude was predicated upon a fear that a precedent would be set for an Asian country to do something the United States felt was inimical to its interests. In the spring of 1940, the United States successfully pressured Canada to abandon a preemptive occupation of Greenland planned in the wake of the German conquest of Denmark. In this instance, Washington feared that Japan would seize upon any Canadian precedent to stage a preemptive strike of its own against the Netherlands' East Indies. See David G. Haglund., «'Plain Grand Imperialism on a Miniature Scale': Canadian-American Rivalry over Greenland in 1940», *American Review of Canadian Studies*, 11, Spring 1981, p. 15-36.

43. E.J. Dosman, «Northern Sovereignty and Canadian Foreign Policy», *The Arctic in Question*, p. 6.

44. See note 16.

45. The American worry (shared to a degree by the Soviets) is that extension of territorial seas from three to twelve miles would enclose more than 100 straits, which are wider than six but narrower than 24 miles. This, according to the former head of the US UNCLOS III delegation, «could seriously impair the flexibility not only of our conventional forces but of our fleet ballistic missile submarines, which depend on complete mobility in the oceans and unimpeded passage through international straits. Only such freedom makes possible the secrecy on which their survivability is based». Elliot L. Richardson, «Power, Mobility and the Law of the Sea», *Foreign Affairs*, 58, Spring 1980, p. 905.

46. Convention, Art. 38.

47. For a good discussion of the issue, see Donat Pharand, with Leonard H. Legault, *Northwest Passage: Arctic Straits*, Dordrecht, Vartinus Nijhoff, 1984.

48. Roger D. McConchie and Robert S. Reid, «Canadian Foreign Policy and International Straits», *Canadian Foreign Policy and the Law of the Sea*, p. 170.

49. *Citizen* (Ottawa), April 12, 1986, p. 43.

50. Convention, Art. 234. According to this article, «coastal states have the right to adopt and enforce non-discriminatory laws and regulations for the prevention, reduction and control of marine pollution from vessels in ice-covered areas within the limits of the exclusive economic zone, where particularly severe climatic conditions and the presence of ice covering such areas for most of the year create obstructions or exceptional hazards to navigation, and pollution of the marine environment could cause major harm to or irreversible disturbance of the ecological balance».

51. The «functional principle» is arguably one of the hallmarks of Canadian foreign policy in this century, having been especially prominent in connection with Canadian Law of the Sea policy. The principle is associated with the substitution of «custodianship» for full sovereignty, and with the concomitant delegation of powers for the performance of specific duties. For a comprehensive analysis, see A.J. Miller, «The Functional Principle in Canada's External Relations», *International Journal*, 35, Spring 1980, p. 309-328. For functionalism and Law of the Sea matters, see John W. Holmes, *Canada: A Middle-Aged Power*, Toronto, McClelland and Stewart, 1976, p. 66-70; and Georges Antoine Léger, «Droit de la mer: La contribution du Canada au nouveau concept de la zone économique», *Études internationales*, 11, September 1980, p. 421-440.

52. Maxwell Cohen, «The Arctic and the National Interest», *International Journal*, 26, Winter 1970-1971, p. 52-81.

53. «[The] impetus for Canadian policy came from internal public pressure, pressure motivated largely by jurisdictional and not environmental concerns. The basis for these concerns was the planned Arctic voyage of the American supertanker *Manhattan*, a voyage that aroused far greater fears of loss of sovereignty than of environmental destruction.» R. Michael M'Gonigle and Mark W. Zacher, *Pollution, Politics, and International Law: Tankers at Sea*, Berkeley, University of California Press, 1979, p. 280.

54. One of the biggest impediments to Canada's obtaining full-sovereignty status in the Arctic waters, of course, remains the attitude of the United States. In a policy statement released in the aftermath of the Gulf of Sidra fighting of March 1986, the State Department affirmed that «the United States is committed to the exercise and preservation of navigation and overflight rights and freedoms around the world [...] Examples of the types of objectionable claims against which the United States has exercised rights and freedoms are *unrecognized historic waters claims*, territorial sea claims greater than 12 nautical miles, and territorial sea claims that impose impermissible restrictions on the innocent passage of any type of vessels [...]», Ottawa, US Embassy, «US Committed to Free Passage Rights», *Text*, March 27, 1986 (emphasis added).

55. For a discussion of the impact of Canadian Arctic legislation on international law, see Donat Pharand, «La contribution du Canada au développement du droit international pour la protection du milieu marin: Le cas spécial de l'Arctique», *Études internationales*, II, September 1980, p. 441-466.

56. Peter C. Dobell, *Canada's Search for New Roles: Foreign Policy in the Trudeau Era*, London, Oxford University Press, 1972, p. 77.

57. R. Michael M'Gonigle and Mark W. Zacher, «Canadian Foreign Policy and the Control of Marine Pollution», in *Canadian Foreign Policy and the Law of the Sea*, p. 113.

58. Buzan, «Canada and the Law of the Sea», p. 156.

59. The argument that the functional approach constitutes a «back-door means» to sovereignty in the Arctic is made in Michael Tucker, *Canadian Foreign Policy: Contemporary Issues and Themes*, Toronto, McGraw-Hill Ryerson, 1980, p. 181.

60. «Twenty-five years ago, nearly all the world's nickel came from either Sudbury, Ontario, or New Caledonia, off the Australian coast. Even though production has increased in absolute terms, Canadian-based mining now represents a far smaller share of the total market and, very significantly, competes for world trade with the output of mines around the world [...]» W.E. Cundiff, *Nodule Shock? Seabed Mining and the Future of the Canadian Nickel Industry*, Occasional Paper No. 1, Montréal, Institute for Research on Public Policy, 1978, p. iii.

61. The argument is not that Canada must lose what it has gained in the matters of fisheries, offshore hydrocarbons, or Arctic pollution control power should the seabed mining talks ultimately fail. Rather, the concern is that inability to resolve this issue might «lead to a much less comprehensive and less widely supported Law of the Sea Convention, and therefore result in a less stable law of the sea regime than Canada had hoped for.» Buzan and Middlemiss, «Canadian Foreign Policy and the Exploitation of the Seabed», p. 46.

62. Elliot L. Richardson, «Law of the Sea», *Naval War College Review*, May-June 1979, p. 9. The phrase, «common heritage of mankind», is from a 1967 speech by Arvid Pardo, Malta's then-representative to the United Nations.

63. Victor Prescott, «The Deep Seabed», *The Maritime Dimension*, p. 65. «The importance of the debate can be roughly measured by the fact that in the *Informal Composite Negotiating Text* there are 34 pages dealing with the deep seabed, which is only one page less than the space occupied by the text dealing with the territorial seas and contiguous zone, straits used for international navigation, archipelagic states, the exclusive economic zone and the continental shelf.»

64. William Safire, «The Great Ripoff», *New York Times*, March 19, 1981.

65. An account of American concern over mineral supplies is found in Alfred E. Eckes, Jr., *The United States and the Global Struggle for Minerals*, Austin, University of Texas Press, 1979.

66. Bohdan O. Szuprowicz, *How to Avoid Strategic Materials Shortages: Dealing with Cartels, Embargoes, and Supply Disruptions*, New York, John Wiley & Sons, 1981, p. 60. For a review of American mineral dependence since World War II, see John Drew Ridge, «Minerals from Abroad: The Changing Scene», *The Mineral Position of the United States, 1975-2000*, ed. Eugene N. Cameron, Madison, University of Wisconsin Press, 1973. A useful corrective to some of the more melodramatic assessments of US dependence is Bruce Russett, «Dimensions of Resource Dependence: Some Elements of Rigor in Concept and Policy Analysis», *International Organization*, 38, Summer 1984, p. 481-499.

67. *New York Times*, March 15, 1981.

68. The Director of the Ontario Government's Division of mineral resources succinctly stated his province's view that «anything that postpones the eventual competition for Sudbury is a good thing». *The Globe and Mail*, May 18, 1981.

69. For the production ceiling, see UN Convention, Art. 151.

70. V.E. McKelvey, «Seabed Minerals and the Law of the Sea», *Science*, 25, July 1980, p. 471. The ceilings for cobalt and manganese would amount to, respectively, 116 and 47 % of world demand by 2000.

71. This interpretation of Canadian ocean initiatives is given in A.E. Gotlieb, «Canadian Diplomatic Initiatives: The Law of the Sea», *Freedom and Change: Essays in Honour of L.B. Pearson*, ed. M.G. Fry, Toronto, McClelland and Stewart, 1975, p. 136-151.

72. Barbara Johnson and Mark W. Zacher, «An Overview of Canadian Ocean Policy», in *Canadian Foreign Policy and the Law of the Sea*, p. 362.

73. «The Diversity of United States interests and lines of influence makes the negotiation of a single national policy as difficult, if not *more* difficult [sic], as negotiating the policy internationally.» Ann L. Hollick, «Canadian-American Relations: Law of the Sea», *Canada and the United States: Transnational and Transgovernmental Relations*, ed. Annette Baker Fox, Alfred O. Hero, and Joseph S. Nye, Jr., New York, Columbia University Press, 1976, p. 180. (Emphasis in original.)

74. The argument that Canada possesses certain structural bargaining advantages vis-à-vis the United States – stemming principally form the smaller size of its «governmental machinery» – is made in Gilbert R. Winham, «Choice and Strategy in Continental Relations», *Continental Community? Independence and Integration in North America*, ed. W. Andrew Axline *et al.*, Toronto, McClelland and Stewart, 1974, p. 230-231. For a generalized application of this structural observation, see Robert O. Keohane and Joseph S. Nye, *Power and Interdependence: World Politics in Transition*, Boston, Little, Brown, 1977, p. 53: «States with intense preferences and coherent positions will bargain more effectively than states constrained by domestic and transnational actors.»

75. The bureaucratic (or governmental) politics model is elucidated in Graham T. Allison's now-classic *Essence of Decision: Explaining the Cuban Missile Crisis*, Boston, Little, Brown, 1971, p. 144-184. An interesting grafting of Allison's approach to the parliamentary system is Kim Richard Nossal's «Bureaucratic Politics and the Westminster Model», *International Conflict and Conflict Management*, ed. Robert O. Matthews, Arthur G. Rubinoff and Janice Gross Stein, Scarborough, Prentice-Hall of Canada, 1984, p. 120-127.

76. Denis Stairs, «The Foreign Policy of Canada», *World Politics: An Introduction*, ed. James N. Rosenau, Kenneth W. Thompson and Gavin Boyd, New York, Free Press, 1976, p. 185.

77. For an example of the application of this model to Canadian UNCLOS diplomacy, see Barry Buzan and Barbara Johnson, «Canada at the Third Law of the Sea Conference: Strategy, Tactics, and Policy», *Canadian Foreign Policy and the Law of the Sea*, p. 255-310.

BIBLIOGRAPHY

ALEXANDER, Lewis M. «Organizational Responses to New Ocean Science and Technology Development», *Ocean Development and International Law*, 9, 1981, p. 241-268.

BARRY, Donald. «The Canadian-European Community Long-Term Fisheries Agreement: Internal Politics and Fisheries Diplomacy», *Journal of European Integration*, 9, Autumn 1985, p. 5-28.

BARRY, Donald. «The US Senate and the Collapse of the East Coast Fisheries Agreement», *Dalhousie Review*, 62, Autumn, 1982, p. 495-503.

BARSTON, R.P. and BIRNIE, Patricia, eds. *The Maritime Dimension*, London, George Allen & Unwin, 1980.

BEESLEY, J.A. «The Law of the Sea Conference: Factors Behind Canada's Stance», *International Perspectives*, July-August 1972, p. 28-30.

BREEN, James H. «The 1982 Dispute Resolving Agreements: The First Step toward Unilateral Mining Outside of the Law of the Sea Convention», *Ocean Development and International Law*, 14, 1984, p. 201-234.

BROWNE, Evan. «Sovereignty Questions Remain After Century in the Arctic», *International Perspectives*, July-August, 1980, p. 7-11.

BUZAN, Barry. «Canada and the Law of the Sea», *Ocean Development and International Law*, 11, 1982, p. 149-180.

BUZAN, Barry. *Seabed Politics*, Praeger Special Studies in International Politics and Government, New York, Praeger, 1976.

COHEN, Maxwell. «The Arctic and the National Interest», *International Journal*, 26, Winter 1970-1971, p. 52-81.

CUNDIFF, W.D. *Nodule Shock? Seabed Mining and the Future of the Canadian Nickel Industry*, Occasional Paper No. 1, Montréal, Institute for Research on Public Policy, 1978.

DARMAN, Richard G. «The Law of the Sea: Rethinking US Interests», *Foreign Affairs*, 56, January 1978, p. 373-395.

DOSMAN, E.J., ed. *The Arctic in Question*, Toronto, Oxford University Press, 1976.

GARCIA AMADOR, F.V. *The Exploitation and Conservation of the Resources of the Sea*, Leyden, Sythoff, 1963.

GORDON, Michael R. «Companies Ready to Stake Out Claims for Mineral Wealth Beneath the Seas», *National Journal*, 9, August 1980, p. 1312-1315.

GOTLIEB, A.E. «Canadian Diplomatic Initiatives: The Law of the Sea», *Freedom and Change: Essays in Honour of L.B. Pearson*, ed. by M.G. Fry, Toronto, McClelland and Stewart, 1975.

GREENE, Stephen and KEATING, Thomas. «Domestic Factors and Canada-United States Fisheries Relations», *Canadian Journal of Political Science*, 13, December 1985, p. 731-750.

HAGE, Robert E. «The Third United Nations Conference on the Law of the Sea: A Canadian Retrospective», *Behind the Headlines*, July 1983.

HAGLUND, David G. «La nouvelle géopolitique des minéraux: une étude sur l'évolution de l'impact international des minéraux stratégiques», *Études internationales*, 13, September 1982, p. 445-471.

HOLLICK, Ann L. «Canadian-American Relations: Law of the Sea», *Canada and the United States: Transnational and Transgovernmental Relations*, Ed. by Annette Baker Fox, Alfred O. Hero and Joseph S. Nye, Jr., New York, Columbia University Press, 1976, p. 162-187.

HOLLICK, Ann L. «The Origins of 200-Mile Offshore Zones», *American Journal of International Law*, 71, July 1977, p. 494-500.

HOLLICK, Ann L. *US Foreign Policy and the Law of the Sea*, Princeton, Princeton University Press, 1981.

JOHNSON, Barbara and ZACHER, Mark W., eds. *Canadian Foreign Policy and the Law of the Sea*, Vancouver, University of British Columbia Press, 1977.

LÉGER, Georges Antoine, «Droit de la mer: la contribution du Canada au nouveau concept de la zone économique», *Études internationales*, 11, September 1980, p. 421-440.

LOGAN, R.M. *Canada, the United States, and the Third Law of the Sea Conference*, Montréal, Canadian-American Committee, C.D. Howe Research Institute, 1974.

LYON, Peyton V. and TOMLIN, Brian W. *Canada as an International Actor*, Canadian Controversies Series, Toronto, MacMillan of Canada, 1979.

M'GONIGLE, R. Michael and ZACHER, Mark W. *Pollution, Politics and International Law: Tankers at Sea*, Berkeley, University of California Press, 1979.

McKELVEY, V.E. «Seabed Minerals and the Law of the Sea», *Science*, July 25, 1980, p. 464-472.

MANGONE, Gerard J. *The United Nations, International Law, and the Bed of the Seas*, Newark, University of Delaware Press, 1972.

MILLS, Hal. «Georges Bank and the National Interest», New *Directions in Ocean Law, Policy and Management*, 1, February 1981, p. 4-5.

NEATBY, L.H. *In Quest of the North West Passage,* Toronto, Longman, Green, 1958.

PHARAND, Donat. «La contribution du Canada au développement du droit international pour la protection du milieu marin: le cas spécial de l'Arctique», *Études internationales,* 11, September 1980, p. 441-466.

PHARAND, Donat. *The Law of the Sea of the Arctic (With Special Reference to Canada),* Ottawa, University of Ottawa Press, 1973.

PHARAND, Donat. «The Legal Regime of the Arctic: Some Outstanding Issues», *International Journal,* 39, Autumn 1984, p. 742-799.

PHARAND, Donat and LEGAULT, Leonard H. *Northwest Passage: Arctic Straits,* Dordrecht, Martinus Nijhoff, 1984.

RICHARDSON, Elliot L. «Law of the Sea», *Naval War College Review,* May-June 1979, p. 3-10.

RICHARDSON, Elliot L. «Power, Mobility and the Law of the Sea», *Foreign Affairs,* 58, Spring 1980, p. 902-919.

SANGUIN, André-Louis. «La zone canadienne des 200 milles dans l'Atlantique: un exemple de la nouvelle géographie politique des océans», *Études internationales,* 11, June 1980, p. 239-251.

SZUPROWICZ, Bohdan O. *How to Avoid Strategic Materials Shortages: Dealing with Cartels, Embargoes, and Supply Disruptions,* New York, John Wiley & Sons, 1981.

WANG, Erik B. «Canada-United States Fisheries and Maritime Boundary Negotiations: Diplomacy in Deep Water», *Behind the Headlines,* April 1981.

26

Canadian Immigration and Refugee Policies

Freda Hawkins
University of Warwick – United Kingdom

Immigration and refugee policies and programs, as well as the staff and structures required to implement and manage them, have made a major contribution to Canada's external relations and overseas image in the postwar period. This fact is very often ignored by our academic authorities on international affairs, as well as by many politicians and senior officials who have always accorded much greater prestige to those who are involved in conventional diplomatic activities, however unimportant these may be, or who manage Canada's trade relations, or overseas aid programs, or other areas of public policy involving foreign operations. To manage the flow of human beings to Canada which has had such an important influence on population growth and economic development, on the life and vitality of Canadian cities and on the range of skills and talents which our labour force can offer has been regarded, for the greater part of the postwar period and even to some extent today, as a second class and non-prestigious activity.

Equally, when the dissemination of information about Canada in foreign countries is acknowledged as very difficult to do, the fact that our overseas immigration officers (working in 59 overseas offices and 44 countries) do it all the time, either in direct personal contact with would-be immigrants, or by responding to enquiries and applications with printed material (often reaching the applicant's friends and relatives also) is rarely mentioned. The intangible but very important international migration grapevine is another factor of great significance relating to our international image. Across air space in all directions, go the satisfactions and critical comments of countless immigrants, and often refugees, who are reporting back on their experience in Canada, and describing the new country they have chosen to settle in or where chance has placed them. In the field of international communication, these private channels are critical. Only perhaps in relation to refugees, beginning with the Ugandan Asian Refugee Movement in 1972-1973 and confirmed by the large-scale Indochinese Movement which is still continuing, have we begun to appreciate what a potent instrument for international goodwill our policies and programs in this field can be. Our standing in the international community as a generous and responsible country of permanent settlement for refugees does more for us than any official public relations and information exercise could ever do.

POSTWAR POLICY EVOLUTION

Canada has admitted 4,5 million immigrants and refugees since the end of World War II. This compares with 3,5 million for Australia and approaching 11 million for the United States, the other two major immigrant receiving countries in recent times. Table 1, presented at the end of the chapter, shows Canada's annual intake of immigrants and refugees between 1946 and 1981.

The critical dates in the evolution of Canadian postwar immigration policy are 1947, 1962, 1966-1967 and 1976-1977. Each marks the beginning of a significant new stage in policy development and/or management. In 1947, Prime Minister Mackenzie King made an important statement outlining the major features of the Liberal Government's postwar immigration policy – essentially a continuation of the interwar «White Canada» policy. This was followed, however, by the creation of a new Department of Citizenship and Immigration in 1950 and a new Immigration Act which was passed in 1952. In 1962, in the new Immigration Regulations of that year, the Diefenbaker Government abandoned an immigration policy based on racial discrimination in favour of a universal policy based on skills and talents, family reunification and compassionate considerations mainly relating to refugees. In 1966-1967, immigration became part of a new, high-priority Department of Manpower and Immigration with a mandate to upgrade and develop the skills and mobility of the Canadian labour force. Special Immigration Regulations issued in 1967 contained an entirely new «Canadian point system» for the selection and admission of immigrants, which had been worked out by Canadian immigration officials, and would later be adopted in a modified form by Australia.

In the years 1976-1977, a new Immigration Act was passed by Parliament, introducing significant changes in immigration and refugee policy and management. It had been preceded by a major review of Canada's immigration and population policies, which began in the fall of 1972, followed by a Green Paper on Immigration Policy tabled in the House of Commons in February 1975. This led to the appointment in March of a Special Joint Committee of the Senate and the House of Commons to examine the Green Paper and to hold public hearings across Canada on the fundamental questions it raised of immigration policy and population growth and distribution. The Committee produced an excellent report to Parliament eight months later. 60 out of 65 of the Committee's recommendations were accepted by the Liberal Government and they formed some of the major elements in the new Immigration Act passed by Parliament in the following year. In August 1977, the Employment and Immigration Reorganization Act received royal assent. It provided for the amalgamation of the Department of Manpower and Immigration and the Unemployment Insurance Commission to form a new and very large quasi-independent agency, the Canada Employment and Immigration Commission with a small supporting Department of Employment and Immigration. The Commission had a regional structure which consisted initially of ten regions, organized mainly on provincial lines, and an eleventh region formed by Manpower and Immigration's Foreign Service. In April 1981, however, as part of the accelerated process of consolidation of Canada's overseas operations, made known by the Prime Minister on March 21, 1980, it was announced that the Foreign Service, consisting of some 350 immigration officers, would be transferred to the Department of External Affairs.

We will examine each of these stages in turn, recalling in each case some of the critical issues of the day. We will also look at the parallel development of refugee policy; at Canada's involvement with UNHCR (Office of the United Nations High Commissioner for Refugees) and ICEM (Intergovernmental Committee for European Migration), now known as ICM (Intergovernmental Committee for Migration); and at our response to the world refugee explosion of recent years.

THE EARLY POSTWAR PERIOD, 1946-1962

As the war in Europe ended, it became obvious that something would have to be done about Canada's existing immigration policy, law and management, all of which appeared to be inadequate for the postwar world. In addition, it was clear that some kind of major response would have to be made to the critical situation involving millions of displaced and homeless persons in Europe. On December 14, 1945, David Croll, then Liberal Member for the Toronto riding of Spadina, raised the question of immigration in the House, urging that this be studied immediately with a view to the development of a short-term and long-term immigration policy for Canada. The Minister of Mines and Resources, J.A. Glen, then responsible for immigration, responded by saying that the Government was studying the matter, but had to give first priority to the repatriation and re-establishment in Canada of service personnel. Early in 1946, however, a Cabinet sub-committee was formed to consider the whole question of postwar immigration to Canada and an interdepartmental committee was established at the same time to consider its domestic implications.

At that point, the admission of immigrants to Canada was governed by an order-in-council of March 31, 1931 (P.C. 695) which restricted it to: 1. British subjects defined as «British by reason of birth or naturalization in Great Britain or Ireland, Newfoundland, New Zealand, Australia and the Union of South Africa; 2. Citizens of the United States; 3. The wife and unmarried children under 18 and fiancé(e)s of legal residents of Canada; and 4. «Agriculturalists having sufficient means to farm in Canada». Under an order-in-council of September 16, 1930 (P.C. 2115), what was called «Asiatic immigration» (excluding the Chinese) was restricted to the wife and unmarried children under 18 of any Canadian citizen resident in Canada who was in a position to receive and care for his dependents. Under the revised Chinese Immigration Act of 1923, all persons of Chinese ethnic origin, except merchants, were prohibited from admission regardless of their nationality or religion. The term «merchant» was narrowly defined to mean «a person who devoted his undivided attention to mercantile pursuits, who had not less than $2,500 invested in an enterprise importing to Canada or exporting to China goods of Chinese or Canadian origin or manufacture and who had conducted such a business for at least three years».

During the first few years after the war, the following moves were made by the Liberal Government, under Mackenzie King until November 1948 and then under Louis St. Laurent, to define Canadian citizenship, to establish immigration and management policy on an acceptable and effective basis; and to respond to the refugee and displaced persons crisis in Europe:

- In 1946, Paul Martin, then Secretary of State, introduced a Citizenship Bill to revise and consolidate naturalization and citizenship laws, and to introduce the concept of «Canadian citizenship» in place of «British nationality». It was enacted during that year, proclaimed on January 1, 1947 and subsequently amended several times. It was eventually replaced by a new Citizenship Act which became law in 1976;

- The established categories for the admission of relatives were cautiously widened in 1946, 1947 and 1949, mainly because of the many families separated by war;
- Emergency measures were introduced to bring refugees and displaced persons to Canada. These were announced by Prime Minister Mackenzie King in the House of Commons on November 7, 1946. Arrangements were made with the International Refugee Organization to facilitate this movement. By March 1947, two immigration teams were in action in Europe and the first displaced person sailed for Canada a month later. On June 6, 1947, provision was made for the admission of 5 000 displaced but later this number was substantially increased. Eventually, a total of 165 697 displaced persons were admitted to Canada between 1947 and 1952;
- Arrangements were made to admit three special movements of immigrants, two in 1946 and one in 1947, consisting of Polish ex-servicemen then in Britain and Italy; Netherlands farm workers (following an approach by the Netherlands Government); and Maltese immigrants (following representation from the British Government);
- Farm workers, miners and loggers – if coming to assured employment – were added to the admissible classes in view of the urgent need for labour in Canada's primary industries;
- It was decided to repeal the Chinese Immigration Act of 1923 and to place the Chinese with other Asians under the still very restrictive provisions of P.C. 2115. A Bill to repeal the Chinese Immigration Act was introduced in the House on May 2, 1947;
- A postwar immigration policy for Canada was formulated. This was outlined by Prime Minister Mackenzie King in the House on May 1, 1947. This was the critical date mentioned earlier;
- By order-in-council in June 1949, citizens of France were placed in the same category for admission to Canada as British subjects (as defined) and US citizens;
- A new Department of Citizenship and Immigration was created, which opened its doors to the public on January 18, 1950.

The famous Mackenzie King statement on immigration policy of May 1947 served as the official formulation of Canadian immigration policy until 1962[1]. It was a sober and unenthusiastic document, originally drafted by Gordon Robertson in the Prime Minister's office, redrafted by Jack Pickersgill, then the Prime Minister's special assistant and later a Minister of Citizenship and Immigration, and submitted to the Prime Minister and Cabinet. It spoke very plainly first of the Government's intention to use immigration judiciously for population growth and economic development while keeping it under firm control; and secondly of the Government's determination to preserve the basic character of the Canadian population as it was then and to prevent any disturbing changes which might result from mass immigration, particularly from Asia.

The main body of the statement is divided into two parts: consideration of the Government's short-term («measures designed for immediate application») and long-term programs. In the first part, the Prime Minister outlined the steps which had already been taken and which have been described above. In the second part, he established six major premises as the basis for Canada's long-term immigration program. There is no comparable statement in official pronouncements or in subsequent law and regulations until we get to the Immigration Act of 1976 which contains, in Part I, a list of ten basic principles and objectives of immigration policy. There is a world of difference between the two, and an examination of both documents provides a valuable measure of the extent to which attitudes and objectives in Canadian immigration changed over that 30-year period.

Mackenzie King's basic premises were as follows:

- The objective of Canada's immigration policy must be to enlarge the population of the country. It would be dangerous for a small population to hold «so great a heritage as ours»;
- If properly planned, immigration will improve the Canadian standard of living. A larger population will help to develop Canada's resources, enlarge its domestic market, and reduce its dependence on the export of primary products;
- It is essential that immigrants be selected with care;
- It is of the utmost importance to relate immigration to absorptive capacity [...] the serious losses of population in the past through emigration – particularly of young people educated and trained in Canada – were a warning that absorptive capacity should not be exceeded;
- Immigration is a matter of domestic policy and is subject to the control of Parliament. Objectionable discrimination should be removed from existing legislation, but Canada is perfectly within its rights in selecting the immigrants it wants. An alien has no «fundamental human right» to enter Canada. This is a privilege;
- The people of Canada do not wish to make a fundamental alteration in the character of their population through mass immigration. The Government is therefore opposed to «large-scale immigration from the Orient» which would certainly give rise to social and economic problems which might lead to serious international difficulties. The Government has no intention of changing the regulations governing Asiatic immigration «unless and until alternative measures of effective control have been worked out». However, the Government is ready to negotiate special agreements with other countries for the control of immigration based on complete equality and reciprocity.

Although under Section 95 of the BNA Act, immigration is a concurrent jurisdiction of the Federal Government and the provinces, there was no reference to the provinces or to their immigration interests and responsibilities in this statement. And, as the Opposition spokesman, E. Davie Fulton, pointed out, there was no indication of any kind as to how these principles would be carried out. Where would these immigrants come from? How would they be selected? Which countries was the Government prepared to negotiate with? And what kind of assistance, if any, would be provided for immigrants[2]? No one in the Liberal administration had any answer to these questions.

The new Department of Citizenship and Immigration survived for fifteen years and is the only example we have so far of a federal department devoted primarily to the development and management of immigration. It also had an Indian Affairs

Branch and a small Citizenship Branch, transferred from its original home in the Department of the Secretary of State. The theory behind this collection of responsibilities, devised by the Department's two principal architects: Dr. Hugh Keenleyside, formerly Deputy Minister of the old Department of Mines and Resources, and Jack Pickersgill, was that it would be advantageous if Canada's human as opposed to natural resources were managed by one department. This thought was expressed by Prime Minister St. Laurent on November 26, 1946, when moving resolutions in the House that Bills be presented to create three new departments, a Department of Resources and Development, a Department of Mines and Technical Surveys and a Department of Citizenship and Immigration.

«It was felt, the Prime Minister said, that it would have some psychological effect to say that these three activities dealing with human beings, and which are designed to bring those human beings to the status of full citizenship as rapidly as possible, were under one head. Having citizenship, immigration and Indian affairs in the one department would indicate that the purpose of the activities of that department was to make Canadian citizens out of those who were born here, of the original inhabitants of the territory and of those who migrated to this country[3].» It was a rather shallow concept, taking no account of the very different needs of native peoples and immigrants and the different kinds of knowledge and expertise required in each policy area; and the association did not work well.

The Department of Citizenship and Immigration was a small and uninfluential department with very limited resources, working always in its overseas activities in the shadow of and with very little encouragement from the Department of External Affairs, and battling at home with the purely labour market approach to immigration of the Department of Labour. Overseas, it would be a long time before immigration officers would be accorder rank, pay and privileges approaching those of the employees of External Affairs and Trade and Commerce. Nevertheless, the Department's achievements were not inconsiderable, given that this was the first federal department of its kind. Perhaps its major achievement was to lay the foundation for a professional immigration service and to create a sense of dedication to it as well as increasing expertise in this field among its officers.

When the new department first began to function in the early months of 1950, with only a skeleton staff in Canada and a small energency organization overseas, it had to deal with some urgent problems. Thousands of European immigrants were anxious to emigrate to Canada, but eligibility had to be created for them. A decision had to be taken on the admission of the Germans and Japanese as immigrants. The new multiracial Commonwealth was also presenting a distinctly award problem to the Liberal Government which had been so explicit about its rejection of Asian immigration. And a wholly new legal basis had to be created for the management and control of a very much larger immigration movement than Canada had known for 20 years; and that meant a new Immigration Act.

Steps were taken quickly to deal with these issues. By an order-in-council of June 9, 1950, the admissible classes of European immigrants were enlarged to include any immigrant «who satisfied the Minister that he is a suitable immigrant having regard to the climatic, the social, educational, industrial, labour or other conditions or requirements of Canada; and that he is not undesirable owing to his probable inability to become readily adapted and integrated into the life of the Canadian community and to assume the duties of Canadian citizenship within a reasonable time after his entry». Three months later, the Germans were placed on the same footing as other Europeans, the Japanese remaining enemy aliens until July 1952. In January 1951, a very minor token gesture was made to India, Pakistan and Ceylon whereby 150 Indians, 100 Pakistanis and 50 Ceylonese would be admitted to Canada annually, as well as the immediate families of Canadian citizens resident in Canada of these countries of origin. Finally, a new Immigration Act was passed in 1952 and became law on June 1, 1953.

IMMIGRATION ACT OF 1952

The Immigration Act of 1952 did some useful and necessary things but was, on the whole, an inadequate and illiberal piece of legislation reflecting attitudes and using terminology of the prewar period. It is most unfortunate that it remained the basic statute in immigration for so long – 24 years – simply because of a lack of political will and sufficient determination to change it. The Act, whose weaknesses were quickly appreciated, was modified or bypassed from time to time by immigration regulations – often because politicians found it easier to change the regulations than the Act – but its basic provisions in the area of control and enforcement remained valid until the mid-1970s. Among its many provisions, it established the right of admission for Canadian citizens and persons with Canadian domicile, and defined Canadian domicile for immigration purposes. It exhaustively listed what were called «the prohibited classes» and established the right of examination of immigrants. The prohibited classes included a long and mournful list of unacceptable persons including idiots, imbeciles, morons, the insane, psychopathic personalities, epileptics, cases of tuberculosis, persons who had been convicted of or admitted having committed any crime involving moral turpitude (an old American term which lent itself to very subjective interpretation); prostitutes, homesexuals, pimps, professional beggars, vagrants, chronic alcoholics and persons who were or might become, in the opinion of the Special Inquiry Officer, public charges. The Act also laid down conditions for the arrest, detention and deportation of immigrants and would-be immigrants and for examinations, inquiries and appeals. It also privided for «reports in certain cases» on persons other than Canadian citizens who were associated with subversive organizations and were undesirable for other specified reasons. In addition, it dealt with offences and penalties in immigration law and attempted to provide some protection for immigrants against exploitation. It provided penalties for exploitation and corruption in the Immigration Service. It also provided that loans could be granted to immigrants to cover the cost of transportation and expenses en route – in sum a mixed bag of positive and harsh provisions.

The Act had, however, two fundamental defects, both of which did a great deal of damage to the management of immigration in Canada in the ensuing years. The first was the degree of uncontrolled discretionary power which it vested in the Minister of Citizenship and Immigration and his officials. The Act gave to the Governor-in-Council, for example, the all-embracing power to prohibit or limit the admission of persons by reason of:

- Nationality, citizenship, ethnic group, occupation, class or geographical area of origin;
- Peculiar customs, habits, modes of life, or methods of holding property;

- Unsuitability having regard to the climatic, economic, social, industrial, educational, labour, health or other conditions or requirements existing temporarily or otherwise, in Canada or in the area or country from or through which such persons came to Canada;
- Probable inability to become readily assimilated or to assume the duties and responsibilities of Canadian citizenship within a reasonable time after admission.

Any would-be immigrant from any part of the globe could be excluded on one or other of these grounds.

This and other provisions of the Act gave the Minister potentially the last word on every individual case and this, as the Department rapidly learned, meant that Ministers were deluged with representations requesting a personal decision. When Jack Pickersgill, who became Minister of Citizenship and Immigration in July 1954[4], appeared before the Special Committee on Estimates the following year, he said that he was spending 90 % of the time which he devoted to immigration on marginal cases. He did not think that this was the real purpose of the Immigration Department which was, he felt, as Mackenzie King had said, to increase the population of Canada by immigration[5]. The flood of correspondence on individual cases was as time-consuming for the Department and its officials – at home and overseas – as it was for the Minister, and prevented both from spending sufficient time on planning and on other aspects of management. It contributed also to the fact that this portfolio was never a popular one among candidates for Cabinet office.

These substantial discretionary powers which devolved upon immigration officials also, together with the high degree of subjective interpretation involved in administering the Act, undoubtedly created an initial bias against and suspicion of immigration officers, since it was felt that such substantial powers could only lead to abuse. Members of Parliament, members of the legal profession as well as the press were particularly critical on these grounds for many years. In addition, the Act itself, with its punitive tone and heavy emphasis on exclusion, helped to create a rather negative climate in immigration, hindering public understanding of the real difficulties of managing this complex and sensitive area of public policy. We cannot record here all the efforts – most of them half-hearted – to change the Act, except that the first one occurred in 1955, when Jack Pickersgill secured Cabinet's approval in principle for certain substantive changes in the Act, but failed to follow this up. The last effort, and the only one which had real heart in it, began in 1972 when Robert Andras became Minister of Manpower and Immigration and initiated a major review of Canada's Immigration and population policies. This effort, which resulted in the new Immigration Act of 1976, will be described in detail later in this chapter.

With the exception of the Hungarian Refugee Movement of 1956, which was managed with vigour and enthusiasm, the Liberal Government did very little to improve immigration policy and management after the initial moves which have just been described. There was a continuing lack of consultation with the provinces in this area of common jurisdiction. Little thought was given to the development of adequate services for immigrants in Canada, beyond meeting their basic welfare and medical needs for one year after arrival. There was no public participation and almost no funding of voluntary agencies providing services to immigrants. Overseas, the Immigration Branch had to make do with very limited resources, weak support from Ottawa and almost no help from other overseas departments. At the same time, some serious problems were building up in immigration through the 1950s which were not tackled until the Progressive Conservatives under John Diefenbaker won the 1957 and then the 1958 federal elections, the latter giving them a comfortable majority. On May 12, 1958, Ellen Fairclough became Minister of Citizenship and Immigration, retaining this portfolio for just over four years. For the last two years of her tenure, her Deputy Minister was George F. Davidson, a very able public servant who has had a distinguished carrer in Ottawa and at the United Nations. Together they tried to deal with some of the most urgent matters. In this, it must be said, they had very little encouragement from the Prime Minister whose imagination and interest were never caught by immigration, despite a posture of great warmth and friendship towards ethnic communites.

The first problem to emerge soon after Mrs. Fairclough became Minister was the sponsorship question – the first appearance on a large scale of the perennial problem of sponsored relatives, which is one of the most politically sensitive issues in immigration and one which is very difficult to control. A very substantial movement of mainly rural immigrants from Southern Europe to Canada took place in the 1950s. They came chiefly from Southern Italy and from the poorer regions of Greece and Portugal and were followed by an equally substantial movement of relatives, facilitated by an order-in-council (P.C. 785) introduced by the Liberal Government in May 1956, in response to a judgement of the Supreme Court of Canada in the Brent case[6]. Applications poured in to the European immigration offices who reported mounting backlogs which their staffs could not handle. By February 1959, the total backlog in all countries reached 131 785. In 1958, E. Davie Fulton, who was Acting Minister of Citizenship and Immigration for eleven months prior to the appointment of Mrs. Fairclough, had agreed to some administrative controls on the escalating sponsored movement. As the situation worsened, however, Mrs. Fairclough and her officials decided that drastic action was required and in March 1959, an order-in-Council (P.C. 310) was introduced, limiting the admission of relatives to the immediate family. It was done almost surreptitiously, with no advance information or publicity, obviously in the hope that no one would notice it. But the Liberals did notice it and in a fighting speech in the House of Commons, Jack Pickersgill, the former Minister, accused the Government of «an unnecessary and cruel act» in attempting to prevent the reunion of families and of perpetrating «a grave affront to Parliament» in the secretive manner in which the whole affair was handled. In the political uproar which followed involving the Opposition, the press, ethnic organizations, MPs with heavily immigrant ridings and even the Government of Ontario (concerned with its standing among a large immigrant population), the Conservative Government backed down. Mrs. Fairclough was obliged to announce that the new order-in-council would be rescinded – pending revisions in the Immigration Act which she hoped to suggest in a few months' time. Much of the political furore around this incident was, to put it mildly, dishonest. Even if the Fairclough order-in-council was somewhat too restrictive – and certainly undiplomatically handled – the escalating sponsored movement had to be controlled in some way and the backlogs in the overseas immigration offices reduced. This was done quietly by administrative means in the ensuing months.

At the same time, another problem of equal if not greater complexity arose to plague the Conservative Government and Mrs. Fairclough; and it also proved very difficult to resolve. It concerned the large illegal movement of Chinese immigrants from Hong Kong to the United States and Canada which came to light in the mid-1950s. Illegality, like the potential for escalation in the numbers of sponsored relatives, is a standing problem in immigration. For every legal immigration movement, there is generally an illegal one somewhere in the background; and there is little to match the determination of human beings to overcome the increasingly tough barriers to migration, if they decide or are persuaded to do so. Illegal immigrants will brave the gunboats and sometimes shark-infested waters off the shores of Hong Kong. They will cross the English Channel at night in midwinter in frail rowing boats, and they will let themselves be concealed in oil drums or hidden under the floorboards of trucks to get across the US-Canadian border. And all this is grist to the mill of the ancient commerce of migration which flourishes today more vigorously than ever, due to rapid communications and varied modes of transport. Among illegal operators, however, there have been few to match the Chinese – facing very fierce discrimination in the major receiving countries in this century – for sheer ingenuity and a remarkable degree of success.

In the mid-1950s, the American authorities in Hong Kong became aware of the existence of a major conspiracy to evade the immigration laws of the United States. This involved an organized operation for the sale and purchase of false identities, enabling almost any Chinese to enter the United States though ineligible under existing immigration laws. This was the famous system of «paper families» in which fictitious Chinese families were created in the United States to sponsor so-called relatives in Hong Kong; or fictitious slots were arranged in existing Chinese families in the US, into which fictitious relatives could be fitted. It was very successful and very lucrative. At that time, American citizenship could be purchased in Hong Kong for approximately $3 000 with $500 down and the balance after arrival in the United States. Some 40 firms were thought to be involved. The system was also based on a vast network of misrepresentation in the United States and in Hong Kong which made a return to legality very difficult. Shortly afterwards, the British authorities in Hong Kong obtained information on a large organized ring of immigration agents in Hong Kong, New Zealand, Australia, the United States, Canada and South America. And the Canadians, already alerted to the fact that the paper family system probably involved Canada also, were able to obtain the necessary proof that this was the case in August 1959. Further investigation by the Hong Kong police and the RCMP confirmed the existence of a very large and well-established illegal immigration movement from Hong Kong to Canada.

Faced with this dilemma, the Conservative Government behaved in a liberal and proper manner, but made no attempt to match subtlety with subtlety. In June 1960, Mrs. Fairclough announced an amnesty for all Chinese who had entered Canada illegally before July 1, 1960 and said that it was not the intention of the Government «to prosecute or deport from the country any Chinese presently in Canada who have not themselves engaged in assisting other Chinese, apart from their own relatives, to enter Canada illegally». This amnesty was later extended by one of her Liberal successors, René Tremblay, by a «period of tolerance» which continued up to September 1, 1964. Mrs. Fairclough also announced the introduction of the Chinese Adjustment Statement Program which was modelled on the American Truthful Statement Program for the Chinese which had not been a conspicuous success. The Canadian Program called upon the Chinese who had entered Canada illegally «to come forward and make complete and honest statements pertaining to the circumstances under which they had entered Canada, together with truthful information concerning their family backgrounds. In return, these illegal immigrants would have their cases reviewed by the Minister of Citizenship and might be permitted to remain in Canada if they were of good moral character and had not been systematically engaged in illegal immigration».

The Chinese Adjustment Statement Program lasted for over ten years and finally petered out in the early 1970s. Between June 1960 and July 1970, 11 569 Chinese came forward and had their status adjusted. Nevertheless, the Program was generally felt to have been of limited value, but although several attempts were made to terminate it they were unsuccessful. Ironically, it was the Chinese community itself, with the aid of several members of Parliament, who insisted that the Program be preserved as a matter of good faith on the Government's part. The following is a brief quotation from the author's discussion of this question in *Canada and Immigration: Public Policy and Public Concern.*

> Although many Chinese came forward in the spirit of the program and it was helpful to those who did so, the Program itself did not get at the heart of the problem which was organized crime on a large scale, high profits and very flexible operations. The firms and agents soon became familiar with the Adjustment Statement Program and coached their clients in it. Truthful statements in Canada frequently implicated relatives and others in Hong Kong, or led to the revelation of vast areas of earlier misrepresentation. The «paper families» had a tenacious strength of their own[7].

At one point, British officials in Hong Kong actually requested that the Program be terminated as it involved too many legal problems. The issue of the illegal Chinese immigration movement was eventually solved or very greatly reduced in importance by a combination of quite different factors: the new non-discriminatory immigration policy which Mrs. Fairclough was to introduce in 1962; the Canadian point system for the selection and admission of immigrants adopted in 1967, as well as the increasingly high educational and skill levels among would-be immigrants in Hong Kong, enabling them to qualify and enter Canada in the regular way. This is not to say, however, that the illegal migration industry in Hong Kong is wholly a thing of the past.

THE WHITE-CANADA POLICY ENDS

Although the years of Conservative administration produced some interesting policy developments, they were bleak times for immigration generally and for the Immigration Service. It was a period of recession with high unemployment rates; and financial austerity and a low key approach to immigration were the order of the day. From early 1960 onwards, the Department of Citizenship suffered serious financial cutbacks, there was a freeze on staff hiring, no money for promotion and none for improvements in the overseas offices, some of which were described by Mrs. Fairclough at this period as «a disgrace». As shown in Table 1, immigration intake declined to its lowest point in the postwar period in 1961 when only 71 689 immigrants were admitted.

Policies, however, could be changed and the most important change and the main achievement of Mrs. Fairclough's ministry occurred in 1962 when new immigration regulations were introduced, removing racial discrimination as the major feature of Canada's immigration policy[8]. From then on, immigration policy would be based on the three major criteria of skill and contribution to the labour force; family reunion; and compassionate considerations mainly relating to refugees. Canada was the first of the three major receiving countries, all of which had «white» immigration policies in the 20th century, to make this move. The United States followed with the Kennedy amendments to the Immigration Act of 1965 which established a non-discriminatory policy and became effective in 1968, and Australia announced the end of her White-Australia policy in 1973[9].

The Canadian Immigration Regulations of 1962 contained one remaining discriminatory clause (31 d) confining the sponsorship of relatives by immigrants from Asia and African countries (excluding Egypt) to the immediate family, whereas all other immigrants could sponsor a range of more distant relatives also. This clause was inserted at the last minute because of a fear on the part of senior officials in the Department, including the Deputy Minister, of an influx of unskilled sponsored relatives from Asia similar to the one which had been taking place from Southern Europe. This clause was removed in the Immigration Regulations of 1967.

As we have seen, Fairclough had announced her intention of making significant changes in the Immigration Act itself. In his 1957 election campaign, Diefenbaker had promised that a Conservative Government would apply a vigorous immigration policy in cooperation with the provinces. «The Immigration Act, he said, would be overhauled – Canada must populate or perish[10].» The 1958 Annual Report of the Department of Citizenship and Immigration stated that a thorough review of immigration policies and procedures was now underway. Speaking in the House on the sponsorship issue in April 1959, Fairclough said that when this review had been completed and proposals drafted, she intended to consult with ethnic groups and the ethnic press and to seek the advice of immigrant aid agencies, labour, business, the churches and welfare groups. Out of all this she hoped they could produce «a new deal in immigration matters: positive approaches, democratic programming, raising of standards, flexible practices for selective immigration to replace the rigid restrictions in the present act and regulations[11]. In the fall of 1960, the Speech from the Throne referred to the expectation that a revised Immigration Act would be placed before Parliament; and Fairclough referred to this again in the debate on the estimates in February 1961, although she sounded a cautious note, implying that there was still a great deal of work to be done. From then on, the prospect of a new Act receded. The Diefenbaker Government, now in considerable difficulties, seemed less and less inclined to take this on. Within the Department, where a draft Immigration Bill was being prepared, work on it was discontinued in the summer of 1961. In an interview with the author several years later, Mrs. Fairclough said that her Deputy Minister, Dr. Davidson, advised her that they really did not need a new act. They could achieve what they wanted by changing the regulations[12].

It is interesting to examine the reasons and pressures which lay behind the major change in immigration policy embodied in these new immigration regulations. There had been no vigorous public debate on the issue of racial discrimination in immigration policy, such as the one which took place in the United States in the 1950s over the provisions of the McCarran-Walter Act of 1952, which perpetuated the principle of racial discrimination in immigration and had been passed by Congress over President Truman's veto. No reform groups appeared, as they did in Australia, to pressure the Government in this direction[13]. Parliament did not show any substantial concern over Canada's discriminatory immigration policy and it is doubtful whether the Canadian public was even aware of its existence.

This fundamental policy change was largely the work of a group of senior officials in the public service, including Dr. Davidson, consisting particularly of those who were involved in Canada's external relations. Only they were really aware of the damage done to Canada's reputation in the international community by the «White Canada policy» and the extent to which it diminished the positive role Canada was attempting to play on the international scene and within the growing multiracial Commonwealth. It was very fortunate that they acted when they did. The 1960s was a critical decade, marking the final ending of empires and the emergence of a number of new independent countries who were to speak with an increasingly firm voice at the United Nations. Race relations and racial discrimination became sensitive international issues. By removing racial discrimination from immigration policy at this point (relatively quietly), Canada did not become known around the world for its White-Canada policy. Australia, on the other hand, whose racially-discriminatory immigration policy lasted only eleven years longer than its close counterpart in Canada, did get saddled with this unenviable reputation.

THE MANPOWER ERA, 1966-1976

There were no further policy developments of any consequence during the remaining period of Conservative Government. Richard Bell, the third Minister of Citizenship and Immigration in the Diefenbaker administration – Mrs. Fairclough became Postmaster-General in a Cabinet reshuffle in the summer of 1962 – did manage, however, in the short time he had, to inject some renewed life and vigour into the Department whose morale had sunk to a very low point with the continuing financial stringency, lack of adequate resources and obvious lack of interest and concern in Cabinet. In a process which became known as «Bell's Resurrection», he managed almost single-handedly to turn this state of affairs around, and to set the department off on a really active promotion and recruiting program overseas.

Bell was a perceptive analyst of the state of affairs in immigration at that time. In an interview with the author, he said that during his short tenure of office, he had been very impressed with the need for creative development in immigration planning and administration. Neither ministers nor officials in this department had been sufficiently organization-minded in his view, and this was what the Department really needed, together with strong support from Cabinet. He felt that it was a very difficult ministry and former ministers shared his view. «So often as Minister, he said, one got bogged down in difficult cases and cases which were potentially politically dangerous», which was very time-consuming. On Parliament and on the Overseas Service, he said:

> Very little help could be expected from the House of Commons. The House was indifferent to immigration, apart from a small group of MPs, with immigrant ridings, most of whom had very narrow concerns but exercised a disproportionate influence. Nor were the attitudes of the Department of External Affairs and Trade and Commerce helpful or constructive at that time. Both departments wanted to keep immigration very firmly in third place in relation to status, pay and allowances. He was appalled by the classification of immigration officers when he first saw it[14].

The Liberals under Lester B. Pearson won the federal election of April 1963 but without an overall majority, and a rapid procession of Liberal Ministers of Citizenship and Immigration and Manpower and Immigration followed Richard Bell. As can be seen from Appendix I, most of them held this portfolio for very short periods only. The second of these ministers, René Tremblay, was however an energetic developer of the Richard Bell kind. After six months in office, he and his department produced a blueprint for reorganization and development – some 30 proposals in all – which he presented to the House on August 14, 1964. It had Treasury Board support and was offered as a new deal in immigration with a major emphasis on administrative improvements. It should be noted that the Canadian economy, which had started to gain momentum again from 1961 onwards, was now in a buoyant state and there was money in the bank for this kind of development.

The 30 proposals included new plans for the Overseas Service which were described as follows:

- A new regional office in Europe to supervise immigration programs in the sixteen countries where we maintain offices.
- A new immigration staff unit to look after immigration from the Western Hemisphere, Asia and the Pacific. Increased support and attention would be given to immigration from these sources.
- A greatly increased promotional campaign overseas.
- A new establishment structure for immigration personnel abroad as a first step in plans to ensure better classifications. A career-foreign service must be developed, it was said, with «opportunities as fully rewarding as any comparable post in the public service».
- Improved immigration offices, better working conditions, and facilities to create a better image for Canada overseas and to enable it to compete more effectively in immigration with other countries.

Tremblay also discussed the question of a new Immigration Act. He proposed to initiate detailed studies over the whole field after which he would introduce a revised Act for the consideration of Parliament as soon as possible[15].

Most of these plans went forward, although Tremblay was not there, after February 1965, to see them through. The Department was reorganized into five principal divisions with a separate directorate for the Overseas Service. New senior staffs were recruited. A new Canadian Immigration Affairs Officer Series was created for the Overseas Service with distinctly higher classifications. Plans were made to open a European regional office in Geneva. Increasing efforts were put into promotion activities and public relations staffs were hired for Ottawa and the major overseas offices. Two special firms were commissioned, one to promote immigration overseas and the other to attract private business to Canada. Newspaper advertising was greatly increased in Britain and introduced for the first time in the Netherlands. Admission figures began to rise: 112 606 in 1964, 146 758 in 1965 and 194 743 in 1966. At the same time, the detailed studies mentioned by Tremblay were started by the Department's new Policy and Planning Division. On December 31, 1964, Prime Minister Lester B. Pearson announced – rather too soon – that a White Paper on immigration policies, practices and administration, presumably leading to legislation, would be prepared for presentation to Parliament in 1965.

In the midst of these developments, without any prior consultation with or warning to department officials, with the single exception of the Deputy Minister, came a major announcement in Parliament on December 17, 1965 by the Prime Minister of a large-scale Government reorganization including a number of new departments. From this it was learned that the Department of Citizenship and Immigration would very shortly cease to exist. Immigration would become part of an important new Department of Manpower planned to be one of the «key economic ministries». The Prime Minister also announced that Jean Marchand would become Minister of Citizenship and Immigration, eventually taking charge of the new department. On January 1, 1966, Tom Kent, who had been principal Secretary and Policy Adviser to the Prime Minister and a major architect of the new Manpower development policy, took over as Deputy Minister of Citizenship and Immigration on the same temporary basis, with a mandate to create the new Department of Manpower and get it in working order. At the same time, the Indian Affairs Branch was transferred temporarily to the Department of Northern Affairs and National Resources. Important sections of the Department of Labour, including the National Employment Service, were transferred temporarily to Citizenship and Immigration; and a little later the Citizenship Branch was transferred to the Department of the Secretary of State.

On May 9, the Prime Minister introduced in the House a Government Organization Bill providing for the establishment of a number of new departments including a Department of Manpower and a Department of Indian Affairs and Northern Development, describing this as the most extensive change in the administrative organization of government ever made in peacetime. In the debate on the Bill, former Minister Richard Bell was the principal spokesman for the Opposition. He said that submerging immigration in what was basically a labour portfolio was a grave error of national policy. The branches of the Department of Labour which were to be integrated (with immigration) in the new Department of Manpower had persistently sought to cut immigration back. Wherever there was a marriage of immigration and labour, immigration was subdued. At the same time, he and other Opposition spokesmen urged that citizenship should not be divorced from immigration. The two areas of public policy complemented each other and should be managed together. None of this was of any avail however and the Bill was duly passed. During the debate, a motion was moved to include the word «Immigration» in the title of the new Department. This was accepted by the Government and carried unanimously[16]. On October 3, 1966, the new Department of Manpower and Immigration opened its doors to the public and the former offices of the National Employment Service became Canada Manpower Centres.

The pressures which made manpower development a major concern of the Pearson Government had been building up for some time. In November 1960, as an outcome of high levels of unemployment from 1957 onwards, a Special Committee of the Senate on Manpower and Employment was appointed «to study and report upon the trends in manpower requirements and utilization in Canada, with the object of exploring the possibilities of maintaining and extending a high level of employment». In its final report of June 1961, the Senate Committee noted a number of trends with which we are all too familiar today, including the growing incidence of unemployment among young people, the unskilled and the inadequately educated. The Committee recommended that a much larger proportion of Canada's resources be devoted to education and training of all kinds and that a thorough study be made of the adequacy of the National Employment Service, its organization and procedures, in the light of present-day conditions[17]. In 1964, the Economic Council of Canada pointed out, in its first *Annual Review,* that effective labour market policies must be developed to promote more efficient use of Canada's manpower resources. The main agency for this would be the National Employment Service which must have the means «to promote the occupational, industrial and geographical mobility of the labour force to meet the requirements of a changing industrial economy»[18]. During this period also, the OECD reported that the Canadian labour force was one of the least skilled among industrialized countries. Within Canada, there was increasing dissatisfaction with the NES-Manpower development was in fact becoming a fashionable cause and expectations of what could be achieved by large-scale labour force training, upgrading and mobility programs were rising. Tom Kent, who was an economist by training, became a passionate advocate of this approach to some of Canada's most urgent economic problems, including unemployment and effective response to technological change.

Thus, immigration entered the manpower era and became what was then regarded as an indispensable branch of manpower activities. Many immigration officers felt at this time that it was being «downgraded to a manpower policy» and inevitably its policies and programs acquired a stronger labour market orientation. The new Department of Manpower and Immigration, however, was a much larger and more influential department than the former Department of Citizenship and Immigration, with a stronger voice in Cabinet and a much larger budget. It was also organized on a regional basis with five major regions which were named Atlantic Provinces, Québec, Ontario, Prairie Provinces and Northwest Territories (British Columbia and the Yukon). The association of immigration with manpower, which has continued to the present day, proved in fact to have both substantial advantages and disadvantages.

The next two years were a very creative period in immigration as well as manpower. Improvements continued in Overseas Service which would now be known as the Foreign Branch of the Department of Manpower and Immigration. A White Paper on Immigration Policy was tabled in the House of Commons on October 14, 1966, followed by the appointment of a Special Joint Committee of the Senate and the House of Commons to study it and make recommendations. On March 23, 1967, an Immigration Appeal Board Act was passed, creating a wholly independent Appeal Board, whose decisions were final, subject only to appeal to the Supreme Court of Canada on matters of law, and which could hear appeals against all deportation orders and appeals from some classes of sponsors (determined by the Governor-in-Council as Canadian citizens only)[19]. On August 16, new Immigration Regulations were introduced outlining for the first time the precise criteria to be used in the selection of immigrants – the Canadian point system. On December 21 of the same year, a Canada Manpower and Immigration Council Act was passed, establishing a Canada Manpower and Immigration Council and four Advisory Boards to advise the Minister on «all matters to which his duties, power and functions extend».

The White Paper of 1966 was a curious document and the Special Joint Committee was a singularly casual parliamentary committee which failed to produce a final report. They are worth mentioning only because they inadvertently led to the adoption of the point system. The White Paper was, in a way, a piece of leftover business for the new Manpower and Immigration administration. A final draft was presented to the new Deputy Minister early on and was then rewritten for greater «saleability». Although it appeared only eleven days after the opening of the new Department, the White Paper said next to nothing about immigration's new environment, and provided only limited information about Canada's existing immigration law and practice. It did have a major objective, however, which was not frankly acknowledged, and that was once again to try and control the movement of sponsored relatives, particularly in the light of Canada's increasing need for skilled manpower and the real difficulties experienced by the unskilled in the Canadian labour market. It was proposed that whereas all immigrants could bring their immediate family to Canada, only Canadian citizens should have the right to sponsor a wider range of relatives provided that these relatives were literate, had a reasonable level of education or were qualified occupationally. Exactly half the White Paper is concerned with arguments relating to this proposal.

The Special Joint Committee was, however, hostile to this idea. It felt, in part, that it attached a utilitarian value to citizenship which they found objectionable. But it was also hostile to the image of a technological society in which unskilled labour was at a serious disadvantage and reluctant to accept any adjustment to it. Because of their rejection of this proposal, the Department of Manpower and Immigration had to think again. A four-man task force of experienced immigration officials was appointed to devise admission categories in which the sponsored stream would be divided into dependent and non-dependent relatives, and new criteria would be developed on the basis of a point system (an idea which had already been put forward within the department) and on the principle of universality. They produced the Canadian point system which was outlined in the new Immigration Regulations of 1967. This system of immigrant selection has been remarkably useful and successful although it needs more careful monitoring and periodic adjustment than it received in the next few years. It was finally revised and improved in the most recent Immigration Regulations of 1978 which complemented the new Immigration Act of 1976. The present point system is set forth in Appendix II.

The next four years following these developments were years of considerable frustration for the Immigration Division. In 1968, the innovative if not always percipient team of Marchand and Kent moved on, and, with the exception of Bryce Mackasey who was Minister of Manpower and Immigration for eleven months only in 1972, the ministers and deputy ministers who replaced them in the next four years were far less concerned and energetic. Immigration officials felt swamped by their numerous Manpower colleagues who often had seniority; by the weight given to the views of manpower economists; and by the short-term approach and often complete lack of interest in immigration shown on the manpower side. Important settlement responsibilities for immigrants in Canada had been lost when the Citizenship Branch moved back to the Department of the Secretary of State[20]. In addition, a wholly absurd management structure had been introduced in the Department of Manpower and Immigration whereby, in the interest of coordination in a very large department, all operational activities were confined to a central Operations Division reducing the others, including immigration, to impotence. To give only one example, senior immigration officials could no longer communicate directly with or give orders to the field, in an area of public policy where day-to-day contact and decision-making are vital. From 1970 onwards, there was also evidence that a serious illegal immigration movement was building up, as a result of a generous but, in view of accumulated experience, hazardous provision in the 1967 Immigration Regulations permitting non-immigrants to change their status in Canada.

THE DRIVE FOR A NEW IMMIGRATION ACT AND A POPULATION POLICY FOR CANADA

During the debate in May 1966 on the Government Organization Bill creating the Department of Manpower and Immigration, Jean Marchand strenuously denied that Immigration would suffer as a result of the merger with Manpower and argued that the conduct of immigration affairs really depended on the attitude of the Minister. In November 1972, a minister appeared on the scene who had all the necessary drive and enthusiasm and was to make a lasting contribution to the development of Canadian immigration policy and law. This was Robert Andras who was first elected to Parliament as Liberal member for Thunder Bay-Nipigon in 1965 and jointed the Trudeau Cabinet in 1968, serving in various capacities until he took over the Manpower and Immigration portfolio. Within a few months, he had acquired a Deputy Minister of like-mindedness – Alan Gotlieb, then a senior official in the Department of External Affairs and later to become its Under Secretary – and for four years, these two men were to form a very influential political partnership.

Bob Andras was determined to get a new Immigration Act – it was well known that almost every previous minister in the postwar period had tried to do this and failed. He had also become responsible for population policy by agreement with the Prime Minister. Population issues, which had hitherto aroused at most only luke-warm interest in Canada, were becoming the subject of increasing international concern. 1974 had been designated by the UN General Assembly as World Population Year and a World Population Conference was to be held in Bucharest in Agusut of that year. When he arrived to take up his new assignment, however, Bob Andras found not only an urgent immediate problem to deal with – the new critical illegal immigration movement – but also that the Department itself was in very poor shape. In an interview with the author, he described this as «a terrible mess»[21]. The major developments which had taken place in both manpower and immigration from 1966 onwards had not been followed by a period of effective consolidation. There had been a high turnover of deputy ministers as well as ministers. The internal organization structure was disastrous and morale was very low. In immigration, the new point system had never been properly reviewed and provided no control over numbers. In addition, the Unemployment Insurance Commission, for which he was also responsible, was at its lowest ebb.

From November 1972 onwards, these problems were attacked in a vigorous and creative way, beginning with the illegal immigration movement. We cannot examine this in detail here, but it is a classic case of the unforeseen consequences which can occur in immigration as a result of new or untried laws and regulations, and the extreme care which has to be taken in areas like internal change of status. In this case, it was not long after 1967 before commercial operators in many parts of the world began to appreciate the opportunities offered by the combined use of Section 34 of the 1967 Immigration Regulations (permitting internal change of status), and the new Immigration Appeal Board set up in the same year with authority to make final and binding decisions on deportation. Anyone who had been ordered deported had the right to appeal to the new Board, no matter what his or her status under the Immigration Act might be.

Within less than two years, floods of visitors began to arrive in Canada on organized flights from Europe, Asia, Latin America, the Caribbean and elsewhere with the obvious intention of staying, applying for landed immigrant status and, if refused, submitting an appeal to the Immigration Appeal Board which had the power to permit them to stay in Canada on compassionate or humanitarian grounds. The longer they stayed and the more successfully they settled in, the more compelling those grounds would obviously be. In 1970, approximately 45 000 visitors in Canada applied for landed immigrant status. And both the number of visitors arriving at Canada's international airports and the number of appeals made to the Immigration Appeal Board were increasing alarmingly. By October 1972, as many as 4 500 visitors arrived at Toronto International Airport during one week-end. By the end of the year, the backlog of cases before the Immigration Appeal Board was over 12 000 and increasing by 1 000 a month, a caseload which the Board simply could not handle with its existing resources.

The Liberal Government moved quickly from November 1972 onwards to bring this situation under control. On November 3, 1972, Section 34 of the 1967 Immigration Regulations was revoked and two months later, regulations were introduced requiring registration of all visitors staying in Canada for more than three months, as well as employment visas for all those seeking jobs. But something had to be done also about the huge number of cases before the Immigration Appeal Board and about the thousands of visitors already in Canada and no longer able to apply for landed immigrant status. A great many of these visitors had been told and genuinely believed that this was an entirely proper way of emigrating to this country. The first problem was dealt with by new legislation, introduced in June 1973, providing for the appointment of additional temporary members of the Immigration Appeal Board when necessary and for the modification of existing appeal rights, confining them in future to permanent residents, those who had a valid immigrant or non-immigrant visa when applying for admission to Canada, and those who had a substantial claim to refugee status or Canadian citizenship. The second problem was dealt with by the introduction in the same month of what was called the «Adjustment of Status Program» which offered the opportunity to those caught by the November 3 announcement, as well as to the many people who were believed to have lived in Canada possibly for years without legal status, to regularize their status within a 60-day period. It was a remarkably successful program, carried out with great verve and imagination, and when it ended on October 15, it was found that some 50 000 people from more than one 150 countries had obtained landed immigrant status. There was a fair amount of pressure on the Government to extend and later on to repeat the program, but this has been resisted.

When the Adjustment of Status Program was well underway, the next step, as the Minister and his senior officials saw it, was to initiate a thorough review of existing immigration and population policies and programs leading to a Green Paper on the subject, to public debate on the issues involved and to a new Immigration Act. They then proceeded to get this process going, beginning with an official announcement of the review made by Bob Andras in the House on September 15. He said that a special task force (later given the name of the Canadian Immigration and Population Study) was being created within the Department of Manpower and Immigration to carry out this review and to study policy options, under the direction of a senior official on loan from the Department of External Affairs. The task force would be supported by a group of non-government experts and consultants. The provinces would be consulted and over 100 organizations would be invited to present briefs. A Green Paper on immigration policy would be published in the spring, followed by intensive public discussion. The aim would be to establish a forward-looking immigration policy backed by new legislation to be presented to Parliament as soon as possible.

The Green Paper did not appear for fifteen months instead of the six originally envisaged, as the task force encountered many difficulties, due mainly to inexperience and to the sheer dearth of readily-available studies and other useful material relating to immigration and population. It was finally completed and tabled in the House of Commons by the Minister on February 3, 1975. It consisted of four separate volumes and eight supplementary studies, written either by academic consultants or officials, several of which appeared a little later. Volume One was the critical volume, however, and it contained a short essay on contemporary immigration policy in which the important issues which the Government and its principal policy-makers wished to put before the public were discussed or mentioned briefly. Unfortunately it was not an impressive piece of work and did not really live up to the occasion, presenting a rather narrow and depressing view of the immigration scene in Canada. This had a clearly negative impact on the public debate which followed, but did not prove significant in the long run, since the next stage in the process proved to be much more constructive.

As we have seen, the publication of the Green Paper was almost immediately followed by the appointment of another Special Joint Committee of the Senate and the House of Commons (in March 1965) which proceeded to examine and invite the views of the public on the issues involved. In contrast to its predecessor of 1966-1967, this committee proved to be an able, dedicated and hard-working one which was fortunate in its chairmanship and strong staff support. It held nearly 50 public hearings in 21 Canadian cities, in each of Canada's five regions and in the Northwest Territories, heard some 400 witnesses and received briefs and letters from more than 1 800 hundred organizations and individuals, and all within a period of about five months. It then produced an excellent report to Parliament in November of the same year and, as we have seen, a majority of its recommendations were, rather thankfully and very warmly, accepted by the Government. They now form some of the major elements in a new Immigration Act which was constructed during the following year and had its first reading in the House on November 22, 1976.

From 1972 onwards, the Andras-Gotlieb team had four major objectives. The first was to get a new Immigration Act in which, with the aid of the Special Joint Committee and other contributors to the public debate in 1972, they were remarkably successful. The second was to improve the overall process of immigration management and in particular to involve the provinces in this process in a much more effective way than in the past. This was achieved through special provisions in the Immigration Act and through new bilateral agreements on immigration which have been signed with some but not yet all of the provinces. The third was to encourage the development of a more specific population policy for Canada; and initially to persuade the provinces to establish, in collaboration with the Federal Government, a set of agreed guidelines on population growth and distribution which could be a useful basis for planning and development at the federal and provincial levels. When tabling the Green Paper in the House, Bob Andras announced that the Federal Government was taking a series of steps «to foster the widest possible measure of agreement about Canada's population future» and had appointed a Demographic Policy Steering Group of deputy ministers in Ottawa, as well as creating a National Demographic Policy Secretariat. Immediately after this, he began a tour of the provinces to discuss the proposed guidelines, but met with an unexpectedly cool reception. Only Québec and Alberta responded positively. The other provinces were simply not prepared to get involved at this stage in looking ahead and trying to plan Canada's demographic future. Here all that could be achieved was a minor demographic input in the Immigration Act. The final objective, and one about which Bob Andras himself became very convinced early on, was to provide better overall labour market policies and programs through the amalgamation of the Department of Manpower and Immigration and the Unemployment Insurance Commission. This was achieved through new legislation which followed the Immigration Act of 1977 in which created a very large, new quasi-independent agency, the Canada Employment and Immigration Commission, with a small accompanying Department of Employment and Immigration which exists primarily to give the new Commission a voice in Cabinet. It was an outstanding effort in a period of only four years.

THE IMMIGRATION ACT OF 1976

We will now look briefly at the major provisions of the new Immigration Act and then at refugee policy in Canada, particularly in the past decade when some important new policy developments have taken place and an increasing number of refugees have been admitted.

Canada's new Immigration Act is an innovative, liberal and effective piece of legislation and a vast improvement on the 1952 Act. Few laws are perfect and there are a few mainly lesser provisions of this Act which could be improved, but on the whole it has received very little criticism since it became law on August 5, 1977. As the Minister[22] said when originally tabling the Bill in the House of Commons, the Act explicitly affirms, for the first time, the fundamental principles of Canadian immigration law: family reunion, non-discrimination, concern for refugees and the promotion of Canada's demographic, economic, social and cultural goals. It removes inequities in the present law; it provides a modern, flexible framework for the future development of immigration policy; and it makes future immigration levels a matter for open decision and public announcement in advance by government. The following are some brief comments on several of its most important provisions:

Canadian Immigration Policy

The Special Joint Committee had recommended that a new Immigration Act should contain «a clear statement of principles and objectives». This statement is contained in Part I of the Act which will be found in Appendix III. It includes a commitment to a continuing policy of non-discrimination in immigration on grounds of race, national or ethnic origin, colour, religion or sex, as well as a commitment «to fulfill Canada's international legal obligations with respect to refugees and to uphold its humanitarian tradition with respect to the displaced and the persecuted». The statement also links immigration policy and the attainment of demographic goals respecting «the size, rate of growth, structure and geographic distribution of the Canadian population».

Immigration Planning and Management

One of the most important innovations in the new Act relates to an entirely new process of consultation with the provinces and voluntary sector prior to the annual announcement of immigration levels in Parliament. Section 109 of the Act makes consultation with the provinces by the Minister mandatory and also enables him to enter into agreements with a province or group of provinces relating to immigration. Section 7 requires the Minister, after consulting with the provinces and «such other persons, organizations and institutions as he deems appropriate», to announce annually in Parliament the number of immigrants which the Government proposes to admit during any specified period of time. There have now been five annual announcements of forthcoming immigration levels and in 1981, a three-year planning cycle was introduced.

Inadmissible Classes

Part 3 of the Act which deals with «Exclusion and Removal» begins with a wholly revised section on what are now called «inadmissible classes». Substantive changes have been made in the new Act reflecting far more liberal and sensible attitudes to the question of exclusion. The Act simply identifies certain broad classes of persons whose entry to Canada might endanger public health, welfare, order, security or the integrity of the immigration program. Grounds for exclusion now include a degree of health impairment, judged on an individual's total health profile, which would constitute a threat to public health or safety, or cause excessive demands to be made on health or social services; the lack of means of support or evident capacity to acquire them; criminal offences of a severe character without evidence of rehabilitation; involvement in criminal activity (such as organized crime); or in espionage, subversion or acts of violence (such as terrorism and hijacking).

Control and Enforcement

The Immigration Act makes some major changes in the control and enforcement area, including provisions which seek: 1. to improve the conduct of inquiries relating to persons subject to removal from Canada by the introduction of a new adjudication system; 2. to provide new ways to protect the fundamental rights of persons subject to an inquiry; and 3. instead of simple deportation in all cases requiring removal, as laid down in the 1952 Act, to offer three different instruments for removal depending on the gravity of the case, namely a deportation order, an exclusion order and a simple departure notice. Among a number of other important provisions in the Act, which also incorporates a revised version of the Immigration Appeal Board Act, there are some entirely new procedures in relation to refugees which will be discussed in the next section.

REFUGEE POLICY AND REFUGEE MOVEMENTS

During the postwar period, Canada has admitted refugees on an individual basis – almost 34 000 individual refugees were admitted between 1959 and 1981 – and in smaller and larger movements, most of them occurring in the 1970s when there was a rapid, world-wide escalation in the total number of refugees, who were appearing for the first time on all continents. Canada has also been associated with the two major international organizations caring for refugees since their foundation – UNHCR (the Office of the United Nations High Commissioner for Refugees) which was founded in 1950 and ICEM, the Intergovernmental Committee for European Migration (now ICM, the Intergovernmental Committee for Migration), founded in 1951. Canada has been an active member of the Executive Committee of member nations of UNHCR throughout the postwar period. It unwisely withdrew from ICEM membership during the Diefenbaker administration (supposedly on grounds of expense), but has recently resumed its association with this organization but not yet as a full member.

Before 1970, there were only two refugee movements to Canada of any size: the Hungarian Refugee Movement in 1956 which brought 37 566 refugees to Canada by the end of December 1958, and the Czech Refugee Movement which involved the admission of 11 153 Czech refugees in 1968-1969. It is in the 1970s, however, that we see one large Refugee Movement following another, the most recent being the Indochinese Refugee Movement which is still continuing, and which has been a major agent of change in a number of countries and in the international organizations involved. In round figures only, the substantial Canadian refugee movements of the 1970s have been as follows, beginning with the Uganda Asian refugee movement in 1972: Uganda Asians (7 000), Chileans (6 500), Lebanese (10 800), Haitians (4 500), Portugese Returnees (mainly from Angola and Mozambique) 2 000 and the Indochinese, nearly 81 000 by the end of June 1982. Recently we have also been admitting substantial numbers of refugees from Eastern Europe, particularly from Poland. The policy and procedural changes embodied in the Immigration Act and Regulations, which are examined below, as well as some more recent policy developments, are a response to these events. They reflect in part an effort to introduce an element of advance planning and more careful control into refugee management, an area which is obviously highly unpredictable and difficult to manage; and also an effort to establish voluntary efforts for refugees, which can be of great value, on a more satisfactory basis.

Canada has also made a considerable financial contribution in this area, providing a total of approximately $52 million in world refugee assistance in 1981, as well as many millions more through our food aid programs and financial support for non-governmental organizations. To give some examples, in Africa where there are now some five million refugees, Canada contributed $22,4 million in 1981 for UNHCR programs and emergency food aid, as well as $10 million for Afghan refugees, $7,4 million for Palestinian refugees and over $6 million for relief operations in Indochina, bringing Canada's total contribution in that region to over $23 million since 1979.

The new Immigration Act and Regulations contain some entirely new provisions relating to refugees, including the important principle and commitment in Part One of the Act. Refugees are now, for the first time, an admissible class in their own right selected according to special criteria and not as part of the general immigration movement. In addition, displaced persons who are *de facto* refugees, but do not qualify under the present official definition of a refugee, can be admitted as a specially-designated class or group of refugees. A third important innovation provides for a much more effective and wider range of voluntary sponsorship of refugees, which has proved to be invaluable for the Indochinese Refugee Movement and, a little later, for the Polish refugees. Under these provisions, any group of not less than five Canadians or any national or provincial incorporated organization may sponsor a refugee family on condition that they make provision for lodging, care, maintenance and resettlement assistance for these refugees for one year. In the case of the Indochinese Refugee Movement which evoked a very warm, spontaneous response from the Canadian community[23], the majority of refugees admitted in 1979 (80) were sponsored by individual Canadians or by Canadian organizations, and these voluntary sponsorships still account for well over 2 000 refugee admissions annually.

The Act also established an official Refugee Status Advisory Committee to advise the Minister on the determination of refugee status in individual cases, replacing an unofficial committee which had been in existence for some years. Under the Act, persons whose claims to refugee status have been rejected by the Committee can appeal their case to the Immigration Appeal Board. Refugee status has now become a very desirable objective for many would-be immigrants, as it obviously facilitates entry, and claims for refugee status have increased recently from 1 500 in 1980 to a projected 3 700 in 1982. A great many claims are not well-founded and rejection rates have been high. Decision-making in this area – attempting to decide who is a genuine refugee and who is not, whose life is really endangered and how much weight should be given to the often desperate needs of the «economic refugee» – is very difficult, and the process set up under the Act has not been working particularly well and has proved rather slow and cumbersome. On September 15, 1981, a Task Force on Immigration Practices and Procedures, established by the Minister a year earlier, submitted a report on *The Refugee Status Determination Process*[24] and made a number of recommendations to speed up and improve these procedures. Thus far, the Minister has responded by establishing new guidelines to assess the credibility of claimants to Convention refugee status[25], providing better information for claimants at ports of entry and immigration centres, and by appointing additional independent members of the Refugee Status Advisory Committee in order to overcome delays in processing claims.

Beginning late in 1978, the first annual refugee plan was developed with a target of 10 000 refugees for 1979, including 5 000 Indochinese, 2 300 East Europeans, 500 South Americans and 200 Convention refugees, as well as a contingency reserve of 2 000. This plan was discussed with the provinces at a federal-provincial meeting on March 2, 1979, but had to be abandoned because of the rapid escalation of the Indochinese Refugee Movement in the summer of 1979. However, it was agreed then that future refugee consultations would take place, whenever possible, at the same time as the consultations required under the Act on immigration levels; and that, as part of these consultations, the Federal Government would ask the provinces how many refugees they felt they could absorb at that time and would also provide advance notice of the arrival of refugee groups whenever feasible. In the 1981 *Annual Report* to Parliament on immigration levels, a refugee plan was presented again. This called for the acceptance of a total of 16 000 government-assisted refugees from Indochina, Eastern Europe, Latin America and the Caribbean, Africa and other areas, plus a projected number of 5 000 private sponsorships, making a total of 21 000. It included a contingency reserve of 2 500. In the 1982 plan, however, the total number was reduced to 14 000 plus private sponsorships and, in the 1983 plan tabled in the House on November 1, 1982, there was a further reduction of 12 000 government-assisted refugees plus possible private sponsorships of between 2 and 3 000. A contingency reserve of 2 000 is included. Cabinet, however, has approved funding for only 10 000 government-assisted refugees so far and extra funding will have to be found if the reserve numbers are used. Refugee policy, like immigration (as we shall see) and other areas of public policy, has fallen, for the time being at least, on harder times.

Major changes have taken place since the mid-1970s, therefore, in the ways in which Canada manages its refugee policies and programs and, because of the world refugee explosion of recent years – there are now an estimated 12,6 million known refugees mainly located in developing countries –, refugees are forming a larger share of our annual immigration movement. As a result of the provisions of the Immigration Act of 1976, there is now much more consultation on the subject of refugees between the Federal Government and the provinces and between these levels of government and the voluntary sector. As an outcome also of the new system of private sponsorships and as a response to the critical world refugee situation, we now have in Canada a much larger and more active public which is interested in and well-informed about refugees and their needs. We also now have a Standing Conference of Canadian Organizations Concerned for Refugees, brought together in the first instance by the representative in Canada of the UN High Commissioner for Refugees; and during its brief period in office in 1979, the Clark Government created a Canadian Foundation for Refugees whose primary purpose initially was to raise and distribute funds to Canadian individuals and organizations who wished to sponsor refugees, but did not have the means to do so. The Foundation has recently undertaken a major review of its operations, however, and in addition to fund-raising, has now decided to make public education, i.e., «to sensitize the Canadian public to the whole subject of refugees» its first priority. In addition to an initial grant of $450 000, most of which has now been distributed among refugee projects, the Federal Government provides the Foundation with free office space in Ottawa plus financing for a staff of three.

In his 1982 report to the United Nations Economic and Social Council, the UN High Commissioner for Refugees, Paul Hartling, noted that there were indications that: «Governments in different parts of the world are adopting an increasingly restrictive approach in granting durable asylum and in identifying persons to be regarded as refugees of concern to the international community [...] Moreover, the economic recession in a number of countries has encouraged the view that all aliens – including refugees – were potential competitors for limited or decreasing economic opportunities. This in turn has resulted in an identification of refugees with ordinary aliens and thereby overlooking their special situation[26].» It is not only in Canada, therefore, that refugees and refugee organizations are feeling the impact of harsh economic times. Here, as we have seen, the admission of government-assisted refugees has been cut back from 16 000 in 1981 to a projected 12 000 in 1983, but no restriction has been placed, thus far, on private sponsorships.

In an interesting speech in a debate in the House on refugee policy in June 1981, the Minister Axworthy suggested the possibility of a new dimension in Canadian refugee programs, particularly in the light of what he called the «very strong and forward-thinking constituency of Canadians who are active and interested in the problems and plight of refugees» which has been built up in recent years. He suggested that in addition to admitting refugees for permanent settlement, Canada should now focus on developing programs in refugee camps around the world. Government would be sympathetic to providing support and assistance, he said, for «the outward reach of Canadians to deal with the refugee problem where it is most serious and drastic», that is, in the camps themselves. He quoted the case of Somalia, one of the poorest countries in the world, which now has close to one million refugees in camps within its borders[27]. Churches and certain voluntary agencies are, of course, already engaged in at least some programs of this kind. It will be interesting to see if more Canadians and more voluntary groups can become involved in an «outward-reach» approach to these critical refugee problems.

IMMIGRATION IN THE 1980s

Immigration policy is inevitably tied to the state of the economy and today, with a much better immigration planning process than we have had in the past and with much more intergovernmental consultation, we are in a position to integrate these areas of public policy more effectively. Immigration figures today clearly show the effect of the recession, although a slight upswing was projected for 1985. The following are the immigration levels which have been planned for the years 1983-1985:

IMMIGRATION LEVELS *

1983	105 000 to 110 000
1984	115 000 to 125 000
1985	120 000 to 135 000

* Annual Report to Parliament on Immigration Levels 1983, Ottawa, Employment and Immigration Canada, November 1982, p. 24.

These figures are lower than those which the Special Joint Committee of the Senate and the House of Commons on Immigration Policy, in their report to Parliament in November 1975, thought desirable from the point of view of Canada's population needs. Difficult decisions clearly lie ahead in immigration in the light of what will probably be, for a variety of reasons, rather high and continuing levels of unemployment. Given our very high level of emigration at the present time (75 000 per *annum* is the estimated figure), population goals and the need for special skills and talents – more than we can train quickly here – can only be met by higher levels of immigration than we have now. At the same time, it may be increasingly difficult from now on for some family class immigrants, who now comprise close to half our annual immigration movement, and refugees to find jobs. It might be pointed out here that Canada today has only the most sketchy of population policies and that this area urgently requires the detailed investigation which it failed to get in the 1970s.

Another dilemma faces us in the coming years. Since we abandoned our «White Canada» immigration policy and opted for a universal, non-discriminatory policy in 1962, we have managed to achieve over time a very reasonable representation, in a world sense, in our annual immigration movement. During the 1970s, Europe, the Americas including the Caribbean, and Asia – Africa with Oceania [28] –

each accounted for close to one-third of our annual intake of immigrants. (Large refugee movements tend to alter this balance temporarily.) Appendix IV contains two tables wich illustrate this fact. Table1 shows immigration by world area for the periods 1965-1969 and 1975-1979. Table 2 shows the principal countries of last permanent residence of immigrants for fiscal year 1979-1980 which gives some indication of the wide range of nationalities and ethnic origins among immigrants now being admitted to Canada. For many reasons, however, having nothing to do with discrimination, it may be difficult to maintain this balance and to do so will require very good and careful management.

Perhaps the area which should give us most concern, however, is not immigration policy and law in which we have made some major advances and improvements, but immigration management for which Government has shown a quite surprising lack of concern. In addition, our services and programs for immigrants and refugees in Canada are still not adequate, at a time when we have a great many newcomers who need them, but this is too detailed a question to explore here. In relation to immigration management, we now divide this in four ways: between the Federal Government and the provinces and between the Canada Employment and Immigration Commission, the Department of External Affairs and the Department of the Secretary of State which is a far from satisfactory arrangement.

First, immigration is a concurrent responsibility of the Federal Government and the provinces under Section 95 of the BNA Act and, as we have seen, the provinces are now much more involved in immigration and refugee planning and programs. Two provinces, Ontario and Québec, have had their own special immigration operations and programs for a long time. In relation to the public service, the Canada Employment and Immigration Commission is responsible for the overall direction and internal management of immigration, including the short-term settlement and adjustment of immigrants and refugees, plus a small residual responsibility for population matters. The Department of External Affairs, in what can only be described as a major empire-building effort relating to the integration of Canada's overseas operations and services, has now absorbed the very efficient former foreign branch of the Immigration Service, thus dividing that service down the middle. And the Department of the Secretary of State is responsible for the longer-term settlement and adjustment of immigrants and refugees, as well as for citizenship and multiculturalism. It is an extraordinary exercise in compartmentalism and, while some of these elements are brought together in the annual consultation process described earlier, the effect of this scattered and divided management on the longer-term settlement of immigrants and refugees, on the provision of services for them, on the coordination of immigration, settlement services and multiculturalism, as well as on the national awareness and discussion of immigration issues, has been dismal to say the least.

We have attempted in this chapter to record the development and evolution of Canada's immigration and refugee policies in the postwar period, as well as the attitudes and objectives of the principal policy-makers involved. As we have seen, immigration and refugee policies have both changed substantially and improved greatly during this period, and in our Immigration Act of 1976, we have created a very good and liberal piece of legislation. But immigration is an ongoing process, at least for the foreseeable future, and much still remains to be done, particularly in the areas of management, coordination and the settlement and adjustment of immigrants and refugees in Canada.

TABLE 1
Canada: Immigration 1946-1981

1946	71 719	1964	112 606
1947	64 127	1965	146 758
1948	125 414	1966	194 743
1949	95 217	1967	222 876
1950	73 912	1968	183 974
1951	194 391	1969	161 531
1952	164 498	1970	147 713
1953	168 868	1971	121 900
1954	154 227	1972	122 006
1955	109 946	1973	184 200
1956	164 857	1974	218 465
1957	282 164	1975	187 881
1958	124 851	1976	149 429
1959	106 928	1977	114 914
1960	104 111	1978	86 313
1961	71 689	1979	112 096
1962	74 586	1980	143 117
1963	93 151	1981	128 111

Source: Canada Employment and Immigration Commission.

NOTES

1. Canada, House of Commons Debates, Vol. 3, 1947, p. 2644-2647.

2. *Ibid.em*, p. 2646 ff.

3. *Ibidem*, Vol. 3, 1949, p. 2284-2297.

4. See «Appendix One» for a list of ministers and deputy ministers responsible for immigration from 1950 to the present.

5. Canada, House of Commons, Special Committee on Estimates, Minutes of Proceedings and Evidence, No. 2, February 25, 1955, p. 48-49.

6. In the Brent case, the Supreme Court of Canada ruled that in delegating the power to decide admissibility to Special Inquiry Officers (who were then ruling on most doubtful cases), the Governor-in-Council had exceeded its legal authority. As a result of this decision, it was decided to spell out the precise classes of persons who were admissible to Canada. Among other provisions, this order-in-council permitted the admission of a wide range of sponsored relatives from Europe, America, Egypt, Israel, Lebanon and Turkey.

7. Freda Hawkins, *Canada and Immigration: Public Policy and Public Concern*, Montréal, McGill-Queen's University Press, 1972, p. 133.

8. The new regulations were tabled in the House by Mrs. Fairclough on January 19, 1962 and came into force on February 1.

9. Australia was the first to establish a racially discriminatory immigration policy which was done in the Immigration Restriction Act of 1901. The United States and Canada began to exclude non-White (generally non-European) immigrants after World War I.

10. Toronto Telegram, April 26, 1957.

11. Canada, House of Commons Debates, Vol. 3, 1959, p. 2937-2938.

12. See Freda Hawkins, *Canada and Immigration: Public Policy and Public Concern*, Chap. 5.

13. A number of Associations for Immigration Reform were organized on a state basis in Australia during the 1960s. An active Immigration Reform Group which produced several publications on the subject was also founded at Melbourne University in 1959.

14. *Freda* Hawkins, *Canada and Immigration: Public Policy and Public Concern*, p. 136.

15. Canada, House of Commons Debates, Vol. 7, 1964, p. 6817-6826.

16. Canada, House of Commons Debates, Vol. 5, 1966, p. 4872-5435, Vol. 6, 1966, p. 5730-5731.

17. Canada, Senate, Special Committee on Manpower and Employment, Final Report, June 1961.

18. Economic Council of Canada, *First Annual Review: Economic Goals for Canada to 1970*, Ottawa, 1964.

19. An Immigration Appeal Board had been established on March 1, 1956 but its powers were very limited. They were somewhat enlarged in the 1962 Immigration Regulations. Joseph Sedgwick, an eminent Toronto lawyer, commissioned by the Pearson Government in 1964 to look into the areas of control and enforcement, as well as the exercise of ministerial discretion under the Immigration Act, recommended, however, that the Immigration Appeal Board should be vested with final authority subject to a right of appeal to the courts, and should be truly independent.

20. A very unsatisfactory agreement had been reached in 1966 between the two departments whereby the Immigration Division would be responsible for the immediate reception and settlement of immigrants (usually for one year or less), while the Citizenship Branch looked after longer-term settlement. No funds were provided to the Branch for this purpose, however, with the result that nothing was done. This agreement contributed substantially to the fact that, although there has been some development in this area, immigrant services are still the weakest part of immigration management in Canada.

21. The author had a series of interviews with Bob Andras between 1976 and 1979.

22. The Bill was introduced by Bud Cullen, who became Minister of Manpower and Immigration on September 5, 1976, replacing Bob Andras who had become President of the Treasury Board at the urgent request of the Prime Minister.

23. In a debate in the House of Commons on April 23, 1980, the Minister of Employment and Immigration, Lloyd Axworthy, spoke of an «enormous outpouring of generosity towards refugees by private Canadians through church organizations and voluntary organizations». He described it as one of the «great success stories in this country». Hansard, Vol. 124, No. 8, p. 338.

24. Task Force on Immigration Practices and Procedures, *The Refugee Status Determination Process*, Ottawa, Supply and Services Canada, November 1981.

25. Convention refugees are those who come within the mandate of UNHCR.

26. Report of the United Nations High Commis-
    sion for Refugees, N.W. Economic and Social
    Council. Second Regular Session, May 1982.
27. Hansard, Vol. 124, No. 212, p. 10662.
28. Mainly the smaller islands.

BIBLIOGRAPHY

ADELMAN, Howard. *Canada and the Indochinese Refugees,* Weigl Educational Associates, Regina, 1982.

BRETON, R., REITZ, J.G. and VALENTINE, V. *Cultural Boundaries and the Cohesion of Canada,* The Institute for Research on Public Policy, Montréal, 1980.

CANADA. Department of Manpower and Immigration, *Canadian Immigration Policy,* White Paper on Immigration, Ottawa, 1966.

CANADA. Department of Manpower and Immigration. *Green Paper on Immigration Policy,* 4 Vol., Ottawa, 1975.

CANADA. *Report to Parliament,* Special Joint Committee of the Senate and the House of Commons on Immigration Policy, Ottawa, 1975.

CANADA. Department of Citizenship and Immigration. *Annual Reports, Immigration Statistics,* Ottawa, 1950-1965.

CANADA. Department of Manpower and Immigration. *Annual Reports, Immigration Statistics,* Ottawa, 1966-1976.

CANADA. Employment and Immigration Commission. *Annual Reports, Annual Reports to Parliament on Immigration, Levels, Immigration Statistics,* Ottawa, since 1977.

DIRKS, Gerald. *Canada's Refugee Policy: Indifference or Opportunism,* Montréal, McGill-Queen's University Press, 1978.

GREEN, Alan G. *Immigration and the Post-War Canadian Economy,* Toronto, Macmillan, 1976.

HAWKINS, Freda. *Canada and Immigration: Public Policy and Public Concern,* Montréal, McGill-Queen's University Press, 1972.

HAWKINS, Freda. *Immigrants and Refugees: The Canadian and Australian Experience,* Submission to the Committee on the Judiciary, Sub-Committee on Immigration, Refugees and International Law, Washington, D.C., US House of Representatives, 1979.

HAWKINS, Freda. *Immigration Law and Management in the Major Receiving Countries Outside the Arab Region,* Paper for the United Nations Economic Commission for Western Asia, Conference on International Migration in the Arab World, Nicosia, May 1981.

KALBACH, Warren E. *The Effect of Immigration and Population,* Supplementary Study for the Green Paper on Immigration Policy, Department of Manpower and Immigration, Ottawa, 1975.

LACHAPELLE, Réjean and HENRIPIN, Jacques. *The Demolinguistic Situation in Canada: Past Trends and Future Prospects,* Montréal, The Institute for Research in Public Policy, 1980.

RICHMOND, Anthony H. and KALBACH, Warren E. *Factors in the Adjustment of Immigrants and Their Descendants,* Ottawa, Statistics Canada, 1980.

STONE, Leroy O. and MARCEAU, Claude. *Canadian Population Trends and Public Policy through the 1980s,* Montréal, The Institute for Research on Public Policy, 1977.

WARD, W. Peter. *White Canada Forever,* Popular Attitudes and Public Policy Towards Orientals in British Columbia, Montréal, McGill-Queen's University Press, 1978.

APPENDIX I

MINISTERS AND DEPUTY MINISTERS RESPONSIBLE FOR IMMIGRATION
1950-1981

Department of Citizenship and Immigration

Ministers	Date Appointed
Hon. Walter Harris	January 18, 1950
Hon. J.W. Pickersgill	July 1, 1954
Hon. E.D. Fulton (Acting)	June 21, 1957
Hon. Ellen L. Fairclough	May 12, 1958
Hon. R.A. Bell	August 9, 1962
Hon. Guy Favreau	April 22, 1963
Hon. René Tremblay	February 3, 1964
Hon. J.R. Nicholson	February 15, 1965

Deputy Ministers	
Laval Fortier	January 18, 1950
George F. Davidson	April 26, 1960
H.M. Jones (Acting)	February 11, 1963
C.M. Isbister	November 4, 1963

Department of Manpower and Immigration

Ministers	
Hon. Jean Marchand	December 17, 1965
Hon. Allan J. MacEachen	July 6, 1968
Hon. Otto E. Lang	September 24, 1970
Hon. Bryce Mackasey	January 28, 1972
Hon. Robert Andras	November 27, 1972
Hon. Bud Cullen	September 15, 1976

Deputy Ministers	
Tom Kent	January 1, 1966
Louis Couillard	July 16, 1968
Jacques DesRoches	April 7, 1972
Alan Gotlieb	April 19, 1973
J.L. Manion	June 2, 1977

Canada Employment and Immigration Commission and Department of Employment and Immigration

Ministers	
Hon. Bud Cullen	August 15, 1977
Hon. Ron Atkey	June 4, 1979
Hon. Lloyd Axworthy	March 3, 1980

Chairmen and Deputy Ministers	
J.L. Manion	August 15, 1977
J.D. Love	October 1, 1979

APPENDIX II

IMMIGRATION SELECTION CRITERIA
A Summary of the Point System

Factors	Criteria	Max. Points	APPLICABLE TO			
			self-employed	entre-preneurs	assisted relatives	others
1. Education	One point for each year of primary and secondary education successfully completed.	12	•	•	•	•
2. Specific Vocational Preparation	To be measured by the amount of formal professional, vocational, apprenticeship, in-plant or on-the-job training necessary for average performance in the occupation under which the applicant is assessed in item 4.	15	•	•	•	•
3. Experience	Points awarded for experience in the occupation under which the applicant is assessed in item 4 or, in the case of an entrepreneur, for experience in the occupation that the entrepreneur is qualified for and is prepared to follow in Canada.	8	•	•	•	•
4. Occupational Demand	Points awarded on the basis of employment opportunities available in Canada in the occupation that the applicant is qualified for and is prepared to follow in Canada.	15	•		•	•
5. Arranged Employment or Designated Occupation	Ten points awarded if the person has arranged employment in Canada that offers reasonable prospects of continuity and meets local conditions of work and wages, *providing* that employment of that person would not interfere with the job opportunities of Canadian citizens or permanent residents, and the person will likely be able to meet all licensing and regulatory requirements; *or* the person is qualified for, and is prepared to work in, a designated occupation and meets all the conditions mentioned for arranged employment except that concerning Canadian citizens and permanent residents.	10				•

Factors	Criteria	Max. Points	self-employed	entre-preneurs	assisted relatives	others
6. Location	Five points awarded to a person who intends to proceed to an area designated as one having a sustained and general need for people at various levels in the employment strata and the necessary services to accommodate population growth. Five points subtracted from a person who intends to proceed to an area designated as not having such a need or such services.	5	•	•		•
7. Age	Ten points awarded to a person 18 to 35 years old. For those over 35, one point shall be subtracted from the maximum of ten for every year over 35.	10	•	•	•	•
8. Knowledge of English and French	Ten points awarded to a person who reads, writes and speaks both English and French fluently. Five points awarded to a person who reads, writes and speaks English *or* French fluently. Fewer points awarded to persons with less language knowledge and ability in English or French.	10	•	•		•
9. Personal Suitability	Points awarded on the basis of an interview held to determine the suitability of the person and his/her dependants to become successfully established in Canada, based on the person's adaptability, motivation, initiative, resourcefulness and other similar qualities.	10	•	•	•	•
10. Relative	Where a person *would* be an assisted relative, *if* a relative in Canada had undertaken to assist him/her, and an immigration officer is satisfied that the relative in Canada is willing to help him/her become established but is not prepared, or is unable, to complete the necessary formal documentation to bring the person to Canada, the person shall be awarded five points.	5	•	•		•

APPENDIX III

IMMIGRATION ACT 1976
Part 1
CANADIAN IMMIGRATION POLICY

Objectives

3. It is hereby declared that Canadian immigration policy and the rules and regulations made under this Act shall be designed and administered in such a manner as to promote the domestic and international interests of Canada recognizing the need.

   a) to support the attainment of such demographic goals as may be established by the Government of Canada from time to time in respect of the size, rate of growth, structure and geographic distribution of the Canadian population;

   b) to enrich and strengthen the cultural and social fabric of Canada, taking into account the federal and bilingual character of Canada;

   c) to facilitate the reunion in Canada of Canadian citizens and permanent residents with their close relatives from abroad;

   d) to encourage and facilitate the adaptation of persons who have been granted admission as permanent residents to Canadian society by promoting cooperation between the Government of Canada and other levels of government and non-governmental agencies in Canada with respect thereto;

   e) to facilitate the entry of visitors into Canada for the purpose of fostering trade and commerce, tourism, cultural and scientific activities and international understanding;

   f) to ensure that any person who seeks admission to Canada on either a permanent or temporary basis is subject to standards of admission that do not discriminate on grounds of race, national or ethnic origin, colour, religion or sex;

   g) to fulfil Canada's international legal obligations with respect to refugees and to uphold its humanitarian tradition with respect to the displaced and the persecuted;

   h) to foster the development of a strong and viable economy and the prosperity of all regions in Canada;

   i) to maintain and protect the health, safety and good order of Canadian society; and

   j) to promote international order and justice by denying the use of Canadian territory to persons who are likely to engage in criminal activity.

APPENDIX IV

TABLE 1
Canada: Immigration by World Area

	1965-1969 (%)	1975-1979 (%)
Europe (including United Kingdom)	68,8	34,8
Africa and the Middle East	2,2	5,6
Asia and the Pacific	12,4	31,1
Western Hemisphere	16,4	28,5
(USA only)	(10,4)	(10,8)
Other Countries	0,2	—
Total	100,0	100,0

TABLE 2
Canada: Principal Countries of Last Permanent Residence of Immigrants in Fiscal Year 1979-1980

Europe

Britain	14 280
Portugal	3 815
France	1 914
USSR	1 842
Italy	1 772
Netherlands	1 593
Germany Fed. Rep.	1 352
Greece	1 140
Poland	1 085
Others	6 156
Total for Europe	34 949

Australasia

Australia	789
New Zealand	618
Others	8
Total for Australasia	1 415

North & Central America

USA	9 186
Jamaica	3 076
Haiti	1 259
Trinidad and Tobago	828
Others	1 772
Total for N. and C. America	16 121

South America

Guyana	2 538
Chile	1 141
Argentina	477
Peru	336
Ecuador	244
Others	964
Total for South America	5 700

Africa

South Africa, Rep. of	1 393
Tanzania	545
Egypt	542
Kenya	326
Rhodesia	213
Morocco	178
Others	903
Total for Africa	4 100

Asia

Vietnam	26 115
China (incl. Hong Kong)	7 947
Laos	7 088
India	5 487
Philippines	4 330
Kampuchea (Cambodia)	1 885
Lebanon	1 739
Iran	1 140
Pakistan	1 034
Other Asia	5 936
Total for Asia	62 701

Oceania

Fiji	494
Mauritius	212
Others	17
Total for Oceania	723

Not Stated	36
Grand Total	125 745

Source: Canada Employment and Immigration Commission.

27

The International Food Policies of Canada

Roger Young
North-South Institute

INTRODUCTION

Canada is to a significant extent a trading nation and in large measure trade was originally initiated on the basis of exports of staple goods (fish, forest products, raw materials, animal skins and then agricultural products) in exchange for the processed materials and manufactured goods from trading partners. The opening of the Canadian frontier and the exploitation of its natural wealth through international trade have had a dramatic impact upon Canada's attempts at nation building.

The international food policies of Canada have reflected the Federal Government's attempts at nation building: the colonial inheritance as a member of the British Empire; the growing dependence, interdependence and at times competition, primarily with the United States but also the global economy; and now the desire to differentiate itself as a smaller power in both economic and political relations with the rest of the world.

This paper addresses itself to the competing claims upon Canada's international food policies during the past 40 years. It is during this period that dramatic changes in world food production and consumption became more apparent and during which claims upon Canada as a food surplus nation in a hungry world brought into focus the self-interest, growing international interdependence and humanitarian objectives which foreign policy has attempted to mediate. The focus of the paper will be on Canada's food policy relations with developing countries.

Canadians are constantly reminded that the face of human misery in the developing world is most often that of a hungry person. Televised news account of relief camps in Ethiopia, the Sudan and drought in the Sahel, are the most recent reports of the debilitating and seemingly persistent misery of poverty, and the inability of all individuals to have command over the most basic of human needs, a satisfactory diet.

International commissions and inquiries by experts agree that as few as 450 million people and as many as one billion persons may currently be without sufficient caloric and protein intakes on a daily basis to sustain normal mental and physical development in the societies in which they live. The majority of these persons live in South Asia (India, Indonesia, Bangladesh and Pakistan) with perhaps 150 million of them living in sub-Saharan Africa and Latin America. For the world's most populous nation, China, it is generally believed that widespread malnutrition is not a major feature, although access to complete information by external observers has been constrained.

While the consequences of «world hunger» have been enshrined in various reports and given a degree of statistical sophistication, the causes of inadequate food consumption by so many people remain highly controversial despite intensive efforts of theoretical and applied study. Thomas Malthus' original prediction of a century ago that the world's food supply would fail to keep pace with the growth of world population because of the declining fertility of land and the unregulated fertility of human beings has been proven conclusively to be false by the application of science and technology to agriculture and the response of human behaviour to changing economic conditions. Nevertheless, new «Cassandras» abound with predictions concerning the inexorable pressure of a growing world population on global food supplies leading to differing degrees of chaos, economic decline and international instability. If one wishes to disclaim these predictions, there are others prepared to argue that the deterioration of climate, the environment or the exploitative activities of multinational agribusiness are sufficient to produce the disaster which may have been avoided by the «natural play» of food and population forces.

Any discussion of international development, or of North-South relations, is inevitably focused on world food issues and hunger. The quest for world food security occupies the work of several international organizations, some donor agency officials and of course the political leaders and citizens of the Third World countries most directly concerned. The term has been given different interpretations, ranging from national food self-reliance to increasing world food production in the medium term, to avoiding sharp shortfalls in food consumption in any one year. The efforts to achieve it encompass a broad range of issues: increased food production and more equitable food consumption principally in the Third World; international trade in cereal grains and oilseeds; measures to stabilize the international wheat market in particular; the holding of international and national food stocks to dampen world price fluctuations and meet emergency consumption needs respectively; and the provision of food aid from food-surplus to food-deficit countries. Each of these issues, in turn, relate to Canadian interests and foreign policy objectives.

Canada's position as a «food-surplus» nation, producing grains in excess of domestic demand, as a major food aid supplier, and its long-standing participation in various world food bodies, such as the Food and Agriculture Organization of the United Nations, has given it an influence in international discussions of food problems far in excess of its normal, middle-level power status. As the world's second largest wheat exporter and food aid provider (well behind the United States in both respects), Canada has had substantial influence in the deliberations of the World Food Programme, the World Food Council and the International Wheat Council, bodies whose mandates in varying degrees can have a direct impact on the availability and distribution of food in the world.

Yet, it is people and not nation-states who are either well-fed or hungry and no discussion of world food issues is complete without consideration of the nature of farming in the Third World and the constraints to its improvement. Too, the public policies of Third World governments which affect the price and distribution of domestic food crops and the development goals of income growth and distribution must be considered.

This paper will review the issues related to the current state of world food production, consumption and trade by tracing the major trends in the past three decades, examining the range and relationship among these factors and reviewing the nature of Canadian foreign policy goals related to food trade and aid.

While this treatment of international trends and institutional structures in sections one and two may seem to be a diversion away from discussing Canada's international food policies, such a detour is required in order to set the context into which these policies are set. Canada's foreign policy objectives as related to agricultural issues combine national economic and political interests with a desire to contribute to multinational efforts towards solving a major world problem. The context then provides the requisite background information with which to describe how these objectives pursued.

TRENDS IN WORLD FOOD PRODUCTION AND TRADE

A great deal has been written of the instability of international grain markets, the impact of rising international wheat prices at certain times on the balance of payments difficulties of developing countries, and of the potential use of the food weapon as a policy tool of the North American governments which «monopolize» the world's wheat trade[1]. It is important to note, however, that the majority of the world's food is grown and consumed within national boundaries. Food imports account for only a modest, though growing, proportion of even the Third World's own food production and consumption.

The world's major food crops: corn, rice, wheat and other cereal grains, legumes – such as peas, beans and lentils –, livestock and fisheries are normally cultivated, bred or culled and consumed within narrow geographical limits. Global cereals production, trade and food aid can be placed in perspective by considering these figures for the crop year ended July 1985: of the 1,78 billion metric tons produced worldwide, about 210 million tons were traded among nations and 11,6 million tons were provided as food aid from all sources. It is these figures which provide the strong evidence that the success or failure to overcome the world's food gap will take place on the farms in the developing world.

Agriculture in the Third World can be characterized, in general terms, as being carried out on numerous small farms with low levels of total output per farm. This has been referred to as traditional agriculture in contrast to the modern farming techniques in the developed world where large commercial farms produce high volumes based on the intensive application of scientific inputs such as seeds, fertilizer and herbicides and the extensive use of farm machinery and fossil fuels.

Why has farming in the Third World remained traditional? A variety of theoretical explanations compete for expository veracity and it is not possible to do justice either to the individual models or their comparative strengths in a short article[2]. There is however a consensus of opinion among agricultural economists that technological developments in tropical agriculture, which provide the basis for improving crop yields and income, must be complemented with broad public policy changes to encourage more farmers to adopt new farming practices.

The development of agriculture in the now high-income industrialized countries was achieved through the application of scientific knowledge and more capital-intensive technology, leading to increased yields of selected cereals and livestock. This development implied falling per unit food prices. This process engendered a significant movement of labor out of, and capital into, the agricultural sector. Such development was not without significant political, economic and social cost given the sizeable adjustment which took place in a relatively short space of time. In Canada in 1941, 28 % of the population was listed as engaged in agricultural activities; by 1985, this figure had fallen to less than 4 % of the population, a movement of some 600 000 households out of direct agricultural production. They were able in large part to move into the expanding manufacturing and service sectors of the economy and these developments were true also for other developed countries.

In contrast, the depressed state of agriculture in many developing countries can be attributed to two sets of constraints. The first concerns the inadequate application of scientific knowledge and technological innovation. The use of high-yielding varieties of corn, wheat and rice, sensitive to the use of inputs such as water, fertilizer, pesticides and sophisticated management practices can have demonstrable and substantial impact on crop yields and farm incomes. In large part, this technological change with its attendant economic and social changes, has not taken place throughout enough of the Third World. Selective and important exceptions do of course exist, in certain areas of Mexico, Colombia, the Philippines, India and Bangladesh[3].

The second set of constraints may be termed those domestic policies which distort the incentives farmers perceive as the economic return to their efforts and which can discourage them from adopting those new practices which would lead to increased output of their food crops. To a significant extent, agriculture is undervalued in many developing countries. The majority of rural families are poor, organized in small and often remote villages; they have little political voice with urban bureaucracies or politicians. Indeed, the political process in many developing countries has bypassed democratic procedures, foreclosing one avenue of pressure for the agricultural sector. If rural families can be ignored, the urban poor cannot. Politicians desire low food prices for urban consumers partially to stimulate labor absorption by industry which they equivalate with modern development and, in part, because the urban poor are often the most visible and potentially the most threatening force to political stability.

Agricultural policy in developing countries has been characterized by the American economist Theodore Schultz, as the victory of «politics over economics». To achieve their political goals of lower food prices, politicians intervene in the agricultural sector to control and often depress food prices for certain «essential» commodities, and to institute marketing boards to control the supply of food and export, cash crops. Export-crops earn an often overvalued foreign exchange and export-crop farmers may therefore be provided with special incentives to maximize output and foreign earnings.

The consequences of these interventions are harmful to the large numbers of subsistence farm families and may often be perverse given the goals they are intended to achieve. The rational response of farmers to controlled prices on food crops is to shift into the production of uncontrolled commodities in order to earn higher returns to their efforts. Often, the economic return to farmers from producing coffee, tea and cotton exceeds that from food crops such as rice, wheat and maize. Controlling food prices to satisfy poor urban consumers can lead to a deterioration in national food production and may lead to an eventual rationing of a stagnating domestic supply of food as the urban population increases[4].

Such food-deficit countries will then have to rely on increased food imports to satisfy demand. In the face of a rising food import bill, a nation's leaders may call for increased food aid to reduce commercial imports and ease the pressure on their nation's treasury. Food aid, gladly given when a food surplus exists in the donor countries, may serve to depress local food prices in the recipient country below those which would have prevailed in the case of either lower food imports or in the absence of the food aid. Indigenous farmers receive incorrect signals to respond to fluctuations in the domestic food market and may not bring forth the increased food supplies in the following crop year which would have followed rising domestic food prices[5].

This relative stagnation of agriculture in parts of the Third World has been part and parcel of a striking change in the production and trade of global food supplies in the last half century. Reference is often made to the relative food self-sufficiency of the world's major regions prior to World War II. Since that time, despite dramatic increases in world food production, differential rates of output growth and food demand have meant that the period since 1960 has been characterized by growing food surpluses in North America and Oceania, and rising food deficits for many countries of Eastern Europe, Asia, Africa and Latin America.

To understand the current concern with food gaps and security, it is necessary to sketch these developments. World wheat production has trebled from 1949 to the present and world cereals production has more than doubled during the same period. The late 1950s and most of the 1960s were characterized by record harvests to that time and wheat, in particular, was considered to be in chronic oversupply. The major wheat producing nations (such as Canada) acted individually and through consultation to protect their domestic economic interest against falling international wheat prices. They attempted, at various times, to store this excess supply, to limit wheat production, to develop new overseas markets for wheat and to institute programs of food aid to food-deficit developing countries[6].

In the Soviet Union and the countries of Eastern Europe, economic development was being achieved through industrialization, and this growing income led to a sustained increase in the demand for an improved diet, particularly meat, which required increasing volumes of feedgrain. Agriculture in this region, always subject to large production variation because of the climate, lagged behind this new demand. By the early 1970s, the Soviet Union and Poland in particular, had become major grain importers. When harvests turned poor in general in 1972-1973, the Soviet import demand had a dramatic and disruptive impact on world grain prices. Future Soviet import demand while unpredictable, will be potentially very large and likely put increased pressure on world grain stocks and prices[7].

Japan's vigorous economic growth after World War II, also based on industrialization, meant that by the 1970s, it became the world's second largest food importer, accounting for 13 % of all grain imports in 1983, some 25 million metric tons.

In Western Europe, renewed industrialization after the war also led to increased income and an increasingly meat-based diet requiring heavy imports of grain.

Despite sustained and costly efforts, beginning in the late 1960s, policies to protect European agriculture from the competitiveness of North American and Australian farmers, had led by 1979 to grain imports of 23 million tonnes[8]. Rapid output increases in the 1980s, encouraged by these subsidies, led to the European Community being self-sufficient in most commodities and a significant exporter of wheat, butter and dairy products.

The Third World became a major food importing region. Although income per capita grew consistently in the postwar period, stating from a much lower base and being more unevenly distributed than in the developed countries, absolute import volumes grew more slowly than Japan, Europe or the USSR. Nevertheless, by 1985, the developing countries, including China, accounted for 50 % or some 108 million metric tons of grain imports. China, Brazil, Egypt, South Korea and Mexico are the largest grain importers in the Third World, and the Third World market, in total, became the fastest growing market for the wheat exporting countries of the United States, Canada, France, Argentina and Australia.

Some caution is required however in interpreting these figures lest the impression be left that grain imports are the dominant factor in discussing world food issues and, thus, that Canada as a grain exporter has some significant power to affect food supply or prices. Of 1984-1985 world wheat production of 512 million tons, the Soviet Union accounts for 25 % of world supply, the US 13 %, China 10 %, and Canada 5 %. Of the 102 million tons entering world trade in wheat, the US represents 40 % of exports, Canada 20 %, Australia 10 % and Argentine 10 %. For the coarse grains (corn, oat, barley for example), the proportions are roughly similar. Of nearly one billion tons of world supply, some 100 million tons enter trade. The US represents 30 % of world supply (but 64 % of world export trade), Canada 3 and 12 % respectively, the Soviet Union 20 % and Europe 12 % of supply and Australia, Argentina and Europe 4, 6 and 10 % of world cereal exports[9].

The significance of these statistics is compelling. Despite the current circumstances of rising international grain production and increasing Third World grain imports, the Prairies of Western Canada and the mid-Western and Southern United States will not be, and cannot be, a «breadbasket» for the world. The world's food problem is principally a problem of food production and consumption within the developing world and primarily amongst the poorer food-deficit countries of the Third World.

THE INTERNATIONAL FOOD REGIME

If the hypothesis is in large measure true that the gap between food supply and demand in the Third World will have to be resolved through increased production and improved consumption within those countries, then, it also seems true that the policies to accomplish the necessary change will have their impact only in the medium term, perhaps ten to 20 years from now. Developing, testing and introducing new varieties and technologies appropriate to the varying agro-climatic conditions in the Third World and instituting policies that will reverse the undervaluation of agriculture while absorbing the social and economic costs associated with large-scale structural change, will not be accomplished easily or without substantial political strain.

Few, if any, countries have the resource endowments to be self-sufficient in a wide range of temperate and tropical food-stuffs. There is a strong argument to suggest that the costs of trying to become so are not justified. The comparative advantage of the major grain producers in the developed world and the sugar cane and tropical fruit and beverage producers of the developing world serve as examples. This economic lesson is as true for the developed as the developing countries[10].

International agricultural trade will continue to play a significant part in the pattern of world food production and consumption. In the model of unfettered free trade, producers with an international comparative advantage would have free access to those markets where production is relatively less efficient. However, because food is deemed to be such a strategic element of individual and collective well-being and because its production is subject to fluctuations induced by external factors such as climate, food policies have become an integral part of public policies within and between nation-states.

This interrelationship among national and international policies of agricultural trade, food aid and foreign aid became striking at the time of the World Food Conference of 1974 held in Rome. The Conference was called following the doubling of the international wheat price in 1973-1974, the decline in carry-over stocks of cereal grains to what was considered dangerously low levels, and the double shock to the poorest developing countries, in particular, of the oil price increase declared by OPEC.

The Conference helped to galvanize action and political commitment on behalf of the poorest countries of the world after international food prices had risen dramatically and food aid levels had fallen precipitously. Despite some political and diplomatic scuffling over who should be held responsible for the confluence of circumstances affecting the international economy in the mid-1970s, progress was achieved in relieving the immediate impact upon the low-income developing countries. The foreign assistance loans of these «most seriously affected» countries were converted to grants by some donors, Canada among them, to provide some relief to their balance of payments difficulties; increased food aid commitments were made and Canada made one of the most generous pledges by providing one million tons for each of the three subsequent years 1975-1978. Two new institutions, the World Food Council and the International Fund for Agricultural Development, were created to heighten political awareness of the food issue and to contribute directly to Third World agricultural development, respectively.

Absent from the programme of action – the *sine qua non* of such international conferences – was any substantial action with respect to international agricultural trade. In part, this was due to the commitment by governments to discuss these trade issues in other fora, such as the General Agreement on Tariffs and Trade (GATT) and the multilateral trade negotiations. Through UNCTAD, the Third World was to renew its call, within the framework of the New International Economic Order, for the stabilization of world grain prices and for wheat in particular.

The discussion of stabilizing international wheat prices was to be carried forward from the Conference through the International Wheat Council. No resolution in the form of an agreement binding on both importing and exporting nations has been achieved and the prospects for even renewed discussion within such a framework remain dim. The major conflict revolves around the desirability and ability of nation-states to stabilize prices within some range. The developing countries, as importers, are requesting the creation of an international buffer stock agency to accumulate and sell off wheat stocks in order to maintain prices within a band of approximately $80 per ton[11]. As importers, they are likely to be the beneficiaries of such stabilization, particularly as prices now appear poised for a significant short-term rise. The developed country importers (Western Europe and Japan are the main actors involved) have also supported price stabilization although they believe price bands must be wider to encourage exporter agreement. The exporting countries, Canada, the United States, Argentina and Australia, strongly influenced by their own domestic wheat producers, have resisted price stabilization and a binding agreement to achieve it. The exporters have not resisted, however, the temptation for consultation amongst themselves, in part to ensure prices do not fall below the «cost of production», which could become a disguised version of price support[12].

The exporting countries also recognize that the Soviet Union, not a party to these discussions within the International Wheat Council, would be the major beneficiary of price stabilization. One estimate places their benefit as high as 28 % of the consumer benefit to be achieved through price stabilization[13]. It seems clear that economic, political and strategic factors have dominated the Western exporters' view on price stabilization.

The issue of grain price instability is a complex issue. Some of the destabilizing influence on grain prices derives from year-to-year production changes caused by climatic factors; some influence derives from the supply management policies of certain regions (in particular the European Economic Community's common agricultural policy guaranteeing Community grain producers above-world prices and subsidizing their surplus production for export promotes price instability); fluctuating world prices derive still further from the unpredictable import demand from a major market such as the Soviet Union where imports can rise of fall by 20 million tons from one year to the next; and finally, the supply management and occasional domestic pricing policies of major producers and exporters such as Canada and the United States, seeking to protect domestic farmers from income declines and consumers from rising food prices, can transmit instability onto international grain markets. Added to this list is the view that the speculative activities of major grain trading companies, such as Cargill, and Dreyfus, seeking to buy cheap and sell dear in the market, produce fluctuations greater than that which could be anticipated from annual supply and demand shifts.

The negotiations within the International Wheat Council to create greater price stability had broken down by early 1979. No agreement could be reached on the price stabilization formula, the holding of an international buffer stock or the right of developing countries to preferential access to reserve stocks when stocks would be falling as prices rose. The talks adjourned without any consensus as to the framework or timing of renewed discussion. The agreement now in force and dating from 1971 has been renewed through June 1986 and there is little prospect for renewal of the negotiation of what is termed «an agreement with economic provisions», *i.e.* binding agreement to maintain prices within some specific range. Under the 1971 agreement, importers and exporters agree only to consult, and to take action tied to a set of indicators surrounded by three price bands relative to the previous year's average. If the world price of wheat passes the innermost band, consultation would take place. If the price continued to rise past the second set of trigger points, an internationally-coordinated reserve stock would be accumulated or released; beyond the third set, exporters and importers would again consult on appropriate modifications to agricultural and trade policies.

Discussions since February 1979 have focused on the development of a «flexible» response to the developing world's stabilization proposals. A small, perhaps 12 million-ton «food security» reserve would be accumulated by producing countries (importers and exporters), allowing for preferential access by developing countries. Outside this safety net reserve, countries would not be found by specific economic provisions but would consult more frequently should prices fluctuate significantly. This flexibility could be interpreted as deliberate vagueness by the developed countries which are being careful to avoid any binding agreement.

If the developing countries are to find only limited relief through the international wheat agreement from rising grain prices, now expected in the coming year, can some solace be found from food aid and agricultural development assistance?

Apart from the national food aid and foreign aid programs of donor countries – Canada's policies and programs are discussed in part four of this chapter –, there are six significant international institutional mechanisms for providing or coordinating food aid and agricultural development assistance. (Five of these institutions are discussed below; the sixth, the World Food Programme is discussed in the fourth part of this chapter).

The United Nations Food and Agriculture Organization (FAO) founded in 1945 at Québec City with active Canadian support and participation has a varied program of technical and policy support for world agriculture. In the past decade, it has become a strong supporter of the Third World's food security needs, with some loss of credibility among certain developed country members. In 1979, the FAO adopted a Five-Point Plan of Action as an interim measure towards world food security until a new International Wheat Agreement could be concluded. In summary form, the Plan contains the following elements: national cereal stocking policies would be adopted by all member-countries but managed so as to not disrupt international markets; food aid would be increased to 10 million tons in 1980 and possibly 15 million tons by 1985; countries would adopt national food policies to improve food production and consumption within their territories; developed countries would be called upon to increase and improve their development assistance for Third World food production.

Some progress has been made towards achieving some elements to the Plan; however, the coordinated approach envisaged has not taken place. In part, this derives from the deliberately vague, and at time conflicting, aspects of the Plan and in part from the fact that it does not, and could not, given that importing and exporting countries are its members, directly confront the issue of international grain prices and the negotiations.

The World Food Council, created at the time of the World Food Conference in 1974, is a 36-member ministerial body whose objectives are to maintain political cognizance of the world food problem and to seek political commitment at the national and international levels to the eradication of hunger and malnutrition. The Council, of which Canada has been a member since its creation, has called for greater attention to food questions in food-deficit countries. It has proposed the adoption of national food strategies to increase investment in the agricultural sector, and the developed countries have been requested to increase and improve their official development assistance to the low-income food-deficit countries. A number of countries have indicated their commitment to implementing such a strategy and Canada and other donor countries have agreed to provide a small amount of technical assistance to these countries.

It is, however, the specific policy recommendations of the Council which have proved to be more controversial and on which agreement has yet to be reached. The Council had called for increased international assistance for investment in agriculture in the «food priority» countries reaching US $8,3 billion (1975 dollars) by 1980, of which US $6,5 billion should be on concessional terms. (An FAO study, *Agriculture: Toward 2000*, estimates the required investment to be US $57 billion (1975 dollars) by 1990 of which external resources would have to supply US $12,7 billion).

These formidable objectives are well beyond the present or probable commitment of donor agencies with respect to development assistance. While these remain benchmarks for investment needs, the Council has had to turn its attention to more limited means of achieving short-term food security and this development threatens to become an increasing preoccupation of the international community.

The Conference of 1974 also brought to fruition a new international agricultural investment organization, the International Fund for Agricultural Development (IFAD) with an initial capitalization of $1 billion. The Fund, consisting of OPEC and Western funds, provides grants and loans to the poorer developing countries for their agricultural sector. At first constrained by a lack of fundable projects, the IFAD is now commiting over $250 million annually for these purposes and now faces problems of adequate capitalization from its contributing members.

The World Bank remains the largest source of financing for Third World agricultural development. Following Robert MacNamara's address to the Bank's Board of Governors in Nairobi in 1973, the Bank reoriented its focus to provide for the basic needs of lower-income members of Third World countries. The Bank's earlier emphasis upon roads and other infrastructural development was changed to provide more funds for direct food production increases by small-scale farmers in the developing world. By fiscal year 1985, the Bank and its affiliate, the International Development Association (IDA), were providing some $3,4 billion of a total commitment of $15,5 billion for agriculture and rural development purposes – up from $500 million in 1969[14].

The World Bank's approach to Third World rural development can be viewed as facilitating the entry of peasant producers to the market economy. The basic elements of the strategy call for increasing the productivity of small holder agriculture through improved pricing policies, reformed tenancy and improved credit, water, technology and extension services in the agriculture sector of Third World countries.

Under the joint sponsorship of the World Bank, FAO and UNDP, the major international research and technical assistance agencies are grouped together through the Consultative Group on International Agricultural Research (CGIAR). Its members include the International Centre for Wheat and Corn Improvement (CIM-MYT, Mexico) and the International Rice Research Institute (IRRI, Philippines), the two centres where much of the research related to the «Green Revolution» was conducted. The 12 member-institutes of the CGIAR account for some $1 billion of annual research and consultancy services related to farming activites in the Third World. Its work is financed by 41 donor countries, international agencies and foundations.

CANADIAN AGRICULTURAL POLICIES

The Canadian response to the development of these factors in world food production and trade has been conditioned by domestic agricultural interests. However, with an open economy seeking to take advantage of the opportunities offered through international trade and at the same time subject to the pressures of international competitiveness, the degree of autonomy in framing domestic policy is constrained by international developments. This brief review of Canadian agricultural policies is intended to shed light on the relationship between national and international interests. In turn, it provides some insight to the development of foreign policy objectives as they relate to agriculture.

Two principal features of national economic development have shaped Canada's domestic agricultural policies since World War II. The first is the structural economic change resulting from increased industrialization – requiring an expanded labour force drawn in part from a dwindling farm population. Secondly, this process has affected and in turn been affected by the conflicting short-run economic interests of different regions within Canada. Thus, for example, the National Policy of 1879, which influenced the development of Central Canada as a manufacturing region and Western Canada as a supplier of raw materials (originally agricultural and forest products but more recently of oil, gas, potash and uranium in addition to these «traditional» commodities), has had a continuing influence upon the development of a national economy. The Federal Government's policies have attempted to arbitrate differing regional interests and perceptions. It is beyond the limited scope of this paper to detail the development and impact of these national economic development policies; however, in assessing the nature and objectives of Canada's agricultural policies, one must be cognizant of the wider dimension of the pursuit of a national economic development policy.

The Federal Government has, often at one and the same time, sought to provide a measure of protection to both food producers and food consumers through its agricultural pricing, transportation and marketing policies. A short-term conflict of economic interest can arise between high grain prices for Western Canadian producers and low bread prices for Central Canadian consumers. (Although the interests of the Central Canadian farming population with more varied production of livestock, dairy, and food crops have also been evident, they are not dealt with in this chapter[15].) These policies have had a direct impact upon the quantity of grains and oilseeds which Canada was able to make available to the world market.

Furthermore, with wheat such a dominant feature of Prairie agriculture, and with wheat exports a growing share of that supply, Canadian wheat policies offer a particular insight to the competing claims on government. Policies have been advanced to protect producers (or assist them during times of strong world demand) against the vagaries of an often turbulent international market. As noted previously, Canada is one of the few nations consistently producing cereal grains well in excess of domestic demand, notwithstanding the fact that on a per capita basis, Canadians are among the largest meat consumers in the world. Livestock, poultry and hogs are, of course, intensive intermediate consumers of grain.

The goals of Canadian wheat policy have been twofold and often at conflict: to assist Canada's international competitiveness with respect to wheat exports and to protect wheat producers and Canadian consumers from sharp shifts in the world price of wheat. The policy thrusts pursued over the course of the last three decades and summarized below indicate some of the conflict between these objectives.

The Canadian Wheat Board, created in 1935, has been the sole marketing agency for Prairie grown wheat since 1943. By setting a delivery quota for each farmer, with the aggregate quota level based on estimates of domestic consumption, export sales and working reserve requirements, the Board controls marketing and influences production decisions at the farm level. The Federal Government, acting through the Board, also provides a measure of price support, and assists Prairie producers by providing advance payments for deliveries in the form of interest-free loans. These assistance programs have been supplemented since 1976 by the Western Grain Stabilization Act. Funded by producer and government contributions, the Act ensures that the net cash flow (the total receipts minus cash costs) of participating Prairie grain and oilseed producers does not fall below the previous five-year average.

Even in the absence of significant levels of price support, surplus stocks of wheat were a persistent problem throughout the 1950s and 1960s and led to measures intended to lessen or more equitably distribute the surplus burden. The Federal Government, between 1956 and 1973, assumed the cost of carrying Canadian Wheat Board stocks of wheat in excess of 178 million bushels. The program was terminated in 1973, as Board stocks fell below the level specified in the legislation, and has not been reactivated. Food aid shipments, while approaching neither the absolute nor relative importance of similar American programs, did reflect in large part the Canadian wheat supply situation and prospects for commercial exports. In contrast to the American experience, however, the Canadian Government has sought to reduce the acreage planted to grains only once. The LIFT (Lower Inventories For Tomorrow) program, implemented in 1970 in response to the record carry-over stocks of the previous year, paid Prairie farmers $6,00 for each acre diverted from wheat to fallow. Under its previsions, two million acres of land were left idle during the following year[16].

Two additional facets of government involvement in the Canadian wheat industry, the maintenance of a domestic consumption price, and the regulation of grain transportation rates, have also affected the availability of Canadian wheat on the world market. In the case of the former, the price of wheat destined for human consumption in Canada has been maintained by the government in isolation from world price levels since 1969. Initially enacted in the wake of the breakdown of the 1967 International Grains Arrangement, the two price systems initially sought to ensure that farmers received a remunerative price for at least a part of their output. The price set by government regulation, $1,95 per bushel, was approximately 25 cents per bushel above prevailing world price levels. With the rapid wheat price increases of 1973 and 1974, however, the objectives and character of the program reversed. Seeking to protect the consumer from rapid price increases, the 1974 Two-Price Wheat Act established $3,25 per bushel as the price at which sales to Canadian millers were to take place. A corresponding producer subsidy of up to $1,75 per bushel was also provided, to compensate producers for revenue foregone. Recent amendments to the program have established a price range for domestic sales of wheat and have dropped the subsidy paid to producers.

In contrast, government involvement in the transportation of wheat to export markets is long-standing, and in large part the recent controversy surrounding the transportation system relates to the Crow's Nest Pass system of freight rates, first enacted in 1897[17]. Given the relatively long distances to overseas customers, some form of transportation subsidy was, and has been, seen to be essential to maintain Canada's competitive position in the world wheat market. In exchange for a government subsidy to the CPR for railway construction, statutory rates applying to the transportation of wheat and certain personal effects of homesteaders were established, rates which were then applied to the movement by rail of all export grain and grain moving east through the port of Thunder Bay. The impact of the rate structure has long been the subject of debate which is difficult to capsulize. At the heart of the issue is the current reluctance, or inability, of rail companies to transport grain at rates which have remained essentially unchanged since 1925. While a number of measures to ease transportation bottlenecks were announced in the late 1970s, it was not until 1893 that measures were introduced to restructure the system of grain transportation rates. Arduous negotiations among governments, producers and the railways were previously left off the political agenda because of the cost such a change could impose on farmers and the uncertain implications the change could have for the structure of Prairie economic life.

These domestic pricing, marketing and transportation policies for cereal grains have been formed with one eye turned to national policy concerns and another turned to Canada's dependence upon developments in international markets. Fluctuations in world cereal prices and shifting patterns of foreign demand for Canadian grains have a direct, visible effect upon the economic fortunes of the Prairie population. So too do they, albeit in a more indirect sense, upon the consumers of Central and Eastern Canada.

Thus, Canada's agricultural policies have had to be determined in light of both national and international developments. The expression of Canada's foreign policy objectives, comprising national and international interests too, has been no less influenced by this complex, and often conflicting, conjuncture of interests.

AGRICULTURE, TRADE AND AID POLICIES

What are the objectives, economic and political, of Canada's foreign policy with respect of international food trade and aid? Is there either a special role or responsibility for Canada, as a middle-size economic and political power but a major grain producer and trader, in the efforts to achieve greater world food security? Are Canadian interests, domestic or foreign policy objectives, coincident with, or distinct from, those of either the United States, as another major grains exporter, or the lower-income food deficit countries of the Third World? Is the food weapon, in light of the United States attempt to restrict grain sales to the Soviet Union in 1980 an appropriate policy tool for Canada and would it represent well Canada's own foreign policy interests?

With significant economic interest in international cereal grains and oilseeds, livestock trading and a dependence on international prices, a long-standing and significant contribution to food aid transfers to developing countries, Canadian foreign policy with respect to food trade and aid bears directly on the interests of Canadian food producers and consumers.

Previous sections of this chapter have attempted to indicate the often vexing role of the political process in all countries in arbitrating the competing short-term interests of food producers and consumers. Much as it is called upon in establishing domestic agricultural policies, the Federal Government in pursuing foreign policy objectives with respect to international agricultural issues must asses and weigh the relative claims of furthering national economic interests and enhancing its international political image by contributing to the resolution of international problems.

One may distinguish between the legitimate interest of a nation-state to pursue its own economic well-being in the conduct of international relations, and the wider objectives of its foreign policy which may embody both self-interest (strategic and military aspects could be considered here) and its mutual interest deriving from increased global interdependence in greater international prosperity and stability. World food issues, in turn, encompass each of these aspects of foreign policy.

The calculus, however imprecise and imperfect, in determining Canadian foreign policy with respect to international agricultural issues, has attempted to meet each of these competing claims. It would be inaccurate though to suggest that in all cases these interests are mutually exclusive. Canada does have a clearly definable interest in increased grain exports, and in the coming decade there is strong evidence to suggest that the Third World will remain (and likely will grow as) an important market for Canadian grain production. Therefore, the ability of these countries to pay for these exports, whether inhibited by poor economic growth, foreign exchange and debt contraints or political difficulties, relates directly to Canadian interests in expanded grains trade.

In addition to its international recognition as a grains exporter, Canada is known as a major provider of food aid. Since the mid-1960s, Canada has been a relatively generous contributor of food aid, both bilateral and multilateral, although its overall share has been modest, overwhelmed by the much larger absolute volume of food aid from America. Canada has for some years been the second largest single bilateral food aid donor and the second largest single contributor to the World Food Programme, the major outlet for multilateral food aid. (The major share of Canada's contribution to the WFP is tied to the use of Canadian commodities, although a cash pledge for administrative and shipping costs is also provided.)

Canada began to give food aid in the 1950s but it was not until the mid-1960s that disbursements reached substantial levels. Food aid disbursements and food aid as a percentage of total Canadian official development assistance are shown in Table 4, at the end of this chapter.

Several trends become readily apparent in reviewing the table. The proportion of foreign aid accounted for by food aid grew to over one-half by the mid-1960s. Food aid, while still a significant component of foreign aid, has fallen relative to overall development assistance in the past decade and in real dollar terms fell between 1975 and 1980 before rising again. This has occurred at the same time that Canadian commercial grain exports to the Third World have risen steadily. Over the period 1971-1975, food aid disbursements in dollar terms rose markedly but in volume terms fell sharply as unit costs were rising. With grain in short supply worldwide and strong demand in export markets, it is likely that Canadian exports displaces food aid transfers over this period. In the mid-1970s, following Canada's generous commitment to provide one million tons of food aid over the three years following the World Food Conference in 1974, dollar disbursements rose dramatically between 1975 and 1978. Between 1978-1980 however, volume and disbursement levels fell again as commercial sales to the Third World were strong and political commitment to food aid slipped following the 1974 Conference. With rising food needs among the poorest developing countries, and Africa in particular, Canadian food aid spending rose substantially in the 1980s with a near 50 % increase between 1982-1985.

Bilateral Canadian food aid has been concentrated upon relatively few recipients. India received over 60 % of the value of Canadian bilateral food aid between 1966 and 1972 and as much as 44 % in 1975-1977. Bangladesh, India, Sri Lanka, and Tanzania accounted for up to two-thirds of Canada's bilateral food aid in the 1970s. About one-half of bilateral food aid was directed to Africa in 1984-1985.

Multilateral food aid has represented since its inception in 1963 until recently a growing proportion of Canadian food aid. In 1966-1967 it accounted for 9 % of food aid but grew steadily to reach a peak of some 50 % in 1975-1976. It is often argued that multilateral food aid is more effective than bilateral food aid as expertise is high, administrative costs lower and international institutions can respond flexibly to perceived food aid to the use of Canadian foodstuffs.

The most important outlet for Canada's multilateral food aid is its contribution to the World Food Programme, an umbrella organization of the United Nations and the Food and Agriculture Organization. Established in 1963, partly at the insistence of the US which sought a sharing of the food aid burden at the time, the WFP is heavily involved in project aid, with shipments closely tied to well-defined development projects in recipient countries. Canada is the second largest contributor to the WFP. For the biennium 1984-1986, Canada will provide some $300 million of which $270 million is in the form of Canadian commodities. A Canadian, Garson Vogel, was until early 1981 Executive Director of the WFP.

The support of small food aid programs of non-governmental organizations such as the Mennonite Central Committee's Food Bank, the NGO-Skim Milk Powder Program and the Provincial Governments' Voluntary Agriculture Development Assistance Program, complete Canada's food aid funding. These NGO and Provincial Government programs amounted to $10,4 million of Federal Government food aid contributions in 1983-1984, the last year ago food aid was programmed separately. Their total value is of course complemented by the organizations' own resources.

Canadian food aid cannot be divorced from domestic food production and trade policies. While direct causality may be difficult to establish and speculation hazardous, there is general agreement among observers that food aid commitments are likely to be residual, to be determined once domestic supply forecasts and trade prospects have been established[18].

Throughout the 1950s and again in the late 1960s, all major grain exporting countries were concerned with surplus wheat stocks. The high costs associated with grain storage and the prospect of future oversupply led to producing-country policies to limit grain production and lower inventories through increased exports and food aid. The US Public Law 480 of 1954 (Agriculture Trade Development and Assistance Act) – the major single piece of legislation to arise from these circumstances – , was seen as a temporary measure to help rundown a burdensome American agricultural surplus. By 1975, P.L. 480 had become a permanent feature, and had supplied $25 billion worth of agricultural commodities equivalent to 16 % of US agricultural exports.

The significant Canadian policies during this period, the Temporary Wheat Reserves Act (1956), the Two-Price Wheat Program (1969) and the Lower Inventories For Tomorrow Program (LIFT, 1970) were symptomatic of this concern with reducing high carryover stocks and maintaining domestic farm incomes in the face of low prices (oversupply) and relatively weak world demand for cereal exports. The Reserves Act was intended to take excess supply out of the market and thereby support the price of wheat. It did not lapse until 1973 by which time oversupply had apparently vanished in the view of governments. The Two-Price Wheat Program, separating domestic and international markets, was introduced in light of low world prices following the breakdown of exporter-importer collaboration under the 1967 International Grains Arrangement. LIFT, which paid farmers not to grow wheat, was applied in similar pursuit of domestic farm-income maintenance and stock-reduction objectives.

The belief that food aid is dependent on domestic output and farm-income variables is evidenced by the fact that just prior to the LIFT initiative, Canadian food aid shipments reached their highest level to date. Furthermore, except for 1975-1978, and for Bangladesh in the mid-1980s, it has been government policy to make annual single-year commitments of bilateral food aid, and to commit only financial resources, not food aid volumes, on a two-year basis to the World Food Programme.

Canada has also used food aid as a market development tool and as a means to support the diversification of the Western Canadian agricultural economy into new varieties and to promote further processing of food within Canada. Theodore Cohn has suggested that the government's desire to promote the rapeseed crushing industry in Canada and to develop India as a significant potential market for Canadian rapeseed oil exports formed important components of food-aid policy in the mid-1970s[19]. One-third of Canada's processed wheat flour exports have been channelled through the World Food Programme.

However strong commercial interests may be in forming food-aid policy, foreign policy and even developmental concerns have also played a role in policy formulation. Canada has played a strong and largely constructive role in multilateral fora dealing with international food questions. In part this derives from a strong sense of self-interest in expanding cereals trade and providing food aid. Two recent examples, however, point to significant generosity by Canada. The 1974 pledge at the World Food Conference of one million tons of food aid for three years with 20 % channelled through multilateral sources, coming at a time when commercial sales could reasonably have been expected, was a significant gesture. (This may be a case of food aid displacing commercial exports.)

After some equivocation, Canada decided in 1979 to support proposals aimed at furthering renegotiation of the Food Aid Convention (FAC). Discussions had broken down on a grain reserve proposal within the Wheat Trade Convention of the International Wheat Agreement. Canada supported initiatives to separate the aid and trade discussions paving the way to a renewal of the FAC with minimum commitments at new, record levels.

A potentially significant foreign policy issue to face Canadian policy-makers in the future is the use of the «food weapon», a deliberate attempt to exact economic or political concessions from a trading partner by withholding supplies of food. Earlier broached as a means to retaliate against OPEC – «a barrel of oil for a bushel of wheat» –, the «trade embargo» enacted by the Carter administration against the Soviet Union in 1980-1981 is the most recent example we have of the use of such a policy tool[20].

It is instructive to review briefly the facts surrounding the embargo as a way to gage its appropriateness for Canadian foreign policy. The US and USSR signed in 1975 a six-year accord by which the USSR agreed to buy a minimum 6 million tons of American grain annually, and to obtain American approval for any purchases above 8 million tons. In February 1980, President Carter announced that as an indication of American disapproval of the Soviet presence in Afghanistan, the United States would, *inter alia,* suspend the sale of American grain to the USSR above the already-committed purchase of 8 million tons. The President requested that other grain exporters to the Soviet Union, Canada included, respect the spirit of his policy by limiting sales to the USSR to «traditional» levels. (Because import demand varies significantly from year to year, the interpretation of traditional levels gave rise to some debate in Canada with the Conservative and Liberal federal governments of 1980, holding two different views as to Canada's traditional level of sales.)

Was the embargo successful in limiting grain sales to the Soviet Union? Although the answer to this question provides only a limited response to America's foreign policy objectives in implementing the embargo, a negative answer would suggest that even this narrow objective was not achieved and thus the policy would appear ineffective and inappropriate[21].

It is believed that the Soviet Union purchased 28 million tons of grains on international markets in 1979-1980, up from 15 million tons the previous year. Despite the reduced American sales and the explicit cooperation of Canada and Australia, the USSR was able to increase its purchases from Argentina, Brazil and Western Europe and to a more limited extent, India, to satisfy a growing import demand that year. What these figures reveal is that exporter cooperation is a necessary and vital condition of a grains embargo or any variation of the use of the food weapon, and that securing such cooperation is unlikely to be forthcoming. The existence of an import demand, and even more strongly so when that demand can cope with increased prices, will, it appears, evoke a supply response from one (or more) exporting country whose immediate economic gain is recognized in making that supply available. In 1981, in response to US producer pressure, President Reagan lifted the US embargo with the USSR.

It appears that the same response by food-exporting countries were one or more of the major exporters to try to drive grain prices up through monopoly practices, whether it be to force an OPEC style cortel to bargain differently or to threaten an unfriendly or uncooperative international power. Nor is it at all clear that the populace of these countries, and their own farmers in particular, would tolerate for very long the application of such a policy that would deny food to another country.

In the search for a renewed commitment on the part of the developed world to the advancement of the developing world, much has been written of the mutual interest of the North and the South in more vigorous and more just economic development in the Third World. In part, this may be interpreted to mean that states, such as Canada, can pursue simultaneously a self-interested and an altruistic foreign policy by strengthening their commitment to world development. Policies need not be framed in a world of exclusivity, between «our» and «their» interests.

It should be clear that Canada's international agricultural policies have struggled with this search for an accomodation of interests. The future of world agriculture suggests that a world of delicate supply-demand balances, unstable prices and perhaps heightened concern for the poorer, food-deficit countries will bring into even sharper focus, the potential conflict between Canadian self-interest and perceptions of international responsibility. Enlightened policy has the opportunity to contribute to Canadian self-interest (through expanded exports of agricultural products) and to meet the major challenges of international development, such as increased food self-reliance. Developing countries experiencing rapid growth in income and food production have been the fastest growing importers of food[22], thus providing the evidence that Canadian opportunities and obligations can be self-reinforcing principles of foreign policy.

TABLE 1
Cereals Production by Region (million tons)

	1970	1975	1979	1984
World	1 242	1 366	1 538	1 780
Developed	423	481	549	619
Developing	370	417	439	591
Africa	43	45	46	44
Latin America	70	79	85	106
Near East	43	53	53	55
Far East	215	240	255	319
Other	25	31	50	67

Source: FAO: Production Yearbook. Various.

TABLE 2
Net Trade in Cereals by Region (million tons)

	1970	1975	1979	1984
Developed	+ 25,6	+ 68,6	+ 84,9	+ 83,5
Developing	− 14,9	− 37,7	− 40,4	− 74,2
Africa	− 3,5	− 8,0	− 10,8	− 31,0
Latin America	+ 4,1	− 3,5	− 4,3	− 2,1
Near East	− 5,2	− 10,5	− 14,0	− 22,5
Far East	− 10,0	− 15,5	− 11,1	− 18,0

Source: FAO: Trade Yearbook. Various.

TABLE 3
Canadian Agricultural Exports by Value ($ million can.)

1960	988
1970	1 869
1975	4 112
1980	8 202
1985*	10 300

* Preliminary

Source: Statistics Canada: Exports by Commodities. Various.

TABLE 4
Canadian Food Aid and Official Development Assistance ($ million can.)

	ODA	Food Aid	Bilateral Food Aid	Multilateral Food Aid	Food Aid as a % of ODA	Bilateral Food Aid as a % of Total Food Aid
1962	51	12,5	12,5		24,5	—
1970	349	104	87	17	29,8	83,5
1975	910	222	117	105	24,5	52,6
1980	1 210	183	85	98	15,1	46,4
1985	2 100	363	223	139	17,2	61,5

Source: CIDA: Annual Report. Various.

NOTES

1. Data on international grain trading is published annually by the FAO. See *Trade Yearbook* (FAO Rome). The most comprehensive research about the activities of the major multinational grain trading companies is to be found in Dan Morgan, *Merchants of Grain*, Harmondsworth, 1980.

2. Two competing and widely cited explanations can be found in T.W. Schultz (ed.), *Distortions of Agricultural Incentives*, Bloomington, 1978, and F. Moore-Lappé and Joseph Collins *Food First: Beyond the Myth of Scarcity*, Boston, 1977.

3. Several references could be cited on the impact of the so-called Green Revolution. The Moore-Lappé book already cited provides evidence of the regressive socio-economic impact. The more optimistic view can be found in *Changes in Rice Farming in Selected Areas of Asia*, IRRI, Manila, 1978.

4. Some excellent case studies, including Mexico, Egypt and the Philippines, illustrating this potential development are described in B. Huddleston and J. McLin (eds.), *Political Investments in Food Production, National and International Case Studies*, Bloomington, 1979.

5. A comprehensive and well-balanced analysis of the causes and consequences of food aid for donor and recipient countries, focusing on Africa, is presented in Christopher Stevens, *Food Aid and the Developing World, Four African Case Studies*, London, 1979.

6. See T.K. Warley, *Agriculture in an Interdependent World, US and Canadian Perspective*, Montréal, 1977, for a concise review of these policies.

7. See Padma Desai, *Estimates of Soviet Grain Imports in 1980-1985: Alternative Approaches*, IFPRI, Washington, 1981. Average annual import requirements for food and feed grains could reach as high as 18-20 million tons or 10 % of world import demand. In 1981, Canada reached a long-term agreement to supply the USSR an average of 5 million tons of grain for 1981-1986. By the mid-1980s, the USSR was importing 45 million tons of grain for all sources.

8. The Community's Common Agricultural Policy (CAP) is designed to protect domestic producers against lower-priced imports and to subsidize the cost of exporting expensive Community grains. The CAP is critically analyzed in «Reforming the CAP», *The Economist*, May 19, 1979, p. 63-69.

9. Annual market share for grain trading and production can be calculated from the FAO's *Trade Yearbook* and *Production Yearbook* respectively.

10. For an excellent statement of the economic implications of more liberalized agricultural trade, and the corresponding costs of barriers to that trade, see Theodor Heidhues, *World Food, Interdependence of Farm and Trade Policies*, London, 1977.

11. For a review of this stage of the negotiations, see Theodore Cohn, «The 1978-1979 negotiations for an international wheat agreement: an opportunity lost?», *International Journal*, Volume XXXV, No. 1, Winter 1979-1980.

12. See the communiqué issued following the consultations among the major wheat exporting nations held in Saskatoon on July 1979 and Melbourne on June 1980. Canadian and American senators had talked of the need for an exporters cartel to protect their domestic farm interests, although no formal negotiations towards that end are known to have been held.

13. See Lance Taylor, A. Sarris and P.C. Abbott, *Grain Reserves Emergency Relief and Food Aid*, Bloomington, 1981. For the parameters used in arriving at this estimate, see Appendix F, p. 129 ff.

14. World Bank, *Annual Report 1983*, Washington, D.C., 1984.

15. The most comprehensive review of the commodity and institutional aspects of Canadian agriculture can be found in *An Agri-Food Strategy for Canada*, Ottawa, Department of Agriculture, 1981.

16. See OECD, *Agriculture Policy in Canada*, Paris, 1973, p. 44-45.

17. See David R. Harvey, *Christmas Turkey or Prairie Vulture? An Economy Analysis of the Crow's Nest Pass Grain Rates*, IRPP, Ottawa, 1980, for a good synthesis of the costs and benefits of this policy. The «Crow's Rate» remains the most controversial transportation issue in Canada involving both senior levels of government in Canada, the railways, farmers and grain marketers. Reviews of the rate structure have been the subject of several special commissions, for example, *Commission into the Cost of Moving Grain by Rail Report*, Ottawa, Queen's Printer, 1977.

18. This argument is made by Theodore Cohn, *Canadian Food Aid, Domestic and Foreign Policy Implications*, Denver, 1980.

19. *Ibidem*, Chapter 3.

20. An excellent survey of trade sanctions and embargoes, their rationale and utility is presented by Margaret Doxey, «Oil and Food as International Sanctions», *International Journal*, Vol. XXXVI, No. 2, Spring 1981, p. 311-334.

21. For contrasting views of the embargos' success, see the articles by Znores Medvedev and Steven Larrabee, *New York Times*, February 10, 1981.

22. B. Huddleston, *Closing the Cereals Gap with Trade and Food Aid*, Washington, D.C., IFPRI, 1984.

BIBLIOGRAPHY

CANADA. *Challenge for Growth: an Agri-Food Strategy for Canada,* Ottawa, Agriculture Canada, Agr-6-81DP, 1981.

CANADA. *Commission into the Cost of Moving Grain by Rail,* Report, 2 volumes, Ottawa, Department of Supply and Services, 1976.

CANADA. *Grain Handling and Transportation Commission,* Report, 2 volumes, Ottawa, Department of Supply and Services, 1977.

COCHRANE, Willard W. and RYAN, Mary E. *American Farm Policy – 1948-1973,* Minneapolis, University of Minnesota Press, 1976.

COHN, Theodore. *Canadian Food Aid, Domestic and Foreign Policy Implications,* Denver, University of Denver, Graduate School of International Studies, 1980. «The 1978-1979 negotiations for an international wheat agreement: an opportunity lost?», *International Journal,* Vol. XXXV, No. 1, Winter 1979-1980.

CONNORS, Tom. *The Australian Wheat Industry: Its Economics and Politics.* Armidale, Australia, Gill Publications, 1972.

EATON, David J. and STEELE, W. Scott, eds. *Analyses of Grain Reserves: A Proceedings.* Washington, D.C., US Department of Agriculture, Economic Research Service, and National Science Foundation, 1976.

EHRHARDT, R. *Canadian Development Assistance to Bangladesh,* Ottawa, North-South Institute, 1983.

ENGLISH, P. *Canadian Development Assistance to Haiti,* Ottawa, North-South Institute, 1984.

FISHER, Lewis A. *Canadian Agriculture and the World Food Problem,* Montréal, C.D. Howe Research Institute, 1976.

FRAENKEL, Richard, M. *et al.,* eds. *The Role of US Agriculture in Foreign Policy,* New York, Praeger, 1979.

GERRARD, C. *Promoting Third World Agriculture,* Ottawa, North-South Institute, 1983.

GITTINGER, J. Price. *North American Agriculture in a New World,* Montréal, Canadian-American Committee, 1970.

HATHAWAY, Dale E. «Grain Stocks and Economic Stability», *Analyses of Grain Reserves: A Proceedings.* Edited by David J. Eaton and W. Scott Steele, Washington, D.C., US Department of Agriculture, Economic Research Service and National Science Foundation, 1976.

HEIDHUES, Theodor. *World Food, Interdependence of Farm and Trade Policies,* London, Trade Policy Research Centre, 1977.

HILLMAN, J.S. and SCHMITZ, Andrew, eds. *International Trade and Agriculture: Theory and Policy,* Boulder, Colorado, Westview Press, 1979.

HOPKINS, Raymond F. and PUCHALA, Donald, J. eds. *The Global Political Economy of Food.* Madison, University of Wisconsin Press, 1979. Also appeared as the Summer 1978 issue of *International Organization,* Vol. 32, No. 3.

HUDDLESTON, Barbara and MCLIN, J.B., eds. *Political Investments in Food Production, National and International Case Studies.* Bloomington, Indiana University Press, 1979.

HUDDLESTON, Barbara. *Closing the Cereals Gap with Trade and Food Aid,* Washington, D.C., IFPRI, 1984.

International Journal (Spring 1-81). Food and Fuel Canadian Institute of International Affairs, Toronto, 1981.

INTERNATIONAL FOOD POLICY RESEARCH INSTITUTE. *Food Needs of Developing Countries: Projections of Production and Consumption to 1990.* Research Report 3. Washington, D.C., 1977.

JOHNSON, D. Gale. «The Food and Agriculture Act of 1977: Implications for Farmers, Consumers and Taxpayers», *Contemporary Economic Problems 1978,* Project Director, William Fellner, Washington, D.C., American Enterprise Institute for Public Policy Research, 1978.

JOHNSON, D. Gale. *Forward Prices for Agriculture,* Chicago, Chicago University Press, 1947.

JOHNSON, D. Gale. «Increased Stability of Grain Supplies in Developing Countries: Optimal Carryovers and Insurance», *New International Economic Order: The North-South Debate,* edited by J.N. Bhagwati, Cambridge, Mass., MIT Press, 1977.

JOHNSON, D. Gale. «Limitations of Grain Reserves in the Quest for Stable Prices», *The World Economy,* Vol. 1, No. 3, June 1978.

JOHNSON, D. Gale. The *Soviet Impact on World Grain Trade,* Montréal, British-North American Committee, 1977.

JOSLING, Tim. *Developed Country Agricultural Policies and Developing Country Supplies: The Case of Wheat.* Washington, D.C., International Food Policy Research Institute, 1980.

JUST, Richard E. «Theoretical and Empirical Possibilities for Determining the Distribution of Welfare Gains from Stabilization». *American Journal of Agriculture Economics,* Volume 59, No. 5, December 1977.

KONANDREAS, Panos, HUDDLESTON, Barbara and RAMANGKURA, Virabongsa. *Food Security: An Insurance Approach.* Research Report 4, Washington, D.C., International Food Policy Research Institute, 1978.

MAXWELL, S.J. and SINGER, H.W. «Food Aid to Developing Countries: A survey», *World Development,* Vol. 7, No. 3, 1979.

MCCALLA, Alex F. and SCHMITZ, Andrews. «Grain Marketing Systems: The Case of the United States versus Canada», *American Journal of Agricultural Economics,* Vol. 61, No. 2, May 1979.

MCLIN, J. «Surrogate International Organization and the Case of World Food Security, 1949-1969», *International Organization,* Vol. 33, No. 1, Winter 1979.

MCNERNEY, J.J. *Developments in International Food Policy,* Commonwealth Economic Paper No. 9, London, The Commonwealth Secretariat, 1978.

NORTH-SOUTH INSTITUTE. *Canada North-South 1977-1978,* Vol. 4: *World Food and the Canadian Breadbasket,* Ottawa, 1978.

ORGANIZATION FOR ECONOMIC COOPERATION AND DEVELOPMENT. *Agricultural Policy in Canada,* Paris, OECD, 1973. *Agricultural Policy in the US Paris, OECD, 1974. Recent Developments in Canadian Agricultural Policy,* Paris, OECD, 1978. *Recent Developments in United States Agricultural Policies,* Paris, OECD, 1976. *Review of Agricultural Policies in OECD Member Countries,* 1978, Paris, OECD, 1979.

PRESIDENTIAL COMMISSION ON WORLD HUNGER. *Overcoming World Hunger: The Challenge Ahead,* Report of the Presidential Commission on World Hunger, Sol. M. Linowitz, Chairman, Washington, D.C., US Government Printing Office, 1980.

REUTLINGER, Shlomo. *Simulation of World-Wide Buffer Stocks of Wheat,* World Bank Staff, Working Paper No. 219, Washington, D.C., International Bank for Reconstruction and Development, 1975.

REUTLINGER, Shlomo and KNAPP, Keith. *Food Security in Food Deficit Countries,* World Bank Staff, *Working Paper* No. 393, Washington, D.C., International Bank for Reconstruction and Development, 1975.

ROYAL SOCIETY OF CANADA. Agricultural Institute of Canada. *Proceedings, Symposium on Canada and World Food,* Ottawa, n.p., 1977.

SCHULTZ, T.W., ed. *Distortions of Agricultural Incentives,* Bloomington, Indiana University Press, 1978.

STEVENS, Christopher. *Food Aid and the Developing World, Four African Case Studies,* London, Croom Helm, in association with the Overseas Development Institute, 1979.

UNITED NATIONS. Food and Agriculture Organization. *Agriculture: Toward 2000,* (c. 79/24), Rome, RAO, 1979. FAO *Production Yearbook.* FAO, annual. *FAO Trade Yearbook,* Rome, FAO, annual. *Food Reserve Policies for World Food Security: A Consultant Study on Alternative Approaches,* ESC: CSP/75/2, Rome, FAO, 1975. *The Stabilization of International Trade in Grains,* Commodity Policy Studies, No. 20, Rome, FAO, 1970.

UNITED STATES. *The Global 2000 Report to the President,* Washington, D.C., US Government Printing Office, 1980.

VALDES, Alberto and HUDDLESTON, Barbara. *Potential of Agriculture Exports to Finance Increased Food Imports in Selected Developing Countries,* Occasional Paper, 2, Washington, D.C., International Food Policy Research Institute, 1977.

VALDES, Alberto, ed. *Food Security for Developing Countries,* Boulder, Colorado, Westview Press, 1981.

WARLEY, T.K. *Agriculture in an Interdependent World: US and Canadian Perspectives,* Montréal, Canadian-American Committee, 1977.

WASSERMAN, Ursula. «International Grains Arrangement 1967», *Journal of World Trade Law,* Vol. 2, No. 2, March-April 1968.

WASSERMAN, Ursula. «International Grains Arrangement 1967», *Journal of World Trade Law,* Vol. 5, No. 3, May-June 1971.

WILSON, C.F. *A Century of Canadian Grain, Government Policy to 1951,* Saskatoon, Western Producer Prairie Books, 1978.

WORLD BANK. *World Development Report,* annual, Washington, D.C.

WORLD FOOD COUNCIL. *Current World Food Situation,* Note by the Executive Director (WFC 1985, Rome, 1985. *Current World Food Situation,* Note by the Executive Director (WFC/1979), Rome, 1979. World Food Security for *the 1980s,* Report by the Executive Director (WFC/1979/5), Rome, 1979.

YOUNG, R. *Canadian Development Assistance to Tanzania,* Ottawa, North-South Institute, 1983.

28

Canada and the Non-Proliferation of Nuclear Weapons: The History of a Dilemma

Michael Tucker
Mount Allison University

Canada's approaches to the problem of the «horizontal» proliferation of nuclear weapons (an increase in the number of states possessing a military nuclear capability) have over the past four decades been shaped by three factors: first, and foremost, Canada's role on the economic front as a supplier of nuclear fuel, equipment and technology for peaceful (and, down to 1965, military) purposes; second, Canada's lengthy involvement at the diplomatic front with multilateral efforts towards the establishment of an international non-proliferation and safeguards regime; and third, in the defence policy realm, Canada's situation as a member of two alliances, NATO and NORAD which, from the time of their respective establishment in 1949 and 1958, have always relied primarily upon the nuclear defence and deterrent capabilities of the United States. Throughout the post-1945 period these factors, either alone or in any particular combination, have posed sufficient problems for Canada's commitment to non-proliferation to make that foreign policy priority a dilemma. Canada's involvement with the military atom during World War II foreshadowed the essences of that dilemma.

THE MANHATTAN CONNECTION

The story of this early involvement with the atom has been ably told elsewhere[1]. There is, thus, no need to recount here Canada's wartime partnership, such as it was, with the United States and Great Britain in the Manhattan Project and the subsequent development of the atomic bomb. Rather, it is more useful for purposes of this brief study to attempt only to extrapolate from the historical record the military, economic and diplomatic themes which seem to emerge from this period and which appear to have cast their shadows over Canada's quest for a stable international non-proliferation regime.

On the military side, it is well to remember that the development of the atomic bomb during World War II was largely an American undertaking. The Canadian role was probably never crucial to the American programme, but it was certainly useful. Canada's foremost contribution was as a source of uranium, possessing the largest known deposits in the world outside the Belgian Congo at the Eldorado Gold

Mines in the Great Bear Lake area. Canada also served as a sanctuary for Anglo-American scientific collaboration on atomic research; initiated during 1941 in the United Kingdom, this research was transferred in 1942 to the Montréal laboratory of the National Research Council and, later, to Chalk River. Third was Canada's technological contribution itself, which included work on a chemical separation process whereby weapons-grade plutonium could be extracted from uranium irradiated in a reactor. Fourth, and not least, was Canada's willingness in the person of the indomitable Minister of Munitions and Supply, C.D. Howe, to collaborate with the United States and Britain on the Combined Policy Committee established at the 1943 Québec Conference with the object of producing «as quickly as possible» an atomic bomb for use during the war[2].

There is no evidence of any qualms harboured by those few in Ottawa who knew of this dimension of Canada's war effort – the first but not the last of Canada's contributions towards the proliferation of nuclear weapons. Nor of course could or should there have been any such qualms, given the prevailing fear in the capitals of the «ABC» powers that the unlocking of the atomic secret might first be achieved by Nazi Germany. Yet nor is there any evidence of Canadian expressions of doubt about the desirability of a continuation after 1945 of the wartime military atomic collaboration between the three Anglo-Saxon powers. In Ottawa, this was seen as both natural and necessary. It was natural in the sense that, failing the attempted establishment of international controls over atomic energy by 1948, Canada's great Anglo-Saxon allies should continue to share their atomic secrets; it was necessary because of the onset of the Cold War, and the related and very real fear that the Soviet Union would soon detonate its own atomic device. Thus it was that the British, while keenly interested in plutonium research after the war, did not make their decision to «go nuclear» until 1948, but Canadians were not troubled by this proliferation move. Collaboration was also seen as necessary because of the prohibition imposed on the sharing of atomic information between the ABC powers by the United States MacMahon Act of 1946 – the second unilateral measure in the annals of non-proliferation, following upon the Canadian decision of December 1945 not to go nuclear. At stake, as a consequence of this Act, was Anglo-American amity, a historic principle and pillar of Canadian foreign policy.

Atomic relations between the United Kingdom and the United States had been difficult at times during the war years, despite the 1943 Tripartite Québec Agreement. They were all the more so after the United States breached this agreement in 1946. Canada was present in the middle, as it were, at the first signs of strain in the transatlantic partnership caused by non-proliferation politics, and this was not to be the last time that Canadians were to find themselves so embroiled. In early 1949, after Britain's announced its intention to build an atomic bomb, Ottawa pressed for a strengthened Anglo-Canadian collaboration in the atomic energy field, particularly in relationship to defence cooperation arrangements. This was seen in Ottawa as a bargaining chip to elicit from Washington a greater exchange of information on atomic research and development. To this end, for the sake of Anglo-American harmony and, it could well be added, for the sake of Canada's own atomic energy programme, the principle of non-proliferation was secondary. There is, thus, some truth to the otherwise harsh judgement that Canada in the early postwar period was more concerned with ways and means to promote rather than control atomic energy[3]; the Canadian situation at this time, as it related to the powerful Canadian interest in the development of an indigenous and sophisticated atomic energy programme, was not unlike that of certain industrialized and developing «near nuclear» states of the contemporary era with whose atomic aspirations Canada has not been entirely unsympathetic. To this point we return below.

While scientists and nationalists shared visions of Canada's future role in the development of the peaceful atom, some in Ottawa, particularly the few senior members of the Department of External Affairs who were aware of Canada's wartime «complicity» in the making of the bomb, were indeed concerned about the problem of nuclear proliferation[4]. This, as they saw it, was one of «uncontrolled» proliferation beyond the North Atlantic triangle, and which would ensue not from a diversion of technology and material from peaceful to military uses, but from the dissemination of knowledge about the atomic secret itself. And while those in the policy community responsible for Canada's atomic programme exhibited a preference for sovereign control over Canadian nuclear research and production facilities, the DEA looked forward to the establishment of international control as the only possible means of averting wide-scale proliferation and as a means of strengthening the pestige and authority of the newly-established United Nations security system. Here they presumed that Canada's apparent near great-power status in the postwar atomic energy field would confer diplomatic leverage of a functional kind. Alas these officials were, for the most part, wrong in this presumption; Canada's leverage in the domain of international non-proliferation diplomacy has never been that strong, despite its significant role as a supplier of uranium and nuclear technology.

Canada, it is true, was propelled into the forefront of middle powers in the postwar negotiations for control over atomic energy. Because of its involvement in the Manhattan Project, Canada earned a seat at great-power diplomatic tables, first at the Washington Conference of November 1945, and then in January 1946, at the United Nations Atomic Energy Commission. The heads of governments of the ABC powers, President Truman, Prime Ministers Attlee and Mackenzie King began the Washington Conference on November 11, 1945, aboard the US naval vessel the *Sequoia* as it set sail, in Lester B. Pearson's words, «in damp and misty weather [...] down the Potomac about noon»[5]. The weather notwithstanding, the Conference achieved its aim, a draft declaration on atomic energy – the first comprehensive multilateral statement of the problems of and the prospects for, the non-proliferation of nuclear weapons. This statement enshrined the basic principle of the non-proliferation regime as it exists today, that for both economic and arms control reasons, the benefits of the peaceful atom should be universally shared under safeguards. That is to say, the three atomic powers would be prepared to share their secret for peaceful purposes if recipient states would in turn forswear the military nuclear option. Canadian officials, by their own admission, had done very little by way of preparation for the Washington talks; nor had they been encouraged to do so. Yet the Canadian role was not negligible. It was Mackenzie King who suggested the incorporation of the above non-proliferation principle into the American draft declaration. At the end of the sentence «We are not convinced that the spreading of the specialized information regarding the practical application of atomic energy, before it is possible to devise safeguards [...] would contribute to a constructive solution of the problem of the atomic bomb», King proposed the inclusion of the following:

> On the contrary, we think it might have the opposite effect. We are, however, prepared to share on a reciprocal basis with other United Nations detailed information concerning the practical industrial application of atomic energy just as soon as effective and forcible safeguards against its use for destructive purposes can be devised[6].

The Tripartite Agreed Declaration on Atomic Energy thus looked forward to the establishment of a United Nations commission, composed of the five permanent members of the UN Security Council and Canada. The commissions's task was to make specific proposals: a) for the exchange of basic scientific information for peaceful purposes; b) for the control of atomic energy to the extent necessary to ensure its use only for peaceful purposes; c) for the elimination of atomic weapons from all national armaments; and d) for the establishment of effective safeguards by means of inspection to guard against evasion. The Soviet Union accepted these non-proliferation principles and the UN Atomic Energy Commission began its work in January 1946.

The key clause was the latter, the quest for effective safeguards. To this end, the United States had initially proposed the establishment of an International Atomic Development Authority, which would have the power of ownership, management, research, licensing and inspection of all matters nuclear within signatory states. To this, the Chief American delegate to the UN AEC, Bernard Baruch, added two provisions of his own: the imposition of sanctions or «condign punishment» for violators, who would be deprived of recourse to Security Council veto power over the implementation of that punishment; and that a control system should be established in stages, only upon the completion of which would the United States submit to its jurisdiction[7].

Despite these provisions in the «Baruch Plan» for international control over atomic energy, it is unlikely that the Soviet Union would have submitted to the pervasive jurisdiction of the IADA in the face of a continued American monopoly of the atomic bomb. Yet, Baruch insisted that his proposal, submitted to the UN General Assembly in the form of a resolution on December 5, 1946, be voted upon by December 20. «This peremptory demand», wrote the New Republic, «raised a storm – small, but significant nonetheless as a clue to latent unrest and uneasiness. The opposition was led by the Canadian delegate, General McNaughton, a military man of some independence who had a distaste for submitting to pressure from any source»[8]. As McNaughton was later to put it, the Baruch Plan was «insincerity from beginning to end»[9].

It is now a matter of history that the Soviet Union did not support this scheme and that, as a consequence, the first international attempt at controlling the spread of nuclear weapons was stillborn. Ottawa feared the potential diplomatic consequences of McNaughton's flair for independence and sent word to New York that Canada was to go no further than the United States on the inspection issue; the General was at liberty only to attempt to change Baruch's stand on the veto question. Failing that, and in the final analysis, Canada was to vote with the United States[10]. This diplomatic posture must be understood in the political context of the Cold War, as it overshadowed any meaningful international effort at controlling the atom. Yet, it was hardly an auspicious beginning for Canada's multilateral non-proliferation diplomacy; the words uttered in September 1945 by the Canadian diplomat-diarist C.S.A. Ritchie were quickly to ring true. «If Canada were a great power», he wrote in a memorandum entitled Control of the Atomic Bomb by the United Nations Organization, «its monopoly [sic] of the indispensable component of the atomic bomb might put this country in a position to determine decisions as to the future use and control of the bomb; but as Canada is not a great power, her possession of uranium is perhaps more likely to expose her to embarrassments and difficulties[11].»

The most enduring legacy of Canada's wartime atomic partnership was not to be in the fields of military defence or diplomacy, troublesome as they were, but in the realm of peaceful nuclear transfers. Canadian scientific work at Chalk River with the design and operation of nuclear reactors, led to the construction of the Zero Energy Experimental Pile (ZEEP). On going critical in September 1945, ZEEP became the first operational reactor outside the United States. This prodigious feat of Canadian technology was soon to be matched by Canadian work on a unique NRX heavy-water moderated research reactor which went critical on July 22, 1947. The Canadian peaceful nuclear industry was born on that date; it came of age in 1962, when a demonstration reactor at Rolphton, Ontario, generated electric power for Ontario Hydro.

During the early postwar years, there were two aspects of the Canadian experience with the peaceful atom which were later to prove to be of considerable significance to Canada's non-proliferation policies and diplomacy. The first was a powerful governmental (as well as private) commitment to Canada's nuclear industry. In attitudinal terms, this, as intimated above, found expression in the efforts of political leaders like C.D. Howe to bring all facets of this industry under sole Canadian control; in organizational terms, this found expression in the establishment of the Atomic Energy Control Board (AECB) in 1946, mandated to sustain indigenous reactor research, and the establishment in 1952 of Atomic Energy Canada Limited (AECL) whose mandate similarly was to encourage the indigenous use of nuclear power in order to reduce Canada's dependence on external sources of energy. As C.E.S. Franks has noted, Canada thereby developed a «powerful internal group supporting the faith and dedicated to development» in atomic energy; the «insulation of these activities from normal political control processes contributed to the perpetuation of the powerful fervour raised by atomic energy. Atomic energy partook of the qualities of a vision, and to believers retains these qualities to this day»[12.]

In its early years, this nationalistic commitment to nuclear energy was heightened by the passage of the American McMahon Act of 1946 and by Canada's first unilateral contribution towards the non-proliferation of nuclear weapons: the decision of December 1945, to focus on the peaceful rather than the military uses of atomic energy. As C.D. Howe described this decision to the House of Commons: «We have not manufactured atomic bombs, we have no intention of manufacturing atomic bombs[13].» While this decision effectively had the status of policy, it was not the product of a conscious or conscientious agonizing based upon strategic or arms control grounds; it simply reflected a mainstream understanding in Ottawa that with the American nuclear «guarantee», Canada had no real need to go nuclear for military security reasons. It has been said that this perception and this reality delimited Canada's ability to fully understand the incentives which less secure countries have held (and continue to hold) for keeping a nuclear option open.

The second aspect of Canada's involvement with the peaceful atom, clearly related to the commitment of successive Canadian governments to an indigenous nuclear industry, was the development of the export incentive. Foreign sales of Canadian uranium, equipment and technology were (and are) needed to achieve the economies of scale to sustain the domestic bureaucratic and technological infrastructure developed during and after World War II; these sales were (and are) also needed to «assure the legitimacy and acceptance of Canada's unique reactor design in the domestic market»[14]. By the early 1950s, this economic motive dovetailed rather fortuitously with international developmental *cum* arms control thinking that, despite the absence of any effective international safeguards regime, potential supplier states should export to countries wanting nuclear power for developmental reasons partly in order to offset the development of indigenous military nuclear capabilities – and, with any luck, the incentive thereto. These interests and assumptions were all inherent in Canada's first (outside the orbit of the North Atlantic triangle) and most troublesome foray into the highly competitive international nuclear marketplace.

Under the Commonwealth Colombo Plan, Canada in 1956 agreed to provide India with a research reactor – the CIR (Canada-India Research Reactor). This arrangement was not subject to stringent safeguards but governed only by an Indian pledge that the CIR would be used for «peaceful purposes». As became all too clear by 1974, when India detonated a nuclear device using plutonium derived from the CIR, Canada would have been well advised in 1956 to have reached an explicit understanding with Indian authorities as to what was meant by this phrase. Canada did require the right to inspect the spent fuel rods but this right lapsed in 1960 when India supplied its own fuel. From a non-proliferation standpoint, however, the shortcomings of the CIR deal were not all that apparent at the time because of the prevail-ing political climate in the Canadian-Indian relationship and because of Western attitudes in general towards peaceful nuclear «aid» programmes[15].

Canada's nuclear relationship with India during the mid-1950s was in step with a growing flexibility in American and British attitudes towards safeguards on the export of nuclear equipment. President Eisenhower's famous 1953 «Atoms for Peace» proposal was quickly followed by a relaxation of the provisions of the McMahon Act; the 1955 UN Conference on the Peaceful Uses of Atomic Energy declassified and released for public consumption considerable data on reactor technology, and the following year Canada, the United States and the United Kingdom jointly declassified information on all phases of a nuclear fuel cycle, including the design and operation of chemical separation or reprocessing plants.

This trend towards liberalism in the nuclear aid programmes of Western suppliers was accurately reflected in the Canadian-Indian relationship. The personal inclinations of Canadian political leaders and Atomic Energy officials to develop closer relations with their Indian counterparts marked the beginning of Canada's nuclear commitment to India which lasted down to and even beyond 1974.

In the 1950s, Canada's expressed sympathy with the developmental aspirations of member states of the Commonwealth, many just emerging from colonial status, was reflected in the Colombo Plan and in «Swami» Pearson's close links with one of the Commonwealth's most articulate Third World leaders – Pandit Nehru of India. India's need for development assistance and the pacifist strain in Nehru's policy of positive neutralism were not alien to the internationalist tradition in Canadian foreign policy during the St. Laurent-Pearson era. This tradition helped to underwrite the CIR deal; so too did the perspectives of the then senior vice-president of AECL, W. Bennett Lewis. Lewis had developed a close working relationship with the Chairman of the Indian Atomic Commission, Dr. Homi Bhabba, and feared that India would develop a nuclear explosion capability if its development needs were shunned by the world community. Lewis was correct in his fear about the development of that capability, but wrong in his assumption that it could be offset by a Canadian (and international) willingness to supply India with nuclear aid. This misperception was widely shared at that time, however.

Eisenhower's Atoms for Peace proposal led to the establishment in 1957 of the Vienna International Atomic Energy Agency and, thereby, to the internationalization of safeguards. Ottawa saw in this agency a useful mechanism to encourage the worldwide peaceful uses of atomic energy, and thus actively participated in the drafting of the IAEA statute during 1955-1956 and in the peparatory commission appointed to arrange for the first session of the agency's general conference in 1957. In tandem with these diplomatic efforts and as Canada's reactor technology developed, Ottawa entered into agreements with West Germany, Switzerland, Japan and Sweden for the transfer of Canadian technology and for the export of Canadian uranium. As with the Indian experience, these sales were covered by «peaceful uses» clauses in addition to bilateral and/or IAEA verification measures. It is to be noted that in 1959, Canada consummated its first power-generating reactor sale with Pakistan – an arrangement that was to prove almost as troublesome as the Indian deal.

From the standpoint of effective Canadian control over these exports, the process by which the decisions were made can best be described as «untidy»[16]. The domestic actors included Eldorado Nuclear, AECL, AECB, and the Economics Division of the DEA. It was not until 1968 that one body, the AECL, was given a control over Canadian nuclear exports. Yet, outside the United Nations Division of the DEA, few in Canada were troubled about this untidy process – or the potential conflict between Canada's commitment to the principle of non-proliferation under the IAEA system and the commitment to the export of nuclear fuel and equipment. In 1959, officials in the UN Division of the DEA who had responsibility for Canadian disarmament policy harboured some doubts about the effectiveness of the safeguards over the CIR and over Canadian uranium exports, and they looked forward to the establishment of a distinct science and disarmament section in their division with the apparent aim of wresting authority over Canada's nuclear transfers away from the Economics Division. The idea for such a section led to the establishment of a separate Disarmament Division within the DEA in 1961; yet, this Division was not given authority over Canada's non-proliferation and safeguards policies, in large measure because of strong opposition from the Economics Division and from the AECL and AECB[17]. This gap in the mandate of the Disarmament Division had somewhat less than salutary implications for Canada's non-proliferation diplomacy during the 1960s.

NON-PROLIFERATION AND CANADIAN DEFENCE POLICY, 1957-1963

At its Heads of Government meetings in December 1957, NATO re-affirmed the ministerial decisions of 1954 and 1955 to equip alliance forces with tactical nuclear weapons. Under the military plan MC-70 of December 1957, alliance members agreed to the deployment in NATO Europe of nuclear-armed air strike forces, nuclear missiles and artillery for the direct support of NATO land forces, nuclear missiles for air defence, and nuclear depth charges for ASW operations under SACLANT. In addition, nuclear weapons were to be stockpiled in Europe for use under the «two keys» system with the United States and IRBMs were to be deployed for use by SACEUR. The stated rationale for MC-70 was the need to offset the numerical superiority of the Warsaw Pact conventional forces; the unstated rationale was to strengthen the commitment of the United States to NATO Europe by «coupling» the US strategic deterrent to American-controlled tactical nuclear systems positioned in Western Europe. This commitment had been called into question by some of the European allies because of the development of Soviet long-range nuclear missiles which could by 1957 strike at the American homeland.

Canada subscribed to NATO's decision of December 1957 and, along with its European allies, initiated discussions with the United States whereby their assigned NATO forces would assume nuclear roles. In 1959, an agreement was reached under which the CF-104 Canadian air squadron in Europe would assume a nuclear strike-reconnaissance role and Honest John nuclear rocket batteries would be used in a support role by the Canadian infantry brigade. These agreements coincided with the most heated Canadian defence policy debate of the post-1945 era, touched off by the arrival of Howard Green to the External Affairs portfolio in 1959[18]. For a mix of reasons which are beyond our purview here, Green fastened onto nuclear disarmament as his primary foreign policy goal and saw the adoption of a nuclear role by Canada as a fetter upon his quest for disarmament through the United Nations[19]. As a consequence of the Minister's vehement if principled opposition to nuclear arms, Canada did not fulfill its nuclear commitments to NATO until 1963, when the Diefenbaker Government and Green were defeated at the polls partly as a consequence of their «indecision» over the direction of Canadian defence policy.

In 1958, the Diefenbaker Government agreed to initiate service-to-service discussions with the United States for the emplacement of American nuclear weapons on Canadian soil under NORAD. In 1959, pressure mounted in Ottawa for the need of a response by the Government on this matter, a pressure heightened by the Government's decision to adopt the Voodoo interceptor and the Bomarc surface to air missile for its NORAD forces, both of which were designed to carry nuclear weapons. It was in fact Canada's nuclear commitments under NORAD rather than NATO to which Green objected most strongly, because the former cut more clearly across his image of Canada as a non-nuclear power independent of the United States in both the foreign and defence policy decision-making fields. Indeed, the former Minister claimed in retirement that he did not oppose a Canadian nuclear role in Europe, being no more prepared than most Canadians to seriously question the military-strategic logic of Canada's tactical nuclear commitments in that theatre – much less question NATO's military force plan, MC-70.

One question which might otherwise have arisen in Canadian thinking about this plan, whether or not a «limited» nuclear war could (or should) be fought in the European theatre without escalation to the strategic level, was deflected by the mainstream Canadian assumption that in battlefield terms there was little distinction between tactical nuclear and conventional weapons systems. In NATO, Canada did not question the increasing reliance on nuclear weapons by the alliance until the establishment of the Nuclear Planning Group (NPG) in 1967; domestically, serious questions of a military-strategic kind about Canada's nuclear roles in Europe – or in North America for that matter – were never raised. This is not to say, however, that questions about these roles did not arise. They did, and with some vigor and political effect, but along the line of whether or not Canada was, through its alliance relationships, aiding and abetting the proliferation of nuclear weapons.

The Diefenbaker Government justified its failure to fulfill Canada's nuclear commitments to NATO and NORAD as a non-proliferation measure. The Prime Minister's comment to the House of Commons in early 1963 had in essence been reiterated on a number of previous occasions. «We shall not, so long as we are pursuing the ways of disarmament, Diefenbaker declared, allow the extension of the nuclear family into Canada [...] We do not intend to allow the spread of nuclear weapons beyond the nations which now have them[20].» Both the NDP and, down to late 1962, the Liberals concurred with this position. As Lester B. Pearson put it, when Leader of the Opposition: «There should be no extension of the nuclear club[21].»

The issue of the relationship between Canada's nuclear defence policy dilemmas and its commitment to the principle of non-proliferation did not come to the fore until late 1960. That November, Ireland placed on the agenda of the UN General Assembly a resolution calling upon nuclear-weapon states to refrain, as a temporary and voluntary measure, from «relinquishing control» over nuclear weapons to states not possessing them; this Irish Resolution, as it came to be known, also called upon non-nuclear weapon states to refrain, on a similar temporary basis, from manufacturing nuclear-weapons and «from otherwise attempting to acquire them». Because of the ambiguity of the phrase «control over nuclear weapons», the issue as to whether NATO's planned nuclear sharing arrangements were consistent with the Irish Resolution became a matter for much debate, in Paris and in Ottawa. Did proliferation mean only «exclusive» or «independent» control over nuclear weapons, or could it be interpreted more broadly so as to include nuclear sharing between a nuclear and (ostensibly) non-nuclear power under which the nuclear weapon power retained ultimate control over the nuclear weapons in question while the non-nuclear power had some degree of control over their possible use in war? A majority of the NATO allies abstained on the Irish Resolution, while Canada temporized in its support for it. Behind these abstentions and Canadian temporizing lay a recognition, if implicit, that nuclear sharing within an alliance constituted a form of proliferation.

It is unlikely that Canada would have differed with its European allies and the United States over this resolution, had Howard Green not been Minister for External Affairs, and had Canada not found support from Norway and Denmark, its close arms control allies within NATO. The Minister had the support of disarmament officials in the UN Division of the DEA and his recently-appointed Adviser and Chief Negotiator for Disarmament, General E.L.M. Burns. Indeed, it was these officials who impressed upon Green their view that a Canadian acceptance of a nuclear weapon role would be inconsistent with the Irish Resolution. Ironically, it was because they also held to this view that defence officials in Ottawa argued against Canada's supporting the resolution; to do so would be to prejudge the outcome of Canada's nuclear sharing negotiations with the United States under NORAD and in NATO. These officials won from Green a public commitment that a continued Canadian support for the principle of non-proliferation as embodied in the Irish Resolution would be conditional upon progress in the broader field of disarmament. Thus, the Minister conceded that, although Canada had refrained from «acquiring» nuclear weapons, his Government would «reserve its right to adopt such measures for the preservation of Canada's security as might be considered necessary [...]»[22].

With the fulfillment in 1963 of Canada's nuclear commitments, by the Pearson Government, it appeared as though Canada's security requirements had finally supplanted its non-proliferation sensibilities. Yet, officially, Ottawa decreed that Canada's acceptance of a nuclear capability did not constitute proliferation because Canada had not acquired an «independent» control over the nuclear weapons available to it under the two-keys arrangement with the United States. As the

Minister of National Defence, Paul Hellyer, attempted to explain to sceptical parliamentarians, «acceptance by Canada of the strike role for the air division and the acquisition of the Honest John rocket for our brigade in Europe has committed us to signing a bilateral agreement whith the United States to permit the immediate availability of nuclear devices. This does not make us a member of the "Nuclear Club". It only fulfills the general undertaking given by us and other member countries at the Heads of Government meeting in December 1957, and the specific undertaking of Canada in 1959 to accept the strike role [...] I know some honourable members are concerned about the moral aspects of these assignments. It is a matter of concern to all of us. As a member of NATO, we have agreed to a strategy of deterrence. As long as we remain a member of the alliance we cannot separate ourselves, morally, from the general policy»[23].

Before the ink was dry on Canada's nuclear commitments, however, the Pearson Government promised the Canadian people that it would attempt to separate this country, morally and otherwise, from «the general policy». For Pearson, the reaons for this promise were perhaps both moral and personal; Green never forgave Pearson for this *volte-face* or «betrayal» of late 1962, and when in 1963 Pearson implemented his decision to accept Canada's nuclear commitments, he incurred the stinging criticism of the Prime Minister to be, Pierre E. Trudeau[24]. Independent control or not, Trudeau argued, Canada had contributed to the proliferation of nuclear weapons. Yet if Canadians, public and official, thought this way, so might others outside Canada. If unfounded in diplomatic reality, the belief that Canada's influence as an advocate of non-proliferation had been reduced as a consequence of the 1963 decision was in some measure responsible for the subsequent re-thinking and ultimate reversal of that decision. As Burns noted in his diary before the 1963 decision, Canada «will be discredited as an earnest advocate of disarmament if it takes nuclear arms and uses weasel arguments to justify them»[25].

CANADA AND THE MULTILATERAL NUCLEAR FORCE

The emplacement of nuclear weapons on Canadian soil and the adoption of a nuclear role for Canada's forces in Europe were not the only defence policy issues to cut across Canada's non-proliferation agenda of the early mid-1960s. A third issue was the ill-fated MLF proposal.

The idea of a Multilateral Nuclear Force (MLF) originated in the late 1950s among European hands in the US State Department. The plan was devised with a view towards offsetting West European, and particularly West German, fears that the United States would not risk the destruction of its homeland by coming to the aid of its European allies in the event of a Soviet continental aggression. By giving NATO European members a greater say in alliance nuclear decision-making, the MLF, a force of mix-manned surface vessels capable of firing 100 Polaris nuclear-tipped IRBMs, was to have cemented the American nuclear guarantee to Europe.

When the idea was first mooted in alliance circles, Canadian officials were almost unanimously opposed to the scheme. Some doubted the political wisdom of a Canadian involvement in yet another field of alliance nuclear endeavour; some feared that the MLF might reduce SACEUR's control over the NATO nuclear deterrent in a moment of crisis, while others feared the possible absence of effective political control over a new and powerful weapons system. Arms control officials in Ottawa, and General Burns in particular, unequivocally opposed the idea of MLF because of what they saw as its proliferation undertones. Accordingly, Burns argued that Canada should actively discourage alliance adoption of the scheme. Only a few within Ottawa's officialdom saw possible arms control merits to the scheme, that it could offset any tendency towards greater West European collaboration in the military nuclear field and that it might, as a substitute for land-based nuclear delivery systems, lead to the establishment of a nuclear free zone in Central Europe. Ironically, it was this view which prevailed as the basis of official Canadian policy on the MLF issue down to 1963 – that it was in the Canadian interest to support NATO discussions over the scheme as an alternative to the proliferation of national nuclear forces[26].

When the Pearson Government entered office in 1963, it was approached, as Burns records, «by the American MLF-promotion team to persuade us to join the project, but had wisely decided to stand aside». When Pearson visited Kennedy shortly after the election, the Prime Minister explained Canada's decision not to participate in the MLF but agreed to Kennedy's request that Canada not «take a position opposing it, in NATO or publicly[27]». It was perhaps a commentary on a lack of effective orchestration between politicians and civil servants over the making of Canadian arms control policy that General Burns found out about this commitment through the Under Secretary of State for External Affairs, Norman Robertson, that November – some three months after the Pearson-Kennedy meetings. This, however, was the least of Burns' embarrassments over the MLF affair. In NATO, Canadian officials remained silent when the issue was discussed; when it was debated at the Geneva Eighteen-Nation Disarmament Conference (ENDC) in the context of discussions over a non-proliferation treaty, General Burns was compelled by his own sense of diplomatic responsibility to defend the MLF.

The Soviet Union, fearing a West German finger on the MLF nuclear trigger, opposed the plan on the grounds that it constituted a form of nuclear proliferation. Down to the mid-1960s, when the United States tacitly dropped the scheme, Soviet opposition to the MLF was the main stumbling block to progress on a non-proliferation treaty. Effectively, Soviet draft treaties for an NPT precluded any form of alliance nuclear sharing. Burns, in his private thoughts, was not unsympathetic with Russian fears over the MLF; publicly, however, he could not endorse Soviet proposals which undermined alliance as well as Canadian defence policy sharing arrangements. These, he advised the ENDC, did not constitute proliferation:

> The Soviet Union and its allies are strongly opposed to certain multinational arrangements which have been made, or are presently contemplated, providing for the participation of several members of the NATO defensive alliance in the creation of a joint nuclear deterrent. The Soviet Union and its allies have been arguing that such arrangements would be contrary to the principle of non-dissemination. As far as the Canadian Government is concerned, arrangements which are at present in effect for the control of nuclear weapons within the Western alliance and arrangements which are at present under discussion are consistent with the terms of the Irish Resolution[28].

As noted above, the MLF was devised with a view towards offsetting West European and especially West German concerns about the steadfastness of the American nuclear guarantee to NATO Europe. When the United States quietly dropped the plan during 1966, and as the United States and the Soviet Union moved towards a mutual understanding that they shared a strong interest in the non-proliferation of nuclear weapons, the security fears of NATO Europe were only heightened. The West European allies, and again the Germans in particular, feared that the United States would ignore their security interests in its efforts at reaching accommodation with the Soviet Union over an NPT – a fear sharpened by early 1967 when the United States violated normal NATO consultative procedures and informed alliance members *ex post facto* that it had reached agreement with the Soviet Union on a number of important provisions for the NPT. This intra-alliance contretemps over how, or whether, the security of NATO Europe could be provided for under a super-power-sanctioned non-proliferation regime provided a very real dilemma for Canada's non-proliferation diplomacy. The essence of this dilemma was that Canada in NATO was neither a North American nor a European country, but both. As a consequence, Canada was at once sympathetic towards and impatient with West European security concerns[29].

Down to 1967, when the main stumbling block to an NPT had been Soviet opposition to proposed alliance nuclear sharing arrangements, Canadian spokesmen tended to express strong sympathy with the West European and particularly the West German desire to have a more meaningful say in the direction of alliance nuclear strategy. Yet arms controllers in Ottawa and General Burns in particular were always somewhat circumspect about the depth of that desire, especially in view of the West German insistence upon a hardware MLF-type solution to the nuclear sharing problem. This circumspection was heightened in 1966, when it appeared that the FRG would not accept the idea of a nuclear planning group committee as an alternative to the MLF. As a consequence, Canada's sympathy with the European perspective diminished; this trend, when coupled with a fear that, partly because of West European opposition, there might well be no non-proliferation treaty at all, led Canada by 1967 to fully support the United States in its efforts to reach agreement over an NPT with the Soviet Union. While Ottawa was aware of the paradox that any effective non-proliferation treaty would require the signatures of the West European powers, it moved in the direction it did for arms control's sake and, as far as can be gathered, largely upon the advice of General Burns.

CANADA AND THE ORIGINS OF THE NON-PROLIFERATION TREATY SAFEGUARDS REGIME

The disagreements which had been expressed during the mid-1960s in NATO and in the Geneva ENDC over a non-proliferation treaty seemed to suggest that the ability or the willingness of non-nuclear states to avail themselves of the nuclear-weapons option was the crux of the matter. In fact, this was by no means entirely the case. It is true that the essential arms control component of the Non-Proliferation Treaty which was agreed upon by the United States and the Soviet Union on July 1, 1968, lies with a commitment by signatory non-nuclear states not to acquire national control or possession of nuclear weapons; by the same token, signatory nuclear-weapon states agreed not to transfer nuclear weapons to non-nuclear powers, or otherwise assist those powers develop a nuclear weapon capability. Yet the basic bargain of the NPT was and remains a willingness on the part of nuclear-weapon and other signatory states with advanced civilian nuclear capabilities to supply the benefits of the Peaceful Atom under safeguards in return for a commitment by recipient states not to develop a military nuclear capability. In the Geneva negotiations which led up to the NPT, and in the NATO discussions over the treaty during 1967, the question of safeguards was very much at the heart of the debate.

Article III of the NPT provides that each non-nuclear weapon state party to the treaty must undertake to accept «safeguards» negotiated with the Vienna Agency «for the exclusive purposes of verification of the fulfillment of its obligations assumed under this Treaty with a view to preventing diversion of nuclear energy from peaceful uses to nuclear weapons or other nuclear explosive devices». It is unlikely that the aligned and nonaligned non-nuclear states that objected to the NPT/IAEA safeguards provisions did so because these provisions prevented these states from going nuclear. These provisions did not and do not prevent such activity; the inspection clause was designed only to deter states from going nuclear by providing for the «timely detection» of a diversion of nuclear material from peaceful to military uses. At best, the NPT safeguards were to provide a symbolic reminder to states of their treaty obligations, as no sanctions against violators were provided for in the NPT regime. As arms control, Article III did little more than set a legal seal on state practice; prior to 1968, the only known nuclear transfers which did not carry safeguards provisions were the French sale of the Dimona research reactor to Israel and the Canadian-Indian CIR arrangement.

In fact, the thrust of the objections of a number of non-nuclear states to the safeguards article lay with a fear that for reasons of red tape and costs, IAEA inspections might inhibit indigenous atomic research and development and give nuclear-weapon states whose peaceful nuclear programmes were not under the treaty subject to international inspection a competitive edge over all other states[30]. Moreover, the NPT appeared at precisely the time a number of industrialized non-nuclear countries were approaching a «takeoff» phase in the development of nuclear energy technologies. This was particularly true of a number of the European members of NATO who were also party to EURATOM, the European nuclear common market. IAEA inspection of EURATOM facilities under the NPT would have denied the European agency one of its few effective functions. Apparent American acquiescence by 1966 in the Soviet position that only IAEA inspections would be acceptable under the NPT was very much at root of the thorny debates over non-proliferation in NATO during 1966-1967.

We have already seen that by this time, arms controllers in Ottawa and General Burns in particular were impatient with the arguments being put forward by some of the NATO European members that the NPT would prejudice their military security; Canadian officials were all the more impatient with arguments from such alliance quarters that IAEA inspection of EURATOM countries under the NPT would prejudice the development of their nuclear energy programmes. Indeed, to some extent, Canadian officials felt such arguments were only stalking horses being used by opponents of the treaty[31].

If Canada's arms control community misperceived the depth of European reservations about the NPT/IAEA safeguards, atomic energy officials in Ottawa did not. They shared these reservations for similar economic and technological reasons, and as a consequence of which it was not until 1972 that Canada agreed to open all its nuclear energy facilities to IAEA inspection. During the NPT debates, General Burns was «muzzled» by atomic energy officials in Canada in his effort to secure the universal application of IAEA safeguards over the nuclear energy programmes of signatory non-nuclear weapon states[32]. Furthermore, these officials were not unsympathetic with the position of EURATOM countries, but for reason of Canada's economic interest. Through EURATOM they hoped to reopen sales of Canadian uranium to France, a market closed to Canadian uranium producers in 1965 when the Pearson Government, in a landmark decision for Canada's non-proliferation policy, refused to sell the French Government uranium for its expanding military nuclear programme and declared that future Canadian uranium exports would be for peaceful purposes only[33]. Largely for economic reasons, thus, Canada was not a prime mover in the debates which led up to the NPT for a universally-binding safeguards regime. That quest, as a hallmark of Canadian non-proliferation diplomacy, would await the Canadian reaction to the Indian nuclear explosion of May 1974.

CANADA, THE NPT AND THE PROBLEM OF VERTICAL PROLIFERATION

In September 1945, Charles Ritchie observed, somewhat presciently, that: «If the effective control of the atomic bomb is to be vested in the Great Powers or to be shared between the two great Anglo-Saxon powers and the Soviet Union, a hegemony of power would result which would be intolerable to the other states of the world and might drive them into competitive experimentation and making of such weapons[34].» To date, Ritchie's prognosis has proven to be only partially true: the horizontal proliferation of nuclear weapons has not come about to the degree that many feared that it would. Yet, «the other states of the world», particularly but not exclusively in the Third World, have indeed expressed their sense of grievance over the perpetuation of the great power nuclear hegemony, a grievance which has been used by important «near nuclear» states such as India as a reason for not signing the NPT. As yet another *quid pro quo* for the signatures of non-nuclear states to the discriminatory NPT, the major nuclear powers promised in Article VI of the treaty that they would in earnest attempt to reduce their own nuclear arsenals. To date, these powers have not done so; indeed, with the qualitative and quantitative advancements in their nuclear armour, they have brought about the problem of «vertical» proliferation.

In the debates which led up to the NPT, Canada was as ambiguous on this issue as on the safeguards article. The Canadian dilemma here, however, did not stem from domestic interests but rather from the nature of the international debate itself. During the mid-1960s, Canada was at times among the most forthright of non-nuclear powers in demanding of the major nuclear powers that they enter into a firm and binding commitment to limit and reduce their nuclear arms; failing this, Canadian spokesmen frequently argued, it could not be expected that aligned and nonaligned non-nuclear states would maintain that status in perpetuity[35]. Accordingly, Canada proposed that the NPT, after it had entered into force, be subject to review every five years. It may be that this country came to regret that particular initiative; the 1980 NPT Review Conference, in what was perhaps a sorry commentary on the contemporary state of the non-proliferation regime, could not reach a consensus on a final communiqué because of the expressed disillusionment on the part of a number of states with the failure of the nuclear powers to live up to the spirit and letter of Article VI[36].

Yet, for diplomatic reasons, Canada wavered in its call for a superpower commitment to nuclear disarmament as part of an NPT regime. In recognizing that for political and strategic reasons it was not possible for the nuclear powers to arrive at the sort of *quid pro quo* a number of non-nuclear states seemed to be demanding, Canada once again began to fear for an NPT and took the position that at best all that could be expected of the nuclear powers was a declaration of intent to disarm at a future date. It was never clear, moreover, that the demand for a halt to the vertical proliferation of nuclear arms, much less nuclear disarmament, was much more than a «diplomatic charade»[37]. The superpowers, of course, did not put this possibility to the test; yet the hard questions remain. How could the demand made during the NPT debates for strengthened superpower commitments to insecure non-nuclear states be reconciled with the demand for superpower disarmament? What was the nature of the relationship between the nuclear armaments of the superpowers and the security interests of those states who opposed the NPT as a discriminatory attempt by the armed to disarm the unarmed? Were superpower strategic arms the essence of the threat to insecure states in instable regions such as the Asian subcontinent, the Middle East or South America? Was India, for instance, serious in its call for Soviet and American nuclear disarmament when in logic the major threat to Indian security was a nuclear-armed China which was not even party to the NPT negotiations?

It remains to be seen whether a «halt» to vertical proliferation would strengthen the existing non-proliferation regime by increasing the number of adherents to the NPT. What is known is that a number of the states which are not signatories to the treaty are insecure «threshold» states, proliferation-prone in essence. This is a major flaw in the existing non-proliferation regime. What is also known is that vertical proliferation continues apace, potentially undermining not so much the existing inhibitions on horizontal proliferation but the stability of the strategic balance of power. This is the other major flaw in the existing non-proliferation regime. During the 1970s, Canada attempted to address the latter problem through a «diplomatic activism», a criticism of the pace and substance of superpower negotiations for such measures as a comprehensive test-ban treaty and a strategic arms convention[38]. Canada attempted to address the former problem by moving into the forefront of supplier states with its rigorous safeguards over its nuclear transfers.

NON-PROLIFERATION AND THE EARLY TRUDEAU YEARS

There can be no doubt about the depth of Pierre Elliot Trudeau's concern over Canada's «complicity» in the proliferation of nuclear weapons. Whether this concern stemmed from an instinctive dislike of nuclear weapons, a fear of the likely untoward implications of further horizontal proliferation for international stability, or a desire that Canada's assumed international image as «peacekeeper» not be unduly tarnished, is difficult to say and probably beside the point. Trudeau had expressed strong misgivings about Pearson's nuclear defence policy decision of 1963 and when he became Prime Minister in 1968, moved in the name of the non-proliferation of nuclear weapons to rid Canada of its nuclear roles under NATO and NORAD[39]. And there can be no doubt that Canada's vanguard non-proliferation and safeguards policies of 1974 and 1976, following upon the trauma of India's nuclear explosion of May 1974, bore the marks not of prime ministerial making but certainly of prime ministerial consecration. Yet a shadow of doubt remains over the prime ministerial commitment to non-proliferation, in the form of a conflicting commitment to Canada's nuclear industry.

During a 1969 internal review of Canada's arms control and disarmament policies, serious consideration was given to what some officials felt, rightly, was Canada's «solemn obligation» to deny nuclear aid to countries which were unwilling to forego the nuclear weapons options – a forebearance which could only have been signalled to the international community by subscription to the NPT. The NPT does not, as well it might, demand of signatory supplier-states that they provide nuclear assistance only to signatory recipients. Yet, as a result of strong pressures from Canadian nuclear interests, this internal review concluded on the note that such a policy move would conflict with Canadian commercial interests and could well have important political repercussions on Canada's overall relationships with nuclear partners such as India, West Germany and Japan. Implicitly, this review recognized the importance of the nuclear connection in many of Canada's bilateral relationships – a point which has gone largely unrecognized in the academic study of Canadian foreign policy. The review process established the Canadian policy that each nuclear transfer would be examined on its merits, in which NPT obligations would be accorded full weight[40].

This internal review of Canada's arms control approaches was part and parcel of the broader foreign policy review which Trudeau had initiated in 1968. The primary «foreign policy» theme which was enunciated by government spokesmen during (and in the White Paper which emanated from) this review process was Canada's economic well-being. The foreign policy review process, in emphasizing this theme, brought to the fore the commercial considerations which had historically been behind Canada's nuclear transfer programmes and heightened the policy relevance of these considerations in any future calculations about Canada's approaches to the problem of nuclear proliferation.

Because of the unique nature of the Candu system and because of the perceived importance of the uranium industry to the Canadian economy, successive Canadian governments consciously attempted to foster their development. As the heavy-water moderated Candu became increasingly vulnerable to worldwide competition from the American-designed light-water reactor system and with the closing of the American market to Canadian uranium, the Trudeau Government felt that it could not be an exception to this practice. Indeed, to the extent that it has been evident at all, the «economic nationalism» of this government has been most visible in the nuclear industry sphere. «Several years ago, Trudeau recollected in 1975, I asked Canadians to pay less attention to the siren song of buying back investment now held in foreign hands. I argued then and shall continue to do so, that buying back the past was not the answer – that we should, instead, ensure that industries of the future were developed by Canadians in the Canadian interest. The nuclear industry was foremost in my mind as a future industry, and as one that will require immense amounts of capital.» The Prime Minister, echoing in effect the thoughts and aspirations of C.D. Howe, had in mind «the fostering of a competitive Canadian industry in all its stages – of exploration, mining, processing, fabrication, design and sales»[41].

To this end, extensive funding was given to Eldorado Nuclear Limited, the Crown corporation charged with uranium procurement, to seek out fresh equity investment in Canada's uranium industry. From 1972 to 1975, the Trudeau Government involved itself in a highly secret uranium cartel whose aim was to ensure equitable and stable prices for producers of that commodity[42]. As noted earlier, the Crown corporation AECL was in 1968 given exclusive jurisdiction over Canada's nuclear reactor and technology exports, an autonomy in effect which some years hence caused the Trudeau Government a degree of embarrassment when it came to light that AECL, unknown to the Minister of Energy, Mines and Resources, stood to lose some $130 million from the sale of a Candu to Argentina[43].

During the 1970s, a number of attentive Canadians became critical of the extent to which the Trudeau Government seemed intent upon making Canada's non-proliferation commitments subservient to its economic interests. Down to 1974, however, such criticism was almost non-existent, save for that of a few in academic circles and within the Department of External Affairs who worried that Canada's safeguards requirements were not sufficiently rigorous. In the House of Commons, the Government was attacked on the grounds that it was not doing enough to foster Canadian nuclear exports, and this criticism came from within all three political parties. Those calling for increased sales based their case on purely domestic considerations, the promotion of Canadian nuclear technology and expertise and the maintenance of high employment in the uranium mining industry. There is no evidence that parliamentarians considered these issues from the standpoint of nuclear proliferation[44].

By 1974, three international events conspired to dramatically alter these attitudes and interests, as a consequence of which members of Parliament became influential in shaping the course of Canada's non-proliferation and safeguards policies. This constituted a rare moment in which Canada's legislative branch had a perceptible influence upon Canadian arms control policy-making.

The first event was the oil embargo instituted against Western countries during the 1973 Middle East war by the Arab oil-producing members of OPEC; the second event was the subsequent quadrupling in the price of crude oil on the international market. Both events sharpened the increasing sense of vulnerability shared by energy-importing nations to the vagaries in the supply and cost of oil; both stimulated a greater interest in nuclear power as a viable alternative energy source. For nuclear exporters, these events provided both promise and constraint. The promise, or so it seemed at the time, was an increased power to shape the international non-proliferation regime on their terms by using, if need be, their privileged access to nuclear material, equipment and technology as a form of economic sanction. The constraint was a heightened interest in and potential access to the technological bases of a «plutonium economy» which were fast coming on stream – enrichment facilities, fast-breeder reactors and especially reprocessing plants – and which would effectively diminish the leverage of supplier-states keen on a strengthened non-proliferation regime. The third event which, above all, stimulated the Canadian interest in non-proliferation was India's nuclear explosion in May 1974.

THE INDIAN CATALYST

In November 1963, the Canadian-Indian nuclear relationship was strengthened with the sale to India of a Candu reactor (RAPP I). As was the case with the CIR deal, this sale provided that the reactor would be used for peaceful purposes only; the safeguards were strengthened, however, to include Canadian inspection of the fuel rods and the possibility of IAEA inspection. This latter provision was implemented in 1971 as RAPP I was due to begin operation in 1972 and as the IAEA was fully organized by this time to conduct such inspections. Yet, the Trudeau Government wanted these safeguards to apply also to a commissioned second RAPP and, retroactively, to the CIR; Canada was becoming somewhat concerned about statements emanating out of India that the Gandhi Government planned to detonate a nuclear explosive device[45].

In 1970, the Canadian embassy in New Delhi reported to Ottawa that the signs pointed to a gradual buildup of an Indian nuclear capability, including the possibility of underground explosions. Yet Ottawa proceeded in fulfilling its nuclear commitments to India, including the export of technology and financial assistance for RAPP II. It may well be that senior political and atomic energy officials in Canada did not believe that India would, or could, conduct a nuclear explosion. Yet in a sense, Canada had no reason not to proceed with its nuclear assistance programmes provided India agreed to IAEA inspection over the two RAPP reactors. This India agreed to, conditional upon a continuation of Canadian nuclear aid. Yet this conditional clause, coupled with Canada's sense of commitment to India, offered both promise and constraint insofar as Canada's peaceful nuclear diplomacy was concerned, a situation which was to be an enduring feature of that diplomacy throughout the 1970s.

The promising element in this situation was a carrot and stick approach to non-proliferation: a guarantee of continued assistance if India adhered to Canada's safeguards requirements, coupled with a threat to review that assistance if India conducted a nuclear explosion. The constraint upon Canadian maneuverability was India's right to disallow inspection of the RAPP reactors if Canada discontinued its nuclear aid programme. The bribe of 1971 worked, as India allowed IAEA inspection on the RAPP reactors; the threat of sanctions did not work, as India's indigenous technological capability in the nuclear field was developing apace and as other nuclear supplier states lurked in the background, waiting it would seem to fill a void left by Canada.

In May 1974, India detonated a «peaceful» nuclear device. The plutonium came from indigenous Indian uranium irradiated in the CIR. The heavy water used in the reactor came either from the United States or an Indian heavy water plant of German design. The plutonium was separated from the spent fuel rods in a French-built reprocessing plant at Trombay. Clearly, Canada was not alone among supplier states in helping India go nuclear (the NPT proscribes nuclear explosions as a form of proliferation, as it is not possible on a technical level to distinguish between their peaceful and military applications). Yet, as testimony to the strength of Canada's commitment to non-proliferation, this country suspended its nuclear assistance to India and, in December 1974, strengthened its safeguards beyond the international norm.

These comparatively stringent safeguards covered the export of all nuclear material, equipment facilities and technology of Canadian origin, and were binding on all states, nuclear and non-nuclear alike. They were to apply to all new and existing agreements, a re-negotiation clause which was to prove troublesome for the Trudeau Government shortly thereafter. The provisions of the new policy comprised a set of «binding commitments» that: 1. Canadian supplies would be used only for «peaceful» non-explosive purposes; 2. Canadian supplies would be covered by IAEA safeguards and, should these not be applied because a recipient state withdrew from the NPT, then Canada had a right to apply «fall-back» safeguards; 3. The «contagion principle» should apply through Canada's right of prior consent over the re-transfer, reprocessing or enrichment of Canadian-supplied material[46].

In August 1974, the Zangger Committee of the IAEA provided a «trigger list» of sensitive or proliferation-prone items which should be safeguarded by the Vienna agency. Canada's safeguards were an advance upon the recommendations of this committee in that the December policy imposed controls on all nuclear materials and equipment of Canadian origin. Canada also required controls over the export of its technology, a safeguard not required by the IAEA/NPT system. Yet Canada's 1974 safeguards did not cover the entire nuclear fuel cycle of recipient states. This was the major gap in these provisions, which could only be closed efffectively with the support of all other supplier countries. The limits to Canadian unilateralism in the safeguards field, and the need for a consensus among supplier states on the establishment of full-scope safeguards, were sharpened with the advent of the new nuclear technologies of the mid-1970s. Indeed these technologies, as much as the Indian explosion itself, were a cause of Canada's new safeguards of 1974.

CANADA AND THE NEW TECHNOLOGIES: WHITHER NON-PROLIFERATION DIPLOMACY?

The challenge posed to the NPT/IAEA non-proliferation regime by the new technologies can be understood only partly in terms of the technical inadequacies of existing safeguards. In other words the challenge was, and is, of a political as much as a technical kind – a matter of incentives as well as capabilities to go nuclear. During the 1970s, however, this fact does not appear to have been widely appreciated, perhaps largely because of the concern aroused by the advent of the new technologies themselves[47].

In technological terms, the major challenge came from the proposed sales of facilities which could produce weapons-grade nuclear materials to countries which had no visible economic need for them[48]. It may well be, ironically, that the developed interest of certain Third World countries in enrichment facilities and reprocessing plants (and eventually fast-breeder reactors) was stimulated by both the uranium cartel and the tightening of safeguards to which Canada was party; in pushing recipient countries to search for independent and assured sources of supply, states such as Canada may have if inadvertently propelled certain states ever closer towards a nuclear weapon capability[49]. This challenge came to a head in 1975, with the sale by West Germany of an entire nuclear fuel cycle comprised of reactors, enrichment and reprocessing facilities to Brazil. This sale bred fears that the world was entering a new plutonium economy with which the existing IAEA/NPT safeguards system could not cope. It could not provide a «timely warning» of the possible diversion of plutonium stocks to weapons use.

The NPT, as noted, prohibits party non-nuclear weapon states from making or acquiring an independent control over nuclear weapons or otherwise acquiring nuclear explosive devices. It does not prohibit, however, such states from acquiring, developing or exporting under safeguards the materials or technology from which a military nuclear capability could be derived. The IAEA/NPT safeguards, as they were refined by the Vienna agency when the NPT came into force in 1970, are comprehensive in the sense that they cover to the extent possible the entire fuel cycle of the nuclear programmes of non-nuclear weapon states party to the treaty. Yet the NPT does not require, at the risk of enhancing its discriminatory nature, that non-nuclear states be a party to it as a condition of their receiving nuclear aid. The fact that key threshold states (such as India, Pakistan, Brazil and Argentina) remain outside the treaty regime yet are still eligible for such aid is a major shortcoming of the contemporary non-proliferation regime. Non-party recipient states must submit to IAEA or «equivalent» safeguards; but these do not cover the full fuel cycle in these states, only the particular transfer in question.

During the 1970s, major supplier states attempted to address this shortcoming by two means: through a diplomatic consensus to be arrived at in the London Suppliers' Club that suppliers would not undercut competitors by reducing safeguards requirements; and through technical understandings arrived at in the post-1977 International Nuclear Fuel Cycle Evaluation (INFCE) that certain «highly sensitive» technologies would not be transferred[50]. Both efforts met with a limited measure of success.

In the autumn of 1975, the London Club or Nuclear Suppliers' Group (NSG) arrived at four guidelines to cover nuclear exports: IAEA safeguards would be applied to exports of nuclear *technology;* nuclear transfers could not be used for «peaceful» nuclear explosives; such transfers would have to be covered by «adequate» physical protection; and these requirements would be binding on nuclear transfers to third parties. The NSG arrived at these guidelines largely at the behest of Canada and the United States, although they fell short of Canadian expectations. Throughout 1975, Canada attempted to persuade its fellow members in the Club to subscribe to the desirability of recipient-state adherence to the NPT as a precondition for nuclear assistance, and to the need of full-scope safeguards on nuclear transfers. Canada also called for the collective imposition of sanctions against deviant states[51]. These efforts marked the zenith of Canada's non-proliferation activism at the multilateral level, a diplomatic temper whetted by the international embarrassment and domestic debates caused by the Indian explosion of 1974. That the Canadian Government did not follow up the advice of domestic critics and impose a unilateral moratorium on Canadian transfers until the London Club concurred with Ottawa's safeguards suggestions was only partly due to countervailing economic considerations, however.

The first NPT review conference was held in 1975, during which member states were duly reminded of the basic bargain of the treaty: that in return for a legal obligation not to develop or acquire nuclear weapons, non-nuclear states were entitled to share in all the benefits of the peaceful atom on a non-discriminatory basis. It seemed, to some at least, that an elitist suppliers' club, through multilateral consensus, and particular states such as Canada, through unilateral fiat, were attempting to revise this bargain on their terms. Member states at the Review Conference were also duly reminded that the existing nuclear weapon powers had not lived up to their promise to negotiate in earnest an end to vertical proliferation. Yet Canada, as we have seen, was troubled by the paradoxes inherent in the NPT debates. To support the treaty was to confer a greater recognition upon the dangers of horizontal than of vertical proliferation; it was to risk the further alienation of those states on the threshold of nuclear weapons development who opposed the discriminatory treaty. To support these near nuclear states was to recognize their demand for a less than intrusive safeguards system on peaceful nuclear transfers; it was also to accept their burdensome demand which might well have placed the very prospects for a treaty in jeopardy, that explicit curbs on the weapons programmes of the nuclear powers be incorporated into an NPT. Canada supported the superpower treaty, and was among the first of the near nuclear to sign and to ratify it. Yet Canada's sympathy with the development aspirations and frustrations of aligned and nonaligned non-nuclear states was rekindled during the 1975 Review Conference debates, in sufficient degree to make Ottawa doubtful about the arms control wisdom of flatly denying assistance to states which were reluctant to subscribe to Canada's 1974 safeguards provisions.

During 1975-1976, Canada attempted to re-negotiate its pre-1974 nuclear agreements in accordance with these provisions. It is to be noted that a number of these agreements were with countries that are usually considered to be highly proliferation-prone, most notably India and Pakistan, but also Argentina, South Korea and Taiwan. Canadian negotiations with the latter three were successful: the 1969 research reactor, heavy water and fuel agreement with Taiwan and the 1973 Candu reactor, heavy water and technology agreement with Argentina were covered by the December 1974 policy, and South Korea, as a condition of the consummation of the 1973 Candu sale, agreed in 1976 to become a party to the NPT. The negotiations with India and Pakistan were not successful, however.

Throughout 1975, Canada attempted to persuade the Indian Government to accept full-scope safeguards on all Canadian-supplied nuclear material, equipment and technology. This effort was to no avail; India would only accept what it had agreed to in 1971, IAEA inspection of the RAPP reactors. In March 1976, the Canadian Government, on the advice of senior officials in the DEA and AECL, decided to renew its nuclear commitments to India, partly out of fear that New Delhi would abrogate the 1971 agreement. Yet two months later, largely in response to domestic pressures, Ottawa terminated the lengthy Canadian-Indian nuclear relationship. Some nine months later, the Canadian nuclear relationship with Pakistan was similarly terminated because of compelling evidence that Pakistan, refusing to submit to Canada's strengthened safeguards requirements, was following the Indian nuclear path.

In December 1976, Canada cut off its supplies of fuel for the KANUPP reactor which it had sold Pakistan in 1959. In 1969, upon Canadian insistence, this reactor was placed under IAEA safeguards and began commercial operation in 1972. Ottawa's fears that these safeguards were not sufficient seemed justified when in 1980, Pakistan announced that it could make its own fuel rods from natural uranium bought from Niger and Libya. These rods could well be irradiated in the KANUPP, removed while the reactor still operates, and then reprocessed to yield plutonium in the small plant which Pakistan built from the blueprints for a French reprocessing plant which Paris agreed to but did not sell Pakistan because of American pressures. As this would be a clear duplication of the Indian route to a nuclear explosive capability, the IAEA has requested (but has not been granted) the right to inspect more closely the KANUPP operation[52]. It would like to install «bundle counters» at this operation, which would record automatically the number of fuel rods being installed and removed. These were developed and tested in Canada under the 1978 Canadian Safeguards Research and Development Program, the object of which is to assist the Agency in the development of safeguards for the proliferation-prone Candu reactor.

As a consequence of Canada's nuclear experiences with Pakistan and India, and the related embargo decisions of 1976, Ottawa that December strengthened its safeguards requirements still further. The new safeguards prescribed that Canadian nuclear exports to non-nuclear weapon states would henceforth be restricted to countries which ratified the NPT or otherwise accepted full-scope safeguards over their entire nuclear fuel cycles. Canada would also terminate automatically reactor or uranium shipments to any non-nuclear country which detonated a nuclear device. Canada, thus, became the first major supplier to require that safeguards on its transfers to non-NPT states were as stringent as those required of party states. Alas, however, a number of Canada's most important uranium customers, most notably Japan and member states of the European Community, objected to Ottawa's full-scope safeguards requirements and its demand for a right of prior consent over the reprocessing of Canadian uranium. These were deemed to be too strong an intrusion upon national sovereignty and an effront to the integrity of EURATOM. Nevertheless, Ottawa placed an embargo upon its nuclear transfers to these countries[53].

The thorny issue of nuclear transfers provided a centerpiece for a number of Canada's most important bilateral relationships during 1977. Not the least of these was the West German relationship, the Federal Republic having been a key country in Canada's successful quest for a «contractual link» with the European Community in 1976 as well as being dependent upon Canada for some 40 % of its uranium supplies. Indeed, it was as a consequence of the summit meetings between Prime Minister Trudeau and the West German Chancellor, Helmut Schmidt, in mid-1977 that Ottawa began to seriously consider the possibility of a relaxation of its embargoes and its rigorous safeguards requirements. These were relaxed that December, as external and domestic economic pressures mounted, when Ottawa agreed to interim supplies of uranium to fill current European Community needs pending the results of the international nuclear fuel cycle evaluation begun that October, and when Ottawa also agreed to replace its demand for a veto over the reprocessing of Canadian-supplied uranium with a process of «consultation».

The interim accords reached between Canada and most of its major nuclear customers at a formal level in January 1978 were consistent with guidelines for nuclear exports established by the London NSG that month. In brief, these guidelines provide that «sensitive» items in a nuclear fuel cycle be covered by IAEA safeguards in non-nuclear states, whether party to the NPT or not, that formal assurances be given by such recipient states that nuclear transfers will not be used for explosive purposes, and that original suppliers of such sensitive «trigger list» items as heavy water production technology, reprocessing and enrichment facilities seek assurances that the re-transfer to third parties of these items be covered by IAEA safeguards. The proximity in the timing between the interim agreements reached between Canada and its uranium customers (many of which were members of the NSG) and the consensus arrived at in the London Club is suggestive of Canadian influence behind the promulgation of the guidelines, the high-point to date in international cooperation for the establishment of safeguards over nuclear exports. Through a seemingly deliberate carrot and stick policy of negotiating transfers while threatening sanctions, Ottawa was able to help shape a more effective non-proliferation regime while bringing to the fore of international attention its two primary concerns: the ability of recipient states to develop a nuclear explosive capability through «peaceful» transfers; and the inherent dangers involved in the wide-scale reprocessing or enrichment of uranium through the less than adequately safeguarded sale or re-transfer of sensitive technologies. Canada has yet to secure international agreement on the need for the imposition of full-scope safeguards on the nuclear programmes on states not party to the NPT, however, much less secure agreement on the desirability of the imposition of sanctions against countries which violate their non-proliferation commitments. It is present Canadian policy, thus, that Ottawa has gone as far as it can, or intends to go, in attempting to shape the international non-proliferation *cum* safeguards regime through unilateral design or restraint[54].

THE PRESENT DILEMMAS

Canada's post-1978 non-proliferation and safeguards approaches must be understood in the light of the findings of the two-year INFCE study. Despite the powerful Canadian interest in nuclear exports, Ottawa had in January 1978 decreed that it would undertake future long-term commitments to its customers only if the results of this fuel-cycle evaluation pointed to the efficacy and the desirability, in arms control terms, of a continued international nuclear commerce in light of the advent of the new technologies. The consensus arrived at by the members of the INFCE study, in February 1980, was ambiguous on the matter of the technical or safeguards problems inherent in these technologies, particularly reprocessing and high-enrichment facilities. It did not, however, negate their use or transfer; instead, it accented the need for effective safeguards in view of a perceived increasing demand for nuclear energy. While billed as a technical study, INFCE drew the essentially political conclusion that assurances of supply and assurances of non-proliferation are complementary desiderata. This principle, of course, is hardly novel; it was and remains the basic bargain of the NPT.

On the basis of the INFCE findings, Canada entered into long-term agreements with a number of its most important nuclear customers. The post-1980 arrangements with the United States, Sweden and EURATOM, for instance, were justified by Ottawa in terms of the INFCE principle that a clear linkage exists between the evolution of an effective non-proliferation regime and a «secure» and «predictable» international nuclear commerce[55]. If specious, one can be marginally sympathetic with Canadian reasoning here: Ottawa's insistence on maintaining in all of its bilateral arrangements fallback and full-scope safeguards, including the right of prior consent over the reprocessing and high enrichment of fuel of Canadian origin, constitute a significant Canadian contribution and commitment to the evolution of an international non-proliferation regime. Canada's salutary efforts in the safeguards field notwithstanding, however, the historic arms control and economic dilemmas underlying Canadian non-proliferation approaches still remain.

The arms control shortcomings of the contemporary non-proliferation regime are widely reported, and need only brief mention here. In short, these appear to be technical but are essentially of a politico-strategic nature. The quest for a technical «fix» through safeguards to the problem of proliferation has been both heightened and made more difficult by the advent of the new technologies. Yet the contemporary international safeguards regime can and is intended to do no more than the safeguards of yesteryear: detect and thus hopefully deter but not prevent the possible diversion of the peaceful atom to military uses. Those who can and want to proliferate will do so, presumably for security reasons[56]. The problem of and the solution to the proliferation of nuclear weapons reside in the incentives more than the capabilities which states possess to «go nuclear». In this sense there is some truth to the judgement that there are only sensitive countries, not sensitive technologies, a point somewhat veiled by the contemporary fixation of international non-proliferation diplomacy with safeguards[57].

One is tempted to suggest that a «solution» to the problem of the incentives of states to go nuclear lies beyond the purview of the peaceful nuclear diplomacy of middle powers such as Canada. In the final analysis, this is undoubtedly true; as the NPT debates of the 1960s signified, a solution, if it is to be found at all, lies with great power security guarantees to insecure non-nuclear states or, failing the granting or acceptance of such guarantees, a great power ordinance against the proliferation of nuclear weapons. Indeed, this issue remains as the only arms control area in which the United States and the Soviet Union are still clearly at one[58]. Yet, in terms of the question of what middle-power supplier states such as Canada can do to mitigate the problem of incentives to proliferation, three points must be recognized. The first is that the international non-proliferation regime is no more but yet no less stable than in previous decades; the once-feared widespread proliferation of nuclear weapons has not, thankfully, materialized. The handful of insecure threshold states once seen as prime candidates for nuclear proliferation has not increased in number despite the dispersion of nuclear technology and know-how. Yet neither has that number decreased; the potential proliferators of yesteryear remain as a threat to the existing non-proliferation regime.

The second and related point is that the development of a capability to go nuclear may or may not help create the incentive to do so. The Indian experience, coupled with widespread suspicions within the international non-proliferaton community about the aims underlying the «peaceful» nuclear programmes of such countries as Pakistan, Iraq, Brazil and Argentina, suggests that supplier states would have done well to err on the side of safety in deciding whether or not to proffer nuclear assistance to such states. A refusal to accept safeguards, full–scope or ortherwise, is not of course necessarily indicative of the intentions of a state to go nuclear, any more than is acceptance of safeguards, however stringent, a guarantee that a state will be deterred or prevented from developing a military nuclear capability. And a refusal by a supplier state to proffer nuclear assistance to a country which has not expressly declared its intentions to go nuclear is a violation of the spirit of and the norms which underlie the present non-proliferation regime[59]. Yet if the threat of proliferation does exist, given the possible disposition of insecure threshold states to go nuclear and the flaws in the existing safeguards regime, it could be argued that supplier states such as Canada would do well in the name of arms control to make the hard decision to opt out of the realm of peaceful nuclear commerce. This would entail a recognition of the third point, that the assumed complementary relationship between the willingness of supplier states to provide nuclear assistance and the willingness of recipient states not to go nuclear has probably never existed[60]. This is a misperception or myth which has been perpetuated from the time of the Tripartite 1945 Declaration on Atomic Energy down to and beyond the 1980 INFCE study. Most states seeking and acquiring nuclear assistance have shown no disposition to go nuclear; the very few that have shown that disposition have already gone or may soon go nuclear, regardless of the willingness of supplier states to proffer nuclear assistance. It is to be noted that such willingness has not been, since the time of the Atoms for Peace proposal, in short supply[61].

For Canada, the hard decision to opt out of the nuclear export business would involve a recognition of another misperception or myth: that the linked policy aims of sustaining the domestic nuclear industry while strengthening the international non-proliferation regime can be achieved through the establishment of a secure and predictable international nuclear commerce. This is a myth not because Canada's non-proliferation and safeguards policy are lax, which they are not by international standards, but because the degree of predictability in international nuclear commerce needed to sustain the Canadian nuclear industry has not in fact existed. Only a minority of states have, on balance, been attracted to the presumed benefits of the Peaceful Atom and, despite the fears of energy shortages so prevalent in the 1970s, the international nuclear marketplace is shrinking dramatically[62]. Developing states have as a whole never seen nuclear energy as a panacea for their economic woes and, increasingly, developed states fear the environmental risks associated with nuclear reactors[63]. Supplier states who remain in the nuclear export market may soon find themselves, if they are not already, hostage to a few recipient countries whose economic interests in the Peaceful Atom are suspect. Caught in that hostage situation, supplier states such as Canada would lose that limited leverage which once seemed to be theirs to shape a non-proliferation regime on their terms[64]. Because of the shrinking international marketplace, Canada's historic relationship with the Peaceful Atom can now be seen in its true light, as a high-cost, low-payoff venture in both economic and arms control terms.

NOTES

1. The best accounts are to be found in John W. Holmes, *The Shaping of Peace: Canada and the Search for World Order 1943-1957*, Vol. I, Toronto, 1979, and James Eayrs, In Defence of Canada, Vol. III: *Peacemaking and Deterrence*, Toronto, 1972, and Vol. IV: *Growing up Allied*, Toronto, 1979.

2. A succinct survey of the Canadian contribution is in Peter G. Mueller, *On Things Nuclear: The Canadian Debate*, Toronto, 1977.

3. Eayrs, Growing up Allied, Toronto, p. 267.

4. Evidence of this concern is to be found in departmental memoranda from this period. See for instance the following items in the DEA File 211-G(S), October 1946-April 1949: C.S.A. Ritchie, «Control of the Atomic Bomb by the United Nations Organization», September 8, 1945; «Canada's position in the development of atomic energy, memorandum from Hume Wrong to Lester B. Pearson, November 3, 1945; and Lester B. Pearson, «Canadian Memorandum on Atomic Warfare», November 8, 1945.

5. L.B. Pearson to the Secretary of State for External Affairs, November 21, 1945, in the DEA File 211-G(S).

6. Debates, House of Commons, December 17, 1945.

7. For a more detailed account of the Baruch Plan, see John Spanier and Joseph Nogee, *The Politics of Disarmament: A Study in Soviet-American Gamesmanship*, New York, 1962. Accounts of Canada's involvement in the commission are to be found in Eayrs, *Peacemaking and Deterrence, op. cit.*; George Ignatieff, «General A.G.L. McNaughton: a soldier in diplomacy», *International Journal*, XXII, Summer 1967; Frederick Osborn, «Negotiating on atomic energy, 1946-1947», in Raymond Dennett and Joseph Johnson, eds., *Negotiating with the Russians*, Boston, 1951; and John Swettenham, *McNaughton III: 1946-1966*, Toronto, 1969.

8. Cited in Swettenham, *op. cit.*, p. 116.

9. Confidential interviews.

10. Eayrs, *Peacemaking and Deterrence*, p. 295.

11. Cited in Holmes, The Shaping of Peace, p. 197.

12. C.E.S. Franks, «Peaceful Nuclear Energy», *International Journal*, XXXIV, Spring 1979, p. 192.

13. Cited in Holmes, *op. cit.*, p. 219.

14. Ted Greenwood, Harold Geiveson and Theodore Taylor, *Nuclear Proliferation: Motivations, Capabilities, and Strategies for Control*, New York, 1977, p. 87.

15. For a fuller account, see Barrie Morrison and Donald Page, «India's option: the nuclear route to achieve goal as world power», *International Perspectives*, July-August 1974, and Ashok Kapur, *India's Nuclear Option*, London, 1976. See also our *Canadian Foreign Policy: contemporary issues and themes*, Scarborough, 1980, p. 203-206.

16. J.E. Hodgetts, *Administering the Atom for Peace*, New York, 1964, p. 109 ff. For a more recent treatment, see the relevant articles in G. Bruce Doern and Robert W. Morrison, eds., *Canadian Nuclear Policies*, Montréal, 1980.

17. Confidential interviews.

18. The best treatment of the defence debates of the Diefenbaker period is still J. McLin, *Canada's Changing Defense Policy 1957-1963*, Baltimore, 1967.

19. See Peyton V. Lyon, *Canada in World Affairs 1961-1963*, Toronto, 1968, p. 80 ff. See also our «Canada's roles in the disarmament negotiations 1957-1971», Unpublished Ph.D. thesis, University of Toronto, December 1977.

20. Canada, Department of External Affairs, *External Affairs*, XV, Ottawa, February 1963, p. 114.

21. Robert Spencer, «External Affairs and Defence», in John Saywell, ed., *Canadian Annual Review for 1961*, Toronto, 1962, p. 107.

22. H. Green, «Canadian efforts in the world today», *Statements and Speeches* 61/5, April 26, 1961.

23. Hellyer, «Speech to the Opening Session of the Special Committee on Defence», Statements and Speeches 63/15, June 27, 1963.

24. See Bruce Thordarson, Trudeau and Foreign Policy: a study in decision-making, Toronto, 1972, p. 46, 75.

25. E.L.M. Burns, *Diaries*, November 3, 1960, File MG-31, Manuscripts, Ottawa, Division, Public Archives Canada. Material in this chapter on Burns' role as Canada's disarmament negotiator during 1960-1968 has been drawn in part from this file.

26. E.L.M. Burns, *A seat at the table*, Toronto, 1972, p. 208-211. On the MLF see also Michael Sherman, Nuclear proliferation: the treaty and after, Toronto, 1968.

27. Burns, *A seat at the table*, p. 209.

28. Eighteen-Nation Disarmament Conference, Geneva, Verbatim Records, 201, July 23, 1964.

29. See our «Canada's roles in the disarmament negotiations», p. 300-314. On the implications for Canada of this split between the United States and NATO Europe, see also Klaus Knorr, «Curbing Nuclear Proliferation: some problems for Canada and the United States», Report of the Canadian-American Assembly on Nuclear Weapons, Scarborough, 1967.

30. See especially Lawrence Scheinman, «Political Implications of Safeguards», in Mason Willrich (ed.), *International Safeguards and Nuclear Industry*, Baltimore, 1973.

31. Confidential interviews.

32. Ibidem.

33. On this decision, see Knorr, op. cit., p. 6-7; Thomas Hockin, «External Affairs and Defence», in John Saywell (ed.), *Canadian Annual Review for 1965*, Toronto, 1966, p. 215 ff.

34. Ritchie, «Control of the Atomic Bomb by the United Nations Organization», September 8, 1945, DEA File 211-G(S), October 1946-April 1949.

35. For a flavour of this sentiment see Lester B. Pearson, «The Prevention of Nuclear Proliferation», *Statements and Speeches*, 66/30, June 25, 1966, and Donald S. McDonald, «Toward the Control of Nuclear Weapons», ibidem, 67/22, June 18, 1967..

36. See «The NPT Review Conference», *Arms Control Today*, February 1981.

37. «Reflections on the Quarter», ORBIS, Spring 1967, p. 9.

38. See our «Canada and arms control: perspectives and trends», *International Journal*, XXXVI, Summer 1981, p. 645-650.

39. Ibidem. See also Harald von Reikhoff, «The impact of Prime Minister Trudeau on foreign policy», *International Journal*, XXXIII, Spring 1978.

40. Confidential interviews.

41. See our *Canadian foreign policy*, p. 201-203.

42. See Larry Stewart, «Canada's role in the international uranium cartel», *International Organization*, Autumn 1981.

43. See *Debates*, House of Commons, November 25, 1976, p. 1364-1365.

44. See Nancy Carroll, «Canada's national interests and nuclear safeguards policy», Unpublished honours graduating essay, Mount Allison University, Sackville, N.B., May 1978.

45. For a detailed account of this episode, see Ashok Kapur, «Canadian-Indian Nuclear Negotiations: some hypotheses and lessons», *World Today*, August 1978; see also Roberta Wohlstetter, «US Peaceful Aid and the Indian Bomb», in Wohlstetter *et al.*, *Nuclear Policies: fuel without the bomb*, Cambridge, Mass., 1978.

46. On the development of Canada's safeguards policies during the 1970s, see Canada, Department of External Affairs, *Foreign Policy Texts*, 82/2, «Canada's Nuclear Non-Proliferation Policy». See also James Keeley, «Canadian nuclear export policy and the problems of proliferation», Canadian Public Policy, Autumn 1980.

47. The challenge posed by these technologies is treated in Lewis Dunn, «The Proliferation Policy Agenda: Taking Stock», Report of the World Peace Foundation, Dedham, Mass., December 1977; George Quester (ed.), «Nuclear Proliferation: breaking the chain», Special Issue, *International Organization*, Winter 1981; Gerard Smith and George Rathjens, «Reassessing nuclear non-proliferation policy», *Foreign Affairs*, Spring 1981. See also and especially the influential volume issued by the US Nuclear Energy Policy Study Group entitled *Nuclear Power: Issues and Choices*, Cambridge, Mass., 1977.

48. Joseph Nye, «Maintaining a non-proliferation regime», in Quester, *op. cit.*, p. 19.

49. Ibidem. See also Daniel Poneman, «Nuclear policies in developing countries», *International Affairs*, Spring 1982, p. 572. While Canada is not opposed to reprocessing in principle, officials in Ottawa have long doubted the economic feasibility of a plutonium economy unless it can be written off against a weapons programme (confidential interviews).

50. The original members of this club were Britain, Canada, France, Japan, West Germany, the United States and the Soviet Union. In 1975, its membership was expanded to include Belgium, Czechoslovakia, East Germany, Italy, the Netherlands, Poland, Sweden and Switzerland. On the INFCE, see Philip Gummett, «From NPT to INFCE: developments in thinking about nuclear non-proliferation», *International Affairs*, Spring 1982.

51. On Canada's role in the London Club, see the official «Canada's Nuclear Non-Proliferation Policy», *Foreign Policy Texts*, 82/2, loc. cit.

52. David K. Willis, «On the trail of the A-Bomb Makers», *The Chritian Science Monitor*, December 1, 1981.

53. A more detailed account of this episode is to be found in our Canadian Foreign Policy, p. 209-212.

54. Mark MacGuigan, «Arms control and disarmament agreements essential to world peace», *Statements and Speeches*, 82/17, July 16, 1982.

55. Canada, Department of External Affairs, *Communiqué*, 126, «Canada/Sweden exchange letters of nuclear cooperation»; 127, «Canada/EURATOM exchange letters of nuclear cooperation», December 18, 1981. See also P. David Lee, «Views from Canada», *Nuclear Non-Proliferation and Safeguards*, Paris, 1981.

56. Unless their nuclear facilities are destroyed by a suspicious neighbour. On Israel's regrettable if novel approach to non-proliferation, see Richard Betts, «Nuclear proliferation after Osirak», *Arms Control Today*, September 1981.

57. P. Gummett, «From NPT to INFCE», *loc. cit.*, p. 567.

58. Joseph W. Clifford, «Where the US and the USSR can get together on arms control», *The Christian Science Monitor*, December 27, 1982.

59. One could argue, for instance, that the prohibition in 1980 by Canada's AECB of a sale by Eldorado Nuclear Limited of processed uranium to an NPT signatory, Iraq, because the Board thought this material might be used to manufacture weapons-grade fuel, was a violation of the spirit if not the letter of the treaty. On the prohibition, see *International Canada*, October 1980, p. 228.

60. See especially Peter Clausen, «Nuclear supply policies after Osirak», *Arms Control Today*, September 1981.

61. Canada has of late, it should be noted, maintained a rather lonely non-proliferation vigil. It was deserted in 1980 by its hitherto closest ally on the safeguards issue, the Carter administration in the United States. In early 1980 that administration, whose 1978 Non-Proliferation Act was in many ways a carbon copy of Canada's 1974 and 1976 policies, reversed its earlier stand and resumed shipments of nuclear fuel to India. This exemption, granted to a non-signatory of the NPT, understandably dismayed Ottawa. See *International Canada*, June 1980, p. 111.

62. See Amory Lovins, L. Hunter Lovins and Leonard Ross, «Nuclear Power and Nuclear Bombs», *Foreign Affairs*, Summer 1980; «French nuclear industry running out of steam», *The Christian Science Monitor*, December 30, 1982; «Nuclear power in US: fission fizzles», *The Christian Science Monitor*, January 4, 1983; «Dismal years forecast for reactor sales», *The Times-Transcript*, Moncton, February 2, 1983.

63. Poneman, «Nuclear Policies in Developing Countries», *loc. cit.*, p. 569.

64. See especially Thomas Neff and Henry Jacoby, «Non-proliferation: strategies in a changing nuclear fuel market», *Foreign Affairs*, Summer 1979, p. 1136-1138.

29

Le Canada et l'espace

Nicolas M. Matte
M.L. Stojak
Université McGill

I. LES FONDEMENTS DU PROGRAMME SPATIAL CANADIEN

Le lancement du satellite *Alouette I* en 1962 marquait l'entrée du Canada dans l'ère spatiale. Déjà à cette époque, deux objectifs fondamentaux du programme spatial canadien avaient été identifiés:

1. d'encourager l'utilisation des technologies spatiales qui contribueraient à la réalisation des objectifs nationaux;

2. de développer au Canada une industrie autonome de fabrication de matériel spatial[1].

L'atteinte de ces deux objectifs a été assurée par l'adoption d'une politique spatiale dynamique, poursuivie assidûment par les divers gouvernements.

À la suite du succès d'*Alouette I*, le Canada et les États-Unis entreprirent un programme conjoint de recherches ionosphériques, connu sous le nom d'International Satellites for Ionospheric Studies (ISIS[2]). Un mémorandum d'accord fut signé en 1963 entre la Commission de recherches de la défense (CRD) du Canada et la National Aeronautics and Space Agency (NASA[3]) des États-Unis, prévoyant la construction de quatre satellites entre 1964 et 1969. Un vote parlementaire spécial accorda les fonds nécessaires pour financer ce programme, sous réserve cependant que la recherche et le développement de la technologie spatiale soient transférés des laboratoires du gouvernement à l'industrie canadienne[4]. Cette décision visait à encourager le développement de l'industrie canadienne dans le milieu spatial, et servirait, dans les années à venir, à donner naissance au Canada à une industrie de fabrication de matériel spatial[5].

En 1966, le Secrétariat de la Science du Conseil privé nommait un groupe de recherche, pour passer en revue la recherche et le développement financés par le Canada et ayant trait à l'espace et à la haute atmosphère. Le groupe de recherche, présidé par John H. Chapman (souvent appelé le «père du programme spatial canadien»), devait évaluer l'importance des divers projets quant à leur contribution à la connaissance scientifique, à l'enseignement, à la formation technologique ainsi qu'aux intérêts économiques du pays, présents et de longue portée. De plus, il devait établir les principaux thèmes qui, en raison de la situation géographique, de la tradition ou des talents spéciaux, s'appliquaient particulièrement au Canada et pourraient donc servir de principes directeurs quant aux futurs programmes[6].

Après de nombreuses consultations auprès des agences gouvernementales, des universités et de l'industrie impliquées dans la recherche spatiale au Canada, Chapman et ses collègues publiaient, en 1967, un rapport intitulé *Upper Atmosphere and Space Programs in Canada – Special Study No. 1*[7]. Trois recommandations méritent une attention particulière, en raison de leur influence sur l'avenir du programme spatial canadien.

L'adaptation de la technologie spatiale aux priorités canadiennes – idée motrice de toute politique spatiale canadienne – était d'une importance primordiale. Dans un pays comme le Canada – qui est le deuxième plus vaste pays au monde, dont la population se retrouve en grande partie le long de la frontière canado-américaine et qui compte de nombreuses localités éloignées des grands centres et peu peuplées –, les communications spatiales faisaient partie de ces forces fondamentales qui tiennent ensemble les diverses parties du pays. La première recommandation du rapport était donc de prendre les mesures nécessaires pour assurer que le Canada établisse et contrôle son système national de satellites. De plus, le gouvernement devait adopter une politique sur l'utilisation des satellites de télécommunications pour les communications intérieures, qui assureraient un contrôle canadien et un emploi maximum de ressources canadiennes pour la conception et la fabrication de ces systèmes de satellites[8].

Soulignant la nature fragmentée du programme spatial[9], le rapport recommandait également la création d'un organisme central qui pourvoirait à la coordination de la recherche spatiale, et serait autorisé à contracter avec d'autres agences spatiales de ce genre[10].

Finalement, en ce qui a trait aux véhicules et aux installations de lancement, il fut recommandé de ne pas investir des grosses sommes d'argent dans ce domaine, mais plutôt de faire appel aux services de lancement de pays étrangers, selon des conditions jugées raisonnables[11].

1. Programme de satellites de communications

Le potentiel de la technologie des satellites pour les télécommunications à travers le vaste territoire canadien fut vite constaté par les scientifiques et les politiciens. Déjà, en 1966, le ministère des Transports avait signé un contrat avec la Northern Electric Company pour une étude des problèmes techniques et d'autre nature que pouvait poser la mise sur pied d'un réseau de satellites canadiens de télécommunications[12]. À la suite du rapport Chapman, le gouvernement du Canada entreprit une étude sur la nécessité et la praticabilité d'un tel système de satellites. En 1968, C.M. Drury, ministre de l'Industrie, rendait public le rapport, publié sous la forme d'un livre blanc[13], qui recommandait la création et l'exploitation d'un système national de satellites de télécommunications. Ce système assurerait l'extension des services français et anglais de télévision partout au Canada, l'extension de la télévision et de la téléphonie dans le Grand Nord, et la satisfaction de la demande accrue pour les communications Est-Ouest en général[14].

De plus, le livre blanc soulignait qu'il était urgent de mettre en place un système national de satellites de télécommunications, étant donné les difficultés éventuelles quant à l'obtention de fréquences radioélectriques appropriées, ainsi que de positions orbitales[15].

Une exploitation efficace et équitable de ces ressources limitées que sont les fréquences et les emplacements sur l'orbite géostationnaire, ainsi que l'orbite synchrone, exigent une mesure considérable de consultation et de coordination technique entre les pays responsables des divers systèmes de communications par satellites. Les emplacements sur l'orbite et les fréquences sont de nature essentiellement internationale, en ce sens qu'elles ne peuvent être l'apanage d'un seul pays donné [...] Dans la plupart des cas d'utilisation de fréquences radioélectriques, la reconnaissance internationale officielle des exigences des pays a tendance à se faire selon la formule «premier arrivé, premier servi». Par conséquent, on se rend compte de l'urgence qu'il y a à ce que la planification d'un système national canadien aille de l'avant [...][16].

Finalement, le livre blanc contenait certaines suggestions quant à la structure d'un éventuel organisme responsable du système national de communications par satellites.

D'abord, le système devait être une entreprise nationale relevant du gouvernement canadien. Ensuite, les satellites et stations terrestres devaient être contrôlés par un seul organisme afin de faciliter l'échange de nouvelles technologies et d'assurer la réussite financière de l'entreprise. Enfin, l'organisme devait pouvoir vendre ses services efficacement et de façon concurrentielle, et se financer adéquatement[17].

Après avoir pesé le pour et le contre de créer une propriété publique ou privée, le livre blanc recommandait la participation d'intérêts privés dans la future société, «pour peu que la structure de propriété et de contrôle permette le contrôle réel du gouvernement sur les questions d'intérêt national»[18].

Un an plus tard, en 1969, Télésat Canada[19], une corporation (publique) de la couronne, fut créée en vue de mettre sur pied des systèmes de satellites de télécommunications fournissant sur une base commerciale des services de télécommunications, premièrement entre les régions du Canada et deuxièmement, conformément aux arrangements intergouvernementaux appropriés, au-delà des frontières canadiennes.

La Loi de la Télésat Canada préconise également, dans la mesure du possible, l'utilisation du personnel canadien pour la technique, la conception et la fabrication lors des travaux de recherche et de développement portant sur ses systèmes de satellites. Cette disposition confirmait le désir du gouvernement du Canada d'encourager la création d'une industrie canadienne spatiale viable. La formation de Télésat Canada représentait également un changement d'orientation dans la politique spatiale du gouvernement: dorénavant, les recherches spatiales se pencheraient vers des programmes techniques de satellites plutôt que sur des études ionosphériques.

A. Anik-A

L'exploitation du système Télésat a débuté en 1972 avec le lancement du satellite *Anik A-1*[20]. C'est ainsi que le Canada est devenu le premier pays au monde à se doter d'un système national de communications utilisant des satellites géostationnaires[21]. Les satellites *Anik A-2* et *Anik A-3*, qui complètent la série A, furent lancés respectivement en avril 1973 et en mai 1975.

Ces trois satellites de la série A ont été construits par la compagnie américaine Hughes Aircraft Corporation, avec la participation de sous-traitants canadiens[22]. Cette même compagnie allait d'ailleurs fabriquer les satellites de la série B et C[23]. Plusieurs députés aux Communes ont souligné que la participation minimale du Canada dans la construction des satellites *Anik-A*, *B* et *C* ne permettrait pas de développer la technologie spatiale au Canada[24]. C'est ainsi qu'en 1975, le gouvernement décida de doter le Canada d'un maître d'œuvre en vue de la construction d'un satellite canadien[25], et demanda à la compagnie canadienne Spar Aerospatiale Ltée de démontrer, dans les meilleurs délais, son potentiel en matière de satellites de communications[26].

Les satellites *Anik* de la série D, commandés par Télésat Canada, ont été les premiers satellites commerciaux dont le maître d'œuvre a été Spar Aérospatiale. La contribution canadienne se chiffrait au-dessus de 50 %, avec Hughes Aircraft agissant à titre de sous-traitant[27]. Une subvention de 19,4 millions de dollars a été accordée par le gouvernement canadien à Télésat Canada, destinée à défrayer les coûts supplémentaires occasionnés par la construction de la série D par un fournisseur canadien[28].

Les retombées économiques de cette décision ne commencent qu'à faire surface. En 1982, le gouvernement brésilien signait un contrat avec Spar pour la construction de deux satellites de télécommunications et des stations terriennes connexes[29]. En 1985, le premier des deux satellites brésiliens, *EMBRATEL*, a été mis en orbite avec succès[30]. Ce projet spatial marquait deux «premières» importantes:

- le premier effort conjoint canado-brésilien visant à procurer au Brésil les avantages des communications par satellites;
- le premier maître d'œuvre canadien pour les satellites et l'équipement au sol connexe à servir les besoins d'un marché international.

Plus récemment, Télésat plaçait une commande auprès de la compagnie Spar pour la construction de la génération des satellites *Anik-E*[31]. Ce contrat ne pourra que rehausser la renommée de Spar et l'aider à augmenter ses services sur le marché international.

B. Hermès et Anik-B

Les satellites *Anik-A* se classaient dans la catégorie des satellites dits de «point-à-point», c'est-à-dire que les signaux sont transportés par les transmetteurs grâce aux moyens conventionnels de communications (micro-ondes ou câbles terrestres) afin d'être reçus par une station terrienne émettrice. À son tour, celle-ci transmet les signaux à un satellite qui les relaie à une station terrienne receveuse chargée d'expédier les messages contenus dans l'émission aux récepteurs individuels et ce, par la voie des moyens conventionnels ci-haut mentionnés. En d'autres termes, les messages de télécommunications doivent passer par les stations terriennes, dont la complexité et le coût ne sont pas négligeables. La nécessité de construire de telles stations complique davantage les communications dans les endroits isolés du Nord canadien.

Dans le but de résoudre ce problème, le Centre de recherches sur les communications (CRC), exploité par le ministère des Communications[32], propose qu'en augmentant la puissance de radiation, la distribution par satellites pourrait être remplacée par la radiodiffusion directe par satellites (RDS). Les signaux émis par RDS seraient reçus par tout poste de radio ou de télévision conventionnel. Ainsi, le besoin de stations terriennes sophistiquées pourrait désormais être éliminé[33].

Afin de prouver ce concept, le Canada embarque sur la mise au point et l'utilisation du satellite technologique de télécommunications, connu aussi sous le nom de *Hermès*. Avec la collaboration de la NASA et de l'Agence spatiale européenne (ESA), ce satellite expérimental de radiodiffusion construit au Canada constitue une première mondiale en utilisant les bandes des 14/12 GHz[34] à des puissances très élevées.

Ayant fait des expériences quant à l'utilisation des bandes 14/12 GHz, le Canada devient le premier État[35] à utiliser ces bandes à des fins commerciales, et ce, avec la deuxième génération de satellites *Anik*. Lancé en janvier 1978, le satellite *Anik-B* est destiné à compléter les capacités opérationnelles de Télésat Canada dans les bandes des 6/4 GHz[36], tout en servant au programme suivi de projets pilotes sur les télécommunications dans les bandes des 14/12 GHz.

C. Anik-C et Anik-D

Les trois satellites nationaux de communications de la série *Anik-C*[37] font usage des bandes de fréquences 14/12 GHz. L'avantage est qu'elles ne sont pas partagées avec les systèmes de télécommunications terrestres à micro-ondes[38]. Ces satellites seront l'organe essentiel des télécommunications Est-Ouest pendant les années 80.

Les deux satellites *Anik-D*[39] fonctionnent dans les bandes 6/4 GHz, et ont été conçus pour «remplacer et étendre les services maintenant remplis par l'intermédiaire des séries de satellites *Anik-A*, dans la bande 4/6 GHz ou *Anik-B*. Les faisceaux de transmission et de réception sur le satellite fourniront une couverture de tout le Canada»[40].

2. Organisation des activités spatiales

Comme il est souligné dans le rapport Chapman, la nature fragmentée du programme canadien de recherche spatiale nécessitait la création d'une agence centrale pour coordonner toutes ses activités. D'après le groupe de recherche, l'absence d'une telle agence avait déjà engendré de sérieux problèmes, puisque aucune délimitation des objectifs technologiques, scientifiques, économiques et sociaux du Canada dans l'espace n'avait été précisée:

> The absence of a national mission-oriented agency with overall responsibility for upper-atmosphere and space activities in Canada has resulted in fragmented programs, divided responsibility, and serious omissions in planning. These deficiencies are bound to become more serious in the future, and could lead to tragic consequences for Canada in loss of technological opportunity, and in gradual erosion on national control over resources and domestic communications[41].

Le 4 juillet 1967, en conformité avec les dispositions de la Loi du Conseil de la science du Canada[42], O.M. Solandt, président du Conseil de la science, soumettait au premier ministre de l'époque, Lester B. Pearson, un rapport intitulé *Report No. 1 – A Space Program for Canada*[43]. Le Conseil, dans le but «d'assurer une approche intégrée de l'utilisation de l'espace pour le bénéfice du peuple canadien»[44], recommandait la création d'une agence centrale relevant du gouvernement du Canada, responsable de l'avancement des connaissances canadiennes dans la science et la technologie de la haute atmosphère et de l'espace; de promouvoir le développement de l'industrie spatiale canadienne; et de planifier et mettre en vigueur un programme spatial canadien[45].

Quant à la structure d'une telle agence, il fut suggéré qu'une corporation de la couronne soit créée, avec un conseil exécutif formé de membres du secteur privé, des universités et de la fonction publique, et ayant comme mandat, *inter alia*:

- d'aviser le ministre responsable sur tout sujet ayant trait à l'utilisation de l'espace par le Canada;
- de planifier et de coordonner tous les projets de recherche et de développement dans le domaine spatial entrepris par des agences ou départements gouvernementaux, ou par les universités et l'industrie pour le gouvernement;
- de coordonner tous les programmes spatiaux scientifiques incluant l'élaboration de procédures et de critères de sélection pour les expérimentations de fusées-sondes et de satellites;
- de promouvoir la collaboration avec d'autres agences (nationales et internationales) pour une utilisation plus efficace de l'espace;
- d'initier et de conclure des contrats sur tout projet dans la haute atmosphère ou dans l'espace, tels qu'approuvés par le ministre responsable[46].

Le Comité interministériel sur l'espace

En 1969, le Cabinet créait le Comité interministériel sur l'espace (CIE) afin d'assurer la coordination des activités spatiales des différents ministères fédéraux[47]. Parmi les ministères membres du CIE, on trouve:

- le ministère des Communications;
- le ministère de l'Énergie, des Mines et des Ressources;
- le ministère de l'Environnement;
- le ministère des Affaires extérieures;
- le ministère des Pêches et des Océans;
- le ministère de l'Industrie et du Commerce;
- le ministère de la Défense nationale;
- le Conseil national de recherches du Canada;
- le ministère d'État aux Sciences et à la Technologie.

De plus, le Conseil du Trésor et le ministère de la Santé et du Bien-Être social participent aux activités du CIE à titre d'observateurs. Jusqu'en 1971, le CIE faisait rapport au Comité du Cabinet sur la science et la technologie. Lorsque ce dernier fut dissout, le CIE allait dorénavant se reporter au nouveau ministère d'État aux Sciences et à la Technologie.

À l'origine, le CIE avait comme mandat d'examiner les activités spatiales canadiennes, incluant celles des ministères et organismes fédéraux, des universités et de l'industrie, et présenter des recommandations relatives à la politique et à la planification du programme à la lumière des intérêts, des besoins et des possibilités du pays[48].

Les fonctions du CIE allaient évoluer parallèlement aux décisions de politiques spatiales prises au fil des années.

En 1974, une politique spatiale canadienne fut adoptée, dont les principes fondamentaux peuvent être résumés ainsi:

- le gouvernement entérine le principe voulant que les installations industrielles canadiennes de conception et de construction des systèmes spatiaux soient conservées et améliorées par le biais d'une politique délibérée de transfert au secteur privé des activités de recherche et de développement spatiaux du gouvernement;
- les politiques d'achat du gouvernement doivent encourager la création d'une capacité viable de recherche, de développement et de fabrication au sein de l'industrie canadienne;
- le Canada doit continuer de faire appel aux autres pays pour le matériel et les services de lancement et doit augmenter les possibilités d'accès à de tels services en participant aux programmes spatiaux des pays fournisseurs;
- les ministères concernés doivent fournir des plans visant à assurer que dans la mesure du possible, les systèmes de satellites du Canada soient conçus et mis au point au Canada, par des citoyens canadiens, à partir d'éléments canadiens;
- le Canada doit avant tout utiliser l'espace pour les applications qui contribuent directement à la réalisation des objectifs nationaux;
- l'utilisation des systèmes spatiaux pour la réalisation de certains objectifs spécifiques doit se faire par des activités proposées et financées par les ministères et les organismes dans le cadre des mandats qui leur sont attribués[49].

Dorénavant, le CIE est responsable de la coordination de l'approvisionnement des engins spatiaux, dans le but de maintenir au Canada une industrie viable de fabrication d'engins spatiaux. De plus, compte tenu du volume de travail de l'industrie, le CIE doit fournir au Conseil du Trésor, à chaque automne, une liste de tous les projets de programmes spatiaux par ordre de priorité. Ce document doit également donner la justification et l'évaluation de leur impact sur l'industrie spatiale canadienne.

Quoiqu'une évaluation au CIE en tant que mécanisme de coordination des activités spatiales canadiennes dépasse le cadre de cet article, il serait bon de souligner que le Conseil des sciences du Canada n'a jamais abandonné sa recommandation de 1967 pour la création d'un organisme central de planification et de mise en œuvre d'un programme spatial canadien[50]. Dans un récent document intitulé *Background Material on the Optimum Size and Scope of the Canadian Space Program*[51], le Conseil des sciences du Canada réitérait le besoin de créer une agence centrale, relevant d'un seul ministère et responsable de l'administration de tous les projets spatiaux. Selon le Conseil, cet objectif était davantage urgent en raison de la décision du gouvernement de participer au projet international de la station spatiale[52]. Selon celui-ci, le CIE ne possède aucune influence quant à la répartition et l'allocation des sommes. En effet, les budgets sont contrôlés par les différents ministères membres du CIE, et – citant un article du *Financial Post* – le Conseil confirme «[...] qu'en pratique, l'établissement des priorités par le CIE équivaut à un exercice de marchandage interdépartemental plutôt qu'à une évaluation rationnelle»[53]. Depuis lors, d'autres propositions ont été avancées dans le même sens, la plus récente étant celle de l'Institut canadien des recherches avancées[54].

À la suite de ces recommandations, il fut annoncé, lors du Discours du Trône inaugurant la deuxième session de la 33e Législature:

> Vu l'importance de la haute technologie dans le développement économique du Canada, mon gouvernement déposera un projet de loi créant une agence spatiale canadienne, qui opérera dans un contexte de coopération internationale, car c'est le plus sûr moyen de réaliser des percées technologiques dans l'exploitation pacifique de l'espace. La nouvelle agence travaillera de concert avec les provinces, l'industrie et les universités, de sorte que les avantages de la participation du Canada à l'aventure spatiale rejailliront sur l'ensemble des Canadiens[55].

Cette déclaration s'inscrit dans le cadre plus général d'une politique scientifique nationale annoncée en mars 1986 par le ministre d'État aux Sciences et à la Technologie, Frank Oberle, selon laquelle, pour la première fois de son histoire, le Canada fixerait ses priorités scientifiques en accord avec les provinces et les milieux scientifiques[56].

3. La coopération

En favorisant le développement des techniques spatiales au sein de l'industrie canadienne, le Canada rejetait une politique reposant sur la dépendance totale vis-à-vis des pays étrangers. Parallèlement, on était conscient que premièrement, certains projets étaient trop onéreux et complexes pour être entrepris par un seul pays, et deuxièmement, que le Canada ne pourrait se permettre de construire des installations de lancement qui lui auraient coûté des millions de dollars par an, pendant de nombreuses années à venir[57]. La politique spatiale du Canada n'a donc pas eu pour but l'autosuffisance complète.

> Cette politique implique que le Canada doit réussir à trouver des partenaires pour ses activités spatiales selon des termes et des conditions qui sont à la satisfaction mutuelle des parties en cause[58].

Par conséquent, le Canada a conclu un certain nombre d'accords bilatéraux ou multilatéraux en vue d'entreprendre des programmes scientifiques et techniques communs. Certaines de ces expériences conjointes dans les domaines clés des activités spatiales du Canada seront discutées ci-dessous[59].

A. Le Canada et les États-Unis

Les États-Unis ont été le principal partenaire spatial du Canada. Depuis le lancement du satellite canadien *Alouette I* en 1962 par la NASA, un certain nombre d'expériences communes ont suivi, et ce, dans différents domaines de l'exploitation spatiale. Les principes de la coopération bilatérale, élaborés la même année, et suivis dans la plupart des projets subséquents, étaient les suivants:

- aucun fonds ne devait franchir la frontière au niveau gouvernemental;
- les tâches étaient définies pour chaque pays;
- chaque pays devait être responsable de sa partie du programme;
- les phases de transition technique, administrative et financière entre les deux pays étaient définies avec beaucoup de soin[60].

Satellites de télécommunications

Dans le domaine des satellites de télécommunications, les deux pays ont entrepris des expériences utiles sur le comportement de l'ionosphère et ce, avec les satellites *Alouette I* et *Alouette II*, lancés en 1962 et 1965 respectivement, de même qu'avec les satellites *Isis* (*I* et *II*) lancés en 1969 et en 1971. Depuis l'automne 1974, le Canada a, en outre, mené une douzaine d'expériences grâce aux satellites d'application de la technologie américaine (ATS-6). Tous les satellites de télécommunications du Canada ont été lancés par les États-Unis[61]. De loin, le projet commun le plus important a été la mise au point et l'utilisation du satellite de technologie et de communications (CTS), connu aussi sous le nom de *Hermès*[62].

Un accord fut signé le 20 avril 1971 entre le ministère des Communications canadien et la NASA en vue d'un programme commun visant, entre autres, les objectifs suivants:

> développer et tester en vol un tube amplificateur mobile à haute puissance, ayant une efficacité de plus de 50 %, avec une production de puissance saturée de 200 watts à 12 GHz; et poursuivre des expériences de systèmes de communications par satellites, utilisant les bandes de 12 et 14 GHz, avec des stations terriennes transportables à bas prix[63].

Le CTS a été mis au point et construit par le Canada. Les États-Unis ont fourni un amplificateur (*travelling wave tube*) de 200 watts et lancèrent le satellite le 17 janvier 1976, en orbite géostationnaire à 116 degrés de longitude ouest. Bien que conçu pour fonctionner pendant une période de deux ans, ce satellite est demeuré actif pendant plus de trois ans, jusqu'au 24 novembre 1979[64]. Les deux États ont mené diverses expériences, en utilisant le satellite selon une alternance quotidienne. Chaque État a construit ses propres terminaux de réception et a choisi les expériences. Celles-ci comprenaient les télécommunications et la télémédecine, de même que des services de santé communautaires, éducatifs, et des services spéciaux.

Le projet CTS a été couronné de succès. Il a fourni une occasion additionnelle de s'assurer de la praticabilité et de la valeur des petites stations terminales terrestres de radiodiffusion[65] aux États-Unis. Étant donné que le CTS avait un contenu canadien à 80 %[66], il a servi à stimuler les possibilités de l'industrie manufacturière spatiale canadienne et lui a permis de devenir compétitive au sein du marché mondial pour la construction de satellites de radiodiffusion. Le CTS a utilisé, pour la première fois, les bandes de fréquences de 14/12 GHz, démontrant ainsi l'opportunité de l'utilisation de ces bandes pour les satellites de radiodiffusion de l'avenir. Par-dessus tout, il a stimulé la création de services de radiodiffusion directe par satellites. Grâce à sa grande puissance de radiodiffusion, seulement de petits terminaux terrestres peu coûteux étaient nécessaires pour fournir des relais de télévision. Encouragé par le succès du projet CTS, le ministère canadien des Communications a prévu d'autres expériences similaires avec le satellite *Anik-B* de Télésat Canada[67].

Programme de satellites de télédétection

La télédétection de la Terre par satellites représente une des plus importantes formes d'exploitation commerciale de l'espace. Cette technologie permet de définir la nature et l'état des ressources naturelles, les éléments et les phénomènes naturels et l'environnement de la Terre au moyen d'observations et de mesures faites à partir de plate-formes spatiales[68]. Les données ainsi obtenues se sont avérées de plus en plus précieuses dans des domaines aussi variés que la cartographie, l'agriculture, la sylviculture, l'océanographie, la géologie et l'hydrologie. On ne saurait trop souligner l'importance de telles données pour un pays comme le Canada, dont l'économie est basée sur l'exploitation des ressources et le commerce.

LANDSAT

Les données fournies par le système de satellites *LANDSAT* des États-Unis peuvent être captées au Canada en vertu de l'accord bilatéral de 1971 entre le Canada et les États-Unis pour l'étude des ressources terrestres[69]. Lancé en juillet 1972, le satellite *ERTS 1* (par la suite appelé *LANDSAT 1*) a été suivi de *LANDSAT 2* et de *LANDSAT 3*, en janvier 1975 et mars 1978 respectivement[70]. L'accord de 1971 a été renouvelé et prorogé d'abord en 1975[71], et ensuite en 1980[72].

Le satellite *LANDSAT 4*, lancé en juillet 1982[73], présente pour sa part une meilleure résolution de la couleur ainsi qu'une meilleure capacité de détails et d'identification. Afin de pouvoir capter ces données, les deux stations terrestres canadiennes de Prince Albert (Saskatchewan) et de Shoe Cove (Terre-Neuve) ont dû être considérablement modifiées[74]. Le dernier satellite, *LANDSAT 5*, a été lancé en mars 1985[75].

Programme d'élaboration du télémanipulateur de la navette spatiale

Le 23 juin 1976, un mémorandum d'accord était signé entre la NASA et le Conseil national de recherches du Canada en vue d'un programme de coopération pour la mise au point et l'acquisition d'un télémanipulateur de navette spatiale[76]. Spar Aérospatiale Ltée a fourni le télémanipulateur CANADARM, un «bras mécanique» utilisé pour déployer et récupérer les instruments, satellites et engins spatiaux de la soute de la navette spatiale[77]. Les avantages d'un tel dispositif ont été clairement démontrés lors de la réparation, dans l'espace, du satellite *Solar Maximum* en avril 1984[78], et du récupérage des satellites *PALAPA-B* et *Westar VI*, en novembre de la même année[79].

Par cette contribution technique au programme de la navette spatiale, le Canada visait à obtenir un accès préférentiel aux services de lancement et à créer un marché à long terme pour les produits fabriqués par le Canada dans le domaine spatial[80].

B. Le Canada et l'Agence spatiale européenne

Désireux d'étendre et de diversifier ses relations avec d'autres États ou groupes d'États, le Canada ne pouvait que considérer favorablement les perspectives que lui ouvrait la création de l'Agence spatiale européenne (ESA). Cette dernière a été formée par une convention signée le 30 mai 1975[81] par onze pays européens[82] et devait remplacer deux organisations européennes établies depuis 1962[83], tout en élargissant le champ d'activités de celles-ci, en vue de doter l'Europe «d'une organisation spatiale européenne unique qui permette d'accroître l'efficacité de l'ensemble de l'effort spatial européen par une meilleure utilisation des ressources actuellement consacrées à l'espace et de définir un programme spatial européen ayant des fins exclusivement pacifiques»[84].

Les premières relations formelles entre le Canada et l'Europe, dans le domaine spatial, ont été établies dès le début des années 70 d'abord dans le cadre du programme de satellites aéronautiques *AEROSAT*[85], et ensuite dans les secteurs des télécommunications[86] et de la télédétection[87].

C'est ainsi que dès la création de fait de l'ESA, le Canada demanda de siéger comme observateur au Conseil de l'Agence. Cette demande a été accordée lors de sa première réunion, en juin 1975. Les contacts entre les organismes gouvernementaux canadiens et l'exécutif de l'ESA[88] se multiplièrent et, en 1977, lors de la première réunion du Conseil, siégeant au niveau ministériel, Jeanne Sauvé, présente à titre de ministre des Communications du gouvernement du Canada, annonçait qu'elle était autorisée «à entreprendre des entretiens exploratoires en vue de définir les termes possibles d'une intensification de nos relations»[89]. Cette démarche, poursuivait-elle, se justifie non seulement par «une convergence entre vos intérêts et les nôtres», mais aussi par «une possibilité réelle de réciprocité et de complémentarité dans nos relations futures», et elle demandait que sa proposition soit placée «dans le cadre de la politique extérieure canadienne visant à intensifier les relations politiques et commerciales entre le Canada et l'Europe»[90].

Outre le souhait de diversifier le champ d'application de ses activités de coopération spatiale, le Canada désirait également s'immiscer, dès le début, dans la planification et la programmation de l'Agence. Tel que souligné par John H. Chapman:

It is our experience that lack of administrative arrangements for cooperation in the early planning stages makes participation in many developing programs at a later time too costly to present a real opportunity.

[...] involvement [...] in the early program planning of the [European Space] Agency [...] would allow Canadian industry as well as user agencies to weigh short-term and long-term costs and benefits at the program-level, as well as in regard to implications for the domestic balance of payments. We have also held preliminary discussions with Japanese agencies with a view to identifying similar long-term planning[91].

L'intervention du ministre canadien ayant été accueillie favorablement, les négociations pour établir le cadre de coopération du Canada dans les activités de l'Agence furent immédiatement entamées par l'Exécutif.

Soulignons que le contexte juridique dans lequel se sont ouvertes les négociations visant à définir le nouveau statut du Canada était quelque peu problématique. La Convention portant création de l'ESA prévoyait, à côté des États «membres», l'existence éventuelle d'États «membres associés». Les premiers sont ceux qui ont signé et ratifié la Convention ou qui y ont adhéré ultérieurement[92]; ils sont tenus de participer aux activités obligatoires et de contribuer aux frais communs fixes de l'Agence[93]. Les seconds sont les États non membres qui s'engagent à coopérer avec l'Agence en contribuant au minimum au financement de projets futurs et pour lesquels les modalités détaillées de l'association sont définies, cas par cas, par le Conseil de l'Agence[94]. La Convention prévoyait de plus l'hypothèse d'une coopération entre l'Agence et un État non membre ou une organisation internationale, d'une façon générale ou dans le cadre d'un programme déterminé auquel un État non membre ou une organisation internationale demande à participer[95]. Une différence fondamentale existe donc entre, d'une part, la qualité d'État membre ou d'État membre associé, qui implique un intérêt pour les activités de l'Agence dans leur ensemble, entraînant des droits et des obligations et, d'autre part, la qualité d'État ou organisation internationale extérieure à l'Agence n'entretenant avec celle-ci qu'un lien de coopération limitée[96].

Le problème qui se posait dans le cas du Canada était qu'il n'avait pas l'intention d'accéder au statut d'«État membre», ni de demander celui d'«État membre associé». En contrepartie, le Canada s'intéressait à certains aspects du fonctionnement de l'Agence et recherchait plus qu'une coopération limitée à des échanges superficiels[97]. Il s'agissait donc «de donner au Canada un statut voisin de celui de membre associé (tel du moins que ce statut pouvait être imaginé à l'époque, faute de précédent) sans pour autant lui reconnaître formellement cette qualité»[98].

Une formule intermédiaire fut finalement adoptée, d'où la signature, le 9 décembre 1978, de l'Accord de l'Agence spatiale européenne et le Canada en matière de coopération[99].

L'accord de 1978

Aux termes de cet accord, le Canada participe aux études générales concernant les projets futurs, études qui font partie des activités de base de l'Agence[100]. La participation du Canada peut également s'étendre à d'autres éléments des activités obligatoires, facultatives ou opérationnelles de l'ESA[101]. Il contribue aux frais d'exécution de ces études à un taux calculé sur la base de son revenu national moyen[102]. En outre, le Canada accepte de verser une contribution de 1 % aux frais communs fixes nets du budget de l'Agence, à titre d'acte tangible de son appartenance à la collectivité. Ce pourcentage est sujet à augmentation en fonction de l'évolution de la participation du Canada aux activités de l'ESA[103].

En ce qui concerne les réunions des organes délibérant de l'Agence, l'article V de l'accord de 1978 prévoit ce qui suit:

- le Canada peut être représenté au Conseil de l'Agence par deux délégués au plus, qui peuvent être accompagnés de conseillers. Ces délégués ont voix délibérative pour les questions relatives aux études de projets futurs ou à toute autre activité de l'Agence à laquelle le Canada pourra participer à l'avenir; ils ont voix consultative pour les autres questions;
- le Canada a voix consultative dans les organes subsidiaires de l'Agence qui sont compétents, à un titre quelconque, pour traiter des activités auxquelles le Canada participe lorsque ces organes examinent des questions relatives auxdites activités; il a voix délibérative lors de la prise des décisions s'y rapportant;
- le Canada est représenté, avec voix délibérative, aux conseils directeurs de programmes de l'Agence pour les activités facultatives auxquelles il participe;
- le Canada peut demander à être représenté en qualité d'observateur aux réunions de tout organe subsidiaire ou Conseil directeur de programme lorsque d'autres questions y sont traitées.

Finalement, l'accord (qui est entré en vigueur le 1er janvier 1979) prévoyait expressément que sa durée d'application serait limitée à cinq ans à partir de cette date (soit jusqu'au 31 décembre 1983)[104]. C'est ainsi que le 9 janvier 1984, le Canada et l'ESA ont signé un accord concernant la coopération entre le Canada et l'Agence spatiale européenne[105], et dont les modalités de coopération sont pour la plupart identiques à celles prévues dans l'accord de 1978, notamment le statut du Canada à titre «d'État coopérant»[106]. Cet accord demeurera en vigueur jusqu'au 31 décembre 1988.

Projets coopératifs

Programme préparatoire européen de satellites de télédétection (ERS)

Tel qu'il est défini, ce programme préparatoire européen de satellites de télédétection a pour principal objectif de préparer le développement du secteur spatial du programme européen par le biais d'études, et, éventuellement, d'activités de prédéveloppement d'éléments critiques de technologie, en tenant compte des travaux réalisés par les États membres de l'ESA dans le cadre de leurs activités nationales de télédétection[107].

En ce qui concerne la télédétection, un programme canadien de satellites d'observation de la Terre (SURSAT) avait été mis sur pied en 1977, afin de contribuer à satisfaire les besoins du Canada en données de télédétection[108]. La participation du Canada au projet ERS lui permettra de partager les coûts des activités des satellites d'observation terrestre, tout en soulignant la nécessité pour le Canada de développer son potentiel industriel pour la réalisation du matériel des satellites d'observation terrestre et des technologies associées.

C'est donc dans ce contexte que le gouvernement du Canada a approuvé sa participation au Programme préparatoire européen de satellites de télédétection de l'ESA[109].

Soulignons que le 16 mai 1986 a eu lieu l'inauguration d'une station de réception à Gatineau. Cette station assure la couverture de l'Est du pays, et recevra des données du satellite français *SPOT*[110] et, plus tard, du satellite européen *ERS-1*.

Programme L-SAT

Ce programme a pour objectif de développer une grande plate-forme poly-valente conçue pour une série d'applications futures dans le domaine des télécommunications, ainsi que la possibilité de développer et de démontrer en orbite une charge utile de télécommunications de pointe. L-SAT consistera en un grand autobus spatial transportant diverses charges de télécommunications pour les États participants.

Le Canada a toujours été très actif dans le domaine des télécommunications, et, en demandant de participer au programme L-SAT, il poursuivait plusieurs objectifs:

- tisser des liens plus solides entre le Canada et l'Europe;
- avoir accès à une grande plate-forme polyvalente afin de l'utiliser dans un programme canadien de satellites de diffusion directe;
- augmenter les exportations du Canada grâce à la collaboration entre les industries canadienne et européenne[111].

De leur côté, les participants européens considéraient que l'acquis technologique et la structure industrielle du Canada constitueraient un apport significatif au programme L-SAT. Le Canada a participé à la phase de définition et à la phase relais du programme L-SAT[112], et intervient actuellement à la phase de développement du programme L-SAT et aux principes de commercialisation ultérieure[113]. En 1983, la compagnie Spar Aérospatiale signait un contrat avec la British Aerospace pour l'exécution d'importants travaux de sous-traitance liés au programme L-SAT[114].

Programme Olympus

Ce programme – également connu sous le nom de «Grand satellite de communications» – a pour objectif le développement d'une grande plate-forme de communications à fonctions multiples, comme la radiodiffusion directe, les communications mobiles et la télédétection[115].

La compagnie Spar Aérospatiale Ltée travaille à l'heure actuelle au programme Olympus, et essaie de déterminer si Olympus pourra être utilisé dans le cadre du programme canadien M-SAT[116].

C. La coopération multilatérale

Outre ces projets bilatéraux, le Canada participe activement à des projets multilatéraux, notamment dans le domaine de l'utilisation des satellites pour des services mobiles[117] à des fins de communications concernant la navigation aéronautique et maritime[118].

AEROSAT

Un mémorandum d'entente fut signé en 1974 par le Canada, l'Agence spatiale européenne et les États-Unis[119], prévoyant l'établissement d'un programme conjoint d'évaluation AEROSAT, afin de déterminer les exigences d'un système opérationnel fournissant des services de télécommunications améliorées entre les aéronefs et les centres de contrôle de la circulation aérienne. Depuis 1974, le programme a été troublé par l'insatisfaction des utilisateurs, ainsi que des retards, des disputes contractuelles et du désenchantement général de la part du Congrès des États-Unis. Un manque de fonds de la part du FAA a entraîné l'abandon de ce programme[120].

SARSAT/COSPAS

Le projet SARSAT/COSPAS est un programme expérimental entrepris en commun par le Canada, la France, les États-Unis et l'Union soviétique[121] pour démontrer l'utilité des engins spatiaux dans la détection et la localisation des signaux d'urgence provenant d'aéronefs ou de navires en détresse. Depuis le lancement du premier satellite en septembre 1982, l'information fournie par le système SARSAT/COSPAS a été utilisée lors de nombreuses détresses[122].

4. Nouvelles initiatives du programme spatial canadien

Le gouvernement a rendu public en mai 1986 son intention d'étoffer davantage le programme spatial canadien[123]: des démarches à long terme visant à assurer une participation suivie des Canadiens aux avantages économiques et sociaux conférés par les progrès de la technologie spatiale. Le nouveau programme canadien est axé sur la coopération internationale en vue d'atteindre cet objectif.

Station spatiale

Une participation canadienne dans le projet américain de station spatiale habitée représente un élément clé du programme canadien[124]. Dans le cadre de ce projet, le Canada développera et construira un centre de service mobile en affinant davantage les techniques mises au point pour le télémanipulateur de la navette spatiale. Un programme de perfectionnement des usagers de la station a été lancé afin de développer les capacités des universités et des industries canadiennes à utiliser le milieu unique qu'est l'espace pour la recherche et la fabrication, dès que la station sera en place, vers le milieu des années 90[125].

Programme d'astronautes canadiens

Ce programme permettra de poursuivre les expériences spatiales qui nécessitent une intervention humaine, et ce, au profit de la communauté scientifique et industrielle[126].

Coopération avec l'Europe

Le Canada compte poursuivre sa coopération avec l'Europe et l'ESA. Il a notamment l'intention de participer au projet *Hermès* de l'ESA. Limitée par la taille, *Hermès* sera une toute petite navette comparée aux modèles américains[127]. Cet avion spatial sera donc capable d'emporter hommes et fret en orbite terrestre et de les ramener au sol.

Communications

Dans le domaine des communications, le programme spatial prévoit l'appui du gouvernement pour un nouveau système commercial de communications, le M-SAT. Ce dernier assurera une plus grande fiabilité aux communications téléphoniques et aux transmissions de données, notamment dans les régions éloignées et isolées du pays[128].

Système de télédétection

Le programme spatial préconise également la poursuite du développement des techniques de télédétection en vue d'une meilleure gestion de nos ressources naturelles et de services d'information améliorés, dans les secteurs agricole, forestier, météorologique et océanique.

Le financement de RADARSAT[129], un système canadien de télédétection, a fait l'objet d'une étude sérieuse au cours de l'année 1987.

II. LE CANADA ET L'ÉLABORATION DU DROIT SPATIAL

Si l'idée de l'exploration et de l'utilisation de l'espace extra-atmosphérique hante l'esprit humain depuis l'Antiquité[130], le lancement par l'Union soviétique, le 4 octobre 1957, du premier satellite artificiel de la Terre, *Spoutnik I*, avec ses implications politiques, militaires, scientifiques et économiques, imposait aux États-Unis, comme à tous les autres États, de définir d'urgence les principes sur lesquels la poursuite des activités dans l'espace devait être fondée. Dans la conjoncture politique de l'époque, le potentiel militaire de cette nouvelle technologie allait motiver les premières interventions. Ce sont donc les Nations Unies qui ont été le berceau dans lequel est né – et continue de se former – le droit de l'espace.

1. Le Comité des utilisations pacifiques de l'espace extra-atmosphérique

Faisant suite à une proposition américaine (fortement secondée par le Canada) de janvier 1957, l'Assemblée générale des Nations Unies recommandait, lors de sa 12e session par sa résolution 1148 (XII), la réglementation, la limitation et la réduction équilibrées de toutes les forces armées et de tous les armements, et l'interdiction de certaines armes de destruction massive[131]. En outre, l'Assemblée générale demandait aux pays intéressés d'«étudier en commun un système d'inspection qui permettrait de s'assurer que l'envoi d'objets à travers l'espace extra-atmosphérique se fera à des fins exclusivement pacifiques et scientifiques»[132].

En vertu des termes de sa résolution 1348 (XIII) de 1958[133], l'Assemblée générale créait un comité *ad hoc* sur les utilisations pacifiques de l'espace extra-atmosphérique, composé de représentants de 18 pays, dont le Canada[134].

Un an plus tard, le comité *ad hoc* fut remplacé par le Comité (permanent) sur les utilisations pacifiques de l'espace extra-atmosphérique (CUPEAA)[135], qui se compose de deux sous-comités, l'un technique et l'autre, juridique. Une sérieuse controverse entre les États-Unis et l'Union soviétique quant à l'effectif et le processus de décision du CUPEAA empêcha ce dernier de fonctionner jusqu'en 1962[136]. Depuis lors, le CUPEAA est le creuset dans lequel s'est effectuée l'élaboration des cinq traités internationaux qui forment la base du droit de l'espace proprement dit.

Le texte le plus important, le Traité de l'espace de 1967[137], constitue la Charte du droit spatial. S'appuyant sur ce traité, quatre autres textes ont été préparés:

- l'Accord sur le retour et le sauvetage des astronautes, et la restitution des objets lancés dans l'espace extra-atmosphérique (1968)[138];
- la Convention sur la responsabilité internationale pour les dommages causés par des objets spatiaux (1972)[139];
- la Convention sur l'immatriculation des objets lancés dans l'espace extra-atmosphérique (1975)[140];
- l'Accord régissant les activités des États sur la Lune et les autres corps célestes (1979)[141].

Tous ces traités sont en vigueur à l'heure actuelle, le Canada ayant ratifié les quatre premiers accords.

La participation active du Canada au développement du droit de l'espace est directement liée à ces accomplissements technologiques dans le domaine spatial. Dans le cadre de sa politique spatiale, le Canada a reconnu, à maintes reprises, que l'utilisation des technologies spatiales doit être:

> renforcée en participant aux activités internationales pour l'utilisation et la réglementation des activités dans l'espace, en négociant des accords qui assureront un accès continu à la science, la technologie et aux installations nécessaires, et en restant au courant des activités spatiales de pays étrangers, afin de pouvoir répondre rapidement au niveau national aux opportunités ainsi qu'aux menaces à la souveraineté nationale[142].

C'est ainsi que la contribution du Canada dans l'élaboration du droit spatial ne constitue pas uniquement une réponse aux préoccupations de diplomates et d'avocats; mais, au contraire, elle «est basée solidement dans la réalisation des intérêts à multiples facettes d'un pays qui possède, *inter alia,* les moyens de fabriquer des objets pour l'espace sans pouvoir les lancer, une plus grande capacité de recevoir des signaux de satellites de radiodiffusion que de produire le contenu de la programmation, et des stations terriennes pour l'interprétation de données provenant de satellites de téléobservation sans pour autant posséder ses propres satellites»[143].

Outre le CUPEAA, le Canada participe activement aux activités de plusieurs autres organisations impliquées dans la formulation du droit de l'espace, comme l'Organisme culturel, scientifique et éducationnel des Nations Unies (UNESCO), l'Organisation mondiale pour la propriété intellectuelle (OMPI) et l'Union internationale des télécommunications (UIT). De plus, le Canada est un État membre de l'Organisation internationale de télécommunications par satellites (INTELSAT)[144] et de l'Organisation internationale de satellites maritimes (INMARSAT)[145]. L'analyse approfondie de la contribution canadienne aux activités de ces organismes dépasse le cadre de cette étude. Nous nous limiterons donc aux différents problèmes discutés au Sous-comité juridique du CUPEAA et, plus récemment, à la Conférence sur le désarmement (CD)[146].

2. La «voie canadienne» et le développement du droit de l'espace

Quatre sujets occupent essentiellement le Sous-comité juridique, les uns de longue date, les autres depuis une époque plus récente. On citera: la délimitation de l'espace, la téléobservation de la terre, la radiodiffusion directe par satellites (RDS) et l'utilisation de sources d'énergie nucléaire dans l'espace (SEN). Le Canada a contribué de façon significative aux discussions portant sur les deux derniers sujets[147].

A. Radiodiffusion directe par satellites (RDS)

En augmentant la puissance de radiation, la distribution par satellites pourrait être remplacée par la RDS. Les signaux émis par RDS peuvent être reçus par tout poste de radio ou de télévision conventionnel, éliminant ainsi le besoin d'antennes complexes ou de stations terriennes sophistiquées.

En 1968, un groupe de travail du CUPEAA sur la RDS fut établi et chargé d'élaborer des principes pour la réglementation de la RDS[148]. Deux écoles de pensée se sont affrontées: les libéraux, partisans de la libre circulation des idées, et les protectionnistes, soucieux du respect de la souveraineté étatique et de la protection de leur identité idéologique et culturelle. Au cours des travaux menant à l'élaboration des projets de principes devant régir la RDS, un nombre impressionnant de propositions ont été soumises au Sous-comité juridique.

Dès 1972, l'Union soviétique présenta un *Projet de Convention sur les principes gouvernant l'utilisation par les États de satellites artificiels aux fins de la télévision directe*[149], lequel tendait à promouvoir le principe du «consentement préalable», de concert avec le contrôle du contenu des programmes. Ces points furent réitérés dans les projets de principes présentés par l'Union soviétique au groupe de travail sur la RDS en 1974[150]. La même année, les États-Unis proposèrent une série de *Principes proposés pour la RDS*[151], revendiquant la «libre circulation de l'information» et tentant d'adopter une approche pragmatique tendant à éviter le besoin de conclure des accords. La proposition canado-suédoise sur les *Projets de principes régissant la radiodiffusion directe par satellites*[152] a essayé de formuler un compromis acceptable entre les positions des superpuissances. Le document canado-suédois liait étroitement le principe du consentement préalable à celui du droit de participation des États récepteurs dans le développement et le fonctionnement de systèmes de RDS devant diffuser sur leur territoire, en tout ou en partie. Il cherchait ainsi à tenir compte des avantages potentiels de la RDS et des différents problèmes de philosophie politique soulevés par la question de la censure de l'information.

Entre 1977 et 1979, le Canada et la Suède tentèrent de réconcilier les opinions diamétralement opposées au sein du CUPEAA[153]. Cependant, le consensus n'a pas été atteint, notamment à cause de l'opposition des États-Unis et de la République fédérale d'Allemagne au principe du consentement préalable[154].

L'impasse juridique dans laquelle se trouvait le CUPEAA et l'absence de consensus a incité l'Assemblée générale à demander au CUPEAA de faire tous ses efforts pour arriver à un accord sur un projet de principes applicables à la RDS pendant sa session de 1982, afin que le projet puisse être examiné par l'Assemblée générale à sa 37e session[155]. Des négociations se sont poursuivies jusqu'au bout afin d'obtenir le consensus, traditionnel en matière de droit de l'espace aux Nations Unies. Finalement, l'Assemblée générale adopta, le 10 décembre 1982, une résolution 37/92 proposant en annexe des principes sur la RDS, prévoyant entre autres «la consultation et l'accord préalable» des États concernés. Le vote a été obtenu par 107 voix contre treize, avec treize abstentions. La majorité des pays occidentaux ont voté contre la proposition. Le Canada s'est abstenu, en soulignant son regret qu'après tant d'années de négociations le consensus n'ait pu être atteint[156].

Cet incident marquait la première fois qu'en matière de droit de l'espace, un texte est adopté sans que soit respectée la pratique du consensus préalable au sein du CUPEAA. L'abandon de cette pratique «pourrait être très grave de conséquences: les nouveaux développements en matière de droit de l'espace risqueraient de s'orienter vers la voie sans issue du droit «déclaratoire»[157].

B. Utilisation de sources d'énergie nucléaire dans l'espace (SEN)

Cette question n'est examinée que depuis peu d'années par le Sous-comité juridique. Le 24 janvier 1978, le satellite soviétique *Cosmos 954* s'est écrasé sur le territoire canadien[158]. Sur la base des travaux effectués par le Sous-comité scientifique et technique[159], l'utilisation des SEN a été inscrite à l'ordre du jour du Sous-comité juridique[160].

Soucieux de la protection de leur sol contre toute sorte de pollution, le Canada fut le premier pays à demander que soit examinée, par le Sous-comité juridique, «la possibilité de compléter les normes du droit international relatives à l'utilisation de sources d'énergie nucléaires dans l'espace extra-atmosphérique». En effet, le Canada voulait voir adoptées des normes plus précises sur la conception même des satellites, les mesures à prendre en cas de retour accidentel dans l'espace, l'assistance et la responsabilité en cas d'accident[161]. Plusieurs autres pays, comme la République fédérale d'Allemagne[162], la Suède[163], la Chine[164], les Pays-Bas[165], le Japon, l'Italie et l'Australie, se sont également rangés du côté canadien.

Lors de la dernière session du Sous-comité juridique en mars 1986, le Canada a déposé un projet de principes sur l'utilisation des SEN[166] afin de permettre au Sous-comité de disposer d'un document de travail au moment où il entreprendrait l'élaboration de tels principes, conformément au nouveau mandat conféré par l'Assemblée générale. Le Sous-comité juridique est parvenu à un consensus sur le texte de deux projets de principes, l'un portant sur le format de notifications préalables d'une rentrée dans l'atmosphère, et l'autre, sur l'assistance aux États en cas d'accident. Toutefois, beaucoup de travail reste à faire. Les négociations se poursuivront durant la prochaine session du Sous-comité juridique.

3. La Conférence du désarmement

Bien que les Nations Unies se soient préoccupées de prévenir une course aux armements dans l'espace extra-atmosphérique dès la fin des années 50, ce n'est que récemment que la Conférence du désarmement (CD) s'est intéressée de près à cette question.

Aux termes de l'article IV du Traité de l'espace, il est interdit de placer en orbite autour de la Terre des objets porteurs d'armes nucléaires ou de tout autre type d'armes de destruction massive. Ce régime de «démilitarisation partielle» de l'espace extra-atmosphérique n'a certes pas empêché les superpuissances d'utiliser ce milieu pour des fins stratégiques[167]. En juin 1979, les États-Unis et l'Union soviétique ont suspendu leurs pourparlers bilatéraux sur les armes antisatellites (ASAT), après un an de débats stériles. Le désaccord portait essentiellement sur les capacités de chaque partie dans ce domaine et sur la nature offensive ou défensive des armes ASAT.

En 1982, à la Deuxième Session extraordinaire des Nations Unies sur le désarmement (UNSSOD II), le premier ministre Pierre E. Trudeau a énoncé la position officielle du Canada sur la militarisation grandissante de l'espace extra-atmosphérique. Il a fait tout particulièrement observer que le Traité de l'espace de 1967 comportait «des vides qui risquent de devenir extrêmement déstabilisateurs», particulièrement en ce qui concernait les armes antisatellites et les lasers antimissiles:

> Je crois que nous ne pouvons plus attendre très longtemps si nous voulons prévenir avec succès les guerres de l'espace. Je propose donc que nous amorcions rapidement l'élaboration d'un traité interdisant la mise au point et le déploiement de toute arme destinée à être employée dans l'espace[168].

Depuis 1982, la prévention d'une course aux armements dans l'espace extra-atmosphérique est à l'ordre du jour de la CD. En 1983 et 1984, le Canada a voté pour les deux résolutions voulant créer un groupe de travail spécial dans le cadre de la CD pour l'étude de cette question. Pendant longtemps, les représentants des 40 nations qui en font partie n'ont pu s'entendre sur le mandat à confier au groupe de travail spécial. Le Canada a activement tenté de promouvoir un accord sur un ordre du jour, en soulignant que l'Assemblée générale avait, à cet égard, attribué une responsabilité fondamentale à la Conférence[169], et à cette fin, a déposé un document de travail décrivant les objectifs souhaitables des pourparlers sur la limitation des armements dans l'espace[170].

Ce n'est qu'en 1985 que l'on s'est finalement entendu sur le mandat à confier au Comité spécial pour la prévention d'une course aux armements dans l'espace. Dans un premier temps, le Comité devait étudier toutes les questions se rapportant à la prévention de cette course aux armements. Il devait également se pencher sur tous les accords et propositions existants, sur les initiatives envisagées, sur le régime légal en vigueur et sur toute activité concernant l'espace extra-atmosphérique[171].

À la suite de la création de ce comité spécial, Joe Clark annonçait que le Canada s'efforcerait concrètement de favoriser un consensus au sujet d'un traité interdisant la militarisation de l'espace extra-atmosphérique et d'en faire comprendre la nécessité[172]. Dans le même sens, l'ambassadeur du Canada à la CD, Alan Beesley, déclarait que la prévention d'une course aux armements dans l'espace constituait l'une des principales préoccupations du Canada[173].

Le Canada a grandement participé aux travaux de ce comité en déposant plusieurs documents dans le but de remédier au manque flagrant de documents concrets dans ce domaine[174].

CONCLUSION

Les programmes spatiaux entrepris par le Canada lui ont appris que la technologie spatiale, bien qu'elle ne soit pas une panacée, peut souvent nous aider à réaliser, sans trop de frais, nos objectifs nationaux. En effet, comme le soulignait l'ancien ministre d'État à la Science et à la Technologie, Donald Johnson, grâce aux politiques adoptées dans le but de développer au Canada une industrie autonome de fabrication de matériel spatial,

> Canada's space industry has been growing at more than 50 % annually with export sales in excess of 70 % of total sales [...] Canada is the only nation in which the national space industry sells more than the Government spends on space[175].

Les attentes des Canadiens pour des services améliorés et plus nombreux, comme par exemple les avantages que la fabrication dans l'espace peut offrir et le rythme accéléré du développement technologique, se conjuguent pour créer des demandes nouvelles de services spatiaux et susciter des propositions nouvelles de la part du gouvernement et du secteur privé pour satisfaire à ces besoins.

De plus, le programme spatial canadien a toujours eu des ramifications internationales. Toutefois – afin que tous puissent profiter des avantages que nous offre la technologie spatiale – il faudra, de plus, s'assurer que l'espace demeure le «patrimoine commun de l'humanité».

NOTES

1. Voir la déclaration de John H. Chapman, ancien sous-ministre, programmes spatiaux, ministère des Communications, Ottawa, dans *International Space Activities*, «Hearings before the Subcommittee on Space Science and Applications», Committee on Science and Technology, US House of Representatives, 95th Congress, 2nd Session, 16 au 18 mai 1978, p. 312.

2. Pour une description détaillée de ce programme, voir J.H. Chapman, P.A. Forsyth, P.A. Lapp et G.N. Patterson, *Upper Atmosphere and Space Programs in Canada, Special Study No. 1*, Secrétariat de la Science, gouvernement du Canada, 1967, p. 11-15. (Ci-après ·désigné sous le nom de «rapport Chapman».)

3. Le mémorandum d'accord – *ISIS* du 23 mai 1963 et l'échange de notes accompagnant ledit mémorandum, daté du 6 mai 1964, sont reproduits dans le rapport Chapman, *ibidem*, p. 138-143.

4. *Ibidem*, p. 11.

5. *Le programme spatial canadien: plan quinquennal 80/81-84/85*, Série n° DOC-6-79 DP, gouvernement du Canada, ministère des Approvisionnements et Services Canada, 1980, p. 8.

6. Rapport Chapman, *supra*, note 2, p. VI.

7. *Ibidem*.

8. *Ibidem*, p. 109 et 111.

9. Pour une énumération des divers organismes gouvernementaux impliqués dans le programme spatial du Canada au cours des années 60, voir *ibidem*.

10. *Ibidem*, p. 110.

11. *Ibidem*, p. 111.

12. L'Union internationale des télécommunications (UIT), 6ᵉ rapport, 1967, p. 25 et s.

13. Livre blanc, *Domestic Satellite Communication Systems for Canada*, l'Honorable C.M. Drury, ministre de l'Industrie, 28 mars 1968, Ottawa, gouvernement du Canada.

14. *Ibidem*, p. 62.

15. Pour une définition de ces deux expressions, voir N.M. Matte, *Droit aérospatial [:] les télécommunications par satellites*, Paris, Éditions A. Pedone, 1982, p. 119 et 132 respectivement.

16. Livre blanc, *supra*, note 13 (traduction des auteurs).

17. N. et M. Mateesco-Matte, éd., *Télésat, Symphonie et la coopération spatiale régionale*, Paris, Éditions A. Pedone, 1978, p. 10-11.

18. P. Trudel, *Droit de l'information et de la communication*, Montréal, les éditions Thémis, 1984, p. 261.

19. *Loi de la Télésat Canada*, S.C. 1968-69, c. 51.

20. Le mot *Anik* signifie «frère» en inuit.

21. Un satellite dans l'orbite géostationnaire (une orbite équatoriale circulaire se situant à une distance d'environ 36 000 km au-dessus de l'équateur) tourne autour de la Terre à une vitesse identique à la rotation de cette dernière et, par conséquent, demeure stationnaire/synchronisé par rapport à un point désigné sur la surface de la planète. Le satellite peut «voir» au moins 1/3 de la surface de la Terre; par conséquent, trois satellites se trouvant sur cette même orbite pourraient assurer un service mondial de télécommunications.

22. RCA (SPAR) pour des éléments de structure et Northern Electric. La participation canadienne n'était que de 13 %; voir *INFOSPAR*, vol. 15, n° 4, décembre 1983, p. 2.

23. Voir N.G. Davies *et al.*, «The Transition from CTS/Hermes Communications Experiments to *ANIK-B* Pilot Projects», Institute of Electrical and Electronics Engineers, *IEEE Communications Magazine*, 1978, p. 331; «Hughes Aircraft dévoile les satellites de télécommunications «*ANIK-C*», *Air et cosmos*, 3 juin 1978, p. 43.

24. Voir Mateesco-Matte, *supra*, note 17, p. 20.

25. *Supra*, note 5, p. 8.

26. *Ibidem*, p. 18.

27. *Supra*, note 22.

28. *Supra*, note 5, p. 8.

29. Les compagnies suivantes se sont jointes à Spar pour la réalisation du projet: Hughes Aircraft des États-Unis, Com Dev and Fleet Aerospace Ltd. du Canada, pour le système de l'engin spatial; SED Systems Ltd. du Canada pour les installations de commande au sol, et Télésat Canada pour le soutien du fonctionnement en orbite.

30. «International Spacecraft», *Aviation Week and Space Technology*, 10 mars 1986, p. 173.

31. «Spar Contract preserves jobs but doesn't create them yet», *The Gazette*, 18 octobre 1986, p. H-3.

32. Voir *supra*, note 5, p. 13.

33. Matte, *supra*, note 15, p. 10-13. Voir aussi *supra*, note 5, p. 10.

34. Matte, *ibidem*, p. 229-230.

35. «Canada First With Commercial Satellite Service in 14/12 GHz Band», *News Release*, ministère des Communications, Ottawa, gouvernement du Canada, 15 septembre 1980.

36. Davies, *supra*, note 23.

37. Deux satellites de la série C ont été lancés: *Anik C-3* en novembre 1982, et *Anik C-2* en juin 1983. Voir *supra*, note 30.

38. J. Almond, «Commercial Communication Satellite Systems in Canada», *IEEE Communications Magazine*, janvier 1981, p. 10.

39. *Anik D-1* a été lancé en août 1982 et *ANIK D-2*, en novembre 1984.

40. Almond, *supra*, note 38, p. 15 (traduction des auteurs).

41. Rapport Chapman, *supra*, note 2, p. 109-110.

42. SRC 1970, c. S-5, articles 11 et 13.

43. *Report No. 1 – A Space Program for Canada*, Science Council of Canada, Ottawa, Queen's Printer, 1967.

44. *Ibidem*, p. 1.

45. *Ibidem*, p. 5.

46. *Ibidem*, p. 6.

47. *Supra*, note 5, p. 16.

48. *Ibidem*.

49. Reproduit dans *ibidem*, p. 17-18.

50. *Supra*, note 43.

51. Science Council of Canada Attachment, «Establish Canadian Space Agency Says Science Council», *News Release*, Ottawa, 23 octobre 1985.

52. Voir *infra*, section I. 1.4., «station spaciale».

53. *Supra*, note 51, p. 1 (traduction des auteurs).

54. *Canada and the Space Station*, A Report to the Government of Canada, The Canadian Institute for Advanced Research, 1985.

55. «Extraits du Discours du Trône», Montréal, *La Presse*, 2 octobre 1986, p. A-8.

56. «Une première politique scientifique pour le Canada», Montréal, *Le Devoir*, 26 mars 1986, p. 1 et 10.

57. *Supra*, note 5, p. 16.

58. Voir *supra*, note 1, p. 312 (traduction des auteurs).

59. Pour une analyse détaillée des expériences conjointes du Canada, voir *ibidem*, p. 313-323. Voir aussi *supra*, note 5.

60. *Ibidem*, p. 311 (traduction des auteurs).

61. *World-Wide Space Activities*, rapport préparé pour le Subcommittee on Science and Technology, US House of Representatives, 95th Congress, 1st Sess., 1977, p. 108.

62. «*Hermes* : The Communications Technology Satellite», ministère des Communications, Ottawa, gouvernement du Canada, 1979; voir aussi *supra*, note 5, p. 8, 10 et 63.

63. Davies, *supra*, note 23, p. 324 (traduction des auteurs).

64. «Canada has lost contact with Hermes», *News Release*, ministère des Communications, Ottawa, gouvernement du Canada, novembre 1979, p. 7. Voir aussi «US-Canadian Comsat Experiment to End This Month», *Flight International*, 27 octobre 1979, p. 1351.

65. D.D. Smith, *Teleservices via Satellite: Experiments and Future Perspectives*, Alphen aan der Rijn, 1978, p. 147.

66. «Canada Being Selective with its Space Funds», *Aviation Week and Space Technology*, 11 juin 1979, p. 203.

67. *Supra*, section I.1.B.

68. Doc. ONU A/AC.105/118 (1978), p. 12, par. 1 (traduction des auteurs).

69. *Remote Sensing from Satellites and Aircraft, Agreement effected by exchange of notes*. Signé à Washington, le 14 mai 1971; entrée en vigueur le 14 mai 1971. 22 UST 684; TIAS 7125; 793 UNTS 69. Reproduit dans S. Gorove (éd.), *United States Space Law – National and International Regulation*, New York, Oceana Publications, 1982, II.B.5, p. 10.

70. «US Spacecraft», *Aviation Week and Space Technology*, 8 mars 1982, p. 134.

71. *Remote Sensing from Satellites and Aircraft, Agreement Amending and Extending the Agreement of May 14, 1971. Effected by exchange of notes*. Signé à Ottawa, les 19 et 22 mars 1976; entrée en vigueur le 23 mars 1976. 27 UST 1075; TIAS 8247. Reproduit dans Gorove, *supra*, note 69, II.B.5, p. 16.

72. *Remote Sensing: Satellites and Aircraft, Agreement Extending the Agreement of May 14, 1971, as Amended and Extended*. Signé à Washington les 20 octobre et 6 novembre 1980; entrée en vigueur le 6 novembre 1980; effective May 14, 1980. TIAS 9934. Reproduit dans Gorove, *ibidem*, p. 22.

73. «US Spacecraft», *Aviation Week and Space Technology*, 10 mars 1986, p. 172.

74. *Supra*, note 5, p. 11. Le Centre canadien de télédétection, à Ottawa, traite les données en provenance de ces deux stations. Il est géré par le ministère de l'Énergie, des Mines et des Ressources.

75. *Supra*, note 61. En 1984, le Congrès américain adoptait une loi intitulée *Land Remote Sensing Commercialization Act of 1984*, public law 98-365 (HR 5155), qui prévoit le transfert du système gouvernemental LANDSAT au secteur privé. Si le Canada désire continuer à recevoir ces données, un nouvel accord devra être conclu.

76. Signé à Washington le 23 juin 1976; entrée en vigueur le 23 juin 1976. Un mémorandum d'accord accompagnant l'échange de notes a été signé les 9 et 18 juillet 1975. 27 UST 3801; TIAS 8400. Reproduit dans Gorove, *supra*, note 69, II.B.5, p. 61.

77. Voir *Space Shuttle Facts – Rockwell International Office of Public Relations*, juin 1982, p. 29.

78. «Orbiter Crew Restores Solar Man», *Aviation Week and Space Technology*, 16 avril 1984, p. 18.

79. «Satellite Retrieval Succeeds Despite Equipment Problems», *Aviation Week and Space Technology*, 19 novembre 1984, p. 16.

80. *Supra*, note 5, p. 8. La responsabilité de ce programme relève du Conseil national de recherches du Canada.

81. *Convention portant création d'une Agence spatiale européenne*, ouverte à la signature le 30 mai 1975; entrée en vigueur le 30 octobre 1980. (Ci-après dénommée «la Convention».)

82. Les onze signataires à l'origine étaient: la République fédérale d'Allemagne, la Belgique, le Danemark, l'Espagne, la France, l'Islande, l'Italie, les Pays-Bas, le Royaume-Uni, la Suède et la Suisse. Depuis, la Finlande a obtenu le statut «d'État membre» à la Convention.

83. L'Organisation européenne de recherches spatiales (CERS/ESRO), créée par une Convention du 14 juin 1962, et l'Organisation européenne pour la mise au point et la construction de lanceurs d'engins spatiaux (CERS/ELDO), créée par une Convention du 29 mars 1967. Le texte de ces conventions est reproduit dans Matte, *Droit aérospatial*, Paris, Éditions A. Pédone, 1969, p. 455 et 476 respectivement. En général, voir, M. Bourély, «L'Agence spatiale européenne», I, *Annales de droit aérien et spatial* 183 (ci-après ADAS),1976.

84. Préambule de la Convention.

85. Voir *infra*, section I.3.C., «AEROSAT».

86. En 1972, la CERS/ESRO et le Canada ont convenu d'exécuter un projet consistant à réaliser et essayer en vol des composants et sous-systèmes faisant appel à des technologies avancées. Ce projet devait s'inscrire dans le cadre du programme expérimental de télécommunications canado-américain CTS. Voir *Accord sous forme d'échange de lettres entre le gouvernement du Canada et l'Organisation européenne de recherches spatiales concernant un projet mis en œuvre conjointement par le ministère des Communications et l'Organisation dans le domaine de la technologie spatiale avancée*, signé le 18 mai 1972. *Mémorandum d'accord entre le ministère des Communications du Canada et l'Organisation européenne de recherches spatiales concernant leur coopération dans le domaine de la technologie spatiale avancée*, entrée en vigueur le 18 mai 1972.

87. Voir *Arrangement entre l'Agence spatiale européenne et le Centre canadien de télédétection*, signé le 21 mars 1977.

88. On entend, par «l'Exécutif de l'ESA», le directeur général de l'ESA et ses collaborateurs chargés de formuler et de mettre en œuvre les décisions du Conseil et des autres organes délibérants de l'Agence.

89. Cité dans M. Bourély, «Le Canada et l'Agence spatiale européenne» IV, *ADAS* 397, 1979, p. 400.

90. *Ibidem*, p. 401.

91. Rapport Chapman, *supra*, note 1, p. 328.

92. Art. (2) de la Convention.

93. Art. (3).

94. Art. XIV (3). L'ESA a signé deux accords conférant la qualité de «membre associé»; le premier avec l'Autriche, le 17 octobre 1979 (révisé le 12 avril 1984), le second avec la Norvège, le 20 avril 1981.

95. Art. XIV (1) et (2).

96. M. Bourély, «Les nouvelles relations entre le Canada et l'Agence spatiale européenne» (1985), X ADAS 201, p. 203.

97. *Ibidem*, p. 204; Bourély, *supra*, note 89, p. 404-405.

98. *Ibidem*.

99. Le texte de cet accord est reproduit dans le Vol. IV des ADAS, p. 706-711. (Ci-après dénommé l'«accord de 1978».)

100. Art. II (1).

101. Art. III.

102. Art. II (2).

103. Art. IV.

104. Art. XIV (1).

105. Le texte de cet accord est reproduit dans le vol. X (1985), *ADAS*, p. 211-215.

106. Pour une analyse approfondie du nouvel accord, voir Bourély, *supra*, note 96.

107. M. Bourély, «La participation du Canada aux programmes de l'Agence spatiale européenne», V, *ADAS* 363, 1980, p. 365.

108. *Supra*, note 5, p. 11.

109. Voir: 1. *Arrangement concernant la participation du gouvernement du Canada au Programme préparatoire européen de satellites de télédétection*, en date du 31 mars 1980, Doc. ESA/LEG/23; 2. *Arrangement concernant la participation du Canada à la phase B du Programme européen de satellites de télédétection de l'Agence spatiale européenne*, en date du 7 février 1983; 3. *Accord entre le gouvernement du Canada et l'Agence spatiale européenne concernant la participation du Canada aux phases de développement et d'exploitation du programme ERS 1*, en date du 8 janvier 1985. Doc. ESA/LEG/68.

110. Le Système probatoire d'observation de la Terre (*SPOT*) est un satellite à résolution détaillée, lancé par la France en avril 1986. Voir F.R. Cleminson, «Multilateralism in the Arms Control Verification Process: A Canadian Perspective», conférence présentée à l'Institut de droit aérien et spatial, Université McGill, 27 mars 1986, p. 15-17 (non publiée).

111. Bourély, *supra*, note 107, p. 369. Voir aussi *supra*, note 5, p. 66.

112. *Arrangement concernant la participation du gouvernement du Canada au programme L-SAT*, en date du 28 juillet 1980. Doc. ESA/LEG/25.

113. *Arrangement concernant la participation du gouvernement du Canada à la phase de développement du programme de grand satellite de télécommunications (L-SAT)*, en date du 25 juin 1982. Doc. ESA/LEG/39.

114. «Spar Aérospatiale décroche un contrat de $65 millions», *La Presse*, 26 avril 1983, p. C 1.

115. P.J. Conchie, «The Olympus Satellite», dans P.M. Bainum et F. von Bun (éd.), *Europe/United States Space activities*, 23rd Goddard Memorial Symposium, vol. 61, «Science and Technology Series», American Astronautical Society Publication, 1985, p. 17.

116. *Ibidem*, p. 20.

117. Un «service mobile» est «un service de radiocommunications entre des stations terrestres et des stations mobiles, ou entre des stations mobiles».

Un «service de satellites mobiles» est «un service de radiocommunications:

• entre des stations terrestres mobiles et une ou plusieurs stations spatiales utilisées pour ce service;

• entre des stations terrestres mobiles par l'intermédiaire d'une ou plusieurs stations spatiales»:

Actes finals de la Conférence mondiale administrative de radio (Genève), 1979 (ci-après cités comme suit: *Actes finals 1979*), n° 3115.

118. Un «service de satellites mobiles aéronautiques» est «un service de satellites mobiles qui utilise des stations terrestres mobiles placées à bord des aéronefs; on peut retrouver, pour ce service, des stations équipées pour assurer la survie et des stations radiophares pour localisation d'urgence, *Actes finals 1979*, n° 3116.

Un «service de satellites mobiles maritimes» est «un service de satellites mobiles qui utilise des stations terrestres mobiles placées à bord des navires; on peut retrouver, pour ce service, des stations équipées pour assurer la survie et des stations de radiophares pour localisation d'urgence. (Traduction des auteurs.) *Actes finals 1979*, n° 3117.

119. *Memorandum of Understanding on a Joint Program of Experimentation and Evaluation Using Aeronautical Satellite Capability Between the United States Department of Transportation (Federal Aviation Administration), the European Space Research Organization, and the Government of Canada*, 2 août 1974; *Exchange of Letters Concerning the Interpretation of the Aerosat Memorandum of Understanding*, 2 août 1974. Voir aussi l'*Arrangement entre l'Organisation européenne de recherches spatiales, le COMSAT General Corporation et le gouvernement du Canada, en vue de la création d'un potentiel du secteur spatial du programme de satellites aéronautiques*.

120. Voir *The US Posture in Space: A Retrospective Assessment*, préparé pour l'Office of Technology Assessment, mars 1981, p. 33-34.

121. En 1979, le Canada, la France et les États-Unis ont signé un Mémorandum d'accord pour l'établissement du projet expérimental SARSAT. Par la suite, les partenaires au projet SARSAT signèrent un Mémorandum d'accord avec l'URSS qui poursuivait un projet expérimental semblable, connu sous le nom de COSPAS. Finalement, en 1980, les quatre pays ont signé un plan de mise en œuvre intitulé COSPAS/SARSAT. Voir «COSPAS/SARSAT services agreement to continue to end of 1990, unless replaced by new international instrument», *ICAO Bulletin*, février 1986, p. 20-23. Récemment, la Norvège s'est jointe à ce programme. Voir «Understanding among the Department of Communications of Canada, the Centre national d'études spatiales of France, the National Aeronautics and Space Administration of the United States of America and the Royal Norwegian Council for Scientific and Industrial Research Concerning Participation by Norway in an Investigation of the Demonstration and Evaluation of an Experimental Satellite-Aided Search and Rescue System», 13 novembre 1981.

122. «Sarsat/Cospas Proves Successful in Rescues», *Aviation Week and Space Technology*, 12 novembre 1984, p. 25.

123. «The Canadian Space Program: New Initiatives», Ministry of State, Science and Technology, mai 1986, reproduit dans *Space Policy*, août 1986, p. 262-265.

124. «Canadian Participation in Space Station», communiqué du Conseil national de recherches du Canada. Voir aussi «Canada Accepts Space Station Co-operation», *Aviation Week and Space Technology*, 25 mars 1985, p. 23.

125. *Supra*, note 123, p. 263. Sur le potentiel de la fabrication de produits dans l'espace, voir National Research Council Canada, *Canadian Participation in Space Station*, Ottawa, 1985, p. 12.

126. *Ibidem*.

127. «*Hermès*: un pas de plus vers la réalisation», *La Presse*, 25 octobre 1986, p. B-8.

128. «M-SAT – An Opportunity for Canada», Ottawa, ministère des Communications.

129. RADARSAT – Communiqué Énergie, Mines et Ressources Canada.

130. N.M. Matte, *Droit aérien-aéronautique* (3ᵉ édition), Paris, les Éditions A. Pedone, 1980, p. 15.

131. Résolution n° 1148 (XII), Assemblée générale des Nations Unies, 14 novembre 1957.

132. *Ibidem*, paragraphe 1(f).

133. «Question de l'utilisation de l'espace extra-atmosphérique à des fins pacifiques», résolution n° 1348 (XIII), Assemblée générale des Nations Unies, 13 décembre 1958.

134. Le comité *ad hoc* se composait des représentants de l'Argentine, de l'Australie, de la Belgique, du Brésil, du Canada, des États-Unis, de la France, de l'Inde, de l'Iran, de l'Italie, du Japon, du Mexique, de la Pologne, de la République arabe unie, du Royaume-Uni de Grande-Bretagne et d'Irlande du Nord, de la Suède, de la Tchécoslovaquie et de l'Union des Républiques socialistes soviétiques.

135. «Coopération internationale touchant les utilisations pacifiques de l'espace extra-atmosphérique», résolution n° 1472 (XIV), Assemblée générale des Nations Unies, 12 décembre 1959.

136. Voir N.M. Matte (éd.), *Space Activities and Emerging International Law*, Montréal, Centre de recherches en droit aérien et spatial, 1984, p. 187-202. L'effectif actuel du CUPEAA est de 53 membres.

137. *Traité sur les principes régissant les activités des États en matière d'exploration et d'utilisation de l'espace extra-atmosphérique, y compris la Lune et les autres corps célestes*, vol. 610, Recueil des traités – Nations Unies, p. 206. Ouvert à la signature le 27 janvier 1967; entrée en vigueur le 10 octobre 1967.

138. *Accord sur le sauvetage des astronautes, le retour des astronautes et la restitution des objets lancés dans l'espace extra-atmosphérique*, vol. 672, Recueil des traités – Nations Unies, p. 119. Ouvert à la signature le 22 avril 1968; entrée en vigueur le 3 décembre 1968.

139. *Convention sur la responsabilité internationale pour les dommages causés par des objets spatiaux*, vol. 24:3, UST, p. 2389. Ouvert à la signature le 29 mars 1972; entrée en vigueur le 9 octobre 1973.

140. *Convention sur l'immatriculation des objets lancés dans l'espace extra-atmosphérique*, vol. 28, UST, p. 695. Ouvert à la signature le 14 janvier 1975; entrée en vigueur le 15 septembre 1976.

141. *Accord régissant l'activité des États sur la Lune et les autres corps célestes*, doc. ONU A/RES/34/58, 14 décembre 1979; entrée en vigueur le 11 juillet 1984.

142. Ministry of State for Science and Technology, Federal Science Activities, 1982/1983 (1982), p. 54 (traduction des auteurs).

143. P. Fauteux, «Canada's Participation in the Development of Space Law: How Well Does the Recent Past Bode for the Future?», rapport non publié, avril 1984, p. 3-4 (traduction des auteurs).

144. Matte, *supra*, note 15, p. 146-190.

145. *Ibidem*, p. 200-206.

146. Pour un inventaire détaillé de la contribution canadienne au sein de l'UIT, voir Matte, *supra*, note 15, p. 115-145. Voir également *Notes pour une allocution de l'hon. Marcel Masse*, ministre des Communications, présenté le 26 mars 1985; et «The Way It Was and Wasn't at WARC '85», *Broadcasting*, 4 novembre 1985, p. 70-72.

147. Pour une analyse exhaustive des discussions du CUPEAA voir Matte, *supra*, note 136, p. 357-505; M. Benkö, W. De Graff et G.C.M. Reijnen, *Space Law in the United Nations*, Martinus Nijhoff Publishers, 1985.

148. Résolution n° 2453 (XXIII), Assemblée générale des Nations Unies, 20 décembre 1968.

149. Voir doc. ONU A/8771 (1972).

150. Voir doc. ONU A/AC.105/WG.3(V)/CRP.8 (1974), appuyé par la Bulgarie, la Hongrie et l'URSS.

151. Voir docs. ONU A/AC.105/WG.3(V)/CRP.2 (1974) et A/AC.105/WG.3(V), CRP.7 (1974).

152. Voir doc. ONU A/AC.105/WG.3(V)/CRP.6 (1974); doc. ONU A/AC.105/WG.3/L.8 (1974).

153. S. Danielson, «An Interdisciplinary Approach in the Regulation by the United Nations of Activities in Outer Space: Some Technical Considerations», dans *Les activités spatiales et leurs implications: d'où vient-on et où va-t-on à l'aube des années 80?*, Toronto, The Carswell Co. Ltd., 1981, p. 103.

154. J. Chapman et G. Warren, «Direct Broadcast Satellites: The ITU, UN and the Real World» IV, ADAS, 413, 1979, p. 426-437.

155. Résolution 36/35, Assemblée générale des Nations Unies, 18 novembre 1981.

156. Doc. ONU A/SPC/L15/Rev. 1, 27 novembre 1982.

157. J.D. de la Rochère, «Attitudes françaises et droit de l'espace» VIII, ADAS, 357, 1983, p. 366.

158. J. Reiskind, «Toward a Responsible Use of Nuclear Power in Outer Space – The Canadian Initiative in the United Nations», VI, ADAS, 461, 1981.

159. À la suite de la résolution 33/16, Assemblée générale des Nations Unies, 10 novembre 1978.

160. À la suite de la résolution 34/66, Assemblée générale des Nations Unies, 5 décembre 1979.

161. A.J. Young, «Legal and Techno-Political Implications of the Use of Nuclear Power Sources in Outer Space», publié dans le volume 12, *Rutgers Computer & Technology Law Journal*, 1987.

162. Document de travail de la République fédérale d'Allemagne, doc. ONU A/AC.105/C.2/L.146, 26 mars 1984.

163. Document de travail de la Suède, doc. ONU WG/NPS(1982)/WP/2, 11 février 1982.

164. Document de travail présenté par le Canada, la Chine, les Pays-Bas et la Suède. Doc. ONU WG/NPS(1984)/WP.4, 29 mars 1984.

165. *Ibidem.*

166. Doc.ONU A/AC.105/C.2/L.154, 25 mars 1986.

167. Pour une analyse exhaustive de la militarisation de l'espace, voir M.L. Stojak, *Legally Permissible Scope of Current Military Activities in Space and Prospects for their Future Control,* thèse de doctorat, D.C.L., Institut de droit aérien et spatial, Université McGill, 1985 (non publié).

168. *Allocution prononcée par le premier ministre à la Deuxième Session extraordinaire des Nations Unies sur le désarmement,* New York, 18 juin 1982.

169. *Conference on Disarmament, Prevention of an Arms Race in Outer Space – Final Records (PV) 1979-1984,* Direction du contrôle des armements et du désarmement, juin 1985, CD/PV.183, 31 août 1982, p. 23.

170. CD/PV.183, 31 août 1982, p. 24.

171. CD/PV.306, 29 mars 1985.

172. Ministère des Affaires extérieures, *Communiqué,* n° 85/46, 9 avril 1985.

173. CD/PV.306, 4 avril 1985, p. 24.

174. En juillet 1985, la délégation canadienne a déposé un document de travail intitulé *Survey of International Law Relevant to Arms Control and Outer Space.* En mars 1986, un recueil de documents issus des débats menés en 1985 par la CD sur l'espace était présenté par le Canada. Enfin, en juillet 1986, le Canada a déposé un document officiel sur la terminologie propre à la limitation des armements dans l'espace.

175. «Minister Announces New Space Plan», *News Release,* Minister of State, Science and Technology, 19 mars 1984.

BIBLIOGRAPHIE

Livres

BAINUM, P.M. et VON BUN, F., éd. *Europe/United States Space Activities*, 23rd Goddard Memorial Symposium, «Science and Technology Series», American Astronautical Society Publication, vol. 61, 1985.

BENKÖ, M., DE GRAFF, W. et REIJNEN, G.C.M. *Space Law in the United Nations*, Martinus Nijhoff Publishers, 1985.

CHAPMAN, J.H., FORSYTH, P.A., LAPP, P.A. et PATTERSON, G.N. *Upper Atmosphere and Space Programs in Canada, Special Study No. 1*, Secrétariat de la Science, gouvernement du Canada, Ottawa, 1967.

Les activités spatiales et leurs implications: d'où vient-on et où va-t-on à l'aube des années 80?, Toronto, The Carswell Co. Ltd., 1981.

MATEESCO-MATTE, N. et M., éd. *Télésat, Symphonie et la coopération spatiale régionale*, Paris, Éditions A. Pedone, 1978.

MATTE, N.M. *Droit aérien-aéronautique* (3e édition), Paris, Éditions A. Pedone, 1980.

MATTE, N.M. *Droit aérospatial [:] les télécommunications par satellites*, Paris, Éditions A. Pedone, 1982.

MATTE, N.M., éd. *Space Activities and Emerging International Law*, Montréal, Centre de recherches en droit aérien et spatial, 1984.

SMITH, D.D. *Teleservices via Satellite: Experiments and Future Perspectives*, Alphen aan der Rijn, 1978.

STOJAK, M.L. *Legally Permissible Scope of Current Military Activities in Space and Prospects for their Future Control*, thèse de doctorat, D.C.L., Institut de droit aérien et spatial, Université McGill, 1983 (non publiée).

TRUDEL, P. *Droit de l'information et de la communication*, Montréal, les Éditions Thémis, 1984.

Articles

ALMOND, J. «Commercial Communication Satellite Systems in Canada», Institute of Electrical and Electronics Engineers, *IEEE Communications Magazine.*, janvier 1981.

BOURÉLY, M. «L'Agence spatiale européenne», I, *Annales de droit aérien et spatial (ADAS)* 183, 1976.

BOURÉLY, M. «Le Canada et l'Agence spatiale européenne» IV ADAS, 1979, p. 400.

BOURÉLY, M. «La participation du Canada aux programmes de l'Agence spatiale européenne», V, ADAS 363, 1980.

BOURÉLY, M. «Les nouvelles relations entre le Canada et l'Agence spatiale européenne», X, *ADAS* 201, 1985.

CHAPMAN, J.H. et WARREN, G. «Direct Broadcast Satellites: The ITU, UN and the Real World», IV, *ADAS* 413, 1979.

CLEMINSON, F.R. «Multilateralism in the Arms Control Verification Process: A Canadian Perspective», texte présenté à l'Institut de droit aérien et spatial, Université McGill, 27 mars 1986 (non publié).

DAVIES, N.G. *et al.* «The Transition from CTS/*Hermes* Communications Experiments to *Anik-B* Pilot Projects», *IEEE Communications Magazine*, 1978.

DE LA ROCHÈRE, J.D. «Attitudes françaises et droit de l'espace», VIII, *ADAS* 357, 1983.

FAUTEUX, P. «Canada's Participation in the Development of Space Law: How Well Does the Recent Past Bode for the Future?», article non publié, avril 1984.

REISKIND, J. «Toward a Responsible Use of Nuclear Power in Outer Space – The Canadian Initiative in the United Nations», VI, *ADAS* 461, 1981.

YOUNG, A.J. «Legal and Techno-Political Implications of the Use of Nuclear Power Sources in Outer Space», 12, *Rutgers Computer & Technology Law Journal*, 1987.

Rapports et documents

Allocution prononcée par le premier ministre du Canada à la Deuxième Session extraordinaire des Nations Unies sur le désarmement, New York, 18 juin 1982.

CANADA. «Canada First With Commercial Satellite Service in 14/12 GHz Band», *News Release*, Ottawa, ministère des Communications 15 septembre 1980.

CANADA. «Canada has lost Contact with *Hermes*», *News Release*, Ottawa, ministère des Communications, novembre 1979.

CANADA. «Hermes: The Communications Technology Satellite», Ottawa, ministère des Communications, 1979.

CANADA. *Le programme spatial canadien: plan quinquennal 80/81-84/85*, série n° DOC-6-79 DP, Ottawa, ministère des Approvisionnements et Services Canada, 1980.

CANADA. *Livre blanc, Domestic Satellite Communication Systems for Canada*, l'Honorable C.M. Drury, ministre de l'Industrie, Ottawa, 28 mars 1968.

CANADA. Ministère des Affaires extérieure. *Communiqué* n° 85/46, 9 avril 1985.

CANADA. Ministry of State for Science and Technology, Federal Science Activities, 1982/1983, Ottawa, 1982.

747

CANADA. «M-SAT – An Opportunity for Canada», Ottawa, ministère des Communications.

CANADA. *Notes pour une allocution de l'hon. Marcel Masse,* ministre des Communications, présenté le 26 mars 1985.

CANADA. RADARSAT. Ministère de l'Énergie, des Mines et des Ressources.

CANADA. *Report No. 1 – A Space Program for Canada,* Science Council of Canada, Ottawa, Queen's Printer, 1967.

CANADA. *Survey of International Law Relevant to Arms Control and Outer Space,* document de travail déposé par la délégation canadienne à la CD, juillet 1985.

CANADA. «The Canadian Space Program: New Initiatives», Ottawa, Ministry of State, Science and Technology, mai 1986.

DIRECTION DU CONTRÔLE DES ARMEMENTS ET DU DÉSARMEMENT. *Conference on Disarmament, Prevention of an Arms Race in Outer Space – Final Records (PV) 1979-1984,* juin 1985, CD/PV.183, 31 août 1982.

ÉTATS-UNIS. *International Space Activities,* Hearings before the Subcommittee on Space Science and Application, Committee in Science and Technology, US House of Representatives, 95th Congress, 2nd Sess., 16-18 mai 1979.

ÉTATS-UNIS. *The US Posture in Space: A Retrospective Assessment,* préparé pour l'Office of Technology Assessment (OTA), Washington, D.C., mars 1981.

ÉTATS-UNIS. *World-Wide Space Activities,* rapport préparé pour le Subcommittee on Science and Technology, US House of Representatives, 95th Congress, 1st Sess., 1977.

THE CANADIAN INSTITUTE FOR ADVANCED RESEARCH. *Canada and the Space Station,* A Report to the Government of Canada, 1985.

SCIENCE COUNCIL OF CANADA. «Establish Council of Canada Attachment», *News Release,* Ottawa, 23 octobre 1985.

Résolutions

1148 (XII), Assemblée générale des Nations Unies, 14 novembre 1957.

1348 (XIII), Assemblée générale des Nations Unies, 13 décembre 1958.

1472 (XIV), Assemblée générale des Nations Unies, 12 décembre 1959.

n° 2453 (XXIII), Assemblée générale des Nations Unies, 20 décembre 1968.

33/16, Assemblée générale des Nations Unies, 10 novembre 1978.

34/66, Assemblée générale des Nations Unies, 5 décembre 1979.

36/35, Assemblée générale des Nations Unies, 18 novembre 1981.

Documents

ONU A/RES/34/58, 14 décembre 1979.

ONU A/8771 (1972).

ONU A/AC.105/WG.3(V)/CRP.2 (1974).

ONU A/AC./105WG.3(V)/CRP.6 (1974).

ONU A/AC.105/WG.3(V)/CRP.7 (1974).

ONU A/AC.105/WG.3(V)/CRP.8 (1974).

ONU A/AC.105/WG.3/L.8 (1974).

ONU A/AC.105/118 (1978).

ONU A/SPC/L15/Rev. 1, 27 novembre 1982.

ONU WG/NPS(1982)/WP/2 (1982).

ONU A/AC.105/C.2/L.146 (1984).

ONU WG/NPS(1984)/WP.4 (1984).

ONU A/AC.105/C.2/L.154 (1986).

CD/PV.306, 29 mars 1985.

CD/PV.306, 4 avril 1985.